BEETLES

of Western North America

BEETLES
of Western North America

Arthur V. Evans

Princeton University Press
Princeton and Oxford

DEDICATION

This book is dedicated to my parents, Ed and Lois Evans, who instilled in me a love for nature and the West; my high school biology teachers Bob Brister and Mike Hanlon, who fueled my passion for field biology; Bob Duff, who first exposed me to the incredible diversity of beetles in western North America; Charlie Hogue, who introduced me to the power of macro photography to illustrate and educate; Elbert Sleeper, for providing me with the academic foundation for all my future studies of the Coleoptera; Chuck Bellamy, who accompanied me on so many field trips throughout the West and beyond; and to my wife, Paula Evans, whose unwavering love and support, combined with her insatiable curiosity for all things beetle, made this book possible.

Published by Princeton University Press
41 William Street, Princeton, New Jersey 08540
6 Oxford Street, Woodstock, Oxfordshire OX20 1TR

press.princeton.edu

All Rights Reserved

Library of Congress Cataloging-in-Publication Data

Names: Evans, Arthur V., author.
Title: Beetles of Western North America / Arthur V. Evans.
Description: Princeton : Princeton University Press, [2021] | Includes bibliographical references and index.
Identifiers: LCCN 2020049834 (print) | LCCN 2020049835 (ebook) | ISBN 9780691164281 (paperback) | ISBN 9780691221373 (ebook)
Subjects: LCSH: Beetles—West (U.S.) | Beetles—Canada, Western. | Beetles—West (U.S.)—Identification. | Beetles—Canada, Western—Identification.
Classification: LCC QL581 .E 2021 (print) | LCC QL581 (ebook) | DDC 595.76097—dc23
LC record available at https://lccn.loc.gov/2020049834
LC ebook record available at https://lccn.loc.gov/2020049835

British Library Cataloging-in-Publication Data is available

Editorial: Robert Kirk and Abigail Johnson
Production Editorial: Mark Bellis
Text Design: D & N Publishing, Wiltshire, UK
Cover Design: Wanda España
Production: Steve Sears
Publicity: Matthew Taylor and Caitlyn Robson
Copyeditor: Lucinda Treadwell

Cover image: *Buprestis aurulenta* © Thomas Shahan
Image previous page: *Pleocoma octopagina* © Arthur V. Evans

This book has been composed in Arial MT (main text) and Avant Garde Gothic PS (headings and captions)

Printed on acid-free paper. ∞

Printed in China

10 9 8 7 6 5 4 3 2 1

CONTENTS

CONTENTS

PREFACE

The companion volume for this book, *Beetles of Eastern North America*, began as an exploration of the beetle fauna that inhabited my newly adopted home state, Virginia. However, *Beetles of Western North America* is more of a homecoming. Its seeds were first sown more than five decades ago during week-long summer camping trips with my family in California on the Central Coast and along the entire length of the Sierra Nevada. Throughout the rest of the year, my parents, Lois and Ed Evans, took my sister Alice and me on weekend excursions to explore the natural wonders and historical sites throughout the Mojave Desert. My parents actively encouraged my interest in insects from a very early age. Later, while on a 4-H field trip to the Entomology Department at the Natural History Museum of Los Angeles County, I learned of the Lorquin Entomological Society that held its monthly meetings at the museum. For several years afterward, my parents made the three-hour round-trip drive numerous times so that I could attend these incredibly influential meetings.

It was during one of my early museum visits that I met Bob Duff, who later invited me to my first insect collecting trip to southeastern Arizona. For several summers, we searched for beetles in the canyons and surrounding environs of the Sky Islands, an archipelago of isolated mountain ranges that connect the southern reaches of the Rockies to the northernmost extent of Mexico's Sierra Madre Occidental. Our trips usually began with brief forays through the mountains and lower desert of southern California, before heading east to cross the Colorado River. On one of these trips, we explored southern New Mexico and drove as far east as western Texas. These expeditions, coupled with Bob's vast entomological knowledge and generous spirit, inspired me to focus my entomological interests on beetles, especially scarabs.

During the summer of 1973, between my sophomore and junior years at Palmdale High School, I enrolled in Field Biology, a class taught by Bob Brister and Mike Hanlon that, to this day, stands as one of my favorite courses ever. In particular, I recall an overnight camping trip in a white fir forest high in the San Gabriel Mountains where we set up lights to attract nocturnal insects, including many beetles whose identities were yet unknown to me, most of which appear in this book.

Upon graduating high school in 1975, I was hired as student worker in the Entomology Department at the Natural History Museum. There I worked with Charlie Hogue, Julian Donahue, Roy Snelling, and Fred Truxal, all of whom instilled in me the importance of fieldwork, maintaining meticulous records, and keeping a well-curated insect collection. Charlie was particularly influential during my early days in entomology and was instrumental in developing my nascent interest in macro photography and writing for a popular audience.

In spring of 1978, I enrolled in the entomology program at California State University, Long Beach (CSULB), for the express purpose of studying beetles with Elbert Sleeper, a noted authority on weevils. Just weeks before the start of the fall semester, I found myself once again in southeastern Arizona. One evening, while I was tending my blacklight sheet in Bog Springs Campground in Madera Canyon, Chuck Bellamy walked out from the shadows and introduced himself. He was enrolled as a graduate student at CSULB with Sleeper as his advisor, and was pursuing a graduate research project on buprestids. This chance meeting marked the beginning of a friendship and numerous field trips together on two continents over a period of 35 years.

My family, along with these friends and mentors, most of whom are now passed, all had a deep and sustained influence on me both personally and professionally. Their collective support and passion for the natural world helped to propel me on a lifelong path of discovery and scholarship in Coleoptera.

ACKNOWLEDGMENTS

Once again, I thank Robert Kirk, publisher at Princeton University Press, for the opportunity to write this book. His continued support, guidance, and, most importantly, patience, were instrumental in its completion. I also appreciate the dedication, expertise, and support of his colleagues including Mark Bellis, Bob Bettendorf, Wanda España, Abigail Johnson, Dimitri Karetnikov, Caitlyn Robson, Steve Sears, Matthew Taylor, and Lucinda Treadwell, as well as David Price-Goodfellow at D & N Publishing.

In addition to my own field experiences and those of others, the information in this book was drawn largely from primary sources, located either in my personal library or through digital libraries, particularly the Biodiversity Heritage Library (BHL) and Journal Storage (JSTOR). These most precious resources have long been invaluable to me for this and countless other research projects. Special thanks to the Boatwright Memorial Library at the University of Richmond in Richmond, Virginia, for providing access to JSTOR and various online journals. Many pertinent publications were generously made available by their authors at ResearchGate.

The taxonomic scope and aesthetic appeal of this book would have been impossible to achieve were it not for the excellent beetle images supplied by talented and dedicated photographers. I am forever grateful to the following photographers for their generosity and support of *Beetles of Western North America*: Alice Abela, Bob Allen, Dave Almquist, Gary Alpert, Bob Anderson, Thomas Atkinson, Paul Bedell, Christoph Benisch, Tom Bentley, Brendon Boudinot, Margarethe Brummermann, Emily Butler, Gary Campbell, Mike Caterino, Patrick Coin, Jillian Cowles, Alan Cressler, Rob Curtis, John Davis, Wendy Duncan, Josef Dvořák, Werner Eigelsreiter, Charley Eiseman, Lynette Elliott, Mike Ferro, Kara Froese, Judy Gallagher, Kevin Gielen, Lucie and Matt Gimmel, Matt Goff, Nicolas Gompel, Henri Goulet, Margy Green, Don Griffiths, Gary Griswold, Joyce Gross, Jeff Gruber, Dennis Haines, Jim Hammond, Guy Hanley, Charles "Chip" Hedgcock, Karl Hillig, Don Hodel, Charlie Hogue (deceased), Jim Hogue, Anna Holden, Tony Iwane, Andrew Johnston, Chris Joll, Scott Justis, Kojun Kanda, Jay Keller, Stanislav Krejčík, Louis LaPierre, Cedric Lee, Mike Lewis, René Limoges, Steve Lingafelter, Ed Lisowski, Nathan Lord, Stephen Luk, Ted MacRae, David Maddison, Crystal Maier, Kirill Makarov, Chris Mallory, Steve Marshall, Kerry Matz, Sean McCann, Gary McDonald, Tommy McElrath, Stephen McKechnie, Andrew McKorney, Charles Melton, Richard Migneault, Graham Montgomery, Jim Moore, Tom Murray, Steve Nanz, Karen Needham, Klaus Bek Nielsen, John Ott, Robert Otto, Loren and Babs Padelford, Tony Palmer, Stewart Peck, Phil Perkins, Merrill Peterson, Darren Pollock, Katy Pye, Mike Quinn, Nikola Rahmé, Jen Read, Jacques Rifkind, Birgit Rhode, Ed Ruden, Phil Schapker, Udo Schmidt, Kyle Schnepp, Aaron Schusteff, Alexey Sergeev, Thomas Shahan, Derek Sikes, Paul Skelley, Barney Streit, Gayle & Jeanell Strickland, Mike Thomas (deceased), Adrian Thysse, Bill Tyson, Matt Van Dam, Salvador Vitanza, Robyn Waayers, Bill Warner, Rick Westcott, Alex Wild, Dick Wilson, Chris Wirth, Hartmut Wisch, and Alex Yelich.

Jennifer Read expertly prepared all 1,500+ images used in this work. She converted JPEGs into TIFFs when needed and, only when absolutely necessary, cropped, sharpened, adjusted exposure, repaired or replaced the occasional missing or damaged appendage, and removed dust and stray hairs so that the subject of each and every image looks its absolute best. Jennifer also rendered the illustrations accompanying the key to families.

The following family, friends, and colleagues afforded invaluable assistance to me in terms of providing logistical support for fieldwork, accompanying me in the field, organizing research and collecting permits, furnishing specimen identifications, sorting out taxonomic issues, providing pertinent literature and images, collecting live specimens to photograph, supplying unpublished biological and locality data, or reviewing portions of the manuscript: Rolf Aalbu, Melissa Aja, Ron Alten, Bob Anderson, Sandy Anderson, Salvador Anzaldo, Allan Ashworth, Brad Barnd, Cheryl Barr and Bill Shepard, Ben Beal, Paul Bedell, Chuck (deceased) and Rose Bellamy, Robert Beiriger, Vassili Belov, Larry Bezark, Pat Bouchard, Allison Boyer, Jeff Brown, Margarethe Brummermann and Randy Kaul, Alan Burke, Susan Burke, Dave Carlson, Chris Carlton, Mike Caterino, Don Chandler, Joe Cicero, Andy Cline, Rich Cunningham, Susan Doniger, Hume Douglas, Eric Eaton, Ilya Enuschenko, Terry Erwin (deceased), Alice Evans, Ed and Lois Evans (both deceased), Paula Evans, Bryan Eya, Zack Falin, Vini Ferreira, Linda Ford, Cristina Francois and John Kraft, Nico Franz, Dave Furth, Steve Gaimari, Rosser Garrison and Natalia van Ellenreider, Michael Geiser, François Geniér, Matt and Lucie Gimmel, Lisa Gonzalez,

Dennis Haines, Gene Hall, Deni and Roger Halterman, Curt Harden, Paul Harrison, Henry Hespenheide, Jim Hogue, Anna Holden, Mike Ivie, Mary Liz Jameson, Charley and Janet Jensen, Paul J. Johnson, Andrew Johnston, Kerry Katovich, Peter Kerr, Bernard Klausnitzer, Jiří Kolibáč, Frank Krell, Jim LaBonte, Paul Lago, John Lawrence, John Leavengood, Luc Leblanc, Rich Leschen, Robin Lesher, Stéphane Le Tirant, Steve Lingafelter and Norm Woodley, Ted MacRae, Crystal Maier, Ed and Lisa Mastro, Blaine Mathison, Adriean Mayor, Tommy McElrath, Sandra McKennon-Volk, Ron McPeak, Rob Mitchell, Ray Nagle, Karen Needham, Al Newton and Margaret Thayer, Alex Nguyen, Dave Numer, Rolf Oberprieler, Charlie O'Brien (deceased), M. J. Paulsen, Stewart Peck, Samuel Perry, Keith Philips, Keith Pike, John Pinto, Darren Pollock, Gareth Powell, Jens Prena, Heidi Preschler, Brett Ratcliffe, Jennifer Read, Mark Readdie, Brady Richards, Jacques Rifkind, Paul Robbins, Steve Roble, Barbara Roth, Dave and Jill Russell, Kyle Schnepp, Paul Schoolmeesters, Owen Shiozaki, Floyd Shockley, Andrew Short, Derek Sikes, Paul Skelley, Aaron Smith, Andrew Smith, Julie Sommers, Charlie Staines, Warren Steiner Jr., Barney Streit and Sandy Hotzakorgian, Celia Stuart, Pat and Lisa Lee Sullivan, Dariusz Tarnawski, Mike Thomas (deceased), Rob Velten, Bernhard von Vondel, Robyn and Gary Waayers, Dave Wagner, Nancy and Ken Walery, Kelli Walker, Marianne and Gary Wallace, Phil Ward, Bill Warner, Ann Washington, Stan Wellso, Rick Westcott, Kirsten and Craig Wilburn, Suzanne Wilcox, Kip Will, Michael Wilson, and Chris Wirth.

Starting in 2010, I undertook six trips to collect and photograph beetles for this book and drove more than 8,000 miles across Washington, Oregon, California, Nevada, and Arizona. I am most grateful to the following individuals and their agencies or institutions for the warm hospitality and numerous kindnesses extended to me during these excursions: Brian Brown (Natural History Museum of Los Angeles County, CA); Jeff Brown (Sagehen Creek Field Station, University of California, Berkeley, CA); Chris Carlton (PPR Research Station, Louisiana State University, Rodeo, NM); Andy Cline (California State Collection of Arthropods, California Department of Food and Agriculture, CA); Cristina Francois (Appleton-Whittell Research Ranch of the National Audubon Society, AZ); Matt Gimmel (Santa Barbara Museum of Natural History, CA); Gene Hall (Department of Entomology, University of Arizona, AZ); Mark Heitlinger (Santa Rita Experimental Station and Wildlife Area, University of Arizona, AZ); Paul G. Johnson (Pinnacles National Park, CA); Dave Numer (Devil's Punchbowl Natural Area and Nature Center, CA); Mark Readdie (Landels-Hill Big Creek Reserve, University of California Santa Cruz Natural Reserve System, CA); Barbara Roth (Southwest Research Station, American Museum of Natural History, AZ).

I thank Dan Young (University of Wisconsin, Madison), whose thorough review and constructive criticism of *Beetles of Eastern North America* proved incredibly useful during the compilation of this volume.

Lastly, I owe a debt of gratitude to the taxonomists, both present and past, many of whom are listed above. For it was their dogged pursuit of describing and diagnosing species that made it possible for others to identify beetles housed in their collections and in the fine images that appear on the following pages. Perhaps this distillation of their dedication and hard work will inspire a new generation of talented and energetic taxonomists. In a world of ever-shrinking natural habitat and financial support for taxonomic research, we need taxonomists now more than ever to help document and conserve beetles.

As with all my previous books, I share the success of this work with all the aforementioned individuals, but the responsibility for any and all of its shortcomings, misrepresentations, inaccuracies, and omissions falls squarely on my shoulders.

9

UPDATES TO *BEETLES OF EASTERN NORTH AMERICA*

The companion volume to this book, *Beetles of Eastern North America* (Princeton University Press, 2014) covers 1,409 species in all 115 families known to occur east of the Mississippi River. Numerous taxonomic changes that have occurred since its publication, along with corrections for errors of identification, are listed below.

p. 71. *Cylindera unipunctata* (Fabricius) is now known as *Apterodela unipunctata* (Fabricius).

p. 75. Species figured is not Rusty Rib-headed Beetle, *Schizogenius ferrugineus* Putzeys, but is the Pale Slope-rumped Beetle, *Clivina pallida* Say.

p. 106. *Helophoris grandis* Illiger is now in the family Helophoridae. *Hydrochus squamifer* LeConte is now in the family Hydrochidae.

p. 141. Species figured is not *Platydracus maculosus* (Gravenhorst), but likely *P. mysticus* (Erichson).

p. 144. *Platycerus virescens* (Fabricius) is now known as *P. quercus* (Weber).

p. 162. *Maladera castanea* is now known as *Maladera formosae* (Brenske).

p. 180. *Cyphon collaris* (Guérin-Ménèville) is now known as *Nyholmia collaris* (Guérin-Ménèville).

p. 181. *Cyphon padi* (Linnaeus) is now known as *Contacyphon neopadi* Klausnitzer.

p. 182. Species figured is not *Prionocyphon discoideus* (Say), but is *P. limbatus* LeConte.

p. 221. *Limonius griseus* (Palisot de Beauvois) is now known as *Gambrinus griseus* (Palisot de Beauvois).

p. 221. *Limonius stigma* (Herbst) is now known as *Gambrinus stigma* (Herbst).

p. 228. *Cardiophorus cardisce* (Say) is now known as *Paracardiophorus cardisce* (Say).

p. 230. *Dictyoptera munda* (Say) is now known as *Punicealis munda* (Say).

p. 241. *Silis bidentatus* (Say) should be *Ditemnus bidentatus* (Say).

p. 260. *Grynocharis quadrilineata* (Melsheimer) and *Lycoptis americana* (Motschulsky) are now in the family Lophocateridae. *Peltis septentrionalis* (Randall) is now in the family Peltidae.

p. 261. *Thymalus marginatus* Chevrolat is now in the family Thymalidae.

p. 272. Species figured is not *Collops quadrimaculatus* (Fabricius), but *C. balteatus* LeConte.

p. 284. *Henotiderus obesulus* (Casey) is now known as *H. centromaculatus* Reitter.

p. 284. Species figured is not *Caenoscelis basalis* Casey, but *C. ferruginea* (Sahlberg).

p. 307. *Hypodacne punctata* LeConte is now in the family Euxestidae.

p. 307. *Murmidius ovalis* (Beck) is now in the family Murmidiidae.

p. 328. Species figured is not *Eustrophopsis bicolor* (Fabricius), but *Synstrophus repandus* (Horn).

p. 349. *Helops aereus* Germar is now known as *Nalassus aereus* (Germar).

p. 363. *Asclera puncticollis* Say is now known as *Ischnomera puncticollis* (Say).

p. 364. *Asclera ruficollis* Say is now known as *Ischnomera ruficollis* (Say).

p. 384. Image is *Elonus gruberi* Gompel, not *E. basalis* (LeConte).

p. 390. *Tragosoma depsarius* (Linnaeus) in North America is now known as *T. harrisii* (LeConte).

p. 446. Species figured is not *Kuschelina gibbitarsa* (Say), but *K. thoracica* (Fabricius).

p. 492. *Larinus planus* (Fabricius) is now known as *L. carlinae* (Olivier).

GEOGRAPHIC COVERAGE AND CLASSIFICATION

Beetles of Western North America covers 1,428 species in 131 families that occur in Canada and the United States west of the Continental Divide (see map below). The classification presented is that proposed by John Lawrence in the revised edition of Beutel and Leschen (2016), supplemented by Gimmel et al. (2019), Kundrata et al. (2014), and Shin et al. (2017). See the Appendix for Selected References (p. 590) and Classification of the *Beetles of Western North America* (p. 564) for complete bibliographic information and the tribal and subfamilial placement of the species that appear in this book, respectively.

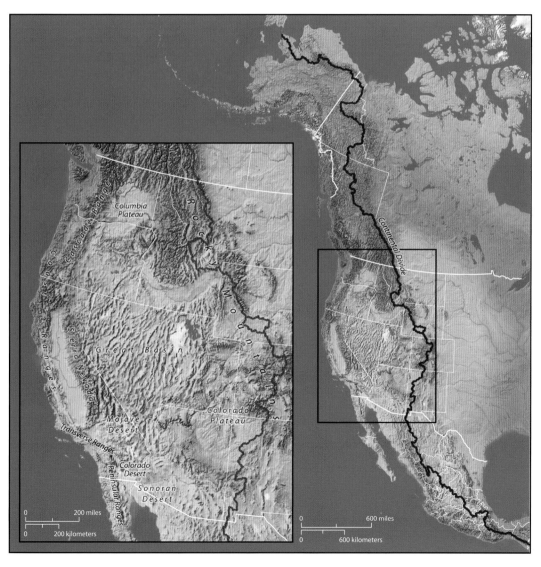

Western North America with inset illustrating major landforms, natural regions, and provincial and state boundaries.

HOW TO USE THIS BOOK

To get the most out of this book, read its introductory sections before venturing out into the field. Once you have become familiar with the lives and bodies of beetles, when and where to look, and the basics of how to collect them, move on to the *family* diagnoses. Learn the diagnostic features that characterize each family, then peruse the individual accounts to get an idea of where and when to look for specific species. Equipped with this information, you will be much better prepared to locate and observe beetles and recognize the specific characteristics that are required for their identification.

ILLUSTRATED KEY TO THE COMMON BEETLE FAMILIES

To assist with the identification of the most commonly encountered beetle families in western North America, a dichotomous key is presented (pp.67–73) consisting of a series of "either-or" choices based on the quality of physical features possessed by a specimen. As with a road map, the reader is directed through a series of junctions called *couplets* that, through a process of elimination, will lead to a smaller and more manageable subset of beetle families. Cross-referenced families in **bold face** are the most likely options, while those in plain text should also be consulted if the bold-faced options don't agree with the specimen in hand.

FAMILY TREATMENTS

Each family treatment includes the family name and its pronunciation, followed by the accepted common name, pronunciation of the scientific family name, a brief overview of the natural history of the species in the family, and a family diagnosis. The *Family Diagnosis* consists of external morphological features that will help to confirm the familial placement of a beetle, including shape, and features of the head, *thorax*, *abdomen*, and appendages. *Similar Families* provides a list of beetle families with species that are superficially similar in appearance, followed by their distinguishing characters. *Fauna* includes the number of

species and genera for each family in Canada and the United States as presented in Marske and Ivie (2003). Updated counts are given, if readily available.

With regard to the pronunciation of family names, I have used Edmund C. Jaeger's *The Biologist's Handbook of Pronunciations* (1960) as a guide. A primer on the proper pronunciation of Latin and Latinized scientific names that addresses the well-known vagaries between North American speakers seldom trained in Latin versus European speakers fluent in one or more Romance languages (and who are generally better versed in Latin), is well beyond the scope of this book. It is understood that Latin is not English, and as Jaeger notes, "It should ever be remembered that while there are formal rules of pronunciation they have not always been observed. Long usage has in certain cases established other ways of sounding some letters, especially vowels, and of placing accents. It is also well to keep in mind that words, especially derived ones, may be pronounced differently by phonetic experts and reputable biologists residing in different countries. The individual preferences are indeed many." In North America, vowels in beetle family names traditionally retain their English sounds, as do consonants, except that "ch" is pronounced "k." It is my hope that readers unfamiliar with beetle family names will find here a foundation on which to learn to pronounce them with a modicum of confidence in the company of North American coleopterists. Following Jaeger, the pronunciations presented in the family diagnoses are indicated by their division into parts (but not necessarily syllables) with hyphens, accents, and diacritical marks pronounced as follows:

â as in far
ā as in bay
ē as in be
ê as in her
ī as in line
ō as in bone
ô as in bore
ū as in blue
û as in urge

SPECIES ACCOUNTS

The species accounts provide the accepted common name (if any), scientific name and authority, length in millimeters, overall form, and color of living beetles. The bright colors (pink, red, orange, yellow, green) of some living beetles frequently fade after death, while metallic colors and iridescence are usually permanent, except in some tortoise beetles (Chrysomelidae). Read the species accounts carefully to discern species-specific features that may not be evident in the photo. As good as the photographs are in this book, they sometimes do not adequately highlight the subtle characters necessary for accurate species identification. Snap judgments based solely on overall appearance and color may result in misidentifications. Information on distinguishing males and females is presented for many species in which the sexes differ markedly from one another externally. Brief notes on seasonality, habitat, food preferences (for adults and occasionally larvae), and distribution are provided and are based, in part, on published accounts and my own field observations. Exotic or adventive species, either purposely or accidentally introduced, are indicated when appropriate. Every effort has been made to ferret out published distributional records and augment them with unpublished data gleaned from websites, local lists, records provided by avocational coleopterists, and specimens examined in select museums. Still, the actual distributions of many species are very likely broader than indicated in this book. When known to me, the total number of species in the genus known to occur west of the Continental Divide is included in parentheses at the end of the account. An accurate count of western taxa within speciose genera was sometimes impractical. In these genera, the number of species is followed by NA to indicate the total number of species in Canada and the United States. These numbers are intended to convey the diversity of the genus and thus alert the reader to the possibility of additional species that are similar in appearance that occur in the region.

IDENTIFICATION

Identifying beetles to genus and species can be challenging. Although many conspicuous species are easily identified by direct comparison with a good photograph, most beetles are small, and the characters necessary for their accurate identification simply cannot be examined without having the specimen in hand. Ideally, it is best to capture and properly prepare a short series of specimens so that

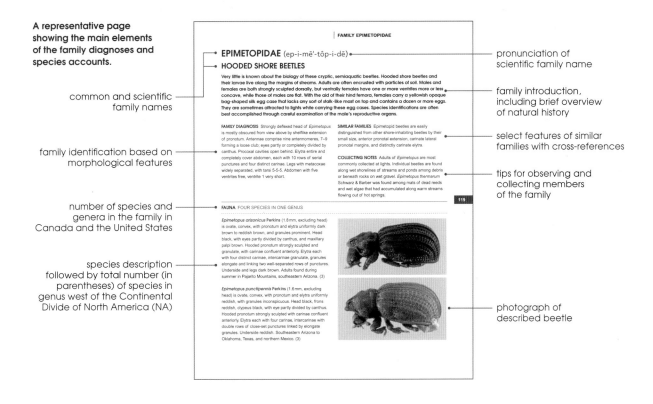

A representative page showing the main elements of the family diagnoses and species accounts.

common and scientific family names

family identification based on morphological features

number of species and genera in the family in Canada and the United States

species description followed by total number (in parentheses) of species in genus west of the Continental Divide of North America (NA)

pronunciation of scientific family name

family introduction, including brief overview of natural history

select features of similar families with cross-references

tips for observing and collecting members of the family

photograph of described beetle

| FAMILY EPIMETOPIDAE

EPIMETOPIDAE (ep-i-mĕ′-tôp-i-dē)
HOODED SHORE BEETLES

Very little is known about the biology of these cryptic, semiaquatic beetles. Hooded shore beetles and their larvae live along the margins of streams. Adults are often encrusted with particles of soil. Males and females are both strongly sculpted dorsally, but ventrally females have one or more ventrites more or less concave, while those of males are flat. With the aid of their hind femora, females carry a yellowish opaque bag-shaped silk egg case that lacks any sort of stalk-like mast on top and contains a dozen or more eggs. They are sometimes attracted to lights while carrying these egg cases. Species identifications are often best accomplished through careful examination of the male's reproductive organs.

FAMILY DIAGNOSIS Strongly deflexed head of *Epimetopus* is mostly obscured from view above by shelflike extension of pronotum. Antennae comprise nine antennomeres, 7–9 forming a loose club; eyes partly or completely divided by canthus. Procoxal cavities open behind. Elytra entire and completely cover abdomen, each with 10 rows of serial punctures and four distinct carinae. Legs with metacoxae widely separated, with tarsi 5-5-5. Abdomen with five ventrites free, ventrite 1 very short.

SIMILAR FAMILIES Epimetopid beetles are easily distinguished from other shore-inhabiting beetles by their small size, anterior pronotal extension, carinate lateral pronotal margins, and distinctly carinate elytra.

COLLECTING NOTES Adults of *Epimetopus* are most commonly collected at lights. Individual beetles are found along wet shorelines of streams and ponds among debris or beneath rocks on wet gravel. *Epimetopus thermarum* Schwarz & Barber was found among mats of dead reeds and wet algae that had accumulated along warm streams flowing out of hot springs.

119

FAUNA FOUR SPECIES IN ONE GENUS

Epimetopus arizonicus Perkins (1.8mm, excluding head) is ovate, convex, with pronotum and elytra uniformly dark brown to reddish brown, and granules prominent. Head black, with eyes partly divided by canthus, and maxillary palpi brown. Hooded pronotum strongly sculpted and granulate, with carinae confluent anteriorly. Elytra each with four distinct carinae, intercarinae granulate, granules elongate and linking two well-separated rows of punctures. Underside and legs dark brown. Adults found during summer in Pajarito Mountains, southeastern Arizona. (3)

Epimetopus punctipennis Perkins (1.6mm, excluding head) is ovate, convex, with pronotum and elytra uniformly reddish, with granules inconspicuous. Head black, frons reddish, clypeus black, with eye partly divided by canthus. Hooded pronotum strongly sculpted with carinae confluent anteriorly. Elytra each with four carinae, intercarinae with double rows of close-set punctures linked by elongate granules. Underside reddish. Southeastern Arizona to Oklahoma, Texas, and northern Mexico. (3)

they are available for detailed microscopic examination. Although 10× or 20× hand lenses are very useful for this purpose, a stereoscopic dissecting microscope with good lighting is ideal. Using a hand lens or microscope to examine specimens takes a bit of practice at first, but once you have mastered these indispensable tools, you will never again waste time by straining your unaided eyes to count tarsomeres and antennomeres or examine genitalia.

Many beetles are positively identified to species only through examination of the male reproductive organs and comparison with detailed illustrations and photos in monographs, or comparison with authoritatively identified specimens that were determined by experts.

Although providing detailed drawings of thousands of beetle reproductive organs is well beyond the scope of this book, it is useful to get into the habit of extracting the male genitalia while the specimen is still fresh and pliable so they can be easily examined by a specialist or compared with literature that depicts the genital structures of closely related species. You can extract the genitalia from the posterior opening of the abdomen by gently pulling them out with fine-tipped forceps or with the aid of a fish-hooked insect pin. Removing genitalia from dried specimens requires that the specimen first be softened in a relaxing chamber, or placed in boiling water with a few drops of dish soap added as a wetting agent. Once the genitalia are extracted, you can leave them attached to the tip of the abdomen by their own tissue, where they will dry in place, or remove them entirely and glue to an insect mounting point placed on the pin between the mounted beetle and its locality label for later examination. Some beetles, especially very small species, require specialized techniques for extracting and preserving their genitalia. Consult the pertinent literature or a specialist before undertaking the dissection of these specimens.

Readers requiring accurate species identification, especially for control of horticultural, agricultural, and forest pests, are encouraged to consult coleopterists affiliated with cooperative extension offices or the entomology department of a museum or university for verification.

INTRODUCTION TO BEETLES

BEETLE MORPHOLOGY

Although colors and patterns are sometimes useful, beetles are classified and more reliably identified based on their morphological features. Therefore, a basic understanding of beetle morphology (Fig. 1) is essential for better understanding of not only their evolutionary relationships, but also the terminology used in the family diagnoses and species accounts that appear in this book.

Figure 1. Dorsal and ventral views, *Harpalus* (Carabidae).

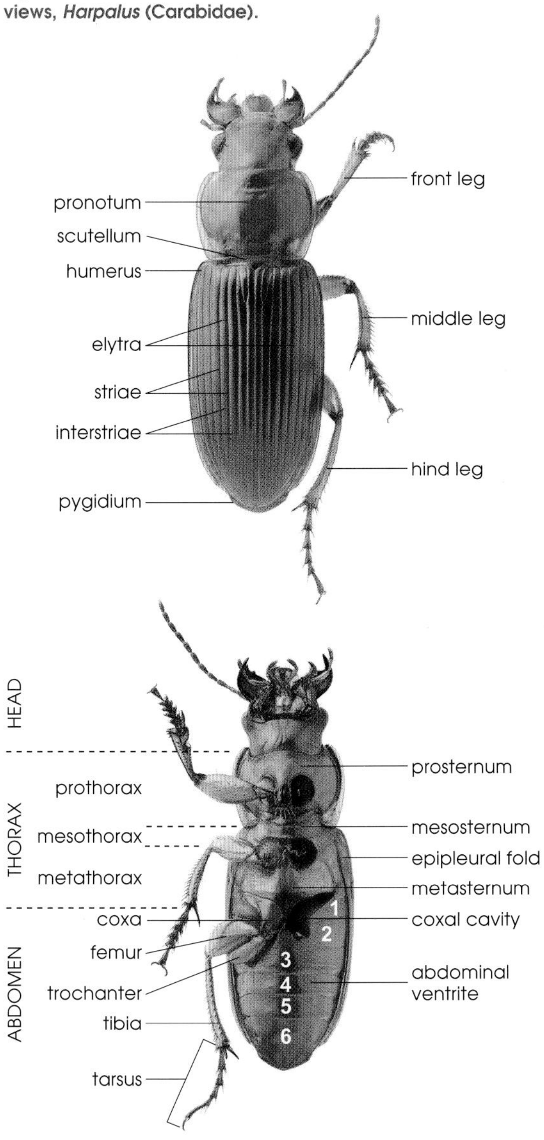

pronotum
scutellum
humerus
front leg
elytra
striae
interstriae
middle leg
pygidium
hind leg

HEAD
THORAX
ABDOMEN
prothorax
mesothorax
metathorax
coxa
femur
trochanter
tibia
tarsus
prosternum
mesosternum
epipleural fold
metasternum
coxal cavity
abdominal ventrite
1
2
3
4
5
6

EXOSKELETON

Adult beetles are protected by a highly modified *exoskeleton* that functions as both skeleton and skin. Internally, the exoskeleton serves as a foundation for powerful muscles and organ systems, while externally providing a platform for important sensory structures that connect beetles to their surrounding environment. The exoskeleton is light, yet durable, and composed of a multilayered structure comprising the polysaccharide *chitin* and the protein *sclerotin*.

The exoskeleton is subdivided into *segments*, some of which are composed of smaller plates, or *sclerites*. The segments are joined into functional units that form three body regions (head, thorax, abdomen) and appendages (mouthparts, antennae, legs). Segments are joined together by membranes of pure chitin or separated by narrow furrows called *sutures*. The division of the exoskeleton into body regions and appendages affords flexibility to beetle bodies, much the way the joints and plates of armor allowed knights to maneuver in battle.

BODY SHAPE

When viewed from above, the basic body shape (Fig. 2) of a beetle is variously described as elongate, oval, triangular, or antlike, among other descriptors. Parallel-sided refers to the straight and parallel sides of the body. Terms like *convex*, *hemispherical*, flat, and flattened are also useful for describing the upper or *dorsal* surface. These descriptors are best determined when beetles are viewed from the side. Lady beetles (Coccinellidae) and some leaf beetles (Chrysomelidae) are sometimes referred to as "hemispherical" because their dorsal surfaces are very convex, while the *ventral* surface or underside is relatively flat. *Cylindrical* is usually applied to elongate, parallel-sided species with convex dorsal and ventral surfaces and suggests that they would appear almost circular in cross section.

SURFACE SCULPTURING

The nature of the outer surface of beetle exoskeletons, or surface sculpturing, is very useful in species identification. Surfaces can be shiny like patent leather or dulled (*alutaceous*) by a minute network of fine cracks resembling those of human skin. The surfaces of the head and legs,

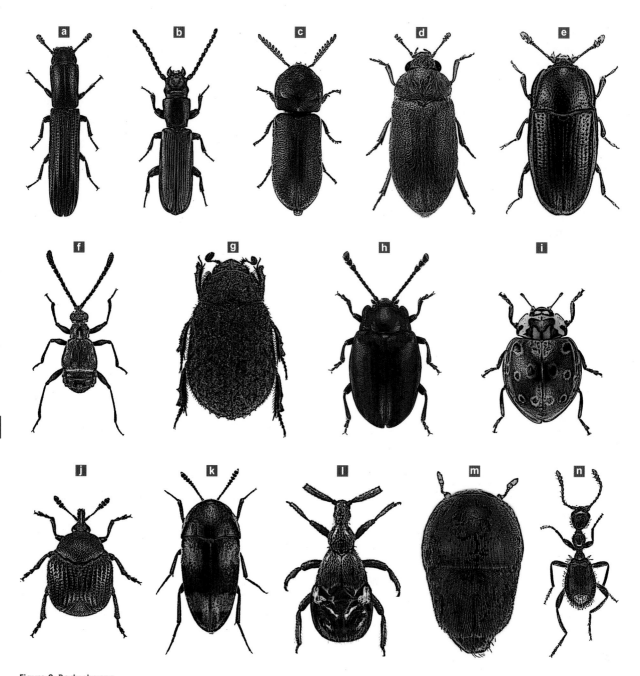

Figure 2. Body shapes.
a. elongate, Zopheridae; b. elongate, Passandridae; c. elliptical, Ptinidae; d. elongate-oval, Byturidae; e. elongate-oval, Cerylonidae; f. elongate-oval, Staphylinidae; g. oval, Trogidae; h. oval, Endomychidae; i. broadly oval, Coccinellidae; j. broadly oval, Brentidae; k. obovate, Tetratomidae; l. triangular, Staphylinidae; m. limuloid, Staphylinidae; n. antlike, Staphylinidae.

especially in burrowing species, are sometimes dulled by normal abrasion as the beetle burrows through soil or wood. Sometimes the surface is *glaucous*, or coated with a grayish or bluish coating of waterproof wax secreted by epidermal glands underlying the exoskeleton. This coating is easily rubbed off or dissolved in chemical preservatives and is usually evident only in freshly emerged individuals.

Shiny or not, many beetle bodies are typically covered to varying degrees with small pits called *punctures*. Punctures range from very small (*finely punctate*) to large (*coarsely punctate*) and may be shallow or deep. The density or distance of punctures from one another is often reported in terms of the degree of separation in relation to the puncture's diameter. *Contiguous* or nearly contiguous punctures are those with their rims in contact with one another, or nearly so. *Cribrate* surfaces are those where irregular punctures are so closely spaced that the surface appears perforated, while *rugose* (rough) surfaces have raised areas formed by small wrinkles, distinct ridges, tubercles, or fingerprint-like whorls. *Granulate* surfaces consist of many small, distinct, and rounded tubercles, like the pebbled surface of a basketball. An *impunctate* surface lacks punctures altogether.

Punctures sometimes bear a single hairlike *seta* (pl. *setae*). Setae are fine or bristly, stand straight up (*erect*), nearly straight (*suberect*), or lie nearly flat on the surface (*recumbent*). Flattened setae, or *scales*, range in outline from nearly round, to *oval* (egg-shaped), *obovate* (pear-shaped), *lanceolate* (spear-shaped) to *linear* (long and slender). Densely setose or scaled surfaces may be partially or completely obscured from view, while the complete absence of setae or scales altogether is referred to as *glabrous*.

HEAD AND ITS APPENDAGES

The capsule-shaped head (Fig. 3) is attached to the thorax by a flexible, membranous neck that is sometimes visible from above (e.g., Meloidae) but usually hidden, along with part of the head, within the first thoracic *segment*, or *prothorax*. In the fireflies (Lampyridae), some hooded beetles (Corylophidae), and other beetle families, the head is completely hidden from above by a hoodlike extension of the dorsal *sclerite* of the prothorax, or *pronotum*.

The compound eyes are usually conspicuous and composed of dozens or hundreds of individual facets or lenses. Awash in light, the lenses of day-active (*diurnal*) beetles are relatively small and flat, while nocturnal species have more convex lenses adapted for gathering all available light. Flightless, cave-dwelling, and subterranean species often have small compound eyes with only a few lenses or may lack eyes altogether. Compound eyes are typically round, or oval to kidney-shaped in outline. The front margins of kidney-shaped eyes may be weakly to strongly notched, or *emarginate*; the antennae of some

species may originate within or near the emargination. The eyes are sometimes partially divided in front by a narrow ridge of cuticle, called the *canthus*. In whirligigs (Gyrinidae) and some throscids (Throscidae) and longhorn beetles (Cerambycidae), the canthus completely divides the eye. Some skin beetles (Dermestidae) and omaline rove beetles (Staphylinidae) also possess a simple eye, or *ocellus*, comprising a single lens located on the front of the head between the compound eyes.

The males of several species of Geotrupidae and Scarabaeidae have horns on their heads modified into spikes and scooped blades that are used in mostly "bloodless" battles with other males of the same species over resources that will attract females. The variation of horn size in males of the same species is of particular interest to scientists who study sexual selection. Environmental factors, especially larval nutrition, may play a more important role in horn development than genetic factors. Although outgunned in battle, less endowed males are still fully capable of mating with females and fertilizing their eggs when the opportunity arises.

The mouthparts of all beetles follow the same basic plan: an upper lip (*labrum*), a pair of *mandibles* and *maxillae*, and a lower lip (*labium*). Although the mandibles of beetles are variously modified to cut and tear flesh (e.g., Carabidae), grind leaves (e.g., Chrysomelidae), or strain fluids (some Scarabaeidae), they also serve other purposes. The outsized mandibles of male *Lucanus mazama* (Lucanidae) and *Archodontes melanopus aridus* (Cerambycidae) are not used for feeding at all, but likely have a role in sexual selection. The relatively short and powerful mandibles of the California Prionus, *Prionus californicus* (Cerambycidae), are used as weapons for defense. Male tiger beetles (Carabidae) use their mandibles to firmly grasp the female during copulation. Attached to the *maxilla* and labium are delicate, flexible, fingerlike structures, or *palps*, that assist beetles in the manipulation of food. The long and conspicuous maxillary palps of water scavengers (Hydrophilidae) are easily mistaken for antennae. Each palp is divided into articles called *palpomeres*. Protecting

17

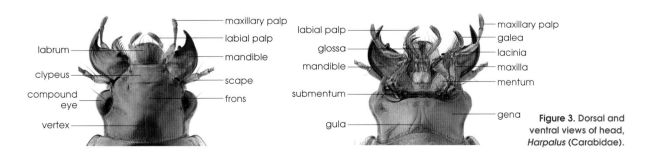

maxillary palp
labial palp
labrum
mandible
clypeus
scape
compound eye
frons
vertex

labial palp
glossa
mandible
submentum
gula
maxillary palp
galea
lacinia
maxilla
mentum
gena

Figure 3. Dorsal and ventral views of head, *Harpalus* (Carabidae).

18

Figure 4. Mouthpart orientation.
a. prognathous head, *Trichocnemis* (Cerambycidae); b. hypognathous mouthparts are directed downward, perpendicular to the long axis of the body, *Chrysochus* (Chrysomelidae); c. rostrate mouthparts are directed downward and are typical of most plant feeding beetles, *Curculio* (Curculionidae); d. maxillae form elongate sucking tube extending posteriorly under body, *Nemognatha* (Meloidae).

BELOW: **Figure 5.**
Parts of the antenna, *Harpalus* (Carabidae).

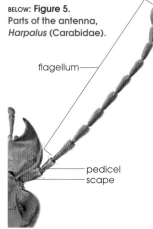

flagellum

pedicel
scape

the mouthparts from above in most beetles is a broad plate of cuticle formed by the leading edge of the head, or *clypeus*. Underneath the head of most beetles is a sclerite analogous with a lower lip called the *labium*. At the base of the labium are two more sclerites: *mentum* and *gula*.

The mouthparts of beetles vary in terms of their orientation related to the long axis of the body (Fig. 4a–d). For example, the mouthparts of predatory and some wood-boring beetles are typically *prognathous*, and are directed forward and aligned with the long axis of the body. *Hypognathous* mouthparts are directed downward and typical of most plant-feeding beetles, including chafers (Scarabaeidae), some longhorn beetles (Cerambycidae), leaf beetles (Chrysomelidae), and weevils (Curculionidae). The hypognathous mouthparts of some net-winged beetles (Lycidae) and narrow-waisted beetles (Salpingidae), and many weevils (Curculionidae) and their relatives are drawn out into a relatively short or elongate *rostrum*.

For most beetles, the primary organs of smell and touch are the *antennae*. These structures are usually attached to the front or sides of the head, often between the eyes and the bases of the mandibles. Although the antennae exhibit an incredible diversity of sizes and shapes, they all consist of three basic parts: *scape*, *pedicel*, and *flagellum* (Fig. 5). Insect morphologists note that only the scape and pedicel have their own internal musculature and thus are the only true antennal segments, while the remaining articles of the flagellum lack any intrinsic musculature and are called *flagellomeres*. Distinguishing segments and flagellomeres to communicate information about the number of antennal

Figure 6. Basic antennal types of beetles.
a. filiform, *Callidium* (Cerambycidae);
b. moniliform, *Cucujus* (Cucujidae);
c. serrate, *Chalcolepidius* (Elateridae);
d. pectinate, *Emelinus* (Aderidae);
e. pectinate, *Euthysanius* (Elateridae);
f. bipectinate, *Zarhipis* (Phengodidae);
g. flabellate, *Ptilophorus* (Ripiphoridae);
h. clavate, *Eurymycter* (Anthribidae);
i. capitate, *Bactridium* (Monotomidae);
j. lamellate, *Polyphylla* (Scarabaeidae);
k. geniculate, *Cactophagus*
(Curculionidae).

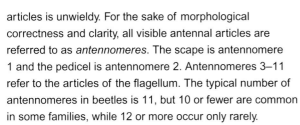

articles is unwieldy. For the sake of morphological correctness and clarity, all visible antennal articles are referred to as *antennomeres*. The scape is antennomere 1 and the pedicel is antennomere 2. Antennomeres 3–11 refer to the articles of the flagellum. The typical number of antennomeres in beetles is 11, but 10 or fewer are common in some families, while 12 or more occur only rarely.

Beetle antennae are generally shorter than the body and somewhat similar in both sexes. In longhorn beetles (Cerambycidae), males are often distinguished by antennae that reach or exceed the elytral apices, while those of the female are distinctly shorter. For example, male pine sawyers in the genus *Monochamus* have long, threadlike antennae up to three times the length of the body, while those of the

female are only slightly longer than the body. In other species, the expanded surfaces of ornate antennal modifications possessed by male *Polyphylla*, *Sandalus*, *Zarhipis*, and *Euthysanius* are packed with sensory pits capable of tracking pheromones released by distant or secretive females.

The principal forms of beetle antennae (Fig. 6) include the following:

- *filiform*, or threadlike, with antennomeres uniformly cylindrical, or nearly so
- *moniliform*, or beadlike, with round antennomeres of uniform size
- *serrate*, or saw-toothed, with flattened, triangular antennomeres

■ *pectinate*, or comblike, with short antennomeres each bearing a prolonged extension (ramus)

■ *bipectinate*, or comblike, with short antennomeres each bearing two prolonged extensions (rami)

■ *flabellate*, or fanlike, with antennomeres bearing long extensions (rami) that fit together like a fan

■ *plumose*, or featherlike, with antennomeres bearing long, slender, flexible extensions (rami)

■ *clavate*, with outermost antennomeres gradually enlarged to form a distinct symmetrical *club*

■ *capitate*, with outermost antennomeres abruptly enlarged to form a round or oval symmetrical club

■ *lamellate*, with outermost antennomeres flat, forming a distinct, lopsided club

■ *geniculate*, or elbowed, with a long, slender scape with pedicel and flagellomeres attached at a distinct angle; pedicel and flagellomeres (including club), are collectively referred to as the *funicle*

THORAX AND ITS APPENDAGES

As with all insects, the beetle thorax is divided into three segments, the *prothorax*, *mesothorax*, and *metathorax*, each bearing a pair of legs. The underside of the thorax is sometimes modified with impressions or distinct grooves that accommodate the antennae or legs.

The prothorax is always exposed and forms the distinctive "midsection" of the beetle body, while the remaining wing-bearing mesothorax and metathorax, collectively known as the *pterothorax*, are hidden beneath the modified mesothoracic wings, or *elytra*. The prothorax is either firmly or loosely attached to the pterothorax. The dorsal sclerite of the prothorax, or *pronotum*, is sometimes hoodlike and extends forward to partially (e.g., Corylophidae) or completely (e.g., Lampyridae) obscure the head when viewed from above. In some males, the pronotal surface is modified with horns, punctures, tubercles, or ridges that are useful in species identification. The sides, or *lateral* margins of the prothorax are partly or completely sharply ridged or carinate (e.g., Carabidae, Gyrinidae, Dytiscidae), or distinctly rounded (e.g., Meloidae, some Cerambycidae). The lateral and posterior margins of the pronotum are sometimes narrowly or broadly flattened (*explanate*), or may have a narrow seam, or marginal bead, along the edge. The portion of the pronotum below the lateral *carina* is called the *hypomeron*, sometimes referred to as the *pronotal epipleuron*. The central portion of the underside of the prothorax, or *prosternum*, is sometimes attenuated into a spinelike structure directed toward the head or backward. The prosternum is flanked on either side

by the *propleuron*. Sometimes the propleuron is divided into two sclerites by the *pleural suture*; the sclerite in front is called the *proepisternum*, while the sclerite behind is the *proepimeron*. A distinct line or suture that delimits the outer portion by separating the propleuron from the *hypomeron* is called the *notopleural suture* in families in the suborder Adephaga, including Carabidae, Gyrinidae, Haliplidae, and Dytiscidae. The front legs are inserted into prothoracic cavities called *procoxal cavities*. Although sometimes very difficult to see, the nature of these cavities is important in the identification of families, subfamilies, and tribes of beetles. If the cavities are enclosed behind by the *proepimeron*, or the junction of the proepimeron and the prosternum, they are said to be "closed behind" (Fig. 7a). If these cavities open directly to the mesothorax, they are said to be "open behind" (Fig. 7b).

The thoracic segments of the pterothorax are broadly united with one another and are covered by the elytra. The mesothorax bears the middle legs below and is evident dorsally in many beetles by the presence of a small

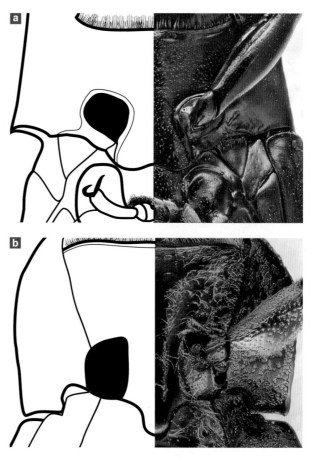

Figure 7. Procoxal cavities.
a. closed; b. open.

triangular or shield-shaped sclerite called the *scutellum*. When visible, the scutellum is always located between the posterior pronotal margin and *elytral suture*, the line straight down the back when the elytra meet one another.

The metathorax bears the hind legs and, if present, the flight wings folded beneath the elytra. The hind coxae are usually wide, or *transverse*. In the adephagan families Carabidae, Gyrinidae, Haliplidae, and Dytiscidae, the hind coxae are immovably fused to the *metasternum* and extend backward past the first abdominal *ventrite*, and thus are said to completely divide the first ventrite. In crawling water beetles (Haliplidae), the hind coxae form broad plates that conceal nearly the entire abdomen, a feature that distinguishes them from all other beetle families. In non-adephagan beetle families, the hind coxae are "free," or not fused to the metasternum and do not extend past or "divide" the first abdominal ventrite. The segments of the pterothorax are usually somewhat shortened in wingless (*apterous*) and reduced-wing (*brachypterous*) species.

The most conspicuous and unique feature of nearly all adult beetles is their possession of modified forewings called elytra (sing. *elytron*) that partially or completely cover the abdomen. The elytra are opaque, soft, and leathery, like those in the elateroid families Lycidae, Phengodidae, Lampyridae, and Cantharidae, or hard and shell-like. At rest, the elytra usually meet over the middle of the back along a distinct and straight line called the *elytral suture*. The tips the elytra, or *elytral apices*, usually meet at the elytral suture, too, although in some species they are slightly divergent. Distinctly diverging elytral apices, such as those of *Lichnanthe* (Glaphyridae) are referred to as *dehiscent*. The bases of the elytra more or less meet at the posterior margin of the pronotum. The outer basal shoulderlike angle of each elytron is called the *humerus* (pl. *humeri*). Punctures irregularly scattered over the elytral surface are referred to as *confused*. Elytra with punctures arranged in rows either are (*punctostriate*) or are not (*punctoseriate*) connected by narrowly impressed longitudinal lines, or *striae*. The spaces between striae are called *intervals* or *interstriae*. The portion of side margins of each elytron that is folded downward is called the *epipleural fold*. Bordering the epipleural fold is a narrow inner edge, or *epipleuron* (pl. *epipleura*) that is of variable width and may or may not extend to the elytral apices. A *pseudepipleuron* is when the lateral elytral *declivity* drops sharply down and inward before the actual epipleuron.

The elytra are typically short in the rove (Staphylinidae), clown (Histeridae), and sap beetles (Nitidulidae), as well as in some genera of longhorn beetles (Cerambycidae). The elytral apices are often *truncate* and straight, appearing as

if they were cut off, or emarginate and flanked or not by one or two tooth- or spinelike projections. The elytra of male *Phengodes* (Phengodidae) are abruptly narrowed apically and oar-shaped, while those of *Ripiphorus* (Ripiphoridae) resemble flaplike scales. In flight, the elytra of most species are lifted and separated when airborne. However, in the fruit chafer genera *Cremastocheilus*, *Cotinis*, and *Euphoria* (Scarabaeidae), and in metallic wood-boring beetles in the genus *Acmaeodera* (Buprestidae), the elytra are partially or totally fused along the elytral suture. When taking to the air, these fast-flying beetles lift their elytra slightly as the membranous flight wings are unfolded and extended through broad notches along the lateral margins near the bases.

The membranous flight wings are supported by a network of hemolymph-filled veins that help them to expand or fold. Some of these veins are hinged so that the wings can be carefully tucked and folded under the elytra. Flight wings are seldom used to identify genera or species, but their venation patterns do offer important clues to the relationships of families. The flight wings of *brachypterous* species are reduced in size, while those lacking these wings altogether are *apterous*. Adult *larviform* females of some Lampyridae, Phengodidae, and Dermestidae may have elytra greatly reduced in size or absent altogether and superficially resemble larvae (Fig. 8).

Beetle legs are subdivided into six segments (Fig. 9). The *coxa* (pl. *coxae*) is generally short and stout, and firmly anchors the leg into the coxal cavity of the thorax while allowing for the horizontal to-and-fro movement of the legs. The *trochanter* is usually small, freely movable in relation to the coxa, but fixed to the femur. The *femur* (pl. *femora*) is the largest and most powerful leg segment and greatly enlarged in jumping species of Scirtidae and Chrysomelidae. The usually long and slender *tibia* (pl. *tibiae*) is sometimes modified into a rakelike structure on the forelegs of burrowing species. The *tarsus* (pl. *tarsi*) is typically divided into multiple articles called *tarsomeres* that lack their own internal musculature, and is terminated by the claw-bearing segment, or *pretarsus*.

The tarsi are of particular value in beetle identification. Each tarsus consists of up to five tarsomeres. The three-digit tarsal formulas used in this book, such as 5-5-5, 5-5-4, or 4-4-4, indicate the number of tarsomeres on the front, middle, and hind legs, respectively. In some species, the penultimate *tarsomere* is small and difficult to see without careful examination under high magnification. The tarsal formulae of these beetles are typically denoted as "appears 4-4-4, but actually 5-5-5". The front tarsi of some male predaceous diving beetles, such as *Cybister*

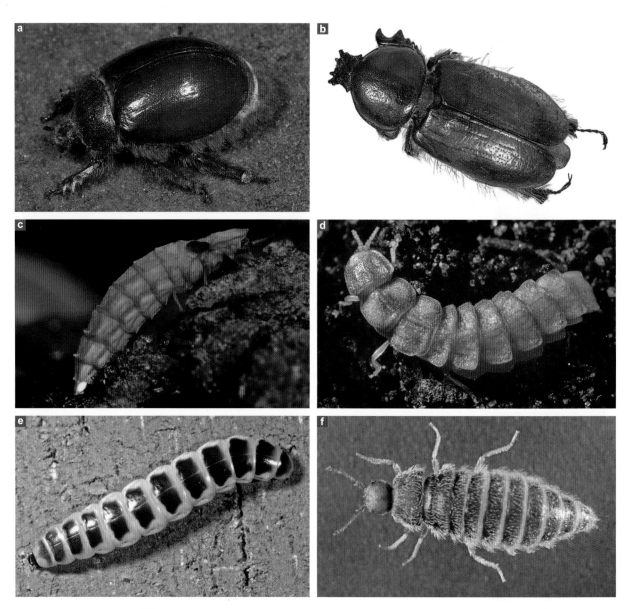

Figure 8. Brachypterous, apterous, and larviform females.
a. *Pleocoma* (Pleocomidae); b. *Diphyllostoma*
(Diphyllostomatidae); c. *Pleotomus* (Lampyridae);
d. *Microphotus* (Lampyridae); e. *Zarhipis* (Phengodidae);
f. *Thylodrias* (Dermestidae).

Figure 9. Hind leg, *Harpalus* (Carabidae).

and *Dytiscus* (Dytiscidae), are highly modified with adhesive pads underneath that enable them to grasp the female's smooth and slippery elytra while mating. In male *Phanaeus* (Scarabaeidae), the front tarsi are absent altogether. The feet of some longhorn beetles (Cerambycidae) and leaf beetles (Chrysomelidae) are equipped with broad, brushy pads underneath that are tightly packed with setae, enabling them to walk on smooth vertical surfaces or cling to uncooperative mates. Cicada parasite beetles (Rhipiceridae) and some click beetles

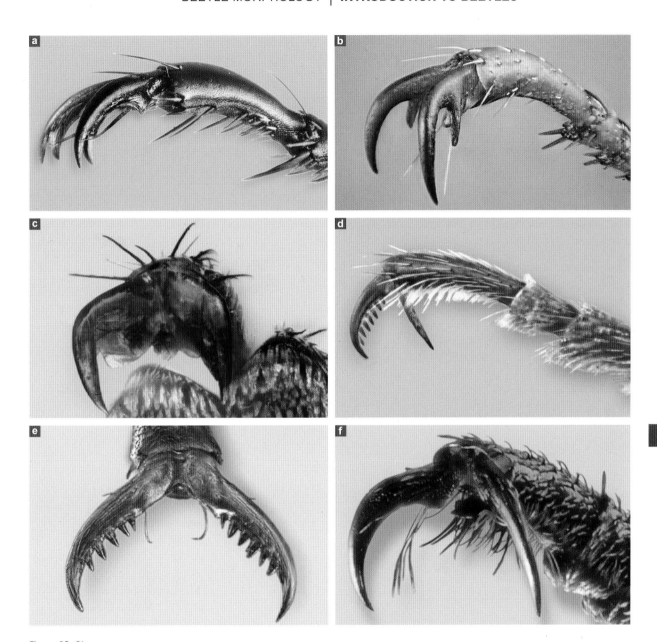

Figure 10. Claws.
a. cleft, *Macrodactylus* (Scarabaeidae); b. toothed, *Polyphylla* (Scarabaeidae); c. appendiculate, *Oberea* (Cerambycidae);
d. pectinate, *Melanotus* (Elateridae); e. serrate, *Synuchus* (Carabidae); f. simple, *Alaus* (Elateridae).

23

(Elateridae) have tarsomeres bearing membranous flaps
that project outward.

The claws of beetles are frequently modified (Fig. 10).
Cleft or *incised* claws are finely split at the apex. *Toothed*
claws have one or more distinct teeth underneath on the
claw blade. *Appendiculate* claws have a broad flange at the
base of the blade. *Serrate* claws have finely notched blades
resembling the teeth of a saw, while *pectinate* claws have
blades with fine, comblike teeth. *Simple* claws, which are
typical of many beetles, lack any such modifications.

ABDOMEN

Beetles typically have 10 abdominal segments, but only five
or six segments are usually visible. Each of these segments
is more or less ringlike and consists of only two sclerites:
a dorsal *tergum* (pl. *terga*) or *tergite*, and the ventral
sternum (pl. *sterna*). Beetle tergites covered by the elytra
are usually thin and flexible, but those exposed in beetles
with short elytra tend to be thicker and more rigid. The
penultimate and ultimate tergites are called the *propygidium*
and *pygidium*, respectively. The pleural membranes are

usually more or less hidden from view. Breathing pores, or *spiracles*, are located in the pleural membrane and/or in the lateral-most regions of the tergites or *ventrites*.

The visible abdominal sternites are called *ventrites*, and each is numbered beginning from the base of the abdomen regardless of the true morphological segment it represents. For example, ventrite 1 is usually abdominal sternite 2 or 3. The ventrites are of varying lengths in relation to one another and are either distinctly or barely separated by deep to shallow sutures or narrow membranes. Ventrites that are fused together, as evidenced by shallow or obsolete sutures, are *connate*, while "free" ventrites are those that are separated by distinct sutures or membranes. In some families, some or all of the ventrites are connate.

The remaining abdominal segments are internal, the most posterior of which are variously modified for reproductive activities: egg laying in females and copulation in males. Long *ovipositors* are characteristic of beetles that deposit their eggs deep in sand or plant tissues, while short and stout ovipositors are indicative of species that deposit their eggs directly on

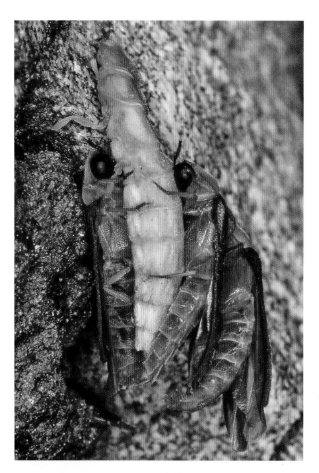

Figure 11. Larviform female pink glowworm with three males, *Microphotus angustus* (Lampyridae).

the surface of various substrates. The often elaborate and distinctive male reproductive organs are of considerable value in species identification and are sometimes the only means of distinguishing closely related species.

BEHAVIOR AND NATURAL HISTORY

The mating behaviors, developmental strategies, and life cycles of all beetles in western North America assure their reproductive success by maximizing their efforts to locate mates, eliminating competition for food and space between larvae and adults, and adapts them to cope with dramatic seasonal shifts in temperatures that typify a temperate climate. With their compact and armored bodies, chewing mouthparts, and modified legs, beetles are equipped to occupy and thrive in diverse habitats. Both adults and larvae chew, burrow, mine, and swim their way through sandy coastal beaches, chaparral, coastal and montane forests, arid desert dunes, backyards, urban parks, and agricultural fields. The ability of most beetles to fly increases their chances of finding food and mates, and affords them opportunities to seek out and colonize new habitats.

MATING BEHAVIOR

With relatively short lifespans lasting only weeks or months, most beetles have little time to waste in finding mates. They have evolved various channels of communication that enhance their efforts at finding a mate, including scent, sight (Fig. 11), or sound. These strategies are often remarkably effective, luring in numerous eager mates from considerable distances. Sex-attractant *pheromones* are used by many species to attract and locate mates over long distances. Males of these species often have longer or more elaborate antennal structures (e.g., Scarabaeidae, Ptilodactylidae, Rhipiceridae, Phengodidae, some Elateridae, Ripiphoridae, Cerambycidae) that provide more surface area for incredibly sensitive sensory pits capable of detecting just a few molecules of the female's pheromone wafting about in the air. These males typically track and locate females by flying in a zigzag pattern until they cross through the female's "odor plume" of pheromone. Once the plume is located, the male follows the increasing concentration of pheromone molecules directly to its source.

The best-known example of visual communication in beetles is that of *bioluminescence*. Bioluminescence is characteristic of some western fireflies, larval and adult female glowworms (Fig. 12), as well as some click beetles. The whitish, greenish-yellow, or reddish light emanating from these insects is produced by special abdominal (e.g., Lampyridae, Phengodidae) or pronotal (e.g., Elateridae) organs. The tissues within these light-producing organs are supplied with oxygen via numerous tracheae. The brightness and duration of the light are controlled by the nervous system that regulates the amount of oxygen reaching these organs and reacting with the pigment luciferin, a chemical reaction sped up by the presence of the enzyme luciferase. The quality of the light produced varies depending on species, as well as temperature and humidity. Bioluminescence in fireflies is virtually 100% efficient, with almost all the energy that goes into the system given off as light. In fact, the light produced by just one firefly produces 1/80,000 of the heat produced by a candle flame of the same brightness. By comparison, notoriously inefficient incandescent lightbulbs lose up to 90% of their electrical energy as heat.

Some male death-watch beetles (Ptinidae) tap their heads against the walls of their wooden galleries to lure females into their tunnels, but most beetles produce sound by rubbing two ridged or roughened surfaces together, a behavior known as *stridulation*. Stridulation generally occurs during courtship, confrontations with other beetles, or in response to other stressful situations, such as attack by a predator. Longhorn (Cerambycidae), June (Scarabaeidae), and bark beetles (Curculionidae) stridulate by rubbing their elytra with their legs or abdomen to create a chirping or squeaking sound when alarmed, possibly to startle predators; some aquatic species stridulate by rubbing their elytra and abdomen together. Stridulatory communication between larvae and adults of the same species occurs, too, possibly as a means to help keep offspring and their parents in close proximity to one another, a theory partly supported by the dependence of some larvae on adults for a steady food supply. For example, hungry *Nicrophorus* larvae are summoned to feed on carrion specially prepared by their parents. These stridulating beetles rub a pair of abdominal files against the underside of their elytra to produce sounds likened to ringing a dinner bell.

Elaborate courtship behaviors in beetles are rare, although some species may engage in nibbling (Cantharidae), licking (Cerambycidae), or antenna pulling (Meloidae) just prior to copulation. In most species of beetles, the male typically mounts the female from above and behind (Fig. 13). Females usually have enormous reserves of eggs awaiting

25

ABOVE: **Figure 12.** Bioluminescent *Zarhipis* (Phengodidae) larva.

Figure 13. Mating jewel beetles, *Gyascutus planicosta* (Buprestidae).

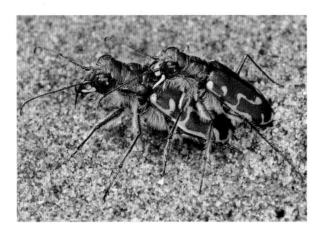

Figure 14. Mate guarding or postinsemination association, *Cicindela hirticollis gravida* (Carabidae).

fertilization, but need to mate only once, despite being courted by numerous enthusiastic males responding to their pheromones. Sperm is usually stored internally in a saclike reservoir called the *spermatheca*. Fertilization does not occur until her eggs travel past the spermatheca, just as they are about to be laid. In these females, it is the sperm of the last male that fertilizes the eggs. To assure their paternity, male tiger beetles (Carabidae) continue to tightly grasp their partners with their mandibles (Fig. 14) after copulation is completed until the eggs are laid, a behavior called *postinsemination association*.

Not all species of beetles must mate to reproduce. *Parthenogenesis*—development from an unfertilized egg—occurs among several families of beetles, including leaf beetles (Chrysomelidae) and weevils (Curculionidae). Males of parthenogenetic species are rare or unknown

Figure 15. *Canthon indigaceus* (Scarabaeidae) on dung ball.

altogether. The females of these species are solely responsible for maintaining the population and do so by producing cloned offspring.

PARENTAL CARE

For most beetles, care of offspring is limited to selection of the egg-laying site by the female. However, some species engage in relatively elaborate behaviors to ensure the survival of their eggs and larvae. For example, some ground beetles (Carabidae) deposit their eggs in carefully constructed cells of mud, twigs, and leaves, while a few water scavenger (Hydrophilidae) and minute moss beetles (Hydraenidae) enclose their eggs singly or in batches within cocoons made of silk secreted by special glands in the female's reproductive system. Depending on the species, leaf beetles (Chrysomelidae) apply a protective coating of their own feces to their eggs that are laced with distasteful chemicals sequestered from the tissues of the host plant. Leaf-mining metallic wood-boring beetles (Buprestidae) and weevils (Curculionidae) provide their offspring with both food and shelter by sandwiching their eggs between the upper and lower surfaces of leaves. Some longhorn beetles provide their larvae with dead wood by girdling, or chewing, a ring around a living tree branch and laying their eggs on the soon-to-be-dead outer tip. Dying branch tips quickly turn brown, a phenomenon called *flagging*, and stand in stark contrast to healthy green foliage. The girdle eventually weakens the branch, causing it to break and fall to the ground where the larvae can feed and develop inside, undisturbed. Female leaf-rolling weevils (Attelabidae) cut the leaf's midrib before laying their eggs in the rolled-up portion of the leaf.

Dung scarabs (Scarabaeidae) and *Nicrophorus* burying beetles (Silphidae) exhibit varying degrees of parental care well beyond the egg stage. Both males and females may cooperate in digging nests for their eggs and provision them with dung (Fig. 15) or carrion, respectively, for their brood. Dung and carrion are rich in nutrients, and competition for these resources can be fierce. Many dung- and carrion-feeding beetles have evolved tunneling or burying behaviors to quickly hide excrement or dead animals from the view of other scavenger species. Burial not only secures food for their young, it also helps to maintain optimum moisture levels for successful brood development. *Nicrophorus* beetles exhibit the most advanced form of parental care known in beetles. They meticulously prepare corpses as food for their young by removing feathers and fur, reshape them by removing or manipulating legs, wings, and tail, all while coating the carcass in saliva laced with antimicrobials that slow decomposition. Females deposit their eggs in the burial chamber and remain with their young larvae as they feed and develop. The brood's first meal consists of droplets of chewed carrion regurgitated by their mother in a broad depression on the carcass.

Ambrosia and bark beetles (Curculionidae) also provide food and shelter for their young, carving elaborate galleries beneath the bark of trees or in galleries that penetrate the sapwood. Adult females cultivate and store *ambrosia* fungus in their *mycangia*, specialized pits on their bodies. As they colonize and tunnel into new trees, they introduce the "starter" ambrosia fungus into the brood chambers, where it will be used as food for both themselves and their developing larvae.

METAMORPHOSIS AND DEVELOPMENT

Beetles develop by a process called *holometaboly*, or complete metamorphosis, that usually involves four distinct stages: egg, *larva*, *pupa*, and adult (Fig. 16). The egg stage is sometimes absent in telephone-pole beetles (Micromalthidae), while the pupal stage may be greatly modified in female glowworms (Phengodidae) and some female fireflies (Lampyridae). Each developmental stage is adapted to a particular season and set of environmental factors that ultimately enhance the individual beetle's ability to survive unfavorable conditions. Adults and larvae are often not found together in the same place at the same time, thereby functioning in the environment as two distinct species. The spatial and temporal separation of the larvae and adults within the same species effectively eliminates competition for the basic resources of food and space.

Females lay their eggs singly or in batches (Fig. 17) through a membranous and sometimes very long tube, or *ovipositor*, usually on or near suitable larval foods. Aquatic species lay their eggs singly or in small batches on submerged rocks, plants, or chunks of wood and other objects. Ground-dwelling beetles that scavenge plant and animal materials often deposit their eggs in soil, leaf litter, compost heaps, dung, carrion, and other sites rich in decomposing organic materials and animal waste. Plant-feeding species drop their eggs at the base of the larval food plant or glue them to various vegetative structures; some species carefully apply a protective coating of their own feces on the eggs. Wood borers, such as longhorn beetles (Cerambycidae), deposit their eggs in cracks, crevices, and wounds of bark.

Most beetle larvae bear little or no resemblance whatsoever to the adults with regard to their form and food preferences. Their growth is typically rapid, and the

Figure 16. Larvae, pupae, and adult mealworm, *Tenebrio molitor* (Tenebrionidae).

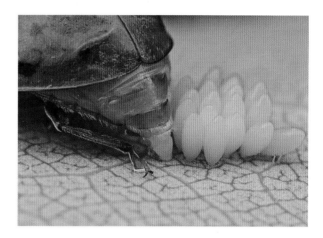

Figure 17. Female *Harmonia axyridis* (Coccinellidae) laying eggs.

27

outgrown exoskeleton is replaced with a new and roomier one secreted by an underlying layer of epidermal cells, a process called *molting*. The stage between each larval molt is called an *instar*. Most species pass through three to five instars, although some may have as few as two (Histeridae) or as many as seven (Dermestidae) or more (Pleocomidae).

Beetle larvae (Fig. 18) are incredibly diverse, although many may be grouped according to their overall body form. The slow and caterpillar-like larvae of lady beetles (Coccinellidae) and some leaf beetles (Chrysomelidae) are called *eruciform*; they typically have well-developed heads, legs, and fleshy abdominal protuberances. Sluggish, C-shaped *scarabaeiform* grubs have distinct heads and well-developed legs suited for burrowing through the soil or rotten wood and are characteristic of scarab beetles and their kin (Lucanidae, Trogidae, Scarabaeidae, etc.). The *elateriform* larvae of click beetles (Elateridae) and many darkling beetles (Tenebrionidae) have long, slender bodies

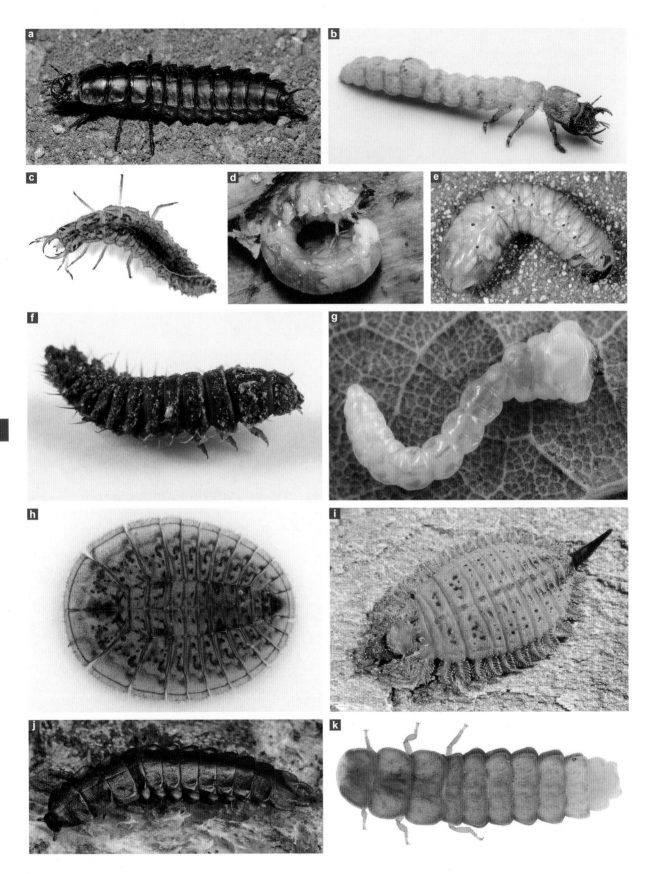

Figure 18. Beetle larvae.
a. *Calosoma* (Carabidae); b. *Amblycheila* (Carabidae);
c. *Tropisternus* (Hydrophilidae); d. *Sinodendron* (Lucanidae);
e. *Cotinis* (Scarabaeidae); f. *Nosodendron* (Nosodendridae);
g. genus unknown (Buprestidae); h. *Eubrianax* (Psephenidae);
i. *Brachypsectra* (Brachypsectridae); j. *Lygistopterus* (Lycidae);
k. *Microphotus* (Lampyridae); l. *Pacificanthia* (Cantharidae);
m. *Alaus* (Elateridae); n. *Anthrenus* (Dermestidae); o. *Harmonia*
(Coccinellidae); p. *Aphorista* (Endomychidae); q. *Coelus*
(Tenebrionidae); r. *Dendroides* (Pyrochroidae); s. *Collops*
(Melyridae); t. *Cypherotylus* (Erotylidae); u. *Aethina* (Nitidulidae);
v. genus unknown (Cerambycidae); w. *Trirhabda* (Chrysomelidae).

with short legs and tough exoskeletons. Thick, legless, maggotlike weevil grubs are called *vermiform*, while the flattened, elongate, and leggy predatory larvae of ground (Carabidae), whirligig (Gyrinidae), predaceous diving (Dytiscidae), water scavenger (Hydrophilidae), and rove beetles (Staphylinidae) are *campodeiform*. The broadly oval, distinctly segmented, turtlelike water penny larvae (Psephenidae) are *cheloniform*, while the sowbug-like larvae of some Silphidae are referred to as *onisciform*. *Fusiform* larvae are broad in the middle and more or less tapered at each end.

Each successive instar is generally like the last in form, just larger in size. The parasitic larvae of cicada parasite beetles (Rhipiceridae), blister beetles (Meloidae), and wedge-shaped beetles (Ripiphoridae) all develop by a special type of holometaboly called *hypermetamorphosis*, a developmental process characterized by two or more distinct larval forms. The first active and leggy instar, or *triungulin*, is adapted for seeking out the appropriate host. Once the triungulin has located a host, it molts into a decidedly less active larva with short, thick legs and begins to feed. This form is followed by a fat, legless grub that eventually develops into a more active short-legged grub that spends most of its time preparing a pupal chamber. Although not parasites, the larvae of telephone-pole beetles (Micromalthidae) also develop by hypermetamorphosis and, under the right conditions, can reproduce additional larvae by laying eggs or giving live birth to another larva. The phenomenon of asexual reproduction by larvae is called *paedogenesis*.

Instead of compound eyes, most beetle larvae possess from one to six simple eyes on each side of the head called *stemmata*, while others lack any visual organs whatsoever and are blind. The mouthparts of most larvae are adapted for crushing, grinding, or tearing foodstuffs. Predatory larvae are liquid feeders and use their mouthparts to pierce and drain prey of their bodily fluids. Some species have sickle-like and grooved mouthparts that channel digestive fluids into insect prey to liquefy their tissues and organs. The antennae of beetle larvae typically consist of only two or four simple segments, but those of Scirtidae (p.114) have long, multisegmented filiform antennae. Giant water scavenger larvae (*Hydrophilus*), known as water tigers, use their sharp, pointed antennae in concert with their mandibles to tear open insect prey.

The beetle larva thorax consists of three very similar segments, the first of which may have a thickened plate across its back. Legs, if present, typically have six or fewer segments. Larvae with legs greatly reduced or absent generally feed inside plant tissues or parasitize other insects.

Figure 19. Larval urogomphi, *Dendroides* (Pyrochroidae).

Most beetle larvae have 9- or 10-segment abdomens that are soft and pliable, allowing their food-filled bodies to rapidly expand without having to molt. Although legless, the abdomen in some terrestrial species possesses segments equipped with fleshy wartlike protuberances that afford the larva a bit of traction as it moves about. The abdomen of some aquatic larvae in several families (e.g. Gyrinidae, Haliplidae, Hydrophilidae, Eulichadidae) possess simple or branched gills laterally or ventrally. The terminal segment of some larvae may end in a pair of fixed or segmented projections called *urogomphi* (Fig. 19).

Many terrestrial beetle larvae live in leaf litter, rotten wood, and various kinds of fungi where they consume a wide variety of organic tissues. *Phytophagous*, or plant-feeding, larvae consume living and decomposing flowers, fruits, seeds, cones, leaves, needles, twigs, branches, trunks, and roots. Leaf-mining species tunnel between the upper and lower surfaces of living leaves, creating discolored blotches, blisters, or meandering tunnels trailing in their wake. Wood-boring larvae tunnel between the bark and wood and, depending on species, either pupate there or tunnel into the sapwood. Still others attack only the heartwood and leave the outer, living sapwood intact. Some larval carrion beetles (Silphidae) feed on accumulations of plant material, while dung-feeding larvae (e.g., some Hydrophilidae and Scarabaeidae) eat plant materials that have been partially decomposed within the digestive tracts of vertebrates.

The fleet-footed *campodeiform* larvae found in several beetle families actively hunt for prey in leaf litter or under bark, while decidedly stationary tiger beetle larvae (Carabidae) ambush prey that stray too close to the entrance of their vertical burrows. Some larval ground beetles and rove beetles (Staphylinidae) actively seek out and consume the pupae of leaf and whirligig beetles, and flies. Glowworm larvae (Phengodidae) overpower millipedes by coiling themselves around the front of a millipede's body (Fig. 20) before biting it just behind and underneath the head. Through its sharp and channeled sickle-shaped mandibles, the larva injects into its victim gut fluids laced with paralyzing toxins and digestive enzymes. Immobilized almost instantly, the millipede is unable to release its noxious defensive chemicals and quickly dies as its internal organs and tissues are liquefied. The phengodid larva consumes all but the millipede's exoskeleton and defensive glands. The larvae of blister beetles (Meloidae) attack underground grasshopper egg masses or invade subterranean nests of solitary bees to raid their stores of pollen and nectar, as well as consume their brood. Rhipicerid and ripiphorid larvae are ectoparasitoids that attack cicada nymphs and various mud-nesting wasps, respectively.

Beetle larvae employ a variety of morphological and chemical strategies to defend themselves. Dermestid larvae (Fig. 21) have clusters of bristly hairlike setae that function as irritating deterrents to predatory mammals, reptiles, and birds. Located on the upper surface of the abdomen, these setae are arrayed like a defensive fan to ward off potential enemies and entangle the mouthparts of ants and other small arthropod predators. These very same structures are common components of household dust and are implicated in triggering allergic reactions and asthma attacks. Tortoise beetle larvae (Chrysomelidae) carry racks of fecal material and old larval exoskeletons over their backs (Fig. 22) under which they can hide, while other leaf beetles construct protective cases from their waste that cover their entire bodies (Fig. 23).

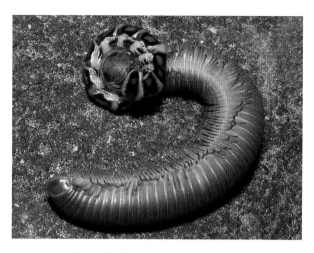

Figure 20. Glowworm larva, *Phengodes* (Phengodidae), attacking a millipede.

Figure 21. *Dermestes* (Dermestidae) larva.

31

Figure 22. Tortoise beetle larvae, *Gratiana* (Chrysomelidae), with defensive rack of fecal material and cast larval exoskeletons.

Figure 23. Case-bearing leaf beetle larva (Chrysomelidae, Cryptocephalinae).

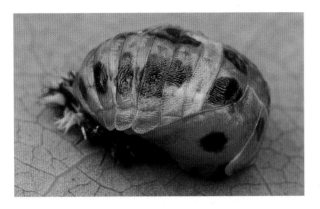

Figure 24. Pupa, *Harmonia* (Coccinellidae).

The last larval instar, sometimes referred to as the *prepupa*, develops into the pupa. Dramatic physiological and morphological transformations take place during the pupal stage (Fig. 24) that marks the end of the larval life adapted primarily for feeding and the beginning of the adult mode of life dominated by reproduction. It is during the pupal stage that the physical details of the adult are revealed. Most beetle pupae are of the *adecticous exarate* type and lack functional mandibles (*adecticous*) and have legs not tightly appressed (*exarate*) to the body. Some species (Ptiliidae, some Staphylinidae, Clambidae, Coccinellidae, some Chrysomelidae) have adecticous pupae with legs that are tightly appressed (*obtect*) along the entire length of the body. Many pupae have functional abdominal muscles that allow for some movement. Some of these species have specialized teeth, or sharp edges along the opposing abdominal segments known as *gin-traps* that snap shut on the appendages of ants, mites, and other small arthropod predators and parasites.

Many beetles overwinter as pupae within chambers located deep in soil, humus, or the tissues of plants where they are less likely to be subjected to freezing temperatures. Some scarab beetle larvae (e.g., *Cotinis*, *Cremastocheilus*, *Dynastes*, *Euphoria*), among others, construct protective pupal chambers from their own fecal material. Leaf beetles (Chrysomelidae) generally pupate in the soil, sometimes inside a *cocoon* within a specially dug chamber, although the larvae of *Ophraella* typically anchor their meshlike cocoons up on their host plant. In glowworms (Phengodidae) and some fireflies (Lampyridae) the females undergo a modified pupal stage and emerge from the pupa, or *eclose*, as an adult that closely resembles the previous larval instar. Adult *larviform* females lack wings or have greatly reduced elytra relative to the male, and are best distinguished from the larvae by the presence of compound eyes externally and reproductive organs internally.

ADULT EMERGENCE

The requisite combination of time, temperature, and moisture triggers adult emergence, or *eclosion*, from the pupa. Freshly eclosed adults are typically soft and pale, or *teneral* (Fig. 25). Their exoskeleton hardens and darkens as it undergoes chemical changes akin to the tanning of leather. Adult beetles are full-grown and never molt again; however, the abdomens of some soft-bodied leaf and blister beetles are capable of limited expansion so they can stuff themselves with food, or become filled with eggs. Once fully developed, adult beetles may or may not feed, but they are ready to mate and reproduce.

FEEDING

Equipped with powerful mandibles, beetles can cut, grind, or chew their way through all kinds of fungal, plant, and animal tissues, living or dead. Most beetles are herbivores and many obtain their nutrition by consuming living plant tissues. Scarabs (Scarabaeidae), blister beetles (Meloidae), leaf beetles (Chrysomelidae), and weevils (Curculionidae) are particularly fond of leafy foliage and will strip leaves of their tissues or completely defoliate plants. Pestiferous beetles in these families hungrily consume turf, garden vegetables, ornamental shrubs, and shade trees as well as agricultural or horticultural crops, while their subterranean larvae frequently attack the roots.

Pollen- and nectar-producing flowers are particularly attractive to some species (e.g., Scarabaeidae, Cantharidae, Lycidae, Meloidae, Mordellidae, Cerambycidae), but the role of beetles as pollinators (Fig. 26) requires further study. Many wood-boring beetles (e.g., Buprestidae, Cerambycidae, Curculionidae) feed on dead or dying wood. Their tunneling and feeding activities in twigs, limbs, trunks, and roots hasten

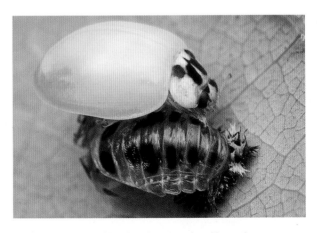

Figure 25. A freshly eclosed and teneral lady beetle, *Harmonia* (Coccinellidae).

32

Figure 26. Flower-visiting beetles that eat pollen.
a. *Eupompha* (Meloidae); b. dasytine melyrid beetles (Melyridae).

decay and attract a succession of additional beetles and
other insects that prefer increasingly rotten wood. Scavengers
prefer their plant foods to be first "cured" by the action of fungi
and bacteria. Dung-feeding beetles (some Hydrophilidae,
Scarabaeidae) consume plant materials already partially
broken down by the digestive tracts of horses, cattle, dogs,
and other vertebrates. Some of these species not only
consume feces, they also bury it as food for their young, and
are among the most beneficial, yet least appreciated insects.

Many beetles are directly or indirectly dependent on fungi.
In fact, the larvae of some wood-boring species are unable
to complete their development in wood unless the tree has
been previously weakened or killed by fungus. To this end,
bark beetles (Curculionidae) introduce fungal spores that kill
twigs and branches, and such infections may eventually kill
the entire tree. Some of these species have special cavities
associated with the head or thorax called *mycangia* that
are specifically adapted for storing fungal spores. Ambrosia
beetles chew chamberlike tunnels in wood and introduce
into them a specific type of fungus that lines the walls,
thus providing food for both themselves and their larvae.
These and other fungi like them are entirely dependent on
beetles for their dispersal and survival. Adults and larvae of
featherwing (Ptiliidae), round fungus (Leiodidae) (Fig. 27),
minute brown scavenger (Latridiidae), and others are
frequently found with mold and other fungi, and slime mold.
Some flat bark (Trogossitidae), pleasing fungus (Erotylidae),
handsome fungus (Endomychidae), some darkling
(Tenebrionidae), and tetratomid beetles (Tetratomidae), and
fungus weevils (Anthribidae), among other families, are also
associated with sac fungi (Ascomycota) and mushrooms,
puffballs, bracket fungi, and their kin (Basidiomycota).

Ground and tiger beetles (Carabidae) are formidable
hunters that rely on speed and powerful mandibles (Fig. 28)

Figure 27. *Agathidium*
(Leiodidae) on fungus.

Figure 28. *Calosoma* (Carabidae) eating a white-lined
sphinx moth caterpillar, *Hyles* (Sphingidae).

33

to overpower and tear apart a broad range of insect and other invertebrate prey. Rove (Staphylinidae) and clown beetles (Histeridae) hunt for maggots, mites, and other small arthropods living among leaf litter, dung, carrion, under bark, in decaying plant and fungal tissues, and sap flows; some are specialists living in bird and mammal nests. Predaceous diving (Dytiscidae) and whirligig (Gyrinidae) beetles both attack aquatic invertebrates or terrestrial insects trapped on the water's surface. Many water scavenger beetles (Hydrophilidae) consume both animal and plant tissues. Predatory scarab beetles (Scarabaeidae) are rare, but adult *Phileurus* have been observed eating various insects, while ant-loving scarabs (*Cremastocheilus*) prey on ant brood. Checkered beetles (Cleridae) and some soldier beetles (Cantharidae) prey on wood-boring and sap-feeding insects, respectively. Lady beetles (Coccinellidae) consume a variety of foodstuffs, especially pollen and molds, but are also predators of aphids, mealybugs, and other plant pests.

Carrion and burying beetles (Silphidae) scavenge freshly dead carcasses, occasionally preying on fly maggots that compete for the same juicy and nutritious resource. Hide beetles (Trogidae) derive most of their diet from keratin-rich feathers, fur, claws, and hooves. Ham beetles (Cleridae) gnaw on dried tissues and will attack dried meats, while skin beetles (Dermestidae) will also infest study skins and insect specimens. Natural history museums around the world enlist the services of select dermestid beetles to clean animal skeletons used in research collections and exhibits, while related species are strictly monitored and controlled as museum pests.

DEFENSE

Beetles are continually beset by various insectivorous predators and parasites, as well as disease-causing agents known as *entomopathogens* that typically infect insects. Birds, bats, rodents, other small to medium-sized mammalian predators (Fig. 29), reptiles, amphibians, and fishes are among the vertebrates that regularly utilize them as food, while spiders, ants, robber flies (Fig. 30), and other beetles rank high among invertebrate predators of beetles. To avoid becoming meals for hungry predators, most beetles rely on morphological and behavioral adaptations. Predation by birds and other diurnal predators is likely to have played a dominant role in the evolution of cryptic and *aposematic* coloration in beetles, while the stridulatory, chemical, and non-aposematic defenses of nocturnal species are especially effective deterrents against mammal, amphibian, and invertebrate predators.

Figure 29. Mammalian carnivore feces packed with beetle remains.

Figure 30. Robber fly, *Diogmites* (Asilidae) preying on a flower chafer, *Euphoria* (Scarabaeidae).

Ground and tiger beetles (Carabidae) back up their bursts of speed to evade predators with sprays of noxious chemical compounds. Tortoise beetles (Chrysomelidae) simply stay put. When attacked, they hunker down by using their oily and bristly feet to cling mightily to the surface of vegetation. Their tortoise-like carapace with broadly flanged edges nearly all around completely covers the beetles' appendages, thwarting the efforts of ants and other predators in their attempts to dislodge it. Adult flea (Chrysomelidae) and some marsh beetles (Scirtidae) have muscular hind jumping legs that propel them out of harm's way in an instant.

Click beetles (Elateridae), false click beetles (Eucnemidae), and throscids (Throscidae) jump by "clicking" themselves away from danger. Elaterids accomplish this feat by contracting ventral muscles that bring a prosternal spine up against a corresponding groove on the mesosternum (Fig. 31). As tension builds, the spine

Figure 31. Clicking mechanism of a click beetle, *Alaus* (Elateridae).

suddenly snaps into the groove with a clearly audible and startling click, propelling the beetle into the air. For some large longhorn beetles (Cerambycidae) and scarabs (Scarabaeidae), size alone—backed up by powerful mandibles, horns, and claws—may be enough to deter all but the most determined predators.

Death feigning, or *thanatosis*, is a behavioral strategy employed by hide beetles (Trogidae), certain darkling beetles (Tenebrionidae), zopherids (Zopheridae), weevils (Curculionidae), and many others. When disturbed, these beetles "play possum" by pulling their legs and antennae up tightly against their bodies; some of these species have special sulci to receive and protect these appendages. Faced with impenetrable bodies that lack any movement, most small predators quickly lose interest and move on.

Other beetle species avoid detection by predators by blending into their backgrounds by employing varying degrees of camouflage. Somber-colored brown or

gray wood-boring beetles and weevils easily blend in with the rough bark and gnarled branches of their food plants. Pale tiger beetles (Carabidae) almost disappear on the sandy shores of beaches, rivers, and streams. Even a few members of the usually brightly colored lady beetles (Coccinellidae) are tan or striped, and thus remain undetected among pine needles. Some seemingly conspicuous bright metallic green beetles (e.g., Scarabaeidae, Buprestidae, Chrysomelidae) also disappear among the needles and leaves of their food plants. Longhorn beetles (Cerambycidae) and fungus weevils (Anthribidae) have markings that make them difficult to find on lichen-covered bark. The small, dark, and chunky warty leaf beetles *Chlamisus*, *Exema*, *Neochlamisus*, and *Pseudochlamys* (Chrysomelidae) hide in plain sight and are often overlooked by predators and collectors alike because of their strong resemblance to caterpillar feces (Fig. 32).

Although incapable of inflicting harm themselves, some beetles mimic the appearance or behavior of stinging insects, a phenomenon known as *Batesian mimicry*. Flower-visiting *Acmaeodera* (Buprestidae) and lepturine longhorns (Cerambycidae) all sport boldly marked and sometimes fuzzy bodies that make them striking mimics of stinging bees and wasps. Some bumble bee scarabs (Glaphyridae) with a bright metallic green prothorax strongly resemble halictine bees as they fly over ribbons of sand winding through willow thickets growing along river courses.

Several species of checkered beetles (Cleridae) are boldly colored to resemble pugnacious ants or wingless wasps known as velvet ants. Their quick, jerky movements further reinforce the charade. But stinging insects are not the only models for beetles seeking protection. Several species of click (Elateridae) and longhorn beetles (Cerambycidae) strongly resemble distasteful fireflies (Lampyridae), soldier (Cantharidae), and net-winged beetles (Lycidae).

Eye spots or sudden flashes of bright colors are thought to startle or confuse would-be predators. The outsized eye spots of eyed click beetles (Elateridae) (Fig. 33) may momentarily confuse a predator, possibly allowing the beetle an extra moment or two to escape. *Trichiotinus* beetles (Scarabaeidae) have bold eye spots on their pygidium that may suggest the face of a stinging wasp to potential attackers. Many dull-colored metallic wood-boring beetles (Buprestidae) and somberly hued tiger beetles (Carabidae) may startle predators by revealing flashes of bright iridescent blue, green, or red on their abdomens when they lift their elytra to take flight.

Some beetles possess chemical arsenals of noxious substances produced by specific glands in their bodies,

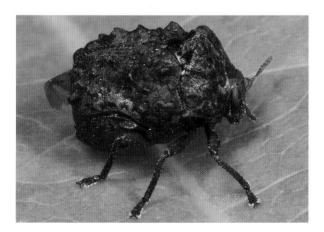

Figure 32. Caterpillar feces mimic, *Neochlamisus* (Chrysomelidae).

35

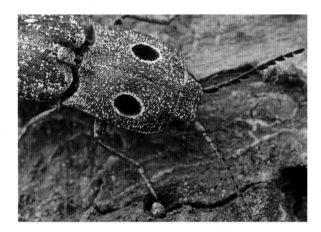

Figure 33. Eye spots on pronotum of an eyed click beetle, *Alaus* (Elateridae).

or extracted from their food and sequestered in special chambers or within their blood (*hemolymph*) that are later employed as repellents, insecticides, and fungicides. Specialized abdominal defensive glands of ground beetles (Carabidae) known as pygidial glands produce hydrocarbons, aldehydes, phenols, quinones, esters, and acids and release them as noxious streams through the anus. For example, aposematically colored bombardier beetles (*Brachinus*) release small, yet potent, boiling clouds of hydrogen peroxide gas laced with hydroquinones and various enzymes, among other components, with considerable accuracy through their anal turret with an audible pop. When attacked, carrion and burying beetles (Silphidae) emit oily, smelly anal secretions with a strong ammonia odor. Most rove beetles (Staphylinidae) and darkling beetles (Tenebrionidae) have *eversible* abdominal or anal glands that produce a wide range of defensive substances. Stink beetles (*Eleodes*) assume a defensive posture by lowering their heads and raising the tip of their abdomens high before releasing defensive chemical compounds with a characteristically noxious odor.

Net-winged (Lycidae), soldier (Cantharidae), lady (Coccinellidae), blister (Meloidae), and milkweed beetles (Cerambycidae) are relatively sluggish insects that boldly display their *aposematic* colors for all to see. Their conspicuously bright and bold patterns warn experienced predators that their bodies contain noxious chemical compounds that render them distasteful. For example, the bright red, black-spotted beetles in the genus *Tetraopes* (Cerambycidae) are specialist herbivores that feed only on milkweeds, plants with tissues containing paralytic toxins known as cardiac glycosides. Undeterred by the presence of this compound, *Tetraopes* larvae feed upon the roots and sequester the milkweed's toxin in tissues destined to become elytra in the adult. Adults eat leaves of milkweed, but limit the amount of cardiac glycosides they ingest by first cutting the leaf's midrib with their mandibles and bleeding off its toxic, milky sap before they start feeding.

Both aposematically colored lady and blister beetles engage in a behavior known as *reflex bleeding* and will purposely exude bright orange or yellow hemolymph laced with noxious chemicals from their leg joints (Fig. 34) to repel

Figure 34. Reflex bleeding from femorotibial joints on oil beetle, *Meloe* (Meloidae).

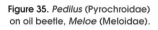

Figure 35. *Pedilus* (Pyrochroidae) on oil beetle, *Meloe* (Meloidae).

36

Figure 36. A pseudoscorpion.

Figure 37. Phoretic mites on burying beetle, *Nicrophorus* (Silphidae).

predators. Cantharidin is an incredibly caustic chemical compound found in the tissues of blister (Meloidae) and false blister beetles (Oedemeridae). It functions as a powerful feeding deterrent to predators and, even in low doses, will blister and burn mucous membranes and other sensitive tissues. Male antlike beetles (Anthicidae) gather cantharidin from dead or dying blister beetles for their own protection and to attract mates. Males pass along large amounts of cantharidin to the females through copulation that—in turn—is passed along to the eggs and larvae as a defensive chemical compound. Other anthicids have thoracic glands that produce chemicals that are particularly distasteful to ants, the primary predators of ground-dwelling insects. *Neopyrochroa* and *Pedilus* (Pyrochroidae) also sequester cantharidin, possibly from blister beetles (Fig. 35) or other natural, yet unknown cantharidin sources.

SYMBIOTIC RELATIONSHIPS

Some beetles have intimate and specialized, or *symbiotic*, relationships with other organisms. Symbiotic relationships that benefit both the beetle and its partner organism are examples of *mutualism*. *Commensalism* is a form of symbiosis where one symbiotic organism clearly benefits while the other is not adversely affected by the relationship. *Parasites*, on the other hand, live at the expense of their hosts.

All plant-feeding beetles, including wood-boring species, are more or less reliant upon mutualistic *endosymbiotic microorganisms*, such as bacteria, fungi, and yeasts that live within special pockets called *mycetomes* in their digestive tracts and assist in digesting the primary component of all plant-based foods, cellulose. The larvae of these species do not begin their lives with these vital organisms in place

and must either obtain them by consuming their eggshells, which were coated by their mothers in residues laden with endosymbionts, or by consuming adult waste (*feces, frass*) that is teeming with them.

Larger species, such as *Polyphylla decemlineata* (Scarabaeidae), *Prionus* species, and *Trichocnemis spiculatus* (Cerambycidae) often harbor one or more pseudoscorpions (Fig. 36) under their elytra, which are occasionally found in killing jars used to dispatch these big beetles. Pseudoscorpions are small scorpion-like arachnids without a stinging tail. They hunt under tree bark for small insect larvae and mites among the chewed galleries and frass left in the wake of wood-boring insects. As their prey populations are depleted, pseudoscorpions seek out and attach themselves to a beetle to hitch a ride to another fallen tree where food is more abundant. Pseudoscorpions depend on their beetle hosts for transportation, a type of commensalism known as *phoresy*. Burying beetles (Silphidae) possess phoretic mites that prey on the eggs of carrion-feeding flies (Fig. 37), thus reducing the competition for their host beetles. Other mite species are not phoretic, but are parasites that feed on the bodily fluids of beetles.

Ant-loving beetles, or *myrmecophiles*, in the families Staphylinidae, Histeridae, Scarabaeidae, and Tenebrionidae, among others, are adapted for living in the nests of ants. Some myrmecophilous beetles may simply be opportunists, living on the fringes of colonies where they scavenge bits of food left behind by the ants (Fig. 38). Other species are much better adapted to living with ants and have evolved various degrees of behavioral, chemical, or tactile mimicry to integrate themselves into the host ants' social system. Host ants tolerate their beetle guests with varying degrees of hospitality, but the benefits derived from the relationship nearly always favor the beetle. Species

Figure 38. *Araeoschizus* (Tenebrionidae) carried by a red harvester ant, *Pogonomyrmex* (Formicidae).

in these and other families similarly adapted to living with termites are referred to as *termitophiles*.

A few beetle larvae are ectoparasitoids of other animals. For example, the larvae of *Brachinus* and *Lebia* (Carabidae) attack the larvae and pupae of aquatic beetles and leaf beetles, respectively. The larvae of cicada parasite beetles (Rhipiceridae) attack cicadas, while those of wedge-shaped beetles (Ripiphoridae) parasitize solitary wasps. Larval passandrids (Passandridae) and bothriderids (Bothrideridae) attack the larvae and pupae of wood-boring longhorn (Cerambycidae) and jewel beetles (Buprestidae). Perhaps the most unusual ectoparasitic beetle known in all North America is *Platypsyllus castoris* (Leiodidae). Both the flattened, louselike ectoparasitic adults and their larvae live on beavers, where they feed on their host's skin and bodily fluids.

AQUATIC BEETLES

Aquatic beetles are variously adapted behaviorally and morphologically for living on the surface of, within, or on the bottom of standing and flowing bodies of water. Winged species are generally good to strong fliers and are, on occasion, attracted to lights at night in large numbers. Based on adult modes of locomotion, water beetles are divided into two basic groups: swimmers and crawlers.

The flattened middle and hind legs of swimmers (Haliplidae, Gyrinidae, Dytiscidae, and some Hydrophilidae) are fringed with setae and used like oars to propel their mostly smooth, rigid, streamlined bodies through standing or slow-moving waters. All but the gyrinids spend most of their adult lives submerged underwater and must regularly bring fresh supplies of air into contact with *spiracles* through which they breathe. Water scavengers (Hydrophilidae) accomplish this by breaking through the surface tension headfirst with their antennae to draw a layer of air over the underside of their abdomen. Crawling water (Haliplidae) and predaceous diving beetles (Dytiscidae) both trap air under their elytra in the *subelytral cavity* by breaching the water surface with the tips of their abdomens. Diving beetles sometimes expose this bubble on the tip of the abdomen where it acts as a physical gill (Fig. 39). For a brief time, oxygen is replenished inside the bubble by passive diffusion.

Whirligig beetles (Gyrinidae) are adapted for life on the surface of standing and slow-moving waters, although they can dive when threatened and remain submerged for short periods of time. They propel themselves with paddlelike middle and hind legs, and steer with the rudderlike tip of the abdomen that bends down almost at a right angle. The compound eyes of gyrinids are completely divided into two functionally different sets of lenses, allowing them to see in both air and water. With special organs in their antennae, whirligig beetles can detect surface vibrations emanating from other gyrinids, predators, and struggling insect prey. Dead and dying insects are grasped with *raptorial*, or grabbing front legs.

Contrastingly, beetles that crawl in the water (Hydraenidae, some Hydrophilidae, Elmidae, Dryopidae, and some Curculionidae) have legs adapted not for swimming, but for clinging, as evidenced by their long pretarsi tipped with well-developed claws. They are partly or wholly clothed in a dense, velvety, and water-repellent *pubescence* called a *hydrofuge* that continuously envelops their bodies in a silvery bubble. This thin layer of air allows a steady supply of dissolved oxygen from the surrounding water to diffuse inward to the spiracles, while permitting the respiratory gas carbon dioxide emitted from the spiracles

Figure 39. A predaceous diving beetle, *Thermonectus* (Dytiscidae) using a bubble of air as a physical gill.

Figure 40. Japanese beetle,
Popillia japonica (Scarabaeidae).

Figure 41. Asian longhorn beetle,
Anoplophora glabripennis (Cerambycidae).

to diffuse outward—a system called *plastron breathing*. Plastron breathing is not very efficient and is largely restricted to sedentary grazers in the families Dryopidae and Elmidae living in shallow, well-oxygenated waters. Once submerged, plastron-breathing beetles seldom, if ever, need to surface or leave the water.

BEETLES AS PESTS

As a group, beetles are among the most beneficial of all animals, but it shouldn't be a surprise when species that have evolved to scavenge animal nests, carrion, dead insects, seeds, and decaying plant materials in nature are also adapted to exploit these very same materials improperly stored in our pantries, warehouses, and museum collections. Beetles in several families infest and damage stores of grains and other cereal products, dried meats and fruits, legumes, nuts, and spices. Others are serious museum pests that destroy often-irreplaceable study skins, and insect and herbarium specimens.

Wood borers are essential for breaking down and recycling nutrients bound up in dead wood, while other phytophagous species help to keep plant populations in check via consumption of reproductive and vegetative structures. However, when these beetles direct their activities to ornamental and horticultural plants, agricultural crops, forests managed for timber, or wood products, the results can be catastrophic. The damage they cause can result in significant monetary losses as a direct result of lost production, trees killed, damaged goods, and pest control efforts. For example, ptinids and bostrichids that normally tunnel into dry wood may severely damage wood carvings, furniture, flooring, and paneling. Both native and adventive bark and ambrosia beetles (Curculionidae) regularly attack

and kill trees in forests and along city streets, usually focusing their efforts on recently dead, injured, or felled trees, or on trees stressed by drought or overwatering. Others attack the roots and branches of fruit and nut trees in orchards, severely impacting crop yields. The tunneling activity of these and other wood-boring beetles disrupts a tree's ability to transport water and nutrients, and introduces debilitating and lethal fungal infections.

Three of the most notorious beetle pests in North America were accidentally introduced from Asia. The Japanese beetle, *Popillia japonica* Newman (Fig. 40) (8.9–11.8 mm) has a coppery green head, pronotum, and legs. Its brown elytra are distinctively flanked by five white abdominal tufts. Adults of this very destructive pest feed on the flowers, fruits, and foliage of more than 300 species of ornamental and landscape plants, garden crops, and commercially grown fruits and vegetables. The larvae consume the roots of turfgrass and other plants, often causing severe damage. Since their discovery in a New Jersey nursery in 1916, Japanese beetles have become established throughout much of the eastern United States and southern Ontario. The grubs are easily transported with roots and soil, while flying adults are known to hitchhike on airplanes, trains, and automobiles, thus posing a serious and continuous threat to agriculture in western North America. Japanese beetles are regularly intercepted in western states, and provinces and several small, isolated infestations in the West have been eradicated.

A native of China and Korea, the Asian longhorn beetle, *Anoplophora glabripennis* (Motschulsky) (12.0–39.0 mm) (Fig. 41) is a large, black longhorn beetle (Cerambycidae) with irregular white spots on the elytra and bluish or white legs. It has long antennae that are ringed in pale blue or white and extend past the elytra by five antennomeres

39

in the male, but by just one or two in the female. The elytra are smooth, shiny, or dull, and only rarely densely spotted or spotless. The tunneling activities of the larvae weaken and kill otherwise healthy trees and threaten millions of street trees and the maple syrup industry. Infestations of this beetle were first reported in New York in 1996, but it was probably introduced about 10 years earlier in untreated wood used to crate heavy equipment. Infestations of this destructive beetle have since been reported from New Jersey, southern Ontario, northeastern Illinois, and Ohio, with additional individuals captured elsewhere, including California. Efforts to eradicate this destructive species involve cutting down, chipping, and burning thousands of trees. This species poses a serious threat to street trees, parks, and forests in western North America. Although this beetle has been intercepted in California, it is not known to be established anywhere in western North America.

The emerald ash borer, *Agrilus planipennis* Fairmaire (Fig. 42) (8.0–14.0 mm), is a slender, bright metallic green, rarely blue-green or violet jewel beetle (Buprestidae), much larger than any species of *Agrilus* native to North America. It also has a distinct ridge down the middle of the pygidium that extends beyond the tip. Emerald ash borers were first discovered in Detroit, Michigan and Windsor, Ontario during the summer of 2002, but they likely arrived in wood packing materials from eastern Asia in the early 1990s. Since then, this species has become established throughout much of the Northeast and upper Midwest. It has destroyed millions of ash trees in Michigan, southern Ontario, and Québec and threatens to destroy ash trees across North America. Ash species are important street trees and a vital source of wood for making furniture, tool handles, and baseball bats. Efforts to control the spread of the emerald ash borer

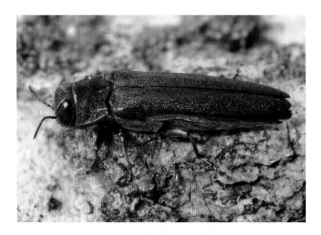

Figure 42. Emerald ash borer,
Agrilus planipennis (Buprestidae).

include quarantines that ban the movement of firewood within and from infested areas, and the introduction of biological control agents imported from China.

Sightings of these beetles anywhere in western North America, preferably supported by specimens or good photos, should be reported immediately to provincial, state, or county departments of agriculture.

BEETLES AS BIOLOGICAL CONTROLS

Biological control involves the use of a pest's natural enemies, such as predators, *parasitoids*, and *pathogens* as control methods, rather than complete reliance on pesticides that may adversely affect wildlife. The modern practice of utilizing predatory insects to control pests using natural enemies from their land of origin began in 1888. Shipments of several species of Australian lady beetles (Coccinellidae) arrived in California and were purposely released in the state to combat the cottony cushion scale, an Australian insect inadvertently introduced into the state that was wreaking havoc with the fledgling citrus industry. The vedalia beetle, *Rodolia cardinalis* (Mulsant), was hailed at the time as a miracle of science and, to this day, continues to help keep the cottony cushion scale in check. The success of this program led to the import of many other coccinellid species, but the benefits of these introductions have been mixed, especially with the Asian multicolored lady beetle, *Harmonia axyridis* (Pallas), that is sometimes viewed more as a nuisance, rather than a beneficial species. The role of these introductions in the observed declines observed in lady beetles indigenous to North America requires further study.

Biological control projects involving beetles are not limited to insect predators, as several species of phytophagous jewel beetles (Buprestidae), leaf beetles (Chrysomelidae), and weevils (Curculionidae) have been imported as biocontrol agents of introduced weeds, especially in rangelands. For example, the St. John's wort beetle, *Chrysolina hyperici* (Forster) (Fig. 43), and its close relative, the Klamath weed beetle, *C. quadrigemina* (Suffrian), were the first insects imported into North America to control *Hypericum perforatum*. This European weed, known in the West as Klamath weed, and elsewhere as goatweed or St. John's wort, is especially detrimental to cattle, but also negatively impacts sheep by displacing palatable forage. In the absence of better forage, livestock forced to graze on Klamath weed become hypersensitive to sunlight. Blisters

Figure 43. Saint John's wort beetle, *Chrysolina hyperici* (Chrysomelidae).

soon develop on areas exposed to direct sun and the animals lose weight as sores develop around their mouths and scabs on their skin.

Chrysolina females lay their eggs on *Hypericum* leaves, either singly or in small clusters. In about a week, the eggs begin to hatch into plump and humpbacked orange larvae that eventually turn grayish pink as they mature. The young larvae completely defoliate plants before they reach maturity by hungrily consuming leaf buds and developing leaves. As a result, the release and subsequent establishment of these beetles to control Klamath weed is generally viewed as effective, especially in warmer, drier habitats.

The application of biological controls to wildland environments, or conservation biocontrol, is more complex than programs targeting invasive species in agricultural systems and rangelands, as evidenced in the effort to

eradicate tamarisk (*Tamarix* species). Also known as saltcedar, tamarisk was introduced from Asia into North America about 200 years ago. Early in the 20th century, they expanded quickly into natural and contrived riparian systems and became associated with the decline of cottonwood-willow woodlands, mesquite bosque, and other native plant complexes west of the Mississippi River, becoming the third most common tree in riparian systems in western United States. The dominance of tamarisk in these habitats is believed by many to increase soil salinity, reduce local water resources, and provide poor habitat for native wildlife relative to displaced native plant communities. To reduce its negative environmental impacts, hundreds of species of herbivorous insects that appeared to feed only on tamarisk were studied to determine which species would become part of a biological control program to suppress tamarisk infestations. Several beetles were selected, including the splendid tamarisk weevil, *Coniatus splendidulus* (Fabricius), and northern tamarisk beetle, *Diorhabda carinulata* Debroschers des Loges (Fig. 44).

The initial success of the northern tamarisk beetle in defoliating tamarisk quickly became controversial. Wildlife agencies became increasingly alarmed that a significant reduction of the tamarisk canopy where federally endangered southwestern willow flycatchers nest would expose the birds to increased temperatures and predation. This concern was exacerbated by the lack of a habitat restoration plan once tamarisk was eliminated. Such conflicts highlight the need for governmental and private agencies charged with conserving wildlife and protecting natural resources to work together. By cooperatively developing a strategic plan early

41

Figure 44. Beetles used as biological controls to eradicate tamarisk.
a. Splendid tamarisk beetle, *Coniatus splendidulus* (Curculionidae);
b. Northern tamarisk beetle, *Diorhabda carinulata* (Chrysomelidae).

in conservation biology programs, science-based monitoring protocols can be developed to assess multiple key parameters that include soil and water dynamics, wildlife habitat use, and habitat restoration.

BEETLES AS INDICATORS OF PAST ENVIRONMENTS

While anthropogenic climate change is likely a contributing factor in a series of widespread droughts that have plagued western North America recently, paleoenvironmental records indicate that such periods of infrequent precipitation are nothing new. Evidence of climate change and its impacts are all around us, but historical records that provide such evidence are less than 200 years old. To fill in this gap, scientists can analyze microfossils consisting of plant and animal remains, especially those of beetles and other insects, to reconstruct ancient climate patterns.

A better understanding of terrestrial paleoenvironments will undoubtedly lead to more accurate predictions of future climatic shifts.

Recent advances in radiocarbon dating make it possible to determine the age of larger insect fragments as far back as 50,000 years. Some dated and identifiable beetle fragments are species of Carabidae and Tenebrionidae that are still extant today. As generalist predators and scavengers, these beetles are not tied to a particular plant or habitat, but instead move into more suitable habitats as temperature, food availability, and other conditions change. As a result, their populations respond relatively quickly to environmental fluctuations, often within a matter of decades rather than centuries, when compared with other groups of organisms, such as plants. For well-documented beetles, knowledge of their life cycles, habitat preferences, and distribution makes them ideal climatic indicators, both present and past, affording researchers with incredibly detailed insights into changing environmental conditions dating back tens of thousands of years.

42

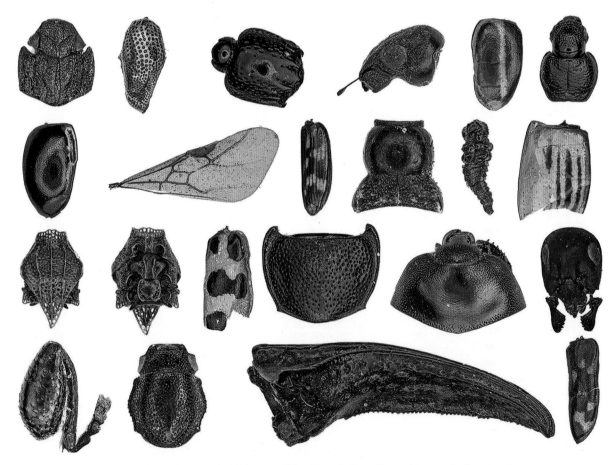

Figure 45. A collection of 44,000-year-old beetle and other arthropod fragments discovered inside the skull of an extinct camel found at Rancho La Brea Tar Pits in California.

For example, a reliably dated cache of 44,000-year-old fragments of insects and other arthropods (Fig. 45) was discovered inside a skull of an extinct camel at the Rancho La Brea Tar Pits in southern California. Careful analysis of this treasure trove revealed, among other things, that the late Pleistocene climate of the Los Angeles Basin was much warmer and drier than previously hypothesized based on plant fossil analysis alone. Further, within this incredible sample were the remains of the nearly cosmopolitan *Necrobia violacea* (Linnaeus), a *synanthropic* species long regarded here in North America as *adventitious*. The discovery of this species' remains in the sample clearly demonstrates that it was established in North America long before the arrival of humans on the continent. This evidence suggests that this beetle is either a Holarctic species that naturally occurs throughout the Northern Hemisphere, or was native to the Nearctic and was subsequently introduced into the Old World by human agency.

THREATENED AND ENDANGERED BEETLES

Habitat loss and fragmentation resulting from urban, commercial, and agricultural development, as well as pesticide use, invasive species, and climate change all contribute to the extirpation or extinction of beetles. In California alone, at least three species or subspecies of beetles are known to have become extinct in the last 150 years: the oblivious tiger beetle, *Cicindela latesignata obliviosa* Casey, the San Joaquin valley tiger beetle, *Cicindela tranquebarica joaquinensis* Knisley and Haines (Carabidae), and the Mono Lake hygrotus diving beetle, *Hygrotus artus* (Fall) (Dytiscidae).

Western North America is particularly susceptible to species loss because of the sheer number of beetles specifically adapted to living in unique and sensitive habitats, especially coastal and desert sand dunes, as well as restricted riparian habitats. Yet only five species of beetles that occur west of the Continental Divide are currently listed as threatened (T) or endangered (E) by the U.S. Fish and Wildlife Service, all of which occur in California: Ohlone tiger beetle, *Cicindela ohlone* Freitag & Cavanaugh (E); delta green ground beetle, *Elaphrus viridis* Horn (T); Casey's June beetle, *Dinacoma caseyi* Blaisdell (E); Mount Hermon June beetle, *Polyphylla barbata* Cazier (E), and valley elderberry longhorn beetle, *Desmocerus californicus dimorphus* Fisher (T) (Fig. 46).

No species of western beetles are afforded federal or provincial protection in Canada. State governments may list additional species as state threatened or endangered, or of special concern.

WHEN AND WHERE TO FIND BEETLES

One of the most appealing aspects of studying beetles is that opportunities to discover and observe unfamiliar species and behaviors abound. You can ramble through backyards, vacant lots, and parks, or explore more distant coastal forests and beaches, chaparral habitats, foothill woodlands, montane forests, and deserts year-round. Visiting familiar areas and habitats throughout the seasons year after year will likely produce a breathtaking diversity of species. Even at higher elevations or in more northern regions, overwintering beetles are found tucked away under snow-covered bark, buried deep in rotten wood or leaf litter, or hiding under boards and other debris to avoid lethal frosts. Many water beetles remain active throughout winter and are sometimes seen swimming under the ice of frozen ponds and lakes; however, some species are adapted to reach peak activity levels in fall and late winter, at least at lower elevations.

Beetles are found year-round in western North America, with the greatest diversity of species most likely to be encountered during the spring and summer months. The beginning of beetle activity varies depending on weather conditions and location, the latter of which is largely influenced by latitude and elevation. Spring conditions arrive later in the north and at higher elevations. As early as January and February, the first sustained periods of warm weather in the coastal plain and low desert of southern California and Arizona will drive many small ground beetles (Carabidae), scarabs (Scarabaeidae), and weevils (Curculionidae), among others, to search for food and mates. As the front of spring progresses northward, brief, yet spectacular bursts of ephemeral wildflowers fueled by rains of the previous winter blanket otherwise parched desert, foothill, and valley landscapes. Among this riot of color are species of beetles with lives as brief as the flowers upon which they feed and mate (Fig. 47). By April and May, coastal forests, chaparral habitats, and inland valleys reach their peak beetle-wise, while June and July mark the first significant levels of sustained beetle activity in coniferous forests at the higher elevations.

Much of the rainfall in the coastal provinces and states of western North America takes place during the fall and

Figure 46. Beetles listed as threatened or endangered in western North America by the U.S. Fish and Wildlife Service.
a. Ohlone tiger beetle (E),
Cicindela ohlone (Carabidae);
b. delta green ground beetle (T),
Elaphrus viridis (Carabidae);
c. Casey's June beetle (E), male and female, *Dinacoma caseyi* (Scarabaeidae);
d. Mount Hermon June beetle (E),
Polyphylla barbata (Scarabaeidae);
e. valley elderberry longhorn beetle (T),
Desmocerus californicus dimorphus (Cerambycidae).

winter, although in some years, heavy rains may persist well into spring, especially along the coast. Fall showers begin sweeping across the Pacific Northwest as early as September, and extend further south in October and November. Winter rains during December and January can be quite heavy at times along the coast, eventually turning into snow as storm systems move eastward across the Coast Ranges, Cascades and Sierra Nevada, and Rocky Mountains. These cold, wet bouts of winter precipitation trigger the activity of select beetle species that are specifically adapted to such conditions. By the middle of June, much of the region is experiencing some level of drought, although summer thundershowers are not unusual in the mountains and deserts. Arizona and adjacent areas typically experience a summer monsoon season that usually begins in July and persists through fall. These late summer thundershowers trigger a new wave of beetle activity across all desert regions of the West.

Time and experience will teach you the best times and places to look for beetles. The following are some of the more productive habitats to search for beetles in western North America. Exploring these and other habitats throughout the day and year will likely reveal a surprisingly diverse fauna that will enhance your enjoyment and appreciation of these fascinating animals. Throughout your explorations, always take care not to damage host plants, and return rocks, logs, and bark to their original positions. Such actions not only keep these sites productive for future visits, but also help to preserve the aesthetics of the habitat for the enjoyment of all.

FLOWERS AND VEGETATION

Spring and summer blooms rich in sweet nectar and high-protein pollen are attractive to flower-visiting beetles, especially scarab (Scarabaeidae), jewel (Buprestidae), sap (Nitidulidae), tumbling flower (Mordellidae), blister (Meloidae), and longhorn (Cerambycidae) beetles. These and other species exploit flowers as sources of food, places to mate and reproduce, or habitats in which to hunt for prey. Carefully examine fruits, seedpods, cones, needles, leaves, and roots of grasses, forbs, vines, shrubs, and trees. The young spring foliage of deciduous shrubs and trees is especially attractive to many plant-feeding species. Some herbivorous beetles are specialists and are seldom found on anything other than the adult or larval host plant.

Slime flux is a bacterial disease of trees and shrubs that forces sap attractive to many species of beetles out of limbs and trunks through freeze cracks, insect emergence holes, and other wounds (Fig. 48). Check not only the nooks and crannies of sap-soaked bark for beetles, but also the sap-drenched soil and litter beneath for smaller species and their larvae.

FRESHLY CUT AND BURNED WOOD

The smell of freshly cut or recently burned wood is especially attractive to beetles, particularly those looking for mates and egg-laying sites. Slash piles (stacks of freshly cut branches) in wooded areas are particularly productive, especially in spring and early summer (Fig. 49). You can also attract beetles with bundles of fresh-cut branches placed in forest openings, along woodland edges, or in canopy-covered habitats that are only partially exposed to sunlight. Inspect the bundles at weekly intervals, day and night, and note which beetles are attracted to the branches of which species of tree. Another technique is to lay branches, bark, or a slab of trunk 10–15 cm thick across the top of a fresh-cut stump in spring and check the top

Figure 47. *Chnaunanthus flavipennis* (Scarabaeidae) on flowers of Spanish needle, *Palafoxia arida*.

Figure 48. *Euphoria leucographa* (Scarabaeidae) feeding at a sapping wound on desert broom, *Baccharis sarothroides*.

45

Figure 49. Piles of freshly cut pine branches are particularly attractive to many wood-boring beetles during spring and summer.

of the stump regularly for beetles that have taken shelter there. Wood smoke, especially that generated by burning pine trees, also attracts wood-boring and bark beetles.

FUNGI, MUSHROOMS, MOSSES, AND LICHENS

Species in several families are found commonly on fungi, slime molds, mosses, and lichens. Carefully inspect fungi with a hand lens and leave them in good condition so they continue to lure new beetles. Fleshy and relatively ephemeral puffballs and mushrooms are also attractive, while more durable woody shelf fungi provide food and breeding sites for other species. Still other species seek out fungal tissues growing on or under bark, or in the soil. In addition to *mycophagous*, or fungal-feeding beetles, predatory rove (Staphylinidae) and clown beetles (Histeridae) frequent fungi infested with insects and mites as hunting grounds. Adults and larval pill or moss beetles (Byrrhidae) are obligate moss feeders that graze on vegetative surfaces or burrow in the soils beneath. Tread very lightly in these habitats so that future visits are equally productive. Only when fungal, moss, and lichen examples are in abundance should samples be collected for microscopic examination or the extraction of specimens.

SNAGS, LOGS, AND STUMPS

Standing snags dry from the top down, and most of their beetles are concentrated at or near the base. Moist rather than dry wood harbors more species. Some species prefer primarily shady habitats, while others prefer more open, sun-drenched wood, although this latter niche dries out more quickly. As the wood decomposes, its quality changes in terms of its suitability as beetle food and egg-laying sites, attracting a progression of beetle species over time. Checking these microhabitats every few weeks over a period of years may reveal an amazing diversity of beetle species.

Recently dead trees with tight-fitting bark are more likely to harbor the adults of smaller or flatter species than those with bark that is easier to remove. As the wood dries and its bark loosens, larger and more robust species can take shelter. Peeling back dead bark, or "barking," is best accomplished during the cooler winter and spring months. Use a broad-blade knife, screwdriver, or dandelion weeding tool to peel back bark and examine all the freshly exposed areas carefully. Whenever possible, replace the bark by nailing or tying it back in place so the site will continue to be colonized by additional individuals and species. Many small species are best found by placing crumbling and rotten wood onto a

light-colored surface for immediate inspection or into a Berlese funnel or some other insect extraction system.

Searching for beetles at night on dead wood with the aid of a headlamp or flashlight on warm spring and summer nights, just as they begin emerging from their hiding to search for mates, is an especially fruitful activity.

STREAM BANKS, LAKESHORES, AND COASTLINES

Plant debris on the surfaces of flumes, streams, and rivers contains flying and crawling beetles trapped by the swirling currents. Some species typically spend their daylight hours hidden under debris washed up on lakeshores and ocean beaches. Flying beetles of all sorts fly—or are windblown—out over lakes and oceans only to drown and be washed back up on shore, sometimes by the thousands. The high waterlines along these shores are often littered with thousands of beetles from various families. Burrowing species that are adapted to living in flat sandy, gravelly, or muddy shorelines are flushed from their burrows by splashing water across the substrate. Ground and tiger beetles (Carabidae) and variegated mud-loving beetles (Heteroceridae) are commonly found on sandy or muddy substrates along the edges of various wetlands.

FRESHWATER POOLS, STREAMS, AND LAKES

While some beetles prefer cold, fast streams, others favor ponds or slow-moving streams. Look for individual *Dineutus* or rafts of *Gyrinus* (Gyrinidae) on the surface of ponds or protected, slow-moving pools scattered along streams. Predaceous diving beetles (Dytiscidae) are often found on gravelly bottoms or beneath submerged objects, while water scavengers (Hydrophilidae), crawling water beetles (Haliplidae), and long-toed water beetles (Dryopidae) are found swimming near emergent plants, crawling among mats of algae, or clinging under logs and rocks. Carefully pick up and examine rocks lifted out of flowing waters for larval water pennies (Psephenidae) and riffle beetles (Elmidae) clinging to their surfaces.

COASTAL AND DESERT DUNES

Various small, sand-loving, or *psammophilic* beetles burrow in flowing sand or hide among plant debris at the bases of dune grasses and other plants. They usually reside down in the moisture layers, or in or under accumulations of *detritus* closer to the surface. Psammophiles typically burrow up and down through the sand as they follow the seasonal moisture and temperature gradients to maintain ideal living conditions, and are active on the surface only for very brief periods of time. These fragile habitats, home to many rare, endangered, poorly known, and undescribed beetle species, are often threatened by off-road vehicles and mining interests.

CARRION

Dead animals provide food and shelter for adult and larval beetles. Look for these beetles on, in, and under the carcass, as well as buried in the soil directly beneath the body. Carrion and burying beetles (Silphidae) feed primarily on fresh, juicy flesh, while most skin beetles (Dermestidae) scavenge dried tissues. Hide beetles (Trogidae) are among the last contingent of insects to visit a carcass and gnaw on the keratin-rich hair, feathers, hooves, and horns. Predatory species (Staphylinidae, Histeridae) seek out and devour the eggs of other carrion-feeding insects and mites. Other beetles are attracted to carrion simply because such microhabitats provide moisture and shelter.

DUNG

The most conspicuous dung-inhabiting beetles in the region belong to the family Scarabaeidae, along with a few species of Hydrophilidae. Native dung beetles are often specialists, preferring the dung of burrowing rodents or deer. Many of the more conspicuous species found in horse and cattle dung originated in Europe and have become widely established in western North America. A few dung scarabs (*Digitonthophagus*, *Oniticellus*, *Onthophagus*, *Onitis*) were purposefully introduced from sub-Saharan Africa to manage cattle waste. Medium and larger species mostly occur in southern Arizona and are drawn to large wet feces produced by cattle, pigs, horses, and humans. Dog and cat feces attract only a few, mostly introduced species of dung scarabs. Clown (Histeridae) and rove beetles (Staphylinidae) are commonly associated with dung as predators of fly eggs and maggots.

BENEATH STONES AND OTHER OBJECTS

Many beetles occasionally or habitually take shelter under rocks, logs, boards, and other debris on the ground, especially in grassy areas and habitats along the edges of ponds, lakes, streams, rivers, and other wetlands. For the benefit of the people following in your footsteps and the organisms living underneath, always return these objects to their original places and positions. Also look for antlike flower (Anthicidae) and false blister beetles (Oedemeridae) under driftwood that has washed up along coastal beaches and river mouths near coastlines, especially along lower reaches that are regularly influenced by the tides.

LEAF LITTER, COMPOST, AND OTHER ACCUMULATIONS OF PLANT MATERIALS

Layers of leaves and needles that gather beneath trees, accumulate along streams and rivers as flood debris, or wash up on beaches and lakeshores after storms frequently harbor all kinds of beetles. Some beetles use these habitats primarily as shelter, while many rove beetles (Staphylinidae), weevils (Curculionidae), and other species spend their entire lives here. During the winter, beetles living in these habitats are collected by placing debris in plastic bags and bringing the samples inside to check for individuals that have become active. Backyard compost heaps, decaying piles of mulch, and other natural or artificial accumulations of decomposing grass, leaves, branches, and other vegetative matter are particularly productive. Some coastal rove beetles and weevils live under decomposing piles of seaweed washed up along the beach.

LIGHTS

Incandescent, fluorescent, and neon lights on porches and storefronts, especially in undeveloped areas, are very attractive to many kinds of beetles. The bright bluish glow of a mercury vapor streetlight is much more attractive to beetles and other insects than the dull yellowish light emitted by their sodium vapor counterparts. Although many beetles will settle on the ground or wall directly beneath or behind the light, others, especially larger species, may prefer to remain on plants and other surfaces just beyond the light's glow.

INDOORS

Look for living and dead beetles on windowsills and in light fixtures inside houses, garages, sheds, and warehouses. Household and structural pests, as well as other beetles trapped indoors, are usually attracted to sunlit windows and other light sources. High numbers of skin beetles (Dermestidae) or pantry pest species are indicative of infested stored foods, skins, plant materials, wood products, and insect collections.

OBSERVING AND PHOTOGRAPHING BEETLES

Making a beetle collection (see p.58) is the best way to learn about beetles. Only by having specimens in hand will you have the opportunity to critically examine the physical features necessary to facilitate accurate species identification and develop an understanding of their classification. However, some readers may prefer instead to simply observe or photograph beetles alive in the wild.

BEETLES THROUGH BINOCULARS

Close-focusing binoculars allow you to observe beetles on flowers or shorelines less than 2 meters away with amazing color and clarity. The larger the diameter of the eyepiece, or objective, the more light that is gathered to form the image. The best binoculars for handheld use are 8 × 42 or 10 × 42. An objective magnification of 8 produces an image as if the viewer were 8 times closer to the subject. A 10-power binocular will make the image larger, but the smaller field of view can make tracking of moving beetles a bit more of a challenge. Lower power binoculars with smaller oculars (e.g., 7 × 36) are also useful. They are smaller and less expensive, but your subjects will not be as magnified or brilliant. When buying a pair of close-focusing binoculars, compare several brands at the same time to determine which model and magnification works best for you and fits your budget. A close-focusing monocular is also useful, less expensive, and easily stowed in your field kit.

A pair of compact binoculars with the front lenses closer together than the eyepiece lenses (reverse Porro prism design) can be modified for close-up beetle watching. Screw a two-element Nikon 5T or 6T close-up lens into a soft lens hood, place the hood with lens in front of the binoculars, and affix them using heavy rubber bands to achieve a close-focusing capability.

BEETLE MACRO PHOTOGRAPHY

Macro, or close-up photography was once the domain of highly proficient photographers using expensive and complex equipment. Today, good quality macro photographs are relatively easy to make, review, and share. Even the most casual photographer can capture good images with relatively inexpensive point-and-shoot digital cameras or smartphones with macro-like capabilities. The very best images, including most of those that grace these pages, were taken with digital single-lens reflex (DSLR) cameras with dedicated macro lenses with focal lengths of 50 mm, 90 mm, or 100 mm that allow focusing on beetles just a few millimeters from the lens. As of this writing, digital single lens mirrorless (DSLM) cameras are becoming more popular with macro photographers.

The distance between the lens and the beetle is called the *working distance*. When fully extended, macro lenses allow you to fill the frame of your photograph with an up to life-size (1:1) image of a beetle. Some beetles are a bit skittish at these close working distances, while others seem not to notice the camera at all. Macro lenses with longer focal lengths (150 mm, 200 mm) have greater working distances and still offer 1:1 capability, but they are bulky, difficult to hold steady, and very expensive. To obtain magnifications greater than life size, 1:2 or more, doublers, teleconverters, and extension tubes of 25 mm or greater are placed between the lens and the camera body. High-quality close-up lenses of varying magnifications screwed on the front of the macro lens can be useful, but will reduce already close working distances and sometimes degrade image quality.

In macro photography, focus is best achieved not by using the camera's autofocus feature, but instead selecting the desired magnification in advance based on the beetle's size and the kind of image you want to make. Once the lens is extended, aim the camera at your subject and look through the viewfinder to compose the shot. Then slowly rock back and forth until the subject is in focus and take the picture. Most beetle images look best when the subject, especially the eyes, and background are both in sharp focus. The depth of focus in a photo, usually referred to as the depth of field, is the distance between the nearest and farthest objects in the photo that are in focus. Think of text on a page photographed at an angle—the sentences in the image that are in focus are indicative of the depth of field. Depth of field is determined by the opening at the back of the lens, or aperture. The aperture is expressed as an *f*-stop; the bigger the *f*-stop number, the smaller the aperture. Decreasing the aperture, or stopping down to $f/16$ or $f/22$, increases the depth of field; however, decreasing the *f*-stop also requires using flash to compensate for the reduced amount of natural light reaching the sensor.

Because of the long barrel of the 100 mm macro lens, the built-in flash on your camera's body will cast a shadow across your beetle and ruin the image; therefore, additional and adjustable external flashes attached to the end of the lens are your best bet. Two adjustable flashes are better than one and always better than the flat lighting provided by a ring flash. Placing these flashes at a 30-degree angle to the long axis of the lens barrel will create the effect of natural morning or afternoon sunlight; however, you may want to adjust one or both flashes to properly expose your subject and its background. Macro photographers often use one flash on the subject while a second flash provides a weaker "fill light" on the nearby background. Distant backgrounds that are underexposed appear dark or black and the overall impression of the photograph is often not pleasing, even if the subject is in perfect focus and properly exposed. The easiest way to compensate for this is by making sure that the background is close enough to the subject to be properly exposed by the flash. Always try to photograph a beetle resting on a leaf or flower rather than one perched on an isolated branch tip. Whenever possible, make sure the background is not so cluttered or busy that it distracts from your subject. Use the highest shutter speed (1/125 sec., 1/250 sec., etc.) possible that synchronizes your camera with the flash system to freeze the action of your subject and mitigate camera movement to make a razor-sharp image.

Take lots of pictures. Experiment with different combinations of apertures, shutter speeds, and flash settings under a variety of conditions, and carefully record these in a small notebook. Compare your notes with the resultant images to establish the settings and conditions that work best for your camera. Carefully review all your images either in camera or on your computer, then select and keep only the very best for each species. There is no point in tying up valuable space on your hard drive with inferior images. Store your images using one of many software applications, and be sure to label each image with locality data and any other pertinent information as if it were a specimen in a collection. This way, your images can be easily retrieved and become part of a permanent record of your travels and observations. Your best images will be those that are well exposed, in focus, and tell a story. The most compelling images of beetles capture them feeding, mating, laying eggs, or otherwise going about their business undisturbed in their own habitat.

There is no one way to photograph a beetle. Every photographer has their own favorite setup and method of working based on a combination of aesthetics, experience, taxonomic interests, available camera equipment, and degree of patience to experiment with said equipment. Most of my images reproduced in this guide were photographed with a Canon EOS Digital Rebel XTi set at ISO 100 with a 100 mm macro lens, up to 50 mm of extension tubes, and a Macro Twin Lite MT-24EX with Meike MK-MT24 diffusers. Each strobe was placed about 90 degrees apart, aimed at about 30 degrees from the axis of the macro lens. I generally used ƒ/16–18 and a shutter speed of 1/125 to

1/200 of a second. Instead of using a tripod to steady the camera, I strap on knee and elbow pads to absorb the shock to my joints produced by hunkering down on the ground, or bracing myself against trees and boulders.

It is important to remember that even the best beetle photographs are often insufficient for accurate identification, especially those species that require careful examination of difficult to see characters and internal structures, such as male genitalia. Thus, is it always desirable to collect beetles after you have photographed them so they are available for further study.

BEETLE CONSERVATION

Commercial and residential development, conversion to agricultural lands, agricultural runoff, grazing, logging, mining, inundation by water impoundments, wetland drainage, indiscriminate use by off-road vehicles, and overuse and abuse of pesticides and herbicides in urban and agricultural areas are just a few of the many human activities that adversely affect, alter, or destroy beetle habitats. The ever-growing list of exotic insect introductions, including those purposely introduced as biological control agents, can inflict unintended and possibly catastrophic consequences on indigenous beetle populations by choking out native food plants or outcompeting native beetles for food, shelter, and egg-laying sites. Climate change, too, will certainly affect many beetle populations, for better and worse.

Beetles restricted to ever-shrinking habitats are particularly susceptible to habitat destruction and competition from invasive species. Populations of *saproxylic*, or rotten-wood-feeding beetles (e.g., Tetratomidae, Melandryidae, Stenotrachelidae, Scraptiidae) in old-growth forests are significantly related to forest structure. The impacts of current forest management practices that fragment these mature growth forests and reduce coarse woody debris could severely impact the availability of food for both the larvae and adults. The coastal and desert dune habitats that support unique beetle species are also under constant threat by mining interests and off-road vehicle use.

Although beetles are among the most conspicuous and charismatic of all insects, our overall lack of knowledge of their biology, ecology, and distribution hampers efforts to identify and protect species in need of conservation. Relatively few species in western North America are recognized as threatened or endangered and afforded legal protection. To find out more about rare, threatened, and

49

endangered beetles in western United States, visit the U.S. Fish & Wildlife Service at fws.gov/Endangered/ and the NatureServe Explorer website at explorer.natureserve.org/.

ETHICS OF BEETLE COLLECTING

Unlike most birds, butterflies, macro moths, dragonflies, and damselflies that are easily identified on sight, many beetles must be in hand for close examination or dissection to facilitate accurate species identifications. Their capture and preservation not only assure identification, but also represent the first important step toward their species' conservation. The data associated with these specimens contribute to our understanding of their habitat preferences, activity period, and distribution. Beetle collecting, collections, and collectors all provide critical information that land managers and other decision makers need to develop and implement the best land-use practices to protect beetle populations.

Whether you are a professional biologist investigating a particular avenue of research, or a student or amateur naturalist who wants to learn more about insects and the natural world, you need not worry that your collecting activities will adversely affect most beetle populations. Such activities pale in comparison to the proficiency demonstrated by hungry insectivorous animals, or to the deleterious effects of pesticide use, mowing, vehicular traffic, artificial lights, and bug zappers. Habitat conversion and destruction, combined with competition from invasive species—not collecting or collectors—pose the greatest threats to beetle populations and habitats throughout western North America.

Beetles with small populations living in sensitive, specialized, or patchy and ephemeral habitats, such as species inhabiting sand dunes and vernal pools, or those dependent on populations of rare plants, should be collected only in small numbers. Elsewhere, the reproductive capacity of most beetles is much greater and differs dramatically from that of vertebrates. Birds, fish, reptiles, amphibians, and mammals all produce relatively few young and must invest enormous amounts of time and effort in nest building and caring for their young to ensure the survival of enough individuals to maintain stable populations. Removal of even a small number of these animals—parents or offspring—can have a major impact on local populations; however, a single female beetle may produce hundreds of young that require little if any parental care at all. Of these, only a few need to survive and reproduce to sustain a thriving population.

Adopt a collecting ethic that embraces the need to conserve beetle populations and their habitats, and

recognizes the rights of landowners. Collecting large numbers of the same species at the same time and place adds little to our knowledge of beetles and does not enhance the diversity that is the mark of a good reference collection. Such a collection, supported by accurate specimen label data and field notes, can only be built over time. The collection of beetles listed as endangered or threatened is strictly regulated, and it is the responsibility of the collector to know which species are afforded protection and to adhere to those regulations. When moving beetles, living or dead, be sure to comply with county, state, and federal agricultural and wildlife regulations. Transporting any living beetles or other insects across county, state, or international borders requires written permission from state or federal agricultural authorities, or both.

Always obtain permission to collect on private lands. Collecting on public lands, such as county, state, and national parks, state and national forests, monuments, and recreational areas, as well as indigenous lands, generally requires written permission, but these requirements may vary depending on locality and the purpose for collecting specimens. Managers of public lands are usually happy to issue permits to individuals conducting beetle surveys or other ecological studies, especially if they are affiliated with museums, universities, and other research institutions. Your efforts will provide data needed to effectively manage and preserve habitats for all wildlife. Always conduct your fieldwork within the conditions set forth in your permit and be respectful of other visitors. Once your project is completed, promptly share your data with the permitting agency and other researchers, and deposit voucher specimens in a permanent museum or university entomology collection.

COLLECTING AND PRESERVING BEETLES

The scientific data generated by professionals and dedicated amateurs collecting beetles are important not only to document the fauna of a given jurisdiction or region, but also to track species diversity and faunal composition over time. The collections of amateur coleopterists working in concert with museum scientists are particularly useful for filling gaps in permanent collections of museums and universities and often provide the basis for both scientific and popular publications. On a more basic level, collecting beetles is a great way to get outside, sharpen your skills of observation, and learn firsthand the biology and ecology of the most diverse group of animals in western North America. Beetle collecting is also an excellent way of getting youngsters outdoors and introducing them to the diversity of nature. Many scientists and educators, including the author of this book, cite the activity of collecting beetles and other insects as the spark that launched their lifelong careers of research and public service.

The initial cost of collecting beetles is minimal, since the basic "tools" required are a sharp pair of eyes, patience, persistence, a few containers, and a bit of luck. Nets, beating sheets, and other collecting equipment listed below are also useful. As your knowledge of the seasonal and habitat proclivities of beetles increases, so will your desire to explore new habitats and try out different collecting equipment and techniques. With time and experience, your collecting activities will become more targeted, and these efforts will contribute to the overall diversity of your collection.

As your expertise develops and research collection grows, you will likely want to know more about curatorial and management topics, including safely preparing shipments of specimens for loans or exchange with other coleopterists. For detailed information on entomological techniques and equipment, consult *Collecting and Preserving Insects and Mites. Techniques and Tools* (Schauff 1986) or *Collecting, Preparing, and Preserving Insects, Mites, and Spiders* (Martin 1977). The Entomological Collections Network (ECN) is a nonprofit organization that promotes entomological science through the preservation, management, use and development of entomological collections and taxonomy. This organization hosts annual meetings and a lively and informative online forum that disseminates best practices information to collection managers and other interested persons worldwide.

BASIC TOOLS FOR HANDLING AND EXAMINING BEETLES

Forceps made of spring aluminum are known as "featherweights." They are extremely useful for picking up small beetles without damaging them, while camel-hair brushes are used to probe for and dislodge beetles from their resting and hiding places.

Aspirators of various designs are useful tools for sucking small beetles from beating sheets, nets, and other substrates into a glass or plastic vial. Protective gauze over the intake tube prevents the accidental inhalation of beetles and other bits, while an inline fuel filter will extract smaller particles, but neither of these protections will completely prevent the inhalation of molds, spores, insect feces, or the noxious defensive odors produced by many beetles.

Blowing aspirators, or those using a suction bulb, do not involve sucking air through a mouthpiece and alleviate these potential hazards, but they are not widely used.

No one who spends any time in the field should be without a good quality hand lens. Available from biological supply companies, hand lenses are small and compact devices for revealing beetle anatomy and other details that might otherwise escape notice by the naked eye alone. Magnifications of 8× or 10× are ideal, with some units employing several lenses in concert to increase magnification. The trick is to hold the hand lens close to your eye and then move in on your subject until it comes into sharp focus.

KILLING JARS AND KILLING AGENTS

Beetles retained as specimens for a collection must be dispatched quickly and humanely. Freezing is an easy and nontoxic method, but the specimens must be kept cool and calm in a small ice chest until they can be placed in a freezer overnight. Using a killing jar with a bit of loosely crumpled paper that is freshly charged with several drops of ethyl acetate or some other killing agent is often a more practical solution. Ethyl acetate is available from biological and scientific supply houses. Although it is relatively safe to use, avoid getting it on your skin, breathing the fumes, or using it near an open flame. The wadded paper toweling not only holds the killing agent, but also absorbs excess fluids produced by your catch and protects your delicate specimens from jostling. Continually opening and closing the killing jar will result in the loss of its potency, so you will have to recharge the killing jar from time to time. A small, 2-ounce squeeze bottle filled with ethyl acetate makes this task easy. Note that ethyl acetate dissolves anything made of styrene, including clear hard plastic bottles and polystyrene foam. Any jar will serve as a killing jar if it has a broad mouth and tight-fitting screw-top lid to retain volatile killing agents. Long cylindrical jars, such as those used for olives, pickled onions, or spices, that are no more than 15 cm tall slip easily into a pocket or collecting bag.

Dark, colorfast beetles with few setae are sometimes killed and temporarily stored by placing them directly in fluid preservative such as 70–95% ethyl alcohol (ethanol) or 70% rubbing alcohol (isopropyl). For long-term storage of larger specimens, pour off the old alcohol and replace it with fresh after a week or two. Although there is no one method for killing beetles for morphological examination, beetles intended for use in tissue studies or molecular analysis must be placed directly in 95% ethanol. Ethanol is generally unavailable to private individuals, except for

51

prohibitively expensive neutral grain spirits, or pure grain alcohol available for purchase in liquor stores. Isopropyl in concentrations of 70% and 91% is readily available in drug and grocery stores, but over time, 91% isopropyl dries out specimens and makes them quite brittle.

NETS

Nets are essential for capturing beetles on the wing, resting on vegetation, or living in aquatic habitats. Flying beetles are best captured with aerial nets with a rim diameter of 30–40 cm and a handle 1 meter long. The net opening is usually reinforced with canvas or some other heavy material to prevent it from tearing. The net bag is made of cotton bobbinet or some other soft and translucent material that will hold its shape and is long enough to easily fold over the rim to trap beetles inside. The tip of the bag is typically rounded, not pointed, so that beetles and other insects are easily removed after capture. These lightweight and durable nets are easily maneuvered when swung through the air. Aerial nets are also used to capture tiger beetles by clapping them over the beetle and then holding the tip of the net bag so that the beetle will climb up into the net. Heavy-duty aerial nets are available commercially and have a net bag that is half canvas and half mesh; these are also used for light-duty sweeping through herbaceous vegetation.

Sweep nets are used to dislodge beetles from the tops of grasses, shrubs, and tree branches. They have shorter, thicker handles, sturdy net rings, and net bags constructed completely of canvas to endure repeated brushing through dense vegetation. Beetles are more likely captured in a sweep net if the rim is kept vertical to the ground. After completing a series of sweeps, swing the net back and forth several times and fold it over the rim to trap the insects inside toward the tip of the net bag. Slowly open the net to release stinging bees and wasps before removing beetles inside by hand, with forceps, or with an aspirator and transferring them to a killing jar.

Aquarium nets are useful for capturing aquatic beetles swimming along the edges of ponds and slow-moving streams. Long-handled dip nets are helpful for scooping beetles swimming in open water further out. D-frame nets have rims that are flat on one side and are dragged along the bottom of standing and moving waters to dislodge specimens resting on rocks and plants. Each of these nets placed vertically on the substrate in moving waters will capture beetles dislodged by lifting stones or disturbing vegetation upstream.

BEATING SHEET

Beating the branches and foliage of trees and shrubs, day or night, is an incredibly productive method for collecting beetles. Beating sheets are typically square sheets of light-colored canvas or ripstop nylon stretched out with two hardwood dowels or plastic tubes as crosspieces, with their ends slipped into reinforced pockets sewn into each corner of the sheet. To collect beetles, place the sheet beneath the foliage and then strike a large branch directly above with another dowel or net handle (Fig. 50). Beetles and other insects and arthropods jarred loose from their perches fall onto the sheet where they are collected using forceps or an aspirator. Beating during the day is most productive in the cooler morning hours in spring and summer. During the heat of the day, beetles often take flight the moment they hit the sheet. Nighttime beating is the best way to find many nocturnal species, including those that are not attracted to lights or baits.

A similar, more targeted method for sampling small flower visitors and other beetles involves using a white plastic pan (Fig. 51) in place of a beating sheet. Such pans have the added advantage of facilitating the extraction of specimens from handfuls of leaf litter, rotten wood, fungi, moss, and other organic materials.

SIEVING

Beetles are extracted from ground litter, fungi, lichens, mosses, soil, and decaying wood samples using various containers fitted with a screened bottom. The size of the mesh is determined by the size of beetles sought. Place the substrate in the container, shake it gently over a white or light-colored pan, sheet, or shower curtain, and collect the beetles with forceps, aspirator, or camel-hair brush. Kitchen strainers work well for sifting beach sand and other fine, dry

Figure 50. Using a beating sheet is an incredibly productive method of collecting beetles.

Figure 51. A white pan is used like a beating sheet or for sorting through handfuls of leaf litter, rotten wood, and other organic materials.

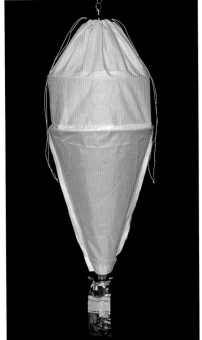

Figure 52. Collapsible Berlese funnel for extracting small beetles and other arthropods from leaf litter.

soils. Beetles and larger pieces of debris retained in the screen are dumped onto a light-colored surface for further sorting, or placed in a Berlese or Winkler funnel.

BERLESE AND WINKLER FUNNELS

The *Berlese-Tullgren funnel* (Fig. 52), or simply *Berlese funnel*, uses the combination of light, heat, and desiccation created by a low-wattage incandescent light bulb to extract beetles from debris samples. Place a piece of coarse screen above the opening of the funnel to prevent debris from falling into the jar. Then fill the funnel with beach wrack, fungi, leaf litter, rotten wood, and other plant debris and place the light bulb above to drive beetles and other arthropod inhabitants downward into a glass jar filled with 70% ethanol or isopropyl as a preservative. The time required to extract all the beetles may be several days, depending on the size and moisture content of the sample.

The *Winkler/Moczarski eclector*, or *Winkler funnel*, is a more portable system. Rather than depending mostly on desiccation of the sample, this method also relies on the movement of beetles and other arthropods within the sample. Litter and rotten wood are collected at the bases of living trees and stumps, alongside logs, or in depressions. These samples are then placed into a Winkler sifter and shaken vigorously through a coarse screen to remove leaves and branches (Fig. 53). Plastic buckets or bins fitted with 6 or 12 mm mesh hardware cloth bottoms will also

Figure 53. A Winkler eclector separates beetles and other small arthropods from larger bits of leaf litter.

facilitate the separation of beetles from these and other coarse plant materials. Beetles and other litter arthropods accumulate within the fine siftate that passes through the screen. The siftate is poured into one or more mesh bags suspended inside the Winkler bag, which is tied off at the top. The large surface area of each mesh bag increases the chances of beetles and other arthropods moving through the sample to crawl through the mesh and fall into a plastic drink cup below that is half-filled with ethanol or isopropyl. Winkler bags are suspended in a well-ventilated place for up to several days so that all the sample's arthropod inhabitants have fallen into the preservative.

FLOATING

Another useful method for separating beetles from plant materials—particularly clumps of grass, but also fungi,

bark, and dung—is to drop the materials into a bucket of water. Beetles and other insects will float to the surface, where they can be scooped up with a small kitchen strainer or collected by hand.

FLUMING

Collecting beetles and other insects from flumes is called fluming. Flumes traversing foothills, particularly along the western slopes of the Sierra Nevada in California, were constructed to divert water from streams and rivers to generate hydroelectricity, irrigate crops, and provide municipalities with drinking water. Functioning as both pitfall trap and conveyor belt, flumes are literally awash in plant debris during the spring and summer that is laden with insects, especially beetles. Sometimes flowing for miles through steep terrain and varied habitats, flumes carry an

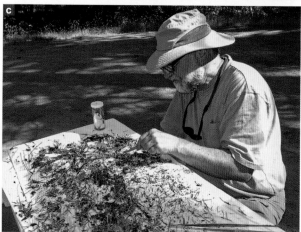

Figure 54. Fluming.
a–b. long-handled pool skimmers are strapped to bridge rails to collect insect-laden plant debris floating down flumes; c. beetles and other insects are sorted from plant debris spread out on a white bed sheet draped over a table.

incredible diversity of trapped insects. Watching the rapidly flowing water to net individual specimens as they float by is not nearly as productive as systematically skimming the water to secure a diversity of beetles. One such method involves employing pool nets to capture debris from the water surface, then hauling the nets out and depositing their contents onto a table covered with a white bed sheet for sorting (Fig. 54).

COLLECTING AT LIGHTS

The most productive method of collecting beetles at night involves attracting them with a light suspended in front of or over a white sheet or polyester shower curtain. Almost any light will attract night-flying beetles, but black or ultraviolet light (Fig. 55) is the most effective. Commercially available black lights operate on house current or 12-volt batteries. Mercury vapor lights using 175-watt bulbs are also very attractive to beetles and other night-flying insects, but require house current or a generator to operate. Note that these bulbs become extremely hot and will break if they come into contact with rain or other sources of moisture. Suspend a freshly laundered sheet between two trees or poles over a ground sheet. Place the light about a foot away and parallel to the upright sheet at about eye level to achieve maximum illumination. Be sure to regularly patrol the ground and nearby shrubs just beyond the illuminated area to find beetles crawling on the ground or wandering about plants, trees, stumps, and logs. Using a headlamp instead of a flashlight will keep both your hands free for

collecting specimens. Warm spring and summer nights (65 °F or higher), especially with little or no moon, are the most productive. Most beetles arrive at lights within two hours after sunset, but some, especially larger species, fly later in the evening. Light traps (Fig. 56) use a black light suspended over a funnel placed over a 3- or 5-gallon bucket. Acrylic or metal vanes help to direct beetles and other insects down the funnel and into the bucket. Supplying the bucket with paper egg cartons or wadded-up paper towels will reduce the wear and tear on beetles and other insects caught in the trap. Always use a collecting jar dedicated to beetles, as mixing them with other insects, especially moths, often results in beetles covered in scales, or other insect specimens damaged by beetle claws.

TRAPPING BEETLES

Methods for trapping beetles, with or without the use of baits, lures, lights, and other attractants, are just as diverse as the beetles themselves. The performance of these traps depends on the selected trap site, time of year, and local conditions. Pitfall traps are designed to capture beetles crawling on the ground. Using a trowel or small shovel, dig a hole just large enough to accommodate a 16-ounce plastic deli or drink cup. Place the cup in the hole so the rim is flush with the surface of the ground. Then place an identical cup within the first cup. Nesting the cups in this fashion allows easy inspection of the trap without having to re-dig the hole each time. Cover the trap with a flat stone or

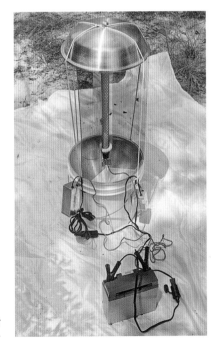

LEFT: **Figure 55.** An ultraviolet light powered by a 12-volt battery suspended in front of an upright sheet to attract beetles and other insects.

RIGHT: **Figure 56.** A 12-volt blacklight bucket trap.

slab of wood raised on small stones, leaving a space large enough for beetles but small enough to keep out larger animals. Place unbaited pitfall traps along natural barriers, such as rock ledges and logs. Otherwise, use wood, metal, or plastic drift fences to increase the effective surface area for each trap (Fig. 57). Pitfalls baited with small amounts of fresh dung, carrion, rotting fruit, or chopped mushrooms will attract and capture beetles over a large surface area without the aid of physical obstacles. Solid and liquid baits are wrapped in cheesecloth or placed in small plastic sauce cups, respectively, and suspended over the trap opening with sticks, wires, or string (Fig. 58). Liquid baits consisting of equal parts molasses and water, or malt with a pinch

of yeast, attract species naturally drawn to sap flows. For traps that are checked daily, place crumpled paper towels or leaves at the bottom to provide beetles with a bit of cover. Pitfalls left out for a week or more are supplied a 50–50 mix of propylene glycol and water to kill and preserve beetles. Unlike ethylene glycol (antifreeze), propylene glycol is not toxic to wildlife. Fruit traps made from plastic drink bottles, cups, or corncob bird feeders (Fig. 59) and hung at various heights in trees and shrubs are very attractive to beetles. Be sure to check these traps regularly and provide a metal or plastic rain guard to prevent specimens from being washed out of the trap. Pan traps, especially bright yellow ones filled with about 50 mm of water (Fig. 60), are

Figure 57. Pitfall trap array.

Figure 58. Pitfall trap with soapy water sunk beneath a stick baited with feces.

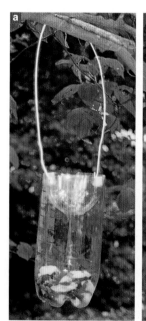

LEFT: **Figure 59.** Fruit traps.
a. trap made from a plastic soft drink bottle;
b. ripe banana placed in a corncob squirrel feeder.

Figure 60. Yellow pan trap filled with soapy water to attract flower-visiting beetles and other insects.

especially attractive to some jewel beetles (Buprestidae), tumbling flower beetles (Mordellidae), and other flower-visiting insects. A drop or two of dish soap added to the water will break the surface tension, making it harder for the beetles to escape.

Flight intercept traps (Fig. 61) generally consist of one or more upright clear plastic panels suspended over a series of pans containing soapy water or propylene glycol. Beetles colliding with the screen fall into the fluid, where they are killed and temporarily preserved. A plastic roof placed over the top of the trap will prevent rainwater from diluting the fluid. A Malaise trap (Fig. 62) is essentially a tent with a wall or partition on the inside. Flying beetles strike the interior walls and fly up into a collecting jar filled with 70% ethanol or isopropyl alcohol. A shallow trough or series of roasting pans filled with fluid are placed under the partition to capture specimens that fall to the ground rather than fly up into the collecting jar. Both traps produce large numbers of diurnal and nocturnal species that are not readily collected via other methods.

Lindgren funnel traps (Fig. 63) consist of a series of four or more black funnels suspended over one another and hung from a branch, rope between two trees, or some other hanger. At the bottom of the funnels is a collecting container that is either dry or partially filled with propylene glycol or some other preservative. The stack of funnels resembles a tree trunk and is attractive to wood-boring beetles and other species that crawl or land on tree trunks. Lindgren funnel traps are sometimes baited with alpha-pinene (a component of turpentine) and ethanol, chemical compounds that mimic those released by injured and dying conifers and hardwoods. Specimens captured in dry collection containers are easily damaged and are best removed every few days, while those with preservative may be inspected weekly or every two weeks.

ABOVE LEFT:
Figure 61.
A V-shaped flight intercept trap.

ABOVE RIGHT:
Figure 62.
Malaise trap.

LEFT:
Figure 63.
Lindgren funnel trap.

TEMPORARY STORAGE OF SPECIMENS

Beetle specimens should be prepared immediately after they are collected and killed, but this is not always possible. Specimens left in killing jars charged with adequate amounts of ethyl acetate will remain relaxed for several days or weeks and can be handled without damage. They can also be transferred to a tightly sealed container and stored in the freezer. For longer periods of storage, carefully place specimens between layers of paper towels moistened with a few drops of ethyl acetate or preserved by adding chlorocresol crystals and store in soft plastic storage boxes with airtight lids. Specimens stored in this manner will keep indefinitely, but delicate colors will fade and setae become matted. Large numbers of beetles collected from Berlese or Winkler funnels, pitfalls, and blacklight traps can be placed in 70% ethanol or isopropyl alcohol. After about a week, replace the fluid with fresh alcohol. Specimens intended for molecular studies must be killed and preserved in 100% ethanol. All specimens preserved in alcohol should be kept cool, especially those intended for subsequent DNA work. Always include basic collecting information (locality, date, collector) inside each container, using pencil or permanent ink on good quality acid-free paper. Samples without this information are of little value and should be discarded.

RECORDS AND FIELD NOTES

Always record the date, place, and collector's name for your specimens. Be sure to include the country, province or state, and county, as well as the name of the nearest city or town, mileage and direction from the nearest road junction, latitude and longitude, and any other locality data that will help fix your collecting locality on a map. These data will become the basis for the locality labels for your specimens and serve as directions to others who may want to retrace your steps to find a specific locality to search for a species.

Dead beetles in collections reveal little of their lives, so it is important to spend some time observing their behaviors whenever possible and record them in your field notes. Your observations should always include time of day, temperature and humidity, plant or animal associations, and reproductive and feeding behaviors; such details are all worthy of note and could easily be new to science. Whenever possible, record these observations in the field, as they are happening. Never trust your memory for long because it is all too easy to confuse bits of information in time and place. With practice, you will settle on a routine for recording your observations.

Maintaining a detailed and accurate field notebook is an important component of a carefully curated beetle collection. The value of the notes is enhanced if they are clearly associated with specific specimens, especially those identified to species. Select a well-bound notebook with acid-free paper that is small enough to pack in your field kit, but large enough not to be easily lost or misplaced, and will withstand the rigors of field use. Pencils and fine-tip marking pens with permanent black ink, such as those manufactured by Prismacolor and Pigma Micron, are available from art supply stores and are the most reliable for taking notes in all sorts of weather.

MAKING A BEETLE COLLECTION

There is still much to learn about the beetles of western North America. Carefully prepared collections, notes, and photographs add enormously to our understanding of their distribution, seasonal activity, and food and habitat preferences and provide a historical record that will offer insights into the possible impacts of climate change. If properly cared for, beetle collections will last hundreds of years to inspire and inform future generations of coleopterists and naturalists. Coleopterists—professionals and amateurs alike—are but temporary caretakers of collections that ultimately belong to the greater scientific community. Should you lose interest, lack adequate storage space, or simply want to preserve the legacy of your hard work long after you are gone, consider donating your collection and its associated records to an appropriate research institution dedicated to housing permanent insect collections and making them available to researchers and students. Below are some tips and tools for building and maintaining a scientifically valuable and aesthetically pleasing beetle collection.

PINNING AND POINTING SPECIMENS

Dead, dried beetles are very brittle, and touching them will result in broken and lost appendages that will make their identification difficult, if not outright impossible. For specimens to be manipulated without damage, they must be mounted on pins that are safely used as handles. Always use black-enameled or stainless-steel insect pins because sewing pins are too short and thick and will corrode. Insect pins are available through entomological supply houses in packets of 100 in several sizes (diameters). Sizes 0–3 are suitable for most of the species found in western North America. Sizes 00 and 000 bend easily and are not recommended for mounting beetles.

Pin beetle specimens when their appendages are still pliable enough to manipulate without damage. Working only with beetles collected at the same place and time, temporarily place your specimens on a folded tissue or paper towel for several minutes to absorb excess moisture. After selecting the appropriate-size pin, grasp your specimen firmly between the thumb and forefinger or brace it on the table with its topside up. With your other hand, push the pin through the base of the right elytron with the pin exiting underneath between the middle and hind legs. Before driving the pin all the way through, check the relative alignment of the specimen

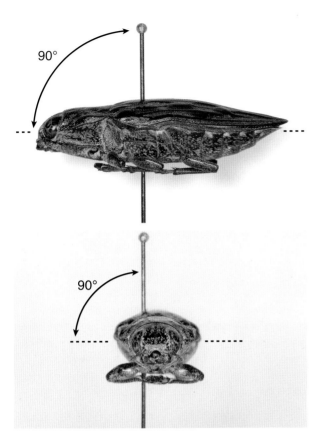

90°

90°

Figure 64. Proper longitudinal and transverse orientation of a beetle specimen on pin.

Figure 65. Pinning block.

Figure 66. Proper longitudinal and transverse orientation of a beetle specimen affixed to a point.

carefully to make sure the shaft of the pin is perpendicular to the long and transverse axes of the body (Fig. 64).

Once the pin is all the way through, use the highest or shortest step of your pinning block to adjust the height of the beetle on the pin so a space of about 25 mm is left between the top of the specimen and the head of the pin. A pinning block (Fig. 65) is a small block of hardwood with three or four fine holes drilled successively deeper in 12 mm increments, beginning with 12 mm. Using this simple tool will enable you to consistently space the head of the pin above the specimen and the intervals between the specimen and its labels underneath.

Specimens that are 5 mm or less or very narrow and likely to be damaged by direct pinning are best preserved on points (Fig. 66). Points are isosceles triangles of acid-free card stock that are about 7 mm long and 2 mm wide at the base. The occasional point can be cut with sharp scissors, but a point punch, available from entomological supply houses, is desirable for making large numbers of uniform points. Push an insect pin (no. 2 or 3) through the broad end of the point and adjust its height on the shaft using the highest step on your pinning block. Using fine-tipped forceps, slightly bend down the tip of the point before attaching it to the specimen. For the sake of convenience, prepare several dozen points in advance to have them ready. Affixing a beetle to a point is best done under well-illuminated magnification provided by an optical visor or binocular dissecting microscope. Place the specimen to be pointed on its back (*dorsum*) or underside (*ventrum*) on a smooth, light-colored surface so the head is to the right and you have unfettered access to the beetle's right-hand side. Then dip the tip of the point into adhesive that is soluble in water (e.g., Elmer's blue gel) or alcohol (shellac, polyvinyl acetate) and affix it to the area of the thorax between the middle and hind legs. Be sure that there is enough glue to securely attach the specimen to the point, but not so much that it spreads and obscures important features needed for identification. Alcohol-soluble adhesives normally thicken with use and can be thinned by adding a bit more alcohol. If too thin, leave the container open for a brief period to allow excess alcohol to volatilize. Once the beetle is glued to the point, minor adjustments can be made so that its body axes are perpendicular to the shaft of the pin.

SPREADING SPECIMENS

Accurate species identification in beetles often requires careful examination of a specimen's appendages, mouthparts, body segments, and genitalia. Familiarity with these features will help guide and improve your efforts to properly prepare and spread specimens. A spreading board (Fig. 67) is the best way to position and set a beetle's antennae and legs in place. Purchase a small sheet of polystyrene foam 2.5 cm thick (30 × 46 × 2.5 cm) from a craft store and wrap it in newsprint to prevent claws and mouthparts of dried specimens from catching on the board's rough surface and breaking off. Start by pinning a temporary locality label in the upper left corner of the spreading board. To the right of the label, push the first pinned beetle into the spreading board so the underside of the body rests directly on the board's surface. Carefully position the legs and antennae with brace pins so that these structures are symmetrical and observable from all angles. Tuck in legs and antennae, since specimens with

outstretched appendages take up valuable space and are likely to be broken. Be sure to keep spread specimens from each locality separate so they can be accurately labeled when they are dry. It may take a week or so for specimens to dry, depending on the size of the specimen and relative humidity. You may want to keep your spreading boards in a protected yet airy space, such as in a covered box, in a cupboard, or on shelves with doors so that your specimens don't get dusty. Once the specimen is dried, carefully remove the brace pins to avoid damaging the now brittle appendages.

LABELING

To be of any scientific value, each specimen must have a permanent, carefully composed, and neatly produced locality label. Using word processing software, type locality labels in columns in a bold sans serif font (Arial, Geneva, Helvetica) at a size of 4- or 5- point size. Each finished label should be no more than 2 cm across and five or six lines long, although some adjustments may be required depending on the length and the nature of the label data. Labels are printed on acid-free 176 g/m^2 card stock with a laser printer set at 1200 dpi or 600 dpi professional. Cut the printed labels into strips and then individually with sharp scissors so that all four sides are neatly trimmed right up to the text.

Locality labels should include the following information on the first line: country (abbreviated as USA or CAN), state or province (e.g., CA for California, BC for British Columbia), and county. The remaining four or five lines of the label include the general locality, specific locality (if applicable), elevation (in feet [ft], or meters [m]), latitude and longitude (preferably in decimal degrees), date (with month spelled out, or as a Roman numeral [eg., vii for July] and full year), collector name(s), and collecting method. A sample locality label is shown below:

> **USA: AZ, Santa Cruz Co.**
> **Santa Rita Mts., Madera Cyn.**
> **Santa Rita Lodge, 4900 ft. elev.**
> **31.7257° N, −110.8804° W**
> **25 July 2021, A.V. & P.G. Evans**
> **at black light**

An additional label may be added to more fully flesh out the method of collection, host plant, and other ecological data, as well as a cross-reference number that connects the specimen to photographs and field notes. Once the beetle is identified to species, a determination label containing the

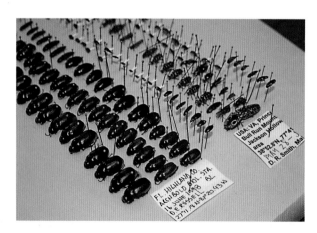

Figure 67. Spreading board with beetle specimens.

species name, name of determiner, and year of determination (as shown below) can be added as the very last label:

Dynastes grantii
(Horn, 1870)
det. A.V. Evans, 2021

Align the pinned specimen and its label so the beetle's head is directed toward the label's left margin. Center the specimen over the label and push the pin partway through. Select the appropriate step on the pinning block to adjust the height of the label on the pin. When labeling pointed specimens, center both the beetle and the point over the label with the point directed toward the label's left margin and the beetle's head off to the right of the point.

RELAXING SPECIMENS

To prepare dried specimens, or to reposition appendages or dissect those already mounted, specimens must first be "relaxed." Beetles that are not delicately patterned or colored, or those lacking any kind of setose or waxy vestiture that could become matted, discolored, or dissolved are placed directly in hot water. Simply bring filtered or distilled water to a boil and then add a drop of dish soap as a wetting agent. After several minutes, specimens submerged in this solution should become pliable enough to manipulate safely; larger and bulkier specimens may take longer.

For delicate specimens with pubescence that should not come into direct contact with water, it is best to use a relaxing chamber. Place a layer of clean sand, cardboard, blotter paper, or some other relatively sterile and porous substrate in a soft (polyethylene) plastic shoe box or

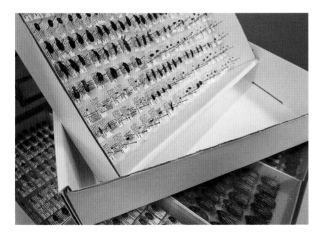

Figure 68. Beetle collections are stored in pest-proof cardboard specimen boxes or glass-topped drawers supplied with unit trays.

food storage container. Saturate the substrate with warm water and pour off the excess. Place dry specimens in a plastic jar lid so they will not come in direct contact with wet surfaces. Add a couple of mothballs to the chamber to discourage mold. Smaller beetles with more delicate bodies will become sufficiently relaxed overnight, but larger, heavier-bodied specimens may take several days to soften. Inspect the chamber every few days for mold that will damage or destroy specimens. Insect pins that corrode in a relaxing chamber should be replaced.

PRESERVING LARVAE AND PUPAE

Larvae and pupae, especially those with ecological data and positively associated with adult voucher specimens, are extremely valuable and should be permanently preserved. Place them in boiling water for several minutes to fix their tissues and kill the microorganisms that will hasten internal tissue decay. Then place them directly in 70% ethanol or isopropyl alcohol. After a day or so, place these specimens (one species per collection) in polyethylene vials with screw caps supplied with a fresh supply of alcohol for permanent storage. Each vial must have its own label inside to be of any scientific value. Long shelf life for wet labels can be problematic because of the effects of preservatives on various papers, ink, and laser-printed text and is still undergoing study. For now, the simplest solution is to use acid-free 100% rag paper with pencil or to print laser labels at 1200 dpi or 600 dpi professional. Before cutting the sheet into individual labels, coat it with clear acrylic spray sealer to increase its durability. Readers interested in building and maintaining extensive collections of beetle larvae and pupae would do well to keep up with published literature and online forum discussions on the latest materials and techniques.

COLLECTION STORAGE

Sturdy, airtight specimen boxes with tight-fitting lids are a must for the permanent storage of beetle specimens. Dermestids, both larvae and adults, and booklice (Psocodea) can slip through the narrowest of spaces and, in a relatively short period of time, reduce pinned beetle collections to dust. Fluctuating temperatures, humidity, and sunlight will also destroy collections over time, so it is important to store them in dark and temperature-controlled spaces.

Storing specimens in tightly sealed glass-topped drawers that are kept in sealed cabinets is the best hedge against light and pest damage, but these systems are expensive. Wooden specimen boxes with tight-fitting lids, known as

Schmitt or Schmitt-type boxes, also provide adequate protection for specimens, but are also pricey. Entomology departments at museums or universities occasionally offer surplus drawers and boxes at reasonable prices. A relatively inexpensive system consists of commercially available cardboard specimen boxes with separate lids and foam bottoms (Fig. 68) that are slipped into 2-gallon resealable plastic bags to keep out pests.

None of these systems is completely effective, especially if beetles left out on spreading boards or open trays become infested with the eggs or larvae of pests and are then introduced into otherwise pest-proof containers. Constant vigilance for fine powder accumulating beneath specimens is essential for identifying those infested with booklice or dermestid larvae. Remove these specimens immediately, take their labels off the pin, and immerse the specimen in alcohol for at least one day. If several specimens within the same box are affected, place the entire box in a very cold freezer for at least a week. This process may need to be repeated, as freezing will usually kill all the dermestid larvae present but may leave unhatched eggs unaffected.

CURATING YOUR COLLECTION

Align your specimens in neat columns and rows using either the label or specimen itself as a guide to create nice, straight rows. Orient each specimen so that the head of the pinned beetle or the tip of the point is directed toward the top of the box. Avoid entangling legs and antennae by not overcrowding specimens. Organize your collection first by family and subfamily, then by tribe, genus, and species (see p.564). A good reference collection not only contains well-prepared specimens accompanied by accurate label data, but is also organized to facilitate the easy retrieval of those specimens. As your collection grows in size and diversity, you might consider adopting a glass-topped drawer system housed in cabinets. These drawers are supplied with interchangeable cardboard trays of various sizes lined with polyethylene foam bottoms called unit trays. Unit tray systems simplify curation and are easily expanded to accommodate the addition of new taxa and specimens. Glass-topped drawers with pinned beetles intended primarily for display must be kept dry and away from extreme temperatures to avoid the growth of mold, and out of direct sunlight to prevent fading. Display cases fitted with UV-filtered Plexiglas will slow, but not prevent, the fading of specimens exposed to sunlight.

BEETLES ON THE WEB

Information on beetles abounds on the Internet. Some of the most useful websites are those maintained by societies and institutions, but there are also helpful sites that are managed by knowledgeable amateurs through social media. The Coleopterists Society website contains not only information about society membership, but also listings of news, events, resources, and other items of interest to those fascinated by beetles.

There are several websites, including BugGuide, iNaturalist, and What's That Bug? where good images of beetles and other insects accompanied by geographic location and other pertinent information may be submitted for identification by knowledgeable members of the community. If you have a beetle that you want to identify, you can also browse images on these websites to search for possible matches. Facebook users can also upload images to several pages that are dedicated to insect identification, including "Pacific Northwest Bugs" and "SW U.S. Arthropods" that focus on insects, including beetles, of western North America.

One of the best ways to identify beetles is to compare them with reliably identified specimens. As it is not always possible to visit a collection in person, several museums have posted high-quality images of identified beetles in their collections online. For example, the Museum of Comparative Zoology at Harvard University has created the MCZBase: The Database of the Zoological Collections. Through online searches, users can locate and examine identified specimens, including holotypes, allotypes, and paratypes, the actual specimens upon which scientists based their original scientific descriptions of those species. Types have a special function in zoological nomenclature in that they serve as the physical standard for species that are formally described in the scientific literature. The Symbiota Collections of Arthropods Network (SCAN) has a collection of images submitted by more than 100 North American arthropod collections for all arthropod taxa, including beetles identified by experts. The New World Cerambycidae is an incredibly useful online resource for identifying longhorn beetles and contains images of types and other specimens that are authoritatively identified.

Access to recently published research articles that monograph beetles, offer identification keys, hypothesize their phylogenetic relationships, and other scientific research are often accessible only through paid subscriptions or to persons with institutional library affiliations. However, some authors immediately post their work at ResearchGate. Older, yet still important publications are often freely available through consortiums such as the Biodiversity Heritage Library (BHL) and Journal Storage (JSTOR).

Details for accessing these and other useful sites are provided in Selected References and Resources (pp.590–593).

KEEPING AND REARING BEETLES IN CAPTIVITY

Live beetles kept at home, in a classroom, or in a laboratory provide numerous opportunities to observe and photograph beetles as they undergo basic life processes. They require little space and are easy to display and maintain. For young students, caring for beetles instills a basic sense of awareness of the natural world by bringing into sharp focus the basic environmental and nutritional needs of organisms. For older students, captive beetles provide opportunities to engage in directed and open inquiry investigations into their behavior. Although few species of live beetles are sold commercially in North America, an amazing diversity of native species is available in nearby vacant lots, parks, and natural areas. Transporting live beetles may be regulated within counties, states, and provinces, and is strictly regulated across state, provincial, and international borders (see Beetle Conservation and the Ethics of Collecting).

TRANSPORT FROM THE FIELD

When transporting live beetles from the field, it is important to remember that even the briefest exposure to direct sunlight or the temperatures inside a closed car at the height of summer will quickly kill them, especially those species adapted to cool or moist habitats. Half- or one-pint deli cups or similar resealable plastic food containers are perfect for transporting beetles so they arrive alive and unharmed. They are inexpensive, lightweight, unbreakable, and easily nested for packing. Before placing beetles in the container, supply it with a piece of paper towel, some leaf litter, or a piece of moss and add a small amount of water to provide a bit of moisture and protect them from the rigors of travel. Always use moistened paper towels or moss when transporting aquatic beetles. Placing them in small amounts of water, even for short periods, may lead to their death by drowning. Then put the containers in an ice chest supplied with one or more frozen water bottles to keep them cool in transit. If the beetles are kept cool and not crowded in their containers, it is not necessary to punch air holes in the lids, especially for day trips.

HOUSING FOR ADULT TERRESTRIAL BEETLES

Keeping beetles in captivity requires some knowledge of their food and moisture requirements so that these conditions can be duplicated in captivity. Supply at least 25 mm depth of a 50–50 mixture of sterile sand and potting or forest soil on the bottom of an appropriately sized terrarium or deep plastic food container. Based on your observations of the beetles in the field, add rocks, bark, chunks of moss, or dried leaves for shelter, and branches and twigs for climbing. Beetles don't require a lot of air, but they do require good ventilation to release heat and control humidity. A secure screened lid attached with binder clips will not only prevent the escape of your animals but also provide plenty of ventilation to minimize the growth of harmful mold and fungi. Regularly mist the enclosure with distilled or filtered water and install a vial of water plugged with cotton and placed on its side. The cotton enables beetles to drink from the vial and acts as a wick that allows moisture to evaporate from the vial into the enclosure to help maintain humidity.

Offer predatory species appropriately sized adult and immature insects as food. Remember that the feeder insects must spend most of their time where they will be found by your beetles. Climbing and flying species are likely to be missed by mostly ground-dwelling predators. Provide plant feeders with fresh cuttings of their host plants placed in small jars or vials of water to maintain freshness as long as possible. Stuffing cotton into the top of the jar to hold the plants in place will prevent beetles from wandering inside and drowning. Some phytophagous species will accept romaine lettuce or other leafy greens, oatmeal, potato slices, and various kinds of fruit. Always remove uneaten plant and animal foods after a day or two to prevent the buildup of mold, mites, and other pests.

Various darkling beetles (Tenebrionidae), *Phloeodes* and *Zopherus* ironclad beetles (Zopheridae), green peach beetles (*Cotinis mutabilis*), western Hercules beetles (*Dynastes grantii*), caterpillar hunters (*Calosoma* species), and tiger beetles (*Cicindela*, etc.) are all relatively large and hardy species that do well in captivity. Green June beetles thrive in a terrarium supplied with several inches of sandy loam, branches to climb, and a variety of soft fruits (peaches, grapes, strawberries, bananas, etc.) to eat. They will mate and lay eggs readily in their enclosure. The C-shaped grubs will develop in a deep, organic substrate supplied with a mixture of leaf litter, grass clippings, and crushed dry dog food. Western Hercules beetles (*Dynastes grantii*) are kept in similar enclosures with thicker branches for climbing and will also eat soft fruits, especially peaches and bananas. They will also accept cotton balls or sponges soaked in a 50–50 solution of water and maple syrup as food. Several caterpillar hunters can be kept together in an open terrarium supplied with branches to climb and plenty of prey. They prefer to eat caterpillars, but will accept commercially available crickets and mealworms. Tiger beetles will do well in a terrarium filled with several inches of clean sand. Keep one corner of the terrarium moist and cover the entire enclosure with a lid fitted with a 40-watt aquarium bulb to supply heat and light. A rock or piece of wood will give them something to burrow under, if they so choose. They will accept a variety of live insects every other day, if the prey items are no larger than the beetles themselves.

SETTING UP AN AQUARIUM

Aquatic beetles are relatively easy to keep in an aquarium and will provide hours of great beetle watching and photography (Fig. 69). A light hood on the aquarium is essential for illuminating your beetles and preventing their escape. Although several filtration systems are available, under-gravel filter systems are particularly easy to maintain for beginners. After assembling and installing the under-gravel filter plate and snapping the clear filter stack pipes in place, place 25 or 50 mm of sealed aquarium gravel on the filter plate. Then half-fill the tank with distilled or filtered water, or tap water that has been allowed to stand in a clean bucket for 24 hours. Add artificial or real plants and some larger rocks, and then top off the water level of the tank. Branches and aquatic vegetation added to the tank may be attractive, but they are likely to introduce unwanted algae to your aquarium.

Whirligig (Gyrinidae) and predaceous diving (Dytiscidae) beetles will eat living or frozen crickets placed on the surface of the water. Mosquito and mayfly larvae are excellent sources of wild insect food, if they are sufficiently available on a regular basis. Hungry predators and scavengers alike readily accept bits of raw meat, fish, and shellfish, but these items will quickly foul the water, requiring frequent water and filter cartridge changes. Water scavenger beetles (Hydrophilidae) will also devour bits of romaine lettuce or aquatic plants. Living aquarium plants or submerged rocks covered with algae will provide food for most herbivorous beetles (Elmidae, Dryopidae), but the presence of algae will require greater vigilance to keep the aquarium clean.

KEEPING BEETLE LARVAE

Unlike butterfly and moth collectors who dedicate much of their time to searching for and rearing caterpillars, coleopterists seldom collect and keep beetle larvae in captivity, partly because of their varied and often specialized feeding requirements, secretive habits, and extended periods of time needed to reach adulthood; however, taking the trouble to rear beetle larvae leads to a better understanding of their biology and is a way of securing adults of species that are otherwise difficult to obtain. The challenge of rearing beetle larvae is in recognizing and duplicating natural conditions in captivity, and maintaining optimal conditions and food quality for the duration of larval and pupal development. Too little moisture results in dehydration that hampers hatching, molting, and pupation, while excess moisture often leads to fatal fungal infections or drowning. Eggs, larvae, pupae, and teneral adults should be handled as little as possible and with great care by using featherweight forceps to avoid inflicting injury.

REARING GROUND-DWELLING BEETLES

Place mating pairs or gravid females of predatory ground beetles (Carabidae) and rove beetles (Staphylinidae) in small transparent plastic containers with lids supplied with about 10 mm depth of moist soil consisting of sand, loam, forest soil rich in organics, or peat moss. The substrate

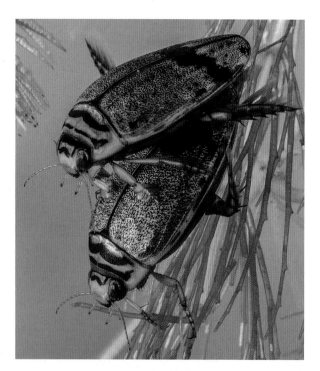

Figure 69. Aquatic beetles are easy to keep and observe in an aquarium.

should be moist enough to remain compacted when squeezed, but without dripping water. To prevent these carnivorous beetles from eating their own eggs, keep their appetites sated with chopped mealworms. Females usually begin laying eggs right away and are removed immediately, or left in the container until the eggs hatch. Place the eggs and young larvae in their own containers to avoid cannibalism. The containers should be kept cool, about 68 °F (20 °C). Check for and remove dead eggs and larvae immediately, especially those attacked by fungi, to avoid spreading infections. Uneaten food should also be removed every other day to limit fungal growth and the proliferation of mites. Species that undergo winter diapause may require an extended cold period to complete their development.

REARING AQUATIC LARVAE

Predaceous diving (Dytiscidae), whirligig (Gyrinidae), and water scavenger (Hydrophilidae) beetles generally lay their eggs on the water's surface or on submerged rocks or vegetation. Their larvae are predatory and require a steady supply of live insect food to complete their development. You can collect feeder insects from natural habitats, or purchase mealworms and flightless fruit flies from dealers or pet shops. Be sure to remove uneaten food to avoid fouling the water. The mature larvae leave the water to pupate in relatively dry subterranean chambers or other protected places just beyond the shoreline. Successful rearing of these beetles requires removing mature larvae and placing them in a container with moist soil, or providing them with the means for crawling out of the tank and into a moist but not wet substrate covered with chunks of wood or moss.

REARING LARVAE FROM DEAD WOOD AND WOODY FUNGI

Rearing beetle larvae from dead wood and woody fungi is often the best way to obtain adult specimens. Although it can be done year-round, late winter and early spring are good times to gather these materials as they frequently contain developing and mature larvae, as well as pupae. Shelf fungi are generally encountered on stumps and snags. Look for weakened branches, or those on dying, recently dead, or injured trees and shrubs, as these are most likely to host wood-boring larvae. Branches exhibiting obvious signs of infestation (exit holes, tunnels exposed by loose bark, etc.) are likely to be past their prime in terms of harboring beetle larvae. Acacia (*Senegalia, Vachellia*), mesquite (*Prosopis*), and oak (*Quercus*) are all favorite larval hosts, as well as fir (*Abies*), juniper (*Juniperus*), and

pine (*Pinus*). As with beetles themselves, the collection and movement of wood, beetle-infested or not, may be strictly regulated by federal, state, and local authorities.

Carefully bundle up fungi and infested branches, and provide each collection with labels indicating locality and date. Place each bundle loosely in its own rearing container. Keeping rearing chambers indoors is likely to speed up the emergence of some beetles, but it may delay those that require a period of cold temperatures to complete their development. Rearing containers must be sealed to prevent desiccation and emerging beetles from escaping, yet breathable to retard the growth of mold, all of which will negatively impact the numbers of beetles emerging from the wood and their collection. Plastic buckets and tubs may require modification by adding screened openings to the lid and sides. Moldy fungi and branches should be removed temporarily until they are dry, while overly desiccated wood can be wetted down. Carefully inspect the contents of each container every one to two weeks during spring and summer for up to two years. The accumulation of wood dust and *frass* on the bottom is a strong indication of larval activity.

Place each living or dead beetle in separate vials that include date and locality information. Accurate records containing locality information, host plant records, and associated parasitoids are important contributions to beetle study, especially for species with biologies that are poorly understood or unknown.

REARING LARVAE FOUND UNDER BARK

The larvae and pupae of species belonging to several beetle families (Lycidae, Elateridae, Pythidae, Tenebrionidae, Stenotrachelidae) are often more commonly encountered than the adults. One method of rearing these larvae is to place them in a covered petri dish containing a small amount of the substrate in which they were collected. Another method involves using glass vials, each filled with approximately 10 mm of compact, moist paper towel covered with 10 mm of loose substrate found under the bark from which the larvae were collected. The size of the vials and type of tree material can be altered depending on species. The tops of the vials are either left open or loosely plugged with crumpled paper towel and kept upright in a lidded box at room temperature. Both the paper toweling and natural substrate not only serve as food, but also help to regulate the moisture content of each vial. Many species require cold before completing their development. These vials are stored in a box and placed in a plastic bag punched with holes and set outside in the fall for exposure to cold winter temperatures. In spring, the larvae are brought back indoors to complete their life cycle. Because the larvae are kept individually, accurate notes can be kept regarding their behavior and length of life cycle with minimal disturbance during examination.

TAKING AN ACTIVE ROLE IN BEETLE RESEARCH

The natural history notes that appear in peer-reviewed journals, newsletters, entomological online forums, and various social media platforms are not only written by professional biologists, but also contributed by observant students and naturalists who keep meticulous notes. The beetles of western North America aren't nearly as well known as the species that inhabit the eastern part of the continent, and there are new genera and species still awaiting discovery and scientific description. Even for species that have been described scientifically, little is known about the various aspects of their lives, including reproduction and development, food preferences and foraging behavior, adult and larval habitat selection, seasonality, number of generations produced annually, and distribution. The bold and distinctive color patterns of some adults have been noted for decades, but little experimental work has been carried out to determine how potential predators of beetles perceive these colors. Geographic variation within beetle populations is poorly documented in most families. Behavioral, ecological, and distributional data gleaned from carefully executed beetle surveys and mark-recapture studies—especially those conducted over a period of several successive years on school grounds, parks, vacant lots, or nearby woods—can be of considerable value. Coordinating such efforts through citizen science organizations working with researchers at universities and natural history museums will facilitate the inclusion of these data into ongoing scientific research.

Traditionally, the study of larvae and of adults have been treated as separate endeavors, but more and more coleopterists today have come to embrace the value of studying both the adult and immature stages simultaneously, especially when studying their evolutionary relationships. Students and naturalists with a knack for rearing beetle larvae associated with reliably identified adults can make enormously important contributions to our understanding of the development of beetles and their evolutionary relationships.

Bioblitzes are popular and expedient ways of gathering beetle and other invertebrate data for national and state forests, parks, and other natural areas that lack this information. Because of their short duration, the findings of these intensive one-day surveys are unduly influenced by season, lunar cycle, local weather conditions, and personnel available to gather samples. As such, these events provide only a snapshot of beetle diversity and thus are not substitutes for well-managed, long-term monitoring efforts. Still, these rapid surveys can generate useful species lists that support efforts to manage and conserve natural resources, and may suggest possible avenues for sustained research programs in the future. Just as importantly, bioblitzes provide opportunities for students and naturalists to meet and collaborate with professional biologists in the field.

Joining an entomological society is a good way to network with professional entomologists and serious naturalists. Membership in The Coleopterists Society (TCS) is essential for anyone studying beetles. Benefits of membership include eligibility to compete for various awards that support undergraduate and graduate research. The Youth Incentive Awards are also available to TCS members. Recipients of these awards receive some financial support and supplies to carry out a research project with a mentor. The entomological societies of America and Canada are also important entomological organizations in North America and provide useful resources to their members. Contact information for these and related organizations are found in the Appendix (p.592).

This key is intended to serve only as a "quick guide" to the most commonly encountered families (**bold** type), while less common families are suggested within square brackets in plain type. As such, the key includes only 91 of the 131 families known to occur in western North America. It should be used in combination with the Similar Families sections included in each family diagnosis for proper family placement. For detailed identification keys to families, subfamilies, tribes, and genera, refer to *American Beetles* (Arnett and Thomas 2001; Arnett et al. 2002).

1. Metacoxae may or may not be enlarged; basal half of hind femora and ventrites clearly visible .... **GO TO 2**
1'. Metacoxae greatly enlarged to conceal basal half of legs and most of first three ventrites:

Haliplidae (p.79)

2. Head without rostrum .... **GO TO 3**

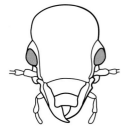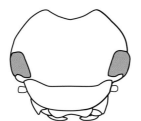

2'. Head with distinctly long or broad rostrum; if rostrum short or absent, then antennae usually geniculate:

Curculionidae (p.539); Anthribidae (p.532); Brentidae (p.539); Attelabidae (p.534)
[see also Cimberididae (p.529), Nemonychidae (p.531); Salpingidae (p.397); Staphylinidae (p.144)]

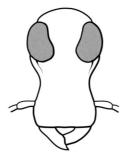

ILLUSTRATED KEY AND GUIDE TO THE COMMON BEETLE FAMILIES OF WESTERN NORTH AMERICA (*CONTINUED*)

3. Hind coxae not immovably fused to metathorax and not dividing the first ventrite....................................**GO TO 4**

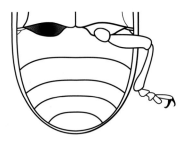

3'. Hind coxae fused to metathorax and dividing the first ventrite:

Carabidae (p.88); Gyrinidae (p.78); Dytiscidae (p.81);
[see also Amphizoidae (p.86); Trachypachidae (p.87)]

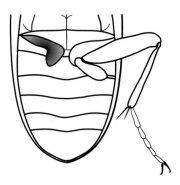

4. Elytra long, covering all or nearly all the abdomen ....**GO TO 5**

4'. Elytra short, exposing two or more terga:

Staphylinidae (p.143); Silphidae (p.140); Histeridae (p.127); Nitidulidae (p.443)
[see also Buprestidae (p.210); Melyridae (p.420); Lampyridae (p.262); Phengodidae (p.271); Cantharidae
(p.265); Ripiphoridae (p.338); Cerambycidae (p.460)]

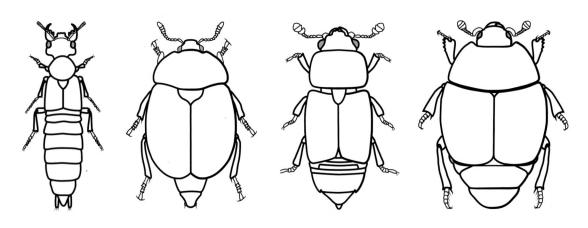

5. Antennae not lamellate ....**GO TO 6**

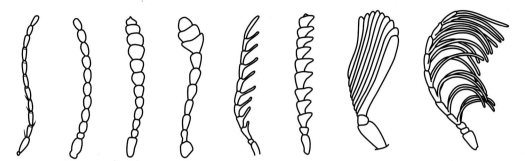

5'. Antennae lamellate with apical three to seven antennomeres forming a distinctly one-sided or asymmetrical club:

Scarabaeidae (p.172)

[see also Pleocomidae (p.153); Geotrupidae (p.156); Trogidae (p.159); Glaresidae (p.162); Diphyllostomatidae (p.163); Lucanidae (p.164); Ochodaeidae (p.167); Hybosoridae (p.169); Glaphyridae (p.170)]

   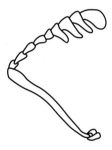

6. Tarsal formula not 5-5-4 ....**GO TO 7**
6'. Tarsal formula 5-5-4:

Tenebrionidae (p.347); Zopheridae (p.340); Melandryidae (p.333); Meloidae (p.378)

[see also Mycetophagidae (p.326); Archeocrypticidae (p.328); Ciidae (p.329);Tetratomidae (p.330); Mordellidae (p.336); Ripiphoridae (p.338); Prostomidae (p.372); Stenotrachelidae (p.372); Oedemeridae (p.374); Mycteridae (p.390); Boridae (p.391); Pythidae (p.392); Pyrochroidae (p.394); Anthicidae (p.400); Ischaliidae (p.396); Salpingidae (p.397); Aderidae (p.406); Scraptiidae (p.408)]

7. Tarsal formula variable; maxillary palps long, usually conspicuous; antennae variable,
   not more than half the length of the body ....**GO TO 8**
7'. Tarsal formula often appears 4-4-4, actually 5-5-5 with small fourth tarsomere surrounded by
   bilobed third tarsomere, or distinctly 5-5-5; maxillary palps short, often not conspicuous;
   antennae never clubbed and more than or less than half the length of body:

Cerambycidae (p.460); Chrysomelidae (p.501)

[see also Megalopodidae (p.498); Orsodacnidae (p.499)]

ILLUSTRATED KEY AND GUIDE TO THE COMMON BEETLE FAMILIES OF WESTERN NORTH AMERICA (*CONTINUED*)

8.   Body with scattered setae or scales, if present at all; head without ocelli .... **GO TO 9**

8'. Body densely covered with setae or scales; head often with one ocellus

    Dermestidae (p.290)

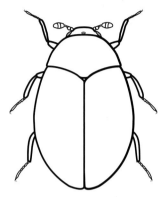

9.   Antennae not clubbed or club not velvety; maxillary palps much shorter than antennae;
    legs not modified for swimming .... **GO TO 10**

9'. Antennae with antennomeres 7–9 forming loose, velvety club; maxillary palps long, always half the length of
    antennae, usually as long or longer; legs often fringed with setae, modified for swimming:

    Hydrophilidae (p.122)

    [see also Helophoridae (p.118); Epimetopidae (p.119); Georissidae (p.120); Hydrochidae (p.121)]

10. Elytra hard and shell-like .... **GO TO 11**

10'. Elytra soft and leathery:

    Cantharidae (p.265); Lampyridae (p.262); Phengodidae (p.271); Lycidae (p.258)

    [see also Omethidae (p.249); Melyridae (p.420)]

11. Ventrites variable, never iridescent or metallic .... **GO TO 12**

11'. Ventrites 1 and 2 fused with no trace of suture between, all iridescent or metallic:

    Buprestidae (p.210)

    [see also Schizopodidae (p.208)]

12. Body variable .... **GO TO 13**

12'. Body strikingly flat:

    Cucujidae (p.453)

    [see also Laemophloeidae (p.458)]

13. Body usually elongate, somewhat flattened or nearly cylindrical; tarsal formula variable .... **GO TO 14**

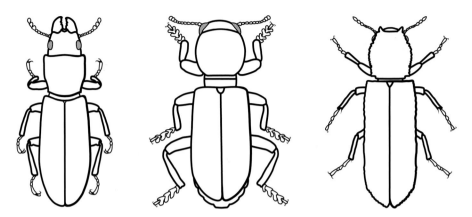

13'. Body typically compact, round, convex dorsally and flattened ventrally; tarsal formula usually appear 3-3-3, actually 4-4-4:

Coccinellidae (p.318)
[see also Erotylidae (p.435); Endomychidae (p.315)]

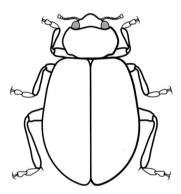

14. Body, legs, and antennae variable .... **GO TO 15**

14'. Prothorax long, loosely articulated with rest of body; antennae usually serrate; legs long, slender:

Elateridae (p.273)
[see also Eucnemidae (p.254); Throscidae (p.252)]

15. Head clearly visible when viewed from above:

Trogossitidae (p.414); Cleridae (p.425); Melyridae (p.420)
[see also Bostrichidae (p.295); Peltidae (p.412); Lophocateridae (p.413); Mauroniscidae (p.418; Rhadalidae (p.419)]

15'. Head hidden from view above by hoodlike prothorax:

Bostrichidae (p.295); Ptinidae (p.299)

BEETLES
OF
WESTERN
NORTH
AMERICA

CUPEDIDAE (kū-ped′-i-dē)
RETICULATED BEETLES

Cupedids are a small and unusual family of primitive beetles. Of the 31 species known worldwide, four occur in North America, two west of the Continental Divide. They are distinguished from all other families of beetle by the elongate elytra with surfaces sculpted with quadrate punctures. Adults are thought to be pollen feeders. The larvae typically bore into firm, fungus-infested wood beneath the bark of limbs and logs and will attack basement timbers of old houses, but are generally not considered to be of economic importance.

FAMILY DIAGNOSIS Adult cupedids are slender, parallel-sided, strongly flattened, roughly sculpted, and clothed in broad and scalelike setae. Prognathous head and pronotum narrower than elytra. Antennae thick, filiform with 11 antennomeres. Prothorax with lateral margins carinate; underneath with (*Prolixocupes*) or without (*Priacma*) distinct sulci to receive front tarsi. Procoxal cavities open behind. Elytra long, broader than prothorax, surface strongly ridged with square punctures between, completely covering abdomen. Tarsi 5-5-5, with simple claws. Abdomen with five ventrites free.

SIMILAR FAMILIES
- net-winged beetles (Lycidae, p.258)—head not visible from above
- some leaf beetles (Chrysomelidae; Cassidinae, pp.505–507)—clavate antennae short, head narrower than pronotum

COLLECTING NOTES Adult cupedids are found in late spring and summer by chopping into old decaying logs and stumps, netted in sunlit patches near infested wood, beaten from dead branches, or at lights. Male *Priacma serrata* are attracted to sheets freshly laundered with solutions containing sodium hypochlorite (e.g., laundry bleach), while *Prolixocupes lobiceps* are sometimes found by sweeping low vegetation early in the evening.

FAUNA FOUR SPECIES IN FOUR GENERA

Priacma serrata (LeConte) (9.6–22.0 mm) is reddish brown or gray with variable pattern of dense black, brown, and gray scales. Antennae scarcely half body length. Underside of prothorax without tarsal sulci. Found in montane forests, especially in association with Douglas-fir (*Pseudotsuga menziesii*). Males fly during day from May through July, especially midafternoon, and are attracted to laundry bleach that acts as a sexual attractant; females seldom encountered. British Columbia and Montana south to southern California. (1)

Prolixocupes lobiceps (LeConte) (7.0–11.0 mm) is pale brown with variable pattern of dark brown or black scales. Head with four large obtuse protuberances, posterior pair nearly twice as large as anterior pair. Antennae long, flattened, usually distinctly longer than half body length and slightly serrate, becoming narrower at apices. Underside of prothorax with tarsal sulci. Adults found under loose bark of California sycamore (*Platanus racemosa*), in decaying stumps of California live oak (*Quercus agrifolia*), on low vegetation at dusk, or at lights. California and Arizona to northern Baja California. (1)

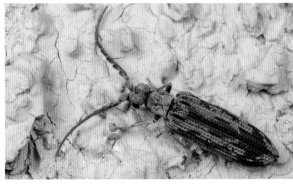

MICROMALTHIDAE (mī-krō-mal'-th-i-dē)
TELEPHONE-POLE BEETLES

The reproductive biology of *Micromalthus debilis* LeConte, the sole representative of Micromalthidae, is utterly bizarre and involves parthenogenesis (reproduction without sex) and paedogenesis (larval reproduction). Under stressful environmental conditions, the highly mobile caraboid larva (so named because it resembles larvae of carabid ground beetles) metamorphoses into a cerambycoid larva (so named because it resembles the larva of a longhorn beetle) that either develops into an adult female or a paedogenetic female- or male-producing larva that gives birth to caraboid larvae. Or the cerambycoid larva can develop directly into a male-producer by laying eggs that hatch into curculionoid (weevil-like) larvae that eventually develop into adult haploid males. The ability to reproduce as both larvae and adults affords micromalthids the opportunity to multiply quickly to fully exploit patchy and ephemeral resources. *Micromalthus* larvae feed and develop in moist, decaying logs and stumps in the red-rotten or yellowish-brown rotten stages of decomposition. Likely indigenous to eastern United States and Belize, isolated populations of micromalthid beetles have become established in the West and other parts of the world, likely because of commerce. Although occasionally attacking rotting telephone poles, *Micromalthus* is not a structural pest, nor is it of any economic importance.

FAMILY DIAGNOSIS Adult micromalthids are elongate, somewhat flattened, with large head and bulging compound eyes broader than pronotum. Head prognathous. Moniliform antennae with 11 antennomeres. Pronotum narrower than head and broadest across in front. Elytra straight-sided, short, leaving five abdominal tergites exposed. Legs slender, tarsi 5-5-5, with simple claws. Abdomen with six ventrites, 3–5 of male each with large seta-filled cavity.

SIMILAR FAMILIES
- rove beetles (Staphylinidae, p.143)—elytra usually shorter, antennae not moniliform
- small soldier beetles (Cantharidae, p.265)—antennae filiform
- soft-winged flower beetles (Melyridae, p.420)—pronotum with well-defined side margins
- checkered beetles (Cleridae, p.425)—antennae never moniliform

COLLECTING NOTES Although sometimes locally abundant, telephone-pole beetles are seldom seen and rarely collected. Adults emerge briefly in large numbers to mate and locate new breeding sites. They are sometimes captured in Malaise or flight intercept traps. Specimens are usually obtained by rearing the small whitish larvae that are sometimes abundant in moist, but not wet, oak or pine logs and stumps in the advanced stages of red-rotten decay. Larvae collected in late winter or early spring and kept indoors usually reach adulthood in a few months.

75

FAUNA ONE SPECIES, *MICROMALTHUS DEBILIS*

Micromalthus debilis LeConte (1.5–2.5 mm) is small, flat, shiny brown to black with yellowish antennae and legs. Head wider than pronotum. Pronotum widest in front and narrowing posteriorly, without carinate lateral margins or grooves on disc. Elytra short, exposing part of abdomen. Rarely seen adults briefly emerge in large numbers, captured in Malaise or flight intercept traps. Larvae sometimes abundant in moist, but not wet, oak or pine logs and stumps in advanced stages of red-rot decay. British Columbia and California; widespread in eastern United States. (3)

HYDROSCAPHIDAE (hī-dro-skā'-fi-dē)
SKIFF BEETLES

Hydroscaphidae comprises 25 species in four genera that are distributed worldwide. Only two species in the genus *Hydroscapha* are found in North America, both west of the Continental Divide. Skiff beetles are small, uncommonly encountered beetles that are sometimes locally abundant along the sides of icy streams and rivers where they feed on filamentous green algae growing on rocks and covered by a thin film of water; they also occur along edges of hot springs. Aquatic larvae also feed on algae, but claims of adults and larvae feeding on cyanobacteria requires confirmation. Females produce one egg at a time and deposit it among algal mats. Pupation occurs in water within the exoskeleton of the last larval instar. Adults carry a bubble of air beneath the elytra, which is held in place by a plastron formed by dense setae on the third abdominal ventrite. Hydroscaphids sometimes turn up in swimming pools, thus confirming their ability to fly. Several populations of *Hydroscapha* found in hot springs in northwestern United States, California, Nevada, may represent distinct species based on differences in their morphology and genetic makeup.

FAMILY DIAGNOSIS Adult hydroscaphids resemble very small tan to brown teardrop-shaped rove beetles, but are distinguished by their distinct notopleural sutures, relatively short legs, and aquatic habits. *Hydroscapha* head prognathous, short, broad, arcuate and distinctly ridged in front, with eyes large, oval, widely separated. Antennae inserted beneath frontal ridge between eyes and base of mandibles, somewhat clavate with eight antennomeres, club consisting of one broad and elongate antennomere. Prothorax short with pronotum wider than head. Procoxal cavities open behind. Elytra smooth, short, exposing 3–5 abdominal segments; flight wings brachypterous or fully developed and fringed with long setae. Abdomen distinctly narrowed and cone-shaped with six visible sternites; third tergite with setae dense, recumbent; tip simply tapered (female) or with two acute and widely separated teeth (male). Legs short; hind coxae widely separated, and enlarged to form plates partially covering hind femora; tarsi 3-3-3. Abdomen with six ventrites free.

SIMILAR FAMILIES

- rove beetles (Staphylinidae, p.143)—terrestrial, 11 antennomeres, underside of prothorax without notopleural suture
- minute moss beetles (Hydraenidae, p.132)—11 antennomeres
- featherwing beetles (Ptiliidae, p.134)—antennal club with two or three antennomeres

COLLECTING NOTES Both adult and larval *Hydroscapha* are found on wet, algal-covered rocks along the edges of cold, well-oxygenated streams and rivers, or among algal mats at the edges of hot springs.

FAUNA TWO SPECIES IN ONE GENUS

Hydroscapha natans LeConte (1.0–2.0mm) is fusiform and brown with fine recumbent pubescence on pronotum and elytra. Eyes not bulging beyond outline of head; antennae with eight antennomeres. Elytra short and truncate, flight wings fully developed and fringed with setae. Metacoxae platelike, covering hind femora. Seldom-seen adults and larvae found year-round among algal mats growing along cold, flowing waters and edges of hot springs. Adults fly at dusk. Southern Idaho to California and Arizona south to Baja California and southern Mexico. *Hydroscapha redfordi* Maier, Ivie, Johnson, and Maddison (1.6–1.8mm) is currently known only from Jerry Johnson Hot Springs in northern Idaho. (2)

SPHAERIUSIDAE (sfē'-rī-ūs-i-dē)
MINUTE BOG BEETLES

Sphaerius, the sole genus of Sphaeriusidae, comprises 23 species distributed on all continents except Antarctica, and needs revision. At least four species occur in North America, three of these west of the Continental Divide. Minute bog beetles are found along the edges of streams and rivers in sandy gravel, mud, under stones, on algae, among roots associated with riparian plants, in moss associated with wetland edges, or in moist leaf litter. Adults breathe underwater by storing oxygen under their elytra. Both adults and larvae feed on green algae. Females produce one large egg at a time.

FAMILY DIAGNOSIS Adult sphaeriusids are very small, broadly oval, convex, smooth and shiny black or brown; underside mostly flat. Head prognathous, short, broad, with prominent eyes, and partly covered by pronotum. Antennae with 11 antennomeres and a cone-shaped club, last antennomere with long setae. Prothorax short, with pronotum narrowed in front and widest at elytra; underside with mesosternum small and fused with metasternum to form a large plate. Elytra very convex and completely covering abdomen, covering membranous flight wings fringed with long setae. Middle legs widely separated at base, hind legs nearly contiguous at bases with coxal plates large and covering femora and first abdominal ventrite, tarsi 3-3-3, with tarsomere 1 much longer than 2, and simple claws unequal in length. Abdomen with three ventrites, ventrites 1 and 3 long, 2 short.

SIMILAR FAMILIES

- minute beetles (Clambidae, p.113)—can partially roll up their bodies
- featherwing beetles (Ptiliidae, p.134)—pronotum less narrowed in front
- minute fungus beetles (Corylophidae, p.314)—head covered by pronotum, clavate antennae with club indistinct
- lady beetles (Coccinellidae, p.318)—antennae club gradual, not distinctly abrupt

COLLECTING NOTES Often overlooked, sphaeriusids are usually found in wet environments, sometimes in association with Hydraenidae (p.132), Hydrophilidae (p.122), and Limnichidae (p.241). Carefully search for them along the edges of bodies of water in wet sandy gravel or mud, among roots, on algae, and under rocks; they can be extracted from plant debris in these microhabitats by using a Berlese funnel.

FAUNA FOUR SPECIES IN ONE GENUS

Sphaerius **species** (0.5–0.6 mm) are shiny black or dark chestnut above, sometimes lighter underneath. Head and eyes large, eyes not prominent; antennal club ovate and narrow; palps pale. Pronotum widest at base near elytra. Underside of thorax forms a large plate with hind coxae. Elytra are strongly convex, long, and completely cover all abdominal ventrites. Legs black or reddish brown. Adults and larvae are extremely small and live among spaces between wet sand grains and gravel and eat algae. Adults are found in damp environments along the shores of wetlands. Washington south to California and Arizona. (3)

GYRINIDAE (ji-rin'-i-dē)
WHIRLIGIG BEETLES

When alarmed, whirligigs gyrate wildly on the surface of water and are the only beetles that use surface tension for support. Using highly specialized antennae, they use surface vibrations to detect the presence of drowning insect prey or to communicate with each other. Their heads are equipped with two separate pairs of compound eyes, each dedicated to seeing above or below the water's surface. Visual information received through the upper pair enables them to maintain their orientation to their surroundings, including other whirligig beetles. Whirligigs move about singly or in large groups in search of mates and insect prey on ponds or along the edges of slow-moving streams, as well as in cattle tanks, canals, swimming pools, even rain puddles. They will briefly dive beneath the surface when threatened. Whirligigs produce defensive secretions from their pygidial glands. Released from the tip of the abdomen, these secretions not only repel hungry predators such as fish, amphibians, and birds, but may also serve as an alarm pheromone to alert nearby whirligigs of approaching danger. This pungent secretion smells like apples and has inspired whirligig nicknames such as "apple bugs," "apple smellers," and "mellow bugs." Recently emerged adults often congregate by the dozens or hundreds in shady or sheltered spots in late summer and fall. Smaller species (*Gyretes*, *Gyrinus*) may climb out of the water onto emergent leaves, twigs, and roots to rest. *Gyretes* prefers shaded undercuts and hollowed-out pockets along the banks of small streams. Females lay eggs singly in rows on submerged vegetation and other objects. Predatory whirligig larvae crawl about the bottom debris of ponds and streams in search of immature insects and other small invertebrates. Mature larvae pupate either on shore (*Dineutus*), or attached to emergent plants above the water surface (*Gyrinus*) inside a case constructed of bits of sand and debris that are glued together by an oral secretion.

78

FAMILY DIAGNOSIS Adult gyrinids are oval, flattened, and uniformly shiny or dull black. Margins of the head, thorax, and abdomen combined form a continuous, hydrodynamic outline. Head prognathous. Antennae short, with 8–11 antennomeres, and clubbed. Compound eyes distinctly divided. Scutellum visible (*Gyrinus*) or not (*Dineutus*, *Gyretes*). Elytra smooth (margins lined with pubescence in *Gyretes*) and do not completely cover the abdomen. Front legs raptorial, adapted for grasping prey. Tarsi 5-5-5, middle and hind legs flattened and paddlelike. Abdomen with six ventrites free.

SIMILAR FAMILIES The completely divided eyes, paddlelike legs, and surface-swelling habit of whirligigs are distinctive.

COLLECTING NOTES Rapidly sweeping an aquatic net through groups of beetles swimming on the surface of ponds and streams is the best way to collect specimens. Individuals may dive beneath the water to avoid capture but will soon resurface. Also investigate shaded undercuts and hollowed-out pockets with trailing roots from terrestrial vegetation along stream and riverbanks. Whirligigs are capable of flight and are sometimes attracted to lights at night.

FAUNA 56 SPECIES IN FOUR GENERA

Dineutus sublineatus Chevrolat (14.0–15.0 mm) is broadly oval, strongly convex, with dorsal surface finely granulate and dull dark olive with a hint of iridescence dorsally, dark to dark reddish brown ventrally. Scutellum not visible. Elytra with sides feebly sinuate, each with nine well-developed striae, sutural angles of both sexes rounded, with apices broadly rounded to somewhat truncate, and marginal serrations and irregularities absent. Forelegs of male with femora distinctly and obliquely toothed, tibiae sinuate. Adults active in summer and found exclusively in permanent stream pools either singly or in small groups; commonly attracted to lights. Southeastern Arizona south to Nicaragua. (1)

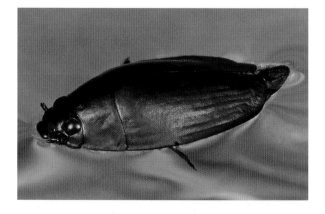

Gyrinus species (3.8–6.4 mm) are small, shiny, dark dorsally, and ventrites sometimes lighter. Adults live on surface of still or slow-moving waters, and have long forelegs. Dorsal and ventral eyes completely divided, inset from lateral margin of head by at least half width of eye. Pronotum and elytra lack setae. Scutellum visible. Elytra with 11 punctostriae. Underside of front tarsi of male with dense brush of setae. Tarsomeres 2–4 on middle and hind legs much broader than long. Identification of species difficult. Adults active spring through early fall. Throughout western North America. (16)

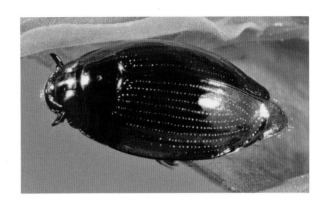

HALIPLIDAE (hal-ip'-li-dē)
CRAWLING WATER BEETLES

Crawling water beetles resemble small, loosely built predaceous diving beetles (Dytiscidae, p.81), but swim by moving their hind legs alternately as if they were walking underwater, like water scavenger beetles (Hydrophilidae, p.122). They are easily distinguished from these and all other aquatic beetles by their enlarged coxal plates that obscure most of the abdomen, and by the broadly tapered head and posterior. Adults typically live along the edges of open and permanent standing or slow-moving freshwater habitats with good water quality, where they crawl over mats of algae and submerged vegetation to graze and/or search for small invertebrate prey. Some species occasionally occupy temporary and vernal pools. *Brychius*, however, prefers flowing streams with oxygen-rich waters. Respiration occurs at the water surface, where they capture air beneath the elytra and hind coxal plate not only to breathe underwater, but also to regulate their buoyancy. Beetles with spent air bubbles must laboriously crawl to the surface to obtain more oxygen. Their legs and bodies are sometimes colonized by protozoans. Despite their common name, crawling water beetles are fair swimmers, relying on long hairlike setae on their middle and hind legs to increase the effectiveness of these limbs as oars. Mating occurs in spring and summer. Eggs are laid on the surfaces of aquatic plants (*Peltodytes*) or in cavities covered in algae or other aquatic vegetation (*Haliplus*) from spring through summer and possibly in fall. The aquatic and herbivorous larvae rely on gills for respiration and feed on algae. When mature, they pupate in a small chamber excavated on shore, usually beneath stones and logs.

FAMILY DIAGNOSIS Adult haliplids are small, yellowish or brownish yellow with black spots, coarsely punctured, oval or broadly ovate, and broadly tapered anteriorly and posteriorly. Head prognathous, small, and elongate, with eyes bulging. Antennae with 11 antennomeres, 1 and 2 short and broad, 3–11 longer and filiform. Pronotum widest at base, with lateral margins arcuate (*Haliplus, Peltodytes*), or parallel-sided (*Brychius*), and carinate; disc unmarked or with two distinct black spots at base (*Peltodytes*). Scutellum concealed. Elytra cover abdomen completely; each punctostriate with large, dark punctures. Legs with tarsi 5-5-5, with long claws minutely serrate to pectinate. Abdomen mostly concealed by large, flattened hind coxal plates that are long and grooved along their posterior margins (*Peltodytes*) exposing only one ventrite, or short with three exposed ventrites.

SIMILAR FAMILIES Haliplids resemble small species of predaceous diving beetles (Dytiscidae) (p.81), and *Berosus* (Hydrophilidae) (p.122) but are easily distinguished from these taxa by their ventrites concealed by expanded hind coxal plates.

COLLECTING NOTES Look for adult haliplids year-round crawling over and feeding among mats of stringy green algae and other submerged vegetation growing in weedy ditches or along the edges of ponds, lakes, or small and slow-moving streams and vernal pools (*Haliplus, Peltodytes*). Lightly sweep a dip net or small aquarium net through algae and aquatic vegetation in these habitats. *Brychius* species prefer coarser substrates along rivers and lakes and are collected by dislodging rocks and catching the loosened material with a D-frame net, or by sweeping the net beneath stream banks. Also drag aquatic vegetation on shore and hand-collect beetles as they attempt to crawl back to the water. All are attracted to lights at night, except the flightless *Haliplus parvulus* Roberts.

FAUNA 67 SPECIES IN THREE GENERA

Brychius hornii Crotch (3.0–4.4 mm) is fusiform, elongate, and pale yellow to brown. Prothorax with sides parallel; underneath with prosternal process nearly parallel before apex. Elytra each with 10 rows of brown/black punctures, intervals micro punctate; ranging from immaculate to a small humeral spot, median lateral spot, with or without apicolateral spot; apical margins acute. Last ventrite sharply pointed. Mostly British Columbia and Alberta south to northern California, Utah, and Wyoming. *Brychius pacificus* Carr (3.3–3.7 mm) similar in form and color; prosternal process with apex distinctly wedge-shaped; boldly marked elytra with apical margins rounded (apices each denticulate), and ventrite blunt. Mostly coastal Oregon to central coast of California. (2)

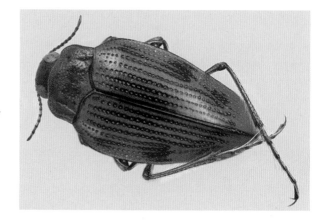

Haliplus concolor LeConte (2.5–3.5 mm) is moderately elongate-oval, broadest near basal quarter of elytra, and more or less uniformly reddish yellow-brown, occasionally with indistinct maculation. Pronotum finely and evenly punctate, without pair of basal spots or plicae; prosternum parallel-sided with sides and apex sharply margined. Elytra with darker infuscations, punctures becoming finer apically, basally, and along suture, with humeri smooth, nearly impunctate. Metasternum with pair of large foveae, and metacoxal plates not margined posteriorly. California to Colorado and Texas, south to Nayarit. *Haliplus tumidus* LeConte (3.0–3.2 mm) metasternum same, elytral maculation sometimes indistinct, with humeri rough. Southeastern California to Texas, south to Guatemala. Genus needs revision. (~18)

Haliplus parvulus Roberts (1.5–2.5 mm) is pale olive green, spindle-shaped, humpbacked, and flightless. Pronotum wider than long, with sides rounded, disc flattened across base, and without large pair of spots on posterior margin. Flight wings reduced to small pads. Males are smaller, with thickened protarsomeres. Localized populations found during spring along edges of ephemeral vernal pools and ponds. Previously placed in *Apteraliplus*, now considered a subgenus of *Haliplus*. Adults and larvae occur in scattered disjunct populations from central Washington and Oregon to central California, possibly in suitable vernal pools in eastern Washington and Oregon; likely in decline. Genus needs revision. (~18)

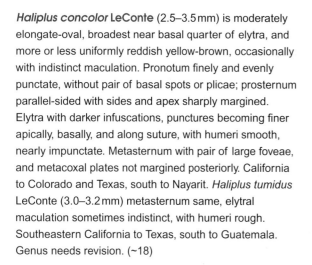

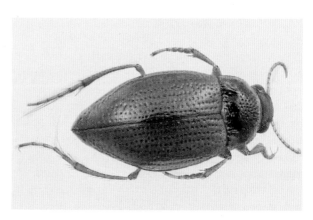

80

Peltodytes callosus LeConte (3.0–3.5 mm) is oval and fusiform, widest just before middle of elytra, and yellowish brown with blackish spots. Pronotum with sides rounded, disc with pair of large spots at base. Elytra with variable black markings, but without subhumeral spots, and a prominent, often black medial tubercle on third stria. Hind femora entirely black or brown. Adults are found in irrigation and roadside ditches, warm springs, and along the edges of ponds, streams, and rivers. Southern British Columbia, Washington, and Idaho south to California and New Mexico. (3)

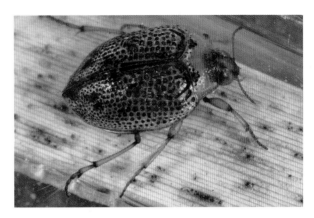

DYTISCIDAE (dī-tis'-i-dē)
PREDACEOUS DIVING BEETLES

Adult and larval dytiscids scavenge and prey on both invertebrate and vertebrate tissues. They occur in a variety of wetland habitats, particularly along the edges of fishless pools, ponds, and slow streams where emergent vegetation grows. A few species prefer cold-water streams, seeps, and springs, or other specialized bodies of water. Adults propel their streamlined bodies through the water with fringed hind legs placed well back on the body to increase speed and maneuverability. Unlike crawling water beetles (Haliplidae, p.79) and water scavenger beetles (Hydrophilidae, p.122) that move their legs alternately as if walking, dytiscids move their legs in unison. Predaceous diving beetles move awkwardly on land because their legs are attached to plates that are tightly fused to the body and incapable of moving up and down like those of terrestrial beetles. Adults respire by rising to the surface with the tip of their abdomen to replenish the bubble of air beneath their elytra. Most species are capable of flight and sometimes migrate in large numbers to new bodies of water. Dytiscids are chemically defended and possess a pair of thoracic glands located just behind the head that secrete steroids that are particularly distasteful to fish. They also have pygidial glands that produce aromatic compounds with antibacterial properties that the beetles apply on themselves in the water and on land. The application of these compounds also increases the beetle's wettability so they can easily reenter the water. Both adults and larvae scavenge and prey on both invertebrates and vertebrates. Females lay eggs singly or in small clutches on aquatic plants and other submerged substrates. Larvae are strong swimmers and actively hunt for larval mosquitoes, biting midges, and other biting insects. The voracious habits of larger species (e.g., *Dytiscus, Cybister*) inspired the common name "water tigers." These larvae obtain air from the surface, while those of smaller species take in dissolved oxygen and release carbon dioxide via cuticular respiration. Mature larvae leave the water to construct oval pupal chambers in mud or damp soil underneath rocks and other objects along the shore. Overwintering typically occurs during the adult stage; beetles are sometimes active in the winter and are observed swimming under the ice.

FAMILY DIAGNOSIS Adult dytiscids are rigid, streamlined, somewhat flattened, oval, broadly oval, or elongate-oval, and usually reddish brown to black or pale, with or without distinct markings. Head prognathous. Antennae moniliform with 11 antennomeres. Pronotum somewhat trapezoidal, broadest at base, with lateral margins more or less arcuate. Procoxal cavities open behind. Scutellum visible or not. Elytra usually smooth and polished, completely covering abdomen, and sometimes sparsely hairy, pitted, or grooved. Legs modified for swimming, flattened and fringed with setae, tarsi 5-5-5, sometimes appear 4-4-4, with simple claws equal or unequal in size. Abdomen with six ventrites connate.

SIMILAR FAMILIES
- whirligig beetles (Gyrinidae, p.78)—eyes divided, antennae clubbed
- crawling water beetles (Haliplidae, p.79)—head small and hind coxae expanded, partly covering

some or most of abdomen
- water scavenger beetles (Hydrophilidae, p.122)—antennae clubbed, maxillary palps long, underside flat, sometimes with a spinelike keel

COLLECTING NOTES Adults are sometimes common at lights in spring and summer. Sweeping an aquatic D-net through exposed and shaded vegetated shallows of permanent ponds, lakes, as well as temporary bodies of water with and without aquatic vegetation on various substrates will produce the greatest diversity of species. Some dytiscids prefer vegetated pools along streams. Aquarium nets and kitchen strainers are handy for sampling wetland margins, rock pools, ditches, and other small aquatic habitats. Baited bottle traps and underwater light traps placed in these habitats, as well as blacklight and mercury vapor lights placed near the shore at night will also attract flying predaceous diving beetles.

FAUNA 513 SPECIES IN 51 GENERA

Agabus lutosus LeConte (6.4–8.4 mm) is mostly black, with frontal spots and anterior margin of clypeus reddish; anterior clypeal margin with continuous bead; labrum, base of antennae, and mouthparts yellowish brown. Lateral pronotal margins narrowly reddish. Prosternal process with lateral bead not expanded behind procoxae. Hind femur with fringe of dense setae on ventral margin near apex; hind coxal lines diverging onto hind coxal lobes. Inhabits warm, temporary ponds and other pools. British Columbia and Baja California Norte to eastern slopes of Cascades and Sierra Nevada. (77)

82

Ilybiosoma regularis (LeConte) (9.2–11.3 mm) is dark reddish brown to brownish black, often with brassy sheen, with appendages reddish. Anterior clypeal bead broadly interrupted medially, with anterior margin of clypeus, frontal margins, and frontal spots pale. Line along anterior pronotal margin interrupted medially; prosternal process with lateral bead not expanded. Elytron with small, oval, sublateral spot sometimes obscure. Hind femur without strong, conspicuous punctation, with a line of closely placed setae near ventral margin apically. California and Baja California. (9)

Ilybius quadrimaculatus Aubé (9.5–11.1 mm) is mostly black with anterior margin of clypeus, labrum, frontal spots, narrow lateral margin of pronotum, and legs dark reddish brown. Antennae reddish, antennomeres 5–11 infuscate apically. Anterior clypeal margin with bead broadly interrupted medially, that of pronotal margin continuous. Elytra usually with distinct small postmedial stripes and subapical crescent-shaped spots. Middle tarsi of male oval, yellow suckers underneath; ventral face of hind tibia with punctation coarse (male), or sparse and fine (female). Among emergent vegetation of ponds and pools along slow-moving streams. British Columbia to northern California, east to southern Alberta and Montana. (9)

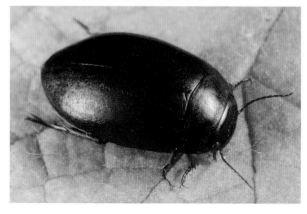

Colymbetes densus densus LeConte (15.7–18.4 mm) is elongate-oval, underside and legs pale. Head black with frons swollen in front of eye and over base of antennae. Pronotum yellowish with dark transverse band often flanked laterally by a small spot, disc microscopically grooved. Front and middle tarsomeres with (male) or without (female) adhesive setae underneath. Elytra pale with transverse black lines, surface sculpted with fine transverse strigae. Reddish legs with femora partly dark. Adults in emergent vegetation along pool margins. Alaska to central Oregon, east to southern Yukon and Wyoming; also in East. Elytra of *C. d. inaequalis* Horn from southern Oregon to California. (7)

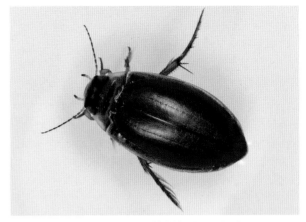

Rhantus gutticollis (Say) (9.8–12.7 mm) is elongate-oval. Head with dark area extending to front of emarginate eye, clypeus and frontal bar or spots pale. Pronotum slightly arcuate laterally, pale disc with pair of infuscate spots medially. Elytra yellow with dark speckles sometimes coalescing to form three lines and a subapical spot on each elytron; disc occasionally mostly black. Underside dark with yellow markings on thorax and lateral margins of ventrites. Male protarsal claws about two-thirds length of adjacent tarsomere. Adults found among vegetation and debris in ponds and quiet pools along small, clear streams. Widespread in western North America, also Wisconsin. (7)

83

Copelatus glyphicus (Say) (4.2–4.6 mm) is elongate, oval, flat, usually uniformly dark or light reddish brown, underside dark brown or blackish, with conspicuously grooved elytra; base of pronotum and elytra without lengthwise grooves. Head with eye margins notched. Pronotum smooth, sides with (female) or without (male) a few fine wrinkles. Scutellum visible. Elytra with 10 striae, alternate striae shorter, intervals inconspicuously punctate. Adults live in shallow permanent and temporary pools, especially over mats of leaves. Oregon and California; also Maritime Provinces and New England to Florida, west to Minnesota, Nebraska, and Texas. (6)

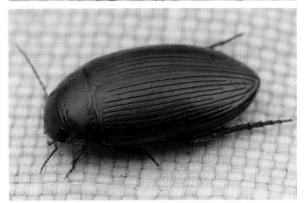

Laccophilus maculosus decipiens LeConte (4.7–6.4 mm) is oval and widest at basal third of elytra, with lateral margins of pronotum and elytra continuous, and body pale yellowish brown with 3–4 pale spots along elytral margins. Elytra with distinct pale spots along basal, lateral, and sutural margins outlined by dense speckles. Underside pale. Middle legs with both apical spurs bifid. Adults found in various pools alongside streams. British Columbia to Baja California, east to Saskatchewan and Colorado. *Laccophilus m. shermani* Leech does not exceed 5.8 mm; occurs in stream pools in coniferous forests from Arizona to western Texas and northern Mexico. (6)

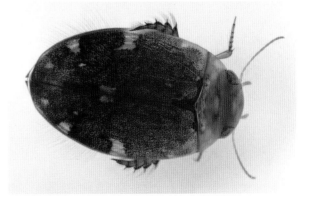

Cybister fimbriolatus (LeConte) (25.5–33.1 mm) is elongate-oval, widest behind middle, black to green, with front of head, lateral margins of pronotum and elytra yellow. Width and length of lateral stripes variable. Females usually with short scratches on sides of pronotum and elytra. Hind femur with apicoventral angles right-angled and often slightly rounded. Hind tarsi single claw (male), female usually with second vestigial claw. Adults in ditches, ponds, and lakes with emergent vegetation; also at lights. Southern California east to southeastern Canada and Florida, to Mexico. *Cybister explanatus* LeConte (24.5–29.0 mm) hind femora with sharply pointed anteroventral angles. Southern Oregon and Nevada through western Mexico to Chiapas. (2)

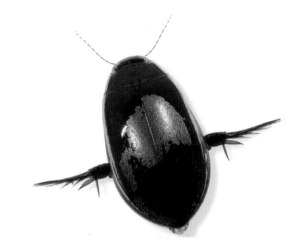

Dytiscus marginicollis LeConte (26.0–33.0 mm) is elongate-oval, black, sometimes with greenish reflections, with broad yellow lateral margins on pronotum and elytra. Large medial yellow chevron not extended to antennal bases, frontoclypeal suture complete, clypeus with anterior margin arcuate medially. Male front tarsi with two large round adhesive pads and a field of smaller ones. Basal yellow pronotal band broadest medially. Yellow elytral margins narrowed apically. Female elytra with field of longitudinal lines basally, with apical half usually densely punctate. Prefers acidic ponds in grassland areas at middle elevations; attracted to lights. Southern British Columbia to California, east to Manitoba and New Mexico; also Mexico. (4)

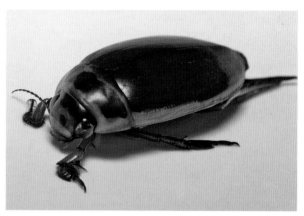

Eretes sticticus (Linnaeus) (12.0–17.0 mm) is broadly oval, pale yellow, with variable black markings dorsally. Head with bilobed spot between eyes. Pronotum with or without black bar or row of spots across middle. Elytra speckled with black punctures coalescing into three spots on each side and feeble apical band; margins behind middle fringed with spines and setae. Male front tarsomeres broad and with setae underneath. Adults in temporary pools, cattle tanks, and ponds; also at lights. Southern United States to Caribbean and northern South America; also Old World. *Eretes explicitus* Miller (southeastern Arizona to Oklahoma and Texas) distinguished only by examining male and female genitalia. (2)

Acilius abbreviatus Mannerheim (12.5–15.5 mm) is elongate-oval, widest behind middle of elytra, and with distinctly punctate surfaces. Head pale with distinct black M on vertex. Pronotum pale with a pair of transverse black bars. Elytra without sulci, yellowish and finely speckled with variable and distinctly pale subapical fascia slightly widened and projecting anteriorly before suture. Front and middle claws unequal in length, anterior claws longer. Underside usually infuscate (southern populations), sometimes partly yellow or completely pale (northern populations). Adults occur in small, deep, and fishless standing waters with dense vegetation. Alaska to southern California, east to Montana, Wyoming, and Colorado. (2)

Graphoderus perplexus (Sharp) (14.0–15.0 mm) is ovate, slightly convex, and yellowish brown with black markings. Head with pale frons contiguous with pale anterior area, or not. Pronotum wider than long, broadest posteriorly, and mostly yellowish brown with transverse black fasciae not reaching either anterior or posterior margins. Elytra yellowish brown. Elytra with lateral black vermiculate spots coalescing on disc to form black mesh enclosing round pale spots. Underside and legs mostly pale. Adults prefer permanent and temporary ponds with emergent vegetation, especially in sunny grassland habitats. Canada and northern United States, in West south to northern California and Utah. (3)

85

Thermonectus marmoratus (Gray) (11.0–15.0 mm) is ovate, slightly convex, and black with bright yellow markings. Head yellow with variable black M-shaped mark between eyes. Pronotum mostly black with yellow lateral margins and transverse medial marks. Elytra widest behind middle, each with a large discal yellow spot near suture and 14–22 smaller yellow spots. Underside bright reddish orange. Male front tarsi with adhesive discs. Adults occur in intermittent pools in desert and mountain canyon streams; also attracted to lights. Southern California to New Mexico, south to Mexico. (4)

Thermonectus nigrofasciatus (Aubé) (11.0–14.0 mm) is pale yellowish and speckled, with variable black M-shaped mark between eyes. Pronotum with narrow black bands sometimes connected laterally, surface smooth (males) or rough (females). Elytra usually with distinct continuous black band behind middle. Front tarsi of males with adhesive discs. Prefers intermittent pools in desert and mountain canyon streams; also attracted to lights. Southern Arizona to western Texas. *Thermonectus intermedius* Crotch elytra black medially, southern California to New Mexico; *T. sibleyi* Goodhue-McWilliams lacks distinct pronotal markings, Arizona, Mexico. (4)

Neoporus undulatus (Say) (3.9–4.5 mm) is broadly or somewhat oval, shiny (male), or dull (female) reddish yellow, with variable reddish-brown markings. Pronotum with front and rear margins dark, and side narrowly explanate. Elytra brownish black with three light irregular bands interrupted at suture. Front tarsi of male expanded. Adults found year-round among emergent vegetation along edges of permanent pools, ponds, small lakes, and margins of slow marshy streams; attracted to lights. Across Canada, south to Oregon; also in east south to Georgia, Arkansas, and Dakotas. *Neoporus superioris* (Balfour-Browne) (4.3–4.8 mm) distinctly striped, Yukon to British Columbia and Montana, east to Ontario and upper Midwest. (2)

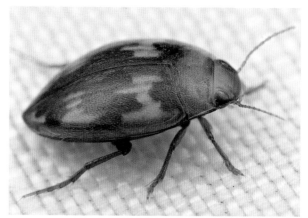

Boreonectes striatellus (LeConte) (3.8–4.7 mm) is broadly oval, variably marked from striped to nearly all black, with surfaces densely punctate and setose. Antennae with antennomeres 1–3 pale, 4–11 infuscate. Pronotum with posterolateral angles distinct, disc lacking distinct longitudinal impressions on either side. Elytra with subsutural striae, plus 1–4 discal striae. Middle coxae narrowly separated. Ventral face of hind tibiae with longitudinal row of coarse punctures. Adults occur in spring-fed pools, beaver ponds, margins of mountain lakes, and along edges of quiet creeks, streams, and rivers with silty or sandy bottoms. Alaska to California, east to Manitoba and western Texas. (12)

86

AMPHIZOIDAE (am-fi-zō'-i-dē)
TROUT-STREAM BEETLES

Trout-stream beetles are a small, distinctive family of semiaquatic beetles that occur in Asia and North America. All five species are included in the genus *Amphizoa*, three of which occur in western North America. They share primitive characteristics with aquatic predaceous diving beetles (Dytiscidae, p.81), as well as with terrestrial ground beetles (Carabidae, p.88), and thus are of considerable interest to evolutionary biologists. Amphizoid larvae and adults are primarily aquatic and inhabit cool and cold streams. Both crawl on submerged rocks, logs, and plants, but adults are sometimes found on emergent objects or clinging to driftwood and other debris that accumulates in backwaters and eddies. Returning to the surface to breathe, adults capture a bubble with their elytra apices, while the larvae use large terminal spiracles. Sluggish by day, these primarily nocturnal insects prey on the naiads of Plecoptera (stoneflies), Odonata (dragonflies, damselflies), and Ephemeroptera (mayflies). Females deposit their large eggs in moist soil or mud along the shore, or in cracks on the underside of submerged wood. The larvae stay close to the surface, clinging to floating debris with head downward, ready to dive after prey. After molting three times, mature larvae leave the water to pupate in mud or sand some distance away from the shoreline. Adults eclose in late summer and are often caked with mud. When handled roughly, trout-stream beetles will secrete a yellow, sticky defensive fluid from their anus that produces an odor akin to overripe cantaloupe, which has antimicrobial properties.

FAMILY DIAGNOSIS The relatively large size, shape, and preferred habitat distinguishes amphizoids from other aquatic families of beetles. Adults are elongate-oval and black. Head prognathous. Filiform antennae with 11 thick antennomeres. Pronotum narrower than elytra, distinctly margined on sides, notopleural suture distinct. Procoxal cavities open behind. Elytra vaguely striate or carinate. Legs not modified for swimming, slender, without long setae, tarsi 5-5-5, tarsomeres and claws simple. Abdomen with six ventrites, 1–3 connate, 1 divided by hind coxae.

SIMILAR FAMILIES
- false ground beetles (Trachypachidae, p.87)— elytra striate, terrestrial
- some ground beetles (Carabidae, p.88)—elytra distinctly striate, terrestrial

- some darkling beetles (Tenebrionidae, p.347)— tarsi 5-5-4, terrestrial

COLLECTING NOTES Look for amphizoid beetles year-round in habitats associated with cold, fast-flowing streams and their waterfalls. Carefully inspect gravel along the shore, or search among accumulations of floating leaves and other plant debris caught against logs, emergent branches, exposed roots beneath undercut banks, or trapped in backwater eddies. Individuals occasionally found in lakes and ponds likely arrived with debris carried by incoming streams.

FAUNA THREE SPECIES IN ONE GENUS

Amphizoa insolens LeConte (10.9–15.0 mm) is broadly elongate-oval, black, with appendages black or reddish black. Pronotum with lateral margins crenulate and parallel behind middle. Elytra convex, surface moderately to coarsely rugose. Alaska to southern California, east to Alberta and Wyoming. *Amphizoa striata* Van Dyke (13.1–14.9 mm) black to tan, with appendages and markings often reddish, pronotum broadest basally, and elytral surface not rugose, British Columbia to Oregon; *A. lecontei* Matthews (11.7–14.2 mm) fifth elytral interval carinate, not depressed between procoxae, Yukon Territory to Oregon, east to Alberta, Montana, and Utah. (3)

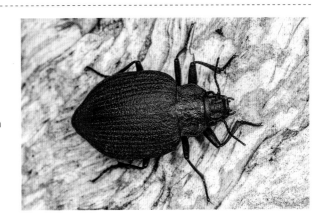

TRACHYPACHIDAE (trak-i-pak'-i-dē)
FALSE GROUND BEETLES

False ground beetles comprise a small, little known family consisting of six species in two genera. The sole genus in the Northern Hemisphere, *Trachypachus*, includes four species, three of which occur in western North America. Both adults and larvae apparently prefer relatively open, dry habitats. They occur on sandy or graveled substrates covered with leaves or needles along riverbanks and slightly shaded areas beneath deciduous and coniferous trees, or on exposed clay banks. Adults are encountered on sunny days running over bare ground and will quickly dive into leaf litter and other debris to avoid danger. Although their feeding preferences are poorly understood, adult and larval trachypachids are likely predators and scavengers of insects and both apparently utilize extraoral digestion.

FAMILY DIAGNOSIS Trachypachids resemble small carabids, but differ in lack of pubescence on their antennae and by the large hind coxae that extend to sides of body. Head prognathous, with eyes moderately prominent. Filiform antennae with 11 antennomeres, 2–11 without pubescence. Prothorax narrower than elytra, each side with three setae, lateral margins carinate and narrowly reflexed. Procoxal cavities open behind. Scutellum visible. Elytra largely smooth, without well-defined punctostriae. Legs short, thick, with large hind coxae reaching the sides of the body; tarsi 5-5-5, males with front tarsomeres 1 and 2, middle tarsomere 1 expanded and setose underneath, claws simple. Abdomen with six ventrites, 1 and 2 connate, posterior margins with one (male) or two pairs (female) of setae.

SIMILAR FAMILIES

■ ground beetles (Carabidae, see below)— antennomeres 3–11 setose, hind coxae not reaching sides of body

COLLECTING NOTES Adult trachypachids are diurnal and found in spring and summer on open, dry, sparsely vegetated soils covered with leaf litter under hardwoods and conifers. *Trachypachus gibbsii* was extracted from duff beneath noble fir (*Abies procera*), while *T. inermis* occurs in landscaped habitats in urban settings.

FAUNA THREE SPECIES IN ONE GENUS

Trachypachus gibbsii LeConte (5.0–6.8 mm) is black with bronze sheen. Pronotum barely narrower at base than middle. Elytra each with 12 rows of micropunctures. Adults active in spring and early summer along dry mountain riverbanks in open, sparsely vegetated habitats, or those covered in dead leaves. Southern British Columbia to southern California, east to Idaho. *Trachypachus inermis* Mannerheim (3.7–5.8 mm) is black, pronotum narrower at base, elytron with 3–9 rows of micropunctures, Alaska to Saskatchewan, south to San Jacinto Mountains of California, and Utah, Colorado; *T. sleveni* Van Dyke (7.0 mm) bronze, with 11–12 rows of coarse punctures on elytron, western Washington and Oregon. (3)

CARABIDAE (kar-ab'-i-dē)
GROUND, TIGER, AND WRINKLED BARK BEETLES

The Carabidae, which include both Rhysodidae (wrinkled bark beetles) and Cicindelidae (tiger beetles) as subfamilies, range in habit from blind and flightless cave dwellers to fully winged beetles with decided preferences for living on the ground or up on trees and shrubs. Most species are shiny and dark, although many species have distinct patterns or metallic reflections. The bright, shiny colors and cryptic markings of tiger beetles help them blend into their background, confounding the efforts of potential predators to track them. Most carabids are fleet of foot and, equipped with long legs and powerful jaws, are perfectly adapted for capturing and killing insect prey. Both adults and larvae attack all sorts of insects and are considered largely beneficial when they prey on pest species. Most adults are opportunistic predators that eat whatever they capture, but some appear to specialize on caterpillars (*Calosoma*, p.91–92) or snails (*Scaphinotus*, p.91). Although frequently characterized as predaceous, some ground beetles (e.g., *Harpalus*, p.105) prefer eating mainly plant materials, especially fruits and seeds. Tiger beetles (p.93–96) hunt mostly during the warmest part of the day, while most other carabids search for prey at dusk or at night. *Clinidium* and *Omoglymmius* (p.99) species spend most of their lives deep inside rotten, fungal-ridden wood, consuming the amoeboid stage of slime molds and possibly the mycelia of other fungi. The mandibles of these beetles are not for chewing, but instead protect special needlelike appendages associated with the maxillae that are adapted for pinning down amoebae, ripping open their cell membranes, and lapping up leaking cellular fluids. Several other aberrant carabids resemble beetles in other families. For example, *Omophron* (p.97) looks like a large crawling water beetle (p.79), while lumbering species of *Metrius* (p.101) bring to mind darkling beetles (p.347). *Psydrus* (p.101) and *Helluomorphoides* (p.111) are somewhat elongate and flattened and have relatively short, thick moniliform antennae. *Fossorial* or burrowing species, such as *Scarites* and *Paraclivina* (p.98), tend to have elongate cylindrical bodies and short legs. Females of the aberrant and myrmecophilous *Pseudomorpha* (p.111) don't lay eggs, but are instead ovoviviparous and carry hatched larvae inside their bodies until they are ready to pupate. Most carabids protect themselves with noxious chemicals. For example, when threatened, *Brachinus* species (p.101) ably defend themselves by releasing noxious fluids from a pair of abdominal glands near the anus with amazing force and accuracy. These smelly and sometimes caustic fluids are produced by pygidial glands located at the tip of the abdomen and contain a potent chemical cocktail of hydrocarbons, aldehydes, phenols, quinones, esters, and acids. Large spring and summer populations of *Calosoma* species and *Tanystoma maculicolle* (p.107) are sometimes a nuisance during their summer flights. Extremely diverse in habits, there is still much to be learned about the ecological roles of carabids, especially their importance as predators in both natural habitats and agricultural systems.

FAMILY DIAGNOSIS Carabids are elongate, flattened to almost cylindrical, seldom clothed in pubescence, but often with sparse erect setae, and somewhat tapered at both ends. Usually uniformly shiny and dark, sometimes brownish or pale, metallic, or bi- or tricolored, often with brightly marked patterns of yellow or orange on the elytra; tiger beetles often with bold white or yellowish, enamel-like markings on otherwise metallic elytra. Mouthparts prognathous. Antennae filiform or moniliform, with 11 antennomeres. Pronotum usually narrower than elytra, with sides sharply margined, less so in tiger beetles. Procoxal cavities open or closed behind. Scutellum visible, except in *Omophron*. Elytra completely covering abdomen, or nearly so, and fused in flightless species; surface smooth, punctured, and often striate. Flight wings fully developed, reduced in size, or absent. Hind trochanter large and offset from femur, tarsi 5-5-5, with claws equal, simple, serrate, or pectinate. Abdomen usually with six ventrites (*Brachinus* has seven or eight) connate, with ventrite 1 divided by hind coxae (p.68).

SIMILAR FAMILIES
- false ground beetles (Trachypachidae, p.87)—antennomeres without pubescence
- some stag beetles (Lucanidae, p.164)—antennae geniculate with lamellate clubs
- bothriderid beetles (Bothrideridae, p.306)—antennae clubbed, tarsi 4-4-4
- colydiine beetles (Zopheridae, p.304)—antennae clubbed, tarsi 5-5-4
- darkling beetles (Tenebrionidae, p.347)—tarsi 5-5-4, antennae sometimes clavate

- comb-clawed beetles (Tenebrionidae: Alleculinae, p.347–366)—tarsi 5-5-4, claws serrate
- dead log beetles (Pythidae, p.392)—tarsi 5-5-4
- narrow-waisted bark beetles (Salpingidae, p.397)—tarsi 5-5-4
- lined flat bark beetles (Laemophloeidae, p.461)—distinct lines along sides of head, pronotum
- *Neandra* (Cerambycidae, p.461)—tarsi appear 4-4-4

COLLECTING NOTES Look for ground beetles under bark, rocks, boards, and logs, especially along the banks of ponds, streams, and rivers. Flush beetles from their hiding places in mud and sand along shorelines by pouring or splashing water over the substrate. Raking leaves and sifting litter in these habitats are productive. Inspect bases of plant rosettes, or within the axils of reeds and grasses growing in wetlands. Beat and sweep vegetation and check tree trunks at night. Pitfall traps, especially those baited with meat, are useful for monitoring some ground beetle populations. Many nocturnal and fully winged species fly to lights. *Clinidium* and *Omoglymmius* are found under loose bark of moist, firm, fungus-ridden logs and stumps, as well as in rotten centers of large, living trees. Tiger beetles are mostly diurnal, extremely alert, and quickly take flight when threatened, fly for a short distance, and land facing the threat. Most are active on hot, bright spring and summer days, especially in sunny, open places along roads and trails, lakeshores, riverbanks, beaches, and mudflats; they hide in burrows under stones, or beneath loose bark at night or during bad weather. Nocturnal species of *Tetracha* are attracted to lights, while those of *Amblycheila* and *Omus* are not.

FAUNA ~2,439 SPECIES IN 208 GENERA

Opisthius richardsoni Kirby (8.5–11.0 mm) is elongate-ovate with head and pronotum relatively narrow, dull black with distinct greenish or coppery luster, with appendage more or less green. Head with frons bearing a pair of setae between very convex eyes; all antennomeres pubescent. Pronotum without lateral setae. Elytra each with four rows of shallow circular ocellate depressions, rows separated by more or less shiny elevations. Diurnal adults fly, are fast runners, and are found on unvegetated soft banks of clay, sand, and gravel along cold streams and rivers. Central Alaska to Sierra Nevada of California, east to central Saskatchewan and north-central Mexico. (1)

Nebria eschscholtzii Ménétriés (9.0–12.0 mm) is elongate-oval and black with pale antennae and legs. Pronotum cordate, lateral margins bulging out immediately from somewhat rectangular posterolateral angles and lacking setigerous punctures. Elytra faintly striopunctate with humeri moderately prominent, lateral margins strongly rounded. Flightless nocturnal adults under stones along wet banks of mountain streams. Northwestern Washington to southern California, east to northeastern Idaho. (53)

Notiophilus biguttatus (Fabricius) (4.7–6.0 mm) is elongate-oval, shiny black with coppery luster, rarely bluish. Head large with prominent eyes, and transverse carinae on frons. Antennae dark with antennomeres 1–4 pale. Elytra finely punctostriate, with interval 2 very broad and smooth, apical declivity sometimes with pale elytral stripes, and each elytron with pair of subapical setigerous punctures. Flight wings fully developed or not. Male front tarsi expanded with setose pads underneath. Femora and tarsi brownish black. Mostly diurnal adults occur on clearings, trails, roads, and other edges in wooded habitats, or hiding underneath leaves and stones. Europe; in West established in British Columbia and Washington. (13)

Cychrus tuberculatus Harris (18.5–25.0 mm) is oblong-oval and dull black. Head elongate, coarsely punctate throughout or only to clypeus, punctures often confluent. Pronotum as long as wide, cordate, roughly punctate. Elytra with humeri rounded, each with three distinct rows of large, convex tubercles and less conspicuous rows of smaller tubercles, separated by area of scattered small, yet distinct granules. Flightless nocturnal adults found during day under rocks and logs in coniferous forests. British Columbia to southern Oregon, possibly northern California. (2)

90

Scaphinotus cristatus (Harris) (11.0–24.0 mm) is oblong-oval and brown or black, seldom with faint blue luster along lateral margins. Head elongate, with deep transverse furrow immediately behind eyes, and frons with elevated crest; long antennae pubescent from antennomere 5. Pronotum cordate, about as long as wide, or slightly wider, with disc convex and smooth or moderately to strongly wrinkled. Elytra with humeri nearly obsolete, each with 17 or 18 wavy and irregular striae. Flightless nocturnal adults found during day under rocks and logs in coniferous forests. Southwestern Oregon to southern California. (29)

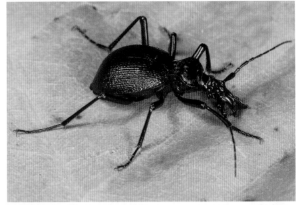

Scaphinotus longiceps Van Dyke (19.0–20.0 mm) is oblong-oval and brown or black with faint purple luster on elytra. Head very long and narrow, about three times longer than wide and longer than pronotum, with convex front transversely wrinkled and lacking carina. Pronotum with strongly convex disc divided by medial line, surface smooth or with fine transverse wrinkles. Elytra each with 14–16 regular striae, intervals moderately convex. Flightless nocturnal adults rare, found during day under rocks and logs in temperate coniferous rainforests. Coastal northern California. (29)

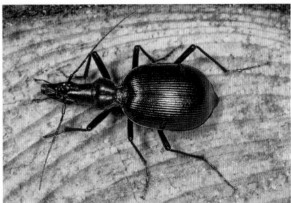

91

Calosoma cancellatum Eschscholtz (16.0–23.0 mm) is dark brown or black, often with green luster or with brilliant green pronotum and elytra. Head densely punctate, slightly wrinkled in front, with confluent punctures near eyes. Pronotum twice as wide as long, sides evenly arcuate. Elytra convex with elytral margins that become slightly wider toward apex, and humeral angles rounded and followed by smooth elytral margin; disc with fourth, eighth, and twelfth bearing pits distinctly wider and more elevated than those on other interstices. Adults found in open, dry habitats in lowlands and mountains. South-central British Columbia to southern California, east to North Dakota and southern Arizona. (25)

Calosoma prominens LeConte (24.0–34.0 mm) is black, often with green or bluish luster in punctures of head and base of pronotum. Head with large, moderately dense punctures becoming confluent near eyes, and stout mandibles somewhat arcuate at apices. Pronotum with strongly angulate lateral margins, angles somewhat sharp, and margins faint to distinct. Elytra slightly wider toward apex, punctostriate with interstices flat. Abdomen with fourth and fifth ventrites lacking setae. Nocturnal adults fly to lights in deserts and dry upland habitats. Eastern California to Baja California Sur, east to central New Mexico and Sonora. (25)

Fiery Searcher *Calosoma scrutator* (Fabricius) (23.0–36.0 mm) has a black head, dark blue or violet pronotum, and brilliant green elytra with metallic reddish or gold margins. Pronotum with broad purple, coppery, or golden green margins. Legs with femora black with blue luster, middle tibiae of male strongly curved, with reddish setal brushes at tip. Adults found in various open habitats and woodland edges on caterpillar-infested shrubs in spring; sometimes common at lights. All *Calosoma* adults release a foul-smelling defensive fluid when disturbed. California and Arizona, south to Venezuela; widespread in eastern North America. (25)

Calosoma semilaeve (LeConte) (17.0–30.0 mm) is dull black with dorsal surfaces finely punctured and wrinkled, sometimes with faint bluish luster. Head and pronotum rough, densely and rugosely punctured. Pronotum twice as wide as long, disc appearing rough, with lateral margins evenly arcuate, hind angles rounded, extending beyond sinuate posterior margin. Elytra dull, basal half appearing scaly with deep transverse wrinkles, humeral angles distinct with adjacent serrated margin, each finely punctostriate with interstices flat. Winged nocturnal and diurnal adults found in various lowland and upland habitats; attracted to lights. Eastern Oregon to southern California, east to southern Arizona. (25)

Carabus nemoralis Müller (21.0–26.0 mm) is black with upper surface more or less metallic, bronze or coppery green, and sides of pronotum and elytra usually broadly bluish or violet. Head finely wrinkled, with fine ridge in front of each eye. Pronotum with broad posterior angles protruding backward. Elytra with rows of widely spaced punctures, spaces between irregularly sculptured, side margins smooth; flight wings reduced. Flightless and nocturnal adults active; found in various disturbed habitats under debris. Adventive from Europe; in western North America from Queen Charlotte Island to central California, east to central Alberta, northern Utah, and southeastern Wyoming. (25)

Carabus serratus Say (15.0–24.0 mm) is elongate-oval, somewhat slender, and black with metallic blue or violet pronotal and elytral margins, and elytra without ridges. Elytra with two or three small notches on sides near base, each with three rows of widely separated punctures, spaces between with three irregular rows of punctures; flight wings fully developed or reduced. Adults active primarily spring and summer, found in various habitats under debris during day; attracted to lights. Across southern Canada and northern United States; in east, south to Georgia, Illinois, and Iowa. (25)

92

Carabus vietinghoffi Adams (20.0–25.0 mm) is black with dorsal surface bluish, sides of prothorax and elytra brilliant green becoming gold. Elytra each with about 15 distinctly interrupted, yet parallel ridges; three primary rows of pits hardly visible. Flightless and nocturnal adults found in more or less open and forested habitats; hide during the day under various debris, as well as logs and stones. Holarctic; eastern Siberia and Seward Peninsula of Alaska to Bathurst Inlet on Arctic coast of Nunavut. (25)

Montane Tiger Beetle *Amblycheila baroni* Rivers (19.0–25.0 mm) is dull black or brown and smooth. Head with prominent mandibles. Elytra convex with large shallow punctures, each with or without one or, rarely, two indistinct longitudinal ridges just above sides. Flightless and nocturnal adults occur on sandy or gravelly washes, dry slopes, and among large boulder fields in juniper-pinyon-oak woodlands during summer monsoons. Central and southeastern Arizona, Sonora; possibly reaching western Texas. Two larger species with three distinct ridges on each elytron, *Amblycheila schwarzi* W. Horn (21.0–28.0 mm) and *A. picolominii* Reiche (24.0–30.0 mm), occur in similar habitats in Mojave Desert and northern Arizona, respectively. (3)

California Night-stalking Tiger Beetle *Omus californicus* Eschscholtz (12.0–23.0 mm) is dull black with dorsal surface coarsely sculptured. Pronotum with anterolateral angles visible from above. Flightless nocturnal adults active in spring in forested habitats. Four subspecies described for populations occurring in coastal forests, western slopes of Sierra Nevada and intervening habitats, and in central and northern California. *Omus audouini* Reiche (14.0–18.0 mm) with anterolateral pronotal angles downturned, coastal forests and grasslands from southern British Columbia to northern California; larger and bronzy *O. dejeani* Reiche (18.0–21.0 mm) is similar in habitat preference and distribution, but reaching only southern Oregon. (6)

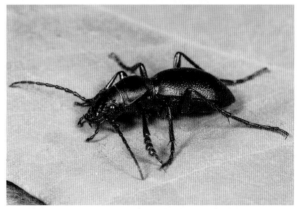

Pan-American Big-headed Tiger Beetle *Tetracha carolina* (Linnaeus) (12.0–20.0 mm) is metallic purple and green with appendages pale yellowish brown. Head broad with prominent eyes and distinct mandibles. Pronotum with front angles forming lobes extending forward. Elytra bright reddish purple, shiny green on sides, with large pale curved markings on apices. Male front tarsi expanded and setose ventrally. Nocturnal adults winged but seldom fly, and found during summer along edges of lakes and rivers, and grassy uplands; attracted to lights. Transcontinental; in West from southern Colorado River Basin east to southern Arizona. (1)

Sonoran Tiger Beetle *Brasiella wickhami* (W. Horn) (7.0–8.0 mm) is small, shiny copper dorsally, usually with greenish reflections. Elytra greenish, markings consist of short lines and small spots. Underside deep metallic blue with greenish reflections. Legs reddish brown with coppery highlights. Nocturnal adults active during summer monsoons, capable of flying short distances, run quickly in grasslands and sparsely vegetated muddy areas along water's edge. Southern Arizona south to Sinaloa. Pygmy tiger beetle *Brasiella viridisticta* Bates (7.0–9.0 mm) is similar in size and reduced markings, habitat preference, and distribution, but dark brown above with shallow elytral punctures distinctly green. (2)

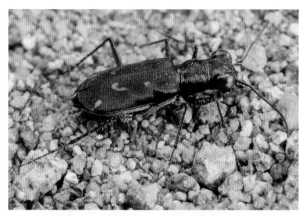

Cicindela hirticollis gravida LeConte (10.0–15.0 mm) is usually brownish green dorsally, sometimes brownish or bluish overall. Sides of prothorax with large tufts of long white setae. Elytra densely pitted with small deep metallic blue punctures, with relatively thick maculation, each with a basal more or less G-shaped maculation; lateral margins of females curved and broadened. Adults active in late spring and summer, restricted to coastal beaches from Santa Cruz, California to Ensenada, Baja California. Nine additional subspecies described across North America. (21)

Western Beach Tiger Beetle *Cicindela latesignata* LeConte (12.0–13.0 mm) is black to blackish green. Head and pronotum with scattered and erect thick white setae. Elytra with very distinct and broad, sometimes coalescing maculation connected along elytral margins. Underside dark metallic green or blue-green. Adults restricted to coastal beaches, bays, estuaries, salt marshes, and sloughs where they often occur in large numbers. Former range reduced by habitat destruction, mostly occurs in protected habitats and military installations. Southern California and Baja California. (21)

Western Tiger Beetle *Cicindela oregona oregona* LeConte (11.0–13.0 mm) is variable, with head, pronotum, and elytra usually uniformly brown, greenish, and purplish to blue or nearly black; some individuals have elytra with different hue. Underside mostly coppery (northern populations) to metallic purple (southern population). Pronotum without large tufts of long white setae. Elytra each with distinctly elbowed middle band, sometimes broken, but lack white marginal line at middle. Diurnal, found along streams and lake shorelines. Southern British Columbia to California, east to Idaho and northern Utah. Three additional subspecies described in region. (21)

Echo Tiger Beetle *Cicindela willistoni echo* Casey (10.0–13.0 mm) is dark brown dorsally. Elytra with broad maculation usually not joined along lateral margins. Underside usually metallic green-blue, rarely coppery. Diurnal adults frequent muddy substrates near seeps, streams, and temporary pools on salt and alkali flats. Great Basin, from southeastern Oregon to northeastern California and southern Nevada, east to southwestern Wyoming and southern Utah. Four additional subspecies of *Cicindela willistoni* are recognized in western North America. (21)

Cicindelidia haemorrhagica LeConte (12.0–4.0 mm) is black, blue-green, or reddish brown dorsally. Elytra usually with maculation complete, each with three distinct narrow to wide bands, and middle band, if present, often not reaching sides; thinner bands sometimes incomplete in eastern Arizona population. Underside dark purple and copper, bright orange abdomen that is clearly visible in flight. Diurnal adults on wet salt flats, wetland edges, and along irrigation ditches. Eastern Washington and Oregon to California, eastward through southern Idaho, northwestern Wyoming, western Utah, and Arizona. Bluish *C. h. pacifica* Schaupp elytra with reduced or no maculation, coastal southern California; *C. h. arizonae* Wickham in bottom of Grand Canyon. (12)

Santa Clara Grasslands Tiger Beetle *Cicindelidia obsoleta santaclarae* Bates (15.0–20.0 mm) is large, dull green, brown, or black, often within a single population. Elytra with thin maculation often reduced to short lines and spots. Diurnal adults active during summer, fly away with an audible buzz; inhabit open grasslands and upland habits with bare ground; often hide under dried cow chips during dry conditions. Southern Colorado to Arizona and western Texas, south to Durango. (12)

Cicindelidia ocellata Klug (9.0–13.0 mm) is brown or dark brown with maculations reduced to spots. Elytra each with four spots. Underside dark coppery green with abdomen usually mostly dark metallic green with last two ventrites orange. Diurnal adults occur in summer on irrigated fields, pastures, and other moist open ground, and often gregarious along edges of stream banks, permanent and temporary pools, and irrigation ditches. Central and southern Arizona to western Texas, Sonora, and Chihuahua. (12)

Chihuahua Tiger Beetle *Cicindelidia punctulata chihuahuae* (11.0–13.0 mm) is bright metallic green, blue-green, bright blue, or dark brown with bronze reflections; population in San Rafael Valley in southern Arizona black. Labrum with single medial tooth. Prothorax narrow. Elytra with maculations sometimes reduced or absent, each with two parallel rows of distinct shallow pits, and apices along suture somewhat dehiscent. Underside metallic green, blue, and copper. Diurnal adults mostly active in summer, found in various habitats with hard-packed soils; attracted to lights. Sometimes considered a separate species. Northeastern Colorado to west-central Nevada, south to Chihuahua. (12)

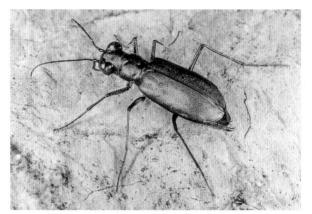

Western Red-bellied Tiger Beetle *Cicindelidia sedecimpunctata* Klug (9.0–11.0 mm) is dark brown. Elytra with broad, yet broken maculations, each with a complete wavy middle band constricted in middle and not reaching margins. Underside of head and prothorax with metallic blue and green inflections, pterothorax dark copper, and abdomen bright orange. Diurnal and highly gregarious adults found during summer along shores of desert streams, lakes, irrigation canals, and persistent rain pools in upland and foothill habitats. Eastern Arizona and New Mexico. (12)

Sigmoid Tiger Beetle *Cicindelidia trifasciata sigmoidea* LeConte (11.0–13.0 mm) is dark olive with coppery reflections. Elytra with distinct maculations that include a narrow S-shaped middle band, non-maculate areas with coarse, metallic green punctures. Underside greenish, dark purple, or black. Diurnal adults occur mostly on coastal beaches and tidal mudflats during late spring and summer, occasionally found along shore of Salton Sea; often attracted to lights. Southern California to Baja California Peninsula. (12)

White-striped Tiger Beetle *Parvindela lemniscata* **(LeConte)** (7.0–9.0 mm) is small and bright metallic orange-red dorsally. Pronotum with line of long, appressed white setae along sides. Elytra each with a bold, more or less straight yellowish-white stripe running along just inside entire lateral margin. Legs entirely reddish, sometimes with metallic reflections. Diurnal and nocturnal adults active during summer monsoons on sandy soils in deserts and open grasslands; often common at lights. Southeastern California and lower elevations in Arizona. (4)

Elaphrus californicus Mannerheim (6.3–8.0 mm) is dull greenish to brassy above, metallic green below. Elytra with large purple impressions. Tibia and part of femora reddish, hind femur with long whitish setae on broad dorsal surface near apex. Males with front tarsi 1–3 dilated. Adults somewhat gregarious and found running over sparsely vegetated wet ground, muddy edges of ponds and lakes, and silted shores of streams and rivers year-round, especially in late spring and summer; overwinter in higher, drier habitats. Throughout North America; in West from Alaska to southern California, east to Alberta, Montana, Wyoming, and Nevada. (16)

Omophron dentatum LeConte (5.4–7.1 mm) is oval and pale, with maculations on head, pronotum, and elytra bright metallic green, and pale M-shaped mark on head. Irregular transverse pronotal band nearly extending to sides. Elytron with 15 punctostriae moderately impressed and three distinct irregular fasciae. Underside dark, with legs pale. Nocturnal adults inhabit wet shorelines of streams, rivers, and lakes. Southern California and Baja California Peninsula. *Omophron solidum* Casey (5.8–7.8 mm) with pale frontal mark V-shaped, punctostriae deeply impressed, middle and apical fascia in contact. Southwestern Oregon, northern California. (7)

Omophron obliteratum Horn (5.9–7.3 mm) is oval, with maculations on head, pronotum, and elytra dark metallic green. Pale area on head V-shaped. Pronotum mostly dark with irregular pale lateral margins and coarsely punctured disc. Elytra each with 14 punctostriae, with dark maculations more extensive than pale areas. Nocturnal adults occur on sandy or gravelly beaches along streams and rivers. Southern California to western Texas, south to Zacatecas. *Omophron americanum* Dejean (5.1– 7.0 mm) superficially similar, elytron with 15 punctostriae. Widespread from eastern North America to northeastern Arizona. (7)

Pasimachus californicus Chaudoir (22.0–38.0 mm) is robust and uniformly dull black, with broad head, prominent mandibles, and filiform antennae. Pronotum broad, widest before middle, and narrowly attached to body. Elytra smooth and convex. Hind tibia of male with dense golden setae on apical half of inside margin. Flightless nocturnal adults especially active during summer monsoons in grasslands and open woodlands; hide in burrows or under rocks, dry cow chips, and other debris; sometimes encountered on overcast days. Utah and Arizona east to southeastern Nebraska and eastern Kansas, south to Michoacán. (5)

Pasimachus viridans LeConte (24.0–28.0 mm) is robust, somewhat elongate-ovate, and dull black with brilliant metallic green pronotal and elytral margins. Head broad with prominent mandibles and filiform antennae. Pronotum broad, widest before middle, and narrowly attached to body, with anterior margin mostly black. Elytra smooth and convex, with humeri more or less green. Nocturnal and flightless adults encountered during summer monsoons in open upland habitats, sometimes active on overcast days or after thundershowers. Southeastern Arizona south to Durango. (5)

Tunneling Large Pedunculate Beetle *Scarites subterraneus* Fabricius (15.0–30.0 mm) is elongate, robust, parallel-sided, with forebody loosely attached to rest of body. Head with large mandibles, antennomeres 8–10 moniliform. Pronotum somewhat square, widest near middle, with hind angles rounded. Elytra without carinae at humeri, each with six complete and widely separated shallow grooves, outermost groove next to side margin incomplete. Front tibiae with one small tooth followed by three large ones. Adults most active spring and summer; attracted to lights. Throughout North America; in West from southern California and Baja California east to Colorado and New Mexico. (1)

Two-spot Slope-rumped Beetle *Paraclivina bipustulata* (**Fabricius**) (6.0–7.5 mm) is elongate, cylindrical, mostly brown or black with antennae, middle and hind legs reddish. Head and prothorax loosely attached to rest of body. Pronotum nearly smooth, without punctures. Elytra deeply punctostriate with basal and preapical red spots nearly reaching suture. Legs with middle tibiae with preapical pegs absent. Nocturnal adults are burrowers, found year-round, especially in spring and summer, and occur among layers of leaf litter, roots of shore grasses, or decaying plant debris, especially along shorelines; often attracted to lights. Southeastern Arizona east to Ontario and Florida. (2)

Akephorus marinus LeConte (5.7–6.3 mm) is uniformly dull reddish brown, with pronotal and elytral surfaces with meshed microsculpture. Anterolateral margins of pronotum with setigerous punctures. Elytra fused, without subapical setigerous punctures. Nocturnal and brachypterous adults are slow runners and prey on small crustaceans. Occur during spring and summer under debris or in burrows under debris in moist sand on exposed Pacific beaches. San Mateo County, California, south to Baja California Peninsula. (2)

Akephorus obesus (LeConte) (5.0–6.5 mm) is tricolored and dull, with pronotal and elytral surfaces with meshed microsculpture. Head dark brown. Pronotum orange-brown, with anterolateral margins lacking setigerous punctures. Elytra dark metallic green, fused, and without subapical setigerous punctures. Nocturnal and brachypterous adults are slow runners and prey on other small rove beetles. Occur during spring and summer under debris or in burrows under debris in moist sand on exposed Pacific beaches. Southern British Columbia to central California. (2)

Clinidium calcaratum LeConte (5.8–8.1 mm) is elongate, somewhat parallel-sided, dark reddish brown to black. Pronotum with two marginal sulci and one long middle sulcus on disc. Elytra deeply sulcate, punctures not distinct, with interstriae almost carinate and apical setae absent. Underside with metasternum between middle and hind legs lacking complete median sulcus. Hind tibial apices of male with hooklike calcars. Adults found year-round under bark of decaying Douglas-fir (*Pseudotsuga menziesii*) and other conifers in humid coastal forests of southern British Columbia to northern Coast Ranges and central Sierra Nevada in California. (1)

Omoglymmius hamatus (LeConte) (6.2–6.8 mm) is elongate, somewhat parallel-sided, reddish brown to black. Head deeply grooved dorsally, eyes large, somewhat circular and granulate. Pronotum twice as long as wide, disc sparsely punctate with three long sulci. Elytra each deeply and distinctly punctostriate with punctures regular, intervals convex, and apices appearing pinched. Legs with middle and hind tibiae each with a single apical spur, hind tibial apices of male with hooklike calcars. Adults found under bark of decaying conifers, such as pine (*Pinus*) and Douglas-fir (*Pseudotsuga menziesii*). Washington to southern California, east to Idaho and southeastern Arizona. (1).

Promecognathus crassus LeConte (10.9–16.0 mm) is black, with appendages lighter, and strongly protruding mandibles nearly straight. Head with irregular furrows not converging, antennal insertions visible dorsally. Anterolateral pronotal margin with single setigerous puncture. Elytral humeri prominent. Flightless and nocturnal adults hunt millipedes on moist or dry soils enriched with humus in foothill and mountain canyons. Southwestern British Columbia to central California. *Promecognathus laevissimus* Dejean (8.0–14.0 mm) with two or three setigerous punctures on each lateral pronotal margin and somewhat rounded humeri; Oregon to central California and northwestern Nevada. (2)

Zacotus matthewsii **(LeConte)** (12.0–17.0 mm) is elongate and bright copper with greenish reflections, metallic green, violet, or dull purple. Head rugose. Pronotum longer than wide with posterior angles rounded, disc shallowly impressed medially with longitudinal line. Elytra each with eight very fine, shallowly impressed striae becoming obsolete laterally. Underside dark reddish brown, legs darker. Nocturnal and flightless adults found in spring and summer, occurring under decaying logs on moist soils covered with a thick layer of needles in coniferous forests and surrounding habitats. Southern British Columbia to northwestern California, east to southwestern Montana. (1)

Bembidion flohri **Bates** (3.9–5.0 mm) is elongate, and somewhat flattened, with head and pronotum brownish black with golden green luster, elytra pale yellowish brown with dark markings, and appendages reddish. Head with mentum toothed. Pronotum with acute rectangular or somewhat obtuse posterior angles. Elytra long and parallel-sided, with pair of small dark spots around anterior setal punctures, followed by broad incomplete fascia behind middle, and a pair of spots before apices. Nocturnal adults occur along edges of saline lakes and ponds; attracted to lights. Central British Columbia to southern California, west to Manitoba, Colorado, and Utah, south to Mexico. (253 Nearctic)

Mioptachys flavicauda **(Say)** (1.5–1.8 mm) is very small, blackish brown, with apical third of elytra and all appendages pale. Head without grooves. Pronotum wider than long, margins broad and pale. Elytra each usually with 1–4 punctostriae. Diurnal adults found year-round under loose bark of dead or dying trees and logs, especially hardwoods. Most individuals capable of flight and occasionally attracted to lights in spring and summer. Widespread in North America; in West from southern British Columbia to southern California, east to southeastern Arizona. (1)

Tachyta kirbyi **Casey** (2.6–3.0 mm) is small and dull black. Head with area between furrows somewhat convex at middle, antennomere 2 longer than 3, underneath with plate behind mouthparts without pits. Pronotum with lateral margins shallow and briefly sinuate in basal half, posterolateral angle slightly obtuse. Elytra each with three seta-bearing punctures, one at base next to scutellum, and with apical punctostriae flanking suture curved upward along lateral margins. Males with front tarsomeres 1–2 expanded with setose pads underneath. Adults found nearly year-round under bark of fallen trees; attracted to lights. West-central British Columbia, south to northwestern Oregon and south-central New Mexico, east to Québec and Massachusetts. (5)

Patrobus longicornis (Say) (9.0–15.0 mm) is shiny black with reddish-brown antennae and paler legs. Head and pronotum narrower than elytra. Eyes each with two setae above. Antennae half as long as body. Pronotum with sides sinuate behind middle, with deep furrow across front and down middle, and basal impression deep and coarsely punctate. Elytra lack margin across bases; flight wings developed or reduced. Nocturnal adults active mostly spring and summer on shores of various water bodies; attracted to lights. In West from British Columbia and southern Northwest Territories to southeastern Arizona and New Mexico. (7)

Psydrus piceus LeConte (5.5–6.2 mm) is dull brownish black to black with reddish-brown appendages. Head small and flat with coarse punctures. Pronotum with anterior lateral setae set wide apart, lateral margins densely setose, setae short. Elytra without humeral tooth, disc punctostriate, and lateral margins somewhat densely setose. Male protarsomeres 1–3 strongly dilated with setal brushes beneath. Nocturnal and gregarious adults hide under loose bark (*Larix*, *Tsuga*); occasionally attracted to lights. Produces *Brachinus*-like sound and strong odor. British Columbia to southern California, east to southwestern New Mexico. (1)

101

Metrius contractus contractus Eschscholtz (12.0–13.0 mm) is elongate-ovate, dull dark brownish black to nearly black dorsally, with raised, beadlike microsculpture dorsally. Lateral pronotal margins broad, occasionally lighter, with disc moderately impressed posteriorly. Elytra weakly punctostriate. Middle male tibiae with setal brushes. Nocturnal and flightless adults in coastal and montane coniferous forests; emits *Brachinus*-like sound and strong odor when disturbed. British Columbia to southern Coast Ranges and Sierra Nevada of California. *Metrius contractus planatus* Van Dyke at Lake Tahoe and Yosemite, California. *Metrius explodens* Bousquet & Goulet (11.0–11.5 mm) mostly brownish, microsculpture flat; occurs in Idaho. (2)

Goniotropis kuntzeni (Bänninger) (15.0–18.0 mm) is elongate and parallel-sided with prominent mandibles. Front tibia with prominent, hook-like antennal cleaning notch. Head without antennal depression beneath anterior margin of eye, with dorsal surface of mandibles impunctate. Pronotum broad, wider than head. Elytra shallowly impressed, with posterolateral marginal notch followed by apical flange. Nocturnal adults search for arthropod prey on trunks of mature, often hollowed Emory oak (*Quercus emoryi*) during summer. Southeastern Arizona, Sonora, and Durango. *Goniotropis parca* (LeConte) (9.0–12.0 mm) pronotum narrower; distribution similar, also Baja California. (2)

Brachinus mexicanus **Dejean** (7.5–9.6mm) is distinctly bicolored with head and prothorax reddish brown and uniformly dull blue elytra. Head with antennomeres entirely dark from 3 on. Elytra with sloped humeri, costae distinct or not, pubescence restricted to depressions 6, 7, 8, and across apical sixth. Underside dark. Legs uniformly reddish brown. Larvae ectoparasites of *Eretes* (p.84) and *Tropisternus* (p.124) pupae. Nocturnal adults found year-round on edges of permanent and temporary ponds and streams; attracted to lights. Washington to Baja California Sur, east to northern Illinois and Guatemala. (19)

Poecilus lucublandus **(Say)** (9.0–14.0mm) is greenish or coppery, bluish, or black above. Antennomeres 2–3 somewhat flattened and finely ridged. Pronotum without distinct marginal bead along sides, outermost impression at base indefinitely delimited. Elytra with deep and sometimes fine punctures; flight wings slightly reduced, occasional flier. Abdomen with two (male) or four (female) setae near tip. Underside black. Adults active mostly spring and summer in various wild and disturbed habitats; attracted to lights. Southern Canada south to Oregon, northern New Mexico and western Texas, and northern Georgia. (10)

Pterostichus lama **(Ménétriés)** (18.0–28.0mm) is large, black, with head and pronotum finely alutaceous and shiny, while elytra more coarsely so, appearing dull. Head broad, mandibles not protruding. Pronotum wide, broadest across prominent anterior angles, with lateral margins finely crenulate. Elytron with dentate humerus, and eight finely impressed punctostriae with strial punctures fine. Male with hind femora not angulate and medially carinate on last ventrite. Hind basal tarsomere with outer surface not grooved. Nocturnal and flightless adults found under bark of damp logs or hunting on ground in dark coastal and montane coniferous forests. Southern British Columbia to southern California and northwestern Nevada. (~140 Nearctic)

Panagaeus sallei **Chaudoir** (12.0–13.0mm) is distinctly bicolored, black with elytra mostly orangish red, coarsely punctured, and moderately clothed in erect setae. Head small, with convex eyes. Pronotum wider than long, broadest before base. Elytra punctostriate, punctures deep, black across base, and irregular fascia behind middle broken at suture. Tarsi with short reddish-brown setae underneath. Nocturnal adults active primarily during summer monsoons on dry leaf litter in woodlands; attracted to lights. Central Arizona and western, south-central Texas south to central Veracruz and Federal District in Mexico; also Baja California Peninsula. (1)

Chlaenius cumatilis LeConte (11.6–13.6 mm) is blue, blue-black, or violet dorsally, occasionally tinged with violet, with appendages orangish brown to reddish brown. Head somewhat shiny, with antennomeres 4–11 darker than 1–3. Pronotum as long as wide, broadest before middle, usually moderately cordate. Elytra dull, flattened to slightly convex, sides evenly rounded, not parallel, and striae with fine punctures; hind wings fully developed. Underside black, with abdomen glabrous. Femora elongate and slender. Nocturnal adults shelter under stones and other debris along lowland, foothill, and mountain streams. Southern California and Baja California Peninsula, and southeastern Arizona. (27)

Chlaenius sericeus (Forster) (11.4–16.1 mm) is bright metallic green dorsally, occasionally with a bronze or bluish luster; appendages reddish brown. Head shiny, with mandibles short and curved, with two seta-bearing punctures above each eye. Antennomeres 1–3 not or only slightly lighter than 4–11. Pronotum less shiny, slightly wider than long, sides slightly sinuate behind middle, hind angles obtuse with a single puncture bearing a long seta. Elytra dull with shallow striae with fine punctures; hind wings fully developed. Underside black. Legs of male with front tarsomeres broad and setose underneath. Widely distributed in North America. (27)

Badister neopulchellus Lindroth (5.0–6.2 mm) is bicolored with distinctly iridescent head and pronotum. Head black and right mandible crossed with deep notch, left mandible normal. Pronotum and elytra orange or yellowish brown. Pronotum narrowest at base, broadly notched in front, with front angles rounded and not protruding, and base distinctly margined within hind angles. Elytra shallowly grooved, spaces between flat; flight wings developed. Front tarsomeres expanded, tarsomere 5 on all tarsi setose underneath. Adults found along edges of standing waters; attracted to lights. In West, from southwest British Columbia to central California eastward. (5)

Diplocheila striatopunctata (LeConte) (12.5–17.9 mm) is black, sometimes with even elytral intervals brown or reddish. Left mandible with small tubercle usually visible from side. Lateral pronotal margins straight or slightly sinuate behind middle; posterior angles broad. Elytral punctostriae deep, intervals slightly convex with one or no seta-bearing punctures. Adults active mostly spring and summer on banks of ditches, canals, and other permanent standing water; fly to lights. Southern British Columbia to central-eastern California and southern Arizona, east to Nova Scotia and northeastern New Jersey. (3)

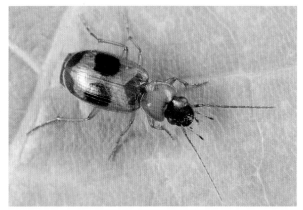

Anisodactylus alternans (Motschulsky) (7.9–10.8 mm) has a black head, sometimes with double reddish spot, first antennomere light or dark, and clypeus with one setigerous puncture at each outer distal angle. Pronotum black, lateral margins sometimes narrowly pale. Elytra uniformly brownish black or black, or extensively pale along base and sides (Great Basin Desert). Nocturnal adults winged; hides under debris along wetland edges. Southeastern British Columbia to southern California, east to Colorado. Bicolorous *A. sanctaecrucis* (Fabricius) (7.9–11.2 mm) lacks reddish spot on head, with two or four setigerous punctures on clypeus; in West from southern British Columbia to central Sierra Nevada of California, eastward. (15)

Cratacanthus dubius (Palisot de Beauvois) (7.5–11.5 mm) is blackish to black, glabrous dorsally, ventral surface paler, with appendages pale to dark reddish brown. Head broad with triangular process before eye projecting over antennal bases, and angulate mandibular ridge. Lateral pronotal margins broadly rounded and sinuate posteriorly. Elytral striae impunctate, with interstriae slightly convex. Tarsi not or only slightly expanded. Nocturnal adults active during summer, capable of flight or not; found in open, sandy, or disturbed habitats; attracted to lights. In West from southeastern Alberta to southern Arizona; also Mexico. (1)

Dicheirus dilitatus dilitatus (Dejean) (17.3–23.5 mm) is somewhat oblong-oval, reddish brown to brown: appendages sometimes paler. Head densely punctate with two or three long setae on each clypeal angle. Pronotum moderately densely punctate. Pronotum wider than long, broadest just before middle, with posterolateral margins nearly straight to broadly rounded posterior angles. Elytral setae usually short and erect. Legs with middle and hind tibiae lacking prominent tubercles at base of spines along sides. Nocturnal adults inhabit dry open grasslands and hillsides in spring. California. *Dicheirus d. angulatus* Casey acute or rounded posterior pronotal angles, elytral setae long; extreme southern California, Baja California. (5)

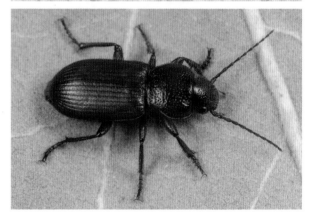

Euryderus grossus (Say) (10.5–16.5 mm) is robust and somewhat shiny black with mouthparts, appendages, and side margins lighter brown. Eyes each with one seta above. Lateral pronotal margin with seta at middle and rear angle. Elytra each with two rows of several deep punctures, each with a single long seta. Front tibiae with long, thick, fingerlike projection on side at tip. Adults active late spring and summer in mostly open habitats; attracted to lights. In West from southern British Columbia to northeastern Oregon and southern Arizona, east to Georgia. (1)

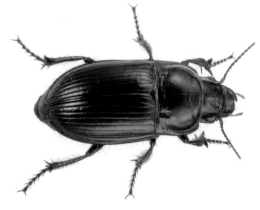

Geopinus incrassatus (Dejean) (13.0–17.0 mm) is robust, convex, and mostly pale reddish yellow-brown. Head short, not narrowed behind eyes. Pronotum mostly smooth, wider than long, widest in front of middle; front and base of equal width, sides sinuate just before hind angles. Elytra distinctly punctostriate, intervals slightly convex. Front tarsomeres 2–4 of male with spongy setose pads underneath. Nocturnal adults active year-round, feeding on seeds and caterpillars, found walking on or burrowing in sparsely vegetated sandy soils, wet sand, and dunes, especially along rivers and streams; attracted to lights. In West from southwestern Idaho to northwestern Nevada and northern Arizona, east to western Colorado. (1)

Harpalus caliginosus (Fabricius) (14.0–35.0 mm) is mostly black with male shinier than female; antennomeres 1–2 and tarsi reddish brown. Head with punctures coarser and denser near eyes. Pronotum distinctly wider than long, as wide as base of elytra, and with hind angles squared. Elytral punctostriae deep, with intervals convex, third interval without seta-bearing punctures. Adults active nearly year-round in open habitats on ground, or under debris where they feed on insects, pollen, and seeds; sometimes attracted to lights in large numbers. They stridulate and release pungent odor in smokelike cloud when threatened. Widespread across southern Canada and United States. (46)

Notiobia purpurascens (Bates) (7.7–10.4 mm) is elongate-oval and black, dull brown to dark reddish brown dorsally, with elytra faintly purplish or bluish, and yellow-brown appendages sometimes reddish. Head large with prominent eyes, distinctly toothed mentum, and labial palpomere 2 setose. Lateral pronotal margins not thickened, strongly converging posteriorly, with posterior angles broadly flattened. Elytron with humeri not toothed and single discal puncture. Hind tarsomere 1 as long as 2 and 3 combined, front and middle tarsomeres of male expanded and setose underneath. Adults under stones and litter in various habitats; attracted to lights. Northern California to central Missouri, southwestern Alabama, south to Mexico. (4)

Polpochila erro (LeConte) (12.5–17.0 mm) is robust, somewhat elongate, reddish brown to black. Head broad. Pronotum wider than long, broadest just before broadly concave anterior margin, lateral margins narrowly explanate, with posterior angles obtuse. Elytra shallowly striate. Legs yellowish brown with darker joints. Nocturnal adults active during summer around densely vegetated pond edges; also attracted to lights. Southern Arizona to western Texas, south to Durango and Sinaloa. (3)

Stenolophus comma (Fabricius) (5.3–7.7 mm) is yellowish brown with spot on elytra; appendages pale except antennomeres 3 or 4–11 darker. Head blackish. Pronotum reddish brown, with or without dark spot at center, sides in front of middle not sinuate, and hind angles broadly rounded. Scutellum flanked by short elytra striae. Elytra each with dark spot extended forward only on second interval out from suture that is about same color as sides. First hind tarsomere not ridged, not distinctly longer than 2. Across North America, south to southeastern California, South Carolina, and northern Alabama. (16)

Stenolophus lineola (Fabricius) (7.0–9.1 mm) is pale reddish yellow with a dark mark between the eyes and two distinct spots on pronotum. Elytra with outer and inner margins of dark areas closest to base. Adults active from spring through early fall, found in various habitats, and eat insects and corn seeds; occasionally a pest in cornfields. Commonly collected at lights and in pitfall traps. Across southern Canada and United States. (16)

106

Stenolophus ochropezus (Say) (4.8–6.7 mm) is blackish with all margins on pronotum and elytra pale. Pronotum with broad, shallow, distinctly punctate impressions at base. Elytra distinctly iridescent. Legs and first two or three antennomeres pale yellowish brown. Adults are active from spring through fall in various habitats and commonly attracted to lights, sometimes in large numbers. Southern California to Baja California Sur, east to southeastern Saskatchewan, Nova Scotia, and Florida (16)

Stenomorphus californicus (Ménétriés) (12.0–14.8 mm) is elongate, more or less parallel-sided, and reddish brown. Pronotum much longer than wide. Elytra distinctly striate. Legs with front femur not dentate, middle femur obtusely dentate near apex, middle tibia densely setose at apex, hind femur distinctly long and slender. Nocturnal adults found mostly during summer monsoons; hide during day under debris; also attracted to lights. Southeastern Arizona and southwestern New Mexico. *Stenomorphus sinaloae* Darlington (10.9–16.5 mm) similar in form and distribution, hind tibia shorter, broader. *S. convexior* Notman (10.0–13.7 mm) with pronotum relatively shorter, middle femur more or less sharply dentate near apex; southern Arizona and Mexico. (3)

Lachnophorus elegantulus Mannerheim (5.5–6.0 mm) is bristling with pale erect setae, dorsal surfaces of head and pronotum coarsely alutaceous, dull, and uniformly dark metallic green. Eyes prominent. Pronotum long as wide, broadest before middle, abruptly narrowed posteriorly, with fine medially impressed line on disc. Elytra shiny, disc punctostriate, punctures coarser at base, mostly whitish with irregular basal and medial metallic brown fasciae, and apices somewhat obliquely truncate. Legs yellow brown, front and middle femora distinctly infuscate at bases, tarsi darker. Adults on creek banks, also at lights during summer. Southwestern Oregon to southern California, east to Kansas and Texas, south to Costa Rica. (1)

Calathus ruficollis Dejean (7.4–10.9 mm) is elongate-ovate, bright reddish to black dorsally, shiny or dull, with head and pronotum sometimes lighter; appendages mostly orangish brown. Pronotum broadest before middle, impunctate posterolaterally, with posterior lateral setigerous puncture not in contact with margin. Elytral humerus not toothed, intervals 2 and 3 with six punctures or fewer. Femoral apices, tibiae, and tarsi darker, with middle femur bearing a row of three or more setigerous punctures beneath anterior surface. Nocturnal and brachypterous adults on moderately dry soil under rocks near streams and lakes. Coastal northern California to northern Baja California; also southern Arizona. (8)

Rhadine species (8.0–16.0 mm) are elongate, more or less slender, uniformly light to dark reddish brown. Head somewhat elongate, constricted behind small eyes to form a neck. Pronotum as long as wide or longer, chordate with flanged margins or not. Elytra with humeri not evident, striae more or less evident. Legs long, slender. Nocturnal and flightless adults found under rocks, logs, and other debris in moist habitats, or inhabit caves, cellars, animal burrows, and rock crevices; also desert dunes. Throughout western North America. Genus needs revision. (11)

Tule Beetle *Tanystoma maculicolle* (Dejean) (5.9–9.1 mm) is brown with sides of pronotum and elytra yellowish brown. Elytral disc with central dark area abruptly expanded laterally to stria 6, while basal and apical portions reach only about stria 4. Flight wings developed or vestigial. Claws simple, middle tarsi lack well-developed dorsal sulcus. Large summer flights sometimes a nuisance. Prefers moist, open woodland habitats in lowlands and foothills. Southern Oregon to northern Baja California. *Tanystoma cuyama* Liebherr (6.1–8.2 mm) with pale elytral margins even; southern Coast and Peninsular Ranges, California. (4)

Perigona nigriceps (Dejean) (2.0–2.5 mm) is somewhat flattened, and pale brownish-yellow with brownish-black head; pronotum sometimes darker. Eyes prominent. Pronotum wider than long, with sides straight to slightly sinuate posteriorly, and posterior angles broadly rounded and weakly explanate. Elytra faintly iridescent, with striae barely developed, each with three discal setigerous punctures, and apices often infuscate, sometimes also dark along suture. Crepuscular and nocturnal adults found along shores of ponds, lakes, and rivers; flies to lights. Southern Asia, nearly cosmopolitan; established in Oregon and California. (1)

Colliuris lioptera (Bates) (8.0–9.3 mm) is mostly uniformly dark brown to brownish black. Head long and rhomboidal, with two pairs of suborbital setae. Antennomeres 8–9 whitish, much paler than 5–7 and 11. Pronotum cylindrical. Elytra punctostriate, each mostly black with one small preapical spot on intervals 5–8 or 6–8. Legs brown with femora yellow at basal half and tibiae with pale yellow submedial band. Adults found along vegetated streams; also at lights. Southeastern Arizona south to Honduras. *Colliuris pilatei* (Chaudoir) (6.0–7.8 mm) with two pairs of suborbital setae and antennomeres 5–11 unicolorous, southern Arizona south to Baja California Sur, Mexico, and Costa Rica. (4)

Colliuris pensylvanica (Linnaeus) (5.8–8.2 mm) has a long, black rhomboidal head and cylindrical pronotum. Head with two pairs of suborbital setae. Dull reddish or yellowish elytra punctostriate, with median band of three spots, diamond-shaped medial spot sometimes extending forward, and apices black. Legs yellowish brown with dusky or black "knees". Adults along wetland edges under logs and stones, or among plants and roots; also at lights. In West from southeastern Arizona to Mexico. *Colliuris lengi* (Schaeffer) (6.5–7.0 mm) head and pronotum shorter, frons with 20–30 long setae, uniformly dark reddish black to black; in grass clumps in dry montane oak forests. Southeastern Arizona and Sonora. (4)

Apenes hilariola Bates (9.0–10.0 mm) is somewhat flattened and dull, with head and pronotum reddish brown, elytra brown with distinct pale pattern, appendages lighter. Head moderately punctured, punctures confluent. Pronotum as wide as long, broadest before middle, with fine transverse wrinkles divided by distinctly impressed midline. Elytra with humeral, lateral, and subapical markings yellow-brown, and truncate apices. Adults at lights along water courses and wooded mountain canyons. Southeastern Arizona south to Baja California Norte, Morelos, and Colima. (4)

Calleida decora (Fabricius) (7.0–9.0 mm) is moderately elongate, somewhat parallel-sided, tricolored dorsally, with head black, pronotum and appendages red, and elytra green. Head glabrous, with large, prominent eyes. Pronotum longer than wide, broadest just before middle, and barely wider than head. Elytra moderately striate with fine punctures, intervals nearly flat. Legs with femoral apices infuscate, and tarsi brown, with upper surfaces flattened and more or less sulcate medially. Male with pro- and mesotarsi somewhat broadened with double series of adhesive setae underneath. Mostly diurnal adults found on plants on sunny days, sheltering under bark and other debris during cool, overcast conditions; occasionally attracted to lights. Southeastern Arizona east to south-central North Dakota and Florida, south to Bahamas and Nicaragua. (2)

Calleida platynoides Horn (10.5–12.5 mm) is moderately elongate, somewhat parallel-sided, dark reddish brown or dark brown, with head, pronotum, and appendages shiny and somewhat lighter. Head sparsely punctate, with frons wrinkled laterally. Pronotum longer than wide, broadest just before middle, and barely wider than head. Elytra dull, weakly and finely striate, indistinctly punctured. Legs with upper surface of tarsi flattened and more or less sulcate medially; male with front and middle tarsi somewhat broadened with double series of adhesive setae underneath. Southern California to Baja California, east to northern Sonora and southeastern Texas. (2)

Lebia analis (4.3–6.0 mm) has mostly a black head slightly narrower than pronotum, with fine grooves between eyes, and palps and mandibular apices darkened. Antennomeres 1–3 pale, 4–11 mostly darker with apices lighter. Pale pronotum wider than long and narrower than elytra. Elytra entirely dark to extensively pale with epipleura pale, striae distinct, interstriae moderately convex, with suture modified apically and apices obliquely truncate. Abdomen mostly pale, darker apically. Legs pale, claws pectinate. Adults mostly diurnal and crepuscular, active spring and summer in various lowland and montane habitats; occasionally attracted to lights. Southeastern Arizona east to southern Ontario and Florida. (28)

Lebia fuscata Dejean (4.3–7.7 mm) is small, bicolored, with head almost as wide as pronotum, which is narrower than elytra. Head black, finely wrinkled or punctate next to eyes. Pronotum black, twice as wide as long, with side and sinuate posterior margins pale. Elytra distinctly striate, interstriae somewhat convex, with pale brownish-yellow lateral margins, and apices obliquely truncate, sinuate. Appendages pale, antennae with outer antennomeres darker. Claws pectinate, front tarsomeres 1–3 broad with adhesive pads below in male. In West, from British Columbia to central California, east to southern Manitoba and east-central Texas. (28)

Lebia viridis Say (4.6–6.6 mm) is uniformly shiny green or dark purplish blue. Antennae mostly blackish, antennomeres 1–3 greenish. Underside and legs blackish. Head with fine grooves along sides. Pronotum narrower than elytra, side margins flattened and narrow, except at distinct hind angle. Elytral punctostriae very fine, interstriae somewhat flat to slightly convex, with apices obliquely truncate, sinuate. Claws pectinate, male with front tarsomeres 1–3 expanded, adhesive pads underneath. Mostly diurnal adults active late spring and summer, on flowers and vegetation; attracted to lights. Widespread in North America south to Guatemala. (28)

Plochionus timidus Haldeman (6.5–7.5 mm) is mostly dark brown to blackish with pale pronotal and elytral margins. Pronotum wider than long, broadest basally, with lateral margins arcuate, fine wrinkles on disc, and fine longitudinal impression medially. Elytra with striae deep and impunctate, interstriae glabrous and convex, and apices truncate. Male protarsomeres 1–3 broad and setose ventrally; tarsomere 4 of both sexes deeply notched. Adults prey on caterpillars, and shelter under tree bark in lowland deciduous forests; attracted to lights. In West from central and southern California to Baja California Peninsula, east to central Texas. (1)

Pseudaptinus tenuicollis (LeConte) (5.2–5.5 mm) is uniformly yellowish brown, punctate and pubescent, with appendages uniformly paler. Head with distinct neck three-fifths as wide as distance across eyes, antennomeres 2 and 3 short. Pronotum somewhat longer than wide, slightly constricted in front, then broadly arcuate, and truncate and narrower than elytra at base. Elytra more finely punctured than head and pronotum, each with eight finely impressed impunctate striae and rounded humeri. Washington to southern California, east to Kansas, Arkansas, and southern Texas, south to Oaxaca. Genus needs revision. (4)

Galerita mexicana Chaudoir (15.5–18.0 mm) is tricolored with head black, pronotum reddish, and elytra dark blue. Head slightly shorter than wide, with a distinct neck and reddish-brown spot between small, yet prominent eyes. Pronotum as long as wide, broadest just before middle, narrowest just before rounded posterior angles. Elytra punctostriate, with interstriae flat and uniformly decumbent setae directed posteriorly. Legs uniformly black. Nocturnal adults found in wet or dry habitats and are fleet of foot, defending themselves with an acrid odor; attracted to lights. South-central Arizona to southeastern Nebraska, Oklahoma, and Texas, south to Costa Rica. (5)

Helluomorphoides latitarsus Casey (13.5–17.9 mm) is elongate, somewhat flattened, parallel-sided, uniformly reddish brown, and setose dorsally. Head finely, densely, and evenly punctate with terminal maxillary palpomere broad. Pronotum slightly shorter than wide, coarsely and densely punctate except along broad, shallow, and longitudinal medial impression. Bases of hind tarsomeres broadly angulate. Elytra with punctostriae broad and shallow, with punctures usually confused. *Helluomorphoides ferrugineus* (LeConte) (12.2–16.0 mm) terminal maxillary palpus slender, punctures mostly confused; *H. papago* (Casey) (11.0–14.5 mm) smaller, terminal segment of maxillary palpus very broad, elytral punctures usually paired. All species attracted to lights, southeastern Arizona to western Texas, south to Mexico. (3)

Pseudomorpha species (6.5–10.3 mm) are elongate, more or less parallel-sided, moderately flattened or slightly convex, and reddish brown to black, with dorsal surface punctate or not and short legs. Head with or without transverse row of coarse punctures across vertex, underneath with short antennal grooves in front of angulate eyes. Pronotum wider than long. Elytra shiny or dull, with rows of sometimes setigerous punctures. Myrmecophilous adults occur among leaf litter during summer; attracted to lights. Throughout drier regions in West, from Oregon and California east to Idaho, Utah, and New Mexico; one species in Southeast. Genus needs revision. (27)

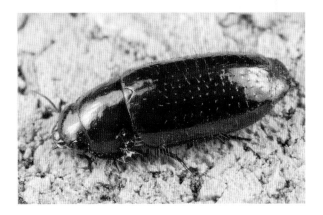

EUCINETIDAE (ū-sin-ēt'-i-dē)
PLATE-THIGH BEETLES

The common family name is derived from the distinctively large coxal plates at the bases of the hind legs. When disturbed, plate-thigh beetles are capable of jumping. The fungus-feeding adults are typically found in association with decaying wood and leaf litter. Eucinetids sometimes occur in aggregations, along with their larvae, under bark of decaying logs and feed on slime molds (many *Eucinetus*) or basidiomycete fungi (*Nycteus*, some *Eucinetus*).

FAMILY DIAGNOSIS Adult eucinetids are elongate-oval or narrowly oval, brownish yellow to black, sometimes with elytral apices reddish. Head small, not visible from above, with mouthparts strongly directed downward and backward and resting on bases of forelegs. Antennae with 11 antennomeres, more or less filiform (*Eucinetus*, *Nycteus*), or with a feeble club (*Euscaphurus*). Prothorax short, wide, with procoxal cavities open behind. Elytra completely cover abdomen, disc punctate, sometimes with punctures arranged in fine transverse *strigae* (*Eucinetus*) or rows (*Euscaphurus*, *Nycteus*), with epipleuron sometimes short (*Eucinetus*, *Nycteus*). Hind legs with coxal plates large and oblique, partially covering legs and first abdominal sternite; femora short, and tibiae tipped with pair of long spurs, middle and hind tarsomeres tipped with rings of dark spines; tarsi 5-5-5. Abdomen with five (*Euscaphurus* males with very small sixth) or six ventrites free or connate.

SIMILAR FAMILIES Plate-thigh beetles resemble species in several other families that are compact and elliptical in outline, but the combination of their enlarged hind coxal plates and ability to jump are distinctive.

COLLECTING NOTES Look for adults beneath bark of decaying logs or in fungi; they also fly to lights and are captured in Malaise traps.

FAUNA FOUR SPECIES IN THREE GENERA

Eucinetus terminalis LeConte (3.0–4.0 mm) is elongate-oval, narrowed posteriorly, shiny black with appendages and about apical one-fourth of elytra yellowish brown, and clothed in fine decumbent pubescence. Head finely punctate, strongly deflexed with antennae filiform. Pronotum small and transverse, and finely punctate. Elytra with eight more or less impressed striae in addition to distinctive sutural striae, and fine transverse strigae. Front coxa long and conical, hind tarsomere 4 longer than 5. Abdomen with six ventrites. In West from British Columbia to Oregon, east to Idaho. (1)

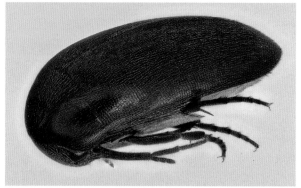

Nycteus infumatus (LeConte) (4.0–4.5 mm) is brownish to blackish, with appendages lighter. Head strongly deflexed, with antennae filiform. Pronotum small, transverse. Elytra densely punctate, vaguely striate, without strigae, weakly narrowed behind, and apices broadly rounded. Front coxa conical, hind tarsomere 4 longer than 5. Abdomen with six ventrites. Adults and larvae found under loose bark of decaying spruce. British Columbia, Washington, and Oregon. *Nycteus testaceus* LeConte (3.5 mm) elongate-ovate, yellowish brown, with densely punctate elytra, and more narrowed behind. *Nycteus punctulatus* LeConte (2.5–2.9 mm) yellowish brown, elytra finely and densely punctate, with striae only along suture. (3)

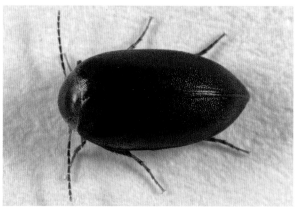

CLAMBIDAE (klamb'-i-dē)
MINUTE BEETLES

Very little is known about the natural history of minute beetles. Adults and larvae found in leaf litter, rotting wood, and other accumulations of decomposing plant debris likely feed on microfungi. Other species are found on the fruiting bodies of sac fungi, mushrooms, and slime molds, where they probably feed on hyphae and spores. Adults are sometimes seen flying above the forest floor at dusk.

FAMILY DIAGNOSIS Adult clambids are very small, oval, convex, yellowish brown to black, and capable of partially rolling up into a ball; surface of pronotum and elytra clothed in pubescence. Hypognathous head strongly deflexed downward, not visible from above, and with eyes partially or completely divided. Abruptly capitate antennae with 10 antennomeres attached closely to eyes, 9–10 forming club. Pronotum short, broader than head, with lateral margins explanate, and slightly overlapping elytra; procoxae externally open. Elytra at widest point slightly broader than prothorax, completely covering abdomen, flight wings fringed with setae. Legs with hind coxal plates expanded, partially covering hind legs, femora swollen, tibiae and tarsi slender, tibiae without apical spurs, tarsi 4-4-4, and claws simple. Abdomen with five ventrites free.

SIMILAR FAMILIES
- pill beetles (Byrrhidae, p.233)—antennae with 11 antennomeres, cannot roll up into ball, tarsi 5-5-5
- minute fungus beetles (Corylophidae, p.314)—cannot roll up into ball, antennal club usually with three antennomeres, hind coxae not enlarged, tarsi 5-5-5
- shining fungus beetles (Phalacridae, p.456)—ball-rolling ability more developed, antennal club with three to five antennomeres, hind coxae not enlarged, tarsi 5-5-5
- *Cybocephalus* (Cybocephalidae, p.459)—head almost as wide as pronotum, antennal club with three antennomeres, hind coxae not enlarged

COLLECTING NOTES Look for adult clambids in accumulations of rotting vegetation, on fruiting bodies of various fungi, flying in wooded areas at dusk, or at lights.

FAUNA 13 SPECIES IN THREE GENERA

Clambus **species** (0.9–1.1 mm) are very small, moderately to very convex, shiny, with or without pubescence above, and brownish, sometimes with lighter margins. Head broad, with side margins dividing eyes. Antennae attached close to eyes, with 10 antennomeres, first and last two enlarged. Scutellum well developed. Adults and larvae found in decaying plant matter feeding on fungal spores, especially those of slime molds (Myxogastria) and sac fungi (Ascomycota). (4)

SCIRTIDAE (skûr'-ti-dē)
MARSH BEETLES

Adult marsh beetles are terrestrial, short-lived insects commonly found on vegetation growing near marshes, ponds, streams, rivers, and other wetlands. Species of *Scirtes* have greatly enlarged hind femora and are capable of jumping. *Cyphon* species are drab and difficult to identify. Scirtid larvae are found in flowing and standing waters. *Elodes* larvae occur in small streams and clear ponds, while those of *Cyphon* are associated with aquatic plants growing along margins and shallows. *Scirtes* larvae prefer to feed and develop in water-filled tree holes. These larvae are quite active and feed on vegetable detritus (*Sacodes*), dead leaves and insects (*Prionocyphon*), or duckweed (*Scirtes*). Pupation occurs in cells in damp soil and among dead moss and leaves, while *Scirtes* pupae are attached to aquatic vegetation. This family is very much in need of revision.

FAMILY DIAGNOSIS Adult scirtids are elongate-oval to nearly circular, somewhat convex, black, brown, yellowish brown to pale yellow, sometimes with red or orange markings. Hypognathous head large, deflexed, with eyes bulging on sides and usually concealed by pronotum. Antennae filiform or somewhat serrate with 11 antennomeres. Pronotum always short, with lateral margins explanate. Procoxal cavities open behind. Scutellum triangular. Elytra punctate, covering abdomen, with apices jointly rounded. Legs with hind femora sometimes enlarged (*Scirtes*), tarsi 5-5-5 with fourth tarsomere bilobed and claws simple. Abdomen with five ventrites, ventrites 1–2 usually connate.

SIMILAR FAMILIES
- plate-thigh beetles (Eucinetidae, p.112)—hind coxae expanded
- ptilodactylid beetles (Ptilodactylidae, p.245)—scutellum heart-shaped

- minute fungus beetles (Corylophidae, p.314)—antennae clubbed
- some lady beetles (Coccinellidae, p.318)—antennae clavate
- hairy fungus beetles (Mycetophagidae, p.326)—antennae clubbed, pronotum longer, often with a pair of pits near posterior margin
- sap beetles (Nitidulidae, p.443)—antennal club with three antennomeres
- shining mold beetles (Phalacridae, p.456)—antennae clubbed
- flea beetles (Chrysomelidae, p.523)—head clearly visible from above

COLLECTING NOTES Adult scirtids are swept or beaten from herbaceous vegetation, shrubs, and trees growing near swamps, ponds, streams, canals, ditches, damp areas, and other wetland habitats. They are also attracted to lights in these habitats and are sometimes captured in light traps in large numbers.

FAUNA ~50 SPECIES IN 11 GENERA

Elodes apicalis LeConte (3.9 mm) is oblong, mostly yellowish brown dorsally, with vertex, broad anteromedial pronotal spot, and elytral apices dark brownish black, and moderately densely clothed in pale recumbent setae. Antennal bases pale. Pronotum wide with sides and anterior angles broadly arcuate, broadest behind middle, and posterior margin sinuate. Elytra with suture infuscate, sometimes broadly at base. Underside of thorax dark. Abdomen of male with last ventrite broadly, but distinctly marginate. Front legs and at least middle coxae yellowish brown. Adults found in montane riparian habitats during summer. British Columbia to California and Nevada. (4)

Herthania concinna (LeConte) (2.8–4.5 mm) is oblong-oval, shiny black, with each elytron variably marked at base with prominent red spots, and clothed in somewhat decumbent setae. Head and pronotum densely punctate. Pronotum wide, with sides weakly arcuate or straight and somewhat narrowed anteriorly, hind angles broad. Elytra scarcely or wider than pronotum, disc more coarsely punctate, with maculations elongate and may or may not reach suture. Legs with tarsi yellowish brown. British Columbia and Alberta to California and Idaho. Best distinguished from *H. yoshitomii* Klausnitzer in same region by careful examination of male genitalia. (1)

Scirtes species (2.5–5.5 mm) is broadly oval, more or less convex, uniformly shiny brown to black, sometimes bicolored, and moderately densely clothed in recumbent setae. Head deflexed, with slender antennae about half as long as body. Pronotum wide, with sides arcuate. Elytra confusedly and densely punctate. Front and middle legs normal, hind legs with coxae meeting along full length of midline with hind margins joining to form a somewhat rectangular plate, and femora greatly enlarged. Abdomen with intercoxal process not on same plane as plate formed by posterior margins of hind coxae. Genus needs revision. (~1).

115

NOSODENDRIDAE (nō-sō-den'-dri-dē)
WOUNDED TREE BEETLES

The North American nosodendrid fauna consists of two species, of which only one, *Nosodendron californicum* Horn, occurs in montane forests in the West. Groups of adults and larvae (p.28, Fig. 18f) inhabit fermented flows of conifer sap teeming with microorganisms known as slime flux. Adults are attracted to slime fluxes that form in larger frost cracks and, to a lesser extent, smaller logging wounds of large Douglas-fir (*Pseudotsuga menziesii*), grand fir (*Abies grandis*), and white fir (*A. concolor*) in stands of old-growth forest. Although once thought to prey upon fly larvae and other small arthropods occupying the same niche, more recent observations suggest that nosodendrids are more likely to feed on bacteria, fungi, and other products of sap fermentation.

FAMILY DIAGNOSIS Adult nosodendrids are oval, compact, convex, black, with ability to retract appendages tightly against the body, flattened front legs with tibiae held in front of femur at rest. Head prognathous, capitate antennae with 11 antennomeres, 9–11 forming distinct club, with three antennomeres protected in cavities underneath the prothorax between the prolegs and sides. Prothorax broadest posteriorly, underneath with hypomeron excavate to receive antennal club and prolegs, procoxae open behind. Elytra entire, completely covering abdomen. Tarsi 5-5-5. Abdomen with five ventrites free.

SIMILAR FAMILIES
- marsh beetles (Scirtidae, p.114)—antennae filiform to weakly serrate
- round fungus beetles (Leiodidae, p.137)—antennae loosely clavate
- pill beetles (Byrrhidae, p.233)—antennae filiform or clavate, dorsal surface scaled
- death-watch beetles (Ptinidae, p.299)—antennae longer, club asymmetrical
- *Hyporhagus* (Zopheridae, p.340)—elytra with rows of punctures

- pleasing fungus beetles (Erotylidae, p.435)—elytra with rows of punctures
- sap beetles (Nitidulidae, p.443)—elytra short with abdominal tergites exposed, front tibiae not expanded

COLLECTING NOTES Look for *Nosodendron* in slime flux flows on trunks of Douglas-fir, and grand and white firs; also inspect below these flows for beetles in sap-soaked needles and soil.

FAUNA TWO SPECIES IN ONE GENUS

Nosodendron californicum Horn (4.5–5.4 mm) is broadly oval, moderately convex, dorsal surface alutaceous, weakly shiny black. Head moderately coarsely punctured, with antennae capitate, brown club comprising three antennomeres. Pronotum less densely punctured than head or elytra, with lateral margins weakly arcuate. Elytra densely, deeply, and irregularly punctate, punctures smaller and denser laterally, with line of small reddish-brown setal tufts on lateral and apical areas. Abdomen with sutures deep. Adults and larvae found in slime fluxes in running or weeping wounds of mature Douglas-fir, firs, and black oak in spring and summer. British Columbia to Transverse Ranges of southern California, east to Idaho. (1)

116

DERODONTIDAE (der-ō-dont′-i-dē)
TOOTH-NECK FUNGUS BEETLES

Derodontids are uncommonly encountered beetles that inhabit moist, cool forests, where both adults and larvae are typically found together. *Derodontus* graze on the fruiting bodies of basidiomycete fungi and are generally more abundant in cooler seasons. *Peltastica* eat fungi and other nutrients suspended in sap flows. *Laricobius* prey on conifer-feeding adelgid aphids. *Laricobius erichsoni* Rosenhauer, a European species, and the native *L. nigrinus* Fender, both of which occur in the Pacific Northwest, were introduced into eastern North America as biological control agents to combat the balsam woolly adelgid (*Adelges picea*) and hemlock woolly adelgid (*A. tsugae*), respectively.

FAMILY DIAGNOSIS Adult derodontids are somewhat convex dorsally and flat ventrally. The combination of a pair of ocelli on head, antennae with loose club of three antennomeres, and serrate pronotal side margins (*Derodontus*), coarse surface sculpturing, rows of large and close-set punctures on elytra, and open middle coxal cavities are distinctive. Tarsi 5-5-5 (*Derodontus*) or 4-4-4 (*Laricobius*), tarsomeres 1–3 lobed underneath (*Laricobius*), with simple claws. Abdomen with five ventrites free (*Derodontus*) or with 1 and 2 connate (*Laricobius*).

SIMILAR FAMILIES
- minute bark beetles (Cerylonidae, p.309)—lack ocelli
- hairy fungus beetles (Mycetophagidae, p.326)—lack ocelli

- fruitworm beetles (Byturidae, p.410)—lack ocelli and distinct rows of punctures on elytra
- shield beetles (Peltidae, p.412)—lack ocelli, much larger
- silken fungus beetles (Cryptophagidae, p.449)— lack ocelli and quadrate elytral punctures

COLLECTING NOTES Derodontids are infrequently collected. *Derodontus* is usually found on fungi, under loose bark, and in Lindgren funnel traps during the cooler seasons of the year. *Laricobius* adults are typically encountered overwintering at the base of conifers infested with adelgids, or beaten from the branches of coniferous trees in spring and early summer. Look for *Peltastica* at fermenting sap under bark of conifers, especially Douglas-fir, and on fresh cuts on logs and stumps.

FAUNA FIVE SPECIES IN THREE GENERA

Peltastica tuberculata Mannerheim (3.3–4.1 mm) is oblong, parallel-sided, somewhat flattened, virtually glabrous, and yellowish brown tinged with dark brown. Antennal insertions hidden from above and antennal sulci underneath. Pronotum broadest behind middle, with sides arcuate, finely serrate, and broadly explanate. Elytra explanate basally, coarsely tuberculate with four or five rows of smooth ivory, black, and brown tubercles, with more or less distinct V-shaped band across basal one-fourth, and about 10 irregular punctostriae. Adults attracted to fermenting sap under bark, and freshly cut logs and stumps of Douglas-fir, *Pseudotsuga menziesii*, possibly other conifers, in spring. Southern Alaska to northern California, east to southwestern Idaho. (1)

Derodontus trisignatus (Mannerheim) (2.5–2.8 mm) is elongate-ovate, reddish yellow-brown, with head and pronotum coarsely punctate, and elytra punctostriate, punctures coarse and deep. Head with large, somewhat triangular ocelli, each of which is connected to two cuticular bridges, and antennal articulations visible from above. Pronotum with sides narrowly explanate, lateral margins arcuate, and armed with four or five sharp teeth, and large punctures underneath. Elytra each with 11 distinct punctostriae, intervals convex, plus a short stria-flanking scutellum, and irregular oblique blackish mark sometimes united across suture, forming basal to medial chevron. Found on fungi (*Hericium, Pholiota*). Southern Alaska to northern California and northern Idaho. (1)

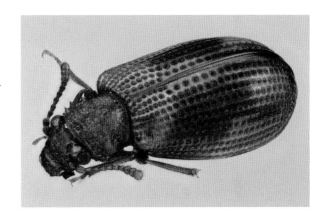

Laricobius nigrinus Fender (2.0–2.7 mm) is elongate-ovate, uniformly black (male) or brownish (female), dorsally clothed in moderately long, erect setae. Pronotum wide, with a large, pitlike puncture near each anterior angle, lateral margins smooth, with anterior margin narrower than posterior margin. Elytra each with 10 punctostriae, plus a short stria flanking scutellum, with punctures large and deep, and intervals one puncture in width or less. Tarsi lobed, with tarsomere 4 strongly reduced. British Columbia to Oregon and northern Idaho. *Laricobius laticollis* Fall has head and scutellum much darker than pronotum or elytra. *Laricobius erichsoni* Rosenhauer reddish, with elytral sutures and sides black. (3)

HELOPHORIDAE (hel-ō-fôr'-i-dē)
HELOPHORID WATER BEETLES

Adult helophorids are sometimes abundant in freshwater habitats, although some coastal species may tolerate or prefer more brackish water. They feed on the softer portions of dead grass and decomposing green algae along the edges of slow-flowing streams, ponds, marshes, swamps, and ephemeral pools with layers of rotting leaves, needles, and twigs on the bottom. Submerged beetles replenish their air supplies by bringing the back of their heads in contact with the surface and raising their antennae to form a funnel through which a parcel of air is drawn and held underneath the body. Capable of flight, helophorids are sometimes attracted in large numbers to lights in spring. Their bag-shaped egg cases topped with variable stalk-like masts and containing several eggs are buried in soil or debris near water. These cases are sticky and often covered with bits of surrounding debris and soil. The terrestrial larvae live on soil and among decaying vegetation strewn along the shoreline and prey on the larvae and pupae of flies and other small organisms. Upon reaching maturity, they excavate small chambers in the soil in which to pupate. A single genus, *Helophorus*, occurs in North America. Most helophorid species are remarkably similar to one another and exhibit a high degree of intraspecific variability, thus making species identification challenging.

FAMILY DIAGNOSIS Helophorids are somewhat elongate, more or less parallel-sided, and slightly convex beetles with prominent eyes that are not emarginate anteriorly. Surfaces of head and pronotum distinctly granulate; labrum not emarginate; antennae comprise eight or nine antennomeres, the last three forming a loose, pubescent club. Pronotum narrowed toward base with obtuse posterior pronotal angles, usually with seven distinct and more or less sinuate longitudinal sulci (*Helophorus arcticus* has one medial sulcus; *H. tuberculatus* Gyllenhal is distinctly granulate), including those along each lateral margin; underneath with distinct antennal sulci on hypomeron. Procoxae open behind. Scutellum small, almost circular. Elytra completely cover abdomen, surface distinctly punctostriate. Legs slender, not modified for swimming, tarsi 5-5-5 with tarsomeres unequal in length, and tarsomere 5 long. Abdomen with five ventrites free.

SIMILAR FAMILIES Helophorid beetles are easily distinguished from species of Hydrochidae (p.121), Hydraenidae (p.132), Elmidae (p.235), and Dryopidae (p.239) by their pronotal sculpturing.

COLLECTING NOTES Look for adult *Helophorus* along grassy margins of shallow temporary or permanent pools, roadside ditches, ponds, swamps, marshes, and slow-moving streams, especially those with decaying vegetation on the bottom. They are often attracted to lights near wetland habitats during their spring dispersal period.

FAUNA 41 SPECIES IN ONE GENUS

Helophorus species (2.0–6.3mm) are more or less elongate, moderately convex, sometimes with metallic luster. Head with distinctly Y-shaped suture dorsally, and abruptly narrowed behind prominent, undivided eyes; antennae comprise eight or nine antennomeres, last three forming loose club. Pronotum typically with seven sulci running lengthwise, rarely granulate or with median sulcus only, with lateral margins serrate, and distinct antennal sulci underneath. Elytra each with 10 punctostriae, with or without additional short stria flanking scutellum, and intervals with or without tubercles. Tarsi with tarsomere 1 usually shorter than second. Mostly in freshwater habitats. Genus needs revision. (~36)

118

EPIMETOPIDAE (ep-i-mē'-tôp-i-dē)
HOODED SHORE BEETLES

Very little is known about the biology of these cryptic, semiaquatic beetles. Hooded shore beetles and their larvae live along the margins of streams. Adults are often encrusted with particles of soil. Males and females are both strongly sculpted dorsally, but ventrally females have one or more ventrites more or less concave, while those of males are flat. With the aid of their hind femora, females carry a yellowish opaque bag-shaped silk egg case that lacks any sort of stalk-like mast on top and contains a dozen or more eggs. They are sometimes attracted to lights while carrying these egg cases. Species identifications are often best accomplished through careful examination of the male's reproductive organs.

FAMILY DIAGNOSIS Strongly deflexed head of *Epimetopus* is mostly obscured from view above by shelflike extension of pronotum. Antennae comprise nine antennomeres, 7–9 forming a loose club; eyes partly or completely divided by canthus. Procoxal cavities open behind. Elytra entire and completely cover abdomen, each with 10 rows of serial punctures and four distinct carinae. Legs with metacoxae widely separated, with tarsi 5-5-5. Abdomen with five ventrites free, ventrite 1 very short.

SIMILAR FAMILIES Epimetopid beetles are easily distinguished from other shore-inhabiting beetles by their small size, anterior pronotal extension, carinate lateral pronotal margins, and distinctly carinate elytra.

COLLECTING NOTES Adults of *Epimetopus* are most commonly collected at lights. Individual beetles are found along wet shorelines of streams and ponds among debris or beneath rocks on wet gravel. *Epimetopus thermarum* Schwarz & Barber was found among mats of dead reeds and wet algae that had accumulated along warm streams flowing out of hot springs.

119

FAUNA FOUR SPECIES IN ONE GENUS

Epimetopus arizonicus Perkins (1.8 mm, excluding head) is ovate, convex, with pronotum and elytra uniformly dark brown to reddish brown, and granules prominent. Head black, with eyes partly divided by canthus, and maxillary palpi brown. Hooded pronotum strongly sculpted and granulate, with carinae confluent anteriorly. Elytra each with four distinct carinae, intercarinae granulate, granules elongate and linking two well-separated rows of punctures. Underside and legs dark brown. Adults found during summer in Pajarito Mountains, southeastern Arizona. (3)

Epimetopus punctipennis Perkins (1.6 mm, excluding head) is ovate, convex, with pronotum and elytra uniformly reddish, with granules inconspicuous. Head black, frons reddish, clypeus black, with eye partly divided by canthus. Hooded pronotum strongly sculpted with carinae confluent anteriorly. Elytra each with four carinae, intercarinae with double rows of close-set punctures linked by elongate granules. Underside reddish. Southeastern Arizona to Oklahoma, Texas, and northern Mexico. (3)

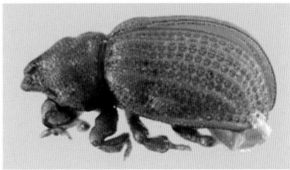

Epimetopus thermarum Schwarz & Barber (2.2–2.8 mm, excluding head) is dark brown, except for lighter reddish-brown legs, and most of apical half of elytra. Head with eyes completely divided by canthus. Hooded pronotum strongly sculpted with carinae confluent anteriorly. Elytra each with four distinctly granulate carinae and paler V-shaped band across middle and apical third of elytra. Arizona and Texas, south to Venezuela. (3)

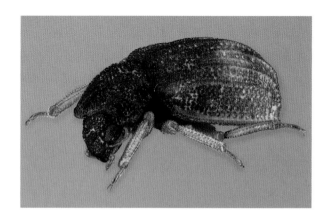

GEORISSIDAE (jē-ō-ris'-i-dē)
MINUTE MUD-LOVING BEETLES

Georissidae comprises solely the genus *Georissus*. Both the adults and larvae are riparian, living along stream edges with permanent deposits of wet silt and debris. The cryptic adults are usually encrusted with fine sand or mud that prevents the opening of the elytra, thus hindering flight. One generation is produced annually. Females bury their silken, bulb-shaped egg cases in moist soil with the masts exposed. Larvae are typically present during late spring and summer. Based on studies of *G. californicus* LeConte, the larvae have three instars. The North American *Georissus* are in need of revision. Some researchers have noted that *Georissus pusillus* LeConte exhibits a great deal of variability, raising suspicions that *G. californicus* might be a synonym.

FAMILY DIAGNOSIS Georissids are small, short, and broadly oval, with dorsal surfaces strongly convex and finely rugose. Hypognathous head obscured from above by anterior margin of pronotum, with eyes small, emarginate in front. Antennae usually with nine antennomeres, 1 and 2 stout, 7–9 forming short, oval club. Lateral margins of pronotum and elytra each distinctly rounded. Pronotum triangular and widest behind middle, with lateral margins rounded; underneath antennal grooves on hypomeron, and procoxal cavities open behind. Scutellum small, nearly hidden. Elytra entirely cover abdomen, each with eight punctostriae. Legs with front coxae large and nearly contiguous, while middle and hind coxae are widely separated; tarsi 4-4-4. Abdomen with five ventrites free, 1 is greatly enlarged.

SIMILAR FAMILIES
- hooded water beetles (Epimetopidae, p.119)—eyes partly or completely divided by canthus, dorsal surfaces distinctly sculptured, pronotum hooded, with lateral margins sharp, elytral surfaces carinate
- bostrichid beetles (Bostrichidae, p.295)—terrestrial, larger, elongate, anterior of hooded pronotum usually rough
- death watch beetles (Ptinidae, p.299)—terrestrial, antennal club not short and oval, legs contractile
- some weevils and bark beetles (Curculionidae, p.538)—geniculate antennae, weevils with mouthparts rostrate

COLLECTING NOTES Adult *Georissus* are found on mud and in debris along mountain streams during spring and summer, and are also attracted to lights. Select riparian sediments are washed through fine sieves or screens for specimens; coarser materials should be carefully inspected with the aid of magnification.

FAUNA TWO SPECIES IN ONE GENUS

Georissus pusillus LeConte (1.4–2.0 mm) is dull black, glabrous, and broadly oval. Head irregularly sculptured; sides and posterior margin of pronotum, sides of elytra, meso- and metasternum, and first ventrite all tuberculate. Pronotum somewhat longer than wide, with more or less distinct impression across base of anterior lobe and fine, longitudinal medial impression. Elytra distinctly punctostriate. Adults active late winter through summer. Pacific Northwest. *Georissus californicus* LeConte (1.8 mm) similar but, according to LeConte, distinguished by having a more distinct pronotal impression and larger, more distinct elytral punctures. Throughout montane California, apparently absent from Central Valley, east front of Sierra Nevada, and southeastern deserts. (2)

HYDROCHIDAE (hī-drok'-i-dē)
HYDROCHID WATER BEETLES

Hydrochidae comprises the single genus *Hydrochus*, of which little is known of the species' biology. All life stages are aquatic and they live among the roots or branches of plants growing at the edges of ponds and sluggish bodies of water. Adults amble slowly across the substrate, consuming algae and decomposing plant tissues, but the food preferences of the larvae remain unknown. To obtain oxygen, hydrochids surface headfirst with their unwettable antennal clubs held out in front of their eyes to break through the surface tension. They then draw in fresh air and capture it as a thin bubble across the hydrofuge underneath their body. When threatened, adult hydrochids feign death. Females produce small silken egg cases that bear a mast. Due to their intraspecific variability, species are difficult to identify without careful examination of the male's reproductive organs. The family is in need of revision as many new species await scientific description.

FAMILY DIAGNOSIS Hydrochid beetles are somewhat elongate-oval to narrowly elongate, somewhat flattened to moderately convex, with dorsal surface granulose, often with metallic reflections. Head strongly narrowed in front of and behind bulging eyes, dorsally with or without Y-shaped suture; antennae with seven antennomeres, 5–7 forming loose club. Pronotum widest in front of middle, distinctly narrower posteriorly than elytra, and surface granulose with seven shallow pitlike depressions (not grooves), three anteriorly and four posteriorly. Procoxal cavities closed behind. Scutellum very small. Elytra each with 10 punctostriae, surfaces with shallow, bilaterally symmetrical elevations and depressions. Underside with meso- and metasternum densely pubescent. Legs with metacoxae narrowly separated; tarsi 5-5-5 with 5 as long as combined lengths of 1–4. Abdomen with five ventrites, each with base transversely elevated, and 5 with apex bearing semitransparent plate with several stout setae.

SIMILAR FAMILIES Hydrochid beetles are distinguished from species of Helophoridae (p.118), Elmidae (p.235), and Dryopidae (p.239) by their antennal configuration and the setal plate on apical margin of ventrite 5. From Hydraenidae (p.132), hydrochids are distinguished by the antennal club comprising three antennomeres and abdomen with five ventrites free.

COLLECTING NOTES Look for hydrochid beetles along the shallow, vegetated edges of ponds. They are frequently attracted to lights placed nearby.

Hydrochus squamifer LeConte (3.3–4.2 mm) is elongate, moderately convex, surface of head and pronotum densely granulose, dark reddish black to blackish above with more or less metallic reflections; appendages mostly reddish yellow-brown, tip of maxillary palps dark. Head with Y-shaped suture on frons and distinct neck behind protruding eyes. Pronotum about as long as wide. Elytra inconspicuously granulose, with punctostriae coarsely and distinctly punctured, and long, metallic stripes. Adults found along edges of lakes, ponds, swamps, marshes, and roadside ditches; also sphagnum bogs. Transcontinental; in West, British Columbia south to California.

HYDROPHILIDAE (hī-drō-fil'-i-dē)
WATER SCAVENGER BEETLES

Hydrophilidae is one of the largest families of aquatic beetles, second in number of species only to the Dytiscidae. Adults are sometimes common along the vegetated edges of ponds and lakes, slow-moving streams, and springs; a few are tolerant of brackish water. They are often among the first to arrive at rain pools and other temporary aquatic habitats. Most species crawl over aquatic vegetation, but some are fair swimmers and propel themselves through the water by moving their legs in an alternate fashion, unlike predaceous diving beetles (Dytiscidae, p.81) that move their legs in unison. While underwater, some hydrophilids (e.g., *Hydrochara, Hydrophilus, Tropisternus*) breathe fresh air from a bubble of air stored beneath their elytra and trapped by the hydrofuge, a dense layer of pubescence on the underside of their bodies. This supply of atmospheric air is recharged when the beetle breaks through the surface film with an antennal club clothed in dense pubescence. Hydrophilids often take flight in search of new habitats. They are occasionally drawn to shiny car surfaces and blue tarps during the day, and are sometimes attracted to lights in large numbers at night. Hydrophilid larvae are mostly predatory, attacking invertebrates and small vertebrates. Adults are primarily vegetarians or omnivores, consuming spores, algae, and decaying vegetation. Larger species prey on snails and other invertebrates, small fish, and tadpoles. Mature larvae construct their pupal chambers of mud near the shore, either buried in the soil or tucked beneath a rock or other object. Despite the common name for the family, some hydrophilids are semiaquatic, riparian, or terrestrial. Species of Sphaeridiinae inhabit very wet dung and compost, while members of the Chaetarthriinae live in mud along stream margins.

FAMILY DIAGNOSIS Adult hydrophilids are typically broadly oval, distinctly convex dorsally and flattened ventrally. Dorsal surface black, sometimes with brownish markings, or rarely greenish or with pale markings. Head hypognathous, with maxillary palps of aquatic species often exceeding length of antennae, but usually equal in length or shorter in terrestrial species. Antennae with 6–10 antennomeres, last three forming a variable club usually nested within a cup-shaped antennomere. Pronotum broader than head and usually wider than long. Procoxal cavities open behind. Scutellum visible. Elytra widest at middle and broader at base than pronotum, surface smooth or rough, sometimes punctostriate, and completely conceal abdomen. Tarsi 5-5-5, 5-4-4 (*Cymbiodyta*), rarely 4-5-5 (male *Berosus*); claws generally simple, with front tarsi sometimes modified in males (*Berosus*). Abdomen usually with five, rarely six ventrites free.

SIMILAR FAMILIES

- predaceous diving beetles (Dytiscidae, p.81)—antennae filiform, mouthparts inconspicuous, body not flattened underneath
- dung beetles (Scarabaeidae, p.172)—antennal club with lamellae
- shining flower beetles (Phalacridae, p.456)—small (1.0–3.0 mm), maxillary palps short, tarsi 5-5-4

COLLECTING NOTES Hydrophilids are collected by sweeping an aquatic net along shallow, vegetated margins of ponds, lakes, and slow-moving streams; searching among submerged organic debris and algae in these habitats is also rewarding, especially with a flashlight at night. Another technique is to disturb aquatic substrates and vegetation to dislodge small, non-swimming species that become trapped on the surface film. Organic debris raked up on shore in an open patch of sand or on a white shower curtain will reveal numerous beetles as they attempt to escape back into the water. Place small amounts of debris into a white pan for careful sorting. Look for terrestrial species by picking through wet leaf litter, moist cow dung, decaying vegetation on shores, or under very rotten carcasses. A Berlese funnel or Winkler eclector is useful for removing individuals from leaf litter. Well-lit storefronts, streetlights, and UV light traps near bodies of water will attract dispersing aquatic species.

FAUNA 188 SPECIES IN 20 GENERA

Berosus punctatissimus **LeConte** (6.5–8.0 mm) is narrowly ovate and mostly pale with variable spots. Head coarsely and deeply punctate, black with strong metallic reflections and eyes prominent. Pronotum coarsely, deeply punctate with longitudinal carina down middle flanked by broad, parallel and oblique black macula with metallic reflections. Scutellum black with metallic reflections. Elytra with numerous brown spots, each with 10 narrow striae, interstriae coarsely punctate, apices emarginate with outer angle spinose. Posterior abdominal margin emarginate with two medial spines. Legs with femoral bases black and pubescent, while rest of leg mostly yellow and glabrous. Washington to Baja California, east to Nevada and Arizona. (21)

Hydrobius fuscipes **(Linnaeus)** (5.4–8.0 mm) is oblong-oval, somewhat convex, finely and densely punctate, and dark brown to blackish with faint metallic luster. Maxillary palps and antennae yellowish brown, tip of last maxillary palpomere usually dark. Elytra sometimes becoming gradually pale on sides, each with 10 distinct punctostriae extending nearly to base. Legs reddish yellow-brown with femora darker, and tarsi 5-5-5. Adults active spring and summer, found in shallow pools, swamps, and sphagnum bogs; attracted to lights. Widespread in northern hemisphere, south to Oregon and South Carolina. (1)

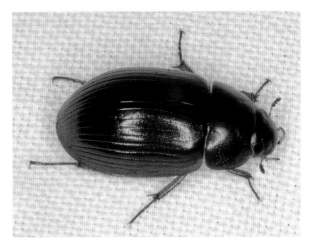

Hydrochara lineata LeConte (13.5–17.0 mm) is moderately broadly oval, and distinctively pale yellowish green to blue green. Antennae reddish yellow-brown with club more or less dark brownish to brownish black. Lateral beads of pronotum narrower than those of elytra. Elytra with serial punctures large, coarse, and very distinct. Legs dark with various green markings and somewhat paler tarsi. Adults found primarily during spring and summer in various habitats in shallow rocky stream pools, mineralized waters, hot springs, and occasionally in swimming pools in mountains and foothills. Northern California to Baja California, east to southern Utah and New Mexico. (3)

Hydrophilus triangularis Say (28.0–38.0 mm) is large, elongate-oval, shiny black with greenish-blue or purplish luster. Antennae yellowish brown to black becoming paler toward apices. Prosternal spine thorax hoodlike behind head. Elytra smooth, each with five rows of punctures, third row out from suture abbreviated at both ends, and apices not toothed. Underside of abdomen brownish black to black, ventrites with lateral white spots. Legs dark with tarsi usually paler. Adults found year-round in deep, vegetated ponds and lakes; attracted to lights. Large, cocoonlike egg cases with a mast float or are attached to submerged objects. Across southern Canada and United States. (2)

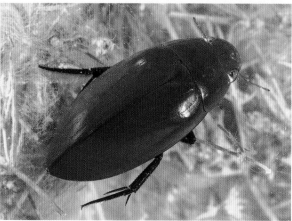

Tropisternus lateralis humeralis Motschulsky (8.0–9.5 mm) is narrowly oval, moderately convex, and shiny black with metallic luster and pale yellowish-brown side margins only on pronotum and elytra; inner edge of elytral band with single incision in basal portion. Prothorax with channel before coxae closed anteriorly by prominent ridge. Underside with keel between middle and hind legs projecting over first visible abdominal sternite as a sharp spine. Fifth ventrite with spine on tip. Adults found year-round in various wetlands; attracted to lights. Southern British Columbia to Baja California. *Tropisternus lateralis marginalis* Motschulsky similar, inner margin of elytral band irregular, extending medially across base. (4)

Laccobius species (2.3–3.5 mm) is convex, narrowly to broadly oval. Head with labrum usually slightly emarginate apically, antennae with eight antennomeres. Terminal maxillary palpomere longer than penultimate palpomere. Pronotum short with medial macula. Elytra without striae. Abdomen with six ventrites. Legs with hind tibia curved, hind trochanters large, and tarsi 5-5-5 with first tarsomere short. Species live in standing and running water. Throughout western North America. Species best identified by careful examination of male genitalia. (7)

124

Cercyon fimbriatus Mannerheim (2.0–3.8 mm) is variable in color, somewhat flat, with head dark, and pronotum and elytra yellowish, pronotum sometimes darker at middle with variable yellow lateral margins. Head and pronotum moderately, densely punctate. Elytra variably marked with narrowly dark suture and deeply impressed striae nearly reaching base. Underside dark with middle portions of thoracic sterna variably lighter. Appendages pale. Adults restricted to ocean beaches, living under rotting seaweed, driftwood, and other debris. Pacific Coast, from southern Alaska through British Columbia to Baja California (21)

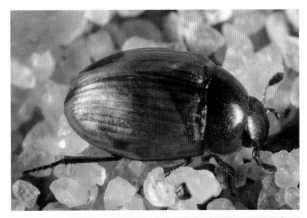

Cymbiodyta acuminata Fall (3.5–4.7 mm) is narrowly oval, moderately convex, dark brownish black to nearly black. Head and pronotum coarsely punctate. Head uniformly dark with pale antennae and mouthparts. Pronotum dark, becoming broadly pale along sides, with anterior and posterior margins narrowly pale, lateral margins nearly straight, and hind angles nearly rectangular. Elytra almost uniformly reddish brown-black, with little or no trace of punctostriae. Mesosternum with middle portion strongly elevated to form long, robust spurlike tooth. Legs dark, with short, glabrous area on hind femur. Across southern Canada and northern United States, in West south to Washington. (5)

Enochrus hamiltoni (Horn) (4.3–6.1 mm) is narrowly oval, moderately convex, and yellowish to brownish black or black. Pale specimens with head dark basally and pronotum disc with variable macula. Dark specimens with clypeus black or paler in front of eyes. Clypeal emargination evenly arcuate, last maxillary palpomere shorter than penultimate. Elytral margins not explanate or reflexed. Underside dark, ventrite 5 entire apically, and fringed with fine dark setae. Legs reddish yellow-brown with paler tarsi and darkened femora. Male front claws unequal and lobed basally, inner lobe larger than outer lobe. Adults occur in various aquatic habitats. Widely distributed in North America. (5)

Sphaeridium scarabaeoides (Linnaeus) (4.0–7.1 mm) is black with reddish and yellowish markings. Lateral pronotal margins reddish at least near apical angles. Elytra with variable dark reddish humeral spots and common yellowish apical spot narrowly divided by dark sutural stripe and extended along lateral margins. *Sphaeridium lunatum* Fabricius (4.3–7.0 mm) with pronotal margins dark, humeral markings less distinct, and divided apical elytral markings scarcely or not extended along lateral margins. *Sphaeridium bipustulatum* Fabricius (3.9–5.2 mm) apical elytral spot entire. All in cow, horse, and other mammal feces. Europe; widespread in North America, except deserts. (3)

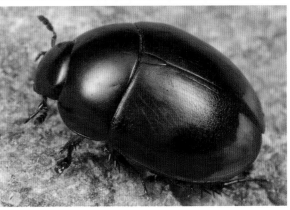

SPHAERITIDAE (sfē-rīt'-i-dē)
FALSE CLOWN BEETLES

Sphaeritidae comprises solely the genus *Sphaerites* that contains five species restricted to temperate forests and alpine habitats in the Northern Hemisphere. Adults are typically associated with decaying organic matter and may be locally common on dung, carrion, feces, fungi, fermenting fruit, sap of dying trees and stumps, and compost. Feeding habits of the adults and larvae are unknown, but their mouthparts are similar to those of predatory histerid beetles (p.127), suggesting that they eat soft insect prey such as fly maggots. As with many histerids, adult *Sphaerites* feign death when disturbed. Only one species, *S. politus*, occurs in North America.

FAMILY DIAGNOSIS False clown beetles are broadly oval and convex. Head deflexed, less than half as wide, not deeply inserted in prothorax, eyes oval, weakly geniculate antennae with 11 antennomeres, scape relatively long, curved, 9–11 forming large densely setose club. Prothorax broad, not tightly joined to pterothorax and freely movable; procoxae transverse, prominent, contiguous, and open. Scutellum moderately large. Elytra long, convex, and truncate apically, with pygidium exposed. Legs with front and middle coxae contiguous, femora swollen, tibiae robust with small spines along outer edges, tarsi 5-5-5. Abdomen with five ventrites free.

SIMILAR FAMILIES

- hister beetles (Histeridae, p.127)—more compact, head and legs more retractile, antennae geniculate, truncate elytra less snug fitting, abdomen tightly fused to thorax
- carrion beetles (Silphidae, p.140)—surfaces without metallic luster
- scarab beetles (Scarabaeidae, p.172)—antennae lamellate

COLLECTING NOTES Adult false clown beetles are sometimes locally abundant in carrion, decayed fungi, bear dung, under bark, and in or near compost. They are also found in unbaited pitfall and flight traps in old-growth conifer forests.

FAUNA ONE SPECIES, *SPHAERITES POLITUS*

Sphaerites politus Mannerheim (3.6–7.0 mm) is broadly oval, convex, black, moderately shiny with faint blue-green metallic reflections, with vestiture generally absent except on appendages. Elytra long, convex, truncate, surfaces each with nine rows of punctures visible from above becoming irregular at base and apex. Legs with hind trochanters spinose. Larvae unknown. Adults active in summer, found typically associated with carrion, bear dung, in or near compost, and in unbaited pitfall and flight traps in old-growth conifer forests; sometimes locally abundant. Southern Alaska to northern California, east to Alberta, Idaho, and western Montana. (1)

HISTERIDAE (his-ter'-i-dē)
HISTER BEETLES

The biologies of most adult and larval histerids are largely unknown, but many are likely to be primarily carnivorous and prey on insects, although adults of some species are reported to feed on fungal spores. Saprophytic species, such as those in the genera *Atholus, Hister, Margarinotus, Omalodes, Saprinus, Spilodiscus,* and *Xerosaprinus* typically prey on fly and beetle larvae inhabiting dung, carrion, or decaying plants. Species of *Hololepta, Platysoma,* and *Platylomalus* are xylophilic. Their small and/or flat bodies are adaptations for moving easily under the bark of dying trees or through decaying tissues of yuccas and common sotol (*Dasylirion*). Cylindrical species of *Teretrius* are adapted for hunting insect prey in the galleries of wood-boring beetles, especially those of bark beetles (Curculionidae, p.539). Psammophilous species, such as *Hypocaccus* and others, inhabit the sandy shores of rivers, lakes, and oceans. Coastal wrack inhabitants likely prey on a diverse fly fauna that breeds in decaying seaweed. The burrows of kangaroo rats (*Dipodomys*), ground squirrels (*Spermophilus*), and prairie dogs (*Cynomys*) all harbor *Eremosaprinus, Geomysaprinus,* and *Onthophilus* species, respectively. Species of histerids that are restricted to these habitats feed mostly on fly eggs and maggots developing in mammal dung. Other *Onthophilus* species have been reported in wasp and ant nests, but myrmecophilous species of *Haeterius* are found only in ant nests, where they scavenge or prey on the immature stages of their hosts. The nests of *Aphaenogaster, Formica, Lasius,* and *Pogonomyrmex* are collectively inhabited by a diverse histerid fauna. When threatened, adult histerids pull their heads inside their prothoraces and tuck their legs tightly beneath their shiny, round, compact bodies. The larvae are unusual among beetles in that there are only two instars. With legs that are small and not particularly useful for walking, histerid larvae move by contracting and relaxing their abdominal muscles. They feed on liquids and must digest their food extraorally with the aid of digestive fluids.

127

FAMILY DIAGNOSIS Adult histerids are mostly small, oval to elongate-oval, convex or flat, compact, shiny black, sometimes with distinct red markings, or reddish, occasionally with metallic blue or green luster, and have retractile appendages. Head usually hypognathous (prognathous in *Hololepta, Iliotona*), with prominent and relatively large mandibles. Geniculate antennae with 11 antennomeres, 9–11 fused to form a compact club often clothed in patches of sensory hairs. Prothorax sometimes with scutellum usually visible. Elytra usually distinctly striate and/or punctured, and short, often truncate apically, exposing last two abdominal tergites. Coxae widely separated, tarsi 5-5-5 or 5-5-4, usually with simple claws equal in size. Abdomen with five ventrites.

SIMILAR FAMILIES
- some water scavenger beetles (Hydrophilidae, p.122)—elytra completely covering abdomen, antennal club not as compact, maxillary palps often long
- false clown beetles (Sphaeritidae, p.126)—less compact, head and legs less retractile, truncate elytra less snug fitting, pronotum not tightly fused to pterothorax
- some round fungus beetles (Leiodidae, p.137)—antennal club long, antennomere 8 usually smaller than 7 and 9

- shining fungus beetles (Staphylinidae, p.143)—antennae weakly clubbed, long, and not tucked under body, abdomen tapered posteriorly
- *Pseudocanthon* (Scarabaeidae, p.179)—antennae lamellate
- short-winged flower beetles (Kateretidae, p.441)—antennae not geniculate
- sap beetles (Nitidulidae, p.443)—antennae not geniculate, tarsi usually expanded and hairy beneath, fourth tarsomere reduced

COLLECTING NOTES Some histerids are attracted to pitfall traps baited with decaying meat or feces. Species in rotting vegetation and fungus are extracted using Berlese funnels, Winkler eclectors, or sorted in a light-colored pan. Examine decaying wounds on trees, cacti, agave, and sotol for other species. Species living under the bark of dead or dying hardwoods and conifers, or in bark beetle tunnels in tree branches, can be trapped in Lindgren funnels baited for bark beetles. Coastal histerids shelter under wrack just above the tide line. Psammophilous species are sifted from sand among the roots of sand-loving plants growing along lakeshores and banks of rivers and streams. Myrmecophilous histerids are collected under rocks in association with their host ants.

FAUNA 431 SPECIES IN 65 GENERA

Plegaderus sayi Marseul (1.4–1.8 mm) is broadest behind elytral base, reddish-brown to black, with deep punctures. Pronotum with distinct lateral furrows, lateral lobe with four or five rows of punctures at transverse groove that divides disc into smaller anterior and larger posterior portions; underside with posterior lobe of prosternum longer than wide, narrower at apex than that of anterior lobe. Elytra flat, punctures round and larger than on pronotum, with surface not appearing finely scratched. Pygidium coarsely punctured across anterior half. Adults under bark of dead conifers (*Pinus*, *Larix*). Pacific Northwest; also in East. (10)

Teretrius cylindrellus Casey (1.6–2.2 mm) is elongate-oblong, cylindrical, and brownish black, with underside, pygidium, and appendages reddish. Head moderately convex and finely, deeply punctate. Pronotum densely and finely punctate; prosternal lobe lacking. Elytral punctures small and deep, with smooth oblong callus. Propygidium more densely punctured than elytra, while evenly convex pygidium less so. Likely in beetle-infested hardwood branches. California. *Teretrius montanus* Horn (2.5–2.8 mm) more robust, prosternal carinae shorter, and basal half of pygidium with punctures less rounded. British Columbia and Alberta, south to California and Colorado. (2)

Platylomalus aequalis (Say) (3.0–3.5 mm) is flat, shiny, and dark reddish-brown to black. Pronotum sparsely punctured. Elytra sparsely punctured down middle, punctures slightly coarser along sides, all but one partial groove at base indistinct or absent, and no groove present along suture. Prosternum with more or less parallel grooves. Adults found under bark of deciduous trees, especially oak (*Quercus*), ash (*Fraxinus*), sycamore (*Platanus*), maple (*Acer*), and aspen and cottonwood (*Populus*). British Columbia east to Québec, south to Kansas and Florida. (1)

Platysoma leconti Marseul (2.5–3.5 mm) is elongate, wide, oval, flat, shiny, and black. Pronotum with anterior marginal groove complete behind head, not interrupted at middle, and punctures becoming coarse at sides. Elytron with three entire striae and two shorter striae that nearly reach apex. Front tibiae with four denticles along outer edge. Adults are found under bark of dead trees, typically in bark beetle galleries. Widely distributed in North America, from Northwest Territories south to northern California, east to Nova Scotia and northern Florida. (1)

Haeterius wagneri Ross (2.7 mm) is robust, broadly oval, mostly smooth dorsally, shiny dark reddish brown, and without any vestiture except along lateral pronotal margins. Head sparsely punctate, antennal scape expanded apically and nearly triangular, labrum without setae. Pronotum with anterior pronotal lobes rugulose. Prosternum flat with marginal carinae converging anteriorly, but not meeting at apex. Elytra tricarinate before humeri. Legs with tibiae broad, flat, with dorsal surfaces sculpted to accept tarsi, front tibiae without apical spurs. Presumably associated with ants, most likely species of *Formica* or *Lasius*. California. (19)

Atholus bimaculatus (Linnaeus) (4.0–4.8 mm) is broadly oblong and shiny black with broad orangish or reddish elytral spot covering posterolateral surface. Antennal club with distinct annuli. Pronotum with single lateral striae to basal third, with lateral depression near each anterior angle, and row of fine and coarse punctures along posterior margin; underside with hypomeron glabrous. Elytra each with four complete sulci. Propygidium finely, sparsely punctate; pygidium with finer punctures. Legs with front tibial sulcus straight. Adults occur in dung and rotting vegetation. Europe; widely established in North America. *Atholus falli* (Bickhardt) (3.5–4.5 mm) lacks lateral pronotal depressions; in West from British Columbia to California. (2)

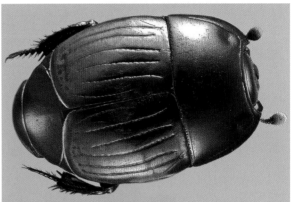

Hister furtivus J.E. LeConte (5.0–8.0 mm) is uniformly shiny black. Pronotum with pair of lateral striae on each side, outer stria entire or nearly so, inner obsolete at posterior half or third; underneath with prosternum with lobe truncate (female) or emarginate (male). Elytra each with three entire, weakly crenulate sulci, fourth restricted to apical half, fifth restricted to apical fourth. Pygidium finely reticulate, moderately coarsely punctured, punctures mostly separated by their own diameters. Adults on carrion, dung, rotting mushrooms, and compost. Widespread across North America; in West from British Columbia south to Arizona and New Mexico. (3)

Spilodiscus sellatus (LeConte) (5.6–7.0 mm) is black with a large, red, boot-shaped spot on each elytron. Head with mandibles prominent. Pronotum between lateral margins and striae with confused strioles, at least in anterior third. Legs with middle and hind femora uniformly dark. Elytra with short striae restricted to basal third or absent, lateral margins and inflexed portion reddish or dark reddish. Anterior portions of propygidium and pygidium usually with fine punctures medially and coarser ones laterally. Adults found during spring and early summer in sandy habitats from ocean beaches to montane streams; coastal populations in decline. Washington to northern Baja California. (2)

Hololepta vernicis Casey (6.5–7.0 mm) is elongate and oblong, somewhat flattened, and smooth, shiny black with reddish appendages. Head with slightly prominent mandibles, longer than (male) or equal (female) in length to head, and frons without strioles. Pronotum with sides moderately coarsely punctate, and posterior margin bisinuate medially; underneath with prosternum lacking short, impressed line inside each lateral emargination. Elytra each with two striae, inner stria half elytral length or entire, outer stria about a one-third elytral length, and reflexed portions of lateral margins rugulose. Pygidium smooth medially and coarsely, deeply punctate on sides. Legs with tibiae dentate, front tibiae quadridentate, middle and hind tibiae tridentate. Adults associated with dying *Dasylirion* and *Agave*. Southeastern Arizona. (3)

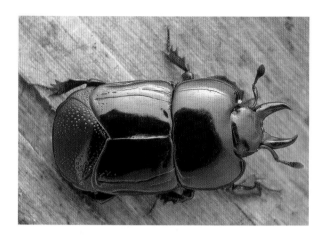

Iliotona cacti LeConte (4.5–8.5 mm) is more or less elongate and oblong, somewhat flattened. Head with mandibles prominent, without teeth, not expanded at their bases. Pronotum with lateral margin grooved only at apical third and a median sulcus extending from apical third to bisinuate posterior margin, and prosternum produced to a nearly acute V underneath head. Elytra each with two striae, inner stria deep and entire, outer stria short and not reaching middle. Pygidium margined. Legs with tibiae dentate, front tibiae quadridentate, middle and hind tibiae tridentate. Larvae and adults found in rotting cactus, where they prey on fly eggs and larvae. Southern California to Texas, south to Mexico. (1)

Omalodes grossus Marseul (8.3–9.0 mm) is broadly oval, convex, and shiny black. Frons shallowly punctate and foveate medially, frontal margin complete. Pronotum without pits, with anterior angles strongly projected forward, and narrowly punctured before complete lateral striae; prosternal apex rounded and margined laterally. Elytra each trisulcate, sulci oblique and finely impressed, outermost sulcus long. Propygidium smooth medially and distinctly punctate laterally. Front tibiae with apical spurs and sinuate tarsal sulcus on dorsal surface. Adults found in rotting cactus, among decaying plant material associated with *Agave* rosettes, occasionally beneath carcasses. Southeastern Arizona to Texas, south to Panama. (1)

Onthophilus lecontei Horn (2.5–3.7 mm) has a densely punctured pronotum with six carinae, outer two carinae diverge posteriorly, outermost carina reaching posterior margin; prosternal lobe with small punctures, surface strigulate. Lateral pronotal margins weakly arcuate. Elytra at base broader than pronotum, costae equally distinct and entire, intercostae weakly bicostate, costae separated by a row of coarse, widely spaced punctures. Propygidium and pygidium both convex and coarsely punctate. First ventrite with large punctures along margin and distinct, punctulate semicircular median area. Nests of harvester ants (*Pogonomyrmex*) and yellowjackets (*Vespula*); under decaying vegetable matter. Coastal California. (3)

Euspilotus scissus (LeConte) (1.6–2.4 mm) is shiny dark brown to brownish black. Frons finely punctured. Pronotum finely punctate, except along posterior margin, with lateral punctures coarser, and without impressions behind anterior angles. Elytra each with four distinct striae barely reaching middle, disc coarsely punctate between striae 1–4, with sutural stria posteriorly, but erased on anterior third or fourth and basal arc. Propygidium and pygidium finely punctate, Pygidium without marginal sulcus, punctures across anterior half sparser than on propygidium. Under decaying seaweed. British Columbia to Baja California. (10)

Hypocaccus bigemmeus (LeConte) (2.0–3.3 mm) with transverse ridge on head. Pronotum coarsely punctate except for triangular area on disc; prosternum with preapical foveae not connected by transverse sulcus. Elytra with sutural stria distinct at basal half, surface between punctures distinctly carinulate, surface between basal arc and elytral base densely strigose-aciculate. *Hypocaccus fraternus* (Say) (2.5–4.2 mm) similar, elytral surfaces between punctures flat or slightly carinulate, surface between basal arc and elytral base smooth. Both under debris on coastal beaches, sandy river shores, occasionally under carrion; British Columbia to California. (6)

Neopachylopus sulcifrons (Mannerheim) (4.5–6.3 mm) with pronotum nearly smooth, coarse punctures mostly across base along posterior margin; prosternum without anterior lobe or foveae, but with an acutely carinate keel. Lateral surfaces of metatibia with about six rows of spines, and front tarsi underneath with two rows of flattened translucent setae (male) or not (female). Coastal wrack on dry sand at high tide. *Neopachylopus aeneipunctatus* (Horn) (2.8–4.0 mm) pronotum coarsely punctate over entire surface, and lateral surfaces of metatibia with three or four rows of spines. Both species British Columbia to California. (2)

Saprinus lugens Erichson (4.8–7.2 mm) is shiny black, without metallic luster. Pronotum with shallow impressions behind anterior angles, lateral marginal bead about same width from apex to base; hypomeron without setae noticeable from above. Elytra coarsely and densely punctate except for broad smooth area behind scutellum delimited laterally by four oblique striae, punctate area distinctly aciculate and not extending anteriorly along suture, with sutural stria usually widely interrupted at basal fourth and not joined with any discal stria. Adults found with carrion and dung, also recorded on foul-smelling flowers of *Dracunculus* and *Suaromatum*. Widely distributed throughout North America from southern Canada south to Mexico. (3)

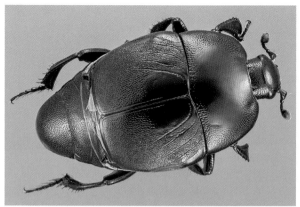

Xerosaprinus lubricus (**LeConte**) (2.4–4.0 mm) is broadly oval, with head black and legs reddish brown. Underside of antennal club with four slitlike sensory structures. Pronotum reddish brown along lateral margins and brownish black on disc, very finely punctured, with coarser punctures on sides and narrowly along posterior margin. Elytra reddish brown with smooth areas darker and sharply delimited posteriorly, demarcation somewhat oblique, and flanked by four oblique striae extending posteriorly to about middle. Pygidium densely, coarsely punctate in anterior half. Adults associated with dung and carrion. Widely distributed in western North America south to California. (11)

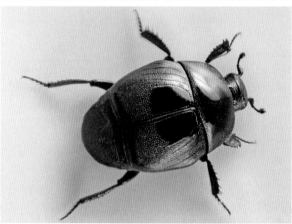

132

HYDRAENIDAE (hī-drēn′-i-dē)
MINUTE MOSS BEETLES

Hydraenids are small, mostly aquatic, non-swimming beetles that live along the margins of permanent and temporary wetlands, including brackish waters. The adults and larvae of some species are reported to graze on microorganisms from the surfaces of wet stones, sand grains, and plant matter. Adults are found among wet vegetation or sand, burrowing in damp sand and soil on shore, or clinging to rocks and chunks of waterlogged wood in streams. Hydraenids are often abundant in these microhabitats and likely play an important role in recycling plant detritus. Eggs are generally laid singly in damp places out of water on leaves, rocks, and algae along the edges of water bodies and are secured to these substrates with silklike strands. The larvae are semiaquatic and are usually found along damp margins of aquatic habitats that also harbor adults. The underside of their bodies is clothed in dense setae that form a plastron to trap a bubble of air, allowing them to breathe underwater. The effectiveness of the plastron is enhanced by an exocrine secretion delivery system. *Exocrine glands* on the head and prothorax produce secretions that are applied to the plastron and other cuticular structures to increase their overall effectiveness in underwater respiration. Adult *Hydraena*, *Limnebius*, and *Ochthebius* utilize setal leg patches to distribute these secretions on respiratory surfaces when they are out of the water. Although the function of these secretions is not completely understood, it appears they also contain antimicrobial properties that prevent microorganisms from colonizing body surfaces, and possibly serve as a wetting agent on nonrespiratory surfaces to facilitate the beetle's entry into the water. Males of some species of *Hydraena* stridulate, but whether this behavior serves a defensive or courtship function remains unknown.

FAMILY DIAGNOSIS Adult hydraenids are black to yellowish brown, sometimes with metallic reflections. Head hypognathous, with maxillary palps long, and eyes prominent. Antennae with nine antennomeres, last five forming club clothed in velvety pubescence. Pronotum broader than head, usually with impressions or grooves (not in *Limnebius*), and lateral margins hyaline or not. Hypomeron with surface modified to protect antennal club and facilitate respiration underwater. Procoxal cavities open or closed (*Hydraena*) behind. Scutellum small and visible. Elytra completely conceal abdomen, surface punctostriate or not (*Limnebius*). Legs short and stout to long and slender; tarsi 5-5-5, with first four tarsomeres short, last tarsomere long, and claws simple. Abdomen with seven ventrites, sometimes 7 completely concealed by 6.

SIMILAR FAMILIES Hydraenid beetles are distinguished from species of Helophoridae (p.118), Hydrochidae (p.121), Elmidae (p.235), and Dryopidae (p.239) by having an antennal club comprising five antennomeres and six or seven ventrites.

COLLECTING NOTES Look for hydraenids along the margins of streams and ponds and stir the sand and gravel at the waterline to flush beetles to the water surface. Also check leaf packs, matted roots, moss-covered rocks, and other wet plant materials along the splash zones of cascades, rills, and waterfalls. Potholes, submerged rocks, and other debris also harbor hydraenids. Multiple genera are sometimes found together in abundance within relatively stable sandy or gravelly stream banks with substrates segregated into layers of different particle sizes resulting in interstitial spaces. One species, *Neocthebius vandykei* (Knisch) (1.6–1.7 mm), is intertidal and occurs in rock crevices from British Columbia to California.

FAUNA 94 SPECIES IN SIX GENERA

Hydraena species (1.0–2.0 mm) are elongate or elongate-oval, somewhat flattened, coarsely punctate, and black-brown, or yellowish brown with pronotal macula, sometimes with lighter appendages. Ocelli present. Antennae with nine antennomeres and shorter than maxillary palps, palpomere 2 very long, slender. Pronotum broader, with lateral margins explanate and somewhat angulate at middle. Elytra at base wider than pronotum, each usually with 10 punctostriae between suture and humerus, intervals flat to carinate. Abdomen with six ventrites, surfaces of 1–4 and anterior half of 5 pubescent. Most adults occur along montane streams, a few along edges of coastal ponds. Throughout North America. (14)

Ochthebius species (1.3–2.5 mm) are elongate-oval to ovate, usually moderately convex, and mostly dark brown with some metallic copper or purplish reflections. Ocelli absent. Antennae with nine antennomeres and longer than maxillary palps, palpomere 2 not particularly elongate. Pronotum variable, sometimes with lateral margins sinuate or deeply incised, often with all margins narrowly or broadly translucent. Elytron with six punctostriae between suture and humerus. Abdomen with seven ventrites, 1–5, sometimes 6, pubescent. Legs moderate in length, slender or stout, with front tarsi of males sometimes having adhesive pads underneath. Adults inhabit wetland edges in coastal and montane regions. Throughout North America. (38)

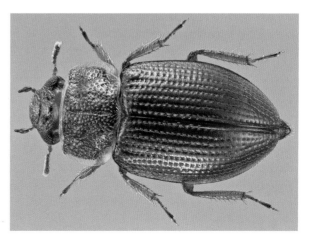

PTILIIDAE (ti-lī'-i-dē)
FEATHERWING BEETLES

Featherwing beetles are the smallest of Coleoptera, with the adults of some species reaching only 0.3 mm in length. They typically have well-developed compound eyes, wings, and body pigmentation, while vestigial forms have eyes, wings, and other structures greatly reduced or absent. Their common name reflects the featherlike form of their flight wings that may extend more than twice their body length. Each wing consists of a central thin and curved shaft bearing long setae on each side that serve to increase its surface area. In addition to their small size and unique flight wing structure, featherwing beetles are also notable because males of some species are unknown and the females reproduce asexually by parthenogenesis. Eggs are typically produced and laid one at a time. Larvae and adults are usually found in moist, decaying organic matter that supports fungal growth in a wide variety of habitats and niches, where they both consume hyphae and spores. Species identification requires mounting specimens on microscope slides. The family needs revision as there are numerous species awaiting scientific description.

FAMILY DIAGNOSIS Adult ptiliids are minute, moderately to strongly convex, yellow, brown, reddish brown, or blackish, and somewhat pubescent. Head prognathous. Antennae with 8–11 antennomeres, antennomeres 1–2 enlarged, with last two or three forming a loose club, each clothed in a whorl of setae. Procoxal cavities open behind. Elytra long, completely covering abdomen, or short and exposing three to five abdominal tergites. Tarsi 3-3-3, tarsomere 1 short, 2 very small, 3 long and slender, with simple claws equal in length, or nearly so. Abdomen with six ventrites.

SIMILAR FAMILIES
- minute beetles (Clambidae, p.113)—capable of partly rolling up
- *Scaphisoma* beetles (Staphylinidae, p.147)—abdomen tapered apically
- minute fungus beetles (Corylophidae, p.314)—pronotum usually conceals head

COLLECTING NOTES Ptiliids are nocturnal and often overlooked. Search for them in rotten wood, clumps of moss, forest canopies, leaf litter, mammal nests, dung middens and piles, logs and stumps rife with fungal growth, tree holes, beach wrack, and fungi—wherever organic materials accumulate. *Actidium* and *Motschulskium* adults and larvae are found under piles of seaweed, while *Actidium* also occur on bare sand and gravel bars along streams. These shore-inhabiting beetles are best collected by flotation. *Cylindrosella* and *Porophila* found in spore tubes on the underside of shelf fungi (Polyporaceae) are picked off with the wetted tips of forceps as they run across the fungal surface.

FAUNA 120 SPECIES IN 29 GENERA

Acrotrichis **species** (0.9–1.1 mm) are oblong or ovate, convex, usually black, brown to reddish brown, with appendages sometimes paler, and clothed in golden or silvery pubescence. Antennae with 11 antennomeres, 9–11 forming club. Pronotum scarcely to much wider than elytra, broadest basally, with posterior angles distinct or not and posterior margin straight. Elytra somewhat short with apices truncate, exposing three to five tergites. Adults found in various habitats, ranging from dung and decaying fungi to leaf litter and mammal nests. Widespread in North America. (35 NA)

Ptenidium pusillum **(Gyllenhal)** (1.0–1.5mm) is ovate, convex, and mostly shiny blackish with long, sparse, silvery pubescence and yellowish appendages. Pronotum short, widest behind middle, sides rounded, with surface distinctly punctate and deep, transverse groove on each side at base. Elytral apices broadly reddish yellow-brown. Inhabits tree holes, forest leaf litter, mammal nests; found on decaying green cracking russula mushroom, *Russula virescens.* North America and Europe. (12+ NA)

AGYRTIDAE (aj-ir′-ti-dē)
PRIMITIVE CARRION BEETLES

Only scant information is available on the natural history of agyrtids in western North America. Most larvae and adults apparently scavenge carrion or decaying organic material. Adults are found in cool, wet habitats primarily when temperatures are cooler. They are often associated with drift along beaches and rivers, mountain stream margins, and high-elevation snowfields. Adults and larvae of *Ipelatus latus* (Mannerheim) are detritivores that inhabit forest litter associated with dead conifer logs. *Lyrosoma opacum* Mannerheim, a flightless species restricted to the Aleutian Island coastlines, feeds on decaying seaweed and kelp in habitats that are at times completely submerged by incoming tides. *Agyrtes longulus* (LeConte) is apparently winter active and has been found in numbers on snow. Virtually nothing is known of *Pteroloma nebrioides* Brown, other than that it lives under stones near streams or in mossy habitats. All species of *Apteroloma* live at high elevations. Although initially thought to feed on decaying vegetation, species in both these genera are now believed to be insect predators.

FAMILY DIAGNOSIS Primitive carrion beetles are plain, oval to elongate-oval, slightly flattened, and brownish. Prognathous head sometimes slightly deflexed. Antennae have 11 antennomeres and are filiform or clavate with weak club formed by last four or five antennomeres. Pronotum broader than head and is distinctly margined laterally. Procoxal cavities open behind. Scutellum visible. Elytra completely cover abdomen, each with 9–10 punctostriae. Tarsi 5-5-5, with simple claws equal in size. Abdomen typically with five ventrites.

SIMILAR FAMILIES
- ground beetles (Carabidae, p.88)—antennae not clubbed
- carrion beetles (Silphidae, p.140)—elytra never striate, abdomen with six ventrites

COLLECTING NOTES Primitive carrion beetles are difficult to find and rarely collected. *Necrophilus* is attracted to carrion-baited traps during the cooler parts of the year. Sifting through river debris, fungi, or material under rotting bark in forested habitats may produce specimens of *Agyrtes* or *Ipelates. Apteroloma* is found among beach drift, amid gravel and moss on the banks of mountain streams, or under rocks at the edges of high-elevation snowfields.

135

FAUNA 11 SPECIES IN SIX GENERA

Agyrtes longulus (LeConte) (5.0–7.0 mm) is elongate and shiny dark reddish brown to black. Head with clypeus broadly rectangular, longer than labrum, mandible lacking preapical teeth, with antennae clavate, club composed of four antennomeres. Pronotum wider, less narrowed anteriorly, with posterior angles sharp. Elytra each with 10 distinct punctostriae, epipleural ridge sinuate, and epipleuron glabrous. Adults active during cooler months in forested habitats, associated with plant debris. Southern Alaska to southern California, east to Idaho. *Agyrtes similis* Fall (5.0–7.0 mm) antennal club composed of five antennomeres, pronotum more narrowed anteriorly, with posterior pronotal angles rounded, and epipleuron pubescent. Coastal Ranges of central and southern California. (2)

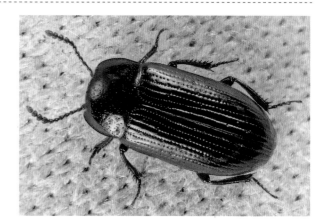

Ipelates latus (Mannerheim) (4.0–6.0 mm) is ovoid, shiny reddish brown, with appendages, and lateral pronotal and elytral margins lighter; lateral margins narrowly reflexed and translucent. Mandibles lacking preapical teeth. Antennae clavate with antennomeres 7–10 grooved at apices, and nearly reach base of pronotum. Pronotum wide with lateral margins narrowly explanate, almost as wide as elytral base. Elytron with nine punctostriae, intervals lacking distinct microsculpture. Hind coxae contiguous. Adults among moist leaf litter and decayed mushrooms at base of conifers, or occasionally under bark of decaying trees along streams. Alaskan Panhandle and Northwestern Territories to central California, east to western Alberta, Idaho, and Montana. (1)

Necrophilus hydrophiloides Guérin-Méneville (10.0–13.0 mm) is somewhat ovoid and brownish. Head with antennae clavate, antennomeres 7–11 forming club, 7–10 each with apical groove. Pronotum with lateral margins broadly explanate. Elytra each with nine distinct punctostriae, punctures small and shallow, intervals convex and impunctate, and lateral and apical margins narrowly reflexed. Hind coxae contiguous. Adults and larvae are scavengers on decaying plant and animal tissues; adults active primarily November through May and encountered at carrion, or in garbage and rotting vegetable material. Alaskan Panhandle south to southern California. (1)

Apteroloma tahoecum (Fall) (5.5–6.5 mm) is ovoid, shiny reddish brown. Mandible with one or two preapical teeth on inner margin, antennomeres lacking apical grooves. Pronotum broadest basally, without basal impressions. Elytral epipleura impunctate, and suture without apical tooth. Adults occur under plant debris in wet habitats, and along shorelines. Oregon to southern California. *Apteroloma caraboides* (Fall) (8.0–10.0 mm) pronotum relatively narrow, elytral suture with distinct subapical tooth. British Columbia and Idaho south to northern California. Species with punctate epipleura: *A. arizonicum* (Van Dyke) posterior pronotal angles obtusely angulate, Arizona; *A. tenuicorne* (LeConte) posterior pronotal angles rounded, Pacific Northwest south to California and Colorado. (4)

LEIODIDAE (lī-ōd'-i-dē)
ROUND FUNGUS BEETLES

Leiodids are a diverse family of small and secretive insects known commonly as round fungus, small carrion, and mammal nest beetles. Many species are detritivores that scavenge organic matter among various habitats and niches. For example, blind and flightless species of *Catopocerus* scavenge fungi growing in moist forest litter and soil, rotten logs, and occasionally caves. Detritivores feed on carrion and dung, and similar accumulations of decaying organic matter, while mycophagous species consume only fungus and/or slime molds. *Leiodes*, and probably *Colon*, also feed on subterranean fungi in forest litter. *Agathidium* eat mostly the fruiting bodies and plasmodia of slime molds, but also feed on fungi, while the closely related *Anisostoma* is a slime mold specialist. Eyeless and flightless *Pinodytes* live in the soil and likely feed on subterranean fungi. A few species are commensals that live in the nests of invertebrates or vertebrates. For example, *Ptomaphagus setiger* lives with *Pogonomyrmex* and *Aphaenogaster* ants, while species of *Platycholeus* inhabit the nests of both ants and termites. The mouse nest beetle *Leptinus occidentamericanus* is a nest inquiline that occupies nests of various rodent species. Three species in the genera *Platypsyllus* and *Leptinillus* are true ectoparasites of aquatic and semiaquatic rodents.

137

FAMILY DIAGNOSIS Most adult leiodids are best distinguished from other small, oval beetles by antennomere 8 being noticeably smaller than antennomeres 7 or 9. Broadly oval to somewhat elongate, slightly flattened to very convex, with prothorax and elytra often granular or finely and transversely striate. Head partly visible from above, with distinctly clubbed antennae, club usually with five antennomeres and interrupted (not in *Colon*) by reduced antennomere 8. Prothorax with lateral margins carinate; procoxae open behind. Elytra long, covering abdomen (except *Platypsyllus*). Legs usually with front tarsi expanded (male) or narrow (female), tarsi usually 5-5-5, sometimes 3-3-3; also 5-5-4 or 4-4-4. Abdomen with six ventrites free, rarely with 1–2 connate.

SIMILAR FAMILIES The combination of body shape and clavate antennae with typically reduced antennomere 8 that is smaller than antennomeres 7 and 9 are distinctive.

COLLECTING NOTES Look for leiodids primarily in wooded habitats among leaf litter and in association with various fungi. Winged species are captured in pitfall traps baited with dung and carrion, and in Malaise or flight intercept traps. Sweeping low vegetation in the evening along forest roads and trails can be productive. Flightless species are extracted from leaf litter by using Tulgren or Berlese funnels, or Winkler eclector. Check fungi for beetles in the field, or gather fungal material and slime molds, spread them across a white background under the heat of a desk lamp to flush out spore-covered beetles. *Leptinus* occur in nests of rodents, while *Platypsyllus* are combed from the fur of freshly dead or captive beavers using a flea comb. The troglobitic *Glacicavicola bathyscioides* occurs in moist habitats in lava tubes and limestone caves. Baited pitfall traps placed in deep rock crevices or in talus slopes may capture other "cave" species.

FAUNA 382 SPECIES IN 38 GENERA

Pinodytes newelli **Peck & Cook** (1.6–2.6 mm) is elongate and light to dark reddish brown. Head without eyes, antennae with antennomere 2 slightly longer than 3, 5 slightly larger than 4, and 6, 8 smaller than 7. Pronotum with disc finely punctured with reticulate microsculpture, posterior lateral margins more or less parallel to about middle, then converging anteriorly, and posterior margin straight. Elytra moderately, coarsely punctate, with a few striae weakly indicated near suture. Hind tibiae narrow basally and widened apically (male) or uniformly slender (female). Adults probably associated with sporocarps of subterranean fungi. Coastal Ranges of Washington and Oregon. (37)

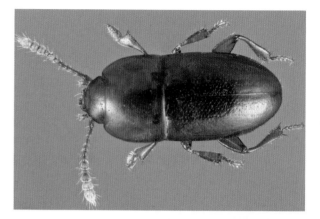

Ice Cave Beetle *Glacicavicola bathyscioides* **Westcott** (5.9–6.0 mm) is elongate, slender, antlike, mostly glabrous, and yellowish brown. Eyeless, with antennae very long with long setae, antennomere 1 longest, 8 not distinctly shorter or narrower than 7 or 9. Pronotum long, broadest at middle. Elytra with apices each narrowly rounded. Abdomen with five (female) or six (male) ventrites. Legs very long, with somewhat swollen femora, tibiae each with pair of apical spurs, and tarsi 5-5-5, each with pair of long sickle-shaped claws. Adults inhabit cold lava tubes or live under rocks in wet, limestone caves. Snake River Lava Plains of southern Idaho to western Wyoming. (1)

Catops basilaris **(Say)** (3.0–4.1 mm) is oblong, brown, surface granular and pubescent, with head, pronotum, and elytral apices darker. Back of head sharply margined, antennae barely reaching evenly arcuate pronotal base, with antennomere 8 reduced, asymmetrical and pointed on one side. Abdomen of female with penultimate ventrite variously emarginate medially on posterior margin. Legs with tibial spurs long, not finely notched, tarsi 5-5-5. Adults active mostly early fall to late spring, found under carrion and owl pellets, or in decaying fungus and leaf litter; sometimes in the nests of moles, shrews, and rodents. Alaska and Canada, south to California, Arizona, Alabama, and South Carolina. (10)

Agathidium species (4.0–6.0 mm) are broadly round, very convex, shiny, uniformly reddish brown to black, glabrous dorsally, and can roll up into a ball. Head with supraocular ridge and antennal grooves underneath. Antennomeres 7 and 8 reduced before abrupt club with three antennomeres. Pronotum expanded laterally. Elytra wide as long, and usually impunctate. Metasternal fovea bearing long tuft of golden setae in male. Front and middle tarsomere 1 moderately expanded laterally and densely setose underneath. Tarsi of male 5-5-4, 5-4-4, 4-4-4, or 4-3-3; female 5-4-4, 4-4-4, or 4-3-3. Adults on slime molds and fungi. Widespread in forested habitats across North America. (34)

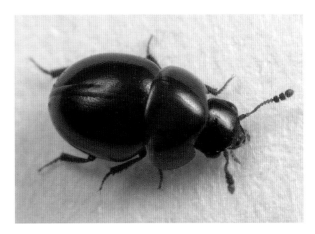

Leiodes assimilis (LeConte) (2.8–4.5 mm) is oval, and shiny reddish brown to nearly black. Head with antennal grooves underneath, antennomeres 7–11 forming long, loose club. Pronotum wider than long, broadest slightly behind middle, posterior margin straight with moderately rounded angles, with disc finely to coarsely densely punctate. Elytra long, slightly wider than pronotum, with disc punctostriate. Front tibiae strongly widened apically, front and middle tarsi moderately dilated in male, with tarsi 5-5-4 in both sexes. Adults trapped in flight intercept and Malaise traps, also at lights in forested and open habitats. Transcontinental; in West from Alaska and Yukon Territory south to Oregon and Colorado. (33)

Beaver Beetle *Platypsyllus castoris* Ritsema (1.9–2.2 mm) is flealike, yellowish brown with darker markings, and is eyeless and flightless. Antennomeres 3–11 short, compact, and partly enclosed in scoop-shaped antennomere 2. Pronotum is about equal in length to short, flaplike elytra. Front tarsus of male with underside densely clothed in setae. Adults and larvae are true ectoparasites of beavers; single record on an otter likely an accidental occurrence. Adults live in fur, with more than 60% of beavers in some populations harboring up to nearly 200 beetles. Distribution likely mirrors that of its host, occurring across southern Canada and most of United States; also Eurasia. (1)

SILPHIDAE (silf'-i-dē)
BURYING AND CARRION BEETLES

Adult burying and carrion beetles are often large, conspicuous insects found in association with carrion, and are sometimes encountered in large numbers. Burying beetles (*Nicrophorus*) have long attracted attention because they work in pairs to prepare carcasses as food for their young, thus exhibiting some of the most advanced parental care behaviors known in beetles. They often harbor predatory mites (p.37, Fig. 37) that help them to compete with other insect scavengers. Adults and larvae of carrion beetles, such as *Necrodes*, scavenge carcasses as they find them and may supplement their diets by feeding opportunistically on maggots. A few genera are phytophagous. For example, species of *Aclypea* feed exclusively on living plants and may become minor crop pests. *Heterosilpha* species scavenge decomposing plant materials and are often encountered on wet lawns. Adult carrion-feeding silphids defend themselves by oozing or spraying a dark, foul-smelling fluid from their anus that smells like rotting flesh and apparently serves as a deterrent to predators and some collectors.

FAMILY DIAGNOSIS Adult silphids are slightly to strongly flattened, ovate or somewhat elongate, and mostly black, sometimes with yellow, orange, or reddish markings on the pronotum and elytra. Head prognathous; antennae clavate or capitate, antennae with 11 antennomeres, and clubs covered with velvety setae. Pronotum broader than head and with lateral margins carinate. Procoxal cavities broadly open behind. Scutellum visible. Elytral surface not striate, either smooth (*Nicrophorus*), or rough, sometimes with three longitudinal costae or branched ribs (Silphinae). Apices of elytra either more or less rounded, sometimes somewhat produced posteriorly at suture (Silphinae), or truncate and exposing one or more abdominal tergites (*Nicrophorus*). Tarsi 5-5-5, with simple claws equal in size. Abdomen with six (female) or seven (male) ventrites free.

SIMILAR FAMILIES
- primitive carrion beetles (Agyrtidae, p.135)—elytra distinctly striate

COLLECTING NOTES Look for silphids in association with animal remains or decaying vegetable matter. Check for beetles under dead animals, or deliberately set out whole animal carcasses to attract them. Pigs, rabbits, chickens, or juvenile turkeys are inexpensive and purchased from farms and butchers. Pitfall traps baited with squid, fish, chicken legs or wings must be secured with chicken wire, and covered with plywood weighed down with rocks to keep out predators such as raccoons, skunks, and coyotes. Covering traps not only keeps out predators, but also prevents rain from entering the trap and rendering the bait less attractive. Look for *Heterosilpha* on well-watered lawns. *Necrodes* and *Nicrophorus* species are sometimes attracted to lights at night.

FAUNA 30 SPECIES IN EIGHT GENERA

Aclypea bituberosa (LeConte) (14.0–17.0 mm) is black or brown, usually clothed in yellow to black pubescence. Labrum deeply notched. Anterior pronotal margin thick, lateral margins elevated, areas behind eyes not impunctate. Elytra each tricostate with deep punctures separated by less than their own widths, often confluent near base. Adults and larvae feed on native chenopods, and are sometimes considered pests of cultivated crops. Western Canada east to upper Midwest. *Aclypea opaca* (Linnaeus) (12.0–15.0 mm) similar, pronotum usually impunctate behind eyes and lateral margins not raised, elytral punctures shallow and rarely separated by less than their own widths. Alaska and extreme northwest of Northwest Territories. (2)

140

Garden Carrion Beetle *Heterosilpha ramosa* (11.0–18.0 mm) is dull black and finely, densely punctate. Each wing cover has three shiny, branched ribs running lengthwise. Elytra each tricostate, apices of female produced. Legs of males with front and middle tarsomeres expanded, densely punctate underneath. Adults and larvae scavenge decaying plants and insects. Adults active spring through fall in damp lawns, fields, and mountain meadows. Western North America south to Baja California and Sonora. *Heterosilpha aenescens* (10.0–15.0 mm) elytra sometimes appear metallic, with male tarsi not expanded or densely setose underneath, and female elytral apices gradually rounded. Southern Oregon to northern Baja California. (2)

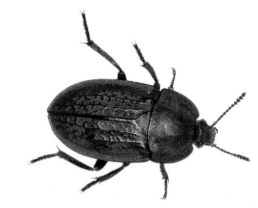

Red-lined Carrion Beetle *Necrodes surinamensis* **(Fabricius)** (12.0–24.0 mm) is mostly black with red markings on apices of costate elytra. Head with eyes large. Pronotum shiny, circular, and widest at middle. Elytra each tricostate, intercostae rough, with variable band of reddish spots near apices sometimes extending up sides. Hind leg of male with expanded femora and curved tibiae. Nocturnal adults active spring and summer, prey on maggots, scavenge carrion, and sometimes attracted to lights. In West from British Columbia to Oregon, east to Alberta Colorado, and Utah, possibly New Mexico. (1)

Thanatophilus lapponicus **(Herbst)** (9.4–14.0 mm) is dull black. Head and pronotum clothed in dense gray pubescence. Elytra black, each tricostate with intervals distinctly tuberculate, apices broadly rounded (male) or sinuate and produced at suture (female). Adults active in spring through early fall, found in open montane habitats on carcasses as both scavengers and predators. Throughout western North America south to southern California, Arizona, New Mexico; also northern Europe and Asia. (5)

Thanatophilus truncatus **(Say)** (10.5–15.9 mm) is uniformly dull black with small dense punctures, each with short, black, recumbent setae. Antennae with clubs gradually widening apically and black. Elytra smooth, without tubercles or costae, with dense punctures and truncate apices in male and female. Adults active late spring through fall in various habitats and are attracted to carrion, feces, and rotting garbage. Arizona to southwestern Kansas south to Mexico. (5)

Nicrophorus defodiens Mannerheim (12.0–18.0 mm) has entirely black antennal clubs. Pronotum quadrate, with broad margins along sides and base. Elytra with medial transverse red markings not reaching suture, sometimes reduced or separated into two spots; epipleura black with red in middle; metasternum with dense yellow pubescence. Hind tibiae straight. Adults active late spring and summer in montane and coastal forests, bury carrion under leaves, not in soil; attracted to lights. Alaska south to central coast of California and Rocky Mountain states; also Northeast south through Appalachian Mountains. (7)

Nicrophorus guttula Motschulsky (14.0–20.0 mm) has black antennal clubs, or with basal antennomere black and remaining three antennomeres orange. Pronotum cordate, broadest anteriorly, with narrow lateral and wide posterior margins. Elytra variably marked with orange, or solid black with a small spot flanking each humerus. Metasternum clothed in dense yellow pubescence. Anterior face of front coxae with long setae on basal half, hind tibiae straight. Active spring through summer in dry forests, prairies, and deserts on carrion and dung. Southern British Columbia to Baja California, east to Saskatchewan and New Mexico. (7)

142

Red and Black Burying Beetle *Nicrophorus marginatus* Fabricius (13.9–22.0 mm) is shiny black with two broad, orange red marks on each elytron, and similarly colored spot on head. Antennal club orange red. Pronotum strongly cordate, broadest anteriorly, with narrow lateral margins and wide posterior. Metasternum densely clothed in yellow pubescence. Hind tibia slightly curved. Nocturnal adults active in summer and prefer open fields, montane meadows, grasslands, and desert woodlands. Adults feed exclusively on fly larvae on carrion. Transcontinental; in West from southern Alberta and most of western North America south to mainland Mexico. (7)

Nicrophorus mexicanus Matthews (13.9–22.0 mm) has antennal clubs with basal antennomere black and remaining three antennomeres orange. Pronotum subquadrate with lateral and posterior margins wide. Elytra each with two transverse orange spots, anterior spots joined at suture, but not apical markings; epipleuron orange with black band and black spot just behind humerus. Metasternum densely clothed in dark brown pubescence. Metepimeron with small patch of brown setae. Nocturnal adults attracted to lights from late spring through early fall. Southern Rocky Mountain states south to El Salvador. (7)

Black Burying Beetle *Nicrophorus nigrita* Mannerheim (13.0–18.0 mm) is nearly all black. Antennae with apical three antennomeres of club orange. Pronotum quadrate with lateral and posterior margins wide. Elytra immaculate. Metasternum densely clothed in brown pubescence has a brownish patch of setae on the underside of its thorax. Nocturnal adults mostly active from late winter to late fall, mostly in coastal forests; also attracted to lights. Southern British Columbia southward to northern Baja California. (7)

STAPHYLINIDAE (staf-i-lin'-i-dē)
ROVE BEETLES

Rove beetles are the largest family of beetles in North America, yet biological information is available for relatively few species. They are found in nearly every type of terrestrial habitat, especially in forests and woodlands, and typically eat almost everything except living tissues of higher plants. Most species prey on insects, mites, and other small invertebrates, but there are several subfamilies with species that feed entirely on fungi or decaying organic matter. Although a few large and conspicuous species are found on carrion and dung, most are decidedly more secretive. They live under rocks and plant debris, or inhabit leaf litter, mosses, and rotting vegetation, especially in woodlands or along the shores of ponds, lakes, streams, and other wetlands; a few species are restricted to ocean beaches. Still others are found under bark, on living plants and fungi, and in the nests of animals. When disturbed, most rove beetles are quick to take to the air. Many run on the ground with their abdomens waving menacingly in the air as if they could sting, but they cannot. Depending on the species, staphylinid larvae are predaceous, mycophagous, or scavengers and live in habitats similar to those of the adults. Staphylinids are challenging to photograph alive, much less identify, and thus are underrepresented in this book. Accurate species identification typically requires the examination of carefully prepared specimens with the aid of detailed monographs.

FAMILY DIAGNOSIS Adult staphylinids are incredibly diverse in form and habit. Most species are distinguished from other families of beetles by their long, slender, nearly parallel-sided, and flexible abdomens, filiform or clavate antennae, and short elytra exposing five to six abdominal tergites. *Baeocera* and *Scaphidium* are small, broadly oval, compact, and leggy with elytra exposing one or two abdominal tergites. Other very small species are elongate-oval with distinctly clubbed antennae, more compact and rigid bodies, with short elytra generally exposing three to five abdominal tergites (Pselaphinae), or covering the abdomen entirely (Scydmaeninae). Head prognathous or hypognathous, with or without distinct neck. Procoxal cavities open or closed behind. Tarsi usually 5-5-5, 3-3-3 (e.g., Pselaphinae), sometimes 4-4-4, 2-2-2, 4-5-5, or 4-4-5. Abdomen with six, sometimes seven ventrites free.

SIMILAR FAMILIES Several other families (Micromalthidae, Cleridae, Cantharidae, Phengodidae, Nitidulidae, Meloidae, Cerambycidae) have species with short elytra exposing just a few abdominal tergites, but overall appearance and form of their antennae will usually distinguish them from most staphylinids.

COLLECTING NOTES Look for rove beetles on dung, carrion, under bark, in fungi, beneath objects and debris on the ground, especially in riparian habitats along wetland habitats, and under wrack on ocean beaches. Sweeping flowers and other herbaceous vegetation, or beating foliage of trees and shrubs are also productive. Some species are best located by sifting leaf litter and detritus, or extracted from these and other substrates gathered in suitable habitats by using Berlese funnels or Winkler eclectors. Many species are attracted to lights at night.

143

FAUNA 4,628 SPECIES IN 567 GENERA

Amphichroum maculatum (Horn) (4.5–6.0 mm) is elongate, somewhat parallel, shiny, pale to dark yellowish brown, with surface alutaceous, densely punctate, and moderately pubescent. Head with pair of ocelli, narrower than prothorax medially, sides behind eyes with stout bristles in male, antennomeres 1–2 mostly glabrous, 7–10 not truncate apically, and apical maxillary palpomeres more or less conical in both sexes; gular sutures separate. Elytra not punctostriate, each sometimes paler with oblique oval spot. Hind tarsomere 5 longer than combined lengths of 1–4, 4 not distinctly bilobed and with apical fringe. Pollen-feeding adults found on flowers of herbs, shrubs, and trees. British Columbia to California. (3)

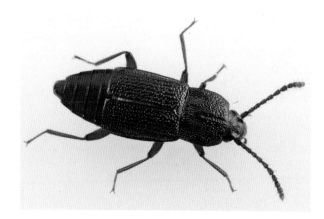

Phlaeopterus cavicollis (Fauvel) (6.3–9.2 mm) is elongate-oval, somewhat flattened and moderately punctate, and brown to dark reddish brown, with elytral basal and pronotal margins, and legs sometimes lighter. Head with pair of ocelli, inner margins of mandible with tooth and irregular row of setae, and antennomeres uniformly pubescent. Pronotum cordate, with lateral margins equally explanate before and after lateral pit. Elytra with humeral angles broadly rounded, not carinate in front. Adults under rocks at edges of snowfields, and on snow, feeding on windblown flies and other insects. Flight wings usually fully developed. Alaska to California, east to Colorado. (18)

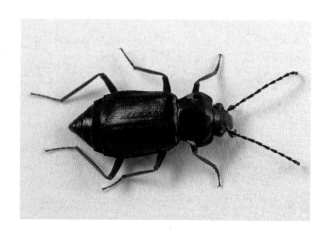

Tanyrhinus singularis Mäklin (4.2–5.4 mm) is elongate-ovate, robust, coarsely punctured, and shiny reddish brown, with paler legs and mouthparts. Head greatly elongate with distinct beak in front of moderately protruding eyes, then somewhat parallel behind, antennomeres 7–11 darker and somewhat expanded. Pronotum trapezoidal, widest at broadly arcuate base. Elytra long and somewhat inflated, each with nine deeply impressed punctostriae with coarse punctures, and conjointly oval apices exposing two or three tergites. Tarsi 5-5-5, front tarsomere 5 longer than 1–4 combined. Uncommon yet distinctive adults found in litter and moss, under logs, and on decaying mushrooms; also attracted to lights. Alaska to central California, possibly Arizona. (1)

Eusphalerum pothos Mannerheim (1.8–3.4 mm) is oval, mostly yellowish brown. Head with pair of ocelli, postocular carinae, and antennomeres 6–11 transverse. Lateral pronotal margins arcuate, narrowly reflexed, and disc with medial longitudinal groove. Elytra rugosely punctate, with apices truncate. Metasternum usually brownish. Male ventrites mostly black, 6 emarginate posteriorly. Hind tarsomere 5 longer than 1–4 combined, each somewhat dilated with long setae underneath. Pollen-feeding adults on flowers in forested habitats, especially during summer. Transcontinental; in West from Alaska to California, east to Alberta and Arizona. (19)

Lordithon kelleyi Mäklin (4.4–5.9 mm) is narrow, tapered posteriorly, smooth and shiny, and mostly yellowish to reddish yellow, with head and scutellum black, most of pronotum dark with pale margins. Basal three or four antennomeres pale. Elytra with dark, triangular scutellar spot extended along suture, with deeply notched medial spot. Abdomen usually dark with apex and bases of tergites 7–8 pale. Adults on fruiting fungal bodies, especially in spring. Transcontinental; in West south to Oregon and Wyoming. *Lordithon fungicola* Campbell (4.6–6.9 mm) elytra lack common scutellar spot; transcontinental, widespread in West. (9)

145

Sepedophilus species (1.2–3.2 mm) are broadly elongate-oval, usually uniformly brownish to reddish brown to blackish, broadest across pronotum or base of elytra, and clothed in dense pubescence. Elytra along suture longer or shorter than pronotum. Abdomen without ridges along sides, apex notched (male) or not (female). Front tibiae with distinct row of spines along outer margins. Adults, and probably larvae, eat fungus found in moldy forest litter and other decaying debris, under loose bark or on fleshy and polypore fungi. Some species run rapidly when disturbed, while others remain immobile. Transcontinental. (7)

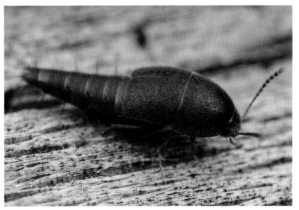

Tachinus basalis Erichson (4.0–5.5 mm) is moderately convex, dark brownish black to black with appendages and elytra paler. Eyes large and temples covered by anterior pronotal angles. Pronotum with microsculpture shallowly impressed with short, fine, and transverse waves. Elytral margins somewhat darker, apical margin irregularly so. Abdomen narrow, posterior margin of sternite 8 deeply notched (male) or with six fimbriate lobes separated by deep emarginations (female). In dung, rotting fungi, and carrion, especially during summer. Alaska to central California, west to Rockies; also in East. (26)

Habrocerus capillaricornis Gravenhorst (2.5–3.0 mm) is somewhat limuloid, compact, smooth, and shiny dark reddish brown with scattered long setae. Head without neck, antennal insertions on sides of labrum and concealed from view above, antennomeres 3–11 very slender. Elytra with epipleural carina. Abdomen with five (male) or six (female) segments visible. Hind femora concealed by metacoxae, tarsi 5-5-5. Adults occur in disturbed habitats among grass piles and compost heaps, in forest leaf litter and woody debris, and on fungi. Europe; widely established in North America. (1)

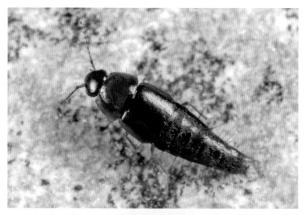

Aleochara pacifica (Casey) (4.0–8.0 mm) is narrowly slender and black with tarsi, labial and maxillary palps, and abdominal apex brown; appendages and elytra sometimes rusty brown. Head, pronotum, and elytra with hexagonal microsculpture distinctly convex. Adults on sea beaches in decaying seaweed, possibly carrion, teeming with fly larvae. Southern British Columbia to northern Baja California. *Aleochara littoralis* (Mäklin) (3.5–7.0 mm) similar in form and habitat preference, antennomeres 6–10 more transverse and more than twice as wide as long; microsculpture only slightly convex; last ventrite of male rounded posteriorly. Pacific and Atlantic coasts. (39)

146

Pontomalota opaca (LeConte) (2.5–3.5 mm) is elongate and mostly pale brownish yellow with a dark abdominal tergite on posterior half in population south of Point Conception, becoming darker overall northward. Pronotum with setae along midline directed longitudinally, not laterally. Elytra short, about as long as pronotum. Tarsi 4-5-5. Adults found on wet sand at night or under kelp wrack during day on ocean beaches, especially in summer, and prey on small fly larvae or scavenge dead arthropods. Alaska to southern California. (3)

Xenodusa reflexa (Walker) (5.3–6.4 mm) is robust, flattened, parallel-sided, finely pubescent and uniformly pale to dark reddish brown. Head half as wide as pronotum, eyes moderately sized, and antennomeres 3–10 cylindrical and subequal in length, 11 longest. Elytra at base as wide as prothorax, longer than pronotum. Abdominal tergites 3–5 with well-developed trichomes laterally, and long erect setae ventrally along sutures. Legs long, slender, with tarsi 4-5-5. Adults and larvae likely associated with ants (*Formica*, *Camponotus*). Transcontinental; in West south along Coast Ranges and Sierra Nevada of central California, and Rocky Mountains to Arizona and New Mexico. (3)

Trigonurus rugosus LeConte (4.5–5.0 mm) is elongate, flattened, somewhat parallel-sided, rugosely punctate, and moderately shiny reddish brown. Head coarsely, irregularly punctured, eyes moderately prominent, and antennae surpassing posterior pronotal angles. Pronotum densely rugosely punctate throughout, and not narrowed posteriorly; hypomeron coarsely punctate throughout. Elytra with irregular rows of punctures, especially posteriorly, with stria 8 punctures very confused and extending from apex nearly to humerus. Tarsi 5-5-5. Mountains above 1,500 meters. *Trigonurus caelatus* LeConte (4.0–5.0 mm) similar, pronotum not rugose on disc, with rows of punctures reaching elytral apices, stria 8 barely extending beyond middle. Western foothills and slopes. Both in Sierra Nevada of California. (5)

Scaphisoma castaneum Motschulsky (2.3–3.0 mm) is narrowly oval, and shiny black or reddish brown, with appendages, underside, and extreme apical portion of elytra reddish. Head more finely punctate than pronotum or elytra. Antennae slender, with outer six antennomeres elongate, antennomere 3 very short and narrowed basally. Pronotum wide. Scutellum not visible. Elytral punctures not seriate, sutural stria extending about halfway to humerus. Associated with fungi, including *Auriporia*, *Fomitopsis*, *Ganoderma*, *Pleurotus*, and *Polyporus*. British Columbia to California, west to Idaho and Utah. *Scaphisoma exiguum* Casey (0.7 mm) reddish brown, with elytra gradually paler behind middle, and legs pale. Oregon. (2)

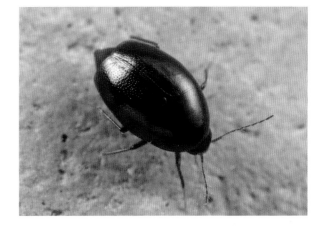

147

Batrisodes species (1.7–2.7 mm) are antlike and shiny reddish brown. Head with eyes present, a pair of deep pits connected by a curved sulcus, and antennal club of three antennomeres, apex with (male) or without (female) blunt tooth. Pronotal disc smooth between two or three longitudinal sulci, with a transverse groove connecting three posterior pits. Elytra short and convex. Abdomen rigid, segments fused. Legs long, femora clavate, hind tibiae bearing apical bundle of setae, and tarsomere 1 short, 2 and 3 long, and claws simple. Adults in decaying wood, mosses, leaf litter, or with ants; some attracted to lights. Widespread in western North America. (72 NA)

Piestus extimus Sharp (3.7–5.2 mm) is flat and moderately shiny light brown to black, with reddish-brown appendages and elytra. Head not narrowed behind eyes, with distinct V-shaped sulcus on frons. Antennae long (male), or barely surpassing elytral apices (female). Pronotum broader than head, lateral margins abruptly narrowed basally, and disc distinctly impressed along midline. Elytra quadrate and sulcate. Paratergites on tergites 1–5. Anterior tibiae spinose internally, tarsi 5-5-5, 5 about as long as 1–4 combined. In decaying cacti, *Dasylirion*, *Yucca*, and under bark of decaying logs. Southern Arizona to southern Mexico. (1)

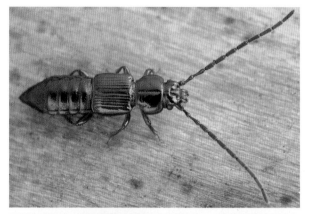

Bledius fenyesi Berhauer & Schubert (2.7–5.0 mm) is subcylindrical, with geniculate antennae. Mandible tridentate, antennomeres 3–7 rounded, without carina circling their apices. Pronotum with lateral margins narrowed posteriorly, and disc coarsely punctured with medial longitudinal impression; procoxal fissure closed, and prosternum lacking setigerous pit in front of each procoxa. Flight wings fully developed. Tibiae spinose and tarsi 4-4-4. Adults in well-decayed seaweed on beaches. San Francisco Bay, California, south to Baja California Sur. *Bledius monstratus* Casey (3.7–5.1 mm) similar, with elytra shorter and flight wings reduced. Coastal British Columbia to central California. (90 NA)

Bledius ferratus LeConte (4.0–8.0 mm) is subcylindrical, light to dark reddish brown, or yellowish brown with appendages somewhat paler, and sparsely punctured dorsally. Head darker, with mandibles bidentate and geniculate antennae. Pronotum with medial longitudinal impression and pubescence of varying lengths; procoxal fissure closed and prosternum lacking setigerous pit in front of each procoxa. Elytra with epipleural ridge present only on apices. Tibiae spinose and tarsi 4-4-4. Prefers moist, salt-encrusted mudflats populated by pickleweed (*Salicornia*). Coastal southern California to Baja California, western Mexico; also Mojave and Sonoran Deserts to western Texas. (90 NA)

Anotylus rugosus (Fabricius) (4.0–5.0 mm) is elongate, black, with reddish-brown appendages, pronotum and elytra sometimes brownish; appendages reddish brown. Head with opaque square area in front. Pronotum with four ridges, pair in middle divergent in front. Elytra combined wider than long, longer than pronotum. Abdomen basolateral ridges on tergite 1. Tarsomeres 1 and 2 nearly equal in length. Adults found on dung, carrion, and decaying vegetable matter. Europe; established from Pacific Northwest south to California; widespread in eastern North America. (18 NA)

Stenus comma LeConte (4.0–5.5 mm) is subcylindrical, coarsely and densely punctured, shiny black with distinct red or orange spot behind middle of each elytron, and tarsi dark brown. Head broad, eyes large, with protrusible labium. Antennae inserted on vertex, last three antennomeres forming weak club. Pronotum narrower than head, narrowed posteriorly, with lateral margins carinate. Elytra short and quadrate. Abdomen unmargined. Hind coxae conical, not expanded laterally. Adults on vegetation and rocks, or in debris in riparian habitats; specialist predators of springtails and other small arthropods. In West south to Oregon and Idaho. (167+ NA)

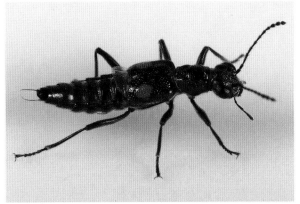

Astenus species (3.0–4.0 mm) are very slender and coarsely punctured dorsally. Head rectangular with distinct neck, labrum bidentate, eyes prominent, barely protruding and smaller than temples, with antennae filiform and apical maxillary palpomeres small. Prothorax oval, broadest subapically, with sides not carinate; prosternum expanded beneath and behind coxae. Elytra scarcely or longer than pronotum, carinate laterally. Paratergites on anterior abdominal segments, with male ventrite 6 deeply incised apically. Tarsi 5-5-5, 4 bilobed. Fleet-footed adults found in lakeshore litter and compost in various habitats and are often attracted to lights. Widespread in West. (7)

Lathrobium species (4.5–7.4 mm) are slender, narrowed posteriorly, and brown or black, sometimes with appendages lighter. Head and pronotum shiny and distinctly punctate without microsculpture. Temples length of small to moderately sized eye. Pronotum necklike in front, distinctly longer than wide, with disc impunctate at midline. Elytra without epipleural carinae. Abdomen with tergites 1–3 or 1–4 each weakly to strongly impressed basally. Hind tibiae with well-developed apical combs and front tarsomeres of males dilated. Adults mostly riparian, found among moss or damp forest litter; occasionally attracted to lights. Widespread in North America. (~10)

Paederus littorarius Gravenhorst (4.0–5.5 mm) is elongate, slender, sparsely clothed in erect setae, and bicolored reddish yellow and black. Head dark with distinct pale neck. Antennae blackish in middle, pale at base and very tip. Pronotum elongate, convex, slightly narrower than head, finely punctate, and sides slightly arched. Elytra with dark blue sheen, punctures coarse, deep, and dense. Abdomen narrower than elytra, parallel-sided, with last two tergites black. Legs with tarsomere 4 bilobed underneath. Under rocks in damp habitats in spring; produce defensive skin irritant, paederin. Canada and northern United States. (6)

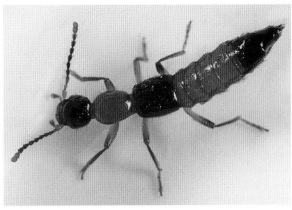

Gyrohypnus fracticornis (O.F. Müller) (6.4–8.2 mm) is elongate, parallel-sided, coarsely punctate, brownish black to black, elytra faintly metallic and, along with abdomen, often paler, especially abdominal apex and sides. Eye small, half as long as tempora, vertex impunctate, with antennae reddish brown, and mouthparts reddish. Pronotum long, slightly narrowed posteriorly, with lateral rows of coarse punctures. Elytra equal in length to pronotum at suture, each with two irregular rows of lateral punctures. Tarsi paler. Adults in decaying plant matter, including mammal droppings, grass clippings, and compost. Palearctic; widely distributed in North America. *Gyrohypnus angustatus* Stephens (5.0–7.0 mm) paler. British Columbia to southern California. (2)

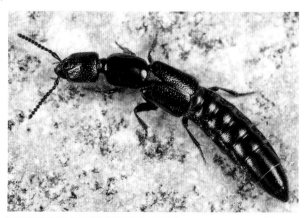

Cafius canescens Mäklin (6.0–10.0 mm) is elongate, robust, somewhat shiny black, with golden pubescence. Head densely alutaceous throughout. Pronotum not longer than wide, with two lines of coarse punctures on disc. Elytra coarsely and densely punctate. Abdomen with sternites 4–6 similarly punctured. *Cafius seminitens* Horn (9.0–11.0 mm) similar in form, slightly larger, with disc of head shiny, shorter antennae, sternite less densely punctured than 5 and 6, and silvery pubescence. Adults of both species active year-round, especially during spring and summer, found under wrack on sandy sea beaches. Alaska to Baja California Sur. (8)

Cafius luteipennis Horn (5.5–7.0 mm) has uniformly yellow-brown elytra. Head less finely and densely punctured dorsally than ventrally. Pronotum long, with areas outside of irregular double row of punctures sparsely punctate. Adults especially active during winter. *Cafius lithocharinus* LeConte (6.0–9.0 mm) head coarsely and sparsely punctured equally dorsally and ventrally; pronotum uniformly and densely punctate, with elytra pale along epipleural and apical margins, sometimes most or all of disc lighter. Adults active during summer. Both species under wrack along rocky coastal beaches from Washington to Baja California. (8)

Hairy Rove Beetle *Creophilus maxillosus villosus* Gravenhorst (11.0–23.0 mm) is large and shiny black with grayish vestiture on back of head, anterior pronotal angles, and pterothorax; abdominal tergites 4–5 mostly whitish gray. Pronotum smooth. Threatened beetles produce an irritating defensive chemical at tip of abdomen. Adults typically appear on carcasses in open, wooded, coastal, urban, and suburban habitats in late spring, again in late summer, and prey on maggots; rarely at dung or light; occasionally of forensic importance. North America to northern Central America. (1)

Dinothenarus saphyrinides Newton (10.0–15.0 mm) is elongate and robust, with dorsum of head, pronotum, and elytra metallic blue or purplish; basal antennomeres, legs, and last two abdominal segments reddish yellow-brown. Head and pronotum coarsely and densely punctate with fine, impunctate line medially. Elytra with punctures fine and dense. Southern British Columbia to California. *Dinothenarus luteipes* (LeConte) similar, but with head, pronotum, and elytra dark metallic green with abdomen mostly dark. California. (6)

Hadrotes crassus Mannerheim (11.0–17.0 mm) is elongate, robust, parallel-sided, mostly smooth and shiny, reddish brown to dark brownish black, and flightless. Head widest behind dorsal eyes. Pronotum nearly as long as wide, with lateral carinae distinct. Elytra quadrate, alutaceous, and finely wrinkled. Legs with tibiae spined on outer edges, tarsi 5-5-5, tarsomeres reddish, 1–4 dilated, hind tarsomeres 1 and 5 long, about equal in length. Nocturnal adults and larvae prey on crustaceans and insects. Adults found year-round on sea beaches, especially in spring and fall, under stones and large masses of rotten seaweed. Alaska to Baja California. (1)

Ocypus olens (Müller) (11.0–20.0 mm) is large, elongate, narrowed in front and back, and black with very short elytra. Prothorax underneath without distinct translucent process behind base of leg. Elytra shorter than pronotum at midline; flight wings reduced, scarcely longer than elytra. Flightless adults active year-round, especially in spring, found in open and forested habitats, often around human dwellings; attracted to carrion. Europe and Middle East; widespread in western North America; also New England to New York. *Ocypus aeneocephalus* (De Geer) (11.0–15.0 mm) with pubescence lighter, abdomen with setal bands and not reddish apically. Europe; British Columbia and Washington. (2)

Philonthus caeruleipennis (Mannerheim) (12.0–15.0 mm) is shiny black with shiny blue or green elytra; antennae and legs dark brown. Round, black head with few punctures, a distinct neck, and wide or wider than pronotum. Pronotum slightly longer than wide, lateral and posterior margins rounded, narrowing toward head. Elytra equal or slightly wider than pronotum, not overlapping, widest at apices. Abdomen iridescent, finely and densely setose. Adults active in summer, associated with fungi, compost, and decaying vegetation in or near wooded habitats; attracted to carrion pitfall traps. Widespread in North America and Europe. (114 NA)

Philonthus cruentatus **(Gmelin)** (5.8–8.3 mm) is elongate, moderately shiny brownish black to black. Head slightly wider than long, parallel-sided behind eyes. Pronotum about as long as wide, narrowed anteriorly, with discal rows containing five punctures; front coxae uniformly dark or inconspicuously, narrowly paler ventro-medially. Elytra coarsely punctate, each with medial apical reddish spot. Male front tarsomeres 1–4 dilated. Adults associated with cow and horse dung, also carrion. Widespread in North America. *Philonthus varians* (Paykull) (5.3–7.4 mm) elytra with red stripe parallel to suture, front coxae light reddish brown, and male front tarsomeres 1–3 dilated. Pacific Northwest to southern California. Both species native to Palearctic. (114 NA)

Quedius plagiatus **Mannerheim** (5.5–9.0 mm) is elongate, black or brownish black, pronotum and abdomen more or less iridescent, with tip of abdomen, apical margins of tergites, and appendages often reddish brown. Head broader than long, eyes convex and prominent, and antennae short with outer antennomeres transverse. Pronotum as long as wide or slightly shorter. Elytra at sides distinctly longer than pronotum at midline. Abdominal punctation on dorsum dense, save for impunctate area on middle of tergite 1. Adults found under bark of injured conifers, and prey on bark beetles. Holarctic; in West, south to mountains of central California, Arizona, and New Mexico. (91 NA)

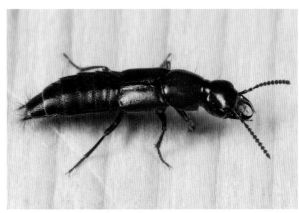

Pictured Rove Beetle *Thinopinus pictus* **LeConte** (12.0–22.0 mm) is a flightless, pale yellowish-brown rove beetle with striking black markings and elytra overlapping along suture. Variable cryptic coloration matches sand, with lighter beetles found on light beaches, and dark individuals found on darker sand. Larva similar to adult, except mandibles lack teeth, elytra absent, and thorax mostly black. Nocturnal adults and larvae found year-round on upper beaches, preying on beach hoppers and other small invertebrates; days spent in burrows or under wrack and debris. Alaska south to California. (1)

PLEOCOMIDAE (plē-ō-kōm-i-dē)
RAIN BEETLES

Pleocomids, all in the genus *Pleocoma*, are commonly known as rain beetles. The flightless, heavy-bodied females (p.22, Fig. 8a) of these apparently ancient insects are among the largest beetles in North America. Following sufficient amounts of rain or snow melt, the fully winged males take to the air in search of mates and track them by following the scent of pheromones released by the females waiting at the entrance of their burrows. Males engage in these mating flights at dawn or dusk, during evening rain showers, and occasionally late mornings or afternoons on sunny days following measurable amounts of rainfall or snowmelt. The timing of this activity varies depending on species, weather conditions, and elevation. Dozens of males may attempt to mate with the same female on the ground or down inside her burrow. Lacking functional mouthparts and the ability to feed, males draw their energy from fat stores acquired during the larval stage to maintain a high body temperature in cold damp weather. They attain an internal temperature of 95 ºF by shivering or vibrating their thoracic muscles. Males have only enough fat stores to afford them a few hours of flight time and die soon after mating, while the more sedentary females require less energy and may live for several months. After mating, the female crawls back down to a depth of 3 meters or more to lay 40–50 eggs in a spiral pattern at the end of the burrow. The newly hatched grubs use their powerful legs and jaws to tunnel through hard, compact soils as they feed externally upon roots of grasses, shrubs, and trees. The larvae of several Oregon species are pests of strawberries (*Fragaria*), pears (*Pyrus*), apples (*Malus*), and cherries (*Prunus*). *Pleocoma dubitabilis* Leach larvae are considered pests on Christmas tree farms. Other rain beetle larvae are sedentary feeders and must continually enlarge their smooth, hard-walled burrows to accommodate their increase in size. As they feed, the damaged rootlets form enlarged nodules, thus supplying the larvae with a sustained food supply. Unlike most scarab beetles (Scarabaeidae, p.172), which have three larval instars, *Pleocoma* grubs molt seven or more times, sometimes taking up to 13 years to reach maturity. Pupation occurs in a simple, elongate chamber in late summer or early fall. The thick layer of setae covering the underside of adult pleocomids probably functions to protect them from abrasion as they burrow up through the soil with their powerful, rakelike legs. *Pleocoma* are found mostly in mountainous habitats from southern Washington to northern Baja California. Because the females are flightless, their populations are more or less restricted to areas that were never subjected to glaciation or inundation by inland seas during the past two or three million years. The presence of rain beetles around San Francisco Bay, the Santa Monica Mountains, inland valleys, and some coastal areas of California subject to previous water inundation suggests that they somehow must have migrated into these areas.

FAMILY DIAGNOSIS Rain beetles are robust, broadly elongate-oval (male) or broadly oval (female), convex, shiny, and densely pubescent ventrally; smaller, fully winged males are easily distinguished from much larger and heavier flightless females. Males often uniformly reddish brown to black, sometimes bicolored; females generally uniformly reddish brown or bicolored. Head of male with clypeus deeply notched, armed with horn or tubercle; antennae with 11 antennomeres, club large (male) or small (female), antennomeres 4–8 lamellate and opposable. Functional mouthparts lacking. Prothorax with pronotum broad, evenly convex or somewhat depressed in front, and lateral margins carinate. Procoxal cavities open behind. Scutellum visible. Elytra convex, shiny, surface appearing smooth, ribbed, or leathery, with faintly or distinctly geminate (pairs of) punctostriae. Pygidium exposed. Legs with prominent, conical procoxae, rakelike protibiae; tarsi 5-5-5, with simple claws equal in size. Abdomen with six ventrites free.

SIMILAR FAMILIES The combination of their large size, densely pubescent undersides, horned heads, lamellate antennae with 11 antennomeres, open procoxal cavities, and activity during fall and winter rains and melting snow readily distinguish male pleocomids from all other scarabaeoid beetles.

COLLECTING NOTES When collecting rain beetles, expect conditions to be cold, wet, and uncomfortable. Mountain roads passing through their habitats may suddenly become impassable due to flooding, landslides, and fallen trees. Search for crepuscular or nocturnal males in flight during or just after the second or third soaking rains in fall, or later in winter when snow begins to melt. Although sometimes abundant with emergences consisting of hundreds of individuals, rain beetle colonies are often localized and easily overlooked. Day fliers are captured on the wing, while beetles flying during predawn or evening hours are readily attracted to black lights, streetlights, lit storefronts, and illuminated house windows. They are frequently attracted to the shimmering surfaces of rain puddles and swimming pools. Caged females releasing pheromones will also attract males. Females in their burrows are best located by following searching males.

FAUNA 29 SPECIES IN ONE GENUS

Southern Rain Beetle *Pleocoma australis* Fall (males 24.0–29.8 mm) is shiny black, with reddish-brown setae underneath. Antennal club with four long, curved lamellae. Pronotum with posterior angles distinct, rounded. Scutellum sparsely punctate. Elytral intervals finely, sparsely punctate, surfaces more or less rugose. Larvae feed on roots of canyon live oak (*Quercus chrysolepis*), possibly other trees, shrubs, and grasses. Males fly in coniferous forest, oak woodland, and chaparral habitats from predawn to dusk, or after dark in fog, light drizzle, or heavy showers during early fall rains in October and November. Transverse and Peninsular Ranges of southern California. (29)

Behren's Rain Beetle *Pleocoma behrensii* LeConte (males 21.0–27.0 mm) is black with a slightly brownish pronotum and clothed underneath with long yellowish or brownish-yellow setae. Antennal club with five long, curved lamellae; apex of antennomere 11 not reaching tip of 10. Pronotum coarsely punctate. Scutellum sparsely punctate. Elytra with geminate striae distinct, intervals rugose. Larvae eat roots of chaparral broom (*Baccharis pilularis*). Adult males fly after soaking rains in late October and November. Coast Ranges in San Francisco Bay region of northern California. (29)

Pleocoma dubitabilis leachi Linsley (males 22.0–23.0 mm) is bicolored, with pronotum chestnut black, and distinctly costate elytra light reddish brown. Antennal club with seven long lamellae. Pronotum glabrous medially. Scutellum setose. Elytral intervals confluently punctate, almost rugose. Southeast of Portland. Oregon rain beetle *Pleocoma oregonensis* Leach (males 19.0–25.0 mm) is similarly bicolored with relatively smooth elytra, and five lamellae in club. East of Cascades in northwestern Oregon. *Pleocoma dubitabilis dubitabilis* Davis (males 20.0–29.0 mm) uniformly dark brown to black. Larvae pests of strawberries and Christmas trees. Willamette Valley region in northwestern Oregon. Males of both subspecies fly from predawn to early evening during fall rains. Oregon. (29)

Pleocoma octopagina Robertson (males 21.0–31.0 mm) is clothed ventrally with dense reddish-golden pubescence, bicolored and shiny dorsally, with brownish-black elytra, and reddish-brown head, pronotum, and legs. Antennal club distinctively comprises eight lamellae. Pronotum slightly flattened anteriorly, with brownish-black infuscations on disc. Elytra finely, sparsely, and irregularly punctate, with vague striae. Male pre-dawn flights triggered by winter rains and snow in December and January in San Gabriel and Sierra Pelona Mountains along San Andreas Fault in various habitats, including chaparral, chaparral mixed with California live oak or piñon pine, and Jeffrey pine forest. Southern California. (29).

Black Rain Beetle *Pleocoma puncticollis* Rivers (males 26.0–31.0 mm) is uniformly shiny black with black or rusty black setae underneath. Antennal club with four long, curved lamellae. Posterior pronotal angles distinct. Scutellum sparsely punctate, glabrous. Geminate elytral striae indicated by rows of shallow, widely spaced punctures, intervals not rugose. Larvae feed on roots of ceanothus (*Ceanothus*). Males fly before dawn or on evenings during or after soaking rains from late November through early January. Chaparral habitats of Santa Monica, Santa Ana Mountains, Peninsular Ranges, and southern coastal plain of San Diego County, from southern California to northern Baja California. (29)

Pleocoma tularensis Leach (males 23.5–28.5 mm) is shiny black dorsally, and clothed in long brown pubescence ventrally. Antennal club of four lamellae preceded by two shorter platelike extensions and nearly reaching base of scape, with antennomere 3 nearly three times as long as 2. Pronotum more angulate laterally. Elytra with weakly developed geminate striae. Southern Sierra Nevada foothills. Fimbriate rain beetle *Pleocoma fimbriata* LeConte (males 27.0–34.0 mm) antennomere 3 barely twice length of 2, with antennal club shorter than base of scape, and pronotum more rounded laterally. Central Sierra Nevada foothills. Males of both species fly with onset of first fall rains in California. (29)

GEOTRUPIDAE (jē-o-trūp'-i-dē)
EARTH-BORING SCARAB BEETLES

Most adult geotrupids in western North America are nocturnal and are often attracted to lights. Their secretive lives are typically characterized by digging deep, nearly vertical burrows into the soil with entrances often marked by conspicuous "push-ups," or piles of soil or sand excavated from below. These burrows usually have one or more blind chambers that branch off and are supplied with plugs formed from fine bits of fungi, leaf litter, and other vegetation as food for the developing larvae. Adults do not care for their young and, once provisioned, soon leave the nest. Both the adults and larvae of most species can produce sound by stridulation. Little is known about the natural history of species in the Bolboceratinae. The subfamily Geotrupinae is represented in western North America by a single species known as the gopher beetle, *Ceratophyus gopherinus* Cartwright. Gopher beetles dig winding tunnels several feet in depth before excavating a horizontal chamber at the end, in which they pack dry surface sand, leaf litter, and twigs of chamise (*Adenostoma fasciculatum*), manzanita (*Arctostaphylos*), and California-lilac (*Ceanothus*). Although western geotrupids are typically of no economic importance, the gopher beetle was initially discovered in 1962 because it was damaging lawns and golf courses with its burrowing activities at Vandenberg Village, north of Lompoc in Santa Barbara County, California. The remaining 11 species of *Ceratophyus* all occur in the Old World and are distributed throughout the Palearctic Realm from Spain to China. It was initially thought that the gopher beetle was inadvertently introduced into California from Europe or Asia via ship's ballast, but it has never been found in either Europe or Asia. Recent research suggests that *Ceratophyus* once had a much broader distribution and that *C. gopherinus* is likely a relict species and is the only member of the genus that occurs in the New World.

156

FAMILY DIAGNOSIS Adult geotrupids are oval, broadly oval, or elongate-oval (*Ceratophyus*), strongly convex or almost hemispherical, usually uniformly yellowish or orangish brown, dark brown, sometimes black, or distinctly bicolored (*Bolbocerosoma pusillum townesi* Howden), never with metallic reflections. Head prognathous; often with distinct horn, tubercle, or ridge; mandibles conspicuous. Antennae with 11 antennomeres, 9–11 lamellate and opposable, with 9 large and cup-shaped, club equal in length or about half as long (*Ceratophyus*) as all previous antennomeres. Pronotum broad, convex, wider or subequal in width to base of elytra, with or without tubercles, costae, horns, grooves, and excavations; procoxae closed. Scutellum visible. Elytra convex, striate, and completely concealing abdomen. Legs adapted for digging, tarsi 5-5-5, with simple claws equal in size. Abdomen with six ventrites free.

SIMILAR FAMILIES
- rain beetles (Pleocomidae, p.153)—male antennal club with 4–8 long antennomeres, females flightless
- sand-loving scarab beetles (Ochodaeidae, p.167)—antennae with 10 antennomeres, eyes bulging, middle tibiae with edge of one spur pectinate
- hybosorid beetles (Hybosoridae, p.169)—antennae with 10 antennomeres
- scarab beetles (Scarabaeidae, p.172)—antennae with 10 or fewer antennomeres

COLLECTING NOTES Adults of nocturnal earth-boring scarab beetles (*Bolboceras*, *Bolborhombus*, *Eucanthus*, and *Odonteus*) are attracted to lights. *Bolbocerosoma* is sometimes found during the day flying low in grassland habitats in southeastern Arizona. *Bolbocerastes* and *Bolborhombus* sometimes burrow into soil at the base of buildings beneath night lights to which they are attracted. Look for push-ups that mark the burrow entrances of *Bolbocerastes*, *Bolbelasmus*, *Ceratophyus*, *Eucanthus*, and *Odonteus* along paths, track roads, and other open patches of ground, especially in sandy habitats after spring and summer thundershowers.

FAUNA 56 SPECIES IN 11 GENERA

Bolbelasmus hornii Rivers (9.8–14.0 mm) is oval, very convex, light to dark reddish brown, shiny. Head with clypeal margin unevenly arcuate, almost truncate; eye not completely divided by canthus; frons with long cylindrical or short conical horn (male), or transverse carina (female). Pronotum with four tubercles, inner pair in front of outer pair (male) or with median arched ridge flanked by pair of round tubercles (female). Elytra with seven striae between suture and humeri. Legs with middle coxae narrowly separated. Nocturnal adults attracted to lights in late winter and early spring. Chaparral habitats from northern California to northern Baja California. (1)

Bolbocerastes imperialis Cartwright (11.0–19.0 mm) is oval, very convex, and shiny yellow-brown to reddish brown, and pubescent ventrally. Male clypeal horn nearly cylindrical in cross section, narrowly truncate at tip; female with anterior horn narrower than median horn, back of median horn punctate. Pronotum without pair of distinct ridges on each side. Elytral bases margined, first striae terminate at scutellum. Middle and hind tibiae obliquely truncate apically. Burrows marked by push-ups near bases of creosote bush (*Larrea tridentata*) and honey mesquite (*Prosopis glandulosa*) from spring through summer; also at lights. Deserts of southern California and Baja California to Utah, Colorado, and western Texas, south to Mexico. (2)

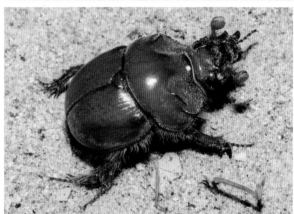

157

Bolbocerastes regalis (Cartwright) (10.0–20.0 mm) is oval, very convex, yellow-brown to dark brown, shiny, setose ventrally. Male clypeal horn is flat, not round in cross section, broadly truncate at tip; female with broad anterior and median horns equal in width, back of median horn smooth. Pronotum with distinct pair of sharp ridges on each side, inner ridge doubly angulate. Base of elytra distinctly margined, first striae ending at scutellum. Middle and hind tibiae obliquely truncate apically. Push-ups in moist sand appear from late winter through summer, most common in spring; attracted to lights. Desert habitats of southern California, Arizona, Nevada, and northwestern Sonora. (2)

Bolborhombus angulus Robinson (7.0–11.0 mm) is oval, very convex, reddish yellow-brown, shiny. Head without median frontal horn in both sexes, clypeus distinctly ridged along anterior margin, anterior angles not connected to horns by ridges; mandibles rounded externally. Pronotum with sharp ridge approximately parallel to anterior margin, space between with pit located behind each eye; lateral margins serrate. Elytra not margined at base, first two striae end at scutellum. Nothing is known of larval habits. Nocturnal adults attracted to lights in summer. Grasslands and oak-juniper woodlands. Southeastern Arizona and Big Bend region of Texas; likely in adjacent Mexico. (3)

Bolborhombus sallei (Bates) (11.0–18 mm) is oval, very convex, and dull reddish yellow to dark brown. Head without median frontal horn in both sexes, clypeus not distinctly ridged along anterior margin, parallel ridge connects anterior angle with tip of horn; mandibles rounded externally. Pronotum with rounded ridge approximately parallel to anterior margin, space between with pit located behind each eye; lateral margins serrate. Elytra not margined basally, striae 1 and 2 interrupted by scutellum. Adults attracted to lights in oak-juniper woodlands during summer. Southern Arizona, east to Kansas and Texas, south to Mexico. (3)

Eucanthus greeni Robinson (9.7–13.4 mm) is broadly oval, convex, light to dark reddish brown, smooth and shiny between punctures. Eye partially divided by canthus; canthus with anterior margin nearly straight, outer angle not produced forward. Antennal club longer than ventral portion of eye. Pronotum with outer third of anterior margin virtually straight; coarse punctures mostly along margins and impressed areas; impressed midline not extended past median transverse ridge. Elytra each with five punctostriae before humerus. In burrows and at lights in open habitats, grasslands during summer. Alberta and Manitoba to southeastern Arizona and New Mexico. (2)

Eucanthus lazarus (Fabricius) (6.4–14.0 mm) is broadly oval, convex, uniformly orange-brown to dark red-brown, smooth and shiny between punctures. Eye partially divided by canthus; canthus with anterior margin nearly straight, outer angle not produced forward. Antennal club longer than ventral portion of eye. Pronotum with outer third of anterior margin evenly curved; coarse punctures mostly along margins and impressed areas; impressed midline not extended past median transverse ridge. Elytra each with five punctostriae before humerus. Attracted to lights in late spring and summer in open habitats. Arizona to South Dakota, Ontario, and northern Georgia. (2)

Odonteus obesus LeConte (6.5–12.0 mm) is oval, very convex, dark reddish brown to black, shiny, with long golden pubescence on underside, legs, and margins of head and pronotum. Head with eyes entirely divided by canthus, with slender curved horn sometimes extending backward over pronotum to scutellum (male), or low transverse ridge (female). Pronotum with ridge on each side and U-shaped protuberance across middle (male) or four swellings (female). Adults burrow in wooded areas marked by push-ups; attracted to lights at night year-round, especially in spring and early summer. Forested montane habitats from British Columbia to California, east to Colorado. (1)

Gopher Beetle *Ceratophyus gopherinus* Cartwright (15.0–23.0 mm) is elongate-oval, black, moderately shiny, and very setose underneath. Male with sharp, upturned clypeal horn opposing equally sharp, forward-protruding pronotal horn; horns less developed in female. Mandibles conspicuous with apices deeply bidentate. Pronotum wide, sides broadly rounded. Elytral striae moderately deep between suture and humeri. Legs long, protibiae with six teeth, middle and hind tibiae curved. Nocturnal adults dig deep, winding tunnels in winter and spring and provision them with plant materials as food for their young. Known only from scrub oak thickets in western Santa Barbara County, California. (1)

TROGIDAE (troj'-i-dē)
HIDE BEETLES

Trogids are dull, costate or warty, brownish, grayish, or blackish beetles that are often covered with mud and mites. They are unique among all scarabaeoid beetles in that they feed primarily on keratin, a fibrous protein that is a key structural component of not only fur and feathers, but also the sheaths covering horns and hooves. Both adults and larvae of most *Omorgus* and *Trox* scavenge this protein from the dry remains of animal carcasses during the final stage of decomposition. Some species, however, appear to prefer accumulations of feathers or hair associated with bird nests or rodent burrows, or fur-laden owl pellets and carnivore feces. When alarmed, adults feign death by pulling in their legs and remaining motionless for long periods of time to avoid detection. Encrusted with debris, they look very much like a pebble, clump of earth, or some other inanimate object. Adults in both genera stridulate when disturbed, making chirping sounds by rubbing a patch of ridges on the *propygidium* against the inner margin of the elytra. Eggs are laid beneath carcasses where the developing larvae dig vertical burrows into which they drag bits of skin, fur, and other keratin sources to feed.

FAMILY DIAGNOSIS Adult hide beetles are oval to elongate-oval, strongly convex, roughly sculptured, and black, usually *tomentose*, with a coating of reddish-brown or brown-gray, matted, woolly setae, or *tomentum*, and frequently encrusted with dirt; underside flat. Head hypognathous with mandibles inconspicuous; eyes not divided by canthus; antennae with 10 antennomeres, 8–10 lamellate and opposable, with club compact and velvety. Pronotum quadrate or rectangular with lateral margins carinate. Procoxal cavities closed behind. Scutellum visible, arrowhead- or hatchet-shaped (*Omorgus*), or more or less oval (*Trox*). Elytra completely conceal abdomen, surfaces with complete or broken carinae, occasionally covered with rows of raised, sometimes shiny, wartlike tubercles. Legs with tarsi 5-5-5, with simple claws equal in size. Abdomen with five ventrites free.

SIMILAR FAMILIES

- enigmatic scarab beetles (Glaresidae, p.162)—very small, eyes divided by canthus
- scarab beetles (Scarabaeidae, p.172—abdomen with six ventrites

- *Eleates*, *Megeleates* (Tenebrionidae, p.360)—tarsi 5-5-4, antennae not abruptly clubbed

COLLECTING METHODS *Omorgus* and *Trox* are most commonly found at lights, or under old, dried carrion. Check the soil carefully beneath carrion or hair-packed owl pellets and carnivore scats for larval burrows and soil-encrusted adults. A few species are found only in association with the nests and burrows of birds and mammals, respectively.

FAUNA 51 SPECIES IN TWO GENERA

Omorgus carinatus (Loomis) (12.0–15.0 mm) elongate-oval, coarsely sculptured dorsally, and dull black with tomentose patches on pronotum and elytra. Head with two distinct tubercles in front. Pronotum tomentose, with distinct ridges, tubercles, and deep depressions on disc, and posterior angles distant from prominent elytral humeri. Scutellum arrowhead-shaped. Elytra without tubercles, each with four distinct and uninterrupted carinae extending from base to apical declivity. Middle and hind legs with tarsomeres carinate and rugose, excavated ventrally and on sides basally. Adults attracted to lights. Southern Arizona east to southwestern Texas, south to Chihuahua. (9)

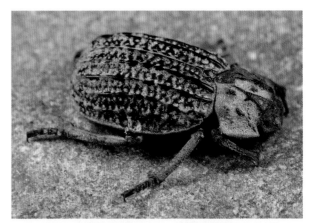

Omorgus punctatus (Germar) (10.5–15.0 mm) is elongate-oval, mostly black, with grayish tomentum sometime reddish. Head with two tubercles. Pronotum distinctly sculptured with ridges and deep depressions, with sides notched just before base, or not. Scutellum arrowhead-shaped. Elytra patchily tomentose, each with three elevated rows of large, shiny black tubercles. Middle and hind tarsi ridged and rugose, sometimes weakly or at base only. Montana to eastern California, south to central Mexico. *Omorgus tessellatus* (LeConte) (14.0–17.0 mm) head with tubercles fused, all elytral tubercles about equal in elevation, and tarsomeres smooth. Both species attracted to carrion and light. Arizona to Kansas and Texas, south to Mexico. (9)

Omorgus suberosus (Fabricius) (11.1–14.1 mm) is elongate-oval, convex, and mostly covered in grayish tomentum with rows of alternating shiny black and pale patches on odd elytral intervals. Head with two tubercles. Pronotum relatively smooth and without ridges anteriorly; margins fringed with moderately long, fine setae and notched laterally just before posterior angle. Scutellum arrowhead-shaped. Elytra almost smooth with weakly developed intervals and bare tubercles appearing tessellated, with humeri distinct. Western United States. (9)

Trox atrox LeConte (6.0–8.5 mm) with clypeus finely, but not densely, punctured. Pronotum glabrous and smooth, usually without trace of median depression, and posterior angles acute, with margins fringed with reddish yellow-brown setae, each longer than width of elytral intervals. Scutellum oval. Elytra with intervals equally flat, each with single row of equidistant yellowish setae, and reflexed lateral margins glabrous. Hind tibiae with serrations continuous to apex. At lights; associated with nests of ground squirrels and burrowing owls; occasionally at carrion. Western North America south to Durango. (9)

Trox gemmulatus Horn (9.2–11.8 mm) with head lacking tubercles and base of antennae with reddish setae. Scutellum oval. Pronotum tomentose with pair of prominent longitudinal ridges separated by distinct depression, sides not constricted basally, posterior margin sinuate before angles. Elytra each with four distinct and sharp costae from base to declivity. Adults emerge after late fall rains to feed and mate on coyote scat in coastal chaparral habitats. Larvae dig vertical burrows beneath fur-laden scat. Southern California to Baja California. (9)

Trox plicatus Robinson (7.5–9.0 mm) has pair of tubercles on head, sometimes faint. Pronotum with prominent pair of medial longitudinal ridges, lateral margins fringed with long setae. Scutellum oval. Elytra shiny or tomentose, all intervals with regular clumps of pale-yellow setae, intervals 3 and 5 weakly, narrowly, and continuously convex, with upturned lateral margins without tubercles and fringed with bunches of 2–10 setae. On owl pellets and at lights during summer in montane habitats. Southeastern Arizona to western Texas, south to Puebla and Veracruz. (9)

Trox scaber (Linnaeus) (5.0–7.0 mm) with pronotal impressions distinct and antennal club reddish brown. Elytral interval 3, sometimes 5, slightly elevated at least basally, with alternating intervals of longer and shorter patches of reddish-brown setae. Hind tibia weakly emarginate before apex. On carrion, owl pellets, feathers; in nests. Widespread. *Trox fascifer* LeConte (5.5–7.0 mm) setal fringe short on weakly sculpted pronotum, elytral setal clumps uniform in size, and hind tibia strongly emarginate before apex. British Columbia to California. *Trox aequalis* Say (5.0–6.0 mm) similar, hind tibia feebly emarginate before apex. Rocky Mountain states. (9)

GLARESIDAE (gla-rēs'-i-dē)
ENIGMATIC SCARAB BEETLES

The family Glaresidae includes about 55 similar species, all in the genus *Glaresis*, that are distributed on all major continents except Australia. They are enigmatic because only the adults are known, and little else of their habits, other than they are nocturnal, usually found in dry, sandy habitats, and are attracted to lights. When handled, they can produce a faint squeaking sound. An examination of their mouthparts suggests that the adults are likely to eat subterranean fungi. Once part of the family Trogidae, Glaresidae is believed to be one of the most primitive families of scarabaeoid beetles. Western glaresids are sometime abundant at lights in arid, sandy desert habitats, but some species occur in chaparral and coniferous forests.

FAMILY DIAGNOSIS Adult glaresids are small, oblong-oval, and light brown, with moderately dense, short setae. Head without horns or tubercles, mandibles barely projecting beyond clypeus; clubbed antennae with 10 antennomeres, 8–10 lamellate and opposable, with club velvety and compact; eyes divided by canthus. Procoxal cavities closed behind. Scutellum visible. Elytra convex, long and fully concealing abdomen, each with 10 distinct carinae. Wings fully developed. Legs with meso- and metatibiae with two apical spurs, metafemora and metatibia enlarged and obscuring abdomen; tarsi 5-5-5, with simple claws equal in size. Abdomen with five ventrites free.

SIMILAR FAMILIES
- earth-boring scarab beetles (Geotrupidae, p.156)—larger; 11 antennomeres
- hide beetles (Trogidae)—larger, eyes not divided by canthus (p.159)
- sand-loving scarab beetles (Ochodaeidae, p.167)—eyes not divided by canthus, one mesotibial spur pectinate
- scavenger scarab beetles (Hybosoridae, p.169)—club antennomeres fold tightly together

COLLECTING NOTES Look for *Glaresis* at lights at night, especially in dry, sandy habitats in deserts, as well as chaparral and coniferous forests in late spring and summer.

FAUNA 25 SPECIES IN ONE GENUS

Glaresis ecostata Fall (3.5–5.2 mm) is oblong-oval, convex, reddish brown, with short, stout setae dorsally. Head smooth with few small tubercles; anterior clypeal margin straight, upturned, angles bluntly pointed. Outer margin of middle tibiae sinuate with six spines from middle to apex. Hind leg with outer margin of tibia bearing a large projection; posterior margin of trochanter with two large teeth and one small tooth. Adults attracted to lights mostly in spring. Sandy desert habitats from southern California to New Mexico and Sonora. (21)

Glaresis inducta Horn (2.7–3.3 mm) is oblong-oval, convex, reddish brown, with short, stout setae dorsally. Head with tubercles; anterior clypeal margin slightly emarginate, slightly upturned. Middle leg with outer margin of tibia sinuate with strong spines from middle to apex. Hind leg with outer margin of tibia with strong projection; posterior surface of trochanter with two spines, inner larger than outer, sometimes variable. Adults are attracted to lights in summer. Sandy habitats from Arizona to Wisconsin, Indiana, and Texas. Most widespread Nearctic species of *Glaresis*. (21)

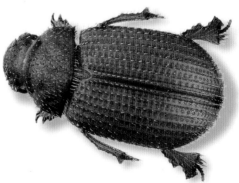

DIPHYLLOSTOMATIDAE (dī-fil-ō-stōm-at'-i-dē)
FALSE STAG BEETLES

This small family of beetles consists of the single genus *Diphyllostoma*. All three known species of diphyllostomatids are endemic to the western foothills of California's Sierra Nevada. Very little is known of their natural history. The diurnal males are sometimes found on early spring and summer mornings perched on vegetation waving their antennae or flying low in a zigzagging pattern as they apparently search for the flightless females. Female diphyllostomatids (p.22, Fig. 8b), with their shorter legs, vestigial wings, and greatly reduced eyes, probably release a pheromone to attract males. The larvae are undescribed and likely develop in the soil.

FAMILY DIAGNOSIS Adult false stag beetles are elongate, somewhat cylindrical, and more or less uniformly dark brown to reddish brown (*D. fimbriatum*) or bicolored (*D. linsleyi*, *D. nigricollis*) with dark head and pronotum with lighter elytra. Head prognathous; mandibles prominent, extending past labrum, and notched (*D. fimbriatum*, *D. nigricollis*) or rounded (*D. linsleyi*) apically; eyes large (male) or small (female); eye canthus absent; antennae straight with 10 tomentose antennomeres, 8–10 lamellate and not opposable. Pronotum plain, weakly convex, base narrower than elytral base. Procoxal cavities closed. Scutellum visible. Elytra long (male) or elongate-oval (female), somewhat convex, and concealing abdomen, with surface weakly punctostriate; wings well developed only in male. Legs long, with fore tibiae without apical spurs, serrate on outer margins; hind tarsi longer (male) or shorter (female) than tibiae; tarsi 5-5-5, with simple claws equal in size. Abdomen with seven ventrites free.

SIMILAR FAMILIES
- stag beetles (Lucanidae, p.164)—antennae usually geniculate, abdomen with five ventrites
- scarab beetles (Scarabaeidae, p.172)—lamellae of club opposable, abdomen with six ventrites

COLLECTING NOTES Although sometimes locally abundant, diphyllostomatids are seldom encountered. Search for males flying low over the ground during the day in late spring and summer, especially early in the morning, in late afternoon, and at dusk. They are occasionally attracted to lights or may stumble into pitfall traps. Inspecting debris floating down flumes and streams flowing through diphyllostomatid habitats may produce males. Females are found by following males, or by searching under debris.

163

FAUNA THREE SPECIES IN ONE GENUS

Diphyllostoma linsleyi (Fall) (5.0–9.0 mm) male is elongate, cylindrical, sparsely pubescent dorsally with fringe of long setae along sides of prothorax and elytra, and dark brown with elytra reddish brown. Head with frontal ridges converging anteriorly, and mandibles distinctly rounded apically. Pronotum narrowly margined along sides, disc finely and sparsely punctate. El Dorado County. *Diphyllostoma nigricollis* (Fall) (6.5–8.0 mm) similarly bicolored, with mandibular apices notched, and tarsomeres more than three times longer than wide; Fresno County. *Diphyllostoma fimbriata* (Fall) (7.0–7.5 mm) uniformly dark or reddish brown, with mandibles less strongly notched, and tarsomeres less than three times longer than wide; Tulare County. All species in California. (3)

LUCANIDAE (lū-kan'-i-dē)
STAG BEETLES

The common name "stag beetle" is derived from the large antlerlike mandibles found in some males, such as the giant stag beetle in eastern North America, *Lucanus elaphus*. Mandible size varies within a species, is directly proportionate to the size of the body, and is regulated by genetic and environmental factors. Males use their oversized mouthparts to engage in grappling contests with rival males to mate with a nearby female. In western North America, most stag beetles are restricted to coastal forests in moist, wooded mountain canyons where dead, decomposing wood is plentiful. A few species are adapted for living in arid sagebrush or dune habitats with plenty of decaying wood. Females lay their eggs in crevices of logs and stumps, and among roots of both deciduous and coniferous trees. The C-shaped grubs eat only decaying wood and thus are not a threat to homes or other structures. While most species of lucanids prefer to breed in hardwoods, the larvae of both western species of *Ceruchus* utilize conifers.

FAMILY DIAGNOSIS Adults lucanids are elongate, somewhat flattened (*Lucanus, Platyceroides, Platyceropsis, Platycerus*) to nearly cylindrical (*Ceruchus, Sinodendron*), usually dull, shiny black or reddish brown, sometimes with a hint of a coppery or bluish sheen (*Platyceroides, Platycerus*). Head prognathous, mandibles prominent and visible from above (except *Sinodendron*) and somewhat more developed in males; ocular canthus present; antennae with 10 antennomeres; antennae straight (*Ceruchus, Sinodendron*) or geniculate (*Lucanus, Platyceroides, Platyceropsis, Platycerus*); last three or four antennomeres lamellate and not opposable; club thick and velvety (except *Ceruchus, Sinodendron*). Pronotum narrower at base than elytra, and somewhat convex, or with transverse ridge or prominence (*Sinodendron*); procoxae closed. Scutellum visible. Elytra finely or coarsely punctate, with or without distinctly impressed striae. Legs with outer margin of front tibiae dentate or serrate, tarsi 5-5-5, with simple tarsal claws equal in size. Abdomen with five ventrites (portion of sixth visible in *Platycerus*) free.

SIMILAR FAMILIES
- ground beetles (Carabidae, p.88)—antennae filiform
- scarab beetles (Scarabaeidae, p.172)—club lamellae fold to form compact club
- powderpost beetles (Bostrichidae, p.295)—antennal club not elongate, mouthparts hypognathous, pronotum usually with tubercles or small horns
- bark-gnawing beetles (Trogossitidae, p.414)—antennal club symmetrical

COLLECTING NOTES Western stag beetles are active from late spring through midsummer in moist, wooded habitats, especially near bodies of water, and occasionally in open sandy spaces and coastal beaches. Some species are encountered during the day resting on vegetation (*Platyceroides, Platycerus*), while others fly at dusk and early evening (*Lucanus*), or are found walking on downed logs, climbing up tree trunks, or crawling over the ground at night. Both adults and larvae are found in decaying wood, especially beneath the loose bark of rotten logs and stumps. Adults are usually collected by hand, netted on the wing, or beaten and swept from vegetation; a few are occasionally attracted to lights at night. *Platyceroides agassii* is attracted to fresh asphalt.

FAUNA 33 SPECIES IN NINE GENERA

Punctate Stag Beetle *Ceruchus punctatus* LeConte
(8.0–16.0 mm) is elongate, cylindrical, and shiny black.
Head as wide as pronotum, mandibles prominent,
especially in male; lamellate antennae straight. Pronotum
twice as wide as long, coarsely punctured, sides straight
(male) or somewhat arcuate (female). Elytra parallel-sided,
coarsely punctured with 2–3 fine, weakly impressed striae
near suture. Adults and larvae found beneath loose bark
of decaying white fir (*Abies concolor*) and ponderosa pine
(*Pinus ponderosa*) logs. Coniferous forests of Cascades
and Sierra Nevada from British Columbia to California, also
Rockies in Idaho and Colorado. (2)

Striated Stag Beetle *Ceruchus striatus* LeConte
(13.0–19.0 mm) is elongate, cylindrical, and shiny black.
Head is as wide as pronotum, mandibles prominent,
especially in male; lamellate antennae straight. Pronotum
twice as wide as long, coarsely punctured, sides straight
(male) or somewhat feebly sinuate (female). Elytra deeply
striate, interstriae convex and coarsely punctured. Adults
and larvae found under loose bark of decaying mountain
hemlock (*Tsuga mertensiana*) and coast redwood (*Sequoia
sempervirens*) logs. Coastal coniferous forests from
southern British Columbia to northern California. (2)

Rugose Stag Beetle *Sinodendron rugosum* Mannerheim
(11.0–18.0 mm) is elongate, cylindrical, and shiny black
with pronotum and elytra coarsely and irregularly punctate.
Head with well-developed horn (male) or tubercle
(female); mandibles not projecting in front of head in
either sex; lamellate antennae straight. Pronotum with
distinct transverse ridge with (male) or without (female) a
medial tubercle. Adults and larvae found beneath bark of
wet, rotten hardwood logs, especially alder (*Alnus*), ash
(*Fraxinus*), maple (*Acer*), California laurel (*Umbellularia
californica*), and oak (*Quercus*). Adults occasionally fly on
warm summer afternoons. Coastal forests and wooded
mountain canyons from British Columbia to southern
California, east to Idaho. (1)

Cottonwood Stag Beetle *Lucanus mazama* (LeConte) (24.0–32.0 mm) is elongate, weakly convex, glabrous dorsally, and dull (male) or moderately shiny (female), and black or reddish black. Head coarsely (male) or rugosely punctate (female), with eye partly divided in front by canthus, lamellate antennae strongly geniculate; mandibles larger, more arcuate in male. Pronotum wider than long, with lateral margin angulate at middle. Elytra finely punctured. Adults and larvae found in rotting oak stumps in Mexico. Adults begin flying at dusk and are attracted to lights. Utah and Arizona, east to Colorado and New Mexico, south to Sonora and Chihuahua. (1)

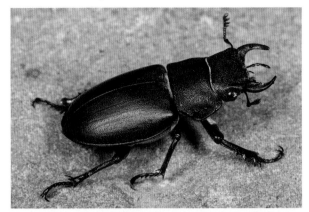

Oregon Stag Beetle *Platycerus oregonensis* Westwood (8.3–10.3 mm) is elongate-oval, moderately convex, head black, pronotum and elytra shiny blue or blue-black. Mandibles distinct. Antennal clubs each with three (female) or four (male) lamellae. Elytra punctostriate, interstriae punctate. Middle and hind tibiae without spines. Adults and larvae beneath loose bark of decaying *Acer*, *Alnus*, *Arbutus*, *Eucalyptus*, *Fraxinus*, *Heteromeles*, *Quercus*, and *Umbellularia*. Diurnal adults encountered flying or resting on vegetation in summer. Coastal forests and interior oak woodlands from British Columbia to central California. (4)

Platyceroides keeni (Casey) (9.8–14.0 mm) is oblong, convex, and shiny dark chestnut. Head with mandibles small, geniculate antennae lamellate. Pronotum broadest at middle, coarsely and sparsely punctate; lateral margins oblique or slightly sinuate to obtuse posterior angles. Elytra punctostriate, interstriae convex, humeri obtuse. Both sexes flightless. Middle and hind tibiae robust, armed with short spines. Larvae in decaying alder (*Alnus*) and poplar (*Populus*) logs washed up on coastal dunes. Adults on or under driftwood, or burrowing under logs in spring. Coastal southern British Columbia to Humboldt Bay, California. (16)

Platyceroides latus (Fall) (9.0–11.0 mm) is elongate-oval, convex and coarsely punctate dorsally. Head and mandibles small, confluently punctured, with antennae geniculate, clypeus thickened anteriorly, strongly declivous before labrum, and width across eyes and genae subequal in male. Pronotum broadest just behind middle, with posterior angles rectangular or slightly acute. Elytra not distinctly striate, with punctures somewhat arranged in rows. Middle and hind tibiae long, narrow. Flight wings present (male) or absent (female). Larvae develop in incense-cedar (*Libocedrus decurrens*). Adults fly at dusk and in evening. Sierra Nevada of northern and Central California. (16)

OCHODAEIDAE (ok-ō-dē′-i-dē)
SAND-LOVING SCARAB BEETLES

Ochodaeids resemble small bolboceratine earth-boring scarab beetles (Geotrupidae, p.156), but are easily distinguished by their antennal and metatibial spur characters. About 80 species and 12 genera of ochodaeids are found in all biogeographic regions except Australasia. Nearly all of the 21 species of North American ochodaeids are nocturnal and prefer sandy soils in arid or semiarid habitats, such as deserts and grasslands. However, the distinctly bicolored and seldom encountered *Parochodaeus californicus* Horn is diurnal and occurs in chaparral habitats of the southern California coastal plain. Very little is known of ochodaeid natural history, which is surprising given that the adults are often abundant at lights. They are capable of stridulation and burrow into the soil, where it has been suggested that they might feed on fungi. For example, adult *Pseudochodaeus estriatus* were found to have numerous spores of a basidiomycete fungus resembling those of puffballs in their digestive tracts. The larvae of all ochodaeids, except for *Pseudochodaeus estriatus*, remain unknown. In this species, the larva's worn mandibles, well-developed legs and claws, and body setation all suggest that its food is not provided by an adult, as is the case with some scarabaeoid beetles.

FAMILY DIAGNOSIS Adult ochodaeids are more or less round or elongate (*Pseudochodaeus*), somewhat convex, reddish brown, and covered with short erect hairs. Head prognathous, with mandibles distinct and eyes bulging; clypeus with or without central tubercle. Antennae with 10 antennomeres, 8–10 lamellate and opposable with 8 somewhat cup-shaped and surrounding 9, club compact and velvety. Procoxal cavities closed behind. Scutellum visible and rounded. Elytra with one (*Pseudochodaeus*) or more punctostriae; apices toothlike and interlocking with corresponding tubercles on posterior margin of propygidium (*Parochodaeus*), or not so modified. Middle and hind tibiae both with outer spurs pectinate (*Pseudochodaeus*), or with pectinate outer spur on middle tibia only. Tarsi 5-5-5, claws simple, equal. Propygidium plain (*Codocera, Cucochodaeus*), long with parallel-sided groove medially (*Xenochodaeus*), or short with groove trapezoidal, with edges converging posteriorly (*Neochodaeus*). Abdomen with six ventrites free.

SIMILAR FAMILIES
- earth-boring scarab beetles (Geotrupidae, p.156)— antennae with 11 antennomeres, outer metatibial spur not notched
- scarab beetles (Scarabaeidae, p.172)—outer metatibial spur not notched

167

COLLECTING NOTES Adult sand-loving scarabs are typically nocturnal and attracted to lights in summer, although some specimens are found in Malaise trap and leaf litter samples. Individuals are occasionally dug from burrows marked by push-ups of soil on bare ground along forested trails and road tracks. The diurnal *Parochodaeus californicus* (Horn) is netted on the wing or captured in Malaise traps during spring. The southeastern *Neochodaeus frontalis* (LeConte) is attracted to traps baited with amyl acetate in Florida.

FAUNA 22 SPECIES IN SIX GENERA

Codocera gnatho (Fall) (5.5–7.5 mm) is elongate-oval, convex, light yellowish brown, with mandibles strongly projecting forward. Head broad with mandibles less developed in female; anterior clypeal tubercle present (female), usually absent or weakly developed (male); mentum with ventrally produced plate in male; 10 antennomeres. Elytra indistinctly punctostriate, punctures without setae; apices not toothed. Propygidium plain, without modifications. Nocturnal adults at lights in spring and summer. Desert habitats from southern California to western Texas, south to Baja California and Durango. (1)

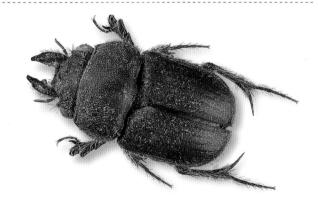

Cucochodaeus sparsus (LeConte) (4.5–8.5mm) is ovate, convex, light yellowish brown, with dorsal surface clothed in short, nearly erect yellowish setae. Head densely, setigerously punctate; clypeus with tubercle or short, erect, cone-shaped horn; frons without transverse ridge; mandibles large with outer margins weakly to strongly angulate; nine antennomeres. Pronotum densely, setigerously punctate; anterior margin slightly projecting forward behind eyes. Elytra indistinctly punctostriate, punctures without setae; apices not toothed. Propygidium without modifications. Middle and hind tibiae without teeth. Nocturnal adults at lights in spring and summer. Arid habitats in southern California to Colorado, western Nebraska, and southwestern Texas; also Chihuahua. (1)

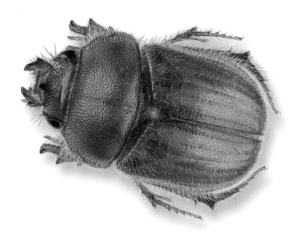

Neochodaeus praesidii (Bates) (6.3–8.5mm) is ovate, convex, light to dark yellowish brown, dorsal surface with short, nearly erect yellowish setae. Head without tubercle or horn, anterior margin of clypeus asymmetrical with a sharp ridge behind, antennae with 10 antennomeres, 8–10 forming compact, somewhat oval club with 8 cup-shaped; mentum underneath flat. Pronotum convex with anterior margin simply concave; surface granular, granules associated with setigerous punctures. Elytra indistinctly punctostriate, punctures without setae; apices not toothed. Propygidium short with medial trapezoidal groove. Nocturnal adults at lights in spring and summer. Arizona to Texas, south to Sinaloa and Durango. (3)

Parochodaeus biarmatus complex (3.5–4.2mm) are ovate, convex, and moderately shiny yellowish brown or brown. Head with vertex not carinate, and antennae with 10 antennomeres; males with pair of tubercles on frontal margin or tooth on posterior margin of hind femur at apical third sometimes lacking. Pronotum coarsely punctate medially along anterior margin. Elytra punctostriate, with sutural apices dentate, interlocking with pair of tubercles on apical margin of propygidium. Front tibia with basal tooth closer to middle tooth than to base of tibia. Adults attracted to lights. Colorado to Arizona, east to Kansas and Texas, south to Durango. Genus needs revision. (~3)

168

Xenochodaeus ulkei (Horn) (5.9–7.0 mm) is ovate, convex, moderately shiny reddish brown, clothed in erect yellowish setae. Head simple and antennae with 10 antennomeres; mentum with distinct longitudinal impression flanked anteriorly by pair of hornlike projections. Pronotum moderately granulate-punctate, with anterior margin concave, not produced behind eyes. Elytra finely striate, striae unipunctate, punctures not setose, with intervals flat and irregularly triseriate with setose punctures, and sutural apices not dentate. Propygidium elongate with somewhat parallel sulcus. Male hind femur without apical tooth and hind tibia slightly expanded medially. Adults attracted to lights. British Columbia south to Oregon, also Nevada and Utah. (4)

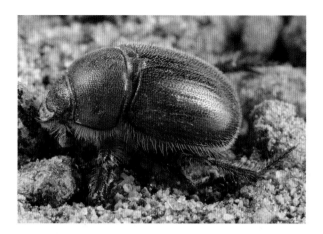

Pseudochodaeus estriatus (Schaeffer) (5.5–9.5 mm) is elongate, convex, light brown to dark reddish brown, densely clothed in short erect yellow setae, setae longer ventrally. Head with clypeal margin upturned; eyes not divided by ocular canthus; antennae with 10 antennomeres, 8–10 forming compact club, with 8 cup-shaped. Pronotum evenly convex with median longitudinal impression. Elytra completely covering abdomen, each with one punctostria. Legs with middle and hind tibial apices expanded, both with outer spurs pectinate; middle tibia with (female) or without (male) setal patch. Nocturnal adults attracted to lights in summer. Mostly open oak-pine forest habitats of Cascades and Sierra Nevada. Southern Oregon to central California. (1)

169

HYBOSORIDAE (hī-bo-sôr'-i-dē)
SCAVENGER AND PILL SCARAB BEETLES

The hybosorid fauna of western North America includes only two species, one adventive and one native, and little is known of their life histories. *Hybosorus illigeri* Reiche is an Old World species that is widely distributed in temperate Europe, sub-Saharan Africa, and from the Middle East to China and Vietnam. Introduced to eastern North America possibly as early as the 19th century, this species has become established across the southern third of the United States, as well as in Mexico, Central and northern South America, and parts of the Caribbean. In Florida, the larvae develop in the soil and are collected among the roots of plants, including fennel (*Foeniculum*) and Bermuda grass (*Cynodon dactylon*). The adults are sometimes considered nuisances in golf courses because of the small mounds of soil produced as a result of their burrowing activities. They are also found at carrion, dung, and lights where they are known to scavenge or prey on insects. The larvae have yet to be formally described. The other species, *Pachyplectrus laevis* LeConte, is native to the Nearctic Realm and occurs in scattered sandy desert habitats in the Colorado, Mojave, and Sonoran Deserts of California and Arizona. The adults are usually found under debris or walking on sand dunes at night, while the larvae remain unknown.

FAMILY DIAGNOSIS Adult hybosorids are oval, convex, and shiny yellowish brown to dark reddish brown to black. Head with mandibles and labrum prominent; antennae with 10 antennomeres, 8–10 lamellate and opposable with 8 somewhat cupuliform and surrounding 9, club compact and velvety. Procoxal cavities closed behind. Scutellum visible. Elytra smooth or punctostriate, completely covering abdomen. Legs with meso- and metatibial spurs simple, with tarsi 5-5-5, and simple claws equal in size. Abdomen with six ventrites free.

SIMILAR FAMILIES
- earth-boring scarab beetles (Geotrupidae, p.156)—antennae with 11 antennomeres

- scarab beetles (Scarabaeidae, p.172)—first club antennomere not cupuliform

COLLECTING NOTES *Hybosorus* is collected in carrion, dung, and at lights. *Pachyplectrus* is found walking on dunes at night, hiding under debris in sandy desert habitats, and is occasionally attracted to lights.

FAUNA FIVE SPECIES IN FOUR GENERA

Hybosorus illigeri Reiche (7.0–9.0 mm) is oval, convex, shiny dark reddish brown to almost black. Head coarsely punctate, without tubercle; mandibles and labrum prominent, apical margin of labrum with 7–11 teeth; mandibles narrow, evenly rounded externally, and sickle-shaped. Pronotum smooth between punctures. Elytron with nine punctostriae between scutellum and humerus. Adults are collected in carrion and dung, or at lights where they sometimes prey on or scavenge remains of other beetles. Old World; established from southeastern California to Kansas and Florida; also Mexico to northern South America and the Caribbean. (1)

Pachyplectrus laevis LeConte (4.8–6.9 mm) is oval, smooth, glabrous, and shiny brown or yellowish brown. Head with medial pyramid-shaped tubercle; mandibles and labrum prominent; mandibles wide, outer margin angular; labrum without teeth. Elytra with only sutural striae distinct. Nocturnal adults active primarily from March through May, found walking on dune crests, or under carrion, owl pellets, and other debris in dry sandy habitats; occasionally at lights. Fragments of dead beetles found in burrow of Merriam's kangaroo rats, *Dipodomys merriami*. Sandy desert regions of southern California east to Utah and Arizona, likely in adjacent northwestern Mexico. (1)

GLAPHYRIDAE (gla-fir'-i-dē)
BUMBLE BEE SCARAB BEETLES

Fuzzy and sometimes partly metallic bumble bee scarabs are strong, fast, and agile fliers that resemble bees in flight. Glaphyridae is a small family comprising seven genera distributed throughout much of the Holarctic region. Of these, only *Lichnanthe* occurs in North America, with eight species restricted to far eastern and western states. The larva of one species, the cranberry grub, *Lichnanthe vulpina* (Hentz), is a pest of commercially grown cranberries in northeastern United States, where it attacks the roots. *Lichnanthe lupina* LeConte, a possibly extinct species from coastal New Jersey and New York, is the most aberrant of the North American glaphyrid fauna because its elytra meet along their entire length, unlike other species of *Lichnanthe* that have dehiscent elytra. Of the six species of *Lichnanthe* that inhabit western North

America, only *L. rathvoni* LeConte is widespread; the remaining five species are all restricted to California. Bumble bee scarabs are often abundant, yet patchily distributed in sand dunes along the northern and central coast of California, or live inland along rivers and streams in sandy riparian habitats populated with thickets of willow (*Salix*). Several of these species characteristically have two- or three-color forms. Both species of *Lichnanthe* that are restricted to coastal dunes, *L. albipilosa* Carlson and *L. ursina* (LeConte), are considered Species of Concern in California because there is currently not enough biological information available to support their state or federal listing as threatened or endangered. Adult *Lichnanthe* reach their peak activity from midmorning to midafternoon and are sometimes observed hovering near flowers and foliage or flying over sandy areas. Both *L. apina* Carlson and *L. rathvoni* LeConte have been observed on the blossoms of yarrow (*Achillea*), but it is not clear whether or not they actually feed, even though their mouthparts appear to be adapted for eating pollen. Females release pheromones to attract males, and mating takes place on the ground or on vegetation. After mating, or at the end of the daily flight period, adults take shelter by burrowing into the sand. The larvae feed among damp layers of decaying leaf litter and other plant debris that has accumulated in sandy depressions and at the bases of trees along the banks of streams and rivers.

FAMILY DIAGNOSIS Adult glaphyrids are elongate, yellowish brown to black, often with metallic reflections, and clothed in long yellowish, yellowish-orange, or black setae; some species have two- or three-color forms. Head somewhat hypognathous; clypeal margin incised at base, exposing antennal bases. Antennae with 10 antennomeres, 8–10 lamellate and opposable, velvety club with lamellae longer (male) or shorter (female) than funicle. Pronotum somewhat rectangular and convex. Procoxal cavities closed behind. Scutellum triangular. Elytra short, smooth, somewhat transparent, and usually dehiscent (diverging) halfway to two-thirds along suture, completely exposing pygidium. Tarsi 5-5-5, with claws equal in size and toothed at base. Abdomen with six ventrites free.

SIMILAR FAMILIES

- scarab beetles (Scarabaeidae, p.172)—elytra never divergent apically, pygidium usually not completely visible from above

COLLECTING METHODS Bumble bee scarabs are encountered on the wing, crawling on the ground, or perching on vegetation in riparian habitats. Species inhabiting coastal dunes are generally found on the leeward side where they are protected from the wind, often flying or resting near dune crests. All species typically reach their peak of activity between late morning and early afternoon hours on sunny or slightly overcast days during the summer. Some beetles are occasionally found on flowers of yarrow (*Achillea*).

171

FAUNA EIGHT SPECIES IN ONE GENUS

Lichnanthe apina Carlson (9.7–14.5 mm) is elongate, convex, typically with long yellow-orange setae underneath, with two-tone hind femora; black form rare. Pronotum bright metallic green, occasionally coppery gold or blue green, posterior margin with complete bead. Elytra dark reddish brown with black setae, slightly dehiscent apically. Hind femora metallic green ventrally, nonmetallic black or dark brown dorsally. Abdominal ventrites metallic in male. Adults fly among willow thickets (*Salix*) and herbaceous plants during June and July. Mating occurs on ground or on vegetation. Sandy riparian habitats in Coast, Transverse, and Peninsular Ranges, Great Central Valley, and southern coastal plain of California. (6)

Lichnanthe rathvoni (LeConte) (10.6–16.6 mm) is elongate, convex, variable with three distinct forms based on color of abdominal setae: pale yellow, orange, or black. Pronotum dark metallic green, posterior marginal bead obsolete medially. Elytra brown, setae yellow to black, yellow and orange forms with correspondingly colored setal patches in irregular rows. Legs not metallic, uniformly dark reddish brown. Hind femora uniformly colored, not metallic. Adults active mostly in June and July in riparian habitats, occasionally found in coastal dunes and sandy habitats away from water. Southern British Columbia to California, east to western Idaho and western Nevada; also northern Baja California. (6)

Lichnanthe ursina (LeConte) (12.9–17.2 mm) is elongate, convex, and clothed in long pale or black setae; pale form most common. Elytral setae black or brown and white, apices notched. Legs with metatibial spurs unequal in length. Males typically encountered in May and June near crest of dunes flying close to the surface of the sand as they search for mates. Coastal sand dunes from Sonoma County to San Mateo County, also reported inland Los Angeles County, California. *Lichnanthe albipilosa* Carlson (13.5–17.5 mm) similar, setae white; elytral dehiscence more acute, apices entire; coastal sand dunes in San Luis Obispo County, California. (6)

172

SCARABAEIDAE (skar-a-be'-i-dē)
SCARAB BEETLES

Scarabaeidae is among the most diverse beetle families in western North America and includes species that have long attracted attention because of their large and colorful bodies, conspicuous and interesting behaviors, and abundance. Several genera (e.g., *Serica*, *Amblonoxia*, *Phobetus*, *Listrochelus*, *Phyllophaga*, *Polyphylla*, *Cyclocephala*, and *Tomarus*) are already familiar to homeowners living in suburbs and mountain communities because they are attracted to porch lights at night, sometimes in large numbers. The roles of scarab beetles as bioindicators, recyclers, and pollinators are often underappreciated, but it is well known that some species are important garden and agricultural pests. For example, the grubs of some *Ataenius* and masked chafers (*Cyclocephala*) are turf pests, especially in parks and golf courses. Adults of several genera (*Hoplia*, *Serica*, *Dichelonyx*, *Diplotaxis*, and *Polyphylla*) may defoliate potted plants, deciduous garden shrubs, vegetable crops, and orchard trees as well as conifers in managed forests. Their larvae, along with those of *Tomarus*, feed on the tender roots of potted plants, seedling trees, and shrubs and are sometimes especially destructive in nurseries. The large, back-crawling, C-shaped grubs of fig or peach beetles, *Cotinis mutabilis* (Gory & Percheron) (p.28, Fig. 18e), commonly inhabit and significantly contribute to the decay of piles of manure, grass clippings, and compost. The big, buzzing adults emerge to feed on soft, ripe fruit including grapes, figs, apricots, peaches, plums, and tomatoes. Small dung beetles, such as *Aphodius* and its relatives, most of which are native to Europe, are often common in herbivore dung, especially of cattle, horses, and other domestic animals. Larger dung beetles (*Canthon*, *Copris*, *Dichotomius*, *Euoniticellus*, *Phanaeus*, and *Onthophagus*) are sometimes encountered on or under cow and horse dung, especially in southeastern Arizona. *Onthophagus taurus* (Schreber) is not an uncommon inhabitant of residential areas, where it eats dog feces in parks and backyards. The activities of dung beetles are important in reducing breeding sites of pestiferous flies and recycling nutrients. In spring, desert annuals may harbor several diminutive species in the genera *Chnaunanthus* (p.45, Fig. 47), *Gymnopyge*, and *Oncerus* that may serve an important role as pollinators for these ephemeral plants. A few genera, such as *Cremastocheilus* and *Valgus*, are typically found in association with ants or termites, respectively.

FAMILY DIAGNOSIS Adult scarabs are oval or elongate-oval, convex or somewhat flattened dorsally, and mostly black, brown, yellowish brown, occasionally green, metallic, or scaled with blotched or striped patterns. Head weakly hypognathous with mandibles visible or not; sometimes with a small tubercle, transverse carina, or distinct horn (*Copris*, *Euoniticellus*, *Liatongus*, *Onthophagus*, *Strategus*, *Xyloryctes*, *Hemiphileurus*, *Phileurus*, *Dynastes*, *Megasoma*); antennae with 8–10 antennomeres, last 3–7 antennomeres lamellate and opposable, forming a compact, sometimes fanlike, usually bare or velvety (Aphodiinae, Scarabaeinae) club. Pronotum variable, with or without horns, tubercles, and excavations; sides always distinctly margined. Procoxal cavities closed behind. Scutellum visible, partly obscured by medial lobe of posterior pronotal margin (*Cotinis*, *Gymnetina*, *Hologymnetis*), or completely hidden (*Canthon*, *Pseudocanthon*, *Copris*, *Canthidium*, *Dichotomius*, *Euoniticellus*, *Digitonthophagus*, *Onthophagus*, *Phanaeus*). Elytra somewhat oval to parallel-sided, with surfaces smooth, irregularly punctured, faintly to deeply punctostriate, or covered with scales, and completely covering abdomen (dung scarabs) or with pygidium partially exposed. Legs strong, adapted for burrowing, with tarsi usually 5-5-5 (protarsi absent in male *Phanaeus*), claws equal or unequal in size, and simple, toothed, cleft, serrate, or pectinate underneath. Abdomen with six ventrites free.

SIMILAR FAMILIES
- rain beetles (Pleocomidae, p.153)—antennae with 11 antennomeres, procoxal cavities open behind
- earth-boring scarab beetles (Geotrupidae, p.156)—antennae with 11 antennomeres, first club antennomere cupuliform
- hide beetles (Trogidae, p.159)—roughly sculptured, abdomen with five ventrites
- enigmatic scarab beetles (Glaresidae, p.162)—abdomen with five ventrites

- false stag beetles (Diphyllostomatidae, p.163)—club antennomeres not opposable, abdomen with seven ventrites
- stag beetles (Lucanidae, p.164)—antennae usually geniculate, club antennomeres not opposable
- sand-loving scarab beetles (Ochodaeidae, p.167)—mandibles exposed, first club antennomere cup-shaped, outer spur on middle tibiae pectinate
- scavenger and pill scarab beetles (Hybosoridae, p.169)—first club antennomere cup-shaped
- bumble bee scarabs (Glaphyridae, p.170)—elytral apices dehiscent, exposing tergites

COLLECTING METHODS Adults scarabs are diurnal, crepuscular, or nocturnal. Most nocturnal species are strongly attracted to lights. Others are found by sweeping, beating, and searching vegetation at night (*Diplotaxis*, *Serica*, *Phyllophaga*, *Coenonycha*, *Dichelonyx*, and *Megasoma*). Diurnal species are commonly found on, in, or under fresh dung (*Aphodius* and relatives, *Canthon*, *Copris*, *Dichotomius*, *Euoniticellus*, *Onitis*, *Phanaeus*, *Onthophagus*), sapping tree wounds (*Cotinis*, *Euphoria*), on foliage (*Dichelonyx*, *Cotalpa*, *Paracotalpa*) and flowers (*Chnaunanthus*, *Gymnopyge*, *Hoplia*, *Euphoria*), or flying over open ground and low vegetation (*Phobetus*, *Paracotalpa*, *Cremastocheilus*). Female *Cotinis* and *Euphoria* are often found flying over turf, compost, and dung heaps in search of egg-laying sites. Scarab burrows in sandy soils in road tracks and along trails are often marked by conspicuous mounds of sand called push-ups. Very small psammophilous species (*Aegialia*, *Odontopsammodius*, *Neopsammodius*, *Geopsammodius*, *Leiopsammodius*, and *Tesarius*) are sifted from sand at the base of plants or among accumulations of vegetation along rivers and in coastal and desert dunes. Hanging traps baited with rotting fruit or malt and molasses are attractive to some species, especially sap feeders (*Megasoma*, *Cotinis*, and *Euphoria*). Dung beetles are attracted to pitfall traps baited with human, pig, sheep, horse, or cow feces.

FAUNA ~1,800 SPECIES IN 170 GENERA

Aegialia crassa LeConte (4.0–5.0 mm) is oblong-oval, convex, and very broad posteriorly, glabrous, and reddish brown to black. Head broad, densely granulate without punctures. Pronotum wider than long, broadest behind middle, without posterior marginal line, with discal punctures mixed in size and sparse, becoming impunctate or minutely punctate laterally. Elytra strongly convex with striae weakly impressed, strial punctures fine and shallow, and intervals slightly convex. Legs with protibiae tridentate, middle and hind tibiae short and robust, and hind tibial spurs spatulate. Flightless adults occur at base of plants in coastal sand dunes. Southern British Columbia to Baja California. (17)

Aphodius fimetarius (Linnaeus) (6.5–9.5 mm) is oblong, robust, and black with red elytra. Head black with three sharp tubercles across front, clypeus with lateral margins (genae) slightly protruding, semi-oval, and widest in front of middle. Pronotum with anterior angles reddish yellow, and frontal depression at middle in male. Scutellum small, triangular. Subapical areas of elytra dull and smooth. Adults active during early summer. *Aphodius pedellus* (De Geer) very similar; genae protruding, moderately to distinctly semicircular, and widest near middle; subapical elytral areas shiny, rough; active early summer, then early fall. Both species in cattle dung. European; widely established across North America. (2)

174

Calamosternus granarius (Linnaeus) (3.4–6.0 mm) is usually black, sometimes with obscure reddish margins on sides of pronotum; occasionally head and pronotum black with dark brown elytra. Head trituberculate, middle tubercle prominent; clypeus rugose and transversely carinate. Pronotum with line across posterior margin. Scutellum pentagonal, depressed. Elytral surface smooth, shiny, without sharp humeral tooth. Upper surface of front tibiae smooth, without punctures; middle and hind tibiae fringed with small spines of about equal length. Adults found year-round in dung, carrion, decaying plant materials, prairie dog burrows; occasional turf pest; attracted to lights. Europe, now cosmopolitan; widely established in North America. (1)

Cinacanthus militaris (LeConte) (4.8–6.1 mm) is mostly pale yellowish brown to dark reddish brown, elytral suture dark brown. Head with clypeal margin straight or emarginate between teeth. Pronotum with fine, barely visible punctures mixed with coarse punctures increasing in size toward lateral margins. Elytral intervals with two rows of irregular coarse punctures. Nocturnal adults active spring through summer, associated with burrows of California ground squirrels (*Spermophilus beecheyi*) and pocket gophers (*Thomomys bottae*); common at lights. Pacific Northwest to California and Nevada. (1)

Coelotrachelus rudis (LeConte) (6.2–7.5 mm) is glabrous, shiny pale to dark reddish brown, with underside paler. Clypeal emargination flanked by distinct teeth. Pronotum laterally explanate, with posterior margin noticeably sinuate and produced at angles, and impunctate or finely punctate with coarse punctures on posterior half of disc sometimes more widely dispersed. Elytra shallowly and finely punctostriate, and intervals with distinct, yet very small punctures. Male protibial spur short, thick, abruptly curved, and blunt with small tooth on inner angle that is lacking in female. Adults in rodent burrows, especially pocket gophers; attracted to lights. Southern Colorado to mountains of southern Arizona and New Mexico. (1)

Diapterna hamata (Say) (5.5–8.3 mm) is dull, bicolored, pale brownish, usually with yellow and brown elytra. Head lacking tubercles or depression behind clypeal margin. Pronotum with distinct line along posterior margin obsolete medially and at posterior angles. Scutellum long, slender. Elytra also entirely yellow or brown. Male protibia with broad, flat inner spur, basal tarsomere of metatarsus with large recurved process. Larvae feed on roots. Adults active late spring, early summer, common in cattle dung. Across southern Canada, northern United States; in West to montane northeastern California, northwestern Nevada, and northern Arizona. (3)

Labarrus pseudolividus (Balthasar) (3.5–5.8 mm) with head brown to blackish with variable amounts of yellowish brown on sides of clypeus; male trituberculate with middle tubercle prominent. Pronotum brown with yellowish-brown sides and pale membrane across front, without bead along posterior margin. Scutellum pentagonal, depressed. Elytra yellowish brown and suture dark, punctostriate with intervals flat, each with brown stripe down middle. Male with longest metatibial spur slender, gradually narrowed apically, and subequal to or longer than first tarsomere. Adults common in herbivore dung and at lights. California eastward. (2)

Otophorus haemorrhoidalis **(Linnaeus)** (4.1–5.5 mm) is bicolored black and red. Head trituberculate, tubercles less prominent in female. Pronotal surface with mixture of fine and coarser punctures. Scutellum coarsely punctured, triangular, longer than one-sixth of elytra. Elytra black with deeply striate and shiny intervals, and apex red, or apex and humeral spots red. Metatibial apices fringed with small spines of equal length. Adults prefer herbivore dung deposited in open, unshaded pastures, or open savanna or woodland habitats. Palearctic; widely established in North America. (1)

Pardalosus pardalis **(LeConte)** (4.3–6.0 mm) is shiny, pale yellowish brown with yellow elytra, yellow distinctly marked with brown spots. Clypeus broadly rounded with medial emargination. Fine and coarse pronotal punctures sparse (male) or dense (female). Metatibial apex fringed with short, unequal spinules; metatarsus long as metatibia, basal tarsomere longer than superior tibial spur. Detritus feeder. Mostly west of Cascade-Sierra Nevada Mountains, from southern British Columbia and southern Idaho to central California. *Pardalosus pseudopardalis* Gordon & Skelley; metatibiae with long, unequal spinules, basal tarsomere shorter than superior tibial spur; California. (4)

Planolinellus vittatus **(Say)** (3.0–4.4 mm) is mostly shiny black, pronotum and elytra marked with red. Head with clypeal apex semicircular and lacking teeth, trituberculate with medial tubercle prominent. Pronotum margined along lateral and posterior margins, with obscure red spot near each side. Elytra punctostriate, intervals flat, usually pale red with faint brown stripe along sutural and lateral margins, sometimes entirely red or dark reddish brown. Found mostly in cow and horse dung, especially in open pastures; occasionally at lights. Southern Canada, most of United States, and northern Mexico; also Old World. (1)

Stenotothorax ovipennis **(Horn)** (6.6–8.2 mm) head lacks a frontal suture, with clypeus finely and densely punctured, never granulate, and apical margin broadly emarginate with rounded angles. Posterior pronotal margin narrower basally, lateral margins explanate anteriorly, large coarse punctures unevenly distributed and coalescing in lateral third, with posterior marginal bead complete. Lateral elytral margins broadly rounded, broadest behind middle, with strial punctures indistinct. Flightless, nocturnal adults reared from pocket gopher burrows. Found under dry carrion, walking on snow during winter and spring. Southern Coast, Transverse, and Peninsular Ranges of southern California. (21)

Teuchestes fossor (Linnaeus) (8.0–12.0 mm) is relatively large and completely shiny black. Head trituberculate with median tubercle prominent, mostly impunctate. Pronotum with fine punctures moderate in density, coarse punctures umbilicate and sparse. Scutellum triangular, elongate, scarcely punctured. Elytra shallowly punctostriate with intervals flat and sparsely punctate. Adults active spring, then late summer and fall, especially on cow dung; will also utilize feces of horse, sheep, and other herbivores deposited in open pasture habitats. Palearctic; across southern Canada and northern United States, in West south to northern California. (1)

Black Turfgrass Ataenius *Ataenius spretulus* **(Haldeman)** (3.6–5.5 mm) is shiny black with legs and clypeal margins reddish. Clypeus wrinkled in front. Pronotum coarsely, sparsely punctured, punctures becoming slightly denser at sides, with base distinctly margined. Elytra longer than wide, punctostriate, with humeri sharp and toothlike. Front femora mostly smooth posteriorly, with few if any coarse punctures; hind femoral line extending halfway from knee to trochanter, tibia usually with apical fringe of five setae, first tarsomere longer than and not articulated between tibial spurs. Turf pests, occasionally at dung; attracted to lights. Ontario; widespread in United States. (27)

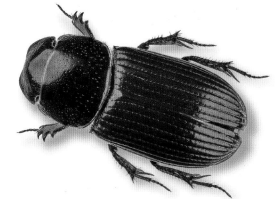

Trichiorhyssemus riparius (Horn) (2.7–3.1 mm) is roughly sculptured, mostly reddish black to black, clothed dorsally with short, erect setae, and ventrally (including hind femora) with scalelike setae. Head tuberculate, tubercles evenly distributed. Pronotum with transverse ridges and furrows not sharply defined, furrow between ridges 3 and 4 widely interrupted. Elytra broadest just behind middle, with all intervals costate. Adults at lights. Southern California to southern Nevada and Arizona. (1) *Rhyssemus californicus* Horn (3.0–4.2 mm) similar in form, but larger and lacking setae dorsally and scalelike setae ventrally. Central California to Arizona. (1)

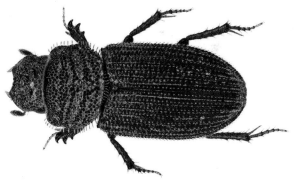

Dichotomius colonicus Say (19.0–28.5 mm) is robust, broadly oval, very convex, shiny black, with rows of dull tomentum on elytral apices. Clypeus transversely wrinkled, with distinct tubercle and ridge in front of eyes (male), or short horn nearly between eyes (female), and parabolic anterior margin slightly emarginate medially. Pronotum sloping in front. Elytra each with six deep punctostriae between suture and humerus. Attracted to lights in grasslands; excavations under cattle dung marked by large push-ups of soil. Southern Arizona to southern Texas, south to Panama. (1)

Copris arizonensis Schaeffer (14.0–22.0 mm) is robust, oval, convex, and shiny black. Major male with long slender horn, pronotum deeply excavate in front, with lateral ridge and bilobate process medially; female with short truncate horn, pronotum not deeply excavate, without distinct medial protuberance. Larvae develop in brood balls fashioned by adults from woodrat (*Neotoma*) dung. Nocturnal adults disperse from *Neotoma* nests with onset of summer monsoons; at lights. Oak-juniper woodland and pine forest habitats of southeastern Arizona to western Texas, south to Chihuahua, Durango, and Jalisco. (3)

Copris lecontei Matthews (10.0–15.0 mm) with horn of major male long and slender, pronotum excavate with ridges and medial tubercles; female with short, truncate horn. Middle, hind tarsi not broadly expanded, tarsomeres longer than wide. Nocturnal adults utilize cow dung, grasping chunks with front legs and dragging them backward down burrow; attracted to lights, traps baited with human feces or cow dung. *Copris macclevei* Warner (9.0–14.0 mm) similar, middle and hind tarsi broadly expanded, middle three tarsomeres as wide as long; occurs in *Neotoma* nests, also at lights during summer. Desert grasslands in southeastern Arizona and Sonora. (3)

Canthon floridanus Brown (11.5–17.5 mm) is dull black, with dorsal surfaces coarsely granulate, granules raised. Head bidentate. Lateral pronotal margins angular just behind middle, posterior margins broadly angulate. Middle and posterior tibiae slender and curved, scarcely enlarged apically; hind leg with femur margined in front and tibia with single spur. Adults search for dung and mates on hot, sunny days, especially after rain. Prefers habitats with sandy soils, using cattle dung to form brood balls; also utilizes feces of other animals. Southern Arizona to central Texas, south to adjacent Mexico. Formerly known as *C. imitator* Brown. (5)

Canthon indigaceus LeConte (8.5–12.0 mm) is oval, convex, shiny metallic green or dark blue, clypeal margin broadly black. Dorsal surfaces finely granulate with scattered fine punctures. Head bidentate. Legs with middle and posterior tibiae slender, curved, scarcely enlarged apically; hind femur margined in front, tibia with single spur. Adults active on hot, sunny days in search of dung and mates, especially during summer monsoons. They prefer cattle dung to form brood balls, but also utilize horse, human, and pig feces. Arizona and Texas, south to along west coast of Mexico to Jalisco. (5)

178

Canthon simplex LeConte (5.0–9.0 mm) is uniformly dull black, sometimes with elytral humeri reddish. Dorsal surfaces finely granulate. Head quadridentate. Prothorax without denticle on ventral margin, subhumeral striae not carinate. Hind femur not margined in front, tibia with single spur. Adults inhabit coastal chaparral, desert scrub, oak woodland, and pine forests up to elevation of 2,700 meters. Utilizes cattle dung or rolls pellets of California ground squirrel (*Spermophilus beecheyi*) and yellow-bellied marmot (*Marmota flaviventris*). Only native dung-rolling scarab along Pacific Coast. British Columbia to Baja California, east to Alberta, Montana, and Colorado. (5)

Pseudocanthon perplexus (LeConte) is shiny black, sometimes with metallic greenish or purplish tinge. Head with clypeus quadridentate, vertex without fine and transverse ridge, and antennae with nine antennomeres. Pronotum with lateral margins rounded. Scutellum hidden. Elytra finely and shallowly striate, with intervals broad and flat. Pygidium lacks basal transverse carina. Legs reddish with middle and hind tibiae slender, curved, and only slightly expanded apically, and hind tibia each with single apical spur. Possibly associated with rodent nests; at lights. Southeastern Arizona east to Wisconsin, Virginia, and Florida, south to South America. (1)

Euoniticellus intermedius (Reiche) (7.0–9.0 mm) is elongate-oval, somewhat flattened, and light brown. Head with (male) or without (female) blunt horn. Pronotum coarsely punctate with distinctive symmetrical markings, swollen anteriorly in male. Scutellum visible. Elytra lighter with several pale spots. Legs mostly pale with tibial apices and tarsi dark. Diurnal adults search for fresh cattle dung pads to construct nests directly beneath pad or dig branched galleries below, and fashion pear-shaped brood balls. Sub-Saharan Africa; established in southern California, Arizona, Texas, Florida, south to Baja California Sur and Chiapas. (1)

Liatongus californicus (Horn) (11.0–12.0 mm) is oblong, dull black, head armed with an erect horn in front (male) or blunt process between eyes (female); eight antennomeres. Pronotum coarsely punctured, depressed anteriorly with median tubercle (male), or somewhat convex with small tubercle (female). Scutellum visible. Elytra each with seven punctostriae before humerus, intervals alutaceous, punctate. Middle and hind tibiae abruptly expanded apically. Adults on horse and cattle dung in spring and summer. East of Cascades in southern Oregon to western Sierra Nevada foothills in central California, east to southwestern Idaho and southwestern Utah. (1)

Onitis alexis Klug (12.0–20.0 mm) is robust, broadly oblong, shiny, with metallic green or coppery head and pronotum and light brown elytra. Head with small tubercle between eyes in both sexes. Pronotum with two distinct pits at base. Scutellum visible. Elytra striate, interstriae convex. Male hind femora each with single hooklike spine. Adults active at dusk in spring and summer, attracted to fresh cattle dung and light at night. Introduced to control dung-breeding flies and reduce dung pats in pastures. Africa and southern Europe; patchily established in coastal plain and adjacent foothills in San Diego County, California. (1)

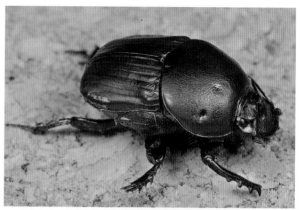

Digitonthophagus gazella (Fabricius) (6.0–13.0 mm) is greenish brown to coppery black with yellowish-brown markings. Head, most of pronotum, portions of underside and tibiae, and large oval spots on middle and hind femora mostly greenish or coppery black. Male with pair of slender, curving horns on head; female with distinct transverse ridge. Pronotum with pale margins at side and base. Elytra light brown, with or without dark markings. Larvae primarily in cow dung, sometimes dog feces. Nocturnal adults under dung and attracted to lights from spring through fall. Southern African species now established across southern third of United States; also Central and South America, Australia, and Japan. (1)

Onthophagus arnetti Howden & Cartwright (6.6–8.6 mm) is distinctly bicolored with dark metallic green pronotum, and dull black elytra finely alutaceous with small tubercles bearing fine punctures at bases. Head with eyes somewhat convex. Pronotum with anterior angles broadly rounded, posterior angles more sharply rounded. Nothing is known of biology, but suspected to be associated with pack rat (*Neotoma*) nests. Seldom encountered adults active in summer, attracted to lights at night. Southeastern Arizona, likely in Sonora. (7)

Onthophagus nuchicornis (Linnaeus) (6.3–8.1 mm) is oval, dull black with tan or brown elytra mottled with black. Male with horn on top of head between eyes. Female with small hump on pronotum just behind head. Pronotum coarsely punctate, spaces between very finely wrinkled. Scutellum not visible. Elytra with punctostriae not deeply impressed, interstriae not distinctly convex. Front legs with tarsi; middle and hind tibiae widened at apices. Adults found on cow and horse dung in summer. Europe; established across southern Canada and northern United States; in West south to Oregon, northern Idaho, and western Montana. (7)

180

Onthophagus taurus (Schreber) (7.0–11.2 mm) is dark brown to black with faint purplish or greenish luster, elytra sometimes paler. Distinctive major male with pair of long curved horns. Pronotum finely granulate in between scattered punctures, with lateral impressions to receive horns (male), or evenly convex (female). Elytral punctostriae not deeply impressed, interstriae not distinctly convex. Adults active in summer, usually found in vertebrate feces, especially dog, cow, and horse; often found in neighborhoods and parks. Old World; established across southern half of United States. (7)

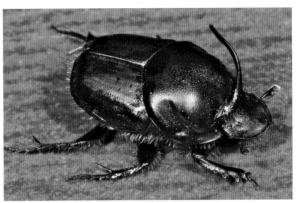

Phanaeus quadridens (Say) (13.0–23.0 mm) is broadly oval, robust, and dark metallic green, sometimes with bluish highlights. Major male with long horn curved over pronotum; pronotum flat, green, coarsely wrinkled, and shieldlike with broadly rounded posterior angles diverging backward; female without horn, pronotum rough, and somewhat convex, not shieldlike. Elytra shallowly striate. Larvae develop in burrows supplied with dung by adults. Adults fly during summer monsoon season, especially in areas above 1,500 meters where cattle graze. Grassland and mixed forest-grassland habitats in southeastern Arizona and southwestern New Mexico, south to Jalisco and Tlaxcala. (3)

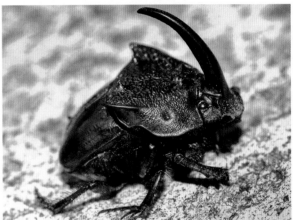

Phanaeus vindex Macleay (11.0–22.0 mm) is bright metallic green with coppery red pronotum. Major male with long horn curved over pronotum; pronotum flat, coarsely wrinkled, and shieldlike with angular posterior angles diverging backward; female with short, truncate process, pronotum rough, somewhat convex, not shieldlike. Elytra costate, interstriae coarsely wrinkled. In various habitats supporting cattle. Southeastern Arizona to South Dakota, Massachusetts, and Florida; also Chihuahua. *Phanaeus amithaon* Harold (13.0–25.0 mm) uniformly green with coppery highlights, elytra punctostriate, interstriae smooth and convex; Santa Cruz River Valley, Arizona, to Mexico. (3)

Acoma mixta Howden (4.8–7.5 mm) male is elongate-oval, reddish brown to brown dorsally, with appendages and underside lighter. Head between eyes deeply, roughly punctate, clypeofrontal junction tumid, with clypeus rounded or truncate, and moderately reflexed anteriorly, less so laterally. Antennae with antennomeres 7–9 forming club. Convex pronotum glabrous, broadest medially, with anterolateral margins straight, and anterior angles obtuse and slightly rounded. Elytral setae short, inconspicuous, typically no longer than widths of obsolete intervals indicated by irregular rows of punctures. Male at lights; females unknown and likely flightless. Southern Arizona. (6)

Chnaunanthus chapini Saylor (3.5–4.1 mm) is elongate-oval, convex, shiny, with head and pronotum reddish brown to brownish black, and elytra yellowish or reddish brown, sometimes with bases darker, to uniformly brownish black. Clypeus parallel basally, gradually narrowed and emarginate anteriorly; labrum beneath clypeus; antennae with nine antennomeres, 7–9 forming small oval club. Pronotum with disc glabrous. Elytral striae impressed. Abdominal sutures indistinct medially, convex (male) or slightly concave (female) when viewed from side. Protibiae tridentate with small apical spur, all claws incised. Diurnal adults on spring flowers, including composites and mallows. Eastern Oregon and California, east to Nevada and northwestern Arizona. (2)

Chnaunanthus flavipennis (Horn) (3.9–4.1 mm) is elongate-oval, convex, shiny, with head dark, pronotum reddish brown, and variable elytra. Clypeus gradually narrowed from base and deeply emarginate in front; labrum beneath clypeus; antennae with nine antennomeres, 7–9 forming small oval club. Pronotum with discal punctures setigerous. Elytra relatively smooth and pale yellow, or darker with vague striae. Abdominal sutures indistinct medially, convex (male) or slightly concave (female) when viewed from side. Protibiae tridentate with small apical spur, all claws incised. Diurnal adults on flowers of spring composites, including Spanish needles (*Palafoxia arida*). Central eastern California, Utah, and northwestern Arizona, south to Baja California. (2)

Coenonycha ampla Cazier (10.0–13.0 mm) is elongate, robust, and uniformly light to dark reddish brown with short, scattered recumbent setae; flight wings fully developed. Head coarsely punctured; clypeus finely granulate, anterior margin more broadly upturned than sides. Pronotum with anterior angles acute, partially covering eyes. Elytra with sides somewhat parallel; humeri prominent; surface finely alutaceous with faint narrow impunctate interstriae, and irregular and setose punctures. Legs long with incised claws appearing entire from sides. Nocturnal adults feed and mate on California juniper (*Juniperus californica*) in spring; attracted to lights. Juniper woodlands, southern Coast Ranges and interior slopes of Transverse Ranges, California. (32)

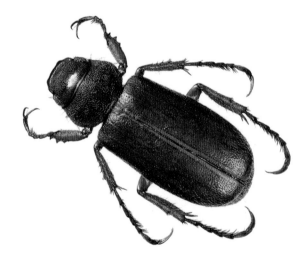

Coenonycha lurida Cazier (7.4–11.0 mm) is uniformly pale yellowish brown. Head with anterior clypeal angles prominent and not toothlike, margin more broadly upturned than sides. Lateral pronotal margins obtuse, not angulate, straight behind middle and narrowly converging. Elytra parallel-sided, translucent with folded flight wings visible, and interstriae obscure. Nocturnal adults feed and mate on white bur-sage (*Ambrosia dumosa*) and burrobush (*Hymenoclea salsola*); attracted to lights. Northern and western reaches of Colorado Desert, California. *Coenonycha pallida* Cazier (8.0–10.5 mm) is similar, clypeal angles sharper; Mojave Desert, California. (32)

Coenonycha testacea Cazier (7.0–11.0 mm) is mostly yellowish brown; flight wings fully developed. Head with anterior third of clypeus rugose medially, anterior clypeal margin more broadly upturned than sides. Pronotum with anterior angles acute, partially covering eyes. Elytra translucent, folded flight wings visible. Nocturnal adults on chamise (*Adenostoma fasciculatum*) and buckwheat (*Eriogonum fasciculatum*) in early spring; at lights. Coastal plain and foothill areas in San Luis Obispo, Santa Barbara, Ventura, and Los Angeles Counties, with similar undescribed species found elsewhere in California. (32)

183

Dichelonyx backii Kirby (6.5–12.2 mm) with body and legs ranging from black to reddish or brownish yellow with elytra usually metallic green, ranging from metallic blue to bronze, purple, gray, or blackish. Clypeus with angles rounded to angulate, anterior margin rounded, truncate, or emarginate, and weakly to strongly reflexed. Pronotum convex, without medial longitudinal sulcus. Legs with apical tibial spurs unequal, acute apically. Abdomen of male concave in side view. Diurnal adults on various conifers, especially ponderosa pine (*Pinus ponderosa*) during summer; at lights. Montane coniferous forests throughout western North America. Genus needs revision. (13)

Dichelonyx muscula Fall (5.8–8.0 mm) is black and moderately clothed in pale decumbent pubescence, pronotum and elytra with bronzy or faintly metallic green luster. Clypeal angles and anterior margin both broadly rounded, margins not strongly reflexed. Pronotum without median sulcus. Elytra with lateral margins pale, pubescence directed posteriorly. Legs black or brownish black, with apical tibial spurs unequal and acute in both sexes. Adults on chamise (*Adenostoma*), ceanothus (*Ceanothus*), and mountain mahogany (*Cercocarpus*); at lights. Coastal central and southern California. (13)

Dichelonyx pusilla LeConte (7.0–9.0 mm) is elongate-oval, blackish, with brown elytra usually marked with discrete stripes of white setae. Head with clypeus angulate, strongly upturned anteriorly, clothed in short, reclined, yellowish-white setae. Pronotum with median longitudinal sulcus. Elytra with lines of white setae separated by equally wide glabrous areas. Abdomen of male concave. Legs blackish to brown; hind tibial spurs unequal, acute apically; male hind claws incised. Adults found on chamise (*Adenostoma fasciculatum*), ceanothus (*Ceanothus*), and mountain mahogany (*Cercocarpus*) in spring and summer; at lights. Coastal sage and chaparral communities of central and southern California to Baja California. (13)

Dichelonyx truncata LeConte (5.6–8.1 mm) is elongate-oval, black with elytra grayish, blackish, to pale yellowish brown, tinged with bronze or greenish sheen. Clypeus truncate or slightly emarginate, broadly upturned, angles distinct. Pronotum convex. Elytra densely clothed in reclining white setae; lateral margins pale. Legs pale yellowish brown to blackish; hind tibial spurs unequal, acute (male) or blunt (female); male hind claws incised. Adults on pine (*Pinus*), ceanothus (*Ceanothus*), willow (*Salix*), mountain mahogany (*Cercocarpus*), sage (*Artemisia*), and flannelbush (*Fremontodendron californicum*) in late spring, early summer; at lights in sage brush, chaparral, and oak-pine woodlands. Washington to California, east to Dakotas, Nebraska, and Arizona. (13)

Dichelonyx vicina Fall (8.5–14.5 mm) is elongate-oval, reddish brown to brown, with brilliant metallic green elytra. Head coarsely punctate, clypeal angles broadly rounded. Pronotum narrowly impunctate along sides of median sulcus. Elytra with sides pale, somewhat parallel; surface densely clothed in short, reclining, pale setae. Abdomen of male concave in side view. Legs pale yellowish brown; hind tibial spurs dissimilar (male) or similar (female) in size; male hind claws simple. Adults found on pines (*Pinus*) and white fir (*Abies concolor*) in summer; also at lights. Coniferous forests of Rockies, Cascades, Sierra Nevada, Transverse, and Peninsular Ranges. British Columbia to California and western Nevada. (13)

Gymnopyge hopliaeformis Linell (5.0–6.0 mm) is oval, somewhat flattened above, finely granulate, coarsely punctured with scattered long and pale reclining setae; male smaller, black, sometimes with brown elytra, female larger, reddish brown. Labium distinct, below clypeus. Antennae with nine antennomeres, 1–6 reddish, 7–9 lamellate forming short, oval, black club. Pronotum convex, lateral margins rounded. Elytra short, exposing abdomen; striae weakly impressed, intervals weakly convex; apices slightly diverging. Ventrites not narrowed medially, sutures distinct. Claws deeply incised. Larvae unknown. Diurnal adults found on spring annuals, including desert-sunflower (*Geraea canescens*) and mallow (*Sphaeralcea*) in Mojave and Colorado Deserts. California. Genus needs revision. (4)

Diplotaxis moerens moerens LeConte (8.0–12.0 mm) is elongate-oval, convex, shiny, reddish brown to black. Head without depressions, uniformly punctured, clypeus scarcely upturned; labrum deeply concave. Pronotum flat with deep furrows along sides. Elytra with punctures larger than pronotum, costae indistinct with dense shallow punctures smaller than interstriae punctures. Nocturnal adults attracted to lights in late spring and summer. Desert scrub habitats in Arizona, Nevada, Utah, southern California, and the northern half of the Baja California Peninsula. *Diplotaxis subangulata* LeConte (6.0–9.0 mm) smaller, reddish brown or black, head crossed by ridgelike swelling; on shrubs and at lights, late spring and summer; widespread. (100+ NA)

Diplotaxis sierrae Fall (11.0–14.5 mm) is large, elongate-oval, glabrous, convex, shiny, dark reddish brown or black. Head with labrum visible, beneath clypeus; 10 antennomeres, 8–10 forming lamellate club. Anterior pronotal margin membranous; anterior angles obtuse. Elytra punctostriate, interstriae coarsely, confusedly punctate. Ventrites equal, sutures distinct; pygidium small, fifth abdominal ventrite fused to propygidium. Hind femora punctate between rows of setigerous punctures; opposing claws equal in size, toothed after middle. Montane habitats, western Nevada and California (absent along coast). Nocturnal adults feed on pine (*Pinus*); at lights. *Diplotaxis insignis* LeConte (11.0–15.0 mm) similar, anterior pronotal angles acute; hind femora impunctate between rows of setigerous punctures; also Utah. (100+ NA)

Grapevine Hoplia *Hoplia callipyge* LeConte (5.7–10.5 mm) is elongate-oval, slightly flattened, yellowish brown, reddish yellowish brown, to brown. Dorsal scales brown, sometimes iridescent pastel, dense (contiguous) to almost completely absent; scales dense ventrally. Erect, dense setae usually brown, or absent. Elytra without distinct pattern, scales oval or elongate. Hind tarsus with single claw. Adults feed on rose (*Rosa*), ceanothus (*Ceanothus*), lupine (*Lupinus*), willow (*Salix*), owl's clover (*Castilleja*), California buckeye (*Aesculus californica*), and yerba santa (*Eriodictyon*) in spring and summer. Various coastal, interior valley, foothill, and mountain habitats from southern British Columbia to northern Baja California, east to Idaho and Utah. (5)

Hoplia dispar LeConte (6.0–9.0 mm) is elongate-oval, slightly flattened, reddish yellowish brown to brownish. Dorsal scales dense, round, uniformly light yellow, pale green, orange, reddish yellowish brown, to brown, sometimes superimposed with faint to heavy dark patterns. Pygidium and underside with scales dense, pearly to silvery green. Diurnal adults active May through July, especially on flowers of Ceanothus; also yarrow (*Achillea millefolium*), buckwheat (*Eriogonum*), and rhododendron (*Rhododendron*). Montane habitats in Cascades and Sierra Nevada in southern Oregon to central California. (5)

Isonychus arizonensis Howden (10.0–11.0 mm) is oval, convex, tan to brown, and covered with whitish setae with patches of brown setae on elytra. Head with apical clypeal margin feebly emarginate; antennae with nine antennomeres, 7–9 forming lamellate club. Pronotum with lateral margins arcuate, convergent anteriorly, anterior angles sharp. Scutellum as wide as long. Elytra each with 10 shallow striae; white and brown setae all decumbent; brownish patches faint in older individuals. Fore tibiae bidentate; hind tarsi much longer than tibiae; claws incised, toothed. Adults at lights during summer monsoon season. Oak-pine forest. Southeastern Arizona and Mexico. (1)

Macrodactylus uniformis Horn (9.0–11.0 mm) is elongate-oval, convex, reddish brown dorsally, mostly blackish ventrally, and densely clothed in recumbent yellowish to grayish-yellow setae. Pronotum hexagonal, with anterior angles not reaching eyes. Legs long, glabrous, reddish brown; middle and hind tarsi much longer than associated tibiae. Diurnal adults found on various plants during summer, including mullein (*Verbascum*), and various fruit trees and shrubs in the rose family; occasionally attracted to lights at night. Southeastern Arizona to western Texas, south to Sonora and Chihuahua. (1)

Amblonoxia carpenteri (LeConte) (16.5–25.4 mm) is reddish yellow-brown, with dense whitish and brown scales, brown setae on head and pronotum, whitish setae on elytra. Apical maxillary palpomere teardrop-shaped, less than half length of antennal club. Antennal club with three antennomeres. Ventrites smooth medially, sutures effaced. Protibiae tridentate. Coastal southern California. *Amblonoxia riversi* (Casey) (15.7–22.7 mm) reddish, posterior pronotal margin with dense setal fringe, maxillary palpomere broadest apically, dorsal scales reddish tan; Pomona Valley, California. (6) *Plectrodes pubescens* Horn (15.2–22.0 mm) oval, ventrites uneven medially; Great Central Valley, California. (1)

Dusty June Beetle *Amblonoxia palpalis* (Horn) (16.0–26.0 mm) is robust, elongate-oval, light reddish brown with white, golden, or brown narrow scales above, long and dense yellowish setae below; females more oval with scales sparse dorsally. Head with last maxillary palpomere more than half to subequal length of antennal club; club with three antennomeres, male club about equal to antennomeres 1–7. Anterior tibiae tridentate. Males commonly attracted to lights in residential areas in summer; females seldom attracted to lights. Coastal plain of southern California. *Amblonoxia harfordi* (Casey) (16.0–25.0 mm) similar; last maxillary palpomere longer than antennal club; northern California. (6)

187

Dinacoma sanfelipe Gillett, Osborne, Reil, & Rubinoff (16.5–21.3 mm) male reddish yellow-brown, and clothed dorsally in dense whitish and yellowish scales, and ventrally with long pale yellowish setae. Antennal club with three antennomeres, about twice length of pedicel. Anterior tibiae bidentate, including apical tooth; posterior femora not enlarged. Males attracted to lights in June. San Felipe Valley, San Diego Co., California. *Dinacoma marginata* Casey (15.1–21.1 mm) male with anterior tibiae tridentate, including apical tooth. Scattered coastal chaparral communities in southern California. Both possibly of conservation concern; unknown females presumed flightless. Genus needs revision. (3+)

Polyphylla cavifrons LeConte (22.5–22.6 mm) is robust, elongate-oval, uniformly reddish brown, with pronotum and elytra without stripes even along suture, clothed in minute and narrow tan scales of varying densities; pruinose in freshly emerged individuals. Antennal club with five short (female) or seven long and curved (male) lamellae. Pronotum, save for edges, without setae. Protibiae tridentate. Nocturnal adults attracted to lights in summer in Colorado River Basin. Southern Nevada to southeastern California and southern Arizona; also northern Baja California and Sonora. Genus needs revision. (17)

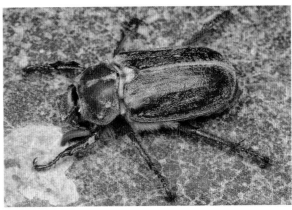

Ten-lined June Beetle *Polyphylla decemlineata* (Say) (18.0–31.0 mm) is black to dark brown, with distinct white elytral stripes smooth-edged, interstitial scales often yellow. Antennal club with five short (female) or seven long and curved (male) lamellae. Pronotum without discal setae. Adults, especially males, fly at dusk and evenings, and at lights in wooded foothills and mountains. Across Western North America. *Polyphylla crinita* LeConte olive brown to black, pronotum without (male) or with (female) erect setae, and distinct and smooth-edged white stripes; primarily Coast Ranges of British Columbia to northern California. Both species lack erect elytral setae. (17)

Polyphylla hammondi LeConte (24.8–45.0 mm) mostly reddish brown, with continuous white elytral stripes smooth, rough-edged, or reduced to discontinuous clumps of scales; interstriae with minute yellow scales. Antennal club with five short (female) or seven long and curved (male) lamellae. Pronotum glabrous on disc. Elytra sometimes unicolorous yellowish brown to deep brown with only sutural stripe; interstriae with yellowish scales. Protibiae tridentate. Attracted to lights at night during summer. Southeastern California to North Dakota and Texas, south to central Mexico; isolated populations east of Mississippi River from Wisconsin to Mississippi. (17)

Polyphylla nigra Casey (21.0–30.2 mm) is robust, elongate-oval, elytra black with continuous white elytral stripes slightly rough-edged, interstriae with yellow scales. Antennal club with five short (female) or seven long and curved (male) lamellae. Pronotum reddish brown with long erect setae in male and female. Protibiae slender, bidentate. Larvae significant pest of commercially grown fruits cultivated in sandy soils. Adults occasionally fly during day, feed on conifers; attracted to lights on summer nights. Northern Coast and Transverse Ranges of California; also Washington, Oregon, and northern Baja California. (17)

Polyphylla sobrina Casey (21.0–28.0 mm) is robust, elongate-oval, with base color distinctively light reddish brown. Antennal club with five short (female) or seven long and curved (male) lamellae. Pronotum with scattered hairlike setae. Elytra without hairlike setae, with stripes ranging from continuous and hard-edged to nearly absent in some females. Protibiae slender and bidentate. Both sexes, especially males, are attracted to lights, primarily Sierra Nevada in general vicinity of Lake Tahoe and Yosemite. California and western Nevada. (17)

European Chafer *Amphimallon majale* (Razoumowsky) (13.0–15.0 mm) is uniformly light reddish brown. Head with labrum notched medially and distinctly separated from clypeus; antennae with nine antennomeres, 7–9 forming lamellate club. Pronotal surface appears silky. Elytra with weakly raised interstriae. Larvae eat roots of wild grasses; pests of turf, clover, small grains, soybeans, and containerized nursery stock. At lights in summer. Europe; established from southwestern British Columbia to Oregon; also in East, New England and Quebec to Connecticut, west to Ontario, Indiana, and West Virginia. (1)

Listrochelus xerophilus (Saylor) (12.0–15.0 mm) is shiny reddish brown with pruinose elytra, and long, dense, pale yellowish setae underneath. Front claws toothed and pectinate basally. Nocturnal adults on rockrose (*Purshia tridentata*) in spring in juniper woodlands of southern California. *Listrochelus stohleri* (Saylor) (*Juniperus*; eastern CA, NV), *L. reevesi* Saylor (Death Valley, CA), *L. sociatus* (Horn) (Pacific Northwest) distinguished by male genitalia. *Listrochelus mucorea* (LeConte) (12.5–19.0 mm) distinctly carinate between eyes, setae white underneath; active in spring on palo verde (*Parkinsonia*). Southeastern California to western Texas. Genus needs revision. (38 NA).

Phyllophaga anxia LeConte (18.0–21.0 mm) is elongate-oval, shiny, glabrous dorsally, reddish brown to brown. Antennae with 10 antennomeres, 8–10 forming club. Lateral pronotal margins weakly serrate, not fringed with long setae. Pygidium large, propygidium and ventrite separated by suture. Male hind tibiae with apical spurs unequal. Nocturnal adults eat leaves of various trees and shrubs in late spring and summer; attracted to lights. In West from Northern Territory to northern California and Utah. *Phyllophaga errans* (LeConte) (Pacific Northwest) and *P. sequoiana* Saylor (central Sierra Nevada) smaller (15.0–19.0 mm), best distinguished by checking male genitalia. Genus needs revision. (~175 NA)

Phyllophaga bilobatata Saylor (15.0–18.0 mm) is elongate, somewhat parallel-sided, glabrous, and shiny dark reddish brown to brownish black. Head with clypeus broad, narrowly and deeply emarginate medially, frons deeply punctate, and antennae antennomeres 8–10 forming short club. Lateral pronotal margins smooth, not crenulate. Pubescence on metasternum long, sparse, and pale brown. Elytra moderately rugosely punctured, and costate along suture. Male ventrite 5 flattened at middle and coarsely punctate. Tibial spurs both long, slender, and freely movable. Tarsal claws cleft apically, with upper blade slightly longer Adults on oak (*Quercus*), and at lights. Arizona. (~175 NA)

Phyllophaga vetula **(Horn)** (13.0–19 mm) is elongate-oval, reddish to dark brown, pruinose, and coarsely punctured dorsally with scattered erect setae. Head with clypeus weakly emarginate, margin slightly upturned; antennae with 10 antennomeres, 8–10 forming club. Pronotum with sides weakly serrate, sparsely fringed with setae. Elytra with very long erect setae at base and along suture. Pygidium large, propygidium and ventrite separated by suture. Legs with opposing claws equal in size, toothed before middle. Adults feed on oak (*Quercus*) leaves; at lights. Arizona to Louisiana, south to southern Mexico. (~175 NA)

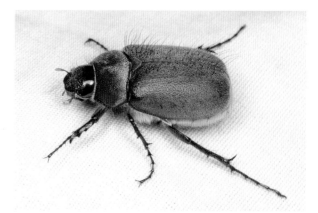

Phobetus comatus **species complex** (12.0–17.0 mm) are variably yellowish brown, head and pronotum darker, with thick, long, yellowish pile underneath. Antennae with antennomeres 8–10 lamellate. Pronotum coarsely punctate anteriorly; anterior and posterior margins with long, pale, erect setae; disc with variable reddish-brown cloud. Sutural and apical margins of elytra often dark. Abdominal ventrites narrowly translucent posteriorly. Male middle tibia with apical hook; hind tibial spurs divided by tarsal articulation. Diurnal, occasionally attracted to lights just after dark in spring in chaparral and oak woodlands. British Columbia and northern Idaho to southern California. Genus needs revision. (8)

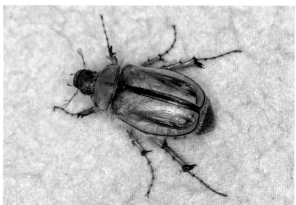

Phobetus humeralis **Cazier** (14.0–16.0 mm) is elongate-oval, yellowish brown with thick, long, yellowish pile underneath. Head reddish brown; antennae with 10 antennomeres, terminal three lamellate. Pronotum sparsely, finely punctured, anterior margin without setae, mostly reddish brown. Elytra translucent, reddish brown along base and suture. Abdominal ventrites narrowly translucent posteriorly. Middle tibia of male hooklike at apex; hind tibial spurs divided by tarsal articulation. Nocturnal adults on hoaryleaf ceanothus (*Ceanothus crassifolius*) in spring; sometimes at lights in southern Coast and western Transverse Ranges, California. (8)

Phobetus mojavus **Barrett** (14.0–17.0 mm) is pale yellowish-brown with thick, long, white pile underneath. Head and anterior margin of pronotum dark reddish brown. Antennae with nine antennomeres, terminal three lamellate. Pronotum sparsely, finely punctured, anterior margin without setae. Elytra translucent with folded flight wings visible. Abdominal ventrites narrowly translucent posteriorly. Middle tibia of male hooklike apically; hind tibial spurs divided by tarsal articulation. Nocturnal, often found feeding and mating on white bur-sage (*Ambrosia dumosa*) in spring, and at lights in Mojave Desert. Southern California. (8)

Phobetus saylori Cazier (11.0–12.0 mm) is black, with long, dense white pile underneath and pale, translucent elytra with black margins. Antennae with nine antennomeres, last three or four lamellate. Pronotum coarsely punctate anteriorly, anterior and posterior margins with long, pale, erect setae. Posterior margins of ventrites narrowly translucent. Middle tibia of male hooklike apically; hind tibial spurs divided by tarsal articulation. Diurnal males fly in search of females from late winter through early spring in desert foothills and juniper-piñon woodlands in southeastern Sierra Nevada, Transverse and Peninsular Ranges of California. (8)

Serica perigonia Dawson (7.5–8.5 mm) is oval, reddish brown, dull, with light grayish bloom, faintly iridescent. Labrum fused to anterior margin of clypeus. Antennomeres 7–9 lamellate. Elytra weakly punctostriate, with interstriae vaguely convex, and fine and irregular strial punctures sometimes bearing a seta. Hind tibial spurs flank base of first tarsomere. Nocturnal adults often found on flowers of California buckwheat (*Eriogonum fasciculatum*), and at lights during late spring and early summer. Southern California, Nevada, and Utah. Identification of *Serica* requires examination of male genitalia. Genus needs revision. (~50)

Anomala arida Casey (8.0–11.0 mm) is shiny and pale yellowish brown. Head dark reddish brown, with clypeus wider than long and apical margin straight, and frons with metallic green luster. Pronotum with crown-shaped dark patch from anterior margin extending past middle, and finely alutaceous with scattered punctures. Elytra translucent, with margins dark, broadly so beneath humeral umbone; sutural stripe extending only to scutellar apex; lateral and apical margins membranous. Claws unequal. Nocturnal adults active during summer monsoons and commonly attracted to lights in mesquite woodlands. Central and southeastern Arizona. (15)

Anomala delicata Casey (8.5–12.5 mm) is elongate-oval, moderately convex, mostly yellowish brown. Head brown, coarsely punctured; clypeus wider than long, apical margin straight. Pronotum anteriorly with large, somewhat quadrangular spot; finely alutaceous with scattered punctures. Elytra translucent, humeri sometimes dark, dark sutural stripe extending only to scutellar apex, with lateral and apical margins membranous. Tibial apices dark; claws unequal. Nocturnal adults active during summer monsoons, on vegetation, commonly attracted to lights in oak-juniper woodlands. Southeastern Arizona to western Texas. (15)

Anomala digressa Casey (9.0–12.0 mm) is shiny, mostly pale yellowish brown. Head brown, coarsely punctured; clypeus wider than long, apical margin straight. Pronotum brown except for yellowish-brown sides punctuated by a small dark spot, and a narrow line down middle; finely alutaceous with scattered punctures. Elytra translucent, pale yellowish brown, with dark sutural stripe narrow or broad extending around scutellum to posterior pronotal margin; lateral and apical margins membranous. Tibial apices dark and claws unequal. Nocturnal adults on vegetation and commonly attracted to lights during summer in oak-juniper woodlands. Central and southeastern Arizona, south to Mexico. (15)

Anomala flavilla flavilla Bates (6.5–10.0 mm) is shiny and pale yellowish brown. Head brown, coarsely punctured; clypeus wider than long, apical margin straight. Pronotum with distinct pair of quadrate patches. Elytra translucent, lateral and sutural margins dark, sutural stripe extending around scutellum to posterior pronotal margin, with lateral and apical margins membranous. At lights. Lower Colorado River Basin of California and Arizona to central Mexico. *Anomala f. coachellae* Potts with pronotum immaculate or with only faint or small paired pronotal markings; Coachella Valley, Riverside County, California. (15)

192

Anomalacra clypealis Schaeffer (8.0–11.0 mm) is shiny yellowish brown with variable dark markings on pronotum and elytra. Clypeus narrow, somewhat parabolic anterior margin moderately reflexed. Pronotum with distinct medial patch, sometimes nearly all dark. Claws unequal, front tarsomeres enlarged with inner front claw incised (male) or not (female). Larval and adult feeding habits unknown. Nocturnal adults active during summer monsoons; attracted to lights in oak-juniper woodlands. Southeastern Arizona, south to Chihuahua and Durango. (1)

Leptohoplia testaceipennis Saylor (5.0–6.0 mm) with labrum fused to clypeus, nine antennomeres, 7–9 forming club, and mentum with thick erect bristles. Front tibia without apical spur; hind claws unequal, long and very short. Adults, especially males, appear on dunes in late afternoon and early evening during summer, flying low in search of females; only fleetingly attracted to lights. Larger, heavier-bodied females attract numerous males with pheromones. Southeastern California and adjacent Arizona. (1) *Anomala carlsoni* Hardy (5.0–8.5 mm) similar in form, distribution, season; labrum free, with protibial spurs, and hind claws paired, short claw half length of long claw. (15)

Strigoderma pimalis Casey (7.3–12.4 mm) is robust, oval, convex, with head, pronotum, and scutellum black with bright green or violaceous luster. Pronotum narrower than elytra, feebly indented, metallic green with pale sides (male) or pale with light greenish luster (female). Elytra each with eight striae between humerus and suture, entirely pale or pale with dark brown or black ridges. Adults are commonly found in Arizona in July and August on various flowering plants, especially mule fat (*Baccharis glutinosa*), hairy senna (*Senna hirsuta*), Arizona prickly poppy (*Argemone arizonica*), and willow (*Salix*). Northwestern Arizona to Sonora, east to southwestern New Mexico, and Chihuahua. (1)

Chrysina beyeri (Skinner) (26.0–35.0 mm) is robust, oval or elongate-oval, convex, shiny, and bright apple green. Elytra with distinct anterior humeri and faintly indicated punctostriae; lateral margins expanded at middle (female). Legs with tibiae and tarsi lavender. Larvae develop in decaying logs. Adults feed on oak (*Quercus*) leaves, rest on trees or hide in leaf litter during day, fly to lights at night, and occasionally fly on hot, humid afternoons during summer monsoon season in oak-juniper woodlands of select mountain ranges in southeastern Arizona and southwestern New Mexico, south to Sonora and Chihuahua. (3)

Chrysina gloriosa (LeConte) (22.0–30.0 mm) is robust, oval, convex, and bright shiny green, sometimes legs with slight yellowish tinge, rarely with strong reddish or purplish tinge overall. Elytra each with four more or less complete silver stripes. Larvae develop in decaying Arizona sycamore (*Platanus wrightii*) and other hardwood logs and pupate in soil. Adults feed on juniper (*Juniperus*) foliage, fly to lights at night, and occasionally fly on hot, humid afternoons during summer monsoon season in juniper and oak-juniper woodlands. Arizona east to western Texas, south to Sonora and Chihuahua. (3)

Chrysina lecontei (Horn) (18.0–27.0 mm) is robust, oval, convex and shiny dark green with clypeus, underside, and legs coppery; female larger. Underside densely clothed in tan setae. Anterior clypeal margin somewhat trapezoidal. Elytra distinctly punctostriate, interstriae convex. Abdomen and legs with greenish highlights. Adults eat pine (*Pinus*) needles, and fly to lights at dusk and early evening during summer monsoon season in pine forests. Arizona and New Mexico, south to Sinaloa and Durango. (3)

Cotalpa consobrina Horn (18.0–22.0 mm) is robust, pale yellow to yellowish brown, with pronotum sometimes slightly coppery. Sides of opaque elytra angulate in female. Legs yellowish brown with dark metallic green tarsi. Adults occur along river bottoms lined with Fremont cottonwood (*Populus fremontii*); commonly attracted to lights. Southeastern Arizona and Sonora. *Cotalpa flavida* Horn (22.0–26.0 mm) legs orangish brown with black tarsi, on cottonwood and willow (*Salix*) in late spring, also at lights along Colorado River and tributaries. Southern Utah, Nevada, Arizona, and California. *Cotalpa ashleyae* La Rue (17.0–18.0 mm) elytra translucent, tarsi yellowish brown; Sonoran Desert in western Arizona. (3)

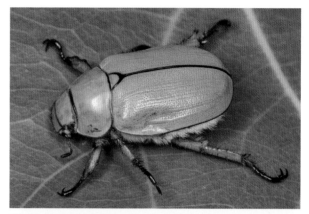

Parabyrsopolis chihuahuae (Bates) (23.1–31.5 mm) is robust, usually reddish brown, sometimes with weak metallic green reflections. Head with dense, confluent large and small punctures, mandibles visible from above, clypeus rounded apically. Pronotum coarsely punctate, with obsolete medial groove, especially in front. Elytra with some shallowly impressed punctostriae, intervals moderately to densely punctate. Pro- and mesotarsal claws usually cleft (male) or simple (female). Food preferences unknown. Adults fly at dusk and early evening, and at lights in pine-oak forests. Huachuca and Patagonia Mountains, southeastern Arizona, south to Michoacán and Mexico. (1)

Paracotalpa deserta Saylor (14.5–19.0 mm) is robust, coarsely punctured, entirely black, with long white pubescence ventrally. Head, pronotum, pygidium, and legs with bluish tinge. Clypeus with sides parallel, apical margin truncate, angles rounded. Pronotum with anterior margin distinctly bisinuate. Elytra without striae. Diurnal adults emerge in afternoon from bases of *Larrea tridentata* and *Ambrosia* to feed and mate on leaves and blossoms of desert annuals, including *Abronia villosa* and *Chylismia claviformis* in February and March. Southwestern Colorado Desert, California to Baja California. (5)

Paracotalpa puncticollis (LeConte) (17.5–22.0 mm) is robust, sparsely clothed in white pubescence, with coarsely punctate bright metallic green head and pronotum, and lemon-yellow elytra. Clypeus green (male) or brick red (female). Elytra faintly striped. Diurnal adults on junipers (*Juniperus*), taking flight at dusk. Juniper woodlands in southern California, Nevada, Arizona, and New Mexico. *Paracotalpa granicollis* (Haldeman) (13.0–18.0 mm) with dark metallic green head and pronotum rugose, and brick red elytra; on juniper. Eastern Washington and Oregon, east of Sierra Nevada of California, eastward to southeastern Idaho, Colorado, and northwestern New Mexico. (5)

Paracotalpa ursina species complex (10.0–23.0 mm) is robust and variable in color and setation. Head and pronotum black, sometimes with greenish or bluish tinge, blue, or green. Clypeus rounded. Pronotum not obscured by setae. Elytra reddish, brown, yellowish, or black. Adults fly on warm spring days; found on chamise (*Adenostoma*), sagebrush (*Artemisia*), and other shrubs. Grassland and chaparral habitats of central and southern California. *Paracotalpa leonina* (Fall) with coarsely punctured dark blue pronotum nearly obscured by long, erect, white setae. Active late winter and early spring. Mojave Desert of California, Nevada, Arizona. Genus needs revision. (5)

Pelidnota lugubris LeConte (15.0–24.0 mm) is completely glabrous, entirely black, legs sometimes with purplish or dark green sheen. Head with outer margin of mandible bidentate; frontal clypeal suture absent. Base of scutellum depressed. Male with apical protarsomere and inner claw enlarged; protarsi of females not modified. Larvae likely in decomposing wood. Nocturnal adults active mostly during summer monsoons, sometimes found on foliage of honey mesquite (*Prosopis glandulosa*) during day; at lights in desert scrub and Mexican oak woodlands. Southeastern Arizona and southwestern New Mexico, south to Sonora. (1)

195

Pseudocotalpa andrewsi Hardy (13.7–17.6 mm) is robust, pale yellowish brown with elytra lighter; dense, pale pubescence ventrally. Clypeus deeply concave, and frontoclypeal suture narrowly arcuate medially. Posterior pronotal angles well defined. Males fly briefly over low dunes in search of females just after sunset in April and May; briefly attracted to lights. Algodones Dunes in southeastern California, south to Baja California. *Pseudocotalpa sonorica* Hardy (20.0+ mm) vicinity of dune peaks, Algodones Dunes in southeastern California and Mohawk Dunes, Arizona, south to Baja California. *Pseudocotalpa giulianii* Hardy (14.0–25.0 mm) Amargosa Desert, Nevada. (3)

Ancognatha manca LeConte (14.0–22.0 mm) is black with chestnut elytra and legs, or reddish black with various yellowish-brown markings on sides of pronotum, bases of elytra, scutellum, pygidium, legs, and underside. Clypeal apex broadly parabolic, slightly upturned. Posterior pronotal margin with weak marginal bead. Elytra punctostriate, geminate rows usually indistinct. Legs with protarsi of males enlarged, large claw split at apex. Nocturnal adults active primarily in summer and are commonly attracted to lights in oak-pine woodlands. Arizona and New Mexico, south to Guerrero and Mexico. (1)

Cyclocephala hirta pilosicollis Saylor (10.5–14.0 mm) is uniformly pale yellowish brown, with long, erect setae dorsally; females less setose. Clypeus narrowly upturned and arcuate apically. Ten antennomeres. Bead on posterior pronotal margin sometimes faint in females. Elytra opaque, striae incomplete, and interstriae coarsely punctate. Male protarsal claw enlarged and incised. Adults swarm over grassy areas; at lights. Northern California to San Gabriel Valley. *Cyclocephala h. hirta* LeConte darker overall, occasionally with faint pronotal and elytral infuscations (not in Arizona), and less densely setose dorsally. California to Baja California, east to Nebraska, Texas; Mexico. (7)

Cyclocephala longula LeConte (11.0–14.3 mm) is glabrous dorsally, with head and pronotum slightly darker than elytra. Head reddish to yellowish brown, dark between eyes; clypeus trapezoidal, truncate apical margin upturned; antennal club longer (male) or shorter (female) than pedicel. Bead on posterior pronotal margin sometimes weak or absent medially. Elytra opaque, yellowish brown, with surface sculpturing indistinct. Male protarsal claw enlarged, not incised. Hind tarsus subequal (male) or shorter (female) than tibia. Common at lights in deserts and foothills. Southern British Columbia, throughout western United States, south to Chihuahua. (7)

Cyclocephala melanocephala (Fabricius) (9.0–15.0 mm) is glabrous dorsally, and distinctly bicolored. Dark reddish brown except for black frons, or black; yellowish-brown elytra. Head with antennal club shorter than antennomeres 1–7 (pedicel) combined. Pronotum without posterior marginal bead. Large front claw of male incised. Hind tarsus shorter than tibia in male, more so in female. Adults found during day deep inside flowers of Jimson weed (*Datura*) in summer; flies to lights. Southern California east to Kansas and Mississippi, south to Baja California Sur, Argentina, and Paraguay. (7)

Cyclocephala pasadenae Casey (9.2–15.2 mm) is mostly yellowish brown, mostly glabrous dorsally; slightly darker, more convex, and less hairy than *C. hirta*. Antennal club as long as (male) or shorter than (female) pedicel. Pronotum yellowish brown, usually with submarginal spot on each side before middle, without posterior marginal bead. Elytra weakly punctostriate, intervals shallowly and coarsely punctate, a few on sides and apices bearing setae. Root-feeding larvae sometimes damage turf. Adults common at lights in residential areas during summer. California to North Dakota, Arkansas, and Texas, south to Guerrero. (7)

Dyscinetus laevicollis Arrow (17.4–21.1 mm) is robust, convex, finely shagreened, and black. Head with clypeal surface transversely wrinkled, or rugose. Pronotum nearly impunctate, punctures moderately large and becoming denser on sides. Legs with protarsi of males with greatly enlarged claws. Elytra shallowly punctostriate, and with lateral apical margins swollen in female. Larvae undescribed, live in soil, and likely feed on plant detritus. Nocturnal adults active in summer and attracted to lights. Southeastern Arizona and southwestern New Mexico, south to Mexico; also Jamaica and Dominican Republic. Previous records of *D. picipes* (Burmeister) in Arizona refer to this species. (1)

Western Hercules Beetle *Dynastes grantii* Horn (37.0–56.0 mm) is large, robust, and black with pronotum and elytra shiny gray with irregular dark spots. Head with horn long, toothed near apex, projecting forward and curving upward (major male), short and toothless (minor male), or absent (female). Pronotal horn projecting forward in males, long (major) or short (minor), or absent (female). Elytral surface smooth (major male) or small punctures moderate in density (minor male, female). Adults active mostly late summer, feed on velvet ash (*Fraxinus velutina*) branches during day, attracted to lights at night. Southwestern Utah and Arizona, east to New Mexico, south to Sonora and Chihuahua. (1)

Megasoma punctulatum Cartwright (25.0–35.0 mm) is dull black, with (major male) or without (female) recurved forked horn on head. Acute anterior pronotal angles present (major male), or absent (female). Elytra somewhat wrinkled. Protibia tridentate, basal tooth distant from apical teeth. Males on bare trunks of honey mesquite (*Prosopis glandulosa*) at night during summer; females occasionally at lights. Mesquite woodlands of southeastern Arizona; probably Sonora. *Megasoma sleeperi* Hardy (24.8–30.5 mm) on palo verde (*Parkinsonia microphylla*) during summer; at lights. Colorado and Mojave Deserts of southern California and southern Nevada. (2).

Ox Beetle *Strategus aloeus* (Linnaeus) (31.0–60.9 mm) is large, robust, and dark mahogany to black. Head with pair of tubercles, and mandibles visible from above. Male pronotum with three blunt to sharply pointed horns; female unarmed. Elytra mostly smooth, with deep sutural stria in both sexes. Front tibiae with five teeth. Females lay eggs in rotten wood where larvae feed and develop. Nocturnal adults active mostly in late spring and summer; attracted to lights, especially females. Arizona to Georgia and Florida, south through Central America to central Brazil and Bolivia. (2)

Strategus cessus LeConte (24.5–41.0 mm) is robust and shiny chestnut to black. Head with clypeus narrowly rounded, almost acute apically, mandibles nearly square. Pronotum of both male and female unarmed, surface punctures large, moderately deep and becoming coarser anteriorly, with a broad, somewhat deep fovea medially. Nocturnal adults are active in summer, especially after monsoon rains, and attracted to lights in Mexican oak and juniper woodlands. Arizona and New Mexico, south through the Sierra Madre Occidental of Sonora and Chihuahua to Jalisco. (2)

Xyloryctes thestalus Bates (23.5–43.0 mm) is robust and shiny black. Head with long, slender recurved horn extending to just below pronotal surface (major male) or sharp tubercles at center (female), clypeus bilobed, strongly upturned at apex. Pronotum anteriorly declivous (male) or convex (female). Elytra with distinct sutural striae, surface distinctly punctostriate. Legs with protibiae with three teeth, metatibiae with 7–8 small teeth at apex. Adults of both sexes attracted to velvet ash (*Fraxinus velutina*) and lights during summer. Larvae found in soil beneath leaf litter, likely feeding on roots or fungi. Mostly southern Utah and Arizona, east to Colorado and western Texas, south to Chiapas. (1)

198

Anoplognatho dunnianus Rivers (20.7–29.0 mm) is robust and shiny chestnut to black. Head with narrowly rounded or somewhat truncate clypeal apex, a distinct and weakly curved carina behind clypeus, and large, almost semicircular mandibles; antennae with nine antennomeres (antennomere 5 subdivided, appearing to have 10 antennomeres). Legs with tarsi distinctly shorter than tibiae. Nocturnal adults become active after first summer rains in mesquite bosques or Mexican oak and juniper woodlands, often found walking on ground or burrowing into soil; attracted to lights at dusk. Southern Arizona, New Mexico, and Texas, south to Sonora and Durango. (1)

Coscinocephalus cribrifrons (Schaeffer) (20.0–23.0 mm) is robust, dark brown or black, with long legs. Head with a tubercle; clypeus not strong, narrowed apically, apex distinctly emarginate; antennae with 10 antennomeres. Elytra each with six punctostriae between humerus and suture, punctures moderate in size, weakly navel-like. Long legs apparently adapted for living in trees. Larvae probably feed on oak (*Quercus*) roots. Nocturnal adults briefly abundant after summer rains in oak-pine woodlands; not common at lights. Males swarm briefly at dusk, running rapidly up and down tree trunks, eventually ascending upward to females probably releasing pheromones. Southeastern Arizona to Sierra Madre Occidental of Sonora and Chihuahua. (1)

Orizabus clunalis (LeConte) (19.0–27.0 mm) is robust, dark reddish brown to blackish. Clypeus extending beyond subapical carina bearing widely separated teeth. Anterior pronotal margin usually with bead, triangular medially with broad depression behind (male) or obtusely angulate without depression (female). Elytra punctostriate, punctures deep, navel-like. Front tibiae bladelike (males) or with three broad teeth (females). Nocturnal adults active during summer in pine/oak/juniper woodlands, feed on needles of Apache pine (*Pinus engelmannii*), also in prairie habitat; attracted to lights. Sympatric with *O. ligyroides* at middle elevations. Arizona to Texas south to Guatemala, western Honduras, and northwestern El Salvador. (5)

Orizabus ligyroides Horn (19.0–27.5 mm) is robust, reddish brown. Head with clypeal apex not extending beyond clypeal carina bearing two narrowly separated teeth. Anterior pronotal margin medially with distinct erect tubercle (male) or weak to strong swelling (female), surface with shallow foveae (male) or not (female). Elytra punctostriate, punctures deep, navel-like. Legs with front tibiae bladelike (males) or with three broad teeth (females). Nocturnal adults active during summer in desert grasslands, prairies, and oak-juniper woodlands; also at lights. Sympatric with *O. clunalis* at middle elevations. Arizona to western Texas and southwestern Kansas, south to northern Mexico. (5)

Oxygrylius ruginasus (LeConte) (14.3–18.6 mm) is light to dark reddish brown. Clypeus with single tooth reflexed at apex, and mandible tridentate. Anterior pronotal margin with shallow pit and small tubercle in front, and posterior margin without bead. Elytra with seven variably complete punctostriae between humerus and suture. Parameres nearly square apically. Adults attracted to lights mostly in summer. Desert regions of southern California east to west Texas, south to state of Mexico. *Oxygrylius peninsularis* Casey (14.5–18.2 mm) parameres with "horns" before apex; Colorado Desert of California and Baja California Peninsula. (2)

Carrot Beetle *Tomarus gibbosus* (De Geer) (10.0–17.0 mm) is robust and reddish brown to black. Clypeus narrowed, with two small upturned teeth (*Oxygrylius* with single upturned tooth); mandibles with three outer teeth. Front pronotal margin with tubercle at middle. Surface of front tibia outside long row of coarse setae-bearing punctures with fine to coarse punctures. Adults commonly attracted to lights in spring and summer. Larvae develop in soils rich in organic matter or in sandy soils feeding on the roots of many plants. Widespread across southern Canada and United States. (1)

Hemiphileurus illatus (LeConte) (15.9–25.0 mm) is robust, shiny dark brown to black, and parallel-sided. Head with deep (major male) or shallow (minor male, female) pit with a short horn (male) or distinct tubercle (female) on either side. Pronotum coarsely and densely punctate, especially on anterior half. Elytra deeply punctostriate, navel-like punctures oval. Nocturnal adults active mostly in summer and prey on larvae of cutworms, longhorn beetles, and other insects; attracted to lights. Colorado and Mojave Deserts of southern California and southern Arizona; also Baja California Peninsula and west coast of mainland Mexico to Jalisco. (1)

Triceratops Beetle *Phileurus truncatus* (Palisot de Beauvois) (28.5–39.3 mm) is large and black, with cephalic horns erect or sometimes curving backward in both sexes. Pronotum with long, broad, shallow furrow widest anteriorly. Elytra shallowly punctostriate with punctures oval and navel-like, and intervals weakly convex. Larvae live in rotten, fungus-infested logs and stumps. Nocturnal adults active in summer, prey on insects in captivity; attracted to lights, but seldom common. Occasionally enter homes in East through chimneys, suggesting possible association with tree holes. Woodlands and forests from southeastern Arizona to Virginia and Florida, south to Panama. (1)

Euphoria fascifera (LeConte) (11.5–15.0 mm) is usually shiny with distinctly banded elytra and dark legs. Head black. Pronotum usually with four black spots. Elytra light orange with three black bands. Diurnal adults sometimes fly in large numbers after heavy summer thundershowers, resembling bumble bees in flight. Attracted to sapping desert broom (*Baccharis sarothroides*), honey mesquite (*Prosopis glandulosa*), and others, also fruit and malt traps. Larvae develop in nests of pack rats (*Neotoma*). Desert mountains and flats of southeastern California, Arizona, southeastern New Mexico; also Baja California Peninsula, northwestern Mexico. (11)

Bumble Flower Beetle *Euphoria inda* (Linnaeus) (11.1–16.1 mm) has dull or shiny elytra, and quadrate clypeus lacking apical teeth. Pronotum black, sometimes with yellow-brown markings. Elytra light to dark yellowish brown with variable, sometimes dense black mottling. Adults fly low over piles of plant debris during spring and summer. Found at ripe fruits, sap flows, and flowers of various plants, including thistle (*Cirsium*). Larvae in rotten wood, thatched ant (*Formica*) nest, and other accumulations of plant debris. Widespread in western United States, except Nevada and most of California. (11)

Euphoria leucographa (Gory & Percheron) (11.2–13.7 mm) is shiny brown with variable metallic luster. Clypeus strongly (male) or moderately (female) reflexed. Pronotum with whitish or yellowish cretaceous bands along lateral margins. Elytra with small to medium kidney-shaped, wormlike, or irregular cretaceous markings. Sides of abdomen with irregular white cretaceous markings. Larvae in nests of *Atta mexicana* ants in Mexico. Adults on flowers and sap flows of desert broom (*Baccharis sarothroides*) (p.45, Fig. 48) in mesquite woodlands, oak (*Quercus*), and other woody shrubs during summer. Southeastern Arizona and southwestern New Mexico, south to Guatemala. (11)

Euphoria monticola Bates (12.1–17.3 mm) is bright to dark or bluish green. Antennal club as long as (male) or shorter than (female) head. Scutellum impunctate. Elytra occasionally with small cretaceous markings. Diurnal adults attracted to sap flows on desert broom (*Baccharis sarothroides*) and oaks (*Quercus*) in various desert, scrub, and forested habitats at onset of summer monsoons; captured in Malaise traps and Lindgren funnel traps baited with various lures. Southeastern Arizona and southwestern New Mexico; also western Mexico south to Jalisco. Formerly known as *E. holochloris* Fall. (11)

201

Euphoria quadricollis Bates (9.7–13.4 mm) is robust, dull (male) or shiny (female) yellowish brown. Pronotum with two dark lines and semicircular spots on each side of midline. Elytra with black, irregular markings sparse (male) or dense (female). Adults active in summer, mostly early in monsoon season; found on flowers or vegetation of desert broom (*Baccharis sarothroides*), Emory oak (*Quercus emoryi*), California brickellbush (*Brickellia californica*), lotebush (*Ziziphus obtusifolia*), and prickly poppy (*Argemone*); also attracted to sapping oak (*Quercus*). Southeastern Arizona and southwestern New Mexico, south to Chihuahua and Durango. (11)

Euphoria verticalis Horn (10.6–13.3 mm) is robust and entirely shiny black or reddish brown. Head with clypeal apex emarginate and two strongly reflexed teeth anterolaterally, frons with moderate to well-developed protuberance. Elytra with apex strongly rounded. Larvae unknown, probably develop in rodent burrows or ant nest. Adults found in late summer feeding on sap and flowers of mule fat (*Baccharis salicifolia*), and roots of common sunflower (*Helianthus annuus*) and tithonia (*Tithonia*); apparently breed in nests of white-throated woodrats (*Neotoma*). Central and southeastern Arizona, southwestern New Mexico, and Sonora. (11)

Cremastocheilus angularis species complex (13.0–14.0 mm) is oblong, flattened, sparsely clothed in thick brown setae, dull black with scattered patches of whitish tomentum, and elytral punctation and form of tarsomeres variable. Head underneath with posterior margin of cup-shaped mentum entire. Pronotum with anterior oblique angles facing inward and posterior angles large and slightly reflexed, with tomentum underneath. Elytra with patch of tomentum at base and irregular transverse lines along sides, and elongate punctures on disc widely separated and open behind. Legs with hind tarsi about three-fifths as long as tibiae, compressed and tapering, and tarsomere 2 as wide as long. California. (22)

Cremastocheilus armatus species complex (10.0–13.0 mm) is oblong, flattened, dull black with patches of yellowish tomentum on elytra behind pronotal posterior angles. Front of head broadly, evenly rounded. Pronotum not divided; anterior angles obliquely facing inward, limited behind with slight transverse impression; posterior angles large, upturned. Elytral punctures broadly oval, occasionally with scattered patches of whitish tomentum. Hind tarsi shorter than tibiae, tarsomeres longer than wide. Adults active in spring; associated with *Formica* ants. British Columbia and Montana south to California. *Cremastocheilus angularis* species complex similar; elytral punctures long, narrow; second hind tarsomere as long as wide; with *Messor* ants; California. (22)

Cremastocheilus constricticollis Cazier (11.0 mm) is dull reddish brown-black with head and legs reddish, with long setae on head, and sides of pronotum and elytra. Head with transverse impression in front of eyes clothed in long, dense, golden pile, and clypeus with median carina. Pronotum slightly more than half width of elytra, with acute posterior angles. Elytra with elongate punctures. Tarsi 5-5-5. Associated with *Myrmecocystus depilis*. Southeastern Arizona and southwestern New Mexico, likely in adjacent Mexico. *Cremastocheilus opaculus* Horn (8.0–10.5 mm) with setal tuft on ocular canthus, pronotum three-fourths as wide as elytra, elytral punctures forming long scratches. Southeastern California and Baja California. (22)

Cremastocheilus planatus species complex (14.0–18.0 mm) is oblong, flattened, and dull black with long legs. Head densely punctate with distinct ridge beside each eye. Pronotal surface not divided; anterior and posterior angles node-shaped, each flanking a deep, trichome-filled pit; sides evenly rounded in front. Elytral punctures elongate. Front tarsus with third tarsomere attached to fourth at its extreme outer corner of posterior margin, fourth and fifth tarsomeres swollen, fifth tarsomere flattened laterally. Adults generally active in spring, associated with *Camponotus* ants. California east to southern Arizona and southeastern New Mexico; likely in northern Mexico. (22)

Cremastocheilus planipes Horn (12.0–14.0 mm) is oblong, flattened, dull, reddish black or black, with dark red legs. Head not densely punctate; clypeus with median ridge. Pronotum with anterior and posterior angles each flanking a deep, trichome-filled pit; divided into unequal thirds; raised lateral areas narrowing into smooth, shiny posterior angles. Elytra without sculpturing between long punctures bearing a seta. Legs with anterior tibiae and femora broad and flattened. Adults become active with first heavy summer rains, associated with *Aphaenogaster* ants. Arid and semiarid habitats between 1,200 and 1,400 meters from southeastern Arizona to Davis Mountains, Texas. (22)

Cremastocheilus quadratus Fall (12.5–14.0 mm) with mentum cup-shaped. Pronotum with scalelike setae, anterior and posterior angles flanking trichome-filled pits, widest across posterior angles, which are widest across disc. Elytral punctures oblong. Tarsomeres concavely compressed laterally. Adults fly in spring; possibly associated with *Messor* ants. Arid southern California and Arizona. *Cremastocheilus schaumi* LeConte mentum flat, pronotum widest medially with long setae; hind tarsi scarcely half length of tibiae, tarsomeres compact, not concavely compressed; central and southern California. *C. westwoodi* Horn similar, hind tarsus two-thirds length of tibia, tarsomeres loosely articulated; foothill and montane habitats, California. (22)

Genuchinus ineptus (Horn) (12.0–13.8 mm) is narrowly elongate-oval, black, with some whitish markings dorsally and ventrally. Clypeus narrowly reflexed. Pronotum hexagonal, without distinct posterior angles. Elytra flat, without costae. Tarsomeres smooth, not overlapping distally. Adults and larvae in decaying plant debris at base of stalk and leaves of sotol (*Dasylirion wheeleri*). Suitable sites for larval development possibly initiated by mining activities of larval *Thrincopyge* (p.218). Adults fly with onset of summer rains; prey on insects. Southeastern Arizona. (1)

Lissomelas flohri Bates (22.0–25.0 mm) is elongate-oval and flattened, smooth with few scattered punctures, and dull black. Head sometimes faintly punctate between eyes, with clypeus deeply impressed, clypeal margin acute, vaguely tuberculate; antennal scape with dorsal surface concave at middle. Pronotum convex, anterior angles normal and posterior angles rounded, none associated with a deep excavation. Legs with tarsomeres overlapping distally, sculpted with numerous evenly spaced longitudinal carinae. Larvae are unknown, but presumably develop in accumulations in leaf litter and other plant debris. Rarely encountered adults fly low over ground mornings after summer thundershowers. Southeastern Arizona, Durango, Distrito Federal, Mexico. (1)

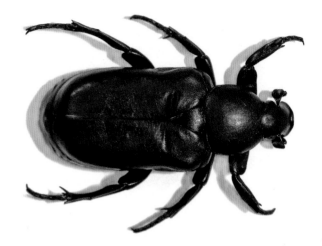

Cotinis impia (Fall) (15.3–21.2 mm) is robust, oval, and uniformly dull velvety black, sometimes with a reddish cast, or reddish tan. Head with narrow ridge down middle; clypeal horn usually short, broad, and bilobed. Pronotum with posterior margin extended medially, covering scutellum. Pronotum and elytra, except for lateral margins, smooth. Underside shiny brownish black, sometimes with greenish reflections. Larvae found in nests of pack rats (*Neotoma*). Diurnal adults active in summer, beaten from or found resting on leaves of oaks (*Quercus*) and other woody shrubs. Southern Arizona and New Mexico south to Sonora and Chihuahua. (2)

Green Fig or Peach Beetle *Cotinis mutabilis* (Gory & Percheron) (19.2–37.5 mm) is robust, oval, and variably dull green and tan dorsally. Head with distinct frontal and clypeal horns. Pronotum and elytra range from green, to mostly green with variable tan margins or mostly tan. Larvae have well-developed legs, but crawl on their backs and develop in compost and dung heaps. Diurnal adults fly noisily and clumsily through yards, orchards, parks, and mesquite woodlands primarily in summer. Adults attack peaches, figs, nectarines, and other fruits on trees damaged by birds or that have fallen on ground. Coastal plains, Antelope Valley, and Great Central Valley of California to southern Nevada, southwestern Utah, Arizona, Colorado, to western Texas, south throughout Mexico to northern South America. (2)

Gymnetina cretacea (LeConte) (19.0–26.8 mm) is shiny black with white markings. Pronotum moderately punctate, with broad lateral bands. Elytra with lines of punctures, each usually with two large spots, sometimes spots fused or with only outer spots. Pygidium with pair of triangular spots. Ventrites 1–4 with posterolateral spots. Southeastern Arizona, southwestern New Mexico, south to Mexico. *Gymnetina howdeni* Warner & Ratcliffe similar, pronotum and elytra sparsely punctured, each with a crescent, two spots or, rarely, one spot, and at least one ventrite pair of lateral spots. Southern Arizona to Durango. *Gymnetina borealis* Warner & Ratcliffe mostly black dorsally and ventrally. Central Arizona and New Mexico. (3)

Hologymnetis argenteola (Bates) (13.5–20.5 mm) is robust and velvety dusky olive brown to olive green. Head without horn. Posterior margin of pronotum lobed medially, obscuring most of scutellum. Elytra with scattered crescent-shaped punctures. Underside bright metallic pale yellow-green with brassy green and coppery reflections. Front tibiae with three somewhat equally spaced teeth in both sexes. Larvae likely develop among accumulations of plant materials. Diurnal adults drink sap from desert broom (*Baccharis sarothroides*) and fly primarily during summer monsoon season. Southeastern Arizona, Sonora, and Chihuahua to Durango. (1)

205

Trichiotinus assimilis (Kirby) (8.0–11.5 mm) is beelike, shiny black, and clothed in long grayish or yellowish setae. Elytra usually with distinct, pale lines obliquely crossing surface and flanking apices of suture, even intervals sparsely punctate with punctures large, odd intervals flat. Pygidium clothed in dense, long setae. Larvae develop in decaying hardwood branches, logs, and stumps. Diurnal adults are fast-flying flower visitors that feed on pollen in summer. Southern British Columbia, eastern Washington and Oregon, Idaho, Utah, and northern Arizona and New Mexico, east to central Alberta, Nova Scotia, and Pennsylvania. (1)

Valgus californicus Horn (8.0–9.0 mm) is dull black or reddish brown, flattened dorsally, with lateral pronotal margins sinuate, not serrate, and short elytra exposing abdomen. Abdomen with (female) or without (male) a short, recurved pygidial spine. Larvae beneath pine (*Pinus*) bark on stumps and logs in moist frass of dampwood termites (*Zootermopsis angusticollis*). Adults under pine bark, or in blind ends of termite galleries in dry wood during spring and summer; rarely encountered in flight. Cascades, Sierra Nevada, and Coast, Transverse, and Peninsular Ranges. Southern Oregon and California. (1)

DASCILLIDAE (da-sil'-i-dē)
SOFT-BODIED PLANT BEETLES

Very little is known about the habits of soft-bodied plant beetles. Soil-dwelling *Dascillus* larvae are found in moist sandy soil or under rocks and are thought to feed on the roots of living plants, both native and introduced, including fruit trees. However, studies of *Dascillus* larvae in Ireland suggest that they feed primarily on decaying plant materials and thus are detritivores. In California, adult *Dascillus* emerge in spring and are found on vegetation, including grasses and fruit trees. Although male *Anorus* commonly fly to lights in the drier foothills and deserts of southern California, the brachypterous females are flightless and rarely seen. The few female specimens known were apparently found in association with termite-infested conditions, such as within a buried root of a dead catclaw acacia (*Senegalia greggii*) inhabited by desert dampwood termites, *Paraneotermes simplicicornis*.

FAMILY DIAGNOSIS Dascillid males are elongate, somewhat convex, brownish, mottled gray-brown, or black, with dense decumbent vestiture sometimes obscuring surface and intermixed with longer, erect setae. Head broadly triangular, slightly deflexed, narrower (*Dascillus*) or nearly as wide or wider (*Anorus*) than pronotum, eyes moderate (*Dascillus*) or large (*Anorus*) in size, with mandibles stout and curved. Antennae long, comprising 11 antennomeres. Pronotum moderately convex with carinate borders. Procoxal cavities open behind, with procoxae large and separated (*Dascillus*) or contiguous (*Anorus*). Scutellum visible. Elytra punctostriate, completely covering abdomen (*Dascillus*, male *Anorus*), or short (female *Anorus*). Tarsi 5-5-5, tarsomeres 1–4 lobed underneath, and claws simple. Abdomen with five distinct ventrites free.

SIMILAR FAMILIES
- forest stream beetles (Eulichadidae, p.246)—larger, with scutellum densely covered in white setae
- *Perothops* (Eucnemidae, p.254)—prothorax with hind angles extending backward
- click beetles (Elateridae, p.273)—prothorax is loosely hinged to rest of the body, with posterior angles extended backward

COLLECTING METHODS Inspect fruit trees, native shrubs, and nearby grasses in early spring for *Dascillus*. *Anorus* males are attracted to lights in late spring and early summer in desert habitats and surrounding foothills. Observing and following male *Anorus* between dusk and dawn may result in the discovery of flightless females, as may setting pitfall traps in known habitats during peak activity periods.

FAUNA THREE SPECIES IN TWO GENERA

Davidson's Beetle *Dascillus davidsoni* LeConte (10.0–20.0 mm) is elongate-elliptical, robust, dull brown or blackish, with moderately dense fine light-gray setae variously abraded, with or without zigzag pattern; female larger than males. Head with prominent mandibles strongly curved apically. Pronotum wider than long, with sides broadly arcuate and narrowed anteriorly, anterior margin truncate, and posterior margin bisinuate. Elytra usually with variable irregular subbasal and subapical fasciae, disc punctostriate with interstriae convex. Adults found on grasses and fruit trees in spring. Mostly northern California. *Dascillus plumbeus* Horn, a junior synonym of *D. davidsoni*, tends to be darker and more abraded. (1)

Anorus piceus LeConte (7.0–10.0 mm) is elongate, brownish, and clothed in short recumbent pale pubescence. Head with mandibles prominently curved. Pronotum wider at posterior angles than anterior angles. Scutellum setose. Elytra cover abdomen of male (*left*) but not female (*right*). Males at lights in late spring, early summer in deserts and adjacent foothills; flightless females associated with termites (*Paraneotermes simplicicornis*). Southern California and Nevada to Baja California Norte. *Anorus parvicollis* Horn with anterior and posterior pronotal margins subequal in width, setae long and erect dorsally, and scutellum glabrous. Deserts of southeastern California and southern Nevada to Sonora. *Anorus arizonicus* Blaisdell is a junior synonym of *A. parvicollis*. (2)

RHIPICERIDAE (rip-i-ser'-i-dē)
CICADA PARASITE OR CEDAR BEETLES

In North America, rhipicerids are represented solely by species in the genus *Sandalus*. Very little is known about *Sandalus* biology, except for *S. niger* Knoch in eastern North America. This species gathers in mating aggregations in late summer on the trunks of American elm (*Ulmus americanus*), shingle oak (*Quercus imbricarius*), and other hardwoods. During these aggregations, males and females are found crawling or copulating on the bark, or resting on nearby grass, or flying in the immediate vicinity. After mating, females lay large numbers of eggs in the holes and cracks of bark, presumably in areas where there are plenty of cicadas, using an ovipositor that is nearly as long as their body. The subterranean larvae are ectoparasitoids of cicadas and develop by hypermetamorphosis. After hatching, the highly active triungulin makes its way through the soil in search of young cicada nymphs. The larval stages between the triungulin and pupa are unknown. A single pupa with a shed larval exoskeleton of *S. niger* was found inside the hollowed-out exoskeleton of a cicada nymph, revealing the pre-pupal stage to be a sedentary, grublike larva. *Sandalus* species are less commonly encountered in the West, but there are instances known where they have also been associated with cicadas. The genus needs revision as there are species still awaiting scientific description.

FAMILY DIAGNOSIS Adult rhipicerids are elongate, convex, coarsely and deeply punctured, reddish-brown to black beetles. Head hypognathous with well-developed mandibles. Antennae with 11 antennomeres and flabellate (males) or more or less serrate (females). Pronotum narrowed behind head, becoming wider behind, but narrower than base of elytra. Procoxal cavities open behind. Scutellum visible. Elytra long, completely concealing abdomen, surface vaguely costate and coarsely punctured. Legs with procoxae conical, tarsi 5-5-5, each tarsomere distinctly heart-shaped, with a pair of pale membranous lobes underneath, and simple claws equal in size. Abdomen with five ventrites.

SIMILAR FAMILIES The flabellate antennae of the male, elongate body form, and paired membranous tarsal lobes are distinctive.

COLLECTING NOTES Search for diurnal adults on tree trunks or flying in spring and early summer, or in fall; individuals are occasionally captured in Malaise traps.

FAUNA SEVEN SPECIES IN ONE GENUS

Sandalus californicus LeConte (16.0–17.0 mm) is elongate-oval, convex, coarsely punctate dorsally, sparsely pubescent with short and erect setae, and somewhat shiny black, sometimes with elytra yellowish brown (male). Head and pronotum finely punctate. Antennae inserted on prominent tubercles on sides of head, male antennae flabellate. Pronotum finely punctate with some coarser punctures intermixed, and lateral margin carinate only at base, straight and converging anteriorly, with posterior margin sinuate medially. Elytra coarsely and rugosely punctured, irregularly punctostriate, each with three faint costae. Slender tarsomeres weakly emarginate, lobes small and inconspicuous. Oregon to California, east to Idaho and Nevada. (3)

Sandalus cribricollis Van Dyke (19.0 mm) is elongate-oval, convex, coarsely punctate dorsally, clothed in long grayish pubescence, and black with reddish elytra. Head and pronotum cribriform, with coarse, deep punctures. Pronotum slightly shorter than wide, sides straight and slightly convergent anteriorly, with posterior angles blunt, and disc with coarse punctures intermixed with fine punctures. Elytra punctostriate, with strial punctures coarse and deep, and vague carinae most distinct at base. Tarsi slender, with tarsomeres weakly emarginate, lobes small and inconspicuous. California. (3)

SCHIZOPODIDAE (skiz-op'-ōd-i-dē)

FALSE JEWEL BEETLES

Schizopodidae are known to occur only in southeastern California, southern Nevada, southwestern Arizona, and Baja California, Mexico. Commonly known as false jewel beetles because the adults resemble jewel or metallic wood-boring beetles (Buprestidae, p.210), they are distinguished by their deeply bilobed fourth tarsomere. Schizopodids are typically found feeding on spring-blooming desert flowers, clinging to dry grasses (*Schizopus*), or on foliage of oaks (*Dystaxia*) and junipers (*Glyptoscelimorpha*). Little is known about their natural history. Eggs are probably laid in the soil, and the larvae are thought to be external root feeders.

FAMILY DIAGNOSIS Schizopodid beetles elongate-oval to somewhat oval, more or less stout, and strongly convex. Head hypognathous. Antennae somewhat serrate with 11 (*Schizopus*) or 12 (*Dystaxia*, *Glyptoscelimorpha*) antennomeres. Prothorax wider than head and narrower than base of elytra; pronotum convex and with (*Schizopus*) or without (*Dystaxia*, *Glyptoscelimorpha*) impressions. Procoxal cavities open behind. Scutellum visible. Elytra coarsely punctured (*Schizopus*) or relatively smooth (*Dystaxia*, *Glyptoscelimorpha*), sometimes faintly costate, and always completely covering abdomen. Legs moderately slender (*Schizopus*), or short and stout, with tarsi 5-5-5, with 4 deeply bilobed, and simple or toothed tarsal claws equal in size. Abdomen with five (female) or six (male) ventrites, with 1–2 connate, and apex of 6 deeply emarginate.

SIMILAR FAMILIES

- metallic wood-boring beetles or jewel beetles (Buprestidae, p.210)—fourth tarsal segment of adult not deeply notched or distinctly bilobed
- click beetles (Elateridae, p.273)—body distinctly flexible between prothorax and elytra

COLLECTING METHODS Look for adults during the day on desert flowers in the Mojave Desert, or clinging to dry grasses and herbs (*Schizopus*) during spring and summer in select foothills of California's Central Valley. Beating vegetation of coast live oaks, scrub oaks, and junipers is productive for collecting *Dystaxia* and *Glyptoscelimorpha*.

FAUNA SEVEN SPECIES IN THREE GENERA

Dystaxia murrayi LeConte (9.5–17.0 mm) is robust, oval, iridescent green to dark copper, with finely punctured dorsal surfaces clothed in slender flattened setae. Antennomeres 5–11 elongate. Pronotum convex, without impressions. Claws bifid. Adults on rabbitbrush (*Ericameria nauseosus*) and Nuttall's scrub oak (*Quercus dumosa*). Northern Coast Ranges to Transverse and Peninsular Ranges, also foothills of southern Sierra Nevada. *Dystaxia elegans* Fall (10.5–14.5 mm) similar, with antennomeres 5–11 strongly triangular. Adults on leaves of coast live oak (*Q. agrifolia*) and scrub oak (*Q. berberidifolia*). Southern Coast, Transverse, and Peninsular Ranges. Both California species active in late spring and summer. (2)

Glyptoscelimorpha viridis Chamberlin (6.2–8.7 mm) is elongate-ovate, somewhat cylindrical, moderately robust, iridescent green to coppery, dorsal and ventral surfaces finely punctate with yellowish or whitish lanceolate and recumbent setae. Antennae with antennomeres uniformly yellowish brown, extending to elytral humeri. Pronotum wider than long, broadest posteriorly, with posterolateral margins carinate and somewhat arcuate. Elytral disc with irregular setal patches. Underside with setae dense, somewhat obscuring surface. Legs short, stout, yellowish brown with tarsal claws simple. Adults on California juniper (*Juniperus californica*) during summer in Transverse and Peninsular Ranges. Southern California. (3)

209

Glyptoscelimorpha marmorata Horn (6.9–9.5 mm) is uniformly brassy bronze, with irregular setal patches dorsally, and long lanceolate yellowish and whitish recumbent setae dense ventrally. Antennae extending to posterior margin of pronotum, mostly yellowish brown, last antennomere black. Pronotum wide, broadest posteriorly, with posterolateral margins carinate and somewhat arcuate. Lateral elytral margins parallel to basal five-eighths, apices conjointly rounded, and disc with fine and shallow punctures and irregular setal patches. Legs yellowish brown, with claws simple. On California juniper (*Juniperus californica*) in Coast and western Transverse Ranges, Tehachapi Mountains. California. (3)

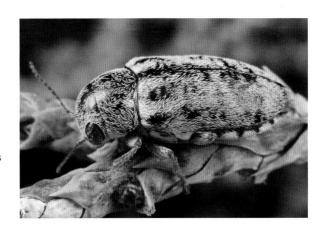

Glyptoscelimorpha juniperae juniperae Knull (8.1–11.7 mm) is elongate-ovate, somewhat cylindrical, robust, light brown, sometimes with hint of iridescent green confined to clypeus, and moderately clothed in pale lanceolate scales. Antennae extending to basal quarter of pronotum. Pronotum wide, broadest posteriorly, with posterolateral margins carinate, somewhat parallel. Elytra moderately convex with disc finely, shallowly punctate. Claws toothed. Adults on juniper (*Juniperus californica*) along northern and western edges of Colorado Desert. *Glyptoscelimorpha j. viridiceps* Nelson similar, mostly light brown, with head and usually pronotum iridescent green, on Utah juniper (*J. osteospermae*) in eastern Inyo and San Bernardino Counties. Both subspecies occur in southern California. (3)

Schizopus laetus LeConte (9.9–18.0 mm) is robust, elongate-oval, coarsely punctate dorsally, and brassy green, green, or blue with elytra same color (female), or yellow-orange or red-orange with green suture (male). Pronotum convex with distinct posterolateral impressions. Adults feed on desert-sunflower (*Geraea canescens*) and brittlebush (*Encelia farinosa*) in deserts. California, Nevada, Arizona, and Baja California. *Schizopus sallei sallei* Horn (9.0–19.5 mm) mostly dark yellowish brown, eastern edge of Great Central Valley; *S. s. nigricans* Nelson female black, western edge of Great Central Valley (San Benito, San Luis Obispo Counties). Both subspecies on dry grasses in spring. Central California. (2)

210

BUPRESTIDAE (bū-prest'-i-dē)
METALLIC WOOD-BORING OR JEWEL BEETLES

The common names applied to this family are apt descriptions of the beautiful iridescent colors that often adorn many buprestids. These streamlined beetles resemble click beetles, but their rigid bodies and metallic colors underneath immediately distinguish them from elaterids. Adult buprestids are most active on hot, sunny days and feed on foliage, pollen, or nectar; flower visitors are likely to play a significant role in pollination. Many are strong fliers and readily take to the air when threatened, often with a loud buzzing noise. Females run rapidly over tree trunks and branches, stopping briefly here and there to probe the bark and wood with their ovipositors extended in preparation for laying eggs in crevices. Eggs of leaf miners are glued to leaves of their host plants. Although a few of the wood-boring species attack healthy trees, most prefer to breed in trees or shrubs weakened by drought, fire, injury, or infestations by other insects. Emerging adults leave behind distinctive elliptical or oval emergence holes in trunks and branches. Even though buprestids are among the most destructive of borers in managed timber regions, they are an important link in the recycling of dead trees and downed wood. The usually flattened and always legless larvae often have broad and flat thoracic segments (p.28, Fig.18g) that give them a "square nail" look. The larvae of many buprestids mine the sapwood of branches, trunks, and roots, whereas others bore extensively into the heartwood; some species work both. Their galleries are relatively wide and flat, form long linear or meandering tracts beneath the bark or in the heartwood, and can hasten the death of already weakened trees. Galleries are usually tightly packed with wood dust and frass frequently arranged in thin layers defined with finely reticulate ridges resembling fingerprints. A few species are known to attack seasoned wood (*Buprestis*). Depending on the species involved, *Agrilus* larvae produce swellings along stems known as galls, or girdle twigs as they feed. Girdlers construct spiral galleries around small stems, killing the terminal end of the branch. Still other species (*Brachys, Pachyschelus, Taphrocerus*) are stem and leaf miners of both herbaceous and woody plants, while one species of *Chrysophana* utilizes pine cones.

FAMILY DIAGNOSIS Adult buprestids are elongate, broadly flattened or narrowly cylindrical, and have rigid bodies; usually metallic, or black with yellow markings above, and typically iridescent ventrally. Head hypognathous and inserted into slightly broader prothorax. Antennae serrate with 11 antennomeres. Procoxal cavities open behind. Scutellum visible or not. Elytra smooth, costate, or sculptured and usually almost completely conceal abdomen. Legs with tarsi 5-5-5, claws equal in size and simple, appendiculate, or cleft. Abdomen with five ventrites, with 1–2 connate.

SIMILAR FAMILIES
- false jewel beetles (Schizopodidae, p.208)—fourth tarsal segment of adult deeply notched or distinctly bilobed
- false click beetles (Eucnemidae, p.254)—never metallic, body distinctly flexible between prothorax and elytra
- click beetles (Elateridae, p.273)—body distinctly flexible between prothorax and elytra
- lizard beetles (Erotylidae, p.436)—antennae clubbed

COLLECTING METHODS Buprestids are most active during the hottest parts of the day and often found resting on tree trunks, flowers, or foliage of plants in which their larvae feed and develop. Forest and woodland species (*Chalcophora, Chrysobothris, Dicerca, Polycesta*) are sometimes found sunning themselves on dead or dying tree trunks and limbs. These and other species are frequently drawn to freshly cut wood, especially recently felled trees and slash cut by logging operations (p.45, Fig. 49). *Acmaeodera* are commonly attracted to flowers, especially the yellow blooms of composites and mustards, and may be captured in yellow pan traps (p.56, Fig. 60). Beating and sweeping vegetation during the early morning hours is also very productive. Using an aspirator will allow sucking up beetles quickly and easily from the beating sheet before they have a chance to escape. As the heat of the day increases, dislodged beetles will fall on the sheet and quickly fly away before they can be captured. Rearing jewel beetles from infested wood is also productive (see p.65).

FAUNA 788 SPECIES IN 53 GENERA

Mastogenius robustus Schaeffer (3.2–3.7 mm) is elongate, robust, somewhat flattened dorsally and ventrally, coarsely punctate, and somewhat shiny black with brassy luster. Eyes with inner margins converging dorsally. Pronotum broadest medially, with posterior margin straight. Elytra at base as broad as prothorax, with moderately dense, fine setae, with apices conjointly rounded. *Mastogenius arizonicus* Bellamy (3.9–4.1 mm) slender, uniformly black with purplish luster, pronotum broadest medially. Southeastern Arizona. *Mastogenius puncticollis* Schaeffer (3.0 mm) robust, black and bronzed, pronotum widest just behind middle, and elytra glabrous. Southern California and Arizona. Adults of all species on oak (*Quercus*). (3)

Acmaeodera acanthicola Barr (6.2–7.5 mm) is elongate-cuneate, somewhat flattened, and uniformly bluish black with pair of red postmedian elytral patches. Pronotum wider than long, narrower at base than elytra; distinctly margined on sides; posterior margin rasplike; front margin of prosternum with stout teeth on each side. Scutellum not visible. Elytra with strial punctures on disc small, elongate, and deep; patches oblique, broadest at lateral margins, not reaching suture. Larvae develop on *Celtis ehrenbergiana*; adults on flowers of *Vachellia*, *Senegalia*, and *Parkinsonia*. Southeastern California, Arizona, Texas; also, Mexico. *Acmaeodera bivulnera* Horn similar, black, with prosternal apex lobed and broadly emarginate. (~150 NA)

Acmaeodera amplicollis LeConte (9.0–13.0 mm) is elongate-cuneate, with metallic greenish luster. Pronotum wider than elytra; sides with a broad yellow stripe just before expanded lateral margins, stripes not reaching anterior angle, and posterior margin rasplike; front of prosternum sinuate. Scutellum not visible. Elytra yellow with irregular black markings, costate basally, each with black stripe reaching to about middle, behind with irregular bands that reach suture or not. Underside greenish, with suture between ventrites 1 and 2 not visible. Adults on flowers of composites, including *Baileya*, *Gaillardia*, *Gutierrezia*, *Gymnosperma*, *Helianthus*, *Heterotheca*, *Xanthisima gracilis*, *Senecio*, *Verbesina*. Southeastern Arizona and New Mexico; also Chihuahua, Durango, Mexico. (~150 NA)

Acmaeodera angelica Fall (6.5–11.0 mm) is elongate-cuneate, robust, clothed in long erect brown and silvery setae, has brownish black with bronze luster, and variable elytral markings. Pronotum unicolorous, with pronotal margin rasplike. Scutellum not visible. Elytra moderately sinuate behind humeri, with sublateral and discal rows of punctures sometimes coalescing into narrow, transverse lines not reaching suture; posthumeral spots seldom coalescent or obsolete, and sublateral markings sometime reddish. Suture between ventrites 1 and 2 not visible. Adults on flowers of chamise (*Adenostoma*), buckwheat (*Eriogonum*), acacia (*Senegalia*), desert mallow (*Sphaeralcea*); also scrub oak (*Quercus*). Oregon to California, east to Nevada and Arizona; also Mexico. (~150 NA)

Acmaeodera cazieri Knull (4.4–7.8 mm) is elongate-cuneate, robust, clothed in erect pale pubescence, with elytra each with irregular yellow stripe extending from humeral umbone to apex. Head convex, coarsely and densely punctate, with median carina on vertex. Pronotum wider than long, broadest behind middle, with sides arcuate, and disc uniformly dark and depressed medially before rasplike posterior margin; prosternum broadly emarginate. Scutellum not visible. Elytra at base narrower than prothorax, with humeri prominent and depressed in between, sides parallel to apical third, margins serrate on apical three-quarters, strial punctures large and nearly contiguous, and intervals convex. Suture between ventrites 1 and 2 not visible. Adults on many kinds of flowers. Ventrites sometimes with bluish tinge. Arizona. (~150 NA)

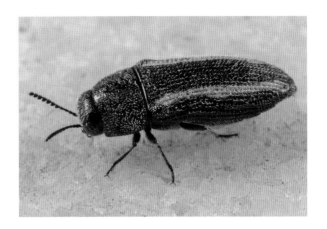

Acmaeodera connexa LeConte (7.2–13.0 mm) is elongate-cuneate, somewhat flattened, and with metallic luster. Pronotum slightly wider than elytra, widest in front of base, without lateral spot; front margin of prosternum sinuate, posterior margin rasplike. Scutellum not visible. Elytra black, each with basal spots coalescing to form irregular oblique mark; two interstriae carinate at base. Suture between ventrites 1 and 2 not visible, 5 with subapical elevation or plate. Larvae mine injured oaks (*Quercus*). Adults on various flowers, including encelia (*Encelia*), fleabane daisy (*Erigeron*), yerba santa (*Eriodictyon*), rose (*Rosa*), sage (*Salvia*), and globemallow (*Sphaeralcea ambigua*) in summer. Eastern Washington to southwestern Oregon, California, and Nevada. (~150 NA)

Acmaeodera disjuncta Fall (9.0–12.0 mm) is elongate-cuneate, coarsely punctate and clothed in dark pubescence dorsally, and black without metallic luster, with yellow and red elytral markings. Pronotum slightly wider than elytra; sides with a yellow stripe abruptly narrowed just before anterior angles, and posterior margin rasplike; apex of prosternum sinuate. Scutellum not visible. Elytra punctostriate, with strial punctures distinct, intervals not carinate, and disc with a few large spots and fasciae, and apical reddish spots on sides. Suture between ventrites 1 and 2 not visible. Adults on various flowers, especially Asteraceae. Arizona and New Mexico, south to Mexico. (~150 NA)

Acmaeodera gibbula LeConte (10.0–12.0 mm) is elongate-cuneate, somewhat flattened, and shiny black with bold yellow and red spots. Head and pronotum with greenish or purplish luster. Pronotum with pair of yellow spots on each side; front margin of prosternum rectangular, angles lobed, and posterior margin rasplike. Scutellum not visible. Elytra with bluish luster, sides usually with at least three prominent red spots. Suture between ventrites 1 and 2 not visible. Larvae in dead limbs of mesquite (*Prosopis*), catclaw (*Senegalia*), ironwood (*Olneya tesota*), palo verde (*Parkinsonia*), and willow (*Salix*). Adults eat pollen and foliage of various plants, including desert twinbugs (*Dicoria canescens*). Desert habitats from southern California to southwestern Utah and Texas; also, Baja California Peninsula, Coahuila and Durango. (~150 NA)

Acmaeodera hepburnii LeConte (6.0–12.0 mm) is elongate-cuneate, somewhat flattened, and yellow and black with bronze luster. Pronotum widest at base, as wide as elytra at base; sides not expanded, each with a small yellow spot near base; front of prosternum somewhat sinuate, and posterior margin rasplike. Scutellum not visible. Elytra with irregular yellow markings most extensive on basal half with smaller bands apically; lateral margin from humerus to indentation yellow. Ventrites bronze, suture between 1 and 2 not visible. Larvae develop in oak (*Quercus*). Adults found on various flowers, including yarrow (*Achillea*), yerba santa (*Eriodictyon*), fleabane daisies (*Erigeron*), buckwheat (*Eriogonum*), woolly sunflowers (*Eriophyllum*), gilia (*Gilia*) in summer. Western Oregon and California. (~150 NA)

Acmaeodera labyrinthica Fall (6.1–10.5 mm) is elongate-cuneate, stout, somewhat flattened, clothed in long, erect pubescence, and black with bronze luster, and intricately irregular yellow pattern on elytra. Pronotum with disc uniformly dark, rarely with small spot, and depressed medially before rasplike posterior margin; apical margin of prosternum usually emarginate, sometimes faintly trisinuate. Scutellum not visible. Elytra with strial punctures coarse. Last ventrite with subapical carinae small, rarely lacking. Suture between ventrites 1 and 2 not visible. Larvae develop in oak (*Quercus*), California laurel (*Umbellularia*). Adults on various flowers, including pincushion (*Chaenactis*), brittlebush (*Encelia*), and woolly sunflower (*Eriophyllum*). Oregon and California, east to Utah and Arizona. (~150 NA)

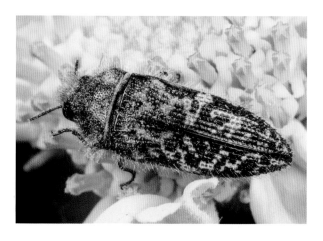

214

Acmaeodera latiflava latiflava Fall (7.0–9.5 mm) is moderately elongate-cuneate, clothed in long, erect, silvery pubescence, and brownish black with bronzy luster, with mostly pale yellow elytra. Pronotum wide, with posterolateral margins yellowish. Scutellum not visible. Elytra moderately sinuate behind humeri, disc pale yellow except for humeral umbone, narrow sutural stripe, and one or two spots on apical third. Larvae develop in flowering stalks of *Agave*, *Hesperoyucca*, and *Yucca*. Adults on flowers, including chamise (*Adenostoma*), brittlebush (*Encelia*), yerba santa (*Eriodictyon*), mesquite (*Prosopis*), and desert mallow (*Sphaeralcea*). California to Nevada and Arizona. *Acmaeodera l. lineipicta* Fall similar, with a stripe behind each umbone almost reaching apex, on *Baileya*. Arizona. (~150 NA)

Acmaeodera prorsa Fall (6.5–11.0 mm) is broadly elongate-cuneate, moderately robust, slightly flattened and clothed dorsally in moderately long brown pubescence, that of underside whitish, and blackish brown with yellow marking along sides of elytra. Pronotum unicolorous, broadest and strongly arcuate behind middle. Elytra at base slightly narrower than prothorax, each with three or four lateral spots, those in middle largest and transverse. Underside bronzed. Abdomen with last ventrite without thick subapical crest. Adults on scrub oak (*Quercus*), also on flowers of yerba santa (*Eriodictyon*), rose (*Rosa*), and sage (*Salvia*). California. (~150 NA)

Acmaeodera pubiventris lanata Horn (7.5–10.5 mm) is elongate-cuneate, somewhat flattened, clothed in long, pale, erect setae, and shiny black with purplish luster and yellow stripes. Pronotum uniformly black, not wider than elytra; front margin of prosternum distinctly toothed on either side, and posterior margin rasplike. Scutellum not visible. Elytra each with pair of irregular yellow stripes sometimes broken into irregular spots. Suture between ventrites 1 and 2 not visible, 2 more distinctly, finely, densely punctate medially than 1. Larvae develop in *Ephedra*. Adults on *Eriogonum*, *Eriodictyon*. California to Utah and Arizona; also Mexico. (~150 NA)

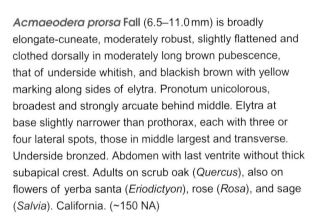

Acmaeodera resplendens Van Dyke (9.5–12.0 mm) is elongate-cuneate, somewhat flattened, distinctly punctate with large punctures, and uniformly greenish bronze, or brilliant green or bluish green. Head finely and densely punctate between eyes, with coarse punctures on vertex. Pronotum wider than long, with angles prominent, with sides broadly arcuate behind, then straight and convergent anteriorly, disc flat, and posterior margin rasplike. Scutellum not visible. Elytra punctostriate, with strial punctures coarse and slightly transversely rugose, and carinate with third interval briefly carinate, fifth interval carinate to basal two-thirds, and disc along suture flat. Suture between ventrites 1 and 2 not visible. Adults on composite flowers, including *Helianthus nuttallii*; also *Verbena gooddingii*. Southeastern Arizona south to Chihuahua and Durango. (~150 NA)

Acmaeodera rubronotata Laporte & Gory (7.0–12.0 mm) is elongate-cuneate, coarsely punctate with erect pubescence dorsally, and black with bronze luster, with yellow, white, and red elytral markings. Pronotum wider than long, sides broadly and evenly arcuate, disc without markings, with median triangular impression flanked posteriorly by a pair of foveae, and posterior margin rasplike. Scutellum not visible. Elytra black, with humeral umbones prominent, sparse yellow spots basally, red markings apically, and three intervals on sides convex and tuberculate behind middle, marginal interval moderately serrate. Suture between ventrites 1 and 2 not visible. Larvae in oak (*Quercus*); adults on various flowers. Idaho, Nevada, and Arizona, east to Colorado and Texas, south to southern Mexico. (~150 NA)

Acmaeodera scalaris Mannerheim (9.5–11.0 mm) is elongate-cuneate, robust, coarsely punctate and pubescent dorsally, and black with yellow and white elytral markings. Pronotum with metallic luster, more or less as wide as base of elytra, with sides white, lateral margins narrow and not reflexed, and posterior margin rasplike; apex of prosternum trisinuate. Scutellum not visible. Elytra punctostriate, strial punctures small and shallow, with intervals not costate, whitish lateral margins medially, and more or less striped basally with a few large spots and fasciae apically. Suture between ventrites 1 and 2 not visible. Adults on flowers of sweet acacia (*Vachellia*) and palo verde (*Parkinsonia*), as well as asters and *Sphaeralcea*. Southeastern Arizona to southern Texas, south to Mexico and Central America. (~150 NA)

Acmaeodera solitaria Kerremans (8.0–11.0 mm) is elongate-cuneate, coarsely punctate and pubescent dorsally, head and pronotum with greenish luster, and elytra with black and yellowish spots and fascia. Pronotum with sides arcuate and margined in yellow in more than basal half, posterior margin rasplike. Scutellum not visible. Elytra at base not wider than prothorax, with sides gradually narrowed to apical third, strial punctures fine, intervals on disc flat, while those on sides convex, three outer intervals tuberculate behind middle, outermost interval serrate. Suture between ventrites 1 and 2 not visible, 5 with subapical elevation. Adults on various composites and other flowers. California to New Mexico, south to Mexico. (~150 NA)

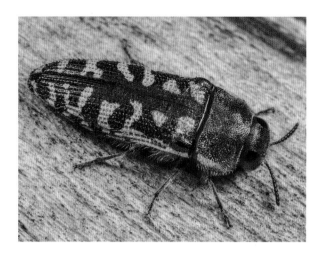

Anambodera nebulosa (Horn) (6.0–7.0 mm) is elongate-cuneate, robust, sparsely setose, and brownish black with weak bronze luster on head, prothorax, and abdomen. Head cribrately punctured, sparsely setose, and frons not impressed. Pronotum wider than long, uniformly dark, without any indication of side margins. Elytra at base not wider than prothorax, lateral margins serrulate at apical third, with disc deeply and narrowly punctostriate, strial punctures coarse, pale markings reticulate, and setae short. Suture between ventrites 1 and 2 readily visible, 5 without subapical plate. Adults on small yellow flowers, including *Camissoniopsis*. Central California. *Anambodera geminata* (Horn) with irregular brown elytral stripes. Western North America. (6)

Polycesta aruensis Obenberger (9.0–22.9 mm) is elongate, shiny black with bronze luster. Front of head flat and punctate with short smooth ridge above each antennal base. Pronotum densely punctured, with narrow median impression flanked by narrowly smooth surfaces; posterior margin bisinuate. Scutellum somewhat rectangular and convex, smooth. Elytra at base subequal to width of pronotum; lateral margins sinuate at middle. Ventrites 2 through 4 with posterior margins more or less truncate. Larvae develop in Texas ebony (*Ebenopsis ebano*) and willow (*Salix*). Adults on desert baccharis (*Baccharis sergiloides*), acacia (*Vachellia*), blue palo verde (*Parkinsonia florida*), mesquite (*Prosopis*), and smoke tree (*Psorothamnus spinosus*) in summer. Desert habitats from southern California to Texas. (9)

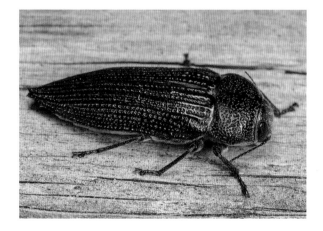

Chrysophana placida (LeConte) (6.0–10.5 mm) is elongate-oval, bright metallic green or blue with broad, reddish, longitudinal stripe on each elytron. Head with coarse, deep punctures almost touching; antennae black, dark purple, or blue. Pronotum finely punctate, punctures separated by less than their own diameters. Underside bright shiny green. Larvae mine limbs, stumps, and dead or dying conifers, especially pines (*Pinus*). Common, yet seldom-seen adults are not of economic importance. Southern British Columbia to California, east to Alberta, South Dakota, and New Mexico. *Chrysophana conicola* Van Dyke (9.0–12.0 mm) with shiny underside coppery; larvae in cones of pines (*Pinus*). (2)

Thrincopyge ambiens (LeConte) (16.2–22.5 mm) is slender-elongate, parallel-sided, flattened dorsally, convex ventrally, and usually green with coppery luster, with narrow yellow markings on sides of pronotum and elytra. Pronotal and elytral punctures moderately coarse. Elytra punctostriate. Larvae mine stalks and leaf bases of sotol (*Dasylirion*). Adults on sotol and beargrass (*Nolina*). Southeastern Arizona to western Texas; Coahuila. *Thrincopyge alacris* (LeConte) (16.0–23.0 mm) usually deep blue, elytra without striae, usually with two pairs of yellow bars before middle and pair of elongate spots apically that are variable; on sotol. Southeastern Arizona to western Texas, south to Chihuahua and Guanajuato. Species possibly hybridize with one another. (2)

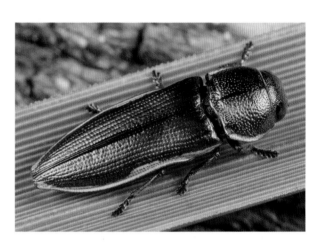

Paratyndaris olneyae (Skinner) (6.0–11.0 mm) is robust, cylindrical, blackish, and densely clothed in short, pale setae. Pronotal midline narrowly impunctate. Elytra each with two small orange spots arranged transversely before middle, spots sometimes larger and joined; punctostriate, intervals convex, with lateral margins indented, and apices distinctly toothed. Second ventrite with broad median lobe extending one-third (female) or two-thirds (male) across ventrite 3. Larvae develop in catclaw (*Senegalia*), palo verde (*Parkinsonia*), ironwood (*Olneya tesota*), and mesquite (*Prosopis*) branches. Adults on larval food shrubs in summer. Desert habitats from southeastern California to southwestern Utah; also Baja California Peninsula, Sonora. (5)

Sculptured Pine Borer *Chalcophora angulicollis* **(LeConte)** (22.0–31.0 mm) is shiny, irregularly sculptured dorsally, and black with bronze luster. Protibia with two strong ridges on posterior face. Elytra with costae irregularly expanded; posterolateral margins of elytra weakly serrate or crenulate. Larvae develop under bark of pine (*Pinus*), fir (*Abies*), and Douglas-fir (*Pseudotsuga menziesii*). Adults on conifer trunks exposed to full sun camouflaged by their pronotal and elytral sculpturing, especially after fire; slow-flying, produce loud buzz when flying. Common in coniferous forests throughout western North America, from Northwest Territories and British Columbia to California, east to Alberta, Montana, western Nebraska, and New Mexico. (1)

Nanularia brunneata **(Knull)** (6.8–12.0 mm) is covered with thick powdery coating, clothed in moderately dense, erect white setae, with head, pronotum, and underside coppery. Inner margins of eyes parallel, and antennomeres 4–10 compact, not flattened. Lateral pronotal margins carinate. Elytra brownish with apices not bidentate. Larvae in woody stems and roots of *Eriogonum elongatum*, *E. fasciculatum*, and *E. inflatum*. Adults found on buckwheat May through September. Xeric desert and montane habitats, southern California to Idaho, Utah, and Arizona. (7).

Dicerca hesperoborealis **Hatch & Beer** (16.0–20.0 mm) is brassy, coppery, or dark coppery, with small black elytral patches, and coppery elytral apices and underside. Head coarsely, rugosely punctured with irregular, elevated smooth ridges, and recurved white setae. Pronotum coarsely and confluently punctured, especially laterally, with median channel deeply impressed anteriorly and posteriorly. Elytra wider than prothorax, striae more impressed toward suture, and apices strongly produced. Processes between hind coxae sulcate medially. Hosts include birch (*Betula*) and alder (*Alnus*). British Columbia to northern California, east to Alberta, Montana, and Utah. (10)

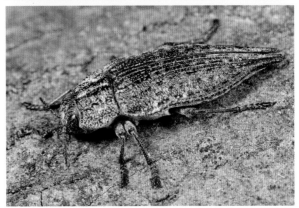

Dicerca hornii hornii **Crotch** (14.0–22.0 mm) is brassy reddish or greenish with a coppery luster ventrally. Antennomere 2 shorter than 3. Elytra with numerous small, smooth, raised areas; striae well defined toward suture; interstriae carinate apically; apices entire or weakly emarginate and slightly produced. Male metatibia with sharp tooth. Last female ventrite entire. Larvae in injured deciduous trees; adults on larval hosts. British Columbia to Baja California east to Idaho, Utah, and Arizona. *Dicerca h. nelsoni* Beer is bright copper, with male metatibial tooth short and blunt; Inyo County, California. (10)

Flat-headed Poplar Borer *Dicerca tenebrica* (Kirby) (14.5–26.0 mm) is elongate, moderately convex, bronze or copper to black, sometimes with bluish tint dorsally and coppery ventrally; elytra apices strongly produced. Head rough with irregular smooth areas; second antennomere subequal in length to third. Pronotum with distinct median channel, punctures becoming coarser laterally. Elytral apices entire, divergent. Male middle tibia with tooth. Last ventrite of female tridentate. Adults active March through November; eggs laid on sun-drenched trunks of cottonwoods and aspens (*Populus*). Widespread across Canada and United States. Best separated from *D. hesperoborealis* Hatch & Beer (British Columbia, Pacific Northwest states) by examination of male genitalia. (10)

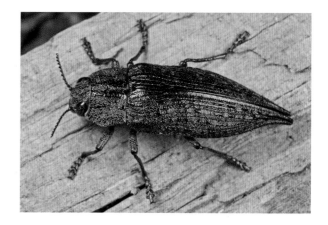

Dicerca tenebrosa (Kirby) (17.0–19.0 mm) is elongate, convex, black with coppery tints, and numerous prominent, smooth, black raised areas on elytra. Two long smooth raised areas on vertex between eyes; second antennomere distinctly shorter than third. Lateral pronotal margins parallel basally, broadest before middle, then converging toward anterior angles; disc with median channel distinct. Elytra with setae short, and moderately produced apices entire. Middle tibiae of male toothed. Last ventrite of female tridentate. Larvae in conifers; adults attracted to freshly cut logs. Widely distributed across Canada and northern United States. *Dicerca crassicollis* LeConte and *D. sexualis* Crotch similar, lateral pronotal margins more strongly expanded. (10)

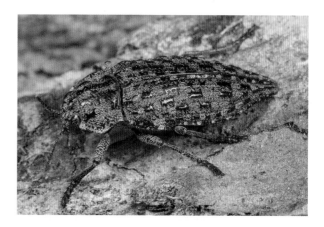

Gyascutus caelatus (LeConte) (18.0–30.0 mm) is robust, convex, surface coarsely and irregularly sculptured with raised purplish blue callosities surrounded by brassy punctate areas; yellow powdery coating easily rubbed off. Head with inner margins of eyes converging; antennomeres 4–10 compact, strongly flattened, and unicolored (female) or bicolored (male). Raised posterior pronotal margin continuous across middle. Elytral apices notched, bidentate. Protibiae curved. Larvae and their plant hosts are unknown. Adults are usually found on whitethorn (*Vachellia constricta*) and viscid acacias (*V. vernicosa*) in summer. Southeastern Arizona to western Texas, south to Sonora, Durango, and Coahuila. (8)

Gyascutus planicosta planicosta (LeConte) (8.4–20.4 mm) is robust, convex, irregularly sculptured, and dark blue with distinct elytral costae; yellow powdery coating easily rubbed off. Head with inner margins of eyes converging; antennae reaching posterior angles, antennomeres 4–10 elongate, somewhat serrate, flattened. Pronotum with prominent raised areas, raised posterior margin interrupted at middle. Elytral apices bidentate. Adults associated with various desert shrubs in summer, including creosote bush (*Larrea tridentata*). Low deserts of southeastern California, southern Nevada, southwestern Arizona, and northern Baja California. Two additional subspecies brassy green with moderate (*G. p. obliteratus* [LeConte] more eastern) or no (*G. p. cribriceps* Casey, more northern) elytral costae. (8)

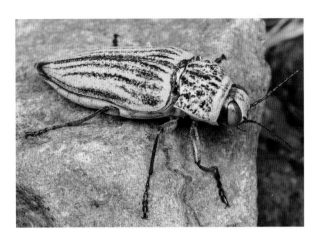

Hippomelas planicauda Casey (16.0–29.0 mm) is moderately robust, convex, uniformly sculptured without conspicuous callosities and black with bluish to slightly brassy tint dorsally. Inner margins of eyes converging; antennae reaching posterior angles, antennomeres 4–10 elongate and flattened, parallel-sided in males. Elytral bases narrowly covered with yellow waxy powder; epipleuron not toothed. Protibiae straight; front trochanter without distinct tooth; male with metatibiae enlarged apically, tarsomere 1 shorter than 5. Adults on mimosas (*Mimosa dysocarpa*, *M. aculeaticarpa*) and viscid acacia (*Vachellia vernicosa*) during summer monsoons. Arizona to western Texas, south to Sonora and Sinaloa. (4)

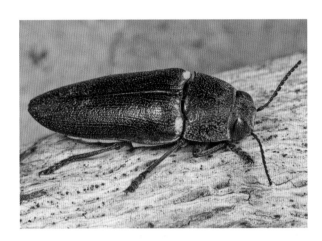

221

Hippomelas sphenicus (LeConte) (12.0–33.0 mm) resembles *H. planicauda*, but is black with a brassy tint dorsally, with elytral bases narrowly covered with orangish waxy powder, and male with metatibiae slender. Adults primarily on mesquite (*Prosopis*), occasionally on *Senegalia*. Arizona to western Texas, south to Sinaloa and Tamaulipas. *Hippomelas parkeri* Nelson (14.5–18.5 mm) is similar, but smaller, less shiny with a bluish tint, more densely punctate dorsally, and elytral bases narrowly covered with yellow waxy powder. Adults usually found on fairyduster (*Calliandra eriophylla*). Southern Arizona. *Hippomelas martini* Nelson (15.0–22.1 mm) also small, brassy green, with male hind tibia somewhat enlarged apically. Southeastern Arizona south to Nayarit. (4)

Lampetis webbii **(LeConte)** (13.0–32.0 mm) is dark bluish black dorsally with brassy green punctures. Anterolateral pronotal margins straight and converging anteriorly. Elytra weakly striate with isolated, finely punctate depressions; apices usually dark blue. Larvae purportedly in blue palo verde (*Parkinsonia florida*). Adults on various trees in summer. Southeastern Arizona to western Texas, south to Sonora and Durango. *Lampetis drummondi* (Laporte & Gory) (14.0–38.0 mm) with anterolateral pronotal margins rounded. Elytra with numerous finely punctate depressions contiguous in lines or patches; apices usually green or brassy. Southeastern Arizona to Colorado and Louisiana; also northeastern Mexico. (2)

Poecilonota cyanipes **(Say)** (10.4–16.0 mm) is dark coppery gray with elytral apices brightly bronzed. Head finely, sparsely pubescent, densely punctate with groove down middle, antennal base coppery. Pronotum broadest medially with smooth raised line down middle, sides coarsely, densely punctate. Scutellum short, wide, straight behind with angles distinct. Elytra punctostriate, punctures irregular, interstriae with irregular smooth spots, and prolonged apices with edges denticulate or serrulate. Underside bronze. Larva in cottonwood (*Populus*) and willow (*Salix*). Yukon Territory to Arizona, east to New Brunswick and Louisiana. (7)

Actenodes calcaratus **Chevrolat** (15.0–17.0 mm) is broad, somewhat flattened, coarsely punctured, bronzy black with faint coppery reflections, with coppery zigzag fascia on elytra usually prominent, sometimes faint or not apparent. Eyes separated dorsally by one-half or less their own widths. Pronotum moderately convex with vague depressions, with lateral margins diverging posteriorly to divergent posterior angles. Elytra wider than prothorax, vaguely depressed before middle, with fine punctures becoming rugose basally and laterally. Associated with *Vachellia*, *Parkinsonia*, and *Prosopis*. Arizona to Louisiana, south to South America. (4)

Anthaxia (*Melanthaxia*) **species** (2.8–6.0 mm) are broadly elliptical, somewhat flattened, often moderately pubescent with short white, brown, or black recumbent setae, and variably dull brown or black with dark bronze or coppery luster, sometimes with bluish or greenish margins. Pronotal disc with polygonal cells containing central granules or not, sometimes finely wrinkled laterally. Elytra punctate to granulate, and broadly rounded apically. Larvae in conifer branches. Adults usually on flowers in coniferous forests, including *Achillea*, *Ceanothus*, *Encelia*, *Eriodictyon*, *Erysimum*, *Lupinus*, *Rhamnus*, *Rosa*. Western North America. Genus needs revision. (~36)

Agaeocera gentilis (Horn) (9.0–15.0 mm) is elongate-cuneate, somewhat cylindrical, uniformly shiny green with coppery luster dorsally. Head black with weak greenish luster, with large eyes not prominent, and antennae short with outer antennomeres transverse. Pronotum wider than long, sides converging anteriorly and parallel posteriorly, disc coarsely punctate, becoming more so laterally, with weak impression before scutellum. Elytra as wide as or slightly narrower than prothorax, with punctures small and deep, and costae scarcely visible. Larvae develop in *Sphaeralcea*. California to Texas, south to Mexico. *Agaeocera scintillans* Waterhouse with elongate pronotal foveae, and distinctly costate elytra. Adults on pelotazo (*Abutilon incanum*). Arizona, Texas, and Mexico. (2)

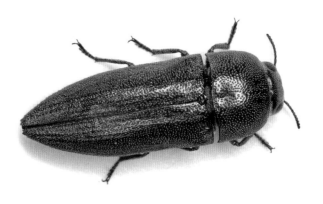

Golden Buprestid *Buprestis aurulenta* Linnaeus (12.0–22.0 mm) is mostly iridescent green to blue-green with distinct bright coppery reflections along elytral suture. Head, pronotum, and elytra without markings. Protibial apices of male without teeth. Elytra each with five, rarely six impunctate costae. Larvae associated with pitchy scars and wounds in living branches, stumps, exposed roots, and logs of conifers, especially ponderosa pine (*Pinus ponderosa*) and Douglas-fir (*Pseudotsuga menziesii*); typically require up to four years to complete development. Adults emerging from infested lumber damage wooden storage tanks and structural timbers. Pine forests from southern British Columbia to southern California, east to Manitoba, Montana, and New Mexico. (14)

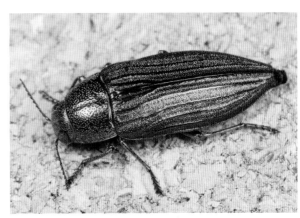

Buprestis confluenta Say (13.0–17.0 mm) is elongate-oval, golden green to blue or purple, with numerous, small, irregular isolated or more or less confluent yellow spots scattered on elytral surface distinctive. Head with green or coppery antennae. Elytral interstriae uniformly elevated; apices sometimes with coppery margins. Abdomen with middle of first ventrite grooved. Underside green to coppery, prosternum often yellow, with coxae, legs, and sides of thorax and ventrites sometimes spotted. Larvae develop in quaking aspen and cottonwoods (*Populus*). Adults found on injured, dead, and dying larval host trees in summer. British Columbia to California, east to Québec, Michigan, and Texas. (14)

Buprestis gibbsii (LeConte) (14.5–20.0 mm) is elongate-cuneate, and metallic green to bluish purple, with six yellow or orange spots on elytra. Pronotum moderately and shallowly punctured. Elytra punctostriate, strial punctures small, intervals moderately elevated, with pair of large, elongate spots before middle sometimes divided at or encircling humeri, followed by a pair of fascia sometimes divided into four spots, and a pair of subapical transverse spots sometimes tinged orange laterally, last two pairs of markings reach sides, never suture. Underside green without markings, ventrite 1 not sulcate medially. Larvae develop in oaks (*Quercus garryana*, *Q. kelloggii*). British Columbia to southern California. (14)

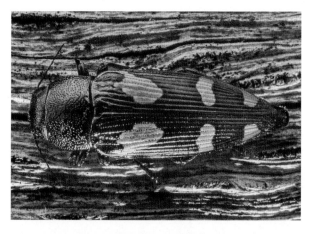

Buprestis laeviventris (LeConte) (14.0–23.0 mm) is black with orange markings, usually with four more or less transverse elytral bands broken at suture. Head, anterior pronotal angles and margin marked, posterior angles unmarked. Underside of thorax without markings. Elytral markings joined lengthwise near suture; alternate interstriae more strongly elevated. First ventrite with distinct longitudinal grooves medially; last ventrite only with orange spots. Larvae mine dead conifers. Adults on trunks during summer. Southeast British Columbia to southern California, east to South Dakota and New Mexico. *Buprestis nuttalli* Kirby (12.5–21.0 mm) similar, posterior pronotal angles and underside of thorax distinctly marked, elytral markings not joined lengthwise. (14)

Buprestis viridisuturalis Nicolay & Weiss (11.0–22.0 mm) is mostly green or blue, with elytra mostly yellow, sometimes tinged with red laterally, especially on apices. Elytra with suture narrowly green with single subapical band (male), or broadly green with two variable and irregular bands behind middle sometimes reaching lateral margins (female). Underside uniformly green, blue, or purple; last ventrite sometimes with pair of yellow spots. Front tibia with single tooth and margined internally (male) or simple (female). Larvae mine cottonwoods (*Populus*), willow (*Salix*), and white alder (*Alnus rhombifolia*). Adults common during summer in riparian woodlands. Washington to Nevada and southern California; possibly southern British Columbia. (14)

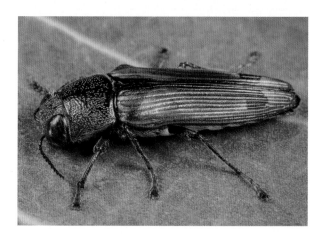

Spectralia cuprescens **(Knull)** (10.0–12.5 mm) is elongate-cuneiform, convex, and uniformly coppery, with head and pronotum slightly greenish. Head clothed in white pubescence, most antennomeres elongate-triangular. Pronotum wider than long, broadest just behind middle, with lateral margins obsolete anteriorly, and disc coarsely punctured, becoming denser laterally. Elytra slightly wider than prothorax, disc punctostriate, with intervals coarsely and irregularly punctured, punctures smaller than those on pronotum, and apices emarginate and sharply bidentate. Larvae develop in desert honeysuckle, *Anisacanthus thurberi*. Arizona. *Spectralia purpurascens* (Schaeffer) (8.0 mm) elytral apices more deeply emarginate and spinose; larvae and adults on beloperone (*Justicia californica*). Southern California and Baja California. (2)

Western Cedar Borer *Trachykele blondeli blondeli* **Marseul** (11.0–20.0 mm) is elongate-cuneiform, coarsely punctured dorsally, and bright shiny emerald green, sometimes with golden luster. Pronotum irregularly convex, with lateral margins strongly angular. Scutellum not visible. Elytra sometimes with several slightly impressed dark spots. Larvae in western red cedar (*Thuja plicata*), cypress (*Cupressus*), juniper (*Juniperus*), and possibly incense-cedar (*Calocedrus decurrens*); sometimes pest in managed trees. Adults emerge in spring and feed on foliage of tree crowns through summer. Southern British Columbia to northern California; also Arizona, New Mexico to Mexico. *Trachykele opulenta* Fall (16.0–20.0 mm) similar, less coarsely punctate, and sides of pronotum moderately angulate. Oregon and California. (4)

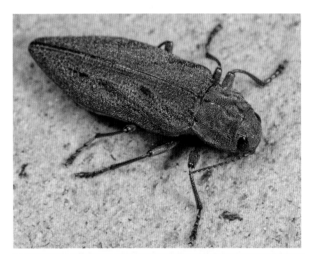

225

Trachykele nimbosa **Fall** (15.0–17.0 mm) is sparsely clothed in somewhat scalelike setae, and dull black to violet bronze. Pronotum wider than long, with lateral margins expanded and sharply elevated medially, and disc irregular with broad concavities. Elytra with numerous irregular and impressed smooth black spots, each with three or four more or less interrupted costae, and disc alutaceous and moderately closely punctate. Underside conspicuously pubescent, with ventrites brilliantly shiny copper bronze. Larvae develop in fir (*Abies*) and hemlock (*Tsuga*). British Columbia to central California, east to Idaho. (4)

Flat-headed Apple Tree Borer *Chrysobothris femorata* **(Olivier)** (7.0–16.0 mm) is elongate-oblong, slightly flat, black with coppery or bronze reflections, and indistinctly marked with dull spots and irregular bands. Head with clypeus sharply notched at middle and round sides, male with bright green face. Larvae feed and develop in many species of hardwoods, including maple (*Acer*), apple (*Malus*), pear (*Pyrus*), peach (*Prunus*), willow (*Salix*), oak (*Quercus*), and elm (*Ulmus*). Adults found in late spring and summer on sunlit tree trunks, under bark; also in Malaise traps. Throughout North America. (101)

Chrysobothris helferi Fisher (6.5–9.0 mm) with head and middle of pronotum coppery, and elytra with coarsely punctate areas coppery, sometimes with waxy bloom. Pronotum broadest medially, sides parallel, with disc finely, sparsely, and irregularly punctate medially, coarsely and confluently punctate laterally. Elytral bases abruptly angulate medially and transverse laterally, with broad, transverse callosities between humeri and across middle. Ventrites with lateral callosities. On juniper (*Juniperus*). California. *Chrysobothris texana* LeConte (7.0–13.5 mm) similar, elytra costate with bases evenly rounded. California east to Idaho, North Dakota, Nebraska, Oklahoma, and Texas; south to Mexico. (101)

Pacific Flat-headed Borer *Chrysobothris mali* Horn (6.0–11.0 mm) is brownish black to reddish coppery dorsally, with distinct coppery spots on elytra. Head with vague chevron and two small spots on front. Pronotum flattened with indistinct midline impression. Elytra indistinctly pubescent, each with three or four costae, costa closest to suture distinct along entire length, outermost costa indistinct; posterolateral margins serrate. Larva mines inner bark and outer sapwood, sometimes disfiguring small broadleaf trees and shrubs; adults on larval hosts in spring and summer. Southern British Columbia to California, east to Manitoba, Colorado, and Texas. (101)

Chrysobothris merkelii Horn (15.0–19.5 mm) is shiny brownish black with faint purplish or bronzy reflections dorsally, coppery with a greenish tinge ventrally. Pronotum broadest at anterior third, disc convex with three vague depressions on each side. Elytra wider than prothorax, each bearing four distinct and smooth costae, with 1 running entire length, 3 short and arcuate, and 4 most obscure, following lateral margin and joining 2 near apex. Larvae and adults associated with acacia (*Vachellia*), mesquite (*Prosopis*), and other thorn trees. California east to Nevada and Texas; also Mexico. (101)

Chrysobothris monticola Fall (12.0–15.0 mm) is moderately elongate, flattened dorsally, coarsely and deeply punctate, with smooth elevated spaces shiny brownish black, depressed areas brownish coppery, and underside uniformly purplish coppery. Head with antennae copper. Pronotum wide, densely punctate, with median depression flanked anteriorly with broad, smooth, elevated spaces. Elytra wider than prothorax, disc uneven with numerous large, irregular, and smooth patches, each elytron with four more or less distinct carinae, sutural carinae distinct, others sinuate and variously interrupted by densely punctate areas, and apices separately rounded. Larvae and adults associated with pines (*Pinus*). British Columbia to California, east to Alberta, Montana, and Colorado; also Mexico. (101)

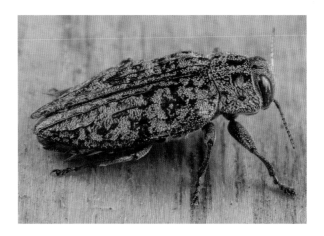

Chrysobothris octocola LeConte (10.2–17.0 mm) is elongate, flattened dorsally, brassy or coppery brown with shiny green or golden elytral spots. Clypeus deeply emarginate. Pronotum convex, without distinct median depression or raised areas. Elytral surface without setae. Sides of last abdominal segment serrate; ventrites with smooth raised areas laterally. Front and middle tibiae of male curved, anterior tibia with numerous small teeth near apex; posterior femur not dentate in both sexes. Larva mines acacia (*Vachellia*), mesquite (*Prosopis*), palo verde (*Parkinsonia*), and willow (*Salix*). Adults on acacia, catclaw, and mesquite in summer and fall. Desert habitats from California and Nevada to Colorado and Texas. (101)

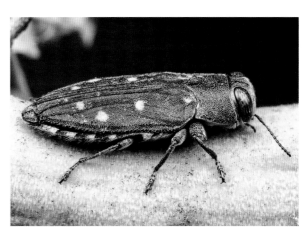

227

Chrysobothris quadrilineata LeConte (12.5–14.0 mm) is broadly elongate, flattened dorsally, black, with depressed punctured areas grayish with bronze luster, smooth surfaces shiny. Head coppery, front densely clothed in long, white setae, and with four raised diagonal ridges; clypeus broadly, shallowly emarginate; antennae gradually narrowed toward apices, dark bronzy green, becoming black toward outer margins. Pronotum wider than long, with deep groove down middle; prosternum with median lobe. Elytral base surface without setae. Sides of last abdominal segment serrate. Anterior tibia of male without small row of teeth along inner margin. Adults on juniper (*Juniperus*) in summer. Oregon and southern California to South Dakota and Texas. (101)

Chrysobothris viridicyanea Horn (7.0–11.0 mm) is broadly elongate, flattened dorsally, coarsely and sparsely punctate, and uniformly brilliant green with faint golden or bluish tinge, to violet blue, with underside even shinier. Head golden green, with longitudinal occipital carina, inconspicuous pale setae, and coppery antennae. Pronotum wide, broadest anteriorly, and disc without smooth callosities. Elytra slightly wider than prothorax, broadest behind middle, irregularly punctate with transverse smooth areas, with humeral depressions shallow, and basal depressions deep. Larvae in limbs and smaller branches of incense cedar (*Calocedrus decurrens*), western juniper (*Juniperus occidentalis*), and Rocky Mountain juniper (*J. scopulorum*); adults on various conifers. Oregon, California, and Nevada. (101)

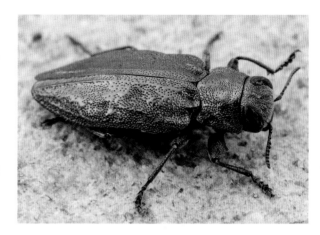

Knowltonia biramosa Fisher (8.0–10.5 mm) is broadly elongate, somewhat convex, and bright green or coppery brown, without pubescence or conspicuous surface sculpturing on elytra. Male antennae biramose, rami of antennomeres 5–11 subequal in length, 5–10, and usually 11 symmetrical, or nearly so. Pronotum wider than long, moderately rugose anteriorly. Elytra with violaceous spots. Profemoral tooth narrow and acute apically, not serrate. Ventrites green or dark, rarely violet or bluish. California east to Idaho, Utah, and Arizona. *Knowltonia calida* (Knull) abdomen black with metallic luster, male antennomeres 4–10 asymmetrical. Colorado Desert of California, Arizona, and Baja California. Both species associated with *Atriplex*. (3)

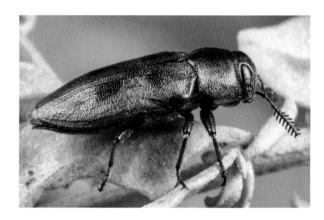

Sphaerobothris ulkei (LeConte) (14.0–17.0 mm) is broadly elongate, somewhat convex, and iridescent brassy green. Head with eyes separated on vertex about twice width of eye. Pronotum twice as long as wide, distinctly narrower anteriorly than posteriorly, broadest at posterior third, without depressions, with posterior margin broadly rounded medially. Elytra barely wider than prothorax, with sides mostly parallel, punctures coarse and weakly rugose, and marked with two pairs of indistinct purplish spots apically. Underside bluish. Arizona to Texas, also Mexico. *Sphaerobothris platti* (Cazier) uniformly iridescent deep green or brownish, with shallow punctures fine and sparse. Southeastern California. Adults of both species on *Ephedra*. (2)

Juniperella mirabilis Knull (19.0–21.0 mm) is elongate-oval, stout, mostly glabrous, head and underside bearing short setae and broadly banded elytra. Head and pronotum coarsely punctate. Metallic green pronotum broadest basally. Elytra dark greenish black with yellow bands not reaching suture. Larvae mine roots and thick trunks of California juniper (*Juniperus californica*), boring under bark and outer sapwood. Rarely encountered adults emerge from large, elliptical holes hidden by bark at bases of trunks in summer, and rest among dense foliage; fly with loud buzz. Juniper woodlands along foothills of Transverse and Peninsular Ranges in California. (1)

Melanophila acuminata (De Geer) (7.0–13.0 mm) is elongate-oval and uniformly dull black. Pronotum broadest before middle, with disc reticulate-granulate and finely punctate medially, punctures distinct and shallow laterally. Elytra broader than prothorax, glabrous, surface with dense, irregular, and weak elevations, and apices acute. Larvae develop in pine (*Pinus*), fir (*Abies*), spruce (*Picea*), cedar (*Cupressus*), and arborvitae (*Thuja*). Adults attracted to fires and scorched timber; occasionally at lights. Holarctic; transcontinental in coniferous forests. Note: mesothorax with (*Melanophila* species) or without (*Phaenops* species) pits adjacent to coxal cavities. (6)

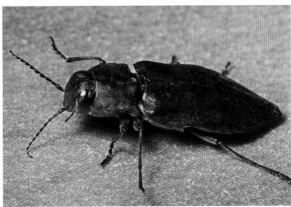

Charcoal Beetle *Melanophila consputa* LeConte (8.0–13.0 mm) is dull black dorsally and ventrally, with five or six yellow spots on each elytron. Pronotum broadest before middle, lateral margins broadly arcuate, and disc convex, with reticulations becoming more distinct laterally. Elytra broader than prothorax, glabrous, and granulate-punctate. Adults attracted to wood smoke and cement plant fumes; occasionally at lights. Washington to California, east to Idaho, Colorado, Utah, and Arizona. *Melanophila notata* (Laporte & Gory) with only three to four spots on elytron. Widespread in West, south to Central America; West Indies. (6)

Phaenops drummondi drummondi (Kirby) (8.0–12.0 mm) is completely black, with three or four yellow spots on each elytron. Pronotum broadest before middle, lateral margins weakly arcuate, and disc finely strigose. Elytra broader than prothorax, each with three faint costae or not, and numerous fine, short setae. Mesothorax without pits adjacent to coxae. Larvae in injured, mistletoe-infested, fire-killed, or recently felled conifers. Alaska, western Canada and United States. *Phaenops lecontei* (Obenberger) (10.0–11.2 mm) similar, pronotal disc coarsely strigose and punctate. On fir (*Abies*) and pine (*Pinus*). British Columbia and western United States. (7)

229

Phaenops gentilis (**LeConte**) (8.0–14.0 mm) is elongate-oval, flattened, densely punctured, and distinctively green or blue-green to purplish dorsally, and coppery to greenish ventrally. Pronotum wide, broadest before middle, with lateral margins evenly arcuate, and disc convex. Elytra broader than prothorax, weakly divergent laterally, with surface weakly undulating at basal two-thirds, and short setae. Underside shiny, weakly granulate, with last ventrite acutely rounded (female), or emarginate male. Larvae develop in pine (*Pinus*) bark. Adults attracted to injured, downed, or felled trees. Western British Columbia and throughout western United States. (7)

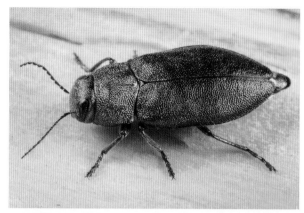

Phaenops vandykei (**Obenberger**) (7.3–11.5 mm) is elongate-oval, flattened, and dark coppery or bronze, with elytra immaculate. Pronotum wide, broadest just behind middle, with disc coarsely strigose, and coarse confluent punctures laterally. Elytra broader than prothorax, weakly costate on apical half, and with numerous scattered short setae. Larvae and adults associated with ponderosa pine (*Pinus ponderosa*). Adults prey of crabronid wasp, *Cerceris completa*; parasitized by sarcophagid fly, *Senotainia trilineata*. Oregon to southern California. Genus needs revision. (7)

230

Xenomelanophila miranda (**LeConte**) (13.5–16.0 mm) has boldly tricolored elytra. Head with five smooth, raised callosities. Pronotum broadest medially, lateral margin obliterated anteriorly, and sinuate just before posterior angle, with seven raised and smooth callosities on disc. Elytra at base wider than prothorax, mostly yellow with basal and lateral margins red, and large black submarginal and discal spots, with posterolateral margins becoming serrate. Underside greenish. Adults associated mostly with juniper (*Juniperus*), frequently attracted to smoldering stumps and branches. British Columbia to California, east to Idaho, Colorado, and Texas; also Mexico. (1)

Goldspotted Oak Borer *Agrilus auroguttatus* Schaeffer (9.0–12.0 mm) is slender, and dull black with metallic blue and green luster. Pronotum wide, narrower at base than apex, clothed in golden-yellow pubescence behind anterior angles, and sides weakly sinuate before rectangular posterior angles. Elytra sinuate behind humeri, with six yellow pubescent spots, and apices each narrowly rounded and serrulate. Larvae chew meandering tunnels on surface of sapwood on trunks of oaks (*Quercus agrifolia*, *Q. engelmannii*, *Q. kelloggii*). Southeastern Arizona and Baja California Peninsula; adventive pest in southern California. (75)

Agrilus cavatus Chevrolat (8.2–14.5 mm) is reddish or bronzy coppery dorsally, brassier ventrally. Head with deep, longitudinal depression between large, broadly oblong eyes that are more rounded below. Pronotum as wide as elytra, with deep median impression expanding posteriorly. Elytra each with raised suture and vague, relatively smooth carina, and a pair of pubescent spots on apical third, sides briefly parallel behind humeri then broadly arcuate before middle, and broadly rounded apices coarsely serrulate. Ventrites 1–4 densely pubescent laterally, 3 with additional pubescent patch. On *Acaciella*. Arizona east to Oklahoma and Texas; south to South America. (75)

Agrilus heterothecae Knull (5.6–7.0 mm) with head and pronotum coppery, and granulate-punctate elytra dull black or bluish black and clothed in short setae. Head with medial depression shallow, not quite reaching occiput, with antennae black, and antennomere 3 triangular. Pronotum almost quadrate, with deep arcuate impressions laterally, and less deeply impressed before scutellum. On *Heterotheca*. Arizona, Mexico. *Agrilus huachucae* Schaeffer (7.0–9.5 mm) with deep depression on head reaching occiput, antennae metallic green, antennomere 3 elongate, with stronger pronotal depression before scutellum. On *Brickellia* and *Quercus*. Arizona, New Mexico, south to Mexico. (75)

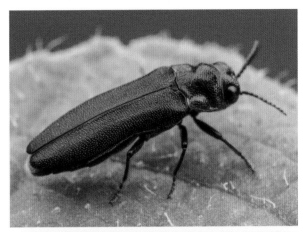

Common Willow Agrilus *Agrilus politus* (Say) (5.0–8.5 mm) is variably green to coppery or metallic gray. Antennae becoming serrate at antennomere 4, 7–11 wider than long. Elytra unmarked, and apices not prolonged. Pygidium without projecting carina. Front tarsal claws with inner teeth not turned inward. Larvae producing galls as they girdle branches of maple (*Acer*) and willow (*Salix*). Across most of Canada and United States. *Agrilus burkei* Fisher (6.0–9.0 mm) very similar, except deep blue to bluish green. Larvae in alder (*Alnus*). Western provinces and states. (75)

Agrilus pulchellus Bland (5.5–12.0 mm) with male head brassy coppery in front, with pronotum and elytral suture brassy green; these surfaces bluer in female. Both sexes with long, broad coppery elytral stripe laterally. Male with metasternum broadly, densely pubescent laterally; pubescent patches on first two ventrites broadly connected. Abdomen with distinct black glabrous and white pubescent patches laterally. Larvae mine roots of fleabane (*Erigeron*). Adults on various flowers during summer. Southeastern Arizona to North Dakota and Texas, south to Sinaloa and Durango. (75)

Agrilus walsinghami Crotch (9.0–13.0 mm) is elongate, subcylindrical, somewhat flattened dorsally. Bronzy brown head and pronotum, and brassy elytra with purplish tint (male), greenish blue (female). Elytra each with three fine, irregular, faint costae; distinctly marked with white pubescent spots. Underside of both sexes bronzy green with prominent white pubescent patches and coppery legs. Rubber rabbitbrush, *Ericameria nauseosa*, is presumed larval host plant. Distinctive adults found on flowers or stems of larval host from mid-July to mid-September. British Columbia to California, east to Idaho, Colorado, and New Mexico. (75)

Brachys aerosus Melsheimer (3.0–6.3 mm) is broadly ovate, triangular, bicolored, with pubescence variably gray to reddish brown and gold. Head with tubercle above eye not prominent. Scutellum small. Elytra black with bluish, purplish, or brassy luster, especially humeral region; apical setae mostly gold. Abdomen underneath with tip of last ventrite straight in both sexes. Larva mines leaves of oak (*Quercus*) and many other deciduous trees. Adults active late spring and summer, found on Columbia hawthorn (*Crataegus columbiana*), black birch (*Betula occidentalis*), and quaking aspen (*Populus tremuloides*); other hardwoods recorded in eastern part of range. Widespread across Canada; in West, south to Washington and Montana; also Arizona. (5)

Pachyschelus secedens Waterhouse (3.0 mm) is broadly obovate; flattened, and bicolored with shiny black head, pronotum, and scutellum, and shiny blue-black elytra. Pronotum with lateral margins brassy. Scutellum large, triangular. Abdomen with posterior margin of last ventrite acute with setose medial projection (male) or emarginate medially with downturned teeth (female). Legs with broad, flattened tibiae with apices dilated. Larvae mine the leaves of San Pedro ticktrefoil, *Desmodium batocaulon*. Adults found during summer monsoons resting and mating on leaves of larval host plant. Colorado and Arizona, south to Guatemala. (1)

232

BYRRHIDAE (bir'-i-dē)
PILL OR MOSS BEETLES

Adult and larval byrrhids feed primarily on mosses and, on occasion, liverworts. The larvae of most species burrow through the tissues and underlying substrate as they feed, but those of *Cytilus alternatus* (Say) are surface grazers and consume bits of dead wood, lichen, moss fragments, and leaves. Most adults are nocturnal and are strictly surface grazers, but will feed during the day in conditions of low light or under the cover of debris. One species, *Amphicyrta chrysomelina* Erichson, feeds on the succulent stems and leaves of vascular forest plants. Both the adults and larvae are sometimes minor pests of ornamental lilies and vegetables grown commercially and in home gardens, and are abundant in weedy lawns in the Pacific Northwest. Most byrrhids can withdraw their legs into recesses when disturbed. Remaining motionless, some pill beetles strongly resemble seeds or mammal feces. Byrrhids capable of flight take to the air in spring and early summer, and are sometimes found washed up on shores among lines of debris.

FAMILY DIAGNOSIS Adult byrrhids are broadly oval, convex above and below, compact, with dorsal surface often clothed in scales, setae, or bristles. Head hypognathous and frequently concealed from view above. Antenna with 11 antennomeres and clavate, capitate, or somewhat filiform. Prothorax with lateral margins carinate. Procoxal cavities open behind. Elytra cover abdomen. Underside usually with depressions or sulci to receive appendages. Tarsi 4-4-4, 5-5-5, tarsomeres 1–3 usually increasing in size distally, 4 small, 5 long, simple or with pads underneath; claws simple. Abdomen with five ventrites, with 1–2 connate.

SIMILAR FAMILIES
- wounded-tree beetles (Nosodendridae, p.115)— flattened fore legs
- round fungus beetles (Leiodidae, p.137)—dorsal surface without setae or scales
- some dermestid beetles (Dermestidae, p.290)— have ocelli and distinctly clubbed antennae
- death-watch beetles (Ptinidae, p.299)—antennal club asymmetrical
- minute fungus beetles (Corylophidae, p.314)— underside flat
- *Hyporhagus* (Zopheridae, p.344)—mouthparts directed forward, upper surface without setae or scales, antennal club distinct, tarsi 5-5-4
- some darkling beetles (Tenebrionidae, p.347)— bases of antennae hidden from above
- seed beetles (Chrysomelidae: Bruchinae, p.502)— usually with short beak on head, pygidium visible
- small fungus weevils (Anthribidae, p.532)—usually with short, broad beak, pygidium visible

COLLECTING NOTES These infrequently collected beetles are most often found in moss, among roots of grasses growing in moist habitats, beneath debris, under bark, or along lake beaches in drift. Some species are occasionally attracted to lights.

FAUNA 35 SPECIES IN 15 GENERA

Amphicyrta dentipes Erichson (5.0–10.0 mm) is broadly ovoid and occasionally inflated posteriorly, strongly convex, smooth and glabrous dorsally, and dark reddish brown without metallic luster. Head small, with antennae filiform, terminal antennomeres barely enlarged and compressed. Elytron with epipleuron distinct at base only, becoming obsolete at middle. Legs short, with tarsomeres 1–3 lobed. Larvae and adults feed on succulent leaves and stems of forest and prairie herbs from southwestern Oregon to southern California. *Amphicyrta chrysomelina* Erichson (8.0–12.0 mm) more elongate, reddish brown with coppery sheen, occasionally with greenish reflections. Coastal coniferous forests from Oregon to northern California. (2)

233

Byrrhus eximius LeConte (5.5–7.0 mm) is oval, convex, with pubescence simple and appressed, and black with antennae and tarsi somewhat reddish. Mandibles concealed underneath by prosternal lobe. Elytra finely punctostriate, with punctures dense and usually coalesced, rugulose. Elytra somewhat tessellate with black and grayish pubescence, with grayish or brownish transverse mark across middle, and margins lacking stout, blunt bristles. Legs retractile, with tibiae somewhat broad and flat, evenly rounded externally. Alaska, western Canada, south to northern California and Colorado. (6)

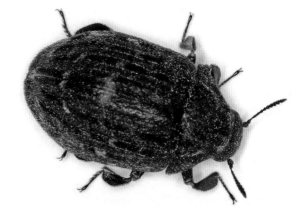

Cytilus alternatus (Say) (4.0–6.5 mm) is black and gray with bronze luster, and has clavate antennae. Head, pronotum, and underside with appressed reddish-brown to golden setae. Scutellum with golden pubescence. Elytra punctostriate, disc finely rugosely punctate, with tessellated pattern of black, grayish, and golden pubescence, often with alternating bronze stripes. Nocturnal adults on mat-forming mosses. In West, south to California and Utah; also Europe. *Cytilus mimicus* Casey more elongate and parallel-sided, elytra with greenish iridescent patches or intervals, pubescence grayish, rarely tessellate. Montane western North America. (2)

234

Morychus oblongus LeConte (4.1–4.1 mm) is shiny copper or metallic green and clothed in reddish-brown and white setae dorsally, and black ventrally, with appendages reddish. Antennae short and clavate. Elytra confusedly punctate. Abdominal sutures arcuate. Legs short, tarsomere 4 with membranous ventral lobe. *Morychus aeneolus* LeConte (3.9–4.3 mm) is brownish black, often with greenish reflections and clothed in intermixed brownish and whitish setae dorsally, latter prominent along lateral margins, and reddish ventrally. Tarsal lobe vestigial. Both species on mosses (*Ceratodon, Polytrichum*) in montane western Canada and United States. (2)

Lioon simplicipes (Mannerheim) (3.2–4.1 mm) is ovoid-globose, strongly convex dorsally, depressed at pronotal-elytral juncture, with short, fine, erect pubescence that is easily rubbed off, and shiny black to brownish with metallic luster dorsally; underside and appendages paler. Antennae clavate, with antennomeres 6–11 forming flat, elongate club. Elytra fused, with epipleuron broad and flat, and length of elytron. Legs not retractile. Flightless adults on mosses. Southeastern Alaska to coastal northern California. *Lioon nezperce* Johnson (2.9–3.6 mm) occurs in northern Idaho and northwestern Montana. (2)

Chaetophora spinosa (Rossi) (0.9–2.1 mm) is strongly oval, convex, and clothed above only with distinctly clubbed bristles. Head tucked under prothorax. Antennae short and distinctly clubbed. Elytra with rows of shallow punctures. Legs retractile and capable of being completely withdrawn into sulci on underside of thorax. Adults associated with mosses and algae in moist and disturbed habitats. Europe; established in British Columbia and Idaho; also in east from Maritime Provinces and Québec to Maryland, west to Ontario and Ohio. (1)

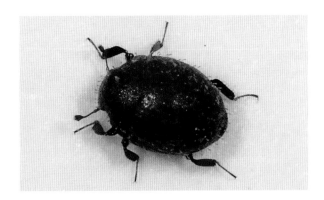

ELMIDAE (elm'-i-dē)
RIFFLE BEETLES

Elmids are associated with clean, permanent streams and their presence is an indication of good water quality. Elmid larvae are strictly aquatic and are found crawling over, under, and between submerged substrates. When ready to pupate, they crawl out of the water to pupate in small cells in moist sand beneath rocks, under loose bark, in wet moss, or in other protected sites near the water's edge. Adults typically emerge from their pupal cells at dusk during summer and crawl back to the water or take to the air. Individuals of species capable of flight do so only once in their lifetime to disperse and are frequently attracted to lights. In most species, the adults live together with their larvae among the rocks and cobble of shallow rapids or riffles of streams and may be present in large numbers. These hard-bodied adults are completely clothed in a dense, velvety, and water-repellent pubescence known as the *hydrofuge*. Once submerged, the hydrofuge continuously envelops the elmid's body in a silvery bubble. This thin layer of air allows a steady supply of dissolved oxygen from the surrounding water to diffuse inward to their spiracles, while permitting the respiratory carbon dioxide emitted from the spiracles to diffuse outward—a system called *plastron breathing*. Once submerged, elmids seldom, if ever, need to go to the surface or leave the water. These adults are long-lived, and it is not unusual to find them caked in mineral and organic deposits, or covered with small aquatic organisms. The exception is the xylophagous species *Lara avara* LeConte. The larvae live and feed on surfaces of submerged decaying wood, likely consuming a mixture of algae and wood-rotting microbes mixed with decaying wood. They take nearly four or more years to complete their development before leaving the water to pupate in moss growing along the shore. The relatively soft-bodied adults are pubescent, but lack a plastron, and live for only about three weeks. Riparian, rather than aquatic in their habits, *Lara* adults live on damp wood just above the waterline.

FAMILY DIAGNOSIS Adult elmids are elongate or oval, with long legs and large claws, and underside clothed in thick silvery gray pile, or not (*Lara*); elytra with faint or distinct yellowish or reddish markings in some species. Head hypognathous and often hidden from view above. Antennae long, filiform or clavate, with 8–11 antennomeres. Prothorax broader than head, irregularly quadrate, with posterior angles acute, and disc variously smooth, punctate, sulcate, rugose, or carinate, or a combination thereof. Procoxal cavities open behind. Scutellum small, suboval, triangular, or pentagonal. Elytra punctate, rugose, sometimes carinate, and completely conceal abdomen. Legs generally long and not modified for swimming; tarsi 5-5-5, first tarsomere nearly subequal to remaining tarsus, with large and equal claws sometimes toothed. Abdomen with five ventrites free.

SIMILAR FAMILIES
- minute moss beetles (Hydraenidae, p.132)— maxillary palps long; antennae short
- long-toed water beetles (Dryopidae, p.239)— antennae short, most antennomeres wider than long
- travertine beetles (Lutrochidae, p.240)—antennae short with articles 1–2 long and broad

235

- minute marsh-loving beetles (Limnichidae, p.241)—body covered with colorful scales
- water penny beetles (Psephenidae, p.244)—strongly oval in form, antennae flabellate or serrate, elytra soft

COLLECTING NOTES Elmids are found year-round. Look for them on vegetation and debris in the riffle areas of small gravelly and rocky streams, or on emergent portions of logs (*Lara*). Stir up stream bottoms by overturning or kicking rocks so the current will wash the dislodged beetles into a net or screen placed immediately downstream. Dump the net's contents into a shallow, light-colored pan so the small, dark-colored larvae and adults are easily seen. Use a Berlese funnel to extract beetles from submerged plant debris. Freshly emerged adults are often attracted in large numbers to lights placed near streams.

FAUNA ~100 SPECIES IN 26 GENERA

Lara avara avara LeConte (6.0–8.1 mm) is finely pubescent dorsally and ventrally, and dark brownish black. Pubescence of head and pronotum erect. Elytra wider than pronotum, with pubescence lighter and denser on alternate intervals, appearing as olivaceous lines. Femora sometimes partly reddish brown. Associated with cold foothill and mountain streams. Most of western North America. *Lara a. amplipennis* Darlington with pronotum longer, posterior angles more acute, and elytra uniformly pubescent. British Columbia to central California. *Lara gehringi* Darlington (5.5–6.5 mm) very similar, but elytral pubescence uniform. Washington to southern California. (2)

Ampumixis dispar (Fall) (1.8–2.2 mm) is elongate-oval, stout, very convex, nearly glabrous, and brownish black or black with basal third and apices of elytra lighter. Antennae with 11 antennomeres. Pronotum wide, with disc abruptly convex medially, sides barely arcuate, and flaring briefly at posterior angles. Elytra broadest medially, each with nine punctostriae, punctures coarse and deep medially, with intervals flat or nearly so, and lateral margin arcuate before apex. Apical half of tibiae fringed with tomentum, and claws simple. On sandy or gravelly bottoms of cold, clear foothill and mountain streams. Washington to California. (1)

Atractelmis wawona Chandler (2.0 mm) is elongate-oval, convex, nearly glabrous and brownish black. Antennomeres 9–11 forming barely enlarged club. Pronotum with sides nearly straight and converging anteriorly, disc bulbous posteriorly, sublateral carinae flanking transverse sulcus, and posterior margin broadly lobed in front of scutellum. Elytra broadest at basal third, humeri prominent, sides broadly arcuate to apices, with humeral patches extending posteriorly along suture, and elongate-oblique subapical spots. Last two posterior ventrites without longitudinal sutures. Adults in fast, clear, small to medium-sized mountain streams. Oregon and Idaho to California. (1)

Dubiraphia giulianii (Van Dyke) (2.1–2.3 mm) is elongate, subparallel, convex, and shiny brownish black with elytral markings. Head with 11 antennomeres and four maxillary palpomeres. Pronotum slightly wider than long, convex and evenly punctured, anterior lobe distinct, sides broadly arcuate. Elytra smooth, with strial punctures coarse, sides straight along basal two-thirds, then diverging slightly, then straight and oblique to apex, with yellowish humeral spot on disc extending posteriorly toward suture, and oblique subapical stripe reaching just behind middle. Oregon and Idaho to northern California. *Dubiraphia brunnescens* (Fall) (1.8–2.5 mm) uniformly dark brown, occasionally elytra with faint humeral or subapical spots. California. (2)

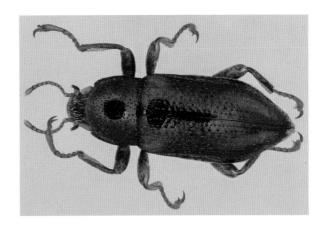

Heterlimnius koebelei Martin (2.0–2.5 mm) is broadly oval, broadest behind middle, convex, somewhat parallel-sided, sparsely setose, and brownish black with elytral bases and apices lighter. Antenna with 11 antennomeres, 1–8 yellowish brown, 9–11 darker and forming distinct club. Pronotum shiny, broadest posteriorly, with disc finely and sparsely punctate, with sublateral foveae. Elytra punctostriate, punctures distinct, intervals convex, with dark median band extended anteriorly and posteriorly along suture. Found in fast-flowing mountain streams. British Columbia to northern California. *Heterlimnius corpulentus* (LeConte) (2.6–2.9 mm) brown or black, elytra base sometimes reddish, with 10 antennomeres. British Columbia to California, east to Montana, South Dakota, and New Mexico. (2)

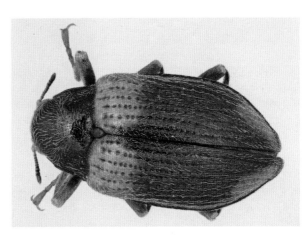

Narpus concolor (LeConte) (3.2–3.4 mm) is elongate, convex, with sides arcuate, and brownish black with elytra black to reddish, usually with dark median band. Antennae with 11 antennomeres. Maxillary palp with three palpomeres. Pronotum evenly punctured, without sublateral carinae. Elytra punctostriate, with coarse, deep strial punctures obscured apically. Front tibiae with fringe of tomentum, hind coxae transverse. Adults in gravel bars and leaf litter along small streams. Western North America. *Narpus arizonicus* (Brown) (3.4 mm) black with bronze luster, sides arcuate; Arizona. *Narpus angustus* (Casey) (3.0–4.0 mm) also black, slenderer, sides nearly parallel; found along larger rivers in coastal mountains. Northern California. (3)

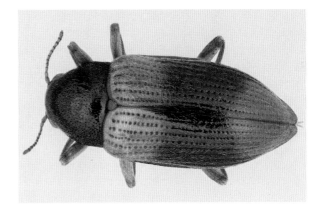

Optioservus quadrimaculatus (Horn) (1.8–2.2 mm)
is elongate, relatively broad, somewhat convex, and
dark brownish black with relatively large orangish elytral
markings. Antennae with 11 antennomeres, 9–11 forming
club. Pronotum distinctly narrower than elytra. Elytra
with strial punctures becoming obsolete apically, sides
somewhat rounded, and humeral spot broad, often reaching
second stria. Ventrite 5 evenly rounded apically. Claws large
and curved. *Optioservus seriatus* (LeConte) very similar,
prothorax barely wider than elytra, sides of elytra typically
subparallel, and humeral spot narrower, not reaching
second stria. Both species occupy gravelly stream bottoms;
widely distributed in western North America, except
Arizona. (6)

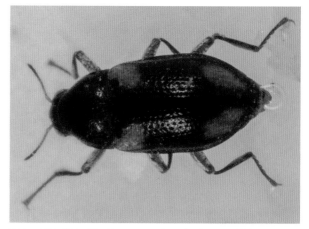

Ordobrevia nubifera (Fall) (2.1–2.7 mm) is elongate,
slender to robust, parallel-sided, with sculpturing and
granulation slight to very coarse, granules on head and legs
elongate, and uniformly brown to yellowish brown with a
transverse yellow band across middle of elytra. Pronotum
usually wider than long, broadest behind middle, narrower
than elytra, with lateral margins sinuate and weakly serrate,
and disc densely covered with granules and punctures.
Elytra punctostriate, with strial punctures becoming obscure
at apical third and obsolete on apices. Legs with front tibiae
lacking fringe of tomentum. Washington to California. (1)

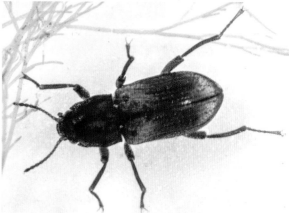

Zaitzevia parvula (Horn) (1.9–2.5 mm) is elongate,
narrow, dark brownish black, sometimes with appendages
paler. Antennae very short, with 8 distinct antennomeres,
8–11 forming long club. Pronotum with short median
sulcus flanked posteriorly by short, longitudinal sulci.
Elytra punctostriate. Hind coxae transverse. Male with last
ventrite about half as wide at apex as at base, granulate,
and narrowly biconic apically. Adults in riffles of mountain
and foothill streams. Yukon to California, east to Alberta,
Montana, Nebraska, and New Mexico. *Zaitzevia posthonia*
Brown similar, male with last ventrite not conspicuously
granulate and broadly rounded apically. Adults found
in clean riffles at lower elevations. British Columbia to
California. (2)

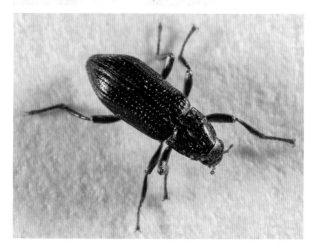

DRYOPIDAE (drī-ōp'-i-dē)
LONG-TOED WATER BEETLES

Dryopids live in both shallow rapids and riffles of streams and in slow-moving water. Their common name is derived from their unusually long claws, or "toes." Adult *Helichus* live underwater and walk about on aquatic vegetation and submerged debris, while their larvae live in moist sand several feet from the edge of streams where they probably feed on roots or decaying vegetation. Adult *Helichus* have a plastron, a dense layer of short setae that covers their bodies and traps a silvery blanket of air that allows them to acquire and dispose of respiratory gases underwater; however, the very pubescent *Pelonomus* lack a plastron altogether. Females have well-developed egg-laying tubes with blades that enable them to place their eggs in the soil or in plant tissues, and their flight muscles slowly atrophy with age. Larval development requires two or more years and pupation takes place on land. *Helichus* pupae have special abdominal structures called gin-traps that probably serve to anchor the pupae within the cast exoskeleton of the last larval instar to help facilitate adult emergence. Newly emerged adults fly or crawl to water.

FAMILY DIAGNOSIS Adult dryopids are elongate, oval, dull dark gray, brown, or nearly black, and densely clothed in coarse or fine setae; upper surfaces often encrusted with minerals. Head hypognathous and distinctly retracted into prothorax. Antennae short with 11 antennomeres, 4–11 expanded sideways to form a loose club. Pronotum wider than head, without broad projection in front. Procoxae open behind. Scutellum visible. Elytra completely conceal abdomen. Legs long, slender, not modified for swimming, tarsi 5-5-5, last tarsomere long with unusually long and simple claws. Abdomen with five ventrites free, with sutures sometime interrupted medially.

SIMILAR FAMILIES
- minute moss beetles (Hydraenidae, p.132)—maxillary palps elongate
- riffle beetles (Elmidae, p.235)—antennae long, with most antennomeres longer than wide
- travertine beetles (Lutrochidae, p.240)—small, oval, antennae short with antennomeres 1–2 long and broad
- minute marsh-loving beetles (Limnichidae, p.241)—body covered with short, scalelike hairs
- water penny beetles (Psephenidae, p.244)—oval, antennae flabellate or serrate, elytra soft

COLLECTING NOTES Dryopids are usually found clinging to logs and debris in stream riffles. Specimens are collected by stirring up the bottom of riffles or submerged plant debris and letting the current wash the dislodged beetles into an aquatic net or screen placed just downstream. Dump the net's contents into a shallow, light-colored pan where the dark-colored adults will stand out against the light background. Search stream pools for active adults at night with a flashlight. Dryopids are also extracted from plant debris using a Berlese funnel. Recently emerged adults in both genera are attracted to lights placed near these habitats at night.

239

FAUNA 13 SPECIES IN FIVE GENERA

Dryops arizonensis Schaeffer (3.5–4.5 mm) is elongate-oval, slightly convex, moderately clothed in short, fine pubescence, and uniformly brownish, with tarsi slightly paler. Head moderately densely punctate, with very short antennae comprising 11 antennomeres. Pronotum wide, with distinct sublateral sulci, and lateral margins narrowing anteriorly from acute posterior to anterior angles. Elytra confusedly punctate with punctures becoming finer apically, with intermixed short and long setae. Adults found just above waterline in stream debris clinging to branches, or on emergent rock surface in riffles; also attracted to lights. Central and southern Arizona, Texas; also Mexico. (1)

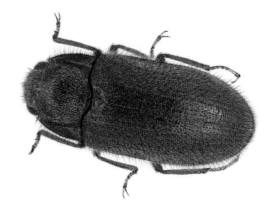

Helichus striatus LeConte (4.5–6.3 mm) is oblong, convex, not uniformly clothed in fine, silky pubescence, with bare areas shiny brown to black. Pronotum wide, gradually depressed behind middle, with a fovea on each side behind middle, and without glabrous area in front of scutellum. Elytra each with alternate intervals more convex or raised, and apices received within lateral grooves on last tergite. Last ventrite with pubescence not matching previous ventrites, often appearing bare. Legs with tarsomere 5 nearly as long as combined length of 1–4, and large claws. Adults in fast-flowing streams with rocky or gravelly bottoms. Widespread in western North America. (4)

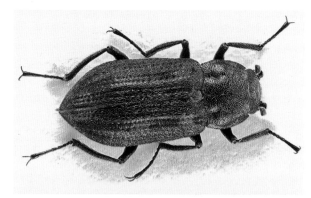

Postelichus species (5.2–8.0 mm) are very similar to *Helichus*, but larger. Terminal maxillary palpomere in both sexes with long or very long invaginated sensory pit before apex. Scutellum flattened. All ventrites uniformly clothed in dense recumbent tomentum. Adults are commonly found on debris and under rocks in valley, foothill, or mountain streams. Three species of *Postelichus* occur in western North America (*P. confluentus* Hinton, *P. immsi* Hinton, and *P. productus* LeConte) and are difficult to identify without careful examination of male genitalia. California east to Utah and Texas, south to Mexico. (3)

240

LUTROCHIDAE (lū-trok-i-dē)
TRAVERTINE BEETLES

Both adults and larvae are aquatic and found on travertine (calcareous) deposits along the edges of shallow, fast-flowing warm springs and streams, where they feed on algae and waterlogged wood. The larvae overwinter and, when their development is completed, pupate in protected sites just above water level. One generation is produced annually.

FAMILY DIAGNOSIS Adult lutrochids are obovate, strongly convex, compact, yellowish, and densely pubescent and punctate. Head hypognathous and broad. Antennae short, with 11 antennomeres, 1 and 2 broad, conspicuously setose, and subequal to combined length of remaining antennomeres. Pronotum wider than head, but narrower than base of elytra. Procoxal cavities open behind. Elytra densely punctate and setose, and completely cover abdomen. Legs with femora grooved to receive tibiae, tarsi 5-5-5, last tarsomere long, and claws simple. Abdomen with five ventrites, with 1–2 connate.

SIMILAR FAMILIES
- minute moss beetles (Hydraenidae, p.132)—maxillary palps elongate
- riffle beetles (Elmidae, p.235)—antennae long, with most antennomeres longer than wide
- minute marsh-loving beetles (Limnichidae, p.241)—body covered with short, scalelike setae
- water penny beetles (Psephenidae, p.244)—oval, antennae flabellate, serrate, elytra soft

COLLECTING NOTES Adult *Lutrochus* are found on travertine deposits at or near the waterline of fast-moving streams on the wet, downstream surfaces of rocks and other objects emerging from the water. They are sometimes found in large numbers in these habitats and are quick to fly when disturbed.

Lutrochus arizonicus Brown & Murvosh (3.0–3.7 mm) is obovate, strongly convex, and densely clothed in fine recumbent yellowish pubescence. Head about two-thirds width of pronotum, with apical clypeal margin straight, and antennae short. Pronotum wider than long, broadest at base, and convex, with feebly sinuate lateral margins slightly carinate, and narrowing anteriorly to weakly explanate angles. Elytra very convex, humeri weakly protuberant, and disc without any indication of striae or tubercles. Legs pubescent, except middle tibia, upper surface of middle tarsus, and all apical tarsomeres glabrous; hind coxa deeply grooved to receive femur, and all femora grooved to receive tibiae. Arizona. (1)

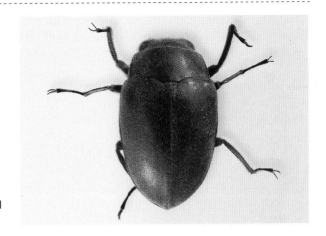

LIMNICHIDAE (lim-nik'-i-dē)
MINUTE MARSH-LOVING BEETLES

Little is known about the biology and natural history of limnichids. Adults and larvae are both terrestrial and most species are riparian, occurring along margins of streams on wet sand or loam (*Limnichius*), among well-vegetated shorelines of lakes and streams, or in emergent vegetation and wood (*Limnichites*). *Physemus minutus* LeConte inhabits drying mud or muddy banks of streams and rivers, while *Throscinus crotchii* LeConte prefers wet sand beaches and intertidal mudflats. Limnichid larvae develop in damp soil or debris in these habitats and probably feed on decaying plant materials. Pupation also occurs in these larval habitats.

FAMILY DIAGNOSIS Adult limnichids are oval or elongate (*Throscinus*), uniformly brownish to blackish, or colorful and clothed in fine grayish pubescence or scalelike setae. Head hypognathous, small, and deeply inserted inside prothorax, with eyes visible from above (*Limnichites*) or not (*Eulimnichus*). Antennae short and clavate, with 11 antennomeres, most antennomeres broad, 2 large, 3–8 smaller and nearly moniliform, 9–11 gradually larger and forming loose club (clavate). Pronotum convex with sides sharply margined and converging toward head, with (*Physemus*) or without deep excavation on each side of head to receive antennae. Procoxal cavities open behind. Elytra punctate and completely cover abdomen, with setae on disc either uniform in texture (*Eulimnichus, Limnichites*), or a mixture of reclining and erect setae (*Limnichoderus*). Underside with depressions for reception of legs or not (*Throscinus*). Legs slender, tarsi 5-5-5. Abdomen with five ventrites free.

SIMILAR FAMILIES
- some small water scavenger beetles (Hydrophilidae, p.122)—maxillary palps conspicuous
- minute moss beetles (Hydraenidae, p.132)—maxillary palps elongate
- moss beetles (Byrrhidae, p.233)—antennae clubbed, strongly convex
- riffle beetles (Elmidae, p.235)—antennae long, with most antennomeres longer than wide
- travertine beetles (Lutrochidae, p.240)—small, oval, antennae short, antennomeres 1–2 long, broad
- water penny beetles (Psephenidae, p.244)—oval, flabellate or serrate antennae
- some small lady beetles (Coccinellidae, p.318)—antennae clubbed, tarsi 4-4-4 or 3-3-3

COLLECTING NOTES Look for adult limnichids in riparian habitats on streamside plants, or at the waterline on the downstream side of emergent rocks, wood, and vegetation. Beating and sweeping vegetation in riparian habitats can be productive. *Physemus* are found by splashing water over muddy banks of rivers and streams, or captured as they run across drying mud. *Throscinus* occur in coastal intertidal mudflats covered by high tides. Adults often fly to lights.

FAUNA 28 SPECIES IN SIX GENERA

Throscinus crotchii LeConte (2.0–2.5 mm) is black with bronze luster, and densely clothed in short suberect, grayish pubescence. Head not strongly retracted into prothorax, with oval eyes widely separated on vertex, and antennomeres 6–11 forming club. Pronotum as broad as elytra, disc very convex anteriorly, with sides gradually diverging to bisinuate posterior margin; anterior lobe of prosternum extending beneath head. Scutellum large and triangular. Elytra finely and confusedly punctate. Underside without sulci to receive legs. Inhabits coastal intertidal mudflats. Southern California south to Baja California and Nayarit. (1)

Eulimnichus analis (LeConte) (2.1–2.7 mm) is shiny black with coarse and dense punctures, and moderately dense, uniformly recumbent gold and gray pubescence. Eyes largely concealed from view above, with surfaces flat and vertical. Pronotum wide, anterior margin deeply emarginate, anterior angles prominent, lateral margins carinate and narrowed anteriorly; prosternal process sulcate. Elytra confusedly punctate, with punctures becoming shallower laterally and apically. Washington to California, east to Idaho, Oklahoma, and Texas; south to Sonora. *Eulimnichus californicus* (LeConte) (1.8–2.0 mm) with dorsal surface dull between punctures; Oregon to southern California. (4)

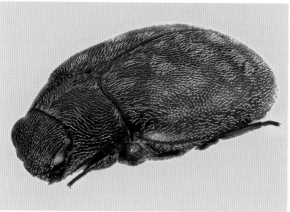

HETEROCERIDAE (het-êr-o-ser'-i-dē)
VARIEGATED MUD-LOVING BEETLES

Heterocerids are small, flat, and distinctively shaped beetles, often with a zigzag pattern on the elytra. Both adults and larvae live in galleries dug in sand or mudflats along the shores of ponds, lakes, and streams and consume algae, zooplankton, and other organic debris that washes up on shore. Adults use their rakelike forelegs to clear sediment away from the head and move it to the sides and rear, often leaving behind chimneylike piles of soil on the surface. They sometimes inhabit cracks and crevices that occur naturally as mud dries. At dusk on warm summer evenings, the adults leave their shoreline burrows and are often attracted to lights in enormous numbers. The relatively stationary larvae are much more likely to succumb to dehydration or inundation than are the highly mobile adults. Young larvae initially use the tunnels dug by the adults, but soon construct their own. Pupation occurs within a sealed chamber and the adults emerge in about three to six days. Heterocerids are an important prey item for birds and frogs, and apparently play a significant role in seed dispersal and burial in sandy soils.

FAMILY DIAGNOSIS Adult heterocerids are long, robust, somewhat flattened, usually dark (*Tropicus pusillus* is pale), covered with dense silky pubescence, and often with contrasting dark and light zigzag markings on elytra. Head prognathous with prominent, flattened mandibles, especially males. Antennae short, usually with 11 (*Augyles*, *Heterocerus*) or nine (*Tropicus*) antennomeres, last seven forming an oblong, serrate club. Pronotum broader than head and narrower than or equal to base of elytra. Procoxal cavities open behind. Scutellum visible. Elytra completely cover abdomen, with (*Augyles*, *Heterocerus*) or without (*Tropicus*) three irregular transverse bands. Metathoracic coxal lines present (*Augyles*) or absent (*Heterocerus*, *Tropicus*). Legs, especially front pair, with rakelike rows of spines, tarsi 4-4-4, claws large, slender, and simple. Abdomen with five ventrites free, first ventrite with or without distinctly curved lines behind the hind coxae.

SIMILAR FAMILIES The protruding mandibles, flattened body, zigzag patches of setae on the elytra, and spiny, rakelike legs are distinctive.

COLLECTING NOTES Adults are sometimes found in large numbers along the muddy banks of streams, ponds, and lakes during the warmer months and commonly attracted to lights near the shoreline. Splashing water onto sandy banks may drive the beetles from their underground galleries into plain view; this technique is of limited value on muddy shores.

FAUNA 34 SPECIES IN THREE GENERA

Heterocerus fenestratus (Thunberg) (3.5–5.3 mm) is elongate, distinctly blotched, and blackish brown with dense setae. Antennae with 11 antennomeres, 5–11 forming oblong serrate club. Pronotum distinctly pale, finely punctate, and posterior margin finely notched. Elytron irregularly trifasciate, with distinct and elongate pale blotches, some reaching pale margins; turned-under rim pale. Tarsi pale. Adults active in summer; attracted to lights. Widespread in North America. (5)

Heterocerus mollinus Kiesenwetter (3.9–5.6 mm) is dark with three distinct reddish-brown zigzag bands across each elytron, bands sometimes forming spots or are vague in older specimens. Front angles of pronotum pale or blackish. Elytra irregularly trifasciate. Lines behind bases of middle legs present and in contact with bases. Males with mandibles elongate, clypeus long in some specimens. Adults attracted to lights. Arizona eastward to Manitoba, Québec to Florida

Tropicus pusillus (Say) (2.0–3.0 mm) is small and uniformly pale sooty-brown, dull yellow, or orange-brown, and densely clothed in short yellowish pubescence, sometimes with a broad darker band running down middle from head to elytral apices. Mandible of male with process that overlaps labrum. Antennae with nine antennomeres. Elytra smooth and without transverse spots or markings. Epiplurae and legs pale. Adults sometimes attracted to light in very large numbers along drainage ditches, sandy ponds, and intermittent creeks. Throughout United States south to Central America; also Québec, Ontario, and Caribbean. (1)

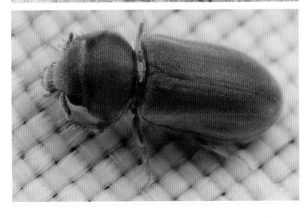

PSEPHENIDAE (sef-en'-i-dē)
WATER PENNY BEETLES

The larvae of *Acneus*, *Eubrianax*, and *Psephenus* are all aquatic and known as water pennies. They are so named because of their distinctly oval, flat, and often golden brown (p.28, Fig. 18h) color, resembling small, segmented coins. Their low body profile, along with very powerful claws, enables them to cling to smooth, rocky surfaces exposed to rapidly flowing water in high-quality streams, where they graze on algae. When mature, the larvae of all North American species leave the water to pupate on the smooth underside of rocks and logs along the streamside. Pupation occurs under the protective cover of the last larval exoskeleton. The terrestrial adults have reduced mouthparts, do not feed, and thus are relatively short-lived. Adult males are typically encountered on boulders or other objects protruding from the water, or resting on nearby vegetation. Almost immediately after mating, adult females crawl into the water to lay their flat eggs under stones. They obtain oxygen from a layer of air trapped by their "hairy" body surface and die soon after oviposition.

FAMILY DIAGNOSIS Adult psephenids in North America are oval, slightly flattened, brownish to blackish, and soft-bodied. Head hypognathous and partly retracted inside prothorax, with mandibles concealed. Antennae long and moniliform, serrate, or pectinate, with 11 antennomeres. Procoxal cavities open behind. Scutellum visible. Elytra soft and leathery, completely covering abdomen. Tarsi 5-5-5, with claws equal in size and simple, toothed, or cleft. Abdomen with five ventrites free.

SIMILAR FAMILIES
- marsh beetles (Scirtidae, p.114)—tarsi with fourth tarsomere deeply lobed
- ptilodactylid beetles (Ptilodactylidae, p.245)—larger and elongate, antennae inserted below eyes

COLLECTING NOTES Adult psephenids are often found during the day on exposed rock surfaces among stream riffles. Others are found on nearby vegetation and are captured by beating or sweeping riparian shrubs and trees.

244

FAUNA 16 SPECIES IN FIVE GENERA

Eubrianax edwardsii (LeConte) (3.0–4.5 mm) is broadly ovate, somewhat flattened, and black, with elytra and appendages reddish brown. Head typically hidden under broadly expanded pronotum, with antennae pectinate (male) or serrate (female). Pronotum broadly arcuate anteriorly with pair of pale and somewhat translucent marginal spots, broadly explanate laterally, with posterior margin bisinuate and smooth. Scutellum large and black. Elytra with striae irregularly punctured, weakly punctostriate from apical quarter to apices, and interstriae narrow and more or less flat. Tarsi slender, claws not toothed at base, but with basal membranous appendage nearly reaching claw apices. Adults on sunny boulders along streams during summer. Oregon, California, and Nevada. (1)

Acneus quadrimaculatus Horn (3.5–4.5 mm) is broadly ovate, moderately shiny brownish black with appendages, lateral margins, and elytra markings lighter, with fine crenulations along pronotal and elytral bases. Antennae about half body length, serrate (female) or flabellate (male). Pronotum short and broad; prosternum depressed between coxae. Elytra about as wide at base as pronotum, not much longer than wide, broadest at apical third, each with pair of orangish-brown spots not reaching suture, sometimes spots joined and sutural intervals lighter. Claws with basal tooth (male) or not (female). Pacific Coast, Washington to California. *Acneus oregonensis* Fender similar in size, with elytra pale, each with seven dark spots. Oregon. (4)

Psephenus falli Casey (3.3–5.1 mm) is more or less oblong, somewhat flattened, and weakly shiny brownish black, with elytra usually dark brown, and antennomere 2, legs, and underside sometimes lighter. Antennae slender and reaching humeri (male) or not (female), antennomeres 4–10 about as long as wide and subequal in length. Pronotum broad, uniformly dull (female) or partly shiny (male). Ventrite 5 with apical margin weakly (female) or deeply (male) emarginate. Elytra at base as wide as pronotum, broadest toward apex, with apices dehiscent and broadly rounded. Legs uniformly dark. Oregon to California, east to Idaho. (5)

PTILODACTYLIDAE (til-ō-dak'-til-i-dē)
PTILODACTYLID BEETLES

Adult ptilodactylids are terrestrial and some are thought to feed on microfungi growing on leaf surfaces. In western North America, the food preferences of both *Anchycteis velutina* Horn and *Araeopidius monachus* (LeConte) are unknown, although the latter is often found on the flowers of various shrubs. Ptilodactylid larvae are terrestrial, semiaquatic, or aquatic and feed on decaying vegetation and wood. The larvae of both *Anchycteis velutina* and *Araeopidius monachus* are truly aquatic and live in mud, gravel, or sand along the bottom of fast-flowing streams, where they feed on the roots of emergent vegetation. *Araeopidius* larvae have plastron plates along the sides of their bodies that, along with dorsally placed terminal spiracles, are likely adaptations that enhance their ability to survive seasonal flooding in riparian habitats. Pupation for both species likely occurs on land. There is still much to be learned about the classification and natural history of this family.

FAMILY DIAGNOSIS Adult ptilodactylids are elongate-oblong, nearly parallel-sided, uniformly brown to brownish-black and moderately clothed in dense setae. Head hypognathous, mostly concealed from view above, with bulging eyes. Antennae with 11 antennomeres, pectinate (male *Anchycteis*), filiform, or serrate (*Araeopidius*). Pronotum broad, with lateral margins distinctly carinate (*Anchycteis*) or not (*Araeopidius*), and posterior margin crenulate. Procoxal cavities open behind. Scutellum somewhat triangular, with basal margin finely notched. Elytra punctostriate, never costate, rounded apically, and completely covering abdomen. Legs slender, with tarsi 5-5-5 and claws simple. Abdomen with five ventrites free.

SIMILAR FAMILIES

- some death-watch beetles (Ptinidae, p.299)—base of pronotum not carinate
- comb-clawed beetles (Tenebrionidae: Alleculinae, p.365)—tarsi 5-5-4, antennae filiform

COLLECTING NOTES Look for ptilodactylids in the immediate vicinity of riparian, semiaquatic, and aquatic habitats. Adults are collected by beating or sweeping vegetation along streams, rivers, and other bodies of water. They are attracted to lights, found in flight intercept and Malaise traps, and skimmed from floating debris washing down mountain flumes.

FAUNA 19 SPECIES IN SIX GENERA

Anchycteis velutina Horn (9.5–10.5 mm) is oblong-oval, robust, clothed in extremely fine brown pubescence, finely punctate dorsally, and uniformly dull black. Head deflexed, with antennae serrate (female) or pectinate (male) with processes as long as or longer than antennomeres. Pronotum broad and convex, with lateral margins carinate, and slightly flattened before scutellum. Scutellum heart-shaped and concave. Elytra each with 10 feebly impressed punctostriae, 6–9 obsolete at basal third. Middle coxae twice as widely separated as front coxae. Adults on rocks and vegetation near streams. Southwestern Oregon to northern California. (1)

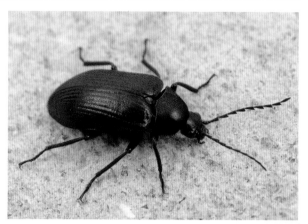

Araeopidius monachus (LeConte) (8.5–10.0 mm) is elongate, dark brown, densely clothed in decumbent pale brownish or grayish setae. Antennae serrate. Pronotum wide, broadest at base, with anterior margin forming hood over head, lateral margins nearly obsolete, and posterior angles acute in dorsal view. Elytra finely punctate, each with about 10 weakly impressed striae with larger punctures, and sutural stria deeply impressed at base, with setae frequently rubbed off to form mottled or irregularly banded patterns. Adults on flowers, including cowparsnip (*Heracleum lunatum*) and western mountain ash (*Sorbus sitchensis*). British Columbia to California, east to Montana. (1)

EULICHADIDAE (ū-lik-ad'-i-dē)
FOREST STREAM BEETLES

The Eulichadidae include only two genera, *Eulichas* with approximately 30 species from India east to China and the Philippines, and the monotypic *Stenocolus* that is restricted to the Sacramento and San Joaquin Valleys of northern and central California. *Stenocolus* larvae are found year-round under moderate to large rocks and leaf packs in small streams and rivers at lower elevations. They burrow into the substrate, feed on fine particulate organic matter, and require at least two years to complete their development. The distinct and branched gill-like structures located on the undersides of abdominal segments 1–7 are not respiratory in nature, but are instead osmobranchiae that have an osmoregulatory function. Mature larvae emerge from the water to pupate in the soil streamside beneath nearby objects. Adults do not feed, live only weeks, and are found on leaves and branches of riparian vegetation on hot summer afternoons in habitats that support the larvae.

FAMILY DIAGNOSIS Eulichadids are elongate and resemble loosely built click beetles with a round scutellum clothed in dense white setae. Head prognathous, slightly inserted into prothorax, with eyes and mandibles prominent. Antennae with 11 antennomeres and serrate, especially in male, with antennomere 1 slightly conical, 2 small and rounded. Prothorax twice as wide as long, sides strong-margined and converging toward head, posterior margin bisinuate, with angles acute. Procoxal cavities open behind. Scutellum distinctly round and densely covered with white setae. Elytra shallowly punctate, completely covering abdomen. Legs with tibial spurs short, long slender tarsi 5-5-5, tarsomeres 1–4 slightly pubescent underneath, 5 as long as 2–4 combined; claws simple. Abdomen with five ventrites free, with 5 longer.

SIMILAR FAMILIES

- soft-bodied plant beetles (*Dascillus*, Dascillidae, p.206)—smaller, scutellum not clothed in white setae
- ptilodactylid beetles (Ptilodactylidae, p.245)—mandibles not prominent, scutellum not clothed in white setae
- *Perothops* (Eucnemidae, p.255)—scutellum not clothed in white setae, claws pectinate
- click beetles (Elateridae, p.273)—scutellum not clothed in white setae, fore body loosely attached to rest of body, rear angles of pronotum directed backward

COLLECTING NOTES Seldom-encountered adults are usually found on hot afternoons by beating or sweeping riparian vegetation and are also attracted to lights at night.

FAUNA ONE SPECIES, *STENOCOLUS SCUTELLARIS*

Stenocolus scutellaris LeConte (10.0–21.0 mm) is elongate, narrowed at both ends, parallel-sided, dark brownish black, and moderately clothed in short, depressed tan pubescence, pubescence sometimes rubbed off; females larger and darker. Head with somewhat prominent eyes partly obscured by pronotal angles, antennae strongly (male) or slightly (female) serrate. Pronotum wider than long, strongly narrowed anteriorly, sides angulate, then sinuate to acute posterior angles. Scutellum densely covered with white setae. Elytra faintly costate, intercostae finely and confusedly punctate. Underside with dense, gray pubescence. Adults occur on riparian vegetation, mostly along streams flowing into the San Joaquin and Sacramento Valleys up to about 1,200 meters. Northern California. (1)

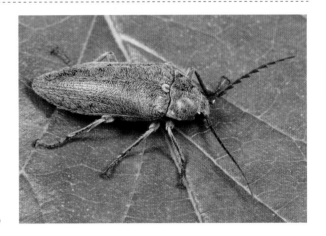

247

ARTEMATOPODIDAE (âr-tē-mat-ō′-pōd-i-dē)
ARTEMATOPODID BEETLES

Very little is known about the biology and natural history of artematopodids. Adults are usually found resting on understory growth in wooded habitats, especially along waterways. Species of *Eurypogon* and *Macropogon* are closely associated with mosses. The larvae and pupae of *M. sequoiae* Hopping were found among rhizoids in mixed mats of mosses dominated by species of *Grimmia* growing on boulders in the Sierra Nevada of California. An adult of *Allopogonia villosus* (Horn) was found beating branches of scrub oak (*Quercus*).

FAMILY DIAGNOSIS Adult artematopodids are elongate, strongly convex, and clothed in erect setae. Head with antennal insertions visible from above. Antennae filiform or subserrate, antennomeres 2–4 very short and combined not longer than 5 (*Macropogon*), or 2–3 short and combined equal to 4 (*Eurypogon*). Prothorax with lateral margins sharply defined (*Brevipogon*) or not. Prosternum in front of coxae with (*Brevipogon*, *Eurypogon*, *Macropogon*) or without paired ridges (*Allopogonia*). Procoxal cavities open behind. Elytra with 11 or 12 rows of punctures. Tarsi 5-5-5, two or more tarsomeres lobed beneath, with simple claws. Abdomen with five ventrites, 1–2 connate.

SIMILAR FAMILIES

- ptilodactylid beetles (Ptilodactylidae, p.245)—males with pectinate antennae
- rare click beetles (Cerophytidae, p.250)—hind trochanters very long
- throscid beetles (Throscidae, p.252)—antennae clavate

- click beetles (Elateridae, p.273)—forebody loosely attached to rest of body, rear angles of pronotum directed backward
- fruitworm beetles (Byturidae, p.410)—tarsomeres 2–3 lobed underneath

COLLECTING NOTES Artematopodid beetles are collected by beating or sweeping vegetation along streams, rivers, and other bodies of water. They are also attracted to lights, found in flight intercept and Malaise traps, and skimmed from floating debris washed down mountain flumes.

FAUNA NINE SPECIES IN FOUR GENERA

Allopogonia villosus (Horn) (5.0–6.0 mm) is oblong, convex, parallel-sided, uniformly brown with underside and appendages reddish, and sparsely clothed dorsally and ventrally in long erect brown setae. Head rugosely punctate, mandibles without subapical tooth, antennae not reaching middle of elytra, with antennomere 2 small, 3–10 distinctly serrate in male. Pronotum broad, coarsely and densely punctate; prosternum in front of coxae without paired ridges. Elytra punctostriate with strial punctures coarse, and interstriae narrow. Ventrites 2–4 with patches of glandular setae. Tarsomeres 2–4 lobed underneath and claws simple. Adults collected on scrub oak (*Quercus*) and in Malaise traps. Central California to northern Baja California. (1)

Eurypogon californicus Horn (4.0–5.0 mm) is oblong, moderately shiny dark brown with appendages paler, and sparsely clothed in suberect golden pubescence. Head coarsely and sparsely punctate; somewhat serrate antennae, with antennomeres 2–3 short with 2 oval and 3 longer, their lengths combined equal length of 4. Pronotum trapezoidal, broadest at base, with posterior angles projecting slightly over humeri; prosternum prolonged, meeting mesosternum and limited on each side by elevated and divergent line. Elytra wider than pronotum, punctostriate with punctures fine. Underside sparsely punctate underneath. Adults attracted to lights and extracted from Malaise trap samples. California, Colorado, and New Mexico. (1)

Macropogon testaceipennis Motschulsky (4.5–8.0 mm) is elongate, parallel-sided, black with bicolored elytra, and prothorax and elytra densely clothed in long, golden, suberect setae. Antennomeres 2–4 approximately as long as wide (male), or 2 much shorter than 3 or 4 (female). Pronotum widest at base, disc shiny black and densely punctured. Elytra punctostriate, variably reddish brown with suture or all margins narrowly black, or black with reddish humeri. British Columbia to southern California. *Macropogon piceus* LeConte (5.0–6.0 mm) black with appendages lighter, British Columbia to Oregon, east to Montana, also in East; *M. sequoiae* Hopping (5.0–7.5 mm) has uniformly brown elytra and more slender antennae. California. (3)

OMETHIDAE (ō-meth'-i-dē)
FALSE SOLDIER, FALSE FIREFLY, AND LONG-LIPPED BEETLES

Very little is known about the natural history of omethids. The apparently short-lived adults are seldom encountered, except when observed resting on vegetation or captured in traps. The larvae are entirely unknown, as are the feeding habits of the adults. Most of the species in western North America, some of which resemble Lycidae (p.258), Lampyridae (p.262) and Cantharidae (p.265), are diurnal and active in spring and early summer, and occupy forested regions from British Columbia to northern California. Recent molecular and morphological studies have resulted in the inclusion of long-lipped beetles as a subfamily, Telegeusinae, within the family Omethidae. The common name "long-lipped" beetle is inspired by the long terminal segments of the labial and maxillary palps in *Telegeusis*. The telegeusines are restricted to the New World and represented north of Mexico by three species, all within the genus *Telegeusis*. Two species, *T. nubifer* Martin and *T. schwarzi* Barber, occur west of the Continental Divide in southern Arizona. As with all other species of *Telegeusis*, these two taxa are known only from adult males intercepted at dusk or captured in Malaise, flight intercept, and light traps. The females are completely unknown and are thought be flightless, or possibly larviform.

FAMILY DIAGNOSIS Adult omethids are narrowly elongate to broadly ovate, and somewhat flattened. Head with clypeus apparent or not, eyes protruding, apical maxillary palpomere flat and elongate (*Telegeusis*) or not. Antennae filiform, serrate, or pectinate, with 11 antennomeres. Pronotum wider than long, with lateral margins carinate. Procoxal cavities open behind. Elytra soft and short (*Telegeusis*), or about as long as or longer than abdomen, and usually without costae (weakly costate in *Matheteus*). Legs more or less long and slender, tarsi 5-5-5, with tarsomeres slender, 3 and 4 with deeply bifid and ventral membranous lobes, 1 and 2 sometimes with fine, setose pads underneath, and claws simple, appendiculate, or with reduced basal tooth. Abdomen with seven or eight ventrites free.

SIMILAR FAMILIES
- rove beetles (Staphylinidae, p.143)—antennae long
- net-winged beetles (Lycidae, p.258)—elytra with network of raised costae
- some soldier beetles (Cantharidae, p.265)—antennae long, clypeus membranous and not distinct, tarsomere 4 bilobed
- glowworms (Phengodidae, p.271)—male with bipectinate antennae, females larviform
- some checkered beetles (Cleridae, p.425)—antennae long
- some longhorn beetles (Cerambycidae, p.460)—antennae long

COLLECTING NOTES Adult male long-lipped beetles become active just before dusk and are sometimes attracted in numbers to lights. They are also captured in Malaise and flight intercept traps. Both omethine and matheteine adults rest on vegetation during the day in

spring and early summer. They are collected by sweeping low herbaceous growth along streams and rivers, or sorted from floating debris skimmed from mountain flumes.

FAUNA 13 SPECIES IN EIGHT GENERA

Telegeusis nubifer Martin (4.6–8.0 mm) is elongate, slender, and yellowish with faintly bicolored elytra. Head with elongate palps not exceeding length of antennae, terminal palpomeres yellow. Elytra infuscate at truncated apices, each three times as long as wide, extending past apices of hind coxae. Found at lights during summer monsoons in mountain canyons of southeastern Arizona. *Telegeusis schwarzi* Barber (5.0–8.0 mm) is yellow with palpi, apices of elytra, and pronotal margins whitish; elytra shorter, truncate, each almost as long as wide, not extending past apices of hind coxae; central Arizona. (2)

Matheteus theveneti LeConte (10.0–11.5 mm) is broadly oval, black with rose-red pronotum and elytra, and clothed mostly with suberect golden pubescence. Head concealed from view above, yellowish in front of eyes, antennae pectinate with rami longer in male, each broadly attached to and arising more or less medially from antennomere. Pronotum transverse, without anterior or posterior angles, with or without broad black spot on disc that is sometimes divided medially. Elytra broadest at apical third, with outer margins explanate, especially at base, each with four costae. Abdomen with distinct paratergites. Tarsomeres 3 and 4 lobed underneath. Short-lived adults active mostly in spring. Southwestern Oregon to central California. (1)

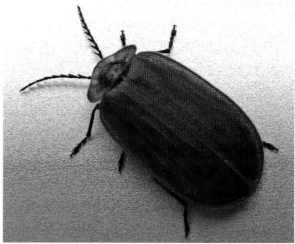

CEROPHYTIDAE (ser-ō-fīt′-i-dē)
RARE CLICK BEETLES

In North America, Cerophytidae is represented by two species in the genus *Cerophytum*, of which one, *C. convexicolle* LeConte, occurs west of the Continental Divide. Very little is known about the natural history of these uncommon beetles, although the larvae of a European species are associated with decaying layers of xylem in deciduous hardwoods. Like other "clicking" beetles (Elateridae, Throscidae, Eucnemidae), adult rare click beetles have the ability to "jump"; however, unlike the thoracic clicking mechanisms of these other families, the clicking mechanism of cerophytids is very poorly developed and their jumping ability is not well understood.

FAMILY DIAGNOSIS Adult cerophytids are elongate, somewhat convex, and moderately clothed in dark setae. Head hypognathous, bulging between eyes, deeply set inside prothorax and partly visible from above. Antennae with 11 antennomeres, strongly serrate (female) or

pectinate (male), bases narrowly separated on bulge between eyes. Prothorax convex and loosely connected to body. Procoxal cavities open behind. Scutellum small and triangular. Elytra long, straight-sided, with rows of deep and rectangular punctures; abdomen completely covered.

Legs do not retract into sulci; hind trochanters very long, almost as long as femora; tarsi 5-5-5, tarsomeres 2–4 with pads underneath, 3 shallowly and 4 deeply notched; claws pectinate. Abdomen with five ventrites, with 1–4 connate.

SIMILAR FAMILIES Cerophytids are superficially similar to the following families but easily distinguished by their body form and long hind trochanters:

- artematopodid beetles (Artematopodidae, p.247)
- throscid beetles (Throscidae, p.252)
- false click beetles (Eucnemidae, p.254)

- click beetles (Elateridae, p.273)
- death-watch beetles (Ptinidae, p.299)

COLLECTING NOTES Adult cerophytids are seldom collected. They occur in forested and chaparral habitats and are usually encountered at lights or discovered in Malaise trap samples. Individuals are also captured on the wing, under bark, in decaying wood, or swept from vegetation. Additional specimens have been sifted from leaf litter and other plant debris on the ground.

FAUNA TWO SPECIES IN ONE GENUS

Cerophytum convexicolle LeConte (6.5–7.0 mm) is elongate-oblong, dull black with legs brownish, and sparsely clothed in reddish pubescence. Head with large, prominent round eyes, prominent mandibles sharp, with antennae pectinate (male) or serrate (female). Pronotum broad with lateral margins rounded, and posterior angles somewhat prominent; prosternum lobed in front with sutures simple, arcuate. Elytra broadest across prominent humeri and wider than prothorax, punctostriate with strial punctures coarse and close, with intervals flat and finely but not densely punctured with somewhat transverse wrinkles, and lateral margins arcuate and narrowing at apical third. Legs moderate in length, with front femur grooved to receive tibia. Southwestern Oregon and California. (1)

BRACHYPSECTRIDAE (brak-ip-sekt'-ri-dē)
TEXAS BEETLES

Brachypsectridae is a small family with a widely disjunct global distribution and is represented in North America by a single species, *Brachypsectra fulva* LeConte. The apparent rarity of these beetles is the result of their preference for cryptic microhabitats with accumulations of small arthropods that serve as prey for the predatory larvae. Adult males are short lived, while most of the known female specimens were reared from larvae collected under loose bark, in lava rock cracks, among leaf bases of agavaceous plants, beneath loose bark of eucalyptus, mesquite, and pine, or under leaf litter and other plant debris on the ground. Rather than favoring particular plants, these beetles apparently prefer secure habitats that harbor large numbers of sheltering insects and other arthropods. The peculiarly oval and flattened larvae (p.28, Fig. 18i) capture small arthropods (spiders and other arachnids, ants, beetle larvae) by arching their backs and trapping prey between the articulated spine at the end of the abdomen and their channeled mandibles, adapted for sucking out bodily fluids. Small papillae covering their backs are suspected to produce chemical compounds that are attractive to potential prey. Mature larvae pupate within a coarsely meshed silken enclosure constructed with white silk attached to the upper and lower surfaces of their retreat.

FAMILY DIAGNOSIS Adult brachypsectrids are relatively small, lightly sclerotized, and nondescript beetles that resemble small, primitive elateroids, but lack a thoracic clicking mechanism. Head somewhat broad and deeply inserted in prothorax. Antennae with 11 antennomeres, 5–10 somewhat pectinate (males) or weakly serrate (females). Prothorax with prosternum large, forming "chin piece" below head. Procoxal cavities broadly open behind. Tarsi 5-5-5, tarsomere 4 slightly smaller and weakly lobed underneath, with simple claws. Abdomen with five ventrites free.

SIMILAR FAMILIES

- soft-bodied plant beetles (Dascillidae, p.206)— not flattened, antennae filiform or serrate from antennomere 3 to apex
- rare click beetles (Cerophytidae, p.250)—antennae pectinate in males, serrate in females from antennomere 3 to apex

- throscid beetles (Throscidae, p.252)—antennal club with three antennomeres
- false click beetles (Eucnemidae, p.254)—antennae filiform or serrate from antennomere 3 or 4 to apex
- click beetles (Elateridae, p.273)—rarely flat, clicking mechanism present, antennae serrate in both sexes

COLLECTING NOTES Adult male brachypsectrids are attracted to lights at night, while females are occasionally found in larval breeding sites beneath loose bark or at bases of leaf blades of agavaceous plants in desert scrub and upland habitats.

FAUNA ONE SPECIES, *BRACHYPSECTRA FULVA*

Brachypsectra fulva LeConte (3.7–6.3 mm) is oblong, somewhat elongate and flattened, yellowish brown lighter on elytra and underside, with dorsal surface sparsely clothed in bristly setae. Male with antennomeres 5–10 pectinate, projections not acute. Pronotum wider than long, sides sinuate near base with narrowly acute posterior angles carinate, extending backward. Elytra striate with sides nearly parallel. Adults and larvae found in and under loose bark, cracks in rocks, and other microhabitats with accumulations of small arthropod prey. Nocturnal males attracted to lights in summer; females occur in microhabitats suitable for larval development. California to Colorado and central Texas, south to Baja California and Sonora. (1)

THROSCIDAE (throsk'-i-dē)
THROSCID BEETLES

Throscids resemble very small and stout click beetles (Elateridae, p.273) with rigid bodies. Very little is known about their natural history, including the food preferences of both the larvae and adults. The larvae live and develop in decaying logs in association with fungi, in fungus-infested soil samples and in clumps of grass. *Pactopus* larvae have been found under a log in a forested habitat impacted by fire. The short-lived throscid adults are commonly found on flowers and vegetation on warm days in spring and early summer and are sometimes attracted to lights. When disturbed, some species retract their legs and antennae into special sulci on the underside of the thorax, remain motionless, and strongly resemble seeds. Despite their rigid bodies, throscids do possess a clicking mechanism like that of click beetles and can propel themselves several centimeters into the air.

FAMILY DIAGNOSIS Adult throscids are elongate-oblong to somewhat elongate, moderately convex, reddish brown to black, and covered with fine, pale pubescence. Head

hypognathous, deeply inserted in prothorax, with eyes coarsely faceted and deeply notched, sometimes nearly divided, or only slightly emarginate (*Pactopus*). Labrum distinct. Antennae with 11 antennomeres, only slightly expanded apically (*Pactopus*) to loosely clavate, antennae received by sulci on underside of prothorax. Prothorax tightly fitted against base of elytra and narrowed anteriorly, posterior angles directed backward. Procoxal cavities open behind. Scutellum small, triangular. Elytra shallowly grooved and punctured, rounded at apices, and completely covering abdomen. Underside of metathorax smooth on sides (*Trixagus*), or with deep oblique sulci to accommodate middle tarsi (*Aulonothroscus*). Legs tightly retracting against body, tarsi 5-5-5, tarsi slender (*Pactopus*) or with tarsomere 4 lobed underneath, claws equal and simple. Abdomen with five fused ventrites free, with simple depressions that accommodate tarsi, or deep and oblique sulci (*Pactopus*).

SIMILAR FAMILIES

- metallic wood-boring beetles (Buprestidae, p.210)—usually larger, antennae usually serrate, metallic ventrally
- false click beetles (Eucnemidae, p.254)—usually larger, generally broadest at prothorax, antennae never clubbed
- click beetles (Elateridae, p.273)—prothorax loosely hinged to rest of body
- fruitworm beetles (Byturidae, p.410)—tarsi lobed
- false skin beetles (Biphyllidae, p.411)—posterior pronotal angles not extended
- silken fungus beetles (Cryptophagidae, p.449)—posterior pronotal angles not extended

COLLECTING NOTES Adult throscids are sometimes common in open, vegetated habitats. Beating and sweeping flowers and foliage of deciduous hardwoods along roads and trails in wooded areas are the best ways to collect adults. Strong fliers, they are also netted during late afternoons and early evenings on warm days. Some species are captured in numbers in Malaise and flight intercept traps, while nocturnal species are attracted to lights. Still others occur in moss and leaf litter, and are extracted using a Berlese funnel or Winkler eclector.

FAUNA 20 SPECIES IN THREE GENERA

Aulonothroscus validus LeConte (2.5–5.0 mm) is oblong, robust, and dark brown with pronotum sometimes darker, dorsal surface with mixed fine and coarse punctures, and clothed in fine recumbent setae. Head convex without carinae, eyes small, feebly emarginate at antennal insertion, and antennae capitate with antennomeres 9–11 forming club. Pronotum convex; prosternal striae short and parallel. Elytra distinctly punctostriate with strial punctures coarse. Underside of metasternum with deep oblique sulci to receive middle tarsi. Tarsomere 4 lobed underneath. Adults on vegetation during spring and summer; attracted to lights. British Columbia to California, east to Nevada. (1)

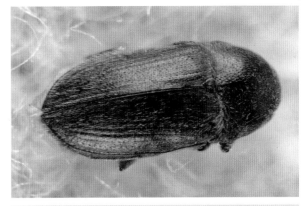

Pactopus hornii (LeConte) (2.7–6.0 mm) is oblong-oval, reddish to dark brown with appendages and humeri often paler, and clothed in short fine decumbent gray setae. Head not carinate, nearly round eyes entire, and antennae not distinctly clubbed. Pronotum coarsely punctate, lateral margins more (male) or less (female) sinuate, with posterior angles strongly produced backward, embracing humeri. Elytra distinctly punctostriate with interstriae flat, with lateral margins straight (male) or slightly arcuate (female). Metasternum and abdominal ventrites 1–3 with deep oblique tarsal sulci. Tarsi slender. Adults on vegetation during spring and summer; attracted to lights. British Columbia to California, east to Idaho; South Dakota. (1)

Trixagus carinicollis (Schaeffer) (2.1–3.3 mm) is oblong-oval, dull reddish to black with long yellowish or grayish pubescence. Head with a pair of parallel ridges, eyes deeply divided by a narrow depression, and antennae capitate with antennomeres 9–11 forming club. Pronotum wider than long with posterior angles distinct and projecting backward, and each bearing a narrow ridge. Elytra with dense fringe of long setae on sides just behind middle (male) or not (female). Underside with metasternum lacking deep tarsal sulci. Tarsomere 4 lobed underneath. Adults active spring and summer, found resting on vegetation; attracted to lights. Pacific Northwest; also Maritime Provinces to Virginia, west to Ontario, Iowa, and Kentucky. (4)

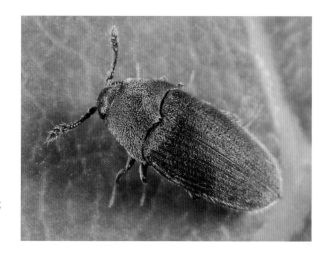

EUCNEMIDAE (ūk-nēm′-i-dē)
FALSE CLICK BEETLES

Most "false" click beetles can "click" as well as elaterids, and a few species have enough flexibility between the prothorax and elytra that they can flip themselves into the air. Their clicking mechanism is the same as that of Elateridae and likewise is thought to startle predators. Adults are active in spring and summer and found resting on vegetation or on tree trunks during the day. Although little is known of their habits, eucnemids likely play an important role in the interactions between trees, fungi, and forest regeneration and could be used as important indicators of forest diversity. Eucnemid larvae lack legs, have mandibles with their grinding surfaces on the outside, and resemble the larvae of metallic wood-boring beetles because the first thoracic segment is wider than the rest of the body. They are sometimes called "cross-cut borers" because they typically mine across the wood grain. Rather than constructing galleries, most eucnemid larvae force their wedge-shaped heads through soft wood with the aid of special plates on their abdomens. Although some species prefer coniferous trees, most eucnemid larvae develop in decaying hardwoods infected with fungi that cause white rot. They apparently feed on fungus, not wood, and must first vomit digestive juices that break down fungal tissues into nutritious juices that are then sucked into the mouth.

FAMILY DIAGNOSIS Adult eucnemids are long, convex, sometimes nearly cylindrical, brownish to blackish beetles. Head partially retracted inside prothorax, with hypognathous mouthparts. Antennae with 11 antennomeres and moniliform, filiform, or with last seven or eight terminal antennomeres serrate or pectinate. Prothorax broader than head and elytra, hypomera plain, or with antennal sulci. Procoxal cavities open behind. Scutellum visible, oval to broadly oval, or triangular. Elytra parallel-sided, rows of punctures with smooth spaces between, rounded at apices, and completely cover the abdomen. Tarsi 5-5-5, tarsomere 4 sometimes lobed, with claws equal, simple, toothed, or comblike. Abdomen with five ventrites connate, 5 longer.

SIMILAR FAMILIES
- metallic wood-boring or jewel beetles (Buprestidae, p.210)—most species shiny or metallic underneath
- rare click beetles (Cerophytidae, p.250)—hind trochanters very long
- throscid beetles (Throscidae, p.252)—antennal club typically comprising three antennomeres
- click beetles (Elateridae, p.273)—labrum visible, abdomen with three, four, or five fused ventrites
- lizard beetles (Erotylidae, p.436)—antennae clubbed

COLLECTING NOTES Eucnemids are seldom as common as click beetles. Some species are beaten or swept from vegetation, whereas others are found beneath loose bark

254

of their host trees. A few species are netted on the wing at dusk or are attracted to lights. Additional species and specimens are captured in flight intercept, Malaise, and Lindgren funnel traps.

FAUNA 85 SPECIES IN 37 GENERA

Perothops witticki LeConte (9.0–22.0 mm) is oblong, parallel-sided, robust, reddish brown, and clothed in fine yellowish-gray pubescence. Suprantennal ridges nearly transverse and separated in front. Pronotum wide, broadest behind middle, sides rounded and sinuate before sharp and divergent posterior angles; triangular hypomeron simple, prosternal process abruptly declivous behind coxae. Elytra striate, interstriae slightly convex. Protibia with two apical spurs, tarsomeres short and pubescent underneath, and claws pectinate. Diurnal adults on mature oaks (*Quercus*) in late spring, early summer. *Perothops cervinus* Lacordaire (11.0–20.0 mm) with long, acute, and divergent posterior angles; prosternal process longer, gradually sloping behind coxae, elytral interstriae more convex. Both in California. (2)

Anelastes californicus Muona (5.7–10.2 mm) is oblong, slightly flattened, and uniformly light brown, with surface finely granulose and sparsely clothed in short golden recumbent pubescence. Antennae simple, slightly stouter in female, 11 narrowed apically. Pronotum with lateral ridge complete, weakly sinuate before posterior angles; triangular hypomeron simple. Elytra punctostriate with punctures deep, interstriae convex. Protibia with two apical spurs, and claws simple. California and Baja California Peninsula. *Anelastes desertorum* Muona (5.1–10.5 mm) similar, Oregon and Idaho to Texas; *A. drurii* Kirby (7.5–13.0 mm) dark brown, with lateral pronotal ridge faint and obliterated just before posterior angle, throughout West. (3)

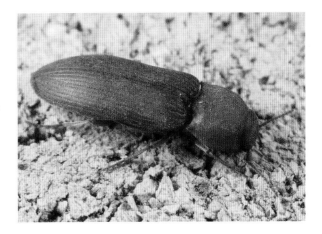

255

Palaeoxenus dohrni Horn (13.0–19.0 mm) is oblong, somewhat parallel-sided, convex, and distinctively bicolored black with head, pronotum, humeri, elytral apices, and most of underside dull to bright red, with surfaces moderately clothed in fine recumbent pubescence the same color as surface. Pronotum wider than long, lateral margins moderately arcuate, gradually narrowed at apical third with posterior angles prolonged posteriorly; hypomeron simple. Elytra punctostriate with intervals convex basally and becoming flatter posteriorly, slightly broader behind middle. Adults and larvae found under bark low on conifer snags and stumps, such as incense cedar (*Libocedrus decurrens*) and sugar pine (*Pinus lambertiana*). Transverse Ranges of southern California. (1)

Sarpedon scabrosus Bonvouloir (5.0–7.0 mm) is elongate, cylindrical, densely punctate and partly granulose dorsally, black, with anterior pronotal margin always and sometimes other margins and appendages variably lighter. Antennomeres 4–10 bipectinate (male) or biserrate (female). Pronotum slightly longer than wide, lateral margins straight, complete, and serrate, with medial impression on disc flanked by shorter longitudinal impressions; antennal depression faintly indicated on hypomeron. Protibia with single apical spur, meso- and metatibiae without spines or combs, and claws simple. Elytra punctostriate. Adults on *Populus*, in Malaise traps. British Columbia to California, east to Colorado; also in eastern North America. (1)

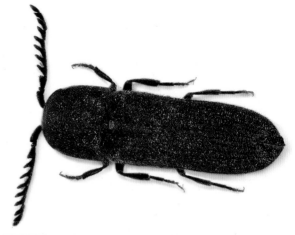

Microrhagus pectinatus (LeConte) (3.0–5.0 mm) dark brown or black, legs and parts of antennae, anterior pronotal margin, elytra, and abdomen lighter, and moderately clothed in yellowish recumbent pubescence. Antennae deeply serrate (female) or pectinate (male), insertions narrowly separated, antennomere 3 longer than 4. Pronotum broad, lateral margin divided, posterior ridge short and extending up one-third of pronotum, and narrow medial groove on disc; triangular hypomeron with notosternal antennal groove. Elytral apices simple. Protibia with single apical spur, meso- and metatibiae without spines, metacoxal plates narrowed laterally, and claws simple. Larvae in rotten hardwoods. Adults at lights, in Malaise and Lindgren funnel traps. British Columbia; widespread in East. (1)

Melasis tsugae Hopping (6.5–9.5 mm) is elongate, somewhat cylindrical, moderately shiny black with appendages brown. Frons without transverse carina. Antennae serrate (female) or pectinate (male) with rami long, that of 6 abruptly longer than 5. Pronotum narrow and broadest just behind anterior margin, with short basal impression just before scutellum. Elytra distinctly striate, striae with punctures most evident apically, and interstriae granulose. British Columbia to northern California. *Melasis rufipalpus* Chevrolat (6.5–8.5 mm) similar, with male rami shorter; Arizona. *Melasis rufipennis* Horn (7.2–13.0 mm) elytra reddish brown, frons usually with transverse carina: British Columbia to southern California, and Nevada. (3)

Xylophilus crassicornis Muona (2.9–4.0 mm) is elongate, cylindrical, and black with abdomen, appendages, part of clypeus, pronotal margins, and elytra reddish brown. Antennomeres 4–10 wider than long. Pronotum sparsely punctate; hypomeron simple and triangular. Pronotum convex with lateral margins rounded. Elytra coarsely and confusedly punctate, sometimes with linear infuscations. Adults uncommonly collected in Malaise and Lindgren funnel traps. Washington; widespread in eastern United States. *Xylophilus cylindriformis* (Horn) (3.0–7.1 mm) similar, sometimes uniformly dark brown, antennomeres 4–10 as long as or longer than wide, pronotum mostly densely punctate. Most commonly encountered *Xylophilus*. British Columbia to California, east to Nevada; also Northeastern United States. (2)

Proutianus americana (Horn) (6.5–8.5 mm) is elongate, robust, slightly flattened, dark brown to black with appendages and lateral pronotal margins sometimes lighter, and sparsely clothed in inconspicuous vestiture. Flattened clavate antennae short, antennomeres 9–11 enlarged. Acute posterior pronotal angles acute, slightly produced backward; hypomeron with lateral antennal sulci closed at base. Elytra with distinct striae impunctate and flat interstriae. Protibia with one spur, middle and hind legs with apical spurs, hind tibia flat with upper and lower surfaces sharply defined, and tarsomere 4 simple. Mesosternum without tarsal sulci. Uncommon; collected flying at night and in turpentine trap in redwood forest. British Columbia to California. (1)

257

Hemiopsida robusta (Van Dyke) (6.0–8.0 mm) is elongate, robust, dark brown to black with appendages and underside reddish, and sparsely clothed in fine reddish-yellow pubescence. Dorsal pronotal and elytral contours not distinctly continuous. Mandibles slender. Antennae slender and surpassing pronotum, antennomeres 9–11 not enlarged, each more or less equal in length to others. Pronotum barely wider than long with carinate lateral margins simple; hypomeron unmodified. Elytra with punctostriae variably distinct with strial punctures inconspicuous, interstriae flat. Legs slender, protibia with one spur, middle and hind tibiae each with single spine on lateral surface, and tarsomere 4 simple. California. (1)

LYCIDAE (lis'-i-dē)
NET-WINGED BEETLES

The possession of lightly sclerotized exoskeletons presents net-winged beetles with at least two major challenges. First, their pliable bodies provide a poor framework for flight muscles. With their elytra spread, lycids generally fly only short distances, slowly fluttering mothlike through the air. Second, their thin cuticles increase their chances of desiccation, limiting the distribution of many species in western North America to relatively moist, wooded habitats. However, species of *Lucaina* have apparently adapted to living in desert environments, in part, by restricting adult activity to the summer monsoon season. Lycids are typically encountered resting singly on leaves or decaying wood, but *Lycus* regularly gather in large and conspicuous mating aggregations on flowering shrubs and trees. Their bold and aposematically colored bodies, a feature shared with many other lycids, presumably serve to warn potential predators of the beetles' chemical defenses. When disturbed, they produce bitter and malodorous drops of yellowish hemolymph from their appendages and elytral margins that serve as feeding deterrents to vertebrate and invertebrate predators alike. Distasteful net-winged beetles are mimicked not only by other beetles (e.g., Cleridae (p.425), Chrysomelidae (p.501), and Cerambycidae (p.460)) but also by moths, true bugs, and other insects. Most adult lycids apparently do not feed and are short-lived, although flower-visiting species such as *Lycus* do consume nectar. Larval lycids live under bark and in decaying wood, where they feed on fluids and soft tissues associated with fungal growth.

FAMILY DIAGNOSIS Adult lycids are soft-bodied and flattened, with coarsely sculptured and loose-fitting elytra often boldly marked with red or orange. Head prognathous, sometimes extended beaklike, and partially covered by pronotum. Antennae with 11 flattened antennomeres, weakly to strongly serrate or pectinate (*Caenia*). Pronotum flattened, bell-shaped, margins distinct, concealing head from view above. Procoxal cavities open behind. Elytra nearly straight-sided or expanded past the middle and extend well beyond outline of abdomen; surface with network of long costae connected by less distinct cross-ridges. Legs with coxae widely separated; tarsi 5-5-5, tarsomeres 1–4 with dense pubescence underneath, claws simple and equal. Abdomen with seven (female) or eight (male) ventrites free.

SIMILAR FAMILIES
- reticulated beetles (Cupedidae, p.74)—head exposed
- fireflies (Lampyridae, p.262)—elytra without costae; abdomen sometimes with two or three yellow and bioluminescent ventrites
- soldier beetles (Cantharidae, p.265)—elytra without costae; head distinct from above
- glowworms (Phengodidae, p.271)—male antennae bipectinate, mandibles distinct, and elytra without costae
- some leaf beetles (Chrysomelidae: Cassidinae, p.501)—hard-bodied, antennae short and weakly clubbed

COLLECTING NOTES Sweeping and beating vegetation during the day in spring and summer will produce net-winged beetles. Pupae and freshly eclosed adults are sometimes found under the loose bark of snags, stumps, and logs. Look for species of *Lucaina* and *Lycus* on flowers during the day in late spring and summer. *Dictyoptera*, *Greenarus*, *Punicealis*, and *Plateros* are usually found on vegetation or under loose bark on decaying logs and stumps. Some species (*Caenia*) are attracted to lights at night, while still others are captured in Malaise and flight intercept traps.

FAUNA 78 SPECIES IN 20 GENERA

Dictyoptera simplicipes (Mannerheim) (6.5–12.5 mm) is black with bright red pronotum, elytra, femora, and tibiae. Diamond-shaped median pronotal cell complete and black. Elytral pubescence short, concentrated on carinae, intervals nearly glabrous with two rows of cells. Abdomen black. Montane mesic forests. *Dictyoptera aurora* (Herbst) (6.5–11.0 mm) pronotum black with red margins and black legs. Both in western North America. (2) *Punicealis hamata* (Mannerheim) (10.0–15.5 mm) uniformly scarlet red or orangish dorsally, elytral pubescence evenly distributed, legs mostly reddish; Alaska to Washington, east to Idaho. (1)

Greenarus thoracicus (Randall) (5.0–8.5 mm) is elongate, somewhat parallel-sided and flattened, black with bicolored elytra, and moderately clothed in short recumbent setae. Pronotum pentagonal, lateral margins rarely reddish, and disc with median diamond-shaped cell complete. Elytra with humeri reddish, spot small, not reaching margin, and sometimes extending to middle, each with three carinae and four double rows of rectangular cells. Underside and legs black. Widespread in southern Canada and United States. (1)

Lucaina greeni Ferreira & Ivie (5.0–7.5 mm) elytra orangish with black oval spot across apical half, or entirely bluish black. Rostrum length equivalent to half distance between eyes; clypeal suture not evident. Pronotum usually with median spot or stripe. On *Prosopis, Senegalia* flowers. Southeastern California, southern Nevada to Texas, south to Mexico. *Lucaina marginata* Gorham (4.5–7.0 mm) black with lateral pronotal and elytral margins narrowly orange, rostrum length about one-quarter distance between eyes; southeastern Arizona, western Texas. *Lucaina milleri* Ferreira & Ivie (4.3–5.6 mm) black, with basal one-third to half of elytra yellowish; on *Eriogonum, Prosopis* flowers. Southern California and Baja California. (3)

Lygistopterus dimidiatus LeConte (7.0–10.0 mm) is red and black, with head not rostrate, and elytra with anterior margins of blue-black areas oblique. Southeastern British Columbia to central Sierra Nevada, California, east to Idaho and western Nevada. *Lygistopterus slevini* (Van Dyke) (8.0–10.0 mm) elytra with anterior margins of dark area transverse. Coastal California. *Lygistopterus fervens* (LeConte) (8.0–9.0 mm) elytra uniformly reddish; British Columbia and Alberta to Oregon, east to South Dakota. *Lygistopterus ruficollis* (LeConte) (7.0–9.5 mm) elytra black; Oregon and Colorado to Arizona and New Mexico. (5)

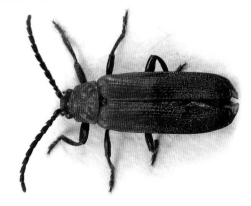

Lygistopterus ignitus (Green) (7.0–11.0 mm) is densely pubescent, with dorsal surface mostly reddish orange, and head, middle of pronotum, scutellum, elytral apices, and appendages black. Mouthparts not rostrate. Pronotum somewhat pentagonal, and broadest basally. Elytra broadest at apical fourth, each with four carinae most evident basally, with outer two relatively weak. On flowers of *Ceanothus* and other woody shrubs at high elevation. *Lygistopterus apicalis* (Green) (6.5–8.3 mm) is similar in form, color, and habitat, except dorsal surface of pronotum entirely black. Both species known only from southeastern Arizona. (5)

Macrolygistopterus rubripennis (LeConte) (10.0–14.0 mm) is black with scarlet red elytra. Head with short, blunt rostrum, and slender antennae slightly compressed in male, with antennomere 2 short and as long as wide, 3 triangular and as long as 1, and 4–11 each longer than wide and subequal in length to 3. Pronotum broadest posteriorly, lateral margins straight before diverging and narrowly rounded posterior angles. Elytra broadest at apical third, finely punctate without costae, and densely clothed in coarse, recumbent setae. On vegetation; occasionally at lights. Arizona to Colorado and New Mexico. (1)

Caenia amplicornis LeConte (7.0–10.5 mm) is flat, broadest at apical third of elytra, and mostly black. Sides of pronotum and basal half of elytral margins pinkish red. Antennae flat, and pectinate (male) or serrate (female). Anterior pronotal margin narrowly curved medially. Elytron with four carinae, sutural interval with a single row of cells, except toward apices. At lights in montane forests of southeastern Arizona, southwestern New Mexico in summer. *Caenia dimidiata* (Fabricius) (8.5–13.5 mm) antennae pectinate in both sexes, basal half of elytra orange with large scutellar black spot; Chiricahua Mountains, Arizona. New species await description. (2+)

Lycus arizonensis Green (13.0–18.5 mm) is elongate-oval with elytra mostly orange with apical one-fourth black. Head with rostrum relatively short, not more than twice the distance between the eyes. Elytra expanded apically, especially in males, with anterior margin of apical band not notched where it meets humeral costa. Femora mostly orange with apices black. Tibiae distinctly (male) or scarcely (female) curved. Adults commonly found on various flowering shrubs during summer in mountain canyons. Southeastern Arizona. Compare with *L. fernandezi*. (10)

Lycus fernandezi Dugés (10.0–18.0 mm) is elongate-oval with elytra mostly orange with apical one-fourth black. Head with rostrum longer and slender, length more than twice the distance between the eyes. Elytra expanded apically, especially in males, with anterior margin of apical band typically notched where it meets humeral costa. Femora entirely orange, sometimes with apices dusky or black. Tibiae distinctly (male) or scarcely (female) curved. Adults commonly found on various flowering shrubs during summer. Southeastern Arizona. Compare with *L. arizonensis*. (10)

Lycus fulvellus femoratus (Schaeffer) (10.0–14.0 mm) is elongate-oval with uniformly orange elytra. Head, most of antennae, and ventral surface black. Pronotum pale with small median dark spot, disc alutaceous and dull. Legs and femoral apices black, while trochanters and femora mostly reddish orange. Elytra with alternating costae distinctly more elevated, especially on apical half. Underside of thorax black, abdomen mostly dusky to black with lateral margins and the two most posterior ventrites orange. Adults on flowers of *Ceanothus* in high-elevation mountains during summer. Southeastern Arizona. (10)

Lycus loripes (Chevrolat) (10.0–13.0 mm) is elongate-oval, somewhat shiny, and orange. Head with rostrum long and slender, length about two and one-fifth distance between eyes. Antennae, except for basal three antennomeres, black. Pronotum smooth and shiny medially. Tibiae vary from entirely dark to entirely pale and strongly (male) or weakly (female) curved. Adults on flowering shrubs, such as mule fat (*Baccharis salicifolia*), mimosa (*Mimosa*), and mesquite (*Prosopis*) during summer in mountain canyons. Southeastern Arizona to Texas. Compare with *L. simulans*. (10)

Lycus sanguinipennis Say (9.0–13.5 mm) is mostly black, moderately clothed in short pubescence, with explanate lateral margins of pronotum and elytra dull red, and scutellum and broad scutellar spot at base of elytra dusky to black. Rostrum short and stout, length equivalent to nearly one-half the distance between the eyes. Adults on flowers of *Ceanothus* in high-elevation mountains of southeastern Arizona and New Mexico. *Lycus sanguineus* (Gorham) (11.5–14.5 mm) scarlet, sparsely setose, abdomen covered by long elytra (male) or exposed by short and narrow elytra (female), with apical fourth or fifth black. Males often found clinging to grasses. Arizona to Texas. (10)

Lycus simulans (Schaeffer) (10.0–12.0 mm) is elongate-oval and orange with mostly black antennae, tibiae, and tarsi. Head with rostrum stout and relatively short, less than about one and a half times distance between eyes. Antenna with first three antennomeres pale. Tibiae vary from entirely dark to entirely pale and strongly (male) or weakly (female) curved. Metatibial spurs similar in size and sharp apically. Adults found on flowering shrubs during summer in lower Madrean woodlands. Southeastern Arizona. *Lycus minuta* Green similar in appearance, and distribution, but less than 10 mm in length; usually only first antennomere pale. Compare with *L. loripes*. (10)

Plateros species (3.7–8.0 mm) are elongate, almost parallel-sided, slightly wider at elytral apices, dull black, and pronotum reddish brown with spot on middle, and front of head very short and mouthparts directed down. Antennae simple and slender. Pronotum widest at base, without ridge down middle or oblique ridges on sides, front margin and angles broadly rounded. Elytra with costae all similar height. Species are most reliably distinguished by examination of male genitalia; females best identified by capture in copula with male. Adults active during summer and are attracted to lights in wooded habitats in middle elevations. Arizona. Genus needs revision (8).

LAMPYRIDAE (lam-pir'-i-dē)
FIREFLIES, LIGHTNINGBUGS, AND GLOWWORMS

Lampyrids are soft-bodied beetles that are mostly tropical and subtropical in distribution, but a few species (e.g., *Microphotus* and *Pterotus*, and some *Pleotomus*) are restricted to decidedly more arid habitats in western North America. Adult females of some bioluminescent species are larviform and are called glowworms. Nocturnal, light-producing species spend their days hiding beneath bark, in leaf litter, or resting on leaves. Diurnal fireflies with weak or no light-producing organs (*Ellychnia*, *Lucidota*, *Pyropyga*) are generally found on flowers or streamside vegetation. The feeding habits of adult fireflies are poorly known and many species appear not to feed at all. Lampyrid larvae are predators of snails, slugs, earthworms, and small insects. They paralyze and kill their prey with the aid of chemical compounds pumped through channeled mandibles. Steroidal compounds called lucibufagins chemically protect fireflies by making them distasteful to predators. Whether the adult glows or not, all known eggs, larvae, and pupae of fireflies are bioluminescent, which serves as an aposematic warning to potential predators of their distastefulness. Adults benefit from this defensive strategy as well, in addition to utilizing bioluminescence as a means of locating potential mates (p.22, Fig. 8c; p.24, Fig. 11). Adult females of several lampyrid species in western North America are unknown and are presumed flightless and/or larviform.

FAMILY DIAGNOSIS Soft-bodied lampyrids are flattened, with hypognathous head covered by pronotum. Eyes large, especially in male. Antennae with 11 antennomeres and are filiform, serrate, or pectinate. Pronotum flattened, with lateral margin distinctly carinate. Procoxal cavities open behind. Scutellum visible. Elytra with surface sometimes weakly costate, with side margins nearly parallel, broadest at middle, and usually almost or completely conceal abdomen. Tarsi

5-5-5, tarsomere 4 heart-shaped; claws equal in size and usually simple. Abdomen with seven (female) or eight (male) ventrites free.

SIMILAR FAMILIES
- false soldier beetles (Omethidae, p.249)—labrum distinct, antennae separated by nearly twice diameter of antennal pits, abdomen without light-producing organs
- net-winged beetles (Lycidae, p.258)—head exposed from above, elytral costae usually connected by distinct but less conspicuous cross-veins (except in *Calochromus*, *Lygistopterus*, *Macrolygistopterus*), abdomen without light-producing organs
- soldier beetles (Cantharidae, p.265)—head exposed, not covered by pronotum, abdomen without light-producing organs
- adult male glowworms (Phengodidae, p.271)—head clearly visible, antennae bipectinate, sicklelike mandibles visible, elytra short

■ **COLLECTING NOTES** Bioluminescent *Photinus*, mostly males, are captured at night by hand or with a net as they are flashing; flashing females, both winged and wingless, are generally found on foliage or on the ground. Adults of *Ellychnia* and *Pyropyga* are sometimes found during the day resting on vegetation where they are collected by beating or sweeping. Species that are not bioluminescent are usually found under bark, drinking sap from freeze cracks on tree trunks, resting on vegetation, or flying during the day. Lampyrids are occasionally attracted to lights, especially males of *Microphotus*, *Pleotomus*, and *Pterotus*. Look for bioluminescent and larviform female pink glowworms (*Microphotus*) on rock walls, road and trail cuts, and other vertical surfaces in foothill and mountain habitats.

FAUNA 124 SPECIES IN 16 GENERA

Microphotus angustus LeConte (6.5–12.0 mm) male is elongate-elliptical, somewhat parallel-sided, granulate-punctate and sparsely pubescent dorsally, often with pinkish tinge. Eyes ventrally briefly contiguous, or nearly so, posteriorly. Antennae short, usually with nine, sometimes 10 antennomeres. Pronotum pale, wider than long, broadest at base, with lateral margins somewhat parallel or slightly diverging posteriorly, translucent above eyes, median longitudinal line not impressed, and posterior margin truncate. Elytra more than three times length of pronotum, and dark brown. Weakly bioluminescent; attracted to lights. Bioluminescent adult larviform female (p.22, Fig. 8d) pinkish and granular dorsally, and produces greenish light. Oregon to southern California. (7)

Paraphausis species (4.0–7.0 mm) males are elongate-elliptical, with sides somewhat parallel, and dorsal surfaces granulate. Eyes small, antennae approximate, with 11 short, stout antennomeres, completely covered by semielliptical pronotum when retracted. Pronotum with anterior angles obliterated and posterior angles rectangular, and sides broadly explanate. Elytra long with posterior abdominal tergite exposed, and vestiture dual. Legs short, stout, and compressed. Diurnal, resting on vegetation, also in flight intercept traps. At least two California species await description. *Paraphausis eximius* Green is black with reddish pronotum, scutellum, and posterior abdominal segment. Southeastern Arizona. (1+)

Ellychnia californica Motschulsky (9.5–16.0 mm) is coarsely punctate dorsally, and mostly black with bicolored pronotum. Eyes small, with antennae slender and not strongly compressed, antennomere 3 similar in length to 4, 11 without minute apical appendage. Elliptical pronotum with anterior angles obliterated, posterior angles rectangular, and lateral black margins uniformly narrow, with broad pinkish-red sublateral stripes, and a median, distinctly edged black stripe divergent posteriorly to basal lobes just before margin. Legs short, stout, and compressed. Diurnal adults fully winged, found on flowers and vegetation. California. (12)

Photinus knulli Green (7.5–8.0 mm) is finely, coarsely granulate-punctate dorsally. Eyes separated medially by less than (male) or more than (female) eye diameter. Pronotum quadrate or slightly wider, with sides slightly converging posteriorly, and rosy pink area divided by irregular median longitudinal stripe reaching posterior margin, becoming broader, then diffuse and coarsely punctate anteriorly. Elytra brownish black with margins pale yellow and narrower along suture than sides. Both sexes winged and bioluminescent. Males flash synchronously in leks; at lights. Riparian canyons of southeastern Arizona, likely in adjacent Sonora. (1)

264

Pyropyga nigricans Say (6.5–8.0 mm) is black or dark brownish black with bicolored pronotum. Eyes small. Antennae similar in both sexes, slender, compressed, with antennomeres 3–11 parallel-sided. Pronotum with black borders sometimes wanting, with median longitudinal stripe approximately one-third of entire pronotal width and flanked by trapezoidal orangish-red patches. Elytra with dual pubescence absent basally, with abdomen sometimes exposed. Last ventrite arcuately emarginate (male), or angularly notched (female). Legs short with claws simple. British Columbia to Baja California, east to Saskatchewan, and south to Mexico; also northeastern United States. (1)

Pleotomus pallens LeConte (9.4–20.0 mm) male is dull red, with head, antennae, and elytra dull black. Eyes very large, antennae short and robust, and mandibles slender apically. Antennae bipectinate with 13–14 antennomeres, branches short. Abdominal spiracles ventral. Flightless females with greatly reduced elytra. Adult males occasionally at lights. Males variable in form and color, becoming paler in the eastern and southern parts of its range; Southwestern form known previously as *P. nigripennis* LeConte. Southern California east to Utah, Kentucky, and Texas; south to southern Mexico. (1)

Pterotus obscuripennis (LeConte) (9.5–12.0 mm) male is elongate, somewhat parallel-sided, soft-bodied, and orange with black head, antennae, elytra, most of tibiae, and tarsi. Head partly covered by pronotum; mandibles not visible; antennae long with 11 antennomeres, 3–10 each with single threadlike compressed branch. Elytra long, narrow, rough, costate, not covering last abdominal segment. Unlike adult male, larva and larviform female bioluminescent. Males attracted to lights in spring and early summer in Coast ranges, foothills, and chaparral habitats. Washington to northern Baja California. *Pterotus curticornis* Chemsak (11.0–12.0 mm) antennae shorter with rami shorter and broader, pronotum narrower, legs orange and reddish; western edge of Colorado Desert, California. (2)

CANTHARIDAE (kan-thâr'-i-dē)
SOLDIER BEETLES

The natural history of most cantharids is poorly known. Adults are *univoltine*, short-lived, and frequently encountered feeding on flowers, resting on foliage during the day, or at lights at night. *Chauliognathus* are primarily pollen and nectar feeders and, along with other cantharids that visit flowers regularly, may be important pollinators. Some adult Cantharini and Podabrini prey primarily on aphids and other nectar-feeding insects, but will also imbibe nutrient-rich nectar. Some species possess narrowly notched lateral pronotal margins (*Ditemnus*, *Silis*) or highly modified abdominal segments (*Malthodes*) that likely function in courtship behavior and mate recognition. The larvae, pupae, and adults of some species produce defensive secretions from their abdominal glands. Contrasting color patterns, or aposematism, especially in adult cantharids, serve to warn potential predators of their bad taste. Beetles in other families mimic the color patterns of distasteful soldier beetles to discourage attacks by predators. When disturbed, some cantharids quickly withdraw their legs, drop to the ground, and become lost in the tangle of plants and debris below. Dead and contorted soldier beetles with their mandibles embedded in stems or leaf edges are likely infected by fungal pathogens in the genera *Eryniopsis* and *Zoophthora* that also attack other insects. The open wings and contorted bodies of the fungal victims have been dubbed "violent deaths" in the literature and are thought to enhance dispersal of spores of the killer fungus. Nocturnal cantharid larvae (p.29, Fig. 18l) are often velvety in appearance and develop under bark or in damp areas beneath stones, logs, or other debris. Most are liquid-feeding predators that utilize channeled mandibles, an oral filter, and *cibarial pump* to draw fluids from earthworms, slugs, caterpillars, maggots, and grasshopper eggs. Some species are somewhat omnivorous and will graze on grasses and other plant materials, too. Numerous genera need revision; many species of *Podabrus* will eventually be transferred to *Dichelotarsus*.

FAMILY DIAGNOSIS Adult cantharids are long, soft-bodied beetles, many of which resemble fireflies (Lampyridae), but its head is not completely concealed under the pronotum. Heads are prognathous, sometimes deflexed, with labrum membranous or hidden under clypeus. Antennae long, usually filiform, sometimes serrate or pectinate (*Tytthonyx*), with 11 antennomeres. Pronotum flat, usually broader than and partially conceals head (e.g., *Chauliognathus*, *Pacificanthia*, *Rhagonycha*) or not (e.g., *Dichelotarsus*, *Podabrus*), with lateral margins distinctly carinate and sometimes notched or otherwise distinctly modified (*Ditemnus*, *Silis*). Procoxal cavities broadly open behind, nearly absent. Soft elytra are short (*Malthinus*, *Trypherus*), or long and nearly or completely conceal abdomen. Tarsi 5-5-5, tarsomere 4 deeply notched and heart-shaped, claws equal in size, and simple, toothed, or lobed. Abdomen without bioluminescent organs, with seven (female, some males), or eight (most males) ventrites free.

265

SIMILAR FAMILIES

- false soldier beetles (Omethidae, p.249)—labrum distinct, tarsomeres 3 and 4 lobed, abdomen without glandular openings
- net-winged beetles (Lycidae, p.258)—labrum evident, elytral costae connected by distinct but less conspicuous cross-ridges (except in *Calochromus, Lygistopterus, Macrolygistopterus*)
- lightningbugs, fireflies (Lampyridae, p.262)—head covered by pronotum, labrum evident, abdomen sometimes with bioluminescent organs
- adult male glowworms (Phengodidae, p.271)—antennae bipectinate, mandibles distinct and sickle-shaped

- false blister beetles (Oedemeridae, p.374)—prothorax without distinct lateral margins, tarsi 5-5-4
- blister beetles (Meloidae, p.378)—bodies more cylindrical, head with neck, tarsi 5-5-4
- some longhorn beetles (Cerambycidae, p.460)—tarsi appear 4-4-4, but are 5-5-5

COLLECTING NOTES Cantharids are typically found feeding on flowers and resting among foliage during the day and easily hand-picked or collected by sweeping. They are sometimes especially abundant on vegetation in meadows and riparian habitats. Species in several genera are attracted to lights on warm nights during the spring and summer.

FAUNA 473 SPECIES IN 25 GENERA

Cantharis grandicollis (LeConte) (8.0–11.0 mm) is mostly black with orangish-red head, pronotum, and abdomen, and clothed in fine, simple pubescence of equal length. Head with black vertex sometimes reduced to broad triangular spot; eyes and mouthparts black, mandibles simple, and antennae mostly dark with antennomeres 1–3 lighter. Pronotum broader than head, reddish orange, and immaculate. Elytra coarsely granulate-punctate. Front femora sometimes partly pale, tarsomeres broad and lobed, 3 deeply emarginate, with 4 inserted before apex, and claws toothed. On flowers in montane habitats, especially Sierra Nevada. Southern Oregon and California. (22 NA)

Chauliognathus lecontei Champion (14.0–17.5 mm) is elongate, parallel-sided, and mostly red with eyes, most of mouthparts, basal two or three antennomeres, apical third or quarter of elytra, tibiae, tarsi, and all but bases of femora black. Pronotum wider than long, disc dull and with or without a pair of elongate black spots. Elytra with apical quarter black. Underside with last ventrite black. Adults occur on flowers of *Baccharis* and other flowering asters during summer in southeastern Arizona and southwestern New Mexico. (11)

Chauliognathus lewisi Crotch (8.0–10.0 mm) is mostly yellow with black markings. Head black with sides in front of eyes and mandibles yellow, antennae and mouthparts mostly black. Pronotum with large black M- or urn-shaped discal spot. Scutellum black. Elytra with or without distinct narrow black band across base that does not reach lateral margins and extends more or less continuously to but not reaching apices. Underside mostly yellow; legs black with bases of femora, trochanter, and coxae yellow. On summer flowers in mountains. Southeastern California to western Texas. (11)

Chauliognathus limbicollis LeConte (9.5–13.0 mm) is elongate, parallel-sided, and orange with black markings. Head black. Pronotum somewhat wider than long, with anterior margin broadly rounded, disc black and margins broadly orange. Elytra with triangular scutellar spots and apical third black. Underside with metathorax black, ventrites mostly pale (male) or mostly black with sides and apices more or less broadly pale (female). Legs black with front tibiae reddish brown. Adults occur on various flowers during summer in mountains of Idaho to eastern Arizona, east to Kansas and Texas. (11)

Chauliognathus misellus Horn (9.5–13.0 mm) is elongate, mostly pale yellow or pale orange-yellow with sparse black markings dorsally; appendages mostly black. Head black with sides in front of eyes and antennal sockets yellow. Pronotum nearly as long as wide, with pale margins and reddish-yellow disc usually immaculate, or sometimes with a pair of small spots. Elytra each with small round to transverse spot not reaching margins. Underside mostly yellow, with metasternum black posteriorly, with subtriangular mark extending anteriorly to about middle of metathorax. Adults on various flowers during late summer in mountains of northern, central, and southeastern Arizona. (11)

267

Chauliognathus obscurus Schaeffer (7.5–11.0 mm) is elongate and mostly reddish brown with darker markings and appendages. Head with a pair of large triangular dark brown or black spots between eyes that are sometimes broadly coalescent. Pronotum longer than wide, reddish orange with sides pale yellow, and a pair of small black spots or medial pair of broad dark brown or black stripes. Elytra brownish black with lateral and sutural margins pale to about middle. Underside mostly reddish orange with legs black with coxae, trochanters, and most of femora pale. Adults on various flowers during summer in montane habitats of southeastern Arizona. (11)

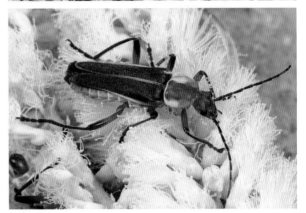

Chauliognathus omissus Fall (8.0–11.0 mm) is orangish, with head black, often sides below antennae pale. Pronotum with variable M- or urn-shaped spot. Elytra narrowed behind middle, with triangular basal spots meeting along suture, occasionally extending to elongate apical black spots forming uneven stripe; apical spots not reaching margins, sometimes extending to middle. Metathorax yellow and black. Abdomen mostly yellow (male) or with black spot(s) (female). Legs black. On *Gaillardia* and other asters. Southeastern Arizona. *Chauliognathus arizonensis* Fender (7.0–9.5 mm) metathorax entirely black, with diamond-shaped frontal impression on head; southeastern Arizona. (11)

Chauliognathus profundus LeConte (14.0–17.5 mm) is reddish orange and black dorsally, with appendages mostly black. Head black, sometimes with sides of clypeus pale. Pronotum immaculate, or with two or three black oval spots across middle; three black spots sometimes coalesce into a lobed band. Elytra with apical third black. Underside reddish orange with apical ventrite black. Coxae, trochanters, and femoral bases reddish orange. On flowers of *Baccharis* and other flowering shrubs during summer. Southeastern Arizona. (11)

Cultellunguis perpallens (Fall) (8.0–9.0 mm) is uniformly pale yellowish brown, elytra slightly paler. Pronotum with anterior margin broadly rounded, anterior angles obliterated, and broadly rounded posterior angles rectangular. Finely granulate elytra clothed in pale, recumbent setae. Claws simple (female), or with inner front claw incised (male). Coastal southern California. *Cultellunguis larvalis* (LeConte) (8.0–8.5 mm) darker, occipital spots often broadly expanded between eyes, pronotum with broadly rounded anterior angles and at least an indication of median "M," dusky elytra with margins partly darker, and dark underneath. Coastal northern and central California. Both on vegetation; at lights. (11)

Brown Leatherwing Beetle *Pacificanthia consors* **(LeConte)** (12.0–20.0 mm) is mostly orange with elytra uniformly brownish gray. Eyes large, antennae filiform and dusky, antennomeres 4–11 each with (male) or without (female) glabrous sulcus. Pronotum broadest across apical third, with anterior margin arcuate. Elytra with short velvety pubescence. Long, slender legs with femoral apices dark, tibiae and tarsi dusky, and outer claws with blunt tooth especially prominent on front leg. Male hind tibia with inner curved spur covered by conspicuous apical projection. Nocturnal adults prey on mealybugs and emit musty odor when threatened. At lights; California. (1)

Podabrus latimanus Motschulsky (10.0–12.0 mm) is black dorsally, with front of head and sides of pronotum orange. Head with eyes small, without frontoclypeal suture, and distinctly constricted behind eyes. Antennae mostly dusky with basal antennomeres pale. Pronotum wider than long, with anterior margin truncate. Elytra long, finely rugose, and faintly carinate. Last male tergite somewhat triangular. Legs mostly orangish brown with apices of tarsomeres darker, male protibia distinctly laminate inwardly, less so in female. Claws in both sexes armed with long, sharp tooth. Adults on flowers. Washington to central California. Genus needs revision.

Downy Leatherwing Beetle *Podabrus pruinosus pruinosus* LeConte (9.0–14.0 mm) is mostly orange with elytra uniformly brownish gray. Head with eyes small, but not prominent, without frontoclypeal suture, and distinctly constricted behind eyes. Antennae pale or with antennomere 4 dusky. Pronotum wider than long, with anterior margin truncate. Elytra finely rugose with moderate pubescence, and vaguely carinate. Male abdomen with last tergite somewhat triangular. Male hind coxae modified. Adults on flowers. Washington to northern California. *Podabrus pruinosus diversipes* Fall with antennae black with basal antennomeres pale, and legs with tarsi and tibiae, or at least apical portions, black. Pacific Northwest. Genus need revision.

Frostia laticollis (LeConte) (2.0–2.5 mm) is inconspicuously clothed in short pubescence, and dark brown, with orangish-brown pronotum, and short elytra. Head pale in front, black behind antennae, with mandibles not dentate internally but with acute tooth on inflexed outer margin, and antennae reaching elytral apices in male. Pronotum narrower than head across eyes, with anterior angles infuscate, moderately reflexed lateral margins, with moderately deep (male) or shallow (female) impressions. Elytra confusedly and rugosely punctured, each with apices rounded and only vaguely paler; shorter in female. Diurnal adults on vegetation. California. (5)

Discodon abdominale Schaeffer (9.0–11.0 mm) is slightly wider posteriorly, mostly orangish dorsally and ventrally, with moderate pubescence pale and erect. Head with bisinuate mark between eyes, antennae and palps black. Pronotum somewhat broad, disc sometimes with infuscations, anterior margin strongly curved, lateral margins somewhat parallel and incised medially in male, and posterior angles sharply rectangular. Last two ventrites black. Legs orange with femoral apices, tibiae, and tarsi black. Outer claws of tarsi cleft in male. Adults at lights during summer. Southeastern Arizona. (3)

Discodon flavomarginatum Schaeffer (14.0–15.0 mm) is mostly black with black appendages. Pronotum wider than long, pale yellow, with elongate medial black mark flanked on each side by rose stripes, with sides straight and divergent posteriorly. Elytra black with margins brown, surface rough, and lateral margins only slightly divergent past humeri. Underside, except for portions of head and prothorax, black. Legs with outer claw of front and middle legs broadly lobed (male) or simple (female). *Discodon bipunctatum* Schaeffer (10.0–12.0 mm) elytra somewhat parallel-sided, without pale lateral margins. Both species at lights during summer in southeastern Arizona. (3)

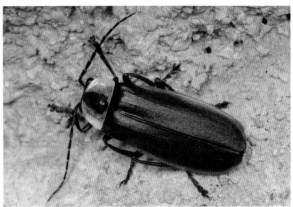

Ditemnus abdominalis (Schaeffer) (4.0–5.0 mm) is elongate, mostly black with prothorax and legs mostly orange. Head black with front pale, antennae black, antennomere 1 and mouthparts mostly pale, with terminal palpomeres black. Pronotum with lateral margins modified and excavated, forming angular processes. Underside with metathorax black and abdomen variously dusky, with sides and middle of ventrites pale, last ventrite with narrow U-shaped emargination. Legs with tibial apices and tarsi dusky. Adults attracted to lights. *Ditemnus howdeni* (Green) (3.5–4.5 mm) and *D. nigerrima* Schaeffer (6.0–6.5 mm) black, former with posterior process of pronotal armature continuous with posterior margin obscuring hind angles, latter with process well in front of hind angles. Southeastern Arizona. (5)

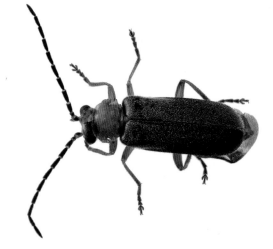

Silis carmelita Green (5.0–6.0 mm) is elongate, parallel-sided, inconspicuously clothed in fine, recumbent pubescence, and brownish black to black with prothorax mostly red. Pronotum wider than long, broadly explanate along anterior and lateral margins, lateral margins notched just before base with posterior process terminating in hairlike spine, and disc with partial or complete medial black stripe with irregular margins broadest at base, then narrowing anteriorly before abruptly expanding over explanate anterior border; stripe often wanting on anterior third or half. Elytra coarsely granulate-punctate. Last ventrite with deep V-shaped emargination. Adults found on foliage, flowers, and at lights. Northern coastal California. (~65)

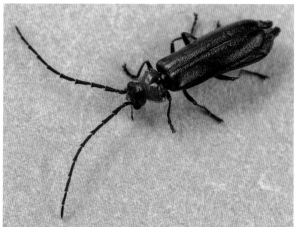

Tytthonyx bicolor (LeConte) (7.5–8.0 mm) male is elongate, clothed in short, recumbent brown setae, and red, with antennae, elytra, wings, and most of legs black. Head broad and black between eyes, with antennae long, antennomeres 3–10 pectinate, extensions elongate-oval and flat. Pronotum wider than long, with angles rounded, anterior margin more or less straight, and lateral and posterior margins distinctly beaded. Scutellum red. Elytra short, less than half abdominal length, deeply dehiscent, with surface rugosely punctate and costate, each attenuate and narrowly rounded apically. Diurnal adults found resting on foliage of various shrubs. Southeastern Arizona. (1)

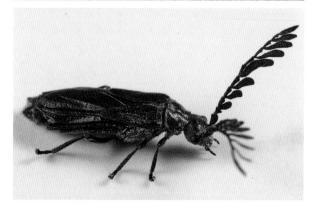

PHENGODIDAE (feng-ôd'-i-dē)
GLOWWORMS

A relatively small family restricted to the New World, the Phengodidae are most diverse in the Neotropical Realm. All genera known to occur in Canada and the United States are represented in the Southwest, including *Cenophengus*, *Distremocephalus*, *Paraptorhodius*, *Phengodes*, *Stenophrixothrix*, and *Zarhipis*. The soft-bodied males resemble other beetles, but their elytra tend to be short, exposing the hind wings and abdomen. The elytra are usually less than half as long as the hind wings. The antennae are often elaborately plumose or bipectinate (p.19, Fig. 6f). The long, fingerlike appendages, or rami, are covered with specialized chemoreceptors adapted for detecting and tracking attractant pheromones produced by the larviform female (p.22, Fig. 8e). Once in close proximity, the male visually homes in on the location of the female's bioluminescence. All known developmental stages (eggs, larvae, pupae) of phengodids, as well as both adult males and females, are bioluminescent. Larvae and adult females of *Phengodes* and *Zarhipis* (p.25, Fig. 12) have lateral spots and transverse bands of yellow-green light produced by pairs of light-producing organs on thoracic and abdominal segments. The arrangement of these organs suggests the illuminated windows on a train car, hence the common name "railroad worms." Adult males are weakly bioluminescent, too, but their lights are difficult to see. Adults apparently do not feed, while the known larvae all prey on small invertebrates. The larvae of both *Phengodes* and *Zarhipis* are millipede predators. Upon finding a millipede, the larva will run alongside its victim for a short distance before climbing onto its back and coiling itself around the millipede's body (p.31, Fig. 20). The phengodid larva then reaches under the millipede's head and uses its sicklelike mandibles to sever its prey's ventral nerve cord to paralyze it and deliver a lethal dose of digestive enzymes. The millipede soon dies and the digestive enzymes liquefy its internal tissues. If the attack occurs aboveground, the larva must drag the millipede into the soil by its antennae before it begins feeding. The larva pushes its way into the millipede's body cavity as it feeds, leaving in its wake a series of disarticulated exoskeletal rings. It may take several days for a phengodid larva to finish its millipede meal.

271

FAMILY DIAGNOSIS Adult males are relatively flat and soft-bodied. Head prognathous and not covered above by pronotum, and narrower (*Phengodes*, *Zarhipis*), or as broad as pronotum, with sickle-shaped mandibles well-developed (*Phengodes*, *Zarhipis*), small (*Distremocephalus*, *Paraptorhodius*, *Stenophrixothrix*), or reduced (*Cenophengus*), with eyes large and convex. Antennae with 12 antennomeres, 4–11 bipectinate, each sometimes with rami long and curled (*Phengodes*, *Zarhipis*). Pronotum flat, wider than long or subrectangular, with lateral margins rounded (*Cenophengus*, *Paraptorhodius*), or carinate. Procoxal cavities open behind. Scutellum visible, pointed (*Phengodes*, *Zarhipis*) or transverse apically. Elytra short, not punctostriate or carinate, exposing three or more abdominal segments. Tarsi 5-5-5, claws equal and simple, toothed, or pectinate (*Stenophrixothrix*). Abdomen with seven ventrites free. The larviform adult females are distinguished from larvae, in part, by their compound eyes.

SIMILAR FAMILIES
- false soldier beetles (Omethidae, p.249)—antennae with 11 articles and not bipectinate, mandibles not visible
- *Caenia* (Lycidae, p.260)—antennae with 11 antennomeres and not bipectinate, head and mandibles not conspicuous, elytral carinae usually connected by less conspicuous cross-veins
- *Pterotus* (Lampyridae, p.265)—antennae with 11 antennomeres and not bipectinate, mandibles not visible
- *Tytthonyx* (Cantharidae, p.270)—antennae with 11 antennomeres and not bipectinate, mandibles not visible
- *Dendroides* (Pyrochroidae, p.396)—male antennae with 11 antennomeres and not bipectinate, elytra cover abdomen, tarsi 5-5-4

COLLECTING NOTES Males are readily attracted to lights during spring and summer in desert and relatively arid, wooded habitats. Raking moist soil from underneath plants where millipedes are active during winter may reveal larvae and larviform females. Look for them under cover boards and other flat objects placed on the ground, or in covered pitfall traps fitted with drift fences.

FAUNA 23 SPECIES IN SIX GENERA

Phengodes arizonensis Wittmer (12.0–23.0 mm) male is elongate, flattened, and uniformly orangish brown with bases of antennomeres 4–11 black. Frons impressed between antennal insertions. Pronotum densely and conspicuously punctate medially, wider than long, with lateral margins narrowly explanate and parallel or slightly diverging toward protruding and acute posterior angles. Elytra short, abruptly narrowed distally with apices rounded. *Phengodes inflata* Wittmer similar, with lateral pronotal margins broadly explanate. *Phengodes mexicana* Wittmer elytra with dusky to black apices. *Phengodes fenestra* Wittmer mostly black with pair of pale spots on pronotum and orange abdomen. Males attracted to lights during summer in mountain habitats. Arizona. (4)

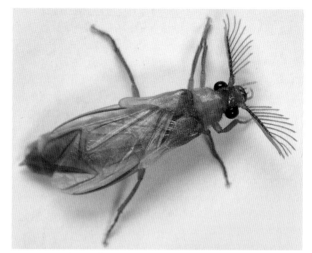

Zarhipis integripennis (LeConte) (12.0–23.0 mm) male is elongate, flattened, with head orange to mostly black, pronotum orange, and elytra black. Abdomen orange or orange with last 1–2 segments black, or mostly reddish black. Head with mandibles distinct, widely separated eyes, with antennal rami five times length of antennomere. Elytron parallel-sided along most of length. Pacific Coast and southwestern United States, and Baja California. *Zarhipis truncaticeps* Fall (12.0–16.0 mm) elytra long, narrowed, and dehiscent apically; southern Mojave, Colorado, and Sonoran Deserts, California and Arizona. *Zarhipis tiemanii* Linsdale (17.0 mm) dehiscent narrow elytra short; Mojave Desert of Arizona, California, and Nevada. Males of all species attracted to lights in spring. (3)

Distremocephalus californicus (Van Dyke) (7.0 mm) male is elongate, somewhat narrow, mostly dull blackish, appendages and sometimes head and pronotum paler, and rugosely punctate dorsally with sparse erect black and brown pubescence. Head broadly rounded behind large, finely granulated, and widely set eyes, with vertex wide as long, and bipectinate antennae with rami short and flat. Pronotum distinctly wider than long, angles rounded in front with posterior angles broadly rectangular. Elytra nearly half as long as abdomen. First tarsomere on front and middle legs with distinct setal comb. Attracted to lights on summer nights in wooded coastal and foothill habitats. California. (4)

272

Distremocephalus opaculus (Horn) (4.5–7.0 mm) male is elongate, narrow, dull orangish with elytra infuscate, and last two segments of dusky abdomen and appendages pale. Head somewhat quadrate behind finely granulated and widely separated eyes, with vertex as wide as long, and bipectinate antennae with rami short and flat, and large. Pronotum slightly wider than long, rounded in front with posterior angles rectangular. Elytra nearly half as long as abdomen. First tarsomere on front and middle legs with distinct setal comb. Attracted to lights during summer nights in wooded upland habitats. Arizona. (4)

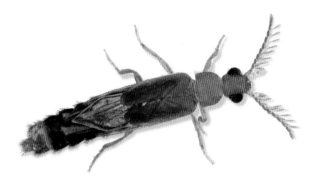

Distremocephalus texanus (LeConte) (6.0 mm) male is elongate, narrow, dull yellowish brown with abdomen often dusky, densely, and finely punctate dorsally with sparse erect yellowish pubescence. Head broadly rounded behind large, finely granulated and wide-set eyes, with vertex as wide as long, and bipectinate antennae with rami short and flat. Pronotum slightly longer than wide, rounded in front with posterior angles rectangular. Elytra about a third as long as abdomen, rounded and dehiscent apically. First tarsomere on front and middle legs with distinct setal comb. Attracted to lights in deserts. Nevada and Arizona, east to Texas. (4)

Stenophrixothrix fusca (Gorham) (8.0–9.2 mm) male is elongate, flattened, mostly brownish, and moderately clothed in short, erect, brownish setae on appendages and margins of pronotum and elytra; legs and underside paler. Head short and broad, without conspicuous mandibles, with eyes nearly meeting underneath and bipectinate antennomeres 3–10 with rami five times longer than antennomere and setose. Pronotum wide, somewhat convex, with lateral margins carinate, but not explanate, with disc shiny and almost glabrous, and slightly obtuse posterior angles. Elytra exceeding half length of abdomen, gradually narrowed and dehiscent apically. Tarsi with setose combs, with all claws finely pectinate. Southeastern Arizona to French Guiana. (1)

273

ELATERIDAE (el-å-ter'-i-dē)
CLICK BEETLES

Click beetles are commonly found on vegetation or under bark during the day, or at lights at night. Adults feed on rotting fruit, flowers, nectar, pollen, fungi, and sapping wounds on shrubs and trees. Some prey on small invertebrates, especially wood-boring insects and plant hoppers. When finding themselves lying on their backs, elaterids attempt to right themselves by tucking their prosternal spine into the mesosternal groove on the underside of the thorax with an audible click, thus inspiring the common name for the family. The sudden change in the beetle's center of gravity resulting from the spine snapping into place flips the insect into the air. This action can be executed from any position and is employed primarily as a means of escape, although it may startle some predators, too. The tough, slender larvae are commonly called wireworms. Many live in rotten wood, while others inhabit soil, rich humus, or decaying plant materials. Some wood-dwelling species are predators, while others scavenge fungi. Soil-dwellers are opportunistic predators and/or root feeders. Herbivorous larvae of *Agriotes*, *Limonius*, *Melanotus*, and *Selatosomus* attack sprouting seeds and roots of young grasses. Some wireworms are economically important and damage the seeds and roots of a variety of crops and garden plants. Three to five molts over a period of three years may be required to reach maturity. Pupation usually takes place in a cell in soil or rotten wood. Both adults and larvae overwinter in the ground, under bark, or in rotten wood. Several Holarctic genera that have been treated separately in the Nearctic and Palearctic Realms are currently being reevaluated. Thus, changes in the generic classification of North American elaterids are to be expected.

FAMILY DIAGNOSIS Adult elaterids are extremely uniform in appearance and are long, somewhat flattened, and mostly brownish or black, although many are quite colorful, sometimes with distinct markings, or with a metallic upper surface (*Chalcolepidius*, *Nitidolimonius*); often clothed in setae or scales; prothorax is large and loosely hinged to rest of body. Head hypognathous or prognathous, with mandibles exposed or not, clypeus absent, and labrum distinct. Serrate to pectinate antennae with 11 antennomeres, and attached near eyes. Prothorax flattened, with lateral margins more or less carinate, and posterior angles projecting, occasionally with depressions or sulci underneath to receive appendages; sometimes with pair of bioluminescent organs on pronotum (*Vesperelater*). Procoxal cavities open behind. Scutellum visible. Elytra smooth, costate, usually with hairlike setae or scaly, and always concealing the abdomen. Legs with tarsi 5-5-5, tarsomeres simple or lobed, claws equal and simple, toothed, or pectinate (*Glyphonyx*, *Melanotus*). Abdomen with five ventrites, 1–4 connate.

SIMILAR FAMILIES

- metallic wood-boring or jewel beetles (Buprestidae, p.210)—body rigid, most species shiny or metallic underneath
- throscid beetles (Throscidae, p.252)—antennae clubbed, rarely serrate
- false click beetles (Eucnemidae, p.254)—labrum not visible; abdomen with 5 fused ventrites
- some false darkling beetles (Melandryidae, p.333)—tarsi 5-5-4
- lizard beetles (Erotylidae: Languriinae, p.436)—antennae capitate

COLLECTING NOTES Forests and woodlands in multiple stages of succession and woodland/wetland edges harbor the greatest diversity of click beetles. Sweep and beat vegetation in these and other habitats for adults. Many species are found beneath the bark of snags, logs, and stumps. Others take shelter beneath stones, boards, or debris, or in riparian sand or gravel, especially in spring. Most nocturnal species are frequently beaten from vegetation and are also attracted to lights. Additional species are captured in Malaise, flight intercept, and Lindgren funnel traps.

FAUNA 1,015 SPECIES IN 102 GENERA

Danosoma brevicorne (LeConte) (13.0–16.0 mm) is dull reddish brown with irregular blotches of tan scales. Pronotum densely, coarsely punctured, broadly and deeply impressed at base near middle and at sides near midlength, hind angles divergent, rounded, and depressed; underneath with antennal, but without tarsal sulci. Elytra densely, coarsely, and irregularly punctured. Claws without basal setae. Predatory larva develops under bark. Adults found under bark in summer in coniferous forests and mixed woodlands. Across Canada, and montane western North America; in east from Maritime provinces and New England to Massachusetts, west to Minnesota. (1)

Lacon rorulentus (LeConte) (11.0–16.0 mm) is elongate, broad, stout, reddish, coarsely and irregularly punctate with punctures large, and covered with broad golden-yellow and brown scales in no discernible pattern. Pronotum with pronounced longitudinal furrow medially. Hypomeron with tarsal sulci indistinct, medial margin deeply sulcate for more than half its length. Mesepimeron in contact with mesocoxal cavity. Claws lacking setae. Adults under bark of rotting pine (*Pinus*) logs and stumps. British Columbia to California, east to Montana. *Lacon pyrsolepis* (LeConte) similar in form, but with distinct tarsal sulci on hypomeron. Arizona and New Mexico. (5)

Lacon sparsus (Candèze) (12.0–15.0 mm) is elongate, broad, stout, black, coarsely and irregularly punctate with punctures large, and covered mostly with broad black scales, with a few white scales intermixed. Pronotum with pronounced longitudinal furrow medially. Hypomeron with tarsal sulci distinct and deep, medial margin deeply sulcate for more than half its length. Mesepimeron in contact with mesocoxal cavity. Claws lacking setae. Adults under bark of rotting pine (*Pinus*) logs and stumps. British Columbia to California. (5)

275

Aeolus livens LeConte (5.7–7.5 mm) is elongate, robust, and clothed in recumbent yellowish setae, and mostly light reddish brown with head, pronotal and elytral markings black; underside entirely light colored. Antennae serrate in both sexes. Pronotum longer than wide, about as broad as elytra, deeply punctured, with medial stripe sometimes wanting, and posterior angles well developed and divergent; underneath with prosternal suture closed anteriorly. Scutellum flat. Elytra with pair of elongate black spots basally and transverse fascia behind middle sometimes coalescent. Tarsomere 4 with dense setose pad underneath, and claws simple. Adults under bark and at lights. Oregon and California, east to Colorado and Texas. (2)

Pasture Wireworm *Conoderus exsul* (Sharp) (10.0–13.0 mm) is somewhat elongate, moderately broad, robust, slightly flattened dorsally, clothed in short, fine, recumbent reddish-yellow pubescence, and uniformly brownish black with appendages lighter. Pronotum wide, broadest behind middle, finely and densely punctured, with posterior angles distinctly produced, slightly divergent, and bicarinate. Elytra deeply striate, with intervals flat and finely rugulose, each with emarginate apices bluntly bidentate. Tarsomere 4 broadly lobed underneath. Larvae feed on grass roots. Adults attracted to lights. Native of New Zealand; established across southern United States; Hawaii. (4)

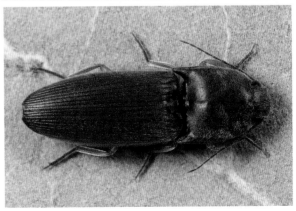

Southern Potato Wireworm *Conoderus falli* Lane (6.0–9.0 mm) is usually somewhat shiny brown, occasionally blackish, with sparse pubescence; appendages tan. Pronotum wider than long, widest in rear, with punctures of two sizes, hind angles short, stout. Elytra with rows of punctures and faint markings often not visible without magnification. Legs with tibiae with spurs on apices, tarsomere 4 with broad, membranous lobe underneath, and claws with basal setae. Subterranean larva eats seeds, roots, stems, and tubers of crops. Adults active spring and summer, found during day under debris; attracted to lights. Neotropical; established from Virginia to Florida, west to California. (4)

Anthracalaus agrypnoides (Van Dyke) (26.5–31.0 mm) is dull black, glabrous, with head and pronotum coarsely punctate, and reddish-brown appendages. Antennae with 11 antennomeres, reaching posterior pronotal angles, 2 small, about half length of 3, 4–10 serrate. Pronotum long, convex, lateral margins broadly arcuate, prominent posterior angles divergent and blunt, with distinct tubercle in front of scutellum; underneath without antennal sulcus. Elytra punctostriate, intervals convex basally, becoming flat posteriorly, with sides gradually tapering to apices. Tarsi not lobed, with thick pile of golden setae ventrally, and claws simple with basal setae. Adults attracted to lights. Southeastern Arizona. (1)

Lanelater schottii (LeConte) (14.0–26.0 mm) is brown, and sparsely clothed in fine, whitish, strongly curved setae. Antennae with 11 antennomeres, 3 longer than 2, and becoming serrate at 4; longer in male. Pronotum with discal punctures large, lateral margins sharply carinate posteriorly, becoming faint anteriorly, supramarginal carina faint and becoming obsolete at about middle, with posterior angles moderately diverging and truncate; antennal sulci along entire length of prosternal suture. Elytra punctostriate, with lateral striae sulcate on basal half. Front tibia without anterior carina dorsally. Claw with basal setae. Adults at lights. Arizona to western Texas, south to Mexico. (1)

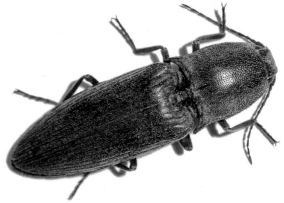

Vesperelater arizonicus (Hyslop) (17.0–25.0 mm) is clothed in short, appressed brown pubescence, and uniformly shiny brown, except for a pair of yellowish luminous spots just before posterior pronotal angles. Antennae reaching (female) or surpassing (male) posterior pronotal margin. Pronotum parallel-sided, with anterolateral margins strongly rounded, and posterior angles acute, divergent, and carinate; luminescent organs equidistant from and not reaching margins, and conspicuous median tubercle on posterior margin compressed laterally. Southeastern Arizona to New Mexico, south to Mexico. (1)

Western Eyed Click Beetle *Alaus melanops* LeConte (21.0–33.0 mm) is elongate, narrow, parallel-sided, black, and clothed in short black or dark gray and whitish setae, with a pair of small round or elliptical velvety black eye spots on pronotum. Pronotum longer than wide, broadest anteriorly with eye spots surrounded by a narrow band of pale scales. Elytra weakly punctostriate, interstriae more or less flat, and black with small, sparse patches of whitish scales. Underside moderately clothed in whitish setae. Adults and larvae found under bark of pine (*Pinus*) logs and stumps; adults occasionally attracted to lights. Widespread in western North America. (3)

Alaus zunianus Casey (34.0–39.0 mm) is elongate, broad, parallel-sided, black, with short, very dark blue scalelike setae intermixed with irregular patches of long white or yellowish-white setae. Pronotum longer than wide, strongly convex, with round velvety black eye spots equidistant between lateral margin and midline, or closer to midline. Elytra black, each with three larger whitish patches and some smaller whitish spots. Legs and underside black, with whitish spot on hypomeron and before sides of ventrites. Adults on sycamore (*Platanus*). Southeastern Arizona. *Alaus lusciosus* (Hope) (35.0–41.0 mm) similar, eye spots closer to lateral margins; underside, including hypomeron and legs, white. Southeastern Arizona to Oklahoma and Texas. (3)

Chalcolepidius apacheanus Casey (32.0–42.0 mm) is elongate, broad, parallel-sided, and shiny dark brown to black, with pronotal and elytral discs clothed in very short, flat, metallic blue or bluish scales. Antennae moderately (female) or strongly serrate (male). Pronotum longer than wide, sides strongly narrowed at anterior quarter, slightly narrowed before angles, with lateral white bands about a quarter of pronotal width, interior margins broadly arcuate. Elytra lateral margins narrowly clothed in white setae, with intervals flat along their entire length. Underside with hypomeron and sides of ventrites black. Adults on oak (*Quercus*). Southern Arizona to Utah and New Mexico, south to Mexico. (5)

Chalcolepidius lenzi Candèze (20.0–40.0 mm) is elongate, elliptical, and shiny black, with very short, flat, metallic olive, grayish to bluish-green scalelike setae; colors sometimes differing dorsally and ventrally. Antennae serrate (female) or strongly serrate (male). Pronotum much longer than wide, disc strongly convex, with lateral margins broadly rounded, narrowly explanate, and narrowed anteriorly and posteriorly before divergent angles. Elytra with intervals flat along their entire length. Adults found on mesquite (*Prosopis juliflora*). Southern Arizona, south to Colima and Veracruz. (5)

Chalcolepidius smaragdinus LeConte (20.0–37.0 mm) is shiny dark brown to black, with very short, flat, metallic green scalelike setae with yellow, blue, or violet reflections; occasionally setae predominantly blue, with colors sometimes differing dorsally and ventrally. Appendages metallic violet or blue. Antennae pectinate (female) or flabellate (male). Lateral pronotal margins straight before narrowing anteriorly. Elytra with intervals flat along their entire length. On desert broom (*Baccharis sarothroides*) and mesquite (*Prosopis juliflora*). Southern Arizona to New Mexico, south to Sonora. (5)

Chalcolepidius tartarus Fall (21.0–36.0 mm) is shiny dark brown to black, with pronotal and elytral discs clothed in very short, flat, metallic blue or bluish scalelike setae. Antennae moderately (female) or strongly serrate (male). Lateral pronotal margins straight before narrowing at anterior quarter, and lateral white bands about a quarter of pronotal width, interior margins more or less straight. Elytra narrowly clothed laterally with white setae, with intervals convex along their entire length. Underside with hypomeron and sides of ventrites white. On desert broom (*Baccharis sarothroides*). Southern Arizona to New Mexico. (5)

278

Chalcolepidius webbii LeConte (25.0–33.0 mm) is shiny dark brown to black, and clothed dorsally and ventrally with very short, flat, metallic blue scalelike setae. Antennae moderately (female) or strongly serrate (male). Lateral pronotal margins slightly narrowed anteriorly and posteriorly before angles, and lateral white bands about a third of pronotal width, interior margins sinuous. Elytra with intervals flat along their entire length, and white lateral margins about three interstriae wide; white lateral margins of *C. apacheanus* and *C. tartarus* narrower, about two interstriae wide. On willow (*Salix*). Southern California to New Mexico, south to Mexico. (5)

Athous species (5.5–22.0 mm) are elongate, slender, sparsely pubescent with setae slender, and various shades of brown to black, sometimes with pronotal and elytral markings, or distinctly bicolored. Head often with anterior clypeal margin distinctly raised and a prominent triangular depression on frons. Antenna with 11 antennomeres, usually serrate in both sexes. Prothorax longer than wide, with posterior margin more or less straight. Prosternal suture single and not excavated anteriorly. Legs with tarsomeres 2 and 3 usually lobed, occasionally with setose pads underneath, and claws not pectinate or serrate, without basal setae. On vegetation and at lights. Montane western North America. (~25)

Hemicrepidius obscurus (LeConte) (14.0–17.0 mm)
is elongate, parallel-sided, somewhat shiny black, and
clothed in short black pubescence. Head with frontal margin
depressed medially to plane of labrum. Pronotum as long
as wide, sparsely punctate medially, becoming moderately
dense laterally, lateral margins arcuate, with bicarinate
posterior angles acute and somewhat divergent; below with
hypomeron without large smooth surface posteriorly. Elytra
punctostriate with punctures fine and interstriae convex.
British Columbia to California, east to Utah. (6)

Tetralimonius ornatulus LeConte (4.2–6.5 mm) is elongate,
somewhat convex, and clothed in suberect yellow setae.
Head reddish brown to black, with antennomeres 2 and
3 combined slightly longer than 4, antennae extending
to posterior pronotal angles by one antennomere or less.
Pronotum black with posterior angles yellow or yellow with
large black spot in middle, lateral margins mostly parallel
and not carinate; underneath with prosternal suture not
sulcate anteriorly and mesal margin of hypomeron with
raised bead. Elytra uniformly pale brown to black with apical
third orange. Abdomen with ventrites reddish brown to
black. Adults found on trees and woody shrubs, including
Ceanothus and *Eriodictyon*. Washington to California. (2)

279

"Ctenicera" protracta (LeConte) (13.0–20.0 mm) is
elongate, flattened or somewhat so, black and slightly
metallic, or yellowish brown, and uniformly clothed in
usually pale pubescence. Antennomeres 3–11 cylindrical.
Pronotum more sparsely punctate down middle than
along sides, not canaliculate medially, with sides gradually
narrowed in front of sharp and divergent posterior angles.
Elytra punctostriate, punctures fine, with intervals nearly
flat, punctured, and shiny. Adults found in meadows and
other moist, grassy areas. British Columbia to northern
California. Species will be transferred to another genus.

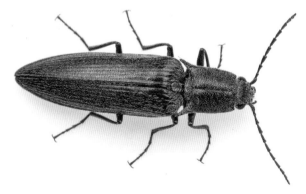

Hadromorphus glaucus (Germar) (7.4–9.1 mm) is stout,
uniformly dull dark brown or black, and moderately clothed
in recumbent white setae. Head broad, half as wide as
pronotum. Antennae not surpassing posterior pronotal
apices and slightly longer in male; antennomeres short and
cylindrical, with 2 and 3 bearing indistinct punctures and only
a few long setae, while 4–11 finely and densely pubescent.
British Columbia to California, east to Alberta, Idaho, and
Utah. *Hadromorphus callidus* Brown (British Columbia) and
H. inutilis Brown (coastal northern California) similar,
antennomeres 2–11 similar in punctation and vestiture, with
reddish-brown appendages, distinguished from one another
only by examination of male genitalia. (3)

Hypoganus rotundicollis (Say) (10.0–13.0 mm) is elongate, somewhat flat, parallel-sided, clothed in short and very fine pubescence, somewhat smooth and shiny, and is uniformly black, sometimes with lateral margins or entire pronotum red. Antennae short, not reaching posterior pronotal angles, antennomere 3 somewhat cylindrical, always longer than 2, with distal antennomeres not elongate, and moderately serrate in male. Pronotum wider than long, convex, with posterior angles narrow, peglike, and abruptly divergent. Elytra with intervals flat or barely convex, and minutely punctured. Adults attracted to lights. British Columbia to northern California. (2)

Neopristilophus maurus (LeConte) (12.7–21.5 mm) is elongate, somewhat feebly shiny black, with appendages sometimes paler. Head half as wide as pronotum, with strongly serrate antennae shorter, not attaining apices of posterior pronotal angles, antennomere 2 not longer than wide, about half as long as 3, and 3 shiny and narrowly triangular. Pronotum equally long as wide, with discal punctures dense, becoming more or less confluent laterally. Elytra with striae distinctly impressed with intervals usually weakly convex and somewhat rugose. British Columbia to California, Arizona, and New Mexico. *Neopristilophus cribrosus* (LeConte) (11.3–19.0 mm) black, shinier, with antennae longer, antennomere 3 distinctly triangular and similar to 4. Washington to northern California. (3)

Nitidolimonius resplendens (Eschscholtz) (11.0–14.0 mm) is elongate, narrow, brilliant metallic green to deep copper, and clothed in fine recumbent pale setae. Antennomere 3 as long as 4. Pronotal punctures uniformly coarse and dense and posterior bicarinate angles acute; hypomeron with mesal margin notched anteriorly. Elytral interstriae slightly convex. Larvae in decaying stumps and surrounding leaf litter. In West, Alaska and British Columbia south to Sierra Nevada of California and Rockies. *Nitidolimonius breweri* (Horn) (10.5 mm) is black, darkly bronzed, antennomere 3 longer than 4; southern Sierra Nevada. *Nitidolimonius weidti* (Angell) brilliant green, finely punctate, antennomere 3 shorter than 4. Cascades of Pacific Northwest. Genus needs revision. (3)

Prosternon bombycinum (Germar) (10.0–15.0 mm) is broadly elongate, clothed in golden pubescence, with head and pronotum brownish black, and elytra and legs dull reddish brown, with femora often dark brown. Antennae serrate in both sexes, intermediate antennomeres distinctly longer than wide, with 3 slightly shorter than 4. Pronotum with setae moderately whorled, sides moderately to strongly arcuate and weakly sinuate before carinate and deplanate hind angles that are stout and not or scarcely divergent. Elytra with pubescence strongly whorled. Claws slender. British Columbia to Oregon, east to Alberta, Montana, and Colorado. *Prosternon mirabilis* (Fall) (8.4–11.0 mm) densely clothed in whorls of orange pubescence obscuring head and pronotum. (5)

Pseudanostirus nigricollis Bland (10.0–12.0 mm) is elongate, weakly convex, black with reddish-brown appendages, and four variable maculae on reddish-orange elytra, and clothed mostly in short, fine, yellowish pubescence. Antennae long, extending well beyond posterior pronotal angles. Pronotum distinctly longer than wide, narrowed anteriorly from middle. Elytra punctostriate, punctures coarse, each with broad oblique band before middle not reaching margins, and a triangular spot posterior to middle. British Columbia to eastern northern California, east to Michigan. (9)

Pseudanostirus tigrinus Fall (9.0–11.2 mm) is elongate, weakly convex, black, clothed in fine silvery pubescence, with three variable brown transverse bands across pale brown elytra. Antennomere 3 subequal to 5 in length, and 4–10 angulate anteroventrally, with antennae surpassing explanate posterior angles in male. Pronotum with four round black pubescent spots; mesal margin of hypomeron excavate anteriorly. Elytral bands with black pubescence. Adults on conifers. Oregon and California. *Pseudanostirus nebraskensis* Bland (9.0–11.0 mm) pronotum sometimes with pair of indistinct circular spots. Western North America. *Pseudanostirus triundulatus* Bland (6.3–8.0 mm) with antennomere 3 shorter than 5. Across Canada, south through Sierra Nevada, Rockies, and New England. (9)

281

Selatosomus edwardsi Horn (11.0–17.0 mm) with head, prosternum, and abdomen always black, prothorax and abdomen often both black, and appendages always reddish brown or dark brown. Head coarsely punctate. Broad, red lateral pronotal margins almost always reaching anterior, but not posterior margins, with posterior margins smooth and angles truncate; hypomeron black, sometimes red. Elytra black or with variable reddish-yellow markings, those at base with transverse bar broken into spots. Metacoxae deeply excavated to receive hind femora, and tarsi slender without pads. On vegetation in montane forests of Sierra Nevada. California. (12)

Selatosomus suckleyi (**LeConte**) (13.0–19.0 mm) is shiny black with bicolored elytra, and glabrous. Head coarsely punctate. Pronotum with disc moderately coarsely and closely punctate near apical and lateral margins, fine and sparse on posterior declivity, with posterior margins smooth and angles truncate. Elytra striopunctate, interstriae flat and sparsely punctate, each bimaculate with yellow spots, including basal crescent starting laterally from humerus to middle before crossing transversely toward suture, and a postmedian spot, neither reaching suture; spots sometimes reduced. Metacoxae deeply excavated to receive hind femora, slender tarsi without pads. British Columbia to Oregon. (12)

Melanactes densus LeConte (17.5–27.0 mm) is moderately shiny black or reddish black, with appendages somewhat lighter. Head densely punctate laterally, antennae with 11 antennomeres, 2 small and shorter than 3, 4–10 serrate. Pronotum quadrate, appearing slightly longer than wide, coarsely and deeply punctate, punctures becoming confluent anteriorly and laterally, with sides somewhat parallel and posterior angles carinate, not diverging. Scutellum glabrous. Elytra broadest at apical third, punctostriate with punctures separated by about twice their diameters, interstriae flat. Claw without setae at base. California. (1)

Pityobius murrayi LeConte (21.0–35.0 mm) is shiny black, and sparsely clothed in recurved black setae. Head coarsely punctate, antenna with 12 antennomeres, 4–11 serrate (female) or bipectinate (male). Pronotum unevenly convex and coarsely punctate, with deep postmedial impression; underneath with posterior margin of hypomeron more or less straight. Elytra deeply punctostriate, intervals convex and sparsely punctured, and slightly broader behind middle in female. Tarsomeres 1–4 with membranous pads underneath, claws without setae, each with small basal tooth. Adults found under pine (*Pinus*) bark, resting on trunks, or crawling on ground. Oregon and California. (1)

282

Negastrius ornatus (LeConte) (2.9–5.4 mm) is oblong, robust, densely clothed in fine appressed grayish setae, and dull black with elytra as figured, with pair of apical spots, or black. Antennae short. Pronotum strigose with fine median line flanked by two impunctate spots, smooth posterior margins, and carinate angles not divergent. Scutellum elliptical. Elytra punctostriate, intervals flat or slightly convex basally. Tibiae and tarsi sometimes lighter, tarsi and claws simple. Southern California. *Negastrius stibicki* Wells similar, pronotum rugosely tuberculate. British Columbia to California, east to Montana. Both in flood debris on sandy river beaches. (5)

Oedostethus femoralis LeConte (4.2–4.7 mm) is clothed in pubescence, smooth and moderately punctate, and dark brown to brownish black, with bases of tibiae and tarsi lighter. Antennae with antennomeres 2 and 3 equal in length. Pronotum strongly convex, with lateral margins rounded and completely carinate; with posterior angle small, sharp, diverging, and carinate; underneath with prosternal sutures curved. Elytral striae deep, fine, and impunctate. Tarsal claws each with broad basal flange extending to midpoint. At lights. Across southern Canada and northern United States; in West, south to Oregon, Nevada, and Utah. (1)

283

Paradonus species (2.2–3.6 mm) are elongate-obovate, somewhat flattened, robust, pale yellowish brown to brown with more or less distinct markings and infuscations, or not. Antennae short, antennomeres 2 and 3 somewhat equal in length. Posterior pronotal angles short, stubby and carinate, carinae scarcely longer than hind angles; prosternal sutures curved. Elytra without striae. Tarsomeres simple, with tarsomeres 1–4 gradually becoming shorter, and 5 longer than length of 3–4 combined. At lights; occasionally on flowers. Widespread across western North America. Genus in need of revision. (5+)

Euthysanius lautus LeConte (18.0–25.0 mm) male (top) is reddish brown, moderately clothed in suberect yellow setae, with striate elytra long. Mandibles visible. Antennae pectinate with long rami, and antennomere 11 longer than 12. Pronotum coarsely punctured along sides, less so medially, with lateral margins rounded anteriorly and distinctly divergent posteriorly. Tibial spurs short and indistinct. At lights. Flightless female (bottom) up to 36.0 mm in length, somewhat cylindrical, pronotum almost as wide as long, elytra combined barely longer than wide and not extending beyond first visible abdominal segment, with apices obliquely truncate. Southern California. (9)

Aplastus species (11.0–17.0 mm) are elongate, slender, somewhat convex, moderately clothed in recumbent setae, and uniformly reddish brown, brown, or brownish black. Mandibles visible when closed. Antennae serrate in both sexes. Pronotum more or less as long as wide, with sides converging anteriorly, and posterior angles long and sharp. Scutellum elongate, somewhat rectangular. Elytra long, finely and shallowly punctostriate, mostly straight-sided, and gradually attenuated posteriorly (male), or short and exposing abdomen (flightless female). Legs long, with tibial spurs short and indistinct, tarsi slender, and claws simple. Males attracted to lights. Genus needs revision. California to Utah and Arizona. (15)

Octinodes schaumii (LeConte) (11.0–13.0 mm) is elongate, slender, pale brown or brown, and clothed in recumbent yellowish pubescence. Head with eyes not prominently hemispherical, antennae with 11 antennomeres, serrate (female) or pectinate (male) with rami three to four times longer than their antennomeres. Pronotum finely and shallowly punctured, with sides arcuate in front, with carinate posterior angles strongly divergent. Elytra somewhat shiny and irregularly and rugosely punctate. Southern California. *Octinodes amplicollis* Van Dyke similar, but with each side of coarsely punctured pronotum bearing an abrupt winglike process. Central California. Adults of both species attracted to lights in foothills and adjacent habitats. (12)

284

Scaptolenus fuscipennis Fall (13.5–16.5 mm, excluding mandibles) male is elongate, attenuated posteriorly, dark reddish brown, with long legs and dense yellowish pubescence underneath. Mandibles visible, antennae somewhat serrate, antennomeres 2 and 3 combined shorter than 4. Pronotum strongly rounded in front, with lateral margins straight from middle to posterior angles. Elytra broadest across humeri, somewhat costate, with apices broadly dehiscent. Front tibia expanded apically and at midlength, distinctly dentate; tarsi slender without pads or dense setae underneath, and claws simple. Flightless female robust with shorter legs. Males fly after summer thundershowers day and night and found on vegetation or at lights. Southeastern Arizona. (1)

Agriotes ferrugineipennis (LeConte) (9.0–12.0 mm) is elongate, slightly robust, conspicuously clothed in whitish or yellowish-gray pubescence, with head, pronotum, and abdomen usually black, elytra light to dark brown, posterior pronotal angles and abdomen often dark brown, and appendages reddish brown. Pronotum longer than wide, unicolorous, with disc closely punctured, punctures deeper than on sides, usually not contiguous, and posterior angles long and slender. Lateral pronotal carinae joining anterior margin at pronotosternal sutures. Elytral intervals usually rugose, sometimes smooth, dull, and very finely punctate. Tarsi and claws simple. Adults on vegetation. British Columbia to northern California, east to Alberta, Montana, Wyoming, and Utah. (21)

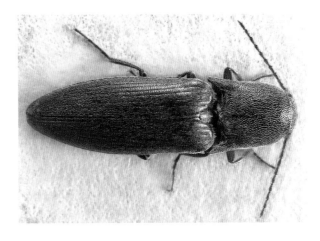

Dalopius species (5.0–9.0 mm) are narrowly elongate, narrow, closely punctured, clothed in fine pubescence, and more or less brown, sometimes with elytral margins variably darker, especially along suture. Distinct suprantennal carinae widely separated, not connected by distinct anterior clypeal margin. Pronotum longer than wide, with lateral pronotal carina entire, more or less straight, and joined to anterior margin above pronotosternal margins. Metacoxal plates narrowed laterally. Tarsi slender, and tarsomeres without membranous ventral pads or projecting lobes, 3 and 4 with setose pads underneath. Adults attracted to lights. Identification requires examination of male genitalia. Widespread in western North America. Genus needs revision.

285

Ampedus cordifer (LeConte) (9.2–11.0 mm) is elongate, elliptical, dull black with bright orange elytra partly black at apex, and clothed in suberect black pubescence on pronotum and elytral spot, yellow on elytra and underside. Pronotum densely punctate and narrowed anteriorly. Elytra with lateral margins somewhat parallel to about apical third, then rounded to apex, with a pair of small, subbasal spots, and an apical heart-shaped black patch reaching margin only at apex near suture. Adults associated with rotting wood of hardwoods and pine. Eastern Oregon and California. *Ampedus behrensi* Horn (9.0–13.0 mm) similar, elytra with apical patch transverse anteriorly and without basal spots. (33)

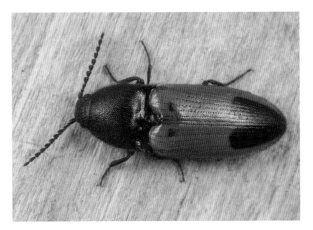

Anchastus bicolor LeConte (6.0–7.5 mm) is elongate, elliptical, clothed in setae, and bicolored with head, prothorax, and underside reddish, elytra black. Frontal margin elevated and projecting over labrum, with antennomere 2 half as long as 3, but slightly shorter than 4. Pronotum longer than wide, disc with punctures fine and dense, lateral margins rounded at apical quarter and more or less straight to prominent bicarinate posterior angles that project directly from hypomera; underneath prosternal suture excavate anteriorly and posterior margin of hypomeron arcuate. Tarsomeres 4 with membranous lobes underneath, with claws toothed. Southeastern California and Arizona, south to Baja California. (6)

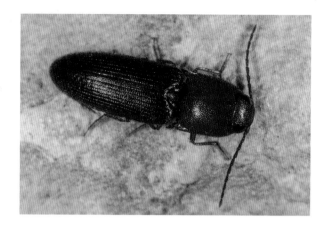

Dicrepidius corvinus Candèze (14.5–20.0 mm) is elongate, slender, densely clothed in brown recumbent setae, and uniformly very dark reddish brown to black, with appendages lighter. Antennae serrate (female), or pectinate (male). Underneath clypeus with two carinae converging anteriorly to clypeal margin. Pronotum long as wide, coarsely punctate, with well-developed posterior angles acute and divergent; prosternal suture excavate anteriorly. Elytra with strial punctures fine. Middle and hind tarsomeres 2 and 3 distinctly lobed, with claws simple, lacking setae. Adults attracted to lights, also under bark of stumps. Southwestern United States. *Dicrepidius serraticornis* Champion with antennae serrate in both sexes. Southeastern Arizona. (2)

Melanotus similis (Kirby) (7.9–12.8 mm) is elongate, somewhat slender, equally clothed in yellowish pubescence on pronotum and elytra, and usually uniformly reddish brown. Head coarsely punctate with hexagonal punctures, with frontal margin well defined, mandible without lateral pit, and antennae with 11 antennomeres, 4 is one and a half times longer than wide and much wider than 3. Pronotum wide, posterior angles acute and carinate, disc with large punctures about same size as head, separated by less than their own diameter. Elytra with strial punctures moderately deep, quadrate. Claws pectinate. Adults on vegetation; attracted to lights. Southern California to Arizona; widespread east of Rockies, also Mexico. (5)

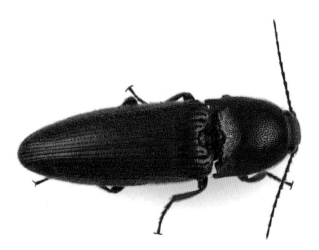

Diplostethus opacicollis Schaeffer (20.0–22.0 mm) is elongate, robust, convex, coarsely punctate, uniformly clothed in medium-length brownish recumbent setae often rubbed off, and dark reddish brown. Moderately serrate antennae nearly reaching (female) or surpassing (male) apex of posterior pronotal angle. Lateral pronotal margins mostly straight, with posterior angles long, acute, and carinate; prosternal process distinctly notched, followed by subapical tooth when viewed laterally. Elytra faintly striate. Southern Arizona to southwestern New Mexico, south to Sinaloa. *Diplostethus arizonensis* (Schaeffer) (12.0–14.5 mm) light reddish brown, clothed in yellowish pubescence, elytra distinctly striate, and prosternum with a single preapical tooth only. Southern Arizona to Texas, south to Sonora. (2)

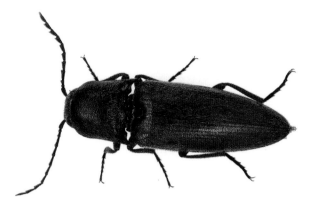

Dolerosomus silaceus (Say) (6.0–8.5 mm) is very elongate, slightly convex, light yellowish to yellowish brown, with pronotum sometimes black, and posterior angles, legs, and mandibles lighter than dorsal surface; underside darker, and densely clothed in short suberect yellowish pubescence. Head with eyes protruding, antennae filiform, longer and extending to basal third of elytra, with antennomeres relatively short, 2 shorter than 3, 2 and 3 combined much shorter than 4. Pronotum distinctly longer than wide, rugosely punctate, with lateral margins slightly sinuate before slightly diverging and bicarinate posterior angles. Elytra punctostriate with punctures large and almost flat interstriae. Oregon and California; also eastern North America. (3)

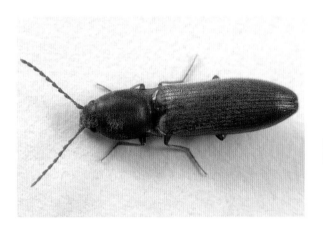

287

Elater lecontei (Horn) (21.0–31.5 mm) is elongate, robust, slightly convex, reddish brown to dark brown dorsally, somewhat lighter ventrally, and sparsely clothed in short brown suberect setae directed posteriorly. Antennae deeply serrate, longer than pronotum, extending to (female) or beyond (male) pronotum. Pronotum barely longer than wide, with faint median impression, with anterior margin carinate at lateral third, and lateral margins distinctly carinate and abruptly narrowed at anterior fourth. Scutellum bell-shaped. Elytra broader than prothorax, punctostriate with punctures not bearing setae, interstriae alutaceous with double rows of punctures, and sutural stria complete along entire length of elytra. Southern California to southern Arizona. (3)

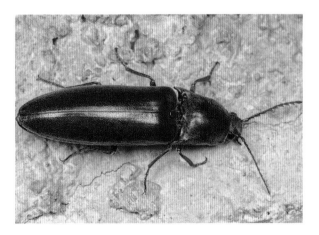

Orthostethus infuscatus **(Germar)** (28.0–35.0 mm) is very elongate, robust, narrowly tapered posteriorly, dark reddish brown to brown, and uniformly clothed in appressed yellowish-brown setae. Antennae not reaching apex of posterior pronotal angle, more deeply serrate in male. Pronotum longer than wide, with lateral margins slightly explanate and rounded at anterior third, then parallel to prominent, bicarinate, and acute posterior angles that are slightly divergent. Elytra finely, densely punctate, more so than pronotum, apices with minute tooth directed away from suture. Sides of mesosternal cavity declivous and prosternal process straight. Adults attracted to lights in wooded habitats. Arizona east to Kansas, Indiana, and Maryland, south to Brazil. (2)

Orthostethus pecticornis **(Champion)** (24.0–43.0 mm) is very elongate, robust, moderately convex, narrowly tapered posteriorly, dark reddish brown, and sparsely clothed in short yellowish setae uniformly arranged and directed posteriorly. Antennae pectinate (male) or serrate (female), extending one antennomere past posterior pronotal angle. Pronotum longer than wide, lateral margins slightly explanate, rounded before apical third and diverging to prominent, bicarinate, and acute posterior angles that are slightly divergent. Elytra more finely and densely punctate than pronotum, apices with very minute tooth. Sides of mesosternal cavity declivous and prosternal process straight. Adults attracted to lights in wooded habitats. Southeastern Arizona south to Sonora and Chihuahua. (2)

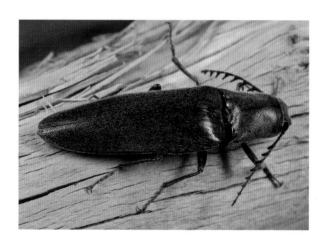

Megapenthes aterrimus **(Motschulsky)** (9.5–18.0 mm) is elongate, slender, uniformly dull black, and clothed in suberect black pubescence. Suprantennal and frontal carinae form complete arcuate margin. Antennomeres 2 and 3 equal in length and diameter. Pronotum coarsely punctured, with posterior angles unicarinate; underneath without antennal groove, prosternal lobe arcuate, and prosternal process between coxae deeply channeled. Scutellum arcuate anteriorly. Elytra finely punctostriate, interstriae coarsely punctate, each sometimes with white spot near apex. Slender tarsi without membranous pads, simple claws lacking setae. Coastal British Columbia to California. *Megapenthes tartareus* (LeConte) narrower and more tapered, prosternal lobe almost truncate, prosternal process slightly channeled. Adults on vegetation. California. (22)

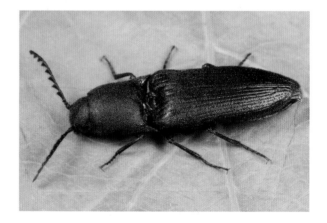

288

Megapenthes caprella LeConte (5.4–7.5 mm)
is elongate, dark brown to black with variable pale
markings on elytra, moderately clothed in suberect brown
pubescence, and brown or reddish-brown appendages.
Suprantennal and frontal carinae form complete arcuate
margin. Antennae not setose, antennomeres 2 and 3
equal in length and diameter. Pronotum finely punctured,
with posterior angles unicarinate and sometimes lighter;
hypomeron somewhat granulose. Scutellum arcuate
anteriorly. Elytra each with arcuate macula at base and
transverse mark at apical third. Tarsi narrow, without
membranous pads or lobes, with simple claws lacking
setae. California to New Mexico. *Megapenthes stigmosus*
(LeConte) similar, hypomeron coarsely punctate, antennae
setose. Pacific Northwest. (22)

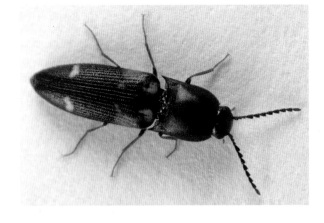

Megapenthes turbulentus (LeConte) (11.0–14.0 mm)
is elongate, slender, brown to black with variegated
elytral pattern, moderately clothed in suberect brown
pubescence, with blackish appendages sometimes
reddish. Suprantennal and frontal carinae form complete
arcuate margin. Antennomeres 2 and 3 equal in length and
diameter. Pronotum black or sometimes yellowish, rugosely
punctured, with posterior angles unicarinate; underneath
without antennal groove, prosternal lobe arcuate. Anterior
margin of scutellum arcuate. Elytra yellowish with two
or three irregular black bands, and punctostriate with
punctures deep. Tarsi narrow, without membranous pads
or lobes, with simple claws lacking setae. California to New
Mexico. (22)

Cardiophorus brevis (Champion) (6.5–8.0 mm) is
elongate, robust, sparsely clothed in short yellowish
pubescence, and reddish orange dorsally with variable
black markings on pronotum and elytra, with head,
prosternum, pterothorax, and abdomen black. Pronotum
very convex, with or without variable median black stripe
on anterior half. Scutellum heart-shaped. Elytra deeply
striate, with intervals convex, with black either restricted to
a broad sutural stripe, or expanded to cover all but humeral
umbones. Claws simple, with small basal flange. Adults
found on vegetation, including mimosa (*Mimosa*). Arizona
and Mexico. (62)

Cardiophorus edwardsi Horn (8.5–9.0 mm) is elongate, shiny black, and elytra partly red with suture and apex more or less black or reddish black, and clothed in fine, moderately dense pubescence. Antennae black, sometimes with basal antennomeres paler, those of male longer and thicker than female, exceeding posterior pronotal margin. Pronotum longer than wide, moderately convex with fine groove down middle. Elytra distinctly (male) or slightly (female) wider than prothorax. Legs black or partly or completely reddish brown. Tibia with very short fine pubescence, middle and hind tarsi with first tarsomere longer than last. British Columbia to California, east to Nevada. (62)

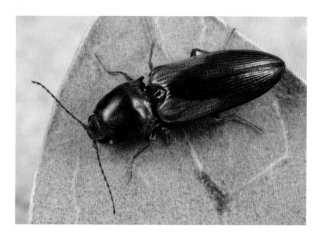

Horistonotus simplex LeConte (6.0–8.5 mm) is somewhat elongate, moderately robust, sparsely clothed in short yellowish pubescence, and somewhat shiny, ranging from uniformly reddish to dark brown, with appendages lighter. Pronotum about as wide as long, bipunctate with small punctures in between larger punctures, sides only margined and not narrowed posteriorly, posterior angles flattened, with posterior margins narrowly notched, or plicate, before each angle. Scutellum heart-shaped. Elytra wide as prothorax, strial punctures coarse and closely set, with intervals convex at apices. Claws rectangularly dentate at base to about middle. Adults attracted to lights. California to Colorado and Texas, south to Baja California Peninsula and Sonora. (5)

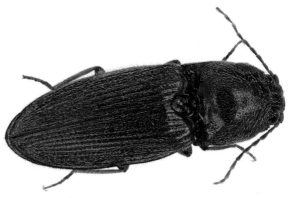

290

DERMESTIDAE (dêr-mes'-ti-dē)
SKIN BEETLES

Well known as pests of stored products and museum collections, skin beetles occur in many habitats and reach their greatest diversity and abundance in arid and semiarid regions. Both the adults and larvae are largely scavengers of protein and are often associated with fur, feathers, spider webs, organic debris in animal nests, or carcasses. Some of these species also prey on viable insect eggs or consume injured larvae and pupae. A few species feed on plant materials and may become pests when they infest stores of seeds, grains, and other cereal products. The larvae of *Orphilus* feed and develop within fungus-infested wood, while the adults feed largely on pollen and nectar. The ability of dermestids to tolerate dry conditions pre-adapts them for infesting dry stores of animal- and plant-based foods in homes, warehouses, and museums. *Dermestes* and *Thylodrias* larvae and adults damage stored products, but only the larvae of *Anthrenus* (p.29, Fig. 18n), *Attagenus*, and *Trogoderma* are of economic importance. Adult *Anthrenus* and *Attagenus* enter homes and other buildings during spring and summer to lay their eggs, where their larvae will hatch and infest woolen materials, carpets, silk products, and dried meats. Their larvae will also attack museum specimens, including study skins and insect collections. Household reinfestations may stem from undetected natural reservoirs immediately outside, such as bird, mammal, or paper wasp nests. Indoors, dead insects in spider webs, windowsills, and light fixtures may become dermestid breeding grounds. Species of *Dermestes* are used by natural history museums around the world to clean animal skeletons before placing them in research collections or putting them on display. Most dermestid larvae (p.31, Fig. 21) are defended with dense stiff setae that can cause skin irritation and respiratory issues in some people.

FAMILY DIAGNOSIS Adult dermestids are usually oblong or oval, rarely elongate (male *Thylodrias*), compact, robust, and clothed in black, brown, tan, and white scales (*Anthrenus*) or setae (*Cryptorhopalum*). Head small, not strongly deflexed, and retracted within prothorax, with or without (*Dermestes*) ocellus. Antennae with 11 (nine in *Dearthrus*) antennomeres, 9–11 usually forming loose or compact club, or not (*Thylodrias*). Pronotum broader than long, narrowed to head, underside with or without defined depression to receive antennae. Procoxal cavities open behind. Elytra completely covering abdomen, clothed in setae or scales, or entirely absent (female *Thylodrias*). Hind legs with coxae excavated to receive femora, tarsi 5-5-5, and simple claws equal in size. Abdomen with five or seven (*Thylodrias*) ventrites free.

SIMILAR FAMILIES No beetles similar in form have an ocellus.
- plate-thigh beetles (Eucinetidae, p.112)—antennae filiform, not clubbed
- marsh beetles (Scirtidae, p.114)—antennae not clubbed
- wounded-tree beetles (Nosodendridae, p.115)—front tibia broad, flat
- death-watch beetles (Ptinidae, p.299)—antennae long, club antennomeres asymmetrical
- *Hyporhagus* (Zopheridae, p.344)—elytra with rows of punctures, tarsi 5-5-4
- seed beetles (Chrysomelidae: Bruchinae, p.501)—head elongate, rostrum short, pygidium exposed

COLLECTING NOTES *Orphilus* and other small, flower-visiting dermestids are commonly hand-collected or swept from plants, especially those with dense clusters of flowers, such as yarrow (*Achillea*), spirea (*Spiraea*), buckbrush (*Ceanothus*), and others in carrot family (Apiaceae). *Anthrenus* and *Attagenus* are found indoors on windowsills of homes and other buildings with infested animal products. All stages of *Dermestes* are found on or underneath carcasses, whereas the adults are occasionally taken at lights.

FAUNA 121 SPECIES IN 15 GENERA

Black Larder Beetle *Dermestes ater* **De Geer** (7.0–9.0 mm) is oblong, shiny black or dark reddish brown, with antennae and tarsi paler, and dorsum dominated by black setae with some scattered paler setae. Pronotum wide, broadest at basal third, with lateral margins rounded. Elytra with broad shallow striae indistinct, and punctures similar to those on pronotal disc. Underside with golden setae, abdomen with ventrites 3 and 4 with (male) or without (female) medial tufts of setae. Both adults and larvae feed on various animal- and plant-based materials; also prey on insects. Old World; California, more common in East. (14)

Dermestes caninus **Germar** (5.5–8.5 mm) is elongate-oblong, black, with dense black, gray, and reddish-brown pubescence on pronotum and elytra. Pronotum completely covered with pubescence, disc sometimes with diffuse white spots. Elytra often with reddish-brown pubescence wanting. Thorax clothed in dense white setae, abdomen less so with black spots on sides. Middle and hind femora with a white ring. Adults and larvae found on carcasses in various habitats; adults attracted to lights. Widely distributed in southern Canada and United States. (14)

291

Dermestes frischii Kugelann (6.0–10.0 mm) is oblong, shiny black to dark reddish brown, with dense white or yellowish recumbent setae on sides of head and pronotum, and most of underside. Pronotum with lateral and anterior margins clothed in broad band of white or yellowish setae that becomes narrow in front. Elytra indistinctly striate, with apical margins not serrate, and rounded at suture. Ventrites with dark anterolateral patches. Hide beetle *Dermestes maculatus* De Geer similar in size and color, but apical elytral margins serrate and spinose at suture. Both Old World species widely distributed in southern Canada and United States. (14)

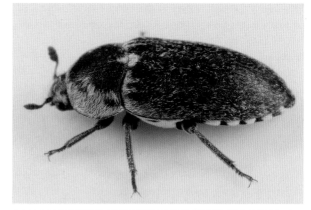

Larder Beetle *Dermestes lardarius* Linnaeus (5.0–9.0 mm) is oblong, black, clothed in setae, with basal three-fifths of each elytron with dense grayish setae enclosing three dark broad spots; underside and legs black, clothed in fine yellowish pubescence. Antennae clubbed. Pronotum dark, plain, without sharp ridges along sides, and completely clothed in dark pubescence. Abdomen underneath with five ventrites. Bases of front legs large and touching; hind femora clearly received in coxal groove. Adults and larvae found on nearly any dry or decomposing animal products and sometimes a minor to significant household pest. Widespread in North America. (13)

Common Carrion Dermestid *Dermestes marmoratus* Say (10.0–12.5 mm) is oblong, black or dark reddish brown, and clothed in alternating patches of golden brown and black setae. Pronotum with three small white patches of setae across disc. Elytra with broad band of dense grayish-white setae across base becoming narrower medially. Underside with dense white setae, abdomen with ventrites 3 and 4 with (male) or without (female) medial tufts of setae. Common on carrion, sometimes considered a minor pest in cereal warehouses, where it likely feeds on dead insects. Widespread in western and central North America. (13)

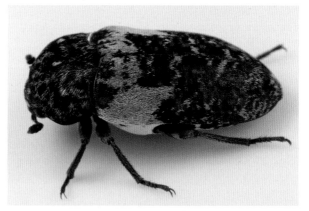

Dermestes talpinus Mannerheim (5.0–8.0 mm) is oblong, black or dark brown, and clothed in variegated black, grayish, and light reddish-brown pubescence. Pronotum with reddish pubescence more abundant than black. Elytra with grayish and reddish setae forming numerous short irregular transverse patches. Underside with ventrites 1–4 white, each with lateral black spot, and 5 black with three white setal patches. Alaska to California, east to Northern Territories, Alberta, and Texas. *Dermestes undulatus* Brahm pronotum with black setae more numerous than golden, with patch of yellow setae on each side. Europe; in West, Idaho and Colorado. Adults on dry carrion. (13)

Odd Beetle *Thylodrias contractus* Motschulsky is narrowly subparallel (male, 2.0–3.0 mm) or obovate (female 3.0–5.1 mm), pale yellowish brown, and densely clothed in short setae. Head with ocellus, antennae with nine (female) or 10 (male) antennomeres, and 6–9 (male) or 7–9 (female) each elongate. Males have soft posteriorly dehiscent elytra, and most with reduced flight wings; larviform females lack both elytra and flight wings. Both sexes with seven ventrites. Strictly associated with humans, both adults and larvae feed on skins, hides, fur, feathers, silk, wool, and other materials of animal origin. Sometimes minor pest in homes, markets, butcher shops, and insect collections. Rare; collections usually consist of larvae or individual males. Old World; established throughout North America. (1)

Orphilus subnitidus LeConte (2.8–3.8 mm) is oval, dull black with dark reddish-brown appendages, glabrous, confusedly punctate, with punctures becoming elongate apically on elytra. Head with median ocellus, and capitate antennae with 11 antennomeres, 9–11 forming club. Pronotal punctures finer than those of elytra, with posterior margin extended medially. Elytra broadest across humeral calluses, with punctures separated by their diameters basally and becoming more distant apically. Larvae develop in small dry branches infested with fungus (*Trametes*). Adults found on flowers of *Achillea*, *Ceanothus*, *Chrysolepis*, *Hydrangea*, *Spiraea*, and various umbelliferous species. British Columbia to California, east to Wyoming, Nebraska, and New Mexico. (1)

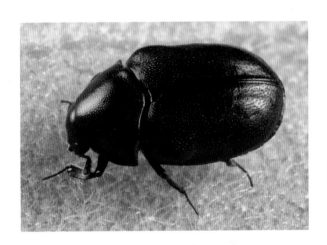

293

Attagenus brunneus Falderman (2.9–5.0 mm) is oblong, light brownish to black, appendages somewhat lighter, and clothed in recumbent black pubescence. Head with median ocellus, antennae with 11 antennomeres, 9–11 forming compact club, and terminal antennomere of male about six or seven times the combined length of two proceeding antennomeres. Pronotum with posterior band of light golden-brown setae, sometimes with additional light setae on other margins, and coxae distinctly separated by narrow prosternal process. Elytra with golden setae absent or limited to base. First tarsomere of hind leg half as long as second. Larvae occasionally household pests. Adults found on flowers, attracted to lights. Widespread in North America. (8)

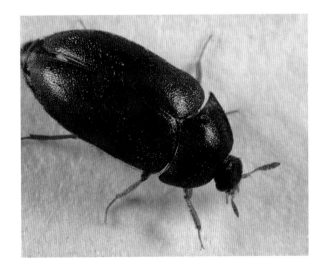

Anthrenus lepidus LeConte (2.6–3.7 mm) is oblong-oval, moderately convex, black with dark reddish-brown appendages, with variable patterns of round scales. Head with nearly all scales dark brown or black, eyes with inner margins emarginate, antennae with 11 antennomeres, 9–11 forming club. Pronotum with lateral pale scales behind middle surrounding small patch of yellowish or black scales. Elytra with only isolated patches of white scales on basal third, sutural stripe white at base or bicolored with orange, with continuous sutural stripe of pale scales sometimes incomplete on apical two-fifths. Larvae seldom of economic importance, adults pollen feeders. Widespread in North America. (8)

Varied Carpet Beetle *Anthrenus verbasci* (Linnaeus) (2.0–3.0 mm) is oblong-oval, moderately convex, with variable patterns of long, narrow scales twice as long as wide. Eyes with inner margins entire, antennae with 11 antennomeres, 9–11 forming club. Most individuals covered with white, yellowish, and dark brown to black scales; occasionally with few or no yellow scales, or with mostly white and golden scales. Elytral bands, if present, include yellowish scales and patches of white scales. Larvae consume preserved insects and remains in spider webs; reared from mud dauber wasp nests, occasional pest in alfalfa leaf-cutting bee nests. Adults eat pollen. Widespread in North America. (8)

Cryptorhopalum species (2.0–3.0 mm) are small, ovate, evenly convex, sparsely pubescent, blackish or black, with retractable appendages. Head with ocellus, underneath with mouthparts mostly covered by prothoracic process. Antennal club with two antennomeres. Pronotum punctate on either side of basal lobe, underneath with deep grooves for accepting antennae bound in rear by thin ridge. Hind coxae excavated to receive femora. Adults feed on pollen and nectar and are collected on many flowering plants and shrubs. Females best identified to species through association with males. Widespread in western North America. (17)

Megatoma variegata (Horn) (3.5–6.1 mm) is elongate-oval, mostly black, and moderately densely clothed in erect or recumbent golden-brown pubescence, and black and white setae. Terminal antennomere subequal to (female) or distinctly longer than (male) preceding antennomeres combined. Prothorax with antennal cavity on hypomeron broadly open posteriorly. Elytral vestiture forming a distinct pattern, cuticle underneath bands distinctly paler. Adults and larvae scavenge dead insects; a pest in museum insect collections. British Columbia to California, east to Alberta, Idaho, and Colorado. Genus needs revision. (8)

Trogoderma glabrum (Herbst) (2.0–3.9 mm) is oblong-oval, dark brown or black, coarsely pubescent, with narrow golden-brown and white pubescent bands across elytra. Head with eyes shallowly emarginate to slightly sinuate on inner margin and ocellus on front of head. Antenna with 11 antennomeres, 3–10 gradually wider in male, with 3 less than half as wide as 2. Band at base of elytron looped or appearing as vague humeral spot, middle band often uninterrupted and expanded at suture. Legs with first hind tarsomere as long as second. Once a major pest of granaries, now kept in check by a parasitic wasp, *Mattesia trogodermae*. Europe; widely established in North America. (8)

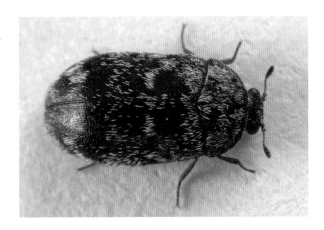

BOSTRICHIDAE (bos-trik'-i-dē)
BOSTRICHID BEETLES

Bostrichids, also known as twig or branch borers and powderpost beetles, develop in dead branches, living trees, or fire-killed wood. Some species prefer old wood, whereas others attack cut and seasoned timber. The tunneling activities of some larvae are particularly damaging to old dwellings and furniture. Others mine living limbs of weakened cultivated trees or tunnel through green shoots of living plants. Because of their tendency to bore into wood products, bostrichid beetles are widely distributed around the world through commerce. Some species (*Rhyzopertha*) cause considerable damage to stored products, especially dried roots and grains. The feeding galleries of adults and larvae of many species are filled with coarse dust mixed with waste and wood fragments. The fine "post" of powdery frass left behind in the tunnels of some species (*Lyctus, Trogoxylon*) suggested the common name powderpost beetles. The closely placed round exit holes of some species inspired another common name, "shot hole borers." Many bostrichids maintain intracellular bacteria in special organs called mycetomes located inside the midgut that aid in the digestion of wood. Larval bostrichids are especially tolerant of extremely low-moisture environments.

FAMILY DIAGNOSIS Most adult bostrichids are distinguished from other beetles in western North America by their narrow to broadly cylindrical bodies, strongly convex and hoodlike pronotum, and deflexed head not visible from above. Powderpost beetles (*Lyctus, Trogoxylon*) have completely exposed heads with a somewhat flattened prothorax with distinct lateral margins carinate. Head with mandibles exposed. Clubbed antennae with 8–11 antennomeres, club antennomeres often asymmetrical. Hoodlike pronotum sometimes rough, toothed, or with hornlike projections in front and without carinate lateral margins, or with margins carinate (*Lyctus, Trogoxylon*). Procoxal cavities open or closed behind. Elytra parallel-sided, coarsely or finely punctate, with rows of punctures or costae, sharp tubercles or spines on apices, and completely conceal abdomen; apices may or may not appear abruptly cut off. Tarsi 5-5-5, claws equal in size, toothed. Abdomen with five ventrites free.

SIMILAR FAMILIES
- some death-watch beetles (Ptinidae, p.299)—antennae serrate or flabellate
- minute tree-fungus beetles (Ciidae, p.329)—antennae with symmetrical club
- cylindrical bark beetles (Zopheridae: Colydiinae, p.344)—mandibles concealed, tarsi 5-5-4
- bark or ambrosia beetles (Curculionidae, p.560)—antennal club compact

COLLECTING NOTES Adult bostrichids are commonly found at lights, netted on the wing, or occasionally beaten from infested dead branches. Wood- and bark-feeding species are procured by gathering infested materials and storing them in rearing chambers. Check wooden furniture for exit holes and powdery residue. Bostrichids emerging indoors are attracted to sunny windows and found dead on windowsills.

FAUNA 77 SPECIES IN 26 GENERA

Melalgus confertus LeConte (7.0–13.0 mm) is elongate, cylindrical, with suberect pubescence, and brown. Head clearly visible from above, eyes separated by six times their own diameter when viewed from front, and frons similar in both sexes. Antenna with 10 antennomeres. Pronotum not distinctly wider than long. Elytra granulose toward sides and apices. Protibia deeply emarginate apically. Larvae develop in small, dead twigs of hardwoods, including orchard trees. Oregon to California. *Melalgus megalops* (Fall) (5.0–7.0 mm) similar, with large prominent eyes separated by three times eye diameter, pronotum distinctly wider than long, and elytra granulose toward sides and apices. Southern California. (2)

Polycaon stoutii (**LeConte**) (10.0–24.0 mm) is elongate, somewhat cylindrical, and dull black. Head clearly visible beyond prothorax, and pronotum without tubercles. Antennae with 11 antennomeres, 3 distinctly shorter than 4. Protibia not emarginate apically. Elytral apices simple. Larvae develop in hardwoods, including orchard trees, but seldom considered pests. Adults are attracted to lights on warm nights in wooded mountainous regions. British Columbia to California, east to Texas, and south to Mexico. *Polycaon granulatus* Van Dyke (8.0–10.0 mm) similar, with 10 antennomeres, more granulose dorsally, elytral apices of male incised and bidentate, with antennae, tarsal claws, and lateral elytral margins reddish brown. Northern California. (2)

Giant Palm Borer *Dinapate wrightii* **Horn** (30.0–52.0 mm) is large and shiny black, sometimes with a reddish tinge, and underside and appendages dark reddish brown. Head reflexed, deeply inserted into prothorax. Short antennae with 10 antennomeres, 1 and 2 cup-shaped. Pronotum without lateral margins. A native of palm oases, now a pest of planted palms. Females tunnel into palm crown to lay 400 to 500 eggs and yellowish larvae develop in dead and dying trunks. Chewing inside trunks heard from several feet away. Adults emerge from dime-sized emergence holes in summer. California and Baja California Peninsula, east to Utah, Arizona, and western Mexico. (1)

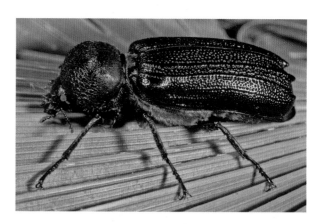

Amphicerus cornutus (Pallas) (8.5–14.0 mm) is elongate, cylindrical, and uniformly brownish black with reddish-brown antennae and tarsi. Head small and deflexed, deeply inserted in prothorax, and antennae with 10 antennomeres, 8–10 forming club, each with longitudinal grooves on surface. Pronotum as long as wide, broadest medially, strongly declivous anteriorly with broad, rasplike tubercles, and four or five semierect tubercles on each side; lateral margins strongly converging to hooklike anterior angles that are more developed in males. Lateral elytral margins parallel, and sutural margins slightly elevated just past declivity. Larvae in mesquite (*Prosopis*); adults at lights. Across southern United States south to Caribbean and northern South America. (2)

Apatides fortis (LeConte) (9.0–20.0 mm) is elongate, cylindrical, and black with reddish tinge. Head small and deflexed, deeply inserted in prothorax, with frons transversely elevated between eyes. Ten antennomeres. Pronotum as long as wide, broadest medially, strongly declivous anteriorly, with large scalelike granules on disc, and lateral margins strongly converging anteriorly to a pair of hooklike projections. Elytra with rows of coarse, deep punctures, and apices each thickened with (male) or without (female) a tuft of yellow setae. Larvae in dead mesquite (*Prosopis*). At lights. Southern California east to Utah and Oklahoma; south to Mexico. (1)

297

Lichenophanes fasciculatus (Fall) (7.0–12.0 mm) is elongate, cylindrical, coarsely and deeply punctate dorsally, and shiny blackish brown, with moderately long and recumbent yellowish-brown setae and numerous pointed and thick tufts of erect black setae. Head deeply inserted in prothorax, not visible from above. Pronotum as long as wide, and strongly but not densely tuberculate across front with two hooklike processes. Elytra deeply and almost cribrately punctate, without costae, and with thick tufts of black setae. Legs short. Southeastern Arizona, Baja California Sur. Possibly synonymous with a Mexican species. (4)

Dendrobiella aspera (LeConte) (5.0–7.5 mm) is dark reddish brown; appendages, except front tibiae, brownish yellow. Head deflexed, deeply inserted into prothorax, front coarsely granulose (male) or sparsely punctate (female). Antennae with 10 antennomeres, three club antennomeres with sensory depressions. Pronotum convex, without distinct lateral carinae. Elytra convex, punctate, with punctures coarse and deep near apical declivity, and apices each with a pair of spinose tubercles. Larvae in palo verde (*Parkinsonia*), mesquite (*Prosopis*), and tamarisk (*Tamarix*). Adults at lights. Southern California and Arizona to Baja California Sur. (1)

Xyloblaptus quadrispinosus (LeConte) (2.7–4.0 mm) is robust, cylindrical, and dark reddish brown, with bases of elytra and pronotum reddish, and appendages brownish yellow. Head not visible from above. Pronotum wider than long, anterior half irregularly and densely dentate, semierect rasplike teeth variable in size, largest near each anterior angles. Elytra with pair of broad tubercles on outer margin of apical declivity only rarely acute, never with spinose apices. Ventrites 1–4 narrowed medially in female. Legs short. On *Parkinsonia*, *Prosopis*, and *Senegalia*. Colorado Desert of California to western Texas. *Xyloblaptus prosopidis* Fisher (2.7–4.0 mm) with elytral tubercles spinose, on *Prosopis*, Mojave Desert, California. (2)

Psoa maculata (LeConte) (6.0–11.0 mm) is elongate, cylindrical, clothed in erect pubescence, and forebody black with purplish or greenish tinge. Head narrow, not concealed by prothorax. Pronotum wide, broadest medially, sides broadly arcuate, moderately flattened, and coarsely punctate. Elytra parallel, with apices each narrowly rounded, punctures confused, and black with variable reddish, yellow, or tan markings sometimes forming irregular stripes. Develops in hardwoods. California. *Psoa quadrisignata* (Horn) (6.6–9.0 mm) pronotum shiny and sparsely punctate, broadest anteriorly, with posterolateral margins convergent posteriorly, and black elytra with variable reddish markings, or mostly red with six spots. Develops in coyote brush (*Baccharis pilularis*). British Columbia to California. (2)

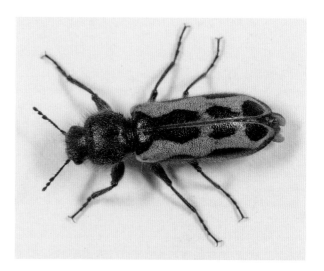

Rhyzopertha dominica (Fabricius) (2.0–3.0 mm) is elongate, cylindrical, clothed in yellowish setae, shiny, and uniformly dark reddish brown to brownish black; appendages sometimes lighter. Head slightly convex, partly covered by prothorax, not visible from above. Pronotum distinctly and uniformly convex, widest near middle; front half with arched rows of broadly rounded teeth, those nearest front forming a raised and notched ridge, rear half with flattened granules. Elytra at base almost equal in length to pronotum, with rows of coarse, deep punctures. Adults and larvae infest stored grains and various vegetable foods, especially cereals. Cosmopolitan; throughout southern Canada and United States. (1)

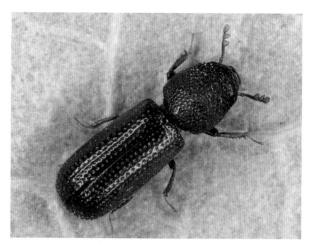

298

Brown Powderpost Beetle *Lyctus brunneus* (Stephens)
(2.2–7.0 mm) is elongate, slender, somewhat parallel-sided,
and moderately clothed in fine, recumbent setae, and
brown. Head barely declivous, narrower than prothorax,
with distinct notch between frontal and postclypeal
lobes. Pronotum broadest across anterior quarter, with
lateral margins finely denticulate, somewhat sinuate, and
narrowing posteriorly, disc coarsely and densely punctate
with slight median Y-shaped depression. Elytra broader
than prothorax, punctostriate with intervals bearing a single
row of punctures. Ventrite 4 of female without thick fringe
of silky setae. Larva develops in dead, dry hardwood
branches; also attacks hardwood flooring, cabinets, and tool
handles. Southern Canada and United States. (6)

Southern Lyctus Beetle *Lyctus carbonarius* Waltl
(2.5–6.0 mm) is elongate, slender, somewhat straight-sided,
and clothed in fine, recumbent setae. Head visible, barely
declivous, narrower than pronotum, antennal club stout,
antennomere 10 wider than long. Pronotum shallowly
punctate, slightly wider than long, narrower than elytra,
with sharply defined side margins, interstriate distinct hind
angles, and a deep groove down middle at base. Elytra
punctostriate, interstriae with two rows of punctures. Larva
develops in dead, dry hardwood branches; also attacks
hardwood flooring, cabinets, and tool handles. Southern
Canada and United States. Formerly known as *Lyctus
planicollis* LeConte. (6)

PTINIDAE (tin'-i-dē)
DEATH-WATCH AND SPIDER BEETLES

The family Ptinidae was formerly known as Anobiidae. The common name "death-watch" beetle is
based on the behavior of the European furniture beetle, *Anobium punctatum* (De Geer), in which the
males strike their heads against the pronotum to produce a series of audible clicks that were often heard
during hushed, deathbed vigils. Important ptinid pests of stored products include the cigarette beetle,
Lasioderma serricorne (Fabricius), and the drugstore beetle, *Stegobium paniceum* (Linnaeus). Both species
cause considerable economic damage by infesting drugs, tobacco, seeds, spices, cereals, and leather.
Larval ptinids attack hardwoods and softwoods, boring into bark, dry wood, twigs, seeds, woody fruits,
and galls. A few species eat woody fungi, puffballs, or young stems and shoots of growing trees. Some
species store symbiotic yeastlike organisms in special pouches in their midgut that enhance their ability
to digest wood. Spider beetles have inflated elytra that are conspicuously wider than the pronotum, giving
them a spiderlike appearance. Most spider beetles feed on accumulations of plant and animal materials,
especially in nests, including those of solitary bees, and in animal dung. They are sometimes household
pests, infesting stored flour, cereal products, wool, and other similar dried plant- or animal-based materials.

FAMILY DIAGNOSIS Adult ptinids are short with
hypognathous heads covered with hoodlike prothorax, or
spiderlike with hypognathous heads, head and prothorax
either narrower than elytra or about the same width, very

convex elytra, and long, slender legs and antennae; legs often received into sulci on underside. Often clothed in fine scales or setae. Antennae usually with 11 antennomeres; club, if present, asymmetrical, especially in male. Procoxal cavities open behind. Elytra with surface smooth or rough, with punctostriae present or absent. Tarsi 5-5-5, claws equal and simple. Abdomen usually with five ventrites, with 1–2 or 1–3 connate.

SIMILAR FAMILIES

- skin beetles (Dermestidae, p.290)—antennae with symmetrical club
- bostrichid beetles (Bostrichidae, p.295)—antennae short with compact club
- minute tree-fungus beetles (Ciidae, p.329)—antennae with symmetrical club
- bark beetles (Curculionidae: Scolytinae, p.560)—geniculate antennae with symmetrical club

COLLECTING NOTES Death-watch beetles are usually collected in small numbers, either at lights, by beating and sweeping vegetation, or by rearing from infested wood and fungus. Spider beetles living indoors infest stored organic products and related debris. Outdoors, some spider beetles might be collected using techniques similar to those used to obtain death-watch beetles, as well as sorting through abandoned animal nests and dried dung, or in pitfall traps.

FAUNA 471 SPECIES IN 67 GENERA

Ptinomorphus granosus **(LeConte)** (3.0–4.5 mm) is elongate-oblong, punctate-granulose dorsally, sparsely clothed in short recumbent grayish and darker setae, and brownish black. Antennae as long as (male) or shorter than (female) body. Pronotum nearly as long as wide, somewhat constricted in front, narrower than elytra. Elytra with somewhat diffuse and irregular transverse fasciae. Breed in old twigs of coast live oak (*Quercus agrifolia*); larvae pupate within loose silk cocoons. California. *Ptinomorphus angulatus* (Fall) (4.0 mm) slightly slenderer, elytra smooth with two distinct and irregularly angulate pale fasciae; on live oak. Southern California. *Ptinomorphus semivittatus* (Van Dyke) (6.0 mm) with elytral stripes, on black oak (*Quercus kelloggii*). Central California. (3)

Northern Spider Beetle *Mezium affine* Boieldieu (2.3–2.5 mm) is broadly oval, with elytra strongly convex and shiny dark reddish brown or black. Forebody and appendages densely setose. Medial pronotal groove broad, shallow, and parallel-sided, with weak basal swellings on each side. Elytra smooth, impunctate, nearly glabrous, with basal setose collar complete on each side. Flightless adults in decaying animal and plant matter. North Africa; across southern Canada, northeastern United States. American spider beetle *Mezium americanum* (Laporte de Castlenau) (1.5–3.5 mm) pronotal groove deeper, with a prominent basal swelling on each side, and basal setose collar deeply interrupted laterally. Uncommon. Cosmopolitan; across United States. (2)

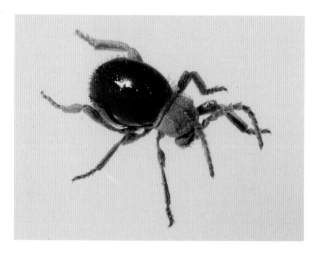

Niptus giulianii **Aalbu & Andrews** (2.6–2.9 mm) is broadly oval, and densely setose, with reddish-brown elytra strongly convex and shiny. Eyes large, frons narrow and flat between antennal fossae (pits), their dorsal rims not distinctly carinate nor elevated laterally. Elytra with strial punctures obsolete; intervals 3 and 5 with long and erect setae longer than single interval, and intervals 2 and 4 with short, recurved setae. Female ventrite 5 with patch of scalelike setae. Femora short and clavate, and tibiae stout. Adults associated with rodent burrows, especially near or on sand dunes. Central eastern California east to Utah and Arizona. (9)

Ptinus fallax **Fall** (2.5–3.3 mm) is moderately elongate, somewhat convex, clothed in bristling erect and suberect brownish setae, and dark reddish brown with broad brownish-black band across elytra. Head with eyes of male relatively small, separated in front by distance much greater than their vertical diameter. Antennae of male not as long as body, and serrate, with antennomeres elongate and triangular. Scutellum clothed in white setae. Elytra with strial punctures fine, with median oblique bar extending to fourth interval, and base and apices, including suture, reddish; outline similar in both sexes. Last ventrite of male lacking distinct apical tubercle. British Columbia to southern California. (15)

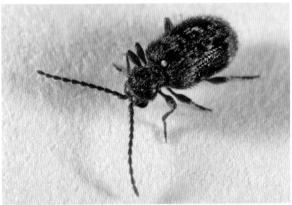

Ptinus gandolphei **Pic** (3.0–3.5 mm) is elongate, somewhat parallel-sided (male) or elongate-oval (female), somewhat convex, moderately clothed in recumbent reddish-yellow setae, and uniformly light reddish brown. Males resemble *P. verticalis*. Male antennae exceeding length of body, antennomeres 3–11 long. Pronotum narrow, with median line not prominent posteriorly. Elytra with strial punctures setose, setae small; male moderately clothed in coarse yellowish setae; each interval with rows of short inclined and recurved bristlelike setae in both sexes; female elytra with setae denser, alternate intervals with rows of long, fine, erect setae. Adults associated with seed and animal feed. California. (15)

Ptinus paulonotatus **Pic** (2.2–3.0 mm) is elongate, somewhat parallel-sided, clothed in long suberect yellowish or brownish-yellow setae, and usually uniformly reddish brown. Head granulate, broader than prothorax across convex eyes, with antennae of male somewhat serrate and shorter than body. Pronotum with disc granulate. Elytra distinctly punctostriate, intervals slightly wider than strial punctures, each stria with series of erect setae, with pale narrow subbasal fascia closer to sides and subapical transverse bands nearly reaching suture. Colorado to Arizona, east to Texas; also Mexico. (15)

Ptinus verticalis LeConte (2.0–3.0 mm) is elongate, somewhat parallel-sided (male) or elongate-oval (female), somewhat convex, moderately clothed in recumbent light reddish-brown scalelike setae, and uniformly reddish brown. Males resemble *P. gandolphei.* Head and pronotum nearly equal in width. Elytra about twice as wide as prothorax, punctostriate, with intervals each with a row of pale bristlelike setae that are not recurved in females, and alternate intervals wider. California. (15)

Episernus trapezoidus (Fall) (3.0–4.0 mm) is narrowly elongate, parallel-sided, moderately convex, clothed in fine recumbent pubescence, and yellowish brown with head and underside darker. Head across eyes wider than pronotum, eyes large and convex in male, antennomere 1 relatively long, and 8–10 forming slender club. Pronotal sides straight, weakly margined, convergent anteriorly from base, and posterior angles evident. Elytra broader than prothorax, finely punctate. Legs slender, with femora thickened, but not clavate. Adults on branches of dead conifers. California to Colorado. *Episernus champlaini* (Fisher) black, with head not wider than prothorax, eyes smaller, and tibiae and tarsi paler; on dead limbs of *Pinus flexilis.* Colorado. (2)

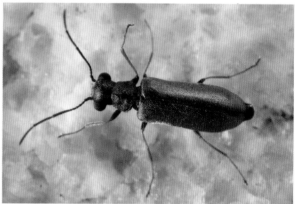

Ozognathus cornutus LeConte (1.3–3.3 mm) is oblong, stout, sparsely clothed in short, pale recumbent setae, and moderately shiny blackish brown. Mandibles with (male) or without (female) large horns emerging from base. Antennae reddish, antennomeres 9–11 forming black club. Pronotum convex, with sides rounded, and margins nearly parallel then sinuate before posterior angles. Elytra more finely punctate than pronotum. Legs reddish, femora sometimes blackish. Larvae in *Gnorimoschema* galls; adults on twigs. California. *Ozognathus dubius* Fall (2.4–2.7 mm) less stout and shiny, somewhat more finely punctate, more conspicuously pubescent. Arizona, Colorado. (2)

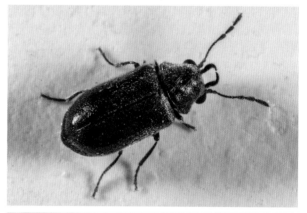

Furniture Beetle *Anobium punctatum* (De Geer) (2.7–4.0 mm) is elongate, clothed in short yellowish-gray pubescence lying on surface, and reddish to blackish brown. Antennae filiform, antennomeres all long and cylindrical. Head deeply inserted in prothorax, with prominent bump on top, and mandibles not directed back under body. Pronotum with sides sharply margined and raised behind; underneath with surface concave and bases of forelegs widely separated. Elytra with striae deeply punctate. Abdomen underneath with grooves much more visible laterally than medially. Claws simple. Adults and larvae found in many hardwoods and conifers; also infest beams, flooring, furniture. Europe; widely established in North America. (1)

California Deathwatch Beetle *Hemicoelus gibbicollis* **(LeConte)** (3.5–6.0 mm) is somewhat cylindrical, brown to brownish black, with sparse, appressed pubescence. Antennae not serrate, with 11 antennomeres, 9 as long as (female) or longer than (male) combined lengths of 3–8. Pronotum much narrower than elytra, with disc strongly elevated and compressed, sides bisinuate, anterior angles prominently dentiform, and posterior angles rounded. Elytra punctostriate, punctures large, with pubescence uniform or denser on alternate intervals. Ventrite 2 longer than 5. Alaska to California. (5)

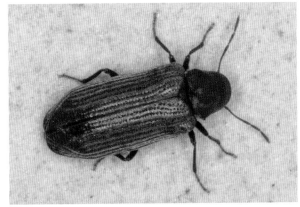

Actenobius pleuralis **(Casey)** (2.9–5.2 mm) is both moderately punctate and clothed in short recumbent pubescence, and dull blackish brown with reddish appendages. Head narrow, inserted in prothorax up to moderately convex eyes. Antennae barely half length of body, serrate in both sexes, with antennomeres 3–10 elongate-triangular. Pronotum broad, finely tuberculate, with sides weakly arcuate, finely serrulate, slightly converging anteriorly, with posterior angles rounded. Elytra as wide as prothorax, weakly punctostriate, with strial punctures becoming obsolete apically. Underside finely punctate and pubescent. On coast live oak (*Quercus agrifolia*). California. (1)

Xeranobium **species** (3.5–7.7 mm) are moderately to densely and uniformly clothed in fine appressed setae ranging from light gray, tan, or dull yellow, occasionally with scattered short, erect setae, with cuticle light to dark brown or black. Large eyes bulging. Eleven antennomeres, with 3–8 serrate to pectinate, and 9–11 very elongate (male), or with 3–8 nearly filiform, serrate, or rarely pectinate (female). Pronotum with lateral carinate margins only evident basally. Elytra with or without distinct punctostriae or costae formed by pubescence. Hind tarsus more than one and a half times length of tibia. Western North America. (11)

Priobium punctatum **(LeConte)** (4.5–6.5 mm) is clothed dorsally in erect, bristly pubescence, and dull black. Head deeply withdrawn into prothorax, nearly covering eyes. Antennae not distinctly clubbed. Pronotum with lateral carinae basally, disc granulate, and posterior angles slightly retracted. Elytra punctostriate, punctures deep and nearly square, with narrow intervals weakly convex. Abdominal sutures obscured medially, with large ring-shaped punctures at middle sparse, less distinct. California east to South Dakota, Nebraska, New Mexico. *Priobium sericeum* Say (4.9–6.2 mm) with pubescence short and recumbent. Arizona east to Wisconsin, Nova Scotia, and Florida. (2)

Cigarette Beetle *Lasioderma serricorne* (Fabricius) (1.8–3.0 mm) is oval, uniformly light yellowish brown to reddish brown, and humpbacked with serrate antennae and smooth elytra. Body clothed in short, dense yellowish pubescence. Elytra with faint rows of erect pubescence. Front legs with tibiae distinctly widened and flattened toward apices. Larvae and adults found in various dried plant products. Larva pupates in silken cocoon. Cosmopolitan. *Lasioderma haemorrhoidale* (Illiger) (2.3–2.7 mm) more elongate, with underside significantly darker than rest of body. Adults on flowers of thistle (*Cirsium*). Mediterranean region; established in California. (2)

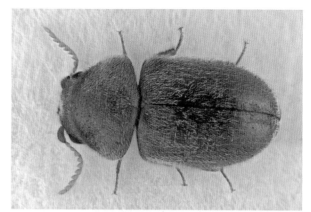

Trichodesma cristata Casey (5.2–6.8 mm) is oblong, robust, convex, coarsely punctate dorsally, sparsely and irregularly clothed in long white, brown, and black pubescence, and brownish black. Pronotum wide, with lateral margins evenly arcuate and converging posteriorly, with disc strongly gibbous and granulate, and dense, almost woolly white vestiture mixed with scattered long, fine, erect setae and tufts. Elytral vestiture not concealing surface, with humerus and basal margin, median and subapical spot, and tufts of erect blackish-brown setae. British Columbia to southern California. *Trichodesma setifera* (LeConte) (3.2 mm) with pubescence uniformly pale. Southern California. (2)

Drugstore Beetle *Stegobium paniceum* (Linnaeus) (2.0–3.5 mm) is oblong, reddish to reddish brown. Head concealed from above by pronotum. Antennal club longer than preceding antennomeres combined, 9–11 each somewhat elongate and slightly expanded at apices. Prothorax with side margins distinctly carinate; underneath with sides concave, and coxae widely separated. Elytra long, distinctly punctostriate, with strial punctures elongate. Common pest in homes, commercial food-distribution and processing facilities. Infests stored foods and dried plant and animal materials, including museum specimens. Cosmopolitan. (1)

Ptilinus acuminatus Casey (2.5–4.0 mm) male is elongate, cylindrical, moderately clothed in short, appressed yellowish pubescence, and dull brownish black, with legs somewhat lighter, and head and pronotum sometimes darker. Head evenly convex, with minute granules. Antennal rami moderate in length. Pronotum about equal in width to elytra, with anterior margin broadly rounded laterally and slightly angulate and reflexed medially, and disc granulate with granules larger anteromedially. Elytra coarsely and sparsely punctate, punctures arranged somewhat serially. On woody shrubs, including *Ceanothus* and *Cercocarpus*. California. (4)

Euvrilletta serricornis White (4.8–6.8 mm) is elongate, cylindrical, parallel-sided, with only short tan appressed pubescence producing a silky sheen, and more or less reddish brown with pronotum clouded with dark brown. Head with eyes large, and antennomeres 4–10 serrate, 9–11 each long, with combined lengths not longer than 2–8 combined. Pronotum wider than long, broadest behind middle, with disc evenly convex and posterior lateral areas depressed. Elytra each with 10 complete punctostriae, plus a short scutellar and subhumeral striae, with strial punctures elongate and impressed, and weakly convex intervals. California and Nevada. (13)

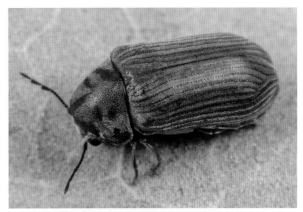

Vrilletta bicolor White (7.2–7.7 mm) is elongate, robust, somewhat parallel-sided, densely clothed in appressed whitish setae not obscuring surface, with head and underside black to dark brown, with dorsal surface mostly reddish or orangish brown. Head minutely granulate-punctate with faint longitudinal ridge. Antennomeres 2–3, 9–10 serrate, and 4–8 pectinate, with 9–11 combined shorter than all preceding antennomeres combined. Lateral pronotal margins arcuate, disc convex. Elytra with interstriae strongly convex, and lateral and sutural margins usually dark. Adults reared from white alder (*Alnus rhombifolia*). California. (8)

Vrilletta decorata Van Dyke (5.2–6.9 mm) is elongate, moderately robust, parallel-sided, and dark brownish black with variable elytral markings. Head granulate-punctate with faint longitudinal ridge, antennomeres 3–8 serrate, 9 and 10 enlarged, serrate. Pronotum wider than long, with sides widely margined. Elytra with striae completely impressed, intervals strongly convex, and several variable yellow stripes sometimes reduced to oblique patch at basal quarter or elongate spot on interval 3. Adults reared from coast live oak (*Quercus agrifolia*). British Columbia to California. (8)

Caenocara species (1.2–2.5 mm) are oval, rotund, resembling bristly seeds, moderately punctate, sparsely clothed in erect or suberect pubescence, and shiny reddish brown to black. Eyes deeply emarginate to almost divided. Antennae completely concealed in repose, with nine antennomeres, antennomere 1 more strongly produced laterally in males, and forming a transverse isosceles triangle in females. Pronotum wide, and broadest basally. Elytra with two distinct sulci above lateral margins, plus a partial third barely reaching middle. Underneath with legs retracting into sulci. Adults on low vegetation in damp habitats, and in puffballs (*Calvatia, Lycoperdon, Sclerodema*). Widespread in North America. (3)

Tricorynus species (1.6–3.9 mm) are oblong, convex, compact, shiny or dull light reddish brown to reddish black, with sparse to dense yellowish or grayish pubescence often rubbed off in patches; appendages paler. Head slanted back, eyes not deeply notched, and antennae clubbed, with 10 antennomeres, antennal bases in front of each eye and far apart. Sides of pronotum sharp, complete. Elytra grooved only at sides near apices. Underside with bases of front legs hidden, front of metasternum grooved to receive middle legs, hind legs capable of tucking between raised posterior margin of thorax and abdomen. Difficult to identify without careful examination of appendages. Adults active in spring and summer; attracted to lights. Widespread in western North America. (32)

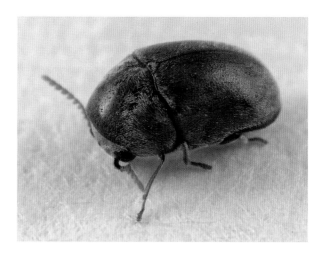

BOTHRIDERIDAE (both-ri-der'-i-dē)
BOTHRIDERID BEETLES

All known larval bothriderids develop by hypermetamorphosis and are external parasites of wood-boring larvae and their pupae. In eastern North America, *Bothrideres* larvae attack those of Buprestidae (p.210), Ptinidae (p.299), Bostrichidae (p.295), Mycteridae (p.390), Cerambycidae (p.460), and Curculionidae (p.539). The larvae of the western *Bothrideres cactophagi* Schwarz are reported to parasitize the larvae and pupae of a large cactus weevil, *Cactophagus spinolae* (Gyllenhal) (p.540), while the adults of some *Sosylus* species prey on ambrosia beetles (Curculionidae) and their larvae. Although bothriderid larvae are currently of little or no economic importance, studies on their parasitic habits may encourage their use as biocontrol agents of wood-boring beetles in managed forests. The larvae of some species of *Sosylus* are known to construct waxen pupal chambers, while those of *Deretaphrus* spin silken cocoons. Adult bothriderids are typically found at the base of long dead and dry trees or among their roots. More or less flattened adults of *Bothrideres* live under bark, whereas the more cylindrical *Deretaphrus* and *Sosylus* generally inhabit the tunnels of their beetle hosts.

FAMILY DIAGNOSIS Adult bothriderids are narrowly elongate and somewhat flattened or subcylindrical. Head slightly deflexed. Antennae with 11 antennomeres, club with two (*Bothrideres*, *Sosylus*) or three (*Deretaphrus*) antennomeres, and insertions visible from above. Prothorax longer than wide. Procoxal cavities narrowly or broadly closed behind. Elytra carinate. Tarsi 4-4-4. Abdomen with five ventrites free.

SIMILAR FAMILIES
- wrinkled bark beetles (Carabidae, p.99)—antennae moniliform, tarsi 5-5-5
- powderpost beetles (Bostrichidae: Lyctinae, p.299)—tarsi 5-5-5
- cylindrical bark beetles (Zopheridae: Colydiinae, p.341)—antennal insertions hidden
- small darkling beetles (Tenebrionidae, p.347)—antennal insertions hidden, tarsi 5-5-4
- small bark-gnawing beetles (Trogossitidae, p.414)—mandibles prominent, tarsi 5-5-5

COLLECTING NOTES Peeling back bark of standing dead conifers at or below ground level is the most productive method for collecting bothriderids. Some species are occasionally associated with fire scars and a few are attracted to lights.

FAUNA 14 SPECIES IN FIVE GENERA

Bothrideres montanus Horn (3.3–6.5 mm) is somewhat convex, shiny dark brown to black, and sparsely pubescent. Pronotum nearly as long as wide, broadest near apical quarter, apical margin sinuate with angles produced, depressions on disc distinct and large, anterior depression twice as large as posterior depression that is closed at base. Elytra with even intervals slightly lower than odd, somewhat polished, and without pubescence, with interval 3 strongly raised at base, much higher than intervals 2 or 4. Adults found under bark at base of ponderosa pine (*Pinus ponderosa*) snags. Arizona to Colorado and New Mexico, south to Mexico. (5)

Deretaphrus oregonensis Horn (6.4–12.9 mm) is elongate, dull dark brown to black, and glabrous. Antenna short and thick, club not abrupt. Pronotum longer than wide, broadest near apical third, disc rugosely punctate with deep medial canal interrupted before middle, with lateral margins convergent and sinuate basally. Elytra convex, each with four distinct costae between suture and lateral margin, intervals with a double row of large, deep, and well-separated punctures. Larvae are ectoparasitoids of wood-boring beetle larvae and pupate within a loose silken cocoon. Adults found under dry bark at base of conifer snags. British Columbia to southern California, east to Montana, Idaho, and Utah. (1)

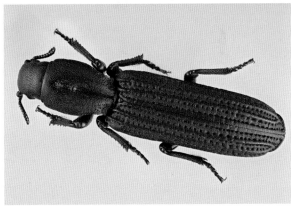

MURMIDIIDAE (mûr-mid-ī′-i-dē)

MURMIDIID BEETLES

Until recently, Murmidiidae were considered a subfamily of Cerylonidae. Most murmidiid species occur in the New World. One Old World species, *Murmidius ovalis* (Beck), now cosmopolitan, is widespread in North America. Although often associated with stored food and other products, this species is not considered a pest. Three additional species are native to North America, one of which, *Mychocerinus arizonensis* Lawrence & Stephan, occurs west of the Continental Divide in southeastern Arizona and southern Sonora, and is found under bark. Both adults and larvae of other species are frequently found under bark of dead trees in early stages of decay. Despite their known habitat associations, the specific food preferences of these beetles remain unclear.

FAMILY DIAGNOSIS Western murmidiids are very small (1.1–1.4 mm), broadly oval, relatively flat (*Mychocerinus*), or convex (*Murmidius*), surfaces rough, clothed in minute setae, and usually shiny reddish brown. Head prognathous, deeply withdrawn into prothorax, with frontoclypeal suture present. Capitate antennae with nine (*Mychocerinus*) or 10 (*Murmidius*) antennomeres, and terminal antennomere forming cylindrical, not flattened, club. Prothoracic antennal cavities dorsal and clearly visible from above (*Murmidius*) or ventral and not visible from above (*Mychocerinus*). Procoxal cavities open behind. Elytra punctoseriate and completely cover abdomen. Tarsi 4-4-4. Abdomen with five ventrites free, ventrite 1 longest, and posterior margin of 5 inflexed and crenulate.

SIMILAR FAMILIES

- round fungus beetles (Leiodidae, p.137)—antennomere 8 smaller than 7 and 9
- small handsome fungus beetles (Endomychidae, p.315)—antennal club with three antennomeres
- hairy fungus beetles (Mycetophagidae, p.326)—pronotum with basal pair of grooves, antennal club usually with three antennomeres

- *Hyporhagus* (Zopheridae, p.344)—much larger, with antennal bases concealed from above by frontal margin, club with three antennomeres

COLLECTING NOTES Adult and onisciform larvae of *Murmidius ovalis* are typically associated with stored products containing fruits, seeds, and various grains in granaries and warehouses. It has also been collected from oak galls, dead leaves, and cut grass. *Mychocerinus arizonensis* is found under dry bark of mesquite (*Prosopis juliflora*) and oak (*Quercus*) bark.

FAUNA FOUR SPECIES IN THREE GENERA

Murmidius ovalis **(Beck)** (1.2–1.4 mm) is oval, strongly convex, shiny brown, and clothed in inconspicuous, sparse, short, fine, recumbent setae. Head with eyes large and finely faceted, antennae with 10 antennomeres, cavities for receiving antennae visible from above. Pronotum twice as wide as long, widest at base, with dorsal cavities along sides to receive antennae clearly visible. Elytra with rows of distinct punctures. Legs with tibiae angles on outer margins and tarsi 4-4-4. Adults found in packages of seeds, rice, and other stored products; also in cut grass, hay, leaves, and other decomposing vegetation. Cosmopolitan; widespread in United States. (1)

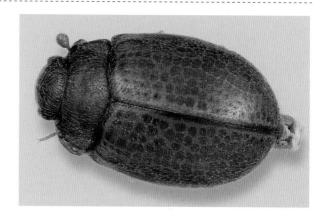

308

TEREDIDAE (ter-ed′-i-dē)
TEREDID BEETLES

Until recently, Teredidae was considered a subfamily of the Bothrideridae. The natural history of this small family is largely unknown. Unlike bothriderid larvae that are ectoparasitoids of beetles and other wood-boring insects, those of teredids are free-living. Some species are believed to consume fungi, including those cultivated by ambrosia beetles (p.539) within their galleries in wood. They are not known to construct cocoons prior to pupation. Western species are found in coniferous forests and are typically associated with dead conifers.

FAMILY DIAGNOSIS Adult teredids are elongate, sparsely pubescent or nearly glabrous. Head prognathous. Antennae with 10 antennomeres, insertions visible from above, with antennal grooves absent. Procoxal cavities narrowly closed behind. Elytra not carinate. Apex of protibia spinose with fixed teeth and subequal protibial spurs; procoxae contiguous, or nearly so, globular and projecting, cavities open externally, with trochanters large and distinct; mesocoxae broadly separated with cavities closed laterally, and tarsi 4-4-4 in both sexes. Abdomen with five ventrites free, with ventrite 1 longer than 2 and narrowly acute between hind coxae.

SIMILAR FAMILIES

- wrinkled bark beetles (Carabidae, p.88)—antennae moniliform, tarsi 5-5-5
- powderpost beetles (Bostrichidae: Lyctinae, p.299)—tarsi 5-5-5
- bothriderid beetles (Bothrideridae, p.306)—11 antennomeres, elytra carinate
- cylindrical bark beetles (Zopheridae: Colydiinae, p.340)—antennal insertions hidden
- small darkling beetles (Tenebrionidae, p.347)—antennal insertions hidden from view above, tarsi 5-5-4

- small bark-gnawing beetles (Trogossitidae, p.414)—mandibles prominent, tarsi 5-5-5

COLLECTING NOTES Both western teredids are found under dead conifer bark, or in samples of dry or slightly moist decayed material found inside or immediately around the bases of snags and stumps. Beetles are then extracted from these samples using Berlese or Winkler extraction methods. *Oxylaemus californicus* is occasionally encountered during evening flights and attracted to lights.

FAUNA TWO SPECIES IN TWO GENERA

Oxylaemus californicus Crotch (3.2–4.4 mm) is elongate, cylindrical, shiny reddish brown, and clothed in short erect pubescence. Pronotum longer than wide, lateral margins somewhat parallel, punctures elongate, with center of disc a variable impunctate line, and large and deep basal impressions near posterior angles becoming narrower and shallower as they extend anteriorly to middle. Elytra with punctostriae not impressed except sutural striae at declivity, punctures large, well-separated, and somewhat elongate. First ventrite with anterior margin narrowly impunctate. Adults under bark of conifers; occasionally attracted to lights. British Columbia to northern California, east to Idaho and New Mexico. (1)

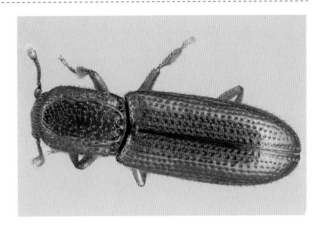

Rustleria obscura Stephan (3.1 mm) is elongate, cylindrical, brown, confusedly punctate, with moderately dense pubescence, setae fine and white. Head strongly deflexed and deeply withdrawn into pronotum, with antennae short, with 10 antennomeres, 10 forming abrupt club. Pronotum longer than wide, obovate, broadest near apical third, with sides rounded and converging posteriorly, and basal half with medial depression flanked by shallow triangular depressions. Elytra finely punctate. Procoxae confluent with their cavities narrowly open behind; mesocoxae narrowly separated, and first ventrite narrowly produced between metacoxae. Single known specimen found in partially rotten ponderosa pine (*Pinus ponderosa*) stump infested with ants at 2,600 meters. Southeastern Arizona. (1)

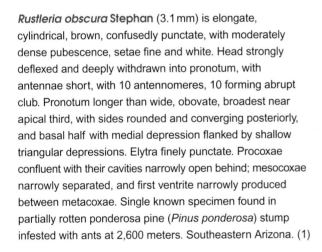

CERYLONIDAE (ser'-i-lon'-i-dē)
MINUTE BARK BEETLES

Cerylonid beetles are collected from various types of fungus-infested bark and wood, leaf litter, and other rotting debris by using mass extraction methods. As a result, little is known of their life cycles or specific food preferences, other than both adults and larvae are mycophagous and consume fungal spores and hyphae. *Cerylon* and *Philothermus* live under bark, while *Mychocerus* is commonly found in leaf litter.

FAMILY DIAGNOSIS Adult cerylonids are elongate, parallel-sided, and flat (*Cerylon, Philothermus*) or compact, broadly oval, and convex (*Mychocerus*), and mostly smooth and shiny. Head with frontoclypeal suture absent. Antennae with eight (*Mychocerus*), 10 (*Cerylon*), or 11 (*Philothermus*) antennomeres, last one or two forming a distinct club, with bases exposed. Prothorax with (*Mychocerus*) or without antennal cavities underneath. Procoxal cavities open or closed behind. Elytra punctostriate. Legs with tarsi 4-4-4, and claws simple. Abdomen with five distinct ventrites, with 1 longest, and posterior margin of 5 inflexed and crenulate.

SIMILAR FAMILIES

- powderpost beetles (Bostrichidae, p.299)—sides of body nearly parallel
- root-eating beetles (Monotomidae, p.438)—tip of abdomen exposed beyond elytra

- colydiine zopherids (Zopheridae, p.341)—antennal bases concealed from above by frontal margin

COLLECTING NOTES In western North America, minute bark beetles are best collected by using Berlese funnel or Winkler extractor methods to obtain specimens from decayed wood and leaf litter. Both *Cerylon* and *Philothermus* are found under bark and are sometimes captured in Lindgren funnels. *Mychocerus discretus* (Casey) is sifted from rotten conifer legs in red rot stage, from western Washington to northern California.

FAUNA 11 SPECIES IN THREE GENERA

Cerylon unicolor (**Ziegler**) (1.8–2.4 mm) is elongate-oval, flattened, glabrous, shiny dark reddish brown. Head without suture across front, clypeus shallowly emarginate in both sexes, antennae with 10 antennomeres, 10 forming club, 3 more than one and a half times longer than 4. Pronotum nearly as wide as long, sides somewhat parallel, slightly divergent (male) or parallel at base, then convergent anteriorly (female), disc distinctly punctured; without antennal sulci, and coxal cavities broadly closed behind. Elytra punctostriate basally, intervals finely punctate. Front tibia dentate at outer apical angle. Adults on fungi under bark of rotten logs; at lights. In West from British Columbia to coastal southern California. (5)

Philothermus occidentalis **Lawrence & Stephan** (1.9–2.3 mm) is elongate-oval, smooth, clothed in short, erect setae, and shiny reddish brown. Antennomeres 10 and 11 forming distinct club. Pronotum wider than long, moderately convex, with lateral margins narrow and somewhat irregular; underneath without antennal cavities and coxal cavities narrowly closed behind. Elytra each with seven punctostriae, punctures more or less equal to those on pronotum, deeply impressed, with intervals smooth, slightly convex, finely punctate. Adults found in moist conifer forest litter, sometimes in association with *Cerylon californicum* Casey (3.0+ mm), which is obviously larger, with distinct vestiture, and intervals almost flat. Northern California. (1)

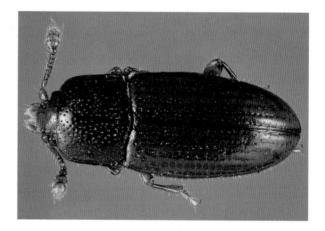

LATRIDIIDAE (la-trid-ī'-i-dē)
MINUTE BROWN SCAVENGER BEETLES

Adult and larval latridiids feed on the reproductive structures of fungi (Zygomycota, Deuteromycota, Ascomycota), plant and animal materials, and slime molds. Species of the subfamily Latridiinae are typically found in leaf litter of various shrubs and trees, while those of Corticariinae are found on dead or dying vegetation. Species in several genera (*Cartodere, Corticaria, Corticarina, Dienerella, Enicmus, Latridius,* and *Thes*) are regularly associated with stored products. Others are also found indoors in moldy situations associated with home air conditioning systems and damp basements. Based on the few known food preferences gleaned from captive adults and larvae, most latridiids likely feed on various fungal structures of a variety of fungi. The larval habits of most species are unknown but, given that they are also mycophages, it is surmised that they inhabit the same microhabitats as the adults.

FAMILY DIAGNOSIS Adult latridiids are small, elongate-oval, usually widest at middle, somewhat convex, sometimes setose. Head prognathous and not hidden by prothorax. Antennae with 10–11 antennomeres, last two or three antennomeres forming a gradual club. Pronotum usually narrower than base of elytra. Procoxal cavities closed behind. Elytra entire, completely covering abdomen, and strongly punctostriate, with humeral angles often rounded. Tarsi 3-3-3, with claws simple. Abdomen with five ventrites free.

SIMILAR FAMILIES
- tooth-neck fungus beetles (Derodontidae, p.116)—antennal club weak, elytra with large punctures, not grooved
- minute bark beetles (Cerylonidae, p.309)—pronotum nearly as wide as base of elytra
- akalyptoischiid scavenger beetles

(Akalyptoischiidae, p.313)—procoxal cavities open behind, tarsi appear 3-3-3, with tarsomere 1 annulated at middle
- hairy fungus beetles (Mycetophagidae, p. 326)—larger; pronotum as wide as base of elytra
- root-eating beetles (Monotomidae, p.438)—elytra shorter, exposing last abdominal tergite
- silken fungus beetles (Cryptophagidae, p.449)—larger; pronotum as wide as base of elytra

COLLECTING NOTES Minute brown scavenger beetles are collected by sifting or applying Berlese techniques to leaf litter, or by sweeping and beating dead, low-lying vegetation. Some species are found on dung and carrion, while a few species are attracted to lights. Adult corticariines such as *Corticaria* and *Melanophthalma* are covered by a waxy substance that must often be removed to ensure accurate species identification.

311

FAUNA 118 SPECIES IN 17 GENERA

Corticaria serrata (**Paykull**) (1.7–2.3 mm) is oblong-oval, somewhat convex, dull reddish yellow to dark reddish brown, with grayish pubescence. Head and pronotum closely punctured, spaces between finely wrinkled. Bulge behind eye short. Pronotum wider than long, sides with small teeth, base at middle with deep round pit, narrower than elytra; underside with distinct pair of setose pits. Elytra coarsely punctate with faint rows of punctures. Adults feed on fungi, found in moldy plant debris, often associated with stored foods in warehouses. Cosmopolitan; widespread in North America. (41 NA)

Melanophthalma picta LeConte (1.3 mm) is oval, somewhat robust, dull reddish yellow, with short pubescence, and dark markings on elytra. Antennal club with two antennomeres. Pronotum slightly wider than head, punctured, without pits at base. Elytra wider than pronotum, oval, with dark band across middle and diffuse patches at base and apices, with surface finely grooved with sparse punctures, spaces between with very fine punctures. Adults active in late spring and early summer, found in damp leaves and tussock mounds associated with coastal and salt marsh habitats. Massachusetts to Florida, west to Indiana and Texas; also Pacific Northwest. (21 NA)

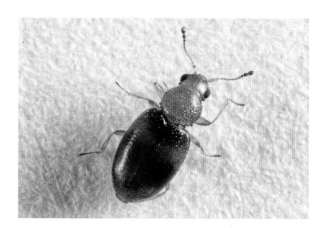

Plaster Beetle *Cartodere constrictus* (Gyllenhal) (1.2–1.8 mm) is elongate-oval, coarsely punctate dorsally, glabrous, and reddish brown to brownish black, with appendages paler. Head rectangular with prominent and finely faceted eyes and temples. Antennae relatively short, barely reaching middle of pronotum, with club abrupt and comprising two antennomeres. Pronotum distinctly constricted at posterior third and disc bicarinate. Elytra carinate, each with three carinae, including one behind each humerus, and intercostae with two rows of large, deep punctures. Adults associated with moldy grain and debris in mills, also in damp basements. Cosmopolitan; widespread in western North America. (1)

Dienerella filum (Aubé) (1.2–1.6 mm) is elongate, somewhat straight-sided and flat, coarsely sculptured with areas without punctures on head and pronotum, shiny, and uniformly reddish brown or yellowish brown. Head lacks paired ridges, eyes small with fewer than 20 facets; antennal club with two antennomeres, antennomere 3 not widest at base. Appendages slightly paler. Pronotum wider than long, sides broadest near front, sinuate at basal third, with a broad, deep groove across base. Elytra each with seven rows of deep punctures. Larvae and flightless adults found in damp, moldy conditions indoors and in nature. Widely distributed. (9)

Enicmus aterrimus (Motschulsky) (1.6–1.9 mm) is dull, blackish or reddish, with densely punctate head and pronotum. Head with well-developed eyes with more than 70 facets. Antennal club with three antennomeres. Pronotum quadrate with anterior angles lobed, sides somewhat parallel and sinuate before posterior angles, and broad, deep depression behind middle; prosternum with carinate process raised above coxae. Elytron with eight indistinct punctostriae. Likely feeds on slime mold (Myxomycetes) spores. Europe; widely distributed in North America. (4)

AKALYPTOISCHIIDAE (ak-al-ip-tō-is-kī'-i-dē)
AKALYPTOISCHIID SCAVENGER BEETLES

Akalyptoischiidae is a small family of beetles comprising 24 species in the genus *Akalyptoischion* and are collectively known from Oregon south to Baja California Sur, east to Idaho, Utah, and western Texas, a range that is likely to expand as more species are discovered. The flightless adults are often found in dry, broadleaf deciduous leaf litter, especially oak, or pine (*Pinus*) and other conifer duff. Others are associated with accumulations of plant debris inside pack rat (*Neotoma*) nests. The larvae are presently unknown. The food preference of both adult and larval *Akalyptoischion*, based on their habitat preferences and close phylogenetic relationship with Latridiidae (p.311), is presumed to be fungi. The limited dispersal abilities of akalyptoischiids living within unique or threatened environments is of potential interest to zoogeographers and conservation biologists.

FAMILY DIAGNOSIS Adult akalyptoischiids are very small, elongate, narrow, and somewhat parallel-sided. Head prognathous, eyes small with few facets and situated on posterior corners, mandibles large and serrate, with labrum large and expanded laterally. Antennae with 11 antennomeres, 3–8 or 9 moniliform, loose club comprising two or three antennomeres. Procoxal cavities broadly open behind. Elytra long, covering entire abdomen. Tarsi 3-3-3, with first tarsomere apparently a composite of two tarsomeres as indicated by an annulation. Abdomen with five ventrites free, first ventrite twice as long as ventrites 2, 3, or 4.

SIMILAR FAMILIES
- tooth-neck fungus beetles (Derodontidae, p.116)—antennal club weak, elytra with large punctures, not grooved
- minute bark beetles (Cerylonidae, p.309)—pronotum nearly as wide as base of elytra
- minute brown scavenger beetles (Latridiidae, p.311)—procoxal cavities closed behind
- hairy fungus beetles (Mycetophagidae, p.326)—larger, pronotum as wide as base of elytra
- root-eating beetles (Monotomidae, p.438)—elytra shorter, exposing last abdominal tergite
- silken fungus beetles (Cryptophagidae, p.449)—larger, pronotum as wide as base of elytra

COLLECTING NOTES Berlese and Winkler sampling in leaf litter from beneath various woody broadleaf shrubs and trees in coastal, chaparral, montane, and desert habitats, including oak (*Quercus*), toyon (*Heteromeles*), sugar bush (*Rhus*), chamise (*Adenostoma*), sycamore (*Platanus*), mountain mahogany (*Cercocarpus*), buckbrush (*Ceanothus*), mesquite (*Prosopis*), and desert almond (*Prunus*); also associated with Joshua (*Yucca*), pine (*Pinus*), redwood (*Sequoia*), and cypress (*Cupressus*). Pitfall traps placed in these microhabitats are also productive.

313

FAUNA 24 SPECIES IN ONE GENUS

Akalyptoischion quadrifoveolata (Fall) (1.2–1.3 mm) is elongate, slender, convex, and uniformly reddish brown, coarsely and rugosely punctured, and sparsely clothed in short recumbent setae of equal length. Head with small eyes consisting of four facets, antennal club comprising three antennomeres. Pronotum broadest at middle, with lateral margins evenly arcuate, scarcely explanate with ~12 tubercles bearing short decumbent setae, and disc rugose. Elytra wider than pronotum, suture fused, each with six punctostriae with strial punctures large, and sparsely setose with short decumbent setae of equal length. Central California, New Mexico. (24)

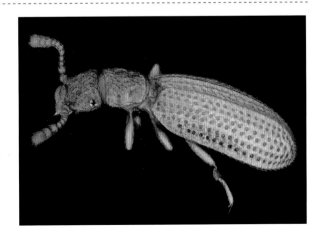

ANAMORPHIDAE (a-na-môrf'-i-dē)
ANAMORPHID FUNGUS BEETLES

Anamorphidae was, until recently, considered a subfamily of Endomychidae, but was elevated to family status based primarily on larval characters, as well as internal features of the adults. In North America, all but the widespread *Symbiotes gibberosus* (Lucas) are restricted to eastern Canada and United States. Anamorphid larvae and adults probably feed on fungal spores, as the mandibles possessed by several genera are modified to function as "spore mills."

FAMILY DIAGNOSIS Anamorphids are strongly oval or elongate-oval (*Symbiotes*) and convex, and clothed in long, fine, suberect setae. Head prognathous and deeply retracted within prothorax, with eyes placed on sides. Capitate antennae with 10 or 11 (*Symbiotes*) antennomeres, with 9–11 forming club. Pronotum with deep sulci near each lateral margin. Procoxal cavities open behind. Legs with tarsi usually 3-3-3 or 4-4-4 (*Symbiotes*), with claws simple (*Symbiotes*) or dentate basally. Abdomen with five ventrites free, ventrite 1 longest.

SIMILAR FAMILIES
- handsome fungus beetles (Endomychidae, p.315)—elongate-oval species much larger, with front angles of pronotum usually distinctly produced anteriorly

COLLECTING NOTES Search for *Symbiotes gibberosus* under bark of decaying oak (*Quercus*) and among various accumulations of plant debris.

FAUNA 11 SPECIES IN SIX GENERA

Symbiotes gibberosus (Lucas) (1.5–1.8 mm) is elongate-oval, convex, moderately densely clothed in long, bristling, pale setae, and uniformly shiny yellowish to reddish brown. Head broad, finely and sparsely punctate, with long antennae, antennomeres 9–11 forming loose, parallel-sided club. Pronotum wide, lateral margins narrowly explanate, finely crenulate, and parallel basally, with disc abruptly convex between triangular sulci. Scutellum small and transverse. Elytra broadest near basal third, with sutural stria strongly curved before scutellum, and apical tubercle in male. Tarsi 4-4-4. Adults under bark on decaying oak (*Quercus*), or in bird nests, moldy grain, and tree hole litter. Europe; western North America; also in East. (1)

CORYLOPHIDAE (kôr-il-of'-i-dē)
MINUTE HOODED AND FUNGUS BEETLES

The common name "minute hooded beetles" is derived from their small size and the broad, shelflike anterior margin of the pronotum projecting over the head of many species and concealing it from view above. Most adult and larval corylophids eat the spores and hyphae of molds and other microfungi. They are typically found under bark, on leaf surfaces, and in accumulations of decaying plant material. *Orthoperus* feeds on mold, while *Sericoderus* has been found on various gilled fungi. *Arthrolips* and *Orthoperus* have also been recorded feeding on bracket fungi. *Clypastraea* live among fungi and mold in rotten wood and under the bark of dead trees. Adults of *Aenigmaticum californicum* Casey have been found on the inflorescences of an unidentified flower.

FAMILY DIAGNOSIS Adult corylophids in western North America are very small, mostly elongate-oval or elongate (*Aenigmaticum*), and somewhat flattened. Head often obscured from view above by front margin of pronotum. Clubbed antennae with 9–11 antennomeres, last three forming distinct club. Pronotum with anterior margin completely covering head, or emarginate with head exposed (*Aenigmaticum*), and anterior angles absent or not produced anteriorly. Procoxal cavities closed behind. Elytra often truncate apically and exposing pygidium, with sutural stria present and variable in length. Front coxal cavities closed. Tarsi 4-4-4, with simple claws. Abdomen with six ventrites free, ventrite 1 usually longer than 2.

SIMILAR FAMILIES Many families have species with similar body form, but none have the pronotum extending over the head *and* distinctly clubbed antennae. *Aenigmaticum californicum* resembles a very small Latridiidae (p.311), but has tarsi 4-4-4.

COLLECTING NOTES Look for corylophids under bark, on flowers and foliage, and in accumulations of rotting vegetation, including leaf litter, haystacks, cut grass, root masses, dead twigs and branches, and the moldy remains of tent caterpillar nests.

FAUNA 61 SPECIES IN 10 GENERA

Sericoderus lateralis Gyllenhal (0.7–1.1 mm) is oval, pubescent, and shiny pale yellowish or reddish brown, with appendages yellowish. Head with eyes prominent, with antennomeres 8–10 forming dusky club. Pronotum convex, somewhat produced in front, not semicircular, broadest across sinuate posterior margin, with disc impunctate with anterior medial infuscation, margins sharp and not explanate, and acute posterior angles acute, projecting beyond margin. Scutellum large with apex rounded. Elytra broad, not much longer than pronotum, with sutural striae distinct, and apices each broadly truncate. Tarsi slender on both sexes. Associated with damp molds (*Mucor*, *Penicillium*) and fungus in vegetable debris and under bark. Cosmopolitan. (3)

315

ENDOMYCHIDAE (en-dō-mik'-i-dē)
HANDSOME FUNGUS BEETLES

Endomychid adults and larvae feed on softer fruiting bodies, microhyphae, or spores of many kinds of fungi, especially macro-Basidiomycetes. They are typically found in fungus-infested microhabitats in decaying wood, beneath logs, and on or beneath bark. The larvae of *Lycoperdina ferrugineus* LeConte are specialists that feed inside of *Apioperdon* puffballs. Although *Aphorista morosa* (LeConte) has been found in association with a yellow plasmodium, there is no evidence that they or any other endomychids feed on slime molds. *Lycoperdina ferrugineus* engages in reflex-bleeding when alarmed, secreting a noxious fluid from the leg joints as a defensive measure, as do lady beetles (Coccinellidae, p.318).

FAMILY DIAGNOSIS Adult endomychids are distinguished by a pair of distinct longitudinal sulci that flank the midline of the pronotum and a frontoclypeal suture. They are broadly rounded, oval, or elongate-oval, and sometimes moderately flattened. Head prognathous with eyes set on sides. Antennae with 11 antennomeres, 9–11 forming loose club. Procoxal cavities open behind. Elytra are irregularly punctured, sometimes setose, and completely conceal abdomen. Tarsi usually 4-4-4, sometimes with tarsomere 3 minute, or 3-3-3, and tarsomeres simple or 1–2 strongly bilobed beneath, and usually simple claws. Abdomen with five or six ventrites free, with first ventrite long.

SIMILAR FAMILIES

- minute bark beetles (Cerylonidae, p.309)—last palpomere small or pointed apically, elytra almost always with rows of punctures
- lady beetles (Coccinellidae, p.318)—antennae not as distinctly clubbed, pronotal sulci lacking
- pleasing fungus beetles (Erotylidae, p.435)—front angles of pronotum not extended forward, elytra with rows of punctures, tarsi appear 5-5-5
- some leaf beetles (Chrysomelidae, p.501)—tarsi apparently 4-4-4, but actually 5-5-5

COLLECTING NOTES Look for handsome fungus beetles on fungi on or under bark on snags and logs, especially at night, or by sifting through rotten wood and leaf litter. A few species are captured in Malaise traps or attracted to lights.

FAUNA 33 SPECIES IN 15 GENERA

Epipocus unicolor Horn (5.5–8.0 mm) is elongate-oval, shiny, alutaceous, uniformly reddish brown, and sparsely clothed in long suberect tawny pubescence. Head densely and coarsely punctured. Pronotum wider than long, anterior margin deeply emarginate with angles obtuse, lateral margin rounded in front of and sinuate behind middle, with hind angles acute and discal punctures coarse and sparse between moderately deep and slightly convergent sulci, becoming finer and denser laterally. Abdomen with six ventrites. Male with small interior spur below middle of front tibia. Adults under bark and damp logs, attracted to lights. Arizona to Colorado and New Mexico, south to Mexico. (6)

Aphorista laeta LeConte (5.3–7.8 mm) is elongate-oval, sparsely pubescent, shiny, and light reddish brown; antennae and elytral disc bluish black. Pronotum wider than long, disc finely and sparsely punctate, broadly impressed before middle, anterior margin deeply emarginate with stridulatory membrane, lateral margin beaded and rounded in front of and sinuate behind middle, with two small discal black spots, and posterior margin deeply impressed between deep longitudinal sulci. Elytra with pale margins narrow laterally, broader and irregular basally. Abdomen with five ventrites. Protibia dentate on inner margin at middle (male), or not (female). Adults under bark. British Columbia to California, east to Idaho and Wyoming. (2)

Aphorista morosa (LeConte) (6.2–7.2 mm) is reddish brown, with appendages, pronotal margins, humeri, epipleura, and abdomen lighter. Anterior pronotal margin deeply emarginate with stridulatory membrane, with acute angles, lateral margin beaded and rounded in front of and sinuate behind middle, and posterior margin deeply impressed between deep longitudinal sulci; prosternum not extended posteriorly, coxae globular and narrowly separated. Elytral punctures confused. Abdomen with five ventrites. Small protibial spine on inner margin at about apical third (male). Oregon to California, east to Colorado and New Mexico. (2)

Lycoperdina ferruginea LeConte (4.5–6.0 mm) is oblong-oval, shiny dark reddish brown to nearly black, pronotal disc and elytra sometimes darker. Pronotum with disc alutaceous and finely punctate, anterior margin with stridulatory membrane, and posterior margin deeply impressed between moderately impressed longitudinal sulci; prosternum not extended posteriorly, coxae subcylindrical and contiguous. Antennae with last two antennomeres abruptly widened and flattened. Abdomen with five ventrites. Mostly brachypterous adults are specialist feeders on pear-shaped puffballs, *Apioperdon pyriforme* (Lycoperdales); also attracted to lights and cantharidin traps. British Columbia, Alberta, and Montana; widespread in eastern North America. (1)

Mycetina idahoensis Fall (3.8–4.5 mm) is elongate-oval, shiny black with four orangish-red spots on elytra. Pronotum with lateral margins behind middle straight. Elytra somewhat coarsely punctate, more broadly oval, each with larger triangular humeral spot and smaller transversely oval subapical spot. Posterior tibia of male dilated at apical one-third. Abdomen with five ventrites. Adults found under bark. British Columbia to California, east to Idaho and Montana. *Mycetina hornii* Crotch (3.0–4.0 mm) is similarly marked, with elytra more finely punctate and narrowly oval, and posterior tibia of male not dilated apically. Coast Ranges and Sierra Nevada of central California. (2)

317

Phymaphora californica Horn (3.4–3.6 mm) is oblong and somewhat oval, shiny pale or dark reddish brown and black, and fine punctures with short, inconspicuous setae. Antennal club with four antennomeres greatly modified (male) or somewhat expanded (female); male antennal club equal in length to funicle. Pronotum wider than long, broadest at anterior one-third, lateral margin sinuate before acute posterior angles, and posterior margin deeply impressed in between longitudinal carinae, with median longitudinal infuscation on disc. Elytra broadest about middle, with variable dark suture and broad, black fascia across middle and apices. Abdomen with five ventrites. Southwestern British Columbia to California, east to Nevada. (1)

MYCETAEIDAE (mi-sē-tē'-i-dē)

HAIRY CELLAR BEETLES

The hairy cellar beetle, *Mycetaea subterranea* (Fabricius), is found in cellars, granaries, and warehouses in moldy stored grain products, as well as in tree holes and bird nests. Although sometimes considered a minor pest, it is likely that they feed only on mold and not on the spoiled grain.

FAMILY DIAGNOSIS Adult mycetaeids are elongate-oval, convex, clothed dorsally in long, suberect, pale setae, and light to dark brown with appendages lighter. Head prognathous, with eyes placed on sides, and mentum with small triangular setose tubercle medially. Pronotum with prominent and complete sublateral carinae. Procoxal cavities open behind. Elytra completely cover abdomen. Legs with tarsi 4-4-4, with tarsomere 3 clearly visible. Abdomen with five ventrites free, and first ventrite longer.

SIMILAR FAMILIES The combination of elongate-oval shape, vestiture, sublateral pronotal carinae, and tarsal formula are distinctive.

COLLECTING NOTES Adults and larvae found among moldy stored products, and in bird nests, old tree trunks, caves, and beehives.

FAUNA ONE SPECIES, *MYCETAEA SUBTERRANEA*

Hairy Cellar Beetle *Mycetaea subterranea* (Fabricius) (1.5–1.9 mm) is elongate-oval, moderately strongly convex, coarsely punctate, and moderately clothed in pale pubescence consisting of long erect and short recumbent setae. Antennae clavate, club with three antennomeres. Pronotum wider than long, broadest across middle, with lateral margins strongly arcuate, and strong and complete sublateral carina closer to margin posteriorly than anteriorly. Elytra with setae on intervals longer than those on striae. Adults and larvae feed upon moldy stored products in granaries, mills, warehouses, and basements; also found in association with old tree trunks, caves, and beehives. Adventive species from Europe, widely distributed in North America. (1)

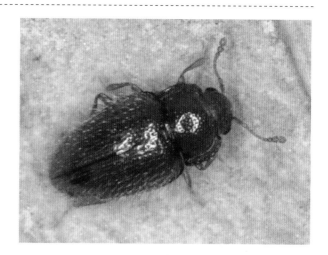

COCCINELLIDAE (kok-si-nel'-i-dē)

LADY BEETLES

Coccinellids, also known as "ladybugs," are among the most familiar and beloved of all insects. They are surprisingly diverse in their feeding habits as adults, ranging from insect predators and fungivores to plant feeders. Most species typically prey on plant pests in the order Hemiptera, especially aphids, psyllids, scale insects, and mealybugs. Prey preferences are determined primarily by nutritional requirements for completing their development and may be influenced by season. Some of these predatory species are generally considered among the most beneficial of insects, and several are commonly reared and released as biological control agents to combat aphids and scales. In the absence of suitable prey, some of these predators will also eat pollen, nectar, or fungi. Species in the genus *Epilachna*, however, are exclusively phytophagous, feeding on the leaves of cucurbits and solanaceous plants, and thus are sometimes considered agricultural and garden pests. *Psyllobora* species are fungivores and consume

318

powdery mildews. Some coccinellids, such as the convergent lady beetle (*Hippodamia convergens* Guérin), are known for their complex periodic migratory and aggregation behaviors associated with food-induced *diapause*. They exhibit seasonal shifts in food preference, switching from aphids to pollen or nectar, and gather in small summer or large winter aggregations in the mountains, such as the Sierra Nevada and Transverse Ranges of California. The bright and contrasting patterns of spots or stripes of many coccinellids serve as aposematic or warning colors that advertise the presence of repellent chemicals in their bodies. The defensive release of yellowish fluid from their femorotibial joints, or "knees," containing bitter-tasting alkaloids is known as reflex bleeding and renders these beetles distasteful to their attackers, especially ants.

FAMILY DIAGNOSIS Many adult coccinellids are conspicuously marked in red and black and are typically oval to elongate-oval, and weakly convex to strongly hemispherical in profile. Head usually prognathous, sometimes hypognathous (Chilocorini), and shallowly or deeply inserted within prothorax. Antennae clavate with 7–11 antennomeres, ending in a loose or compact club. Prothorax convex, wider than long, with lateral margins carinate. Procoxal cavities usually closed behind. Scutellum small and triangular. Elytra without punctostriae, covering abdomen entirely. Underside flat. Tarsi usually 4-4-4, but may appear 3-3-3. Metasternum with or without postcoxal line. Abdomen with five to seven ventrites free, first ventrite with or without complete postcoxal line (absent in *Coleomegilla*).

SIMILAR FAMILIES

- marsh beetles (Scirtidae, p.114)—antennae filiform or serrate
- round fungus beetles (Leiodidae, p.137)—antennae capitate, elytra often striate
- minute fungus beetles (Corylophidae, p.314)—antennae capitate
- handsome fungus beetles (Endomychidae, p.315)—front angles of pronotum distinctly pointed forward
- pleasing fungus beetles (Erotylidae, p.435)—antennae capitate
- shining flower beetles (Phalacridae, p.456)—antennae capitate, tarsi appear 4-4-4, but are 5-5-5, no distinct markings on the elytra, ventrites without lines
- leaf beetles (Chrysomelidae, p.501)—tarsi appear 4-4-4, but are 5-5-5

COLLECTING NOTES Search for lady beetles on herbaceous plants, shrubs, and trees, especially those infested with sap-sucking aphids and scales. Sweeping and beating these plants will reveal a diversity of taxa. A few species are attracted to lights.

FAUNA ~500 SPECIES IN 60 GENERA

Microweisea misella (LeConte) (0.9–1.5 mm) is small, slightly elongate, oval, convex, without pubescence on upper surface, completely dark brown or black; appendages slightly paler. Head finely wrinkled, not set deep inside prothorax; antennal club with three antennomeres. Pronotum strongly punctured with line just inside front angles. Flight wings present. Tarsi 3-3-3. Adults active spring and summer, and prey on armored scales (Diaspididae) on various trees and shrubs. Across southern Canada and most of United States, except Southwest and peninsular Florida. *Microweisea suturalis* (Schwarz) (1.0–1.1 mm) with head and pronotum dark, elytra light yellowish brown except for narrowly dark suture; southern California. (2)

Chilocorus cacti (Linnaeus) (4.0–6.2 mm) is somewhat elongate-oval, not strongly convex, smooth, and shiny black except for a large transverse red spot on each elytron. Underside with thoracic sterna and abdomen yellow or red. California and Nevada east to Florida; widespread in New World. Adults and larvae prey on scale insects on cactus and other plants. *Chilocorus fraternus* LeConte (3.4–4.5 mm) and *C. orbus* Casey (4.0–5.1 mm) similar, and shiny black except abdomen yellow or red; both species Washington to California and separable only by examination of male genitalia. (7)

Cryptolaemus montrouzieri Mulsant (3.4–4.5 mm) is oval, convex, and bicolored with head, prothorax, and apices of elytra reddish yellow, rest of body black or blackish. Head underneath with mouthparts and antennae covered by thoracic plate. Antennomeres 8–10 forming club. Legs with tibial spurs absent, tarsi 3-3-3, claws with broad basal tooth. Abdomen underneath with curved lines on first ventrite reaching sides. Adults and larvae prey primarily on scale insects. A native of Australia, established in California and southern Florida, and patchily distributed in eastern United States. (1)

Scymnus nebulosus LeConte (2.0–2.5 mm) is elongate-oval, convex, plain pale reddish brown to yellowish brown with small dark irregular infuscations, occasionally pronotum and part of elytra black, and moderately clothed in pale pubescence. Head finely punctured, punctures separated by their own diameters or less, and eyes pubescent. Antennae with 10 antennomeres, club uneven on lower margin. Pronotal punctures slightly coarser than head. Elytra smooth, shiny, and broad apically, with punctation much coarser than on pronotum, with pubescence arranged in S-pattern. Underside with pterothoracic and abdominal segments black. British Columbia to southern California, east to Idaho. *Scymnus difficilis* Casey (1.7–2.1 mm) evenly narrowed anteriorly and posteriorly, elytra unmarked; California. (101 NA)

Adalia bipunctata (Linnaeus) (3.5–5.2 mm) is slightly elongate-oval, weakly convex, and mostly red or black with variable maculations pattern. Pronotum wide, covering part of eyes, with medial M or broad macula in dark forms, and arcuate posterior margin without bead. Elytral pattern with one or two medial spots, or diffuse to moderate or heavy transverse markings. First ventrite with postcoxal line complete. Femora not extending beyond sides, middle and hind tibiae tipped with pair of spurs, and tarsal claws each with a quadrate basal tooth. Adults and larvae are aphid and adelgid predators. Europe; established throughout North America; also temperate South America. (1)

Anatis lecontei Casey (7.7–10.5 mm) is broadly oval, orangish red with distinct black markings on pronotum. Pronotum black with white lateral stripes just inside lateral margins, often with two posteromedial spots, and a posterior marginal bead. Elytra immaculate with broadly explanate lateral margins black and distinctly angulate in front of middle, angulations maculate. Underside with prosternum strongly convex medially and protuberant apically. Claws with somewhat quadrate basal tooth. British Columbia to Idaho and California, east to Alberta, Montana, Colorado, and Texas. (3)

Anatis rathvoni (LeConte) (7.5–10.2 mm) is broadly oval, yellowish to red with distinct black markings on pronotum and elytra. Pronotum black with broad white lateral stripes and two posteromedial spots, with posterior marginal bead. Elytra with black spots faintly ringed, lateral margins broadly explanate and distinctly angulate before middle, angulations maculate. Underside with prosternum strongly convex medially and protuberant apically. Claws with somewhat quadrate basal tooth. British Columbia to northern California, east to Saskatchewan. *Anatis mali* (Say) (7.3–10.0 mm) with elytra margins weakly explanate and not angulate, dark elytral spots distinctly ringed with white or yellow. Alaska to Oregon, east Ontario and Virginia. (3)

Calvia quaturodecimguttata (Linnaeus) (4.0–5.5 mm) is oval, not strongly convex, shiny, with extremely variable color pattern; bold dark spots on pale, or pale spots on dark background. Head with eyes partly covered in front with canthus, front corners of clypeus produced forward. Pronotum without any trace of finely wrinkled sculpturing, base without fine groove or bead along margin. Middle and hind tibiae tipped with pair of spurs, tarsal claws each with a quadrate basal tooth. Adults and larvae prey on aphids and psyllids. Holarctic; Alaska, across Canada and northern half of United States. (1)

Coccinella californica (Mannerheim) (5.1–6.8 mm) has nearly immaculate elytra. Head black with two distinct pale spots. Pronotum black with rectangular pale anterolateral patches. Elytra red with basal transverse pale areas flanking small scutellar black spot, and narrowly dark brown to black suture. First ventrite with incomplete postcoxal line. Legs black, with middle and hind tibiae with two apical spurs. Coastal British Columbia to southern California. Resembles immaculate *C. novemnotata* Herbst (4.7–7.0 mm), a widely distributed species that is broadly white between eyes; *C. johnsoni* Casey also similar, but has maculate elytra; coastal Alaska to southern California. (13)

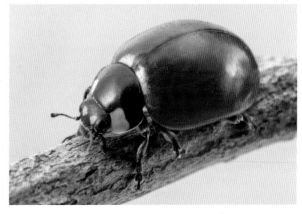

Coccinella monticola Mulsant (5.2–7.0 mm) is broadly oval, convex, and with variable elytral maculations. Head black with two distinct pale spots. Pronotum black with trapezoidal pale anterolateral patches. Elytra red with basal pale areas flanking scutellum, large postscutellar black spot, each with variably heavy markings, medial lateral and discal maculations sometimes coalescent. First ventrite with incomplete postcoxal line. Legs black, with middle and hind tibiae bearing two apical spurs. Widely distributed in western Canada and United States, also northeastern United States. (13)

Seven-spotted Lady Beetle *Coccinella septempunctata* **(Linnaeus)** (6.5–7.8 mm) is broadly oval and convex. Head black with two distinct white spots. Pronotum black at middle of anterior margin with pale, somewhat triangular spots under anterior angles. Elytra red with seven black spots, including shared spot on scutellum. First ventrite with incomplete postcoxal line. Legs black, with middle and hind tibiae bearing two apical spurs. Adults found on vegetation and occasionally at lights. Europe; widespread across southern Canada and throughout the United States. Nine-spotted lady beetle, *C. novempunctata* Herbst (4.7–7.0 mm), is a seldom-seen native species, usually with four black spots on each elytron, plus shared spot. (9)

Coleomegilla maculata strenua (Casey) (6.4–7.0 mm) is somewhat elongate and flattened. Head black with pale triangular patch on front. Pronotum yellowish or pinkish with a pair of large triangular spots and fine posterior marginal bead. Elytra pink or red with six black spots, median spot large, with apical spots touching sutural margin. Underside and legs black, except for yellowish prosternum and lateral abdominal margins. Mesosternum and first ventrite lacking postcoxal lines. Claws with subquadrate basal tooth. Adults on vegetation in spring and summer, where they prey on aphids and eat pollen. Southern California to southern Texas. (1)

Cycloneda polita Casey (3.5–6.2 mm) with anterior pronotal margin completely white with median extension tapering posteriorly in both sexes, and lateral white circles complete or broken. Elytra usually red with pale area, if present, restricted to semicircular spot adjacent to scutellum and not reaching humeri, and somewhat horizontal epipleurae weakly concave. Hind legs black with femoral and tibial apices, tibial base, and tarsi pale. Southern Canada and western United States. *Cycloneda sanguinea* (Linnaeus) (3.2–6.5 mm) nearly circular, with lateral pronotal spot enclosed, and epipleura distinctly concave and steeply descending externally. Southern California to Texas. (2)

322

Multicolored Asian Lady Beetle *Harmonia axyridis* **(Pallas)** (4.8–7.5 mm) is oval, convex, and incredibly variable in elytral color and pattern. Pronotum white with up to five black spots often joined to form an M-shaped mark or a solid trapezoid. Elytra red or orange, each with up to 10 black small or large spots in fully marked individuals, or black with 2–4 red spots, or some other variation; side margin distinctly beaded and not translucent. Sometimes considered a nuisance when they gather on or enter homes and outbuildings in late fall and winter. Adults found year-round on trees and shrubs; attracted to lights. Eurasian; established throughout North America. (2)

Convergent Lady Beetle *Hippodamia convergens* **Guérin** (4.3–7.3 mm) is somewhat elongate-oval. Clypeus with anterolateral angles produced, eyes notched by canthus, and antennae with 11 antennomeres. Pronotum with elongate pale spots converging posteriorly, pale borders along sides more or less even, and base black. Elytron with six small, discrete spots usually present, sometimes reduced in number or absent; margins weakly reflexed along sides. Legs with femur visible beyond elytron and claws cleft. Adults form summer or winter aggregations in mountains. Common across southern Canada and United States. (17)

Hippodamia parenthesis **(Say)** (3.7–5.6 mm) is elongate-oval with black head variably marked with pale spots and antennae with 11 antennomeres. Black pronotal maculation nearly divided basally by white trapezoidal spot. Elytra with black triangular postscutellar spot, humeral spots, and bold, curved apical maculae never reaching suture, each sometimes reduced or broken into two spots. Claws cleft. Widespread. *Hippodamia apicalis* Casey (3.5–4.7 mm) with curved apical spots always crossing suture at apex. British Columbia to southern California, east to Montana and New Mexico; sympatric with *H. expurgata* Casey (3.5–5.0 mm) in Rockies, best distinguished by examining male genitalia. (17)

Hippodamia tredecimpunctata tibialis **(Say)** (4.5–6.4 mm) is elongate-oval, somewhat flattened, glabrous, and shiny red with black maculae. Head mostly black with frons pale, brown clypeus with anterolateral angles produced, eyes notched by canthus, and antennae with 11 antennomeres. Pronotum completely black medially, or with black area broken anterolaterally. Elytron with seven discrete black spots, with scutellar and postscutellar spots sometimes confluent. Mesepimeron entirely yellow. Hind femora visible beyond elytral margins. Middle and hind tibiae each with two apical spurs. Tarsi appear 3-3-3, actually 4-4-4, with claws cleft. Widely distributed in Canada and United States.

Mulsantina picta (Randall) (3.3–5.3 mm) has an M-shaped pattern on pronotum and a stripe down each elytron. Head is yellow with pair of black spots flanking clypeus, each narrowly connected to black top of head. Pronotum distinctively patterned with spot on each side connected to middle black M-shaped mark, all of which are sometimes broken up into smaller spots. Elytral markings vary from heavily marked to no marks at all. Middle and hind tibiae without apical spurs. A predator of adelgids, aphids, and scales, especially those on fir (*Abies*) and pine (*Pinus*). Across Canada and contiguous United States. (3)

Myzia interrupta (Casey) (6.5–8.0 mm) is pale yellowish brown, with brown appendages. Head immaculate. Pronotum immaculate, or with three light brown spots basally. Elytron with three brown stripes often reduced, with lateral margin weakly explanate and rounded apically. On conifers. British Columbia to California, east to Alberta, Nebraska, and western Texas. *Myzia subvittata* (Mulsant) (5.7–8.0 mm) pronotum usually black or brown medially, with broad white lateral borders, elytra with margins broadly explanate in front of middle and acutely tapered apically; British Columbia to California, east to Saskatchewan, Idaho, and Nevada. (2)

324

Ashy-gray Lady Beetle *Olla v-nigrum* (Mulsant) (3.7–6.2 mm) is nearly circular in outline when viewed from above, very convex, and shiny. Two distinct color forms include dorsum mostly black with a large reddish-orange spot on each elytron, or pale grayish yellow with black spots, sometime with basal spots reduced and a large spot just behind middle; dark form predominates in East. Elytra with lateral margins weakly explanate. Legs with middle and hind tibiae each with pair of apical spurs, and all claws with large, subquadrate basal tooth. Adults active spring and summer and prey on aphids in several genera. North America south to Argentina. (1)

Paranaemia vittigera (Mannerheim) (4.5–6.6 mm) is elongate-oval, somewhat flattened, yellowish or reddish dorsally with bold black markings and stripes. Head black with narrow medial stripe. Pronotum with pair of more or less triangular maculations. Elytra with three black stripes. Underside black, except for yellow prosternum. Legs black with middle and hind tibiae each with two apical spurs, femur clearly visible beyond elytral margin, and claws widened basally and not toothed. Metasternum lacking postcoxal line, apical margin ridged and weakly emarginate; first ventrite without postcoxal line. Alberta to Oregon and California, east to Colorado, western Texas; also Mexico. (1).

Psyllobora borealis Casey (2.4–3.1 mm) is similar to *P. vigintimaculata* (below), but more robust. Appendages pale. Head pale with black or brown markings on vertex and front, and black before anterior pronotal margin. Pronotum with four black or pale brown spots. Elytra with spots usually black, humeral spot in contact with basal spot or not, submedian spot on suture distinct from subapical spots, and lateral subapical spot free or narrowly connected to large inner spot. Southern British Columbia to California, east to Montana, Colorado, and New Mexico. (3)

Twenty-spotted Lady Beetle *Psyllobora vigintimaculata* **(Say)** (1.7–3.0 mm) is elongate-oval and pale with black and/or brown markings and spots. Head pale with dark spot in front of anterior pronotal margin. Pronotum always with four dark spots. Elytral pattern variable, usually with nine black spots more or less confluent on a pale background, subapical lateral spot small, narrowly separated from or joined to apical spots; California populations mostly or completely with brown spots. Adults found on vegetation in spring and summer. Some species of *Psyllobora* feed on fungus, especially powdery mildews, e.g., *Erysiphe*. Alaska, southern Canada, and throughout United States into Mexico. (3)

Hyperaspis octonotata Casey (2.3–3.5 mm) is round, convex, with very distinctive pronotal and elytral markings. Antennae with 11 antennomeres. Pronotum black with lateral margins broadly yellowish and anterior margin black (female) or yellowish (male). Elytra each with four reddish maculations, anterior margin of discal spot oblique or emarginate. Postcoxal line is evenly curved throughout and not reaching hind margin of first abdominal sternum. Strictly predators of soft scale insects (Coccidae) and mealybugs (Pseudococcidae). California to Colorado and Texas. (56)

Vedalia Beetle *Rodolia cardinalis* (Mulsant) (2.6–4.2 mm) is somewhat elongate-oval, convex, moderately clothed in suberect setae, and red with bases of head, pronotum, and scutellum black. Head with labrum flat and slightly emarginate anteriorly. Elytra broadest at middle with lateral margins almost parallel, each with two black maculations, and suture variably black with median diamond-shaped pattern sometimes in contact with maculations. Underside of meso- and metathorax dark, as are femora and median area of ventrites 1–2; line behind hind coxae complete. An Australian species famously introduced into California in 1888 to control a citrus pest, the cottony cushion scale (*Icerya purchasi*). California. (1)

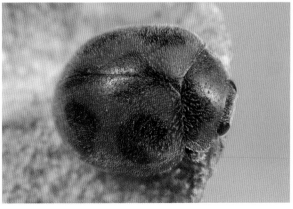

Epilachna tredecimnotata (Latreille) (6.7–10.1 mm) is broadly oval, convex, moderately pubescent with short recumbent setae, and shiny yellowish orange to orange with 14 spots on elytra and yellowish appendages. Head and pronotum unmarked. Elytra each marked with three rows of variable and usually distinct dark spots, anterior and middle rows with three spots, and apex with a single large spot; no spots in contact with suture. Legs entirely yellow. Adults and larvae feed on leaves of plants related to melons and squash (Cucurbitaceae). Arizona to Colombia and Venezuela. (1)

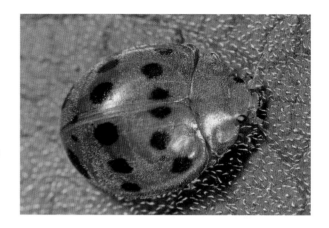

MYCETOPHAGIDAE (mī-sē-tō-faj'-i-dē)
HAIRY FUNGUS BEETLES

Adult and larval mycetophagids, including species of *Mycetophagus*, feed on fungi and are usually found under bark, on mushrooms and shelf fungi, and in moldy, plant-based substrates. The hairy fungus beetle, *Typhaea stercorea* (Linnaeus), and *Litargus balteatus* LeConte, both cosmopolitan species widely established in North America, are frequently found indoors in association with moldy stored plant products. Adults of *Berginus pumilus* LeConte are recorded on the flowers of dodder (*Cuscuta*) and elderberry (*Sambucus*).

326

FAMILY DIAGNOSIS Most adult mycetophagids are oblong to somewhat ovate, slightly flattened, clothed in pubescence, and dark brown, sometimes with orange or yellowish markings on elytra. Head with eyes strongly protuberant and coarsely faceted. Clavate antennae with 11 antennomeres, terminal three to five antennomeres forming loose club. Pronotum with lateral margins carinate, as broad as elytra basally, and usually with a pair of depressions at posterior margin. Procoxal cavities open behind. Scutellum visible. Elytra punctostriate with intervals rugulose, combined apices rounded, and completely covering abdomen. Tarsi 4-4-4, sometimes 3-4-4 (males), with claws simple. Abdomen with five ventrites free.

SIMILAR FAMILIES

- small carrion beetles (Leiodidae, p.137)—weak antennal club with antennomere 8 smaller than 7 and 9
- variegated mud-loving beetles (Heteroceridae, p.242)—antennae filiform or serrate
- minute brown scavenger beetles (Latridiidae, p.311)—prothorax narrower than elytra
- fruitworm beetles (Byturidae, p.410)—color uniform; tarsomeres 2–3 distinctly lobed
- silken fungus beetles (Cryptophagidae, p.449)—colors different, pronotum usually widest at middle

COLLECTING NOTES Look for hairy fungus beetles under fungal-bearing bark, and in moldy plant debris and stored food products. *Berginus pumilus* occurs on flowers. Some species are also attracted to lights.

FAUNA 26 SPECIES IN FIVE GENERA

Berginus pumilus LeConte (1.5–2.0 mm) is elongate-oval, weakly convex, roughly sculptured dorsally, clothed in pale, curved, and recumbent setae and somewhat shiny reddish brown to black with purplish luster. Head with eyes prominently convex, antennae with 11 antennomeres, 10–11 forming club. Pronotum as long as wide or wider, with longitudinal impressions on each side. Elytra wider than prothorax, broadest behind middle, and punctostriate, with punctures coarse and in rows confused by transverse rugae, each with five rows of reddish, scalelike pubescence arising from weak costae sometimes rubbed off. Adults on flowers, including dodder (*Cuscuta*) and elderberry (*Sambucus*). Coastal southern California and Baja California Peninsula. (1)

Litargus balteatus LeConte (1.7–2.4 mm) is oval to elongate-oval, moderately convex, and brownish black or dark with variable pale markings on pronotum and elytra, pronotal punctures weakly raised and annulate, and elytra yellowish brown with incomplete brownish-black band. Antennomeres 9–11 forming club, 11 elongate, as long as 9–10 combined. Densely punctate pronotum with pair of weak and somewhat arcuate subbasal impressions. Elytra with variable undulating medial fascia and apices dark, and paler areas clothed in paler pubescence. Cosmopolitan; widespread in North America. *Litargus nebulosus* LeConte with antennomere 11 slightly longer than 10. Utah to New Mexico, east to Québec, Virginia, and Florida. (2)

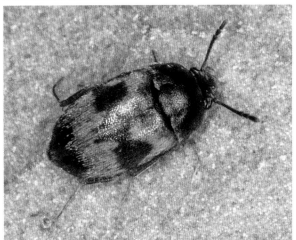

Mycetophagus pluriguttatus LeConte (4.3–4.8 mm) is elongate-oval, moderately convex, and sparsely clothed in short recumbent setae, with dorsal punctures moderately coarse, deep, and moderately dense. Pronotum broadest behind middle, with anterior angles broadly rounded, lateral margins evenly arcuate and weakly convergent posteriorly, and subbasal impressions short and distinct, and evenly distributed punctures moderately coarse and deep. Elytra with punctostriae not very evident; often with pale humeral, post-humeral, post-medial maculations; individuals from coastal populations may have only a pair of subapical spots. Adults found under bark on rotten logs. British Columbia to California, east to Montana and Idaho. (8)

Hairy Fungus Beetle *Typhaea stercorea* (Linnaeus) (2.2–3.2 mm) is oblong-oval, moderately convex, uniformly dull reddish yellow with black eyes, and moderately densely pubescent. Head across eyes narrower than pronotum; antennal club with three antennomeres. Pronotum widest across basal third with posterior angles distinct. Elytra sometimes darker, with fine, erect, yellowish setae. Front tarsi with three (male) or four (female) tarsomeres. Adults and larvae found on moldy stored foods and other decaying organic materials. Adults attracted to lights. Europe, nearly cosmopolitan; widely distributed in North America. (1)

ARCHEOCRYPTICIDAE (ar-kē-ō-krip-tis'-i-dē)
ARCHEOCRYPTICID BEETLES

Adults and larvae are usually found in leaf litter and other plant debris. Adults are collected in rotting flowers in Panama and from wood-rotting fungi in Australia. One species extracted from leaf litter samples at high elevations in southern Mexico, *Enneboeus marmoratus* Champion, was recently discovered in the San Francisco Bay region in California and appears to have become established. Given their preference for moist organic debris, it is possible that these saprophagic or mycophagous beetles were transported in potted plants, possibly in the larval or pupal stages.

FAMILY DIAGNOSIS Adult archeocrypticids in North America are small, oval, moderately to strongly convex, and sparsely clothed in fine, recumbent setae. Antennae clavate with 11 antennomeres with 9–11 forming club. Underside of prothorax with intercoxal processes that extend posteriorly partially closing coxal cavities. Scutellum visible. Elytra with punctostriae distinct or not. Legs moderately long with tarsi 5-5-4, and claws simple. Abdomen with five ventrites, 1–2 free.

SIMILAR FAMILIES
- *Hyporhagus* (Zopheridae, p.344)—ventrites 1–4, connate
- some darkling beetles (Tenebrionidae, p.347)—prothorax without process underneath, partially closing coxal cavities; antennal club large
- some pleasing fungus beetles (Erotylidae, p.435)—antennae capitate

COLLECTING NOTES Archeocrypticids are extracted from leaf litter and other vegetable debris using Berlese funnels and Winkler extractors. They are also attracted to lights at night.

FAUNA TWO SPECIES IN ONE GENUS

Enneboeus marmoratus Champion (3.5–4.0 mm) is elongate-oval, moderately convex, mostly black with diffuse reddish markings, undulating setal pattern on elytra, and reddish-brown appendages. Prothorax with pronotum twice as wide as long, with lateral margins broadly arcuate; male prosternum with medial sex patch consisting of small, round pit containing setae near anterior margin. Elytra with reddish patches on humeri and apical margins, and punctostriae extremely faint. Adults found in moist leaf litter, also attracted to lights at night in summer. (1)

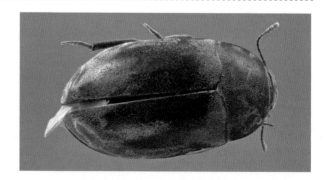

CIIDAE (sī'-i-dē)
MINUTE TREE-FUNGUS BEETLES

Adult and larval ciids are all mycophagous and feed on the fruiting bodies of woody or fibrous wood-rotting fungi growing on logs and stumps, especially in jelly (*Auricularia*), polypore (*Fomes, Ganoderma, Phellinus, Trichaptum*), false turkey tail (*Stereum*), and turkey tail (*Tramea*) fungi. Most species feed on relatively few species, while a few may consume a wider variety of fungi. *Hadraule blaisdelli* (Casey), a widespread species with diverse food preferences, occasionally attacks fungal specimens prepared for scientific study, and thus sometimes considered an herbarium pest. For ciids with known habits, pupation usually occurs within the host fungus, but *Sphindocis denticollis* Fall apparently pupates in the wood of madrone (*Arbutus menziesii*) beneath the sporophores of *Antrodea favescens*. Dried fungi prepared in Asia and imported into the United States for commercial use as food and medicine are occasionally infested with ciids.

FAMILY DIAGNOSIS Adult ciids are small, elongate to oval, convex, cylindrical, with the head more or less hidden from above. Head slightly deflexed with moderately protuberant eyes. Antennae short, with 8–10 antennomeres, last 2–3 forming a loose symmetrical club. Pronotum not or slightly narrower than elytra. Procoxae open or closed behind. Scutellum visible, sometimes reduced. Elytra not striate, and clothed in erect setae. Tarsi 4-4-4, tarsomeres simple, without membranous lobes, tarsomere 3 shorter than 4, with simple protarsal claws. Abdomen with five ventrites, with ventrites 1–2 free (Ciinae) or connate (Sphindociinae).

SIMILAR FAMILIES
- branch and twig borers (Bostrichidae, p.295)—antennal club asymmetrical
- death-watch beetles (Ptinidae, p.299)—antennal club asymmetrical
- cryptic slime mold beetles (Sphindidae, p.434)—elytra coarsely punctostriate
- bark beetles (Curculionidae, p.539)—antennal club large, apparently with one antennomere

COLLECTING NOTES Ciids are commonly found in tunnels chewed into their host fungi. They are easily reared from infested fungi.

329

FAUNA 84 SPECIES IN 13 GENERA

Sphindocis denticollis Fall (3.7–4.0 mm) is elongate, parallel-sided, slightly flattened, distinctly and uniformly punctate dorsally, seemingly glabrous with very minute setae, and shiny reddish brown. Head with prominently convex eyes. Antenna with 11 antennomeres, 9–11 forming club. Pronotum wider than long, with lateral margins broadly arcuate, reflexed, and crenulate, each with several round denticles, with disc densely punctate. Elytra barely wider than prothorax, lateral margins somewhat parallel until apical two-fifths, with apex evenly rounded. Abdomen with ventrites 1 and 2 connate. Adults and larvae associated with fruiting bodies of *Poria* and *Antrodea* fungi. Coastal forests of northern California. (1)

Ceracis californicus (Casey) (1.2–2.1 mm) ranges from uniformly black, black with some red on anterior pronotal margin and elytral apices, to all reddish brown, with paler appendages. Antennae with nine antennomeres. Pronotum not distinctly narrowed anteriorly, and anterior margin with weakly to strongly produced converging, parallel, or diverging lamina with two distinct teeth or horns in male. Elytra with two sizes of coarse and distinct punctures usually separated by less than their own diameters. Adults on various basidiomycete fungi, including *Bjerkandera*, *Coriolus*, *Funalia*, and *Ganoderma*. Washington to California, east to Nebraska and New Mexico, and south to Mexico; also in Northeast. (4)

Hadraule blaisdelli (Casey) (less than 1.5 mm) is elongate, somewhat parallel-sided, and flattened, with head and pronotum light reddish brown, and elytra dark brown. Antennae with nine antennomeres, club with two antennomeres, and first club antennomere barely longer than preceding antennomere. Pronotum slightly wider anteriorly, broadest at anterior quarter, with lateral margins straight and narrowly explanate, barely visible from above; prosternum twice as long in front of coxae than intercoxal process. Elytra darker than pronotum. Adults on various polypore fungi, including *Coriolus* and *Ganoderma*; occasionally an herbarium pest. British Columbia to California, east to Utah and Texas, south to Mexico; scattered records in Northeast. (1)

Plesiocis cribrum Casey (1.8–3.5 mm) is short, stout, convex, with pronotum and elytra coarsely punctate and clothed in short, stout, bristly setae, and reddish brown or paler. Frontoclypeal ridge of male bearing four sharp teeth, with medial teeth widely separated. Antennae with nine antennomeres. Anterior pronotal margin of male produced and emarginate to form a pair of horns or tubercles. Elytra uniformly, coarsely, and densely punctate, and clothed in short, stout bristles. Outer apical angle of front tibia produced and dentate. Adults on polypore fungi in coniferous forests. Across North America and throughout West. (1)

TETRATOMIDAE (tet-ra-tom'-i-dē)
POLYPORE FUNGUS BEETLES

Tetratomids are diverse in appearance and challenging to characterize as a family. Both adults and larvae feed on the softer fruiting bodies of Hymenomycetes fungi growing on decaying wood, especially shelf fungi (Polyporaceae) and pale-spore mushrooms (Tricholomataceae). Larvae bore into fresh or decaying sporophores, while the nocturnal adults are usually found on the surfaces of fungi and dead wood.

FAMILY DIAGNOSIS Adult tetratomids are oblong to ovate, somewhat flattened, and pubescent with notched eyes. Clavate antennae with 11 antennomeres, with apical three to four antennomeres forming loose club, and antennal insertions slightly hidden or visible from above. Prothorax wide, broader than head, and nearly as wide as elytra. Scutellum visible. Elytra completely covering abdomen. Front coxae separated by prosternal process. Procoxal cavities broadly or narrowly open behind. Tarsi 5-5-4, with tarsomeres slender and not lobed underneath, tarsomere 1 long, and simple claws. Abdomen with five ventrites, with 1–2 free or connate.

SIMILAR FAMILIES

- plate-thigh beetles (Eucinetidae, p.112)—hind coxal plates covering part of abdomen, tarsi 5-5-5
- hairy fungus beetles (Mycetophagidae, p.326)—tarsi 4-4-4, 3-4-4
- false darkling beetles (Melandryidae, p.333)—middle tibia as long as femur or first tarsomere, if shorter then spurs at least one-third length of tibia
- comb-clawed beetles (Tenebrionidae: Alleculinae, p.365)—claws pectinate

COLLECTING NOTES Look for tetratomids at night on fungi and on or under bark of fungus-ridden logs and stumps. Some species are captured in Lindgren funnels set in forested habitats, or are attracted to lights.

FAUNA 26 SPECIES IN 10 GENERA

Tetratoma concolor LeConte (3.2–4.2 mm) is oblong-oval, parallel-sided, convex, finely and sparsely pubescent, and shiny yellowish brown to brownish black with reddish tinge, with legs, bases of antennae, and underside somewhat lighter. Head finely punctured, eyes well developed and emarginate in front. Antennomeres 8–11 abruptly dilated, forming loose club, with 8–10 transverse. Pronotum wider than long, sides arcuate, converging anteriorly, and narrowly margined, with posterior angles rounded and obtuse, and posterior margin sinuate with a pair of distinct basal impressions. Elytra confusedly and coarsely punctate. Abdomen with first ventrite about as long as 2–3 combined. Alaska and across Canada, south to California, Colorado, and Arizona. (1)

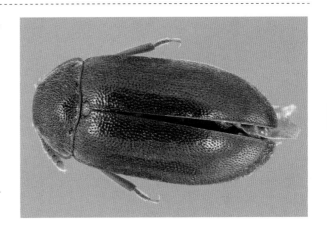

Triphyllia elongata (LeConte) (3.7–4.8 mm) is oblong-oval, parallel-sided, densely punctate, sparsely clothed in fine recumbent pubescence, and brownish black with reddish tinge, with head and pronotum darker. Head finely punctate, with antennomeres 9–11 abruptly transverse, forming loose, parallel-sided club. Pronotum wide and convex, lateral margins arcuate, crenulate, broadly explanate and reflexed, and impressed at posterior third, with posterior angles somewhat rectangular. Elytra at base slightly wider than prothorax, coarsely and confusedly punctate. Ventrites gradually and uniformly decreasing in length posteriorly, with 1 scarcely longer than 2. Adults associated with fungus (*Laetiporus conifericola*) growing on conifers. Alaska to California. (1)

Hallomenus scapularis Melsheimer (4.0–5.0 mm) is elongate, oblong, densely clothed in yellowish setae, and dark reddish brown to blackish with legs and basal angles of elytra yellowish or reddish yellow. Eyes with deep notches distant from antennal bases. Antennomeres short, slightly expanded outward, 3–10 almost equal in length. Pronotum densely punctured with a pair of deep depressions at base. Elytra not striate. Legs with tibial spurs very short. Adults active in summer in coniferous and deciduous forests, found under bark of dead pine (*Pinus*), on pine strobili, and on polypore fungi. Across Canada, in West south to California and New Mexico. (3)

Eustrophopsis arizonensis (Horn) (5.8–7.8 mm) is clothed dorsally in short setae, and uniformly dark dorsally, with underside lighter. Head with eyes moderately widely separated, antennomeres 5–10 broad, 1–4 and 11 light to dark reddish. Pronotum with pair of basal impressions; hypomeron rugosely punctate. Elytra punctostriate. Middle and hind tibiae with oblique, comblike ridges. Montana and South Dakota south to Oaxaca. *Eustrophopsis bicolor* (Fabricius) (4.2–6.5 mm) with antennomeres 5–10 longer than wide, and underside of prothorax relatively smooth. Widespread, most common in East. Both species on polypores and under loose bark of fungus-infested logs. (7)

332

Eustrophus tomentosus Say (4.5–6.0 mm) is dark brown with appendages lighter, with golden sheen produced by short, dense pubescence on pronotum and elytra. Eyes widely separated. Antenna with sensilla interrupted, not ringlike. Pronotum with two somewhat linear impressions basally. Middle and hind tibiae with numerous oblique comblike ridges, and tarsi slender and simple. Nocturnal adults on conifer and hardwood stumps and fungus, or under bark; also at lights. Across North America; in West from British Columbia to California, east to Montana, Utah, and Arizona. (1)

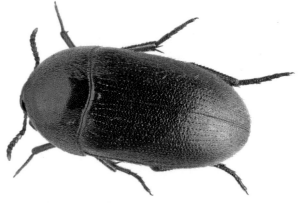

Synstrophus repandus (Horn) (5.6–7.0 mm) is clothed in long conspicuous pubescence, and uniformly blackish brown to black dorsally, with underside slightly lighter. Head with eyes narrowly separated, almost contiguous. Antennae with basal four antennomeres dark reddish brown and distal half of 11 reddish. Pronotum with two somewhat linear impressions basally. Elytra distinctly punctostriate, with punctures coarse. Middle and hind tibiae without oblique ridges, but with scattered spines. Tarsi slender and simple. Nocturnal adults on dead wood and fungus. Widely distributed in North America, more common in East. (1)

MELANDRYIDAE (mel-an-drī'-i-dē)
FALSE DARKLING BEETLES

Little has been published on the biology of North American Melandryidae, especially those species that inhabit the West. Melandryids are found exclusively in forested habitats where the feeding habitats of the larvae are divided into two general categories: those that develop in fungal bodies, and those that develop in rotten soft or hard fungus-infested wood. For example, the larvae of the transcontinental *Orchesia castanea* (Melsheimer) develop in fungi in the genera *Coriolus* and *Lenzites* in eastern North America. The larvae of another transcontinental species, *Melandrya striata* Say, develop in rotting logs of deciduous trees. Species of *Enchodes* are known to develop in hardwood logs with white rot, but adults of the transcontinental *E. sericea* (Haldeman) are found at night on dead or dying conifers. In Europe, species of *Phryganophilus* are usually associated with fungus-infested deciduous trees, but one species may also utilize both hardwoods and conifers. Adults of *Rushia californicus* Fall & Cockerell are also associated with conifers, specifically dead *Pinus* logs. *Serropalpus* larvae prefer the hard wood of recently dead or dying trees, especially fir (*Abies*) and spruce (*Picea*).

FAMILY DIAGNOSIS Adult melandryids in western North America are elongate-slender to elongate-oval. Head moderately hypognathous. Antennae with 11 antennomeres, moniliform or filiform to serrate, with insertions visible from above. Prothorax with lateral margins complete or not. Procoxal cavities open or closed behind. Middle tibia as long as femur or tarsomere 1, or shorter with long tibial spurs one-third or more of length of tibia. Tip of maxillary palp usually large and hatchet- or knife-shaped. Elytra completely covering abdomen. Tarsi 5-5-4 in both sexes, with tarsomeres narrow, or with penultimate tarsomere expanded ventrally, and claws simple or with basal tooth (*Osphya*). Abdomen with five ventrites, with 1–2 connate.

SIMILAR FAMILIES
- ground beetles (Carabidae, p.88)—tarsi 5-5-5
- polypore fungus beetles (Tetratomidae, p.330)—

tarsomeres not lobed underneath; procoxae separated by process
- tumbling flower beetles (Mordellidae, p.336)—humpbacked, abdomen pointed
- comb-clawed beetles (Tenebrionidae, p.365)—pronotum without pits, claws pectinate
- false flower beetles (Scraptiidae, p.408)—head not fitting into prothorax, sometimes with fine, transverse strigae across pronotum and elytra

COLLECTING NOTES Adults are found under loose bark of snags and stumps. They are also found on fresh or decaying fungi or fungus-infested logs at night; some species are regularly attracted to lights. Take note of fungal masses, well-rotted tree holes, dying trees, and snags during the day and revisit these sites at night to search for adults. Melandryids are also captured in Malaise and Lindgren funnel traps.

333

FAUNA 50 SPECIES IN 24 GENERA

Phloiotrya riversi (LeConte) (9.0–11.0 mm) is elongate, narrow, moderately convex, and densely and rugosely punctate, clothed in short pubescence, and reddish brown with appendages somewhat lighter. Head convex, with antennomere 3 as long as 1 and 2, slightly shorter than 4. Pronotum about as long as wide, lateral margins narrowed almost from base to anterior margin, with posterior angles broadly rectangular, and weakly depressed. Elytra not striate, each with three costae faintly indicated. Middle and hind tibial apices squarely truncate and all claws simple. Adults in decaying hardwoods, including madrone (*Arbutus*), and at lights. Washington and Idaho to California. Genus needs revision. (1)

Emmesa testacea testacea Van Dyke (8.0–9.6 mm) is sparsely clothed in short golden pubescence, and yellowish brown with head and pronotal disc black, with outer antennomeres, femora, and underside reddish or brownish black. Vertex depressed. Pronotum broadest at or behind middle. Elytra broadest behind middle, without costae, with apices rounded. On California live oak (*Quercus agrifolia*). *Emmesa t. leeperi* Mäklin refers to uniformly black individuals in northern parts of range. British Columbia and Alberta to northern California. *Emmesa stacesmithi* Hatch with vertex not depressed, and costate elytra. British Columbia. (2)

Melandrya striata Say (7.0–15.0 mm) is elongate-oblong, shiny black, somewhat flattened with elytra striate. Head with eyes vaguely emarginate in front. Antennae reddish brown. Pronotum narrowed toward head with pair of depressions, posterior margin extending loosely over elytra. Elytra coarsely, setigerously punctate, setae dark and recumbent, with at least seven raised intervals. Penultimate tarsomere with short lobe underneath, claws simple. Larvae develop in deciduous logs. Flight wasplike. Adults hide under bark; found in Malaise, Lindgren, and flight intercept traps. Across southern Canada and eastern United States. (1)

Phryganophilus collaris LeConte (10.0–15.0 mm) is black, with pronotum, save for a pair of discal spots, red. Head and pronotum closely punctate. Pronotum broadest just behind middle, with two broad impressions on each side, narrowly and shallowly impressed middle before posterior margin, and basal margins and posterior angles broadly rounded. Elytral surface densely covered with minute punctures and tubercles bearing inconspicuous decumbent setae. Claws simple. Found in coniferous forests. Transcontinental; in West from British Columbia to northern California and Idaho. (1)

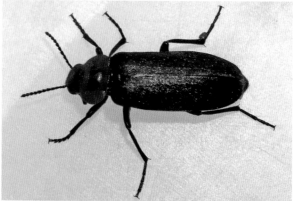

Prothalpia holmbergii (Mannerheim) (3.6–6.1 mm) is clothed in long, recumbent, yellowish setae, yellowish brown to dark brownish black, with three to four strongly sinuate transverse fascial elytra that are sometimes partly confluent. Head nearly black, and finely punctate. Antennomere 3 less than twice length of 2. Pronotum and elytra coarsely and densely punctate. Pronotum broadest just before middle, with rectangular posterior angles flanking a pair of distinct basal impressions and sinuate posterior margin; coxal cavity with outer fissure. Elytra at base broader than prothorax, and yellowish brown with variegated dark markings. Claws simple. Alaska to northern California. (1)

Orchesia castanea (Melsheimer) (4.0–5.8 mm) is elongate, convex, clothed in fine brown pubescence, and uniformly dark chestnut brown with appendages lighter. Head with eyes narrowly separated. Pronotum wider than long and more coarsely and densely punctured at base, basal impressions shallow. Elytra more densely punctured and pubescent at base. Legs with hind tibiae tipped with very long spurs at least one-third length of tibiae, and claws simple. Adults found in summer on vegetation and logs infested with fungi; also at lights. Will jump while attempting to escape. British Columbia; also Newfoundland to South Carolina, west to Manitoba, Indiana, and Texas. (2)

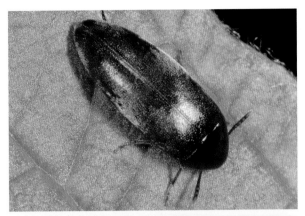

Enchodes sericea (Haldeman) (11.0–15.0 mm) is elongate, slender, tapering toward rear, densely clothed in fine yellowish pubescence, and uniformly brown; appendages paler. Pronotum about as wide as long, with side margins rounded, hind angles prominent, with shallow triangular depression on each side at base. Elytra smooth, shiny, without punctostriae, finely punctate, and evenly tapered from base to tip. Claws simple. Fleet-footed. Nocturnal adults active in summer, found on dead, rotten conifer and hardwood limbs, snags, logs, and trunks, or beaten from dead limbs; also attracted to lights. Across Canada, south to Georgia, Louisiana, and North Dakota. (1)

Serropalpus substriatus Haldeman (9.0–14.0 mm) is very elongate, slightly flattened dorsally, densely clothed in short golden pubescence, and brown with appendages reddish. Head finely and densely punctured, and antennae long, slender, and extending to middle of elytra in male. Maxillary palps with last three palpomeres triangular and serrate. Prothorax long and laterally carinate. Elytra finely punctured, punctures becoming coarser basally and granulate behind humeri, and shallowly striate. Middle and hind tibiae with comblike ridges, and pretarsi expanded in male. Larvae in dead conifers. Adults at lights. Western North America; also in Northeast. (3)

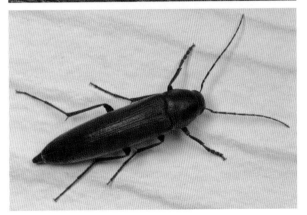

Xylita laevigata (Hellenius) (6.3–8.4 mm) is elongate, densely and rugosely punctate or granulose, and clothed in short decumbent pubescence. Usually with head and prothorax brownish black, with mouthparts, elytra, abdomen, and appendages reddish brown. Head and pronotum rugosely punctate, with terminal maxillary palpomere long, narrow, bladelike. Pronotum broadest about middle, with lateral margins obsolete anteriorly, and posterolateral areas flattened. Elytra granulose, usually without dark sutural streak or lines of punctures. Claws simple. On fungi on conifers, and at lights. Holarctic; in West from Alaska south to Oregon and Idaho. (3)

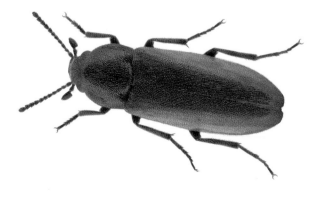

Osphya lutea (Horn) (8.0–10.5 mm) is elongate, clothed in short, recumbent setae, and shiny and uniformly yellowish or reddish brown, with appendages and underside lighter. Filiform antennae long. Apical maxillary palpomeres knife blade-shaped. Prothorax nearly as long as wide. Male with hind femora enlarged, and without abdominal processes. Middle tibia as long as either femur or first tarsomere, tarsomere 3 distinctly lobed, lobes extending beneath 4, claws with large basal tooth. Adults attracted to lights. Southern California. *Osphya essigi* Van Dyke (7.0 mm) distinctly bicolored with head, elytra, and abdomen mostly brownish black, and male with spiny processes on ventrites 1 and 2. Central California. (2)

MORDELLIDAE (môr-del'-i-dē)
TUMBLING FLOWER BEETLES

Tumbling flower beetles are aptly named. When threatened, they rapidly kick their hind legs back and forth, causing them to bounce and tumble unpredictably, or quickly take flight. Mordellids are small, mostly black, sometimes distinctly patterned, wedge-shaped beetles commonly found on flowers, often in great numbers in spring and summer. Adults apparently feed on pollen and nectar of a variety of plants, especially those in the families Apiaceae and Asteraceae. There appears to be little relationship between adult feeding preferences and larval food plants. Herbivorous larvae (Mordellisteni) feed inside the living stems of plants, while others (Mordellini) are saproxylic and bore into compact substrates such as galls, decaying wood, and fungi. Nearly three-quarters of the mordellids known in North America are in the genus *Mordellistena*.

FAMILY DIAGNOSIS The humpbacked and wedge-shaped body form, with elongate and narrow abdomen extending well beyond elytra, and jumping behavior of adult mordellids are distinctive. Adults are mostly black, sometimes with distinct patterns of setae. Head hypognathous and large, nearly as wide as and lying flush against anterior of prothorax. Antennae with 11 antennomeres, antennomeres serrate, clavate, or filiform. Pronotum small, narrowed toward head, with distinct lateral margin. Procoxal cavities broadly open behind. Scutellum visible. Elytra smooth and narrowed behind and completely conceal all but part of the last abdominal segment; surface clothed in fine setae and frequently patterned with lighter-colored setae to form lines, bands, or spots. Pygidium long, slender, and stylelike. Hind legs long, tarsi 5-5-4, claws equal and toothed; outer surface of hind tibiae and first two or three tarsomeres often with distinct ridges. Abdomen with five ventrites free.

SIMILAR FAMILIES
- wedge-shaped beetles (Ripiphoridae: *Macrosiagon*, p.339)—last abdominal ventrite blunt
- false flower beetles (Scraptiidae, p.408)—abdomen not sharply pointed

COLLECTING NOTES Mordellids are wary and escape easily, but they can be picked from flowers by hand, scooped into a container, or collected with a sweep net. Malaise and flight intercept traps produce the greatest diversity of species, especially those that do not visit flowers. A few species are sometimes attracted to lights or to baited Lindgren funnel traps.

FAUNA 189 SPECIES IN 17 GENERA

Hoshihananomia perlineata (Fall) (4.0–4.5 mm) is elongate, moderately attenuate, dull black with grayish margins and stripes. Head broad, with glabrous, finely granulated eyes not reaching occiput, terminal maxillary palpomere broadly triangular, almost knife blade-shaped. Pronotum sometimes with pair of gray parallel stripes. Elytra somewhat flattened on disc, each with suture and four narrow stripes grayish, inner stripe extending only to about middle. Pygidium black with silvery pubescence at base. Underside black with variable bands of gray pubescence denser along sides and posterior margins of ventrites. Arizona and New Mexico. (1)

Mordella atrata Melsheimer (3.5–6.0 mm) is wedge-shaped, robust, clothed dorsally in brownish or slightly grayish black pubescence, and black with tinge of iridescence. Setose eyes large, round, finely granulated, and reaching occiput. Pronotum wide, broadest before posterior margin, slightly broader than elytra at base, with disc finely punctured. Elytral surface reticulate, moderately punctured. Underside brownish to nearly black, with sides and anterior margins of ventrites, and base of anal style with silky grayish setae. Adults on flowers. Pacific Northwest to eastern United States. *Mordella hubbsi* Liljeblad (5.0–6.5 mm) similar, front and middle femora, except for apices, reddish. British Columbia to California and Idaho. (11)

Glipostenoda ambusta (LeConte) (6.7–7.7 mm) is elongate, somewhat parallel, moderately robust, finely punctate, clothed in fine decumbent pale setae, and reddish brown, sometimes with head and pronotum darker, with eyes and some tibial ridges black. Head with setose eyes entire and convex. Pronotum almost as long as wide, finely and completely margined, with sides and angles rounded, and median posterior lobe short and rounded. Elytra long, each with apices rounded. Hind tibia slightly shorter than tarsomeres 1 and 2 combined, middle and hind tibiae with long, oblique ridges, hind tarsomere 1 with three or four ridges, 2 with two or three ridges. Pacific Northwest east to Ontario, Georgia, and Alabama. (1)

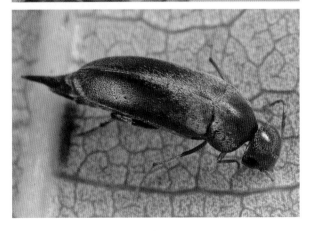

Mordellina pustulata (Melsheimer) (2.5–5.5 mm) is elongate, and mostly dull black with numerous spots of silvery gray pubescent spots interspersed with dark brown pubescence on pronotum and elytra. Pronotum slightly wider than long, finely punctured, and median lobe on posterior margin round and not prominent. Elytra with silvery spots sometimes forming narrow broken bands. Hind legs with tibiae and tarsomere 1 each with three oblique and parallel ridges, tarsomere 2 with two ridges. Larvae reared from branches of ragweed (*Ambrosia*) and cocklebur (*Xanthium*); adults on vegetation, occasionally attracted to lights. Washington to California, east to Idaho and Arizona; widespread in eastern United States. (3)

Mordellochroa scapularis (Say) (4.0–5.8 mm) is dull black, elytra with yellow or reddish-yellow humeral spots not reaching scutellum. Femora black, while tibiae, tarsi, and last abdominal ventrite somewhat reddish yellow. Remaining abdominal ventrites reddish yellow to nearly black. Adults active during summer in woodlands, wet forests, and stands of red spruce (*Picea rubens*). Adults on flowers, such as hawthorn (*Crataegus*) and oaks (*Quercus*). Transcontinental in Canada, south Minnesota, Illinois, and Oklahoma. (1)

RIPIPHORIDAE (rip-if-ôr′-i-dē)
RIPIPHORID BEETLES

Information on the lives of ripiphorids is fragmentary. The short-lived adults are usually found resting on low grasses or in mating swarms on flowers, and their feeding habits are unknown. The mouthparts of adult *Macrosiagon* are greatly prolonged, suggesting they feed on nectar, while the less-developed mouthparts of *Ripiphorus* indicate that they probably do not feed at all. The bipectinate antennae of male ripiphorids suggest they track females emitting sexual pheromones. Nothing is known about the life cycle of *Ptilophorus*. All known larvae are parasitoids of other insects and develop by hypermetamorphosis. *Macrosiagon* larvae parasitize wasps in several families of aculeate Hymenoptera, including Vespidae, Sphecidae, Crabronidae, Tiphiidae, Pompilidae, Apidae, and Halictidae. Species in the genus *Ripiphorus* lay eggs on flowers; the hatching triungulins use their mandibles to attach themselves to solitary bees gathering pollen and are carried back to the bee's nest.

FAMILY DIAGNOSIS Adult ripiphorids in western North America are elongate-oval (*Ptilophorus*), humpbacked, and wedge-shaped, with black and orange, red, or yellow coloration (*Macrosiagon*), or flylike (*Ripiphorus*). Head hypognathous and strongly deflexed. Antennae with 11 antennomeres (10 in some *Ripiphorus* females), antennomeres flabellate, pectinate, or serrate; male antennae typically more elaborate than female and may be biflabellate or bipectinate. Pronotum large, bell-shaped, narrowest behind head, and with lateral margins not carinate. Procoxal cavities broadly open behind. Scutellum visible (*Ptilophorus*), highly modified (*Ripiphorus*), or completely or partly covered by extended margin of the pronotum (*Macrosiagon*). Elytra smooth, cover abdomen entirely (*Ptilophorus*, *Macrosiagon*), with apices sometimes acute and somewhat dehiscent (*Macrosiagon*), or scalelike (*Ripiphorus*). Legs slender, tarsi 5-5-4, hind tibiae never with ridges or spines before tip, claws equal, comblike or toothed. Abdomen with five ventrites free.

SIMILAR FAMILIES

- twisted-winged parasites (Order Strepsiptera)—
  male eyes stalked, elytra short and knoblike,
  abdomen pointed
- false darkling beetles (Melandryidae, p.333)—
  antennae filiform or slightly clubbed
- tumbling flower beetles (Mordellidae, p.336)—elytra
  cover most of the abdomen, antennae filiform or
  serrate, last abdominal ventrite acutely pointed

COLLECTING NOTES Although they may be quite abundant locally, ripiphorid beetles are rare in collections partly because of their short flight period. Collecting the fast-moving adults by hand can be challenging. Sweep or examine flowers and low vegetation closely on late spring and summer days. Females are often seen on flowers with blossoms attractive to bees and wasps, especially buckwheat (*Eriogonum*), milkweed (*Asclepias*), and various asters. Malaise and flight intercept traps may yield additional specimens, especially of those species that do not frequent flowers.

FAUNA 51 SPECIES IN SIX GENERA

Ptilophorus wrightii **(LeConte)** (6.0–9.0 mm) is clothed in short and pale recumbent setae, and blackish brown with appendages, elytra, and abdomen more or less brown. Vertex raised slightly above pronotal margin. Eyes distinctly divided into dorsal and ventral lobes connected by a thin strip. Antennae pectinate (male) or serrate (female). Pronotum narrowed anteriorly, with posterior margin bisinuate and flanked by acute posterior angles. Elytra gradually converging posteriorly to round apex. Internal margin of distinctly expanded metatibial apex deeply incised. Adults on grass and other vegetation. Colorado to southern Arizona, east to Oklahoma and Texas. (1)

Macrosiagon cruenta **(Germar)** (5.0–8.0 mm) with head and thorax variably red and black. Vertex broadly rounded with anterior surface flat or slightly concave. Bipectinate antennae well developed in male. Posterior pronotal margin with narrow median lobe extending over scutellum not elevated or cup-shaped. Elytra almost cover abdomen, dehiscent at apical third, and red or black basally and apically. Abdomen black (male), red (female), or both. Front coxae not separated by spine and nearly contiguous; hind tarsomere 2 longer than 3. On flowers. Southern California east to Saskatchewan, Indiana, New Jersey, and Florida. Genus needs revision. (11 NA)

Macrosiagon flavipennis **(LeConte)** (7.0–11.0 mm) is narrowly wedge-shaped, with black head and thorax. Head and thorax black. Vertex with distinct concavity on front of elevation. Antennae bipectinate and yellowish brown (male), or pectinate and black (female). Pronotum with distinct elevated process on posterior median lobe. Elytra yellow and narrowly dark at base, with (female) or without (male) black apices, and apices dehiscent at about middle. Flight wings more or less brown. Abdomen black (male) or red (female). Tibial spines sharp. Southern California to eastern United States. Genus needs revision. (11 NA)

Macrosiagon pectinata species complex (3.5–8.0 mm) are variable, head and thorax red to black. Vertex rounded and slightly convex in front, and occiput without distinct suture. Antennae pectinate (female) or bipectinate (male). Pronotum with posterior medial process not elevated. Elytra pale with basal and apical markings sometimes coalescent with median spots. Hind tarsomeres 1 and 2 not produced, 2 shorter than 3. Eastern California eastward. *Macrosiagon sayi* (LeConte) and *M. octomaculata* (Gerstaecker) similar, both with vertices flattened or slightly convex, and hind tarsi with apices of tarsomeres 1 and 2 produced or not, respectively. Southern California eastward. (11 NA)

Ripiphorus rex Champion (8.0–11.0 mm) is wedge-shaped, robust, with erect and suberect yellow pubescence, and black with yellow-brown markings. Head with antennae pectinate (female) or biflabellate (male). Prothorax mostly shiny black, finely and irregularly punctured. Elytra short, scalelike, with interior margin sinuate, and mostly yellow-brown with narrowly black bases. Abdomen strongly curved, with tergites narrowly pale and ventrites narrowly black. Legs stout, mostly pale, apices and terminal tarsomeres sometimes dark, with middle tibia serrate, and apex of hind tarsomere 1 obliquely truncate, and claws pectinate. Adults on *Baileya* and other asters. Southern California east to Utah and New Mexico. Genus needs revision. (36 NA)

ZOPHERIDAE (zof-êr′-i-dē)
ZOPHERID BEETLES

When disturbed, adult zopherids often feign death by drawing in their appendages and remaining motionless. *Hyporhagus*, *Usechus*, *Usechimorpha*, *Phloeodes*, and *Zopherus* all possess sulci on the hypomera to receive their antennae. Wing reduction or loss is common and species in the tribes Phellopsini, Usechini, and Zopherini are all flightless. *Phloeodes* and *Zopherus* have incredibly tough exoskeletons and are sometimes called ironclad beetles. Recently, the exoskeleton of *Phloeodes diabolicus* (p.345) has been the subject of intense study by materials scientists attempting to understand the physical properties of these seemingly crush-proof and impenetrable beetles. Adult *Phellopsis*, *Phloeodes*, and *Zopherus* all occur in a variety of woodland, forest, and desert habitats, where they are found under bark on dead, fungus-infested logs and stumps of various deciduous and coniferous trees. Their lightly armored and short-legged larvae are adapted for boring into reasonably sound dead trunks and root crowns infested with white-rot fungi. *Hyporhagus* adults and larvae are found in association with decaying yucca stalks, Joshua trees, and cacti. Adult colydiines enter logs and stumps through preexisting insect tunnels or cracks resulting from injury or desiccation. Flattened species are usually encountered in dead wood, under loose bark, or tunneling in rotten or sound logs and stumps of various conifers or hardwoods. Adults of *Bitoma*, *Namunaria*, and *Synchita* are collected on fruiting bodies of wood-rotting Basidiomycetes. Cylindrical species (e.g., *Aulonium*, *Colydium*) follow the tunnels of bark and ambrosia beetles (Curculionidae) where the adults feed on rotten wood and cambial tissue, but the larvae of *Aulonium longum* LeConte prey on the larvae of *Dendroctonus* bark beetles. Early instars of *Lasconotus subcostulatus* Kraus feed primarily on fungi, yet the third-stage larvae also switch to carnivory and prey on the larvae and pupae of *Ips* bark beetles (Curculionidae). Species of *Colydium* are recorded to prey on bark beetles, too, but more study is needed to confirm their predatory behavior.

FAMILY DIAGNOSIS Adult zopherids are elongate, cylindrical to flattened and parallel-sided or oval (*Hyporhagus*), usually brown or black, with or without subtle patterns of yellow, red, or gray vestiture. Head prognathous, visible from above with eyes usually entire, sometimes shallowly or deeply notched by canthus. Antennae with 9–11 antennomeres, bases concealed from above by anterior margin of head, clavate to capitate with club formed by two or three sometimes fused antennomeres. Pronotum square, elongate or transverse, margins explanate, smooth, finely toothed, or elaborately produced, and hypomeron with or without antennal sulci. Procoxal cavities open or closed behind. Scutellum visible or not. Elytra more or less parallel-sided, completely concealing abdomen; surface sculptured with tubercles, rows of deep punctures, or well-defined carinae, or smooth and oval (*Hyporhagus*). Legs short, slender, tarsi 4-4-4 or 5-5-4 (*Phellopsis*, *Phloeodes*, *Usechimorpha*, *Usechus*, *Zopherus*), with simple claws equal in size. Abdomen with five ventrites; first two, three, or four ventrites mostly connate and separated by indistinct sutures.

SIMILAR FAMILIES
- wrinkled bark beetles (Carabidae, p.88)—antennae moniliform
- lyctine powderpost beetles (Bostrichidae, p.299)—mandibles prominent from above
- root-eating beetles (Monotomidae, p.438)—elytra do not cover tip of abdomen
- silvanid beetles (Silvanidae, p.451)—antennae filiform, tarsi 5-5-5

- bothriderid beetles (Bothrideridae, p.306)—antennal insertions exposed, tarsi 4-4-4
- minute bark beetles (Cerylonidae, p.309)—elytra smooth and without vestiture
- some darkling beetles (Tenebrionidae, p.347)—prosternal process between coxae arched, procoxal cavities usually closed behind, antennae with 11 antennomeres, prothorax underneath without sulci to receive antennae, tarsi usually 5-5-4, sometimes 4-4-4; abdomen with ventrites 1–3 connate; many produce odorous defensive secretions
- ambrosia beetles (Curculionidae, p.539)—antennal club spherical, tarsi 5-5-5

COLLECTING NOTES Zopherid beetles are found year-round beneath the bark or on logs of dead pines (*Pinus*), oaks (*Quercus*), cottonwoods (*Populus*), and other trees with fungus-infested wood. Both *Phloeodes* and *Zopherus* are sometimes abundant in foothill and desert woodlands, where they are found walking on trails in oak woodlands or pine forests late in the afternoon or early evening during late spring and summer. Species in both genera are long-lived and easily kept in captivity on a diet of fungusy wood, apple slices, and oatmeal. *Hyporhagus* are found on rotting yucca stalks, Joshua trees, and cacti at night and are attracted to lights. Adult colydiines are typically found on or under bark, in the galleries of other wood-boring beetles, and occasionally at lights. Beating large dead branches and young dead trees, especially those covered with fungal growth, is also productive.

341

FAUNA 113 SPECIES IN 49 GENERA

Aulonium longum LeConte (4.2–5.5 mm) is strongly elongate, four times longer than wide, subparallel, subcylindrical, and uniformly dark reddish brown. Pronotum in front quarter with a pair of strongly raised knobs (males) and or low callosities (female). Elytra finely punctostriate, punctures dense, intervals finely and very densely punctate. Tarsi 4-4-4. Adults found year-round under bark of ponderosa (*Pinus ponderosa*) and other pines infested with bark beetles. Throughout western North America. (1)

Colydium lineola Say (3.0–7.0 mm) is very elongate and slender, somewhat cylindrical, and shiny reddish brown or blackish. Head with tip of labrum and clypeus setose. Pronotum one and a half times longer than wide, with narrow groove down middle, punctures elongate, and front wider than base. Elytra costate, all but outermost costae distinct all along their entire lengths. Tarsi 4-4-4. Adults found under bark and in tunnels of wood-boring beetles in hardwoods, occasionally pine (*Pinus*) and spruce (*Picea*), especially around base and exposed roots; sometimes attracted to lights. In western North America from British Columbia south to California and Arizona; also in East. (3)

Rhagodera tuberculata Mannerheim (7.0–8.0 mm) is elongate, widest across middle of elytra, and dull black and sparsely covered with elongate scales; often encrusted. Eleven antennomeres with scalelike pubescence, 3 as long as diameter of eye, 9–11 forming weak club. Pronotal disc with pair of median longitudinal carinae. Elytra each with three carinae, 1 and 3 prominent basally, 2 unbroken near apex; beginning at middle of penultimate ventrite, epipleural fold becomes a short, raised carina. Procoxal cavities narrowly open behind. Tarsi 4-4-4. Uncommon; under bark in wooded habitats. Southern California to southern Arizona. (3)

Bitoma ornata (**LeConte**) (2.0–3.0 mm) is elongate, subparallel, slightly less than three times as long as wide, flattened, sparsely pubescent, and black; only native western species with two well-separated red spots on each elytron. Head without distinct antennal grooves; antennae with 11 antennomeres, 10–11 forming abrupt club, 11 slightly narrowed. Pronotum with two pairs of full-length longitudinal carinae. Elytra with carinae moderately raised, sometimes without apical spots. Tarsi 4-4-4. Adults under bark of dead willows and maples in riparian habitats in spring and summer; in flood debris; at lights. Southwestern Oregon to Idaho, south to California, and Sonora. (3)

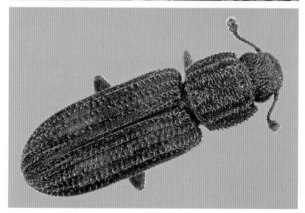

Coxelus serratus Horn (2.0–2.9 mm) is moderately elongate-ovate, dark brown to black, and without dorsal carinae. Pronotal and elytral discs without carinae. Antennae with 11 antennomeres, 10–11 forming distinct club. Pronotum strongly convex with lateral margins broadly explanate, procoxal cavities open behind. Elytra fused, punctostriate, punctures coarse. Tarsi 4-4-4. Uncommon, flightless adults found primarily in spring and summer under bark of dead Douglas-fir and sifted from deep litter of coastal redwood. Southern Coastal, Transverse, and Peninsular Ranges, California. (2)

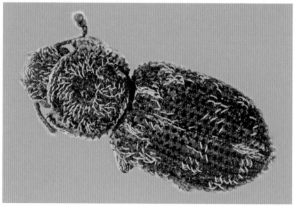

Denophloeus nosodermoides (Horn) (6.0–7.0 mm) is somewhat parallel and cylindrical, dull black, with short, curved pubescence sometimes encrusted. Antennae stout, thick and moderately clothed in setae, with 11 antennomeres, 9 barely reaching prosternal margin, 4–8 each moniliform, 9 wider than 8, 10–11 forming abrupt club, 11 narrowed. Pronotum with margins explanate, widest at apical quarter, with pair of undulating, blunt carinae on disc. Elytra with irregular, blunt, intermittent carinae, and without explanate lateral margins. Tarsi 4-4-4. Under loose bark of conifer stumps in spring and summer. Southern Oregon and northern California. (1)

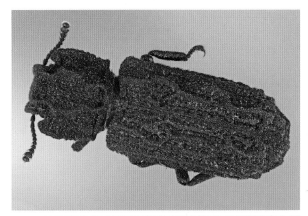

Lasconotus subcostulatus Kraus (2.5–2.8 mm) is elongate-oblong, reddish brown, with carinate pronotum and elytra. Eyes large. Antennae with 11 antennomeres, 9–11 forming distinct club. Pronotum subquadrate, slightly narrower than elytra, lateral margins somewhat parallel, and scarcely converging posteriorly, median impression without median carina, antennal grooves absent, and procoxal cavities closed behind. Elytra somewhat broad. Legs with protibial apices expanded; tarsi 4-4-4. Adults usually encountered in pines (*Pinus*) and spruce (*Picea*) infested with bark beetles. Widespread in western North America. (16)

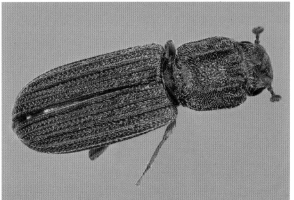

343

Megataphrus tenuicornis Casey (3.5–4.5 mm) is dark brown to black, often encrusted. Kidney-shaped eyes with fewer than 12 coarse facets. Antennomeres 10–11 forming distinct club, 11 subequal to eye. Antennal sulci on hypomeron sharply margined, procoxal cavities open behind. Elytra fused, each with three carinae topped with row of posteriorly curved setae, 1 ending near middle of declivity, 2 and 3 joined near apex, with interstriae striopunctate. Tarsi 4-4-4. Flightless adults sifted year-round from duff of redwood, fir, eucalyptus, laurel; also under bark of stumps. Southwestern Oregon to southern California. (3)

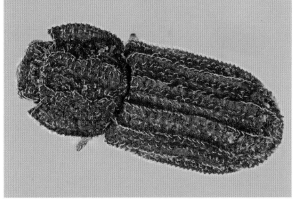

Microprius rufulus (Motschulsky) (3.2 mm) is elongate, somewhat flat, reddish brown, and clothed in minute setae. Head with eyes long and finely faceted; antennae with 11 antennomeres, 10–11 forming club, with long antennal groove. Pronotum with lateral margins parallel, narrowly explanate, and finely serrate; disc with network of connected bifurcating carinae. Elytra carinate, deeply punctate, with punctures regularly arranged in nine rows. Tarsi 4-4-4. Underside with procoxal cavities narrowly open behind and metacoxae narrowly separated. Adults found at lights and under bark of various trees. Old World species established in various habitats and likely to become widespread. Southern California; also Virginia. (1)

Namunaria pacifica (Horn) (4.0–5.0 mm) is elongate, somewhat flat, and black with margins lighter. Head with eyes prominent, finely faceted; antennae with 11 antennomeres, 10–11 forming club. Pronotum smooth, strongly convex, and slightly longer than wide with lateral margins broadly explanate and nearly parallel at middle; underside with antennal grooves short, as long as eyes. Procoxal cavities closed behind. Elytral surface with tufts of setae. Tarsi 4-4-4. Adults under loose bark of dead conifers and hardwoods. Southern British Columbia to central California. (1)

Hyporhagus gilensis Horn (4.5–7.5 mm) is compact, elongate-oval, dull black dorsally, with anterior pronotal, lateral pronotal, and elytral margins, and appendages dark red-brown. Capitate antennae with 10 antennomeres, 8–10 forming club. Pronotum broadest at base, anterior and lateral margins dark reddish brown. Elytra at base slightly wider than pronotum; disc finely punctostriate, with two striae closest to suture obsolete. Tarsi 5-5-4; male protarsomeres 1 and 2 dilated and densely pubescent underneath. Adults in rotting chaparral yucca (*Hesperoyucca whipplei*) stalks and on dead Joshua tree (*Yucca brevifolia*) trunks at night in summer; also at lights. Foothills on edge of Mojave Desert. (3)

Phellopsis porcata (LeConte) (12.0–18.0 mm) is elongate, parallel-sided, dull reddish brown to black, with dorsal surface covered with small, setose tubercles. Capitate antennae with 11 antennomeres, 9–11 forming club. Procoxal cavities narrowly open behind. Scutellum visible. Small elytral punctures obscured by thin, dense setae, with diameter of discal tubercles about half that of punctures. Tarsi 5-5-4, tarsi and claws simple. Adults under bark of large, fungus-infested coniferous logs and stumps year-round in old-growth coniferous forests. Larvae bore in soft wood, feeding on white sheet fungi. Alaska to southern California, east to Alberta, western Montana, and Idaho; isolated Nevada population requires study. (1)

Pycnomerus arizonicus Stephan (3.2–3.8 mm) is elongate-ovate, somewhat depressed, glabrous, and shiny reddish brown with head and pronotum slightly darker. Antennae with 10 antennomeres, 10 forming club; insertion and mandible not separated by carina. Scutellum visible. Elytra with intervals flat, apex rounded. Tibiae with outer apical angle forming tooth, coxae separated by their own width. Tarsi 4-4-4. Adults found under moist bar of rotting ponderosa pine (*Pinus ponderosa*), also at lights. *Pycnomerus quercus* Stephan (3.5–4.0 mm) similar, antennomeres 9–10 forming club, under loose, moist oak (*Quercus*) bark in wet mountain canyons. Both species in southeastern Arizona. (2)

Usechus lacerata Motschulsky (3.1–5.5 mm) is somewhat flattened, brown or blackish, and roughly sculptured with short, sparse, reddish or yellowish scalelike setae. Antennomeres 9–11 forming weak club. Sides of pronotum parallel behind middle, antennal grooves on anterolateral margins. Procoxal cavities narrowly open behind. Scutellum obscured. Elytra costate, interstriae with double rows of punctures, bases undeveloped. Tarsi 5-5-4. Under bark of fungus-infested oak (*Quercus*) and big-leaf maple (*Acer macrophyllum*) logs in moist coastal and inland forests. Northern and central California. *Usechus nucleatus* Casey (2.9–4.8 mm) similar, with basal elytral processes extending over pronotum. Washington and Oregon. (2)

Usechimorpha montanus Doyen (3.9–5.2 mm) is uniformly reddish brown and clothed in coarse golden setae. Head withdrawn into prothorax, antennal club distinct. Lateral pronotal margins angular medially, with antennal sulci reaching angles. Procoxal cavities broadly open behind. Scutellum obscured. Elytral interstriae 1, 2, and 4 regular and evenly setose. Tarsi 5-5-4. On western sulphur shelf (*Laetiporus gilbertsonii*) in coniferous forests of Sierra Nevada, California. *Usechimorpha barberi* Blaisdell (3.2 mm) with interstriae 1, 2, and 4 with dense, setose tubercles; Western Oregon, northern California. (2)

Phloeodes diabolicus (LeConte) (15.0–25.0 mm) is dull pale brown to gray-black dorsally. Antennomere 10 forming weak club. Prothorax narrowed behind; deep sulcus of hypomeron clearly defined posteriorly and completely contains antennae. Scutellum concealed. Elytra usually with arcuate velvety black patches; northern populations with pale, crusty vestiture apically. Legs lack rows of golden setae; tarsi 5-5-4 with narrowly glabrous strip ventrally. Nocturnal adults on logs and stumps, or beneath loose bark of decaying *Quercus*, *Populus*, *Platanus*, *Salix* during day. Woodlands of California Floristic Province. (2)

Phloeodes plicatus (LeConte) (12.0–17.0 mm) is uniformly light brown to chestnut gray dorsally. Antennomere 10 forming a weak club. Antennal sulcus of hypomeron not limited posteriorly. Scutellum concealed. Elytra never with velvety patches, each plicate laterally with a pair of broad carinae, and sculpted apically with three broad knoblike ridges. Legs lack rows of golden setae; tarsi 5-5-4 with well-developed glabrous strip ventrally. Adult habits similar to *P. diabolicus*. Woodlands of California Floristic Province and Baja California; occurrences elsewhere require confirmation. (2)

Zopherus gracilis Horn (11.6–21.7 mm) is robust, elongate, subcylindrical, dull black, and relatively smooth. Antennae appear to have nine antennomeres, with 9–11 fused, forming club. Pronotum sparsely punctate, with deep antennal grooves underneath. Scutellum concealed. Elytra with scattered punctures and randomly arranged wavy lines; intensity of elytral sculpturing increases in northern populations; apical longitudinal costae poorly defined and only slightly swollen. Legs with rows of dense golden setae; tarsi 5-5-4. Nocturnal adults on base of pine (*Pinus*) snags and living alligator juniper (*Juniperus deppeana*) in summer. Northern and eastern Arizona, southwestern New Mexico, and adjacent Sonora. (7)

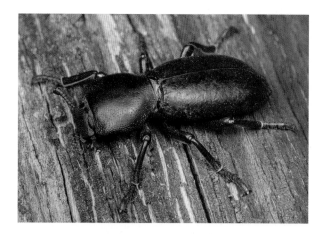

Zopherus granicollis granicollis Horn (12.6–20.5 mm) is robust, elongate, subcylindrical, and dull black. Antennal club with antennomeres 9–11 fused. Pronotum coarse granulate and punctate; hypomera deeply sulcate. Scutellum concealed. Elytra coarsely, contiguously tuberculate. Legs with rows of golden setae. Tarsi 5-5-4. Larvae develop in root crowns of dead pines (*Pinus monophylla*, *P. jeffreyi*) and possibly in living California juniper (*Juniperus californica*). Adults hide under bark year-round, and walk about bases of dead pines and living junipers on spring and summer nights. Transverse and Peninsular Ranges of California; also Baja California. *Zopherus granicollis ventriosus* Casey with finer elytral tubercles; western foothills southern Sierra Nevada, Saline Valley, California. (7)

Zopherus tristis LeConte (10.5–22.0 mm) is elongate, subcylindrical, and dull black with lateral elytral margins mostly parallel and abruptly narrowed at base and apex; sides sometimes encrusted with whitish secretion. Antennal club with antennomeres 9–11 fused. Pronotum usually coarsely punctured; hypomeron deeply sulcate and prosternum coarsely punctured. Scutellum concealed. Elytra with broad tubercles usually flattened, their posterior margins somewhat truncate; apical longitudinal costae distinct. Legs with rows of golden setae. Tarsi 5-5-4. Nocturnal adults found year-round on or under bark of tamarisk (*Tamarix*) and other trees. Primarily Colorado and Sonoran Deserts. Southeastern California, southwestern Arizona, south to adjacent Baja California and Sonora. (7)

TENEBRIONIDAE (tē-neb-ri-on'-i-dē)
DARKLING BEETLES

Tenebrionids are typically hard, dull or shiny brown or black beetles, although a few species are notably covered in pale scales, brightly marked in red, or distinctly metallic. The heavily sclerotized bodies of many flightless, ground-dwelling species adapt them to life in arid and semiarid habitats. Adults are typically crepuscular or nocturnal and spend their days hidden in leaf litter, under rocks and other debris, or down in animal burrows where temperatures are cooler and humidity levels are higher. Others tunnel into soil, decayed wood, and fungi, or live among detritus associated with nests of other animals, including pack rats and ants. Wood-associated species live under bark or in the abandoned galleries chewed by wood-boring insects where they are often dependent on fungi to break down wood into suitable food. Some tenebrionids nibble on the surfaces of polypore fungi, while others graze on algae or lichens growing on rocks, logs, and stumps. Diurnal species are commonly found on various plants resting on stems, leaves, and flowers. Several adventive Old World species are pests of stored food products. When threatened, many darkling beetles produce foul-smelling fluids from their anal glands or feign death.

FAMILY DIAGNOSIS Adult tenebrionids are incredibly diverse in form, ranging from elongate and somewhat cylindrical or slightly flattened, or oblong to strongly oval and strongly convex to nearly hemispherical. Head has kidney-shaped, strongly notched, or completely divided eyes, and clypeus or *epistoma* with clypeolabral membrane exposed or not. Antennae typically with 11 antennomeres and are moniliform or clavate, with bases hidden from view from above by expanded rim on front of the head. Procoxal cavities are closed behind. Elytra completely conceal the abdomen, often fused along suture, with discal surfaces smooth, rough, confusedly punctate, and punctostriate and/or carinate; flight wings fully developed or, in species with elytra partially or completely fused, reduced or absent. Legs are stout or slender, tarsi usually 5-5-4, rarely 4-4-4 (*Anchomma, Rhipidandrus*), with penultimate tarsomere sometimes lobed, and claws equal in size, toothed or pectinate. Abdomen with five ventrites, 1–3 connate.

SIMILAR FAMILIES
- ground beetles (Carabidae, p.88)—tarsi 5-5-5, first abdominal ventrite divided by hind coxae
- minute bark beetles (Cerylonidae, p.309)—very small, tarsi 4-4-4, antennae capitate
- false darkling beetles (Melandryidae, p.333)—winged, pronotum often with two impressions at posterior margin

- zopherid beetles (Zopheridae, p.340)—prosternal process between coxae flat and broad, procoxal cavities open or closed behind, prothorax often with distinct sulci underneath to receive antennae, tarsi 4-4-4 or 5-5-4, abdomen usually with ventrites 2–4 connate
- pleasing fungus beetles (Erotylidae, p.435)—tarsi 5-5-5, antennae capitate, elytra sometimes with bright-colored markings

COLLECTING NOTES Search for darkling beetles under stones and beneath loose bark on snags, logs, and stumps. Thoroughly inspect accumulations of leaf litter at the bases of trees and shrubs or at the edges of rocky outcrops. Sifting sand around the bases of grasses, shrubs, and trees in desert and coastal dunes will reveal numerous species endemic to these habitats. Carefully check woody fungi, as well as soil, rocks, trees, and other lichen-encrusted surfaces in forested habitats at night. Diurnal species are found by inspecting vegetation and beating and sweeping foliage and flowers. Look for flightless crepuscular and nocturnal ground-dwellers wandering along trails and crossing dirt roads. Setting out trails of uncooked oatmeal in these and other open habitats will attract these beetles as they forage for food. Winged nocturnal species are attracted to lights at storefronts, gas stations, and truck stops. Select species are also captured in Lindgren funnel, Malaise, and pitfall traps.

FAUNA ~1,184 SPECIES IN ~191 GENERA

Anchomma costatum LeConte (4.0 mm) is elongate, dull reddish brown or black, coarsely punctate, and sparsely clothed in pale, somewhat erect scalelike setae. Head broadly explanate laterally, with short, thick, setose antennae and divided eyes. Pronotum rectangular, longer than wide, with sides explanate and a pair of elevated carinae on disc; front coxae closed. Ventrites without membranous posterior margins. Front tibia not expanded apically; tarsi 4-4-4. Elytra distinctly margined and sharply costate, with interstriae bipunctate. Adults found under rocks, sometimes in association with *Phiedole* ants, or walking on sandy soil in oak woodlands among columns of *Liometopum*. Coastal and desert regions of southern California. (1).

Microschatia championi Horn (15.7–20.8 mm) is elongate-ovate, robust, black with finely to coarsely punctate pronotum and coarsely to very coarsely punctate or punctate-rugose elytra. Head without tubercles on frons and labrum emarginate, not notched; mentum broadly emarginate with narrow median notch. Pronotum broadest about middle, with lateral margins broad, thick, and granulate, with posterior margin noticeably narrowed with a pair of tubercles, and posterior angles distinct and rectangular; hypomeron punctate. Elytra punctostriate medially with punctures sparse, larger punctures dense, often confluent and rugose, and epipleura becoming wider toward base, epipleural fold distinct along entire length. Adults crepuscular. Extreme southern California to Baja California Sur. (5)

Microschatia inaequalis LeConte (12.0–19.0 mm) is elongate-ovate, robust, and black or brownish black, occasionally with bluish-white margins. Pronotum broadest at middle with posterior margin narrowed, lateral margins narrowly to moderately explanate and crenulate, and disc finely tuberculate-rugose anteriorly, becoming punctate-rugose posteriorly and along lateral margins; hypomeron tuberculate. Elytra very coarsely rugose with overlay of fine tubercles, rugae sometimes forming one or more convoluted and irregular longitudinal costae. Nocturnal and flightless adults found in various arid and semiarid habitats in southern California and Baja California. (5)

Pelecyphorus liratus **(LeConte)** (11.5–13.0 mm) is dull black with coarsely punctured head and pronotum, and sparsely clothed in recumbent scalelike yellowish-brown setae. Pronotum broadest before middle, angles prominent and acute, with anterolateral margins broadly arcuate, posterolateral margins straight and converging, and a medial longitudinal ridge ending posteriorly in a point flanked by dense setal fringe along sinuate posterior margin. Elytron with three discal carinae, inner discoidal carina ending at apical one-third, and outer two at apical one-fourth; shared sutural carina reaching apex. Flightless adults diurnal. Arizona and New Mexico, south to Chihuahua and Durango. (1)

Philolithus actuosus **(Horn)** (14.7–23.4 mm) is dull black, with head finely granulate. Pronotum wide, with anterior margin emarginate with angles acute, sides moderately arcuate and crenulate, disc coarsely punctate laterally, and posterior margin nearly truncate with angles rectangular. Elytra oval, sides carinate, each usually with one distinct, curved carina medially on disc extending two-thirds length of elytron, often with obsolete carina between it and suture. Nocturnal adults found walking or sheltering beneath debris year-round in desert and wooded foothill habitats. California. (22)

Philolithus morbillosus **(LeConte)** (16.5–17.5 mm) is elongate-ovate and very dark reddish-brown to black. Head finely punctate. Pronotum slightly longer than wide, serrate sides broadly rounded and briefly sinuate at rectangular basal angles, disc with large, coarse punctures becoming denser and confluent along sides. Elytra narrow at base, humeri sharply dentate, sides carinate, each with two irregular carinae and intercostae with irregular transverse folds. Flightless adults found walking on ground during day. Arizona and Sonora. (22)

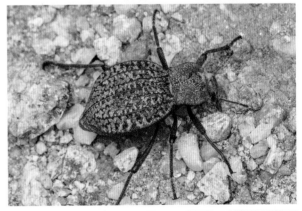

Stenomorpha confluens **(LeConte)** (19.0–26.4 mm) is somewhat shiny black, sometimes coated with bluish-white pruinosity. Pronotum wide, broadest at/or just before middle, narrower than elytra, with sides more coarsely punctured than disc, lateral margins crenulate and elevated, and posterior margin arcuate to truncate. Elytra obovate, disc somewhat flat and impunctate, suture slightly elevated, with single inner costa usually confluent with raised lateral margin basally, and curving toward suture before apex. Flightless and nocturnal adults on desert dunes at dusk primarily during late summer through fall. California and Arizona, south to Baja California and Sonora. (77)

Stenomorpha lecontei (Horn) (15.2–22.8 mm) is elongate-oblong, dull black, and hard bodied with carinate elytra. Pronotum convex, wider than long, sides more coarsely punctate, lateral margins narrow, evenly arcuate, and crenulate, disc evenly and densely punctate. Elytra elongate-oval, somewhat parallel-sided (male) or broadly oval (female), each with sutural, lateral, and two discal costae distinctly elevated, first and second joined about apical one-sixth, third beginning at about basal one-fourth of lateral margin and terminating opposite confluence of first and second. Southern California. (77)

Stenomorpha marginata LeConte (25.4–30.5 mm) is elongate-obovate and dull black with dorsal surface sparsely and finely punctured. Head coarsely punctured. Pronotum wider than long, disc convex, less strongly punctured, sides broadly flat and coarsely crenulate, with arcuate lateral margins crenulate, and posterior margin bisinuate. Elytra sometimes dark reddish brown, with more or less crenulate humeral margins short, reaching just past humeri, or extending just beyond apical declivity, and disc rough with scattered shallow punctures. Nocturnal and flightless adults found walking on ground after dark. California to Texas, south to Sonora and Chihuahua. (77)

Lepidocnemeplatia sericea (Horn) (2.5–3.3 mm) is elongate, moderately convex, reddish brown, and densely clothed in short yellowish, yellowish brown, or grayish slender scales. Front of head strongly emarginate and sharply reflexed between large eyes. Pronotum wider than long, broadest before middle, nearly equal in width to elytra, with posterior margin bisinuate. Elytra at base slightly wider than pronotum, each with 10 punctostriae covered with scales, denuded patches appear as medial and subapical fascia. Front tibia triangular with narrow basal bare spot on inner surface, apical spur large. Winged adults under stones and at lights. Washington to Baja California Sur, east to Nevada, Texas, and Nicaragua. (2)

Cnemodinus testaceus (Horn) (6.0–8.1 mm) is shiny pale yellowish brown. Head with frons moderately punctate between large, slightly emarginate, and coarsely faceted eyes. Pronotum slightly wide, with anterior angles obtuse, sides broadly rounded, posterior angles rectangular, and disc more coarsely punctured laterally. Elytra sparsely punctured with scattered, short, erect yellowish setae. Legs slender and front tibia flattened with apical angle elongate and middle tooth acute. Nocturnal and winged adults at lights during spring in desert habitats. Southern California and Arizona. (3)

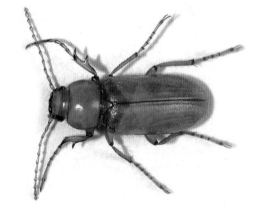

Coelus ciliatus Eschscholtz (5.3–7.5 mm) is strongly convex, shiny black with fringe of long reddish-brown setae along sides. Clypeus elevated, separated from frons by strong ridge. Antennae with 11 antennomeres, barely exceeding blunt anterior pronotal angles. Lateral pronotal margins evenly arcuate and somewhat explanate. Elytra with setose punctures tuberculate. Front tibiae fringed with 8–16 long setae, and tarsomere 1 short, produced ventrally into blunt curved spur. Flightless diurnal adults on coastal dunes; occasionally on sandy soils inland. Southern British Columbia to Baja California. *Coelus pacificus* Fall similar, frons and clypeus on same plane; Channel Islands, California. (5)

Conionitis species (6.3–15.0 mm) are elongate-oval, moderately convex, and dull to moderately shiny black. Labrum distinct, not covered by clypeus. Eyes partly divided by canthus or not. Clavate antennae short, not reaching base of wide pronotum. Elytra more punctate apically and laterally, glabrous or with conspicuous setae, and epipleura gradually narrowing from humerus to apex. Legs stout, protibia more or less cylindrical in cross section, gradually enlarged to apex with pair of spurs, sometimes briefly hooked at outer apical margin, with tarsi spinose underneath. Alaska to Baja California, east Montana, and Colorado. (55)

Eusattus difficilis LeConte (9.0–13.0 mm) is black with faintly costulate elytra. Head with terminal antennomere asymmetrical and angulate apically. Pronotum wide, disc with larger slightly raised punctures becoming denser and more distinct laterally. Elytral disc is variable, ranging from weakly rugose with raised punctures (coastal, western Mojave) to distinctly more tuberculate (Mojave Desert). Outer margins of protibia with row of closely spaced spinules extending to apex. Coastal, desert, and mountain habitats with sandy, clay, rocky substrates. Southern California to Baja California, east to southern Nevada. (12)

Eusattus dilitatus LeConte (11.0–14.0 mm long) is shiny black and densely setose underneath. Antennae short, subequal to front tarsi in length, appearing almost glabrous, with terminal antennomere symmetrically rounded apically. Pronotum with irregular patches of low, rounded and oval tubercles laterally, each subtended by short, declined seta; anterior and posterior margins with dense setose fringe. Elytra rugulose with broad, flat tubercles becoming obsolete basally, and epipleuron narrowing abruptly behind humerus. Middle and hind tibiae strongly bowed. Buried in sand beneath *Larrea* and other shrubs in Colorado and Sonoran Deserts. Southeastern California, southwestern Arizona, and northwestern Sonora. (12)

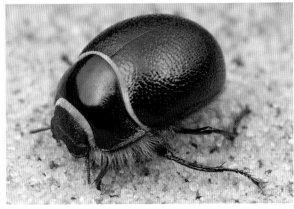

Eusattus muricatus LeConte (11.0–13.0 mm) is subglobular with glabrous or nearly glabrous tuberculate elytra. Head with frons tuberculate, tubercles round or elongate. Antennae subequal in length to front femora, terminal antennomere symmetrical and rounded apically. Pronotum broad, with discal raised punctures becoming tuberculate laterally, anterior and pronotal margins with dense fringe of golden setae. Elytra with disc rugulose and glabrous, epipleuron with small tubercles and setigerous punctures, especially in basal half. Protibia with apical process extending to apex of tarsomere 3 or 4. Adults inhabit major dune systems, including those in Great Basin and Mojave Deserts. Eastern Oregon to eastern California, east to southern Idaho, Colorado, and western Texas. (12)

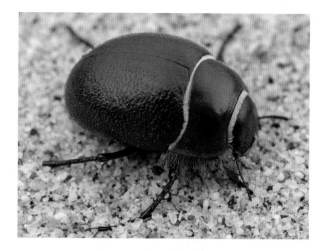

Eusattus reticulatus (Say) (elytra 7.7–13.2 mm long) is very broadly oval, moderately convex, and black with costate-reticulate elytra. Head and pronotum appear impunctate or with widely scattered, shallow, large and small punctures. Terminal antennomere symmetrical and rounded apically. Pronotum broad with sides broadly arcuate and diverging to base. Elytron with irregular depressions sometimes filled with light-colored accretions creating sharply contrasting pattern, and lateral margin arcuate. Front legs with tibiae flat with expanded process apically, tarsomeres cylindrical and truncate apically, and tarsomere 1 more than twice length of 2. Arid grasslands, scrublands, and woodlands, especially along riparian habitats. Utah to Sonora, east to Colorado, Oklahoma, and Chihuahua. (12)

Asbolus laevis LeConte (15.0–20.0 mm) is elongate-oval, dull black or bluish black with pronotum and elytra mostly smooth. Eyes peanut-shaped, antennae flattened in cross section, narrowly oval. Pronotum convex, wider than long, broadest before middle, with lateral margins arcuate. Pseudepipleural margins of elytra each with row of granulate punctures. Tarsomeres with long brushes of setae laterally and apically. Adults walk on desert dunes at night. Southern California to Baja California, east to southwestern Arizona and northwestern Sonora. *Asbolus papillosus* (Triplehorn) similar, pronotum and elytra sparsely and finely granulate, tarsal setation short and spiny ventrally; inland desert dunes of southern California. (3)

Asbolus verrucosus LeConte (19.0–20.0 mm) is elongate-oval, and dull black and rough, often with bluish-white pruinescence. Eyes peanut-shaped, antennae flattened in cross section, narrowly oval. Pronotum wider than long, broadest before middle, with disc rugosely granulate, strongly inflated, forming two distinct lateral lobes, and sides somewhat arcuate. Elytra somewhat globose, intervals studded with tubercles or wartlike protuberances that occasionally form carinae. Tarsal setation short and spinose. Adults found walking at night on dunes and gravel, under debris, or at base of woody desert shrubs. Southern California to Baja California, east to southwestern Utah and southwestern New Mexico. (3)

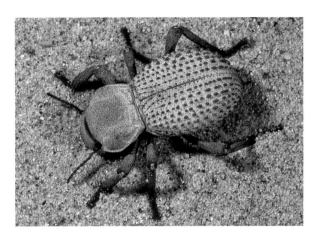

Cryptoglossa muricata (LeConte) (13.9–24.1 mm) is elongate, somewhat parallel-sided, and black with pronotal punctures and low areas on elytra sometimes filled with light-colored accretions. Head with eyes elongate, slightly narrowed on both sides at middle, and antennae broadly oval in cross section. Pronotum broadly convex, appearing somewhat flat, disc with minute to small scattered punctures, lateral punctures larger and denser. Elytral disc appearing rough, studded with short tubercles. Males with elongate tubercle on middle femur that is concave at center. Adults found mostly during spring under stones and other debris in Mojave, Colorado, and Western Sonoran Deserts. California to Baja California, east to Utah, Arizona, and Sonora. (4)

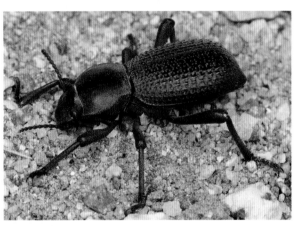

353

Cryptoglossa variolosa (Horn) (11.0–20.1 mm) is elongate, somewhat parallel-sided, and dull black with head, pronotum, and underside deeply, coarsely, and densely punctured, punctures both medium and large. Eyes elongate, slightly narrowed on both sides at middle, and antennae broadly oval in cross section. Pronotum broadly convex, appearing somewhat flat, and widest before middle, anterolateral margins arcuate, posterolateral margins narrowed toward base, disc with large dense punctures laterally. Elytra with large, flattened, raised areas arranged in rows. Nocturnal adults found during day under stones and cactus debris in Sonoran Desert and associated uplands. Extreme southeastern California to New Mexico, south to Sinaloa. (4)

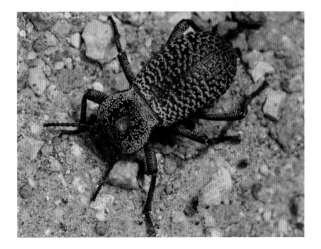

Schizillus laticeps Horn (21.0–25.0 mm) is dull black, with eyes completely divided, antennomere 3 subequal to combined lengths of 4–5, and clypeus strongly deflexed over labrum. Pronotum narrowly convex, disc with small to minute punctures becoming sparse laterally. Elytra elongate-oval, with irregular flat tubercles. Hind femora punctate. Adults nocturnal. Southern California to Baja California, east to Utah and Arizona; isolated population in San Joaquin Valley. *Schizillus nunenmacheri* Blaisdell (18.2–20.0 mm) antennomere 3 subequal to 4–6 combined, clypeus horizontal and flat, hind femora impunctate; southeastern California east to Utah and northern Arizona. (2)

Auchmobius sublaevis LeConte (9.2–10.0 mm) is ovate, robust, dull black with reddish-brown appendages. Head broad, antennae short and stout, not reaching base of pronotum, with antennomeres 2 and 3 elongate and equal in length. Pronotum wider than long, broadest at base, and strongly convex, with sides broadly arcuate, and small, scattered punctures on disc becoming coarser and denser laterally. Elytra convex, each appearing faintly wrinkled, with distinct, somewhat dense punctures. Front tibia with external apical tooth more or less produced. Adults found walking on ground during day or under debris. Southern California. (8)

Chilometopon brachystomum Doyen (4.0–7.0 mm) is pale to dark chestnut brown, often with irregular grayish coating. Head slightly longer than wide, coarsely punctate, with canthus reaching no more than one-quarter across eye, and epistomal lobe short and truncate. Pronotum broadest across middle with apex wider than base. Scutellum broad, merging into elytra. Elytra broadest medially. Wings fully developed or slightly reduced. On flowers in dune habitats spring through summer; at lights. Central California and Nevada, south to Baja California Sur and Arizona. (6)

Edrotes ventricosus LeConte (6.4–10.0 mm) elytra smooth with minute tubercles, shiny or dull black, with four lines of long, erect, pale setae on each elytron. Eyes prominent and coarsely faceted. Anterior pronotal angles acute. Diurnal, flightless adults stridulate; active winter and spring in deserts. Oregon to Baja California Sur, east to Idaho and Sonora. *Edrotes rotundatus* (Say) (5.4–7.5 mm) elytra are rough and coarsely impunctate. Utah and Arizona, east to Colorado, Texas, and Chihuahua. *Edrotes arens* LaRivers (5.2–8.5 mm) elytra tuberculate with short, appressed, scalelike vestiture. Sand dunes. California and Arizona south to Sonora. (5)

354

Triorophus laevis LeConte (7.0–8.0 mm) is elongate-oval, shiny black and glabrous, with relatively long appendages. Head broad, sparsely punctate, with lateral lobes more prominent than eyes. Pronotum sparsely punctate with more or less distinct bead along lateral margins. Elytra with coarse punctostriae becoming obsolete after middle, interstriae and apices impunctate. Legs long and slender. Inhabits dry, often desert habitats. California and Nevada south to Sonora. (17)

Bothrotes plumbeus plumbeus (LeConte) (9.0–10.5 mm) is dull black, with dorsal pubescence or not. Head with supraorbital carinae and abruptly constricted behind eyes. Pronotum with lateral margins broadly arcuate in lateral view, with elevations arcuate (female) or convex (male), and posterior margin bisinuate. Elytra broader than pronotum, broadly rounded apically, faintly costate, and confusedly punctate. California to South Dakota, Kansas, and Texas. *Bothrotes canaliculatus* (Say) (10.8–11.3 mm) coppery, lateral pronotal margins strongly arcuate in lateral view, female with elevations straight. On vegetation and flowers. Arizona to Ohio, south to Mexico. (2)

Lobometopon fusiforme (Casey) (8.2–11.5 mm) is elongate-fusiform, convex, shiny charcoal gray or dark brown, often with a brassy tinge. Head as long as wide, densely punctured, alutaceous between punctures, with eyes not prominent. Pronotum with disc finely and densely punctate, save for narrow impunctate medial line, nearly as long as wide, sides diverging to base, anterior angles acute and prominent, and posterior margin sinuate. Elytra at base not wider than prothorax; disc evenly, confusedly, and densely punctate throughout, each bearing a minute seta. Winged adults on branches of *Baccharis* in summer. Arizona and Sonora. (2)

Metopoloba pruinosa pruinosa (Horn) (10.0–12.2 mm) is elongate-fusiform, convex, shiny brown, and clothed in short, inconspicuous setae; grayish pruinosity forming broken longitudinal lines on elytra on newly emerged beetles is easily rubbed off. Head abruptly constricted behind eyes, each flanked above by a distinct carina. Pronotum smooth and convex in both sexes, sides diverging to base, with posterior margin sinuate. Elytra with disc densely, evenly, and confusedly punctured, and apex narrowly rounded. Winged adults on *Baccharis* and at lights during summer. California east to Utah and Arizona. *Metopoloba p. subseriata* Casey elytra with feebly impressed lines of aggregated coarse punctures; southeastern Arizona to Texas. (1)

Pechalius vestitus (Casey) (11.0–12.0 mm) is elongate-fusiform, convex, shiny with brassy tinge, with uniformly short, thick, moderately dense white appressed setae sometimes rubbed off. Eyes not prominent and lacking adjacent ridge. Pronotum with disc smooth and broadly convex, wider than long, sides diverging to base, posterior margin bisinuate. Elytra at base nearly as wide as pronotum, each with blunt subapical protuberance, and narrowly truncate apex. Hind tarsomeres 1–3 with dense ventral pads of pale setae. Winged adults beaten from oak (*Quercus*) during summer. Southeastern Arizona. *Pechalius dentiger* (Horn) (11.7–12.2 mm) with setae distinctly patchy, elytron with subapical denticle, adults under *Prosopis* bark. Both occur in southeastern Arizona (2).

Polemiotus submetallicus (LeConte) (13.5–16.7 mm) is elongate-fusiform, convex, shiny reddish brown with faint coppery tinge, and uniformly clothed in short, thick appressed setae. Head with sides distinctly lobed in front of eyes, each with inner margin deeply grooved. Pronotum much narrower than elytra, wider than long, broadest just before middle, posterolateral margins subparallel, with disc somewhat flattened and moderately punctate. Elytra convex, humeri prominent and rounded, punctures moderately coarse and confusedly aggregated into weakly impressed lines, with intervals sparse, confused, and with minute punctures. Winged adults attracted to lights during summer. Southeastern Arizona. (1)

Nyctoporis carinata LeConte (13.0–15.0 mm) is elongate, somewhat parallel-sided, convex, dull black, and hard-bodied with dorsal surfaces and appendages coarsely sculptured. Head with eyes coarsely faceted and transversely kidney-shaped. Pronotum slightly wider than long, with sides explanate, disc deeply, coarsely, confluently punctate, and without depressions. Elytra wider than pronotum, crests of elevated costae irregularly crenulate, lower costae consisting of long, closely set tubercles, and intervals with row of coarse, closely set tuberculate punctures. Legs with tarsi bearing long, dense, golden setae underneath. Flightless adults are found in detritus, and under rocks and loose debris in montane habitats. Central and southern California. Genus needs revision. (5)

Araeoschizus species (3.2–5.1 mm) are elongate-oval, more or less shiny light to dark brown, with dorsal surface coarsely sculpted, and covered in scalelike setae. Head large, longer than pronotum, and eyes completely divided with larger portion dorsal. Pronotum short, broadest before middle, with or without longitudinal groove. Elytra costate, intercostae coarsely punctate, with or without scalelike setae. Ventrites flat, slightly concave (male), or somewhat convex (female). Legs short, robust with femora toothed or not. Adults found under stones and in ant nests in arid, sandy habitats in spring and summer. Southwestern Oregon to Baja California, east to Idaho, Wyoming, Colorado, and western Texas, south to Mexico. (28)

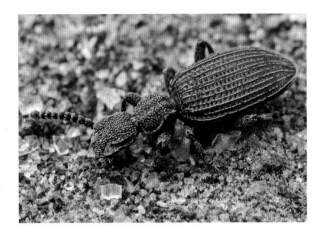

Alaephus species (4.5–7.0 mm) are elongate, somewhat parallel-sided, convex, and moderately dull to shiny and pale yellowish or reddish brown. Head large, more or less prominent and weakly emarginate, with lateral margins reflexed over antennal bases, antennae long. Pronotum wider than long, broadest at or just before middle, with disc coarsely, sometimes confluently punctate, and angulation between dorsum and hypomeron acute. Elytra confusedly punctate, and sparsely clothed in inconspicuous setae. Abdomen without visible membranes. Legs moderately slender with tarsi spinose underneath. Winged and nocturnal adults attracted to lights in mountains and forests. California east to Utah and New Mexico. Genus needs revision. (10)

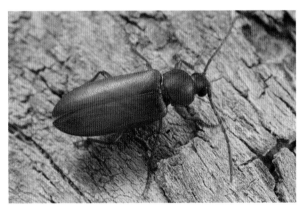

357

Eupsophulus castaneus (Horn) (13.7–15.2 mm) is elongate-oblong, faintly alutaceous, and moderately shiny dark reddish brown. Head with anterior margin of epistoma not reflexed. Pronotal punctures neither dense, nor confluent, and angulation between pronotum and hypomeron obtuse. Elytra sparsely and confusedly punctured, sometimes with very short scattered setae along sides. Legs long, slender with short spinules under tarsi. Nocturnal and winged adults attracted to lights at night during late spring and early summer. California and Baja California, east to Nevada, Texas, Sonora, and Coahuila. *Eupsophulus brevipennis* Casey (9.0–10.0 mm) pronotal punctures denser, with nine longitudinal rows of setae on each elytron; southeastern Arizona. (2)

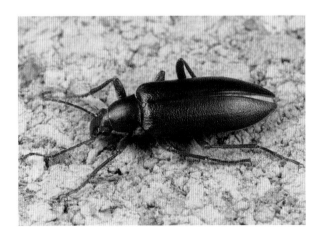

Eleodes armata LeConte (23.5–32.5 mm) is smooth, usually with all femoral teeth long and acute. Pronotum widest just before middle and sinuate to base. Elytra more or less abruptly declivous apically (especially female), at most weakly caudate (male). First three ventrites finely punctured to impunctate. Protarsomere 1 not thickened apically and lacking setal tuft ventrally. Nocturnal adults become active at dusk in dry habitats and deserts. Southeastern Oregon to northern Baja California, east to southwestern Idaho, western Nevada, southwestern Utah, western Arizona, and northern Sonora. (258 NA)

Eleodes obscura sulcipennis Mannerheim (23.0–31.5 mm) is shiny black with distinctly sulcate elytra. Pronotum moderately convex, finely punctate, widest just before middle, with anterior angles barely produced, lateral margins strongly arcuate and narrowed posteriorly. Elytra parallel-sided (male) or slightly inflated posteriorly (female), with humeri obsolete, and rounded laterally, without carinae. Front legs with strong (male) or blunt (female) femoral spine at apical one-quarter, and tarsomere 1 with bulbous ventral lobe. British Columbia to California, east to Montana and Arizona, south to Chihuahua and Durango. (258 NA)

Eleodes osculans (LeConte) (13.0–19.0 mm) is elongate, black, variable in size and punctation, and conspicuously clothed in long, erect, reddish-brown setae. Pronotum constricted at base with posterior angle more or less rectangular. Elytra with large, shallow, and closely spaced punctures each bearing a seta on anterior margin and arranged in rows or not, and interstriae with irregular seta-bearing punctures. Mesotibia armed with distinct tooth at apical one-quarter (male) or not (female). Adults active during spring and summer in various wooded habitats. California and Baja California. (258 NA)

Eleodes tribula Thomas (13.0–19.0 mm) is elongate-ovate, shiny black, and densely clothed dorsally in long, dark brown setae. Pronotum moderately punctate, anterior angles rounded and not produced, and lateral margins arcuate and narrowing posteriorly. Elytra confusedly punctostriate with interstriae lacking tubercles, rounded laterally without marginal carinae, and apices often extended (male) or not (female). Flightless, nocturnal adults on sandy soils in eastern Sonoran Desert of southern Arizona and Sonora. *Eleodes pilosa* Horn (11.6–15.2 mm) more robust, dull with strongly sculptured surfaces, and black setae. Dry habitats throughout western North America. (258 NA)

Embaphion contusum LeConte (14.0–20.5 mm) is elongate and dull black. Head sparsely setose with eyes vertically narrowed. Pronotum minutely punctured, with broad lateral margins strongly flattened, curled upward, and finely, transversely wrinkled. Elytra roughened with minute tubercles and sparsely clothed in dark setae, with sharply elevated lateral margin reaching apex, and apices somewhat extended (male) or not (female). Nocturnal adults found walking on sandy soils or beneath debris in various habitats. Wyoming to Arizona, east to Kansas and New Mexico. (4)

Embaphion depressum (LeConte) (9.6–11.2 mm) is elongate-oval, rugose with coarse punctures, and dull black with reddish-brown appendages. Pronotum broader than long, moderately convex, with narrow lateral margins explanate, but not curled upward, and densely covered with large punctures. Elytra broadly oval with sharply elevated lateral margins rounded, gradually narrowing to apex, and rows of moderately coarse punctures bearing short, somewhat erect setae. Flightless and nocturnal adults found walking on sandy soils or hiding under debris during day in Colorado and Mojave Deserts of California. (4)

Embaphion elongatum Horn (15.2–17.5 mm) is elongate, with surfaces dull black, alutaceous, and clothed in short, somewhat erect dark brown setae. Pronotum with anterior margin deeply emarginate, sides broadly arcuate and finely crenulate, posterior margin truncate. Elytra nearly twice as long as broad, with carinate lateral margins finely serrate, disc weakly convex to flat, suture carinate from basal one-quarter to apex. Flightless and nocturnal adults found walking on sandy soils or hiding under debris during day in various habitats. Oregon to California, east to Idaho and Utah. (4)

Lariversius tibialis Blaisdell (7.0–9.0 mm) is oblong-oval, moderately convex, dull to shiny reddish black to blackish, with sides and legs fringed with long yellow pubescence. Eyes small, transverse, and not prominent. Antennae short and thick. Pronotum somewhat oval with acute anterior angles, disc moderately and evenly convex, and slightly narrower than elytra. Elytra slightly longer than wide, disc roughly and irregularly sculpted with low, large, flat-topped tubercles, laterally and apically, with short setae. Nocturnal and flightless adults are sand dune obligates often found at bases of plants in the southern Great Basin Desert and found year-round. Nevada. (1)

359

Trogloderus vandykei La Rivers (10.0–12.5 mm) is elongate, oblong-oval, dull black, and roughly sculptured with carinate elytra. Pronotum reticulate on disc with a shallow longitudinal furrow down middle, and narrowly tuberculate along lateral margins that are completely serrate and sinuate just before small and acute posterior angles. Elytra elongate-oval, humeri obsolete, distinctly carinate, each with four distinct costae, intercostae smooth and without cross-ridges. Legs short with surfaces scabrous. Adults active during spring on sand dunes from later afternoon onward in Mojave Desert. California and Arizona. (4)

Eleates depressus (Randall) (5.0–7.5 mm) is oblong, convex, and dull brown or black, with fine elytral carinae. Head not deeply hidden in prothorax, eyes completely divided. Pronotum with front angles rounded, front margin not lobed at middle, and sides smooth, not finely serrate. Elytra finely carinate, intervals each with a row of coarse and uniformly distributed punctures. Adults found under bark in association with fungus in coniferous forests and mixed woodlands. In western North America from British Columbia to Oregon. *Eleates occidentalis* Casey (4.5–5.0 mm) similar in form and habit, Sierra Nevada of California. (2)

Megeleates sequoiarum Casey (6.5–7.0 mm) is oblong, strongly convex, parallel-sided, dull black, and glabrous. Head roughly punctate with tuberculiform elevation above each eye and narrower than pronotum. Pronotum wider than long, sides evenly arcuate and distinctly crenulate, and disc coarsely tuberculate and sulcate down middle, sides of sulcus becoming carinate (male) or tumid (female) anteriorly. Elytra about as wide as pronotum, with slightly prominent lateral margins strongly crenulate and not reflexed. Legs coarsely, densely punctate. Adults found in montane habitats on or in association with *Fomes* and *Ganoderma* fungi. Washington to California. (1)

Rhipidandrus peninsularis Horn (3.5–4.0 mm) is short, oblong, robust, convex, coarsely and roughly punctate, and dull brown, with appendages paler. Head reticulate, pubescent, and densely punctured between eyes, with clypeus smooth. Antennomeres 6–10 transverse and forming loose, asymmetrical club. Prothorax wider than long, slightly narrower in front, with sides weakly arcuate, and pronotum evenly convex and finely reticulate. Elytra at base not broader than prothorax, and disc distinctly costate, with intercostae rugose. Tarsi 4-4-4. Adults on fungi; also attracted to lights. Arizona, Texas, and Baja California Sur. (1)

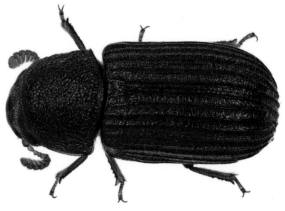

Scotobaenus parallelus LeConte (16.0–19.0 mm) is elongate-oblong, parallel-sided, somewhat depressed, and somewhat shiny black. Head transverse. Pronotum moderately convex, less densely punctate than head, with sides arcuate before becoming sinuate then nearly parallel at basal one-tenth and produced posterior angles acute to nearly rectangular. Elytra not fused, surface with striae narrowly impressed and regularly interrupted. Last ventrite with posterior marginal bead. Tarsomeres 1–4 densely pubescent ventrally, femora distinctly clavate, and meso- and metafemora with (male) or without (female) dense yellow pubescence. Adults under loose pine (*Pinus*) bark during spring and summer. Washington to California. (4)

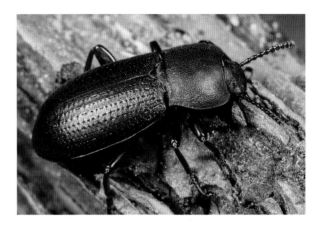

Argoporis bicolor (LeConte) (8.3–14.0 mm) is elongate, somewhat parallel-sided, and dark reddish brown to black, with clypeus and appendages red. Head broad, with frontoclypeal suture only shallowly impressed, and clypeus distinctly protruding and strongly convex medially. Pronotum longer than wide, broadest at middle, with discal punctures minute and moderately dense. Elytra punctoseriate, intervals flat to slightly convex, and slightly more elevated on apical declivity. Dorsal angle of front tibia neither extended nor flattened apically; male hind femur with two or three somewhat equally spaced teeth. Adults on ground or beneath rocks. Southern California and Arizona, south to Baja California and Sonora. (6)

Cerenopus concolor LeConte (14.0–25.0 mm) is elongate-pyriform and dull to moderately shiny black. Pronotum longer than wide, disc duller and punctate or somewhat rugose laterally, with bead along sides seldom interrupted. Elytra with punctostriae impressed, punctures large, moderately deep, and sometimes transverse, with intervals convex and apices narrowly rounded. Legs with dorsal apical angle of front tibia prolonged and hind femur long, reaching or surpassing posterior margin of ventrite 5; front femur abruptly clavate in male. Nocturnal and flightless adults found year-round walking on ground or near light in desert, sand dunes, and chaparral habitats. California, Nevada, Arizona, and entire Baja California Peninsula. (1)

Apsena rufipes (Eschscholtz) (6.0–7.0 mm) is somewhat parallel-sided to oblong-oval, moderately convex or flattened, and dark reddish brown to blackish with appendages and head sometimes reddish. Eyes narrow and kidney-shaped. Antennae somewhat robust and reaching base of pronotum. Pronotum wide, disc coarsely and densely punctate, punctures coalescing into irregular longitudinal lines, with lateral margins narrowly explanate, evenly arcuate, and carinate. Elytra with humeri small and dentiform, basal margin irregular, and disc punctostriate with moderately deep, elongate punctures, and interstriae narrowly costate. Adults under debris in spring. California. (6)

Epantius obscurus LeConte (7.0–8.0 mm) is somewhat flattened and mostly dull black. Head small, with large and prominent eyes, and short, slender antennae. Pronotum wide, disc coarsely and densely punctate, and anterior angles not prominent, with sides broadly arcuate and weakly sinuate just before rectangular posterior angles. Elytra slightly wider than pronotum, lacking distinct costae, with fine erect setae on lateral and apical declivities, and small humeri. On ocean beaches year-round under kelp and sea grass at or above high tide line. California to Baja California. (1)

Helops laetus LeConte (5.0–9.5 mm) is elongate-ovate, and shiny brown with metallic greenish and coppery reflections. Head punctate-rugose, with antennae slender. Pronotum wide, coarsely punctured, strongly reflexed laterally with margins not strongly arcuate, becoming straight and somewhat parallel behind middle. Elytra with sides impressed at basal third, weakly punctostriate, interstriae finely punctate with 1 and 9 coalescing apically. Protibia truncate apically, not produced; males with protarsi strongly dilated. Winged adults under bark of decaying logs in mesic forests. British Columbia to California. Genus needs revision. (24)

Cheirodes californicus (Horn) (3.2–5.0 mm) is oval, robust, moderately convex, dark brownish black, with sides of pronotum and elytra fringed with long yellow setae. Head densely and coarsely punctured, with sides widely dilated, clypeus broadly and deeply emarginate, and eyes deeply emarginate with upper portion small. Antennae short with antennomeres 7–10 forming club. Pronotum short, densely and coarsely punctured. Elytra with basal margin weakly emarginate, and surface coarsely and irregularly punctured. Legs short, robust, with all tibiae broadened apically, outer apical angle of each prolonged. Sandy habitats in spring and summer. Washington to California and Nevada. (1)

Metaclisa marginalis Horn (6.5–7.5 mm) is elongate-oval and shiny dark brown with margins sometime lighter. Head and pronotum coarsely, but not densely punctured. Eyes deeply emarginate anteriorly. Pronotum slightly wider than long, broadest just before middle, sides narrowly explanate, anterolateral margins arcuate, posterolateral margins straight and parallel, and posterior margin broadly lobate medially. Elytra finely punctostriate, punctures close, interstriae flat with small and confused punctures, and pseudepipleurae ending abruptly before elytral apices. Front tibia gradually expanding, outside margin smooth and slightly sinuate before apex. Adults under thick, loose bark of recently dead Jeffrey pine (*Pinus jeffreyi*) stumps and logs. British Columbia to California. (1)

Ammodonus granosus Fall (5.0 mm) is broadly oval, somewhat convex, dull black, and densely clothed in appressed grayish and brownish scales intermixed with nearly recumbent, scalelike setae arranged in rows. Head and anterior portion of pronotum with numerous scattered granules. Elytra mostly gray, each with a small brownish basal spot and a more or less irregular transverse brownish spot medially. Adults attracted to lights in forested and desert scrub habitats in Arizona and Mexico; also Peru. *Ammodonus tropicus* (Kirsch) similar, without granules, with sides of pronotum and elytra fimbriate; California and Arizona south to Colombia and Caribbean. (2)

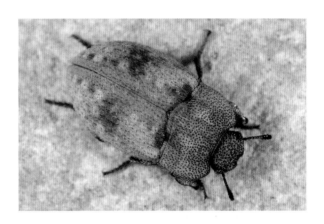

363

Blapstinus species (3.8–7.7 mm) are elongate-oval and pubescent with sides of pronotum and elytra not fimbriate. Antennomeres slender. Pronotum with disc coarsely punctured, lateral margins arcuate, and posterior margin bisinuate. Elytra with striae distinctly impressed or not. Legs with front tibia straight and not externally produced at apex; front and middle tarsi of male often dilated. Winged adults attracted to lights during late spring and summer in dry habitats. Throughout western North America. (17) *Ulus* species (5.6–6.5 mm) similar, vesture coarse and dense, with sides of pronotum and elytra fimbriate, front tibia externally produced apically, and male front tarsi not or barely modified. Across southern United States to Central America. (3) Both genera need revision.

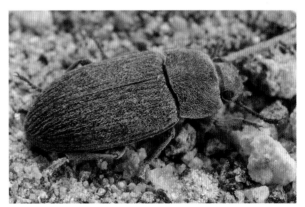

Conibius gagates (Horn) (5.8–7.1 mm) is oblong, robust, convex, strongly alutaceous, smooth, and black, sometimes pruinose, with appendages lighter. Head broad, strongly rounded near completely divided eyes, with antennae robust, antennomeres 4–8 wider than long. Pronotum wider than long, with anterior angles prominent and acute, sides not fimbriate, and obtuse, narrowly rounded posterior angles. Scutellum very broad and short. Elytra elongate-oval, faintly punctostriate with punctures minute and interstriae not raised, with humeri broadly rounded and sides weakly rounded. Legs moderate in length, robust, with front tibia narrow, and front tarsi of male weakly dilated. Flightless adults found under stones. Arizona, Sonora, and Chihuahua. (4)

Trichoton sordidum (LeConte) (6.6–7.7 mm) is oblong-oval, moderately convex, shiny brownish black, and mottled with dense vestiture. Head broad with eyes completely divided. Pronotum wide, broadest behind middle, with anterior angles prominent, sides widely explanate and broadly arcuate, posterior margin deeply bisinuate between somewhat acute posterior angles. Elytra confusedly mottled with patches of short, erect, dark brown setae gradually broadening to their apices and narrow, and flat pale setae. Front tibiae bent (female) or notched (male) apically, with front and middle tarsi with dense setae underneath in both sexes. Flightless, nocturnal adults attracted to lights or hide in rock crevices in dry desert and grasslands. California, Nevada, and Arizona south to Nicaragua. (1)

Ulus crassus (LeConte) (5.0–6.5 mm) is elongate-oval, somewhat flattened, slightly brown or black, and uniformly clothed in fine decumbent golden setae, with lateral pronotal and elytral margins carinate and fimbriate. Head coarsely punctate with some punctures confluent. Pronotum punctate with anterior angles rounded and weakly produced, sides arcuate anteriorly and nearly straight to carinate posterior margin. Elytra shallowly punctostriate, punctures larger than those on rugose interstriae. Front tibial apices dilated with a distinct apical projection. Front tarsomeres 1–3 of male robust with weak pencils of setae underneath. Adults fly to lights. Oregon to California, east to Utah and Texas, south to Mexico. (3)

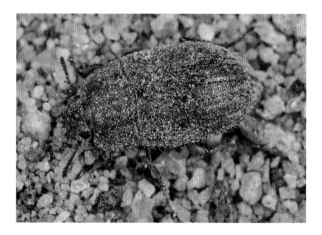

Zophobas subnitens (Horn) (28.0–30.0 mm) is elliptical, straight-sided, and uniformly dull black. Head large, eyes kidney-shaped, basal membrane of labrum exposed, and last antennomere asymmetrical apically. Pronotum wider than long, discal punctures not evident, broadest at middle, and narrower than elytra, with sides broadly arcuate before brief sinuation at somewhat obtuse posterior angle; posterior margin wider than anterior and faintly impressed. Elytra with punctostriae not sulcate, intervals flat. Underside with membranes along posterior margins of ventrites 3 and 4. Tarsi underneath clothed in fine reddish-brown setae. Nocturnal adults found on trunks of oaks (*Quercus*) and at lights. Arizona and Sonora. (1)

Red Flour Beetle *Tribolium castaneum* (Herbst) (3.0–4.0 mm) is elongate and uniformly reddish brown. Head with eyes shallowly notched without ridge above, 3–4 facets wide on sides; antennomeres 8–11 forming a moderately compact club, last antennomere arcuate, not subtruncate apically; underneath with eyes almost reaching base of maxillary palps. Head and pronotum sparsely, finely punctate. Pronotum wider than long, sides somewhat parallel with lateral bead not continuous over anterior margin, and hind angles distinct. Elytra with rows of small punctures, intervals finely and usually distinctly carinate. Adults and larvae associated with stored grain products, seeds, nuts, spices, dry pet food, and dried fruit. Cosmopolitan. (7)

Uloma longula LeConte (8.0–10.3 mm) is elongate, parallel-sided, somewhat flattened, and shiny reddish yellow-brown. Head with anterior margin of clypeus (epistoma) broadly emarginate, with antennae gradually clavate and last antennomere evenly rounded apically. Pronotum is wider than long and finely punctate, with sides and lateral anterior margins narrowly explanate. Elytra with striae finely impressed, intervals somewhat convex, with epipleura ending before apices and briefly exposed pygidium. Protibiae expanded apically with outer margin serrate. Adults under loose bark of conifer stumps and logs. British Columbia to California. (1)

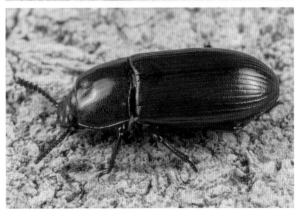

Isomira species (3.0–6.5 mm) are elongate-oval, moderately convex, yellowish-, reddish-, or very dark brown. Head and pronotum densely and contiguously punctate. Antennae filiform. Pronotum wide, broadest just before base. Elytral striae vaguely impressed or not, sutural striae most prominent with others most visible apically. Flight wings fully developed. Legs slender, front coxae widely separated, with ventral surface tarsi pubescent, and claws pectinate. On flowers and at lights in spring and summer. Western North America. (4)

Lystronychus scapularis **Champion** (5.5–8.0 mm) is moderately elongate, somewhat convex, and dull black or reddish black, and clothed in long, erect, scattered setae. Head short, coarsely and rugosely punctate, eyes narrowly separated (male) or not (female), with antennae dark blue or bluish black, reaching middle of elytra (male) or not (female); antennomeres 4–10 long, wide, flattened, and serrate in male. Pronotum transverse, convex, broadest in front of middle, lateral margins narrowed posteriorly, with two or three distinct teeth. Elytra with bluish tinge, each with reddish humeral patch, lines of shallow punctures, and flat intervals. Legs dark reddish black. Adults attracted to lights. Southeastern Arizona to Panama. (1)

Mycetochara procera **Casey** (5.5–6.7 mm) is variable, narrowly elongate, uniformly pale to dark brown with paler appendages. Head moderately coarsely and sparsely punctate, eyes smaller (male) or larger (female), with female antennomeres uniformly wide, 8–11 sometimes faintly narrower than 7. Pronotum transverse, with punctures coarse (male) or fine (female) and separated by one and a half to two times their diameters; elytra moderately (male) to strongly (female) convex, with punctostriae faintly impressed. Underside with procoxae narrowly separated by thin prosternal process. Adults attracted to lights during summer. Southern British Columbia to south-central California, east to northern Idaho and north-central Arizona. (6)

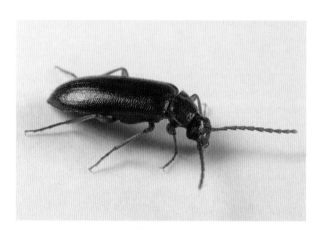

Pseudocistela pinguis **(LeConte)** (7.0–10.8 mm) is elongate-oval, with dorsum moderately shiny black and finely densely punctulate with inconspicuous recumbent pubescence. Antennae strongly serrate in both sexes. Pronotum wider than long, broadest at base, with sides arcuate to anterior margin and oblique before acute posterior angles, with sinuate posterior margin. Elytra each with a scutellar and nine additional striae punctate and finely incised, intervals convex. British Columbia to California, Nevada, and Idaho, and Colorado to New Mexico. *Pseudocistela pectinata* Hopping (7.0–10.8 mm) with antennae subpectinate (male) or weakly serrate (female), posterior pronotal angles almost 90°, elytra deeply punctostriate. British Columbia. (3)

Stenochidus gracilis (LeConte) (7.0–8.0 mm) is elongate-oblong, appearing glabrous, and black with metallic bluish tinge. Head and pronotum densely and somewhat coarsely punctate. Pronotum as long as wide (male) or slightly transverse (female). Elytra not deeply striate, intervals flat. Femora mostly red, rarely entirely black. Adults on flowers of *Adenostoma fasciculatum*. Southern California. *Stenochidus cyanescens* (LeConte) (8.0–9.0 mm) uniformly dull black, with legs entirely black or brown. Found in late spring and early summer on branches of Jeffrey pine (*Pinus jeffreyi*) with staminate cones. Oregon, northern California, and Nevada. *Stenochidus robustus* Schaeffer (10.5 mm) more rubust, with deeply impressed striae and convex intervals. California. (3)

Gondwanocrypticus platensis (Fairmaire) (3.9–4.6 mm) is broadly oval, uniformly dull dark brown to black with pronotum sometimes lighter, and sparsely clothed in very short, fine setae; legs reddish brown. Head with eyes elliptical and antennomeres 1–2 reddish at base, remaining dark, 2 much shorter than 3, apex of 11 asymmetrical. Pronotum widest at base, with anterolateral margins arcuate and posterolateral margins parallel. Elytra vaguely punctostriate with intervals sparsely punctured and humeri evident. Adults active in spring and summer, found in leaf litter, under beach wrack, sandy soil habitats, usually in association with ants. South America; widely established across southern United States, including California. (1)

367

Adelina pallida (Say) (4.5–6.0 mm) is oblong, somewhat straight-sided, very flat, and shiny reddish brown. Male with pair of small triangular horns in front of each eye, one concealed from above by the other, not protruding much beyond clypeus. Antennomeres gradually enlarged apically. Pronotum with sides distinctly sinuate before hind angles and two short, deep lines near sides at base. Elytra with rows of punctures, spaces between sparsely punctate. Adults under bark; attracted to lights. California; also Virginia to Florida, west to Indiana. *Adelina plana* (Fabricius) (3.7–4.5 mm) smaller, male clypeus deeply inserted between protruding horns; pronotum more or less quadrate. Deserts of California and Arizona. (3)

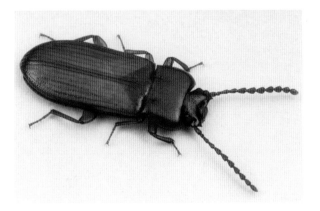

Larger Black Flour Beetle *Cynaeus angustus* (LeConte) (4.5–6.1 mm) is elongate-oval, flattened, and dark brown to black. Head broadest across slightly notched eyes. Antennomeres gradually enlarged apically. Pronotum wide, with anterior margin emarginate, lateral margins strongly arcuate and not narrowed anteriorly, and a pair of pits near slightly sinuate posterior margin. Elytra shallowly punctostriate. On stumps, in plant debris, under driftwood; also at light. Minor pest in mills and poultry houses. Widespread in North America. *Cynaeus depressus* Horn (5.6–7.6 mm) pronotum narrower, anterior pronotal margin nearly truncate, with sides less rounded and converging anteriorly. California and Arizona, south to Baja California. (2)

Diaperis rufipes Horn (5.2–6.8 mm) is oval, strongly convex, and shiny. Head reddish. Pronotum black. Elytra usually reddish orange with two continuous, irregular transverse black bands and narrow sutural stripe, and a pair of reddish apical spots; reddish areas sometimes reduced to narrow basal band and two apical spots. Underside black or reddish. Front femora reddish. On shelf fungus or under bark of *Populus*; at lights. California, Arizona, and New Mexico. *Diaperis californica* Blaisdell (5.0–5.8 mm) elongate-oval, elytra with one continuous black band, on fungi growing on *Quercus*. Central California. (2)

Platydema oregonensis LeConte (4.0–6.1 mm) is broadly ovate, moderately shiny dark reddish brown to black, with appendages reddish brown. Frons unarmed, with longitudinal impression between eyes. Pronotum trapezoidal in shape, sides nearly straight and converging toward distinctly emarginate anterior margin. Elytra each with eight weakly impressed punctostriae, shallow punctures widely and irregularly spaced, outer striae poorly defined basally and apically, plus a short punctostria flanking scutellum. Metatarsomere 1 longer than combined lengths of 2 and 3. Under bark of *Pinus* stumps and logs. British Columbia to California, east to Idaho. (7)

Platydema wandae Triplehorn (5.1–7.8 mm) is broadly oval, moderately convex, and dull velvety brown to black, with appendages uniformly reddish brown. Pronotum minutely punctate, with anterior margin distinctly emarginate. Elytral punctostriae shallowly impressed. Metatarsomere 1 longer than combined lengths of 2 and 3. Nocturnal adults on shelf fungi growing on *Quercus* and other dead trees; at lights. Arizona and New Mexico. *Platydema nigritum* (Motschulsky) (4.6–7.8 mm) similar, antennomeres 1–4 and 11 light reddish brown, 5–10 dark brown to black; southern United States to Central America. (7)

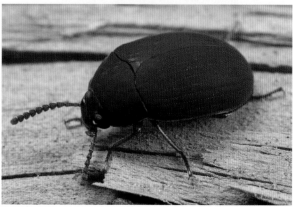

Corticeus substriatus LeConte (4.0–5.7 mm) is elongate, uniformly reddish brown dorsally and ventrally, and glabrous. Pronotum slightly wider than long, and coarsely punctured, with anterolateral angles sharp, lateral margins broadly and evenly rounded, and narrowly explanate along entire length. Elytra confusedly punctate. Adults found year-round in bark beetle galleries under bark of various conifers, including *Pinus*, *Picea*, and *Pseudotsuga*, and likely feed on *Dendroctonus ponderosae* Hopkins (p.560), as well as their fungus and frass. Widely distributed in coniferous montane forests in western North America. (8)

Phaleria rotundata LeConte (5.3–6.8 mm) is elongate-oval, robust, somewhat convex, and shiny pale reddish brown, rarely entirely blackish, with long, dense setae along lateral margins of pronotum and elytra. Head with eyes large, separated ventrally by at least ventral diameter of one eye, antennae not surpassing base of pronotum. Pronotum widest at base. Elytra sometimes infuscate medially. Underside of prothorax (hypomera) with distinct setae. Underside occasionally black. All tibiae spiny, front tibiae expanded. Flightless adults found year-round under decaying seaweed deposited near high tide on Pacific Coast beaches. San Francisco Bay, California to northern Baja California. (1)

Phaleromela variegata Triplehorn (2.6–4.0 mm) is blackish with irregular reddish-brown elytral markings. Small, round eyes widely separated above and below. Antennae surpassing pronotum. Pronotal plicae present posterolaterally. Elytra with pale oblique humeral markings and apical bands or spots, each with eight fine, feebly impressed punctostriae, interstriae convex or flat. All tibiae spiny, protibiae expanded apically. On sandy banks of montane streams and rivers. Yukon and Northwest Territories south to northern California and Idaho. *Phaleromela picta* (Mannerheim) (2.8–3.9 mm) pale with blackish M-shaped elytral markings, without pronotal plicae. Coastal dunes, British Columbia to central California. (4)

Alobates pensylvanicus (De Geer) (20.0–23.0 mm) is oblong, somewhat dull dark brown to black. Underside of head without bright yellow clump of setae. Pronotum slightly wider than long, widest at middle, with lateral margins not carinate. Elytra wider at base than prothorax, with rows of fine punctures, spaces between finely wrinkled with three irregular rows of very fine punctures. Adults found, sometimes in large numbers, under bark of decaying hardwoods, on fungus. Widespread in eastern North America, established in Oregon and California. (1)

Cibdelis blaschkei Mannerheim (13.2–14.2 mm) is elongate-oblong, shiny black, and glabrous with surfaces punctate-rugose. Head rounded in front with epistoma truncate medially. Pronotum densely and coarsely punctured and convex, with anterior margin truncate with angles obtuse, lateral margins arcuate to distinct, but not prominent posterior angles. Elytra faintly punctostriate with small rounded tubercles more or less arranged in rows. Adults found under bark and stones in woodlands where larvae develop in dry, rotten branches of oaks (*Quercus*). California. Genus needs revision. (5)

Coelocnemis dilaticollis Mannerheim (19.0–29.0 mm) is variable, moderately to very robust, convex, and uniformly dull black. Head distinctly and moderately to densely punctate to rugose. Pronotum moderately convex, wider than long, broadest and somewhat angulate at middle, with underside (hypomeron) punctate. Elytra broadly convex, strial punctures may be variously obscured by rugosity, interstriae finely punctate to very coarsely rugose. Tibiae with paired apical narrow longitudinal lines of yellowish pubescence, tarsi underneath with dense yellowish pubescence. Nocturnal adults flightless, found under bark of pine (*Pinus*) stumps during spring and summer. British Columbia to southern California, east to Alberta, Montana, Wyoming, and Utah. (7)

Coelocnemis sulcata Casey (26.0–28.0 mm) is elongate and moderately stout, convex, uniformly dull reddish black to black, and finely to very finely punctate. Head half as wide as prothorax, antennomeres 7–11 asymmetrical. Pronotum as long as wide or slightly longer, broadest just before middle, with underside (hypomeron) smooth. Elytra punctostriate with intervals distinctly convex. Tibiae with paired lines of yellowish pubescence apically, tarsi underneath with dense yellowish pubescence. Nocturnal adults flightless, found walking on ground at night. California east to Idaho, Utah, and Arizona. *Coelocnemis magna* LeConte prosternal process prominent, interstriae flat; California to New Mexico and Baja California. (7)

Iphthiminus serratus (Mannerheim) (16.5–22.5 mm) is somewhat flattened, and moderately shiny black. Head coarsely punctate to punctate-rugose. Pronotum moderately rugose with large, uniform punctures, and lateral margins serrate. Elytra faintly punctostriate, interstriae finely punctate and flat. Nocturnal and flightless adults under loose bark of fungus-infested conifer logs and stumps. British Columbia to California, east to Alberta, Montana, and Nebraska. *Iphthiminus lewisii* (Horn) (18.3–29.2 mm) pronotum smooth, minutely and uniformly punctate, with lateral margins less serrate, and elytra smooth, striae sometimes absent, interstriae convex with punctures minute to absent. On *Pinus* and *Quercus*. Southern California to Wyoming, Colorado, New Mexico, and eastern Texas. (2)

Upis ceramboides (Linnaeus) (13.0–18.6 mm) is elongate with all but elytra dull black. Pronotum coarsely and irregularly punctate with apical angles rounded and depressed, posterior angles obtuse, and posterior margin sinuate. Elytra shiny, with sides diverging to about apical third, with surface sculpted with large, coarse, irregular punctures. Year-round in deciduous and mixed forests on or under bark of *Acer*, *Populus*, and *Betula*; adapted to survive cold temperatures. Holarctic; in West, from Alaska and Yukon Territory south to Oregon, Idaho, and Wyoming. (1)

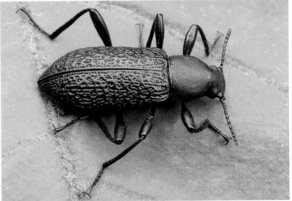

371

Strongylium atrum Champion (15.7–22.6 mm) is elongate, uniformly dull black, with long slender legs. Eyes relatively large, inner margins converging anteriorly. Antennae uniformly black, slightly longer in male. Pronotum lacks lateral margin. Elytra finely punctostriate. Adults in logs, on vegetation, and at lights at night. Southeastern Arizona and New Mexico, south to Durango and Sinaloa. *Strongylium apache* Triplehorn & Spilman (12.7–17.9 mm) eyes relatively small with inner margins subparallel, terminal antennomere reddish yellow, pronotum has distinct, yet fine pronotal margin; adults at lights during summer in southeastern Arizona, southwestern New Mexico, south to Sonora. (2)

Statira pluripunctata Horn (6.0–9.5 mm) is dull blackish brown with forebody, legs, and underside reddish brown. Head scabrous, antennae half as long as body. Pronotum longer than wide, disc finely rugulose, with lateral margins usually distinct only between middle and posterior angles. Elytral striae finely punctate, alternate intervals setigerously punctate, 8–16 on 1, 14–21 on 3, 12–20 on 5, 10–17 on 7, and 12–20 on 9. Meso- and metatibiae both sulcate. Prosternum raised between procoxae. Adults on vegetation and at lights during summer. Utah and Arizona to Texas. (8)

PROSTOMIDAE (pro-stōm'-i-dē)
JUGULAR-HORNED BEETLES

A single species of jugular-horned beetle, *Prostomis mandibularis* (Fabricius), occurs in North America and is restricted to the western portion of the continent. Both larvae and adults occur in the decaying heartwood of large-diameter rotten conifer logs, especially those in the reddish mudlike stage of decomposition.

FAMILY DIAGNOSIS Prostomids are elongate, parallel-sided, and flattened. Head prognathous and bearing large mandibles that are serrate internally. Antennae with 11 antennomeres, 9–11 forming weak club. Pronotum quadrate, with lateral margins rounded and not carinate, posterior margin slightly broader than base of elytra. Procoxal cavities closed behind. Elytra long, parallel-sided, and covering abdomen completely. Legs short, with tarsi 4-4-4 and claws simple. Abdomen with five ventrites, 1–2 connate with suture evident.

SIMILAR FAMILIES *Prostomis* superficially resembles beetles in the families Zopheridae (p.340), some Tenebrionidae (p.347), Silvanidae, (p.451), Cucujidae (p.453), and Laemophloeidae (p.458), but are easily distinguished by the prognathous head bearing large serrated mandibles and tarsi 4-4-4 in both sexes.

COLLECTING NOTES Look for adult jugular-horned beetles under the bark of rotten logs of various conifers. Adults and larvae are known to inhabit dead conifer logs within reddish claylike material between layers of decaying wood fibers.

FAUNA ONE SPECIES, *PROSTOMIS MANDIBULARIS*

Prostomis mandibularis (Fabricius) (4.8–6.2 mm) is elongate, somewhat parallel-sided, flat, shiny yellowish brown to pale reddish brown, and broadest across eyes, gradually narrowing posteriorly. Head prognathous with conspicuous mandibles. Antennae short, not reaching posterior margin of pronotum. Pronotum quadrate, broadest anteriorly, lateral margins more or less parallel, not carinate, with posterior angles minutely angulate. Elytra with combined apices rounded, each with six deep punctostriae between suture and weakly indicated lateral fold, striae weakly impressed except those flanking suture. British Columbia to northern California. (1)

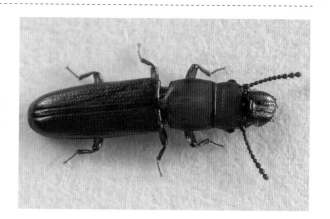

STENOTRACHELIDAE (sten-ō-tra-kēl'-i-dē)
FALSE LONGHORN BEETLES

Little is known about the habits of this small, uncommonly encountered family of beetles. Adults are likely short-lived and are usually found on vegetation. Some species occur on flowers, and their mouthparts are comparable to beetles in other families that feed on pollen and nectar. Known stenotrachelid larvae develop in decaying wood in deciduous and coniferous forests. *Cephaloon* larvae are associated with conifer logs in the red-rot stage preceded by the presence of cellulose-destroying brown-rot fungi. *Stenotrachelus aeneus* (Fabricius) larvae are found under bark or in the wood of dead deciduous trees, including willow (*Salix*), poplar (*Populus*), alder (*Alnus*), and beech (*Fagus*).

FAMILY DIAGNOSIS Adult stenotrachelids are elongate, usually narrowed at both ends, and somewhat convex with usually fine vestiture. Head elongate and diamond- or bell-shaped, narrowed gradually (*Cephaloon*) behind

372

eyes, with distinct neck, prognathous or hypognathous (*Anelpistus canadensis* Mank); eyes notched. Antennae attached between eyes, with 11 antennomeres, usually filiform with apical antennomeres sometimes thickened. Pronotum elongate and bell-shaped (*Anelpistus canadensis*, *Cephaloon*) or quadrate (*Stenotrachelus*), side margins completely carinate (*Anelpistus canadensis*, *Stenotrachelus*), or without distinct margins (*Cephaloon*). Procoxal cavities open behind. Elytra gradually narrowed toward apices, vaguely costate and irregularly punctate, and completely covering abdomen. Legs long and slender, with tarsomeres simple, tarsi 5-5-4, and claws simple (*Anelpistus canadensis*, *Stenotrachelus*) or pectinate with a membranous lobe beneath (*Cephaloon*). Abdomen with five ventrites free, or 1–2 connate.

SIMILAR FAMILIES

- false blister beetles (Oedemeridae, p.374)—pronotum widest toward head, last tarsomere wide, setose underneath
- blister beetles (Meloidae, p.378)—hypognathous head deflexed with narrow neck, broader than pronotum
- fire-colored beetles (Pyrochroidae, p.394)—antennae serrate or plumose
- *Retocomus*, *Stereopalpus* (Anthicidae, p.405)—head with narrow neck, body clothed in setae
- longhorn beetles (Cerambycidae, p.460)—tarsi apparently 4-4-4, actually 5-5-5

COLLECTING NOTES Search for false longhorn beetles during the day resting on flowers or vegetation in moist, wooded habitats. They are also collected by sweeping and beating vegetation, or attracted to lights at night. Individuals are sometimes captured in Malaise and flight intercept traps.

FAUNA 10 SPECIES IN FOUR GENERA

Stenotrachelus aeneus (Fabricius) (11.0 mm) is elongate, black, punctate with silvery setae lying nearly flat on surface, with reddish-black appendages. Head exposed and prognathous, antennae filiform with antennomere 3 elongate. Pronotum punctate, without granulations, and with distinct and complete lateral margins. Elytra irregularly undulate with traces of striae. Adults attracted to lights or found in flight intercept traps in late summer. Larvae develop in decomposing wood. Holarctic; transcontinental from British Columbia east across Canada, and south to Michigan and New Hampshire. (1)

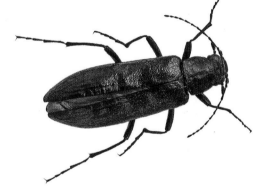

373

Cephaloon bicolor Horn (11.0–16.0 mm) has antennae with last three antennomeres not distinctly thickened, with combined lengths barely exceeding 1.5 mm. Membranous lobes of tarsal claws robust, obtuse, not curved at apices. Male yellowish brown, sometimes with elytral margins and spot on pronotal disc black; ventrite 3 with bifurcate processes short, triangular. Female black to yellowish brown, sometimes with head and pronotum reddish and elytra black (see *C. vandykei* female). *Cephaloon pacificum* Van Dyke (13.0–14.0 mm) with pulvilli very slender, acute, and curved. Females yellowish brown; males with head, antennae, pronotum, and elytral margins black, with no bifurcate process. Both coastal British Columbia to northern California. (4)

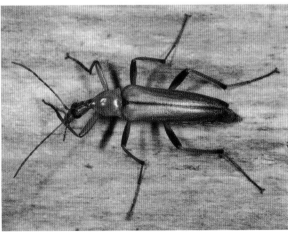

Cephaloon vandykei Hopping & Hopping (10.0–16.0 mm) has antennae with last three antennomeres not distinctly thickened, with combined lengths barely exceeding 1.0 mm. Membranous lobes of tarsal claws robust, obtuse, not curved at apices. Males yellowish brown, ventrite 3 with bifurcate processes shorter, triangular. Female light reddish brown with elytra and metasternum black. Northern Sierra Nevada, California. *Cephaloon tenuicorne* LeConte (11.0–17.0 mm) with similar antennae and membranous lobes, males usually entirely black, sometimes with legs bicolored, bifurcate processes longer, fingerlike; females entirely yellowish brown to black. British Columbia to central California, east to Alberta, Montana, Utah, and Colorado. Both species attracted to lights. (4)

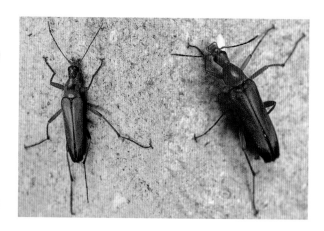

OEDEMERIDAE (ē-de-mer'-i-dē)
FALSE BLISTER BEETLES

False blister beetles not only resemble blister beetles (Meloidae, p.378), some species also produce cantharidin, a chemical capable of producing blisters that range from painless to mildly uncomfortable to extremely painful and slow to heal. When squeezed or crushed against the skin, these beetles defensively secrete this caustic compound via their bodily fluids. Aposematic coloration is found throughout the family, and it is likely that many species possess cantharidin. False blister beetles are most abundant in coastal and moist wooded habitats, where they are usually found resting on foliage, or hiding under driftwood or in moist, rotten logs. Nectar and pollen feeders are frequently found on flowers of perennials, shrubs, and trees. Oedemerid larvae often develop in moist decaying logs, stumps, and roots of hardwoods and conifers, as well as in driftwood washed up along rivers and beaches. Larvae of the wharf borer, *Nacerdes melanura* (Linnaeus), an Old World species established along both the Pacific and Atlantic coasts, are of minor economic importance as they damage wharf pilings and other structural timbers.

FAMILY DIAGNOSIS Adult oedemerids are elongate, slender, and soft-bodied, with colors ranging from black, brown, or gray to yellowish brown, sometimes with yellow, red, or orange pronotum or markings on elytra. Head more or less prognathous and not strongly narrowed behind eyes. Antennae filiform, usually with 11 (12 in *Nacerdes*) antennomeres, males of some species with last antennomere constricted medially, sometimes appearing as if they have 12 antennomeres. Pronotum often longer than wide, usually broadest at anterior one-third and narrowed toward elytra, with anterior margin slightly covering head, lateral margins not carinate and usually sinuate. Procoxal cavities broadly open behind. Elytra broader than posterior margin of pronotum, long, almost or completely concealing abdomen. Tarsi 5-5-4 in both sexes, with penultimate tarsomere distinctly lobed and thickly setose underneath. Abdomen with five ventrites, with 1–2 connate.

SIMILAR FAMILIES
- soldier beetles (Cantharidae, p.265)—lateral pronotal margins carinate, tarsi 5-5-5
- blister beetles (Meloidae, p.378)—head usually wider than pronotum, with a distinct neck, and pronotum not abruptly wider at anterior one-third
- longhorn beetles (Cerambycidae, p.460)—tarsi appear 4-4-4, actually 5-5-5

COLLECTING NOTES Look for adult oedemerids during the day on flowers of various plants, especially woody shrubs and trees. Sweeping vegetation, especially flower heads and leaves, is productive. Check under driftwood along beaches and shores of bays and large rivers. In mesic forested habitats, examine wet and rotten logs, stumps, and roots of hardwoods and conifers. Be sure to carefully search through the litter immediately surrounding these microniches, too. Some species in these and other wooded habitats, as well as deserts and other xeric environments, are attracted to lights. *Calopus angustus* (LeConte) is captured in both Lindgren funnel and flight intercept traps.

FAUNA 87 SPECIES IN 17 GENERA

Calopus angustus **(LeConte)** (15.0–21.0 mm) is elongate and brownish, with long antennae. Eyes deeply notched, with serrate antennae inserted within notch. Antennomere 2 small, 3–11 long and flat, 3–10 four times as long as their width at middle. Mandibular apices notched. Pronotum as long as wide, scarcely widened in front, with disc roughly punctured. Elytra long, coarsely punctate, with apices jointly rounded. Larvae develop in dead and living conifers and hardwoods. Adults found under bark during summer, also in Lindgren funnel and flight intercept traps; attracted to lights. Transcontinental; in West from British Columbia to California, east to Alberta, Idaho, Colorado, and New Mexico. (1)

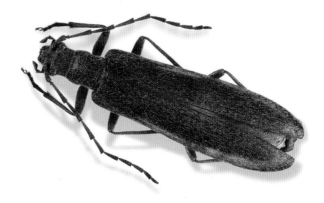

Ischnomera excavata LeConte (5.0–9.0 mm) is elongate, densely punctate, dull, and moderately densely clothed in short, decumbent pubescence. Head short, black, with mandibular apices notched, with antennal insertion between eye and base of mandible. Pronotum red, anterior and posterior margins often black, rugose and punctate or occasionally sparsely punctate and shiny, sometimes variably marked with 1–2 discal spots and/or median discal spot. Elytra black, sometimes with bluish luster, and costate. Front tibia with two apical spurs and all claws with basal tooth. Adults on flowers of buckbrush (*Ceanothus*) and elderberry (*Sambucus*). British Columbia to California, east to Idaho, Utah, and Arizona. *Ischnomera nigra* (LeConte) (6.0–10.0 mm) uniformly black. Pacific Northwest. (5)

Copdita quadrimaculata **(Motschulsky)** (8.0–20.0 mm) is slender, sparsely clothed in fine, short, recumbent pale setae, and brown with head and pronotal markings; elytra, underside, and femoral apices darker. Head with eyes protruding and slightly emarginate, with mandibular apices notched, and antennal insertion approximate to eye. Antennomeres cylindrical, not expanded, with apical antennomere of male constricted medially. Pronotum longer than wide, with four dark spots. Elytra finely rugose. Apical ventrite pale, produced and truncate (male), or evenly arcuate (female). Front tibia with two apical spurs, and claws simple. Adults under driftwood on beaches during summer; also at lights. British Columbia to California, east to Arizona. (1)

Eumecomera cyanipennis (Horn) (7.0–11.0 mm) is metallic blue-green, and clothed in coarse, long, moderately dense pubescence. Head long, mandibular apices notched, with eyes moderately protruding and deeply emarginate. Pronotum long, coarsely punctate, with intermixed black and white setae. Elytra rugose. Posterior margin of apical ventrite shallowly (female) or deeply (male) emarginate. On flowers in Coastal and Transverse Ranges. Oregon to southern California. *Eumecomera bicolor* (Horn) with head black, pronotum orange with light and dark setae, and elytra metallic blue, Oregon and California. *E. obscura* (LeConte) similarly bicolored, pronotal setae pale, California east to Colorado and Texas. (3)

Oxacis subfusca Horn (6.0–9.0 mm) is dusky brown and moderately densely clothed in fine recumbent whitish setae, appearing powdery. Head short, mandibular apices entire; with eyes prominent and slightly emarginate at antennal insertions. Antennomeres 3–11 cylindrical, about three times longer than wide. Prothorax long, disc rugosely punctate, with fine pubescence not obscuring surface. Elytra finely rugose, not costate. Apical ventrite evenly arcuate (male), or only slightly emarginate (female) posteriorly. Claws not toothed basally. At lights during summer in wooded habitats. Utah to Arizona and New Mexico. (5)

Oxacis sericea Horn (5.0–8.0 mm) is elongate, densely clothed in long, coarse, whitish setae, with pale yellowish-brown appendages. Head short, mandibular apices entire, eyes protruding, and slightly emarginate. Antennomeres cylindrical, 3–11 about five times longer than wide. Pronotum long, densely punctured and rugose, and clothed in long, dense, white pubescence that obscures punctures. Elytra not costate. Claws not toothed basally. At lights. Great Basin and Mojave Deserts. Oregon and California east to Idaho and Nevada; also Texas. (5)

Rhinoplatia ruficollis Horn (8.0 mm) is mostly blackish with reddish-orange prothorax, and moderately densely clothed in grayish setae. Head occasionally reddish orange apically, with elongate mandibles entire apically. Filiform antennae inserted midway between eyes and mandibular bases. Eyes oval, not emarginate or protruding. Elytra narrowed apically, densely punctate, sometimes vaguely costate, rarely purplish. On flowers during late spring and early summer. Western Nevada, southern California, and northwestern Arizona. *Rhinoplatia mortivallicola* Arnett (9.0–14.0 mm) narrower, with head, antennae, prothorax, procoxae, and tarsi reddish orange, pronotum glabrous, and sparse black pubescence on elytral apices. Mojave Desert. (2)

Sisenes championi Horn (10.0–12.0 mm) is mostly black with scarlet red elytra clothed in short, fine, dense orange pubescence. Head long and rugose, with mandibular apices notched. Antennae inserted away from eyes, with antennomeres flattened and three times longer than wide. Pronotum long, somewhat expanded anteriorly, with broad orange stripes along sides, and lateral margins slightly sinuate. Elytra costate and rugose. Legs slender and claws simple. On flowers of *Mimosa aculeaticarpa biuncifera* and *Ceanothus greggii* during early summer. Upland and montane habitats in southeastern Arizona. (1)

Xanthochroina bicolor (LeConte) (6.0–9.0 mm) is moderately clothed in recumbent golden pubescence, with head, thorax, and legs orange, and elytra and antennae brown. Head short, with short curved mandibles thin and entire apically. Elongate-oval eyes small with antennae inserted in emarginations. Pronotum wide, disc with punctation similar to that of head. Elytra finely rugose. Legs slender, protibia with pair of apical spurs. Claws simple. Larvae known to infest wood flooring, railroad ties, and mining timbers. At lights during summer. British Columbia to California, east to Idaho, Wyoming, Utah, and western Texas. (1)

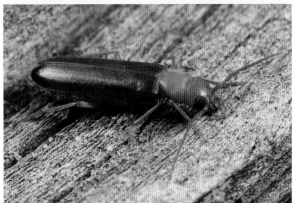

377

Ditylus gracilis LeConte (13.0–23.0 mm) is robust, dull black, punctate-rugose, and clothed in short dark or golden vesture. Small eyes slightly emarginate. Antennomeres 4–10 long, five times longer than wide, not expanded apically. Prothorax long. Elytra moderately rugose, weakly costate. Protibia with two apical spurs. Tarsi tomentose ventrally, metatarsomere 1 longer than 2–4 combined. Claws simple. Larvae in wet rotten spruce (*Picea*) and cedar (*Thuja*) logs. Adults on decayed logs and flowers. Alaska to central California, east to Idaho. *Ditylus quadricollis* LeConte (15.0–21.0 mm) with similar color and vesture, antennomeres 4–10 three times longer than wide. (2)

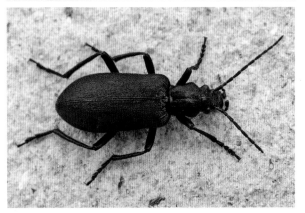

Wharf Borer *Nacerdes melanura* (Linnaeus) (10.0–12.0 mm) is elongate, yellowish orange, and clothed in fine golden pubescence, with elytral apices black and appendages yellowish brown. Head as long as broad with small, elongate-oval, and scarcely notched eyes. Antennae with 12 antennomeres. Pronotum wider than long and coarsely punctate. Legs slender, front tibia with single apical spur, and claws simple. Larvae in damp and decaying driftwood, wharf pilings, and old timber along coast and rivers; can survive tidal immersion. Short-lived adults active in spring and summer. Cosmopolitan; transcontinental, in West from coastal British Columbia to California. (1)

Xanthochroa californica Horn (8.0–12.0 mm) is elongate with head, thorax, and femora orange, and elytra metallic blue-green; antennae, eyes, tibiae, and tarsi black. Head short and sparsely punctate, with large eyes oval and distinctly emarginate, and antennae with apparently 12 (male) antennomeres. Pronotum as wide as long, disc shiny and weakly punctate, underside with prosternum dark. Elytra rugose and weakly costate. Abdomen shiny black with apical ventrite mostly orangish yellow and deeply cleft (male) or not (female). Legs slender, front tibia with single apical spur, and claws simple. Adults attracted to lights during summer in wooded montane habitats of California. (4)

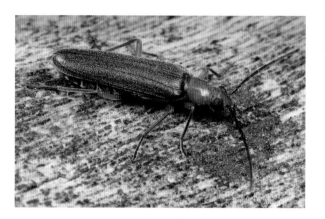

MELOIDAE (mel-ō′-i-dē)
BLISTER BEETLES

Blister beetles are of particular interest because of their medical, veterinary, and agricultural importance. They are so named because their *hemolymph* and soft tissues contain cantharidin, a caustic chemical released through leg joints (p.36, Fig. 34) that irritates and blisters sensitive tissues and discourages predators. Males transfer cantharidin to females while mating, which in turn place it on their eggs, also to deter predators. Some antlike flower beetles (Anthicidae, p.400) and *Pedilus* (Pyrochroidae, p.394) are attracted to cantharidin and often drawn to living or dead meloids. Blister beetles exhibit exceptionally diverse courtship behavior that utilizes chemical, tactile, and visual cues. Most meloids are diurnal, but species in some genera (e.g., *Epicauta, Pyrota*) are active mostly at night. Nearly all adults are phytophagous and especially fond of plants in the families Asteraceae, Convolvulaceae, Fabaceae, Malvaceae, and Solanaceae. Species of *Lytta* and *Pyrota* often gather in conspicuous mating aggregations as they feed. Many meloids eat flowers and their associated tissues, but species of *Epicauta* prefer to eat leaves and may become serious garden and agricultural pests by attacking crops such as alfalfa, beets, potatoes, and tomatoes. The larvae of meloids develop by hypermetamorphosis and prey on either grasshopper eggs (*Epicauta*), or the larvae of solitary bees. The active first instar larva, or triungulin, is physically and behaviorally adapted for actively seeking out the appropriate host. Triungulins of most Nemognathinae and some Meloinae are parasitoids of bee larvae and rely on the bees themselves for transportation back to their subterranean nests filled with brood. The triungulins attach themselves to adult bees as they visit flowers to gather nectar and pollen as nest provisions for their brood.

FAMILY DIAGNOSIS Adult meloids are typically elongate, soft-bodied, black, gray, brownish, metallic blue or green, or a combination of black with yellow, orange, or red markings, with antlike head and short neck. Head hypognathous, deflexed, and strongly narrowed behind eyes to form a neck. Antennae usually filiform or moniliform with 11 antennomeres; middle antennomeres sometimes modified as grasping organs (male *Meloe*). Pronotum usually narrower than both head and base of elytra, with lateral margins broadly rounded. Procoxal cavities open behind. Elytra soft, leathery, rolled over abdomen along sides, usually long and loosely cover most of abdomen, or short and meeting along suture (*Cordylospasta, Lytta sublaevis, Megetra*) or overlapping basally (*Meloe*). Legs long, tarsi 5-5-4, tarsi simple, with pads or bilobed, claws with dorsal and ventral blade, dorsal blade sometimes pectinate. Abdomen with six ventrites free.

SIMILAR FAMILIES
- soldier beetles (Cantharidae, p.265)—tarsi 5-5-5, elytra not rolled over abdomen
- some darkling beetles (Tenebrionidae, p.347)—no neck, elytra not rolled over abdomen
- false longhorn beetles (Stenotrachelidae, p.372)—head narrow, elytra not rolled over abdomen
- false blister beetles (Oedemeridae, p.374)—head lacks neck, elytra not rolled over abdomen

- fire-colored beetles (Pyrochroidae, p.394)—antennae serrate or pectinate, elytra not rolled over abdomen
- some antlike flower beetles (Anthicidae, p.400)—elytra not rolled over abdomen

COLLECTING NOTES Most meloids are commonly found mating and feeding on flowers in spring and summer, while others are encountered wandering on the ground, especially during cooler times of the year. They are carefully collected by hand, or located by beating and sweeping vegetation. Some are attracted to lights, while flightless species are collected in pitfall traps. Avoid skin irritations by carefully washing after handling meloids.

FAUNA 424 SPECIES IN 21 GENERA

Epicauta abadona Skinner (9.0–18.0 mm) is elongate, slender, and tan with striped pronotum and elytra; antennae, femora, tibiae, basal portion of pronotum, and underside orange. Head evenly convex, middle smooth and glabrous in male. Pronotum often with weak pair of stripes. Elytra each with three black stripes, two of equal width near suture and extending posteriorly from humerus, and a narrower faint lateral stripe largely clothed in yellow, not black, vestiture. Legs with spurs of front and middle tibiae curved underneath. Adults commonly attracted to lights, mostly during late summer. Southern Arizona south to Sonora and Sinaloa. (~200 NA)

Epicauta cinctipennis (Chevrolat) (8.0–16.0 mm) is elongate, dull black, and mostly clothed in shorter black pubescence not obscuring cuticle, with longer and dense whitish setae on midline of head and pronotum, and on elytral margins. Head with sparse, pale pubescence around eyes and occiput, with antennae elongate and filiform in both sexes, and antennomeres 4–10 three times longer than wide. Pronotum short, with lateral margins subparallel behind, and converging anteriorly to broad apical collar. Elytral margins occasionally with yellow-orange setae. Adults on lupine (*Lupinus*) and meadow-rue (*Thalictrum*). Arizona, southern New Mexico, and western Texas, south to Mexico. (~200 NA)

Epicauta costata (LeConte) (7.0–20.0 mm) is elongate, slender, light yellowish brown to black, and densely clothed in almost white scalelike pubescence that obscures the surface, save for midline of pronotum and one or two pairs of spots on disc. Male with antennomeres 3–5, and to lesser extent 2, long, slender, and shiny dorsally. Elytra each with four sharply elevated carinae. Adults feed on *Datura*, as well as *Solanum* during summer; also at lights. Arizona to western Texas, south to Durango and Chihuahua. *Epicauta tricostata* (Werner) (7.0–11.0 mm) similar, but elytra with three carinae. These are the only *Epicauta* species with scalelike vestiture and costate elytra. (~200 NA)

Epicauta hirsutapubescens (Maydell) (7.0–12.0 mm) is black or brown and clothed in dense pubescence. Antennomere 1 long, subequal to 2–4 combined, curved over eye in male. Elytron with stripe of dense gray pubescence from humerus almost to apex. Legs reddish with apices of segments and tarsomeres dark, hind trochanter with grayish tuft, and middle femur without fringe underneath. Adults at lights. Arizona to Texas, south to Durango. *Epicauta virgulata* (LeConte) (8.0–12.0 mm) antennomere 1 longer than 2–4 combined, hind trochanter without tuft, middle femur with fringe underneath; on *Olneya tesota*. California and Arizona, south to Baja California Sur and Sinaloa. (~200 NA)

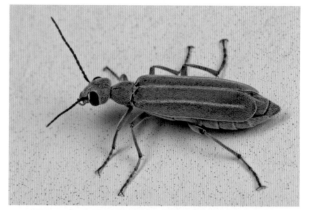

Epicauta ochrea (LeConte) (7.5–15.0 mm) is elongate, reddish brown to dark brown, with elytra lighter. Head densely and deeply punctured with deep median suture, with middle antennomeres thickened in male. Pronotum wider than long, median suture distinct, with sparse pubescence sometimes partially or completely rubbed off. Elytra clothed in silky appressed yellowish pubescence. Male with single curved spur on front tibia. Nocturnal adults associated with *Yucca*, spend their days down in axils; attracted to lights during summer. Utah and Arizona, east to Oklahoma and Texas, south to Mexico. (~200 NA)

Punctate Blister Beetle *Epicauta puncticollis* **Mannerheim** (6.0–13.0 mm) is elongate and shiny black with abundant silky black setae that do not obscure surface. Head coarsely punctate, narrowly sulcate medially, with short reddish-brown line between eyes, and antennae not tapering to apex, antennomeres 1–4 with short vestiture, setae not as long as width of their respective segments. Elytra densely granulate. Tarsal pads of variable extent always present on some segments. Adults found mostly during summer on many kinds of flowers in various habitats, except deserts, including gardens and agricultural fields. Southern British Columbia to northwestern Baja California, east to Montana and Wyoming. (~200 NA)

Epicauta purpurea (Horn) (8.0–15.0 mm) is elongate, dull blackish or dark brownish with dense black or brownish pubescence producing a faint, purplish sheen, and striped elytra. Head large and grayish with pair of elongate black markings. Pronotum gray with a pair of elongate black markings on disc. Elytra black, with margins and discal stripes gray. Underside and legs with less dense gray pubescence. Adults found walking on ground, or feeding on *Desmodium* and *Convolvulus* during summer. Arizona to Sinaloa and Durango. (~200 NA)

Epicauta segmenta (Say) (12.0–20.0 mm) is robust, dull black, and mostly clothed in short black pubescence. Pronotum slightly longer than wide, with posterior pronotal margin fringed with erect white setae. Elytra entirely black. Underside with coxae and posterior margins of abdominal sterna fringed with white setae, sometimes faintly so. Fully winged and diurnal adults feed on *Solanum* and *Datura* during summer. Arizona to Great Plains and western Texas, south to Mexico. Flightless form with inflated elytra occurs from western Texas to Great Plains. (~200 NA)

Epicauta tenuilineata (Horn) (7.0–15.0 mm) is elongate, slender, and tan with sparse, scattered, ashy gray pubescence becoming dense along thin raised lines on elytra. Median sutures of head and pronotum denuded, not sulcate. Head with eyes large and bulging, antennomere 2 longer than 1, 1 and 2 slender and shiny in male. Pronotum slightly longer than wide and bell-shaped. Elytra each with small rubbed spots near scutellum and on humerus, and four very narrow raised lines. Nocturnal adults attracted to lights during summer in Colorado and Sonoran Deserts. Southern California, southern Arizona, and Baja California Sur. (~200 NA)

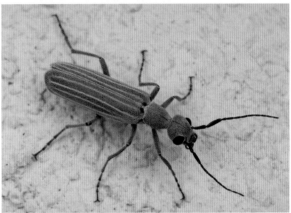

Epicauta wheeleri Horn (6.0–10.0 mm) is elongate, somewhat slender, black, and densely clothed in fine ashy gray to yellowish-gray pubescence, except for deep yellow or reddish-orange patch on pronotal disc. Pronotum slightly longer than wide, sides evenly arcuate. Elytra with black patches flanking scutellum, present or not on humeri. Legs ashy gray with femoral and tibial apices, and tarsi black. Abdomen gray with small black patches medially and laterally on ventrites 2–5. Diurnal adults feed on flowers of *Ericameria*, *Lepidospartum*, and other composites in deserts. Central and southeastern California to southwestern Utah and southeastern Arizona. (~200 NA)

Cordylospasta opaca (Horn) (6.0–19.0 mm) is robust, somewhat shiny black, coarsely rugose, with pronounced sexual dimorphism, and geographically variable in form. Antennae with 11 antennomeres reaching middle of pronotum (female), or attaining posterior pronotal margin (male). Pronotum short. Elytra not overlapping basally, cover abdomen (male), or short and dehiscent apically exposing sometimes enlarged abdomen (female); females apterous, fully winged males capable of flight. Adults feed on plants in diverse families in various habitats from about sea level to 2,000 meters. Southern California and Mojave Desert regions of Nevada and Arizona. *Cordylospasta fulleri* Horn (6.0–19.0 mm) antennae with 8–10 antennomeres. Restricted to Great Basin. (2)

Inflated Blister Beetle *Cysteodemus armatus* LeConte (7.0–18.0 mm) is robust, mostly glabrous, with strongly inflated black elytra fused along suture. Pronotum and elytra sometimes coated with light yellow, white, or whitish-brown encrustation. Elytra may have faint metallic reflections. Pronotum with a single weak or strongly developed lateral spine, disc strongly sloping posteriorly. Flightless adults feed on blossoms of creosote bush (*Larrea tridentata*), composites, and many other spring flowers in the Mojave, Colorado, and Sonoran Deserts. California, Arizona, and Baja California. (2)

Cysteodemus wislizeni LeConte (10.0–15.0 mm) is robust, mostly glabrous, with strongly inflated and fused elytra deep metallic blue, green, and violet. Pronotum with sides angulate or tuberculate, never spined, with disc only slightly sloping posteriorly. Dorsal surfaces never obscured by any coatings or encrustations. Flightless adults feed on late summer and early fall flowers of many plants, including *Aster*, *Solanum*, *Gilia*, and *Tribulus*. Chihuahuan Desert. Extreme southeastern Arizona, New Mexico, western Texas, and south to Durango and Coahuila. (2)

Eupompha elegans elegans (LeConte) (5.5–13.0 mm) is elongate, somewhat slender. Head, pronotum, and legs black. Male with deep cephalic sulcus. Antennae usually somewhat filiform, antennomere 9 at least slightly longer than wide. Has a broad stripe variable in length on each elytron, sometimes accompanied by subapical spot. Elytra variably bicolored, either blue with large reddish-orange and posteriorly attenuated humeral spot, or sometimes a longitudinal and medially sinuate bar extending and gradually expanding posteriorly toward apex or apical spot. Front tarsomeres 1–3 inflated, not sulcate above, and with setal pads below. Diurnal adults feed on spring and summer flowers of composites mostly on coastal plain and adjacent foothills of southern California. (9)

Eupompha elegans perpulchra (Horn) (5.5–13.0 mm) is similar to *E. e. elegans*, but with elytra either entirely dark blue or variably bicolored with more or less rectangular basal and medial patches, and apical spots that sometimes coalesce to form a median longitudinal bark that may or may not be completely traversed by narrow medial black band. Diurnal adults feed on desert flowers in spring and summer, especially composites such as *Chaenactis*, *Encelia*, *Geraea*, *Malacothrix*, and *Palafoxia* in Sonoran and Mojave Deserts northward. California, Nevada, Arizona, Baja California, and Sonora. (9)

Eupompha schwarzi (Wellman) (7.0–10.0 mm) is elongate, slender, with color of head and pronotum varying geographically, and not densely pubescent. Head typically black below eyes and reddish orange above, occasionally all or nearly all black, or almost entirely reddish orange with black eye margins. Pronotum as wide as long, narrowed anteriorly, usually black, sometimes with reddish patches on disc, or mostly reddish with black margins. Elytra entirely orange, sometimes apical half suffused with black. Male front tarsi slightly inflated and dorsally sulcate. Adults eat blossoms of *Encelia*, *Geraea*, and other spring flowers in Mojave and Sonoran Deserts. Southeastern California, southern Nevada, and southwestern Arizona. (9)

Megetra punctata Selander (11.0–18.0 mm) is flightless, shiny black with red markings, with elytra short and abdomen often enlarged. Head and pronotum smooth. Elytra coarsely, confluently punctured, without lateral carinae. On *Amaranthus*, *Boerhaavia*, and *Kallstroemia* in summer. Southeastern Arizona to Durango. Following with elytra carinate laterally. *Megetra cancellata* (Brandt and Erichson) (17.0–30.0 mm) elytra coarsely reticulate, interstices broad. Southeastern Arizona to western Texas; south to central Mexico. *Megetra vittata* (LeConte) (12.0–24.0 mm) elytra finely reticulate, interstices narrow. Central Arizona to southwestern Colorado and western Texas. (3)

383

Phodaga alticeps LeConte (10.0–25.0 mm) is dull black, with medial conelike projection behind eyes. Elytra smooth, nearly glabrous, and somewhat inflated. Abdomen bright red below elytral margins. Legs long and slender; male protarsomere 1 with ventral flange and deep basal pit, and metatibiae inflated with deep ventral furrow. Adults run rapidly on ground with wings raised. On Palmer's crinklemat (*Tiquilia palmeri*) and cleftleaf wild heliotrope (*Phacelia crenulata*) in spring and early summer in Mojave, Colorado, and Sonoran Deserts. (2).

Phodaga marmorata (Casey) (6.0–16.0 mm) is dull black, with antennae short and flat. Inflated elytra broadly expanded behind middle, with faint and irregular raised reticulate pattern variegated with ashy grayish pubescence. Antennae short and flat. Legs long and slender, male protarsomere 1 with ventral flange. Adults eat flowers and foliage of manybristle chinchweed (*Pectis papposa*), Arizona poppy (*Kallstroemia grandiflora*), and puncture vine (*Tribulus terrestris*) in late summer and early fall in deserts. Southern California and Nevada to western Texas, south to Baja California Sur, Sonora, and Chihuahua. (2)

Pleurospasta mirabilis (Horn) (6.0–13.0 mm) is dull reddish brown and pale yellow with tan to brown markings. Head strongly convex between antennae and abruptly depressed behind. Pronotum smooth, weakly convex basally. Elytra costate, each with two (rarely one) spot near scutellum, an irregular fascia just before middle, and a weak, interrupted subapical band. Profemur with internal excavation bearing distinct patch of silky setae. Adults run rapidly, and feed on Palmer's crinklemat (*Tiquilia palmeri*), bristly nama (*Nama hispidum*), and *Cryptantha* in spring in lower Mojave and Sonoran Deserts. (2)

Iron Cross Beetle *Tegrodera aloga* Skinner (14.0–26.0 mm) has a red head and pronotum, and yellowish-orange elytra with large black cells, and irregular black fascia across middle, and dark brown to black suture. Adults eat miniature woollystar (*Eriastrum diffusum*), alfalfa (*Medicago*), and other desert plants. Southeastern California, southern Arizona, and southwestern Sonora. *Tegrodera latecincta* Horn (15.0–26.0 mm) pronotum orange to black, with bold transverse elytral band; Antelope and Owens Valleys northward, California. *Tegrodera erosa* LeConte (13.0–29.0 mm) pronotum orange to black, with faint oblique elytral band; southern foothills of Transverse Ranges, southern California to Pacific coast of Baja California. (3)

Lytta aeneipennis (LeConte) (5.0–12.0 mm) with head and pronotum mostly reddish orange with dark setae, and entirely metallic; rugose elytra. Head broad and setose, with front of head, mouthparts, antennae, and small eyes black; antennae reaching or surpassing posterior margin of pronotum (male) or not (female). Pronotum wide, narrower than head, setose, reddish orange with narrowly dark posterior margin, and two small lateral impressions. Impunctate elytra metallic blue-green, green, or blue. Legs mostly black, femora dark metallic blue or blue-black, with tarsal claws cleft to base, blades free and subequal in length. On spring poppies. Southwestern California. (38)

Lytta auriculata (Horn) (6.0–19.0 mm) is black with faint metallic luster, and clothed in short, erect, and colorless pubescence. Frons with small orange spot, and vertex usually orange with black midline; head sometimes entirely orange or black. Antennae reaching or surpassing posterior pronotal margin (male) or not (female). Elytra dark metallic green or bluish green. Front tibia with two spurs, hind trochanters not spined nor angulate on ventral margin. On flowers in spring and early summer. Southern California and Baja California, east to southeastern Arizona, and north along Colorado River Basin to Utah; Texas. (38)

Lytta biguttata LeConte (7.0–13.0 mm) is usually orange with eyes, mouthparts, antennae, tibiae, and tarsi black, and clothed in pale pubescence of varying lengths. Head sometimes black with orange frontal spot, slightly flattened behind eyes in male, with basal antennomeres sometimes paler. Pronotum sometimes with margins narrowly dark, disc sometimes with a lateral spot just before and after middle. Elytra with suture dark, never with basal spots, immaculate or with small black spot, short stripe, or pair of stripes at apical one-fourth. Legs with first middle tarsomere of male bent. Adults found on various composite flowers during late spring and summer. Colorado and North Dakota to Mexico. (38)

Lytta chloris Fall (7.0–14.0 mm) is brilliant brassy green with pubescence clear (Sierra foothills) or dark, usually with microreticulate sculpturing on all dorsal surfaces. Head with orange spot, male antennomeres elongate and cylindrical. Elytra usually with moderately long or long setae at base and along margin. Male ventrite 6 typically flat, shallowly and evenly emarginate. Adults on composite flowers. Foothills of Coast Ranges and western southern Sierra Nevada, California. *Lytta rathvoni* LeConte (8.0–17.0 mm) elytra metallic violet, greenish violet, or occasionally pure green, with rest of body green or brassy; adults on lupins and poppies. Central Valley to southern western foothills of Sierra Nevada. (38)

Lytta deserticola LeConte (11.0–23.0 mm) is elongate, robust, and shiny black with partly red head, pronotum, and legs, and roughly sculptured elytral surface. Head with inner margins of eyes, mouthparts, and antennae black. Pronotum somewhat circular, disc with two or four black spots across middle. Elytra finely reticulate with network of raised lines, cells clearly visible. Underside black. Legs with femora mostly red, their apices and bases black, and setose pads under tarsi. Adults on flowers during late summer. Southwestern Utah to Arizona and New Mexico, to southern Sonora. (38)

Desert or Master Blister Beetle *Lytta magister* Horn (16.5–33.0 mm) is mostly black with bright orange or reddish-orange head, pronotum, femora, and tibiae. Head not distinctly triangular. Middle antennomeres of male broad. Pronotum hexagonal, with disc more or less flat. Elytral surface coarsely reticulated. Legs with femoral and tibial apices, and tarsi black; tarsi without setose pads ventrally. Deserts, on various soft plants and small shrubs, especially composites, either feeding or in mating swarms during spring. Southern California east to southwestern New Mexico, south to Sonora. (38)

Lytta nuttalli Say (7.0–21.0 mm) with head and pronotum brassy green, and elytra iridescent, usually dark metallic violet, rarely entirely green. Lateral pronotal angles prominent. Elytra finely rugulose, with scattered pubescence longest basally. Femora and tibiae metallic green, blue, or purple. Adults on legumes. Sierra Nevada, California, central Alberta south to Arizona, east to Saskatchewan, South Dakota, and New Mexico. *Lytta cyanipennis* (LeConte) (8.0–20.0 mm) similar, with setae on thoracic sterna uniformly dark. Southern British Columbia to northern California, southern Utah, and southern Wyoming. *Lytta viridana* LeConte (10.0–17.0 mm) setae on thoracic sterna translucent apically, dark basally. Rocky Mountain states and provinces. (38)

Lytta stygica (LeConte) (7.0–15.0 mm) is elongate, robust, and uniformly metallic green or blue, rarely black without luster, with short, dark, inconspicuous pubescence on elytra. Head and pronotum smooth, rarely microreticulate. Elytra rugose and impunctate. Adults on various flowers primarily during spring. Pacific Northwest, California, southern Nevada, and south-central Arizona. *Lytta comus* Selander (7.0–13.0 mm) similar, conspicuously clothed in long, erect setae throughout; adults on flowers of *Ceanothus*, *Cryptantha*, *Eriodictyon*, and *Eschscholtzia*. Coast Ranges and western side of Central Valley. Both species difficult to distinguish from *L. chloris* in southern Coast Ranges. (38)

Lytta sublaevis (Horn) (11.0–20.0 mm) is robust and black with orange frontal spot, often with orange markings on vertex, pronotum, or both, with short elytra, and somewhat swollen abdomen. Small eyes oval. Antennae short. Scutellum exposed, broad. Pronotum broad, hexagonal, and more or less flat. Smooth elytra inflated, exposing last two abdominal terga. Flightless, diurnal adults on grass, *Eschscholtzia*, *Amsinckia*, and composites in foothills of southern Coast Ranges, southern Great Central Valley, and Tehachapi Mountains. Central California. (38)

Meloe barbarus LeConte (5.0–14.0 mm to elytral apices) is black, sometimes with blue luster. Antennomeres 5–7 wide and flat (male) or filiform (female). Scutellum hidden. Pronotum long, coarsely punctate, lateral margins behind angulation somewhat parallel or slightly sinuate, with a distinct subtriangular basal depression; usually a finely impressed median line on basal two-thirds of disc, and posterior margin entirely visible dorsally. Faintly rugose elytra short, overlapping basally. Pygidium broadly rounded. Fall through spring at low and intermediate elevations with mild winters. British Columbia to southern California, east to Idaho, Utah, and Arizona. (15)

Pyrota akhurstiana Horn (12.0–21.0 mm) is elongate, moderately slender, and mostly shiny black with bright red markings on head, pronotum, and elytra. Head continuously red between eyes. Pronotum longer than wide, with large medial triangular red patch in front, often with lateral red patches, an occasional small medial marking at base, and lateral margins abruptly narrowing in front of middle. Elytra black with margins broadly red. Legs long, slender, with front tarsomeres 1–3 of male slightly expanded. Adults commonly attracted to lights during summer; occasionally found in large mating swarms during day. Southeastern Arizona to western Texas, south to Mexico. (8)

Pyrota palpalis Champion (6.0–17.0 mm) is elongate, moderately slender, with bright pale yellow to dull orange head, pronotum, underside, and legs, and three-banded elytra. Eyes, antennae, femoral and tibial apices, and tarsi black. Pronotum sometimes with pair of small spots. Elytra smooth, shiny ivory or cream-colored with basal band often broken into two elongate spots per elytron. Pygidial apex deeply emarginate. Adults eat various composite flowers during summer. Southern California to Utah, western Texas, and Mexico. *Pyrota concinna* Casey (11.0–18.0 mm) elytra microgranulate, yellow with black bands, with extensive black markings on underside. Southern Nevada east to Colorado, Nebraska, Kansas, Arkansas, Texas, and Mexico. (8)

Gnathium caviceps MacSwain (4.0–6.0 mm) is uniformly shiny yellowish orange with black eyes and yellowish-brown antennae and tarsi. Head with impressed impunctate area between eyes, mandibles, and maxillary mouthparts elongate, and apical antennomeres thickened. Pronotum longer than wide, sides broadly rounded, with disc finely and sparsely punctate. Short, unequal setae on elytral disc. Adults on flowers of *Geraea canescens* during spring. Southeastern California and adjacent Arizona. *Gnathium eremicola* MacSwain similar in color, with pronotum long and parallel-sided; active in late summer, Colorado Desert. *G. nitidum* Horn similar, mouthparts shorter, pronotum scarcely broader than long; summer, western Great Basin to Arizona, east to Texas. (8)

Nemognatha nigripennis LeConte (5.0–10.0 mm)
is somewhat parallel-sided, shiny, and clothed in fine,
erect, black pubescence. Head, thorax, and abdomen
reddish orange, while eyes, antennae, mandibular apices,
mouthparts, femoral apices, tibiae, and tarsi black; elytra
and scutellum black to reddish orange. Mandibles evenly
curved, mouthparts long, reaching or surpassing hind
coxae. Pronotum scarcely wider than long. Male abdomen
with transversely oval punctate area on ventrites 4 and
5 each bearing a tuft of setae. Hind legs with tibial spurs
very slender, apices sharp. Adults on flowers, including
Eriogonum and *Achillea*, during spring and summer. Oregon
to Baja California, east to Colorado and Texas. (20)

Nemognatha scutellaris LeConte (5.0–10.0 mm) mostly
yellowish orange to reddish orange dorsally, appendages
and underside brownish black, and clothed in dark
pubescence. Head triangular, black with variable pale spot
behind eyes and mouthparts long, reaching hind coxae.
Pronotum wide and rectangular, sometimes with vague
spots. Scutellum dark brown to black. Elytra moderately
densely rugose-punctate with moderately long, appressed
setae, and narrowly black posterolateral and apical
margins. Hind tibial spurs flattened and concave with
apices acute. Adults on various flowers, including *Achillea*
and *Eriogonum*, in various habitats mostly in spring and
summer. Washington to California, east to Idaho, South
Dakota, and Nebraska. (20)

Nemognatha soror MacSwain (7.5–15.0 mm) is shiny,
with eyes and appendages black, and body varying
from entirely black to black with reddish-orange head,
pronotum, and apex of abdomen, or nearly entirely reddish
orange dorsally with black elytral apices and mostly
black underneath, to entirely reddish orange dorsally and
ventrally. Mouthparts short, scarcely longer than head.
Pronotum somewhat wide, rectangular, with fine punctures
moderately sparse. Elytra finely, densely punctate, rugose,
with dark, appressed setae. Hind tibial spurs flared apically,
outer spurs no more than twice as broad as inner spur.
Adults on yarrow (*Achillea*) flowers during spring and
summer. British Columbia to California. (20)

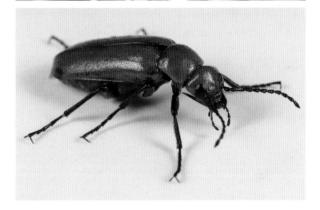

Pseudozonitis brevis Enns (7.0–10.0 mm) is elongate, robust, more or less shiny, with head and pronotum uniformly yellowish or yellowish brown, and antennae, femoral and tibial apices, and tarsi brown. Head not abruptly narrowed behind black eyes. Elytra clothed in moderately dense, short, appressed, white setae, and dull brown with margins and sinuous discal stripes yellowish, or uniformly yellowish brown or pale brown. Adults found at lights during summer. Southeastern California, southwestern Utah, and Arizona. (8)

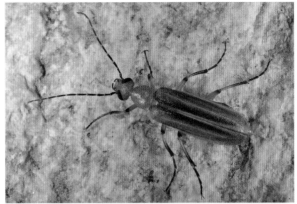

Pseudozonitis vaurieae Enns (10.0–18.0 mm) is weakly shiny with head and pronotum yellowish to yellowish brown. Head large with black eyes and appendages. Pronotum long with broad median pinkish-red patch before middle crossed by broad, transverse band reaching margins. Elytra rugose-punctate, usually black with suture, margins, and sinuous stripes pale, occasionally entirely pale. Distal quarter of femora, distal half of tibiae, and tarsi black. Adults at lights during summer, or on flowers of creosote and rabbitbrush. Southeastern California to Texas, south to Mexico. *Pseudozonitis stroudi* Selander (7.0–11.0 mm) smaller, abruptly narrowed behind head, pronotum with rectangular media reddish spot. Southern Arizona to western Texas. (8)

389

Tricrania stansburyii (Haldeman) (8.0–14.0 mm) is robust, moderately shiny black with red or brick-red elytra; head and pronotum coarsely punctured and clothed in stiff, erect black setae. Head large, broadly triangular with enlarged temples, sometimes with orange-red area on center of vertex. Pronotum somewhat rectangular. Elytra usually uniformly colored, sometimes with variable dark areas. Adults on ground or under logs in spring near the nests of several ground-nesting bee genera that they parasitize; occasionally on flowers of various forbs and shrubs growing in various habitats. Northwest Territories to California, east to South Dakota, Nebraska, Kansas, and Texas. (1)

Zonitis dunniana Casey (7.5–14.0 mm) is pale yellow with slightly greenish elytra, dark eyes, antennae, and tarsi. Long, stout sucking tube no longer than somewhat arcuate mandibles, rarely exceeding hind coxae. Pronotum sparsely punctate, sometimes with pair of pits. Elytra sparsely, coarsely punctate, with faint narrow lines. On various composite flowers in summer and early fall. Arizona and Colorado south to Texas and northern Mexico. *Zonitis sayi* Wickham (8.0–12.0 mm) sucking tube longer than arcuate mandibles, attaining hind coxae. Southern Alberta and Idaho to southeastern Arizona, east to Manitoba, Minnesota, Kansas, and western Texas. (8)

MYCTERIDAE (mik-ter'-i-dē)
PALM AND FLOWER BEETLES

Little is known about the natural history of mycterids. Adults of *Mycterus* are sometimes abundant on flowers and are suspected to eat pollen, but the larval habits of all North American species are unknown. Adults and larvae of *Lacconotus pinicola* Horn are associated with dead branches, mostly those of conifers (*Pinus*, *Abies*, *Picea*), as well as some hardwoods, including poplar (*Populus*) and oak (*Quercus*). The distinctly long, slender, and flat *Hemipeplus marginipennis* LeConte (not included), an adventive species in western North America, was first found in California in Santa Cruz County in 1958. In southeastern United States, this species is attracted to lights and associated with sabal palms. Sabal palms are widely distributed in California as an ornamental, but it is not known if *Hemipeplus* is established in the state.

FAMILY DIAGNOSIS Adult mycterids are somewhat oval and slightly flattened (*Lacconotus*), or stout and convex (*Mycterus*). Head short (*Lacconotus*), or elongate with short rostrum (*Mycterus*). Antennae with 11 antennomeres, each antennomere slightly elongate (*Lacconotus*) or serrate (*Mycterus*). Prothorax subquadrate and parallel-sided (*Lacconotus*, *Mycterus elongata*) or campanulate (*Mycterus*). Procoxal cavities open or closed. Elytra covering entire abdomen. Tarsi 5-5-4, with penultimate tarsomere slightly expanded apically, forming a fleshy lobe, and claws slightly swollen or with small tooth at base. Abdomen with five ventrites, 1–2 connate.

SIMILAR FAMILIES *Lacconotus* and *Mycterus* differ from narrow-waisted bark beetles (Salpingidae, p.397) by their lateral pronotal margins not converging toward elytra.

COLLECTING NOTES Look for *Mycterus* on spring and early summer flowers, especially on *Ceanothus*, *Daucus*, and *Hesperoyucca*. *Lacconotus* is usually beaten from branches of conifers and occasionally from hardwoods. They are also captured in Malaise and flight intercept traps, and are attracted to ultraviolet light.

390

FAUNA 12 SPECIES IN THREE GENERA

Lacconotus pinicola Horn (4.8–7.5 mm) is light brown to nearly black dorsally. Eyes small. Antennomeres 5–10 longer than wide, and subserrate. Elytral punctation fine, inconspicuous. On ponderosa pine (*Pinus ponderosa*), also Engelmann spruce (*Picea engelmanni*), scrub oak (*Quercus turbinella*), and cherry (*Prunus*) in late spring, early summer. Southern British Columbia, California and western Nevada south to northern Baja California, also Utah and Arizona, east to Colorado and New Mexico. (1)

Mycterus canescens Horn (3.0–6.0 mm) is elongate-oval, stout, and convex, densely punctate dorsally with conspicuous silvery white setae, and dull black. Head broadly produced in front, nearly as long as wide, and black (female) or brown (male) in front of eyes. Pronotum bell-shaped with margins arcuate in front, sides more or less parallel, and slightly sinuate before base. Male first ventrite with abruptly raised shiny process between hind coxae. Front and middle legs brown, hind legs with femora black, tibiae and tarsi brown. Adults on spring flowers. Oregon to California, east to Texas. (4)

Mycterus concolor LeConte (3.5–5.0 mm) is elongate-oval, stout and convex, densely punctate dorsally with inconspicuous vestiture, and uniformly dull dark gray (male and female), occasionally with yellowish brown or brownish elytra (female). Head broadly produced in front, black, with mouth parts brown and antennae dark. Pronotum bell-shaped. Elytra sometimes lighter in color than forebody. Male first ventrite with abruptly raised shiny process between hind coxae. Legs black with tibiae and tarsi paler. Adults on spring flowers, including buckbrush (*Ceanothus*) and bushmallow (*Malacothamnus*). British Columbia to California, west Idaho. *Mycterus elongata* Hopping (7.0 mm) elongate, parallel-sided, uniformly reddish brown. Western slopes of southern Sierra Nevada, California. (4)

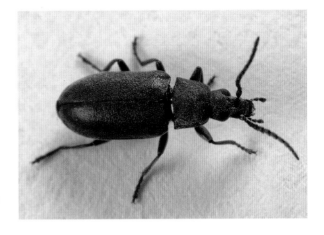

Mycterus quadricollis Horn (5.0–6.5 mm) is elongate-oval, stout, densely punctate, and dull black with clypeus, mouthparts, appendages, and margin of last ventrite brown or yellowish brown. Head broadly produced in front, nearly as long as wide, with antennomeres flattened and bilaterally produced in male. Pronotum subquadrate, nearly as wide as long, disc with variable V-shaped depression. Elytra in both sexes sometimes yellowish brown and shiny. Underside of male with large patch of fine brownish setae on each of ventrites 1–4. Adults typically found on blossoms of chaparral yucca (*Hesperoyucca whipplei*) and Joshua tree (*Yucca brevifolia*). Southern California to New Mexico, south to northern Mexico. (4)

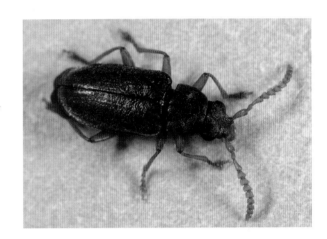

391

BORIDAE (bôr'-i-dē)
CONIFER BARK BEETLES

Both North American species of borids occur in the West. Adults and larvae of *Boros unicolor* Say are found under the bark of standing or leaning dead pine (*Pinus*) snags and logs, especially at ground level. *Lecontia discicollis* (LeConte) is also found in association with dead conifers, especially among moist and decayed root systems of trees killed by fire or bark beetles (Curculionidae, p.539).

FAMILY DIAGNOSIS Adult borids are distinguished by antennal bases hidden from view above, capitate antennae with club comprising three antennomeres, distinctly carinate lateral pronotal margins, and lack of any conspicuous setae on the upper surface of the body. Body elongate, parallel-sided, and distinctly punctate. Head behind eyes parallel-sided (*Lecontia*) or abruptly narrowed with temples (*Boros*). Antennae with 11 antennomeres, 9–11 forming club and each with kidney-shaped sensory patch. Procoxal cavities broadly open behind. Elytra long and completely cover abdomen. Tarsi 5-5-4, tarsomeres slender, not lobed, and setose ventrally, with claws simple. Abdomen with five ventrites, 1–2 connate.

SIMILAR FAMILIES
- some false darkling beetles (Melandryidae, p.333)—antennal bases visible from above
- dead log beetles (Pythidae, p.392)—pronotum with distinct pair of impressions
- fire-colored beetles (Pyrochroidae, p.394)—head usually distinct with narrow neck

- narrow-waisted bark beetles (Salpingidae, p.397)—abdomen with five ventrites free

COLLECTING NOTES Look for *Boros* under bark of pine snags and logs near ground level, as well as in the adjacent forest litter below; also attracted to Lindgren funnel traps. *Lecontia* are found among moist, decayed root systems of trees killed by bark beetles or fire.

FAUNA TWO SPECIES IN TWO GENERA

Boros unicolor Say (11.0–13.0 mm) is elongate, slender, somewhat cylindrical and slightly flattened dorsally, shiny, and uniformly dark brown to blackish. Head abruptly narrowed behind eyes. Pronotum oval, broadest near middle, with lateral margins evenly arcuate and carinae not joining posterior margin. Head and pronotum coarsely, densely punctate, elytra more finely punctured. Pronotum convex, with disc neither flattened nor impressed. Elytral surface confusedly punctate, without trace of striae. Adults and larvae found beneath loose bark of dead pine (*Pinus*) snags and stumps; adults overwinter under bark. Transcontinental; British Columbia east across southern Canada, south to northeastern United States. (1).

Lecontia discicollis **(LeConte)** (12.0–23.0 mm) is elongate, somewhat convex, and blackish. Head with mandibles distinctly protruding from beneath labrum, sides behind eyes somewhat parallel, and moniliform antennae with last three antennomeres broad. Pronotum broadest anteriorly, disc flattened medially and concave on sides, with lateral margins carinate and continuous with posterior margin. Elytra indistinctly striate, interstriae weakly convex, with scattered coarse punctures. Adults and larvae found under bark of fire-killed conifers. Transcontinental; widespread in montane North America; in West, from British Columbia to Oregon, east to Idaho, Arizona, and New Mexico. (1)

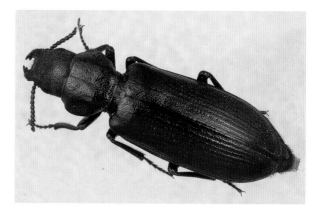

PYTHIDAE (pith'-i-dē)
DEAD LOG BEETLES

Adult pythids are found on and beneath the loose bark of logs. Studies of the adult mandibular structure of both *Pytho* and *Priognathus* suggest a predatory lifestyle, but such behavior has not been substantiated. Nothing is known of the habits of *Trimitomerus riversii* Horn, other than the adults are commonly attracted to lights in desert regions. All known pythid larvae in North America are associated with rotting wood. The somewhat flattened *Pytho* larvae live in conifer (*Pinus, Picea, Abies*) logs within fungus-infested cambial-phloem layer, while those of *Priognathus* prefer red-rotten sapwood. Both adults and larvae of *Pytho* possess relatively high supercooling temperature points and are used in studies examining the physiology of cold tolerance. Larval *Sphalma quadricollis* Horn are found beneath loose bark of cottonwood logs (*Populus*).

FAMILY DIAGNOSIS Adult pythids are elongate, somewhat cylindrical or flattened, the dorsal surface with punctures of various depths. Head prognathous, with eyes small, or large (*Trimitomerus*). Antennae with 11 antennomeres. Pronotum rounded or somewhat square, wider than long and widest at middle, surface evenly convex (*Priognathus*) to slightly flattened with vague or distinct pair of depressions (*Pytho*) with side margins rounded; front coxal cavities open between and behind. Scutellum small, triangular. Elytra elongate, more or less straight-sided, completely covering abdomen, or nearly so, with confused punctures or broadly elevated intervals (*Pytho*). Legs slender, tarsi 5-5-4, tarsomeres slender and simple, with simple claws equal in size. Abdomen with five ventrites free (*Pytho, Priognathus*) or 1–2 connate (*Sphalma, Trimitomerus*).

SIMILAR FAMILIES
- ground beetles (Carabidae, p.88)—tarsi 5-5-5
- comb-clawed beetles (Tenebrionidae, p.366)—claws pectinate
- conifer bark beetles (Boridae, p.391)—pronotum convex, elytra not distinctly striate

COLLECTING NOTES Adults found year-round under the bark of dead conifers such as fir (*Abies*), larch (*Larix*), spruce (*Picea*), pine (*Pinus*), and hemlock (*Tsuga*), especially fall through spring. Large trees that have been dead for at least three or four years with loose but intact bark, not greatly decayed heartwood, and a large amount of cambium-phloem (inner bark) are the most productive. Beetles are sometimes swept or beaten from foliage during summer.

FAUNA SEVEN SPECIES IN FOUR GENERA

Pytho americanus Kirby (7.1–14.8 mm) has rounded later prothoracic margins, side margins widest just before middle. Elytra reddish, blackish, or black with a weak violet sheen to strongly metallic green or blue luster. Abdomen orangish red to blackish. Legs reddish, tibiae and tarsi darker than femora. Transcontinental; in West, from Alaska to California, east to Rockies. The following species are both uniformly nonmetallic dark brown to black. *Pytho niger* Kirby (10.0–12.0 mm) with rounded prothorax widest at middle; Alaska and British Columbia east across Canada, south to Minnesota, Wisconsin, and Virginia; *P. seidlitzi* Blair (9.3–14.8 mm) with prothoracic margins subparallel; western Canada and Idaho. (3)

Priognathus monilicornis (Randall) (8.0–11.0 mm) is reddish brown or blackish with appendages and abdomen paler, and upper surface coarsely punctate, elytra more so in vague rows. Antennae moniliform with antennomeres 8–11 forming indistinct club. Pronotum almost as long as wide, evenly convex. Larvae develop in sapwood in red-rotten conifer logs; adults found under bark. Mountainous regions of western North America; also Maritime Provinces and New England to West Virginia, west to Michigan. (1)

Sphalma quadricollis Horn (6.0–8.6 mm) is elongate, convex, punctate-glabrous, and shiny black with reddish legs. Head broad, cylindrical behind round, and more closely punctate than elytra, with moderately prominent eyes and mandibles not visible from above. Antennae as long as head and prothorax combined, antennomeres 8–11 forming club, with insertions not visible from above. Pronotum wide, with lateral margins arcuate, distinctly carinate, and visible dorsally, with posterior margin sinuate behind distinct basal impressions. Elytra elongate with parallel lateral margins gradually narrowing posteriorly at apical fourth. Larvae under loose bark of black cottonwood (*Populus balsamifera trichocarpa*); adults on trunks. British Columbia to California, east to Idaho. (1)

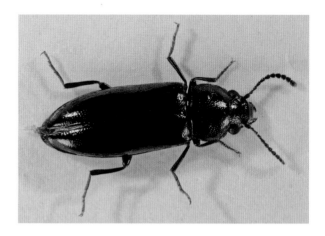

Trimitomerus riversii Horn (7.0–19.0 mm) is elongate, somewhat tapered, dorsally dark reddish brown with brown appendages, pale or yellowish-brown elytra, and black ventrally. Head large, narrowed behind prominent eyes, mandibles prominent, each with a tooth just before apex, and antennae long with antennomeres 9–11 flat and elongate. Prothorax oval, slightly wider than long, with lateral margins rounded and vague posterior V-shaped medial impression on sparsely punctate flattened disc. Elytra widest at base, gradually narrowing posteriorly. Legs moderately long and slender. Posterior margin of apical male ventrite with deep triangular notch. Adults attracted to lights during summer. Southern Arizona. (1)

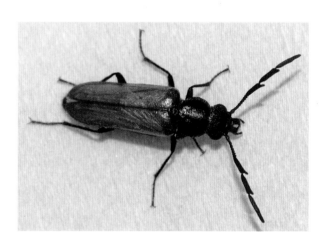

394

PYROCHROIDAE (pī-rok-rō′-i-dē)

FIRE-COLORED BEETLES

Pyrochroid beetles are found in relatively cool, moist, and wooded habitats. Adult *Dendroides* and *Neopyrochroa* are largely nocturnal and spend their days resting on vegetation. *Pedilus* adults are diurnal and found on flowers and vegetation of various plants, including willows (*Salix*), maples (*Acer*), buckeyes (*Aesculus*), alders (*Alnus*), and other plants growing in damp areas. Adult male *Neopyrochroa*, *Schizotus*, and many *Pedilus* are attracted to cantharidin, a chemical compound produced by blister beetles (Meloidae) and some false blister beetles (Oedemeridae). *Pedilus* species are sometimes found on meloids (p.36, Fig. 35). The straight, flat larvae of *Dendroides* and *Neopyrochroa* are commonly found under loose tree bark of rotting hardwood and conifer logs, where they eat bits of fungi and fungus-infested wood and may take several years to complete their development. The larvae of *Dendroides ephemeroides* (Mannerheim) and *Neopyrochroa sierraensis* Young both utilize black cottonwood (*Populus balsamifera trichocarpa*) logs. *Dendroides* larvae usually occur along the sides of the log, while those of *Neopyrochroa* occupy the cooler and wetter underside. *Pedilus* larvae also develop under the bark of rotting trees, while those of *Schizotus* are typically found under mats of moss growing on decaying logs at the edges of bogs and other boreal habitats.

FAMILY DIAGNOSIS Adult pyrochroids are elongate, weakly to moderately flattened, soft-bodied, and yellowish brown to black, often with reddish or orange pronotum. Head somewhat hypognathous, abruptly narrowed behind kidney-shaped eyes with distinct neck, and males with distinct pits (*Neopyrochroa*, *Schizotus*), or not (*Anisotria*, *Dendroides*, *Pedilus*, *Tydessa*). Antennae long, with 11 antennomeres, mostly filiform to pectinate (females) to serrate or plumose (males). Prothorax narrower than elytra, elliptical in outline (*Pedilus*), or somewhat oval, without carinate lateral margins. Procoxal cavities broadly open behind. Elytra usually dark and completely cover abdomen. Metathoracic wings sometimes reduced (*Anisotria*) or absent (*Cononotus*). Legs long, slender, tarsi 5-5-4, claws simple or distinctly toothed at base (*Pedilus*). Abdomen with five or six ventrites free, or 1–2 connate (*Cononotus*). *Neopyrochroa* males distinguished by plumose antennae and deep cranial pits, is represented in the West by two species (not included) that are both restricted to California. The southern Californian *Neopyrochroa californica* (Horn) has a black head and black legs, while those of *N. sierraensis* Young in the Sierra Nevada are orangish.

SIMILAR FAMILIES

- soldier beetles (Cantharidae, p.265)—antennae not pectinate, tarsi appear 4-4-4, actually 5-5-5
- glowworms (Phengodidae, p.271)—antennae

of males bipectinate, sicklelike mandibles conspicuous, tarsi 5-5-5
- false blister beetles (Oedemeridae, p.374)—pronotum widest in front of middle
- blister beetles (Meloidae, p.378)—antennae filiform or moniliform, sometimes modified in middle
- antlike flower beetles (Anthicidae, p.400)—pronotum widest in front, eyes not kidney-shaped
- some longhorn beetles (Cerambycidae, p.460)—without neck, tarsi appear 4-4-4, actually 5-5-5
- orsodacnid leaf beetles (Orsodacnidae, p.499)—without neck, tarsi appear 4-4-4, actually 5-5-5

COLLECTING NOTES Look for fire-colored beetles from late spring through midsummer in wooded habitats. Searching under bark, beating foliage of trees and shrubs during the day, and checking lights at night are the most effective ways of collecting adults; chunks of fruit under bark of decaying trees is also productive. *Neopyrochroa* are attracted to fermenting baits, made with beer and molasses, at night. Males of *Neopyrochroa*, *Schizotus*, and *Pedilus* are drawn to cantharidin bait traps. Some species are also attracted to lights. Species of *Cononotus* are sometimes collected with pitfall traps set in dry, sandy habitats.

395

FAUNA 50 SPECIES IN SEVEN GENERA

Tydessa blaisdelli Pollock (5.9–7.1 mm) is elongate-oval, inconspicuously pubescent on pronotum and elytra, shiny with head and pronotum dark brownish black with elytra somewhat lighter, and basal three to four antennomeres and tarsi light brown. Head with antennomeres filiform, and similar in width to pronotum. Pronotum with lateral margins carinate about half their length, slightly sinuate before posterior margin, and posterior angles indistinct, rounded, and not produced, each with a small pit. Adults associated with decaying logs. Oregon, northern California, and eastern Nevada. (1)

Pedilus flabellatus (Horn) (4.5–8.5 mm) is mostly yellowish brown to orange, with head, pterothorax, and abdomen dark brown, reddish brown, to black. Antennae serrate (female), or flabellate (male) with antennomeres 4–10 each with extension ranging from one to five times the length of its antennomere, and with 11 five times length of 10. Pronotum wide, broadest before middle. On *Pinus*, flying midmorning and at lights; not known to be attracted to cantharidin. British Columbia to southern California, east to western Nevada. *Pedilus parvicollis* (Fall) (6.5–9.0 mm) similar in color, but with male antennae flabellate beginning with antennomere 3. Southern Sierra Nevada in central California. (22)

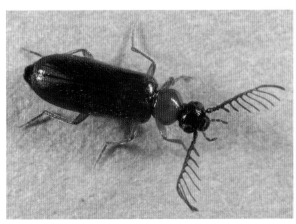

Schizotus cervicalis Newman (5.5–9.0 mm) is mostly black with reddish-orange markings. Head with mouthparts pale, males with a pair of pits behind eyes. Antennae black, serrate in females, weakly pectinate in males. Pronotum with lateral margins not carinate, posterior angles not projecting. Elytra black with yellow or yellowish-orange margins. Legs black with tarsal claws simple. Adults in boreal habitats under bark and on vegetation; not attracted to lights. Larvae typically found in decaying wood and under moss on logs. Transcontinental; across southern Canada and northeastern United States. *Schizotus fuscicollis* (Dejean) with elytra uniformly yellow-orange. Alaska and eastern Russia. (2)

Dendroides ephemeroides (Mannerheim) (11.0–17.5 mm) is elongate, somewhat convex, parallel-sided, and yellowish brown with eyes and mandibular apices black. Head lacking cranial pits, with large convex eyes separated by less than width across top of eye (female) or nearly contiguous (male). Antennae serrate (female) or plumose (male). Pronotum bell-shaped, somewhat convex, shallowly and sparsely punctate. Elytra broader and more distinctly punctate than prothorax. Legs with femora distinctly rugulose and moderately punctate, with punctures separated by more than their diameters. Legs long and tarsal claws simple. Adults on rotten logs and at lights. Alaska to northern California, east to Alberta and Idaho. (3)

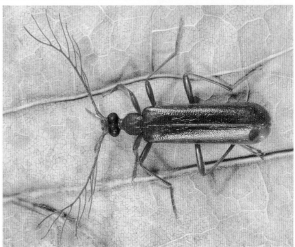

Cononotus bryanti Van Dyke (3.7–4.0 mm) elongate, clothed in coarse gray pubescence that obscures light reddish-brown cuticle. Head with feebly convex eyes about as wide as anterior of prothorax, with antennae reaching base of thorax. Prothorax somewhat conical, narrower anteriorly than long, broadest just before middle. Elytra elongate-elliptical, convex, with fine punctures confused. Flightless adults associated with decaying cacti and dried cow dung; larvae probably develop in decaying flesh of cacti and other succulents. Southern Arizona, Baja California. (6)

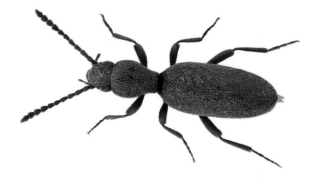

ISCHALIIDAE (is-kal-ī′-i-dē)
ISCHALIID BEETLES

Ischaliidae is a small, poorly known family inhabiting the eastern Palearctic, eastern Oriental and Nearctic Realms, and comprises 45 species in a single genus, *Ischalia*. *Ischalia* was originally placed in the Pedilidae, now a subfamily of the Pyrochroidae. Based on larval characters, it was later moved to the Anthicidae (p.400); however, *Ischalia* is very different from other antlike flower beetles. Although some coleopterists consider Ischaliinae a subfamily of anthicids, *Ischalia* is considered here to represent a distinct family of beetles.

FAMILY DIAGNOSIS Western North American *Ischalia* adults are oblong, somewhat flattened, and bicolored. Head with broad neck. Antennae with 11 antennomeres. Pronotum campanulate, or bell-shaped, with distinct lateral and median longitudinal carinae ending in angular projections along posterior margin. Procoxae open behind. Elytra with distinct, sublateral carinae before almost vertical declivity to lateral margins; flight wings reduced. Legs without tibial spurs, tarsi 5-5-4. Abdomen with five ventrites free.

SIMILAR FAMILIES The pronotal and elytra characters are unique to Ischaliidae.

COLLECTING NOTES Adults are found year-round by inspecting fungal mycelia associated with decaying logs and stumps of both conifers and hardwoods; sifting leaves and other decaying vegetation in the immediate vicinity of these microhabitats may be productive. Specimens are sometimes captured in flight intercept and pitfall traps set in appropriate habitats.

FAUNA THREE SPECIES IN ONE GENUS

Ischalia californica Van Dyke (4.0–6.5 mm) is oblong, parallel-sided, flat, and mostly orange-yellow with bicolored elytra. Eyes and antennomeres 3–9 black. Pronotum campanulate, as long as wide, with median carina and posterior angles produced over margin. Elytra with sublateral carinae, black sutural stripe not reaching apices, abruptly expanded to lateral margins at apical two-thirds, and punctures fine along suture and coarse near lateral carinae. Oregon and California. *Ischalia vancouverensis* Harrington (6.1–7.5 mm) with elytral punctures uniformly coarse, and sutural stripe broadly expanded before apical half, not attaining lateral margins. British Columbia to Oregon, east to Alberta. Adults associated with fungi in old decaying logs. (2)

SALPINGIDAE (sal-pinj'-i-dē)
NARROW-WAISTED BARK BEETLES

Salpingids are difficult to characterize as a family. Species currently included in the family have historically been classified in several other families, and further changes to the present composition of Salpingidae will likely occur as a result of comprehensive phylogenetic studies underway. Adult salpingids are usually found on flowers and foliage, or on decaying twigs and under the bark of logs. The few known larvae are associated with decaying twigs and logs. *Rhinosimus viridiaenus* (Randall) adults chew the bark of dead alder (*Alnus*) branches, while their larvae apparently feed on the inner bark. Adults and larvae of *Aglenus brunneus* Erichson scavenge decaying vegetation, manure, and guano in caves, cellars, stables, granaries, and mills. Adults of *Dacoderus*, found under bark and stones, possess several characters associated with other myrmecophilous and termitophilous beetles. *Elacatis* larvae develop under the bark of decaying logs, while the adults occur on the bark of dead or dying pines; the larvae are not predatory, but the adults seem to have predatory habits. Both the broad, flat larvae and flightless adults of *Aegialites debilis* Mannerheim are likely predators of mites and other small animals living among rock crevices and barnacles in the intertidal zone.

FAMILY DIAGNOSIS Adult salpingids in western North America are elongate and convex, or somewhat flat. Head with (*Rhinosimus*) or without a rostrum, and eyes usually present (absent in *Aglenus*). Filiform or clavate antennae with 11 antennomeres. Pronotum wide to elongate (*Dacoderus*), narrower posteriorly than elytra (except *Aglenus* and *Aegialites*), usually convex, flattened, or slightly concave (*Dacoderus*). Procoxal cavities usually broadly to narrowly open (narrowly closed in *Elacatis*) behind. Scutellum visible. Elytra long and cover abdomen. Tarsi 5-5-4 (4-4-4 in *Aglenus*), with claws simple. Abdomen with five ventrites free.

SIMILAR FAMILIES

- rove beetles (Staphylinidae, p.143)—antennae not clubbed
- zopherid beetles (Zopheridae: Colydiinae, p.340)—eyes present

- *Mycterus* (Mycteridae, p.390)—shiny and metallic, pronotum narrow at base

COLLECTING NOTES Look for narrow-waisted bark beetles on flowers and under bark, or find them by sweeping or beating foliage and decaying twigs of conifers and hardwoods. *Rhinosimus* are beaten from dead branches of red alder (*Alnus rubra*) and bigleaf maple (*Acer macrophyllum*), while *Vincenzellus elongatus* (Mannerheim) are similarly collected from dead conifer branches. *Aegialites* occur along the seashore in the intertidal zone, especially around barnacles. Search for *Dacoderus* under bark or stones, possibly in association with termites or ants, respectively; specimens are also collected in overnight pitfall traps set at the edges of small islands created by mesquite (*Prosopis*) and palo verde (*Parkinsonia*) in dry, desert washes. *Elacatis* are attracted to Lindgren funnel traps baited with bark beetle or *Sirex* woodwasp lures.

FAUNA 20 SPECIES IN EIGHT GENERA

Aegialites debilis Mannerheim (3.0–4.0 mm) is elongate-oval, somewhat convex, with scattered pubescence, and more or less shiny black. Head and pronotum somewhat dull and with only a few inconspicuous punctures. Head broad, with face short, and eyes small, not prominent. Antennae more or less moniliform. Pronotum slightly wider than long, broadest at apical third, with longitudinal line prominent. Elytra striate, but without distinct strial punctures. Underneath with all coxae widely separated. Flightless adults and broad, flat larvae live among rock crevices and barnacles in intertidal zone, presumably feeding on mites and other small animals. Sitka, Alaska. (13)

Aglenus brunneus (Gyllenhal) (1.6–2.2 mm) is elongate, somewhat cylindrical, nearly glabrous, with oval punctures dorsally, and shiny pale to moderately dark reddish brown with pale brownish-yellow appendages. Head without eyes, with antennomeres 9–11 forming loose club. Pronotum broadest at apical fourth, with lateral margins nearly straight and finely carinate, with posterior margin broadly arcuate and finely margined; underneath with procoxae open behind. Elytra covering abdomen, humeri angulate and produced, with confused punctures coarse and dense basally, becoming finer and sparser apically. Tarsi 4-4-4. Adults scavenge in various situations for decaying plant materials. Europe; widely established in North America. (1)

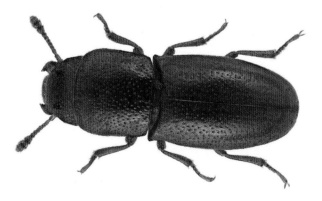

Dacoderus striaticeps LeConte (3.9–4.2mm) is elongate, slender, flattened, glabrous, and shiny dark reddish brown. Head nearly equal in length to prothorax, with deep longitudinal striations, and eyes dorsal, not visible from below. Antennae moniliform. Pronotum with lateral margins interrupted behind middle by distinct swellings, and discal pit without transverse ridge. Elytra with punctation confused. Flightless adults found in pitfall traps, under bark and stones, and in association with various accumulations of plant materials. Southeastern California to southern Arizona, south to Sonora. *Dacoderus sleeperi* Aalbu, Andrews, & Pollock with transverse ridge in discal pronotal pit. Southwestern California to Baja California. (2)

Elacatis umbrosus (LeConte) (3.9–6.0mm) is elongate-oval, subparallel-sided, densely clothed in pale pubescence, setae thick, and variously reddish brown with slight purplish brassy sheen. Eyes strongly convex and large, occupying almost entire space between antennal insertion and anterior pronotal margin. Antenna with elongate loose club consisting of three antennomeres that are sometimes darker than submoniliform antennomeres 1–8. Pronotum moderately convex, with lateral margins carinate with two or three tubercles. Elytra with punctures confused, and dark with well-delimited light areas, especially in light forms. Fleet-footed adults on bark of dead and dying pine (*Pinus*), possibly preying on bark beetles; at lights, Lindgren funnel traps. Western North America. (5)

399

Rhinosimus viridiaenus (Randall) (2.5–4.5mm) is elongate, glabrous, and shiny black with metallic greenish luster; appendages and tip of rostrum reddish yellow. Rostrum nearly two times longer than basal width, expanded apically. Antennal club with four antennomeres, 8–10 moniliform. Pronotum with sides converging posteriorly. Elytra punctostriate, intervals flat. Tarsi 5-5-4. Adults associated with dead hardwood branches. Transcontinental; in West, British Columbia to California. *Rhinosimus pallipes* Boheman (2.2–2.7mm) metallic, rostrum barely longer than basal width, antennomeres 7–10 moniliform; lupines in coastal dune habitats; British Columbia to northern California. Genus needs revision. (3)

Sphaeriestes virescens (LeConte) (2.5–3.0 mm) is elongate, convex, glabrous, and shiny black with appendages partly lighter. Head without rostrum, coarsely and sparsely punctate; antennae slender, the loose and elongate club with three antennomeres. Pronotum as long as wide, broadest across anterior third, then lateral margins converging posteriorly, with disc coarsely and distinctly punctate. Elytra at base wider than prothorax, punctostriae with irregular and fine punctures becoming obscure apically, with intervals punctate. Adults associated with pine (*Pinus*). Transcontinental; across Canada, south to northeastern United States. *Sphaeriestes alternatus* (LeConte) (2.9–3.7 mm) with elytral punctures more conspicuous and intervals impunctate. British Columbia to northern California. (2)

Vincenzellus elongatus (Mannerheim) (3.3–3.6 mm) is elongate, glabrous and coarsely punctate dorsally, and somewhat shiny brownish black with only slight metallic luster. Head produced into short, broad rostrum, with lateral margins indistinctly concave dorsally, impressed supra-antennal margins somewhat parallel before antennal insertions, frons impressed, and antennae slightly clavate with club comprising six antennomeres. Pronotum nearly as long as wide, broadest about apical third, and parallel before posterior angles, with a large, deep fovea on each side before middle. Elytra wider than prothorax, with bases slightly depressed, and punctostriae becoming confused basally. Adults beaten from dead branches of fir (*Abies*) and spruce (*Picea*). Alaska to California. (1)

400

ANTHICIDAE (an-this'-i-dē)
ANTLIKE FLOWER BEETLES

Despite their common name, only species in the anthicid genera *Ischyropalpus, Retocomus, Stereopalpus* visit flowers and feed on pollen and nectar. Most species are omnivorous and scavenge various plant, fungal, and animal materials. A few species prey on small arthropods and their eggs and have been considered possible candidates for biological control agents. Others are found on foliage, in association with decaying vegetation on the ground, or crawling over areas of exposed soil in riparian habitats with nearby ground-hugging vegetation, bits of debris, stones, or clumps of litter under which to hide. Some species are restricted to sand dunes, and shorelines of fresh water and alkali lakes. Species of *Anthicus* and *Notoxus* scavenge dead insects and are attracted to cantharidin in the bodies of dead blister beetles (Meloidae, p.378) and false blister beetles (Oedemeridae, p.374). Adults of *Amblyderus, Malporus,* and *Mecynotarsus* spend their days burrowed into sandy soils or hiding under objects and debris along the coast, or along margins of marshes, lakes, and rivers. The omnivorous larvae live in soil in association with decayed vegetation on the ground, and generally share the same feeding habits as their adults.

FAMILY DIAGNOSIS Adult anthicids are antlike in appearance. Head distinct, with neck. Antennae with 11 antennomeres, usually filiform, serrate, or clavate. Pronotum constricted or narrowed at base, and lateral margins not carinate, with base narrower than base of elytra; *Mecynotarsus* and *Notoxus* have a single prominent horn that projects over head. Procoxal cavities broadly open behind. Elytra covered with short setae and nearly or completely cover abdomen. Tarsi 5-5-4, slender, penultimate tarsomeres narrowly lobed underneath, with claws simple or appendiculate. Abdomen with five ventrites free.

SIMILAR FAMILIES

- antlike stone beetles (Staphylinidae, p.143)— antennal club loosely formed with three or four antennomeres, abdomen with six ventrites, tarsi 5-5-5
- spider beetles (Ptinidae, p.299)—antennae clubbed, tarsi 5-5-5
- fire-colored beetles *Cononotus* (p.396, Pyrochroidae)—pronotum round
- antlike leaf beetles (Aderidae, p.406)—eyes notched next to antennal insertion; first two abdominal ventrites connate
- checkered beetles (Cleridae, p.425)—antennae clubbed, tarsi 5-5-5

- orsodacnid leaf beetles (Orsodacnidae, p.499)— tarsi appear 4-4-4, but are 5-5-5
- leaf beetles (Chrysomelidae, p.501)—tarsi appear 4-4-4, but are 5-5-5

COLLECTING NOTES Look for antlike flower beetles crawling on exposed ground in riparian habitats or along shores and beaches with scattered prostrate plants, stones, and debris, or clumps of litter under which they can hide; wet spots in otherwise dry areas, especially under debris and mats of algae or decaying vegetation are particularly productive. Beating and sweeping vegetation, especially oaks (*Quercus*), willows (*Salix*), and grasses are the most effective methods for collecting *Notoxus* adults. *Anthicus*, *Formicilla*, *Mecynotarsus*, *Notoxus*, and *Vacusus* are attracted to cantharidin traps left in shaded areas, especially in the morning and late afternoon. These traps consist of boxes with recently killed or pinned blister beetles, or small containers of alcohol in which blister beetles have been soaked. Many species of anthicids are attracted to lights, especially in riparian habitats with suitable substrates.

FAUNA 231 SPECIES IN 32 GENERA

Amblyderus parviceps (2.5–3.6 mm) is oblong-oval, robust, with head and pronotum indistinctly granulate, and light orange-brown with elytra sometimes partly or entirely brown. Head strongly triangular. Pronotum broadest at about anterior margin, anterior surface abruptly declivous and flat, and lateral margins evenly converging posteriorly when viewed dorsally. Elytra with humeri prominent. Adults in sand beneath plants on coastal California dunes. *Amblyderus obsesus* Casey (3.7–4.3 mm) uniformly yellowish or orangish, elytra sometimes bluish, and pronotum with short neck anteriorly, and sides briefly parallel at base. Under wrack on sandy Pacific beaches. British Columbia to southern California. Adults of both species flightless. (4)

Anthicus cervinus LaFerté-Sénectère (2.5–3.3 mm) is elongate, variably dull yellowish to reddish brown, with head somewhat straight across base and darker than prothorax, and elytra darker at apical two-fifths. Head stout, broadest behind eyes. Prothorax stout, with pronotum not deeply constricted. Elytra convex, with strongly curved setae only at base, and pale spot on middle of each elytron at apical third sometimes poorly marked. Adults common under debris, especially in sandy habitats, from spring through fall; adults overwinter. Widespread across southern Canada and United States, south to southern Mexico. (19)

Anthicus maritimus LeConte (2.3–3.0 mm) is elongate-oval, stout, convex, minutely reticulate, moderately and densely punctate, with pubescence somewhat long and appressed, and dull reddish, with appendages paler, sometimes with elytra brownish black. Head with eyes moderately large, but not prominent, with antennae short and stout, almost moniliform. Pronotum broadest anteriorly, with collar distinct, and disc somewhat convex and more deeply punctured than head. Elytra oval, broadest before middle, with base partly enveloping pronotum, and without any trace of humeri. Adults found on Pacific beaches above high tide. Legs with front femora stout, broadest beyond middle. Southern California and northern Baja California. (19)

Anthicus punctulatus LeConte (2.5–3.5 mm) is elongate, smooth between coarse punctures, clothed in long, fine, and recumbent pubescence, and usually black with bases of appendages paler than body, or sometimes brown with paler appendages. Head with eyes large, but not prominent, with last five antennomeres slightly thickened, 7–10 somewhat triangular. Pronotum broadest at anterior quarter, followed by straight lateral margins converging, then becoming somewhat parallel before posterior margin. Elytra with humeri prominent, tactile setae erect, and disc somewhat flattened. Adults found on vegetation. British Columbia to southern California, east to Manitoba, Wyoming and Utah. (19)

Cyclodinus franciscanus (Casey) (3.2–3.8 mm) is typically yellowish- or orange-brown with vague to distinct, brown, blotchy, elytral markings at scutellum, middle, and apices; darker specimens with head and pronotum red-brown. Head with base narrowed and somewhat conical posteriorly in dorsal view. Pronotum with distinct collar anteriorly. Elytra with medial blotches rarely meeting to form transverse band. Adults found beneath objects and debris along shorelines and muddy edges; also at lights. San Francisco Bay area and Central Valley, California. Most species in region reliably identified on basis of location and male genitalia configuration. (6)

Formicilla munda LeConte (1.8–2.4 mm) is antlike, polished with few punctures and scattered long tactile setae, and shiny pale to dark reddish brown with elytra darker, with complete transverse bands of variable width at basal fourth and apical three-fourths. Head with eyes round to oval, and base somewhat truncate to rounded. Pronotum distinctly constricted at posterior half and shallowly depressed across dorsum. Elytra with dorsal depression distinct. Adults attracted to lights. California east to Colorado and Texas, south to central Mexico. (1)

Ischyropalpus nitidulus **(LeConte)** (2.6–3.3 mm) is somewhat stout, densely pubescent, and shiny reddish to black with appendages paler. Head with neck thin and smooth. Apices of maxillary palps large, triangular. Pronotum with front collarlike, sides rounded in anterior half, then straight and parallel behind. Elytra impressed across basal fourth, without striae. Adults found on flowers, e.g., milkweed (*Asclepias*); prey on mites on pine (*Pinus*) in West. Widespread in North America. (4)

Omonadus formicarius **(Goeze)** (3.0–3.5 mm) is usually reddish with last three-quarters of elytra darker. Head broad, somewhat box-shaped, and straight along base, deeply grooved, with large, prominent eyes. Pronotum lacks tubercles in front. Side margins of mesosternum nearly straight and lacking a fringe of appressed setae. Adults found in coastal dunes and in association with decaying vegetation; also collected at lights. Old World, now cosmopolitan; throughout southern Canada and United States. (2)

Stricticollis tobias **(Marseul)** (2.6–3.1 mm) is reddish with yellowish appendages. Head with basal margin slightly rounded with notch in middle. Pronotum and elytra flat. Elytra clothed in moderately fine and reclining pubescence, reddish brown to blackish area extending from basal third or quarter to apex, suture entirely pale, and faint pale spot before tip of each elytron. Middle East and India; widespread in North America. (1)

Vacusus confinis **(LeConte)** (2.3–2.8 mm) is smooth between punctures, inconspicuously pubescent with setae not paler than ground color, and uniformly shiny brownish black to black with underside and appendages lighter. Head somewhat truncate basally, with antennae moderately slender and gradually thickened apically. Pronotum longer than wide, broadest at apical quarter. Elytra with sides parallel and disc somewhat flattened, and disc densely and evenly punctured with pubescence slightly longer and less appressed than on pronotum. California east to Idaho and Texas. *Vacusus vicinus* (LaFerté-Sénectère) similar, with contrasting light and dark elytral markings. Across southern United States to Panama; also Greater Antilles. (4)

Mecynotarsus delicatulus Horn (2.0–3.0 mm) is oblong-oval, clothed in pale and slender setae, and mostly pale yellowish brown. Head lacking erect setae on lateral margins of vertex. Pronotum oval with lateral margins convergent posteriorly, with prominent horn with central carina extending anteriorly over head, more than six teeth on each side of horn, and a pair of tactile setae at middle of posterior margin. Elytra minutely punctured and clothed in fine pubescence, with medial infuscation, and lacking longitudinal sulcus at lateral margins. Flightless adults found on dunes at night. Oregon to southern California, east to Idaho, Utah, and Arizona, south to Sonora. (1)

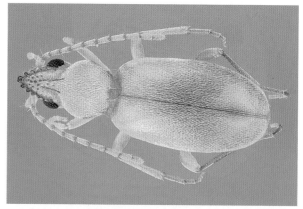

Notoxus conformis LeConte (2.6–3.5 mm) is elongate, reddish brown to brown with appendages lighter, setae appressed, and elytra yellowish to reddish brown with sinuate markings. Lateral margins of vertex with erect setae. Pronotal horn lacking ventrolateral pits, smooth anteriorly but with 0–2 marginal teeth at base, sides parallel to slightly constricted basally, and setose antebasal groove. Elytra with sinuate antebasal and postmedial brown bands sinuate with latter extended anteriorly along suture, and apices darkened. Ventrite 5 rounded to truncate (male), or bluntly triangular (female). Adults on plants and leaf litter. Southern California and Baja California, east to Utah and Arizona. (28)

Notoxus desertus Casey (2.8–4.2 mm) is tan with dark markings on elytra, and pubescent with yellowish and brown setae. Vertex with erect setae laterally. Pronotal horn with broken antebasal pubescent band and without ridge dorsally; ventrally with pits and distinctly raised margins bearing 4–9 teeth. Elytral setae long, with antebasal spots sometimes coalescent, and irregular dark postmedian band with smooth margins extended anteriorly along suture. Ventrite 5 broadly rounded (male) or rounded-triangular (female) apically. Attracted to lights and cantharidin. Pacific Northwest to Nevada and Arizona; also in East. (28)

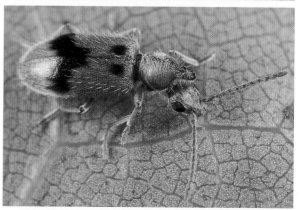

Notoxus lustrellus Casey (2.7–3.6 mm) is elongate, pubescent, and orange to brown, with elytra tan to reddish brown with brown markings. Lateral margins of vertex with erect setae. Pronotum with discal setae distinct, horn lacking ventrolateral pits, margins dentate with 6–10 teeth, margins ending before apex, and antebasal groove with pubescence complete, or with medial separation about equal in width or less than basal width of crest. Elytra with postmedian spots sometimes forming band, and male with apical tubercles. Ventrite 5 rounded (male), or triangular (female). Under driftwood and plants in coastal dunes. California, likely Baja California. (28)

Duboisius arizonensis (Champion) (6.0–8.5 mm) is elongate, coarsely punctate dorsally, and brownish black, with decumbent to suberect brown setae, and pronotal and elytral maculae consisting of small clumps of short, decumbent, white setae. Head equal to or slightly wider than pronotum, with eyes entire or weakly sulcate near antennal insertions, terminal maxillary palpomere shaped like paring knife blade. Pronotum nearly as long as wide, with anterior margin protruding medially, and without median sulcus. Underneath with metasternum not spinose, and ventrite 5 of male with later process pointed and subapically depressed. Adults are attracted to lights. Arizona south to Baja California and Sonora. (4)

Retocomus lindrothi Abdullah (6.5–8.0 mm) is elongate, coarsely punctured, and appearing bristly, with dense pubescence, including erect brown setae and appressed white setae, concealing surface. Head more or less equal in width to prothorax. Pronotum as long as wide, broadest just before apical margin, with median longitudinal sulcus not distinct, and more or less with row of white pubescence. Underneath with metasternum not spinose in either sex, with ventrite 5 deeply emarginate with well-developed long and narrow side arms (male), or tergite 5 with prominent central process (female). Southern California. (30)

Stereopalpus pruinosus LeConte (5.5–9.5 mm) is black, with legs reddish, sometimes black, and uniformly pubescent with dense to very dense silvery white recumbent setae. Head bulging behind large, coarsely faceted eyes, with terminal maxillary palpomeres elongate and parallel-sided. Pronotum quadrate, with anterior margin protruding medially, lateral margins broadly and shallowly concave before posterior angles, and without median line; coxal cavities open externally. Elytra immaculate. Ventrite 5 emarginate (male), or entire (female). Bases of coxae, femoral apices, tibiae, and distal tarsomeres blackish. California to New Mexico and Colorado. (4)

Macratria brunnea Casey (3.9–4.9 mm) is reddish brown, with appendages lighter, and clothed in fine recumbent yellowish pubescence. Head without frontoclypeal suture, and smooth, narrow neck about one-quarter width of head. Terminal antennomere slightly longer than penultimate. Pronotum unarmed, with distinct collar, and lateral margins converging behind middle. Elytra convex, not costate, with narrow longitudinal sulcus along lateral margins. Hind coxae broadly separated by angulate process on anterior margin of ventrite 1. On riparian vegetation; attracted to lights. Arizona to Texas, south to Mexico. (1)

ADERIDAE (a-dēr'-i-dē)
ANTLIKE LEAF BEETLES

Little is known of the biology and natural history of aderids. Adults are found on vegetation, especially on the underside of leaves, and on flowers. Known larvae are found in leaf litter, under bark, and in rotten wood, especially that in the red-rot stage of decay. Some species possibly scavenge dead insects or eat fungi. The immature stages of *Vanonous balteatus* Werner, a species that occurs in south-central United States, were found in the subterranean nests of solitary bees (Apidae) in Chiapas, Mexico. They were apparently opportunistically feeding on fungi growing on masses of old, decaying provisions of pollen and dead bees.

FAMILY DIAGNOSIS Adult aderids are small and antlike in form. Broad head more or less deflexed, constricted at base with neck, with eyes coarsely faceted, notched, and setose. Antennae filiform, clavate, or comblike (some males pectinate), with 11 antennomeres. Procoxal cavities open behind. Tarsi appear 4-4-3, actually 5-5-4, tarsomere 1 long, penultimate tarsomeres very short, with third from last tarsomeres lobed underneath, and claws simple. Abdomen with five ventrites, 1–2 connate.

SIMILAR FAMILIES
- *Pedilus* (Pyrochroidae, p.395)—larger
- antlike flower beetles (Anthicidae, p.400)—eyes not notched, abdominal ventrites 1–2 free
- false flower beetles (Scraptiidae, p.408)—not antlike, abdominal ventrites free
- orsodacnid leaf beetles (Orsodacnidae, p.409)—larger, tarsi 5-5-5
- some leaf beetles (Chrysomelidae: Criocerinae, p.501)—larger, tarsi 5-5-5

COLLECTING NOTES Antlike leaf beetles spend their days on the undersides of leaves and are collected by sweeping and beating the foliage of shrubs and trees, especially deciduous hardwoods such as oak (*Quercus*). They are often collected in Malaise and flight intercept traps. Some species are attracted to lights.

FAUNA 48 SPECIES IN 11 GENERA

Elonus simplex Werner (2.8 mm) is dark brown with deep, flat-bottomed punctures, and clothed in longer, erect, and shorter appressed setae on elytra. Eyes deeply emarginate near antennal insertions and setose, with facets as large as elytral punctures. Elytra red across base, with short appressed setae directed laterally. Hind femora of male without ventral brushes. Adults attracted to lights. Southeastern Arizona, southern New Mexico, and Sonora. *Elonus excavatus* Werner similar, hind femora with large brush in excavation extending across entire surface; southeastern Arizona. *Elonus hesperus* Werner with large femoral brush in excavation divided into two parts; in West from southeastern Arizona to Sinaloa. (3)

"Xylophilus" constrictus (Fall) (1.5–1.5 mm) is oblong-
oval, somewhat flattened, and brownish black, with
appendages lighter. Head with eyes broader than prothorax,
frons swollen. Antennomere 3 elongate. Pronotum with
both anteapical and antebasal sulci. Elytra at base much
broader than prothorax, more coarsely punctate than
head and pronotum, without tactile setae. Legs lack setal
brushes, tarsomere 3 long, subequal in length to 4. Adult on
vegetation in various foothill and mountain habitats during
spring and early summer. *"Xylophilus"* previously in use
(see p.257), thus rules of zoological nomenclature dictate
that this aderid be placed in another, possibly new, genus.
California and Arizona. (1)

Emelinus butleri Werner (3.3–4.3 mm) is elongate, parallel-
sided, sparsely clothed in short gray pubescence, and dark
brown with elytral humeri broadly reddish. Male antennae
flabellate, rami short, most subequal in length and less
than two-fifths of antennal length. Pronotum somewhat
bell-shaped with loose tuft of setae on each posterior angle.
Elytra not as deeply punctate as pronotum, with tactile
setae indistinct, about two-thirds length of recumbent setae.
Underside dark brown with coxae, trochanters, and part of
femora lighter. *Emelinus huachucae* Werner (2.8–3.8 mm)
paler with variegated elytral pattern, and male rami all less
than one-fifth length of antenna. (3)

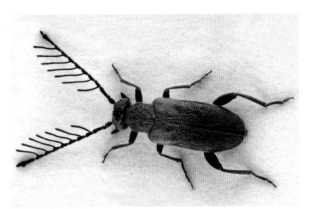

407

Emelinus melsheimeri (LeConte) (2.2 mm) is elongate,
somewhat parallel-sided, pubescent, and mostly tan with
dark zigzag pattern on elytra; antennae, tibiae, and tarsi
dull yellow. Head dark with eyes large, coarsely faceted,
separated by two-fifths their maximum width in males,
with antennae flabellate (male), or not (female). Pronotum
dark, each posterior angle with loose tuft. Elytra with tactile
setae difficult to see, about two-thirds length of recumbent
setae, and three dark uneven bars. Underside dark. Legs
with femora dark. Adults active spring and summer, found
on vegetation. Eastern Arizona, east to Massachusetts to
Florida, and south to Mexico. (3)

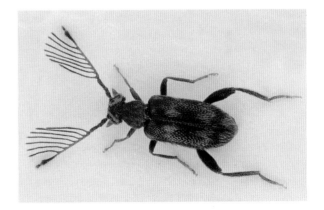

SCRAPTIIDAE (scrap-tī'-i-dē)
FALSE FLOWER BEETLES

This family of beetles comprises two very different subfamilies, Scraptiinae and Anaspinae, whose current members have been variously placed in Melandryidae and Mordellidae respectively. The mostly diurnal adults are commonly encountered on foliage and flowers. The few known larvae of scraptiids are found under the bark of dead snags and in decaying logs.

FAMILY DIAGNOSIS Adult scraptiids are mostly soft-bodied, sometimes distinctly clothed in setae, and have deeply notched eyes. Body elongate, parallel-sided to somewhat ovate, often broadest across pronotal-elytral junction, slightly flattened to moderately convex, with or without distinct vestiture on upper surface. Head hypognathous and not retracted within pronotum. Antenna with 11 antennomeres, moniliform or filiform, and with or without distinct club. Prothorax with lateral margins distinct and carinate, especially posteriorly, sometimes with pair of small depressions near posterior margins, surface sometimes with fine transverse lines, or *strigae* (*Anaspis, Diclidia, Pentaria*). Procoxal cavities broadly open behind. Elytra elongate to somewhat ovate with punctures (*Allopoda, Canifa, Scraptia*) or fine transverse lines (*Anaspis, Diclidia, Pentaria*) and cover entire abdomen. Legs slender with femora slightly swollen midlength, tarsi 5-5-4, penultimate tarsomere with or without fleshy lobes underneath; claws simple or toothed. Abdomen with five ventrites free, those of male *Anaspis* with short, movable appendages.

SIMILAR FAMILIES
- false darkling beetles (Melandryidae, p.333)—head retracted within pronotum
- tumbling flower beetles (Mordellidae, p.336)—last abdominal ventrite long, sharply pointed
- comb-clawed beetles (Tenebrionidae: Alleculinae, p.366)—claws pectinate

COLLECTING NOTES Look for false flower beetles in forests and adjacent open habitats on vegetation and flowers, especially those in the carrot (Apiaceae), buckthorn (Rhamnaceae), and rose (Rosaceae) families. Hand-collecting, sweep-netting, and beating foliage are the most productive collecting techniques; additional specimens are captured in Malaise traps and at lights. *Anaspis* and *Canifa* are especially common on flowers and leaves in open areas; *Canifa* are also encountered on foliage shrubs in woodlands. *Pentaria* are sometimes attracted to lights.

408

FAUNA 46 SPECIES IN 13 GENERA

- -

Anaspis atrata **Champion** (2.7–3.0 mm) is oblong, distinctly tapered posteriorly, and dorsal surface uniformly shiny black, with clypeus, three basal antennomeres, and palpi more or less reddish yellow-brown. Head sharply constricted behind eyes. Antennae short, with antennomeres gradually widening distally. Pronotum and elytra with distinct and transverse strigae. Pronotum one-half wider than long, with posterior angles obtuse. Elytra inconspicuously clothed in adpressed pubescence. Front and middle legs with tarsomere 4 short, about half length of and concealed between lobes of 3. Abdominal ventrite 3 of male with two movable appendages. Adults on flowers, including *Ceanothus* and *Cercocarpus*. Widespread in western North America. (13)

Anaspis collaris LeConte (2.1–2.5 mm) is barely tapered posteriorly, with prothorax pale brown, and elytra black. Head constricted behind eyes, and black with clypeus brown. Antennae mostly black and gradually widened distally, with basal three or four antennomeres pale. Pronotum and elytra with distinct and transverse strigae. Elytra clothed in very fine silky yellowish gray adpressed pubescence. Front legs pale, and middle and hind legs darker (male), or black (female), pro- and mesotarsomere 4 short, about half length of and concealed between lobes of 3. Underside black, with abdominal ventrite 3 of male with two movable appendages. California and Nevada. (13)

Anaspis rufa Say (2.8–4.0 mm) is oblong, distinctly tapered posteriorly, and mostly brownish yellow. Head sharply constricted behind eyes. Antennae short, with antennomeres gradually widening distally, 5–11 black. Pronotum and base of elytra with distinct transverse strigae. Elytra with indistinct adpressed pubescence. Front and middle legs with tarsomere 4 short, about half length of and concealed between lobes of 3. Abdomen black, ventrite 3 of male with widely separated pair of long movable appendages, followed by a shorter pair on 4. Adults on flowers. British Columbia to California, east to Montana. (13)

Pentaria trifasciata (Melsheimer) (3.0–4.0 mm) is elongate and narrowed, with distinct transverse strigae on pronotum and elytra, fine yellowish pubescence, and banded elytra. Head, antennomeres 1–5, base of pronotum, legs, and elytral spots before middle and apices yellowish brown; rest of body pale to dark brown or blackish. Pronotum wide, sides evenly rounded to sharp posterior angles. Elytra with bands sometimes weak, almost entirely yellow-brown, and not covering pygidium. Adults on flowers of trees and shrubs, dogwood (*Cornus*), hydrangea (*Hydrangea*), and black haw (*Viburnum*); also in Malaise traps, at lights. Widespread in North America; in West from British Columbia to California, east to Wyoming, Colorado, and New Mexico. (3)

Canifa pallipes (Melsheimer) (2.0–2.5 mm) is elongate, slender, parallel-sided, punctate dorsally and without transverse strigae, dark brown with appendages pale, and densely clothed in fine yellow pubescence. Head darker with antennae slightly more than half of body length; antennomeres 2–3 short, equal in length. Pronotum wide, with pair of distinct impressions at base. Elytra somewhat rugosely punctate. Adults found on foliage of shrubs and trees, including ponderosa pine (*Pinus ponderosa*) during spring and early summer. Transcontinental; across southern Canada, south to eastern United States. (1)

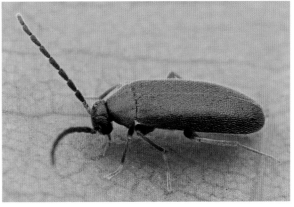

BYTURIDAE (bit-ūr'-i-dē)
FRUITWORM BEETLES

Only two species of Byturidae are known in North America, both of which occur in the West. Adults of the raspberry fruitworm, *Byturus unicolor* Say, emerge from their subterranean pupae in spring and feed on leaves and flowers of various plants. After mating, females probably lay eggs on or near buds, flowers, and developing fruits of avens (*Geum*), blackberry (*Rubus*), and possibly spotted geranium (*Geranium maculatum*). Upon reaching maturity, the larvae drop to the ground to pupate. The larvae of *Xerasia grisescens* (Jayne) have been found on the catkins of oaks (*Quercus*) in California, while the adults have been reported from oak galls.

FAMILY DIAGNOSIS Adult byturids in western North America are robust, usually uniformly yellowish, reddish brown, to blackish, with clubbed antennae, platelike lobes on tarsomeres, and are moderately clothed in long and dense setae. Head prognathous, inserted inside prothorax up to protuberant eyes. Clavate antennae with 11 antennomeres, 9–11 forming loose club. Prothorax wider than head, broadest at base, and almost equal in width to base of elytra, with lateral margins carinate. Procoxal cavities narrowly open behind. Scutellum small. Elytra not striate, with scattered punctures, straight-sided, uniformly colored or sometimes with faint and oblique bands, and completely cover abdomen. Legs with femora moderately swollen, tibiae slender; tarsi 5-5-5, with tarsomeres 2–3 broadly lobed underneath, 4 small, and claws with large basal tooth and equal in size. Abdomen with five ventrites free, ventrite 1 with process projecting anteriorly between coxae.

SIMILAR FAMILIES
- tooth-neck fungus beetles (Derodontidae, p.116)—elytra striate, tarsi not lobed underneath

- throscid beetles (Throscidae, p.252)—hind angles of pronotum extended backward; tarsi not lobed underneath
- skin beetles (Dermestidae, p.290)—tarsi not lobed underneath
- hairy fungus beetle (Mycetophagidae, p.326)—tarsi not lobed underneath
- comb-clawed beetles (Tenebrionidae, p.347)—claws pectinate
- false skin beetles (Biphyllidae, p.411)—tarsomeres 2–3 with lobes underneath slender, ventrite 1 with lines converging between legs
- silken fungus beetles (Cryptophagidae, p.449)—tarsi not lobed underneath

COLLECTING NOTES Adult byturids are hand-picked, beaten, or swept from foliage of various plants in spring and early summer. Look for *Byturus unicolor* on flowering blackberries, avens, and other plants in spring. *Xerasia griscecens* is found mostly on oaks, but is also on conifers, including pines and cypress. Malaise and light traps occasionally produce additional specimens.

FAUNA TWO SPECIES IN TWO GENERA

Raspberry Fruitworm *Byturus unicolor* Say (2.7–4.8 mm) is oblong, somewhat convex, usually uniformly yellowish to reddish brown to blackish, sometimes with prothorax and/or underside of pterothorax darker, with seta-bearing punctures. Antennal club with three antennomeres. Pronotum wider than long. Elytra with very faint, fine costae topped with fine seta-bearing punctures, spaces between with one or two irregular rows of larger seta-bearing punctures. Legs with tarsomeres 2–3 lobed. Adults active in spring, found on leaves of berry shrubs (*Rubus*). Transcontinental; in West from Alaska to Oregon, east to Alberta, Idaho, and Montana. (1)

Xerasia griscecens (Jayne) (2.2–3.9 mm, minus head) is elongate-oval, somewhat convex, yellowish to reddish brown to blackish, and clothed in long, dense, recumbent, mixed whitish and brown setae, appearing unicolorous to having distinct dark bands. Head deflexed and inserted into prothorax, with eyes small, and antennomeres 1–2 much larger than 3–8, 9–11 forming distinct club. Pronotum wider than long, sides somewhat flattened above and below, and disc setigerously punctate. Elytra not costate, widest posteriorly. Front tarsal claws cleft in male. Adults found in association with oak (*Quercus*) and occasionally conifers, especially pine (*Pinus*). Southwestern Washington to southern California, also southeastern Arizona south to western Mexico. (1)

BIPHYLLIDAE (bī-fil'-i-dē)
FALSE SKIN BEETLES

Of the three species of biphyllids known in North America, only one, *Anchorius lineatus* Casey, occurs in the West. Little is known about the biology of this species. The larvae are found under fermenting bark of mesquite (*Prosopis*), while the adults occur on mesquite bark and are attracted to lights. Other species of *Anchorius*, all distributed in the Neotropical Realm, are associated with fungusy logs.

411

FAMILY DIAGNOSIS Adult biphyllids are oblong-oval, somewhat convex, strongly pubescent with a mixture of setae on dorsal surface that lie flat on body surface, or stand more erect in rows on pronotum and elytra, and oblique lines on ventrite 1 that converge between hind legs. Head prognathous and inserted into prothorax up to base of eyes. Antennae with 11 antennomeres, 9–11 forming club, insertions concealed from above. Prothorax broader than head, slightly narrower than elytra at base, with 10 longitudinal carinae on disc, and lateral margins carinate. Procoxal cavities closed behind. Scutellum partly exposed and broad. Elytra punctostriate, lateral margins slightly arcuate, and completely cover abdomen. Legs slender with tarsi 5-5-5, tarsomeres 2–3 with slender pubescent lobes, 4 short, 5 longer than remaining tarsomeres combined, and simple claws equal in size. Abdomen with five ventrites free, ventrite 1 longer than 2 and forming narrowly rounded intercoxal process with pair of strong diverging lines after hind coxae.

SIMILAR FAMILIES
- tooth-necked fungus beetles (Derodontidae, p.116)—elytra striate, tarsi not lobed underneath
- throscid beetles (Throscidae, p.252)—hind angles of pronotum extended backward, tarsi not lobed underneath
- skin beetles (Dermestidae, p.290)—tarsi not lobed
- hairy fungus beetles (Mycetophagidae, p.326)—tarsi not lobed underneath
- comb-clawed beetles (Tenebrionidae, p.347)—claws pectinate
- fruitworms (Byturidae, p.410)—tarsomeres 2–3 with broad lobes underneath, abdominal ventrite 1 without lines
- silken fungus beetles (Cryptophagidae, p.449)—tarsi not lobed underneath

COLLECTING NOTES Look for adult *Anchorius* on mesquite (*Prosopis*) bark and at lights in mesquite woodlands.

FAUNA THREE SPECIES IN TWO GENERA

Anchorius lineatus Casey (3.3–4.1 mm) is oval, somewhat flattened, uniformly light to dark brown, and densely clothed dorsally and ventrally with very fine pale yellow setae. Pronotum wide, disc with 10 longitudinal ridges, and explanate sides broadly arcuate and narrowed anteriorly. Elytra punctostriate and setose, distinctly costate. Ventrite 1 with femoral lines weak, and strong lateral lines extending from posterior angles to hind coxal cavities. Middle and hind femora stout, tarsomeres 2–3 lobed, 2 shorter than 3, and claws simple. Underside uniformly punctate. Larvae develop under fermenting bark of mesquite (*Prosopis*), while adults found in bark and attracted to lights. Southeastern California to southern Arizona. (1)

PELTIDAE (pelt'-i-dē)
SHIELD BEETLES

This family contains the single genus *Peltis* and was formerly considered a subfamily in Trogossitidae. Both adults and larvae feed on the mycelia of wood-rotting fungi. In western North America, three species occur in forests and are associated with *Fomitopsis* and *Polyporus* fungi growing under the bark of pine (*Pinus*), fir (*Abies*), spruce (*Picea*), hemlock (*Tsuga*), and other conifers. The larvae develop inside decaying wood, while the adults live under bark.

FAMILY DIAGNOSIS Shield beetles are broadly oval, flat, coarsely punctate, with dorsal surface mostly glabrous, or with elytral tubercles setose (*Peltis pippingskoeldi*), and lateral margins of pronotum and elytra broadly explanate. Prognathous head small, not concealed by pronotum, with small eyes and a frontoclypeal suture. Antennae with 11 antennomeres, 9–11 forming symmetrical club. Pronotum wide, with anterior margin deeply emarginate, and carinate lateral margin explanate. Procoxal cavities open behind. Scutellum visible. Elytra each with six discal costae. Legs short, tibiae with single hooked spur, with tarsi 5-5-5, and claws simple. Abdomen with five ventrites free.

SIMILAR FAMILIES
- *Grynocharis* (Lophocateridae, p.414)—elytron with four discal carinae
- *Calitys* (Trogossitidae, p.414)—elytron with five discal carinae, 1 and 2 tuberculate
- sap beetles (Nitidulidae, p.443)—elytra not costate

COLLECTING NOTES Look for adults of all three species of *Peltis* beneath bark of conifer logs, snags, and stumps in association with polypore fungi.

412

FAUNA FIVE SPECIES IN TWO GENERA

Peltis pippingskoeldi (Mannerheim) (6.0–12.3 mm) is broadly oval, moderately shiny, somewhat flattened, reddish brown to dark brown with margins lighter, and pale reddish-brown spots on elytra. Head not concealed by pronotum. Pronotum and elytral lateral margins broadly explanate and concave. Pronotum broad and densely punctate. Elytra with costae interrupted with shiny, setose, and sometimes elongate tubercles, even costae more strongly elevated, each with about seven spots. Adults under conifer bark in association with polypores (*Fomitopsis pinicola, Polyporus abeitinus*). British Columbia to southern California, Arizona, and New Mexico. (3)

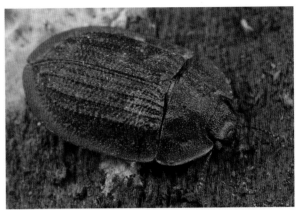

Peltis septentrionalis (Randall) (6.8–12.3 mm) is broadly oval, somewhat flattened, and uniformly shiny dark reddish brown above, paler below, with lateral margins of pronotum and elytra broadly explanate and flat. Head coarsely punctate. Pronotum much wider than long, and sparsely punctate. Uninterrupted elytral carinae not sharply elevated, with sides nearly vertical. Adults under conifer bark in association with polypores (*Fomitopsis pinicola, Oligoporus fragilis*). Alaska, across Canada, northern United States; in West south to California and Arizona. *Peltis fraterna* (Randall) (6.0–9.7 mm) with pronotal margins not or only slightly reflexed, and elevation between lateral elytral margins and disc oblique; western North America south to California, Idaho, and Colorado. (3)

413

LOPHOCATERIDAE (lō-fō-ka-ter'-i-dē)

LOPHOCATERID BEETLES

Lophocaterids, formerly a tribe in Trogossitidae, consist of two genera in western North America. Adults of *Eronyxa* are apparently pollen feeders and found on flowers of *Ceanothus, Prunus,* and other shrubs. *Grynocharis* adults live under bark of conifers, where they and their larvae both feed on mycelia of wood-rotting fungi. *Eronyxa expansus* Van Dyke larvae are presumed predators of the incense cedar scale, *Xylococculus macrocarpae.*

FAMILY DIAGNOSIS Western lophocaterids are oblong, somewhat flat, with dorsal surface pubescent (*Eronyxa*), or glabrous (*Grynocharis*). Head small, not concealed by pronotum, with distinct frontoclypeal suture. Antennae with 11 antennomeres, 9–11 forming loose asymmetrical (*Eronyxa*) or symmetrical (*Grynocharis*) club. Pronotum broad, with anterior margins emarginate (*Grynocharis*) or truncate (*Eronyxa*), and lateral margins explanate. Procoxae open behind. Scutellum visible. Elytra oblong, explanate laterally, with (*Grynocharis*) or without (*Eronyxa*) well-developed costae. Legs with tibiae bearing a pair of apical spurs, tarsi 5-5-5, tarsomere 1 small, and claws simple. Abdomen with five ventrites free.

SIMILAR FAMILIES

- *Peltis* (Peltidae, p.413)—pronotum and elytra with broadly explanate lateral margins, elytron with six discal carinae
- *Calitys* (Trogossitidae, p.415)—elytron with five discal carinae, 1 and 2 tuberculate
- sap beetles (Nitidulidae, p.443)—elytra not costate

COLLECTING NOTES

Look for adult and larval *Grynocharis* in association with mycelia of polypore fungi beneath bark of incense cedar (*Libocedrus decurrens*) and other conifer logs, snags, and stumps. *Eronyxa* adults are found on flowers of *Ceanothus*, *Prunus*, and other trees and shrubs; *Eronyxa pallidus* (Motschulsky) larvae have been reared from dead *Ceanothus* branches.

FAUNA EIGHT SPECIES IN FOUR GENERA

Eronyxa pallidus (Motschulsky) (2.9–6.0 mm) is oblong, moderately convex, and brown except head, pronotal disc, and thoracic sterna black, occasionally all black (males), and long, dense recumbent yellowish setae. Pronotal and elytral lateral margins with erect setae. Pronotum broadest behind middle, and lateral margin broadly explanate. Elytra broad, disc confusedly punctate, with lateral margins narrowly explanate. Adults on flowers of *Ceanothus* and other trees and shrubs. British Columbia to southern California. *Eronyxa angustus* (Casey) less convex, pronotum widest medially, mostly Sierra Nevada and Transverse Ranges of California. *Eronyxa expansus* Van Dyke (4.3–5.7 mm) with pronotal and elytral margins equally explanate. Sierra Nevada of California. (3)

414

Grynocharis oregonensis (Schaeffer) (6.3–10.4 mm) is oblong, flat, glabrous dorsally, and reddish brown. Head small, not concealed by pronotum, with antennae robust. Pronotum much wider than long, broadest at about apical third, with apical angles produced and rounded, lateral margins arcuate, narrowly explanate and reflexed. Elytra each with four prominent discal carinae, intervals with three irregular rows of punctures, and lateral margins broadly explanate, somewhat strongly reflexed. Underside finely setose. Adults under bark of pine (*Pinus*) and incense cedar (*Libocedrus decurrens*). British Columbia to Sierra Nevada in central California, east to Idaho and Nevada. (1)

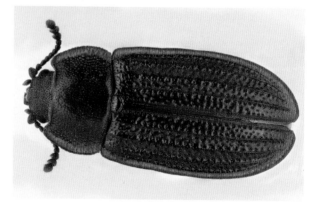

TROGOSSITIDAE (trō-gô-sīt'-i-dē)
BARK-GNAWING BEETLES AND CADELLES

Trogossitids are found under the bark of dead trees, logs, and stumps. Longer, slender, and cylindrical species (*Airora, Corticotomus, Euschaefferia, Nemosoma*) are specialist predators of bark beetles (Curculionidae, pp.559–563), while larger and somewhat flatter species (*Temnoscheila, Tenebroides*) prey on various wood-boring beetles and their larvae. Adults and larvae of the cosmopolitan Cadelle, *Tenebroides mauritanicus* (Linnaeus), infest stored grains and cereals. Both the adults and larvae of the oblong and flat *Calitys* live under bark, where they are associated with mycelia of polypore fungi.

FAMILY DIAGNOSIS Some adult trogossitids are elongate, parallel-sided, and somewhat convex to slightly flattened (*Corticotomus*, *Euschaefferia*, *Nemosoma*, *Temnoscheila*, *Tenebroides*), nearly cylindrical (*Airora*) with head and prothorax narrowly and loosely attached to the rest of the body, or broadly oval and flat (*Calitys*). Head hypognathous, with frontoclypeal suture rarely distinct. Antennae with 11 antennomeres, 9–11 forming loose and symmetrical (*Calitys*) or asymmetrical (*Airora*, *Corticotomus*, *Euschaefferia*, *Nemosoma*, *Temnoscheila*, *Tenebroides*) club. Pronotum wider than head and quadrate, or wider than long, with lateral margins distinctly carinate. Procoxal cavities closed behind. Scutellum visible. Elytra usually completely cover abdomen, or rarely short and exposing abdomen (*Nemosoma championi* Wickham). Tarsi 5-5-5, tarsomere 1 usually very small, with simple claws equal in size. Abdomen with five ventrites free.

SIMILAR FAMILIES

- ground beetles (Carabidae, p.88)—antennae filiform, ventrite 1 divided by metacoxae
- cylindrical bark beetles (Zopheridae, p.341)—tarsi 4-4-4

COLLECTING NOTES Look for bark-gnawing beetles during the day beneath bark of dead conifers and broadleaf trees. Other species are found crawling on dead branches, logs, and stumps at night. *Airora*, *Corticotomus*, *Euschaefferia*, *Nemosoma*, *Temnoscheila*, and *Tenebroides* are occasionally attracted to lights.

FAUNA 50 SPECIES IN EIGHT GENERA

Calitys scabra (Thunberg) (6.6–12.2 mm) is oblong, somewhat flattened, dorsal surfaces roughly sculptured with small tubercles, and black or dark brown-black. Antennal club symmetrical. Pronotum with discal callosities prominent, with sides explanate and serrate. Elytra parallel-sided, costae bearing small, buttonlike tubercles, costae 2 and 3 coalescent apically, 5 on nearly vertical sides. Adults under pine (*Pinus*) bark. Alaska, across Canada and northern United States, in West to southern California and southeastern Arizona. *Calitys minor* Hatch (7.5–8.6 mm) reddish brown, pronotal callosities and elytral carina less evident, carinae 2 and 3 not coalescent, 5 not evident apically; Oregon. (2)

Airora aequalis Reitter (3.7–7.6 mm) is elongate, somewhat cylindrical, moderately shiny light reddish brown to black with head and pronotum sometimes lighter than elytra. Head moderately coarsely and shallowly punctate, antennae short with asymmetrical club. Pronotum with anterior angles rounded, with lateral anterior margins distinct, not angularly reflexed. Elytra with basal angles prominent and produced. Outer tibial margins spined. Under pine (*Pinus*) bark; at lights. British Columbia to California, east to Colorado and western Texas; also, Mexico. *Airora minuta* Schaeffer (3.2–3.6 mm) similar, elytra with basal angles not prominent or produced, with lateral anterior pronotal margins indistinct and angularly reflexed. California, Arizona, and Mexico. (2)

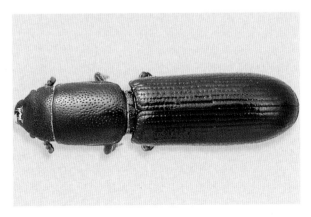

Corticotomus caviceps Fall (3.2–5.3 mm) is elongate, somewhat convex, brownish black with lighter basal patch on each elytron. Head broadly concave and without median groove dorsally, and antennal club asymmetrical. Pronotum without distinct anterior or posterior angles, and sides parallel with distinct marginal beads. Elytra with subhumeral impression, striae evident basally with coarse punctures, interstriae finely punctate. British Columbia to California, east to South Dakota and western Texas. *Corticotomus* with elytra smooth and scarcely punctured: *C. apicalis* Van Dyke (3.6–3.8 mm) bicolored with pronotum not parallel-sided, California; *C. californicus* Van Dyke (2.3–3.3 mm) elytra uniformly colored with parallel-sided pronotum, Oregon to California, east to New Mexico. (3)

Temnoscheila chlorodia (Mannerheim) (8.4–19.8 mm) is elongate, somewhat convex, shiny metallic green, blue, or purple. Head with vertex finely and closely punctate, and frons with distinct longitudinal impression. Antennal club asymmetrical. Pronotum less convex, with anterior angles prominent and sharp, and lateral margins moderately converging posteriorly and angularly deflexed behind middle. Elytra with humeral angles prominent. Adults found under bark of conifers. British Columbia to California, east to South Dakota and Texas, south to western Mexico and Baja California. *Temnoscheila aerea* LeConte similar, head with short longitudinal impression faint or obsolete; California and Arizona. Adults of both species attracted to lights. (7)

Tenebroides crassicornis (Horn) (4.4–10.5 mm) is elongate, broad, somewhat flattened, coarsely but not closely punctate, and reddish brown to brownish black. Head convex, with antennae robust, club asymmetrical with antennomere 8 produced and much smaller than 9, but larger than 7. Pronotum wider than long, narrowed posteriorly, with anterior angles prominent and sharp, lateral margins narrowly rounded and not angularly deflexed behind middle. Elytra punctostriate on disc, interstriae with double row of punctures, and lateral margins slightly arcuate and narrowly explanate basally. Adults mostly associated with conifers, including pine (*Pinus*) and larch (*Larix*). Widely distributed in western North America. (7)

THYMALIDAE (thī-mal'-i-dē)
THYMALID BEETLES

Thymalids, represented across North America by a single species, *Thymalus marginicollis* Chevrolat, were formerly a tribe in Trogossitidae. Adults and larvae feed on and develop in polypore or bracket fungi. In the Northeast, they are most commonly found on *Piptoporus betulinus* growing on birch (*Betula*), but are also recorded on polypores in the genera *Daedalia* and *Trametes*, all of which grow on hardwoods. Adults collected in British Columbia were associated with an unidentified fungus growing on willow (*Salix*).

FAMILY DIAGNOSIS Thymalids, as represented by *Thymalus*, are broadly oval, strongly and evenly convex dorsally, flat ventrally, and clothed dorsally in long pubescence. Head small and prognathous, with frontoclypeal suture absent, and partly concealed from view above by explanate anterior pronotal margin. Antennae with 11 antennomeres, 9–11 forming loose, symmetrical club. Prothorax broad, with angles not evident, and lateral margins explanate. Procoxal cavities open behind. Elytra at base broader than prothorax, with lateral margins and apices explanate, disc vaguely punctoseriate, and completely cover abdomen. Legs with tarsi 5-5-5 and simple, and simple claws equal in size. Abdomen with five ventrites free.

SIMILAR FAMILIES
- lady beetles (Coccinellidae, p.318)—tarsi 4-4-4, appear 3-3-3
- *Peltis* (Peltidae, p.413)—elytron with six discal carinae
- sap beetles (Nitidulidae, p.443)—glabrous dorsally, elytra not punctoseriate
- tortoise beetles (Chrysomelidae: Cassidinae, p.504)—glabrous dorsally, tarsi expanded with setose pads ventrally

COLLECTING NOTES Look for adult and larval *Thymalus* on polypore fungi, especially species in the genera *Piptoporus*, *Daedalia*, *Trametes*, and *Cerrena* growing on hardwoods. Adults are also found in Malaise traps and are occasionally attracted to ultraviolet light, or are found overwintering under loose bark of hardwood logs and stumps.

417

FAUNA ONE SPECIES, *THYMALUS MARGINICOLLIS*

Thymalus marginicollis Chevrolat (4.3–6.2 mm) is broadly oval, convex, clothed dorsally in long, erect pubescence, and shiny pale to dark brown with a brassy luster; margins and underside paler. Antenna with loose club. Head and pronotum closely and coarsely punctured. Margins of pronotum and elytra reddish, flattened, and slightly turned up. Pronotum wide, coarsely punctate, with lateral margins strongly arcuate and broadly explanate. Elytra slightly undulating, with punctures widely separated and coarser than on pronotum. Larvae and adults found on bracket fungi; adults also under bark, sometimes at lights. Transcontinental; across southern Canada, also in eastern United States. (1)

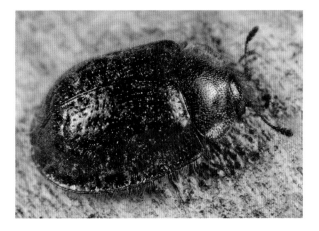

MAURONISCIDAE (môr-ō-nisk′-i-dē)
MAURONISCID FLOWER BEETLES

Mauroniscidae is a small family known only in the New World and was previously treated as part of the subfamily Dasytinae in Melyridae. It is represented by nine species in four genera in the United States, all but one occurring west of the Continental Divide. Nothing is known of their biology, other than that *Mectemycor sericeus* Majer and *Scuromanius facetus* (Casey) are both collected in desert flowers during spring and in late summer–early fall, respectively.

FAMILY DIAGNOSIS North American mauroniscids are elongate, parallel-sided, and convex. Head elongate, with eyes convex and not emarginate, and glabrous (setose in *Dasyrhadus*). Antennae with 11 antennomeres, terminal five or six antennomeres forming weakly developed club, insertions exposed, and mouthparts modified with galea and lacinia elongate and narrow. Prothorax somewhat cylindrical, wider than long or not. Pronotum convex, with lateral margins completely carinate (*Dasyrhadus*, *Mecomycter*, *Scuromanius*), or absent (*Mectemycor*). Procoxal cavities open behind. Elytra irregularly punctate, rounded apically, and completely covering abdomen. Tarsi 5-5-5, tarsomere 1 as long as or longer than 2, with simple claws lacking ungual appendages, except *Dasyrhadus*. Abdomen with six ventrites free, 1 not much longer than 2.

SIMILAR FAMILIES
- soft-winged flower beetles (Melyridae, Dasytinae, p.421)—galea and lacinia not elongate and narrow, usually with ungual appendages

COLLECTING NOTES Look for mauroniscids on desert wildflowers, especially composites (Asteraceae), in the spring and again in late summer, early fall.

FAUNA NINE SPECIES IN THREE GENERA

Mectemycor strangulatus Majer (3.0–5.0 mm) is elongate, with inconspicuous pubescence short, decumbent, and yellowish brown, with head and pronotum darker. Head black, strongly rostrate and constricted laterally. Antennae long, with antennomeres not (male) or weakly (female) transverse. Pronotum elongate and more (male) or less (female) strongly constricted just before middle. Elytral disc tuberculate. Pygidium semicircular. Legs long, with tarsi nearly as long as tibiae (male) or not (female), and claws simple, without ungual appendages. Both *Mectemycor sericeus* Majer and *M. linearis* Fall with pronotum less elongate, former with pronotum more constricted than latter. All likely on desert wildflowers in spring. California. (3)

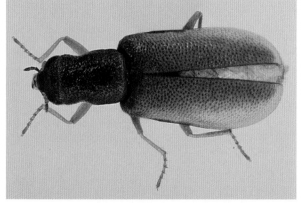

Mecomycter omalinus Horn (2.7–4.0 mm) is obovate, convex, with conspicuous pubescence both decumbent and erect. Head long, with antennomere 5 somewhat triangular. Pronotum longer than wide, broadest at middle, strongly convex, coarsely punctate, and reddish brown, with or without variable black medial patch. Elytra with suture narrowly to broadly dark, especially across base and apical fourth. Claws simple, without ungual appendages. Washington to California, east to Utah. *Mecomycter testaceus* Majer (2.8–3.5 mm) similar in form, uniformly yellow-brown, with antennomere 5 somewhat cylindrical; California. (2)

Scuromanius facetus (Casey) (2.2–3.4 mm) is convex, with decumbent, erect pubescence, and yellowish brown with elytra mostly lighter. Head not rostrate. Antenna with loose club, antennomeres transverse, especially penultimate article. Pronotum somewhat rugose with shallow punctures, with lateral margins more or less angulate medially, and sometimes infuscate on anterior pronotal margin. Elytra with basal infuscation sometimes narrowly extended along suture, expanding at apical quarter. Pygidium semicircular. Claws simple, without ungual appendages. Arizona and New Mexico. *Scuromanius wickhami* Majer more reddish or orange, with lateral pronotal angulation more basal. Inyo Mountains, California. (2)

RHADALIDAE (rad-al'-i-dē)
RHADALID FLOWER BEETLES

Rhadalidae was formerly treated as a subfamily of Melyridae. Little is known about their biology. Adults and larvae of most species are probably predators and feed on small insects, although adults of *Rhadalus* apparently feed on pollen, too. Adults of *Semijulistus* frequently occur at high altitudes, where they visit the flowers of yarrow (*Achillea*) and other plants primarily in spring and early summer. *Semijulistus atrata* (LeConte) is reported to be attracted to the smoke of smouldering pine stumps.

FAMILY DIAGNOSIS Rhadalids are elongate, hard-bodied, convex, lack eversible vesicles, and are uniformly clothed in dense erect pubescence. Head broader than long and partially retracted within prothorax, with coarsely faceted eyes entire or weakly emarginate and glabrous (*Semijulistus*), or setose (*Rhadalus*). Antennae serrate, with 11 antennomeres. Maxillary palps with apical palpomere broadened apically. Prothorax with lateral margins carinate. Procoxal cavities open behind. Legs with tarsi 5-5-5, with tarsomere 1 as long or longer than 2, and tarsal claws variable, most with long membranous appendages.

Abdomen with six ventrites, with 1–2 connate or free (*Dasyrhadus*).

SIMILAR FAMILIES
- soft-winged flower beetles (Melyridae: Dasytinae, p.421)—terminal palpomere *conical*

COLLECTING NOTES *Rhadalus* adults are attracted to lights in chaparral and desert communities from winter through early summer, while those of *Semijulistus* occur on flowers mostly during spring and early summer.

419

FAUNA NINE SPECIES IN THREE GENERA

Rhadalus testaceus LeConte (5.5–6.5 mm) is elongate, convex, somewhat parallel, shiny, dark brown with appendages and underside lighter, and clothed in long erect brown pubescence. Setose eyes separated by three times their own width. Long antennae weakly serrate. Pronotum broad, with sides broadly arcuate and shiny raised patches. Elytra with punctures large and confused and sublateral carinae present. Adults at lights. Southern California and Arizona. *Rhadalus lecontei* Casey (5.8 mm) oblong-oval, pale reddish brown, eyes separated by much less than twice their own widths, and pronotum narrower than elytra. Arizona. (2)

Semijulistus flavipes (LeConte) (3.4–5.8 mm) is oblong, stout and strongly convex, dull black with bluish tinge, and pubescent. Prominent eyes glabrous. Antennae short, appearing loosely clubbed, with antennomeres 7–11 broadly serrate. Pronotum broad, lateral margins evenly arcuate, and serrate. Elytra deeply and confusedly punctate, without sublateral carinae, with very narrow epipleurae not reaching apices; female with a pair of oval, smooth, and shiny callosities on apical third. Legs uniformly yellowish brown. California. *Semijulistus atra* (LeConte) (2.9–4.5 mm) is dull black, with black legs and pale tarsi. Adults on flowers, including yarrow (*Achillea*). British Columbia to Oregon, east to Alberta, Montana, and Colorado. (5)

MELYRIDAE (me-līr′-i-dē)
SOFT-WINGED FLOWER BEETLES

Melyrids feed on both plant and animal materials. Adults are commonly encountered on conifers or flowering plants, where they feed on pollen, look for mates, and possibly prey on small arthropods. Species of *Endeodes* are unusual members of the family in that they all occur along the rocky seashore in the intertidal zone, where they live between stones under dried seaweed and other debris. In agricultural systems, *Collops* species are important predators of crop pests, especially those attacking alfalfa, cotton, and sorghum. Species of Malachiinae are soft-bodied beetles that often have bright, aposematic colors. *Collops* and *Malachius* species have eversible defensive glands or vesicles, balloonlike structures hidden under the prothorax and abdomen that expand like air bags to release noxious odors that deter predators. Some male Malachiinae have incredibly exaggerated antennal features or modified elytra apices that are used in elaborate courtship behaviors. Adult Dasytinae are more compact, hard-bodied, and somberly colored. They often gather in large groups on flowers (p.33, Fig. 26b), feeding on both pollen and nectar. With densely pubescent bodies that trap pollen grains, dasytines are likely significant pollinators. Many of the plants they visit include species grown as food for both human consumption and livestock, as well as for wildlife. The larval biology of soft-winged flower beetles is poorly known. Larval Malachiinae are predators and are usually found in the soil. Nothing is known of the larval habits of North American Dasytinae, other than a mention of *Listrus* larvae found in soil beneath dune vegetation. European dasytine larvae are found mostly in leaf litter or rotting wood, living as detritivores, herbivores, or predators. Some *Malachius* larvae live under bark in association with the galleries of wood-boring beetles, while those of some Old World species are found on plant stems inhabited by tumbling flower beetles (Mordellidae, p.336). All the genera treated here need study.

FAMILY DIAGNOSIS Adult melyrids in western North America are somewhat flat and mostly blue, black, or green, often with contrasting bright red, yellow, or orange markings (Malachiinae), or strongly convex and various shades of gray or brown (Dasytinae). Head large. Antennae with 11 antennomeres, sometimes appearing as 10 because antennomere 2 is partially hidden within 1 (*Collops*). Prothorax variable, more or less quadrate and somewhat broader posteriorly, with lateral margins distinctly carinate, and eversible vesicles (Malachiinae only). Procoxal cavities open behind. Scutellum visible. Elytra soft, loose fitting, and almost always broadest posteriorly. Tarsi 5-5-5, 4-4-5 in male *Collops*, with tarsomeres not lobed, and claws equal and simple, toothed, or with ungual appendages (thin cuticular extensions) from base of claw (most Dasytinae). Abdomen with five or six ventrites free, sometimes with eversible vesicles along sides (Malachiinae).

SIMILAR FAMILIES
- *Ditemnus*, *Silis* (Cantharidae, p.270)—antennae filiform, sides of prothorax notched, tarsi 5-5-5, tarsomere 4 bilobed

420

- checkered beetles (Cleridae, p.425)—
  antennae usually clubbed, occasionally serrate
  or filiform; prothorax with lateral margins not
  carinate; one or more tarsomeres lobed
  underneath
- some leaf beetles (Chrysomelidae, p.501)—
  antennae filiform, prothorax with lateral margins
  not distinctly carinate, tarsi appear 4-4-4, but

actually 5-5-5, tarsomeres 1–3 usually lobed or with
expanded ventral pads

COLLECTING NOTES Most melyrids are collected by hand
from flowers or beaten and swept from trees, shrubs, grasses,
and other herbaceous vegetation. Look for *Endeodes*
running over rocks and driftwood just above high tide line,
as well as under boards and debris in the intertidal zone.

FAUNA 502 SPECIES IN 52 GENERA

Cradytes serricollis **(LeConte)** (4.5–5.5 mm) is densely
clothed in both decumbent and erect pale setae, and black
with elytra partly or wholly reddish brown, reddish brown
with black or brown spots or stripes, brown or black with
reddish-brown stripes, or entirely black. Antennae short.
Lateral pronotal margins serrate, and posterior angles
broadly rounded. Epipleura narrow and broadest basally.
Legs reddish brown, with protibiae with spines along outer
edge, and tarsomere 1 shorter than 2, and claws with well-
developed basal appendages. Male pro- and mesotibiae
with pair of apical spurs, one slender and one spatulate. On
flowers and vegetation. Arizona to Texas. (4)

Eschatocrepis constrictus **(LeConte)** (2.0–3.4 mm)
is convex, inconspicuously clothed in short grayish or
brownish pubescence, and shiny black with bronzy luster;
mouthparts and antennae lighter. Pronotum distinctively and
transversely constricted before anterior margin, with variably
distinct submarginal lines, and angles broadly rounded.
Elytra with sides mostly straight, punctures confused and
somewhat coarser than pronotum, and epipleurae narrow.
Legs yellowish or reddish brown, sometimes with dorsal
femoral surfaces black. Protibiae lacking spines. Claws
with slender symmetrical appendages of equal length. On
various flowers in early spring to early summer in various
lowland and montane habitats. California and Arizona,
south to Baja California. (1)

Eutrichopleurus seriellus **(Casey)** (2.6–3.2 mm) is oblong-
oval, stout, convex, clothed in coarse, decumbent, and
grayish pubescence, without any trace of intermixed erect
setae, and black, with antennae and tarsi reddish. Head
broad, three-quarters as wide as prothorax. Pronotum wider
than long, almost as broad as base of elytra, with short
setal fringe composed of stiff, black setae of even length.
Elytra parallel-sided, jointly rounded apically, and disc
with pubescence denser than that of pronotum. Protibiae
with spines along outer edge. Adults on various flowers,
including thistle (*Cirsium*). California, Nevada, Utah. (115)

Listrus **species** (1.8–3.8 mm) are oblong, more or less parallel-sided, convex, dorsally clothed in simple, decumbent, and sometime patterned pubescence. Eyes glabrous. Pronotum convex, uniformly punctate, with lateral margins minutely serrulate, and anterior angles not produced. Elytral vestiture simple, always uniform in color, with epipleurae narrow and becoming broader, more distinctly defined toward base. Legs short. Protibiae lacking spines. Claws with ungual appendages rounded apically. Adults on many kinds of flowers in spring. Widespread in Western North America. (86)

Attalus **species** (1.5–3.0 mm) are elongate-oval, somewhat flattened, usually with both erect and decumbent setae, with lateral eversible vesicles, and uniformly dark or variably marked with contrasting colors. Antennae with 11 distinct antennomeres, and male antennae serrate. Pronotum more or less quadrate, broader than head. Elytra with humeri lacking tactile setae, expanding posteriorly and broadly rounded apically, and not covering abdomen completely. Abdomen with six ventrites. Protarsi with five tarsomeres in both sexes, male with most tarsomeres bearing apical comb of stout black setae, 2 forming lobe over 3. Diurnal adults usually found on vegetation. Genus needs revision. (54 NA)

422

Collops cribrosus **LeConte** (3.0–4.0 mm) is elongate-oval, shiny, with dorsal surfaces finely, densely, and coarsely punctate, and elytra dark metallic green or blue. Head mostly black with anterior portion pale, with antennomere 2 strongly dilated in male, antennae pale (male), sometimes with terminal antennomeres infuscate in some females. Pronotum either black, often with anterior angles and narrow edge of lateral margins pale, or entirely red, sometimes with central black spot. Elytra oval, narrow at base without humeri. Front legs pale, middle legs variable, and hind legs black. Flightless adults confined to coastal habitats. British Columbia to Baja California. Genus needs revision. (45 NA)

Collops grandis **Champion** (7.0–7.5 mm) is elongate-oval, shiny, and clothed in erect black and recumbent pale setae. Head broad, mostly black with bluish or greenish luster, with clypeus, labrum, and mouthparts yellowish brown. Antennae black with basal segments yellowish brown, antennomere 2 of male expanded with clawlike hook. Pronotum broad, shiny medially. Elytra uniformly metallic blue or bluish green, and densely punctate. Underside mostly red with black metathorax. Legs with femora orangish red, tibiae and tarsi black. Adult found on seepwillows (*Baccharis*) and willows (*Salix*). Southeastern Arizona, likely in New Mexico, south to south-central Mexico. Genus needs revision. (45 NA)

Collops granellus Fall (4.5–5.0 mm) is clothed in erect black and recumbent pale setae. Head and antennae mostly black, with clypeus, labrum, and basal antennomeres pale. Prothorax red. Elytra minutely granulate, each with broad bluish or bluish-green stripe, and pale margins not continuous around apices. Underside entirely red. Legs black (female), or with front and middle femora more or less pale (male). Utah to Mexico. *Collops vittatus* Say (3.4–5.0 mm) similar, pronotal disc with variable spot sometimes divided or lacking, elytra smooth with apical margins often reddish, and legs mostly black. Arizona to eastern United States and Mexico. (45 NA)

Collops histrio Erichson (4.0–5.0 mm) is elongate-oval, coarsely punctate, shiny, clothed in erect black pubescence, and usually mostly red with head mostly black and elytral spots weakly metallic bluish or greenish. Antennae, except for basal antennomeres, black, with antennomere 2 strongly dilated in male. Pronotum without markings, finely punctate and shiny medially, becoming duller and more densely punctate laterally. Elytra moderately and densely coarsely punctate, occasionally mostly black. Underside ranging from almost entirely black to almost entirely red. Tibiae and tarsi black. California and Arizona. Genus needs revision. (45 NA)

423

Collops quadriguttatus Champion (5.0–6.0 mm) is finely punctate dorsally, and sparsely clothed in erect black setae and recumbent pale setae. Head shiny black and sparsely punctate, with clypeus, antennae, and mouthparts pale, and slightly depressed in front. Male antennomere 1 strongly curved and widened apically, 2 with long, curved appendage, 3 serrate, 3–10 decreasing in width. Pronotum mostly black, sparsely and finely punctate, with anterior and lateral margins occasionally reddish. Elytra red with bluish-black humeral and larger apical patches not reaching suture, and surface alutaceous. Front and middle tibiae and tarsi reddish brown, hind femur and tibia infuscate. California. (45 NA)

Collops vittatus (Say) (3.4–5.0 mm) is variably marked, and clothed in long, erect, black setae and short, recumbent, pale setae. Head black with dark metallic blue luster, and mouthparts, basal antennomeres, and all but apical palpomeres pale. Male antennomere 1 longer than wide, with 3 modified. Pronotum red, disc with variable spot sometimes divided or lacking, lateral third minutely rugose and dull, and middle third smooth and shiny. Elytra usually with pair of broad metallic bluish or greenish stripes narrowed at basal third, with suture, lateral, and sometimes apical margins reddish. Legs mostly black. Predatory adults beneficial in cotton and alfalfa fields. Across North America. (45 NA)

Endeodes basalis (LeConte) (3.0–5.0 mm) is slender, with head and pronotum reddish orange, elytra black, and abdomen reddish brown to mostly black. Pronotum broadest at apical third, with anterior margin broadly arcuate, and sides briefly constricted before rounded posterior angles. Rugose elytra nearly half abdominal length. Tibiae and tarsi reddish, tarsi 5-5-5. Under seaweed on sandy beaches. Central California to Baja California. *Endeodes insularis* Blackwelder (3.0–6.0 mm) light reddish brown, abdomen and mandibular apices dark black, and elytra small. North Channel Islands and Central Coast of California. (3)

Endeodes collaris (LeConte) (5.0–7.0 mm) is slender and black, with labrum, pronotum, and abdominal intersegmental membranes reddish. Antennae moniliform. Pronotum slightly wider than long, front and sides broadly rounded, posterior margin straight with slight emargination medially. Elytra small, almost oval, black. Vesicles present on prothorax and between metathorax and abdomen. Tarsi brown, 5-5-5, male protarsomere 2 elongate and swollen with thick, apical comb of black setae. Shelters in cracks of rocks and under debris on coastal beaches below high tide mark in summer and early fall. British Columbia to northern California. (3)

Scarlet Malachite Beetle *Malachius aeneus* (Linnaeus) (6.0–8.0 mm) is broadly oblong, mostly dull, metallic green and clothed in long, dark setae; eversible yellow sacs present behind head and next to hind legs. Head with clypeus and labrum yellowish brown, male with clypeolabral sulcus. Pronotum with anterior angles reddish. Elytra brick red, with posterior margin and broad area along suture extending to apical quarter green. Adults active in late spring and summer, found among cereal crops where they prey on other insects. Europe; established in West from British Columbia to Oregon, east to Saskatchewan, Montana, and Colorado; also Atlantic Provinces and New England. (10)

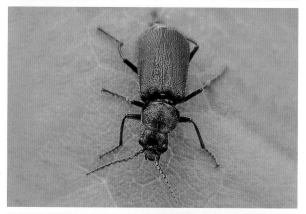

Malachius mixtus Horn (3.0–4.5 mm) is narrowly oblong, shiny, and variable in color. Head mostly black, with clypeus, labrum, and mouthparts yellowish brown. Clypeolabral sulcus evident. Antennae black and pectinate (male) or strongly serrate (female). Pronotum wide, black, sometimes with anterior and/or lateral margins narrowly red, red lateral margin may have small medial spot. Elytra green, blue, or bronze, each sometimes with variable pale yellowish or reddish stripe (Mojave Desert), and apices red. Underside black with metallic luster, sometimes with prothorax and margins of ventrites red. Legs black, with tarsi sometimes lighter. On flowers, including *Yucca*. British Columbia to Oregon, east to Idaho, Nevada, and Arizona. (10)

Malachius thevenetii Horn (4.8–6.0 mm) is narrowly oblong, with only fine decumbent pubescence dorsally, and mostly dull black with bluish-green luster. Anterior margins of clypeus and labrum reddish, with clypeolabral sulcus in both sexes. Antennae strongly serrate or weakly pectinate in male. Pronotum red, with broad medial black stripe on disc. Elytra scabrous, mostly or all blue-green, with sutural apices either emarginate and produced into an acute pale spine at sutural angle (male), or plain and red (female). Legs black with blue luster. Adults on willows (*Salix*), flowers of *Yucca*, and other plants. British Columbia to California, east to Alberta, Montana, and Nevada. (10)

Tanaops species (2.3–4.0 mm) are conspicuously clothed in both erect and recumbent setae. Head sometimes flattened in front and rostrate, with frons simple. Antennae with 11 antennomeres. Prothorax with eversible vesicles below anterior angles. Elytra covering nearly entire abdomen, with apices simple in both sexes. Abdomen with six ventrites, with 4 and/or 5 sometimes sulcate in males. Both sexes with five protarsomeres, male lacking apical combs of teeth, 2 with small, indistinct lobe usually not extending over 3. Often on buckwheat (*Eriogonum*) flowers eating pollen and nectar. Widely distributed in western North America. Genus needs revision. (24)

425

CLERIDAE (klēr'-i-dē)
CHECKERED BEETLES

Adult and larval clerids prey on all life stages of insects, especially beetles. Many species associated with dead wood (*Cymatodera, Enoclerus, Monophylla, Priocera, Thanasimus*) are often found on branches or under bark in tunnels and galleries where they attack the immature stages of bark beetles (Curculionidae), longhorn beetles (Cerambycidae), and metallic wood-boring beetles (Buprestidae). Species of *Enoclerus* and *Thanasimus* are important biological controls of bark beetles and other wood-boring beetles. *Phyllobaenus* species prey on insects that develop in galls, twigs, and stems. *Necrobia* species occur among insect- and mite-infested carcasses and dried meats, or in stored products. Adult *Trichodes* are generalists and prey on various flower-visiting insects and pollen. Their hairy bodies suggest that they may play a role in pollination. The alternating light-and-dark pattern of their elytra gives some species a wasp-like appearance, thus possibly affording them protection from educated predators. Some species (*Chariessa, Pelonides*) appear to be part of mimicry rings involving not only other clerids, but also species of Lycidae, Lampyridae, Cantharidae, and Meloidae. Adults of both *Cymatodera* and *Lecontella* will stridulate when threatened. The larvae of *Cymatodera, Enoclerus, Thanasimus, Pelonium*, and others all prey on wood-boring beetles and their larvae, as well as on other wood-tunneling insects. *Lecontella, Boschella*, and some *Trichodes* larvae develop in the nests of bees, while those of *Aulicus* and some *Trichodes* are reported to prey upon the eggs of lubber grasshoppers.

FAMILY DIAGNOSIS Adult clerids are typically elongate, slender to robust, somewhat flattened or cylindrical, and clothed in bristly pubescence. Hypognathous head often as wide or wider than prothorax, rarely with horns in front

(*Bostrichoclerus bicornis* Van Dyke), with prominent eyes emarginate or not, and are finely or coarsely granulate, and inserted in prothorax. Antennae mostly clavate or capitate, sometimes serrate, pectinate, or flabellate, with 9–11 antennomeres. Pronotum usually longer than wide and with or without lateral carina. Procoxal cavities open or closed behind. Elytra typically broader than prothorax, and almost (*Phyllobaenus*) or completely conceal abdomen. Tarsi 5-5-5, with 4 sometimes very small, 1–3 or 1–4 lobed or densely setose underneath, and claws equal in size and simple, toothed, or cleft. Abdomen usually with six ventrites free, with 1–3 connate.

SIMILAR FAMILIES

- small soldier beetles (Cantharidae, p.265)—antennae filiform
- *Pedilus* (Pyrochroidae, p.395)—head with neck, without coarse, bristly setae
- narrow-waisted bark beetles (Salpingidae, p.397)—head prognathous

- antlike flower beetles (Anthicidae, p.400)—head with neck
- antlike leaf beetles (Aderidae, p.406)—head with neck
- soft-winged flower beetles (Melyridae, p.420)—pronotum with lateral margins carinate, antennae usually serrate

COLLECTING NOTES Flower-visiting clerids are easily collected by hand or gathered in a sweep net or tray. Search trunks, limbs, and twigs of trees infested with, or dead or dying from, bark and wood-boring beetles both day and night. Look under loose bark of living and dead conifers and hardwoods. Also beat infested branches of trees and shrubs and sweep grasses and other soft herbaceous plant growth. Examine carcasses and infested dried meats and meat products for *Necrobia*. Adults of several genera are readily attracted to lights, or collected in Malaise and Lindgren funnel traps baited for bark beetles.

FAUNA ~245 SPECIES IN 37 GENERA

Cymatodera decipiens Fall (3.9–6.5 mm) is elongate, slender, brown with appendages pale reddish brown, and clothed in fine intermixed setae consisting of shorter recumbent and longer erect setae. Head with deeply incised eyes, weakly serrate antennae with 11 antennomeres, antennomeres 2–4 short and subequal in length, 11 circular in cross section and slightly longer than 10, and eyes coarsely granulated. Pronotum long, coarsely and shallowly punctate. Procoxal cavities closed. Elytra with incomplete and irregular transverse anteromedian spot, and distinctly punctostriate at base to about middle. Claws with two strong teeth, basal tooth triangular. Adults at lights. British Columbia to California, east to Idaho. Genus needs revision. (49)

Cymatodera fuchsii Schaeffer (6.0–10.0 mm) is elongate, slender, brown with appendages and underside paler, with dense erect pubescence of mixed lengths. Eyes deeply incised and coarsely granulate. Antennae weakly serrate, with antennomere 11 circular in cross section and slightly longer than 10. Pronotum long, weakly constricted anteriorly and posteriorly, and coarsely punctate. Procoxal cavities closed. Elytra with broad indistinct and irregular pale median fascia, strial punctures large, and striae not extended to apices. Male pygidium with pair of slender upturned processes. Claws bidentate, basal tooth triangular. Adults at lights. California east to Utah and Texas, south to Baja California and Sonora. Genus needs revision. (49)

Cymatodera horni Wolcott (19.0–22.0 mm) is reddish brown to brownish black, and sparsely pubescent. Eyes deeply incised, and coarse. Antennae weakly serrate, antennomeres 2–10 similar in length, 11 longer than 10 and circular in cross section. Procoxal cavities closed. Elytra punctostriate at basal half, striae paired with alternate interstrial broader, each with median reddish-brown fascia, lateral margins nearly parallel (male), and apices rounded. Claws bidentate, basal tooth triangular. Arizona and New Mexico, south to Baja California Sur. *Cymatodera californica* Horn similar, elytral apices sinuate in both sexes, sides of male divergent posteriorly. Southern California. Both at lights. (49)

Cymatodera oblita Horn (11.0–12.6 mm) is elongate, slender, and pale brown with appendages yellowish brown, and sparsely pubescent. Head with deeply incised eye, antennae weakly serrate, antennomeres 2–10 similar in length, 11 longer than 10 and circular in cross section, and eyes coarse. Pronotum broadest in front, not coarsely punctate. Procoxal cavities closed. Elytra with only traces of punctostriae at base, striae equidistant, with apices rounded. Claws with two distinct and strong teeth, basal tooth triangular. Adults attracted to lights. Arizona. Genus need revision. (49)

Cymatodera tricolor Skinner (12.0–16.0 mm) is slender, reddish brown with head, anterior third of pronotum, elytral fascia, apical third of elytra, and ventrites 2–5 brownish black, and median elytra fascia and most or all of ventrite 1 pale yellow, and clothed in moderate pubescence. Eyes coarsely granulate. Antennae weakly serrate, antennomere 11 circular in cross section, slightly longer than 10. Pronotum long, coarsely and shallowly punctate. Elytra with punctostriae not extending to apices. Front and middle legs mostly reddish brown, hind legs mostly darker, with claws bearing two distinct teeth, basal tooth triangular. Adults at lights. Arizona and New Mexico, south to Sonora. Genus needs revision. (49)

Cymatodera vandykei Schaeffer (11.0–12.0 mm) is sparsely pubescent, and brown, with underside and appendages lighter. Head densely punctured. Antennae barely surpassing prothorax. Prothorax constricted before and after middle, with posterior margin broadest. Elytra with humeri indistinct, slightly broader posteriorly, with strial punctures coarse, indistinct pale transverse fascia medially, and apices individually rounded. Ventrite 5 nearly truncate (female), or broadly, very deeply emarginate (male). In coastal sage scrub, chaparral, and oak woodlands. Coast Ranges, California. Flightless *C. angustata* Spinola found inland. Oregon and California, east to Idaho, Nevada, and Arizona. Both flightless. (49)

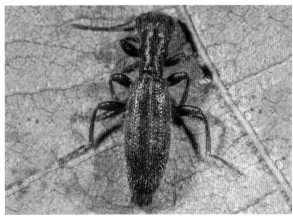

Lecontella gnara Wolcott (7.5–10.2 mm) is light yellowish brown to dark brown, with abdomen lighter. Head across eyes wider than pronotum. Antennae with 11 antennomeres, 2–10 gradually increasing in width, 1–4 cylindrical, 5–10 moderately serrate, and 11 shorter (female) or longer (male) than 10. Pronotum with wide, deep, and coarse punctures. Elytra uniformly colored, coarsely punctured, punctostriae reaching apices. Claws with two distinct triangular teeth. Ventrite 6 broadly rounded (female) or somewhat quadrate and shallowly emarginate (male) posteriorly. At lights. California east to Utah and Texas, south to Baja California and Sonora. (1)

Monophylla californica Fall (4.2–7.0 mm) is slender and pubescent. Head reddish, narrower across eyes than prothorax. Antennae with nine antennomeres, male with 2 robust, 3–6 small and compacted, 7–8 serrate, 9 flat and very long; female with 6–8 serrate, and 9 shorter. Pronotum uniformly brown to almost black with anterior and posterior margins lighter; coxal cavities closed. Elytra light yellowish brown to brownish black, each with pale median transverse spot not reaching suture. Legs bicolored. Adults prey on *Scobicia* and *Lyctus* in oaks. Oregon to California, east to Wyoming and Texas; also Mexico. *Monophylla pallipes* Schaeffer similar, with 10 antennomeres. (3)

Phyllobaenus humeralis (Say) (3.5–5.5 mm) is elongate, narrow, and black to bluish black with reddish humeri sometimes reduced or absent. Head short and, including bulging and weakly emarginate eyes, broader than prothorax. Short antennae comprising 11 antennomeres, 9 as broad as long, 10 swollen and ovate, and 11 very small. Pronotum as wide as long, broadest before middle; anterior coxal cavities closed behind. Elytra broader than prothorax, coarsely punctate, widest at apical third, and covering abdomen. Claw with broad basal tooth. Diurnal adults on foliage and flowers; attracted to lights. Transcontinental; in West from British Columbia to Oregon, east to Montana. (33)

Phyllobaenus scaber LeConte (2.2–3.5 mm) is black with brassy or greenish luster, and densely clothed in erect black and somewhat recumbent pale setae. Bulging eyes weakly emarginate. Pronotum as wide as long; anterior coxal cavities closed behind. Elytra broader than prothorax, finely and densely punctate, narrowed behind middle and covering abdomen; somewhat roughened and tumid apically, with apical margins serrate. Claw with broad basal tooth. Larvae associated with galls, where they prey on various insects and their parasitoids. British Columbia to California, east to Idaho, Wyoming, Kansas, and New Mexico. (33)

Aulicus apachei Barr & Foster (6.1–6.7 mm) is black dorsally, with bold markings on blue-black elytra. Antennae light or partially dark, antennomeres 9–11 forming loose, abruptly enlarged club. Pronotum coarsely punctate, and moderately clothed in suberect white setae. Elytra with a pair of large reddish or yellowish humeral spots with or without small dark spot, and narrowly joined along lateral margins to broad postmedian transverse markings. Abdomen reddish (male) or reddish with blackish margins. Southern Arizona to Texas, and Mexico. *Aulicus antennatus* Schaeffer (5.5–9.1 mm) similar, abdomen mostly black. Oregon and California, east to Idaho, Nevada, and western Arizona. (10)

Enoclerus bimaculatus (Skinner) (10.0–11.0 mm) with head, prothorax, and legs brown, and clothed in coarse, erect, black and gray setae. Eyes deeply emarginate. Antennal club compact. Pronotum as long as wide, anterior transverse depression evident laterally. Procoxal cavities open. Elytra each with medial round ivory spot (pinkish after death) and apical third darker, covered with dense gray recumbent pubescence. Tarsomeres 3–4 about equal in size. Adults prey on *Chrysobothris* adults. At lights in oak-pine-juniper woodlands. *Enoclerus luscus* (Klug) (13.0 mm), with broad medial band abruptly narrowed before suture. Both southeastern Arizona and Mexico. (26)

Enoclerus eximius (Mannerheim) (5.5–10.0 mm) is black with antennal clubs and tarsi brown, elytra orangish red, abdomen red, and clothed in intermixed erect black and gray setae. Eyes deeply emarginate. Antennal club compact. Pronotum as long as wide, anterior transverse depression evident laterally, with a pairs of black pubescent spots. Procoxal cavities open. Elytra with three subbasal spots, and apical two-fifths black, and apices crossed by a broad band of pale pubescence. Tarsomeres 3–4 about equal in size. On conifers infested with beetle borers. British Columbia to California, east to Idaho. (26)

Enoclerus laetus (Klug) (5.0–8.0 mm) is elongate, mostly black with pronotum red or black, and clothed in erect and suberect black and grayish setae. Eyes emarginate. Antenna with club compact. Pronotum as long as wide, with anterior transverse depression evident laterally. Procoxal cavities open. Elytra uniformly punctate and black, with pair of small basal whitish spots followed by a weak transverse band of grayish pubescence, a pair of bold arcuate whitish bands, and a more distinctive subapical grayish band of pubescence. Abdomen black. Tarsomeres 3–4 about equal in size. Adults on flowering plants. British Columbia to California, east to Kansas and Texas; Mexico. (26)

Enoclerus lecontei Wolcott (5.0–9.0 mm) is black with gray markings, and clothed in long erect black setae and short, appressed grayish setae. Eyes deeply emarginate. Antennae capitate with club compact. Pronotum about as long as wide, with anterior transverse depression evident laterally. Procoxal cavities open. Elytra uniformly punctate with weak brassy luster and prominent fascia across near apex. Abdomen black. Tarsomeres 3–4 about equal in size. Adults sun-drenched pine logs. Adults and larvae important predators of adult and larval bark beetles, respectively. British Columbia to California, east to Idaho, Colorado, and New Mexico; also Mexico. (26)

Enoclerus quadrisignatus (Say) (7.0–12.0 mm) is elongate, coarsely punctate, dull reddish brown, clothed in recumbent and erect grayish setae, with appendages dark brown to black. Eyes deeply emarginate. Antennal club compact. Pronotum about as long as wide, with anterior transverse depression evident laterally. Procoxal cavities open. Elytra each with broad whitish band across middle and narrower brown band just before apices, both narrowly interrupted by suture. Tarsomeres 3–4 about equal in size. Adults on hardwood branches infested with bark beetles; also attracted to lights. Southern California east to Colorado, New Jersey, and Georgia, south to Mexico. (26)

Enoclerus sphegeus (Fabricius) (7.5–12.5 mm) is black with brassy or purplish luster with a red abdomen, and clothed in black and yellowish pubescence. Eyes deeply emarginate. Capitate antennae with compact club. Pronotum long as wide, with anterior transverse depression evident laterally. Procoxal cavities open. Elytra uniformly punctate with distinct broad wavy fascia medially, and thin indistinct wavy fascia apically. Tarsomeres 3 and 4 about equal in size. Adults on pine (*Pinus*) logs and slash. Adults and larvae important predators of adult and larval bark beetles, respectively. British Columbia to California, east to Idaho, Colorado, and New Mexico; also Mexico. (26)

Enoclerus spinolae (LeConte) (9.0–13.0 mm) is red with head, thorax, and appendages black, and clothed in erect black and shorter suberect golden pubescence. Eyes deeply emarginate. Antennae capitate with club compact. Pronotum about as long as wide, with anterior transverse depression evident laterally. Procoxal cavities open. Elytra uniformly punctate, with black humeri and broad to narrow postmedial transverse bars that do not reach suture. Tarsomeres 3–4 about equal in size. Adults found on *Yucca* flowers, including Spanish dagger (*Y. schidigera*). California east to Kansas and Texas, south to Mexico. (26)

Thanasimus undatulus (Say) (7.0–10.0 mm) has abdominal sternites wholly or partly black. Eyes finely granulate and deeply emarginate. Antennomeres 7–11 forming loose club. Tarsomeres 3–4 about equal in size. Pronotum with anterior transverse depression prominent laterally. Procoxal cavities open. Elytra coarsely punctostriate basally, becoming obsolete about middle, with setose fascia before middle extending to scutellum. Alaska south to California, east to Montana and New Mexico; also in East. *Thanasimus repandus* Horn (8.5–12.5 mm) entirely red ventrally, setose fascia before middle not extending anteriorly. California. *Thanasimus dubius* (Fabricius) (7.5–9.0 mm) red ventrally, setose fascia before middle extending anteriorly. Adults on trees heavily infested with bark beetles. (3)

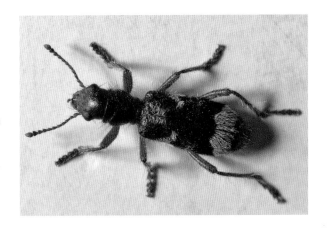

Trichodes ornatus subspecies (4.9–14.2 mm) are elongate, slender to moderately robust, with bicolored elytra. Head and pronotum metallic blue or green. Pronotum strongly constricted at base, disc coarsely punctate, and densely clothed in yellow pubescence. Elytra indistinctly punctate and bicolored, mostly yellow, whitish, or red with umbones nearly always dark, and variable black markings with metallic blue luster, to mostly black with metallic luster. Five subspecies based on body shape, size, color, elytral markings, and vestiture. In Pacific Northwest and Rockies, populations with at least half or more of elytra with dark blue metallic markings. Adults on flowers. Widespread in western North America. (6)

431

Trichodes peninsularis horni Wolcott & Chapin (7.8–16.8 mm) is elongate, moderately robust, and clothed dorsally in yellowish-brown recumbent to erect setae. Head and prothorax with purplish or bluish luster. Pronotum coarsely punctate. Elytra coarsely punctostriate, tricolored with yellow basal band narrow, in contact with scutellum, and disc with mostly brown patches narrowly bordered in black with purplish or bluish luster. Abdomen usually dark. Southern Arizona, southwestern New Mexico, and northern Sonora. *Trichodes peninsularis basalis* Van Dyke (7.8–16.8 mm) with yellow elytral bands significantly expanded and brown patches reduced to apex, abdomen mostly pale, sometimes with dark median spots. Southeastern California and southwestern Arizona. Adults on flowers. (6)

Boschella fasciata (LeConte) (4.0–7.0 mm) is elongate, slender, and mostly reddish brown with elytra and abdomen darker, with suberect brownish pubescence. Finely faceted eyes broadly and deeply notched. Antennal club loose and flat, antennomeres 9–10 flat triangular in female (*left*), more so in male (*right*). Pronotum coarsely punctate, uneven, with lateral margins abruptly expanded at middle. Procoxal cavities broadly open. Elytra long, with faint blue or greenish luster in life, coarsely punctate striae, and with or without fascia before middle. Tarsomere 4 small, set at base of 5. Adults on California bay (*Umbellularia californicus*) and willow (*Salix*). British Columbia to California. (1)

Chariessa elegans Horn (7.0–13.0 mm) is oblong-oval, with forebody, underside and associated pubescence pale red. Elytra more black than blue. Legs mostly reddish with black tarsi. Adults emerge from oak (*Quercus*), madrone (*Arbutus*), and walnut (*Juglans*). British Columbia to California, east to Texas. *Chariessa catalina* Opitz (7.5–14.0 mm) is oblong-oval, with forebody, venter, and associated pubescence crimson and elytra more blue than black. Adults emerge from wood of oak, hackberry (*Celtis*), honey locust (*Gleditsia*), and madrone (*Arbutus*). California east to Utah and New Mexico, south to Mexico. *Chariessa dichroa* (LeConte) (6.5–12.0 mm) slenderer, with black legs. Adults associated with oak. California. (4)

Loedelia maculicollis (LeConte) (3.5–6.5 mm) is convex with erect reddish and black pubescence. Head black, narrower than prothorax. Middle antennomere of club and last labial palpomere each distinctly triangular. Pronotum red with anteromedial black triangle sometimes extended to posterior margin. Elytra deep metallic blue or green, with coarse punctures dense and confused. Abdomen and legs black. Claws cleft. Eastern Oregon and California. *Loedelia discoidea* (LeConte) similar, with medial pronotal spot and legs mostly reddish with black tarsi. Arizona and New Mexico, south to Baja California. Both on flowering deciduous woody shrubs and trees. (2)

Red-shouldered Ham Beetle *Necrobia ruficollis* (Fabricius) (4.0–6.2 mm) is oblong and convex, with upper surface metallic blue or greenish and brownish red. Front of head and apical three-fourths of elytra metallic blue. Base and underside of head and thorax, and base of elytra reddish brown. Elytra with rows of fine punctures. Antennae and abdomen dark brown. Legs with claws toothed at base. Adults found on carrion, where they scavenge tissues and prey on insects. Cosmopolitan; across southern Canada and United States. (3)

Red-legged Ham Beetle *Necrobia rufipes* **(De Geer)**
(3.5–6.0 mm) is oblong and convex, and uniformly metallic
blue or green with legs and antennal bases red. Antennae
mostly dark brown. Pronotum wider than long with sides
broadly rounded. Elytra convex, with rows of fine and widely
separated punctures, spaces between finely punctured.
Adults scavenge carrion and prey on other insects in spring
and summer; sometimes found in stored grains and other
foods where it feeds on insect pests. Cosmopolitan; across
southern Canada and United States. (3)

Black-legged Ham Beetle *Necrobia violacea*
(Linnaeus) (3.2–4.5 mm) is oblong and convex, and uniformly
metallic green or blue, with dark brown to black appendages.
Head and pronotum densely and finely punctate. Elytra with
rows of coarse punctures, spaces between broad with
dense, minute punctures. Adults active in spring and
summer and scavenge on carrion and prey on other insects.
Discovery of this species inside a cache of insects and
other arthropods preserved in the skull of a 40,000-year-old
camel (see p.42) established that it occurred in North
America before humans arrived. Cosmopolitan; across
southern Canada and United States. (3)

Pelonium peninsulare Schaeffer (7.0–11.0 mm) is
elongate, convex, cryptically marked with pale, light and dark
brown markings, and clothed in yellowish-brown pubescence.
Eyes coarsely granulate. Loose antennal club with
antennomeres 9–10 flat and triangular, more so in male. Both
terminal maxillary and labial palpomeres strongly triangular.
Prothorax with deep median and two oblique basal
impressions. Elytra gradually widening toward apex, discal
punctures large and interstitial spaces polished, with broad
pale fascia at middle, two narrow undulate black fascia
bordering pale brownish subapical fascia, and yellowish-white
apices. Adults attracted to lights. Arizona, Baja California
Sur, and mainland Mexico south to Costa Rica. (1)

Pelonides humeralis **(Horn)** (6.0–10.0 mm) is subovate,
flat, and variably red and black, with underside of
pterothorax and abdomen shiny black. Head and antennae
black, antennae with 10 antennomeres, with 8–10 forming
loose and deeply serrate club, more so in male. Pronotum
red, about as long as wide, with broad black stripe down
middle, and sides margined. Elytra finely granulose, and
uniformly black (male), or red or bicolored (female) with
apical third or more mostly black with red triangular humeral
patches extending along sides; discal black margins
sinuous. On flowering woody shrubs, including *Ceanothus*.
Southern Arizona east to Texas, south to Mexico. (1)

SPHINDIDAE (sfin'-di-dē)
CRYPTIC SLIME MOLD BEETLES

Sphididae is a small family of beetles represented in North America by four genera, two of which occur in the West. Little is known of the ecology of sphindids, other than their association with slime molds. Adult and larval sphindids feed on spores and related structures in spore-bearing bodies of slime molds growing on dead trees, logs, and stumps. *Sphindus* and *Odontosphindus* are associated with mature, dry, cushion-shaped spore masses (aethalia) of *Fuligo septica*, commonly known as dog vomit or scrambled egg slime mold. *Sphindus* are also associated with *Arcyria versicolor* and *Stemonitis* species. Adults are sometimes found overwintering under bark and in leaf litter, but their larvae are known only from aethalia.

FAMILY DIAGNOSIS Adult sphindids in western North America are cylindrical and parallel-sided. Head partially visible from above. Antennae clavate with 10 (*Sphindus*) or 11 (*Odontosphindus*) antennomeres, with last two or three antennomeres pubescent and forming club. Pronotum convex, as wide as elytra at base, with lateral margins dentate (*Odontosphindus*), or crenulate (*Sphindus*). Procoxal cavities broadly open, closed, or nearly closed behind. Scutellum visible. Elytra punctostriate. Tarsi 5-5-5 (female) or 5-5-4 (male). Abdomen with five ventrites free.

SIMILAR FAMILIES
- branch and twig borers (Bostrichidae, p.306)—antennal club asymmetrical
- death-watch beetles (Ptinidae, p.299)—antennal club asymmetrical
- minute tree-fungus beetles (Ciidae, p.329)—elytra usually without punctostriae
- bark and ambrosia beetles (Curculionidae: Scolytinae, p.560)—antennae geniculate with club ball-like, comprising one antennomere

COLLECTING NOTES Cryptic slime mold beetles are not often collected, but they can be locally abundant on slime molds growing on dead trees, logs, stumps, and leaf litter. They are best extracted from these substrates by applying mild heat in Berlese funnels. Adults are also found in flight intercept and Malaise traps, or occasionally by sweeping or in light traps.

FAUNA NINE SPECIES IN FOUR GENERA

Odontosphindus clavicornis **(Casey)** (3.0–3.4 mm) is elongate-oval, somewhat parallel-sided, moderately convex, glabrous, and chestnut with legs paler. Head finely and densely punctate, eyes moderately large and convex, with antennomeres 10 and 11 large, 11 twice as long as 10. Pronotum convex, wider than long, surface finely alutaceous and closely ocellate-punctate, lateral margins narrowly explanate and irregularly denticulate, each with 6–7 acute teeth, and anterior angles briefly acute, and posterior angles broadly rounded. Elytron with 10 punctostriae, punctures course, and intervals finely alutaceous. Tarsi 5-5-5 (female) or 5-5-4 (male). Adults on *Fuligo*, *Stemonitis* and other slime molds. British Columbia to central California. (1)

434

Sphindus americanus LeConte (1.5–2.5 mm) is elongate-oval, parallel-sided, somewhat shiny, sparsely pubescent, and brownish black with elytra sometimes brownish. Head with several grooves adjacent to each eye; antennae with 10 antennomeres, two comprising distinct club. Pronotum lacks fine ridge down middle, side margin without teeth. Elytra sometimes with basal angles prominent. Appendages reddish brown. Adults active in summer, found on fruiting bodies of slime molds (*Comatricha, Fuligo, Stemonitis*) growing on old trees and logs; also attracted to lights. Widely distributed in North America. *Sphindus crassulus* Casey antennal club with three antennomeres. (2)

EROTYLIDAE (er-ō-til'-i-dē)
PLEASING FUNGUS AND LIZARD BEETLES

Adult and larval pleasing fungus beetles are usually found on large basidiomycete fungi, including bracket fungi growing on or under the bark of rotten logs, or on mushrooms in the soil associated with roots, and feed on the fruiting bodies. Adults often have contrasting red or yellow markings; these colors may serve to warn predators of their potential distastefulness. Eggs are usually laid on the fungal food of larvae. The larvae feed either by burrowing through fungal tissues or by grazing on the surface. Adults of some species are mostly diurnal (*Cypherotylus, Triplax, Tritoma*), while others (*Ischyrus, Megalodacne*) are primarily nocturnal. One eastern species, *Megalodacne heros* (Say), was possibly introduced into the northern Central Valley of California with firewood. Both adults and larvae are found feeding on bracket fungi growing on almond trees. The larvae of *Cypherotylus californicus* (Lacordaire) (p.29, Fig. 18t) form conspicuous aggregations of up to several dozen or more individuals around fungi growing on the underside of decaying logs in relatively damp, shady locations. They pupate *en masse* head down within the caste exoskeleton of the last larval instar. Phytophagous lizard beetles are frequently found on flowers, and feed on pollen and leaves. Their larvae bore within the stems of plants, especially asters (Asteraceae) and legumes (Fabaceae). Their feeding activities seldom kill the plant, but will weaken stems and cause them to break off. One widespread North American species, the clover stem borer, *Languria mozardi* Latreille, is a minor pest of alfalfa in the West and red clover in the East.

FAMILY DIAGNOSIS Adult erotylids are elongate-oval, broadly oval, or slender and straight-sided, reddish brown or black, sometimes with contrasting colors and markings. Head hypognathous and retracted inside prothorax. Antennae with 11 antennomeres, with terminal three, or four to five (lizard beetles) forming a club. Pronotum variable in shape and distinctly margined. Scutellum visible. Procoxal cavities closed behind. Elytra smooth, sometimes punctostriate, and completely conceal abdomen. Legs with tarsi 5-5-5, with tarsomere 4 sometimes reduced, appearing 4-4-4; first three tarsomeres are more or less broad with brushy pads underneath, and simple claws equal in size. Abdomen with five ventrites free.

SIMILAR FAMILIES

- metallic wood-boring or jewel beetles (Buprestidae, p.210)—usually metallic, antennae not clubbed, and metacoxae with sulci to receive hind femora
- false click beetles (Eucnemidae, p.254)—antennae usually serrate, with clicking mechanism
- click beetles (Elateridae, p.273)—antennae usually serrate, with clicking mechanism
- handsome fungus beetles (Endomychidae, p.315)—front angles of pronotum distinct, extended forward; tarsi 4-4-4, appear 3-3-3
- lady beetles (Coccinellidae, p.318)—antennae without distinct club; tarsi 4-4-4, appear 3-3-3
- *Hyporhagus* (Zopheridae, p.344)—hypomera with antennal sulci; tarsi 5-5-4

- some darkling beetles (Tenebrionidae, p.347)—antennae without distinct club; tarsi 5-5-4
- short-winged flower beetles (Kateretidae, p.441)—elytra usually short, abdomen partially exposed
- sap beetles (Nitidulidae, p.443)—elytra usually short, abdomen partially exposed
- some leaf beetles (Chrysomelidae, p.501)—antennae filiform or clavate

COLLECTING NOTES Look for pleasing fungus beetles on or near woody and soft fungi on snags and logs, or beneath loose bark of fungus-infested logs, especially in moist forests and wooded canyons. Species are also sifted from moist duff beneath trees or extracted by placing leaf litter samples in a Berlese funnel. Some species are captured in Malaise and light traps. Lizard beetles are found on various flowers and vegetation, especially those serving as larval food plants.

FAUNA 49 SPECIES IN 11 GENERA

Acropteroxys gracilis divisa (Horn) (11.0–15.0 mm) is elongate, cylindrical, parallel-sided, and shiny black with a mostly red prothorax. Head black, ocular stria absent. Antennal club symmetrical with five antennomeres. Pronotum with basal half more or less dark, with red and black border sinuate. Elytra black, punctostriate. Underside of thorax red or red with some black, and abdomen black, with apices pointed and slightly separated. Larvae in stems of ragweed (*Ambrosia*). Adults on flowers, including thistle (*Cirsium*). Idaho to southeastern Arizona, eastward to Ontario, Massachusetts, and South Carolina; also Mexico. (1)

Languria convexicollis Horn (9.0–11.5 mm) is elongate, cylindrical, and black with prothorax mostly red. Head sometimes with red, with ocular stria deep and close to eye, extending from antennal insertion to front of eye. Antennal club with six antennomeres. Anterior and posterior pronotal margins variably black. Elytra punctostriate, with intervals sometimes flat, and apices evenly rounded. Pterothorax and abdomen brownish-black. Adults on prickly poppy (*Argemone*). British Columbia to California, east to Utah and Arizona, south to Mexico. Clover Stem Borer *Languria mozardii* Latreille (4.0–9.0 mm) small, with red head and pronotum, club with six antennomeres, and elytral apices evenly rounded. Southern Canada and United States. (4)

Langurites lineatus Laporte (11.0–15.0 mm) is elongate, tapered posteriorly and variably orange and brownish-black. Head orange, often with spot on vertex, and ocular stria distant from eye and shallow, extending from antennal insertion to front of eye. Antennal club symmetrical with five antennomeres. Pronotum with variable medial and lateral stripes. Elytra entirely dark, or dark along suture and apices, or mostly orange; surface punctostriate, intervals with scattered and shallow punctures, and apices each with acute tooth and obliquely notched to suture. Underside orange or black, and legs bicolored with tarsi and tibiae mostly or completely dark. Southeastern Arizona south to South America. (1)

Dacne californica (Horn) (1.9–3.5 mm) is weakly convex, coarsely punctate dorsally and sparsely pubescent, and shiny reddish to blackish brown, with a somewhat distinct basal spot on each elytron. Asymmetrical antennal club longer than wide. Terminal maxillary palpomere cylindrical. Pronotum convex, with anterior margin at middle surpassing angles, posterior margin with fine bead. Elytra becoming gradually lighter apically, with fine basal margins. Tarsomeres 3 and 4 subequal in length. On oyster mushrooms (*Pleurotus ostreatus*) on alder (*Alnus*), other hardwoods. British Columbia to Baja California, east to Idaho and Utah. (4)

Megalodacne heros (Say) (14.0–22.0 mm) is shiny black and reddish orange. Pronotum as wide as long. Elytra with two broad orange-red bands; basal band surrounds two round humeral spots and nearly encloses a short black band just behind scutellum; no punctures on black areas. Adults on and larvae in shelf fungus (*Ganoderma*) growing on almonds and other hardwoods. Adults active during spring and summer, found on logs in moist woods during day, or hiding in cracks of logs and under loose bark; sometimes form large overwintering aggregations. Eastern North America; adventive in northern California. (1)

437

Ischyrus quadripunctatus chiasticus Boyle (5.5–8.6 mm) is somewhat convex, and pale reddish yellow with brownish-black or black spots and bands. Head black with large reddish patch, and large eyes coarsely faceted. Pronotum narrowly black along anterior and posterior margins, with four round spots across middle. Elytra with basal "X-shaped" spot, and irregular band behind middle. Underside black with sides of abdomen yellow. Arizona and Mexico. *Ischyrus aleator* Boyle (6.6–8.6 mm) is light brownish yellow, without spots on pronotum, with discal stripes on elytra running from humeri to apical third. Southeastern Arizona south through western Mexico to El Salvador and Guatemala. Both species at lights. (2)

Triplax californica LeConte (2.7–5.0 mm) is elongate-elliptical, with sides somewhat parallel, and black, with head, prothorax, and appendages (except middle and hind coxae) reddish orange. Head with sides around antennal insertions weakly concave. Pronotum broadest across posterior margin, with discal punctures large, more so laterally, and angle pores very large. Elytra lacking basal margins, and punctostriae with intervals flat with irregular mesh of fine fissures, and punctures slightly more numerous than small strial punctures. On oyster mushroom (*Pleurotus ostreatus*) growing on cottonwood (*Populus*) and alder (*Alnus*). British Columbia to California, east to Nevada. (8)

Cypherotylus californicus (Lacordaire) (12.0–20.0 mm) is broadly obovate, and dull black with elytra somewhat flattened dorsally when viewed from side, and blue or purplish in life, fading to dirty yellowish brown in death. Pronotum somewhat convex, usually broadest basally, with sides evenly arcuate to almost straight, and converging to prominent anterior angles, with irregular shallow impressions on disc. Elytra with numerous irregularly spaced black impressions, and usually with an irregular medial blotch on lateral margins. Adults and larvae on fungi growing on oaks (*Quercus*) and other trees. Wyoming to southeastern Arizona, east to Kansas and New Mexico, south to Mexico. (1)

MONOTOMIDAE (mon-ot-ōm'-i-dē)
ROOT-EATING BEETLES

Many monotomids are found under the bark of dead trees or in decomposing plant materials and are believed to be mycophagous. *Europs* occur under dead tree bark, and are also associated with cultivated plants and attracted to lights. *Hesperobaenus rufipes* LeConte lives under the bark of oak (*Quercus*) and maple (*Acer*), where it presumably feeds on fungus. *Monotoma* adults feed mostly on mold growing among decaying plants in ant nests, compost heaps, haystacks, and fouled stored food products. Their association with artificial accumulations of plants has resulted in their becoming widely established through human agency. *Phyconomus marinus* (LeConte) occurs under decaying seaweed washed up on coastal beaches. *Rhizophagus* live under tree bark and in decaying plant materials where they scavenge dead insects and probably eat fungi, although some European species are reported to prey on xylophagous insects, including *Dendroctonus* larvae.

FAMILY DIAGNOSIS Adult monotomids are elongate, narrow, parallel-sided, with last abdominal segment exposed beyond tip of elytra. Head prognathous, not concealed from view above. Antennae short, stout, appearing to have 10 antennomeres, 10 and 11 fused to form club with one article, or 9 + 10/11 forming club of two articles. Pronotum more or less quadrate to elongate. Procoxal cavities broadly closed behind. Elytra truncate at apex, and short exposing one (female), or two (male) tergites. Legs short, tarsi 5-5-5 (female), or 5-5-4 (male). Abdomen with five ventrites free, 1 and 5 elongate, 2–4 short and subequal in length.

SIMILAR FAMILIES
- zopherid beetles (Zopheridae, p.340)—pygidium not exposed

- palmetto beetles (Smicripidae, p.440)—mandibles clearly visible; clubbed antennae with 11 antennomeres, club with three antennomeres
- sap beetles (Nitidulidae, p.443)—antennae with 11 antennomeres, 9–11 forming club
- silvanid beetles (Silvanidae, p.451)—antennae with 11 antennomeres, 9–11 forming club

COLLECTING NOTES Look carefully for monotomids in rotting wood or under stones. Species that frequent decomposing plant debris may be found in stacks of hay, compost heaps, or grass clippings. Some species living in wooded habitats are attracted to molasses traps. A few species are attracted to lights.

438

FAUNA 55 SPECIES IN 11 GENERA

Bactridium californicum Fall (2.0–2.3 mm) is elongate-oval, weakly shiny, and reddish brown, with appendages yellowish brown. Head sparsely, coarsely punctate, and almost as broad as prothorax. Pronotum about as long as wide, with all angles obtuse, and lateral margins straight and slightly converging posteriorly. Elytra at base broader than prothorax, finely punctostriate with punctures distinct, and diffuse darker scutellar spot and apical third. Pygidium and last ventrite coarsely and densely punctate, with ventrites 2–4 each with single row of coarse, elongate, and closely spaced punctures. Adults under bark of sycamore (*Platanus*). California. Genus needs revision. (8)

Europs striatulus Fall (1.9–2.6 mm) is elongate-oval, setose, and uniformly reddish brown. Head without antennal sulci, antennal club comprises three antennomeres. Pronotum slightly longer than wide, with sides narrowly explanate and parallel to slightly convergent posteriorly, and disc narrowly impunctate medially; front coxae rounded. Elytral disc with setigerous punctures arranged in rows, three along lateral inflections. Ventrite 1 with coxal bead rounded and not triangularly produced, in male without median plaque bearing proportionally long setae. Under bark of dead conifers. Arizona and New Mexico. (1)

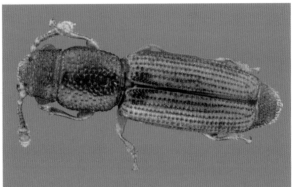

Hesperobaenus abbreviatus (Motschulsky) (2.0–2.8 mm) is reddish brown and yellowish; rarely completely dark. Head with temples longer than half longitudinal diameter of eyes, without antennal sulci. Antennal club with two antennomeres. Anterior pronotal angles produced, disc impunctate medially, punctures subcontiguous laterally; procoxae rounded. Scutellum glabrous. Basal half of elytra distinctly pale, setae arranged in rows, intervals 3 and 5 with just one to four setae basally. Metacoxal bead triangularly produced on ventrite 1, with male ventrite 5 not depressed. Under bark of dead hardwoods. British Columbia to California, east to Idaho, Colorado, and New Mexico. (4)

Phyconomus marinus (LeConte) (3.5–4.8 mm) is somewhat flattened, finely punctured with recumbent pubescence dorsally, and reddish brown. Antennomeres 9–10 forming club. Pronotum broadest across anterior quarter, then sides converging posteriorly, and disc coarsely punctate; front coxa rounded. Elytra with setigerous punctures confused. Ventrite 1 with broadly rounded intercoxal process. Adults inhabit upper tidal zone under seaweed and driftwood washed up on coastal beaches. California and Baja California. (1)

Monotoma bicolor Villa & Villa (1.9–2.5 mm) is elongate and reddish brown to blackish, with head and pronotum darker than elytra. Antennal club with one antennomere, antennomere 3 as long as 2. Pronotum elongate, coarsely punctate with shallow dual impressions, and blunt protruding front angles. Elytra with paired rows of punctures somewhat confused at very base and tip, not covering abdomen and exposing one (female) or two (male) abdominal ventrites. Abdomen underneath with first ventrite longer than rest. Adults active in summer, found in decaying vegetable matter. Europe; widespread in North America, in West from British Columbia to California, east to Arizona. (11)

Rhizophagus minutus Mannerheim (2.0–2.8 mm) is elongate, narrow, with short, sparse setae, and reddish brown with four paler elytral spots. Head without frontoclypeal suture, with antennal grooves, and temple shorter than vertical diameter of eye. Antennae with 10 antennomeres, 10 forming globose club. Pronotum transverse, with anterior angles slightly projected forward, lateral margins narrowly explanate; front coxae transverse. Scutellum exposed and flat. Elytra punctostriate, with apices subtruncate, exposing one (female) or two (male) terga. Ventrite 1 as long as 2–5 combined. Adults under bark of dead coniferous and hardwood trees. British Columbia and Idaho to southern California, east to New Mexico. (8)

440

SMICRIPIDAE (smī-krip'-i-dē)
PALMETTO BEETLES

Smicripidae is a small New World family that occurs from southern United States to the Caribbean and South America. All six currently known species are in the genus *Smicrips*, and numerous species from the Neotropical Realm await description. Very little is known about their biology and natural history, other than an apparent association with palms. The sole representative of the family in western North America is an undescribed species of *Smicrips* known from the Colorado Desert of southern California, where both native and introduced palms occur. This taxon, initially and erroneously identified as *S. hypocoproides* Reitter (a synonym of *S. palmicola* from Florida), was associated with rotting oranges. In Florida, adult *Smicrips palmicola* LeConte are associated primarily with the inflorescences of cabbage palmetto (*Sabal palmetto*). They are occasionally attracted to sap, decaying flowers and oranges, and rotting cotton bolls, and are found in leaf litter. The larvae are usually found in decaying plant matter and leaf litter that accumulates near adult-inhabited palms. Another *Smicrips* from Texas, *S. texana* (Casey), has been collected mostly in pitfall traps, and occasionally in unbaited Lindgren funnel traps and ultraviolet light in the sabal palm (*Sabal mexicana*) forest of the Lower Rio Grande Valley.

FAMILY DIAGNOSIS Adult smicripids are small, elongate, parallel-sided, and flattened, with frontoclypeal suture distinct and curved. Head prognathous and not narrowed behind moderately prominent eyes. Antennae with 11 antennomeres, 9–11 forming distinct and elongate clubs; maxilla with single lobe (lacinia). Procoxae broadly open behind externally, and narrowly closed internally. Scutellum visible. Elytra short and truncate apically, exposing both propygidium and pygidium. Tarsi 4-4-4, tarsomere 3 minute, 4 as long or longer than 1–3 combined, with claws simple. Abdomen with five ventrites free, 1 and 5 elongate, 2–4 equally short.

SIMILAR FAMILIES

- rove beetles (Staphylinidae, p.143)—antennae filiform
- root-eating beetles (Monotomidae, p.438)—antennal club consisting of one or two antennomeres

- sap beetles (Nitidulidae, p.443)—last abdominal ventrite not longer than previous two ventrites combined

COLLECTING NOTES Look for *Smicrips* in decaying fruit and other plant materials, possibly in association with native and ornamental palms, in the Colorado Desert of California. Pitfall and flight intercept traps, as well as light traps placed in these habitats may also be productive.

FAUNA THREE SPECIES IN ONE GENUS

Smicrips **species** (1.0–2.0 mm) are small, elongate, parallel-sided, flattened, and reddish brown. Head with distinct groove between front and clypeus curved, mandibles well developed in male, antennae with antennomeres 9–11 forming club. Pronotum slightly wider than head. Elytra twice as long and barely wider than pronotum, sides broadly rounded, and short, exposing pygidium. Legs with last tarsomere longer than rest of tarsus. Adults found in association with accumulations of decaying plant matter. Southern California. Note that *Smicrips palmicola* LeConte from Florida is figured. (1)

441

KATERETIDAE (ka-ter-et'-i-dē)
SHORT-WINGED FLOWER BEETLES

Both adult and larval kateretids feed and develop in flowers. The larvae develop within the seed capsules, while the adults consume petals and pollen. Whether generalists or specialists, larvae within each genus tend to be associated with host plants in the same family. Although they restrict their reproductive activities to larval host plants, adults are generalized feeders and visit a broad range of flowers.

FAMILY DIAGNOSIS Adult kateretids are small and somewhat elongate-oval. Head prognathous, and maxilla with both galea and lacinia long and narrow. Antennae with 11 antennomeres, 9–11 forming weak round or oval club. Pronotum slightly narrower than elytra. Elytra not punctostriate and short, exposing both propygidium and pygidium. Procoxal cavities open behind. Tarsi 5-5-5, with claws simple or dentate. Abdomen with five ventrites free, 1 as long as or longer than 2 and 3 combined.

SIMILAR FAMILIES

- round fungus beetles (Leiodidae, p.137)—elytra grooved; antennomere 8 smaller than 7 and 9
- minute fungus beetles (Corylophidae, p.314)— head often not visible from above

- hairy fungus beetles (Mycetophagidae, p.326)— body with short pubescence, antennal club less compact
- thymalid beetles (Thymalidae, p.417)—antennal club loose, side margin of pronotum carinate, tarsal claws long
- sap beetles (Nitidulidae, p.443)—antennae strongly capitate, front coxal cavities closed behind externally
- shining flower beetles (Phalacridae, p.456)—dorsal surface shiny, more convex, antennal club less compact

COLLECTING NOTES Adult kateretids are found on flowers and swept from vegetation during spring and early summer.

FAUNA 11 SPECIES IN SEVEN GENERA

Amartus tinctus (Mannerheim) (3.9–5.5 mm) is oval, robust, convex, somewhat dull, moderately clothed in gray pubescence, and blackish with reddish-brown appendages to entirely yellowish brown. Head densely pubescent, and coarsely punctate, more so than pronotum, with antennae weakly clubbed. Pronotum wider than long, distinctly convex and narrower anteriorly than posteriorly, and less punctate with lateral margins weakly arcuate, and posterior angles broadly rounded. Elytral apices somewhat truncate. Claws simple. Oregon to southern California, east to southeastern Arizona. *Amartus rufipes* LeConte (3.2–4.0 mm) less robust, with moderately convex pronotum not narrower apically. Adults of both species on flowers of poppies (*Eschscholzia*). California and Arizona. (2)

Anthonaeus agavensis (Crotch) (3.8–4.5 mm) is oblong-oval, flattened, usually brownish black or black with elytra always yellowish brown. Head much narrower than prothorax, with mandibles bluntly toothed on inner margin. Pronotum wide, with sides strongly and evenly arcuate, and lateral and posterior margins narrowly reflexed. Elytra together longer than wide and becoming broader apically. Propygidium and pygidium exposed, latter with margins narrowly reflexed and, in male, emarginate apically. Claws simple. Adults on flowers of chaparral yucca (*Hesperoyucca whipplei*); larvae likely develop in seed capsules. Coastal southern California. (1)

Brachypterus urticae (Fabricius) (1.5–2.0 mm) is oval, convex, sparsely pubescent, moderately punctate dorsally, and shiny brownish or black, sometimes with brassy tinge. Head narrower than pronotum. Pronotum nearly as wide as elytra, sides broadly arcuate and usually somewhat sinuate basally, with posterior angles obtuse, not rectangular. Elytra slightly more punctate than pronotum, with apices variously truncate. Ventrite 1 at middle longer than 2 and 3 combined. Claws distinctly toothed basally. Adults active in summer, found on the flowers of various plants, including nettles (*Urtica*). Widespread in North America; in West from Alaska and Northern Territories south to California and Colorado. (1)

Heterhelus sericans **(LeConte)** (1.5–2.3 mm) is oval and slightly oblong, feebly shiny, sparsely pubescent, and usually yellowish brown with head and elytra brownish black, occasionally uniformly reddish brown with pale appendages. Pronotum wide, anterior margin not emarginate, sides weakly arcuate (male) or slightly sinuate posteriorly (female), with disc strongly convex and moderately densely punctate. Elytra coarsely and densely punctate, with apices obliquely rounded and somewhat truncate, exposing posterior angles of propygidium and pygidium. Claws simple. Adults associated with flowers of elderberry (*Sambucus*). Transcontinental; in West from British Columbia to southern California, east to Idaho, Utah, and New Mexico. (1)

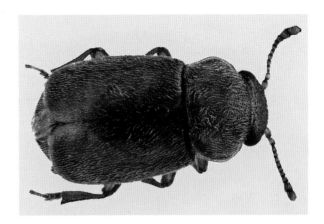

NITIDULIDAE (nit-i-dū′-li-dē)
SAP BEETLES

Nitidulids, variously known as sap, pollen, and picnic beetles, are incredibly diverse in terms of their life histories. These small and mostly compact beetles live in a wide variety of habitats where they are primarily phytophagous or mycophagous, while a few species are necrophagous or predaceous. *Conotelus* species resemble rove beetles (p.143) and inhabit live flowers. Tree sap flowing from wounds attracts species of *Carpophilus*, *Colopterus*, *Cryptarcha*, *Epuraea*, *Glischrochilus*, *Lobiopa*, and *Soronia*, some of which may play a role in the transmission of tree-killing fungal pathogens. The small hive beetle, *Aethina tumida* (Murray), invades European bee hives and solicits food from worker bees, while their larvae (p.29, Fig. 18u) foul the hive as they feed on pollen, honey, and brood. Mycophagous *Stelidota* are associated with fungal hyphae growing in leaf litter, while *Pocadius* and *Thalycra* feed on puffballs and false truffles, respectively. *Pityophagus rufipennis* is found under pine bark, where it presumably preys on bark beetles. The last stages of carrion decomposition attract species of *Omosita* and *Nitidula*, as well as some *Epuraea*. Some nitidulids are commonly encountered as pests of crops and dried goods. Species of *Carpophilus* are minor pests of dried fruits and other stored products. Adults and larvae not only contaminate products with their waste, they also introduce molds and other organisms that further hasten its decomposition.

FAMILY DIAGNOSIS Adult nitidulids are mostly small and elongate and cylindrical, broadly oval and hemispherical, or somewhat flattened, with antennae distinctly capitate, and often with short elytra exposing part of pygidium and one, two, or three additional tergites. Head prognathous. Antennae with 11 antennomeres, 9–11 forming round or oval club. Pronotum wider than long, with lateral margins often thin and explanate, and posterior margin closely united with or overlapping base of elytra. Procoxal cavities open (Cryptarchinae) or closed behind. Elytra short or long, without striae or carinae, with combined apices truncate or individually rounded. Legs short and somewhat stout, with tarsi 5-5-5, tarsomeres 1–3 broad, 1 usually as long as 2, and 4 small, with claws simple or dentate. Abdomen with five ventrites free.

SIMILAR FAMILIES

- marsh beetles (Scirtidae, p.114)—antennae filiform or serrate, elytra completely covering abdomen
- wounded-tree beetles (Nosodendridae, p.115)—tibiae broadly expanded, elytra covering abdomen
- water scavenger beetles (Hydrophilidae, p.122)—long maxillary palps, clavate antennal club
- clown beetles (Histeridae, p.127)—antennae geniculate, elytra short, lined with rows of punctures and cover all but last two abdominal tergites
- round fungus beetles (Leiodidae, p.137)—elytra punctostriate, antennomere 8 smaller than 7 and 9
- some rove beetles (Staphylinidae, p.143)—antennae usually not distinctly clubbed, elytra with rows of punctures or distinctly costate

- pill beetles (Byrrhidae, p.233)—antennae filiform or clavate, club with three to seven antennomeres
- skin beetles (Dermestidae, p.290)—body usually covered with scales or setae
- minute fungus beetles (Corylophidae, p.314)—head often not visible from above
- hairy fungus beetles (Mycetophagidae, p.326)—body with short setae, antennal club less compact
- thymalid beetles (Thymalidae, p.417)—antennal club loose, sides of pronotum sharp, tarsal claws long
- pleasing fungus beetles (Erotylidae, p.435)—elytra completely covering abdomen
- palmetto beetles (Smicripidae, p.440)—mandibles clearly visible, clubbed antennae with 11 antennomeres, 9–11 forming club
- shining flower beetles (Phalacridae, p.456)—dorsal surface shiny, antennal club less compact

- tortoise beetles (Chrysomelidae: Cassidinae, p.504)—head not visible from above, antennae filiform or clavate

COLLECTING NOTES Look for nitidulids in flowers and leaf litter, at sap flows on tree trunks, on decaying fruits and fungi, and under loose bark and carcasses in the advanced stages of decay. Sweeping low vegetation at dusk may capture species associated with subterranean fungi. Species in several genera are attracted to lights. Pitfall traps baited with fermenting malt or molasses are also effective for species known to occur on fungi, including subterranean species. Place about 6 mm of malt or molasses in a metal or plastic container and add enough water so that the mixture is about 25 mm deep. Add a couple pinches of yeast to the solution. Many species are collected in Malaise and flight intercept traps placed in forests and woodlands.

444

FAUNA 175 SPECIES IN 33 GENERA

Cryptarcha concinna Melsheimer (2.0–3.0 mm) is oval, weakly convex, finely pubescent, densely and finely punctate dorsally, with markings variable or absent. Labrum and frons fused with clypeus, and mandibles unequal in male. Pronotum with posterior marginal bead, slightly overlapping base of elytra; prosternum narrow, more or less acutely rounded apically, and not extending beyond middle of mesosternum. Elytra with sutural striae only, each with about eight rows of stout and suberect setae, a median basal spot, and usually with complete sinuous elytral band. At rotting fruit and light. Widespread in North America. *Cryptarcha ampla* Erichson (4.5–7.8 mm) prosternum broadly rounded apically. Widespread, except Southwest. (4)

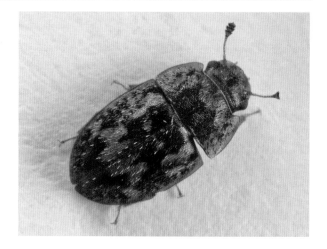

Four-spotted Sap Beetle *Glischrochilus quadrisignatus* **(Say)** (4.0–7.0 mm) is oblong, convex, somewhat shiny black with a pair of yellowish or reddish spots on each elytron. Head large, broad, with labrum and frons fused with clypeus. Pronotum with lateral margins narrowly but distinctly upturned. Elytra with basal spots further from suture than spots behind middle. Adults attracted to decaying and stored fruit and vegetables, and other sweet odors; also attracted to lights. In West, British Columbia to Utah. *Glischrochilus vittatus* (Say) (3.5–6.0 mm) similar in form, with broken pale lines on elytra. Under pine (*Pinus*) bark. Alaska to California and Nevada. (7)

Pityophagus rufipennis Horn (4.4–7.0 mm) is elongate, convex, glabrous, shiny, and usually dark reddish brown with appendages and elytra lighter, rarely uniformly blackish. Head moderately densely and coarsely punctate, with transverse impression across base. Pronotum quadrate, lateral margins nearly straight and slightly converging posteriorly, without posterior marginal bead; procoxal cavities closed. Elytra alutaceous, more finely punctate than pronotum. Pygidial margin strongly elevated. Tibiae distinctly spiny. Adults at slash piles, likely prey on bark beetles. British Columbia to California, east to Arizona. (1)

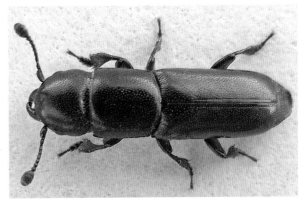

Epuraea luteola (Erichson) (2.0–2.5 mm) is moderately shiny, sparsely pubescent and, except eyes and antennal clubs, uniformly yellowish brown. Head finely and sparsely punctate. Pronotum very wide, narrowly reflexed lateral margins weakly arcuate and narrowed anteriorly, with posterior angles rectangular, slightly explanate, and microsculpture consisting of fine parallel lines. Elytra slightly more sparsely and coarsely punctate than pronotum, with two abdominal segments. Metatibiae simple, with metatibiae abruptly expanded just before middle. Tarsomeres 1–3 bilobed. Pest of dried fruits, mushrooms. Neotropical; established across United States. (14)

445

Small Hive Beetle *Aethina tumida* (Murray) (5.0–7.0 mm) is oval, reddish brown, dark brown, or black. Head with labrum visible and distinct, and eyes with conspicuous setae. Pronotum wider than long, widest at middle. Elytra long, covering all but last abdominal tergite, and slightly narrower than pronotum. Legs with outer edges of middle and hind tibiae with two rows of spines, tarsi 5-5-5. Larvae are serious pest of beehives, ruining combs and contaminating honey. Adults active spring and summer; feed on honey and pollen, usually found in association with beehives. Sub-Saharan Africa; transcontinental, widespread in western United States. (1)

Dried Fruit Beetle *Carpophilus hemipterus* (Linnaeus) (2.0–4.0 mm) is oblong, somewhat flattened, weakly shiny, dark reddish brown to blackish. Head with large eyes and few punctures. Pronotum wide, lateral margins weakly arcuate, with hind angles obtuse. Elytra together wider than long, more finely punctate than pronotum, short, with humeral patches and irregular areas on apices yellowish brown; three abdominal tergites exposed. Minor pest of dried fruit and stored products, attracted to decaying fruits, nuts, and vegetables; also on oak wilt mycelial mats under rotten logs. Nearly cosmopolitan; widespread in North America. (20)

Lobiopa falli Parsons (5.3–6.7 mm) is oval, weakly convex, dull, with scattered thick setae, and pale to dark reddish brown with lateral margins lighter. Eyes not as long as depth of pronotal emargination. Submentum coarsely punctate. Pronotum deeply emarginate anteriorly, with lateral margins arcuate, broadly explanate, and strongly narrowed anteriorly; underneath with antennal grooves parallel. Elytra not costate, with lateral margins explanate, coarse and shallow discal punctures, about seven rows of thick setae, and pale spots; short irregular band across suture apical declivity most visible in lighter individuals. Adults at lights. Southeastern Arizona. (3)

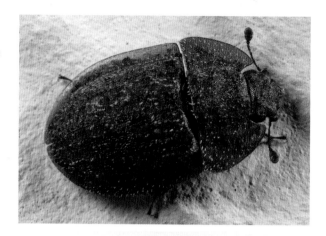

Nitops pallipennis (Say) (2.5–4.0 mm) is oblong-oval, robust, sparsely pubescent, and usually blackish, with appendages paler. Pronotum wider than long, narrowed in front, with sides moderately arcuate, and hind angles broadly rounded, with disc densely punctate. Elytra pale yellowish brown, fimbriate, together slightly wider than long, with surfaces regularly, densely punctate, and pygidium and penultimate tergite exposed. Mesosternum simple. Ventrites 2 and 3 short. Adults common on prickly pear cactus flowers (*Opuntia*) in spring and early summer. Widespread in western North America. (7)

Omosita discoidea (Fabricius) (2.0–3.2 mm) is oblong-oval, moderately convex, sparsely pubescent, and mostly yellowish brown, with head, antennal club, and posterior third of elytra dark. Pronotum wider than long, with lateral margins broad, moderately arcuate, and disc coarsely and densely punctate. Elytra covering abdomen, more sparsely and finely punctate than pronotum, with several pale spots on apices. *Omosita nearctica* Kirejtshuk has darker elytral bases and lighter apices. Both species on carrion and widely distributed in North America. Reports of *O. colon* (Fabricius) from western Canada require confirmation. (2)

Pallodes plateosus Schaeffer (3.6–4.3 mm) is somewhat obovate, strongly convex, shiny, and glabrous, with pronotum yellowish brown, and scutellum and elytra dark reddish brown. Head and antennal clubs reddish black. Pronotum broad, yellowish brown with large, dark, and diffuse central spot flanked on each side by small round spot; underneath antennal sulci short and convergent. Scutellum broadly triangular. Elytra entire, gradually converging posteriorly, exposing only tip of pygidium, and darker laterally and apically, with discal punctation somewhat obsolete. Underside dark reddish brown. Legs yellowish brown, with long metatarsi. On fresh mushrooms; at lights. Southeastern Arizona and New Mexico. (1)

Soronia guttulata **(LeConte)** (5.0–6.0 mm) is weakly convex, faintly shiny, finely and sparsely pubescent, and dark reddish brown, with pronotal and elytral discs nearly black. Head finely and densely punctate, with sinuous impression between eyes. Pronotum wide, anterior margin deeply emarginate, and lateral margins broadly explanate and narrowed anteriorly, with four vague foveae and sometimes median depression on disc; underneath with antennal sulci strongly convergent posteriorly. Elytra maculate, each with five vague costae. Densely punctate ventrally, except sparsely punctate prosternum. Under pine (*Pinus*) bark. In West, British Columbia to California. (1)

Colopterus truncatus **(Randall)** (1.5–2.7 mm) is very flat, sparsely pubescent, and reddish yellow-brown to blackish with an oblique pale spot on each elytron; darker specimens have brownish antennae and reddish legs, paler individuals with yellowish-brown appendages. Head coarsely punctate. Pronotum wide, sparsely punctate, and weakly emarginate anteriorly. Elytra densely punctate. Abdomen with ventrite 5 as long as 1–4 combined. Tarsal claws simple. On fungus, probably under bark during spring and summer. Southern Canada and United States, south to South America. (1)

Conotelus mexicanus **Sharp** (3.2–4.0 mm) is slender, convex, narrowed posteriorly, sparsely pubescent, and dark brown to black, sometimes with elytra lighter. Head broad. Pronotum nearly as broad as elytra. Scutellum transverse and truncate apically. Elytra short, exposing three abdominal terga, and fringed with short setae apically. Hypopygium long and pygidium conical, latter shallowly emarginate in male. Legs short, black, with femora weakly sulcate, tarsi dilated, tarsomere 5 about as long as 1–4 combined, and claws simple. Adults in fresh flowers; larvae develop in fallen corollas. Southern California and Arizona, south to Panama. (1)

Fabogethes nigrescens **(Stephens)** (1.8–2.0 mm) is moderately convex, shiny black, and sparsely pubescent. Head densely punctate with clypeus nearly square, labrum distinct. Prothorax wide, with lateral margins narrowed and more rounded narrowed anteriorly. Elytra densely punctate, and completely covering abdomen. Outer margins of meso- and metatibiae with a row of spines. Claws simple. Larva develops in flowers of clover (*Trifolium*) and other plants in pea family (Fabaceae). Pollen-feeding adults on flowers in various open habitats during spring and summer. Eurasia; in West from British Columbia south to Oregon. (1)

Nitidula flavomaculata Rossi (3.0–5.0 mm) is oblong-oval, moderately depressed, densely and finely pubescent, and blackish with lateral pronotal margins, humeral patches that may or may not be contiguous with a pair of discal spots that are all yellowish brown. Pronotum is wider than long, weakly convex, with moderately arcuate lateral margins narrowly reflexed and slightly converging anteriorly; underneath with antennal grooves strongly convergent posteriorly. Adults associated with carrion and fungi. Eurasia; established in Oregon and California, also on East Coast. (5)

Nitidula ziczac Say (3.0–5.0 mm) is oblong, moderately convex, densely pubescent, and reddish black, with variable yellowish-brown elytral markings sometimes absent. Pronotum with lateral margins very narrowly reflexed and moderately arcuate, obtuse posterior angles, and finely punctate disc; underneath with antennal grooves strongly convergent posteriorly. Elytra finely punctate, typically with basal spots and median sigmoid band. Adults associated with carrion and fungi. Across southern Canada and northern United States. (5)

Pocadius fulvipennis Erichson (2.5–4.2 mm) is oval, moderately convex and shiny, sparsely pubescent, and variably black with red basal spot on each elytron to yellowish brown. Head vertical and coarsely punctate, with eyes glabrous. Pronotum wide, with lateral margins arcuate and narrowed anteriorly, without posterior marginal bead; underneath with prosternum distinctly arcuate in profile. Front tarsi not dilated, hind tibiae without conspicuous spines on outer edge. Elytra covering entire abdomen, each with 10 rows of shallow, quadrate punctures and flat intervals with single row of fine setigerous punctures. Adults on giant puffball (*Calvatia gigantea*) in spring and summer. British Columbia to southern California. (3)

Stelidota octomaculata (Say) (2.2–3.5 mm) is oval, convex, sparsely punctate, and somewhat shiny yellowish brown to reddish black with indistinct pale elytral spots. Pronotal anterior margin deeply emarginate, arcuate lateral margins broadly explanate, widest before bisinuate base; antennal grooves underneath parallel. Elytra with rows of oval punctures with spaces between almost flat. Male middle tibiae neither curved nor abruptly expanded apically. Adults found at sap flows, rotten fruit, and under leaves; occasionally attracted to lights. Southeastern Arizona eastward to Nova Scotia and Florida. *Stelidota strigosa* (Gyllenhal) pronotum anterior pronotal margin weakly emarginate, sides narrowly explanate, and base truncate. Arizona to eastern United States and South America. (2)

448

Thalycra sinuata Howden (2.7–5.7 mm) is moderately convex, punctate and setose dorsally, setae often abraded in males, with lateral margins distinct, and dark reddish brown. Head with punctures coarse, nearly contiguous, especially on clypeus. Pronotum evenly punctate, some punctures oblong. Elytra punctate basally, less so apically. Front tibia bearing 2–3 teeth, front tarsi not expanded, with basal half of male hind tibia usually shallowly sinuate. Five (female) or six (male) ventrites; apical one-sixth of female pygidium glabrous. Adults on *Rhizopogon* fungi in ponderosa pine (*Pinus ponderosa*) forests, also at malt traps and light. British Columbia and Alberta south to southern California, east to Colorado and New Mexico. (11)

CRYPTOPHAGIDAE (krip-to-faj'-i-dē)
SILKEN FUNGUS BEETLES

Most cryptophagids are mycophagous and found in various accumulations of decaying vegetation and other substrates that foster mold growth, where they feed on hyphae, spores, conidia, and other microscopic fungal materials. Some species are associated with plants. For example, *Telmatophilus americanus* LeConte occurs on emergent aquatic plants. Others are scavengers in nests of social insects. *Antherophagus* species are all associated with bumble bees (*Bombus*) and are sometimes found on flowers, in nests, or clinging to the mouthparts, antennae, and legs of foraging bees. *Myrmedophila americanus* (LeConte) lives in the nests of wood ants (*Formica*). Species of *Cryptophagus* and *Henoticus* occasionally occur in small numbers in moldy food products stored in homes, warehouses, and granaries.

449

FAMILY DIAGNOSIS Adult cryptophagids are elongate-oval to oval, robust, and frequently clothed dorsally in long, silky setae. Antennae with 11 antennomeres, usually with 9–11 forming loose club. Head broad, slightly deflexed, with large, protuberant eyes finely faceted and glabrous. Pronotum broad, sometimes with irregular lateral margins, and often with a pair of depressions along posterior margin. Procoxal cavities open or closed behind. Elytra smooth with punctures irregular. Legs usually long and slender, with female tarsi 5-5-5, usually 5-5-4 in male, but 5-5-5 in *Telmatophilus*. Abdomen with five ventrites free, ventrite 1 with or without any coxal lines and about as long as 2 and 3 combined.

SIMILAR FAMILIES
- tooth-neck fungus beetles (Derodontidae, p.116)—elytra with distinct quadrate punctures
- round fungus beetles (Leiodidae, p.137)—club with five antennomeres, 8 usually smaller than 7 and 9
- minute bark beetles (Cerylonidae, p.309)—antennal club with two antennomeres, usually glabrous dorsally

- hairy fungus beetles (Mycetophagidae, p.326)—most species distinctly bicolored, abdominal ventrites all of equal length
- polypore fungus beetles (Tetratomidae, p.330)—antennae weakly clavate if clubbed at all, abdominal ventrites all equal in length
- zopherid beetles (Zopheridae, p.340)—antennal club with two antennomeres, tarsi 4-4-4
- fruitworm beetles (Byturidae, p.410)—abdominal ventrites all equal in length, tarsomeres 2–3 lobed underneath
- false skin beetles (Biphyllidae, p.411)—sublateral lines present on the pronotum, with postcoxal lines on abdomen

COLLECTING NOTES Cryptophagids are usually found in association with mold or moldy substrates, on fungus, and in decaying vegetation. Look under bark of dead trees, in decaying wood and other vegetable debris, or accumulations of plant materials in abandoned nests of small mammals. The most effective collecting methods involve extracting cryptophagids from leaf litter and rotten wood using either Berlese funnels or Winkler eclectors. Some species are collected in flight intercept traps, while others are swept or beaten from vegetation, or attracted to yellow pan traps.

FAUNA 145 SPECIES IN 16 GENERA

Telmatophilus americanus LeConte (2.4–3.0 mm) is oblong-oval, convex, dark reddish brown to blackish with short, fine, gray pubescence and reddish-brown appendages. Pronotum broad, convex, with lateral margins arcuate and finely serrate, and posterior margin with pair of pits and somewhat acute angles. Elytra slightly broader and less densely punctured than prothorax. Male hind legs with external flangelike expansion at base of tibiae, tarsi 5-5-5 with tarsomeres 2–3 markedly lobed. Last abdominal ventrite of male bilobed. Adults found in summer on flowers of bur-reed (*Sparganium*); on arrow-arum (*Peltandrum virginica*) in East. In West from British Columbia to Oregon, east to Alberta and Colorado. (1)

Cryptophagus species (1.6–3.5 mm) are small, oblong, reddish brown to black with distinct and irregular margins on sides of pronotum, and have conspicuous decumbent or suberect setae on pronotum and elytra. Head without groove before clypeus. Pronotum without narrow sublateral grooves before narrow margins, each margin with broad angle in front and small, distinct toothlike projection at middle. Elytra with punctures confused, and distinctly clothed in setae. Adults and larvae occur in habitats promoting fungal growth; some species associated with mammal nests or occasionally infest stored products. Widespread in western North America. Genus needs revision. (25)

Antherophagus ochraceus Melsheimer (3.4–5.0 mm) is oblong, somewhat convex, finely punctate dorsally, densely clothed in appressed yellowish pubescence, and uniformly yellowish brown, with antennae and bases of tibiae dark in male. Head with eyes large and flat eyes, distinct temples, and labrum entire (female), or broadly and deeply emarginate (male). Pronotum broader than long, with fine, dense punctures, and lateral margins smooth, straight, and somewhat parallel, with bead thickened anteriorly. Elytra wide as pronotum, with disc finely and densely punctate. Adults found on various flowers, or clinging to bumble bees; larvae develop in bumble bee nests. In West from British Columbia and Alberta south to Oregon and Colorado. (3)

Caenoscelis ferruginea Sahlberg (1.7–2.3 mm) is elongate-oval, finely and distinctly pubescent, and pale reddish brown. Eyes large with multiple facets. Antennae stout with distinct club, insertions medially approximate on frons, with surface between narrow and minutely carinate. Pronotum broad, convex, narrowed anteriorly, and carinate laterally, with margins entire and strongly arcuate, and posterior margin with feeble median impression. Adults found under bark and in other accumulations of plant material, including pack rat nests. Europe and northern Asia; in West from Alaska and Yukon Territory south to California and Colorado. (4)

Atomaria species (1.0–2.1 mm) are oval-oblong, convex, shiny, distinctly punctate, with decumbent pubescence, and yellowish-, reddish-, or blackish-brown to black. Head with frontoclypeal suture present, antennal club with three antennomeres, and antennal insertions closer to eyes than to each other. Pronotum wider than long, with lateral margins carinate, somewhat parallel or oblique, and more or less narrowed anteriorly; underneath with prosternal process flat, narrow, and without parallel lines. Elytra with punctures confused or in rows. Adults and larvae feed on mycelial fungal growth among accumulations of plant debris. Widespread in western North America. Genus needs revision. (~70 NA)

451

SILVANIDAE (sil-vān'-i-dē)
SILVANID FLAT BARK BEETLES

Both larvae and adults of *Cathartosilvanus, Dendrophagus, Silvanus,* and *Uleiota* are found under bark, where they likely feed on fungi. *Telephanus* species occur on plants, especially among withered, drooping leaves or under plant debris, where they are also probably eating fungi. The biologies of species that are of economic importance are the best known among silvanids. Two genera (*Cathartus, Oryzaephilus*) that occur in the region contain species that are sometimes important pests of stored grains, grain products, nuts, and spices.

FAMILY DIAGNOSIS Adult silvanids are small, elongate, parallel-sided to slightly oval in outline, and somewhat flattened with lateral pronotal margins distinctly margined, wavy, or toothed; most lack conspicuous setae. Head prognathous and broad, usually distinctly narrowed behind eyes. Antennae with 11 antennomeres, usually long and mostly filiform (*Telephanus, Uleiota*), or shorter with moniliform antennomeres and distinct club (*Cathartosilvanus, Oryzaephilus, Silvanus*). Prothorax longer than wide. Procoxal cavities closed or broadly open (*Dendrophagus, Uleiota*) behind. Elytra long, distinctly pitted or rough, and cover abdomen completely. Tarsi 5-5-5 (4-4-4 in *Uleiota*), with simple claws equal in length. Abdomen with five ventrites free.

SIMILAR FAMILIES
- *Adelina* (Tenebrionidae, p.367)—antennal insertion hidden from view above
- root-eating beetles (Monotomidae, p.438)—antennae with 10 antennomeres, with 10 or 9 and 10 forming club
- flat bark beetles (Cucujidae, p.453)—more flattened, antennae not clubbed, pronotum usually wider than long or quadrate, tarsi 5-5-4 in males

■ lined flat bark beetles (Laemophloeidae, p.458)—head and pronotum with distinct lines or ridges along sides

COLLECTING NOTES Look for silvanids on plants, under loose bark of stumps, snags, and logs of hardwoods, especially oaks (*Quercus*). Also search through decaying plant materials, particularly rotting fruit and infested stored products.

FAUNA 32 SPECIES IN 14 GENERA

Dendrophagus cygnaei Mannerheim (5.0–7.0 mm) is elongate, flat, straight-sided, and reddish yellow-brown to dark brownish-black with appendages, especially tarsi, paler. Antennae long, filiform, without club, with elongate scape. Pronotum elongate, with sides smooth and front angles rounded, disc densely punctured with pair of long impressions; underneath with coxal cavities open behind. Tarsi 5-5-5, 1 short, but distinct. Adults found under bark. Alaska and across Canada and northern United States; in West south to California. (1)

Uleiota truncatus Motschulsky (4.2–5.3 mm) is elongate, flat, parallel-sided, and yellowish brown to brownish black with explanate elytral margins and/or appendages sometimes lighter. Head with eyes moderately large, antennae long and filiform, and mandible armed with slender, curved horn in male. Long antennae filiform, without club, with elongate scape. Pronotum with anterior angles prominent and toothed, lateral margins with denticles. Elytra with humeri carinate, each with five punctostriae, and apices somewhat rounded (female) or obliquely truncate (male). Tarsi 4-4-4, with 4 longer than 1–3 combined. Adults under loose bark of dead oak (*Quercus*), alder (*Alnus*), and other hardwoods. British Columbia to southern California. (1)

Telephanus lecontei Casey (3.8–4.2 mm) is elongate-oval, somewhat convex, coarsely punctate, moderately pubescent dorsally, and uniformly dark yellowish brown to brownish black, with head and antennae sometimes reddish and legs paler. Antennae long and filiform, with first antennomere long. Pronotum elongate, broadest about middle and gradually narrowing posteriorly, with lateral margins irregular. Procoxal cavities closed behind. Elytra at base broader than prothorax, disc punctostriate, with pubescence relatively long and denser laterally. Legs moderately long, slender, with femora swollen, especially on hind legs, and tarsomere 4 bilobed. Adults at lights. Southeastern Arizona. (1)

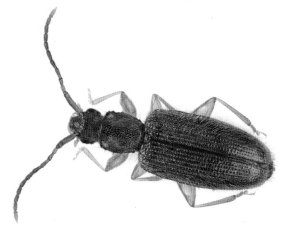

452

Merchant Grain Beetle *Oryzaephilus mercator* (Fauvel) (2.2–3.1 mm) is elongate, flattened, and uniformly brown. Head with surface less coarsely and closely punctate in front of eyes, sides behind eye less than one-third length of eye and sharply and narrowly angular. Sides of pronotum each with six sawlike teeth. Elytra costate, intervals with rows of coarse and close-set punctures. Hind femora each with (male) or without (female) a tooth. Adults and larvae are common pantry pests and associated with cereals, dried fruits, and nuts; adults not cold-tolerant. Old World, now cosmopolitan. (2)

Saw-toothed Grain Beetle *Oryzaephilus surinamensis* (Linnaeus) (2.1–3.2 mm) is elongate, flattened, and uniformly brown. Head with surface close-set coarse punctures throughout and sides behind eye at least half length of eye and not narrow and sharp; club antennomeres quadrate. Sides of pronotum each with six sawlike teeth. Elytra costate, intervals with coarse and close-set punctures. Hind femora each with (male) or without (female) a tooth. Adults and larvae associated with cereals, dried fruits, and nuts, especially in food processing centers; adults cold-tolerant, sometimes found under tree bark. Old World, now cosmopolitan. (2)

Silvanus bidentatus (Fabricius) (2.5–3.5 mm) is elongate, somewhat depressed, inconspicuously pubescent, and dull reddish yellow-brown, with head and pronotum coarsely punctate. Head wider than long, narrower across eyes than across anterior angles of pronotum, with temple about length of two eye facets. Pronotum long, somewhat convex, narrower than elytra, with acute anterior angles produced more laterally than anteriorly. Elytra deeply punctostriate with raised intervals bearing setose tubercles. Male hind trochanter bearing small, distinct spine, ventral side of femur with moderate ridge at basal third, and tibia with no spinules. Adults under bark. Asia; established along West Coast and in Southwest, also Northeast. (3)

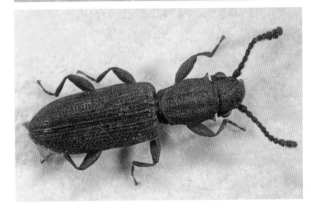

453

CUCUJIDAE (kū-kū'-ji-dē)
FLAT BARK BEETLES

Adult and larval cucujids are typically very flat, an adaptation that makes them well suited for living under the bark of dead and dying trees. In the West, both *Cucujus* and *Pediacus* are associated with conifers. Very little is known about the biology of Cucujidae. The larvae of *Cucujus clavipes puniceus* Mannerheim are reportedly predatory, and their tolerance to extreme cold has made them the focus of numerous studies on cold tolerance. Although both the larvae and adults overwinter, the larvae are better adapted for surviving cold temperatures and are generally encountered more commonly during the winter months. To avoid freezing, *Cucujus* larvae eliminate water from their tissues and seek out favorable microenvironments. They also produce high levels of "antifreeze" in their hemolymph and combine it with special chemical compounds that encourage ice crystal formation between cells, thus avoiding the development of lethal crystals within their cells.

FAMILY DIAGNOSIS Adult cucujids are elongate, conspicuously flat, and somewhat parallel-sided. Prognathous head is broad and triangular, and with (*Cucujus*) or without (*Pediacus*) bulging temples behind eyes. Antennae with 11 antennomeres, and filiform to nearly moniliform, and without a distinct club. Pronotum more or less square to longer than wide. Procoxal cavities open behind. Scutellum visible. Elytra long, completely concealing abdomen, with disc flat and finely punctured. Tarsi 5-5-4 (male) or 5-5-5 (female), with simple claws equal in length. Abdomen with five ventrites free.

SIMILAR FAMILIES

- silvanid beetles (Silvanidae, p.451)—less flattened, antennae clubbed or filiform; pronotum usually longer than wide, tarsi 5-5-5 in both sexes
- lined flat bark beetles (Laemophloeidae, p.458)— head and pronotum with a distinct submarginal line or fine ridge

COLLECTING NOTES Look for adult and larval cucujids under the loose bark of recently dead or decomposing pines and other conifers. Adults are sometimes captured in Lindgren funnel traps.

FAUNA EIGHT SPECIES IN TWO GENERA

Red Flat Bark Beetle *Cucujus clavipes puniceus* Mannerheim (12.5–16.0 mm) is elongate, strongly flattened, somewhat parallel-sided, somewhat dull, and mostly bright red, with eyes, most antennomeres, mandibular apices, and tibiae black. Head distinctly triangular, widest across bulging and broadly rounded temples behind eyes, and coarsely punctate. Antennae thick, nearly filiform, and not clubbed. Basal antennomeres mostly red. Pronotum transverse, angles obtuse, sides irregularly serrate, and coarsely punctate, with medial and sublateral longitudinal impressions on disc. Elytra flat, alutaceous, and relatively smooth. Predatory adults and distinctly flat, segmented larvae found under loose bark of dead pine (*Pinus*). Alaska to California, east to Alberta, Montana, Colorado, and New Mexico. (1)

Pediacus stephani Thomas (2.7–3.6 mm) is elongate, somewhat parallel-sided, flat, coarsely punctured, and yellowish brown. Head triangular, without temples or small distinct denticle behind small eyes, and broadest across eyes. Antennae thick, with antennomeres 9–11 forming loose club. Pronotum transverse, with lateral margins broadly explanate and not inflexed, each with four larger and many smaller marginal denticles, including angles. Elytral surface densely and finely granulate, with large basal punctures coarse, becoming smaller after basal fifth. Tarsomeres not lobed. Adults and larvae usually found underneath bark of dead conifers in montane habitats. British Columbia to California, east to western Nevada. (5)

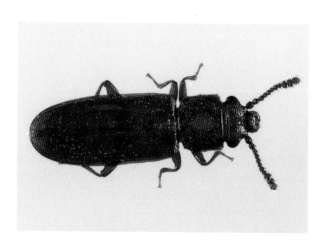

PASSANDRIDAE (pas-an'-dri-dē)
PARASITIC FLAT BARK BEETLES

Passandrids are primarily tropical in distribution, although a few species are found in decidedly more temperate habitats in North and South America. The feeding habits of adult passandrids have not been determined, but the known larvae are unusual in that they are ectoparasitoids of wood-boring larvae and pupae of weevils, longhorns, ambrosia and bark beetles, or wasps. In eastern North America, *Catogenus rufus* (Fabricius) is associated with the pupa of a longhorn beetle, *Anelaphus parallelus* (Newman). The larva of another passandrid widespread in eastern United States, *Taphroscelidia linearis* (LeConte), apparently lives in the galleries of a bark beetle, *Pityophthorus concentralis* Eichoff. Other than occasional attraction of adults to lights, the biology of the sole western representative of the family, *Catogenus thomasi* Ślipiński, remains unknown.

FAMILY DIAGNOSIS Adult passandrids in western North America are elongate, parallel-sided, strongly flattened, dark mahogany brown, with elytra more or less distinctly striate. Head prognathous and carinate laterally, genae produced as rounded plates that conceal maxillae, and confluent gular grooves underneath. Moniliform antennae thick and pubescent, with 11 antennomeres, their insertions hidden from view above by frontal ridges. Sides of head and prothorax distinctly carinate. Pronotum longer than wide, slightly narrower at base than elytra, and carinate laterally, without sublateral lines. Procoxal cavities open behind. Scutellum small, visible. Elytra long and completely covering abdomen, straight-sided, with more or less distinct rows of punctures. Legs short and stout, tarsi 5-5-5 in both sexes, tarsomeres not lobed underneath, with simple claws equal in length. Abdomen with five ventrites free.

SIMILAR FAMILIES
- wrinkled bark beetles (Carabidae, p.99)—pronotum deeply sulcate
- cylindrical bark beetles (Zopheridae, p.341)—antennae capitate
- some darkling beetles (Tenebrionidae, p.347)—antennal insertions hidden from above
- silvanid beetles (Silvanidae, p.451)—antennae not moniliform
- flat bark beetles (Cucujidae, p.453)—flattened, pronotum quadrate, males 5-5-4
- lined flat bark beetles (Laemophloeidae, p.458)—flattened, distinct lines along sides of head and pronotum

COLLECTING NOTES Look for passandrids under bark and at lights. They are sometimes found in Malaise and flight intercept trap samples.

455

FAUNA THREE SPECIES IN TWO GENERA

Catogenus thomasi Ślipiński (8.0–12.0 mm) is elongate, somewhat flat, weakly shiny, and uniformly mahogany brown. Head rugosely punctate, usually with occipital region deeply sulcate, medial longitudinal groove faint and flanked by elongate pits, with eyes small, their diameter subequal to width of scape, and terminal antennomere asymmetrical with smooth keel apically. Pronotum slightly longer than wide, weakly convex, depressed medially, and densely punctured, with vestigial submarginal lines barely visible in basal one-fourth. Elytra sparsely punctured laterally beyond sharp humeral carinae. Last ventrite with preapical sulcus. Adults attracted to lights in desert, thorn scrub, and upland habitats. Arizona and Oaxaca. (1)

PHALACRIDAE (fa-lak'-ri-dē)
SHINING FLOWER AND SHINING MOLD BEETLES

Phalacrids are round, strongly convex beetles with flat undersides and have the ability to foil predators by tucking in their appendages. Their form and behavior not only shield them from attacks, but also allow them to escape danger by rolling off leaves and taking to the air, or simply falling to the ground. Adults feed on either pollen or fungal structures. Some adult and larval phalacrids are associated with fungi that cause diseases in vascular plants, including ergots, rusts, and smuts. They are apparently important natural control agents of these diseases because any spores they ingest become unviable. Despite this apparent beneficial behavior, their use as biological control agents still awaits further study. *Acylomus* adults feed on saprophytic fungi found on dead or dying plant structures, and are often associated with ergot fungi or molds growing on clusters of drying leaves, dead legume pods, and cotton bolls. *Phalacrus* is associated with the spores of smut fungi. *Stilbus* nibbles on molds growing on plant surfaces, especially those of grasses. Pollen-feeding species of *Olibrus* are commonly found on composite flowers in late summer, where their larvae develop in the flower heads on a diet of plant fluids. Examination of male genitalia is usually required for species identification.

FAMILY DIAGNOSIS Adult phalacrids are small, broadly oval to nearly circular with a continuous body outline, very convex above and flat below, shiny brownish or black, and completely glabrous dorsally. Head hypognathous and smooth, and visible from above, with eyes not prominent. Antennae with 11 antennomeres, antennomeres 9–11 forming elongate club, with 11 largest. Scutellum somewhat large, triangular. Elytra completely cover abdomen, with or without one or two striae near suture, and combined apices rounded. Legs with tarsi 5-5-5 (5-5-4 in some, especially males), tarsomeres 1–3 broad and setose underneath, 4 small and obscure, with claws toothed or appendiculate basally. Abdomen with five ventrites free.

SIMILAR FAMILIES
- minute beetles (Clambidae, p.113)—can partially roll up
- marsh beetles (Scirtidae, p.114)—antennae not clubbed
- water scavenger beetles (Hydrophilidae, p.122)—usually more than 3 mm long; mouthparts elongate
- round fungus beetles (Leiodidae, p.137)—antennal club with three to five antennomeres, antennomere 8 usually reduced in size, tibia usually shiny, expanded, spiny
- lady beetles (Coccinellidae, p.318)—antennae short, club with three to six antennomeres, often clothed in setae
- pleasing fungus beetles (Erotylidae, p.435)—rarely as convex, usually black with red, yellow, or orange
- sap beetles (Nitidulidae, p.443)—antennae distinctly capitate, clothed in dorsal setae

COLLECTING NOTES Adult phalacrids are collected by carefully inspecting flowers, beating and sweeping grasses and shrubs, or by searching moldy grass and other vegetation, plants infected with smut, and fungus on decaying logs in forested habitats. Check tree branches broken off by summer storms for clumps of dried leaves that might harbor adult and larval phalacrids within wilted and curled surfaces. Cutting branches of hardwood trees, bundling them up, and then hanging them in shady places will duplicate this microhabitat. Hibernating adults are sometimes sifted from leaf litter or found under boards and stones in open fields and under beach drift from late fall through early spring. Malaise and black light traps will produce additional specimens.

FAUNA 122 SPECIES IN 12 GENERA

Olibrus species (1.0–2.8 mm) are ovoid, with greasy, not iridescent, luster. Eyes with facets similar in size and margins entire, apical margin of clypeus more or less straight. Antennomere 11 top-shaped, or conical. Pronotal posterior angles evident, tightly appressed against base of elytra when at rest. Elytra very shiny, with sutural and one or two discal striae, and punctures indistinct. Middle leg with tarsomere 1 shorter than 2, hind leg with metatibial spurs narrow. Diurnal adults are generalist feeders on pollen, while host-specific larvae feed and develop inside of flower heads of composites. Widespread in North America. Genus needs revision. (28 NA)

Phalacrus species (1.7–3.6 mm) are typically oval, convex, and shiny black. Head with eyes small, clypeal margin not emarginate and concealing antennal bases, terminal antennomere elongate, and mandibles prominent, curved, and pointed. Pronotum very finely punctate and sharply margined basally. Scutellum large, wider than distance between elytral striae. Elytra each with single, distinct sutural stria sometimes greatly reduced, but rarely absent. Legs with tibial spur formula 2-2-2, metatibial spurs short, tarsal formula 5-5-5 in both sexes, and robust tarsi. Adults feed on smut and rust fungi and are found on flowers or swept from vegetation; attracted to lights. Throughout western North America. (13)

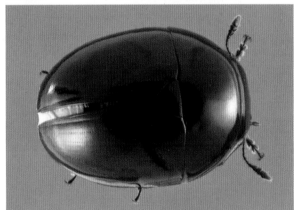

457

Stilbus apicalis (Melsheimer) (1.6–2.4 mm) is relatively elongate, oval, convex, polished brown to black, with apical third of elytra, underside, and appendages yellowish to yellowish brown. Head about half as wide as prothorax, with antennal bases visible from above. Pronotum broad. Elytra each with sutural stria that disappears before reaching scutellum. Legs with tibial spurs small, inconspicuous, hind tarsi short with tarsomere 1 shorter than 2, and all tarsi 5-5-4. Adults and larvae likely graze on molds growing on grasses; adults attracted to lights. Males seldom collected. Transcontinental; in West from British Columbia to California, east to Idaho. Genus needs revision. (22)

LAEMOPHLOEIDAE (lē-mō-flō'-i-dē)
LINED FLAT BARK BEETLES

Little is known about the biology of most laemophloeids. Both adults and larvae are found beneath the bark of logs, usually hardwoods such as oak (*Quercus*). Some feed on fungal spores and hyphae in leaf litter and under bark, or in the galleries of bark beetles (Curculionidae, p.539), while others occur on the fruiting bodies of ascomycete fungi. *Narthecius* is found in galleries under bark and apparently preys on bark beetles. *Cryptolestes curus* Lefkovitch, a native of the Middle East, was apparently introduced into Arizona with date palms and preys on the red date palm scale, *Phoenicoccus marlatti*. The elongate, flattened larvae of laemophloeids are unique among the Coleoptera in producing silk from a pair of prothoracic glands to form a cocoon in which they pupate.

FAMILY DIAGNOSIS Adult laemophloeids are usually flattened or somewhat cylindrical (*Narthecius*), and usually with a pair of fine carinae or grooves along sides of head and pronotum. Head prognathous and broad, with sides bordered by carina or groove (absent in *Lathropus*), widest across round or oval eyes, and mandibles stout to elongate, sometimes visible from above. Antennae usually filiform with 10 antennomeres. Procoxal cavities open to closed behind. Scutellum broad to triangular. Elytra usually with a carina running from humerus, with side margins (epipleural fold) moderate to broad and complete from base to apex. Legs slender, with tarsi 5-5-5 (female), usually 5-5-4 in male, with tarsomere 1 long; and simple claws. Abdomen with five ventrites free.

- powderpost beetles (Bostrichidae: Lyctinae, p.299)—antennae short, club with two antennomeres
- cylindrical bark beetles (Zopheridae, p.341)—antennal club distinct
- *Adelina* (Tenebrionidae, p.367)—no grooves or ridges on head or pronotum
- silvanid beetles (Silvanidae, p.451)—tarsomere 1 longer than 2
- flat bark beetles (Cucujidae, p.453)—antennomere 1 short, tarsi lobed
- parasitic flat bark beetles (Passandridae, p.455)—maxillae hidden; elytra, not pronotum, with distinct lines; tarsi 5-5-5 in both sexes

SIMILAR FAMILIES
- wrinkled bark beetles (Carabidae, p.99)—prothorax with deep grooves

COLLECTING NOTES Adults are found under bark of oak and other deciduous hardwoods, beaten from dead branches, or attracted to lights at night.

FAUNA 52 SPECIES IN 13 GENERA

Laemophloeus biguttatus Say (1.9–3.9 mm) is oblong-oval, flat, densely and coarsely punctate dorsally, conspicuously pubescent, and uniformly reddish brown or blackish with a small, distinct, oval medial spot on each elytron. Appendages and underside paler. Head with distinct frontoclypeal suture, and labrum shallowly emarginate apically. Pronotum with sublateral grooves and lateral margins weakly arcuate with minutely prominent angles. Elytra carinate laterally, each with three discal striae. Ventrite 2 with apex of intercoxal process acute. Adults and larvae eat ascomycete fungi. California east across United States, south to Mexico. *Laemophloeus apache* Thomas darker with basal elytral spot long, mostly in second interval. (4)

CYBOCEPHALIDAE (sib-ō-sef-al'-i-dē)
CYBOCEPHALID BEETLES

The Cybocephalidae, once considered a subfamily of Nitidulidae (p.443), consist of seven genera worldwide. Only five species of cybocephalids, all *Cybocephalus*, occur in North America, two of which are known in the West. They are capable of tightly tucking the head and appendages in against the body so that their mandibles rest on the underside of the thorax. Unlike nitidulids, cybocephalids are exclusively predators and prey primarily on armored scales (Diaspidae), but will occasionally attack whiteflies (Aleyrodidae), mealybugs (Pseudococcidae), and citrus red mites (*Panonychus citri*). Several species have been released in various parts of the world as biological control agents of scale insects. For example, *C. nipponicus* Endrody-Younga was released in Florida to control scale insects on sago palms (*Cycas*) and has been introduced into additional states to prey on other scale insects, too.

FAMILY DIAGNOSIS Adult cybocephalid beetles are ovate, very convex, black or bicolored, and capable of contracting all appendages tight against body. Head prognathous, deflexed, and very broad, nearly as wide as prothorax. Antennae with 11 antennomeres, longer than width of head, with antennomeres 9–11 forming flat club. Pronotum with sides short, margined base covering base of elytra. Underside of thorax impressed to receive middle and hind legs. Procoxal cavities closed behind. Scutellum large, triangular. Elytra long, nearly covering pygidium. Legs with tibiae simple, tarsi 4-4-4, with each tarsomere slightly expanded underneath, tarsomeres 2 and 3 bilobed, and simple claws. Abdomen with five ventrites free.

SIMILAR FAMILIES

- minute beetles (Clambidae, p.113)—antennal club with two antennomeres, clypeus completely covers mouth, hind coxae enlarged
- *Agathidium* (Leiodidae, p.139)—tarsi 5-5-4 (male), 5-4-4 (female)
- lady beetles (Coccinellidae, p.318)—head narrower, inserted in prothorax, tarsi 4-4-4, appear 3-3-3
- shining flower and mold beetles (Phalacridae, p.456)—tarsi 5-5-5; antennal club elongate

COLLECTING NOTES Adults are collected by beating or sweeping sagebrush (*Artemisia*), in Malaise traps, or occasionally in pitfall traps.

459

FAUNA FIVE SPECIES IN ONE GENUS

Cybocephalus californicus Horn (0.9–1.3 mm) is elongate-ovate, smooth, strongly convex dorsally, and shiny black or brown with occasional brassy tinge, with lateral pronotal margins and elytral apices translucent yellow. Serrate antennal club smaller than large, oblong eye, and truncate or slightly emarginate apically. Pronotal angles narrowly arcuate, especially anteriorly, and disc alutaceous and finely punctate. Elytra uniformly punctate, with translucent apices broadly impunctate. British Columbia to California, east to Montana, Colorado, Oklahoma, and Texas. *Cybocephalus randalli* T.R. Smith (1.2–1.3 mm) black, with apex of serrate antennal club rounded. Washington to California, east to Idaho and Utah. Adults of both species on sagebrush (*Artemisia*). (2)

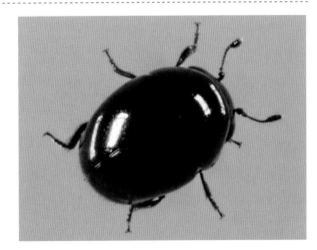

CERAMBYCIDAE (ser-am-bis'-i-dē)
LONGHORN BEETLES

Longhorn beetles are particularly conspicuous because of their long antennae, large size, or bright colors. Adults are commonly found in wooded areas, where they are attracted to freshly painted surfaces, cut wood, flowers, or lights at night. They are commonly found in dead or damaged tree material, twigs, and small branches of woody plants. Bright and contrastingly colored species are typically diurnal flower visitors that look and behave like stinging wasps. Nocturnal species are mostly dull black or brown and spend their days hiding beneath logs and bark, emerging at dusk or in the evening to search mainly for mates. Others are cryptically marked and camouflaged against the bark of trees, allowing them to hide in plain sight. Adults of some species apparently do not feed at all, while others consume twigs, bark, and fibrous inner bark (bast), or eat leaves, needles, cones, fruits, and sap. Flower-visiting lepturine longhorns ingest pollen, stamens, and nectar. Males often have long antennae and use them to guard females while they are ovipositing. Eggs are usually laid in cracks or crevices in bark, or about injuries on trunks or branches. Adult female *Oncideres* prepare food for their larvae by gnawing a channel around small twigs of living trees and shrubs before laying an egg just past the girdle. Girdling quickly kills the outer portion of the branch, thus providing food for the developing larvae. The plump and cylindrical larvae, commonly known as roundheaded borers, are all phytophagous. They typically feed internally, attacking dead and decaying wood, or living trees, shrubs, and other plants by chewing their way into branches, trunks, stems, roots, and cones. *Prionus* larvae attack dead wood, as well as roots of living trees, woody shrubs and vines, even grasses. Larvae of *Styloxus* and *Aneflomorpha* girdle twigs from the inside by consuming their pithy centers, while others induce galls and other abnormal tissue growths as they feed. Larval *Saperda* kill and deform larger branches as they feed, resulting in galls and other abnormalities. *Crossidius* larvae feed internally upon the roots and root crowns of their host plants, while those of *Tetraopes* burrow through the soil to feed externally. The wood-feeding activities of cerambycid larvae contribute to the breakdown of trees weakened or killed by storms, fires, and infestations of other insects, and thus play a critical ecological role in the recycling of nutrients. Species in the genera *Trichocnemis, Prionus, Arhopalus, Asemum*, and *Monochamus* are occasionally pests in managed forests where trees are valued for their lumber. Injured or drought-stressed shade and ornamental trees are particularly susceptible to attack. Phylogenetic studies currently underway that include both Nearctic and Palearctic taxa will likely result in significant changes to the tribal classification presented here (p.580).

FAMILY DIAGNOSIS Adult cerambycids are extremely variable in shape. They are usually robust, broad across base of elytra, with antennae at least half as long as body, sometimes much longer, and usually longest in male. Head prognathous and strongly deflexed, sometimes elongated into a narrow muzzle (Lepturinae), with eyes usually notched around antennal bases. Lateral prothoracic carinae present (*Neandra*), sometimes serrate or coarsely dentate (Prioninae), or absent. Procoxal cavities broadly open to narrowly closed behind. Scutellum visible. Elytra usually long and usually covering all or most of abdomen, or distinctly shortened (*Methia, Molorchus, Necydalis, Styloxus, Ulochaetes*). Tarsi typically appear 4-4-4, but actually 5-5-5 with tarsomere 4 small and tucked between lobes of heart-shaped 3; rarely obviously 5-5-5 (*Neandra, Neospondylis*). Abdomen with five ventrites free.

SIMILAR FAMILIES

- stag beetles (Lucanidae, p.164)—antennal club asymmetrical
- soldier beetles (Cantharidae, p.265)—tarsi distinctly 5-5-5, body and elytra soft
- false longhorn beetles (Stenotrachelidae, p.372)—claws pectinate, tarsi 5-5-4
- false blister beetles (Oedemeridae, p.374)—pronotum broadest in front, tarsi 5-5-4
- orsodacnid leaf beetles (Orsodacnidae, p.499)—antennae short, pronotum widest in front
- some leaf beetles (Chrysomelidae, p.501)—antennae and body short, or pronotum broadest in front, or elytra broadest at apices

COLLECTING NOTES Look for diurnal longhorn beetles on flowers or resting on leaves and stems. Nocturnal species hide under loose bark of logs and stumps during the day, and are attracted to lights placed at night in openings surrounded by woods. Be sure to check for longhorns in the shadows just beyond the light's glow. Beating and sweeping branches and leaves of larval host plants during the day is also productive. Check downed logs and freshly cut wood day and night (p.45, Fig. 49). Beetles will often take cover under green branches placed on freshly cut stumps. Some species are attracted to fermenting molasses and watermelon rinds, while conifer feeders are attracted to fresh paint, turpentine, and other solvents. Another very productive method is to collect sections of larvae-infested wood and place them in a rearing container from which emerging adults cannot escape (p.65).

FAUNA ~958 SPECIES IN ~306 GENERA

Neandra marginicollis **(Schaeffer)** (14.0–22.0 mm, mandibles excluded) is robust, broadly oblong, shiny and smooth reddish brown, with prominent mandibles and short antennae. Eyes emarginate. Pronotum wider in front (male) or not (female), anterior margin nearly straight between angles, with transverse impression deeply impressed laterally. Elytra more finely and sparsely punctured than pronotum. Claws without bristlelike *onychium* in between. Adults found under bark of old stumps of western sycamore *(Platanus racemosa)* and white alder *(Alnus rhombifolia)*; also attracted to lights during summer. Larvae bore into heartwood of these and other hardwoods, leaving the outer, living sapwood intact. Coastal southern California, montane southeastern Arizona. (1)

Trichocnemis pauper **(Linsley)** (45.0–50.0 mm) is large, elongate, two-toned brown with elytra lighter. Mandibles shorter than half length of small head. Antennae slender, surpassing middle of elytra (male), or not (female). Pronotum with deep depressions (male) or not (female); lateral margins with spines generally of equal length. Elytra uniformly pale brown, inner angles of apices without spines. Larvae develop in oaks (*Q. agrifolia*, *Q. chrysolepis*, *Q. kelloggi*, *Q. wislezeni*). Adults, especially females, are attracted to lights during summer. Southern Sierra Nevada, Coast and Transverse Ranges, California. (2)

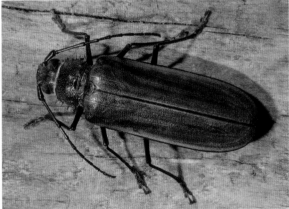

Ponderous Borer *Trichocnemis spiculatus spiculatus* **(LeConte)** (40.0–65.0 mm) is very large, more or less uniformly dark brown, with short mandibles. Antennae slender, surpassing middle of elytra (male), or not (female). Pronotum coarsely punctured with five deep depressions (male) or low calluses (female), with uneven lateral spines on margins. Elytral apices at suture spinose. Larvae in conifer logs and stumps, including *Pinus ponderosa*, *Pseudotsuga menziesii*, *Sequoia sempervirens*, forming broad channels in heartwood packed with coarse frass; emergence holes elliptical. Adults fly at dusk and attracted to lights, especially females. Southern British Columbia to Baja California, east to western Montana. (2)

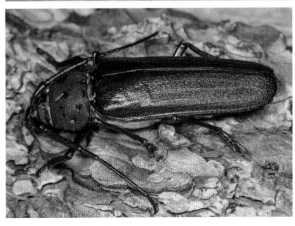

Trichocnemis spiculatus neomexicanus Casey (40.0–65.0mm) is very large, robust, with reddish-brown elytra with concentrated irregular pale blotches between costae, and short mandibles. Antennae slender, surpassing middle of elytra (male), or not (female). Pronotum coarsely punctured with five deep depressions (male) or low calluses (female), with uneven spines on lateral margins. Larvae mine heartwood of pines, forming broad channels in heartwood packed with coarse frass; large emergence holes elliptical. Nocturnal adults attracted to lights, on larval infested logs and stumps, and beneath loose bark of ponderosa pine (*Pinus ponderosa*) snags. Rocky Mountains to southeastern Arizona, New Mexico, and northern Sonora. (1)

Willow Root Borer *Archodontes melanopus aridus* **Casey** (21.0–47.0mm, without mandibles) is large, elongate, parallel-sided, uniformly dark shiny brown with mandibles projecting downward. Head large with relatively long mandibles lacking dorsal carinae, without internal teeth (male), antennae slender, with tubercles obtuse. Pronotum about as long as wide, with lateral margins subparallel, crenulate, rarely serrate or dentate, about as wide as base of elytra. Adults active in summer, flying at dusk around broom (*Baccharis*) or about the larval host plant, willow (*Salix*); attracted to lights. Colorado River drainage in southeastern California and western Arizona. (1)

Hardwood Stump Borer *Mallodon dasystomus* (Say) (20.0–50.0mm) is large, elongate, somewhat flattened, and dark reddish brown. Head large, prognathous, very coarsely punctured; antennae slender, tubercles acute, reaching basal third (male), or shorter (female), prominent mandibles arcuate, setose, not constricted at base, slightly longer than head (male), finely carinate dorsally; antennae not surpassing (male) or attaining (female) middle of elytra. Lateral pronotal margins spinose, disc with polished facets (male) or mostly smooth (female). Elytra appear smooth. Larvae in heartwood of living and recently dead sycamore (*Platanus wrightii*), and other hardwoods. Adults attracted to lights. Southeastern Arizona to Virginia and Florida, south to Colombia. (1)

Southwestern Stump Borer *Nothopleurus lobigenis* Bates (20.0–52.8 mm) is elongate-oblong, flattened, and shiny dark reddish brown. Antennae scarcely surpassing (male) or not reaching (female) middle. Outer margins of mandibles straight or slightly arcuate, distinctly longer (male) or shorter (female) than head, not narrowed basally. Pronotal margins with five or more small spines of equal length. Elytra smooth. Larvae in roots of honey mesquite *(Prosopis glandulosa)* and ornamental hardwoods. Southeastern California to Texas, south to Mexico. *Nothopleurus madericus* (Skiles) (20.0–46.0 mm, with mandibles) mandibles strongly and evenly arcuate externally, male's only slightly longer than head, and abruptly narrowed basally. Arizona and Chihuahua. Both species at lights. (2)

Hairy Pine Borer *Tragosoma harrisii* LeConte (18.0–36.0 mm) is elongate, shiny brown to dark brown. Antennae slender, reaching elytral apices in male, with poriferous area on antennomere 3 on apical third or fourth. Prothorax with single spine on each side, densely hairy in male, less so in female. Elytral surface wrinkled with scattered punctures. Larvae in sapwood of decaying pines *(Pinus)* above 1,500 meters. Adults attracted to lights. Transcontinental; in West from British Columbia south to southern California, and Rockies to Chihuahua. *Tragosoma soror* Laplante poriferous area on antennomere 3 of male covering about apical half. British Columbia to central California, east to western Montana. (4)

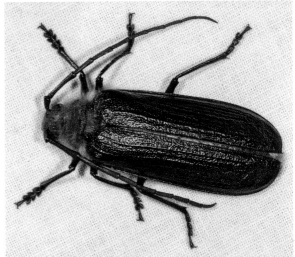

Tragosoma pilosicorne Casey (24.0–28.0 mm) is elongate, shiny pale brown. Head and pronotum nearly glabrous. Elytra coarsely and deeply punctured, apical sutural spines longer than pronotal spines. Larvae develop in sound or rotten dead trunks and fallen limbs of gray *(Pinus sabiniana)* and ponderosa *(P. ponderosa)* pines. Males, occasionally females, at lights during summer in dry habitats. Southern Oregon and throughout California in Sierra Nevada, Coastal, Transverse, and Peninsular Ranges. *Tragosoma spiculum* Casey (23.0–31.0 mm) darker with pronotal and elytral punctation sparser, apical sutural spines half as long as pronotal spines; southern Rockies, breeds in Chihuahua pine *(P. chihuahuana)* in mountains of southeastern Arizona. (4)

463

Palo Verde Beetle *Derobrachus hovorei* Santos-Silva (33.0–70.2 mm) is dark reddish brown. Head prognathous, antennae slender with 11 antennomeres, 3 coarsely granulate, longer than 1 and 2 combined, robust, apical width at least one-third of length, and thickened apically in male. Lateral pronotal margin with three spines, anterior spine divided. Metasternum with long, dense setae. Larvae in *Parkinsonia*, *Prosopis*, *Quercus*, and *Populus*. Mostly males at lights. *Derobrachus leechi* Chemsak & Linsley, antennomere 3 thick, not granulate; mesosternal setae short, sparse. *D. geminatus* LeConte, antennomere 3 narrow, apical width less than one-third of length. All from southern California to southwestern New Mexico; Mexico. (3)

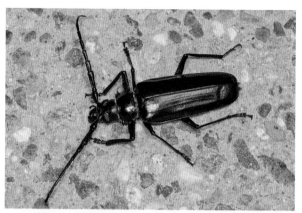

California Prionus *Prionus californicus* Motschulsky (24.0–55.0 mm, with mandibles) is robust and dark reddish brown. Antennae with 12 antennomeres, distinctly serrate, thick and exceeding two-thirds length of elytra (male), or slender, reaching middle (female). Lateral pronotal margins with three spines. Larvae in roots of living and dead *Quercus*, *Populus*, other hardwoods, conifers, and grasses growing in light, well-drained soils. Mostly males at lights in summer, early fall. Western North America, except deserts. *Prionus lecontei* Lameere (52.0–60.0 mm) has 13 antennomeres, with flightless females larger, heavier; larvae in oaks; southern Sierra Nevada, southern California mountains. (3)

Prionus heroicus Semenov (37.0–52.0 mm, with mandibles) is large, very robust, broadly oblong, dark brown to blackish, with appendages and underside often lighter. Males of *P. heroicus* differ from those of *P. californicus* by the meso- and metatibial apices not spined at dorsal margin. Females with metasternum distinctly pubescent laterally, while that of *P. californicus* is usually pubescent throughout. Larvae probably develop in oak (*Quercus*). Adults, especially males, fly late afternoon and at dusk; also attracted to lights. Colorado to Arizona and New Mexico. (3)

Desmocerus aureipennis aureipennis Chevrolat (23.0–30.0 mm) is stout, broad-shouldered, tapered posteriorly, coarsely punctured and nearly glabrous dorsally, with head and body dull black. Antennae about as long as body (male), or shorter (female). Pronotum wider than long, disc coarsely punctate. Elytra entirely orange (male) or bluish green with broad orange margins (female). Larvae mine pithy stem bases of blue elderberry (*Sambucus nigra cerulea*) at elevations above 1,700 meters, and take two years to mature; adults on foliage of larval hosts that have recently bloomed. Klamath Mountains and Sierra Nevada, California. (5)

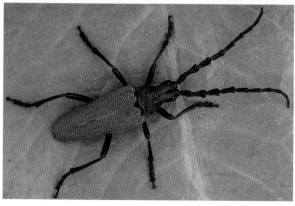

California Elderberry Longhorn Borer *Desmocerus californicus californicus* Horn (13.0–25.0 mm) is stout, broad-shouldered, tapered posteriorly, head and body black, with long pale pubescence. Antennae about as long as body (male), or shorter (female). Head rugose punctate. Pronotum without large irregular wrinkles. Elytra of both sexes mostly blue-black with narrow red-orange borders. Larvae and adults on blue elderberry (*Sambucus nigra cerulea*) in summer. Pacific Coast of California, from central Coast Ranges south to Orange County. Valley elderberry longhorn beetle *D. c. dimorphus* Fisher (p.44, Fig. 46e) is listed as federally threatened. (5)

Desmocerus cribripennis Horn (11.5–21.0 mm) is broad-shouldered, tapered posteriorly, with head and body dull black, pale pubescence, and antennae as long as body (male), or shorter (female). Head punctate-rugose. Pronotum and elytra with equally long setae. Pronotum cribrate. Elytra metallic blue-green with narrow orange margins. Diurnal adults on *Sambucus racemosa* flowers and foliage during summer. Pacific Coast, southern British Columbia to central Coast Ranges of California. *Desmocerus piperi* Webb (14.0–20.0 mm) head mostly punctate, dorsal setae short, male elytra entirely orange; on *Sambucus racemosa* var. *melanocarpa*, southeastern British Columbia and southwestern Alberta, south to eastern Oregon. (5)

Anastrangalia laetifica (**LeConte**) (7.0–13.0 mm) is tapered posteriorly, and sexually dimorphic with male variable in color. Head with temples somewhat parallel and weakly serrate antennae. Male elytra shiny, densely punctate, punctures equal to or smaller than those on pronotum, uniformly black, reddish and black, or brown and black. Female elytra dull, moderately coarsely punctate, and reddish with pair of black sutural spots at basal one-third and near margins at middle. Larvae in pine (*Pinus*). Adults on spring and early summer flowers of annuals and shrubs. Washington and western Montana to southern California. (3)

Cyphonotida rostrata borealis **Linsley & Chemsak** (9.0–16.0 mm) is broad-shouldered and tapering posteriorly. Elongate head black, antennomeres becoming gradually thicker apically. Convex pronotum red, with hind angles rounded. Elytra black, coarse basal punctures becoming finer apically, humeri reddish externally, with apices obliquely truncate to sinuate, external angles angulate to weakly produced. Underside mostly reddish orange. Legs mostly black, meso- and metatibiae partly red. On flowers of *Baccharis*, *Brickellia*, *Guardiola*, *Mimosa*, and *Dalea*. Central and southeastern Arizona to northern Mexico. (1)

Etorofus soror (**LeConte**) (9.0–17.0 mm) is elongate, tapering posteriorly, with pale elytra marked with black bands. Pronotum mostly black with narrowly lighter lateral and posterior margins, disc with deep punctures, densely clothed in somewhat depressed golden setae. Elytra yellowish brown with median transverse bands broad, uniting at suture, apices oblique, outer angle spinose; rarely with subbasal spots. Larvae in pines (*Pinus*). Diurnal adults on spring and summer flowers, including ceanothus (*Ceanothus*), lupine (*Lupinus*), buckwheat (*Eriogonum*), and yarrow (*Achillea*). Sierra Nevada, California. *Etorofus obliteratus* (Haldeman) similar, pale elytra usually infuscate with subbasal spots. British Columbia to western Montana, south to central Coast Ranges of California. (6)

Grammoptera militaris (**Chevrolat**) (4.0–6.0 mm) is small, somewhat parallel-sided, metallic greenish or bluish, with reddish humeri. Head with temples not inflated, convergent to neck; antennae reaching middle (female) or not reaching elytral apices. Pronotum convex, slightly longer than wide, sides barely sinuate, base not impressed across middle. Elytral punctures sparse at reddish humeri, remainder of basal half coarsely, contiguously punctate and becoming finer toward apices, and lateral margins slightly expanding toward apices. Diurnal adults found on various spring and summer flowers, including ceanothus (*Ceanothus*), cowparsnip (*Heracleum*), monkey flower (*Mimulus*), buckeye (*Aesculus*), sumac (*Rhus*), and mesquite (*Prosopis*). Central California to northern Baja California. (4)

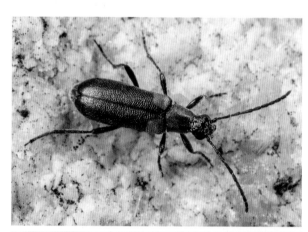

Grammoptera molybdica (**LeConte**) (4.0–7.0 mm) is small, somewhat parallel-sided, metallic greenish or bluish. Head with temples not inflated, convergent to neck; antennae reaching middle (female) or not reaching elytral apices. Pronotum convex, slightly longer than wide, sides moderately sinuate, base not impressed across middle. Elytra with punctures moderately coarse on basal half, becoming finer and more dispersed apically, and lateral margins slightly expanding toward apices. Legs slender, front femora sometimes bicolored. Diurnal adults found on various spring and summer flowers, including ceanothus (*Ceanothus*), dogwood (*Cornus*), Queen Anne's lace (*Daucus*), rose (*Rosa*), buckeye (*Aesculus*), manzanita (*Arctostaphylos*), and buckthorn (*Frangula*). British Columbia to Idaho and southern California. (4)

Lepturopsis dolorosa (LeConte) (9.0–16.0 mm) is robust, tapering posteriorly, and black. Head abruptly constricted behind eyes. Pronotum convex, wider than long, with sides rounder and narrow longitudinal impression on disc. Scutellum lying below surface of elytra, flanked by more or less distinct basal elytral lobes. Elytral apices slightly dehiscent. Larvae utilize Douglas-fir (*Pseudotsuga menziesii*). Diurnal adults on various spring and summer flowers, including buckwheat (*Eriogonum*), yarrow (*Achillea*), ceanothus (*Ceanothus*), chinquapin (*Chrysolepis*), elderberry (*Sambucus*), goldenrod (*Solidago*), spirea (*Spiraea*), and mullein (*Verbascum*). British Columbia and Idaho to central California. (1)

Neobellamira delicata australis Linsley & Chemsak (9.0–11.0 mm) is elongate, broad-shouldered, with sides of elytra arcuate and narrowed apically. Males with head, pronotum, thoracic sterna, antennae, hind tibiae, and tarsi black; elytra yellowish brown with at least apical one-third infuscate, margins black, and each elytron with black basal stripe. Females reddish with elytra partially infuscate, basal dark stripes vague or absent. Elytral apices dehiscent, surpassed by tapered abdomen. Diurnal adults on various flowers, including ceanothus (*Ceanothus*), buckwheat (*Eriogonum*), and chamise (*Adenostoma*) in spring and summer. Transverse and Peninsular Ranges, southern California. *Neobellamira d. delicata* (LeConte), western Oregon to southern Sierra Nevada of California. (1)

Ortholeptura valida (LeConte) (17.0–28.0 mm) is stout, elongate, somewhat parallel-sided, and yellow-brown. Head with eyes coarsely faceted, antennomere 3 subequal to 1 (scape). Pronotum longer than wide, with disc constricted anteriorly and posteriorly, and posterior angles rounded. Elytra each with two or three sets of dark oblique spots, with apices spinose at suture. Larvae develop in decaying conifers (*Abies*, *Pinus*, *Pseudotsuga*, *Tsuga*). Adults at lights during summer. Oregon to southern California. *Ortholeptura insignis* (Fall) (21.0–27.0 mm) is reddish brown, elytra striped with apices subtruncate, rounded, or dentate at suture; coastal California. *O. obscura* (Swaine & Hopping) (21.0–27.0 mm) eastern Washington and Oregon. (3)

Stenostrophia tribalteata sierra Linsley & Chemsak (7.0–
12.0 mm) is moderately robust, tapering, and with bicolored
pronotal and elytral pubescence. Head densely pubescent
and slender antennae dark. Pronotum impressed anteriorly
and posteriorly, sinuate laterally, with dense bristly black
setae on disc, and yellow pubescence along margins.
Transverse yellow elytral bands broader, and apices
obliquely truncate. Legs orangish. Oregon to southern
California. *Stenostrophia tribalteata tribalteata* (LeConte)
similar, pronotum also with long, pale, erect setae (male)
or suberect dark setae (female); east of Sierra Nevada. *S.
t. serpentina* (Casey) sparsely pubescent, vertex glabrous,
with narrow yellow pubescence on pronotal margins, and
black elytral bands broader; Rocky Mountains, central
Nevada. (3)

Stictoleptura canadensis cribripennis (LeConte)
(11.0–24.0 mm) is moderately robust, tapering, and
variably marked. Antennae with 12 antennomeres, 5–10
slightly serrate, 4–8 usually annulated, 8 entirely pale or at
most with apical third dark. Pronotum and elytra coarsely
punctured. Pronotum almost as long a wide, angles
rounded, with apical and basal impressions. Elytra with
basal third to half red (male, left), or almost entirely reddish,
black, or black with basal red spots (female, right); apices
dentate. Diurnal adults on summer flowers (*Chrysolepis*,
Epilobium); larvae develop in conifers, oak (*Quercus*).
British Columbia to northern Sierra Nevada of California,
east to Manitoba and Rocky Mountains to southern New
Mexico. (1)

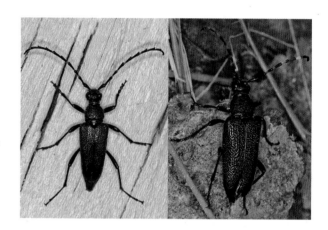

Strophiona tigrina Casey (9.0–15.0 mm) is moderately
robust, tapering. Front of head and abdomen reddish
orange. Pronotum as long as or longer than wide, disc
coarsely punctate and usually obscured by pubescence.
Elytra each with narrow band across humerus, oblique
subbasal band sometimes not reaching suture, elongate
medial spot on side never reaching suture, and broad
subapical and narrow apical bands. Legs yellowish.
Adults on various summer flowers; larvae develop in oak
(*Quercus*). Washington to southern California. *Strophiona
laeta* (LeConte) (10.0–16.0 mm) pronotum wider than
long, with disc finely punctate and usually visible medially;
subbasal elytral band transverse. On summer flowers from
southern British Columbia to southern California, east to
New Mexico. (2)

Typocerus balteatus Horn (9.0–15.0 mm) is moderately robust and tapering. Head elongate, bicolorous. Antennae with 11 antennomeres in both sexes, about as long (male) or shorter (female) than elytra, 1–5 pale and slender, remaining articles dark, thick, and serrate. Pronotum about as long as wide, disc not strongly inflated, with depressed golden pubescence, and apical and posterior bands dense. Elytra yellow, usually with four, sometimes three narrow transverse black bands occasionally reduced to black spots, apices slightly emarginate-truncate. Legs slender, mostly pale, with tarsi sometimes darker. Diurnal adults on various late summer flowers; larvae develop in *Ceanothus*, possibly *Ericameria*. South-central Alberta to east-central California, southern Arizona, and New Mexico. (3)

Xestoleptura crassipes (LeConte) (8.0–15.0 mm) is elongate, tapered (male) or parallel-sided (female). Antennae stout, antennomeres not strongly expanded at apices, as long (male), or half (female) length of elytra. Pronotum convex, lateral margins angulate, disc densely punctate and moderately clothed in erect pubescence. Elytra yellowish and densely pubescent, with two black median spots usually not reaching suture and transverse bands at apical third and apices black. Hind tibia of male with apical plate internally. Larvae in conifers; diurnal adults on flowers. British Columbia to southern California, east to Colorado. *Xestoleptura crassicornis* (LeConte) (10.0–17.0 mm) elytra glabrous, with broad transverse bands. Washington to southern California, east to Rockies. (4)

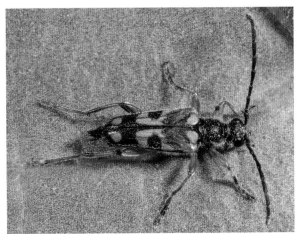

Centrodera spurca (LeConte) (19.0–30.0 mm) is robust, broad-shouldered, shiny pale brownish yellow. Eyes coarsely faceted. Antennomeres longer (male) or shorter (female) than body. Pronotum with lateral tubercles, coarsely punctate, sparsely pubescent. Elytra with basal half coarsely, closely punctate with depressed and recurved pubescence sparse, each with single black marginal spot at middle, apices truncate and toothed at suture. Larvae feed in rotting stumps and roots of oak (*Quercus*), madrone (*Arbutus*), service-berry (*Amelanchier*), and shepherdia (*Shepherdia*). Adults attracted to lights and fermenting bait traps during summer in montane habitats. Southern British Columbia to southern California, western Montana, and Utah. (8)

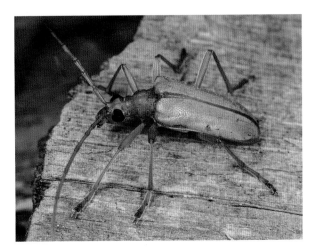

Cortodera cubitalis (LeConte) (6.0–12.0 mm) is slender, elongate, with both sexes either yellowish brown or black with pale humeri, and elytra tapering posteriorly. Short head with entire eyes, and slender antennae extending to middle (female) or apices (male) of elytra. Pronotum and elytra with short, appressed pubescence. Elytra somewhat glabrous and impressed before very sparsely punctate humeral area, punctures behind smaller. Legs with hind trochanters evenly rounded at apices. Adults found on spring and early summer flowers of annuals, shrubs, and trees. Coast Ranges and western foothills of Sierra Nevada, California. (20)

Cortodera falsa (LeConte) (5.0–8.0 mm) is small, elongate, somewhat tapering posteriorly, and bicolored with body dull black, and front of head and prothorax reddish. Antennae reaching elytral apices (male) or not (female). Pronotum more or less as long as broad, sparsely punctate and setose, setae mostly short and depressed. Elytra twice as long as wide, disc with moderately dense pubescence. Abdomen usually black with apex reddish, sometimes all reddish. Adults found on various spring and early summer flowers of annuals and shrubs. Coast Ranges and Sierra Nevada of southern California to Baja California. (20)

Evodinus vancouveri Casey (8.0–13.0 mm) is somewhat tapering, with black body and appendages, and black and ivory elytra. Eyes distinctly emarginate. Antennae nearly reaching elytral apices (male), or not (female). Pronotum long. Elytra somewhat constricted laterally at middle, disc with corresponding light and dark pubescence, and mostly black, with black basal band, subbasal black spots, and lateral dark stripes extending along sides from humeri to lateral medial and subapical spots; apices dark. Diurnal adults on flowers. Mostly south-central Alaska, Yukon Territory, and Alberta south to Idaho and Northern Coast Ranges of California. (1)

Judolia instabilis (Haldeman) (6.0–15.0 mm) is robust, sides tapering, and variable in size and color pattern; populations with high percentages of mostly black individuals in San Jacinto Mountains, southeastern Arizona. Pronotum densely pubescent, distinctly and narrowly margined in front, and broadly depressed across posterior margin. Elytral pattern all black to mostly pale yellow with a few black spots; apices narrowly rounded. Larvae in roots of vetch (*Astragalus*) and lupine (*Lupinus*). Diurnal adults frequently on flowers, especially lupine (*Lupinus*) and buckwheat (*Eriogonum*), in spring and summer. Yukon Territory to Baja California, east to western Manitoba and southern Arizona, and south along Sierra Madre Occidental to Durango. (8)

Judolia montivagans (Couper) (7.0–12.0 mm) is black with yellow elytra with three variable black bands just behind base, middle, and apex. Pronotum convex, appearing dull; coarsely punctate with punctures running together, sparsely pubescent with sharp hind angles. Scutellum notched apically. Elytral apices black, broadly rounded. Metatarsi uniformly dark. Larvae develop in conifers. Adults found on various flowers of annuals and shrubs during summer. Alaska, across Canada, New England; also Rocky Mountains south to New Mexico. (8)

Lepturobosca chrysocoma (Kirby) (10.0–20.0 mm) is moderately sized, tapering posteriorly, with black body and brown elytra usually obscured by uniformly dense, recumbent, bright golden velvety pubescence, sometimes reduced in populations in Rockies. Larvae mine pine (*Pinus*), spruce (*Picea*), aspen (*Populus*), and alder (*Alnus*). Diurnal adults active in summer and found on various meadow flowers, also staminate catkins of Jeffrey pines (*Pinus jeffreyi*). In West from British Columbia south through Cascades of Washington and Oregon, Sierra Nevada and Transverse Ranges of California, and Rocky Mountains to southeastern Arizona, New Mexico, and northern Mexico. *Lepturobosca nigrolineata* (Bland) darker overall, especially along sides of elytra; Colorado, New Mexico. (2)

471

Neanthophylax tenebrosus nigrolineatus (Van Dyke) (11.0–17.0 mm) is dull black, pronotum punctate-rugose, with medial impressions anteriorly and posteriorly, and acute lateral tubercles; rarely with pale elytral stripes; pale pubescence evident. British Columbia to Cascades of Washington and Oregon. *Neanthophylax t. orientalis* Linsley & Chemsak (13.0–18.0 mm) dorsal surface coarsely, deeply, and irregularly punctate; pronotum without impressions, densely punctured, not rugose, obtuse lateral tubercles, and pubescence not evident. Oregon, Utah. *Neanthophylax t. tenebrosus* (LeConte) (11.0–18.0 mm) with shallow transverse impression across posterior margin, elytral rugae moderately coarse. Southern Oregon to Sierra Nevada, California. Diurnal adults on vegetation or flying during summer. (4)

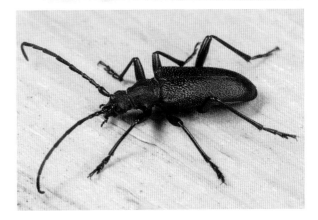

Pachyta armata (**LeConte**) (7.0–22.0 mm) is broad-shouldered, strongly tapering posteriorly, and black with mostly yellow elytra. Lateral pronotal tubercles prominent. Scutellum surrounded by elevated basal margin of elytra. Elytra strongly convex, marginal stripes on apical half narrow or broad, with apices narrowly notched. Larvae mine *Pinus* and *Tsuga*. Diurnal adults on flowers in summer. Northern California beetles smaller with black elytral margins broader. British Columbia to Sierra Nevada of California, western Montana. *Pachyta lamed liturata* Kirby (10.0–17.0 mm) similar, with elytra brownish to infuscate; boreal America, in West south to Sierra Nevada of California, and western Montana to southeastern Arizona and Colorado. (2)

Pidonia gnathoides (**LeConte**) (7.0–9.0 mm) is variably reddish yellow-brown, occasionally with pronotum and elytra black, with dorsum deeply punctate. Large head with swollen temples. Antennomere 3 shorter than 1, 3 and 4 subequal in length. Pronotum deeply punctate, longer in male, weakly constricted apically and basally. Elytra each with reddish-brown or black spot, sometimes infuscate along suture. Legs, especially hind legs, sometimes partially dark. On *Ceanothus* flowers and young conifers (*Pinus*, *Libocedrus*). British Columbia to central Coast Ranges and southern Sierra Nevada, California. (3)

Rhagium inquisitor (**Linnaeus**) (9.0–21.0 mm) is variable in color and size, but short, thick antennae, produced side margins of pronotum, and strongly ridged elytra are distinctive. Eggs deposited in bark crevices in spring and larvae bore through bark and into cambium of various conifers, especially pine (*Pinus*); development takes two years. Pupation occurs in an oval ring of coarse wood fibers under bark. Adults overwinter in pupal rings or under loose bark in winter and early spring; on pine logs in spring and summer. Often collected in Lindgren funnel traps. Northern Hemisphere; widespread in North America. (1)

Stenocorus nubifer (**LeConte**) (9.0–21.0 mm) is uniformly black, reddish brown, or black with reddish humeri, or pale yellowish-brown elytral stripes. Eyes small, finely faceted, and barely emarginate. Antennomere 3 longer than 4. Pronotum densely punctate and pubescent, with sides obtusely tuberculate, posterior margin slightly sinuate. Elytra dull, finely, densely punctate, with fine, dense appressed pubescence; apices obliquely truncate or emarginate. On flowers of *Eriodictyon*, *Ceanothus*, *Lupinus*, *Heracleum*, *Achillea* in spring and summer. Southern British Columbia and Alberta to southern California and Utah. *Stenocorus vestitus* (Haldeman) similar, elytral apices rounded. (6)

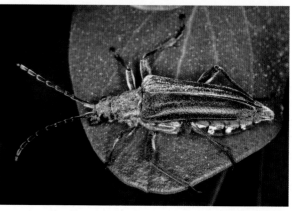

Enoploderes vitticollis (LeConte) (11.0–18.0 mm) is black dorsally with reddish-orange stripes on head and pronotum; pronotum, humeri, and legs sometimes reddish. Antennae extend to about middle (female) or apical third (male) of elytra. Pronotum wide, sides distinctly tuberculate, disc with pair of impunctate median calluses. Elytra densely, deeply, and irregularly punctate. Legs slender, hind femora arcuate. Larvae in hardwoods, including maple (*Acer*), alder (*Alnus*), cottonwood (*Populus*), California laurel (*Umbellularia*), willow (*Salix*), and oak (*Quercus*). Adults active during spring and summer. British Columbia to western Nevada and southern California. (1)

New House Borer *Arhopalus productus* (LeConte) (12.0–25.0 mm) is uniformly dull black with short pale setae that are longer underneath. Slender antennae reaching middle (female) or apical three-fifths (male) of elytra, outer antennomeres becoming gradually shorter, last four combined nearly as long as all three previous antennomeres. Sides of pronotum rounded. Elytra three times as long as wide, each tricostate, one costa indistinct. Legs slender, femora not clavate, posterior tarsomere 3 cleft about half its length, nearly even with apex of 4. Larvae mine dead or dying *Abies* and *Pinus*, especially recently burned trees. Western North America south to Honduras. (5)

Asemum nitidum LeConte (15.0–20.0 mm) is robust, parallel-sided, and somewhat shiny black with brownish pubescence. Antennomeres thick basally, becoming slender and tapering apically, antennomere 1 much longer than 3, 2 as broad as long, apical antennomeres not shorter. Pronotum wide, with sides broadly rounded. Elytra obscurely costate. Legs short, black; anterior tibiae with two spurs. Larvae mine *Pinus*, *Abies*, and *Pseudotsuga menziesii*. British Columbia south to southern California and New Mexico. *Asemum caseyi* Linsley (12.0–16.0 mm) similar, less robust, pale brown to black; antennae uniformly slender, antennomere 2 is one and a half times longer than wide; Pacific Northwest to southern California. (3)

Asemum striatum (Linnaeus) (10.0–18.0 mm) is dull black to brown, parallel-sided, with surface densely, finely pubescent. Eyes finely faceted. Apical antennomeres becoming shorter. Elytral surface faintly costate. Legs short, black, and anterior tibiae with two spurs. Larvae develop in conifers, including *Pinus*, *Larix*, and *Abies*. Nocturnal adults on or under bark, and at bases of larval host trees during day, and at lights during spring and summer. Transcontinental; in coniferous forests across southern Canada and western North America; also eastern United States. (3)

Megasemum asperum (LeConte) (15.0–23.0 mm) is elongate, somewhat cylindrical, and uniformly dull reddish brown to brown with short, fine, pale golden pubescence. Eyes coarsely faceted, broadly and deeply notched. Antennae robust, tapering, attaining basal third (male) or fifth (female) of elytra, and clothed in moderately coarse setae. Pronotum slightly wider than long. Elytra nearly three times as long as wide. Anterior tibiae each with two spurs. Larvae mine Douglas-fir (*Pseudotsuga menziesii*) and fir (*Abies*). Adults attracted to lights during summer. Coniferous forests of western North America. (1)

Atimia confusa dorsalis LeConte (6.0–12.0 mm) is elongate-oval, somewhat convex, with elytral margins gradually tapering apically; pronotum and elytra with coarse, appressed setae and glabrous patches. Antennae shorter than elytra in both sexes, antennomere 2 less than half length of 3. Pronotum wider than long, sides obtuse. Scutellum longer than wide, narrowly rounded apically. Elytral apices obliquely truncate. Legs short. Larvae mine incense cedar (*Libocedrus decurrens*), western red cedar (*Thuja plicata*), redwood (*Sequoia sempervirens*), cypress (*Cupressus*), and juniper (*Juniperus*). Adults active spring and summer. British Columbia south to northern Baja California and Utah. *Atimia c. maritima* Linsley (8.0–12.0 mm), coastal California. (6)

Neospondylis upiformis (Mannerheim) (8.0–20.0 mm) is elongate, robust, coarsely punctate, and shiny black, with long mandibles and short antennae. Eyes weakly notched; mandibles robust with sharp inner edge (female), or thin with dull inner edge (male). Pronotum widest anteriorly, lateral margins rounded. Elytron with two or more faint costae. Tarsi distinctly 5-5-5, tarsomere 4 small. Larvae likely root feeders and develop in larch (*Larix*), spruce (*Picea*), possibly pine (*Pinus*). Diurnal adults fly on sunny days, attracted to shiny surfaces; common in pitfall traps. Transcontinental; across southern Canada, northern United States, in West from southeastern Alaska to southern California, western Montana and New Mexico; also Durango. (1)

Necydalis barbarae Rivers (20.0–28.0 mm) is wasplike, elongate, somewhat robust, sparsely setose, and shiny dark brown or reddish brown, with very short elytra not reflexed apically nor with deep subapical impressions. Pronotum as wide as head, with sides strongly tuberculate. Larvae develop in coast live oak (*Quercus agrifolia*). Uncommon adults active in summer and found resting on vegetation. Pacific Coast, San Francisco Bay region to Santa Barbara. (6)

Necydalis cavipennis LeConte (13.0–24.0 mm) is wasplike with very short elytra reflexed apically, each with deep subapical impressions; with dense appressed golden pubescence. Usually blackish with bicolored elytra (male), or brown (female). Outer antennomeres black. Pronotum with median longitudinal sulcus deeply impressed. Slender metatarsi with tarsomere 1 distinctly narrower than tibial apex. Larvae develop in heartwood of oaks (*Quercus*) and other deciduous trees, especially in stumps or bases of standing trees. Diurnal adults active in summer on larval hosts. British Columbia south to California, Arizona, and northern Mexico. (6)

Lion Beetle *Ulochaetes leoninus* LeConte (17.0–32.0 mm) is subcylindrical, yellow and black, with short, yellow-tipped elytra. Appendages, except tibiae, completely black; resemble bumble bees in appearance and flight behavior. Antennae as long as (male) or shorter than (female) body. Pronotum densely clothed in erect yellow setae. Females lay eggs at base of conifer snags and stumps, especially *Pinus ponderosa* and *Pseudotsuga menziesii*; bluff stinging when threatened. Larvae mine roots and lower trunk. Diurnal adults found on host trunks or flying around midday. Southern British Columbia to northern Idaho, south to Baja California. (1)

Achryson surinamum (Linnaeus) (10.0–23.0 mm) is nearly cylindrical, and yellowish brown with undulating black marks and spots. Head slightly narrower than prothorax; antennae longer (male) or shorter (female) than body, antennomeres not armed with spines. Prothorax with sides broadly rounded. Elytra granulate basally, becoming punctate apically, finely and uniformly pubescent, and apices spinose at or just before suture. Larvae mine woody legumes, including locust (*Robinia*); also elm (*Ulmus*) and hackberry (*Celtis*). Adults at lights spring through summer. Across southern United States to Mexico and Caribbean, south to Argentina and Brazil. (1)

Plinthocoelium suaveolens plicatum (LeConte) (29.0–38.0 mm) is bright metallic green, blue-green, or cobalt, without bronze or coppery caste. Antennae slender, greatly exceeding (male) or shorter than (female) elytral apices. Pronotum with single spine on each side, disc transversely wrinkled. Femora red or reddish brown, apices and rest of leg black. Larvae mine roots of gum bully (*Sideroxylon lanuginosum rigidum*). Diurnal adults active on blossoms and trunks of larval host, or sapping or resting on desert broom (*Baccharis sarothroides*); produces a noxious fluid from between pronotum and elytra when handled. Southeastern Arizona to central Texas, south to Sonora and Tamaulipas. (1)

Callidium antennatum hesperum Casey (9.0–13.0 mm) is violet or blue, rarely greenish, and clothed in erect black pubescence. Antennae one-half to two-thirds as long as body (female), or more or less equal in length (male). Pronotum wide, slightly broader than base of elytra, and narrowed across posterior margin. Elytra densely punctate, with apices broadly rounded. Legs with femora distinctly clavate, tibiae curved. Larvae develop in pine (*Pinus*) branches. Diurnal adults on dead branches of larval host or on pine slash during spring and summer. British Columbia to southern California and Rockies. (13)

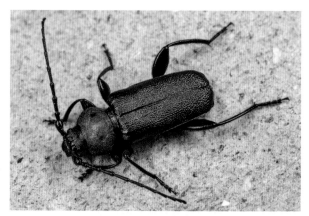

Phymatodes grandis Casey (8.0–15.0 mm) is somewhat flat and parallel-sided, uniformly brown to black, and moderately clothed in short, almost erect brown setae. Eyes deeply notched in front, upper and lower lobes connected by more than three rows of facets. Robust antennae nearly as long as (male) or three-quarters (female) length of elytra. Pronotum shiny, granulate-punctate, with smooth elongate median callus basally. Elytra alutaceous, dull. Femora clavate. Larvae in oak (*Quercus*). Adults at lights in summer, frequently transported indoors in firewood. British Columbia to southern California, Arizona, and Baja California. Formerly *P. lecontei* Linsley. (17)

476

Pseudopilema hoppingi (Van Dyke) (7.0–10.0 mm) is elongate, somewhat cylindrical, and reddish brown. Antennae reaching about three-quarters length of elytra (female) or apices. Pronotum shiny, sparsely punctured, with obtuse lateral tubercles and long, erect setae. Elytra coarsely, but shallowly punctured, with numerous coarse, erect setae; those of female sometimes brown or dark brown. Larvae develop in meandering galleries in heartwood of dead branches of oaks (*Quercus*). Adults found during summer while beating oak branches. Northern Coast Ranges and Sierra Nevada, California. (1)

Xylocrius agassizi (LeConte) (10.0–16.5 mm) is broad, flattened, and black with coarse erect black setae. Antenna with 11 antennomeres, 2 as long as wide, about half (male) or one-third to two-fifths (female) length of body. Pronotum nearly as wide as elytra, sides rounded. Elytra with basal half shiny and coarsely, densely punctate, apical half more densely pubescent, dull and finely punctate. Femora clavate, hind leg tarsomere 1 less than twice as long as wide. Larvae in *Ribes*. Pacific Coast and Rocky Mountains, British Columbia to southern California and New Mexico. *Xylocrius cribratus* (LeConte) (10.0–13.0 mm) elytra coarsely, cribrately punctate, shiny, and uniformly pubescent throughout. Northern California. (2)

Clytus clitellarius (Van Dyke) (7.5–10.0 mm) is elongate, dark brown, with pubescent elytral patterns of yellow and gray. Antennae reaching middle of elytra (male) or not (female). Pronotum lacks transverse carinae, about long as wide, narrower than elytra. Elytra before middle with broad, saddle-shaped pubescent band with irregular margins extending anteriorly along suture, and broken subapical bands often reduced to one or two small spots, followed by apical patch. Male femora slightly clavate, females' scarcely so, or not. Larvae in white fir (*Abies concolor*); diurnal adults on flowers of *Ceanothus* and beaten from dead fir branches during late spring and early summer. Northern California. (6)

Clytus planifrons (LeConte) (6.5–13.0 mm) is black, with bold yellow pubescent bands and brownish appendages. Antennae short, antennomeres 3 and 4 reddish brown, 8–11 darker, not reaching middle (male) or just surpassing subhumeral bar (female). Pronotum lacks transverse carinae, and narrower than elytra. Elytra with subhumeral spots large, with pubescent band before middle extending anteriorly along suture. Abdomen with band of thick appressed setae along all but last ventrite. Legs reddish brown. Larvae in fir (*Abies*); diurnal adults on flowering shrubs and fir branches on sunny ground. Southern British Columbia and southwestern Alberta to southern California. (6)

Megacyllene antennata (White) (12.0–25.0 mm) is elongate, robust, somewhat tapering, and brown or reddish brown with pale yellowish brown or gray pubescence. Antennae longer (male) or shorter (female) than elytra, with long spines on apices of antennomeres 3–6. Pronotum wider than long, unmarked, with pubescence obscuring disc. Elytra with broad, irregular transverse pubescent bands just before and after middle. Larvae develop in dead branches of mesquite (*Prosopis*) and acacia (*Senegalia*). Nocturnal adults attracted to lights, especially during summer. California to Texas, south to Baja California, Sonora, and Sinaloa. (3)

Neoclytus modestus modestus Fall (9.0–13.0 mm) is dark brown to blackish with white bands (male) or black with yellow bands (female). Pronotum with transverse ridges, pale band along anterior margin, and broken medial band present (female) or absent (male). Scutellum densely pubescent. Elytra with short, oblique bands extending forward at suture. Episterna of pterothorax densely clothed in white pubescence. Larvae in *Quercus*. Transverse Ranges and coastal areas of southern California. *Neoclytus m. zebratus* Van Dyke similar, dense white pubescence absent on mesepisterna, female pronotal and elytral bands usually white. Oregon and northern California. (12)

Semanotus amplus amplus (Casey) (5.0–14.5 mm) with antennae reaching mid length (female) or three-fourths to elytral apices (male). Pronotum wider than long, narrowed posteriorly. Basal three-fourths of elytra light to dark orange with pair of black spots, and apices black. Larval hosts *Thuja plicata, Libocedrus decurrens, Juniperus occidentalis*. Adults on larval hosts in late spring and early summer. British Columbia and Idaho to southern California. *Semanotus a. basalis* (Casey) dark between humeri, spots sometimes coalescing at suture; larvae in *Thuja plicata*, northern British Columbia to central California. *S. a. sequoiae* Van Dyke basal one-third of elytral disc light brown to red, apical two-thirds black; larvae in *Sequoia sempervirens*, California. (7)

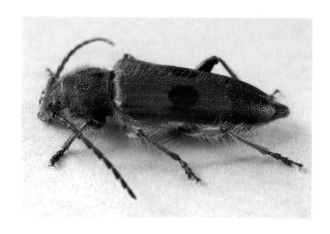

Triodoclytus lanifer (LeConte) (8.0–12.0 mm) is moderately robust, black, clothed in long yellowish setae, and has integumental, rather than pubescent, pale markings on elytra. Head short, coarsely punctate and densely setose, not bicarinate. Antennae tapering apically, with scape robust and without spines, reaching (female) or surpassing (male) middle of elytra. Pronotum round, wider than long, without transverse carinae, and coarsely punctate with long setae. Elytra with distinct light and dark markings, cream medial transverse band sometimes broken or obsolete. Legs with femora weakly clavate. Larvae in *Quercus, Ceanothus, Sambucus, Rhamnus*, and *Pickeringia*; adults on flowers during late spring and summer. Oregon and California. (1)

Xylotrechus insignis LeConte (12.0–18.0 mm) is elongate and robust, and sexually dimorphic with pubescent yellow or yellowish-white markings. Head with frons bearing V-shaped carina, short antennae in both sexes, and unarmed antennomeres. Pronotum as wide as elytra. Elytra gradually tapered to subtruncate apices, with distinct pubescent fascia, subhumeral fascia usually reduced to short bars, subapical pubescent fascia not broadly expanded at suture. Legs elongate, hind femora attaining (female) or surpassing (male) elytral apices. Smaller male (*left*) is reddish brown with reduced yellow markings, while larger female (*right*) is black with bold markings on head, pronotum, and elytra. Larvae in living and dead *Salix*; diurnal adults on vegetation in spring. Oregon to Baja California. (9)

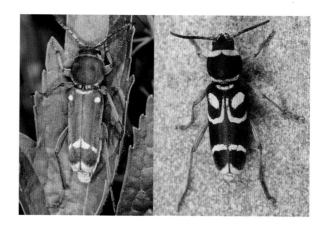

Xylotrechus nauticus (Mannerheim) (9.0–16.0 mm) is robust, cylindrical, black, rarely brownish, with coarse appressed pubescence forming three irregular gray bands across elytra. Head with conspicuous V-shaped frontal carina, antennae short, barely surpassing humeri (female) or reaching basal third of elytra (male). Pronotum slightly wider than long, widest behind middle and abruptly narrowed posteriorly, disc rough. Elytra with apices obliquely truncate, outer angles with distinct obtuse spines. Legs long, hind femora distinctly clavate. Larvae develop in various dying or dead hardwoods (*Arbutus, Quercus, Juglans, Persea*). Adults often emerge from stores of firewood in homes. Washington to Baja California. (9)

Susuacanga falli Linsley (19.0–28.0 mm) is dark brown or blackish with four pairs of small yellow-brown elytral callosities. Head with distinct tubercle above each eye, antennae much longer (male) or shorter (female) than body. Pronotum with low, irregular callosities. Elytra uniformly clothed in short reddish-yellow pubescence, with short, acute apical spine at suture. Femoral apices acutely toothed. Larvae mine heartwood of dead palo verde (*Parkinsonia*). Nocturnal adults on dead larval host trees, or at lights during summer. Southeastern California to southern Arizona, south to Mexico. *Susuacanga ulkei* (Bland) elytra glabrous with basal callosities only. Southern Arizona, south to Baja California and Nayarit. (2)

479

Aneflomorpha parowana Casey (10.0–17.0 mm) is slender, parallel-sided, reddish brown, with coarse white appressed pubescence. Antennomeres each with short apical spine and carina. Pronotum slightly longer than wide, sides impressed basally. Elytra moderately coarsely punctate, moderately dense pubescence fine, depressed, and suberect, and apices emarginate-truncate, usually bidentate. Larval host unknown. Oregon and California to Colorado and New Mexico. *Aneflomorpha lineare* (LeConte) similar, pale yellowish brown, sometimes reddish, elytral pubescence denser, apices shallowly emarginate, not spiniform. Adults of both species nocturnal, attracted to lights. Larvae girdlers of *Quercus* twigs; Oregon to Baja California, east to Nevada. (13)

Anelaphus brevidens (Schaeffer) (11.0–18.0 mm) is clothed in small patches of appressed tawny or yellowish pubescence, coarsely punctate, and brown or brownish black. Antennae as long as (female) or longer than (male) body, antennomeres 3–5 spinose apically. Pronotum nearly as long as wide, coarsely punctate with smooth, median line, and narrower than elytra. Elytral apices not dentiform. Larvae in *Condalia* and *Eysenhardtia*. California to Texas and Baja California. *Anelaphus inflaticollis* Chemsak (13.0–14.0 mm) dorsum more finely punctate, pronotum nearly as wide as elytra; larvae in *Lycium* and *Sarcobatus*; southern foothills of Mojave Desert, southern California. (8)

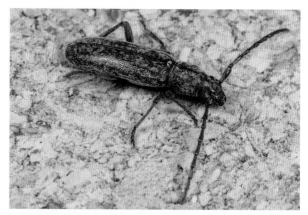

Aneflus prolixus fisheri Knull (24.0–30.0 mm) is reddish brown to brown with coarse, white pubescence. Head with prominent antennal tubercles, antennae shorter than elytra in both sexes, antennomeres 3–7 (male) or 3–8 or 9 (female) spinose at apices and 4–11 expanded externally and carinate. Pronotum long, nearly cylindrical, and clothed in appressed pubescence intermixed with long, erect setae. Elytra coarsely punctured basally, pubescence interrupted by rows of round denuded spots, and apices bispinose. Adults at lights in mesquite woodlands in summer. Southeastern Arizona, New Mexico, and Sonora. *Aneflus p. prolixus* LeConte, southern California and Baja California. (8)

Anoplocurius canotiae (7.0–8.0 mm) is moderately shiny, uniformly brown, and sparsely clothed in suberect pale setae. Forebody with fine network of elevated lines. Antennae with 12 antennomeres, exceeding elytral apices by about 5 (male) or 3–4 (female) antennomeres, antennomere 3 unarmed in male. Pronotum slightly longer than wide. Elytra moderately, coarsely punctate. Larvae in *Canotia holocantha*, *Morus*, *Berberis*; nocturnal adults at lights. Arizona and Sonora. *Anoplocurius altus* Knull with 11 antennomeres, antennomere 3 unarmed in both sexes; larvae in *Quercus*, southern Arizona to western Texas. *Anoplocurius incompletus* Linsley darker, antennomere 3 armed in both sexes; larvae in *Prosopis*, southern California, Baja California. (3)

Astromula nitidum Chemsak & Linsley (14.0–27.0 mm) is elongate, robust, slightly subparallel, slightly flattened, dark reddish brown, and moderately clothed in short golden pubescence. Head narrower than pronotum with antennae short, not reaching middle of elytra in both sexes. Pronotum slightly wider than long, sides broadly rounded. Elytra with base finely and distinctly punctate, becoming finer and denser apically. Legs short and stout. Larvae develop in Joshua tree (*Yucca brevifolia*) trunks; adults attracted to lights in summer. Southern California. (1)

Atylostagma glabra Schaeffer (23.0–28.0 mm) is elongate, subcylindrical, pale reddish yellow, and nearly glabrous. Head with antennae shorter than body in both sexes, with basal antennomeres bispinose, and reaching apical one-fourth (female) or nearly reaching apices (male). Pronotum barely wider than long, coarsely rugosely punctate, except for smooth median line. Elytra shiny, transparent, almost entirely glabrous, each with apices bisetose. Apices of hind femora sharply bispinose. Nocturnal adults attracted to lights during summer. Arizona and Mexico. (1)

Enaphalodes hispicornis (Linnaeus) (27.0–40.0 mm) is elongate, robust, somewhat cylindrical, uniformly dull or faintly shiny reddish to dark brown, and densely clothed in inconspicuous pubescence not obscuring integument. Antennae reach middle of elytra (female), or reach or surpass apices (male). Pronotum wider than long, finely and densely (male), or coarsely and rugosely (female) punctate. Elytra apices emarginate or truncate with sutural spine and outer angle dentiform or not. Underside with ventrites densely clothed in long, pale setae. Larvae develop in oak (*Quercus*). Adults at lights during summer. Transcontinental in United States; in West from California to Idaho, Utah, southeastern Arizona, south to southern Mexico. (5)

481

Enaphalodes niveitectus (Schaeffer) (22.0–27.0 mm) has elytra mottled with patches of dense white pubescence. Antennae reaching (female), or exceeding (male) elytral apices. Pronotum narrower than elytra, uneven, coarsely punctate, with smooth elevated calluses. Larvae in *Quercus emoryi*. Southeastern Arizona. *Enaphalodes cortiphagus* (Craighead) (16.0–27.0 mm) and *E. atomarius* (Drury) (19.0–29.0 mm), also in Arizona, both diffusely mottled with male pronotum as wide as elytra; former with metasternal pubescence mostly white and last female ventrite shallowly notched apically, latter with mostly translucent metasternal pubescence and female ventrite deeply notched apically. (5)

Orwellion gibbulum arizonense (Casey) (15.0–25.0 mm) is reddish brown to brown, with sparse patches of appressed yellowish setae. Head coarsely punctate. Antennae exceeding elytral apices by at least one (female) or three (male) antennomeres. Elytra with large areas not obscured by suberect pubescence, and spinose apically at suture. Larvae in *Salix*, *Populus*, and *Quercus*. Southern Arizona and southwestern New Mexico to Sonora and Chihuahua. *Orwellion occidentalis* (Giesbert & Hovore) (15.0–22.0 mm) lighter, elytra largely obscured by dense, suberect pubescence. Larvae in *Salix*; Lower Colorado River Valley of California and Arizona. Both species at lights in summer. (2)

Brothylus gemmulatus LeConte (12.0–22.0 mm) is elongate, reddish brown, with ocherous pubescence. Head with frontal suture deep. Pronotum slightly wider than long, sides round (male) or tuberculate (female). Elytra granulate, distinctly punctate, with ashy yellow pubescence interspersed with denuded spots. Posterior femora not clavate. Oregon and Utah south to Mexico. *Brothylus conspersus* LeConte (12.0–22.0 mm) is darker and clothed in whitish pubescence, elytra with two polished transverse undulating bands, posterior femora clavate; Oregon to southern California. Larvae of both species bore into dry, dead branches of oaks; nocturnal adults attracted to lights. (2)

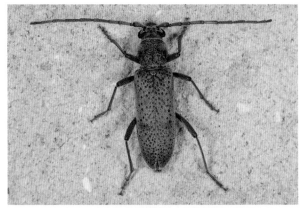

Osmidus guttatus LeConte (15.0–21.0 mm) is elongate, narrow, somewhat parallel-sided, dark brown to blackish, and clothed in short, dense, grayish pubescence. Antennal spines sometimes obsolete. Head closely punctured and pubescent, with frontal suture faint and antennae reaching (female) or surpassing (male) elytral apices. Pronotum oval, about as long as wide, and disc convex with two weak calluses. Elytral pubescence interspersed with small round denuded areas. Legs long, slender. Larvae in *Prosopis*, *Parkinsonia*, *Olneya*; nocturnal adults on larval plant hosts or attracted to lights during summer. Southern California, Nevada, and Arizona south to Baja California, Sonora, and Oaxaca. (1)

Holopleura marginata LeConte (5.0–11.5 mm) is slightly flattened, dull black with head, pronotum, and elytra mostly reddish with variable black markings. Convex eyes and antennae widely separated. Pronotum coarsely punctured. Elytral apices rounded; females with dark band on disc sometimes reduced to oblique bar and lateral spot at apical third. Femora weakly swollen. Larvae in dead branches of *Umbellularia californica*, *Pseudotsuga menziesii*, *Abies bracteata*, and *Pseudotsuga macrocarpa*. Adults active late spring, early summer. Southern British Columbia to Transverse Ranges of southern California. (1)

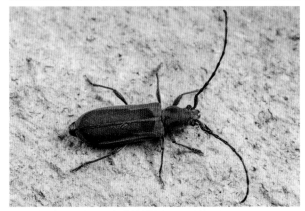

Megobrium edwardsi LeConte (5.0–14.0 mm) is dull brown, and sparsely pubescent with numerous long, erect setae. Head dull, distinctly concave between antennal bases, eyes finely faceted, antennae much longer than (male) or three-fourths length (female) of body. Pronotum with sides and disc tuberculate, finely and closely punctured, sparsely clothed in long erect setae. Elytra with coarse scattered punctures basally and pale V-shaped fascia medially, each separately rounded apically. Procoxae narrowly separated. Femora not strongly clavate. Larvae in *Quercus agrifolia* and *Ceanothus* twigs; adults at lights during spring and summer. Coastal central and southern California. (1)

Styloxus bicolor (Champlain & Knull) (7.0–11.0 mm) is slender, brown to black with short elytra. Head reddish orange, with eyes contiguous. Antennae slightly longer (female) or twice as long (male) as body. Pronotum long, rounded at sides. Elytra longer than pronotum, last two or three abdominal segments exposed. Metafemora clavate. Larvae hollow out pith of juniper (*Juniperus*) and cypress (*Hesperocyparis*) twigs, turning scales brown; adults at lights during summer. Southern California to New Mexico, south to Sonora. *Styloxus fulleri californicus* (Fall) 107.0–18.0 mm) is uniformly brownish yellow, with frons and scape sometimes reddish. Southern Oregon to southern California. (2)

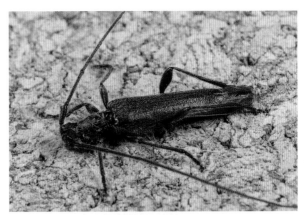

Molorchus longicollis LeConte (4.0–11.5 mm) is slender with short elytra. Head and pronotum coarsely, deeply punctate. Pronotum long, with sides abruptly constricted basally, narrower than base of elytra. Elytra uniformly yellow to reddish brown. Metafemora clavate. Larvae mine dead twigs of deciduous hardwoods and Douglas-fir (*Pseudotsuga menziesii*). Adults on flowers in spring and summer, especially buckbrush (*Ceanothus*), ninebark (*Physocarpus*), and poison oak (*Toxicodendron*). Mostly southern British Columbia to western Montana, south to southern California. *Molorchus eburneus* Linsley (8.5–11.0 mm) finely punctate, elytra each with oblique whitish band. Usually above 1,800 meters, Sierra Nevada and Transverse Ranges of California. (2)

Obrium maculatum (Olivier) (4.0–8.0 mm) is shiny, flattened, pale yellowish brown with distinctive brown elytral markings. Pronotum more strongly narrowed basally. Larvae in branches of hardwood trees and shrubs. Nocturnal adults at lights in spring through early fall. Southern California to eastern North America, south to El Salvador. Pronotum equally narrowed anteriorly and posteriorly: *Obrium californicum* Van Dyke (5.0–7.0 mm) uniformly yellowish brown, central Oregon to central Coast Ranges and Tehachapi Mountains, California; *O. constricticollis* Schaeffer (5.0–6.0 mm) uniformly brown or blackish; southeastern Arizona. *O. discoideum* LeConte (5.0–7.0 mm) pale with cloud on pronotum; southeastern Arizona. (4)

Malacopterus tenellus (Fabricius) (20.0–24.0 mm) is flattened and testaceous. Head coarsely, rugosely punctate. Antennae with 11 antennomeres, each narrowly annulated with black apically, not reaching elytral apices in female. Pronotum with smooth median line flanked by two faint impressions. Elytra with slender costae. Hind leg with tarsomere 1 as long as 2–5 combined. Larvae in *Salix*, *Populus*, and *Celtis*. Adults attracted to lights during summer. California and Arizona. (1)

Oeme costata costata LeConte (12.0–22.0 mm) is elongate, subcylindrical, pale brownish to black; head and prothorax sometimes lighter. Head narrower than pronotum, densely and confluently punctured; antennae slender, as long as (female) or one and a half times length of body (male). Pronotum wider than long. Elytra long, finely pubescent, gradually tapering posteriorly, each tricostate with apices narrowly rounded. Larvae in ponderosa (*Pinus ponderosa*), two needle piñon (*P. edulis*), and lodgepole (*P. contorta*) pines. Adults at lights during summer. Southwestern Montana to California and Texas. *Oeme c. abietis* Chemsak duller, with pronotal disc more finely rugose, elytra more densely pubescent; host *Abies bracteata*. Santa Lucia Mountains, California. (1)

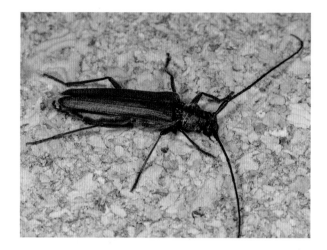

Dicentrus bluthneri LeConte (3.0–7.0 mm) is elongate, dull blackish with brown appendages, with fine, short, mostly pale pubescence. Antennae longer (male) or shorter (female) than body. Pronotum wider than long, sides each with pair of spinose tubercles, median tubercle more developed than posterior tubercle. Elytra each with light brown oval spot and apex. Larvae in smaller twigs of *Pseudotsuga* and *Sequoia*, possibly *Abies*, *Libocedrus*, *Tsuga*; adults active spring and summer. British Columbia to central California. *Dicentrus bidentatus* (Champlain & Knull) (6.0–12.0 mm) uniformly brown with ocherous pubescence sparse, lateral posterior pronotal tubercle more developed; British Columbia and southern Sierra Nevada, California. (2)

Eucalyptus Borer *Phoracantha recurva* Newman (14.0–30.0 mm) is, slightly tapered, and shiny with reddish-brown appendages. Antennae with golden setae, as long as (female) or surpass (male) elytra, and antennomere 3 tipped with recurved spine. Elytra mostly cream, with narrow transverse band between humeri, a pair of irregular discal spots before middle, broad black band across apical half, and rounded apices spinose. Larvae attack injured or stressed *Eucalyptus*; adults in crevices or under loose bark during warmer months. *Phoracantha semipunctata* (Fabricius) (12.0–30.0 mm) antennae bare, elytra mostly dark brown with a central cream-colored band divided by a narrow zigzag band. Australia; in southern California. (2)

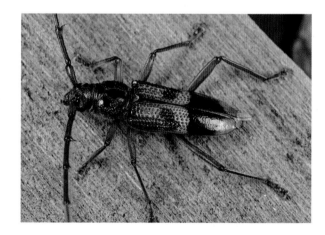

Rhopalophora meeskei Casey (5.5–10.0 mm) is slender, with head, elytra, and legs black, and pronotum red. Antennae reaching well past elytral apices (male) or not (female). Femora clavate. On flowers of *Holodiscus dumosus*, *Heterotheca subaxillaris*, *Achillea millefolium*, *Melilotus officinalis*, *Ceanothus*, *Mimosa grahamii*, and *Baileya pleniradiata* during summer. Southeastern Arizona and New Mexico to Honduras. *Rhopalophora prorubra* Knull (6.4 mm) with red head, pronotum longer than wide, black elytra; southern Arizona. *R. rugicollis* (LeConte) (7.0–10.0 mm) similar, pronotum transversely wrinkled; Arizona and Texas to Guatemala. (3)

Banded Alder or California Laurel Borer *Rosalia funebris* Motschulsky (23.0–40.0 mm) is somewhat parallel-sided, flattened, and black with distinct bands of white or bluish-white pubescence. Antennae annulated with white, slightly (female) or distinctly (male) surpassing elytral apices. Pronotum white with large oval black spot on disc. Variable white elytral bands sometimes reduced to spots. Larvae mine dead trunks of alder (*Alnus*), maple (*Acer*), gum (*Eucalyptus*), ash (*Fraxinus*), sycamore (*Platanus*), coast live oak (*Quercus agrifolia*), willow (*Salix*), elm (*Ulmus*), and California laurel (*Umbellularia californica*). Diurnal adults attracted to drying paint. Alaska to southern California and Rocky Mountains south to Arizona and New Mexico. (1)

485

Callimoxys fuscipennis (LeConte) (7.0–12.5 mm) is small, slender, with bicolored legs and short elytra. Antennae filiform, with 11 antennomeres. Pronotum distinctly punctate, disc black (male) or reddish orange with anterior and posterior margins usually black (female). Elytra narrowed and dehiscent at basal third, exposing abdominal tergites. Legs with femora clavate, hind legs with femora and tibiae bicolored, bases orange and apices dark. Diurnal adults active during spring and summer on numerous flowering shrubs, including *Ceanothus*. Northern Washington to Baja California. (1)

Callimus cyanipennis (LeConte) (5.0–8.0 mm) is small, slender, with bicolored legs and numerous erect setae. Head and antennae black. Pronotum slightly wider than long, orange (female) or black (male). Elytra coarsely punctured and metallic bluish or greenish in both sexes. Abdomen orange. Bicolored legs orange with apices of femora and tibiae black. Larvae mine small limbs of various shrubs; diurnal adults on flowering *Ceanothus* and other shrubs in spring and summer. Previously in the genus *Lampropterus*. Oregon to southern California. (2)

Callimus ruficollis (LeConte) (4.5–8.0 mm) is small, slender, with uniformly colored legs and sparse erect setae. Both sexes similar in color. Head, appendages, and abdomen black. Pronotum as long or longer than wide, partly (male) or entirely (female) reddish. Elytra coarsely punctate, dark metallic blue or green. Larvae mine small limbs of various shrubs; diurnal adults on flowering *Ceanothus* and other shrubs during spring and summer. Previously placed in the genus *Lampropterus*. British Columbia to southern California. (2)

Crossidius coralinus (LeConte) (12.0–21.0 mm) is elongate, polymorphic, red or yellowish brown with black or bluish black elytral markings prominent (females) or reduced (males). Pronotum with acute lateral tubercle. Elytra coarsely punctate basally, finely and closely punctate apically. Abdomen black, red, or clouded with black. Larvae in roots of *Ericameria*; adults on larval hosts in late summer. Thirteen subspecies from Mojave Desert of California to southern Saskatchewan, Wyoming, and New Mexico; *C. c. caeruleipennis* Linsley (female, top) orange, with head, underside of pterothorax, and appendages black; male immaculate or with elytral markings greatly reduced along base and suture; Owens Valley, California. *C. c. ascendens* Linsley (male, bottom) bright red; Antelope Valley, California. Seven species and numerous subspecies of *Crossidius* have been described largely from arid regions in the West, especially the Great Basin and adjacent areas. Regional topography and patchy distribution of larval host plants have resulted in multiple color forms for many species. Larvae are root borers in woody fall-blooming composites, especially *Ericameria*, *Isocoma*, *Artemisia*, and *Gutierrezia*. Diurnal and often brightly colored adults typically emerge in late summer and early autumn to feed and mate on flowers of larval host plants. (7)

Crossidius hirtipes nubilus Linsley (11.0–15.0 mm) is elongate, somewhat parallel-sided, dark reddish brown with head, pronotum, and underside of thorax black, and reddish appendages; dorsum clothed in coarse pubescence. Pronotum rounded, narrower than elytra, sparsely pubescent, and rugosely punctured with sides not strongly tuberculate. Elytra distinctly and coarsely punctured nearly to apices, without prominent discal costae. Larvae in roots of *Ericameria*; adults on larval hosts in late summer. White Mountains in central-east California. Sixteen subspecies of *C. hirtipes* LeConte described from eastern Washington to central-eastern California, east to southwestern Wyoming, Utah, and Arizona. (7)

486

Crossidius testaceus maculicollis Casey (10.0–16.0 mm) is elongate, somewhat parallel-sided, and pale brown. Elytra with reduced discal costae. Larvae in *Isocoma*; adults on larval host plants late summer to early fall. Los Angeles Basin of southern California. *Crossidius testaceus testaceus* LeConte similar, darker, elytral costae more prominent, elytra immaculate (male) or with dark narrow stripe along suture (female); coastal plain of San Diego, California and adjacent Baja California. A third subspecies, *C. t. australis* Linsley, is reddish brown, elytra with distinct shiny discal costae, and black humeral spot and sutural stripe; adults on *Isocoma* flowers during summer. Occurs only near San Quintín, Baja California. (7)

Dendrobias mandibularis mandibularis Dupont (17.0–32.0 mm) is large, shiny yellow and black. Prognathous mandibles (males) sometimes very large; antennae longer than body in both sexes. Lateral pronotal margins each bearing sharp tubercle. Basal and medial elytral bands variable, sutural and lateral margins narrowly or incompletely black. Femora clavate. Larvae mine branches of dead palo verde (*Parkinsonia*). Diurnal adults sap on desert broom (*Baccharis sarothroides*). Arizona to southern Texas, south to Baja California and northern Mexico. *Dendrobias m. reductus* Casey males lack elytral markings, occasionally with sutural spot; females have narrow median band; larvae in willow (*Salix*), southern Colorado River Valley of California and Arizona. (1)

487

Elytroleptus ignitus (**LeConte**) (12.0–16.0 mm) is elongate, flattened, with uniformly orange elytra. Antennae moderately appendiculate (male), or shorter and serrate (female). Elytra tricostate, flared apically. Larvae in oak (*Quercus*) twigs. Predatory adults in Batesian mimicry complex with their prey, *Lycus loripes* (Chevrolat) (p.261) and *L. simulans* (Schaeffer) (p.262), and occur among *Lycus* feeding and mating aggregations. Southeastern Arizona to western Texas, northern Mexico. *Elytroleptus apicalis* (LeConte) orange or reddish orange with apical fifth of elytra black, antennae very appendiculate in male; part of Batesian mimicry complex with prey *Lycus fernandezi* Dugés (p.261) and *L. arizonensis* Green (p.260). Southeastern Arizona and northern Mexico. (5)

Megapurpuricenus magnificus (LeConte) (25.0–38.0 mm) is large, robust, coarsely and confluently punctate, with bold orange-red and black markings. Head with antennae and vertex black, antennae much longer (male) or shorter (female) than body. Pronotum wider than long, variably black, with broad lateral tubercles acute and recurved, elevated median black tubercle flanked by a pair of obliquely connected black tubercles on each side. Elytra black with two variable transverse orange-red bands. Legs slender and black, femora mostly red. Larvae in oaks (*Quercus*). Diurnal adults emerge every three years around larval host trees. Southeastern Arizona south to Chihuahua, and Aguascalientes. (1)

Plionoma suturalis (LeConte) (10.0–16.0 mm) is robust, and black or reddish black, with elytra clothed in uniformly short, dense, white pubescence. Antennae nearly reaching (female) or surpassing (male) elytral apices. Pronotum mostly reddish. Elytral apices each with one sharp, one obtuse spine. Reddish femora clothed in white pubescence. Larvae mine mesquite (*Prosopis*). Adults visit creosote bush (*Larrea tridentata*) and catclaw acacia (*Senegalia greggii*) flowers during summer. Southern California to Texas and northern Mexico. *Plionoma rubens* (Casey) (10.0–12.0 mm) similar, mostly pale reddish with antennae, tibiae, and tarsi black; elytra with conspicuously long, white pubescence; southern California, Baja California to Texas, south to northern Mexico. (2)

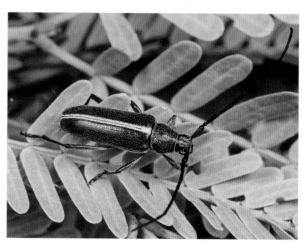

Schizax senex LeConte (12.0–18.0 mm) is elongate, robust, mostly black, and clothed in long, erect, pale setae. Eyes completely divided, antennae longer (male) or shorter (female) than body. Pronotum wider than long and coarsely, roughly punctate, reddish. Scutellum clothed in yellowish-orange setae. Elytral surface more shallowly punctate than pronotum, lateral and sutural margins with narrow line of yellowish-orange setae. Legs long, slender, and reddish. Larvae mine dead branches of mesquite (*Prosopis juliflora*), palo verde (*Parkinsonia florida*, *P. microphylla*), and desert willow (*Chilopsis linearis*). Diurnal adults on spring flowers of larval host, also creosote bush (*Larrea tridentata*). Southern California to western Texas. (1)

Sphaenothecus bilineatus (Gory) (10.0–13.0 mm) is elongate, moderately slender, and shiny black with legs and pronotal disc black or red, and elytra each with a pair of pale yellowish-brown stripes. Antennae of male with 12 antennomeres, much longer than body; female with 11 antennomeres, slightly exceeding length of body. Pronotum longer than wide, flanked by two broad stripes of pale setae. Elytra with coarse punctures, pale stripes narrowly raised and impunctate, and apices each rounded and flanked with pair of small, acute spines. Legs slender, mostly black with red femora. Adults on various flowers, including acacia (*Senegalia*) and desert broom (*Baccharis sarothroides*) during summer. Southern California to Texas, south to Nicaragua. (1)

Stenaspis solitaria (Say) (22.0–35.0 mm) is large, robust, glabrous, and typically uniformly dull black. Antennae much longer than (male) or reaching just behind middle (female) of elytra. Elytral apices rounded. Legs long, slender. Larvae mine branches of mesquite (*Prosopis juliflora*). Diurnal adults on flowering mesquite, catclaw acacia (*Senegalia greggii*), knifeleaf condalia (*Condalia spathulata*), desert broom (*Baccharis sarothroides*), and other flowering trees and shrubs during summer; exude a musty odor when disturbed. Southeastern California to Texas, and Mexico (Baja California Sur, Sonora, Chihuahua, and Durango). (2)

Stenaspis verticalis arizonicus Casey (21.0–32.0 mm) is large, robust, with green or greenish-blue elytra, and glabrous. Head black with red spot on vertex, antennae with basal segments black, remaining antennomeres mostly red with black apices, much longer than body (male) or reaching apical fifth of elytra (female). Pronotum black and more or less posteriorly margined with red. Underside typically mostly reddish brown or black; legs long, slender, and mostly black with red markings. Larval host unknown. Adults feed on flowers of woody shrubs, also found mating and sapping on branches of desert broom (*Baccharis sarothroides*) during summer monsoons in southeastern Arizona. (2)

Tragidion armatum LeConte (20.0–30.0 mm) is black with smooth yellow-orange elytra. Head and pronotum with dense black pubescence. Male antennae with orange rings, extending past elytral apices by no more than two antennomeres; female antennomeres shorter, black. Hind tarsomere 1 not as long as 2 and 3 combined. Larvae develop in chaparral yucca (*Hesperoyucca whipplei*) stalks of plants that reproduce multiple times during their lifetimes. Southern California to Utah, Texas, and northern Mexico. *Tragidion agave* Swift & Ray similar, antennae unicolorous brown, pronotum reddish brown with brown pubescence; larvae in *Agave*, southern California, Baja California. *Tragidion gracilipes* Linsley (20.0–22.0 mm) hind tarsomere 1 longer than 2 and 3 combined, antennomeres 7–11 black; larvae in *Adenostoma* and *Rhamnus*, California. (7)

Tragidion deceptum Swift & Ray (16.5–25.0 mm) is black with costate tawny (male) or red-orange (female) elytra. Head with dense black pubescence, antennae annulated with orange, longer (male) or shorter (female) than elytra. Length of dark basal elytral band twice that of scutellum, costae parallel to suture and ending at apical third. Larvae in oak (*Quercus*). Diurnal adults sap on desert broom (*Baccharis sarothroides*). *Tragidion annulatum* LeConte (17.0–34.0 mm) elytra with basal band not exceeding scutellum, costae extending to apex, and ventral pubescence with metallic blue reflections. Attracted to brush fires in chaparral, desert scrub, and coniferous forests. Southern California to Baja California Sur. (7)

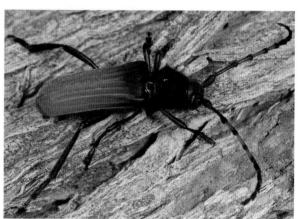

Tragidion densiventre Casey (20.0–28.0 mm) male has reddish-brown head, antennal scape, and legs, with head and pronotum not densely setose. Female forebody and appendages black, with head and pronotum densely setose. Antennae longer (male) or shorter (female) than elytra. Deeply impressed elytra with inner costae slightly bowed inward toward suture, and are tawny (male) or reddish orange (female). Larvae mine honey mesquite (*Prosopis glandulosa*) and catclaw acacia (*Senegalia greggii*). Diurnal adults on flowers of larval hosts and sapping on desert broom (*Baccharis sarothroides*); sometimes found sapping together with *T. deceptum* at lower elevations. Southeastern Arizona to Texas, south to northern Sonora and Chihuahua. (7)

Tylosis maculatus LeConte (10.0–20.0 mm) is mostly reddish orange, with appendages and markings black. Head black. Antennae with 12 antennomeres, with nearly two (female) or six (male) antennomeres extending past body. Pronotum with five small black polished callosities. Elytra with small subscutellar spots well removed from scutellum, with humeral and discal markings faintly bluish or greenish. Prosternum red (female) or black and broadly extending up sides of pronotum (male). Adults on mallows. Arizona to Texas and northern Mexico. *Tylosis puncticollis* Bates (9.0–12.0 mm) with common basal elytral mark enveloping scutellum; Arizona and Mexico. (2)

Acanthocinus obliquus (LeConte) (8.0–17.0 mm, without ovipositor) is reddish brown to blackish with dense, short, and appressed grayish and black pubescence. Antennae twice as long as (female) or two and a half to three times longer than (male) body. Pronotum wide, sides sharply tuberculate behind middle. Elytra with two dark and slightly oblique transverse bands, and dark spots concentrated on distinct costae. Posterior sternite of female distinctly elongate, deeply notched apically, with ovipositor extruded. Larva develops in *Pinus*. Adults at lights. British Columbia to Baja California, east to South Dakota, Colorado, New Mexico, and northern Mexico. (4)

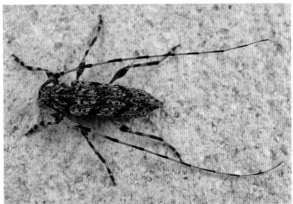

491

Coenopoeus palmeri (LeConte) (18.0–27.0 mm) is usually dull black with extremely variable patches of yellowish-gray pubescence on elytra; occasionally mostly black. Antennae with alternating black and white bands, male with antennomere 6 produced apically. Claws somewhat divaricate. Larvae mine cholla (*Cylindropuntia*) branches, sometimes producing thick black exudate on surface. Nocturnal adults emerge at dusk to feed externally and mate on larval host in late spring, summer; sometimes at lights. Southeastern California and southern Nevada east to Texas, and south to Sinaloa. (1)

Glaucotes yuccivorus (Fall) (12.0–15.0 mm) is robust, somewhat cylindrical, dark reddish brown to blackish, and densely clothed in tightly appressed grayish pubescence. Head with antennae slightly longer (male) or shorter (female) than elytra, antennomeres paler basally. Prothorax wider than long, with sides obtusely tuberculate just behind middle; disc with weak, usually glabrous callosities. Elytra each with 4–5 vague rows of appressed gray setae most evident apically. Elytral surface and legs also moderately clothed in short, semierect yellowish setae. Femora clavate. Larvae in *Yucca*. Adults on larval hosts and at lights in summer. Arizona. (1)

Peritapnia fabra Horn (9.0–13.0 mm) is robust, somewhat flattened dorsally, and dull dark brown to black with underside and appendages reddish. Dorsal surface dulled by dense, shallow micropunctures, with scattered deeper punctures bearing suberect (head, pronotum) or semierect (elytra) black setae. Head short and broad in front, with antennae slightly longer (male) or shorter (female) than body; scape longer than antennomere 3. Pronotum wider than long, disc only faintly callused, with sides broadly angulate. Elytra one and a half times longer than wide, apices rounded. Femora clavate. Adults attracted to lights during summer in montane habitats. Southern Arizona to Baja California and Sinaloa. (1)

Sternidius centralis (LeConte) (5.0–8.0 mm) is reddish brown or blackish, with short, dense, appressed setae brownish, grayish, and black. Antennomere 4 shorter than or equal to 1. Pronotum wider, broadly impressed basally, with disc tricallused and mottled with grayish and brownish setae. Elytra moderately, coarsely punctate basally, disc distinctly costate with dark tufted tubercles, with rounded medial spots on lateral margins not reaching humeri or disc, postmedian spot usually reduced to sutural spots, and apices somewhat truncate. Female with abdominal sternite 5 twice as long as 4. Larvae in mesquite (*Prosopis*); adults at lights. Southern Arizona to Texas. (5)

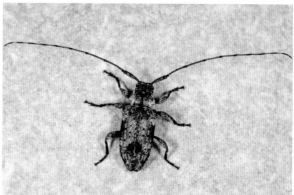

Sternidocinus barbarus (Van Dyke) (11.0–15.0 mm) is somewhat convex and parallel-sided, reddish brown, and clothed in dense grayish pubescence. Head broad, quadrate, and convex (male) or flat (female), with antennae slightly (female) or one-third (male) longer than body. Pronotum shorter than wide, disc with vague elongate medial callus flanked on either side by a shallow callus, and sides with distinct angulate tubercles. Elytra with base narrowly pale brownish, disc with small brownish spots scattered along suture and costae. Legs with femora clavate. Larvae develop in coast live oak (*Quercus agrifolia*), while adults are attracted to lights. Coastal southern California. (1)

Tigrinestola tigrina (Skinner) (11.0–15.0 mm) is clothed in short, appressed uniformly gray setae, and marked with variable black dots and linear dashes. Antennae slightly surpassing elytral apices (male) or not (female), antennomeres mostly clothed in dense gray pubescence, except for black apices. Pronotum with broad lateral tubercles acute, disc often with three black dots. Variable black lines on elytra coalesce behind middle to form irregular transverse fascia. Larvae in *Parkinsonia*. Nocturnal adults on dead branches of *Quercus* and *Acer* during summer; at lights. Arizona and New Mexico to Baja California and Sonora. (1)

Dylobolus rotundicollis (Thomson) (9.0–19.0 mm) is elongate, parallel-sided, and black with head and pronotum orangish red, resembling a firefly. Pronotum broader than long, rounded sides densely fringed with short, erect, golden pubescence intermixed with scattered longer setae. Elytra with lateral margins and suture sometimes narrowly lighter, apices obliquely truncate. Adults on spring and summer flowers of composites and legumes. Southeastern Arizona and Oklahoma to Costa Rica. Formerly in *Mecas*. (1) *Mecas bicallosa* Martin uniformly dark gray; on *Artemisia tridentata*, Washington to Baja California, east to Colorado; *M. menthae* Chemsak & Linsley gray or gray-brown with pale suture; on mint in southeastern Arizona. (2)

Spotted Sawyer *Monochamus clamator latus* Casey (14.0–29.0 mm) is black, sometimes brownish, with dark reddish-brown or black appendages. Antennae much (male) or slightly (female) longer than body, female's broadly ringed in white. Elytra densely, rugosely punctate, with patches of dark brown to black pubescence interspersed with numerous small spots of gray pubescence, and apices narrowly rounded. Larvae develop in conifers (*Pinus*, *Abies*, *Pseudotsuga*); adults at lights. British Columbia to southern California. *Monochamus c. clamator* (LeConte) darker, pubescent patches brownish. Colorado Plateau; *M. c. rubigineus* (Bates) reddish with brownish-orange patches; southeastern Arizona; *M. c. nevadensis* Dillon & Dillon whitish; Nevada and Idaho. (5)

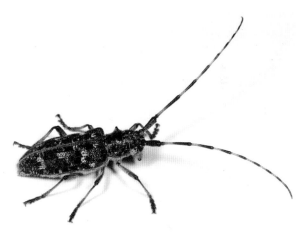

Northeastern Sawyer *Monochamus notatus* (Drury) (23.0–35.0 mm) is reddish brown, surfaces clothed mostly in dense grayish pubescence, and scutellum with off-white setae. Head of female wide, divergent anteriorly. Pronotal tubercles white or off-white at base. Elytra densely pubescent with scattered small patches of black-brown pubescence, reduced or absent in some females; apices angled at suture. Larva develops in dead and dying pine (*Pinus*), also fir (*Abies*), and spruce (*Picea*); Douglas-fir (*Pseudotsuga*) needs documentation. Adults active late spring through summer. In West from southern British Columbia to southern Washington, east to Alberta to Montana. (5)

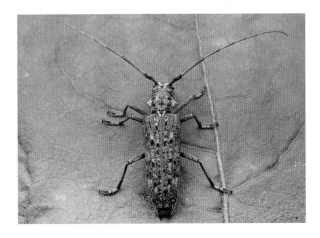

White-spotted Sawyer *Monochamus scutellatus* (Say) (13.0–27.0 mm) is large, striking, shiny black, and sparsely pubescent; populations in Rockies often with a slight metallic caste. Antennae much greater than the length of body in male, shorter with white annulations in female. Scutellum with dense, white appressed setae, midline glabrous. Elytra coarsely punctured, often with small, scattered, white patches of appressed setae, with apices broadly rounded to suture. Larva tunnels in conifers (*Abies*, *Larix*, *Picea*, *Pinus*, *Pseudotsuga*, *Tsuga*); diurnal adults on trunks and injured branches of larval hosts during spring and summer. In West from southern British Columbia to southern California, east to Alberta, Montana, Colorado, and New Mexico. (5)

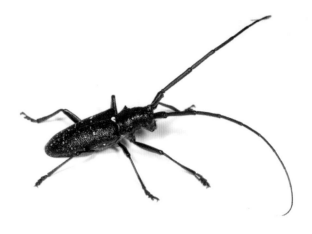

Neoptychodes trilineatus (Linnaeus) (19.0–31.0 mm) is large with smooth-sided pronotum tapered toward front, and with distinctive dense grayish pubescence, brown-orange spots, and white stripes. Head with eyes deeply notched, mouthparts directed downward. Pronotum as long as wide, widest at base, without distinct spines or tubercles on sides. Elytra tapered toward rear, with markings, especially sutural stripe, sometime expanded at middle and spined apices. Larvae develop in fig (*Ficus*), alder (*Alnus*), mulberry (*Morus*), willow (*Salix*), and hackberry (*Celtis*). Adults active in summer, found on trunks of larval hosts. Southeastern Arizona to Florida; across Mexico south to Colombia and Venezuela, also Caribbean. (1)

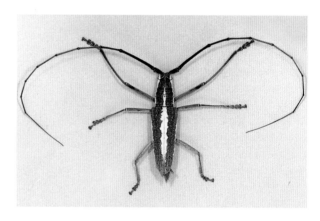

Spotted Tree Borer *Synaphaeta guexi* (LeConte) (11.0–27.0 mm) is robust, broad-shouldered, with antennae as long (female) or longer than (male) body. Elytra with black zigzag stripes and patches of gray and yellow-orange pubescence. Developing larvae leave behind large tunnels filled with loose fibrous shavings. Numerous deciduous trees serve as hosts, including maple (*Acer*), buckeye *(Aesculus),* alder (*Alnus*), cottonwood (*Populus*), willow (*Salix*), California laurel (*Umbellularia californica*); will attack weak and dead fruit and ornamental trees. Nocturnal, cryptic adults encountered on trunks of larval hosts, especially April to July. Southern British Columbia to southern California; recorded from Santa Rita Mountains, southeastern Arizona. (1)

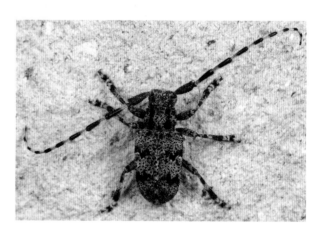

Moneilema gigas LeConte (21.0–34.0 mm) is convex and black. Antennomere 4 with broad white ring. Pronotal spines as long as or longer than antennomere 9. Larvae mine roots and stems of cacti (*Cylindropuntia*, *Opuntia*). Flightless nocturnal adults feed and mate on cactus crowns. Southern Arizona to Sinaloa. *Moneilema semipunctatum* LeConte (15.0–30.0 mm) pronotal spines shorter than antennomere 9. Great Basin, Mojave, Colorado deserts, coastal and desert scrub habitats from southern Idaho to northern Baja California and Arizona. *M. appressum* LeConte (10.0–32.0 mm) lacks pronotal spines, elytra finely wrinkled. Colorado to Arizona, Texas; northern Mexico. (4)

Oberea erythrocephala (Schrank) (10.0–12.0 mm) is mostly dark gray with reddish head and legs. Pronotum without calluses. Introduced from Europe as biocontrol of leafy spurge (*Euphorbia esula*). Adults feed on leaves and flowers during summer; larvae mine stems and root crowns. Established in scattered populations throughout western North America. Native *O. quadricallosa* LeConte (11.0–17.0 mm) with black head, antennae, and elytra; red pronotum with four black calluses, and glabrous femora. Larvae and adults in/on *Populus* and *Salix*. British Columbia to southern California, east to Colorado and Nevada. (2)

Lochmaeocles marmoratus Casey (18.0–33.0 mm) is clothed in dense grayish and orange pubescence. Head with long vertical face, frontal horns at antennal bases well developed, curved downward and inward (male) or moderately produced (female); antennae much (male) or slightly (female) longer than body, and antennomere 3 long and straight. Elytra with numerous glabrous tubercles and narrow transverse whitish band basally, orange spots outlined in gray, and two oblique white bands at middle. Legs long. Larvae in cottonwood (*Populus*) and willow (*Salix*). Adults on larval tree and at lights during late summer. Southeastern Arizona and northwestern Mexico. (1)

Oncideres quercus Skinner (11.0–16.0 mm) is elongate and parallel-sided with dense, appressed gray, orange, and dark brown pubescence dorsally. Head with long, vertical face and orange pubescence around eyes, neck, and vertex; antennae much (male) or slightly (female) longer than body. Pronotum wide, narrowed behind lateral tubercles, with vague median callus on disc. Elytral bases and lateral spots at apical third with dense orangish-brown pubescence, disc with lighter spots raised. Short, stout legs with gray pubescence and erect setae. Larvae in fallen oak (*Quercus*) branches girdled by females. Adults prune oaks during summer. At lights. Arizona and northern Mexico. (2)

Oncideres rhodosticta Bates (11.0–19.0 mm) is elongate and parallel-sided, with three glabrous calluses on pronotum. Head with long and vertical face, antennae much (male) or slightly (female) longer than body. Pronotum wider than long with sides tuberculate behind middle. Elytra with dark brown pubescence at basal and apical thirds and broad median gray band, with orange spots interspersed throughout. Legs short, front femora distinctly transversely carinate over basal half, resulting in a double elevated carina. Larvae develop in branches of leguminous trees (*Prosopis*, *Senegalia*, *Mimosa*, *Parkinsonia*) girdled by females. Adults feed on tender bark and girdle larval host trees in late summer and fall. Arizona to Texas and Mexico. (2)

Hairy Borer *Ipochus fasciatus* LeConte (4.5–10.0 mm) is small, strongly oval and convex, spiderlike, variably reddish brown or dark brown to black, and clothed in long, erect setae. Elytra fused with flight wings underneath absent. Legs short, femora moderately clavate. Flightless adults commonly found year-round under bark of willow (*Salix*), oak (*Quercus*), and many other trees and shrubs, including lemonade sumac (*Rhus integrifolia*), laurel sumac (*Malosma laurina*), toyon (*Heteromeles arbutifolia*), and milk thistle (*Silybum marianum*). Coast Ranges from Monterey Bay southward to the Santa Monica Mountains and coastal foothills of Transverse and Peninsular Ranges, and Channel Islands of California; also Baja California Norte. (1)

Plectrura spinicauda Mannerheim (8.0–13.0 mm) is moderately robust, ovoid, tapering posteriorly, and reddish brown with sparse yellowish patches of pubescence. Pronotum with sharp tubercles on sides. Elytra with glabrous calluses surrounded by coarse, irregular punctures, and apices produced into broad spines. Larvae mine under dead, wet bark, pupating in sapwood of maple (*Acer*), alder (*Alnus*), willow (*Salix*), buckthorns (*Rhamnus*), Douglas-fir (*Pseudotsuga menziesii*), and western red cedar (*Thuja plicata*). Flightless adults found year-round on dead leaves and twigs of larval hosts, or overwinter in bark crevices and loose bark. Pacific Coast, from Alaska to northern California. (1)

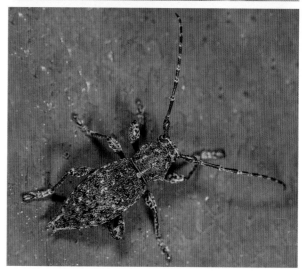

Poliaenus californicus Schaeffer (6.5–11.0 mm) is densely clothed in long, appressed setae. Head with scape slender, antennomere 4 shorter than 3. Pronotum with conical tubercles. Discal elytral costae well developed. Femora clavate. Foothills, mountains of central and southern California. Adult and larvae found on flannelbush (*Fremontodendron californicum*). *Poliaenus obscurus* (Fall) (6.0–9.5 mm) and subspecies similar, costae not well developed; on pine (*Pinus*), California to Nevada and Arizona. *P. oregonus* (LeConte) (6.0–8.5 mm) elytra with broad postmedian band of black pubescence; on conifers, British Columbia to southern California and Rocky Mountains from Idaho and Montana to Colorado and Utah. (4)

Poplar Borer *Saperda calcarata* (Say) (18.0–33.0 mm) is reddish brown to black and clothed in dense, grayish pubescence mottled with pale brown. Head, three pronotal stripes, scutellum, and some lines and spots on elytra with orange-yellow pubescence. Elytra distinctly spined apically. Larvae in poplars (*Populus tremuloides*, *P. deltoides*, and *P. balsamifera*), also willow (*Salix*). Adults feed on foliage, bark, and young shoots in late spring and summer. Transcontinental; in West south to northeastern California, Utah, and Colorado. (4)

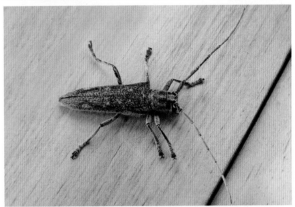

497

Tetraopes annulatus LeConte (8.0–16.0 mm) is robust, stout, and reddish with body densely clothed in short, appressed, grayish pubescence not completely obscuring surface. Pronotal umbone not abruptly elevated, somewhat flattened. Elytral umbones usually shiny, apices usually black. Elytra with humeri dark, subbasal sutural spots, and lateral spots at apical third; scattered short, erect setae on disc. Larvae mine roots of milkweeds (*Asclepias*); diurnal adults on foliage in spring and summer. Eastern Utah and northeastern Arizona to western Colorado and New Mexico. (8)

Tetraopes basalis LeConte (8.0–17.0 mm) is robust, stout, shiny reddish, with black appendages and abdomen, scape and femora often reddish; elytral markings variable. Apical maxillary palpomere elongate, slightly larger than apical labial palpomere. Antennae ringed with grayish pubescence. Pronotal umbone abruptly and distinctly elevated, barely longer than wide, not distinctly delimited laterally. Elytral humeri black, without posthumeral spots, and two black sutural spots present or absent. Larvae mine roots, diurnal adults on foliage of *Asclepias*. Southern Oregon to southern California. *Tetraopes femoratus* LeConte (8.0–19.0 mm) similar, apical maxillary palpomere inflated; pronotal umbone longer than wide, distinctly delimited laterally; Great Basin and Arizona. (8)

Tetraopes discoideus LeConte (6.0–10.0 mm) is small, robust, with head red or black, black pubescence on antennomeres; pronotum mostly reddish or grayish; umbone less elevated. Pronotal umbone abruptly elevated and prominent. Elytra with median chevron, apical chevrons bordered anteriorly by two dark round spots. Adults on *Asclepias subverticillata* during summer. Colorado to Arizona and Texas, south to Guatemala. *Tetraopes skillmani* Chemsak & Noguera (8.0–9.0 mm) with black head; densely gray pubescent antennomeres; pronotum mostly gray with lateral apices reddish, umbone more highly elevated, convex with dense punctation and erect, black setae; elytra without median chevron. Adults on *Funastrum* in summer; southeastern Arizona. *Tetraopes linsleyi* Chemsak with red head and pronotum; central Arizona to Texas. (8)

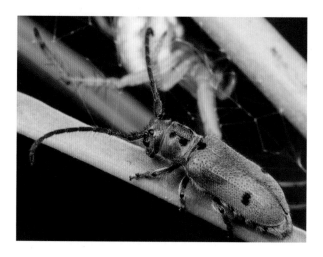

MEGALOPODIDAE (meg-å-lop-ōd′-i-dē)
MEGALOPODID LEAF BEETLES

Megalopodidae is a small family of beetles represented in North America by the single genus *Zeugophora*. Both the adults and larvae are leaf feeders. Little is known of their host plant preferences in the Nearctic, but several species feed on poplars (*Populus*) and willow (*Salix*). The adults feed externally, while their flat, legless larvae mine young leaves and leave large, dark blotches in their wake. Fully developed larvae leave their host plants to pupate in the soil.

FAMILY DIAGNOSIS The short antennae of adult *Zeugophora* are attached low on the head between mandibles and protuberant eyes and are neither directed backward nor set on tubercles. Antennae with 11 antennomeres, 5–11 almost serrate. Pronotum with lateral margins not carinate, and distinctly angulate and constricted posteriorly when viewed from above. Procoxal cavities closed behind. Elytra covering entire abdomen and rounded at apices. Legs with tibiae bearing a pair of apical spurs, tarsi appear 4-4-4, but actually 5-5-5 with tarsomere 4 very small and hidden between lobes of 3; claws equal in size and appendiculate. Abdomen with five ventrites free, 1–4 each somewhat equal in length, 5 longer.

SIMILAR FAMILIES
- orsodacnid leaf beetles (Orsodacnidae, p.499)—prothorax broadly rounded when viewed from above
- leaf beetles (Chrysomelidae, p.501)—conspicuous tibial spurs present or absent, or only on hind legs

COLLECTING NOTES Adults are swept or beaten from the foliage of willow, poplar, and incidentally from other trees and shrubs.

Poplar Black-mine Beetle *Zeugophora scutellaris*
Suffrian (3.5–4.1 mm) is elongate and somewhat parallel-sided, convex, coarsely punctured, sparsely pubescent, shiny, and bicolored. Head, prothorax, and legs reddish orange, while elytra, metasternum, and abdomen black. Antennomeres 1–4 pale, 5–11 somewhat serrate and dark. Pronotum longer than wide, with anterolateral margins narrowed from prominent tubercle to anterior angle. Elytra broader than pronotum, with humeri distinct. Adults on aspen (*Populus*) and willow (*Salix*) in spring and early summer. Holarctic; across Canada and northern United States, in West south to California, east to Montana, Wyoming, and Colorado. Genus needs revision. (7)

ORSODACNIDAE (or-sō-dak'-ni-dē)
ORSODACNID LEAF BEETLES

Four species of orsodacnids occur in North America, three of which occur in mountainous areas of the West. *Orsodacne atra* (Ahrens) occurs throughout the region, while *Aulacoscelis candezei* Chapuis is known from Arizona to Texas; its presence in California, based on a single record from Needles, requires confirmation. The third species, *Janbechynea fulvipes* (Jacoby), is known from southeastern Arizona and Mexico. Little is known about the life history of orsodacnids in North America, other than the adults are often the first phytophagous beetles to emerge in spring (*Orsodacne*), and are sometimes found in flowers (*Orsodacne, Aulacoscelis*) or on oaks (*Aulacoscelis*). Neotropical species of both *Aulacoscelis* and *Janbechynea* are associated with cycads, which are not native in the West. The larvae of all North American orsodacnids are unknown, but it is suspected that those of *Orsodacne* are subterranean and feed either internally or externally on living roots.

FAMILY DIAGNOSIS Adult orsodacnids strongly resemble leaf beetles. Head with distinctly square labrum that projects forward between mandibular bases. Antennae relatively short and weakly serrate, each with 11 antennomeres, attached laterally on head between mandibles and eyes, and are not directed backward or set on tubercles. Pronotum with lateral margins not carinate, and are rounded when viewed from above. Procoxae open behind externally. Elytra cover abdomen entirely, with apices rounded. Legs with all tibiae bearing a pair of apical spurs, tarsi appear 4-4-4, actually 5-5-5 with tarsomere 4 very small and hidden between lobes of 3; claws equal in size and simple (*Aulacoscelis, Janbechynea*) or bifid (*Orsodacne*). Abdomen with five ventrites free, 1 somewhat longer than 2.

SIMILAR FAMILIES
- megalopodid leaf beetles (Megalopodidae, p.498)—lateral margin of prothorax distinctly angled medially when viewed from above
- leaf beetles (Chrysomelidae, p.501)—if present, apical tibial spurs only on hind legs

COLLECTING NOTES Adult *Orsodacne* and *Aulacoscelis* are hand-picked, swept, or beaten from flowers and blooming shrubs. *Orsodacne* is active in early spring. In southeastern Arizona, *Aulacoscelis* and *Janbechynea* occur mostly in montane habitats at high elevation.

FAUNA FOUR SPECIES IN THREE GENERA

Orsodacne atra (Ahrens) (4.0–7.0 mm) is elongate, narrow, somewhat parallel or subparallel-sided, somewhat convex, and variably black, dark red, or brownish yellow; sometimes with stripes or spots. Head is as broad as prothorax. Pronotum with lateral margins neither carinate or upturned, and narrower than base of elytra. Tarsal claws bifid. Larvae are unknown, but may be external root feeders. Adults found in early spring feeding on a wide variety of flowers of deciduous trees and shrubs. Widespread in mountainous regions of western North America; also in East, except for southern states. (1)

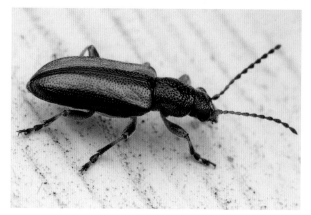

Aulacoscelis candezei Chapuis (6.8–8.8 mm) is elongate, narrow, somewhat flattened, moderately shiny, and variably yellowish to orangish brown with darker elytra, or uniformly brownish, with appendages darker. Antennomeres 8–10 distinctly longer than wide. Pronotum smooth, sparsely punctate, with short longitudinal fold on each side extending from posterior margin to edge of disc, and lateral margins distinctly carinate with narrowly reflexed marginal bead. Elytra sometimes with metallic luster, about as wide at base as at middle, and sparsely clothed in erect setae, each with three or more longitudinal carinae. Tarsal claws simple, tarsomeres 1 and 2 broad in male. Adults on asters, also oak (*Quercus*). Arizona to Texas. (1)

Janbechynea fulvipes (Jacoby) (8.0–8.7 mm) is elongate, somewhat cylindrical, and variably yellowish brown with femoral apices and tibial bases brown to reddish brown with legs and abdominal apex various. Head broader in male. Pronotum wide, with sides constricted at basal third, especially in females, and a pair of basal grooves contiguous to posterior margin, sparse and shallow to dense and deep punctures, especially at anterior angles, and lateral margins carinate with narrowly reflexed marginal bead. Elytra uniformly clothed in dense and appressed pubescence. Legs long and slender, with tarsal claws simple. One record of adult on oak (*Quercus*). Southeastern Arizona and Mexico. (1)

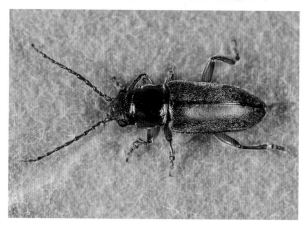

CHRYSOMELIDAE (kris-ō-mel'-i-dē)
LEAF AND SEED BEETLES

Chrysomelids comprise the fourth-largest family of beetles in North America. Most species are small to very small and many are conspicuously colored, possibly warning of their distastefulness to predators. Both adults and larvae typically consume fresh tissues of many kinds of plants growing in sunny habitats. They eat the bark, stems, leaves, flowers, seeds, and roots. The majority of chrysomelids are specialists, feeding only on a single species or on groups of closely related flowering plants, but a few species prefer conifers, ferns, and their allies. Some chrysomelids feed solely on aquatic plants, with adults grazing on leaves and other vegetative structures above the water surface and larvae consuming submerged plant tissues. Larvae either feed out in the open on the surfaces of leaves, mine stems and leaves, or live underground where they feed on roots and other subterranean plant structures. Larvae of Cryptocephalinae inhabit leaf litter, where they consume dead plant materials and live in cases made from their own feces and bits of plant debris. Seed beetle larvae feed and develop inside seeds and seedpods. Many species of chrysomelids are of economic importance, both as adults and as larvae. Garden and crop pests damage plants directly through defoliation, leaf mining, or root boring, or by infecting them with disease. Some seed beetles attack leguminous crops such as alfalfa, beans, lentils, and peas, while others infest stored and dried seeds. However, some leaf beetles, because of their very narrow food preferences and tendency to defoliate host plants, have been pressed into service as biocontrol agents (see p.40) of St. John's Wort, tamarisk, Japanese knotweed, Scotch broom, and other noxious weeds and shrubs.

FAMILY DIAGNOSIS Adult chrysomelids are extremely variable in shape and difficult to characterize as a family. They are long and cylindrical, or compact, square or oval, convex to almost hemispherical, or flattened. Head usually hypognathous, sometimes prognathous. Antennae with 11 antennomeres, usually filiform, sometimes serrate, plumose, flabellate, or clavate. Pronotum triangular or rectangular, broader than head, usually with lateral margins carinate, and sometimes broadly explanate. Procoxae open or closed behind. Elytra conceal abdomen (leaf beetles) or not (seed beetles). Hind legs sometimes enlarged for jumping. Tarsi appear 4-4-4, but are actually 5-5-5, tarsomere 4 small and hidden between lobes of heart-shaped 3; claws usually equal in size, simple or with broad tooth. Abdomen with five ventrites usually free.

SIMILAR FAMILIES
- handsome fungus beetles (Endomychidae, p.315)—tarsi appear 3-3-3, but are 4-4-4
- lady beetles (Coccinellidae, p.318)—tarsi appear 3-3-3, but are 4-4-4
- darkling beetles (Tenebrionidae, p.347)—tarsi 5-5-4
- antlike flower beetles (Anthicidae, p.400)—head with neck, tarsi 5-5-4
- soft-winged flower beetles (Melyridae, p.420)—antennae serrate, tarsi distinctly 5-5-5
- checkered beetles (Cleridae, p.425)—antennae clubbed, tarsi distinctly 5-5-5
- pleasing fungus beetles (Erotylidae, p.435)—antennae with distinct, flat clubs
- longhorn beetles (Cerambycidae, p.460)—pronotum not parallel-sided, widest at middle or behind
- leaf-rolling weevils (Attelabidae, p.534)—antennal club with three antennomeres
- weevils (Curculionidae, p.539)—snout usually longer, geniculate antennae with distinct, antennal club with three antennomeres

COLLECTING NOTES
Look for chrysomelids on the foliage and flowers of trees, shrubs, vines, and herbs growing in all kinds of sunny habitats. Hand-pick adults from plants in gardens, crops, and other sensitive habitats to avoid damaging plants; beating and sweeping are generally more efficient methods of collection elsewhere. Seed beetles are best obtained by collecting seeds and seedpods and placing them in a secure container until the adults emerge.

FAUNA ~1,869 SPECIES IN 218 GENERA

Amblycerus robiniae (Fabricius) (3.8–7.3 mm) is somewhat ovate, arched in profile, mostly reddish brown to black with scattered, black, setigerous pits on pronotum and elytra. Head with eyes large and convex. Pronotum nearly semicircular. Elytra striate with shallow punctures, mostly convex, except for slight depression at scutellum. Pygidium evenly rounded (male) or trilobed (female) apically. Adults on honey locust (*Gleditsia triacanthos*). Mostly in East, with scattered records in western North America. *Amblycerus vitis* (Schaeffer) (2.6–3.7 mm) is uniformly reddish with black eyes, spotless, and with pygidium evenly rounded in both sexes. Adults on wild grape (*Vitis arizonica*). Southeastern Arizona. (2)

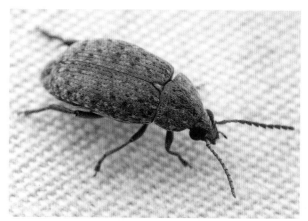

Zabrotes spectabilis Horn (1.3–1.6 mm) is broadly oval, somewhat convex, with dorsal vestiture gray to golden brown to dark brown, white patterns on pronotum, elytra, and pygidium. Eyes deeply emarginate. Antennae expanded distally, reaching middle of elytra, basal antennomere red. Pronotum with a sharply defined white spot on each side and median white stripe on disc. Elytra with pair of white transverse oval spots. Pygidium with medial white stripe. Hind tibiae carinate, spurs equal and movable, with coxae brown and coarsely punctate. Lateral margin of female abdomen with variable patch. Larvae and adults on senna (*Senna*). Oregon and California to Utah and Texas. (11)

Bean Weevil *Acanthoscelides obtectus* (Say) (2.0–3.0 mm) is mostly black with reddish abdomen and legs, and clothed in vestiture of slender yellowish gray and dark brown setae forming three vaguely defined bands across elytra. Head, pronotum, and underside uniformly yellowish gray. Apical and antennomeres 1–4 red. Pronotum bell-shaped. Pygidium with uniformly gray-yellow vestiture, except for denser stripe down median. Lower margin of metafemur with a large tooth, followed by 3–4 smaller teeth; metatibia with carina, apex with triangular process scarcely longer than lateral denticle. First ventrite of male without pit. Larvae and adults primarily associated with beans (*Phaseolus*) and cowpea (*Vigna*). Cosmopolitan. (33)

Algarobius prosopis (LeConte) (2.1–4.1 mm) is elongate-ovate and brownish yellow with eyes, humeri, and female pygidial sulci flanking midline black. Vestiture of fine yellow, white, dark and light brown, and black setae forming variable elytral pattern. Eyes deeply notched. Antennae reach past posterior pronotal margin. Pronotum bell-shaped, convex, with lateral carina weak. Underside clothed mostly with white setae with some yellow spots. Larvae and adults are the most common bruchine associated with mesquite (*Prosopis*) in region. Deserts of southern California to Utah and Texas. (1)

Bruchidius villosus (Fabricius) (2.4–3.2 mm) is mostly black, uniformly clothed in white setae with golden sheen above and white below. Head without frontal carina, eyes deeply notched, and antennomeres 1–4 often reddish; legs sometimes lighter. Elytra without subbasal denticles. Hind femora with tooth on inner lower margin very small, obscure; tibiae slightly bent at base, with apical process. Associated with *Cytisus scoparius* and other leguminous trees and shrubs. Europe; Pacific Northwest, also Northeast. *Bruchidius cisti* (Fabricius) similar, appendages always black, fourth elytral stria with subbasal denticle, hind tibia without process; British Columbia and Montana. (2)

503

Pea Weevil *Bruchus pisorum* (Linnaeus) (3.9–4.9 mm) is black with antennomeres 1–4, protibiae and tarsi, and portions of mesotibiae and tarsi reddish. Vestiture whitish, yellowish brown, dark brown, and black forming distinctive pronotal, elytral, and pygidial patterns. Head without carina. Pronotal apex truncate, sides with median tooth. Pygidium white with dark basal, subapical patches. Hind femur with long tooth on upper margin near apex, usually with small tooth on lower margin. Associated with *Pisum*, *Lathyrus*, and *Vignum*. Adults may emerge from stored peas, but do reproduce indoors. Cosmopolitan. *Bruchus rufimanus* Boheman with femoral angulation only. (2)

Gibbobruchus mimus (Say) (2.3–3.5 mm) is mostly black with dark red patches on elytra. Vestiture of dark brown, orange, white, and yellow setae forming elytral pattern. Antennae reddish yellow, sometimes dusky. Elytra with velvety V-shaped patch on suture near base; occasionally all red. Pygidium without tubercles, but with three glabrous, subapical spots, yellow with bare patch (male) or large, dark heart-shaped spot (female) near apex. Legs mostly reddish, tarsi lighter. Hind femur with median serrate ridge consisting of large tooth followed by a gap and three small teeth. Associated with California redbud (*Cercis orbiculata*). Nevada and Arizona to Maryland and Florida; Mexico. (1)

Megacerus impiger (Horn) (2.1–3.0 mm) is somewhat oval and convex, sides parallel, and reddish brown with diffuse black lateral spots. Males with large eyes and pectinate antennae; female antennae serrate. Pronotum cone-shaped. Elytra with faint diagonal costa extending from prominent humeral bump, strial punctures fine, tenth stria reaches first ventrite, and apices surpassing pygidium with only exposed area sclerotized. Hind femur not enlarged, angulate, toothed or serrate, male hind coxa with broad, polished area. Larvae and adults on false bindweed (*Calystegia*). California to Carolinas and Florida, and Mexico. (5)

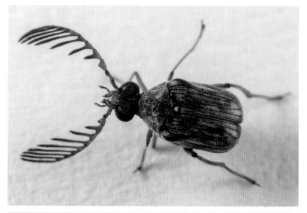

Stator limbatus (Horn) (1.6–2.7 mm) is black with variable marked red and black elytra. Eyes deeply notched. Antennae becoming enlarged apically, with basal four or five antennomeres yellowish brown. Lateral pronotal margins distinctly carinate. Scutellum quadrate, slightly concave. Elytra red to a pattern of small basal and apical red spots on a black background. Pygidium with only exposed area sclerotized. Hind femur with single denticle toward apex. Larvae and adults on various leguminous desert trees, including *Senegalia*, *Prosopis*, and *Parkinsonia*. Southern California to Texas; also Hawaii. (6)

504

Charidotella sexpunctata bicolor (Fabricius) (5.0–7.0 mm) with head completely concealed by pronotum. Underside of pronotum not grooved. Legs with some claws toothed, front claws with broad extension at base. Elytra with front margins smooth, never striped, and very shiny; turns brown after death. Adults active late spring and summer. Both adults and larvae feed on undersides of leaves of sweet potato (*Ipomoea*), bindweed (*Calystegia*), and other morning glories (Convolvulaceae). Larvae carry cast exoskeletons and waste on "anal fork" held over body. Widespread across Canada and United States. (3)

Charidotella succinea (Boheman) (4.0–5.0 mm) is oval, moderately convex with appendages mostly pale yellow. Head hidden from above, antennomeres 8–11 darker. Pronotum with anterior margin broadly translucent and broadly explanate medially, with disc smooth. Elytra with anterior margins smooth, lateral margins narrowly explanate, broadly translucent before base, and disc bright brassy metallic green in life. Underside black. On morning glories. Arizona to Colorado and Texas, south to Central America. *Charidotella bifossulata* (Boheman) similar, margins translucent, pale underneath, elytra each with pair of darkened pits, Arizona. *C. emarginata* (Boheman) black underneath, reddish elytra each with triangular translucent patch on lateral margin; Arizona to Texas and Central America. (4)

Deloyala lecontii (Crotch) (5.0–7.0 mm) is oval, somewhat convex, with appendages mostly pale yellowish brown; mostly black or black with metallic patches. Head hidden from above, antennae long with antennomeres 9–10 black. Pronotum broadly translucent anteriorly with median black patch, or variable transverse figure-8-like marking circumscribing two smaller brassy green patches. Elytra with anterior margins crenulate, lateral margins translucent with narrowly black humeral angles, disc solid black or black with brassy green patches in masklike pattern. Underside reddish brown. Arizona to Texas, south to Mexico. Genus needs revision. (1)

Eggplant Tortoise Beetle *Gratiana pallidula* (Boheman) (5.4–6.1 mm) is oval, not very convex, and mostly pale green-yellow (fades to yellowish brown after death), with pronotal and elytral margins wide and completely translucent. Head hidden from above, antennae short and thick with last three or four antennomeres black. Pronotum without punctures. Elytral bases strongly sinuate and surface with rows of coarse, deep punctures. Spiny pale green larvae feed on nightshade (*Solanum*) and carry defensive fecal shields over back. Adults found in spring and summer on larval host plant. California; widespread in eastern North America. (1)

505

Heliocassis clavata testudinaria (Boheman) (7.0–7.7 mm) is broadly oval with pronotal and elytral margins broadly explanate. Head, appendages, and underside yellow, antennal apices brown. Antennae long, usually held forward. Pronotum with anterior margin broadly translucent, disc smooth, and posterior margin sinuate at base. Elytra brown, except on sides and apices, anterior margins faintly crenulate, disc roughly sculptured with prominent elevation straddling suture just before base. Adults and larvae occur on pepper (*Capsicum*), jimsonweed (*Datura*), nightshade and tomato (*Solanum*). Arizona east to Texas, south to South America. (1)

Anisostena californica Van Dyke (4.1–4.6 mm) is elongate, parallel-sided, coarsely punctured, and uniformly dark metallic blue. Head with frons angulate, impressed medially; eyes finely faceted, not greatly bulging beyond sides; antennae with 11 antennomeres. Pronotum with basal impression, no tooth on anterior angle. Elytra each with three costae and eight punctostriae, plus scutellar stria, and smooth lateral margins. Middle femora strongly curved and serrate on inner margin. Adults found on grasses. British Columbia to California, east to South Dakota and Colorado. (10)

Baliosus californicus (Horn) (4.1–4.5 mm) is elongate, somewhat flattened, wedge-shaped, and yellowish brown. Head with clypeus usually yellow, impunctate with longitudinal sulcus. Pronotum convex, broad, widest at base, with basal impression. Elytra broader than pronotum, with rectangular humeri, and lateral margins serrate and gradually widened posteriorly; elytron with 4 costae, 1 unites with 2, 3 unites with 4, all united at apical one-fifth, costa 1 not branched at base, with 10 punctostriae plus scutellar stria; weakly explanate apically. Legs pale yellow. Adults on ceanothus (*Ceanothus*). Oregon and California, east to Texas. (2)

Brachycoryna longula Weise (2.2–3.1 mm) is elongate, narrow, somewhat convex, parallel-sided, coarsely punctate, and mostly reddish yellow with head, antennae, and bases of legs black. Vertex of head not alutaceous, but with several deep punctures; antennae swollen apically. Surfaces between pronotal and elytral punctures smooth. Elytra each with three costae and lateral margins not distinctly serrate. Adults found on singlewhorl burrobrush (*Hymenoclea monogyra*) and white bur-sage (*Ambrosia dumosa*). California, Nevada, and Arizona, south to Mexico. (5)

506

Microrhopala rubrolineata (Mannerheim) (3.9–5.3 mm) is elongate, somewhat flattened, coarsely punctate, and black with metallic or purplish sheen, with pronotum and elytra usually with orange markings. Vertex of head with medial impression, eyes large, lateral profile of frons not prominent or angulate. Eyes margined behind by row of punctures. Antennomere 3 longer than 2, 5 punctate. Elytra with lateral margins conspicuously serrate. Tarsomere 3 cleft underneath to about two-thirds its length. Larvae on various Asteraceae, including brittlebush (*Encelia*), ragweed (*Ambrosia*), bristleweed (*Hazardia*), goldenbush (*Isocoma*), and goldenrod (*Solidago*). Adults on brickellbush (*Brickellia*) and brittlebush (*Encelia*). California to Texas. (5)

Microrhopala vittata (Fabricius) (5.0–7.0 mm) is somewhat flattened, coarsely punctate, and black with purplish or blue reflections and reddish orange stripes. Head with small eyes separated from mouth by distance equal to length of third antennomere; antennae black, sometimes reddish. Pronotum reddish on sides, anterior margin narrowly transparent, lateral margins somewhat rounded, diverging posteriorly. Elytra punctostriate, punctures coarse and contiguous, with sides undulate or not, never finely serrate (serrulate), widest at apex. Adults on goldenrod (*Solidago*). British Columbia and Alberta to California, Utah, and Colorado; widespread in eastern North America. (5)

Octotoma marginicollis Horn (4.8–6.0 mm) is elongate, somewhat flattened, coarsely punctured, wedge-shaped, and variably yellow with brown and black markings. Antennae as long as head and pronotum combined, with eight antennomeres, 7–8 forming elongate club. Pronotum with lateral margins completely carinate, anterolateral angles projecting forward, posterior margin with pair of broad pits. Elytra with 10 confused punctostriae present at base, plus short scutellar row; disc with irregular, branched carinae most evident on apical half; lateral and apical margins distinctly dentate. Larvae on desert peony (*Acourtia*). Adults on ash (*Fraxinus*), baccharis (*Baccharis*), brickellbush (*Brickellia*), goldeneye (*Viguiera*), and beebalm (*Monarda*). California to Utah and Texas. (1)

Stenopodius flavidus Horn (4.5–5.0 mm) is elongate-oval, somewhat convex, coarsely punctate, and yellow with vertex, eyes, and antennae black, tarsi brown, and dark diffuse markings on pronotum and elytra. Antennae short. Pronotum slightly wider than long, with prominent mostly impunctate medial lobe on anterior margin, and sides somewhat parallel at basal two-thirds. Elytra broader than pronotum, each with 10 punctostriae, punctures in all but 6–7 mostly regular. Larvae on globemallow (*Sphaeralcea*). Adults on larval host plant, hollyhock (*Alcea*), cotton (*Gossypium*), velvetmallow (*Horsfordia*), bushmallow (*Malacothamnus*), mallow (*Malva*), and falsemallow (*Malvastrum*). Washington to California, east to Wyoming, Kansas, and Texas; Mexico. (7)

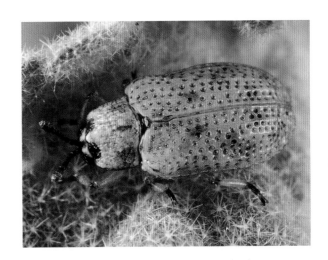

507

Sumitrosis inaequalis (Weber) (3.4–4.2 mm) is elongate, somewhat convex, coarsely punctate, with pale brown and black markings. Vertex with small medial groove and small depression near each eye. Pronotum widest at middle, anterolateral angles narrowly rounded, and pair of black stripes flanking midline. Lateral and apical elytral margins feebly and finely serrate (serrulate), apices rounded and slightly widened. Legs pale. Adults on various plants; larvae mine leaves of asters (*Aster*), baccharis (*Baccharis*), joe pye weed (*Eutrochium*), sunflower (*Helianthus*), coneflowers (*Rudbeckia*), and goldenrod (*Solidago*). British Columbia, Montana, Colorado, Wyoming, and Texas to Maritime Provinces and Florida. *Sumitrosis rosea* (Weber) paler overall, with pronotal angles angulate. (3)

Xenochalepus ater (Weise) (7.2–7.7 mm) is somewhat convex, coarsely punctate, and black with variable reddish-orange markings on pronotum and humeri. Head usually black, vertex with four deep, well-defined grooves; antennomere 3 cylindrical, 4 obconical and sulcate. Lateral margins of pronotum black. Elytra with interval 2 strongly carinate for almost entire length, lateral and apical margins irregularly dentate, apices subquadrate. Underside of thorax black. Larvae on *Glycine* and *Phaseolus*. Adults on *Robinia*, *Rhamnus*, and *Platanus*. Arizona, Texas. *Xenochalepus robiniae* Butte (6.8–7.6 mm) similar, pronotum completely reddish orange; antennomeres 3 and 4 cylindrical, smooth. (2)

Physonota arizonae Schaeffer (11.0–13.0 mm) is oval with translucent lateral pronotal and elytral margins explanate. Head completely concealed from above by rounded anterior pronotal margin. Pronotum widest basally, with long medial dark spot flanked on each side with a shorter marking. Elytra widest basally, tan, disc variously light and dark brown, occasionally with faint creamy white mottling. Ventrites yellow with short transverse lateral dark mark on each sternite. Claws simple, without basal teeth. Larvae and adults on ambrosia leaf bur ragweed (*Ambrosia ambrosioides*) and gentian (*Gentiana*) from late spring through summer. Southern Arizona and Mexico. (1)

Chelymorpha phytophagica Crotch (7.5–10.0 mm) is oblong-oval, coarsely punctate, and orange-red dorsally with short, scattered, erect setae and variable black spots. Distal antennomeres, legs, and underside duskier or brownish. Pronotum with punctures sometimes confluent, and four spots across middle. Elytron with seven or fewer spots, and a small, shared sutural spot behind scutellum. On *Ipomoea*. Arizona to Kansas and Texas; Mexico. Argus tortoise beetle *Chelymorpha cassidea* (Fabricius) (8.5–12.0 mm) is glabrous, brick red, with bold black spots, four to six on pronotum, five on elytron, including shared sutural spot. Transcontinental; Alberta, California, Utah. (2)

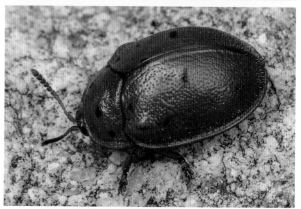

Calligrapha californica coreospivora Brown (5.3–7.0 mm) is elongate-oval, with striped elytra, and dark appendages. Head dark, with basal antennomeres pale. Pronotum pale orangish or reddish with dark, transverse discal mark. Elytra beige with black sutural and entire discal stripes, and pale epipleurae. Underside mostly dark, margins of prothorax reddish. Larvae on *Bidens*; also *Ambrosia* and *Coreopsis*. Across southern Canada, northern United States. *Calligrapha c. californica* Linell similar, except discal elytral stripe obliquely divided behind middle. British Columbia to California, east to Montana. (10)

Calligrapha dislocata (Rogers) (9.0 mm) is oval and convex, with elytra bearing sinuate lines, and underside and appendages dark with metallic green luster. Head black with metallic green luster and moderately punctured. Pronotum black with metallic green luster, disc with scattered deep punctures, especially along sides; hypomeron with distinct suture parallel to lateral margin. Elytra more or less beige, each with distinct sutural and subsutural stripes flanked by another pair of narrow sinuate stripes, outermost in contact with humeral spot; also several smaller spots laterally and apically. Larvae and adults associated with mallows (*Sphaeralcea*) and other Malvaceae. Arizona to Texas, south to Mexico. (10)

Calligrapha multipunctata (Say) (5.9–8.8 mm) is elongate-oval with variable dark markings on pronotum and elytra, and reddish-brown appendages. Head mostly reddish brown or black with greenish luster. Pronotum with anterior and lateral margins broadly pale, darker markings reddish brown or black with greenish luster. Elytra pale, each with a variable stripe along suture and numerous black spots and dashes, except along lateral margins. Underside dark. Larvae feed on willows (*Salix*). Widespread in North America. (10)

Chrysomela confluens Rogers (6.1–8.1 mm) is elongate-oval, parallel-sided, and moderately convex. Head and antennae dark. Pronotum with broad pale lateral margins, each with a distinct black spot, and disc between strongly impressed sulci black with bluish cast; rarely entirely dark. Scutellum dark. Elytra smooth, either entirely deep blue or blue-green, or pale brown with bluish or black sutural stripe, distinct pattern of spots arranged 2-3-3, with median intermediate spots 3.5–4 times longer than wide, and apices produced in female. Legs usually entirely dark, with tibiae sometimes reddish medially or mostly pale. Adults and larvae on willow (*Salix*) and cottonwood (*Populus*). Western Washington to central California, east to Utah. (15)

Chrysomela schaefferi Brown (3.9–6.5 mm) is broadly oval, somewhat convex, and variable in color. Head dark, with antennomeres uniformly dark, sometimes with basal antennomeres pale. Pronotum black and broadly pale, reddish, or reddish orange laterally, with a small dark spot on each margin. Elytra uniformly red, orange, black, or pale brown with darker irregular markings. Legs range from dark yellowish brown to brown or black. Adults and larvae found on willow (*Salix*). Alaska south to California, east to Yukon Territory and Alberta. (15)

Cottonwood Leaf Beetle *Chrysomela scripta*
Fabricius (5.4–10.0 mm) has a greenish-black head with
antennomeres 1, 7–11 dark and 2–6 reddish or dark.
Pronotum greenish black at middle and reddish yellow
outside of broad, distinct groove along each side. Elytra
yellowish with distinct black markings and reddish-yellow
margins. Underside and appendages various colors, legs
with claws simple. Larvae and adults feed on species of
cottonwood (*Populus*) and willow (*Salix*). Adults active spring
through summer; attracted to lights at night. In West from
British Columbia and Alberta to Utah and Colorado. (15)

Red Turnip Beetle *Entomoscelis americana* **Brown**
(6.7–10.0 mm) is oval and red, with black markings,
appendages, and underside. Clypeus, mouthparts, areas
before and behind eyes, and small medial spot on vertex
black. Pronotum with broad median area and small spot
on each side blackish. Elytra with narrow sutural stripe and
two broader discal stripes not reaching base nor apex, with
punctation confused. Claws simple. Posterior margins of
apical ventrite bisinuate (male) or truncate (female). Larvae
and adults minor pests of cabbage, broccoli, mustard, and
radish. In West from Alaska and western Canada south to
Washington, Utah, and Colorado. (1)

Green Dock Beetle *Gastrophysa cyanea* **Melsheimer**
(4.0–5.3 mm) is oval, and entirely brilliant metallic blue or
green, sometimes with bronze luster. Pronotum and elytra
moderately punctured, punctures irregularly scattered.
Pronotum lacks groove along posterior margin. Abdomen
of egg-bearing females greatly enlarged. Tibiae sharply
angled apically, hind femora not swollen, and claws
simple. Larvae and adults on dock (*Rumex*), knotweed
(*Polygonum*), and rhubarb (*Rheum*). Adults overwinter,
emerge in early spring to feed and mate through early
summer. Southern Canada and United States. (4)

American Aspen Beetle *Gonioctena americana*
(Schaeffer) (5.0–6.2 mm) is elongate-oval, somewhat
convex, never metallic, usually with pronotum marked and
elytra spotted; appendages brown. Head reddish brown
with clypeus pale and base black; antennomere 10 not
longer than wide. Pronotum reddish brown and broadly
black at base. Elytra red with rows of punctures, spaces
between finely punctate. Legs with tibiae expanded, each
with tooth near apex. Adults and larvae found on aspen
(*Populus*). Adults briefly active in late spring, overwinter
in leaf litter at base of host. Alaska south to Washington,
Wyoming; across Canada, south to upper Midwest and
northeastern United States. (5)

Colorado Potato Beetle *Leptinotarsa decemlineata* **(Say)** (9.0–11.5 mm) is oval, and strongly convex, and brown-yellow with maculate head and pronotum maculate, and striped elytra. Pronotum with median longitudinal U-shaped mark sometimes broken, flanked on side by five irregular, sometimes confluent spots. Elytron with five distinct black stripes. Legs mostly pale, joints and tarsomeres darker. Larvae and adults on groundcherry (*Physalis*), nightshade and tomatoes (*Solanum*). Southern Canada, United States, and Mexico. *Leptinotarsa tumamoca* Tower (7.3–8.1 mm) smaller, with elytral stripes 2–4 joined at apex; Arizona. *L. peninsularis* Horn (7.3–8.1 mm) with immaculate pronotum, elytron with three bold black stripes, 2–3 joined apically; Arizona, Mexico. (6)

Leptinotarsa haldemani **(Rogers)** (8.8–11.0 mm) is oval, strongly convex, and immaculate with fine punctures dorsally and uniformly deep metallic blue, green, or violet elytra. Head and pronotum uniformly metallic green or dark blue-black. Elytral punctures forming irregular rows. Legs uniformly black. Adults on groundcherry (*Physalis*), nightshade (*Solanum*), and desert-thorn (*Lycium*) during spring and late summer. Southeastern Arizona to Oklahoma and Texas, south to Michoacán and Veracruz. (6)

511

Leptinotarsa lineolata **(Stål)** (7.0–7.7 mm) is oval, and strongly convex, with metallic green or brassy head and pronotum, spots and broken lines on elytra. Head and pronotum immaculate. Scutellum metallic green to brassy. Elytra each with four black stripes with greenish reflections broken at middle, 3 and 4 joined at humerus, and coarse irregular punctures. Legs uniformly light brown. Summer-active adults and black-striped larvae feed exclusively on foliage of singlewhorl burrobrush (*Hymenoclea monogyra*), a low shrub that commonly grows in sandy washes. Southern Arizona to western Texas and northern Mexico. (6)

Leptinotarsa rubiginosa **(Rogers)** (9.3–11.9 mm) is oval, strongly convex, and immaculate with mostly fine punctures dorsally, and uniformly orangish red to red, save for black antennae, mouthparts, and scutellum. Elytral punctures coarse, forming irregular rows. Legs uniformly black, sometimes with partly orangish-red femora and tibiae. Adults on groundcherry (*Physalis*) and nightshade (*Solanum*) during spring and late summer. Southern Arizona to central Texas, south to Puebla and Veracruz. (6)

Longitarsus species (1.7–3.0 mm) are elongate-oval, somewhat convex, shiny, and black, dark brown, or yellowish brown, sometimes darker along elytral suture. Antennae with 11 antennomeres. Pronotum lacking lateral furrows or distinct basal impression. Elytra wider than prothorax, with discal punctation confused and indistinct. Hind femora enlarged. Hind tibia not grooved or expanded along inner margin, and with acute apical spur. Hind tarsus articulated at apex of tibia, and tarsomere 1 at least half as long as tibia. Larvae are root feeders. Adults feed on numerous plants in several plant families. Very challenging to identify to species. Genus needs revision. (17)

Eucalyptus Leaf Beetle *Paropsisterna m-fuscum* **(Boheman)** (6.3–9.5 mm) is broadly oval, moderately hemispherical in profile, without waxy layer, and pale gray to reddish brown with variable brown markings on pronotum and elytra that disappear soon after death. Pronotum much wider than long. Elytra shallowly and confusedly punctate. Middle and hind tibiae with distinct preapical setal brush. Both adults and pale, greenish-gray, caterpillar-like, nocturnal larvae eat leaves and are pests of blue gum trees (*Eucalyptus*). Southeastern Australia; established in southern California. See *Trachymela sloanei* (Blackburn) (p.513). (1)

Plagiodera californica **(Rogers)** (4.2–5.2 mm) is elongate-oval, only somewhat convex, and uniformly dark green with bronze luster. Pronotum with punctures coarser laterally than medially. Elytra with punctures mostly confused, sides strongly curved, epipleuron glabrous and clearly visible in lateral view. Middle and hind tibiae not abnormally expanded apically. Apical tarsomere with acute ventral tooth near base of each claw, and claws simple. California. *Plagiodera arizonae* Crotch (4.7–5.0 mm) prothorax and legs orangish-red. Nevada and Arizona, east to Colorado and Texas. Adults of both species usually found on willow (*Salix*) and occasionally on cottonwood (*Populus*). (2)

Timarcha intricata **Haldeman** (7.0–11.0 mm) is elongate-oval, convex, moderately shiny and uniformly dull black (immature individuals reddish), and rugosely punctate. Head moderately densely punctate. Pronotum broad, lateral margins broadly arcuate, posterior angles rectangular or slightly obtuse; front coxal cavities closed behind. Elytra fused. Male tarsomeres wider than those of female. Flightless, nocturnal adults feed on *Fragaria*, *Rubus*, *Gaultheria*, and *Vaccinium*. British Columbia to California, east to Alberta, Montana, and Idaho. *Timarcha cerdo* (Stål) (5.0–8.0 mm) is shiny reddish or coppery brown. Coastal British Columbia to California. (2)

Eucalyptus or Australian Tortoise Beetle *Trachymela sloanei* (Blackburn) (4.0–7.0 mm) is broadly oval, and yellowish brown to brown with irregular fine blackish mottling that does not fade after death. Pronotum broad, angles obtuse in front and broadly rounded posteriorly, with disc strongly rugulose. Procoxal cavities open behind. Elytra coarsely punctostriate, with narrow interstriae smooth. Middle and hind tibiae with distinct preapical setal brush. Nocturnal larvae and adults notch leaf edges of red gum eucalyptus (*Eucalyptus camaldulensis*); under bark during day. Australia; in California. See *Paropsisterna m-fuscum* (Boheman) (p.512). (1)

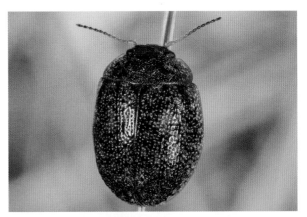

Zygogramma arizonica Schaeffer (5.7–6.5 mm) is broadly oval, often with slight metallic coppery or greenish luster dorsally, and underside and appendages brown. Head and pronotum uniformly brown. Pronotum wide, anterior margin deeply emarginate and flanked by prominent and broad angles; procoxal cavities open behind. Elytra yellowish with epipleurae dark, each with discal stripe sinuous and irregular from humerus to apical third then strongly recurved, sutural and subsutural stripe confluent to about middle, and lateral margins without spots. Claws simple, fused, and contiguous for much of their length. On *Ambrosia*, possibly *Trixis*, and other composites. Arizona. (13)

Zygogramma continua (LeConte) (6.3–7.3 mm) with head, underside, and appendages mostly brown. Pronotum brown with tan markings. Elytra pale, epipleurae dark, two brown or black discal stripes wide, entire, and joined apically, plus confluent sutural and subsutural stripe divergent about middle. Claws simple, mostly fused. On false goldeneye (*Gymnolomia*). Alberta to Arizona, east to Colorado and Texas; south to Mexico. *Zygogramma exclamationis* (Fabricius) (6.5–7.0 mm) elytron with three and a half slender discal stripes, humeral stripe shorter, and sutural and subsutural stripes distinct and reaching apex. On composites. Utah to Arizona, east to Colorado and Texas; Mexico. (13)

Zygogramma piceicollis (Stål) (5.7–7.0 mm) is elongate-oval, moderately convex, slightly bronzed, with head, pronotum, underside, and appendages uniformly brown. Pronotum with anterior margin moderately emarginate and flanked by short, broad angles; front coxal cavities open behind. Elytra pale with epipleurae dark, each with stripes sinuous and broken; humeral and sutural stripe not confluent. Claws simple, and fused for much of their length. On numerous shrubs and trees in several families. Arizona east to Texas; south to Central America. (13)

Zygogramma signatipennis (Stål) (2.5–7.3 mm) is elongate-oval and moderately convex, head and pronotum bluish or greenish black, and underside brown with greenish luster. Pronotum with anterior margin shallowly arcuate between rounded angles; front coxal cavities open behind. Elytra yellowish with black markings with metallic luster, each with humeral and sutural stripes confluent at middle, an oval spot between humeri and scutellum, and four or five spots on posterior half. Tarsal claws simple, fused, and contiguous for much of their length. Adults found on numerous shrubs. Arizona south to Central America. (13)

Asparagus Beetle *Crioceris asparagi* (Linnaeus) (4.7–6.6 mm) is elongate, glabrous and shiny dorsally, with sides of elytra somewhat parallel, with head and most of elytra black, black areas with bluish reflections. Pronotal disc, elytral margins and apices orange. Eyes prominent. Prothorax about as long as wide, distinctly narrower than elytra, with sides rounded; disc sometimes with pair of elongate black spots that meet posteriorly. Elytra with variable light spots, broadly dark along suture. Claws divergent and not touching basally. Adults and larvae feed exclusively on and are pests of asparagus (*Asparagus*). Adults stridulate. Southern Canada and northern half of United States to southern California in West. (2)

Spotted Asparagus Beetle *Crioceris duodecimpunctata* (Linnaeus) (4.9–6.6 mm) is elongate, glabrous, and shiny red-orange dorsally, each elytron usually with six (rarely five) black spots; lighter individuals may have brown rather than black markings. Eyes prominent. Prothorax as long as wide, broadest apically, distinctly narrower than elytra, with sides rounded, and weak transverse depression across basal fourth. Prominent elytral humeri each followed by depression. Femora broadest medially, with claws divergent and not touching basally. *Asparagus* pest. Transcontinental; in West from British Columbia to California, east to Alberta, Montana, Colorado, and Wyoming. (2)

Lily Leaf Beetle *Lilioceris lilii* (Scopoli) (6.3–7.3 mm) is elongate, glabrous and shiny dorsally, sides of elytra somewhat parallel, with black head and red pronotum distinctly narrower than base of red elytra. Eyes prominent. Prothorax about as long as wide, strongly constricted at middle. Elytra with prominent humeri. Legs black with femora broadest medially, claws divergent and not touching at base. Larvae and adults are serious pests of lily (*Lilium*) and fritillary (*Fritillaria*). Europe; in West, established in southern Alberta and Washington. (1)

514

Lema nigrovittata (Guérin-Méneville) (5.0–6.7 mm) is elongate, glabrous and shiny dorsally, and mostly yellow to yellow-orange, with sides of elytra somewhat parallel, with head and pronotum distinctly narrower than base of elytra. Eyes prominent. Prothorax about as long as wide, sometimes with a pair of spots. Elytra each with three prominent stripes, lateral stripes not exceeding sixth and seventh intervals, and prominent humeri; ninth elytral stria without gap. Legs with femora broadest medially, tarsal claws touching at base. Adults and larvae on solanaceous plants, including jimsonweed (*Datura*), groundcherry (*Physalis*), belladonna (*Atropa*), and eggplant (*Solanum*). California to Colorado and Texas. (8)

Lema trabeata Lacordaire (5.2–6.7 mm) is elongate, glabrous and shiny dorsally, sides of elytra somewhat parallel, with head and pronotum entirely black, distinctly narrower than base of elytra. Eyes prominent. Prothorax about as long as wide, constricted at middle. Elytra black with variable pattern of reddish-orange lateral, basal, and apical markings; humeri prominent. Legs with femora broadest medially, tarsal claws touching at base. Adults and larvae on groundcherry (*Physalis*). Southeastern Arizona to Florida. (8)

Threelined Potato Beetle *Lema trivittata trivittata* Say (5.1–7.3 mm) is elongate, glabrous and shiny dorsally, with sides of elytra somewhat parallel, and mostly yellow, yellow-orange to dull orange, with head and pronotum distinctly narrower than base of elytra. Head seldom black between prominent eyes. Prothorax as long as wide, disc with two spots sometimes expanded. Elytra with lateral stripes narrow, about 2–2.5 intervals wide. Femora broadest medially, tarsal claws touching at base. On solanaceous plants, including jimsonweed (*Datura*) and groundcherry (*Physalis*). *Lema daturaphila* Kogan & Goeden (5.7–8.0 mm) very similar, lateral elytral stripes broader, three or more intervals wide. Both species widely distributed. (8)

Oulema arizonae (Schaeffer) (4.9–5.8 mm) is elongate, glabrous dorsally, with sides of elytra somewhat parallel, with reddish-orange head and pronotum sometimes partly dark, distinctly narrower than base of black elytra. Head alutaceous and dull, with antennae and eyes black. Prothorax reddish orange, about as long as wide, constricted close to base. Elytra sometimes with bluish caste, coarsely punctostriate, with ninth stria complete, rarely with gap of one to four punctures. Reddish-orange underside partly to mostly dark. Legs with femora dark reddish to black, and tarsal claws touching at base. Larvae on *Commelina* and *Senecio*. Southeastern Arizona. (4)

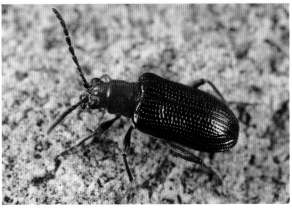

Anomoea rufifrons occidentimutabilis Moldenke (6.0–7.0 mm) is elongate, slender, and dull red and black, without metallic luster. Head and pronotum mostly black. Head with eyes large and distinctly emarginate. Antennae short and serrate. Pronotum wider than long, broadest medially, and more or less impunctate on disc. Elytra red with black suture and broad band across middle, with rows of short setae on disc in male. Legs short and stout (female), or with front tibiae elongate and curved (male). Adults found on woody legumes. Southeastern Arizona south to Jalisco. Genus poorly documented in West and needs revision. (2)

Coleothorpa axillaris LeConte (1.5–2.5 mm) is robust, somewhat cylindrical, widest at humeri, and shiny black without iridescence, densely clothed in appressed white setae dorsally and ventrally, and elytra with red humeri. Pronotum with posterior angles each with a minute spine. Adults found during summer on many plants, including acacia (*Senegalia*) and mesquite (*Prosopis*). Eight subspecies distinguished by elytral pattern and leg color. Western North America south to Mexico. *Coleothorpa vittigera* (LeConte) (4.2–7.3 mm) larger, less pubescence dorsally, and elytra each with broad or narrow reddish-orange stripe. Adults on oak (*Quercus*). Western Canada south to Arizona, New Mexico, and Kansas. *Coleothorpa vittigera arizonensis* (Horn) with humeral patch only. (2)

Megalostomis pyropyga Lacordaire (7.1–13.0 mm) is somewhat cylindrical, with shiny metallic reflections. Front of head and underside densely clothed in appressed dense white setae. Male mandibles longer than clypeus. Head greenish with metallic blue reflections, with eyes distinctly notched. Pronotum wider than long, same color as head except with bronzy area across anterior margin. Elytra with punctation confused, basal half of elytra orange-red, apical half with metallic green or blue reflections and bronzy apicolateral areas. Male forelegs elongate. On *Mimosa* and other legumes. Arizona, New Mexico, and Mexico. (2)

Megalostomis subfasciata (LeConte) (6.0–8.0 mm) is robust, somewhat cylindrical, sparsely pubescent dorsally, and shiny black with a more or less quadrate reddish patch below humerus. Head with eyes distinctly notched. Pronotum clothed in white pubescence. Elytra with punctation confused, less sparsely pubescent than pronotum, pubescence not obscuring pattern, surface with punctures coarse, not dense. Underside clothed in dense white pubescence. Adults found on mimosa (*Mimosa*) and catclaw acacia (*Senegalia greggii*). Baja California, Arizona to Kansas and Texas, south to Sinaloa. (2)

Saxinis saucia LeConte (4.0–7.0 mm) is robust, somewhat cylindrical, and extremely variable; elytra usually metallic blue with red humeri and without pubescence. Pronotal punctures fine. Elytra with sides tapering posteriorly or not, bases extending over basal pronotal margin adjacent to pair of anteromedial depressions. Adults on *Eriogonum* and other plants in late spring and summer. Nine subspecies ranging from southwestern British Columbia to Baja California, east to southwestern Montana, western Colorado, and northwestern Arizona. *Saxinis sonorensis* LeConte (4.0–7.0 mm) light metallic blue with red humeri, densely punctate dorsally. On *Ceanothus*, *Prosopis*, *Senegalia* in summer. Arizona to Texas; Mexico. (9)

Urodera dilaticollis Jacoby (6.5–8.7 mm) is robust, cylindrical, widest at middle of elytra and shiny black with mostly red elytra. Pronotum impunctate, except for coarsely punctured surfaces of broadly explanate lateral margins. Scutellum black. Elytra seriopunctate, immaculate or with V- or Y-shaped black band across middle often broadly interrupted medially. Underside densely clothed in appressed silvery pubescence. Adults associated with mimosa (*Mimosa*), also oak (*Quercus*). Central highlands of Arizona and western New Mexico south to Sinaloa and Durango. (1)

Cryptocephalus atrofasciatus Jacoby (5.0–7.5 mm) is cylindrical, slightly tapered posteriorly. Head light orange to dark brown with long antennae. Pronotum light orange to reddish, with posterior margin crenulate, and usually with lateral basal spot and paler anterior and lateral margins; anterior lateral margin of prothorax straight. Elytra yellowish or orangish with three undulating and transverse black, red, or orange bands, each with eight coarse punctostriae, 5–7 usually entwined, with punctures becoming finer apically. Last ventrite flat, without spines (male), or deeply concave and flanked by curved setae (female). On pines (*Pinus*). Colorado to Arizona and Texas; south to Mexico. (34)

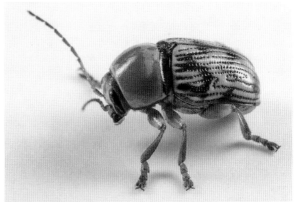

Cryptocephalus sanguinicollis Suffrian (3.2–4.9 mm) is robust, cylindrical, slightly tapered posteriorly. Head coarsely punctured, with long filiform antennae. Pronotum uniformly light to deep red, with punctures small, and posterior margin crenulate; anterior lateral margin of prothorax straight. Elytra uniformly black or dark brown, each with eight coarse punctostriae becoming finer apically, punctures on 5, sometimes 6 and 7, confused. Last ventrite flat medially and without spines (male), or deeply concave and flanked by curved setae (female). On *Adenostoma*, *Eriogonum*, *Arctostaphylos*, *Salix*, and other woody shrubs. British Columbia to Baja California, east to Montana and Utah. (34)

Diachus auratus (Fabricius) (1.8–2.1 mm) is oblong, somewhat cylindrical, tan yellowish-orange with slight bronze luster and alutaceous pronotal and elytral surfaces. Head with eyes shallowly excavated, antennae with 11 antennomeres yellowish brown, 6–11 wider. Pronotum orange laterally, becoming dark bronze medially, with posterior margin crenulate. Scutellum flat, broadly triangular. Elytra finely punctostriate on basal half. Fifth ventrite of female with shallow elliptical depression. Adults found on willow (*Salix*), strawberry, avocado, and numerous other plants, usually restricting their feeding activities to leaf edges. Widespread in North America. (9)

Griburius montezuma (Suffrian) (4.0–6.0 mm) is coarsely punctate, and variably white, black, and red dorsally, and mostly white ventrally. Head black with narrow, transverse white markings above and below eyes. Pronotum black, with anterior margin narrowly white and posterior margin broadly red; prosternum broad, as long as wide. Elytra with black suture flanked narrowly or broadly with white along basal two-thirds or more, and margins black, sometimes with white apical and subapical markings. Legs black and white. Larvae associated with *Neotoma* nests or cave debris inhabited by vultures. Adults on various plants. Arizona east to Maryland and Florida; south to Mexico. (1)

518

Pachybrachis bivittatus (Say) (3.9–5.0 mm) is robust and yellow and brown or reddish brown dorsally. Basal half of antennae pale, antennomere 10 three times as long as wide. Pronotum with indistinct black or reddish M-shaped mark, or completely dark, and posterior margin without bead or crenulations; prosternum narrow, longer than wide. Elytron with two stripes down middle, black or brown, one just above side often broken into three spots, one or more spots sometimes absent. Underside mostly black, tip of abdomen yellow, with ventrite 5 with (female) or without (male) pit. Legs reddish brown, tarsi darker. On *Populus* and *Salix* in summer. Widespread in North America. (37)

Pachybrachis circumcinctus Crotch (3.7–4.2 mm) with dorsal surface nearly lacking any alutaceous surfaces. Eyes separated by two and a half (male) or more than three times (female) length of basal antennomere. Pronotum reddish to reddish-brown with anterior and lateral margins paler, often with three more or less dark spots just before posterior margin lacking bead or crenulations; prosternum narrow, longer than wide. Elytron with single broad discal stripe and black margins. Underside mostly black, with posterior ventrite pale laterally. Tibiae and tarsi usually black. On *Alnus* and *Salix*. Washington to California. (37)

Pachybrachis mellitus Bowditch (3.2–4.2 mm) is compact, robust, somewhat cylindrical, minutely alutaceous, and entirely shiny dark honey-yellow dorsally. Head visible from above and not deeply inserted into prothorax, with antennae longer in male, not surpassing middle of metasternum. Pronotum wider than long, disc sparsely and finely punctate between larger punctures, with posterior margin about as wide as anterior margin and lacking bead or crenulations; prosternum narrow, longer than wide. Elytra with mostly confused punctures, except for two impressed lateral punctostriae. Adults on broom snakeweed (*Gutierrezia sarothrae*) or, rarely, desert twinbugs (*Dicoria canescens*). California east to Utah and Texas. (37)

Pachybrachis thoracicus Jacoby (3.0–5.0 mm) is compact, robust, somewhat cylindrical, and distinctively dull black with bases of pronotum and elytra orangish red, and densely clothed in recumbent, silvery white pubescence, especially on head, pygidium, and underside. Head not deeply inserted into prothorax, with antennae long, black, and not reaching elytral declivity. Pronotum wider than long, with posterior margin lacking bead or crenulations, and orangish-red band broadest laterally. Elytra with basal margins raised. Legs stout, with front femora thickened and hind tibiae without apical spurs. Adults on acacia (*Senegalia*), palo verde (*Parkinsonia*), mesquite (*Prosopis*), and willow (*Salix*). Southern Nevada and Utah to Pacific Coast of central Mexico. (37)

Neohaemonia nigricornis (Kirby) (5.8–7.4 mm) is elongate, with thorax and elytra translucent pale brown in life, and remainder of body black. Head with thick yellowish pubescence interrupted by sometimes brown prominence on vertex. Antennomeres thick. Pronotum narrow with discal punctures along posterior margin; underneath broadly pubescent above coxa. Elytra punctostriate with punctures black, and apices with stout spine on outer apical angle. First ventrite with (male) or without oblong medial depression. All apical tarsi about as long as combined length of preceding tarsomeres, with hind legs long, femora slender and untoothed. Adults on pondweed (*Potamogeton*). Mostly in Northeast, with isolated records in British Columbia and Washington. (1)

519

Plateumaris dubia (Schaeffer) (6.6–8.7 mm) is broad-shouldered, shiny, and coppery, metallic greenish, purple, or black, with appendages entirely metallic or dark; bases of femora, tibiae, and antennomeres sometimes reddish brown. Head finely setose and punctate, often with sulcus between eyes. Pronotum long with prominent calluses, median line, and basal sulcus, and disc transversely rugose. Elytra broader than pronotum, with punctures small, and apical sutural bead narrow. Pygidium sometimes reddish brown apically, truncate (male) or pointed (female) apically. Male mesotibia lacks tubercle, metafemur with single tooth small or absent. Adults on sedges (*Carex, Eleocharis,* probably *Scirpus*). Alaska to Oregon, east to Alberta, Montana, and Colorado. (11)

Western Grape Rootworm *Bromius obscurus* (Linnaeus) (4.0–5.5 mm) is oblong, robust, black, brown, or black and brown, and densely clothed in pale pubescence. Pronotum rounded on sides and much narrower than elytra. Minor grape (*Vitis*) pest; larvae feed externally on roots, while adults chew long, linear cuts in leaves. North American populations reproduce sexually, while European populations are parthenogenetic. Europe; widely distributed in North America. (1)

Colaspidea smaragdula LeConte (2.0–6.0 mm) is oblong, robust, and shiny bronze, green, purplish, or bluish, and densely clothed in fine recumbent pale setae. Head narrower than pronotum, eyes round, with antennomere 1 globose, and 3 longer than 2. Pronotum with postocular lobe at anterior angles, with marginal bead on sides. Elytral punctation confused and shallow. Pygidium without medial longitudinal groove. Legs usually metallic, and tibiae, coxae, and base of femora red-orange or brown, with tarsal claws diverging and bifid. Adults on chamise (*Adenostoma*), buckbrush (*Ceanothus*), mountain mahogany (*Cercocarpus*), flannelbush (*Fremontodendron*), and antelope brush (*Purshia*). Oregon to California, east to Nevada and Arizona. Genus needs revision. (3)

Dogbane Beetle *Chrysochus auratus* (Fabricius) (8.0–13.0 mm) is oblong, robust, glabrous dorsally, and shiny brilliant iridescent green, coppery green, golden green or bluish green. Head retracted into pronotum, with last five antennomeres slightly enlarged. Pronotum variably intermixed with fine and coarse punctures. Adults and larvae associated exclusively with dogbane (*Apocynum*) and milkweed (*Asclepias*); diurnal adults found on leaves of host plant. Hybridizes with *C. cobaltinus* in Yakima Valley, Washington. Transcontinental; in West from south-central British Columbia to north-central Oregon. (2)

520

Blue Milkweed Beetle *Chrysochus cobaltinus* LeConte (6.5–11.5mm) is robust and oblong, glabrous dorsally, and shiny deep cobalt blue, rarely with greenish tinge. Head retracted into pronotum, last five antennomeres slightly enlarged. Pronotum variably intermixed with fine and coarse punctures. Adults and larvae associated exclusively with dogbane (*Apocynum*) and milkweed (*Asclepias*); diurnal adults found on leaves of host. Hybridizes with *C. auratus* in Yakima Valley, Washington. South-central British Columbia to southern California, east to western Montana, northern Nevada, and Utah. (2)

Colaspis nigrocyanea Crotch (4.7–5.5mm) is oblong-oval and convex, coarsely punctured, and shiny bluish-black with greenish or purplish reflections dorsally, metallic blue with purplish reflections ventrally, including legs. Antennae dark with metallic sheen, antennomeres 3–6 brown. Pronotum deeply and irregularly punctate, punctures sometimes coalescent medially, with interstices smooth, and lateral margins evenly arcuate. Elytra with rows of deep punctures somewhat geminate. Adults on climbing milkweed (*Funastrum cyanchoides*). Arizona. (9)

Colaspis viriditincta Schaeffer (5.0–6.0mm) is oblong-oval and convex, with head, prothorax, and underside usually shiny brassy green, and appendages yellowish brown. Head and pronotum densely punctate. Pronotal lateral margins rounded, somewhat angulate behind middle, with posterior angles toothed. Elytra yellowish or reddish brown, each with eight flat costae, and large, brassy interstrial punctures mostly in double rows. Legs with apices of femora and tibiae sometimes darker, with male hind tibiae dilated at middle. Underside with apical ventrite pale. Adults reported feeding on nasturtium, either *Nasturtium*, *Rorippa*, or *Tropaeolum*. Southern Arizona. (9)

Glyptoscelis albida LeConte (6.2–10.5mm) is oblong-oval, stout, convex, with surfaces blackish with bronzy, sometimes purplish-brown luster. Head broad with wide-set eyes, antennae dark brown, extending beyond humeri. Pronotum and elytra evenly and densely clothed in long, appressed pubescence appearing grayish with intermixed white and brown pointed setae. Prothorax broad, pronotum coarsely and contiguously punctate. Elytra slightly depressed in front of scutellum. Underside clothed in fine, silky, white setae. Legs and tarsi short, with claws toothed. Adults found on incense cedar (*Libocedrus decurrens*) and Arizona cypress (*Cupressus arizonica*). In West, British Columbia to southern California, east to Alberta, Montana, and Utah. (19)

Tymnes oregonensis (Crotch) (5.0–7.0 mm) is shiny blue, green, or golden dorsally and ventrally, with appendages usually orange. Head retractile with prothorax up to posterior margin of moderately bulging eyes, and antennomere 3 longer than 4. Pronotum with anterior angles toothed, sides margined and nearly parallel, discal punctures coarsely and densely punctate, and posterior angles distinct. Elytra with humeri not prominent. Pygidium grooved. Elytra with more or less confused round punctures larger than those of pronotum. Male tarsomere 3 dilated, and claws of both sexes appendiculate. On *Calocedrus decurrens* and *Juniperus californica*. Oregon and northern California. (1)

Graphops pubescens (Melsheimer) (3.2–4.4 mm) is oblong-oval, sparsely setose, with shiny metallic bronze or coppery sheen. Pronotum wider than long. Elytra more than twice as long as pronotum, with prominent humeri and fine, inconspicuous setae, and rows of fine punctures. Abdomen with pygidium lacking conspicuous groove down middle. Legs with apices of middle and hind tibiae distinctly notched, front femora each with small tooth, and claws with long inner tooth. Adults on evening primrose (*Oenothera*) in spring and summer. Widespread in western North America. (7)

522

Alder Flea Beetle *Altica ambiens* (LeConte) (4.8–6.3 mm) is oblong, somewhat convex, shiny, and deep metallic blue, including appendages. Head with antennae inserted high on frons near middle of eyes. Pronotum wide, slightly narrower anteriorly than posteriorly, with lateral margins moderately explanate, and posterior transverse impression deeply impressed and terminating in lateral pits. Elytra each with lateral costa high, or prominent and concealing lateral margin. Hind femora strongly swollen, and basal tarsomere enlarged (male) or narrow (female). Larvae feed on leaves of alder (*Alnus*), while adults found on various plants. Widely distributed in western North America. (32)

Sumac Flea Beetle *Blepharida rhois* (Forster) (6.3–7.7 mm) is oval, very convex, and shiny, with head and pronotum uniformly orangish, yellowish, or greenish, and underside reddish brown. Antennae with 11 antennomeres, dark reddish brown, with bases widely separated. Pronotum convex, without impressions, and finely punctate. Elytra mottled or irregularly striped red and white. Elytra punctoseriate, with widely separated punctures coarse. Front and middle femora pale, while tibiae, tarsi, and hind femoral apices dark reddish brown. Hind legs with tarsomeres not inflated, tibiae not grooved, dilated, or serrate, and all claws bifid. Adults on *Rhus* and *Toxicodendron*. Transcontinental, across southern Canada and United States. (1)

Disonycha alternata (Illiger) (6.5–8.5 mm) is oblong-oval, convex, moderately shiny, with red head and pronotum, and striped elytra. Head mostly red with eyes and occiput black. Antennae mostly black with basal antennomere somewhat lighter. Pronotum slightly wider than long, red with pale borders, disc with two, four, or five black spots, and arcuate sides narrowed anteriorly. Scutellum dark. Elytra yellowish, impunctate, parallel-sided, each with narrow black sutural, discal, and submarginal stripes; lateral margins pale. Legs reddish with tibial apices and tarsi black. Adults usually associated with willow (*Salix*); also found incidentally on many other plants. Widespread in North America. (17)

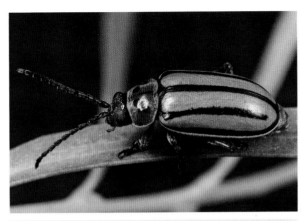

Disonycha tenuicornis Horn (6.0–7.6 mm) is oblong-oval, convex, moderately shiny, with head, pronotum, and striped elytra all orangish red. Head entirely reddish, except for black eyes and mandibular apices. Pronotum slightly wider than long, with two anterior black spots. Elytra impunctate, parallel-sided, each with narrow black or brownish sutural and discal stripes with pale edges; at most with only traces of submarginal stripes; lateral margins pale. Legs reddish with tibial apices and tarsi dark. Adults and larvae on *Salvia*; also reported on willow (*Salix*). Arizona to Texas, south to Mexico. (17)

523

Tobacco Flea Beetle *Epitrix hirtipennis* (Melsheimer) (1.6–2.0 mm) is broadly elongate-oval, robust, and brownish with metallic luster. Head and pronotum light reddish brown, thorax and abdomen brownish, and legs lighter. Head with antennal impression noticeable, either weak or shallow. Antennae yellowish brown, becoming darker apically. Pronotum with surface alutaceous and lateral carinae serrate. Elytra brownish yellow, punctostriate, with sutural stria ending at one-half to apical third, and a single row of setae on intervals. Adults are associated with many species of Solanaceae, including *Capsicum*, *Datura*, *Lycopersicon*, *Nicotiana*, and *Solanum*. Widespread in North America. (5)

Hemiglyptus basalis (Crotch) (3.0–3.5 mm) is elongate-oval, shiny, and dark, with purplish, greenish, or bluish luster, reddish yellow-brown appendages, and sparsely clothed in scattered setae that are easily rubbed off. Pronotum wider than long, disc moderately and deeply punctate, with lateral furrow long, extending to point well beyond juncture of transverse impression, and transverse basal impression arcuate, distinct, and impunctate behind. Elytra with poorly defined punctostriae, intervals 3 and 5 confusedly punctate behind middle, and scattered erect setae. Tibiae each with apical spur. On *Eriodictyon* and waterleaf *Hydrophyllum*. Oregon and California, east to Utah and Arizona. (1)

Kuschelina lugens (LeConte) (4.5–6.0 mm) is oblong-oval, somewhat convex, and uniformly dull black, sometimes with bluish, greenish, or purplish luster, with sparse and fine pubescence ventrally. Head with front flat and tubercles indistinct, eyes small, interocular space half width of head, with antennomeres almost moniliform. Pronotal and elytral margins narrowly reflexed. Pronotum broad, with lateral margins arcuate and narrowed anteriorly. Elytra somewhat smooth and only faintly punctate. Last ventrite and sometimes posterior margins of others yellowish. Metafemora enlarged; femora and all tarsi slightly reddish. Widespread in western North America. (7)

Walterianella durangoensis (Jacoby) (5.0–6.2 mm) is oblong-oval, somewhat convex, feebly shiny and finely punctate, with elytra drab yellow-brown with five or six small black spots on each elytron, and underside yellowish brown and finely pubescent. Head faintly punctate. Antennomeres 1–4 and apex of 11 lighter. Pronotal and elytral margins broadly explanate. Pronotum broad, weakly punctate, with lateral margins arcuately narrowed anteriorly. Elytra with sides nearly parallel, humeri distinct, spots arranged in rows, and explanate margins sometimes slightly reflexed. Metafemora enlarged. On *Chilopsis linearis*. Arizona south to Mexico. (1)

524

Western Striped Cucumber Beetle *Acalymma trivittatum* (Mannerheim) (4.6–5.8 mm) has elytra with three black or dark brown stripes; distinctly punctostriate, punctures mostly in pairs; sutural stripe exceeds costa 1, not reaching apical margin; lateral stripe from base of elytron to apical ninth, covering costae 5–8; pale stripe at middle third covering three or four distinct costae. Dark brown to black legs with pale femoral bases; hind, middle tibiae sometimes pale at middle. On plants in cucumber family. Western North America to Central America. *Acalymma blandulum* (LeConte) (4.3–5.5 mm) sutural stripe includes costa 1, pale elytral stripes including 2–3 indistinct costae. Arizona to Midwest, Mexico. (2)

Western Corn Rootworm *Diabrotica virgifera* LeConte (4.6–5.9 mm) is elongate-oval, with a dark brown or black head, yellowish-orange pronotum and pale greenish elytra, each with black sutural and lateral stripe. Pronotum narrower than elytra, with carinate lateral margins. Elytron with 4–5 weak longitudinal carinae between suture and humeral carina. Males with apical spurs on middle and hind tibiae, females with spurs on all tibiae; claws bifid in both sexes. Adults and larvae are pests of corn; adults on flowers of many plants. Idaho, Utah, and Arizona, east to Ontario, northeastern United States, and Texas. (7)

Western Spotted Cucumber Beetle *Diabrotica undecimpunctata undecimpunctata* Mannerheim (4.8–6.9 mm) is elongate-oval, and black with yellowish-green pronotum and elytra. Pronotum narrower than elytra, with carinate lateral margins. Scutellum black. Elytra with three bands of round black spots. Abdomen black. Legs black, males with apical spurs on meso- and metatibiae, females with spurs on all tibiae; claws bifid. On many plants. Pacific Coast states. *Diabrotica u. howardi* Barber spots larger, legs bicolored, western North America; *D. u. tenella* LeConte less robust, elytral spots smaller and brownish, legs bicolored. Southwestern and south central states. (7)

Galeruca rudis LeConte (7.0–10.2 mm) is ovate, coarsely punctured, glabrous, and dark brown or blackish brown with distinct pale brown elytral margin. Elytron with three or four prominent and entire discal costae, with intercostal areas irregularly, yet distinctly punctate, sometimes with small intercostal ridges. On *Lupinus*. Widespread in montane western North America. *Galeruca browni* Blake (8.0–10.5 mm) similar, intercostal punctures dense and contiguous. On Brassicaceae; western Canada. *Galeruca costatissima* Blake (9.0–12.0 mm) with less prominent intercostal carinae, apparently with 7–8 costae on each elytron. On *Cardaria draba*; Utah to Arizona, east Colorado and New Mexico. (3)

Water Leaf Beetle *Galerucella nymphaeae* (Linnaeus) (4.5–6.0 mm) is somewhat oblong, dull. Head brown, black across top. Pronotum wider than long, reddish brown with three blackish spots; sides each with broad, deep, punctate depression. Elytra brown, suture and sides reddish brown. Bases of front legs not quite touching, narrowly separated by prosternal process; tibiae without spurs. Adults and larvae on floating aquatic plants, chewing irregular trenches on leaves of *Brasenia schreberi*, *Nuphar*, and *Polygonum*. Adults active spring through early fall; at lights. Europe; widely established in North America, except Southwest. (1)

Monoxia debilis LeConte (3.8–5.0 mm) is elongate-oval, dull yellowish brown, and conspicuously clothed in appressed pubescence. Head with terminal antennomeres slightly thicker and dark reddish brown. Pronotum broad, depressed, with lateral margins rounded, and punctures smaller than those of elytra. Elytra coarsely and deeply punctate, more so anteriorly; clothed in short, dense, pale silvery pubescence; short sulcus between humerus and scutellum. Claws simple (female) or bifid (male). On *Chenopodium album* and *Beta vulgaris*. Alberta to Arizona, east to North Dakota, Kansas, and New Mexico. (14)

Black-margined Loosestrife Beetle *Neogalerucella calmariensis* **(Linnaeus)** (3.6–5.6 mm) is elongate, orangish with dark markings on head, pronotum, and elytra. Pronotum with black triangle or broad stripe down middle. Scutellum black. Elytra each with dark, ill-defined broad stripe reaching from base to apical quarter. Ventrite 4 partly or wholly dark. Underside mostly dark. Legs with bases of forelegs not separated by prosternal process, bases of middle legs narrowly separated; femora sometimes dusky. Introduced as biological control of purple loosestrife (*Lythrum salicarium*). Overwintering adults emerge in spring to feed on developing plants. Europe; British Columbia and Alberta, across southern Canada and northeastern United States. (4)

Ophraea rugosa Jacoby (7.5–8.0 mm) is oblong-oval, mostly dull black with pronotum reddish, with pronotal and elytral surfaces coarsely punctate and clothed in very short, scarcely visible pubescence. Head with antennae just surpassing humeri, with antennomeres 3 and 4 subequal in length. Pronotum wider than long, widest behind middle, with anterior angles prominent, and medial elongate black spot. Elytra with faint greenish luster and lateral margins somewhat declivous behind humeri and narrowly explanate. Middle tibiae of male with apical spurs. Adults on leaves of beloperone (*Justicia*). Arizona to Guatemala. (1)

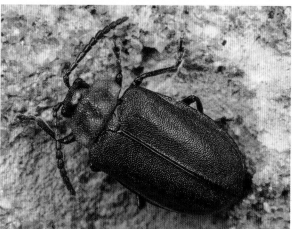

Paranapiacaba tricincta (5.5–7.0 mm) is elongate-oval, convex, and shiny with three black bands across elytra, second and third bands divided by pale suture, and apices black. Antennae slender; antennomere 2 short, 3 twice as long as 2 and nearly as long as 4. Prothorax orange, narrower than elytra, with distinct lateral bead. Elytra with confused punctation, without carinae. Femoral apices, tibiae, and tarsi black, with apical tibial spurs on all legs except front legs of male; claws bifid. Underside of metathorax black, abdomen orange. Adults on several plants in cucumber, aster, and legume families. Utah and Arizona, east to Midwest. (1)

Tricholochmaea punctipennis **(Mannerheim)** (6.0–7.0 mm) is oblong, slightly convex. Head black between eyes, and paler in front. Antennae black and sparsely pubescent with antennomere 4 distinctly longer than 2. Pronotum broadest just before base, lateral margins incised at base and narrowing anteriorly, with dark markings on disc; procoxal cavities open. Elytra entirely black with narrow convexity before lateral margin. Male with broad apical spur on middle tibia. Abdomen with posterior margin of last ventrite excavated (male) or entire (female). Adults on willow (*Salix*), cottonwood (*Populus*), and alder (*Alnus*). Widespread in western North America. (4)

Trirhabda eriodictyonis Fall (5.0–9.0 mm) is elongate, robust, somewhat narrowed posteriorly, and pale yellow brown; males often a third smaller than females. Head coarsely punctate with dark eyes and elongate markings down middle. Pronotum shiny, twice as wide as long, and traversed by three black spots. Scutellum pale, often with dark basal margin. Elytra often with darkened humeral spot occasionally extended into a lateral stripe with greenish metallic luster. Adults and larvae on yerba santa (*Eriodictyon*). Southern California to Utah and Arizona. (19)

Trirhabda flavolimbata (Mannerheim) (5.0–8.0 mm) is oblong-oval, robust, and pale with shiny metallic green or blue markings on dorsal surface. Head with broad metallic band behind eyes. Pronotum broad, traversed medially by three bold dark spots with faint metallic luster. Elytra coarsely and densely punctate, clothed in short pale pubescence, and mostly brilliant metallic green or blue with pale lateral and apical margins; never striped. Adults and larvae on coyote brush (*Baccharis pilularis*); adults on several other plants. Northern California. (19)

Elm Leaf Beetle *Xanthogaleruca luteola* (Muller) (6.0–6.5 mm) is elongate-oval, strongly convex, and yellowish or greenish, sometimes with head, thorax, and legs pale orangish brown. Head with frons between eyes and base of head black. Prothorax narrower than elytra, disc with hourglass mark flanked on both sides with a black spot; front coxal cavities open. Elytra each with short basal stripe and humeral stripe extending almost to apex. Legs without apical tibial spurs. Larvae skeletonize elm (*Ulmus*) leaves as they feed, then pupate on surface of ground or in bark crevices at base of tree. Europe; widely established in North America. (1)

Androlyperus fulvus Crotch (4.5–7.9 mm) is elongate-oval, shiny, somewhat flattened, with head (clypeus, mouthparts sometimes paler), subserrate antennae, scutellum, legs, and underside black; pronotum red, and elytra brownish orange. Pronotum longer than wide, lateral and posterior margins with bead, disc sometimes infuscate. Elytra inconspicuously punctate, sometimes with poorly defined dark spot in apical half; posterolateral margins of male indented. Both sexes with spurs on meso- and metatibiae, but not protibiae. Claws appendiculate. Underside of male abdomen with four long, slender abdominal appendages, last ventrite with short apical lobe. Adults on golden-yarrow (*Eriophyllum confertifolium*) and speckled clarkia (*Clarkia cylindrica*). California. (5)

Scelolyperus lecontii (Crotch) (4.5–5.0 mm) is somewhat elongate, parallel-sided, shiny, convex, with head, pronotum, and underside black, elytra dark metallic blue or green, and legs and antennae reddish brown. Head alutaceous; antennae reaching past middle of elytra, antennomere 2 about half length of 3 or 4. Pronotum finely, densely punctate, wider than long, with anterior angles swollen and posterior angles produced, truncate. Elytra alutaceous, very finely punctate, and sparsely setose. Adults on spreading dogbane (*Apocynum androsaemifolium*) and forest scurfpea (*Rupertia physodes*). British Columbia to California, east to South Dakota and New Mexico. (22)

Western Fruit Beetle *Syneta albida* LeConte (5.0–7.0 mm) is elongate, slender, somewhat convex, and uniformly pale with black eyes, or uniformly dusky to dark brown. Smooth, longitudinal line between eyes, space between antennal bases smooth. Pronotum narrow, sides with obtuse tubercles just behind middle. Elytra with scattered setae of varying lengths. Claws bifid. Last ventrite with (female) or without (male) deep, semicircular and fimbriate excavation. Adults on willow (*Salix*), dogwood (*Cornus*), alder (*Alnus*), maple (*Acer*), and various fruit trees (*Cydonia*, *Prunus*, *Pyrus*). British Columbia to northern California. *Syneta seriata* LeConte (4.0–5.5 mm) with no line between eyes, punctate between more narrowly separated antennae. On oak (*Quercus*). (7)

Syneta hamata Horn (5.5–9.5 mm) is elongate, slender, coarsely punctate, ranging from shiny pale yellowish brown to uniformly reddish or brown, head and pronotum sometimes darker. Pronotum narrow, sides armed with three distinct, slender, spinelike teeth. Elytra glabrous, carinae 2 and 4 strong, elevated. Hind tibiae distinctly hooked (male) or expanded backward much further than inner edge, with pair of apical spurs (female). Claws bifid. Last ventrite with (female) or without (male) deep, semicircular and fimbriate excavation. Adults on many plants during summer, including fir (*Abies*), maple (*Acer*), birch (*Betula*), raspberry (*Rubus*), and hazelnut (*Corylus*). Alaska to California, Idaho, Montana, and Wyoming. (7)

Syneta simplex simplex LeConte (5.0–7.0 mm) is elongate, slender, somewhat convex, and usually more or less reddish brown with suture and legs often paler. Antennae with basal three or four antennomeres pale, remainder dark. Pronotum narrower than base of elytra. Elytral carinae only faintly represented as narrow, smooth, flat lines between punctures, other punctures separated by more than one and a half times their diameters. Claws bifid. Last ventrite with (female) or without (male) deep, semicircular, and fimbriate excavation. Adults on oak (*Quercus*) at lower elevations. British Columbia to northern California. *Syneta s. subalpina* Edwards on fir (*Abies*) at high elevation in Pacific Northwest. (7)

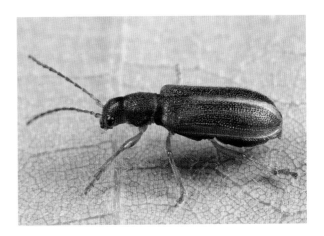

Thricolema anomala Crotch (7.0–9.0 mm) is elongate, somewhat cylindrical, parallel-sided, coarsely punctate dorsally, and uniformly reddish brown with surfaces densely clothed in long, dense, decumbent white pubescence. Prothorax without lateral carinae, with lateral margins angulate, anterior and posterior pronotal angles prominent; procoxal cavities open. Elytral punctation confused, each with single costae originating from prominent humerus not reaching apex. All tibiae without apical spines, claws cleft (males) or simple (females). Adults on incense cedar (*Libocedrus decurrens*), western juniper (*Juniperus occidentalis*), and redwood (*Sequoia sempervirens*) in spring and early summer. Oregon and northern California. (1)

CIMBERIDIDAE (sim-ber-id'-i-dē)
CIMBERIDID SNOUT BEETLES

Cimberidids are a small and seldom collected family of beetles. Once considered a subfamily of Nemonychidae, cimberidids were recently elevated to family, in part, based on their mitochondrial genome. All but two of the 14 North American species occur in coniferous forests of western montane and boreal regions. Although most of these species are associated with pines (*Pinus*), further investigations may reveal that other coniferous genera also serve as hosts. Adults are typically encountered feeding on pollen from male cones, or *strobili*, early in the season, sometimes when snow is still on the ground. Females lay eggs in the strobili, where the larvae feed on pollen until they eventually drop to the ground and pupate in the soil. Additional fieldwork involving extensive collecting over broad ranges, careful recording of host species, and rearing is needed to determine the host preferences and species limits of the North American fauna and possibly identify additional new taxa. Such an undertaking would include cutting small branches containing strobili at least 10 days before or a few days after the pollen is shed, placing them in plastic bags, and storing the samples in a cool place until the adults emerge.

FAMILY DIAGNOSIS Cimberidids are elongate, somewhat flattened dorsally, and clothed in short to moderately long, fine, appressed to recumbent pubescence. Head not fully inserted into prothorax up to eyes. Rostrum straight or curved and narrow, with a distinct labrum and two gular sutures. Mandibles horizontal, armed with a single tooth on inner margin and inserted into the head dorsally (*Cimberis*), or oblique, unarmed (without teeth), and inserted laterally

(*Acromacer*, *Lecontellus*, *Pityomacer*). Straight antennae with 11 antennomeres, 9–11 forming weak club. Pronotum with anterior margin straight or moderately emarginate (*Cimberis*), or deeply emarginate (*Acromacer*, *Lecontellus*, *Pityomacer*), with prosternum in both sexes unarmed. Procoxae narrowly closed behind. Elytra with confused punctures and completely conceal abdomen. Tibiae each with pair of apical spines present. Tarsi appear 4-4-4, actually 5-5-5, tarsomere 2 lobed medially, projecting over 3, 4 small, and claws simple. Abdomen with five ventrites free, with ventrites soft and subequal in length.

SIMILAR FAMILIES

- *Mycterus* (Mycteridae, p.390)—rostrum broad, antennae not clubbed, tarsi 5-5-4
- *Rhinosimus* (Salpingidae, p.399)—rostrum broad, antennae with loose club, tarsi 5-5-5
- pine weevils (Nemonychidae, p.531)—elytra punctostriate, hind tibia with single apical spur, tarsomere 2 truncate medially, not covering 3
- fungus weevils (Anthribidae, p.532)—antennae long, tibiae with spurs on apices, pygidium exposed
- leaf-rolling, tooth-nose, and thief weevils (Attelabidae, p.534)—antennae attached at base of rostrum
- pear-shaped weevils (Brentidae, p.537)—body pear-shaped, trochanter elongate and somewhat cylindrical
- weevils (Curculionidae, p.539)—antennae geniculate

COLLECTING NOTES Look for adults on male strobili producing pollen on pines growing in montane and boreal coniferous forests during late winter and early spring. Cimberidids are occasionally found in Malaise traps.

FAUNA 14 SPECIES IN FOUR GENERA

Acromacer bombifrons (LeConte) (2.8–5.4 mm) is elongate, slightly convex, clothed in long light brown pubescence, and head, rostrum, and pronotum brown, with elytra, legs, and ventral surfaces lighter. Head with mandibles inserted laterally, labrum triangular and pointed at apex, and frons deeply saddled (frons rising vertically above base of rostrum). Pronotum convex, slightly wider than long, broadest just behind middle, disc shiny and densely, deeply punctured, with sides moderately to strongly arcuate. Elytra with punctures confused. Abdomen of female without setal tufts on ventrites. British Columbia to California, east to Alberta, Idaho, and Nevada. (1)

Cimberis bihirsuta (Hatch) (2.5–4.1 mm) is elongate and slightly convex. Rostrum slightly curved, longer (female) or shorter (male) than combined length of head and pronotum, length between antennal insertion and base longer in female, and mandibles inserted laterally and toothed internally. Ventrites 3–4 each with two small white tufts. Femora dark brown. British Columbia to central California, east to Idaho and Wyoming. *Cimberis compta* (LeConte) (2.7–4.2 mm) rostrum shorter than combined length of head and pronotum; femora yellowish, reddish, or dark brown; female ventrites 3–4 with single tuft. British Columbia to California, east to Montana and New Mexico. *Cimberis decipiens* Kuschel (2.8–4.0 mm) black with reddish or brown appendages. British to California, east to Colorado. (3)

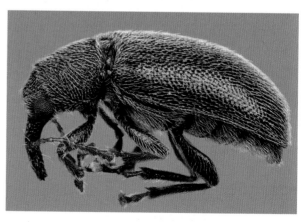

Pityomacer pix Kuschel (3.0 mm) is elongate, slightly convex, with head, pronotum, and underside black, while appendages and elytra are usually dark brown; sparsely clothed dorsally in uniformly short, fine, recumbent gray or golden-brown setae becoming paler laterally. Head with frons convex between eyes. Rostrum weakly curved with mandibles inserted laterally and unarmed internally, and antennae inserted at about middle. Pronotum with anterior margin not deeply emarginate. Elytra confusedly punctate. Ventrites 3–4 of female each with or without two small tufts of white setae. Uncommon. British Columbia to Oregon, east to Alberta and Montana. (1)

Lecontellus byturoides (LeConte) (3.0–5.1 mm) is elongate, slightly convex, with body yellowish, reddish, or blackish, and sparsely clothed in coarse recumbent gray setae. Head coarsely and densely punctured, frons convex and more finely punctured. Rostrum more or less curved, with mandibles inserted dorsally, and antennae inserted before middle. Pronotum wide, globose, with anterior margin deeply emarginate, and disc more strongly punctured in male. Elytra confusedly and coarsely punctured; if dark, then pronotum reddish. Ventrites 3–4 each with (female) or without (male) 1–2 setaceous patches. Adults on ponderosa (*Pinus ponderosa*) and Monterey (*P. radiata*) pines. Central Washington to California, east to Nevada; possibly British Columbia. (1)

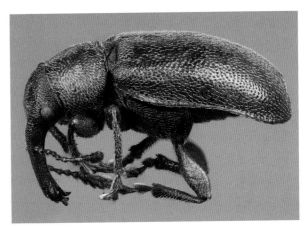

531

NEMONYCHIDAE (nem-on-ik'-i-dē)

PINE FLOWER SNOUT BEETLES

Nemonychidae is represented in North America by a single species, *Atopomacer ites* Kuschel. *Atopomacer* is primarily Neotropical in distribution and its nearest relatives occur in Argentina, Chile, and New Zealand. Based on the habits of two Mexican species in this genus, the adults of *A. ites* are likely found on the male strobili of pines (*Pinus*) growing at high elevations, but this needs confirmation.

FAMILY DIAGNOSIS *Atopomacer* is elongate, somewhat convex, and clothed in dense pubescence. Head inserted in prothorax to eyes. Rostrum long, straight, and narrow, with a distinct labrum and two gular sutures. Mandibles slender with inner margin uneven and armed with indistinct tooth. Straight antennae with 11 antennomeres, 9–11 forming weak club. Pronotum abruptly constricted in front at anterior angles. Prosternum of male armed with "forklike" process. Procoxae narrowly closed behind. Elytra with confused punctures and completely cover abdomen. Front and middle tibiae each with pair of apical spines, hind tibiae with one. Tarsi appear 4-4-4, actually 5-5-5, tarsomere 2 truncate medially, not projecting over 3, 4 small, and claws each with rounded basal swelling. Abdomen with five ventrites free, ventrites soft, with 5 truncate (male) or rounded (female) posteriorly.

SIMILAR FAMILIES
- *Mycterus* (Mycteridae, p.390)—rostrum broad; antennae not clubbed; tarsi 5-5-4
- cimberidid weevils (Cimberididae, p.529)—elytra confusedly punctate; hind tibiae with pair of apical spurs; tarsomere 2 lobed medially and covering 3
- fungus weevils (Anthribidae, p.532)—antennae long; tibiae with spurs on apices; pygidium exposed

- leaf-rolling, tooth-nose, and thief weevils (Attelabidae, p.534)—antennae attached at base of rostrum
- pear-shaped weevils (Brentidae, p.537)—body pear-shaped; trochanter elongate and somewhat cylindrical

- weevils (Curculionidae, p.539)—antennae geniculate

COLLECTING NOTES Adults likely found on male strobili of pine (*Pinus*) growing at high elevations in spring and early summer; rarely at lights.

FAUNA ONE SPECIES, *ATOPOMACER ITES*

Atopomacer ites Kuschel (3.3–3.6 mm) is elongate, slightly convex, uniformly reddish brown, and densely clothed in short, fine, recumbent setae. Eyes small and round, moderately protruding; rostrum slender and gently curved, longer than prothorax, with antennae inserted just behind mandibles. Pronotum broad, with apical and posterior angles rounded; prosternal process of male extended into a forked horn. Elytral striae indistinct. Tarsomere 2 truncate medially, not overlapping base of 3, with hind tibia with single apical spur, and claw lamellate with broad basal flange. Adults likely found on male strobili of pine (*Pinus*) growing at high elevations in spring and early summer. Arizona and Colorado. (1)

ANTHRIBIDAE (an-thri'-bi-dē)
FUNGUS WEEVILS

Anthribids are uncommonly collected and the biology of most species is poorly known. Adults are often encountered on dead or injured branches, clumps of dried leaves, bark, smut-infested grass, and flowers, as well as on fungus. Larvae feed inside twigs and branches, inside polypore fungi, or under the fungus-infested bark of dead and dying trees. Adults of stem-feeding larvae generally eat pollen of their larval host plant.

FAMILY DIAGNOSIS Adult anthribids have a large head that is seldom retracted into prothorax. Rostrum, if readily evident, broad and flat, with stout and curved mandibles, and a labrum. Straight antennae with 11 antennomeres, 9–11 forming weak club. Pronotum sometimes with transverse ridge before posterior margin that may turn forward to form a short, carinate lateral margin. Procoxal cavities closed behind. Elytra with scutellar striae short, not covering pygidium, and always locking into a longitudinal pygidial sulcus across base of exposed pygidium. Legs lack apical spurs and tarsi appear 4-4-4, actually 5-5-5 with tarsomere 4 very small, tarsomere 3 only with spongy pubescent pad underneath, and claws mostly toothed or cleft. Abdomen with five ventrites, with 1–3, 1–4, or 1–5 connate.

SIMILAR FAMILIES
- *Mycterus* (Mycteridae, p.390)—rostrum broad, antennae not clubbed, tarsi 5-5-4
- *Rhinosimus* (Salpingidae, p.399)—rostrum broad, antennae with loose club, tarsi 5-5-5
- cimberidid weevils (Cimberididae, p.529) pygidium covered by elytra
- pine flower snout weevils (Nemonychidae, p.531)—pygidium covered by elytra
- leaf-rolling, tooth-nose, and thief weevils (Attelabidae, p.534)—antennae attached at base of rostrum
- pear-shaped weevils (Brentidae, p.537)—body pear-shaped, trochanter elongate and somewhat cylindrical
- weevils (Curculionidae, p.539)—antennae geniculate

COLLECTING NOTES Anthribids are beaten from fungus-infested dead or diseased branches, clumps of dead twigs or leaves, or tangles of dead vines. Inspect the sheet right away since anthribids are relatively fast and take wing quickly. Other species are found on fungi growing on tree trunks. Sweeping weedy fields with fungus-infected and smutty grasses can be productive, too. Species in several genera are collected in Malaise traps.

FAUNA 88 SPECIES IN 30 GENERA

Eugonus bicolor Valentine (2.5–3.0 mm) is elongate-elliptical, parallel-sided, evenly convex, and reddish brown, with mixed dark brown and straw-colored dorsal pubescence; underside and legs more or less uniformly gray. Head with antennae short, area between eyes densely and roughly punctured, and antennal scrobes strongly produced toward ventral midline. Pronotum broadest at anterior third, lateral carina extending to anterior angle, with basal carina almost entire and area before posterior margin densely punctate. Elytra with distinct basal margin, strial punctures deep, and pale pubescence most evident as irregular spots on basal third, and larger patches above apical declivity broken at suture. Adults attracted to lights. Southeastern Arizona. (1)

Eurymycter fasciatus (Olivier) (6.5–8.0 mm) is broadly elongate-oval, roughly sculptured, dark brown or black, with conspicuous white pubescence on rostrum and band across elytra before apical declivity that reaches sides, and abdomen. Eyes not protruding, with inner margins not carinate, and interocular space flat. Rostrum with lateral carinae distinct and medial carina evident only at base. Pronotum wider than long, disc uneven, briefly and narrowly and transversely sulcate medially at anterior third. Elytra with odd intervals 3, 5, and 7 elevated, and fascia narrow with irregular edges. Ventrites with brown lateral spots. Hind tibia with narrow pale median ring. In west from British Columbia to Oregon, east to Idaho and Utah. (1)

Gonotropis gibbosus LeConte (3.7–6.0 mm) is convex, somewhat ovate, and dull black. Sides of head with dense, fine, white pubescence. Pronotum with broad triangular impression bordered by triangular patch of light brown pubescence. Elytra wider than prothorax, with two prominent tubercles at base, front half with large saddle-shaped patch of pale pubescence, with rows of deep punctures, spaces between raised. Abdomen underneath with tip rounded in both sexes. Adults collected on dead hemlock (*Tsuga*). Alaska and Canada south to Colorado and Pennsylvania. (1)

Trigonorhinus sticticus (Boheman) (2.5–3.0 mm) is oblong, robust, brown, and clothed in dark brown and grayish-yellow setae, rostrum narrowed from base to tip, longer at middle than sides. Eyes notched at bases of antennae. Pronotum convex, brown to blackish, widest in front of or at basal ridge. Scutellum U-shaped. Elytra each with central brown spot and other variable markings. Legs reddish brown, femora dark at middle, tibiae without rings or spots, tarsomere 3 on all feet distinctly lobed. Adults associated with yellow nutsedge (*Cyperus esculentus*) and corn smut (*Utilago maydis*). Transcontinental; in West from British Columbia to California, east to Alberta, Montana, and Utah. (3)

ATTELABIDAE (at-e-lab'-i-dē)

LEAF-ROLLING AND THIEF WEEVILS, AND TOOTH-NOSE SNOUT BEETLES

Attelabids either mine or roll up leaves, or inhabit other plant tissues, especially reproductive structures. Female leaf-rolling weevils (*Synolabus*) lay one or more eggs on a leaf, then use their mandibles to chew and cut the base of the leaf and roll it around the eggs with their front legs. The rolled-up barrel-like leaf serves as both food and shelter for the developing larvae. Thief weevils in the genus *Pterocolus* are so named because the females take over the rolled leaf nurseries of other attelabids by destroying their eggs and replacing them with their own. Tooth-nose snout beetles (Rhynchitinae) have mandibles toothed on the inner and outer margins and their larvae mine dead leaves (*Eugnamptus*) or develop in dead flower heads (*Haplorhynchites*). Most attelabids are of no economic importance, although *Merhynchites*, which develops in buds and shoots, sometimes damages cultivated blackberries, raspberries, and roses.

FAMILY DIAGNOSIS Adult leaf-rolling weevils are more or less stout, broad across elytral bases, and glabrous, while tooth-nose snout beetles are elongate, very small and oval (*Eugnamptus*), or very small and broadly oval (*Pterocolus*). Antennae straight, each with 11 antennomeres, 9–11 forming weak club. Rostrum long and slender (*Eugnamptus*) or short and broad, and mandibles toothed only on inner margin (*Himatolabus, Synolabus*), or on both inner and outer margins. Pronotum distinctly narrower than base of elytra. Procoxal cavities open or closed behind. Elytra cover entire abdomen. Tarsi appear 4-4-4, but are 5-5-5; tarsomere 4 small, partially hidden within lobes of heart-shaped tarsomere 3, claws equal in size and appendiculate or fused (*Himatolabus, Synolabus*) at base. Abdomen with five ventrites becoming progressively shorter posteriorly, 1–2 connate.

SIMILAR FAMILIES

- *Mycterus* (Mycteridae, p.390)—rostrum broad, antennae not clubbed, tarsi 5-5-4

- *Rhinosimus* (Salpingidae, p.399)—rostrum broad, antennae with loose club, tarsi 5-5-5
- cimberidid weevils (Cimberididae, p.529)—rostrum with distinct labrum
- pine flower snout beetles (Nemonychidae, p.531)—associated with male pine cones; rostrum with distinct labrum
- fungus weevils (Anthribidae, p.532)—rostrum broad, antennae long, pygidium exposed
- pear-shaped weevils (Brentidae, p.537)—body pear-shaped, trochanter elongate and somewhat cylindrical
- weevils (Curculionidae, p.539)—geniculate antennae with compact club comprising one to three antennomeres

COLLECTING NOTES Beating shrubs, trees, and vines, and sweeping flowers are the most productive field methods for collecting attelabids, along with searching host plants. Some species are abundant in spring and early summer on oak (*Quercus*), sumac (*Rhus*), and wild rose (*Rosa*).

FAUNA 51 SPECIES IN 11 GENERA

Himatolabus pubescens (Say) (4.0–7.2 mm) is pear-shaped, robust, uniformly dull reddish brown or darker, and irregularly clothed in short, yellowish pubescence. Rostrum short, coarsely punctate in front of antennal bases. Pronotum smooth, coarsely punctate with narrow groove down middle, anterior margin without lobes covering eyes. Elytra without basal tubercles, with strial punctures close-set, and interstriae finely punctate. Adults active mostly in summer, found on oak (*Quercus*). Colorado and Arizona east to Maritime Provinces, Virginia, and Alabama; south to Mexico. *Himatolabus axillaris* (Gyllenhal) (4.1–7.7 mm) is brownish black or black with reddish spots on elytral humeri. Utah and Arizona south to Guatemala. (2)

Synolabus nigripes (LeConte) (3.5–4.5 mm) is pear-shaped, robust, lacks setae, and is mostly reddish with variable dark areas; rostrum and appendages black without bluish tinge. Femora swollen, front femora with one (female) or two (male) blunt teeth. Elytra with basal pale areas and punctures arranged in rows. Underside dull red. On sumac (*Rhus*) and at lights in spring and summer. Females roll up leaves within which their larvae develop. Arizona east to Colorado, Minnesota, Kansas, and Florida. (1)

535

Eugnamptus nigriventris Schaeffer (3.4–6.3 mm) is slightly convex, reddish orange with black or dilute black metathorax, abdomen, and most of hind coxae. Eyes of male larger and closer together than in female. Antennal club and rostral apex sometimes darker. Pronotum as wide as long, with disc coarsely punctate, and narrower than elytra. Elytra with metallic bluish or greenish luster, punctostriate, punctures large, with interstriae wider than striae and flat to weakly convex, and covering pygidium. Abdomen black. On *Quercus* and *Juglans*. Arizona east to Texas. (4)

Deporaus glastinus LeConte (3.5–4.6 mm) is elongate, slightly convex, shiny black with blue luster, and clothed in nearly erect setae. Rostrum in front of eyes shorter than head. Head slightly narrowed behind prominent eyes and longer than prothorax. Only funicular antennomere 1 longer than wide. Pronotum as long as wide, narrower than base of elytra, and not carinate laterally. Elytra somewhat parallel, deeply punctate, punctures arranged in lines, with scutellar striole, and somewhat short, not covering pygidium. Tarsomere 1 longer than 2 and 3 combined. Larvae mine *Quercus* leaves; adults on oaks. Western Washington and Oregon to Baja California, east Colorado and Texas. (1)

Pterocolus ovatus (Fabricius) (2.0–3.7 mm) is broadly ovate, convex and compact, and uniformly deep metallic blue or greenish black with antennae, mandibles, and claws brown. Rostrum straight and shorter than head, with antenna inserted near basal quarter. Pronotum with distinct lateral carina, lateral punctures sometimes fused longitudinally. Punctostriae distinct, punctures moderately deep, interstriae narrow, convex, and widely separated. Rounded apices exposing pygidium. Females use leaves rolled by other attelabids. On many trees and shrubs in spring and summer. Arizona east to Ontario, New England, and Florida; south to Central America. (1)

Haplorhynchites pseudomexicanus Hamilton (4.2–5.7 mm) is clothed in long black setae dorsally and ventrally. Black with appendages and tip of rostrum lighter; elytra with dark metallic blue or bluish-green luster. Antennal club symmetrical in both sexes. Rostrum one-quarter (female) or barely longer (male) than pronotum. Pronotum broad, not carinate laterally, and evenly punctate. Elytra setose along suture in males, with striae distinct, intervals broad and more or less flat, and distinctly punctate with some punctures about one-third as large as strial punctures. Pygidium partly exposed. On *Helianthus*, possibly other Asteraceae. Arizona, Texas. (5)

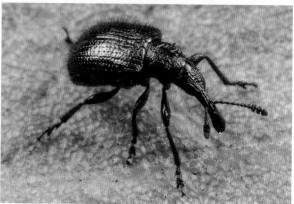

Merhynchites wickhami Cockerell (4.7–8.2 mm) is black with pronotum and elytra red or orangish red. Eyes weakly convex in dorsal view, anterior margins forming 45° angle with rostrum. Rostrum slightly and evenly arcuate (female) or obviously arcuate (male) beyond antennal insertions. Punctostriae indistinct, with intervals minutely rugose. Pygidium partly exposed. Widespread in West. *Merhynchites bicolor* (Fabricius) similar, with eyes prominent, anterior margins forming 90° with rostrum, rostrum straight in both sexes; elytral striae moderately impressed, with interstriae smooth. Across southern Canada and United States. Both species on *Rosa*; larvae develop in buds and hips. (3)

Temnocerus naso (Casey) (2.1–3.7 mm) is bronze to metallic bluish or greenish, with scattered recumbent yellowish setae. Frons with broad medial depression and subequal in length to base of rostrum. Eyes not prominent. Antennae inserted near basal two-fifths (female) or one-third (male) of rostrum. Pronotum broadest at middle, and densely punctate with punctures sometimes coalescent. Elytral intervals with two rows of setigerous punctures, with apices more or less oblique. Pygidium mostly covered by elytra. Adults on *Quercus*, *Juniperus*, *Plagiobothrys*, and *Eriogonum*. Southern California and Baja California. (7)

BRENTIDAE (bren'-ti-dē)
STRAIGHT-SNOUTED AND PEAR-SHAPED WEEVILS

Most western species of brentids are very small and difficult to identify. Their larvae mine stems, developing fruits, and seeds of legumes (Fabaceae), composites (Asteraceae), mallows (Malvaceae), buckwheats (Polygonaceae), umbellifers (Apiaceae), and other flowering plants. The adventive hollyhock weevil, *Rhopalapion longirostre* (Olivier), is found on hollyhock (*Alcea rosea*). A few seed-feeding species (*Exapion*) were purposely imported from Europe into western North America as biological control agents of gorse (*Ulex europaeus*) and Scotch broom (*Cytisus scoparius*). Another European species, *Nanophyes marmoratus* (Fabricius), was introduced into eastern North America to control purple loosestrife (*Lythrum salicaria*).

FAMILY DIAGNOSIS Adult brentids are difficult to characterize as a family, despite their radically different forms that are either pear-shaped or elongate and narrow. In the West, all species are small, more or less pear-shaped, and clothed in scattered scalelike pubescence. Head with rostrum long, slender, cylindrical, and usually longer in females. Antennae straight or geniculate (*Microon*, *Nanophyes*), with a loose or compact club, and inserted on sides at midlength. Procoxal cavities contiguous and closed behind. Legs with trochanter long and somewhat cylindrical, with femur attached to apex of trochanter, and tarsi 5-5-5. Abdomen with five ventrites, with 1–2 connate and combined are much longer and on a different plane than ventrites 3 and 4.

SIMILAR FAMILIES
- cimberidid beetles (Cimberididae, p.529)—antennae attached near tip of rostrum, tibiae with spurs, labrum visible and free
- pine flower snout beetles (Nemonychidae, p.531)—antennae attached near tip of rostrum, tibiae with spurs, labrum visible and free
- fungus weevils (Anthribidae, p.532)—labrum visible, antennae attached at base of rostrum, tibiae without spurs, labrum visible and free
- leaf-rolling weevils (Attelabidae, p.534)—labrum not free
- weevils (Curculionidae, p.539)—geniculate antennae clubbed

COLLECTING NOTES Look for brentids by beating or sweeping flowers and vegetation, especially composites (Asteraceae), legumes (Fabaceae), and mallows (Malvaceae). Some species are attracted to lights.

537

FAUNA 151 SPECIES IN 30 GENERA

Betulapion simile (Kirby) (1.7–2.2 mm) is narrowly elongate-oval, black, and clothed in conspicuous and sparse whitish to yellowish-white long, fine scales. Head with eyes moderately prominent, rostrum slightly curved, slightly longer (male) or one and a half to two times longer (female) than pronotum. Antennae straight. Pronotum barely wider than long at posterior margin. Elytra with striae deep, strial punctures setigerous, with intervals bearing single row of fine scales. Apices of middle and hind tibiae with spinelike processes equal in size. Adults and larvae on paper birch (*Betula papyrifera*). Eurasia; established from Pacific Northwest and Utah, east to Newfoundland and North Carolina. (1)

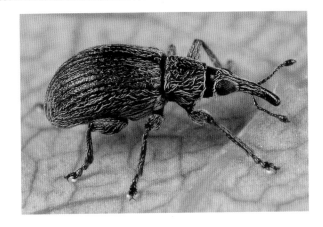

Exapion fuscirostre (Fabricius) (2.0–3.0 mm) is elongate-oval, dull brown or reddish brown with appendages lighter, and clothed in uniformly pale or tan slender scales forming long lateral stripes. Rostrum long, slender, and slightly curved. Antennae straight. Male pygidium with distinct preapical sulcus. British Columbia to California, east to Idaho; also in Northeast. *Exapion ulicis* (Forster) similar in length, gray with brownish-gray legs, and clothed in pale scales sometimes forming faint narrow stripes on elytra. British Columbia to California. Both species introduced from Europe as a biocontrol agents of Scotch broom (*Cytisus scoparius*). (2)

Microon canadense (Brown) (1.2–1.9 mm) is broadly oval, strongly convex, sparsely and evenly clothed in fine and appressed whitish setae, shiny, and uniformly reddish brown, with head and ventral surfaces darker. Antennae geniculate with scape longer than funicle. Rostrum almost as long as head and prothorax combined, feebly curved and finely tricarinate. Pronotum about twice as long as wide, broadest at base with sides straight and strongly converging anteriorly. Elytral humeri prominent, deeply striate, with intervals moderately convex and with distinct sculpturing. Femora unarmed, with claws equal in length and fused basally. Western Canada and Rocky Mountain states south to Arizona. (1)

Hollyhock Weevil *Rhopalapion longirostre* (Olivier) (2.6–3.2 mm) is pear-shaped, black with reddish-brown legs, clothed in grayish pubescence. Rostrum of female very long, twice as long as in male. Antennae straight, antennomere 1 (scape) shorter than next three antennomeres of funicle, funicle with seven antennomeres, club with sutures distinct. Pronotum with vestiture directed toward midline on disc. Pygidium of male without deep groove across tip. Legs with front femora stout, males lacking polished area underneath, middle coxae of both sexes separated by mesosternal processes, and all claws toothed basally. Adults found on hollyhock (*Alcea rosea*) and cotton (*Gossypium*). Eurasia; widely established in North America. (1)

CURCULIONIDAE (kŭr-kū-li-on′-i-dē)
WEEVILS AND SNOUT, BARK, AND AMBROSIA BEETLES

Curculionidae, one of the largest families of beetles, is among the most speciose, diverse, and abundant groups of animals in the world. They occur throughout western North America, from sandy ocean beaches to high-elevation forests to hot, xeric deserts. Weevils feed on the vegetative and reproductive structures of a broad range of plants and, along with the Cerambycidae (p.460) and Chrysomelidae (p.501), are among the largest families of herbivorous beetles. Although most weevils are associated with living

538

terrestrial and aquatic plants, a few scavenge dead plant tissues. Adults of aquatic species can swim, some quite well. Some weevils are adapted for feeding on conifers, especially pines (*Pinus*), but most species and their larvae are associated with flowering plants, both monocots and dicots. Larvae of generalist species feed in the soil on plant roots, sometimes producing characteristically shaped galls as they feed. Larvae of specialists often feed internally in the stems, roots, leaves, or reproductive structures of just one or more closely related plant species. The larvae of a few species graze the surfaces of living or dead leaves, or mine their inner tissues. Most adults eat leaves, pollen, flowers, and fungi, while others attack fruits and nuts, or burrow into wood. Bark and ambrosia beetles live mostly in injured, weakened, or dying trees, shrubs, and woody vines. Bark beetles typically feed on phloem and inner tree bark, sometimes leaving characteristic galleries and tunnels in their wake. Ambrosia beetles cultivate and feed on symbiotic ambrosia fungi within the xylem of the host plant. Some bark and ambrosia beetles are well-known vectors of disease-causing fungi that degrade or kill vast numbers of coniferous trees annually. Blue stain pine is the result of the blue stain fungus that is frequently disseminated by bark beetles. Most weevils are easily recognized by their elongate snout, or rostrum. Females, especially of those species that lay their eggs directly into living plant tissues, often have rostra distinctly longer than those of males. In addition to feeding, they use their long mouthparts to excavate holes in which to deposit their eggs to protect them from predators, parasites, and desiccation. Use of the rostrum in egg-laying by weevils is a key factor in their overall evolutionary success. In the few species known to reproduce without mating (parthenogenesis), males are either rare or entirely unknown. Many important pantry, garden, agricultural, and forest weevil pests in North America were accidentally introduced from Europe, often as stowaways in ornamental plants and stored products. Other exotic species were purposely introduced as biocontrol agents of numerous invasive plants such as puncture vine and saltcedar (see p.41).

FAMILY DIAGNOSIS Adult curculionids are incredibly diverse in form, ranging from broadly oval, long and cylindrical, to strongly hemispherical. Rostrum is long and slender, short and broad, greatly reduced, or entirely absent, sometimes flanked on each side by a deep groove, or *scrobe* that receives scape of antenna with funicle remaining free. Surface sometimes scaled, with varied patterns of black, brown, or gray, sometimes with weak to decidedly metallic reflections. Eyes present, reduced or, rarely, absent. Antennae almost always geniculate with 11 antennomeres, 9–11 forming a compact club. Antennal insertion on rostrum varies, usually inserted between midlength and apex, but sometimes basal (*Cactophagus*, *Rhodobaenus*, *Rhynchophorus*, *Scyphophorus*, *Sitophilus*, *Sphenophorus*, *Yuccaborus*) with scape often reaching beyond anterior pronotal margin. Pronotum long or short, slightly wider than the head, without sharp lateral margins. Procoxal cavities open or closed behind. Scutellum inconspicuous or hidden. Elytra rounded or parallel-sided, almost or completely concealing abdomen. Tarsi appear 4-4-4, usually 5-5-5, tarsomere 4 very small and hidden within lobes of heart-shaped 3, with claws mostly equal in size and simple. Abdomen with five ventrites, 1 and 2 usually connate.

SIMILAR FAMILIES
- bostrichid beetles (Bostrichidae, p.295)—clubbed antennae not geniculate

- minute tree-fungus beetles (Ciidae, p.329)—clubbed antennae not geniculate, tarsi 4-4-4
- *Rhinosimus* (Salpingidae, p.399)—rare, associated with dead wood, antennae straight, body with a distinct green metallic sheen
- cimberidid weevils (Cimberididae, p.529)—elytra confusedly punctate, hind tibiae with pair of apical spurs, tarsomere 2 lobed medially and covering 3
- pine flower snout beetles (Nemonychidae, p.531)—rare, on male pine strobili; antennae straight, club with three antennomeres, labrum distinct
- fungus weevils (Anthribidae, p.532)—beak broad, antennae not geniculate, club faint or absent in species with long antennae, pygidium exposed
- some leaf-rolling weevils (Attelabidae, p.534)—antennae straight, club loose with three antennomeres, elytra nearly as wide as long, covering the abdomen, body never covered with scales, claws lobed or toothed at base
- pear-shaped weevils (Brentidae, p.537)—body pear-shaped, trochanter elongate and somewhat cylindrical

COLLECTING NOTES Look for weevils on developing foliage, especially plants in bloom or bearing fruit. Hand-picking, beating, and sweeping from a wide variety of plants during the day and after dark will reveal a diversity of species. Some species are found in association with dying or dead trees in various stages of decay. Flightless species sometimes take refuge under rocks and other debris. A few species are attracted to lights. When disturbed, many weevils play dead and resemble seeds, buds, and other plant structures. Extracting specimens from leaf litter using Berlese funnels or Winkler eclectors is very productive. Ambrosia and bark beetles are best captured with a net, by hand, or at lights. Look for piles of fine sawdust in bark crevices or on the ground under dead or dying trees and peel back loose bark to search for adults. Rearing ambrosia and bark beetles from infested wood is the most productive method of collection, especially for species that develop in cones, twigs, and branches. Freshly killed trees are more attractive to beetles than those that have been dead for a long time. Malaise traps and Lindgren funnels baited with commercially available lures formulated to attract bark beetles are also productive.

FAUNA 2,919 SPECIES IN 501 GENERA

Yuccaborus frontalis (LeConte) (6.0–18.0 mm, minus rostrum) is cylindrical, and uniformly shiny or dull black or reddish black. Eye separated above by distance equal to basal width of rostrum. Rostrum straight and cylindrical, shorter than pronotum, with mandibles trilobed apically and curving outward. Pronotum coarsely punctured, anterior margin without lobe behind eye. Elytra punctostriate, interstriae nearly flat. Tibiae with small teeth along inner margin, tarsomere 3 deeply bilobed and wider than 1 and 2, and claws widely separated. Nocturnal adults on *Yucca*; at lights. Southern California east to Nevada and western Texas; south to Baja California Sur and mainland Mexico. (1)

540

Cactophagus spinolae validus (LeConte) (15.0–25.0 mm, minus rostrum) is robust, densely and finely punctate, weakly shiny and uniformly black. Rostrum as long as pronotum, evenly arcuate (female) or more arcuate near apex (male). Pronotum long, disc virtually impunctate; front coxae narrowly separated by width of antennal club. Elytra finely punctostriate, punctures small and shallow, with interstriae flat. Male femora without internal apical tooth. Tarsomere 3 broadly spatulate in both sexes, with spongy golden setal brush ventrally. Adults and larvae associated with *Opuntia* and other cacti. California and Arizona, south to Baja California Sur and Sinaloa. (1)

Rhodobaenus tredecimpunctatus (Illiger) (6.0–10.0 mm) is elongate, with a black head, rostrum, underside, and appendages, and mostly red pronotum and elytra. Rostrum long, with basal dilation deeply grooved. Pronotum with black spots round, discrete, and similar in size. Elytral suture and apices red. Legs with femora black, front and hind femora clavate, wider at apex than base. Adults found on sunflower (*Helianthus*) and other composites, while larvae develop inside stems. California to southern Ontario, New York, and Florida; also Mexico. *Rhodobaenus pustulosus* (Gyllenhal) (8.5–13.0 mm) is reddish or blackish with whitish dots. Southeastern Arizona east to Texas, south to Costa Rica. (2)

Palm Weevil *Rhynchophorus palmarum* **(Linnaeus)** (26.0–44.0 mm) is elongate-oval, glossy to dull dorsally and uniformly black. Head with eyes large and elongate-oval, with rostrum shorter than pronotum, cylindrical with reddish setae dorsally (male) or not (female). Pronotum narrower than elytra, with posterior margin broadly rounded. Elytra each with six deep striae. Larvae damage apical growth of Canary Island date palms (*Phoenix canariensis*) and are a significant threat to edible date industry. Southern California, southwestern Arizona, and southern Texas, to South America. *Rhynchophorus vulneratus* (Panzer) (27.0–33.0 mm) red with black markings, or mostly black with red stripe down pronotum; was eradicated from Laguna Beach, California in 2015. (1)

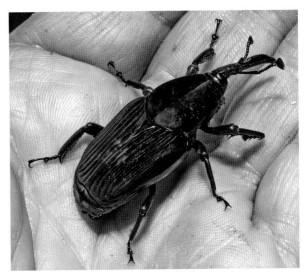

Sisal Weevil *Scyphophorus acupunctatus* **Gyllenhal** (8.0–24.0 mm) is elongate-oval, somewhat flattened, dull black. Eyes large and elongate, separated dorsally and touching ventrally. Rostrum stout, nearly straight with antennae inserted at base. Antennal funicle with six antennomeres, club with spongy apex retracted, concave, and not visible in lateral view. Pronotum nearly as wide as elytra, without postocular lobes. Scutellum visible. Elytral intervals finely and shallowly punctate, with apices truncate. Tibiae with outer apices dentate. Soles of tarsomere 3 glabrous, save for fringe of stiff setae along apical border. Adults on agave (*Agave*). California east to Colorado, Kansas, and Texas; south to South America. (2)

Scyphophorus yuccae **Horn** (8.0–24.0 mm) is elongate-oval, flatter in profile than *S. acupunctatus*, and dull black. Rostrum narrow, nearly straight with antennae inserted at base. Antennal funicle with six antennomeres, club with spongy apex truncate, somewhat carinate and visible in lateral view. Pronotum nearly as wide as elytra, without postocular lobes. Scutellum visible. Elytral intervals deeply punctate in single line, with apices oblique from suture. Tibiae with outer apices dentate. Soles of tarsomere 3 glabrous, save for fringe of stiff setae along apical border. Adults at base of flowering stalks of chaparral yucca (*Hesperoyucca whipplei*). California; also records from Arizona, Texas, and Baja California. (2)

541

Rice Weevil *Sitophilus oryzae* **(Linnaeus)** (2.1–2.8 mm) is somewhat dull reddish-brown to black, upper and lower surfaces densely and coarsely punctured, long rostrum three-fourths length of pronotum, and with elytra of most individuals bearing four reddish spots. Sides of pronotum mostly rounded before head. Elytral humeri prominent and quadrate/angulate, with closely set double rows of punctures. A serious pest of stored grains; larvae feed and develop inside individual grains, eventually hollowing them out. Difficult to distinguish from Greater Rice Weevil *S. zeamais* Motschulsky. Granary Weevil *S. granarius* (Linnaeus) also similar, but with elytral humeri rounded. All species cosmopolitan; widely distributed across southern Canada and United States. (5)

Sphenophorus aequalis pictus **(LeConte)** (9.0–21.0 mm) is bicolored, mostly black dorsally with little enamel-like coating, and white markings underneath. Pronotum with three narrowly separated black stripes. Elytra with one or two complete white stripes or not, striae fine with punctures small and shallow. Coastal southern California to Baja California. *Sphenophorus a. ochrea* (LeConte) bicolored, mostly yellowish, pronotum striped, with elytral punctures oval; eastern California to Utah and Texas; *S. a. discolor* (Mannerheim) uniformly black or dark red with elytral strial punctures deep and mostly round; Oregon to northern California. *S. a. aequalis* (Gyllenhal) almost entirely covered with enamel-like coating, with distinct pronotal stripes; Pacific Northwest, southern Canada, also East. (19)

Sphenophorus australis australis Chittenden (10.0–14.0 mm) is elongate-oval and shiny black. Antennal club longer than wide. Rostrum evenly rounded at base. Pronotal stripes usually distinct. Scutellum triangular, longer than wide, and broadest near base. Elytral intervals with enamel-like coating appearing mottled. East of Sierra Nevada to Idaho and Arizona, eastward. *S. australis abrasa* Chittenden pronotal stripes merged across middle and elytra nearly devoid of coating, except for sides of elytra. Tarsomere 3 narrow, subequal in width to 2, with ventral pilosity restricted to anterolateral areas. Pygidium exposed. Washington and western Oregon to central California. Adults of both subspecies associated with common cattail (*Typha latifolia*). (19)

Sphenophorus costipennis (Horn) (8.0–13.0 mm) is black with gray, yellowish, or reddish enamel-like coating in depressed areas dorsally, and red markings ventrally. Rostrum appearing humped at base and dilated at apical quarter. Pronotum with three broad carinae. Elytra with raised costae nearly reaching apices. Male with ventrite 1 between hind coxae, with longitudinal patches of setae on each side. Hind tarsomere 3 usually long and narrow, barely wider than 1 and 2. Larvae in roots of softstem bulrush (*Schoenoplectus tabernaemontani*), also longhair sedge (*Carex comosa*). Widespread in North America. (19)

Treptoplatypus wilsoni (Swaine) (5.0–5.7 mm) is elongate, slender, cylindrical, parallel-sided, and dark brown with appendages lighter. Head finely and densely punctate with dense, erect golden setae. Pronotum nearly one and a half times longer than wide. Elytra two and a half times longer than wide, with striae narrowly impressed with fine punctures, interstriae and lateral apical angles slightly dentate (female) or strongly produced (male). Underside with thoracic sclerites near hind legs not modified to receive femora. Larvae develop in dying, injured, or cut coniferous trees. Southern British Columbia to California, east to Idaho. (1)

Clover Leaf Weevil *Brachypera zoilus* (Scopoli) (5.0–8.5 mm) is oval, robust, black, and densely clothed in slender gray scales with metallic luster, and short, broader, brown, yellowish-brown, and blackish-brown scales notched on apices intermixed with suberect bristles. Rostrum stout, two-thirds shorter than length of pronotum. Pronotum wider than long, sides parallel, then abruptly narrowed in front. Elytra paler laterally. Ventrite 1 of male impressed and emarginate posteriorly. Adults and larvae pests on alfalfa (*Medicago*), clover (*Trifolium*), and other legumes; larvae pupate in loose cocoons attached to leaves. Europe; established in western British Columbia and western United States. (1)

Lesser Clover Leaf Weevil *Hypera nigrirostris* (Fabricius) (3.5–4.5 mm) is elongate-oval, reddish-brown to black, and densely clothed in greenish hairlike scales, scales on sides notched on tip; appendages reddish brown. Head black, rostrum of male as long as pronotum, antennal scape reaching front margin of more or less elongate-oval eye. Pronotum long, often with pale line down middle, sides rounded behind middle, with base narrower than elytra. Elytra finely punctostriate, interstriae with short, thick, reclining setae, basal angles rounded, and sides parallel. Tibiae without sharp, apical hooks; claws separate, simple. On *Medicago*, *Trifolium*, and grasses in spring and summer. Europe; British Columbia to California, east to Idaho; also in East. (9)

Rice Water Weevil *Lissorhoptrus oryzophilus* Kuschel (2.6–3.8 mm) is oblong-oval, dark beige to dark brown, and densely coated with flat tan and brown scales. Somewhat cylindrical rostrum stout, rugosely punctate, and as long as prothorax. Antenna with base of club large, shiny. Pronotum wider than long and slightly constricted near base. Elytra broader than prothorax, with small strial punctures close set and small tubercles at apical declivity. Mesotibia curved with long slender setae, metatibia with finely notched apical tooth (male) or two simple teeth (female). On cultivated rice (*Oryza sativa*) and other wetland vegetation; at lights. Eastern United States; in California. (1)

Adaleres ovipennis Casey (10.8–14.5 mm) is elongate-oval and densely clothed in smooth, shiny, round gray and brown scales. Eyes oval and flat, rostrum short and robust. Antennae lacking scales, with first three funicular antennomeres elongate. Pronotum nearly smooth, uniformly and densely clothed in scales. Elytra with humeri broadly rounded and intervals flat or slightly convex, especially after apical declivity. Metepisternal suture well defined. Ventrite 1 with posterior margin broadly emarginate medially, 2 much longer than combined lengths of 3–4. Tarsomere 1 with dorsal surface scaled and setose. Flightless adults on *Quercus*, *Ceanothus*, and fruit and nut trees. California. (3)

Vegetable Weevil *Listroderes costirostris* Schönherr (6.4–8.7 mm) is elongate-oval and densely clothed in dark reddish brown, gray, and black scales interspersed with more or less erect pale and dark bristles, appearing shaggy. Rostrum half as long as pronotum. Pronotum nearly as wide as long, broadest before middle, then sides converging posteriorly, with light stripe down middle. Elytra with dark scales forming oblique apical bands, each with conical tubercle before apex. Larvae burrow in fleshy roots, stems, and leaves of wild and ornamental plants, including vegetable crops; adults damage or girdle stems. South America; established in California, western Arizona. (1)

Crocidema californica Van Dyke (8.5–11.0 mm) is narrowly elliptical, convex, shiny dark reddish brown to black, and more or less densely clothed in somewhat iridescent dark scales and long erect setae. Eyes large, but not prominent. Rostrum robust, almost as broad basally as apically. Antennae long, scape with suberect setae, with abrupt and elongate club. Pronotum broadest before middle, with distinct postocular lobes. Elytra lacking distinct basal margin, striae finely and sharply impressed with striae 9–10 joined above metacoxal margin. On vegetation and at lights. Transverse Ranges of southern California. (5)

Dyslobus ursinus (Horn) (5.5–7.5 mm) is elongate-oval, coarsely and roughly punctured on head and pronotum, and clothed in scattered, small, elongate, white scales and somewhat erect brownish setae. Rostrum with strongly elevated median carina extending nearly from antennal insertion to base. Pronotal disc tuberculate with deep grooves between rugae, and sparsely scaled. Elytra with humeri ill-defined, first two striae along suture deeply impressed and others not, large strial punctures deep, interstriae flat, completely covered with light and dark scales, and numerous erect, fine brown setae in two or three rows. British Columbia to Oregon, east to Wyoming and Utah. Genus needs revision. (~35)

Panscopus spantoni Bright (7.7–9.9 mm) is gray to very dark brown or black, clothed in thin, flattened setae, and with pronotum and elytra coarsely and rugosely tuberculate. Antennal scape long and extending to posterior margin of eye; funicle setose, without scales. Pronotum wider than long, but narrower than base of elytra. Strial punctures covered by large, round scales; alternate intervals elevated, with setae thin at apices. Metepisternal suture distinct. Dorsal surfaces of tarsomeres 1–3 setose. With four (female) or five (male) ventrites. On plants in moist forests. Southern British Columbia to western Oregon. (22)

545

Rhigopsis effracta LeConte (4.5–6.5 mm) is dark gray and black, irregularly and coarsely sculptured, and covered dorsally in scales and dense coating. Head with hoodlike tubercle above flat, tear-shaped eye. Clubbed antenna scaled with short funiculum. Rostrum trisulcate dorsally, and well-defined scrobe with upper marginal angle rounded. Ventral edge of postocular pronotal lobe rounded. Elytral bases not carinate, with somewhat oblique humeri tuberculate, disc slightly flattened, intervals with large pits, and sides distinctly carinate. Tarsi spinose ventrally. On *Yucca* and other plants. California, Baja California. (1)

Colecerus dispar (LeConte) (3.5–5.5 mm) is oblong-oval, densely scaly and variably marked dorsally with round blackish, brown, and whitish scales. Head and rostrum combined as long as prothorax. Underside of rostrum with deep, basal transverse sulcus continuous with scrobe. Pronotum rhomboidal, sides gradually narrowing anteriorly, with postocular lobe on anterolateral margin more rounded, and posterolateral angles prominent and briefly margined. Scutellum white. Elytra at base not wider than prothorax, humeri angulate and punctostriate with punctures deep and widely spaced, with intervals slightly convex. Adults on *Prosopis*. Arizona and Texas, also Baja California. (1)

Sesbania Clown Weevil *Eudiagogus pulcher* Fåhraeus (3.9–8.0 mm) is oblong-oval, slender, and densely clothed in brownish black, tan, copper, and greenish metallic scales. Head, except for dark spot at base of rostrum, covered with tan and coppery scales. Rostrum flat dorsally. Pronotum with coppery scales forming cross bars. Elytra with narrow greenish suture flanked by broad black stripes, followed by narrow stripes intersected at middle by transverse stripe to margin. Larva feeds on roots of riverhemp (*Sesbania*) and senna (*Cassia*). Adults on larval host plants during late spring and summer. Southeastern California and southwestern Arizona, also Gulf Coast states. (1)

Trigonoscuta **species** (5.0–10.0 mm) are oval, stout, convex, and densely clothed in smooth, shiny scales and scattered fine erect setae. Eyes oval and convex. Rostrum short, broad, and somewhat cylindrical. Pronotum somewhat wider than long, with anterior and posterior margins straight. Elytra with humeri rounded and oval (male) or broadly oval (female). Nocturnal adults shelter among roots of host plants, including grasses, *Oenothera*, *Ambrosia*, *Atriplex*, and others growing in sandy coastal and desert habitats from southern British Columbia to Baja California. Numerous species and subspecies of questionable validity. Genus needs revision. (65)

Ericydeus lautus **(LeConte)** (7.0–13.0 mm) is somewhat flattened, and densely clothed in gray and brown scales. Head with median sulcus extending onto rostrum, and eye on side of head. Pronotum with sides sinuate after middle and broadest posteriorly. Elytra with prominent humeri, deep punctures, and distinct pattern. Tarsi clothed dorsally in coarse setae. Utah, Arizona, and New Mexico, south to Baja California and mainland Mexico. *Ericydeus placidus* (Horn) (11.0–18.0 mm) slender, uniformly white, with smaller elytral punctures. California and Arizona, south to Baja California. Both species on *Senegalia* and other leguminous woody trees and shrubs. (2)

Fuller Rose Weevil *Naupactus cervinus* (Boheman) (6.0–8.5 mm) is oblong-oval, dark brown, and uniformly clothed in small gray, brown, and pinkish scales, with characteristic, sometimes faint oblique whitish bar behind middle on sides of elytra. Rostrum very short and broad. Sides of body with or without paler scales, never with distinct stripe fringed with darker scales. Pronotum with front and side margins rounded. Elytra with humeri lacking, not wider than base of pronotum. Flightless adults active year-round, found on many plants; parthenogenetic. South American, widespread in North America. (3)

Ophryastes argentatus LeConte (9.5–17.5 mm) is light or dark gray with small dark spots or scattered light blotches on elytra, and densely clothed in flat light or dark gray, tan, dark brown to blackish scales, or black when abraded. Rostrum broadly, deeply impressed basally, trisulcate dorsally with median sulcus moderately wide and deep. Anterior pronotal margin with postocular lobes bearing dense setae, with lateral margins lacking projections. Elytral scales imbricate, strial punctures deep, and equally wide interstriae flat or distinctly convex. On *Larrea*, *Vachellia*, and *Prosopis*. Southern California east to Utah and Arizona; south to Mexico. (36)

Strawberry Root Weevil *Otiorhynchus ovatus* (Linnaeus) (4.5–6.0 mm) is coarsely sculptured, shiny black or dark reddish brown with appendages lighter, and sparsely clothed in short, recumbent yellowish setae. Rostrum flat, coarsely and roughly punctate, with several weak longitudinal carinae. Pronotum narrow, almost round, with deep medial grooves. Elytral punctostriae weakly impressed, punctures deep, with interstriae weakly convex to flat. Femora swollen on apical half and toothed. Profemoral tooth notched, others usually simple. Males unknown. Flightless, parthenogenetic females consume leaves of strawberries and other plants; larvae feed on roots. Europe; widespread in North America. (4)

Rough Strawberry Root Weevil *Otiorhynchus rugoso-striatus* (Goeze) (5.5–8.5 mm) is oblong-oval, roughly sculptured, black to light reddish brown with appendages lighter, and sparsely clothed in curled reddish setae. Rostrum short, with longitudinal depression basally, and Y-shaped carina apically. Pronotum round, wider than long, with disc coarsely tuberculate. Elytra oval, nearly twice as wide as pronotum, interstriae moderately impressed and deeply punctured, and interstriae regularly tuberculate with two rows of small seta-bearing tubercles. Front femora not toothed. Flightless and parthenogenetic females feed on leaves of strawberries and other plants. Europe; widespread in North America. (4)

Black Vine Weevil *Otiorhynchus sulcatus* (Fabricius) (7.5–9.2 mm) is black or brownish black with lighter appendages. Rostrum short, deeply sulcate dorsally, with Y-shaped carina apically. Pronotum oval, longer than wide, lateral margins rounded, and disc coarsely tuberculate. Elytra round, twice as wide as pronotum; punctostriae moderately impressed, punctures deep, interstriae convex and weakly to strongly tuberculate, with scattered clumps of light, slender scales. Flightless and parthenogenetic females on many plants, sometimes pests in greenhouses and nurseries. Europe; widespread in North America. (4)

Aragnomus griseus Horn (3.5–4.5 mm) is oval, robust, convex, with body and appendages densely clothed in grayish scales, intermixed dorsally with variegated pattern of brown scales, and sparse, erect black setae. Head with eyes round and not prominent. Rostrum broader than long, shorter than head, and flattened dorsally. Antenna with scape much shorter than funicle. Pronotum more or less cylindrical, slightly wider than long, bulging at middle, with anterior and posterior margins straight, and broad brownish stripe medially. Scutellum not visible. Claws fused basally. Adults on Utah juniper (*Juniperus osteospermae*). Washington to California, east to Montana, Colorado, and Arizona. (3)

Dysticheus insignis Horn (4.0 mm) is oval and densely clothed in appressed scales and short, stout, erect scalelike setae. Coarsely punctured head and rostrum combined as long as prothorax. Pronotum wider than long, with disc nearly flat in lateral view. Elytra clothed in elongate gray scales irregularly intermixed with darker patches, and striae with closely set punctures deep and quadrate, with two rows of stout setae on flat intervals. Ventrite 2 equal to 3–4 combined. Hind tibial combs present. *Dysticheus rotundicollis* Van Dyke (5.5 mm) elongate, robust, prothorax about as wide as long; elytral declivity with denser, erect setae. Both on *Senecio* and *Gutierrezia*. California. (2)

Eucilinus aridus (Van Dyke) (6.0–6.5 mm) is broadly oval, funicle and tarsi reddish brown, and densely clothed in pearly white appressed scales and long, fine, erect pale setae, more so on lateral margins. Eyes flat. Rostrum short, broad, and gradually narrowed anteriorly. Pronotal disc slightly bulging when viewed laterally, with postocular lobes and setal fringe absent. Elytra with narrow basal margin; striae finely impressed and closely punctured, and intervals flat with irregular setose punctures, setae short. Paired claws fused basally. Nocturnal adults on *Larrea*. Southern California. *Eucilinus mononychyus* Buchanan (3.5–3.8 mm) with single tarsal claw. Utah and Arizona. (3)

Nemocestes horni Van Dyke (6.0–9.0 mm) is oval, and completely clothed in round, recumbent scales intermixed with somewhat erect, flat setae. Scape barely surpassing anterior margin of pronotum, funicular antennomere 7 longer than wide. Anterior pronotal margin broadly arcuate. Scutellar interstriae convex and glabrous, interstria 5 flat apically, with interstrial setae stout. Hind tibia of female armed with pair of spines. Flightless, nocturnal adults on various shrubs. Pacific Coast, from southern British Columbia to northern California; also Northeast. (9)

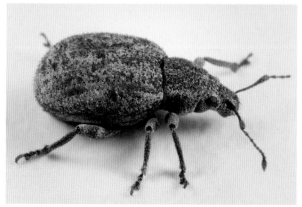

Thricolepis inornata Horn (3.0–5.2 mm) is broadly oval, moderately robust, convex, shiny black with legs reddish brown or darker, and densely clothed in pearly white scales that are easily rubbed off. Head and rostrum longer than prothorax, with surfaces sparsely punctured and not densely scaly. Scales sometimes forming inconspicuous lateral pronotal stripes. Elytra with rows of moderately coarse, closely spaced punctures, with flat intervals bearing rows of short black setae. Adults on *Quercus*, fruit trees, and various shrubs. Western United States to Mexico. *Thricolepis simulator* Horn (3.0 mm) head and rostrum densely scaled and intermixed with very short setae. California. (2)

Pachyrhinus californicus (Horn) (5.0–7.8 mm) is elongate, usually dark reddish brown to blackish with reddish legs, frequently with greenish luster, especially pronotum, and densely clothed in small, recumbent scales. Eyes small, strongly convex. Rostrum with conspicuously curved glabrous callosity extending between antennal insertions. Pronotum wider than long and disc with dense, elongate, recumbent scales and scattered, narrow, semierect scales. Elytra with humeri prominent, and disc mostly brown with suture and sides diffusely mottled with white and brown scales. Adults associated with pine (*Pinus*). British Columbia and Idaho to Baja California and Arizona. Genus needs revision. (6)

Pachyrhinus elegans (Couper) (4.5–7.2 mm) is elongate and clothed dorsally in recumbent, elongate, and metallic green, dull green, brown, golden brown, or gray scales. Eyes small, strongly convex. Rostrum with conspicuously curved glabrous callosity extending between antennal insertions. Pronotum wider than long and disc with dense, elongate, recumbent scales and scattered, semierect narrow scales. Elytra with humeri prominent, and disc sometimes intermixed with elongate golden or green scales, suture and sides pale metallic green, bluish, or dull white. Legs blackish (male) or brownish (female), and claws fused basally. Adults associated with pine (*Pinus*). Western Canada and northwestern United States. Genus needs revision. (6)

Barypeithes pellucidus (Boheman) (2.9–4.0 mm) is oval, stout, light to dark reddish brown or blackish with pale appendages and sparsely clothed in erect setae. Eyes flat. Rostrum very short, broad. Pronotum round, convex, coarsely punctate. Elytra wider than pronotum, elongate-globose, strial punctures large, deep, close-set and setose; interstriae flat with rows of long, recumbent setae. Femora clavate. Flightless adults on *Quercus*, *Ulmus*, *Prunus*, *Crataegus*, *Rubus*, *Fragaria*, and others. Europe; established in British Columbia to California, also in East. (1)

Sitona californicus Fåhraeus (4.2–6.0 mm) is elongate-oval, slender, brown to black, densely clothed in flat, recumbent brownish to whitish scales intermixed with erect dark and pale setae. Eyes large, round, and strongly protuberant. Rostrum short, broad with deeply impressed dorsal sulcus, and distinctly bisulcate on apical third, and mandibles without deciduous scar, but with flat, recumbent scales. Pronotum smooth, much narrower than elytral bases, with fine, shallow, widely separated punctures, and medial white stripe. Elytra with variable indistinct variegated pattern. Adults on *Lupinus, Ceanothus*, and other plants, including fruit trees. British Columbia to Baja California, east to Alberta, Montana, Minnesota, Missouri, and Georgia. (12)

Hadromeropsis opalina (Horn) (6.4–9.5 mm) is elongate, convex, and black with reddish-brown antennae and tarsi; usually densely clothed in brilliant round metallic green scales, sometimes with blue-green, blue, white, or coppery scales. Eyes moderately convex and slightly transverse. Pronotum slightly broader than long, with postocular setae poorly developed or absent. Elytra striate, often missing scales and appearing as if peppered with black; some individuals with somewhat faint elongate pattern of paler scales laterally and beside suture. Front legs larger than middle and hind legs. Adults on fairyduster (*Calliandra eriophylla*) and acacia (*Senegalia*). Arizona to central Mexico. (1)

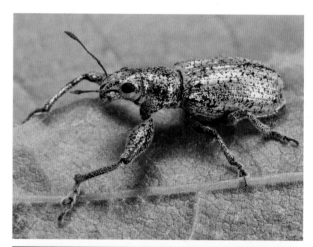

Pandeleteinus submetallicus (Schaeffer) (2.7–4.8 mm) is elongate-oval, clothed entirely in bright metallic green to yellow-green, coppery tan, or nonmetallic tan scales. Head large, spherical, and bulging between small round eyes, with short rostrum broadly emarginate apically, and antennal club slender and pointed. Prothorax as wide or slightly wider than long, broadest anteriorly and medially. Front legs scarcely enlarged, with coxae nearly contiguous. Elytra punctostriate, punctures small and deep, interstriae flat, with humeri prominent. Adults found on juniper (*Juniperus*). California east to Colorado and Texas. Nonmetallic *P. elytroplanatus* Howden (3.0–4.5 mm) with, and *P. lucidillus* Howden (2.8–3.8 mm) without oblique elytral fasciae; both southeastern Arizona. (3)

Pandeleteius robustus Schaeffer (4.3–7.4 mm) is light reddish brown, mottled with noncontiguous whitish, yellowish-brown, and brown scales, with enlarged front legs. Elliptical eyes slightly convex and flattened rostrum arcuately emarginate apically. Pronotum nearly as long as broad, broadest just before posterior margin, with setae arising on margin just inside prominent anterior angles. Prolegs with femora bulging, tibiae curved inward apically, and coxae distinctly separated. Elytra without basal tuft of erect setae, with distinct bump between humeri and scutellum, yellowish-brown suture, and mostly white declivity. On mountain mahogany (*Cercocarpus*). Southeastern Arizona and New Mexico. (8)

Apleurus angularis (LeConte) (5.7–12.2 mm) is elongate-ovate, dark brown, and mottled with dense whitish and brown broad and slender scales. Head with teardrop-shaped eyes prominent and convex, rostrum distinctly longer than head. Pronotum distinctly punctured, expanded laterally just behind anterior constriction, anterior margin with small angle behind eyes. Tarsal claws slender and widely divergent. Elytral suture and odd intervals slightly (macropterous) or, more commonly, markedly elevated (apterous). Tibia with apical ridge sharp, with claws robust and fused at base. On shrubby composites in dry sandy habitats. California eastward to Idaho, Colorado, Oklahoma, and western Texas. (30)

Cyphocleonus achates Fåhraeus (7.0–17.5 mm) is elongate-oval, mottled with reddish-brown and grayish scales, punctuated by numerous and irregular shiny black glabrous tubercles. Rostrum distinctly longer than head, dorsomedially carinate along entire length, with raised lateral margins basally. Pronotum long, dorsally and laterally, with anterior margins straight behind eyes. Elytra faintly striate. Flightless adults biocontrol agents of knapweed (*Centaurea*). Root-feeding larvae initiate galls. Eurasian; southwestern Canada and northwestern United States. (1)

Scaphomorphus quadrilineatus (Chevrolat) (8.3–14.3 mm) is narrow, densely clothed in long, erect, scalelike setae. Eyes elongate-oval. Funicular article 3 as long as wide, about subequal in length to each of 4–7. Rostrum with low median carina dorsally. Pronotum shallowly convex medially, without anterolateral lobe, and postocular bristles unequal in length. Elytra striped. Metatarsomere 3 with pilose pads covering half to two-thirds of ventral surface. Winged adults on woody Rosaceae and Rhamnaceae. California to Nebraska and central Texas. *Scaphomorphus trivittatus* (Say) and *S. placidus* (Csiki) both on legumes; former widespread in western North America, latter California. (13)

Larinus carlinae (Olivier) (7.0–8.0 mm) is broadly oval, dark brown or black with patches of grayish hairlike scales and fine setae; freshly emerged individuals coated with yellow wax. Head and pronotum rugosely punctate. Rostrum elongate, cylindrical, as long as or longer than pronotum, and slightly curved, with ventral edge rounded, lacking longitudinal ridge and groove. Elytra with striae moderately deep. A biocontrol of Canada thistle (*Cirsium arvense*); adults eat vegetation, while larvae consume developing seeds in flower heads. Europe; established in British Columbia, Alberta, Colorado, Oregon, Utah, and Washington, also in East. Formerly *L. planus* (Fabricius). (4)

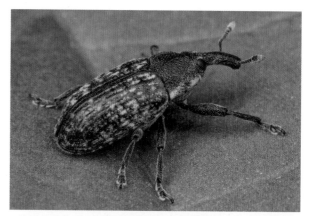

Lixus perforatus LeConte (6.8–10.8 mm) is clothed in gray and brown pubescence, more so laterally. Rostrum longer and narrower than head, with antennae inserted at about middle (female), or stouter with antennal insertions at about apical third, with dorsal median carina. Antennomere 3 of funicle distinctly longer than wide and longer than each of 4–7. Pronotum longer than wide; anterolateral margin with small postocular lobe bearing bristles unequal in length. Elytra slightly wider than prothorax, with scutellar impression broad, shallow. On various plants, including *Ambrosia*. Washington to California, east to Idaho. (9)

Anthonomus haematopus Boheman (2.2–3.4 mm) is brownish black, elytra and abdomen reddish, with sparse and uniform pubescence. Rostrum stout, curved, densely punctate, as long as head and thorax combined. Antennae paler. Pronotum reddish anteriorly, disc coarsely punctate. Elytra one-third wider at base than pronotum, punctostriate, punctures shallow and close-set, intervals nearly flat and finely wrinkled, sometimes with postmedial clumps of white pubescence. Ventrites 2–5 each decreasing in length posteriorly. Profemora with single tooth. Larva in *Salix* stem galls. In West from British Columbia to Baja California; east to Alberta, Idaho, and Utah. (32)

Curculio aurivestis Chittenden (5.0–6.3 mm) is ovate to somewhat elongate-ovate, light brown to reddish brown with underside darker and legs lighter. Rostrum gently arcuate in both sexes, continuous (male) or somewhat continuous (female) with frons, and nearly half (female) to two-fifths (male) body length. Pronotum wide, constricted at apical third, with discal punctures distinct and uniform in size, and narrow median line flanked by darker broad lines. Elytra broader than pronotum, usually with irregular brownish bands evident. Hind femur reaching to elytral apex. Adults on oaks, including canyon live oak (*Quercus chrysolepis*) and Oregon white oak (*Q. garryana*). British Columbia to southern California. (10)

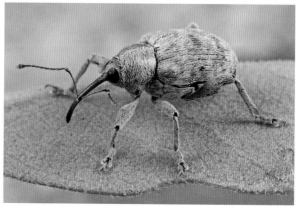

Dorytomus inaequalis Casey (5.4–7.5 mm) is oblong, stout, weakly convex dorsally, and black with elytra mottled with patches of pale setae; sexually dimorphic. Rostrum long, slender, and evenly arcuate, with antennae inserted medially (female) or nearly apical (male). Pronotum transverse and oval (large males), or shorter (females), with discal punctures moderately coarse and deep. Elytra weakly impressed with strial punctures deep, and clothed in patches of sparse, stiff, erect setae. Legs with femora minutely toothed, with toothed claws free at base and widely divergent; male with front legs and front tarsomere 1 elongate. Adults found on cottonwood (*Populus*). Widespread in western North America. (15)

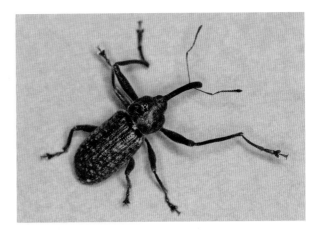

Rhinusa tetra (Fabricius) (2.0–4.5 mm) is broadly oval, very stout, shiny black, and densely clothed in yellowish-gray setae, appearing brassy. Antennal funicle with five antennomeres. Rostrum straight, moderately elongate and tapered apically, with antennae inserted just before middle. Pronotum densely punctate, with lateral margins strongly arcuate. Elytra moderately wider than prothorax, broadest medially, weakly convex, with interstriae weakly visible through dense and somewhat recumbent to erect setae. Pygidium visible beyond elytra. Femora toothed, teeth more prominent in males, with tarsi fused at base. Introduced from Europe as biological control for common mullein (*Verbascum thapsus*). In West from British Columbia to California, east to South Dakota and Texas. (3)

Myrmex lineatus (Pascoe) (6.5–7.5 mm) is elongate-oval, convex, antlike, shiny black with antennae and tarsi dark reddish brown, and densely clothed in recumbent coarse white and finer erect black and white setae. Eyes well developed. Rostrum not received in distinct prosternal channel, without dorsal excavation in both sexes. Pronotum longer than wide, convex, coarsely punctured, and narrower than base of elytra; coxae positioned at middle of prosternum. Elytra with pattern of alternating glabrous and scaly lines. Femora dentate on ventral margin, and claws not fused, each with basal process. Winged adults on flowers and shrubs. Washington to California, east to Idaho, Utah, and Arizona. (14)

Myrmex vandykei Sleeper (7.0–8.5 mm) is antlike, shiny black with antennae and tarsi dark reddish brown, and moderately clothed in recumbent coarse white and finer erect black and white setae. Eyes well developed. Rostrum not received in distinct prosternal channel. Pronotum long, strongly convex, finely punctured, and narrower than base of elytra. Front coxae positioned at middle of prosternum; femur with ventral tooth. Scutellum densely setose. Elytral interstriae clothed in white pubescence. Suture between ventrites 2 and 3 more or less straight. Claws free basally, each with basal process. Winged adults on shrubs, including *Ceanothus*. Arizona. (14)

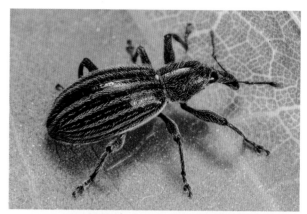

Tachyerges salicis (Linnaeus) (2.2–2.9 mm) is elongate-oval, black with brown tarsi, and mostly reddish-brown antennae. Eyes contiguous. Antennae with seven funicular antennomeres. Pronotum wide, broadest posteriorly, and narrower than elytra. Elytra black, striae coarsely punctured, intervals convex, with two or more transverse, irregularly shaped light bands of scales. Metafemora expanded. Larvae mine willow (*Salix*) and aspen (*Populus*) leaves. Adults jump. *Tachyerges niger* (Horn) black with at most indistinct white elytral band. Alaska, western Canada, Rocky Mountain states, also in East. *T. ephippiatus* (Say) with rostrum and elytral cuticle beneath bands pale; widespread. (3)

Cnemidoprion oblongus (Horn) (4.5–6.0 mm) is dark brown, and densely clothed in erect brown and gray setae. Slender rostrum as long as prothorax, hidden in sternal channel in repose. Funicular antennomere 2 slender, twice length of 3, and one and a half times longer than 1. Pronotum wide, coarsely punctate, not carinate. Mesocoxae separated by apical width of rostrum. Elytra with strial punctures closely set and apices broadly rounded. Outer tibial margins with large serrations or denticles, and hind tibia with apical comb of stout setae. Femora with single tooth, front femur with additional denticle. At lights. Arizona and Baja California. (1)

Poplar and Willow Borer *Cryptorhynchus lapathi* (Linnaeus) (5.6–8.3 mm) is dull black with appendages brown, and densely clothed in sooty black and pale scales intermixed with tufts of erect bristly black scales. Rostrum hidden in sternal channel in repose. Pronotum with pair of tufts of black scales flanking middle of anterior margin, and three across disc just before middle. Elytra with strial punctures large and deep, some wider than intervals, apical one-third with strongly contrasting white scales. Femora each with two distinct teeth. Larvae mine young stems of *Salix*, *Populus*, *Alnus*, and *Betula*. British Columbia to Oregon, east to Alberta, Montana, and Utah. (1)

Zascelis irrorata LeConte (5.0–6.5 mm) is coarsely sculptured, dark reddish brown or black, and sparsely clothed in scattered recumbent scales. Head visible dorsally. Long, slender rostrum slightly arcuate; hidden in sternal channel in repose. Lateral pronotal margins parallel behind middle, with postocular lobe. Scutellum visible. Elytra flattened. Middle coxae separated by width of rostral apex. Outer margins of tibiae with dentate or sharply serrate carina at apical third, with apical comb of stout setae on hind tibiae. Femora armed with single tooth. At lights. California to Baja California, east to Colorado and New Mexico; south to Central America. (1)

Emphyastes fucicola Mannerheim (4.7–6.7 mm) is pale reddish brown, sometimes with median portions of pronotum and elytra faintly darker, and sparsely clothed in minute recumbent pale setae. Eyes round, coarsely faceted, and flat. Rostrum short with dorsal surface at basal two-thirds and sides carinate. Pronotum broadly oval, inconspicuously punctate, without distinct lobes behind eyes on anterior margins. Elytra obscurely punctostriate with intervals convex. Tibial apices each with long paddlelike extension beyond tarsal articulation. Larvae in decaying seaweed; adults under debris on intertidal beaches. Alaska to California. (1)

Lepyrus oregonensis Casey (9.7–15.0 mm) is dull black, tuberculate, and moderately clothed in small brown and whitish scales, latter forming scattered patches on elytra. Eyes round and distinctly convex. Rostrum and pronotum with prominent carinae. Anterior pronotal margin lacking lobes behind eyes. Elytra coarsely granular with scattered patches of white scales, compressed apically with apices somewhat produced, odd intervals distinctly elevated, and strial punctures distinct and irregular in size, depth, and placement. Femora unarmed, tibiae slender. Alaska to California, east to Saskatchewan and Idaho. *Lepyrus gemellus* Kirby (15.0–17.0 mm) elytra with pairs of white lines. (2)

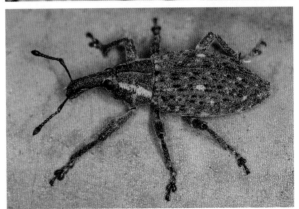

Pissodes schwarzi Hopkins (5.2–6.7 mm) with patches of rusty brown and whitish setae. Slender rostrum slightly shorter or longer than prothorax. Pronotal punctures coarse and posterior angles rectangular. Elytra slightly broader than prothorax, punctostriate with punctures coarse, intervals 3 and 5 distinctly elevated and rugose, basal brown spots moderately large, white spots at declivity fused and forming irregular transverse band not reaching suture. Male metatibia lacking long setal fringe. Adults on *Pinus ponderosa*; larvae in boles and root collars of *Pinus* and *Larix*. British Columbia to California, east to Alberta, Montana, Colorado, and Arizona. Genus needs revision. (13)

Sternechus paludatus (Casey) (5.0–6.8 mm) is broadly oval, strongly convex, shiny black, with sparse pubescence denser posteriorly. Rostrum short, thick, with antennae inserted near weakly dilated apex. Pronotum wide, broadest behind middle, without postocular lobes, with disc coarsely punctate. Elytra broader than prothorax at base, each with a pair of densely pubescent patches, a toothlike posthumeral prominence on lateral margin, rows of coarse round punctures, and a large pubescent tubercle at declivity. Femora not enlarged, dentate underneath, with claws stout and fused along more than basal half. On *Robinia neomexicana*; at lights. Arizona and New Mexico. (1)

Laemosaccus burkei Hespenheide (2.5–4.8 mm) is slightly obovate, robust, somewhat cylindrical, and black with a large red-orange elytral spot on basal two-thirds. Frons with dense, white setae obscuring surface between eyes and on rostrum above antennal insertions. Pronotum strongly convex, with anterior collar densely clothed in silvery setae. Elytra at base broader than prothorax, punctostriate with strial punctures deep, and short, exposing one (female) or two (male) tergites apically. Undersides with large silvery setae obscuring surfaces. On mesquite and other woody legumes. Arizona and Texas; south to Mexico. (7)

Magdalis lecontei Horn (4.5–8.3 mm) is metallic blue, blue-black, black, blue-green, or green, sometimes with purplish reflections, with antennae and tarsi black, and nearly glabrous. Antennae inserted at about basal two-fifths (male) or one-third (female) of rostrum. Pronotum coarsely and densely punctate, with sides arcuate before middle and posterior margins more or less produced or divergent. Elytra alutaceous with punctostriae feeble and widened posteriorly. Femora toothed, front femora slender, and claws simple. Adults found on pines (*Pinus*). Widespread in western North America. (12)

Cosmobaris scolopacea (Germar) (3.0–3.3 mm) is oblong-oval, convex, and black with patches of brownish, whitish, and yellowish scales on sides of pronotum and elytra. Rostrum as long as head and pronotum combined, conspicuously sculptured. Pronotum slightly wider than long with large, dense punctures. Elytra two-fifths (male) or half (female) as long as wide. Underside with band of white scales next to base of elytra. Adults active spring and summer, found on ragweed (*Ambrosia*) and goosefoot (*Chenopodium*); attracted to lights. In West from British Columbia to Baja California, east to Idaho and Texas; widespread in eastern North America. (1)

Trichobaris mucorea (LeConte) (4.0–6.8 mm) is elongate, parallel-sided, and clothed in small gray scales, ventrally with larger white scales. Rostrum constricted basally. Propleural maculae large, usually confluent. Metepisternum visible between pronotum and humerus. Pygidium exposed. Claws fused basally. Male ventrites 1–2 concave, densely clothed in appressed, parallel scales, 3–4 black and glabrous medially with black setae along posterior margins; female posterior margins with white scales. *Trichobaris compacta* Casey (3.7–6.0 mm) and *T. cylindrica* Casey (3.4–4.7 mm) have smaller, discrete propleural maculae, former with pronotum broadest basally, latter broadest before middle. Adults on jimsonweed (*Datura*) and occasionally other flowers. Southwestern United States and Mexico. (3)

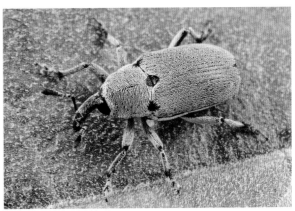

Ceutorhynchus americanus Buchanan (2.1–3.0 mm) is blackish, with brassy reflections, and metallic blue or green elytra. Rostrum slender, curved, more than half again as long as pronotum. Funicle with seven antennomeres before club. Pronotum narrowed anteriorly and constricted just before anterior margin; underneath with short channel between coxae. Elytra with patch of small white scales behind scutellum. Middle and hind femora each with a tooth, tarsomere 5 shorter than combined lengths of 2 and 3. On *Brassica* in spring. North America. Genus needs revision. (26)

Dietzella zimmermanni (Gyllenhal) (2.4–3.2 mm) is densely clothed in black and white scales, with a distinctly bicolored pronotum. Head sometimes completely withdrawn into prothorax, with short rostrum and six antennomeres between elbow and club. Rostrum short, about three times longer than wide. Prothorax barely wider than long with sharp tubercles on sides, front margin with pair of small teeth. Elytra with crosslike markings. Femora unarmed, and claws each bearing long, slender tooth. On *Epilobium*. British Columbia; also Newfoundland and Québec to Georgia, west to Ontario, Wisconsin, Arkansas, and Louisiana. (1)

Lechriops californicus (LeConte) (2.0–3.5 mm) is black, and irregularly clothed in brown and white scales. Large, oval eyes almost touching, bordered with pale scales. Rostrum stout and narrowed apically. Pronotum as wide as long. Elytra slightly wider than prothorax, strial punctures fine, interstriae flat, and distinct white sutural spot behind middle. Femora toothed, metafemora ringed with black. On *Pinus jeffreyi* and *P. ponderosa*. British Columbia and Idaho to Mexico. *Lechriops grisea* Sleeper (3.5–4.5 mm) pronotum with sides clothed in pale setae, elytra much wider than prothorax, suture with prominent light spot and line from declivity to apex. Arizona. (5)

Geraeus patagoniensis (Sleeper) (3.1–5.2 mm) is black, with bases of interstriae 1–2 with well-defined patch of broader scalloped scales, followed by patch of dark scales reduced in size on smaller beetles. Male abdomen depressed with patch of long, erect setae. Southeastern Arizona to Mexico. *Geraeus modestus* (Boheman) (3.6–5.1 mm) reddish brown, clothed dorsally in oval scalloped scales, bases of interstriae 1–2 with ill-defined patch of broad scalloped white scales, followed by patch of dark scales; male with some inconspicuous setae on ventrites. Southeastern Arizona to Texas. Both species on composites and other plants. (7)

Tachygonus centralis LeConte (1.9–2.3 mm) is rhomboid, flattened dorsoventrally, coarsely punctured, and black, with antennae, tibial apices, and last two tarsomeres brown. Antennae not geniculate. Pronotum with small tufts of white pectinate setae on posterior angles. Elytra abruptly broader than prothorax, with conspicuous tuft of suberect white, pectinate setae behind inconspicuous scutellum, deep strial punctures, and prominent humeri. Legs black, with hind femora short, swollen, and dentate along inner margin. Larvae mine *Robinia* leaves. Colorado to Arizona, east to Illinois and Texas. *Tachygonus rhombus* Casey with elytral tufts and bicolored legs, on *Quercus*. Arizona to Panama. (2)

Cylindrocopturus adspersus (LeConte) (2.5–3.5 mm) is elongate-oval, with dorsal surface densely scaled, pronotum and elytra with variable patterns formed by whitish, brown, and black scales. Rostrum short, stout, coarsely punctate. Pronotum long, with sides white anteriorly and posteriorly. Elytra slightly wider at base than prothorax, punctostriate, flat, with indistinct brown spots; scales flat, in pairs interspersed with single elliptical erect scales; abrupt apical declivity, and apices not divergent at suture. Pygidium concealed. Ventrite 2 smooth, not tuberculate. On composites. Southern California east to Missouri and Texas. (20)

Peltophorus polymitus seminiveus (LeConte) (7.5–10.0 mm) is broadly oval, somewhat flattened dorsally and ventrally, and mottled dorsally with dense black and white scales. Large oval eyes nearly contiguous. Pronotum coarsely punctured, punctures never forming prominent longitudinal ridges, with sides convergent anteriorly. Elytra with strial punctures large, each bearing a single suberect scale, and not covering pygidium. *Peltophorus adustus* (Fall) similar, elytra mostly brown with suture pale, pronotum cribrately punctured, sometimes forming longitudinal ridges, and sides mostly parallel before abrupt apical constriction. Both species diurnal, on *Agave*, and occur in southeastern Arizona and New Mexico, south to Mexico. (2)

Cossonus crenatus Horn (3.5–5.5 mm) is slightly flattened dorsally, and black. Head finely and sparsely punctured posteriorly, eyes prominent. Funicular antennomeres approximately equal in width with club at least twice as wide as funicle. Rostrum shorter than half length of pronotum, abruptly dilated apically in dorsal view, with antennal insertions located past mid length. Pronotum long, coarsely punctate, punctures cribrate laterally, with sides broadly arcuate, and posterior margin bisinuate. Elytra as broad as prothorax, with punctostriae slightly broader and deeper basally, with convex intervals narrow. British Columbia to Baja California, east to Idaho and New Mexico. Genus needs revision. (8)

Elassoptes marinus Horn (3.2–3.6 mm) is oblong-oval, shiny brown or reddish brown, without obvious dorsal vestiture. Coarsely faceted eye small, flat, and located on side of head. Funicle comprises seven antennomeres. Rostrum stout, longer than head, and somewhat flattened. Pronotum slightly wider than long, with sides broadly arcuate. Elytral punctures large, with intervals convex and transversely rugose. Femora weakly clavate and flattened; hind tibiae expanded apically, each with stout apical tooth hooklike and inner tooth spatulate and longer than claw. Under driftwood on sandy ocean beaches. British Columbia to Baja California. (1)

559

Rhyncolus cylindricollis Wollaston (3.3–4.2 mm) is cylindrical, coarsely punctured, and shiny black. Funicular antennomere 2 twice as wide as long or wider, imbedded in 1. Rostrum narrowed apically when viewed dorsally and laterally. Pronotum longer than wide, coarsely punctate, with lateral margins broadly arcuate. Inner margins of elytral intervals, especially 4–6, distinctly more carinate; apical costae not prominent, and intervals 7 and 9 coalescent well before apex. Male ventrite 1 without pubescent patch. Under bark of dead conifers. British Columbia to California, east to Idaho and Nevada. Genus needs revision. (13)

Western Pine Beetle *Dendroctonus brevicomis* LeConte (2.5–5.0 mm) is dark brown and stout. Head with epistomal process rounded, eyes ovate and entire, convex frons, and a deep, narrow median groove on vertex reaching upper level of eyes. Antennal club strongly flattened, with funicle comprising five antennomeres. Pronotum wide, with disc smooth and finely, shallowly punctate. Elytra with intervals densely and confusedly crenulate, pubescence on rounded apical declivity uniformly short, and declivital interval 2 weakly impressed between 1 and 3. In *Pinus ponderosa* and *P. coulteri*. British Columbia to California, east to Montana and western Texas; south to Chihuahua. (11)

Mountain Pine Beetle *Dendroctonus ponderosae*
Hopkins (3.5–7.5 mm) is robust, parallel-sided, and more
or less cylindrical, and shiny black when mature. Head with
frons convex and without median frontal groove. Antenna
with strongly flattened club and funicle comprising five
antennomeres. Pronotum wider than long, about half length
of elytra, with discal punctures coarse and dense. Elytra
striate, with basal margins armed and surface of declivity
dull and rugulose. Southern British Columbia to Baja
California, east to South Dakota and New Mexico. Jeffrey
pine beetle *Dendroctonus jeffreyi* Hopkins very similar but
with closer and deeper pronotal punctures. Adults of both
species attack pine (*Pinus*). (11)

Douglas-fir Beetle *Dendroctonus pseudotsugae*
Hopkins (4.4–7.0 mm) is robust, parallel-sided, and more
or less cylindrical, and dark brown to black when mature,
with elytra sometimes lighter. Frons strongly protuberant,
irregularly granulate, with fine, deep punctures, and
without median groove. Antenna with strongly flattened
club and funicle comprising five antennomeres. Pronotal
punctures small. Elytral intervals without fine punctures
among rough sculpturing, and declivital intervals smooth
and shiny, with declivital striae strongly impressed, and
interval 1 strongly elevated. Adults develop in Douglas-fir
(*Pseudotsuga menziesii*), rarely larch (*Larix*) and hemlock
(*Tsuga*). British Columbia and Alberta to California and
Chihuahua. (11)

Spruce Beetle *Dendroctonus rufipennis* (Kirby)
(4.4–7.0 mm) is robust, parallel-sided, and more or less
cylindrical, and dark brown with reddish elytra when
mature; old adults uniformly black. Frons convex, with fine,
dense, deep punctures, and granulate medially. Antenna
with strongly flattened club and funicle comprising five
antennomeres. Elytra with strial punctures large and
shallow, intervals densely and transversely crenulate,
and apical declivity steep and convex, with intervals
nearly smooth, punctate, and median punctures minutely
granulate anteriorly. Develops in spruce (*Picea*). Alaska to
Newfoundland, south to northern California, Arizona, New
Mexico; Great Lakes states and Pennsylvania. (11)

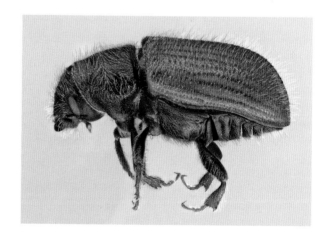

Red Turpentine Beetle *Dendroctonus valens* LeConte (5.3–9.0 mm) is large, stout, cylindrical, and uniformly reddish to reddish-brown. Antennal club semicircular, flattened, and crossed by three curved grooves. Pronotum with dense, shallow punctures becoming smaller laterally. Elytra with punctures small and deep, numerous setae at base, with scattered granule on declivity, and evenly convex apices. Larvae develop primarily in pine (*Pinus*), occasionally in other conifers. Adults attracted to injured, weakened, infested, or dying trees and freshly cut stumps of pines (*Pinus*), fir (*Abies*), larch (*Larix*), and spruce (*Picea*), usually near ground. Across Canada and western United States to Guatemala; also in Northeast. (11)

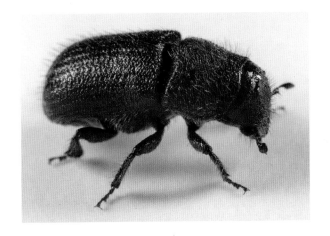

Hylastes macer LeConte (5.1–6.0 mm) is elongate, somewhat cylindrical, dull black, with entire pronotal and elytral surfaces minutely reticulate. Pronotum longer than wide, broadest at middle, with sides broadly arcuate before rounded anterior margin, and punctures small, shallow, and irregular in size and outline. Elytra parallel-sided at basal half, then converging just behind declivity, with most striae weakly impressed, strial punctures moderately large and deep, intervals convex; apical declivity with small scales. Adults construct galleries in phloem tissues of stumps and roots of pines (*Pinus*) and occasionally spruce (*Picea*). British Columbia to California, east to South Dakota and Arizona. (9)

Hylurgops porosus (LeConte) (3.3–4.6 mm) is elongate, somewhat cylindrical, variable in outline, and glossy dark brown or reddish brown to black when mature. Pronotum typically slightly longer than wide, with sides usually moderately arcuate, sometimes nearly straight and parallel basally, and weakly constricted anteriorly; surface smooth between equal numbers of large and small intermixed punctures on disc, and medial impunctate line. Elytra smooth between large, deep, strial punctures, with declivital intervals equal in height bearing erect setae and moderately abundant scales and interstrial setae. Tarsomere 3 broad and bilobed. Develops in various species of pine (*Pinus*). British Columbia to Arizona, east to Saskatchewan and New Mexico. (7)

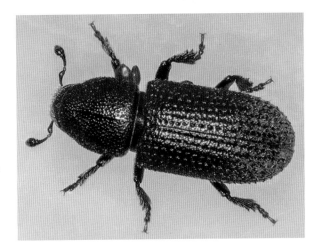

Pseudohylesinus nebulosus (LeConte) (2.3–2.9 mm) is elongate, robust, and dark brown with variegated pattern formed by light and dark scales and setae. Frons about as long as wide, broadly convex, with surface densely punctured. Antennal club with antennomeres 1 and 2 more or less equal in length. Elytra with serrations on basal margin distinctly elevated and sharp, especially laterally, declivital interval 1 and 3 weakly or not elevated, 9 moderately elevated, 1–3 more or less equal in width, all with granulate surface sculpturing. Adults chew longitudinal parental galleries in Douglas-fir (*Pseudotsuga menziesii*), and occasionally hemlock (*Tsuga*). British Columbia and Alberta, south to northern California and Chihuahua. (11)

European Shothole Borer *Anisandrus dispar* (Fabricius) (1.8–3.7 mm) is elongate, robust, and shiny reddish brown. Frons minutely reticulate, dull, and slightly impressed above epistoma on each side of elevated carina. Pronotum with 6–8 prominent asperities on anterior margin. Elytra with strial punctures large and closely set; declivity convex, with all intervals faintly granulate, 1 and 3 elevated, and ridge of 7 acute, elevated, and unbroken, with posterolateral margins lacking denticles, and setae as long as interval width. Develops in various hardwoods. In West in Pacific Northwest provinces and states; also in Northeast. (1)

Pine Engraver Beetle *Ips pini* (Say) (3.3–4.3 mm) is dark reddish brown to blackish. Vertex coarsely punctured, and frons granulate without median tubercle. Pronotum with discal punctures behind summit less dense and smaller than those in postlateral areas, and largest punctures two-thirds diameter of strial punctures. Elytral intervals smooth, with steep apical declivity shiny, broadly scooped out, and bearing four teeth along each side. Attacks thin-barked portions of *Pinus* slash, and dead or dying trees, seldom attacks healthy trees; rarely breeds in *Picea* and *Larix*; brood gallery distinctive. Alaska, across Canada, and western United States south to Mexico; also in East. (17)

Pityokteines ornatus (Swaine) (2.1–2.9 mm) is cylindrical, and reddish brown. Frons convex, especially in female, with surface granulate, punctate, and sparsely pubescent. Antennal club obliquely truncate. Elytra distinctly punctostriate, strial punctures large, with excavated declivity narrow with rounded lateral margins poorly developed apically. Male with edges of declivity more pronounced than female, with basally enlarged spine. In boles of cut, fallen, or dying *Pinus jeffreyi*, usually in trees where *Ips* are established. Southern British Columbia to California, east to western South Dakota, Colorado, and Arizona. (5)

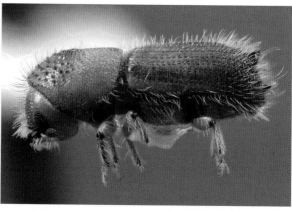

Pityophthorus venustus Blackman (1.7–2.1 mm) is elongate, stout, cylindrical, and somewhat shiny reddish brown. Frons somewhat convex from epistoma to well past eyes, with surface densely, coarsely, and setigerously punctured, setae rather long. Pronotum about as long as wide, with anterior margin distinctly asperate, disc smooth between punctures, and clothed in fine, suberect setae. Elytra smooth between moderately deep strial punctures, declivity steep, narrow and not strongly sulcate, with lateral convexities broadly rounded, minutely granulate, interstriae 3 and 8 not elevated apically, and 2 with tubercles at base. Develop in small branches of pines (*Pinus*). California east to South Dakota and western Texas. (26)

Fir Engraver Beetle *Scolytus ventralis* LeConte (2.5–4.3 mm) is twice as long as wide, usually very dark reddish brown with elytra lighter. Head with frons broadly convex and densely clothed in short fine setae. Antenna with scape shorter than funicle that comprises seven antennomeres. Pronotum slightly wider than long, glabrous except along margins, with punctures separated by 2–4 times their diameters. Scutellum depressed. Elytra barely declivous apically. Male with posterior margin of ventrite 2 vertical and produced into a small, median, carinate tubercle. Develops primarily in boles, tops, and slash of white fir (*Abies concolor*), grand fir (*A. grandis*), and California red fir (*A. magnifica*). British Columbia to California, east to Montana and New Mexico. (12)

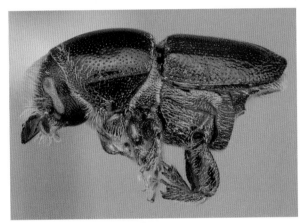

Xyleborinus saxesenii (Ratzeburg) (1.5–2.6 mm) is elongate, cylindrical, and dark brown with appendages lighter. Frons minutely reticulate, punctures and median line faint. Scutellum conical. Pronotum with anterior margin lacking asperities, anterior half densely tuberculate. Elytra with punctures deep, intervals smooth, and declivity dull and steep, occupying less than one-third of declivital length; intervals 1 and 3 slightly raised, 1 tuberculate and 2 unarmed, and apical portion of interval 9 forming lower margin and bearing several acute tubercles. Develops in limbs and boles of weakened deciduous trees, and some conifers (*Libocedrus*, *Pinus*, *Tsuga*). Across southern Canada and United States, south to Mexico. (2)

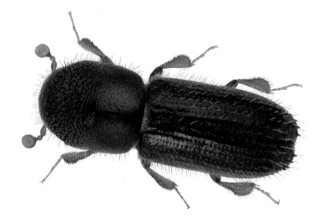

563

Appendix

CLASSIFICATION OF THE BEETLES COVERED IN THIS BOOK

The classification used for this book is based on Beutel and Leschen (2016), Evans and Smith (2020), Gimmel et al. (2019), McKenna et al. (2019), and Vasilikopoulos et al. (2019) (see bibliographic information in Selected References and Resources).

ORDER COLEOPTERA

Suborder Archostemata
    Family Cupedidae (p.74)
        Subfamily Priacminae
            Priacma serrata (LeConte) (p.74)
            Prolixocupes lobiceps (LeConte) (p.74)
    Family Micromalthidae (p.75)
        Micromalthus debilis LeConte (p.75)
Suborder Myxophaga
    Superfamily Sphaeriusoidea
    Family Hydroscaphidae (p.76)
        Hydroscapha natans LeConte (p.76)
    Family Sphaeriusidae (p.77)
        Sphaerius species (p.77)
Suborder Adephaga
    Family Gyrinidae (pp.78–9)
        Subfamily Gyrininae
          Tribe Enhydrini
            Dineutus sublineatus Chevrolat (p.78)
          Tribe Gyrinini
            Gyrinus species (p.79)
    Family Haliplidae (pp.79–81)
        Brychius hornii Crotch (p.80)
        Haliplus concolor LeConte (p.80)
        Haliplus parvulus Roberts (p.80)
        Peltodytes callosus (LeConte) (p.81)
    Family Dytiscidae (pp.81–6)
        Subfamily Agabinae
          Tribe Agabini
            Agabus lutosus (LeConte) (p.82)
            Ilybius quadrimaculatus Aubé (p.82)
        Subfamily Colymbetinae
            Colymbetes densus LeConte (p.83)
            Rhantus gutticollis (Say) (p.83)

Subfamily Copelatinae
    Copelatus glyphicus (Say) (p.83)
Subfamily Laccophilinae
    Tribe Laccophilini
        Laccophilus maculosus decipiens LeConte (p.83)
Subfamily Cybistrinae
    Cybister fimbriolatus (Say) (p.84)
Subfamily Dytiscinae
    Tribe Dytiscini
        Dytiscus marginicollis LeConte (p.84)
    Tribe Eretini
        Eretes sticticus (Linnaeus) (p.84)
    Tribe Acilini
        Acilius abbreviatus Aubé (p.85)
        Graphoderus perplexus (Sharp) (p.85)
        Thermonectus marmoratus (Gray) (p.85)
        Thermonectus nigrofasciatus (Aubé) (p.85)
Subfamily Hydroporinae
    Tribe Hydroporini
        Boreonectes striatellus (LeConte) (p.86)
        Neoporus undulatus (Say) (p.86)
Family Amphizoidae (pp.86–7)
    Amphizoa insolens LeConte (p.87)
Family Trachypachidae
    Trachypachus gibbsii LeConte (p.88)
Family Carabidae (pp.88–111)
    Subfamily Nebriinae
        Tribe Opisthiini
          Opisthius richardsoni Kirby (p.90)
        Tribe Nebriini
          Nebria eschscholtzii Ménétriés (p.90)
        Tribe Notiophilini
          Notiophilus biguttatus (Fabricius) (p.90)

Subfamily Carabinae
    Tribe Cychrini
        Cychrus tuberculatus Harris (p.90)
        Scaphinotus cristatus (Harris) (p.91)
        Scaphinotus longiceps Van Dyke (p.91)
    Tribe Carabini
        Calosoma cancellatum Eschscholtz (p.91)
        Calosoma prominens LeConte (p.91)
        Calosoma scrutator (Fabricius) (p.92)
        Calosoma semilaeve (LeConte) (p.92)
        Carabus nemoralis Müller (p.92)
        Carabus serratus Say (p.92)
        Carabus vietinghoffi Adams (p.93)
Subfamily Cicindelinae
    Tribe Amblycheilini
        Amblycheila baroni Rivers (p.93)
        Omus californicus Eschscholtz (p.93)
    Tribe Megacephalini
        Tetracha carolina (Linnaeus) (p.93)
    Tribe Cicindelini
        Brasiella wickhami (W. Horn) (p.94)
        Cicindela hirticollis gravida LeConte (p.94)
        Cicindela latesignata LeConte (p.94)
        Cicindela oregona LeConte (p.94)
        Cicindela willistoni echo Casey (p.95)
        Cicindelidia haemorrhagica LeConte (p.95)
        Cicindelidia obsoleta santaclarae Bates
          (p.95)
        Cicindelidia ocellata Klug (p.95)
        Cicindelidia punctulata chihuahuae Bates
          (p.96)
        Cicindelidia sedecimpunctata Klug (p.96)
        Cicindelidia trifasciata sigmoidea LeConte
          (p.96)
        Parvindela lemniscata (LeConte) (p.96)
Subfamily Elaphrinae
    Tribe Elaphrini
        Elaphrus californicus Mannerheim (p.97)
Subfamily Omophroninae
    Tribe Omophronini
        Omophron dentatum LeConte (p.97)
        Omophron obliteratum Horn (p.97)
Subfamily Scaritinae
    Tribe Pasimachini
        Pasimachus californicus Chaudoir (p.97)
        Pasimachus viridans LeConte (p.98)
    Tribe Scaritini
        Scarites subterraneus Fabricius (p.98)
    Tribe Clivini
        Paraclivina bipustulata (Fabricius) (p.98)
    Tribe Dyschiriini
        Akephorus marinus LeConte (p.98)
        Akephorus obesus (LeConte) (p.99)
    Tribe Rhysodini
        Clinidium calcaratum LeConte (p.99)
        Omoglymmius hamatus (LeConte) (p.99)

    Tribe Promecognathini
        Promecognathus crassus LeConte (p.99)
Subfamily Broscinae
    Tribe Broscini
        Zacotus matthewsii (LeConte) (p.100)
Subfamily Trechinae
    Tribe Bembidini
        Bembidion flohri Bates (p.100)
        Mioptachys flavicauda (Say) (p.100)
        Tachyta kirbyi Casey (p.100)
Subfamily Patrobinae
    Tribe Patrobini
        Patrobus longicornis (Say) (p.101)
Subfamily Psydrinae
    Tribe Psydrini
        Psydrus piceus LeConte (p.101)
Subfamily Paussinae
    Tribe Metriini
        Metrius contractus Eschscholtz (p.101)
    Tribe Ozaenini
        Goniotropis kuntzeni (Bänninger) (p.101)
Subfamily Brachininae
    Tribe Brachinini
        Brachinus mexicanus Dejean (p.102)
Subfamily Harpalinae
    Tribe Pterostichini
        Poecilus lucublandus (Say) (p.102)
        Pterostichus lama (Ménétriés) (p.102)
    Tribe Panagaenini
        Panagaeus sallei Chaudoir (p.102)
    Tribe Chlaeniini
        Chlaenius cumatilis LeConte (p.103)
        Chlaenius sericeus (Forster) (p.103)
    Tribe Licinini
        Badister neopulchellus Lindroth (p.103)
        Diplocheila striatopunctata (LeConte) (p.103)
    Tribe Harpalini
        Anisodactylus alternans (Motschulsky) (p.104)
        Cratacanthus dubius (Palisot de Beauvois)
          (p.104)
        Dicheirus dilitatus (Dejean) (p.104)
        Euryderus grossus (Say) (p.104)
        Geopinus incrassatus (Dejean) (p.105)
        Harpalus caliginosus (Fabricius) (p.105)
        Notiobia purpurascens (Bates) (p.105)
        Polpochila erro (LeConte) (p.105)
        Stenolophus comma (Fabricius) (p.106)
        Stenolophus lineola (Fabricius) (p.106)
        Stenolophus ochropezus (Say) (p.106)
        Stenomorphus californicus (Ménétriés) (p.106)
    Tribe Lachnophorini
        Lachnophorus elegantulus Mannerheim
          (p.107)
    Tribe Sphodrini
        Calathus ruficollis Dejean (p.107)

565

Tribe Platynini
Rhadine species (p.107)
Tanystoma maculicolle (Dejean) (p.107)
Tribe Perigonini
Perigona nigriceps (Dejean) (p.108)
Tribe Odacanthini
Colliuris lioptera (Bates) (p.108)
Colliuris pensylvanica (Linnaeus) (p.108)
Tribe Lebiini
Apenes hilariola Bates (p.108)
Calleida decora (Fabricius) (p.109)
Calleida platynoides Horn (p.109)
Lebia analis Dejean (p.109)
Lebia fuscata Dejean (p.110)
Lebia viridis Say (p.110)
Plochionus timidus Haldeman (p.110)
Tribe Zuphini
Pseudaptinus tenuicollis (LeConte) (p.110)
Tribe Galeritini
Galerita mexicana Chaudoir (p.111)
Tribe Helluonini
Helluomorphoides latitarsus Casey (p.111)
Tribe Pseudomorphini
Pseudomorpha species (p.111)
Suborder Polyphaga
Superfamily Nosodendroidea
Family Nosodendridae (pp.115–16)
Nosodendron californicum Horn (p.116)
Series Scirtiformia
Superfamily Scirtoidea
Family Eucinetidae (p.112)
Eucinetus terminalis LeConte (p.112)
Nycteus infumatus (LeConte) (p.112)
Family Clambidae (p.113)
Clambus species (p.113)
Family Scirtidae (pp.114–15)
Elodes apicalis LeConte (p.114)
Herthania concinna (LeConte) (p.115)
Scirtes species (p.115)
Series Derodontiformia
Superfamily Derodontoidea
Family Derodontidae (pp.116–17)
Subfamily Peltasticinae
Peltastica tuberculata Mannerheim (p.117)
Subfamily Derodontinae
Derodontus trisignatus (Mannerheim) (p.117)
Subfamily Laricobiinae
Laricobius nigrinus Fender (p.117)
Series Staphyliniformia
Superfamily Hydrophiloidea
Family Helophoridae (p.118)
Helophorus species (p.118)
Family Epimetopidae (pp.119–20)
Epimetopus arizonicus Perkins (p.119)
Epimetopus punctipennis Perkins (p.119)

566

Epimetopus thermarum Schwarz & Barber
(p.120)
Family Georissidae (pp.120–1)
Georissus pusillus LeConte (p.121)
Family Hydrochidae (pp.121–2)
Hydrochus squamifer LeConte
Family Hydrophilidae (pp.122–5)
Subfamily Hydrophilinae
Tribe Berosini
Berosus punctatissimus LeConte (p.123)
Tribe Hydrophilini
Hydrobius fuscipes (Linnaeus) (p.123)
Hydrochara lineata LeConte (p.124)
Hydrophilus triangularis Say (p.124)
Tropisternus lateralis humeralis Motschulsky
(p.124)
Tribe Laccobiini
Laccobius species (p.124)
Subfamily Enochrinae
Cercyon fimbriatus Mannerheim (p.125)
Cymbiodyta acuminata Fall (p.125)
Enochrus hamiltoni (Horn) (p.125)
Subfamily Sphaeridiinae
Sphaeridium lunatus Fabricius (p.125)
Family Sphaeritidae (p.126)
Sphaerites politus Mannerheim (p.126)
Family Histeridae (pp.127–32)
Subfamily Abraeinae
Tribe Plegaderini
Plegaderus sayi Marseul (p.128)
Tribe Teretriini
Teretrius cylindrellus Casey (p.128)
Subfamily Dendrophilinae
Tribe Paromalini
Platylomalus aequalis (Say) (p.128)
Platysoma leconti Marseul (p.128)
Subfamily Haeteriinae
Haeterius wagneri Ross (p.129)
Subfamily Histerinae
Tribe Histerini
Atholus bimaculatus (Linnaeus) (p.129)
Hister furtivus J.E. LeConte (p.129)
Spilodiscus sellatus (LeConte) (p.129)
Tribe Hololeptini
Hololepta vernicis Casey (p.130)
Iliotona cacti LeConte (p.130)
Tribe Omalodini
Omalodes grossus Marseul (p.130)
Subfamily Onthophilininae
Onthophilus lecontei Horn (p.131)
Subfamily Saprininae
Euspilotus scissus (LeConte) (p.131)
Hypocaccus bigemmeus (LeConte) (p.131)
Neopachylopus sulcifrons (Mannerheim) (p.131)
Saprinus lugens Erichson (p.132)
Xerosaprinus lubricus (LeConte) (p.132)

Tribe Onitini
  Onitis alexis Klug (p.180)
Tribe Onthophagini
  Digitonthophagus gazella (Fabricius) (p.180)
  Onthophagus arnetti Howden & Cartwright (p.180)
  Onthophagus nuchicornis (Linnaeus) (p.180)
  Onthophagus taurus (Schreber) (p.181)
Tribe Phanaenini
  Phanaeus quadridens (Say) (p.181)
  Phanaeus vindex MacLeay (p.181)
Subfamily Melolonthinae
  Tribe Acomini
    Acoma mixta Howden (p.181)
  Tribe Chnaunanthini
    Chnaunanthus chapini Saylor (p.182)
    Chnaunanthus flavipennis (Horn) (p.182)
  Tribe Dichelonychini
    Coenonycha ampla Cazier (p.182)
    Coenonycha lurida Cazier (p.183)
    Coenonycha testacea Cazier (p.183)
    Dichelonyx backii Kirby (p.183)
    Dichelonyx muscula Fall (p.183)
    Dichelonyx pusilla LeConte (p.184)
    Dichelonyx truncata LeConte (p.184)
    Dichelonyx vicina Fall (p.184)
    Gymnopyge hopliaeformis Linell (p.185)
  Tribe Diplotaxini
    Diplotaxis sierrae Fall (p.185)
    Diplotaxis moerens moerens LeConte (p.185)
  Tribe Hopliini
    Hoplia callipyge LeConte (p.186)
    Hoplia dispar LeConte (p.186)
  Tribe Macrodactylini
    Isonychus arizonensis Howden (p.186)
    Macrodactylus uniformis Horn (p.186)
  Tribe Melolonthini
    Amblonoxia carpenteri (LeConte) (p.187)
    Amblonoxia palpalis (Horn) (p.187)
    Dinacoma sanfelipe Gillett, Osborne, Reil & Rubinoff (p.187)
    Polyphylla cavifrons LeConte (p.187)
    Polyphylla decemlineata (Say) (p.188)
    Polyphylla hammondi LeConte (p.188)
    Polyphylla nigra Casey (p.188)
    Polyphylla sobrina Casey (p.188)
  Tribe Rhizotrogini
    Amphimallon majale (Razoumowsky) (p.189)
    Listrochelus xerophilus (Saylor) (p.189)
    Phyllophaga anxia (LeConte) (p.189)
    Phyllophaga bilobatata Saylor (p.189)
    Phyllophaga vetula (Horn) (p.190)
  Tribe Phobetusini
    Phobetus comatus LeConte (p.190)
    Phobetus humeralis Cazier (p.190)
    Phobetus mojavus Barrett (p.190)
    Phobetus saylori Cazier (p.191)

Tribe Sericini
  Serica perigonia Dawson (p.191)
Subfamily Rutelinae
  Tribe Anomalini
    Anomala arida Casey (p.191)
    Anomala delicata Casey (p.191)
    Anomala digressa Casey (p.192)
    Anomala flavilla flavilla Bates (p.192)
    Anomalacra clypealis Schaeffer (p.192)
    Leptohoplia testaceipennis Saylor (p.192)
    Strigoderma pimalis Casey (p.193)
  Tribe Rutelini
    Chrysina beyeri (Skinner) (p.193)
    Chrysina gloriosa (LeConte) (p.193)
    Chrysina lecontei (Horn) (p.193)
    Cotalpa consobrina Horn (p.194)
    Parabyrsopolis chihuahuae (Bates) (p.194)
    Paracotalpa deserta Saylor (p.194)
    Paracotalpa puncticollis (LeConte) (p.194)
    Paracotalpa ursina (Horn) (p.195)
    Pelidnota lugubris LeConte (p.195)
    Pseudocotalpa andrewsi Hardy (p.195)
Subfamily Dynastinae
  Tribe Cyclocephalini
    Ancognatha manca (LeConte) (p.195)
    Cyclocephala hirta LeConte (p.196)
    Cyclocephala longula LeConte (p.196)
    Cyclocephala melanocephala (Fabricius) (p.196)
    Cyclocephala pasadenae (Casey) (p.196)
    Dyscinetus laevicollis Arrow (p.197)
  Tribe Dynastini
    Dynastes grantii Horn (p.197)
    Megasoma punctulatum Cartwright (p.197)
  Tribe Oryctini
    Strategus aloeus (Linnaeus) (p.197)
    Strategus cessus LeConte (p.198)
    Xyloryctes thestalus Bates (p.198)
  Tribe Pentodontini
    Anoplognatho dunnianus Rivers (p.198)
    Coscinocephalus cribrifrons (Schaeffer) (p.198)
    Orizabus clunalis (LeConte) (p.199)
    Orizabus ligyroides Horn (p.199)
    Oxygrylius ruginasus (LeConte) (p.199)
    Tomarus gibbosus (DeGeer) (p.199)
  Tribe Phileurini
    Hemiphileurus illatus (LeConte) (p.200)
    Phileurus truncatus (Palisot de Beauvois) (p.200)
Subfamily Cetoniinae
  Tribe Cetoniini
    Euphoria fascifera (LeConte) (p.200)
    Euphoria inda (Linnaeus) (p.200)
    Euphoria leucographa (Gory & Percheron) (p.201)

571

573

Tribe Cnemeplatiini
  Lepidocnemeplatia sericea (Horn) (p.350)
Tribe Cnemodinini
  Cnemodinus testaceus (Horn) (p.350)
Tribe Coniontini
  Coelus ciliatus Eschscholtz (p.351)
  Conionitis species (p.351)
  Eusattus difficilis LeConte (p.351)
  Eusattus dilitatus LeConte (p.351)
  Eusattus muricatus LeConte (p.352)
  Eusattus reticulatus Say (p.352)
Tribe Cryptoglossini
  Asbolus laevis LeConte (p.352)
  Asbolus verrucosus LeConte (p.353)
  Cryptoglossa muricata (LeConte) (p.353)
  Cryptoglossa variolosa (Horn) (p.353)
  Schizillus laticeps Horn (p.354)
Tribe Edrotini
  Auchmobius sublaevis LeConte (p.354)
  Chilometopon brachystomum Doyen (p.354)
  Edrotes ventricosus LeConte (p.354)
  Triorophus laevis LeConte (p.355)
Tribe Epitragini
  Bothrotes plumbeus plumbeus (LeConte)
    (p.355)
  Lobometopon fusiforme (Casey) (p.355)
  Metopoloba pruinosa pruinosa (Horn) (p.355)
  Pechalius vestitus (Casey) (p.356)
  Polemiotus submetallicus (LeConte) (p.356)
Tribe Nyctoporini
  Nyctoporis carinata LeConte (p.356)
Tribe Stenosini
  Araeoschizus species (p.357)
Tribe Vacronini
  Alaephus species (p.357)
  Eupsophulus castaneus (Horn) (p.357)
Subfamily Tenebrioninae
  Tribe Amphidorini
    Eleodes armata LeConte (p.358)
    Eleodes obscura sulcipennis Mannerheim
      (p.358)
    Eleodes osculans (LeConte) (p.358)
    Eleodes tribula Thomas (p.358)
    Embaphion contusum LeConte (p.359)
    Embaphion depressum (LeConte) (p.359)
    Embaphion elongatum Horn (p.359)
    Lariversius tibialis Blaisdell (p.359)
    Trogloderus vandykei La Rivers (p.360)
  Tribe Bolitophagini
    Eleates depressus (Randall) (p.360)
    Megeleates sequoarium Casey (p.360)
    Rhipidandrus peninsularis Horn (p.360)
  Tribe Centronopini
    Scotobaenus parallelus LeConte (p.361)

Tribe Cerenopini
  Argoporis bicolor (LeConte) (p.361)
  Cerenopus concolor LeConte (p.361)
Tribe Eulabini
  Apsena rufipes (Eschscholtz) (p.362)
  Epantius obscurus LeConte (p.362)
Tribe Helopini
  Helops laeta LeConte (p.362)
Tribe Melanimonini
  Cheirodes californicus (Horn) (p.362)
Tribe Metaclisini
  Metaclisa marginalis Horn (p.363)
Tribe Opatrini
  Ammodonus granosus Fall (p.363)
  Blapstinus species (p.363)
  Conibius gagates (Horn) (p.364)
  Trichoton sordidum (LeConte) (p.364)
  Ulus crassus (LeConte) (p.364)
Tribe Tenebrionini
  Zophobas subnitens (Horn) (p.365)
Tribe Triboliini
  Tribolium castaneum (Herbst) (p.365)
Tribe Ulomini
  Uloma longula LeConte (p.365)
Subfamily Alleculinae
  Tribe Alleculini
    Isomira species (p.365)
    Lystronychus scapularis Champion (p.366)
    Mycetochara procera Casey (p.366)
    Pseudocistela pinguis (LeConte) (p.366)
    Stenochidus gracilis (LeConte) (p.367)
Subfamily Diaperinae
  Tribe Crypticini
    Gondwanocrypticus platensis (Fairmaire)
      (p.367)
  Tribe Diaperini
    Adelina pallida (Say) (p.367)
    Cynaeus angustus (LeConte) (p.368)
    Diaperis rufipes Horn (p.368)
    Platydema oregonensis LeConte (p.368)
    Platydema wandae Triplehorn (p.368)
  Tribe Hypophloeini
    Corticeus substriatus LeConte (p.369)
  Tribe Phaleriini
    Phaleria rotundata LeConte (p.369)
    Phaleromela variegata Triplehorn (p.369)
Subfamily Stenochiinae
  Tribe Cnodalonini
    Alobates pensylvanicus (DeGeer) (p.369)
    Cibdelis blaschkei Mannerheim (p.370)
    Coelocnemis dilaticollis Mannerheim (p.370)
    Coelocnemis sulcata Casey (p.370)
    Iphthiminus serratus (Mannerheim) (p.371)
    Upis ceramboides (Linnaeus) (p.371)
  Tribe Stenochiini
    Strongylium atrum Champion (p.371)

579

Subfamily Cassidinae
  Tribe Cassidini
    Charidotella sexpunctata bicolor (Fabricius) (p.504)
    Charidotella succinea (Boheman) (p.504)
    Deloyala lecontii (Crotch) (p.505)
    Gratiana pallidula (Boheman) (p.505)
    Heliocassis clavata testudinaria (Boheman) (p.505)
  Tribe Chalepini
    Anisostena californica Van Dyke (p.505)
    Baliosus californicus (Horn) (p.506)
    Brachycoryna longula Weise (p.506)
    Microrhopala rubrolineata (Mannerheim) (p.506)
    Microrhopala vittata (Fabricius) (p.506)
    Octotoma marginicollis Horn (p.507)
    Stenopodius flavidus Horn (p.507)
    Sumitrosis inaequalis (Weber) (p.507)
    Xenochalepus ater (Weise) (p.508)
  Tribe Ischyrosonychini
    Physonota arizonae Schaeffer (p.508)
  Tribe Mesomphalini
    Chelymorpha phytophagica Crotch (p.508)
Subfamily Chrysomelinae
  Tribe Chrysomelini
    Calligrapha californica coreospivora Brown (p.508)
    Calligrapha dislocata (Rogers) (p.509)
    Calligrapha multipunctata (Say) (p.509)
    Chrysomela confluens Rogers (p.509)
    Chrysomela schaefferi Brown (p.509)
    Chrysomela scripta Fabricius (p.510)
    Entomoscelis americana Brown (p.510)
    Gastrophysa cyanea Melsheimer (p.510)
    Gonioctena americana (Schaeffer) (p.510)
    Leptinotarsa decemlineata (Say) (p.511)
    Leptinotarsa haldemani (Rogers) (p.511)
    Leptinotarsa lineolata (Stål) (p.511)
    Leptinotarsa rubiginosa (Rogers) (p.511)
    Longitarsus species (p.512)
    Paropsisterna m-fuscum (Boheman) (p.512)
    Plagiodera californica (Rogers) (p.512)
    Timarcha intricata Haldeman (p.512)
    Trachymela sloanei (Blackburn) (p.513)
    Zygogramma arizonica Schaeffer (p.513)
    Zygogramma continua (LeConte) (p.513)
    Zygogramma piceicollis (Stål) (p.513)
    Zygogramma signatipennis (Stål) (p.514)
Subfamily Criocerinae
  Tribe Criocerini
    Crioceris asparagi (Linnaeus) (p.514)
    Crioceris duodecimpunctata (Linnaeus) (p.514)
    Lilioceris lilii (Scopoli) (p.514)

  Tribe Lemini
    Lema nigrovittata (Guérin-Méneville) (p.515)
    Lema trabeata Lacordaire (p.515)
    Lema trivittata trivittata Say (p.515)
    Oulema arizonae (Schaeffer) (p.515)
Subfamily Cryptocephalinae
  Tribe Clytrini
    Anomoea rufifrons occidentimutabilis Moldenke (p.516)
    Coleothorpa axillaris LeConte (p.516)
    Megalostomis pyropyga Lacordaire (p.516)
    Megalostomis subfasciata (LeConte) (p.516)
    Saxinis saucia LeConte (p.517)
    Urodera dilaticollis Jacoby (p.517)
  Tribe Cryptocephalini
    Cryptocephalus atrofasciatus Jacoby (p.517)
    Cryptocephalus sanguinipennis Suffrian (p.517)
    Diachus auratus (Fabricius) (p.518)
    Griburius montezuma (Suffrian) (p.518)
    Pachybrachis bivittatus (Say) (p.518)
    Pachybrachis circumcinctus Crotch (p.518)
    Pachybrachis mellitus Bowditch (p.519)
    Pachybrachis thoracicus Jacoby (p.519)
Subfamily Donaciinae
  Tribe Haemoniini
    Neohaemonia nigricornis (Kirby) (p.519)
  Tribe Plateumarini
    Plateumaris dubia (Schaeffer) (p.520)
Subfamily Eumolpinae
  Tribe Adoxini
    Bromius obscurus (Linnaeus) (p.520)
    Colaspidea smaragdula LeConte (p.520)
  Tribe Eumolpini
    Chrysochus auratus (Fabricius) (p.520)
    Chrysochus cobaltinus LeConte (p.521)
    Colaspis nigrocyanea Crotch (p.521)
    Colaspis viriditincta Schaeffer (p.521)
    Glyptoscelis albida LeConte (p.521)
    Tymnes oregonensis (Crotch) (p.522)
  Tribe Typhophorini
    Graphops pubescens (Melsheimer) (p.522)
Subfamily Galerucinae
  Tribe Alticini
    Altica ambiens (LeConte) (p.522)
    Blepharida rhois (Forster) (p.522)
    Disonycha alternata (Illiger) (p.523)
    Disonycha tenuicornis Horn (p.523)
    Epitrix hirtipennis (Melsheimer) (p.523)
    Hemiglyptus basalis (Crotch) (p.523)
    Kuschelina lugens (LeConte) (p.524)
    Walterianella durangoensis (Jacoby) (p.524)
  Tribe Galerucini
    Acalymma trivittatum Mannerheim (p.524)
    Diabrotica undecimpunctata undecimpunctata Mannerheim (p.525)

Tribe Otiorhychini
   Otiorhynchus ovatus (Linnaeus) (p.547)
   Otiorhynchus rugosostriatus (Goeze) (p.547)
   Otiorhynchus sulcatus (Fabricius) (p.547)
Tribe Peritelini
   Aragnomus griseus Horn (p.548)
   Dysticheus insignis Horn (p.548)
   Eucilinus aridus (Van Dyke) (p.548)
   Nemocestes horni Van Dyke (p.548)
   Thricolepis inornata Horn (p.549)
Tribe Polydrusini
   Pachyrhinus californicus (Horn) (p.549)
   Pachyrhinus elegans (Couper) (p.549)
Tribe Sciaphilini
   Barypeithes pellucidus (Boheman) (p.549)
Tribe Sitonini
   Sitona californicus Fåhraeus (p.550)
Tribe Tanymecini
   Hadromeropsis opalina (Horn) (p.550)
   Pandeleteinus submetallicus (Schaeffer)
     (p.550)
   Pandeleteius robustus Schaeffer (p.551)
Subfamily Lixiinae
  Tribe Cleonini
   Apleurus angularis (LeConte) (p.551)
   Cyphocleonus achates Fåhraeus (p.551)
   Scaphomorphus quadrilineatus (Chevrolat)
     (p.551)
  Tribe Lixini
   Larinus carlinae (Olivier) (p.552)
   Lixus perforatus LeConte (p.552)
Subfamily Curculioninae
  Tribe Anthonomini
   Anthonomus haematopus Boheman (p.552)
  Tribe Curculionini
   Curculio aurivestis Chittenden (p.552)
  Tribe Ellescini
   Dorytomus inaequalis Casey (p.553)
  Tribe Mecinini
   Rhinusa tetra (Fabricius) (p.553)
  Tribe Otidocephalini
   Myrmex lineatus (Pascoe) (p.553)
   Myrmex vandykei Sleeper (p.554)
  Tribe Rhamphini
   Tachyerges salicis (Linnaeus) (p.554)
Subfamily Molytinae
  Tribe Cryptorhynchini
   Cnemidoprion oblongus (Horn) (p.554)
   Cryptorhynchus lapathi (Linnaeus) (p.554)
   Zascelis irrorata LeConte (p.555)
  Tribe Emphyastini
   Emphyastes fucicola Mannerheim (p.555)

Tribe Lepyrini
   Lepyrus oregonensis Casey (p.555)
Tribe Pissodini
   Pissodes schwarzi Hopkins (p.555)
Tribe Sternechini
   Sternechus paludatus (Casey) (p.556)
Subfamily Mesoptilinae
  Tribe Laemosaccini
   Laemosaccus burkei Hespenheide (p.556)
  Tribe Magdalidini
   Magdalis lecontei Horn (p.556)
Subfamily Conoderinae
  Tribe Baridini
   Cosmobaris scolopacea (Germar) (p.556)
   Trichobaris mucorea (LeConte) (p.557)
  Tribe Ceutorhynchini
   Ceutorhynchus americanus Buchanan (p.557)
  Tribe Cnemogonini
   Dietzella zimmermanni (Gyllenhal) (p.557)
  Tribe Lechriopini
   Lechriops californica (LeConte) (p.557)
  Tribe Madarini
   Geraeus patagoniensis (Sleeper) (p.558)
  Tribe Tachygonini
   Tachygonus centralis LeConte (p.558)
  Tribe Zygopini
   Cylindrocopturus adspersus (LeConte) (p.558)
   Peltophorus polymitus seminiveus (LeConte)
     (p.558)
Subfamily Cossoninae
  Tribe Cossonini
   Cossonus crenatus Horn (p.559)
  Tribe Rhyncolini
   Elassoptes marinus Horn (p.559)
   Rhyncolus cylindricollis Wollaston (p.559)
Subfamily Scolytinae
  Tribe Dendroctini
   Dendroctonus brevicomis LeConte (p.559)
   Dendroctonus ponderosae Hopkins (p.560)
   Dendroctonus pseudotsugae Hopkins (p.560)
   Dendroctonus rufipennis (Kirby) (p.560)
   Dendroctonus valens (LeConte) (p.561)
  Tribe Hylesini
   Hylastes macer LeConte (p.561)
   Hylurgops porosus (LeConte) (p.561)
   Pseudohylesinus nebulosus (LeConte) (p.562)
  Tribe Scolytini
   Anisandrus dispar (Fabricius) (p.562)
   Ips pini (Say) (p.562)
   Pityokteines ornatus (Swaine) (p.562)
   Pityophthorus venustus Blackman (p.563)
   Scolytus ventralis LeConte (p.563)
   Xyleborinus saxesenii (Ratzeburg) (p.563)

GLOSSARY

abdomen: last major region of beetle body, usually partly or entirely covered by the elytra

adecticous pupa: a pupa without functioning mouthparts

adpressed: laid or pressed to; contiguous

adventitious: not native

aethalium (pl. aethalia): large, thick, cushion-shaped structures of slime molds that contain spores; analogous to fruiting bodies of fungi

alutaceous: surface dulled by a minute network of fine cracks resembling those of human skin

ambrosia: mutualistic fungus grown in tunnels by some bark and ambrosia beetles (Curculionidae) as food

angulate: edge of structure forming an angle

annulate: formed in ringlike articles; ringed

antenna (pl. antennae): pair of jointed sensory appendages on head, attached above or behind mouth

antennomere: article of antenna, including scape, pedicel, and flagellomeres

anterior: in front

anthophagous: flower-feeding

apex: tip of a structure

apical: at or toward the apex

aposematic: possessing distinctive, often contrasting color patterns that serve a defensive purpose by warning predators of unpalatability

appendages: mouthparts, antennae, and legs

appendiculate claw: claw bearing a broad flange at base of claw blade

appressed setae: setae that are in parallel or in contact with body surface

apterous: without flight wings

arcuate: arched or bowlike

band: a marking across the body, from one side to the other

basal: near the base of a structure

bifid: cleft or divided

biflabellate: applied to antennae where each antennomere has pair of extensions

bilobed: divided into two lobes

bioluminescence: production of light involving oxidation of luciferin through the action of luciferase in Lampyridae, Phengodidae, and Elateridae

bipectinate antennae: comblike antennae, with short antennomeres bearing two prolonged extensions

bipunctate: surface with punctures in two sizes

bisinuate: with two sinuations, usually in reference to a margin

brachypterous: flight wings present, but reduced; flightless

calcar: a spinelike process

calcareous: coated with calcium carbonate, or lime

callosity: a rather flattened elevation on surface of exoskeleton

campanulate: shaped like a bell

campodeiform larva: slender, leggy, active beetle larva

canthus: exoskeletal process that partly or completely divides compound eye

capitate antennae: with outermost antennomeres abruptly enlarged to form a round or oval symmetrical club

carina (pl. carinae): a raised narrow ridge or keel along or across a structure

carinate: having a carina

carrion: decaying flesh of dead animal

cercus (pl. cerci): a paired appendage on tip of abdomen

cibarial pump: an organ between mouth and esophagus that draws food into digestive tract

clavate: gradually becoming broader toward apex

claw: typically paired, sharp, hooked structure at apex of tarsus

cleft claw: claw that is finely split or narrowly forked at apex

club: expanded terminal antennomere(s)

clypeus: sclerite typically covering mouthparts of beetles; see epistoma

cocoon: a silken case within which larvae pupate in a few beetle species

Coleoptera: beetles; order of holometabolous insects typically characterized by having chewing mouthparts, and leathery or shell-like forewings called elytra

commensalism: symbiosis in which one organism benefits and the other neither benefits nor is harmed

compound eye: primary organ of sight consisting of multiple facets or lenses

concave: hollowed out, like interior of sphere

confused punctures: punctures not arranged in rows

conical: cylindrical, then tapering to a point

connate ventrites: visible abdominal sternites that are not freely movable, but are fused with sutures in between that are sometimes partly or wholly faint or absent

contiguous: touching

contractile: ability to withdraw appendages tightly against body

convex: rounded, like exterior of sphere

cordate: more or less heart-shaped or triangular, with rounded corners at base, with base not necessarily emarginate

costate: with longitudinal raised ridges coarser than carinae

costulate: ridges less prominent than costate ridges

coxa (pl. coxae): basal segment of leg

crenulate: a margin finely notched with small, rounded teeth

crepuscular: active at dusk or dawn

cribriform: coarsely and densely punctured, appearing like a sieve

cuneate: wedge-shaped

cupuliform: cup-shaped

cylindrical: having the shape of a cylinder; applied to elongate, parallel-sided species with convex dorsal and ventral surfaces, suggesting they appear almost circular in cross section

declivity: downward slope

declivous: sloping downward

decumbent: bent downward from an upright base, applied to a seta

deflexed: abruptly bent downward

dehiscent: separated toward the apex

dentate: toothed, or toothlike

detritivore: eats detritus

detritus: matter decomposed of plant, fungal, and animal material, waste products, and other organic debris

diapause: a period of suspended growth or development characterized by reduced metabolic activity, often during hibernation or aestivation

dicot: a flowering plant in which the embryo typically has two seed leaves, or cotyledons

disc: entire dorsal area contained within pronotal or elytral margins

discal: pertaining to disc

distal: part of an appendage or segment farthest from body

diurnal: active during the day

dorsal: above or on top

eclose, eclosion: in beetles, to emerge from the pupa

ectoparasite: a parasitic organism that feeds externally on its host, but seldom kills it

ectoparasitoid: a parasitic larva that feeds externally on its host and ultimately kills it

elateriform larva: a slender larva with tough exoskeleton, short legs, and very few setae

elongate: long or lengthened

elytral suture: seam down back of beetle where elytra meet when closed at rest

elytron (pl. elytra): leathery or shell-like mesothoracic wing, or forewing of beetles

emarginate: notched, sometimes broadly so, along margin

endoparasitoid: a parasitic larva that feeds internally within its host and ultimately kills it

endosymbiotic microorganism: an organism that lives inside another

entomopathogen: a disease-causing agent that infects insects

epipleuron (pl. epipleura): turned-under fold along lateral edge of elytra

epistoma: oral margin or sclerite behind labrum; see clypeus

erect: upright

eruciform larva: legged beetle larva that is caterpillar-like in form

eversible: capable of being turned outward or inside out.

exarate pupa: pupa with legs and wings free from body and a movable abdomen

exocrine glands: glands that make substances and release them through a duct onto body surface

exoskeleton: protective outer covering of beetles that functions as both skeleton and skin; serves internally as a foundation for muscles and organ systems, while externally providing a platform for sensory and morphological structures

explanate: spread out and flattened, applied to a margin

extraoral: outside of mouth

family: taxonomic subdivision ending in -idae

feces: waste or excrement expelled from anus

femorotibial joint: primary articulation between the femur and tibia

femur (pl. femora): third leg segment from body between trochanter and tibia

filiform antennae: threadlike, with segments uniformly cylindrical, or nearly so

fimbriate: fringed with setae of unequal length, applied to margin or structure

flabellate antennae: fanlike, with segments each bearing a long extension that fit together like a fan

flagellomere: an article of the flagellum

flagellum: antennal articles after the scape and pedicel that lack their own musculature and are not true segments

flume: an inclined human-made channel for water with raised edges built to transport water

fovea (pl. foveae): pit

frass: plant fragments, especially wood, mixed with feces

frontoclypeal suture: transverse suture between frons and clypeus

frons: upper portion of head between eyes and vertex

funicle: part of antenna between antennomere 2 (pedicel) and club

galea (pl. galeae): outer lobe of maxilla

gena (pl. genae): part of head below eye; cheek

geniculate: abruptly bent or elbowed, as in antennae of many weevils in family Curculionidae

gin-trap: defensive pinching device on opposable abdominal tergites of some beetle pupae

glabrous: surface smooth, devoid of setae or sculpturing

glaucous: grayish or bluish, usually with a coating of waterproof wax secreted by epidermal glands underlying the exoskeleton; easily rubbed off or dissolved in chemical preservatives

granulate: surface rough with small grains or granules

gula: a ventral plate on underside of head in prognathous beetles

gular suture: line of division between gula and gena

head: first body region, bearing mouthparts, antennae, and eyes

hemispherical: highly convex dorsally, flat or concave ventrally

hemolymph: beetle blood

herbaceous: small, soft plants without woody tissues

holometaboly: development with four distinct stages (egg, larva, pupa, adult); also called complete metamorphosis

humerus (pl. humeri): outer shoulderlike angle at base of elytra

hyaline: transparent

hydrofuge: dense, water-repellent setae

hypermetamorphosis: type of holometaboly where larvae develop through very different forms, usually found in parasitic beetles (Bothrideridae, Meloidae, Rhipiceridae, Ripiphoridae)

hypognathous: mandibles directed downward

hypomeron: ventral sclerite of prothorax located between pronotum and prosternum

immature: egg, larval, and pupal stages of beetles

impunctate: without punctures

incised claw: claw that is split, or cleft at apex

inflexed: bent or curved inward

infuscate: smoky gray-brown with a blackish tinge

instar: stage between larval molts

intercoxal: between coxae

interval: space between striae on elytra

intraspecific: within same species

iridescent: shimmering metallic colors that change with angle of light

labium: insect mouthpart analogous to "lower lip" and located beneath maxilla

labrum: insect mouthpart analogous to "upper lip" and located over mandibles that is under or extends beyond clypeus

lacinia (pl. laciniae): inner lobe of maxilla

lamellate antennae: with outermost antennomeres flat, and forming a distinctly asymmetrical club; opposable lamellae can be drawn tightly together in Scarabaeidae

lanceolate: oblong and tapering at one end or spear- or lance-shaped; often about shape of scales

larva (pl. larvae): second stage of holometabolous development; sometimes called grub in beetles

larviform: an adult female beetle that lack wings, thus resembling a larva

lateral: referring to side or sides

mandibles: first of two pairs of jaws in beetles, used for chewing

maxilla: second of two pairs of jaws in beetles, used for manipulating food

mentum: ventral head sclerite between mouth and gulum

mesepimeron: rear plate of pleuron of mesothorax

mesepipleuron: pleuron of mesothorax

mesosternum: ventral or sternal portion of mesothorax

mesothorax: middle segment of thorax bearing second pair of legs and elytra

metacoxa (pl. metacoxae): basal segment of hind leg

metasternum: ventral or sternal portion of metathorax

metatarsus: tarsus of hind leg

metathorax: third thoracic segment bearing the third pair of legs and flight wings (if present)

molt: action taken by a larva each time it sheds its exoskeleton to grow

moniliform antennae: antennae with round, beadlike antennomeres of more or less uniform size

monocot: a flowering plant in which the embryo typically has one seed leaf, or cotyledon

mutualism: when two organisms both benefit from a symbiotic relationship

mycangium (pl. mycangia): an exoskeletal pocket-shaped receptacle used to carry symbiotic fungi in bark beetles (Curculionidae)

mycetome: a structure housing intracellular symbiotic bacteria, yeasts, and fungi, often found in gut lining of wood-boring beetle larvae

mycophagous: feeds on fungus

myrmecophile: lives with ants

nocturnal: active at night

notopleural suture: ventral suture separating pronotum from proepisternum in beetles in suborders Archostemata, Myxophaga, and Adephaga

obovate: egg-shaped or ovate, with narrow end directed downward

obtect pupa: legs and wings tightly appressed to body of pupa, abdomen immobile

occiput: back of head

ocellus (pl. ocelli): simple eye in some adult beetles (see stemmata)

onisciform: larva shaped like a sowbug (Subphylum Crustacea, Order Isopoda, Family Oniscidae)

onychium (pl. onychia): various hooklike or padlike pretarsal structures

opisthognathous: ventral mouthparts directed posteriorly resulting from deflexion of facial region

opposable: applied to lamellate antennae; lamellae capable of moving toward and touching one another

osmobranchia (pl. osmobranchiae): branched gill-like structures involved with osmoregulation

osmoregulation: process by which animals regulate amount of water in their bodies to control concentrations of solutes and ions

oval: elliptical, with ends equally rounded

oviposition: act of laying eggs

ovipositor: abdominal structure in female beetles that facilitates oviposition

paedogenesis: production of eggs or larvae by a larva

palp (pl. palpi, palps): fingerlike appendage of mouth associated with maxillae and labia

palpomere: article of a palp

parasite: dependent on another host organism for its existence; usually does not kill host

parasitoid: a parasite that typically kills its host

paratergite: lateral flanges on tergite (dorsal abdominal sclerite, or plate)

parthenogenesis: development from unfertilized eggs

pathogen: a disease-causing organism

pectinate antennae: comblike, with short antennomeres each bearing a prolonged extension

pectinate claw: claw with comblike teeth on blade

pedicel: second antennal segment, located between scape and flagellum

penultimate: next to last

pheromones: chemicals produced by special glands and released into environment to communicate with other members of same species

phloem: vascular tissue in plants that conducts sugars and other metabolic products down from leaves

phoresy: a symbiotic relationship in which a smaller organism is carried by a larger organism strictly for the purpose of transportation

plastron: a thin layer of air trapped in a velvety mesh of dense setae that surrounds the body of some aquatic beetles

plastron breathing: a method of respiration used by some aquatic beetles in which a plastron is used to obtain dissolved oxygen from surrounding water and expel carbon dioxide

pleuron (pl. pleura): lateral sclerites of thoracic and abdominal segments

plicate: appearing folded or pleated

plumose antennae: featherlike, with antennomeres bearing long, slender, and flexible extensions

postcoxal: after or behind coxa

posterior: behind

postscutellar: behind or posterior to scutellum

predaceous: an animal that hunts and feeds on other animals

prepupa: last larval instar

pretarsus: terminal claw-bearing segment borne on apex of tarsus

procoxa (pl. procoxae): basal segment of front leg

procoxal cavity: prothoracic housing for procoxae

prognathous: head and mandibles directed straight forward, or nearly so

pronotosternal suture: suture separating hypomeron of prothorax from prosternum

pronotum: dorsal sclerite of prothorax

propleuron: lateral sclerite of prothorax

propygidium: abdominal tergite before pygidium in beetles

prosternal process: posterior projection of prosternum that may partly overlap mesosternum

prosternum: underside of prothorax, mostly between procoxae

protarsus (pl. protarsi): tarsus of front legs

prothorax: first thoracic segment that bears first pair of legs; midsection of beetle body

protrusible: a body part, such as mouthparts, that can be protruded or extended

proximal: toward base of structure

pruinescence: a waxy bloom or coating

pruinose, pruinosity: appearing as if covered with a fine, dusty coating or waxy bloom, like a plum, and cannot be rubbed off

psammophilic, psammophilous: sand-inhabiting

pseudepipleuron: in some beetles, a strongly turned-under lateral elytral margin before epipleuron

pterothorax: fused wing-bearing meso- and metathorax covered by elytra

pubescence, pubescent: soft, fine, short, loosely set, erect setae

punctoseriate: rows of elytral punctures that occur in line, but not within striae

punctostriate: rows of elytral punctures that occur within striae

punctures: small and/or coarse surface pits. Punctures range from very small (*finely punctate*) to large (*coarsely punctate*) and may be shallow or deep

pupa: stage of holometabolous development between larva and adult

pygidium: last dorsal abdominal tergite in beetles

quadrate: roughly square or rectangular

raptorial: adapted for seizing prey, such as forelegs of Gyrinidae

recumbent: lying down or reclining

reflex bleeding: a defensive release of hemolymph through intersegmental membranes between leg joints and body segments

reticulate: raised network of ridges, as in elytral sculpturing of Lycidae

retractile appendages: capable of being withdrawn, often into ventral depressions or sulci

riparian: narrow band of woodland growing along streams and rivers

rostrum: snoutlike projection of mouthparts (some Lycidae, Mycteridae, and Curculionidae)

rugopunctate: surfaces have punctures so tightly spaced that the surface appears rough

rugose: wrinkled

saprophytic: an organism that inhabits dung, carrion, or decaying plants

saproxylic: an organism that inhabits decaying wood

scale: flattened seta, ranging in outline from nearly round, to oval (egg-shaped), obovate (pear-shaped), lanceolate (spear-shaped), or linear (long and slender)

scape: first of two true antennal segments, followed by pedicel

scarabaeiform larvae: C-shaped grub with well-developed head and legs

scavenger: feeds on decaying plant and fungal tissues and carrion

sclerite: small exoskeletal plate surrounded by sutures or membranes

scrobe: in adult Curculionoidea, a groove on each side of rostrum in which antennae can rest

scutellum: small, often triangular sclerite at base of and between elytra

segment: subdivision of body or appendage distinguished by joints, articulations, or sutures

serrate antennae: saw-toothed, with flattened, triangular antennomeres

serrate claw: claw with jagged, saw-toothed edge

seta (pl. setae): sclerotized hairlike structure arising from single cell; setae are fine or bristly, stand straight up (*erect*) or nearly so (*suberect*), are curved (*decumbent*), or lie nearly flat on the surface (*recumbent*); complete absence of setae or scales is referred to as *glabrous*

setigerous: bearing setae

setose: covered with setae

shagreened: surface finely wrinkled, appearing dull

simple claw: claw without teeth or other modifications

sinuate: wavy, specifically applied to margins

species: basic biological unit of classification; a group of sexually reproducing beetles that can potentially reproduce with one another and is reproductively isolated from other species

spermatheca: a female organ that stores and nourishes sperm until fertilization and oviposition

spinule: a small spine

spiracle: external opening of tracheal system

spur: movable or socketed spine located at tip of leg segment

stemmata: simple eyes in larval beetles

sternite: a subdivision of the sternum

sternum (pl. sterna): underside of a thoracic or abdominal segment

stria (pl. striae): an impressed groove along length of pronotum or elytron, with or without punctures

stridulation: act of sound production by rubbing one body surface against another, usually filelike spines or tubercles across a carina or series of carinae

striga (pl. strigae): a narrow, impressed transverse line

striole: a rudimentary stria

stripe: a marking that runs along the long axis of body

strobilus (pl. strobili): cone; a male or female reproductive structure in gymnosperms

subapical: just before apex of structure

subelytral cavity: a space beneath elytra used by aquatic beetles to store air and bring it in contact with thoracic and abdominal spiracles; also serves in thermoregulation in terrestrial species living in dry habitats

subequal: more or less equal

sulcate: having a sulcus

sulcus (pl. sulci): a groove

suprantennal: above base of antennae

surface sculpture: raised or impressed markings on surface of exoskeleton

sutures: membranes of pure chitin joining segments, seen as narrow furrows separating them

symbiotic: an organism living in association with another, does not imply nature of relationship (see commensalism, mutualism, parasitism, phoresy)

synanthropic: living in close association with humans

tarsal formula: shorthand for number of tarsomeres on front, middle, and hind legs, respectively; 5-5-5, 5-5-4, 4-4-4, etc.

tarsomere: an article of the tarsus that does not bear claws

tarsus (pl. tarsi): foot, penultimate segment of leg attached to apex of tibia, bears pretarsus, and comprises up to five tarsomeres

temple (pl. temples): area of head formed by an abrupt constriction behind compound eyes; sometimes called tempus (pl. tempora)

teneral: freshly eclosed pale and soft-bodied adult

tergite: dorsal sclerite of beetle abdomen; tergum

tergum (pl. terga): dorsal sclerite of beetle abdomen; tergite

terminal: on the tip

termitophile: lives with termites

tessellate: light and dark color pattern or surface sculpturing resembling a checker board

thanatosis: act of playing dead as a defensive tactic so that predators lose interest

thorax: middle body region, bearing legs and wings, subdivided into three segments (pro-, meso-, and metathorax)

tibia (pl. tibiae): fourth segment of leg from base, located between femur and tarsus

tomentose: having tomentum

tomentum: pubescence characterized by short, matted, woolly setae

toothed claw: claw with one or more teeth underneath

travertine: white or light-colored calcareous rock

triseriate: in rows of three

trituberculate: with three tubercles

triungulin: small campodeiform larva that develops by hypermetamorphosis

trochanter: second leg segment from body, located between coxa and femur

truncate: appearing cut- or squared-off

tubercle: small raised bump or knob

ungual: pertaining to a claw, as in ungual appendages

unicarinate: with a single carinae

univoltine: having one generation annually

urogomphus (pl. urogomphi): a fixed and paired, sometime articulated process on apex of larval abdomen in some species

ventral: below or underside

ventrite: visible abdominal sternite; in beetles, first ventrite is usually second abdominal sternite

vermiform larva: legless, almost wormlike beetle larva

vertex: top of head

vesicle: a small, bladderlike sac

vestigial: a small remnant of something once much larger or more conspicuous

xeric: having little moisture; adapted to dry conditions

xylem: vascular tissue in plants that conducts water and minerals up from roots

xylophagous: wood eating

xylophilic: wood loving

SELECTED REFERENCES AND RESOURCES

GENERAL INFORMATION ON NATURAL HISTORY AND BEHAVIOR

Bouchard, P. (ed.). 2014. *The Book of Beetles. A Life-Size Guide to Six Hundred of Nature's Gems*. Chicago: University of Chicago Press. 656 pp.

Crowson, R.A. 1980. *The Biology of the Coleoptera*. London: Academic Press. 802 pp. (out of print).

Evans, A.V., and C.L. Bellamy. 2000. *An Inordinate Fondness for Beetles*. Berkeley: University of California Press. 208 pp.

Evans, A.V., and J.N. Hogue. 2004. *An Introduction to California Beetles*. Berkeley: University of California Press. 299 pp. (out of print).

Klausnitzer, B. 1981. *Beetles*. New York: Exeter. 213 pp. (out of print).

Marshall, S. 2018. *Beetles. The Natural History and Diversity of Coleoptera*. Richmond Hill, ON, Canada: Firefly Books. 784 pp.

Stehr, F. W. (ed.). 1991. *Immature Insects*. Vol. 2. Dubuque, IA: Kendall/Hunt. 973 pp.

BEETLE CLASSIFICATION

Beutel, R.G., and R.A.B. Leschen (eds.). 2016. *Handbook of Zoology. Arthropoda: Insecta. Coleoptera, Beetles. Morphology and Systematics. Archostemata, Adephaga, Myxophaga, and Polyphaga partim*, Vol. 1. 2nd ed. Berlin: Walter de Gruyter. 684 pp.

Bouchard, P., Y. Bousquet, A.E. Davies, M.A. Alonso Zarazaga, J.F. Lawrence, C.H.C. Lyal, A.F. Newton, C.A.M. Reid, M. Schmitt, S.A. Ślipiński, and A.B.T. Smith. 2011. Family-group names in Coleoptera (Insecta). *ZooKeys* 88: 1–972. doi. org/10.3897/zookeys.88.807

Evans, A.V., and A.B.T. Smith. 2020. On the tribal classification of the Nearctic Melolonthinae (Coleoptera: Scarabaeidae), with descriptions of new species of *Acoma* Casey, 1889. *Zootaxa* 4748 (1): 51–77.

Gimmel, M.L., M. Bocakova, N.L. Gunter, and R.A. Leschen. 2019. Comprehensive phylogeny of the Cleroidea (Coleoptera: Cucujiformia). *Systematic Entomology* 44: 527–558. doi.org:/10.1111/syen.12338

Kundrata, R., M. Bockova, and L. Bocak. 2014. The comprehensive phylogeny of the superfamily Elateroidea (Coleoptera: Elateriformia). *Molecular Phylogenetics and Evolution* 76: 162–171. doi.org/10.1016/j.ympev.2014.03.012

Lawrence, J.F., A. Ślipiński, A.E. Seago, M.K. Thayer, A.F. Newton, and A.E. Marvaldi. 2011. Phylogeny of the Coleoptera based on morphological characters of adults and larvae. *Annales Zoologici* 61(1): 1–217. doi. org/10.3161/000345411X576725

Leschen, R.A.B., and R.G. Beutel (eds.). 2014. *Handbook of Zoology. Arthropoda: Insecta. Coleoptera, Beetles. Vol. 3: Morphology and Systematics (Elateroidea, Bostrichiformia, Cucujiformia partim)*. Berlin: Walter de Gruyer. 675 pp.

Leschen, R.A.B., R.G. Beutel, and J.F. Lawrence (eds.). 2010. *Handbook of Zoology. Arthropoda: Insecta. Coleoptera, Beetles. Vol. 2, Morphology and Systematics (Phytophaga)*. Berlin: Walter de Gruyer. 786 pp.

Marske, K.A., and M.A. Ivie. 2003. Beetle fauna of the United States and Canada. *Coleopterists Bulletin* 57(4): 495–503. doi.org/10.1649/663

McKenna, D.D., S. Shin, D. Ahrens, M. Balke, C. Beza-Beza, D.J. Clarke, A. Donath, H.E. Escalona, F. Friedrich, H. Letsch, S. Liu, D. Maddison, C. Mayer, B. Misof, P.J. Murin, O. Niehuis, R.S. Peters, L. Podsiadlowski, H. Pohl, E.D. Scully, E.V. Yan, X. Zhou, A. Ślipiński, and R.G. Beutel. 2019. The evolution and genomic basis of beetle diversity. *Proceedings of the National Academy of Science* 116(9): 24729–24737. doi. org/10.1073/pnas.1909655116

Shin, S., D.J. Clarke, A.R. Lemmon, E.M. Lemmon, A.L. Aitken, S. Haddad, B.D. Farrell, A.E. Marvaldi, R.G. Oberprieler, D.D. McKenna. 2018. Phylogenomic data yield new and robust insights into the phylogeny and evolution of weevils. *Molecular Biology and Evolution* 35(4): 823–836. doi. org/10.1073/pnas.1909655116

Vasilikopoulos, A., M. Balke, R.G. Beutel, A. Donath, L. Podsiadlowski, J.M. Pflug, R.M. Waterhouse, K. Meusemann, R.S. Peters, H.E. Escalona, C. Mayer, S. Liu, L. Henrich, Y. Alarie, D.T. Bilton, F. Jia, X. Zhou, D.R. Maddison, O. Niehuis, and B. Misof. 2019. Phylogenomics of the superfamily Dytiscoidea (Coleoptera: Adephaga) with an evaluation of phylogenetic conflict and systematic error. *Molecular Phylogenetics and Evolution* 135: 270–285. doi.org/10.1016/j. ympev.2019.02.02

NORTH AMERICAN BEETLE IDENTIFICATION

Anderson, R. S., and S. B. Peck. 1985. *The Insects and Arachnids of Canada and Alaska, part 13. The carrion beetles of Canada and Alaska (Coleoptera: Silphidae and Agyrtidae).* Publ. 1778. Ottawa: Research Branch, Agriculture Canada. 121 pp.

Arnett, R. H., Jr., and M. C. Thomas (eds.). 2000. *American Beetles.* Vol. 1: *Archostemata: Myxophaga, Adephaga, Polyphaga: Staphyliniformia.* Boca Raton, FL: CRC Press. 443 pp.

Arnett, R. H., Jr., M. C. Thomas, P. E. Skelley, and J. H. Frank (eds.). 2002. *American Beetles.* Vol. 2: *Polyphaga: Scarabaeoidea through Curculionidae.* Boca Raton, FL: CRC Press. 861 pp.

Bousquet, Y. 1990. *Beetles Associated with Stored Products in Canada: An Identification Guide.* Publ. 1837. Ottawa: Research Branch, Agriculture Canada. 214 pp.

Bousquet, Y., P. Bouchard, A. E. Davies, and D. S. Sikes. 2013. *Checklist of Beetles of Canada and Alaska.* 2nd ed. Pensoft Series Faunistica 109. Sofia, Bulgaria: Pensoft. 402 pp.

Bousquet, Y., and S. Laplante. 2006. *The Insects and Arachnids of Canada and Alaska, part 24. Coleoptera, Histeridae.* Ottawa: National Research Council Press. 485 pp.

Bousquet, Y., S. Laplante, H. E. J. Hammond, and D. W. Langor. 2018. *Cerambycidae (Coleoptera) of Canada and Alaska. Identification Guide with Nomenclatural, Taxonomic, Distributional, Host-plant, and Ecological Data.* Prague: Nakladetelství Jan Farkač. 300 pp.

Bright, D. E. 1976. *The Insects and Arachnids of Canada and Alaska, part 2. The Bark Beetles of Canada and Alaska. Coleoptera: Scolytidae.* Publ. 1576. Ottawa: Research Branch, Agriculture Canada. 241 pp.

Bright, D. E. 1987. *The Insects and Arachnids of Canada and Alaska, part 15. The Metallic Wood-Boring Beetles of Canada and Alaska. Coleoptera: Buprestidae.* Publ. 1810. Ottawa: Research Branch, Agriculture Canada. 335 pp.

Bright, D. E. 1993. *The Insects and Arachnids of Canada and Alaska, part 21. Weevils of Canada and Alaska. Volume 1. Coleoptera: Curculionoidea, excluding Scolytidae and Curculionidae.* Publ. 1882. Ottawa: Research Branch, Agriculture Canada. 217 pp.

Bright, D. E., and P. Bouchard. 2008. *The Insects and Arachnids of Canada and Alaska, part 25. Coleoptera, Curculionidae, Entiminae. Weevils of Canada and Alaska. Volume 2.* Ottawa: National Research Council Press. 327 pp.

Brown, H. P. 1972. *Aquatic Dryopoid Beetles (Coleoptera) of the United States.* Biota of Freshwater Ecosystems Identification Manual No. 6. Water Pollution Control Research Series. Cincinnati, OH: US Environmental Protection Agency. 82 pp. (reprinted in 1976).

Erwin, T.L. 2007. *A Treatise on the Western Hemisphere Caraboidea (Coleoptera). Their Classification, Distributions, and Ways of Life. Vol. 1 (Trachypachidae, Carabidae-Nebriiformes).* Sofia, Bulgaria: Pensoft. 365 pp.

Erwin, T.L. 2011. *A Treatise on the Western Hemisphere Caraboidea (Coleoptera). Their Classification, Distributions, and Ways of Life. Vol. 3 (Carabidae-Loxomeriformes, Melaeniformes).* Sofia, Bulgaria: Pensoft. 412 pp.

Erwin T.L., and D.L. Pearson. 2008. *A Treatise on the Western Hemisphere Caraboidea (Coleoptera). Their Classification, Distributions, and Way of Life. Vol. 2 (Carabidae-Nebriiformes 2-Cicindelitae).* Sofia, Bulgaria: Pensoft. 365 pp.

Evans, A.V. 2014. *Beetles of Eastern North America.* Princeton, NJ: Princeton University Press. 560 pp. jstor.org/stable/j.ctt6wpzmc (accessed 17 August 2020).

Klimaszewski, J., D.W. Langor, R. Batista, J. Dorval, G.G. Majka, G.G.E. Scudder, and Y. Bousquet. 2012. *Synopsis of Adventive Species of Coleoptera (Insecta) Recorded from Canada. Part 1: Carabidae.* Pensoft Series Faunistica No. 103. Sofia-Moscow: Pensoft. 96 pp.

Klimaszewski, J., A. Brunke, V. Assing, D.W. Langor, A.F. Newton, C. Bourdon, G. Pelletier, R.P. Webster, L. Herman, L. Perdereau, A. Davies, A. Smetana, D.S. Chandler, C. Majka, G.G.E. Scudder. 2013. *Synopsis of Adventive Species of Coleoptera (Insecta) recorded from Canada. Part 2: Staphylinidae.* Pensoft Series Faunistica No. 104. Sofia-Moscow: Pensoft. 360 pp.

Klimaszewski, J., D.W. Langor, H.E.J. Hammond, G. Pelletier, Y. Bousquet, C. Bourdon, R.P. Webster, L. Borowiec, G.G.E. Scudder, and C.G. Majka. 2015. *Synopsis of Adventive Species of Coleoptera (Insecta) Recorded from Canada. Part 3: Cucujoidea.* Pensoft Series Faunistica No. 113. Sofia-Moscow: Pensoft. 171 pp.

Klimaszewski, J., D.W. Langor, A.B.T. Smith, E.R. Hoebeke, A. Davies, G. Pelletier, H.B. Douglas, R.P. Webster, C. Bourdon, L. Borowiec, and G.G.E. Scudder. 2017. *Synopsis of Adventive Species of Coleoptera (Insecta) Recorded from Canada. Part 4: Scarabaeoidea, Scirtoidea, Buprestoidea, Byrrhoidea, Elateroidea, Derodontoidea, Bostrichoidea, and Cleroidea.* Pensoft Series Faunistica No. 116. Sofia-Moscow: Pensoft. 215 pp. doi.org/10.3897/ab.e50613

Klimaszewski, J., E.R. Hoebeke, D.W. Lango, H.B. Douglas, L. Borowiec, H.E.J. Hammond, A. Dacies, C. Bourdon, K. Savard. 2020. *Synopsis of Adventive Species of Coleoptera (Insects) Recorded from Canada. Part 5: Chrysomeloidea (Cerambycidae, Chrysomelidae, and Megalopodidae).* Advanced Books. doi.org/10.3897/ab.e50613

Pearson, D.L., C.B. Knisley, and C.J. Zakilek. 2015. *A Field Guide to the Tiger Beetles of the United States and Canada. Identification, Natural History, and Distribution of the Cicindelidae.* 2nd ed. Oxford: Oxford University Press. 251 pp.

White, R.E. 1983. *A Field Guide to the Beetles of North America.* Boston: Houghton Mifflin. 368 pp.

BEETLE IDENTIFICATION FOR WESTERN NORTH AMERICA

Evans, A.V., and J.N. Hogue. 2006. *Field Guide to Beetles of California*. Berkeley: University of California Press. 334 pp. jstor.org/stable/10.1525/j.ctt1pp9kc (accessed 21 March 2021).

Hatch, M.H. 1953. *The Beetles of the Pacific Northwest. Part I. Introduction and Adephaga*. Seattle: University of Washington Publications in Biology 16: 340 pp. (out of print).

Hatch, M.H. 1957. *The Beetles of the Pacific Northwest. Part II. Staphyliniformia*. Seattle: University of Washington Publications in Biology 16: 384 pp. (out of print).

Hatch, M.H. 1962. *The Beetles of the Pacific Northwest. Part III: Pselaphidae and Diversicornia I*. Seattle: University of Washington Publications in Biology 16: 503 pp. (out of print).

Hatch, M.H. 1965. *The Beetles of the Pacific Northwest. Part IV. Macrodactyles, Palpicornes, and Heteromera*. Seattle: University of Washington Publications in Biology 16: 268 pp. (out of print).

Hatch, M.H. 1971. *The Beetles of the Pacific Northwest. Part V: Rhipiceroidea, Stemoxi, Phytophaga, Rhynchophora, and Lamellicornia*. Seattle: University of Washington Publications in Biology 16: 662 pp. (out of print).
Note: All five parts of Hatch's work are available here: ir.library.oregonstate.edu/catalog?q=Beetles%20of%20the%20Pacific%20Northwest&search_field=dspace_collection (accessed 21 March 2021).

Hogue, C.L. 2015. *Insects of the Los Angeles Basin*. 3rd ed. Los Angeles: Natural History Museum of Los Angeles County. 474 pp.

Peterson, M.A. 2018. *Pacific Northwest Insects*. Seattle: Seattle Audubon Society. 520 pp.

COLLECTING, PRESERVING, AND REARING TECHNIQUES

Martin, J.E.H. 1977. *The Insects and Arachnids of Canada. Part 1. Collecting, Preparing, and Preserving Insects, Mites, and Spiders*. Ottawa: Biosystematics Research Institute. 182 pp. (also available in French; out of print). esc-sec.ca/wp/wp-content/uploads/2017/03/AAFC_insects_and_arachnids_part_1_eng.pdf (accessed 21 March 2021).

McMonigle, O. 2012. *The Ultimate Guide to Breeding Beetles. Coleoptera Laboratory Culture Methods*. Landisville, PA: Coachwhip. 206 pp.

Schauff, M. (ed.). 1986. Collecting and preserving insects and mites. Techniques and tools. ars.usda.gov/ARSUserFiles/80420580/CollectingandPreservingInsectsandMites/collpres.pdf (accessed 21 March 2021).

INFORMATION ON RARE AND ENDANGERED SPECIES

Natureserv Explorer. An authoritative source for information on more than 70,000 plants, animals, and ecosystems of the United States and Canada that includes in-depth coverage of rare and endangered species. explorer.natureserve.org (accessed 21 March 2021).

United States Fish and Wildlife Service Endangered Species. Includes an interactive map with endangered species information by state. fws.gov/endangered/ (accessed 21 March 2021).

BEETLE SOCIETIES

The Coleopterists Society: An international organization devoted to the study of all aspects of systematics and biology of beetles of the world; publishes the quarterly *Coleopterists Bulletin*; archive for various beetle newsletters. coleopsoc.org (accessed 21 March 2021).

NATIONAL ENTOMOLOGICAL SOCIETIES

Entomological Society of America
entsoc.org (accessed 21 March 2021).
Entomological Society of Canada
esc-sec.ca (accessed 21 March 2021).
Entomological Collections Network (ECN)
ecnweb.net (accessed 21 March 2021).
Xerces Society for Invertebrate Conservation
xerces.org (accessed 21 March 2021).

ENTOMOLOGICAL SOCIETIES AND CLUBS IN WESTERN NORTH AMERICA

Entomological Society of Alberta
entsocalberta.ca (accessed 21 March 2021).
Entomological Society of British Columbia
entsocbc.ca (accessed 21 March 2021).
Lorquin Entomological Society
facebook.com/lorquinsociety/ (accessed 21 March 2021).
Mile High Bug Club
milehighbugclub.org (accessed 21 March 2021).
Pacific Coast Entomological Society
pcentsoc.org (accessed 21 March 2021).
Santa Barbara Entomological Club

facebook.com/groups/sbEntomology/ (accessed 21 March 2021).

Society of Southwestern Entomologists sswe.tamu.edu (accessed 21 March 2021).

BEETLES OF WESTERN NORTH AMERICA ON THE WEB

Biodiversity Heritage Library (BHL). The Biodiversity Library makes biodiversity literature openly available to the global biodiversity community. biodiversitylibrary.org (accessed 21 March 2021).

BugGuide. An outstanding resource for identified beetle images, taxonomic information, and other online resources. bugguide.net (accessed 21 March 2021).

Cerambycoid. Primary types of the Smithsonian Institution: An online searchable database for primary type specimens of longhorn beetles that includes types of Casey and others. smithsoniancerambycidae.com (accessed 21 March 2021).

Entomology Type Collection (CAS-TYPE) at the California Academy of Sciences. This online database contains records and images of the primary types housed in one of the largest entomology collections in western North America. The beetle types of Blaisdell, Van Dyke, and others are housed here. monarch.calacademy.org/collections/misc/collprofiles. php?collid=15 (accessed 21 March 2021).

The Ground Beetles of Canada: Images and catalogue of Canadian species. cbif.gc.ca/eng/species-bank/ground-beetles-of-canada/?id=1370403266120 (accessed 21 March 2021).

iNaturalist. A joint initiative of the California Academy of Sciences and the National Geographic Society, iNaturalist is a community consisting of millions of naturalists and scientists that record and share observations of nature and facilitate animal and plants identifications, including beetles. inaturalist.org (accessed 21 March 2021).

Journal Storage (JSTOR). An online collaboration with the academic community that connects libraries with students, faculty, and independent researchers. Academic journal articles, books, and other primary sources are provided at low cost or for free. jstor.org (accessed 21 March 2021).

MCZBase: The Database of the Zoological Collections at the Museum of Comparative Zoology, Harvard University. This online database contains records and images of the primary types housed in one of the most important entomology collections in North America. The beetle types of LeConte, Horn, Fall, and others are housed here. mczbase.mcz. harvard.edu (accessed 21 March 2021).

Pacific Northwest Bugs. A public Facebook page where people can upload identification requests, images, videos, observations, links, and other content related to the arthropods of southern British Columbia and Alberta, Washington, Oregon, Idaho, Wyoming, Montana, and northern California. facebook.com/ groups/904079732957442/ (accessed 21 March 2021).

ResearchGate. Provides a platform for researchers to share their publications and to connect and collaborate with colleagues, peers, co-authors, and specialists around the world. researchgate.net (accessed 21 March 2021).

SW U.S. Arthropods. A public Facebook page where people can upload identification requests, images, videos, observations, links, and other content related to the arthropods of Southwestern United States and Northwestern Mexico. facebook.com/groups/SWInsects/ (accessed 21 March 2021).

Symbiota Collections of Arthropods Network (SCAN). Contains specimen records and images of all arthropods contributed by more than 100 North American arthropod collections. The focus is North America, but the scope is global. scan-bugs. org (accessed 21 March 2021).

What's That Bug? A popular webpage where users can upload insect photographs for identification and other information. whatsthatbug.com (accessed 21 March 2021).

BEETLE BOOKS, COLLECTING EQUIPMENT AND SUPPLIES

Atelier Jean Paquet Matériel Entomologique, 4656, route Fossa-mault, Sainte-Catherine-de-la-Jacques-Cartier, Québec G3N 1S8 CANADA; phone 418-875-2276; fax 418-873-1866; atelierjeanpaquet.com (accessed 21 March 2021).

BioQuip Products, Inc., 2321 Gladwick Street, Rancho Dominguez, CA 90220; phone 310-667-8800; fax 310-667-8808; bioquip.com (accessed 21 March 2021).

FIGURE AND PHOTO CREDITS

Map, Dimitri Karetnikov. Fig. 1, Henri Goulet; Figs. 2a–m, Jennifer Read, based on images by Nicolas Gompel, 2n based on image by John Ott; Fig. 3, Henri Goulet; Figs. 4a–c, Arthur V. Evans; Fig. 4d, Joyce Gross; Fig. 5, Henri Goulet; Fig. 6a, Joyce Gross; Fig. 6b, Graham Montgomery; Fig. 6c, Arthur V. Evans; Fig. 6d, Nicolas Gompel; Figs. 6e–h, Joyce Gross; Fig. 6i, Tommy McElrath; Figs. 6j–k, Arthur V. Evans; Fig. 7, Jennifer Read; Fig. 8a, Arthur V. Evans; Fig. 8b, William H. Tyson; Fig. 8c, Joseph Cicero/Alex Yelich; Fig. 8d, James N. Hogue/California State University, Northridge; Fig. 8e, K. S. Matz; Fig. 8f, James N. Hogue/California State University, Northridge; Fig. 9, Henri Goulet; Fig. 10, Jennifer Read; Fig. 11, Arthur V. Evans; Fig. 12, Thomas Shahan/Oregon Department of Agriculture; Figs. 13–15, Arthur V. Evans; Fig. 16, James N. Hogue/California State University, Northridge; Fig. 17, Christopher C. Wirth; Fig. 18a, Charles Melton/nearfamous.com; Fig. 18b, Christopher C. Wirth; Fig. 18c, Salvador Vitanza/USDA APHIS (PPQ); Fig. 18d, Arthur V. Evans; Fig. 18e, James N. Hogue/California State University, Northridge; Figs. 18f–g, Joyce Gross; Fig. 18h, Arthur V. Evans; Fig. 18i, Jeffrey P. Gruber; Fig. 18j, Arthur V. Evans; Fig. 18k, Salvador Vitanza/USDA APHIS (PPQ); Fig. 18l, James N. Hogue/California State University, Northridge; Fig. 18m, Arthur V. Evans; Figs. 18n–o, Christopher C. Wirth; Fig. 18p, Stephen P. L. Luk; Fig. 18q, Alice Abela; Fig. 18r, Christopher C. Wirth; Fig. 18s, Alice Abela; Fig. 18t, Arthur V. Evans; Fig. 18u, © 2021 Alex Wild, used with permission; Fig. 18v, Joyce Gross; Fig. 18w, Alice Abela; Fig. 19, Arthur V. Evans; Fig. 20, Alan Cressler; Fig. 21, James N. Hogue/California State University, Northridge; Fig. 22, Christopher C. Wirth; Fig. 23, Richard Migneault; Figs. 24–25, Christopher C. Wirth; Fig. 26a, James N. Hogue/California State University, Northridge; Fig. 26b, Arthur V. Evans; Fig. 27, Joyce Gross; Fig. 28, Christopher C. Wirth; Figs. 29–32, Arthur V. Evans; Fig. 33, Christopher C. Wirth; Fig. 34, Arthur V. Evans; Fig. 35, Alan Cressler; Fig. 36, Arthur V. Evans; Figs. 37–38, Christopher C. Wirth; Fig. 39, Margy Green/margygreen.com; Fig. 40, Arthur V. Evans; Fig. 41, Charley Eiseman; Fig. 42, Stephen P. L. Luk; Fig. 43, Arthur V. Evans; Fig. 44a, Joyce Gross; Fig. 44b, Alice Abela; Fig. 45, Anna R. Holden; Fig. 46a, Joyce Gross; Fig. 46b, Alice Abela; Fig. 46c, Barney D. Streit; Fig. 46d, Arthur V. Evans; Fig. 46e, Jon Katz and Joe Silveira/USFWS; Fig. 47, Alice Abela; Figs. 48–50, Arthur V. Evans; Fig. 51, Christopher C. Wirth; Fig. 52, BioQuip Products, Inc./bioquip.com; Figs. 53–54a–b, Arthur V. Evans; Fig. 54c, David C. Carlson; Figs. 55–60, Arthur V. Evans; Fig. 61, William B. Warner; Figs. 62–68, Arthur V. Evans; Fig. 69, Margy Green/margygreen.com. Key illustrations, Jennifer Read.

PHOTO CREDITS

ADERIDAE

Elonus simplex, Emelinus butleri, E. melsheimeri–Nicolas Gompel; "*Xylophilus*" *constrictus*–Jeffrey P. Gruber/UW–Madison, Dept. of Entomology.

AGYRTIDAE

Agyrtes longulus–Gary D. Griswold; *Apteroloma tahoecum, Ipelates latus, Necrophilus hydrophiloides*–Joyce Gross.

AKALYPTOISCHIIDAE

Akalyptoischion quadrifoveata–© 2020 Edward L. Ruden, used with permission.

AMPHIZOIDAE

Amphizoa insolens–Joyce Gross.

ANAMORPHIDAE

Symbiotes gibberosus–Joyce Gross.

ANTHICIDAE

Amblyderus parviceps–Alice Abela; *Anthicus cervinus*–Christopher C. Wirth; *Anthicus maritimus*–Alice Abela; *Anthicus punctulatus*–Gary D. Griswold; *Duboisius arizonensis*–Arthur V. Evans; *Formicilla munda*–Salvador Vitanza/USDA APHIS (PPQ); *Ischyropalpus nitidulus*–Joyce Gross; *Macratria brunnea*–Salvador Vitanza/USDA APHIS (PPQ); *Mecynotarsus delicatulus*–Jeffrey P. Gruber/UW–Madison, Dept. of Entomology; *Notoxus conformis*–Alice Abela; *Notoxus desertus*–Tom Murray; *Notoxus lustrellus*–Joyce Gross; *Omonadus formicarius*–Tom Murray; *Retocomus lindrothi*–James N. Hogue/California State University, Northridge; *Stereopalpus pruinosus*–Arthur V. Evans; *Stricticollis tobias*–Tom Murray; *Vacusus confinis*–Graham Montgomery.

ANTHRIBIDAE

Eugonus bicolor–Arthur V. Evans; *Eurymycter fasciatus*–E. Christina Butler; *Gonotropis gibbosus*–Nikola Rahmé; *Trigonorhinus sticticus*–Tom Murray.

ARCHEOCRYPTICIDAE

Enneboeus marmoratus–Lucie Gimmel/Santa Barbara Museum of Natural History.

ARTEMATOPODIDAE

Allopogonia villosus–Arthur V. Evans; *Eurypogon californicus*–Gary Alpert/Northern Arizona University; *Macropogon testaceipennis*–Arthur V. Evans (*l*), Joyce Gross (*r*).

ATTELABIDAE

Deporaus glastinus–Arthur V. Evans; *Eugnamptus nigriventris*–Salvador Vitanza/USDA APHIS (PPQ); *Haplorhynchites pseudomexicanus*–Arthur V. Evans; *Himatolabus pubescens*–Salvador Vitanza/USDA APHIS (PPQ); *Merhynchites wickhami*–Arthur V. Evans; *Pterocolus ovalis, Synolabus nigripes*–Chris Wirth; *Temnocerus naso*–Alice Abela.

BIPHYLLIDAE

Anchorius lineatus–Salvador Vitanza/USDA APHIS (PPQ).

BORIDAE

Boros unicolor–Tom Murray; *Lecontia discicollis*–Michael C. Thomas/Florida State Collection of Arthropods.

BOSTRICHIDAE

Amphicerus cornutus–Joyce Gross; *Apatides fortis*–Arthur V. Evans; *Dendrobiella aspera*–Joyce Gross; *Dinapate wrightii*–James N. Hogue/California State University, Northridge; *Lichenophanes fasciculatus*–Michael C. Thomas/Florida State Collection of Arthropods; *Lyctus brunneus*–Joyce Gross; *Lyctus carbonarius, Melalgus confertus*–Joyce Gross; *Polycaon stoutii*–James N. Hogue/California State University, Northridge; *Psoa maculata*–Joyce Gross; *Rhyzopertha dominica*–Christoph Benisch; *Xyloblaptus quadrispinosus*–Salvador Vitanza/USDA APHIS (PPQ).

BOTHRIDERIDAE

Bothrideres montanus–Christopher C. Wirth; *Deretaphrus oregonensis*–Nathan P. Lord.

BRACHYPSECTRIDAE

Brachypsectra fulva–© 2020 David Maddison, used with permission.

BRENTIDAE

Betulapion simile–Tom Murray; *Exapion fuscirostre*–Lynette Elliott; *Microon canadense*–Guy A. Hanley; *Rhopalapion longirostre*–Joyce Gross.

BUPRESTIDAE

Acmaeodera acanthicola–Jillian H. Cowles; *Acmaeodera amplicollis*–Christopher C. Wirth; *Acmaeodera angelica, A. cazieri, A. connexa, A. disjuncta, A. gibbula, A. hepburnii, A. labyrinthica*–Arthur V. Evans; *Acmaeodera latiflava latiflava, A. prorsa*–James N. Hogue/California State University, Northridge; *Acmaeodera pubiventris lanata*–Arthur V. Evans; *Acmaeodera resplendens*–Jillian H. Cowles; *Acmaeodera rubronotata, A. scalaris, A. solitaria, Actenodes calcaratus*–Arthur V. Evans; *Agaeocera gentilis*–Mike Quinn/texasento.net; *Agrilus auroguttatus*–Mike Lewis/Center for Invasive Species Research; *Agrilus cavatus*–Arthur V. Evans; *Agrilus heterothecae*–Christopher C. Wirth; *Agrilus politus*–Alice Abela; *Agrilus pulchellus*–Christopher C. Wirth; *Agrilus walsinghami*–Ted C. MacRae; *Anambodera nebulosi*–Alice Abela; *Anthaxia (Melanthaxia) species*–Arthur V. Evans; *Brachys aerosus*–Thomas Bentley; *Buprestis aurulenta*–Arthur V. Evans; *Buprestis confluenta*–Ted C. MacRae; *Buprestis gibbsii*–Richard L. Westcott; *Buprestis laeviventris*–R. Dennis Haines; *Buprestis viridisuturalis, Chalcophora angulicollis, Chrysobothris femorata, C. helferi*–Arthur V. Evans; *Chrysobothris mali*–Alice Abela; *Chrysobothris merkelii, C. monticola*–Arthur V. Evans; *Chrysobothris octocola*–Ted C. MacRae; *Chrysobothris quadrilineata*–Arthur V. Evans; *Chrysobothris viridicyanea*–Joyce Gross; *Chrysophana placida, Dicerca hesperoborealis, D. hornii hornii*–Arthur V. Evans; *Dicerca tenebrica*–James N. Hogue/California State University, Northridge; *Dicerca tenebrosa, Gyascutus caelatus, G. planicosta planicosta, Hippomelas planicauda, H. sphenicus, Juniperella mirabilis, Knowltonia biramosa, Lampetis webbii*–Arthur V. Evans; *Mastogenius robustus*–Mike Quinn/texasento.net; *Melanophila acuminata*–Stephen P. L. Luk; *Melanophila consputa*–Arthur V. Evans; *Nanularia brunneata*–Alice Abela; *Pachyschelus secedens, Paratyndaris olneyae, Phaenops drummondi drummondi, P. gentilis, P. vandykei*–Arthur V. Evans; *Poecilonota cyanipes*–Richard Migneault; *Polycesta aruensis*–Arthur V. Evans; *Spectralia cuprescens*–Mike Quinn/texasento.net; *Sphaerobothris ulkei, Thrincopyge ambiens*–Arthur V. Evans; *Trachykele blondeli blondeli*–Joyce Gross; *Trachykele nimbosa*–James N. Hogue/California State University, Northridge; *Xenomelanophila miranda*–Kara L. Froese.

BYRRHIDAE

Amphicyrta dentipes–Joyce Gross; *Byrrhus eximius*–Lynette Elliott; *Chaetophora spinosa, Cytilus alternatus*–Tom Murray; *Lioon simplicipes*–Joyce Gross; *Morychus oblongus*–Werner Eigelsreiter.

BYTURIDAE

Byturus unicolor–Graham Montgomery; *Xerasia griscecens*–Joyce Gross.

CANTHARIDAE

Cantharis grandicollis–Joyce Gross; *Chauliognathus lecontei*–Arthur V. Evans; *Chauliognathus lewisi*–Joyce Gross; *Chauliognathus limbicollis*–Jillian H. Cowles; *Chauliognathus misellus*–Joyce Gross; *Chauliognathus obscurus, C. omissus*–Arthur V. Evans; *Chauliognathus profundus*–Alice Abela; *Cultellunguis perpallens*–Robert L. Allen/Bug Bob; *Discodon abdominale, D. flavomarginatum*–Arthur V. Evans; *Ditemnus abdominalis*–Salvador Vitanza/USDA APHIS (PPQ); *Frostia laticollis*–Joyce Gross; *Pacificanthia consors*–James N. Hogue/

595

California State University, Northridge; *Podabrus latimanus*–Aaron Schusteff; *Podabrus pruinosus pruinosus, Silis carmelita*–Joyce Gross; *Tytthonyx bicolor*–Arthur V. Evans.

CARABIDAE

Akephorus marinus–Alice Abela; *Akephorus obesus*–Joyce Gross; *Amblycheila baroni*–Arthur V. Evans; *Anisodactylus alternans*–Joyce Gross; *Apenes hilariola*–Arthur V. Evans; *Badister neopulchellus*–Tom Murray; *Bembidion flohri*–Christopher C. Wirth; *Brachinus mexicanus*–James N. Hogue/California State University, Northridge; *Brasiella wickhami*–Arthur V. Evans; *Calathus ruficollis*–James N. Hogue/California State University, Northridge; *Calleida decora*–Arthur V. Evans; *Calleida platynoides*–Jillian H. Cowles; *Calosoma cancellatum*–Lynette Elliott; *Calosoma prominens, Calosoma scrutator*–Arthur V. Evans; *Calosoma semilaeve*–James N. Hogue/California State University, Northridge; *Carabus nemoralis*–Lynette Elliott; *Carabus serratus, Carabus vietinghoffi*–Henri Goulet; *Chlaenius cumatilis*–James N. Hogue/California State University, Northridge; *Chlaenius sericeus*–Joyce Gross; *Cicindela hirticollis gravida, C. latesignata, C. oregona, C. willistoni echo, Cicindelidia haemorrhagica, C. obsoleta santaclarae, C. ocellata*–Arthur V. Evans; *Cicindelidia punctulata chihuahuae*–Jillian H. Cowles; *Cicindelidia sedecimpunctata, C. trifasciata sigmoidea*–Arthur V. Evans; *Clinidium calcaratum*–Don Griffiths/Spencer Entomological Collection, Beaty Biodiversity Museum, University of British Columbia; *Colliuris lioptera*–Salvador Vitanza/USDA APHIS (PPQ); *Colliuris pensylvanica*–Joyce Gross; *Cratacanthus dubius*–Arthur V. Evans; *Cychrus tuberculatus*–Andrew McKorney; *Parvindela lemniscata*–Arthur V. Evans; *Dicheirus dilitatus*–Joyce Gross; *Diplocheila striatopunctata*–Henri Goulet; *Elaphrus californicus*–Arthur V. Evans; *Euryderus grossus*–Henri Goulet; *Galerita mexicana*–Arthur V. Evans; *Geopinus incrassatus*–Christopher C. Wirth; *Goniotropis kuntzeni, Harpalus caliginosus, Helluomorphoides latitarsus, Lachnophorus elegantulus, Lebia analis*–Arthur V. Evans; *Lebia fuscata*–Tom Murray; *Lebia viridis*–Christopher C. Wirth; *Metrius contractus*–Arthur V. Evans; *Mioptachys flavicauda*–Christopher C. Wirth; *Nebria eschscholtzii, Notiobia purpurascens*–James N. Hogue/California State University, Northridge; *Notiophilus biguttatus, Omoglymmius hamatus*–Joyce Gross; *Omophron dentatum*–Alice Abela; *Omophron obliteratum*–Christopher C. Wirth; *Omus californicus*–Arthur V. Evans; *Opisthius richardsoni*–Joyce Gross; *Panagaeus sallei*–Arthur V. Evans; *Paraclivina bipustulata*–Joyce Gross; *Pasimachus californicus*–Arthur V. Evans; *Pasimachus viridans*–Charles Hedgcock; *Patrobus longicornis, Perigona nigriceps*–Henri Goulet; *Plochionus timidus*–Christopher C. Wirth; *Poecilus lucublandus*–Henri Goulet; *Polpochila erro*–Arthur V. Evans; *Promecognathus crassus, Pseudaptinus tenuicollis*–Joyce Gross; *Pseudomorpha* species–Arthur V. Evans; *Psydrus piceus*–Graham Montgomery; *Pterostichus lama*–Arthur V. Evans; *Rhadine* species–Joyce Gross; *Scaphinotus cristatus*–Arthur V. Evans; *Scaphinotus longiceps*–Joyce Gross; *Scarites subterraneus*–Patrick Coin; *Stenolophus*

comma–Charley Eiseman; *Stenolophus lineola, S. ochropezus*–Christopher C. Wirth; *Stenomorphus californicus*–Arthur V. Evans; *Tachyta kirbyi*–Henri Goulet; *Tanystoma maculicolle*–Jim Moore; *Tetracha carolina*–Christopher C. Wirth; *Zacotus matthewsii*–Arthur V. Evans.

CERAMBYCIDAE

Acanthocinus obliquus, Achryson surinamum–Joyce Gross; *Anastrangalia laetifica, Aneflomorpha parowana*–Arthur V. Evans; *Aneflus prolixus fisheri*–Alice Abela; *Anelaphus brevidens*–Arthur V. Evans; *Anoplocurius canotiae*–Alice Abela; *Archodontes melanopus aridus*–Steven Lingafelter; *Arhopalus productus*–James N. Hogue/California State University, Northridge; *Asemum nitidum, A. striatum, Astromula nitidum*–Arthur V. Evans; *Atimia confusa dorsalis, Atylostagma glabra*–Joyce Gross; *Brothylus gemmulatus*–Alice Abela; *Callidium antennatum hesperum*–Joyce Gross; *Callimoxys fuscipennis*–Arthur V. Evans; *Callimus cyanipennis, C. ruficollis*–Joyce Gross; *Centrodera spurca*–James N. Hogue/California State University, Northridge; *Clytus clitellarius, C. planifrons*–Joyce Gross; *Coenopoeus palmeri*–Arthur V. Evans; *Cortodera cubitalis*–Joyce Gross; *Cortodera falsa*–James N. Hogue/California State University, Northridge; *Crossidius coralinus caeruleipennis, C. hirtipes nubilus*–Arthur V. Evans; *Crossidius testaceus maculicollis*–Robert L. Allen/Bug Bob; *Cyphonotida rostrata borealis, Dendrobias mandibularis mandibularis, Derobrachus hovorei*–Arthur V. Evans; *Desmocerus aureipennis aureipennis*–Philip A. Schapker; *Desmocerus cribripennis*–Sean McCann; *Dicentrus bluthneri*–Joyce Gross; *Dylobolus rotundicollis*–Arthur V. Evans; *Elytroleptus ignites, Enaphalodes hispicornis, E. niveitectus, Enoploderes vitticollis, Etorofus soror*–Arthur V. Evans; *Evodinus vancouveri*–Judy Gallagher; *Glaucotes yuccivorus*–Arthur V. Evans; *Grammoptera militaris*–Joyce Gross; *Grammoptera molybdica*–Arthur V. Evans; *Holopleura marginata*–Joyce Gross; *Ipochus fasciatus*–Alice Abela; *Judolia instabilis*–Joyce Gross; *Judolia montivagans*–Tom Murray; *Lepturobosca chrysocoma, Lepturopsis dolorosa, Lochmaeocles marmoratus*–Arthur V. Evans; *Malacopterus tenellus*–Jillian H. Cowles; *Mallodon dasystomus, Megacyllene antennata, Megapurpuricenus magnificus*–Arthur V. Evans; *Megasemum asperum*; Patrick Coin; *Megobrium edwardsi*–Arthur V. Evans; *Molorchus longicollis*–Joyce Gross; *Moneilema gigas, Monochamus clamator latus*–Arthur V. Evans; *Monochamus notatus*–Richard Migneault; *Monochamus scutellaris*–Arthur V. Evans; *Neandra marginicollis*–Cedric Lee; *Neanthophylax tenebrosus nigrolineatus*–Arthur V. Evans; *Necydalis barbarae*–Alice Abela; *Necydalis cavipennis*–Joyce Gross; *Neobellamira delicata australis*–Robert L. Allen/Bug Bob; *Neoclytus modestus*–James N. Hogue/California State University, Northridge; *Neoptychodes trilineatus*–Gayle & Jeanell Strickland; *Neospondylis upiformis*–Joyce Gross; *Nothopleurus lobigenis*–Arthur V. Evans; *Oberea erythrocephala*–James N. Hogue/California State University, Northridge; *Obrium maculatum*–Christopher C. Wirth; *Oeme costata, Oncideres quercus*–Arthur V. Evans; *Oncideres rhodosticta, Ortholeptura valida*–Joyce Gross;

Orwellion gibbulum arizonense, Osmidus guttatus–Arthur V. Evans; *Pachyta armata*–Ed Lisowski; *Peritapnia fabra*–Alice Abela; *Phoracantha recurva*–James N. Hogue/California State University, Northridge; *Phymatodes grandis*–Arthur V. Evans; *Pidonia gnathoides*–Joyce Gross; *Plectrura spinicauda*–John Davis; *Plinthocoelium suaveolens plicatum*–Alexey Sergeev; *Plionoma suturalis, Poliaenus californicus, Prionus californicus, P. heroicus*–Arthur V. Evans; *Pseudopilema hoppingi*–Joyce Gross; *Rhagium inquisitor, Rhopalophora meeskei*–Arthur V. Evans; *Rosalia funebris*–Robert L. Allen/Bug Bob; *Saperda calcarata*–Richard Migneault; *Schizax senex*–Charley Eiseman; *Semanotus amplus*–Jim Moore; *Sphaenothecus bilineatus, Stenaspis solitaria, S. verticalis arizonicus*–Arthur V. Evans; *Stenocorus nubifer*–Aaron Schusteff; *Stenostrophia tribalteata sierrae*–Arthur V. Evans; *Sternidius centralis*–Jillian H. Cowles; *Sternidocinus barbarus*–Joyce Gross; *Stictoleptura canadensis cribripennis*–Lynette Elliott; *Strophiona tigrina*–Alice Abela; *Styloxus bicolor, Susuacanga falli*–Arthur V. Evans; *Synaphaeta guexi, Tetraopes annulatus*–Joyce Gross; *Tetraopes basalis, T. discoideus, Tigrinestola tigrine, Tragidion armatum, T. deceptum*–Arthur V. Evans; *Tragosoma harrisii*–Joyce Gross; *Tragosoma pilosicorne*–Arthur V. Evans; *Trichocnemis pauper*–Robert L. Allen/Bug Bob; *Trichocnemis spiculatus neomexicanus, T. s. spiculatus*–Arthur V. Evans; *Triodoclytus lanifer*–© 2021 Robyn J. Waayers, used with permission; *Tylosis maculatus*–Aaron Schusteff; *Typocerus balteatus balteatus, Ulochaetes leoninus*–Arthur V. Evans; *Xestoleptura crassipes, Xylocrius agassizi*–Joyce Gross; *Xylotrechus insignis* female–Aaron Schusteff; *Xylotrechus insignis* male–Joyce Gross; *Xylotrechus nauticus*–Robert L. Allen/Bug Bob.

CEROPHYTIDAE

Cerophytum convexicolle–R. Dennis Haines.

CERYLONIDAE

Cerylon unicolor–Tom Murray; *Philothermus occidentalis*–Museum of Comparative Zoology and Harvard University.

CHRYSOMELIDAE

Acalymma trivittatum–Gary McDonald; *Acanthoscelides obtectus*–Joyce Gross; *Algarobius prosopis*–Christopher C. Wirth; *Altica ambiens*–Merrill A. Peterson; *Amblycerus robiniae*–Christopher C. Wirth; *Androlyperus fulvus, Anisostena californica*–Joyce Gross; *Anomoea rufifrons occidentimutabilis*–Salvador Vitanza/USDA APHIS (PPQ); *Baliosus californicus, Blepharida rhois*–Arthur V. Evans; *Brachycoryna longula*–Joyce Gross; *Bromius obscurus*–Richard Migneault; *Bruchidius villosus*–Christopher C. Wirth; *Bruchus pisorum*–Christoph Benisch; *Calligrapha californica coreospivora*–Joyce Gross; *Calligrapha dislocata*–Arthur V. Evans; *Calligrapha multipunctata*–James N. Hogue/California State University, Northridge; *Charidotella sexpunctata bicolor, C. succinea, Chelymorpha phytophagica, Chrysochus auratus, C. cobaltinus, Chrysomela confluens, Chrysomela schaefferi*–Arthur V.

Evans; *Chrysomela scripta*–Christopher C. Wirth; *Colaspidea smaragdula, Colaspis nigrocyanea*–Arthur V. Evans; *Colaspis viriditincta*–Christopher C. Wirth; *Coleothorpa axillaris*–Salvador Vitanza/USDA APHIS (PPQ); *Crioceris asparagi*–Tom Murray; *Crioceris duodecimpunctata*–Gary Campbell; *Cryptocephalus atrofasciatus*–Arthur V. Evans; *Cryptocephalus sanguinipennis*–Joyce Gross; *Deloyala lecontii*–Christopher C. Wirth; *Diabrotica undecimpunctata undecimpunctata, D. virgifera*–Arthur V. Evans; *Diachus auratus*–Alice Abela; *Disonycha alternata*–Joyce Gross; *Disonycha tenuicornis*–Arthur V. Evans; *Entomoscelis americana*–Adrian D. Thysse; *Epitrix hirtipennis*–Alice Abela; *Galeruca rudis*–Joyce Gross; *Galerucella nymphaeae*–Tom Murray; *Gastrophysa cyanea*–Joyce Gross; *Gibbobruchus mimus*–Graham Montgomery; *Glyptoscelis albida*–Joyce Gross; *Gonioctena americana*–Tom Murray; *Graphops pubescens, Gratiana pallidula*–Arthur V. Evans; *Griburius Montezuma*–Margarethe Brummermann; *Heliocassis clavata testudinaria*–Arthur V. Evans; *Hemiglyptus basalis*–Joyce Gross; *Kuschelina lugens*–Jillian H. Cowles; *Lema nigrovittata*–Arthur V. Evans; *Lema trabeata, L. trivittata trivittata*–Joyce Gross; *Leptinotarsa decemlineata, L. haldemani, L. lineolata*–Arthur V. Evans; *Leptinotarsa rubiginosa*–Alice Abela; *Lilioceris lilii*–Lynette Elliott; *Longitarsus* species, *Megacerus impiger*–Joyce Gross; *Megalostomis pyropyga, M. subfasciata*–Arthur V. Evans; *Microrhopala rubrolineata*–Joyce Gross; *Microrhopala vittata*–Scott Justis; *Monoxia debilis*–Joyce Gross; *Neogalerucella calmariensis*–Tom Murray; *Neohaemonia nigricornis*–Mike Quinn/texasento.net; *Octotoma marginicollis*–Joyce Gross; *Ophraea rugosa*–Arthur V. Evans; *Oulema arizonae*–Joyce Gross; *Pachybrachis bivittatus*–Arthur V. Evans; *Pachybrachis circumcinctus*–Joyce Gross; *Pachybrachis mellitus*–Alice Abela; *Pachybrachis thoracicus*–Jillian H. Cowles; *Paranapiacaba tricincta*–Arthur V. Evans; *Paropsisterna m-fuscum*–Joyce Gross; *Physonota arizonae*–Jillian H. Cowles; *Plagiodera californica*–Joyce Gross; *Plateumaris dubia*–Merrill A. Peterson; *Saxinis saucia*–Arthur V. Evans; *Scelolyperus lecontii*–Jillian H. Cowles; *Stator limbatus, Stenopodius flavidus*–Joyce Gross; *Sumitrosis inaequalis*–Joyce Gross; *Syneta albida, S. hamata, S. simplex simplex*–Arthur V. Evans; *Thricolema anomala*–Joyce Gross; *Timarcha intricata*–© 2021 Robyn J. Waayers, used with permission; *Trachymela sloanei*–Joyce Gross; *Tricholochmaea punctipennis*–Jim Moore; *Trirhabda eriodictyonis*–Arthur V. Evans; *Trirhabda flavolimbata*–Joyce Gross; *Tymnes oregonensis*–Alice Abela; *Urodera dilaticollis*–Arthur V. Evans; *Walterianella durangoensis, Xanthogaleruca luteola*–Joyce Gross; *Xenochalepus ater*–Arthur V. Evans; *Zabrotes spectabilis*–Joyce Gross; *Zygogramma arizonica, Z. continua, Z. piceicollis*–Arthur V. Evans; *Zygogramma signatipennis*–Christopher C. Wirth.

CIIDAE

Ceracis californicus, Hadraule blaisdelli, Plesiocis cribrum, Sphindocis denticollis–Joyce Gross.

CIMBERIDIDAE

Acromacer bombifrons, Cimberis bihirsuta, Lecontellus byturoides, Pityomacer pix–Robert S. Anderson/Canadian Museum of Nature.

CLAMBIDAE

Clambus species–Joyce Gross.

CLERIDAE

Aulicus apachei–Arthur V. Evans; *Boschella fasciata*–Joyce Gross (*l*), Arthur V. Evans (*r*); *Chariessa elegans*–Christopher C. Wirth; *Cymatodera decipiens, C. fuchsia, C. horni, C. oblita, C. tricolor*–Arthur V. Evans; *Cymatodera vandykei*–Jacques Rifkind; *Enoclerus bimaculatus, E. eximius*–Arthur V. Evans; *Enoclerus laetus*–Arthur V. Evans (*l*), Jillian H. Cowles (*r*); *Enoclerus lecontei, E. quadrisignatus, E. sphegeus, E. spinolae*–Arthur V. Evans; *Lecontella gnara*–Lucie Gimmel/Santa Barbara Museum of Natural History; *Loedelia maculicollis*–Joyce Gross; *Monophylla californica*–Lucie Gimmel/Santa Barbara Museum of Natural History; *Necrobia ruficollis, N. rufipes*–Joyce Gross; *Necrobia violacea*–Tom Murray; *Pelonides humeralis*–Arthur V. Evans; *Pelonium peninsulare*–Jacques Rifkind; *Phyllobaenus humeralis*–Christopher C. Wirth; *Phyllobaenus scaber*–James N. Hogue/California State University, Northridge; *Thanasimus undatulus*–Chris Joll; *Trichodes ornatus*–Arthur V. Evans (*l*), Jillian H. Cowles (*r*); *Trichodes peninsularis horni*–Arthur V. Evans.

COCCINELLIDAE

Adalia bipunctata–Joyce Gross; *Anatis lecontei*–Arthur V. Evans; *Anatis rathvoni, Calvia quatuordecimguttata*–Joyce Gross; *Chilocorus cacti*–Stanislav Krejčík; *Coccinella californica, C. monticola*–Joyce Gross; *Coccinella septempunctata*–Christopher C. Wirth; *Coleomegilla maculata, Cryptolaemus montrouzieri, Cycloneda polita*–Joyce Gross; *Epilachna tredecimnotata*–Alice Abela; *Harmonia axyridis*–Tom Murray; *Hippodamia convergens*–Arthur V. Evans; *Hippodamia parenthesis, H. tredecimpunctata tibialis*–Joyce Gross; *Hyperaspis octonotata*–Jillian H. Cowles; *Microweisea misella*–Tom Murray; *Mulsantina picta, Myzia interrupta*–Joyce Gross; *Olla v-nigrum*–Arthur V. Evans; *Paranaemia vittigera, Psyllobora borealis, P. vigintimaculata, Rodolia cardinalis*–Joyce Gross; *Scymnus nebulosus*–Alice Abela.

CORYLOPHIDAE

Sericoderus lateralis–Christoph Benisch.

CRYPTOPHAGIDAE

Antherophagus ochraceus–Tom Murray; *Atomaria* species–Alice Abela; *Caenoscelis ferruginea*–Tom Murray; *Cryptophagus* species–Alice Abela; *Telmatophilus americanus*–Tom Murray.

CUCUJIDAE

Cucujus clavipes puniceus–Graham Montgomery; *Pediacus stephani*–Joyce Gross.

CUPEDIDAE

Priacma serrata–Joyce Gross; *Prolixocupes lobiceps*–Arthur V. Evans.

CURCULIONIDAE

Adaleres ovipennis–Arthur V. Evans; *Anisandrus dispar*–T. H. Atkinson/University of Texas Insect Collection/courtesy of Smithsonian Institution; *Anthonomus haematopus, Apleurus angularis*–Alice Abela; *Aragnomus griseus*–Arthur V. Evans; *Barypeithes pellucidus*–Tom Murray; *Brachypera zoilus*–Thomas Bentley; *Cactophagus spinolae validus*–Arthur V. Evans; *Ceutorhynchus americanus*–Tom Murray; *Cnemidoprion oblongus*–Christopher C. Wirth; *Colecerus dispar*–Arthur V. Evans; *Cosmobaris scolopacea*–Tom Murray; *Cossonus crenatus*–Alice Abela; *Crocidema californica*–Arthur V. Evans; *Cryptorhynchus lapathi*–Tom Murray; *Curculio aurivestis*–Arthur V. Evans; *Cylindrocopturus adspersus*–K. S. Matz; *Cyphocleonus achates*–Lynette Elliott; *Dendroctonus brevicomis*–T. H. Atkinson/University of Texas Insect Collection/courtesy of Smithsonian Institution; *Dendroctonus ponderosae*–Arthur V. Evans; *Dendroctonus pseudotsugae*–T. H. Atkinson/University of Texas Insect Collection/courtesy of Smithsonian Institution; *Dendroctonus rufipennis*–Jennifer Read; *Dendroctonus valens*–Arthur V. Evans; *Dietzella zimmermanni*–Charley Eiseman; *Dorytomus inaequalis*–Lynette Elliott; *Dyslobus ursinus, Dysticheus insignis*–Arthur V. Evans; *Elassoptes marinus, Emphyastes fucicola*–Alice Abela; *Ericydeus lautus*–Arthur V. Evans; *Eucilinus aridus*–Alice Abela; *Eudiagogus pulcher*–Graham Montgomery; *Geraeus patagoniensis, Hadromeropsis opalina*–Arthur V. Evans; *Hylastes macer*–Graham Montgomery; *Hylurgops porosus, Hypera nigrirostris*–Lynette Elliott; *Ips pini*–Pennsylvania DCNR-Forestry, Bugwood.org; *Laemosaccus burkei*–Christopher C. Wirth; *Larinus carlinae*–Arthur V. Evans; *Lechriops californica*–Joyce Gross; *Lepyrus oregonensis*–Lynette Elliott; *Lissorhoptrus oryzophilus*–Graham Montgomery; *Listroderes costirostris*–Christopher C. Wirth; *Lixus perforatus*–Alice Abela; *Magdalis lecontei*–Aaron Schusteff; *Myrmex lineatus*–Alice Abela; *Myrmex vandykei, Naupactus cervinus, Nemocestes horni, Ophryastes argentatus*–Arthur V. Evans; *Otiorhynchus ovatus*–Tom Murray; *Otiorhynchus rugosostriatus*–John Ott; *Otiorhynchus sulcatus*–Arthur V. Evans; *Pachyrhinus californicus*–Alice Abela; *Pachyrhinus elegans*–Joyce Gross; *Pandeleteinus submetallicus, Pandeleteius robustus, Panscopus spantoni, Peltophorus polymitus seminiveus*–Arthur V. Evans; *Pissodes schwarzi*–Joyce Gross; *Pityokteines ornatus*–Michael Caterino/Santa Barbara Museum of Natural History; *Pityophthorus venustus*–T. H. Atkinson/University of Texas Insect Collection/courtesy of Smithsonian Institution; *Pseudohylesinus nebulosus*–Gary D. Griswold; *Rhigopsis effracta*–Alice Abela; *Rhynchophorus palmarum*–Donald R. Hodel; *Yuccaborus frontalis*–Arthur V. Evans; *Rhinusa tetra*–Joyce Gross; *Rhodobaenus tredecimpunctatus*–Arthur V. Evans; *Rhyncolus cylindricollis*–Graham Montgomery; *Scaphomorphus quadrilineatus*–Salvador Vitanza/USDA APHIS (PPQ); *Scolytus ventralis*–T. H. Atkinson/University of Texas Insect Collection/courtesy of Smithsonian Institution; *Scyphophorus acupunctatus*, *S. yuccae*–Arthur V. Evans; *Sitona californicus*–Alice Abela; *Sitophilus oryzae*–Scott Justis; *Sphenophorus aequalis pictus*–James N. Hogue/California State University, Northridge; *Sphenophorus australis*–Jillian H. Cowles; *Sphenophorus costipennis*–Joyce Gross; *Sternechus paludatus*–Jillian H. Cowles; *Tachyerges salicis*–Alice Abela; *Tachygonus centralis*–Christopher C. Wirth; *Thricolepis inornata*–Alice Abela; *Treptoplatypus wilsoni*–Joyce Gross; *Trichobaris mucorea*–Arthur V. Evans; *Trigonoscuta* species–Alice Abela; *Xyleborinus saxesenii*–Kirill Makarov; *Zascelis irrorata*–Arthur V. Evans.

CYBOCEPHALIDAE
Cybocephalus californicus–Joyce Gross.

DASCILLIDAE
Anorus piceus male–Arthur V. Evans, female–Andrew Johnston; *Dascillus davidsoni*–Joyce Gross.

DERMESTIDAE
Anthrenus lepidus–Alice Abela (*l*), Lynette Elliott (*r*); *Anthrenus verbasci*–Joyce Gross; *Attagenus brunneus*–Tom Murray; *Cryptorhopalum* species–Christopher C. Wirth; *Dermestes ater*–James N. Hogue/California State University, Northridge; *Dermestes caninus*, *D. frischii*–Arthur V. Evans; *Dermestes lardarius*–Tom Murray; *Dermestes marmoratus*–Arthur V. Evans; *Dermestes talpinus*–Joyce Gross; *Megatoma variegata*–Lynette Elliott; *Orphilus subnitidus*–Arthur V. Evans; *Thylodrias contractus*–K. S. Matz; *Trogoderma glabrum*–Joyce Gross.

DERODONTIDAE
Derodontus trisignatus–Jennifer Read; *Laricobius nigrinus*–Birgit Rhode, from Leschen, R.A.B. (2011) World review of *Laricobius* (Coleoptera: Derodontidae). *Zootaxa* 2908: 1–44; *Peltastica tuberculata*–Wendy L. Duncan.

DIPHYLLOSTOMATIDAE
Diphyllostoma linsleyi–Joyce Gross.

DRYOPIDAE
Dryops arizonensis–Salvador Vitanza/USDA APHIS (PPQ); *Helichus striatus*–Jeffrey P. Gruber & Nicolas Gompel/UW–Madison, Dept. of Entomology; *Postelichus* species–Joyce Gross.

DYTISCIDAE
Acilius abbreviatus, *Agabus lutosus*–Joyce Gross; *Boreonectes striatellus*–James N. Hogue/California State University,

Northridge; *Colymbetes densus*–Joyce Gross; *Copelatus glyphicus*–Christopher C. Wirth; *Cybister fimbriolatus*–Patrick Coin; *Dytiscus marginicollis*–Gary Alpert/Northern Arizona University; *Eretes sticticus*–Christopher C. Wirth; *Ilybius quadrimaculatus*–Arthur V. Evans; *Laccophilus maculosus decipiens*–Joyce Gross; *Neoporus undulatus*–Christopher C. Wirth; *Rhantus gutticollis*, *Thermonectus marmoratus*–Arthur V. Evans; *Thermonectus nigrofasciatus*–Margy Green/margygreen.com.

ELATERIDAE
Aeolus livens–Joyce Gross; *Agriotes ferrugineipennis*–Jim Moore; *Alaus melanops*, *A. zunianus*–Arthur V. Evans; *Ampedus cordifer*–Joyce Gross; *Anchastus bicolor*–Jillian H. Cowles; *Anthracalaus agrypnoides*–Arthur V. Evans; *Aplastus* species–Joyce Gross; *Athous* species, *Cardiophorus brevis*–Arthur V. Evans; *Cardiophorus edwardsi*–Joyce Gross; *Chalcolepidius apacheanus*–Margarethe Brummermann; *Chalcolepidius lenzi*, *C. smaragdinus*, *C. tartarus*–Arthur V. Evans; *Chalcolepidius webbii*, *Conoderus exsul*, *C. falli*–Joyce Gross; "*Ctenicera*" *protracta*–Graham Montgomery; *Dalopius* species–Rob Curtis/www.theearlybirder.com; *Danosoma brevicorne*–Arthur V. Evans; *Dicrepidius corvinus*, *Diplostethus opacicollis*–Salvador Vitanza/USDA APHIS (PPQ); *Dolerosomus silaceus*–Joyce Gross; *Elater lecontei*, *Euthysanius lautus* male–Arthur V. Evans, female–Robert L. Allen/Bug Bob; *Hadromorphus glaucus*–Joyce Gross; *Hemicrepidius obscurus*–Alice Abela; *Horistonotus simplex*–Salvador Vitanza/USDA APHIS (PPQ); *Hypoganus rotundicollis*–Alice Abela; *Lacon rorulentus*, *L. sparsus*–James N. Hogue/California State University, Northridge; *Lanelater schottii*–Margarethe Brummermann; *Megapenthes aterrimus*–Arthur V. Evans; *Megapenthes caprella*–Joyce Gross; *Megapenthes turbulentus*–Alice Abela; *Melanactes densus*–James N. Hogue/California State University, Northridge; *Melanotus similis*–Salvador Vitanza/USDA APHIS (PPQ); *Negastrius ornatus*–R. Dennis Haines; *Neopristilophus maurus*–Christopher C. Wirth; *Nitidolimonius resplendens*–Adrian D. Thysse; *Octinodes schaumii*–James N. Hogue/California State University, Northridge; *Oedostethus femoralis*–Richard Migneault; *Orthostethus infuscatus*, *O. pecticornis*–Arthur V. Evans; *Paradonus* species–Salvador Vitanza/USDA APHIS (PPQ); *Pityobius murrayi*–Arthur V. Evans; *Prosternon bombycinum*–Lynette Elliott; *Pseudanostirus nigricollis*–Joyce Gross; *Pseudanostirus tigrinus*–Arthur V. Evans; *Scaptolenus fuscipennis*–Joseph (Tony) Palmer; *Selatosomus edwardsi*–Joyce Gross; *Selatosomus suckleyi*–Lynette Elliott; *Tetralimonius ornatulus*–Joyce Gross; *Vesperelater arizonicus*–Arthur V. Evans.

ELMIDAE
Ampumixis dispar, *Atractelmis wawona*, *Dubiraphia giulianii*, *Heterlimnius koebelei*–Crystal Maier/Louisiana State Arthropod Museum; *Lara avara avara*–Joyce Gross; *Narpus concolor*–Crystal Maier/Louisiana State Arthropod Museum; *Optioservus quadrimaculatus*, *Ordobrevia nubifera*, *Zaitzevia parvula*–Joyce Gross.

ENDOMYCHIDAE

Aphorista laeta, A. morosa–Joyce Gross; *Epipocus unicolor*–Arthur V. Evans; *Lycoperdina ferruginea*–Joyce Gross; *Mycetina horni*–Lynette Elliott; *Phymaphora californica*–Joyce Gross.

EPIMETOPIDAE

Epimetopus arizonicus, E. punctipennis–P. D. Perkins; *E. thermarum*–Jennifer Read.

EROTYLIDAE

Acropteroxys gracilis, Cypherotylus californicus–Arthur V. Evans; *Dacne californica*–Joyce Gross; *Ischyrus quadripunctatus chiasticus*–Salvador Vitanza/USDA APHIS (PPQ); *Languria convexicollis, Langurites lineatus, Megalodacne heros*–Arthur V. Evans; *Triplax californica*–Jim Moore.

EUCINETIDAE

Eucinetus terminalis–Jennifer Read; *Nycteus infumatus*–Joyce Gross.

EUCNEMIDAE

Anelastes californicus–Arthur V. Evans; *Hemiopsida robusta, Melasis tsugae*–Robert Otto; *Microrhagus pectinatus*–Tom Murray; *Palaeoxenus dohrni*–James N. Hogue/California State University, Northridge; *Perothops witticki*–© 2021 Robyn J. Waayers, used with permission; *Proutianus americana*–Robert L. Otto; *Sarpedon scabrosus*–Guy A. Hanley; *Xylophilus crassicornis*–Robert L. Otto.

EULICHADIDAE

Stenocolus scutellaris–Arthur V. Evans.

GEORISSIDAE

Georissus pusillus–R. Dennis Haines.

GEOTRUPIDAE

Bolbelasmus horni–James N. Hogue/California State University, Northridge; *Bolbocerastes imperialis*–© 2021 Robyn J. Waayers, used with permission; *Bolbocerastes regalis*–Charles L. Hogue/courtesy of James N. Hogue, California State University, Northridge; *Bolborhombus angulus, Bolborhombus sallei*–Arthur V. Evans; *Ceratophyus gopherinus*–Alice Abela; *Eucanthus greeni*–Arthur V. Evans; *Eucanthus lazarus*–Guy A. Hanley; *Odonteus obesus*–Arthur V. Evans.

GLAPHYRIDAE

Lichnanthe apina–Arthur V. Evans; *Lichnanthe rathvoni*–Joyce Gross; *Lichnanthe ursina*–Arthur V. Evans.

GLARESIDAE

Glaresis ecostata, G. inducta–Guy A. Hanley.

GYRINIDAE

Dineutus sublineatus–Arthur V. Evans; *Gyrinus* species–James N. Hogue/California State University, Northridge.

HALIPLIDAE

Brychius horni–Michael C. Thomas/Florida State Collection of Arthropods, FDACS-DPI; *Haliplus concolor*–Graham Montgomery; *Haliplus parvulus*–Michael C. Thomas/Florida State Collection of Arthropods, FDACS-DPI; *Peltodytes callosus*–Joyce Gross.

HELOPHORIDAE

Helophorus species–Alice Abela.

HETEROCERIDAE

Heterocerus fenestratus–Tom Murray; *Heterocerus mollinus*–Arthur V. Evans; *Tropicus pusillus*–Christopher C. Wirth.

HISTERIDAE

Atholus bimaculatus–Jeffrey P. Gruber/UW-Madison, Dept. of Entomology; *Euspilotus scissus*–Alice Abela; *Haeterius wagneri*–Jeffrey P. Gruber/UW-Madison, Dept. of Entomology; *Hister furtivus*–Guy A. Hanley; *Hololepta vernicis*–© 2021 David Maddison, used with permission; *Hypocaccus bigemmeus*–Alice Abela; *Iliotona cacti*–Michael L. Ferro; *Neopachylopus sulcifrons*–Alice Abela; *Omalodes grossus*–Arthur V. Evans; *Onthophilus lecontei*–R. Dennis Haines; *Platylomalus aequalis, Platysoma leconti*–Christopher C. Wirth; *Plegaderus sayi*–Tom Murray; *Saprinus lugens*–Jeffrey P. Gruber/UW-Madison, Dept. of Entomology; *Spilodiscus sellatus, Teretrius cylindrellus*–Joyce Gross; *Xerosaprinus lubricus*–Arthur V. Evans.

HYBOSORIDAE

Hybosorus illigeri–Arthur V. Evans; *Pachyplectrus laevis*–Guy A. Hanley.

HYDRAENIDAE

Hydraena species–Joyce Gross; *Ochthebius* species–Jeffrey P. Gruber/UW-Madison, Dept. of Entomology.

HYDROCHIDAE

Hydrochus squamifer–Tom Murray.

HYDROPHILIDAE

Berosus punctatissimus–James N. Hogue/California State University, Northridge; *Cercyon fimbriatus*–Alice Abela; *Cymbiodyta acuminata*–Guy A. Hanley; *Enochrus hamiltoni*–Joyce Gross; *Hydrobius fuscipes*–Steve Nanz; *Hydrochara lineata*–Michael Bogan; *Hydrophilus triangularis*–Joyce Gross; *Laccobius* species–Graham Montgomery; *Sphaeridium scarabaeoides, Tropisternus lateralis humeralis*–Arthur V. Evans.

HYDROSCAPHIDAE

Hydroscapha natans–© 2021 David Maddison, used with permission.

ISCHALIIDAE

Ischalia californica–Joyce Gross.

KATERETIDAE

Amartus tinctus–Joyce Gross; *Anthonaeus agavensis*–Kyle Schnepp/Florida State Collection of Arthropods, FDACS-DPI; *Brachypterus urticae*–Tom Murray; *Heterhelus sericans*–Richard Migneault.

LAEMOPHLOEIDAE

Laemophloeus biguttatus–Mike Quinn/texasento.net.

LAMPYRIDAE

Ellychnia californica–Arthur V. Evans; *Microphotus angustus*–Aaron Schusteff; *Paraphausis* species–Joyce Gross; *Photinus knulli*–Arthur V. Evans; *Pleotomus pallens*–James N Hogue/California State University, Northridge (t)/Joe Cicero (b); *Pterotus obscuripennis*–Alice Abela; *Pyropyga nigricans*–Joyce Gross.

LATRIDIIDAE

Cartodere constrictus–Udo Schmidt/CC BY-SA 2.0; *Corticaria serrata, Dienerella filum, Enicmus aterrimus, Melanophthalma picta*–Tom Murray.

LEIODIDAE

Agathidium species–Joyce Gross; *Catops basilaris*–Christopher C. Wirth; *Glacicavicola bathyscioides*–Stewart B. Peck; *Leiodes assimilis*–Tom Murray; *Pinodytes newelli*–Kojun Kanda; *Platypsyllus castoris*–Arthur V. Evans.

LIMNICHIDAE

Throscinus crotchii, Eulimnichus analis–Jennifer Read.

LOPHOCATERIDAE

Eronyxa pallidus–Arthur V. Evans; *Grynocharis oregonensis*–Matthew Van Dam/California Academy of Sciences.

LUCANIDAE

Ceruchus punctatus–Arthur V. Evans; *Ceruchus striatus*–Joyce Gross; *Lucanus mazama*–Arthur V. Evans; *Platyceroides latus*–Joyce Gross; *Platyceroides keeni, Platycerus oregonensis, Sinodendron rugosum*–Arthur V. Evans.

LUTROCHIDAE

Lutrochus arizonicus–Crystal Maier/Louisiana State Arthropod Museum.

LYCIDAE

Caenia amplicornis–Arthur V. Evans; *Dictyoptera simplicipes*–Joyce Gross; *Greenarus thoracicus*–Karl W. Hillig; *Lucaina greeni*–Margarethe Brummermann; *Lycus arizonensis, L. fernandezi, L. fulvellus femoratus, L. loripes, L. sanguinipennis, L. simulans*–Arthur V. Evans; *Lygistopterus dimidiatus*–Jim Moore; *Lygistopterus ignitus*–Arthur V. Evans; *Macrolygistopterus rubripennis*–Jeffrey P. Gruber; *Plateros species*–Arthur V. Evans.

MAURONISCIDAE

Mecomycter omalinus–Lucie Gimmel/Santa Barbara Museum of Natural History; *Mectemycor strangulatus*–Kyle Schnepp/Florida State Collection of Arthropods, FDACS-DPI; *Scuromanius facetus*–Lucie Gimmel/Santa Barbara Museum of Natural History.

MEGALOPODIDAE

Zeugophora scutellaris–Josef Dvořák.

MELANDRYIDAE

Emmesa testacea testacea–Kyle Schnepp/Florida State Collection of Arthropods, FDACS-DPI; *Enchodes sericea*–Rob Curtis/www.theearlybirder.com; *Melandrya striata*–Christopher C. Wirth; *Orchesia castanea*–Tom Murray; *Osphya lutea*–Richard E. Schilk; *Phloiotrya riversi*–Joyce Gross; *Phryganophilus collaris*–Stephen McKechnie; *Prothalpia holmbergii*–Joyce Gross; *Serropalpus substriatus*–Arthur V. Evans; *Xylita laevigata*–Udo Schmidt (CC BY-SA 4.0).

MELOIDAE

Cordylospasta opaca, Cysteodemus armatus, C. wislizeni–Joyce Gross; *Epicauta abadona*–Aaron Schusteff; *Epicauta cinctipennis*–Joyce Gross; *Epicauta costata*, James N. Hogue/California State University, Northridge; *Epicauta hirsutapubescens, E. ochrea, E. puncticollis, E. purpurea, E. segmenta, E. tenuilineata*–Arthur V. Evans; *Epicauta wheeleri*–James N. Hogue/California State University, Northridge; *Eupompha elegans elegans*–Joyce Gross; *Eupompha elegans perpulchra*–Arthur V. Evans; *Eupompha schwarzi*–Joyce Gross; *Gnathium caviceps*–Alice Abela; *Lytta aeneipennis*–Joyce Gross; *Lytta auriculata*–Alice Abela; *Lytta biguttata*–Arthur V. Evans; *Lytta chloris*–James N. Hogue/California State University, Northridge; *Lytta deserticola*–Jillian H. Cowles; *Lytta magister, L. nuttalli, L. stygica*–Joyce Gross; *Lytta sublaevis*–Alice Abela; *Megetra punctata*–Arthur V. Evans; *Meloe barbarus*–Aaron Schusteff; *Nemognatha nigripennis, N. scutellaris, N. soror*–Arthur V. Evans; *Phodaga alticeps*–Joyce Gross; *Phodaga marmorata*–Arthur V. Evans; *Pleurospasta mirabilis*–Joyce Gross; *Pseudozonitis brevis*–Jillian H. Cowles; *Pseudozonitis vaurieae, Pyrota akhurstiana*–Arthur V. Evans; *Pyrota palpalis, Tegrodera aloga*–Joyce Gross; *Tricrania stansburyi*–Alice Abela; *Zonitis dunniana*–Arthur V. Evans.

MELYRIDAE

Attalus species, *Collops cribrosus*–Alice Abela; *Collops grandis*–Arthur V. Evans; *Collops granellus*, *C. histrio*–Arthur V. Evans; *Collops quadriguttatus*–Joyce Gross; *Collops quadrimaculatus*–Arthur V. Evans; *Cradytes serricollis*–Salvador Vitanza/USDA APHIS (PPQ); *Endeodes basalis*–Alice Abela; *Endeodes collaris*–Arthur V. Evans; *Eschatocrepis constrictus*–Hartmut Wisch; *Listrus* species–Joyce Gross; *Malachius aeneus*–Richard Migneault; *Malachius mixtus*–Joyce Gross; *Malachius thevenetii*–Joyce Gross; *Tanaops* species, *Trichochrous seriellus*–Christopher C. Wirth.

MICROMALTHIDAE

Micromalthus debilis–© 2021 Alex Wild, used with permission.

MONOTOMIDAE

Bactridium californicum, *Europs striatulus*–Tommy McElrath; *Hesperobaenus abbreviatus*–Joyce Gross; *Monotoma bicolor*–Tom Murray; *Phyconomus marinus*–Alice Abela; *Rhizophagus minutus*–Joyce Gross.

MORDELLIDAE

Glipostenoda ambusta–Tom Murray; *Hoshihananomia perlineata*–Margarethe Brummermann; *Mordella atrata*–Joyce Gross; *Mordellina pustulata*–Tom Murray; *Mordellochroa scapularis*–Christopher C. Wirth.

MURMIDIIDAE

Murmidius ovalis–Michael C. Thomas/Florida State Collection of Arthropods, FDACS-DPI.

MYCETAEIDAE

Mycetaea subterranea–Christoph Benisch.

MYCETOPHAGIDAE

Berginus pumilus–Chris Mallory; *Litargus balteatus*–Christoph Benisch; *Mycetophagus pluriguttatus*–Joyce Gross; *Typhaea stercorea*–Tom Murray.

MYCTERIDAE

Lacconotus pinicola–Darren A. Pollock; *Mycterus canescens*–Arthur V. Evans; *Mycterus concolor*, *M. quadricollis*–Joyce Gross.

NEMONYCHIDAE

Atopomacer ites–Robert S. Anderson/Canadian Museum of Nature.

NITIDULIDAE

Aethina tumida–James N. Hogue/California State University, Northridge; *Carpophilus hemipterus*–Alice Abela; *Colopterus truncatus*–Tom Murray; *Conotelus mexicana*–Salvador Vitanza/USDA APHIS (PPQ); *Cryptarcha concinna*–Joyce Gross; *Epuraea luteola*–Alice Abela; *Fabogethes nigrescens*–Charley Eiseman; *Glischrochilus quadrisignatus*–Joyce Gross; *Lobiopa falli*–Arthur V. Evans; *Nitidula flavomaculata*, *N. ziczac*–Joyce Gross; *Nitops pallipennis*–Christopher C. Wirth; *Omosita discoidea*–Gary D. Griswold; *Pallodes plateosus*–Joyce Gross; *Pityophagus rufipennis*–Jim Moore; *Pocadius fulvipennis*–Joyce Gross; *Soronia guttulata*–Graham Montgomery; *Stelidota octomaculata*–Tom Murray; *Thalycra sinuata*–Arthur V. Evans.

NOSODENDRIDAE

Nosodendron californicum–Arthur V. Evans.

OCHODAEIDAE

Codocera gnatho, *Cucochodaeus sparsus*–Guy A. Hanley; *Neochodaeus praesidii*–Christopher C. Wirth; *Pseudochodaeus estriatus*, *Xenochodaeus ulkei*–Arthur V. Evans.

OEDEMERIDAE

Calopus angustus–Guy A. Hanley; *Copdita quadrimaculata*–Arthur V. Evans; *Ditylus quadricollis*, *Eumecomera cyanipennis*, *Ischnomera excavata*–Joyce Gross; *Nacerdes melanura*–Arthur V. Evans; *Oxacis sericea*–Joyce Gross; *Oxacis subfusca*–Arthur V. Evans; *Rhinoplatia ruficollis*–James N. Hogue/California State University, Northridge; *Xanthochroa californica*, *Xanthochroina bicolor*–Arthur V. Evans.

OMETHIDAE

Matheteus theveneti–Katy Pye; *Telegeusis nubifer*–© 2021 David Maddison, used with permission.

ORSODACNIDAE

Aulacoscelis candezei–Mike Quinn/texasento.net; *Janbechynea fulvipes*–Charles Melton/nearfamous.com; *Orsodacne atra*–Christopher C. Wirth.

PASSANDRIDAE

Catogenus thomasi–Margarethe Brummermann.

PELTIDAE

Peltis pippingskoeldi–Arthur V. Evans; *Peltis septentrionalis*–Tom Murray.

PHALACRIDAE

Olibrus species–Alice Abela; *Phalacrus* species–Matt Gimmel; *Stilbus apicalis*–Christopher C. Wirth.

PHENGODIDAE

Distremocephalus californicus–Joyce Gross; *Distremocephalus opaculus*–Salvador Vitanza/USDA APHIS (PPQ); *Distremocephalus texanus*–Joyce Gross; *Phengodes arizonensis*–Margarethe Brummermann; *Stenophrixothrix fusca*–Kyle Schnepp/Florida State Collection of Arthropods, FDACS-DPI; *Zarhipis integripennis*–Arthur V. Evans.

PLEOCOMIDAE

Pleocoma australis–© 2021 Robyn J. Waayers, used with permission; *Pleocoma behrensi*–Joyce Gross; *Pleocoma dubitabilis leachi*–Louis LaPierre; *Pleocoma octopagina*–Arthur V. Evans; *Pleocoma puncticollis*–© 2021 Robyn J. Waayers, used with permission; *Pleocoma tularensis*–Joyce Gross.

PROSTOMIDAE

Prostomis mandibularis–Joyce Gross.

PSEPHENIDAE

Acneus quadrimaculatus, Eubrianax edwardsii, Psephenus falli–Joyce Gross.

PTILIIDAE

Ptenidium pusillum–Jennifer Read.

PTILODACTYLIDAE

Anchycteis velutina–Joyce Gross; *Araeopidius monachus*–Andrew McKorney.

PTINIDAE

Actenobius pleuralis–Joyce Gross; *Anobium punctatum*–Christoph Benisch; *Caenocara* species, *Episernus trapezoidus, Euvrilletta serricornis*–Joyce Gross; *Hemicoelus gibbicollis*–Lynette Elliott; *Lasioderma serricorne*–Kevin Gielen; *Mezium affine*–Stephen P. L. Luk; *Niptus giulianii*–Christopher C. Wirth; *Ozognathus cornutus*–Joyce Gross; *Priobium punctatum*–James N. Hogue/California State University, Northridge; *Ptilinus acuminatus, Ptinomorphus granosus, Ptinus fallax, Ptinus gandolphei*–Joyce Gross; *Ptinus paulonotatus*–Jillian H. Cowles; *Ptinus verticalis*–Joyce Gross; *Stegobium paniceum*–Christoph Benisch; *Trichodesma cristata*–Arthur V. Evans; *Tricorynus* species, *Vrilletta bicolor, V. decorata, Xeranobium* species–Joyce Gross.

PYROCHROIDAE

Cononotus bryanti–Nicolas Gompel; *Dendroides ephemeroides*–Richard Wilson; *Pedilus flabellatus*–Joyce Gross; *Schizotus cervicalis*–Tom Murray; *Tydessa blaisdelli*–Darren A. Pollock.

PYTHIDAE

Pytho americanus–Arthur V. Evans; *Priognathus monilicornis*–Tom Murray; *Sphalma quadricollis*–Gary D. Griswold; *Trimitomerus riversii*–Margarethe Brummermann.

RHADALIDAE

Rhadalus testaceus–Salvador Vitanza/USDA APHIS (PPQ); *Semijulistus flavipes*–Joyce Gross.

RHIPICERIDAE

Sandalus californicus–Joyce Gross; *Sandalus cribricollis*–Matthew Van Dam/California Academy of Sciences.

RIPIPHORIDAE

Macrosiagon cruenta–Arthur V. Evans; *Macrosiagon flavipennis*—Alice Abela; *Macrosiagon pectinata*–Arthur V. Evans; *Ptilophorus wrightii*–Joyce Gross; *Ripiphorus rex*–Arthur V. Evans.

SALPINGIDAE

Aegialites debilis–Matt Goff/sitkanature.org; *Aglenus brunneus*–Udo Schmidt/CC BY-SA 2.0; *Dacoderus striaticeps*–Salvador Vitanza/USDA APHIS (PPQ); *Elacatis umbrosus*–Jeffrey P. Gruber/UW–Madison, Dept. of Entomology; *Rhinosimus viridiaenus*–Tom Murray; *Sphaeriestes virescens*–Guy A. Hanley; *Vincenzellus elongatus*–Jaclyn McKeown/Centre for Biodiversity Genomics, University of Guelph.

SCARABAEIDAE

Acoma mixta–Arthur V. Evans; *Aegialia crassa, Amblonoxia carpenteri*–Alice Abela; *Amblonoxia palpalis*–Robert L. Allen/Bug Bob; *Amphimallon majale*–René Limoges/Stéphane Le Tirant; *Ancognatha manca, Anomala arida*–Arthur V. Evans; *Anomala delicata*–Jillian H. Cowles; *Anomala digressa*–Arthur V. Evans; *Anomala flavilla flavilla*–Guy A. Hanley; *Anomalacra clypealis, Anoplognatho dunnianus, Aphodius fimetarius*–Arthur V. Evans; *Ataenius spretulus*–John Ott; *Calamosternus granarius*–Christopher C. Wirth; *Canthon floridanus, C. indigaceus, C. simplex*–Arthur V. Evans; *Chnaunanthus chapini*–Joyce Gross; *Chnaunanthus flavipennis*–Alice Abela; *Chrysina beyeri, C. gloriosa, C. lecontei*–Arthur V. Evans; *Cinacanthus militaris*–Joyce Gross; *Coelotrachelus rudis*–Arthur V. Evans; *Coenonycha ampla*–Guy A. Hanley; *Coenonycha lurida*–Joyce Gross; *Coenonycha testacea, Copris arizonensis, C. lecontei, Coscinocephalus cribrifrons, Cotalpa consobrina, Cotinis impia, C. mutabilis*–Arthur V. Evans; *Cremastocheilus angularis* species complex, *Cremastocheilus armatus* species complex–Joyce Gross; *Cremastocheilus constricticollis*–Alice Abela; *Cremastocheilus planatus, C. planipes, C. quadratus, Cyclocephala hirta, C. longula, C. melanocephala, C. pasadenae, Diapterna hamata, Dichelonyx backii*–Arthur V. Evans; *Dichelonyx muscula*–James N. Hogue/California State University, Northridge; *Dichelonyx pusilla*–Arthur V. Evans; *Dichelonyx truncata*–Guy A. Hanley; *Dichelonyx vicina*–James N. Hogue/California State University, Northridge; *Dichotomius colonicus, Digitonthophagus gazella*–Arthur V. Evans; *Dinacoma sanfelipe*–© 2021 Robyn J. Waayers, used with permission; *Diplotaxis moerens moerens, D. sierra, Dynastes grantii, Dyscinetus laevicollis, Euoniticellus intermedius*–Arthur V. Evans; *Euphoria fascifera*–Charles L. Hogue/courtesy of James N. Hogue, California State University, Northridge; *Euphoria inda, E. leucographa, E. monticola, E. quadricollis*–Arthur V. Evans; *Euphoria verticalis*–Joyce Gross; *Genuchinus ineptus*–Loren J. Padelford; *Gymnetina cretacea*–Arthur V. Evans; *Gymnopyge hopliaeformis*–Alice Abela; *Hemiphileurus illatus, Hologymnetis argenteola, Hoplia callipyge, H. dispar, Isonychus arizonensis*–Arthur V. Evans; *Labarrus pseudolividus*–Joyce Gross; *Leptohoplia testaceipennis*–Guy A. Hanley; *Liatongus californicus*–Arthur V. Evans; *Lissomelas flohri*–Margarethe Brummermann; *Listrochelus xerophilus, Macrodactylus uniformis, Megasoma punctulatum, Onitis alexis, Onthophagus arnetti, O. nuchicornis, O. taurus, Orizabus clunalis, O. ligyroides*–Arthur V. Evans; *Otophorus haemorrhoidalis*–Guy A. Hanley; *Oxygrylius ruginasus, Parabyrsopolis chihuahuae*–Arthur V. Evans; *Paracotalpa deserta*–Charles L. Hogue/courtesy of James N. Hogue, California State University, Northridge; *Paracotalpa puncticollis*–James N. Hogue/California State University, Northridge; *Paracotalpa ursina*–Alice Abela; *Pardalosus pardalis*–Guy A. Hanley; *Pelidnota lugubris*–Arthur V. Evans; *Phanaeus quadridens*–Margarethe Brummermann; *Phanaeus vindex*–Dave Almquist; *Phileurus truncatus*–Arthur V. Evans; *Phobetus comatus*–Aaron Schusteff; *Phobetus humeralis, P. mojavus*–Alice Abela; *Phobetus saylori*–Guy A. Hanley; *Phyllophaga anxia*–James N. Hogue/California State University, Northridge; *Phyllophaga bilobatata, P. vetula*–Arthur V. Evans; *Planolinellus vittatus*–Guy A. Hanley; *Polyphylla cavifrons, P. decimlineata, P. hammondi, P. nigra, P. sobrina, Pseudocanthon perplexus*–Arthur V. Evans; *Pseudocotalpa andrewsi*–© 2021 Robyn J. Waayers, used with permission; *Serica perigonia*–Arthur V. Evans; *Stenotothorax ovipennis*–Guy A. Hanley; *Strategus aloeus, S. cessus, Strigoderma pimalis*–Arthur V. Evans; *Teuchestes fossor*–Paul E. Skelley/Florida State Collection of Arthropods, FDACS-DPI; *Tomarus gibbosus*–Arthur V. Evans; *Trichiorhyssemus riparius*–Salvador Vitanza/USDA APHIS (PPQ); *Trichiotinus assimilis*–Tom Murray; *Valgus californicus*–Joyce Gross; *Xyloryctes thestalus*–Arthur V. Evans.

SCHIZOPODIDAE

Dystaxia murrayi, Glyptoscelimorpha juniperae juniperae, G. marmorata, G. viridis–Arthur V. Evans; *Schizopus laetus*–Tony Iwane.

SCIRTIDAE

Elodes apicalis–Graham Montgomery; *Herthania concinna*–Lynette Elliott; *Scirtes* species–Salvador Vitanza/USDA APHIS (PPQ).

SCRAPTIIDAE

Anaspis atrata–Arthur V. Evans; *Anaspis collaris*–Alice Abela; *Anaspis rufa*–Joyce Gross; *Canifa pallipes, Pentaria trifasciata*–Christopher C. Wirth.

SILPHIDAE

Aclypea bituberosa–Guy A. Hanley; *Heterosilpha ramosa*–Lynette Elliott; *Necrodes surinamensis, Nicrophorus defodiens*–Arthur V. Evans; *Nicrophorus guttula*–Alice Abela; *Nicrophorus marginatus*–Arthur V. Evans; *Nicrophorus mexicanus*–James

N. Hogue/California State University, Northridge; *Nicrophorus nigrita*–Arthur V. Evans; *Thanatophilus lapponicus*–Alice Abela; *Thanatophilus truncatus*–Arthur V. Evans.

SILVANIDAE

Dendrophagus cygnaei–Richard Migneault; *Oryzaephilus mercator*–Gross; *Oryzaephilus surinamensis*–Graham Montgomery; *Silvanus bidentatus*–Gary D. Griswold; *Telephanus lecontei*–Salvador Vitanza/USDA APHIS (PPQ); *Uleiota truncatus*–Joyce Gross.

SMICRIPIDAE

Smicrips species–Michael C. Thomas/Florida State Collection of Arthropods, FDACS-DPI.

SPHAERITIDAE

Sphaerites politus–Arthur V. Evans.

SPHAERIUSIDAE

Sphaerius species–© 2020 David Maddison, used with permission.

SPHINDIDAE

Odontosphindus clavicornis–Joyce Gross; *Sphindus americanus*–Tom Murray.

STAPHYLINIDAE

Aleochara pacifica–Alice Abela; *Amphichroum maculatum*–Joyce Gross; *Anotylus rugosus*–Tom Murray; *Astenus* species–Alice Abela; *Batrisodes* species–Joyce Gross; *Bledius fenyesi, B. ferratus*–Alice Abela; *Cafius canescens*–Joyce Gross; *Cafius luteipennis*–Alice Abela; *Creophilus maxillosus villosus, Dinothenarus saphyrinides*–Arthur V. Evans; *Eusphalerum pothos, Gyrohypnus fracticornis, Habrocerus capillaricornis*–Tom Murray; *Hadrotes crassus, Lathrobium* species–Joyce Gross; *Lordithon kelleyi*–Tom Murray; *Ocypus olens*–Joyce Gross; *Paederus littorarius*–Tom Murray; *Philonthus caeruleipennis*–Arthur V. Evans; *Philonthus cruentatus*–Klaus Bek Nielsen; *Piestus extimus*–© 2020 David Maddison, used with permission; *Phlaeopterus cavicollis*–Joyce Gross; *Pontomalota opaca*–Alice Abela; *Quedius plagiatus*–Tom Murray; *Scaphisoma castaneum*–Joyce Gross; *Sepedophilus* species–Christopher C. Wirth; *Stenus comma*–Joyce Gross; *Tachinus basalis*–Tom Murray; *Tanyrhinus singularis*–Derek S. Sikes/University of Alaska Museum of the North; *Thinopinus pictus*–Arthur V. Evans; *Trigonurus rugosus*–Joyce Gross; *Xenodusa reflexa*–Guy A. Hanley.

STENOTRACHELIDAE

Cephaloon bicolor, Cephaloon vandykei–Joyce Gross; *Stenotrachelus aeneus*–H. E. James Hammond.

TENEBRIONIDAE

Adelina pallida–John Ott; *Alaephus* species, *Alobates pensylvanicus*–Arthur V. Evans; *Ammodonus granosus*–Jillian H. Cowles; *Anchomma costatum*–Alice Abela; *Apsena rufipes*–Aaron Schusteff; *Araeoschizus* species–Christopher C. Wirth; *Argoporis bicolor, Asbolus laevis, A. verrucosus, Auchmobius sublaevis, Blapstinus* species–Arthur V. Evans; *Bothrotes plumbeus plumbeus*–Alice Abela; *Cerenopus concolor*–Arthur V. Evans; *Cheirodes californicus*–Joyce Gross; *Chilometopon brachystomum*–Alice Abela; *Cibdelis blaschkei*–Joyce Gross; *Cnemodinus testaceus*–Margarethe Brummermann; *Coelocnemis dilaticollis, C. sulcata, Coelus ciliatus*–Arthur V. Evans; *Conibius gagates*–Jillian H. Cowles; *Conionitis* species–Arthur V. Evans; *Corticeus substriatus*–Stephen A. Marshall; *Cryptoglossa muricata*–Arthur V. Evans; *Cryptoglossa variolosa*–Alice Abela; *Cynaeus angustus*–James N. Hogue/California State University, Northridge; *Diaperis rufipes*–Arthur V. Evans; *Edrotes ventricosus*–Alice Abela; *Eleates depressus*–Scott Justis; *Eleodes armatus*–Lynette Elliott; *Eleodes obscura sulcipennis*–Arthur V. Evans; *Eleodes osculans*–Alice Abela; *Eleodes tribulus*–Christopher C. Wirth; *Embaphion contusum*–Salvador Vitanza/USDA APHIS (PPQ); *Embaphion depressum*–Joyce Gross; *Embaphion elongatum*–Arthur V. Evans; *Epantius obscurus*–Alice Abela; *Eupsophulus castaneus*–Arthur V. Evans; *Eusattus difficilis*–James N. Hogue/California State University, Northridge; *Eusattus dilitatus*–© 2021 Alex Wild, used with permission; *Eusattus muricatus*–Christopher C. Wirth; *Eusattus reticulatus*–Arthur V. Evans; *Gondwanocrypticus platensis*–Scott Justis; *Helops laeta, Iphthiminus serratus, Isomira* species–Arthur V. Evans; *Lariversius tibialis*–Alice Abela; *Lepidocnemeplatia sericea*–Christopher C. Wirth (*l*), Joyce Gross (*r*); *Lobometopon fusiforme*–Tom Bentley; *Lystronychus scapularis*–Arthur V. Evans; *Megeleates sequoarium*–Aaron Schusteff; *Metaclisa marginalis, Metopoloba pruinosa pruinosa*–Arthur V. Evans; *Microschatia championi*–Joyce Gross; *Microschatia inaequalis*–Alice Abela; *Mycetochara procera, Nyctoporis carinata, Pechalius vestitus, Pelecyphorus liratus*–Arthur V. Evans; *Phaleria rotundata*–Alice Abela; *Phaleromela variegata*–Joyce Gross; *Philolithus actuosus*–Alice Abela; *Philolithus morbillosus, Platydema oregonensis, Platydema wandae, Polemiotus submetallicus*–Arthur V. Evans; *Pseudocistela pinguis*–Alice Abela; *Rhipidandrus peninsularis*–Salvador Vitanza/USDA APHIS (PPQ); *Schizillus laticeps, Scotobaenus parallelus*–Arthur V. Evans; *Statira pluripunctata*–Alice Abela; *Stenochidus gracilis*–Joyce Gross; *Stenomorpha confluens*–Christopher C. Wirth; *Stenomorpha lecontei*–Alice Abela; *Stenomorpha marginata, Strongylium atrum*–Arthur V. Evans; *Tribolium castaneum*–James N. Hogue/California State University, Northridge; *Trichoton sordidum*–Jillian H. Cowles; *Triorophus laevis*–© 2021 Robyn J. Waayers, used with permission; *Trogloderus vandykei*–Alice Abela; *Uloma longula*–Arthur V. Evans; *Ulus crassus*–Alice Abela; *Upis ceramboides*–Richard Migneault; *Zophobas subnitens*–Arthur V. Evans.

TEREDIDAE

Oxylaemus californicus–Brendon Boudinot/ Friedrich-Schiller-Universität Jena; *Rustleria obscura*–Kyle Schnepp/Florida State Collection of Arthropods, FDACS-DPI.

TETRATOMIDAE

Eustrophopsis arizonensis–Arthur V. Evans; *Eustrophus tomentosus*–John Ott; *Hallomenus scapularis*–Tom Murray; *Synstrophus repandus*–Arthur V. Evans; *Tetratoma concolor*–Derek S. Sikes/University of Alaska Museum of the North; *Triphyllia elongata*–Kojun Kanda.

THROSCIDAE

Aulonothroscus validus–Gary D. Griswold; *Pactopus horni*–Joyce Gross; *Trixagus carinicollis*–Tom Murray.

THYMALIDAE

Thymalus marginicollis–Joyce Gross.

TRACHYPACHIDAE

Trachypachus gibbsii–Joyce Gross.

TROGIDAE

Omorgus carinatus, O. punctatus, O. suberosus–Arthur V. Evans; *Trox atrox, T. gemmulatus*–Alice Abela; *Trox plicatus*–Arthur V. Evans; *Trox scaber*–Stephen P. L. Luk.

TROGOSSITIDAE

Airora aequalis–Michael C. Thomas/Florida State Collection of Arthropods, FDACS-DPI; *Calitys scabra*–Arthur V. Evans; *Corticotomus caviceps*–Michael C. Thomas/Florida State Collection of Arthropods, FDACS-DPI; *Temnoscheila chlorodia*–Arthur V. Evans; *Tenebroides crassicornis*–Graham Montgomery.

ZOPHERIDAE

Aulonium longum, Bitoma ornata–Nathan P. Lord; *Colydium lineola*–© 2020 David Maddison, used with permission; *Coxelus serratus, Denophloeus nosodermoides*–Nathan P. Lord; *Hyporhagus gilensis*–Arthur V. Evans; *Lasconotus subcostulatus, Megataphrus tenuicornis*–Nathan P. Lord; *Microprius rufulus*–James N. Hogue/California State University, Northridge; *Namunaria pacifica*–Joyce Gross; *Phellopsis porcata, Phloeodes diabolicus, P. plicatus*–Arthur V. Evans; *Pycnomerus arizonicus*–Nathan P. Lord; *Rhagodera tuberculata*–Alice Abela; *Usechimorpha montanus*–Nathan P. Lord; *Usechus lacerata, Zopherus gracilis, Z. granicollis, Z. tristis*–Arthur V. Evans.

INDEX

Note: Scientific names followed by an asterisk are mentioned in the text, but not illustrated.

607

611

617